Marketing text in the world?

Answer:
Experience. Leadership. Innovation.

MARKETING

Marketing

9/e

Roger A. Kerin
Southern Methodist University

Steven W. Hartley
University of Denver

William Rudelius
University of Minnesota

McGraw-Hill Irwin

Boston   Burr Ridge, IL   Dubuque, IA   New York   San Francisco   St. Louis
Bangkok   Bogotá   Caracas   Kuala Lumpur   Lisbon   London   Madrid   Mexico City
Milan   Montreal   New Delhi   Santiago   Seoul   Singapore   Sydney   Taipei   Toronto

MARKETING

Published by McGraw-Hill/Irwin, a business unit of The McGraw-Hill Companies, Inc., 1221 Avenue of the Americas, New York, NY, 10020. Copyright © 2009, 2006, 2003, 2000, 1997, 1994, 1992, 1989, 1986 by The McGraw-Hill Companies, Inc. All rights reserved. No part of this publication may be reproduced or distributed in any form or by any means, or stored in a database or retrieval system, without the prior written consent of The McGraw-Hill Companies, Inc., including, but not limited to, in any network or other electronic storage or transmission, or broadcast for distance learning.

Some ancillaries, including electronic and print components, may not be available to customers outside the United States.

This book is printed on acid-free paper.
1 2 3 4 5 6 7 8 9 0 WCK/WCK 0 9 8

ISBN   978-0-07-340472-1 (bound edition)
MHID   0-07-340472-1 (bound edition)

ISBN   978-0-07-726589-2 (loose-leaf edition)
MHID   0-07-726589-0 (loose-leaf edition)

Publisher: *Paul Ducham*
Executive editor: *Doug Hughes*
Developmental editors: *Colleen Honan/Gina Huck Siegert*
Editorial assistant: *Kelly Pekelder*
Marketing director: *Krista Bettino*
Digital product manager: *Jared Harless*
Lead project manager: *Christine A. Vaughan*
Lead production supervisor: *Carol A. Bielski*
Lead designer: *Matthew Baldwin*
Senior photo research coordinator: *Jeremy Cheshareck*
Photo researcher: *Mike Hruby*
Media project managers: *Lynn Bluhm and Susan Lombardi*
Cover and interior design: *Keith J. McPherson*
Typeface: *10.5/12 Times Roman*
Compositor: *Aptara, Inc.*
Printer: *Quebecor World Versailles Inc.*

Library of Congress Cataloging-in-Publication Data

Kerin, Roger A.
    Marketing / Roger A. Kerin, Steven W. Hartley, William Rudelius.—9th ed.
        p. cm.—(McGraw-Hill/Irwin series in marketing)
    Previous ed. entered under title.
    Includes index.
    ISBN-13: 978-0-07-340472-1 (alk. paper)
    ISBN-10: 0-07-340472-1 (alk. paper)
    1. Marketing. I. Hartley, Steven William. II. Rudelius, William. III. Title.
HF5415.M29474 2009
658.8—dc22

                                                                    2008002053

www.mhhe.com

A MESSAGE FROM THE AUTHORS

It is difficult to imagine a more dynamic and exciting time for students and instructors, particularly those who are interested in the field of marketing! Each day brings new products, services, technologies, and ideas to the marketplace. You may have observed the growing interest in social networking, environmental sustainability, mobile technologies, the economic growth of China and India, YouTube, iPhones, millennial entrepreneurs, blogs, interactive advertising, social responsibility, and many other new aspects of business. Tomorrow will most certainly add to the list!

As marketing professors we appreciate the opportunity to share our enthusiasm for the field of marketing with you, and to explore the opportunities and challenges the field of marketing will present to all of us as consumers, managers, and students. This edition of *Marketing* is designed to (1) build on the **experience** we've developed during the past eight editions of the text, (2) continue our **leadership** role in exploring new topics and perspectives, and (3) offer pedagogical **innovation** that matches today's educational demands. We have worked diligently to ensure that the time you invest in *Marketing* will provide the most up-to-date, comprehensive, engaging, and integrated learning experience available from any text.

This edition of *Marketing* continues our tradition of using an active-learning approach to bring traditional theories and contemporary concepts to life. You'll find yourself immersed in discussions, examples, and cases based on familiar companies, brands, and products. Feedback from students and instructors from around the world has reinforced our commitment to this approach. We are thrilled that *Marketing* has become the best-selling principles of marketing text in the United States, and, through translations into eight other languages, around the world. The ninth edition strives to exceed the standards set by our past success.

We hope you'll enjoy reading and using our text, and that we've sparked your interest in additional learning and career pursuits in marketing!

Roger A. Kerin
Steven W. Hartley
William Rudelius

Preface

Marketing utilizes a unique, innovative, and effective pedagogical approach developed by the authors through the integration of their combined classroom, college, and university experiences. The elements of this approach have been the foundation for each edition of *Marketing* and serve as the core of the text and it supplements as they evolve and adapt to changes in student learning styles, the growth of the marketing discipline, and the development of new instructional technologies. The distinctive features of the approach are illustrated below:

High Engagement Style
Easy-to-read, high-involvement, interactive writing style that engages students through active learning techniques.

Rigorous Framework
A pedagogy based on the use of Learning Objectives, Learning Reviews, Learning Objectives Reviews, and supportive student supplements.

Marketing
Pedagogical Approach

Personalized Marketing
A vivid and accurate description of businesses, marketing professionals, and entrepreneurs—through cases, exercises, and testimonials—that allows students to personalize marketing and identify possible career interests.

Traditional and Contemporary Coverage
Comprehensive and integrated coverage of traditional and contemporary concepts.

Marketing Decision Making
The use of extended examples, cases, and videos involving people making marketing decisions.

The goal of the Ninth Edition of *Marketing* is to create an exceptional experience for today's students and instructors of marketing. The development of *Marketing* was based on a rigorous process of assessment and the outcome of the process is a text and package of learning tools that are based on experience, leadership, and innovation in marketing education.

EXPERIENCE

Nine editions and more than one million students, as authors.

Ten decades combined and more than 50,000 students taught, as instructors.

This is the experience the Kerin author team brings to the newly updated *Marketing*, 9/e. This experience has shaped the framework for this text and its supplements. How, exactly, do the authors do this in the ninth edition?

- Through the #1 *video case package* in the discipline:

    The Kerin video cases have been praised by users and reviewers for many editions as the most customized, engaging, and relevant video cases available. With the ninth edition, the authors have included nine new video case studies as well as five updated cases to enhance student interest. They present exciting products and companies such as Geek Squad, Starbucks, Best Buy, Rollerblade, BMW, Starbury, The Mall of America, Xerox, and General Mills.

- By integrating assessment tools that allow instructors to meet *AACSB assurance-of-learning requirements:*

  Each chapter begins with learning objectives, includes in-chapter learning reviews, and ends with learning objective summaries. In addition, the *Marketing,* 9/e Test Bank includes learning objective, AACSB learning outcome, and Bloom's Taxonomy designations for each question. The combination of the objectives, outcomes, and taxonomy designation with the specific questions provides an important tool for meeting AACSB assurance of learning requirements.

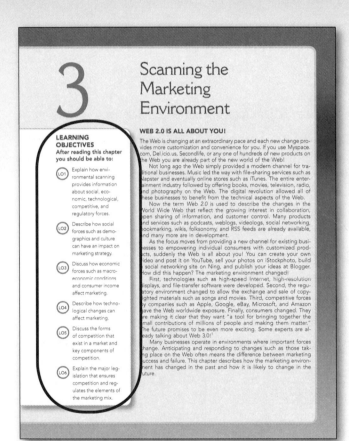

- With the most comprehensive package of *teaching and learning resources:*

  The supplements that accompany *Marketing,* 9/e are a comprehensive and integrated package of resources designed to ensure the highest level of learning for all students, and assist in making an instructor's life easier in the process. The supplements range from online quizzes, to comprehensive PowerPoint slides, to the one-of-a-kind Instructor's Survival Kit, to an integrated Instructor's Manual, to a world-class test bank.

LEADERSHIP

The first custom-made videos to accompany a marketing text.

The first to integrate new content areas such as ethics, technology, and interactive marketing.

The first to utilize active learning approaches in the text and integrated activities.

These are just a few examples that illustrate how the Kerin author team has played a leadership role in the development and delivery of marketing pedagogy. This book is recognized as the market leader in the United States and Canada, and continues to introduce new, leading-edge principles and practices to students and instructors around the world. How does *Marketing*, 9/e continue this tradition of leadership?

- With the inclusion of **Customer Experience Management:**

  Customer experience management reflects contemporary thinking about the way marketers view how customers relate to their organizations and offerings. Students will find that marketing efforts to create a favorable customer experience in the interaction with organizations and the acquisition, use, and disposal of offerings results in mutually beneficial exchange relationships.

- With the focus on **Marketplace Diversity:**

  A diverse mix of buyers and sellers populate today's dynamic marketplace. Students will find that successful marketers are not limited to any particular culture, nationality, race, ethnic group, or gender. Rather, like consumers they serve, marketers mirror society, both domestically and globally. This diversity in today's marketplace is reflected in examples throughout the text.

- By creating the new feature, *Using Marketing Dashboards:*

The use of marketing dashboards among marketing professionals is popular today. Marketing dashboards graphically portray the measures that marketers use to track and analyze marketing phenomena and performance. Students will find commonly used measures applied by successful marketers throughout the text and be exposed to their calculation, interpretation, and application.

Using Marketing Dashboards

Are Cracker Jack Prices Above, At, or Below the Market?

How would you determine whether a firm's retail prices are above, at, or below the market? You might visit retail stores and record what prices retailers are charging for products or brands. This laborious activity can be simplified by combining two consumer market share measures to create a "price premium" display on your marketing dashboard.

Your Challenge Frito-Lay is considering whether to buy the Cracker Jack brand of caramel popcorn from Borden, Inc. Frito-Lay research shows that Cracker Jack has a strong brand equity. But, Cracker Jack's dollar sales market share and pound volume market share declined recently and trailed the Crunch 'n Munch brand as shown in the table.

Borden's management used an above-market, premium pricing strategy for Cracker Jack. Specifically, Cracker Jack's suggested retail price was set to yield an average price premium per pound of 28 percent relative to Crunch 'n Munch. As a Frito-Lay marketer studying Cracker Jack, your challenge is to calculate and display Cracker Jack's actual price premium relative to Crunch 'n Munch. A price premium is the percentage by which the actual price charged for a specific brand exceeds (or falls short of) a benchmark established for a similar product or basket of products. This premium can be calculated as follows:

Price Premium (%)

$$= \frac{\text{Dollar Sales Market Share for a Brand}}{\text{Unit Volume Market Share for a Brand}} - 1$$

Brand	Dollar Sales Market Share	Pound Volume Market Share
Crunch 'n Munch	32%	32%
Cracker Jack	26	19
Fiddle Faddle	7	8
Private Brands	4	8
Seasonal, Specialty, and Regional (S,S,R) Brands	31 / 100%	33 / 100%

Your Findings Using caramel popcorn brand market share data, the Cracker Jack price premium is 1.368, or 36.8 percent, calculated as follows: (26 percent ÷ 19 percent) − 1 = .368. By comparison, Crunch 'n Munch enjoys no price premium. Its dollar sales market share and unit (pound) market share are equal: (32 percent ÷ 32 percent) − 1 = 0, or zero percent. The price premium, or lack thereof, of other brands can be displayed in a marketing dashboard as shown below.

Your Action Cracker Jack's price premium clearly exceeds the 28 percent Borden benchmark relative to Crunch 'n Munch. Cracker Jack's price premium may have overreached its brand equity. Consideration might be given to assessing Cracker Jack's price premium relative to its market position should Frito-Lay purchase the brand.

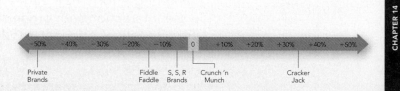

STEP 5: SET THE LIST OR QUOTED PRICE

LO2

The first four steps in setting price covered in Chapter 13 and this chapter result in an approximate price level for the product that appears reasonable. But it still remains for the manager to set a specific list or quoted price in light of all relevant factors.

INNOVATION

What if your research showed that many students in your introductory marketing course don't attempt to read and understand the tables and charts in the textbook? What could you do to increase their interest and involvement? Read on for the answer.

To secure their position in the marketplace, the Kerin author team consistently created innovative pedagogical tools that encourage interaction and match students' learning styles. How did they accomplish this in 9/e?

- With the creation of a *Visually Enhanced Test Bank:*

   The *Marketing* 9/e Test Bank has been completely updated to include the latest concepts and ideas from the textbook. When research by the Kerin author team revealed many students were skipping the tables and charts in the chapter, they decided to do something about it: the Visually Enhanced Test Bank! This moves key tables, charts, ads, and photos from the textbook into the test bank to emphasize their importance and reward students who study these key elements.

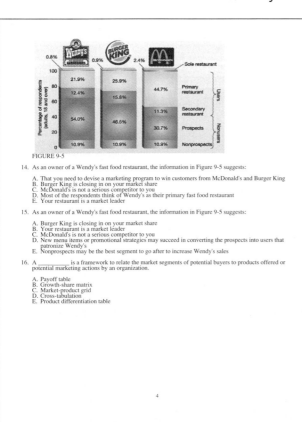

FIGURE 9-5

14. As an owner of a Wendy's fast food restaurant, the information in Figure 9-5 suggests:

   A. That you need to devise a marketing program to win customers from McDonald's and Burger King
   B. Burger King is closing in on your market share
   C. McDonald's is not a serious competitor to you
   D. Most of the respondents think of Wendy's as their primary fast food restaurant
   E. Your restaurant is a market leader

15. As an owner of a Wendy's fast food restaurant, the information in Figure 9-5 suggests:

   A. Burger King is closing in on your market share
   B. Your restaurant is a market leader
   C. McDonald's is not a serious competitor to you
   D. New menu items or promotional strategies may succeed in converting the prospects into users that patronize Wendy's
   E. Nonprospects may be the best segment to go after to increase Wendy's sales

16. A _____ is a framework to relate the market segments of potential buyers to products offered or potential marketing actions by an organization.

   A. Payoff table
   B. Growth-share matrix
   C. Market-product grid
   D. Cross-tabulation
   E. Product differentiation table

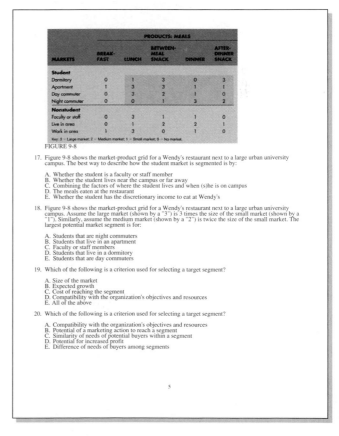

FIGURE 9-8

17. Figure 9-8 shows the market-product grid for a Wendy's restaurant next to a large urban university campus. The best way to describe how the student market is segmented is by:

   A. Whether the student is a faculty or staff member
   B. Whether the student lives near the campus or far away
   C. Combining the factors of where the student lives and when (s)he is on campus
   D. The meals eaten at the restaurant
   E. Whether the student has the discretionary income to eat at Wendy's

18. Figure 9-8 shows the market-product grid for a Wendy's restaurant next to a large urban university campus. Assume the large market (shown by a "3") is 3 times the size of the small market (shown by a "1"). Similarly, assume the medium market (shown by a "2") is twice the size of the small market. The largest potential market segment is for:

   A. Students that are night commuters
   B. Students that live in an apartment
   C. Faculty or staff members
   D. Students that live in a dormitory
   E. Students that are day commuters

19. Which of the following is a criterion used for selecting a target segment?

   A. Size of the market
   B. Expected growth
   C. Cost of reaching the segment
   D. Compatibility with the organization's objectives and resources
   E. All of the above

20. Which of the following is a criterion used for selecting a target segment?

   A. Compatibility with the organization's objectives and resources
   B. Potential of a marketing action to reach a segment
   C. Similarity of needs of potential buyers within a segment
   D. Potential for increased profit
   E. Difference of needs of buyers among segments

- By including **iPod content** for student use:

It has become apparent that student study patterns and practices are changing and evolving. With students being more active and on-the-go than ever, we have created study and prep tools that can be as mobile as they are! Specific chapter quizzes, PowerPoint presentations and video cases can now be viewed and manipulated with any MP3 player.

- Through the **Instructor's Survival Kit:**

This supplement is exactly what it says it is: an instructor's guide to surviving in today's classroom. Instructors create interaction by breaking the classroom into teams that analyze marketing problems presented through In-Class Activities. Students who are kinesthetic learners especially appreciate the hands-on product samples that are tied to the activities and are intended to build on the idea of "cooperative learning."

New and Revised Content

New Innovation Examples and Content. The 3M Post-It Flag Highlighter targeted at college students, opens Chapter 1. This example of new product development and innovation is integrated into the chapter and is featured in the end-of-chapter video case.

Increased Emphasis on the Importance of Marketing in Organizations. Chapter 2 now includes a discussion of the new title for marketing executives – Chief Marketing Officer (CMO) – and the increasingly important role they play. A new Marketing Matters Box describes the diverse activities of CMOs. Chapter 2 also introduces the new Using Marketing Dashboards box.

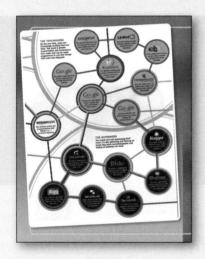

Introduction of Web 2.0 and New Trends in Marketing. Web logs (blogs), social networking, wikis, RSS feeds, and other elements of Web 2.0 are presented in Chapter 3. Recent trends including the concern about global warming, the growing importance of China and India, and the increase in customer-generated content are also discussed. The chapter also includes discussions of hybrid cars, culture jamming, WiMax, generation Y entrepreneurs, and a new case on Geek Squad.

New Detailed Examples of Ethics and Social Responsibility in Marketing. Chapter 4 examples have been expanded to include Anheuser-Busch's new "Responsibility Matters" campaign, Pepsi's reaction to an offer of confidential information, green marketing activities at 3M and Wal-Mart, cause marketing activities at Avon and P&G, and efforts to reclaim and reuse e-waste by Hewlett-Packard.

Updated Consumer Behavior Coverage. Chapter 5 includes a new chapter opening example featuring the importance of and differences in customer experience for men and women when shopping for a new car. It also places increased emphasis on customer experience in the purchase decision process, and includes a new video case on Best Buy.

New Emphasis on Supplier Development and Diversity. New examples of organization buying, including P&G's leadership in supplier development, Lockheed Martin's relationship with NASA, and small business use of business-to-business e-marketplaces have been added to Chapter 6.

Expanded Coverage of Marketing in Developing Countries. The discussion of marketing in developing countries in Chapter 7 now includes an emphasis on the role of entrepreneurship and innovation to promote a higher standard of living and coverage of the "bottom-of-the-pyramid" concept and microfinance. Marketing opportunities in China are also discussed.

Updated Marketing Research Examples and Information. Aging actors in movie sequels like those playing Harry Potter and Indiana Jones are just one of the reasons for marketing research for today's movies, as discussed in Chapter 8. It also covers marketing research aspects of Nielsen ratings of TV shows and websites, data mining, "cool hunters," and toy testing.

New Segmentation and Positioning Coverage. New examples of Zappos online shoes, Wendy's innovations, Apple's new products, and Ann Taylor Loft have been added to the Chapter 9 discussions of segmentation and positioning.

Added Discussion of Sources of New Product Ideas. Where did the idea for Apple's iPhone come from? Chapter 10 opens with Steve Jobs' strategy for developing this revolutionary new product. A new section gives reasons for the huge number of new product failures – ranging from "Groupthink" to not learning lessons from past failures.

Expanded Coverage of Product and Brand Management. Chapter 11 has expanded the discussion of technological substitution using the product life cycle example of cassette tapes, compact discs, and digital music downloads. In addition, customer experience is highlighted through Pepsi, Kleenex, and Kraft packaging examples, and brand personality is highlighted through a Harley-Davidson example. The chapter also includes a new section titled "Contemporary Packaging and Labeling Challenges."

Increased Emphasis on Customer Experience and Customer Experience Management. Given the current focus on enhancing customer experience with products and services this topic is integrated throughout the book. Specifically a new discussion and key term on customer experience management has been added to Chapter 12. New service examples such as Virgin Galactic space tourism, zillow.com, USPS online, and mobile TV have also been added. A new Going Online box discusses Blogwatching as a means of monitoring service failure.

Updated Pricing Coverage. Chapter 13 now opens with a new discussion of StubHub and ticket reselling and includes a comparison of Boeing and Airbus pricing for large passenger jets. The Washburn Guitar video case is completely updated with current products. Chapter 14 emphasizes the distinction between a one-price policy and a flexible-price policy given the advances in information technology. In addition a discussion of the new legal views on the "rule of reason" for vertical and horizontal price fixing and a new video case on the Starbury Collection are included.

New Focus of Channels, Wholesaling, Supply Chain, and Logistics Content. The importance of customer experience management is the focus of Chapter 15 and is discussed in the context of channel management at Apple Stores, in multichannel marketing, and as an element of channel choice. The new title of Chapter 16 also reflects the new focus on the customer. Discussions of IBM, Microsoft, and Hewlett-Packard are included as examples.

Introduction of Social Retailing and Other Retailing Trends. Chapter 17 now opens with a discussion of the growing interest in "social retailing." New discussions of the Macy's mergers, retailer loyalty programs, "site-to-store" services, smack shopping, multichannel marketing, and differences between male and female shoppers have also been added. The new Using Marketing Dashboards box discusses the sales per square foot and same store growth measures.

New Integrated Marketing Communications and Direct Marketing Coverage. Integrated marketing communication is discussed as an important tool in the trend toward customer experience management, and as a means of reaching mobile, multitasking audiences. Examples of media use include social media such as blogs, messaging on cell phones, push and pull advertising, sponsorships, logos, and game-movie partnerships. New company examples include Ford, the Beijing Olympics, Xerox, and State Farm. The chapter also discusses changes in Direct Marketing such as mandatory opt-in requirement in Europe and the possible "do not mail" registry in the U.S.

New Forms of Advertising. Discussion of the growth of new forms of advertising have been added to Chapter 19. The chapter opening example describes new "virtual" world advertising opportunities such as Second Life. Search engine advertising and interactive advertising are also discussed. Examples of ads from Blackberry, Sony, M&Ms, Travelers, the U.S. Army, Diesel, Dasani, Samsung, and Geico are included in the chapter. In addition, the Making Responsible Decisions box discusses the problem of click fraud in online advertising.

Increased Focus on Delivering Customer Solutions. Chapter 20 integrates Xerox and its focus on customer solutions into the chapter opening example and the new end-of-chapter video case. An expanded discussion of the use of technology in selling and sales management is also included.

New Content on Cross-Channel Shoppers and Interactive Marketing. New coverage in Chapter 21 describes "cross-channel" shoppers – the 51 percent of online consumers who research products online but buy in retail stores. New discussions also add emphasis to privacy and security issues in online buying and the impact of interactive marketing on the customer experience. A new Going Online box offers students a web quiz about their use of information and communication technology.

Integrative Summary of the Strategic Marketing Process. Chapter 22 integrates the three phases of the strategic marketing process used throughout the book. It opens by describing the highly successful recent launch of Warm Delights™ – the "indulgent and gooey" microwavable dessert from General Mills. Updated analytical frameworks show how organizations like General Mills, Lockheed's Skunkworks, General Mills, and Dominos Pizza plan, implement, and evaluate effective marketing programs.

New and Updated Career Coverage and Alternate Cases. Appendix C, Planning a Career in Marketing, has been updated to include new salary information, the growing importance of international work experience, and the use of online profiles and networking sites by employers and prospective employees. Appendix D, Alternate Cases, contains more than 50 percent new and updated cases for instructors who elect to assign cases to students.

Organization

The ninth edition of *Marketing* is divided into five parts. Part 1, **Initiating the Marketing Process**, looks first at what marketing is and how it creates customer value and customer relationships (Chapter 1). Then Chapter 2 provides an overview of the strategic marketing process that occurs in an organization—which provides a framework for the text. Appendix A provides a sample marketing plan as a reference for students. Chapter 3 analyzes the five major environmental factors in our changing marketing environment, while Chapter 4 provides a framework for including ethical and social responsibility considerations in marketing decisions.

Part 2, **Understanding Buyers and Markets**, first describes, in Chapter 5, how individual consumers reach buying decisions. Next, Chapter 6 looks at organizational buyers and markets and how they make purchase decisions. And finally, in Chapter 7, the dynamics of world trade and the influence of cultural diversity on global marketing practices are explored.

In Part 3, **Targeting Marketing Opportunities**, the marketing research function and how information about prospective consumers is linked to marketing strategy and decisions is discussed in Chapter 8. The process of segmenting and targeting markets and positioning products appears in Chapter 9.

Part 4, **Satisfying Marketing Opportunities**, covers the marketing mix elements. The product element is divided into the natural chronological sequence of first developing new products and services (Chapter 10) and then managing the existing products (Chapter 11) and services (Chapter 12). Pricing is covered in terms of underlying pricing analysis (Chapter 13), followed by actual price setting (Chapter 14), and Appendix B, Financial Aspects of Marketing. Three chapters address the place (distribution) aspects of marketing: Managing Marketing Channels and Wholesaling (Chapter 15), Customer-driven Supply Chain and Logistics Management (Chapter 16), and Retailing (Chapter 17). Retailing is a separate chapter because of its importance and interest as a career for many of today's students. Promotion is also covered in three chapters. Chapter 18 discusses integrated marketing communications and direct marketing, topics that have grown in importance in the marketing discipline recently. The primary forms of mass market communication—advertising, sales promotion, and public relations—are covered in Chapter 19. Personal selling and sales management are covered in Chapter 20.

Part 5, **Managing the Marketing Process**, discusses issues and techniques related to interactive marketing technologies and the strategic marketing process. Chapter 21 describes how interactive and multichannel marketing influences customer value and the customer experience through context, content, community, customization, connectivity, and commerce. Chapter 22 expands on Chapter 2 to describe specific techniques and issues related to blending the four marketing mix elements to plan, implement, and evaluate marketing programs.

The book closes with several useful supplemental sections. Appendix C, Planning a Career in Marketing, discusses marketing jobs and how to get them, and Appendix D, provides 22 Alternate Cases. In addition, a detailed glossary and three indexes (name, company/product, and subject) complete the book.

Engaging Features

Chapter-opening vignettes introduce students to chapter concepts ahead by using an exciting company as an example. Students are immediately engaged while learning about real-world companies. Chapter 10 discusses *BusinessWeek*'s most innovative company in 2006, Apple.

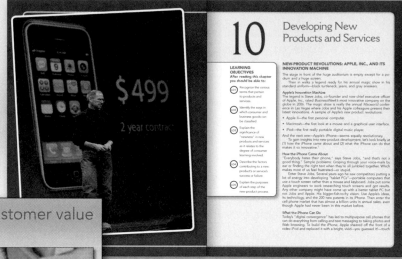

Marketing Matters > > > > > customer value
The Value of a Satisfied Customer to the Company

Customer satisfaction and experience underlie the marketing concept. But how much is a satisfied customer worth?

This question has prompted firms to calculate the financial value of a satisfied customer over time. Frito-Lay, for example, estimates that the average loyal consumer in the southwestern United States eats 21 pounds of salty snack chips a year. At a price of $2.50 a pound, this customer spends $52.50 annually on the company's salty snacks such as Lays and Ruffles potato chips, Doritos and Tostitos tortilla chips, and Fritos corn chips. Exxon estimates that a loyal customer will spend $500 annually for its branded gasoline, not including candy, snacks, oil, or repair services purchased at its gasoline stations. Kimberly-Clark reports that a loyal customer will buy 6.7 boxes of its Kleenex tissues each year and will spend $994 on facial tissues over 60 years, in today's dollars.

These calculations have focused marketer attention on the buying experience, customer satisfaction, and retention. Ford Motor Company has set a target of increasing customer retention—the percentage of Ford owners whose next car is also a Ford—from 60 percent to 80 percent. Why? Ford executives say that each additional percentage point is worth a staggering $100 million in profits.

This calculation is not unique to Ford. Research shows

Marketing Matters boxes highlight real-world examples of customer value creation and delivery and entrepreneurship which gives students further insight into the practical world of marketing.

Making Responsible Decisions > > > > sustainability
Reverse Logistics and Green Marketing Go Together at Hewlett-Packard: Recycling e-waste

Between 20 and 50 million tons of electronic waste find their way to landfills around the world annually. Americans alone are expected to discard 550 million analog TV sets and computer monitors and Japanese consumers will trash 610 million cell phones in 2010. The result? Landfills are seeping lead, chromium, mercury, and other toxins, prevalent in digital debris, into the environment.

Fortunately, Hewlett-Packard has taken it upon itself to act responsibly and address this issue through its highly regarded reverse logistics program. Hewlett-Packard has recycled computer and printer hardware since 1987 and is an industry leader in this practice. The company's recycling service is available today in more than 40 countries, regions, and territories. By 2010, Hewlett-Packard will have recycled over 1 billion pounds of used products to be refurbished for resale or donation or for recovery of materials.

The recycling effort at Hewlett-Packard is also part of the company's Design for Supply Chain program. Among other initiatives in this program, emphasis is placed on product and packaging changes to reduce reverse supply chain and environmental costs. For example, design changes have increased the recycling of its popular ink-jet supplies by 25 percent.

Making Responsible Decisions boxes focus on social responsibility, sustainability, and ethics. These boxes provide exciting, current examples of how companies approach these subjects in their marketing strategy.

Going Online
Are You an Experiencer? An Achiever?: Identifying Your VALS Profile

The VALS™ system run by SRI Consulting Business Intelligence has identified eight unique consumer segments based on a person's primary motivation and resources. The text provides a brief description of each segment.

Do you wish to know your VALS profile? If you do, simply respond to the questions on the VALS survey at www.sric-bi.com/vals. Simply click "VALS Survey." In addition to obtaining your profile in real time, you can examine the characteristics of your and other profiles in greater detail.

Going Online exercises are integrated in the text and ask students to go online and think critically about a specific company's use of the Internet, helping students apply knowledge of key chapter concepts, terms, and topics, as well as evaluate the success or failure of the company's efforts.

building your marketing plan

To do a consumer analysis for the product—the good, service, or idea—in your marketing plan:
1 Identify the consumers who are most likely to buy your product—the primary target market—in terms of (a) their demographic characteristics and (b) any other kind of characteristics you believe are important.
2 Describe (a) the main points of difference of your product for this group and (b) what problem they help

solve for the consumer, in terms of the first stage in the consumer purchase decision process in Figure 5–1.
3 Identify the one or two key influences for each of the four outside boxes in Figure 5–4: (a) marketing mix, (b) psychological, (c) sociocultural, and (d) situational influences.

This consumer analysis will provide the foundation for the marketing mix actions you develop later in your plan.

Building Your Marketing Plan is an end of chapter feature that requires students to go through the practical application of creating their own marketing plan.

INSTRUCTOR RESOURCES

Element	Online Learning Center www.mhhe.com/kerin	IPCD	Other
Instructor's Manual	x	x	
New! Visually Enhanced Test Bank		x	
PowerPoint Presentation	x (basic)	x (enhanced)	
Video Cases			Video DVD
Instructor's Survival Kit (ISK) 0-07-328405-X			Stand-alone kit

- **Instructor's Presentation CD-ROM:**

  The Instructor's Presentation CD-ROM (IPCD) includes a digital version of the Instructor's Resource Manual, PowerPoint slides, and Test Bank. It also contains the EZ Test package.

- **Instructor's Resource Manual:**

  The Instructor's Resource Manual (IRM) to accompany *Marketing*, 9/e is an all-inclusive resource designed to make an instructor's preparation for teaching much easier. The *Instructor's Resource Manual* includes detailed lectures notes, discussions, and a description of all of the individual multimedia assets from which an instructor can construct a custom presentation. Thumbnails in the margin of the IRM help instructors select PowerPoint slides they want to use. The IRM also includes Supplemental Lecture Notes (SLNs) and In-Class Activities (ICAs) that link to sample products in the Instructor's Survival Kit to make marketing come to life in the classroom.

- **Visually Enhanced Test Bank:**

  We offer 5,000 test questions categorized by topic and level of learning (knowledge, comprehension, or application) and correlated to both the Learning Objectives and Bloom's Level of Learning to assist instructors in developing their exams. There are also a number of visually enhanced questions in the test bank that include images and figures from the book itself to ensure student learning and preparation.

- **Test Bank Online**

  A comprehensive bank of test questions is provided within a computerized test bank powered by McGraw-Hill's flexible electronic testing software program EZ Test Online (www.eztestonline.com). EZ Test Online allows you to create paper and online tests or quizzes in this easy-to-use program!

Imagine being able to create and access your test or quiz anywhere, at any time without installing the testing software. Now, with EZ Test Online, instructors can select questions from multiple McGraw-Hill test banks or author their own, and then either print the test for paper distribution or give it online.

Test Creation

- Author/edit questions online using the 14 different question type templates
- Create printed tests or deliver online to get instant scoring and feedback
- Create questions pools to offer multiple versions online—great for practice
- Export your tests for use in WebCT, Blackboard, PageOut and Apple's iQuiz
- Compatible with EZ Test Desktop tests you've already created
- Sharing tests with colleagues, adjuncts, TAs is easy

Online Test Management

- Set availability dates and time limits for your quiz or test
- Control how your test will be presented
- Assign points by question or question type with drop-down menu
- Provide immediate feedback to students or delay until all finish the test
- Create practice tests online to enable student mastery
- Your roster can be uploaded to enable student self-registration

Online Scoring and Reporting

- Automated scoring for most of EZ Test's numerous question types
- Allows manual scoring for essay and other open response questions
- Manual re-scoring and feedback is also available
- EZ Test's grade book is designed to easily export to your grade book
- View basic statistical reports

Support and Help

- User's Guide and built-in page specific help
- Flash tutorials for getting started on the support site
- Support Website: www.mhhe.com/eztest
- Product specialist available at 1-800-331-5094
- Online Training: http://auth.mhhe.com/mpss/workshops/

• WebCT/Blackboard/eCollege/TopClass

You can use *Marketing*, 9/e online material with any online platform-including Blackboard, WebCT, eCollege, TopClass-to expand the reach of your course and open up distance learning options.

• PowerPoint Presentation:

The PowerPoint presentation features slides that can be used and personalized by instructors to help present concepts to students efficiently. The Online Learning Center contains a basic version of the media-enhanced PowerPoint presentation that can be found on the IPCD. The media-enhanced version has video and commercials embedded in the presentation and makes for an engaging and interested classroom lecture.

- **New and Revised Video Cases:**

  A unique series of 22 contemporary marketing video cases is available on DVD. Each video case corresponds with chapter-specific topics and the end-of-chapter case in the text. The video cases feature a variety of organizations and provide balanced coverage of services, consumer products, small businesses, Fortune 500 firms, and business-to-business examples. The ninth edition package includes new videos about Xerox, Starbury, Best Buy, Geek Squad, General Mills Warm Delights, Washburn Guitars, 3M Post-it™ Flag Highlighters, BP (formerly British Petroleum), and Las Vegas.

- **Instructor's Survival Kit (ISK):**

  The Instructor's Survival Kit contains product samples for use in the classroom to illustrate marketing concepts and encourage student involvement and learning, often with teams working on a task for 5 to 15 minutes in class. Today's students are more likely to learn and be motivated by active participative experiences than by classic classroom lecture and discussion. *Marketing*, 9/e utilizes product samples from both large and small firms that will interest today's students. When appropriate, sample print and T.V. ads are included among our PowerPoint presentations.

STUDENT RESOURCES

Element	Online Learning Center www.mhhe.com/kerin	Other
Study Guide 0-07-328410-6		Stand-alone print resource
Student Edition with Video DVD 0-07-723940-7		Optional package bundled with text
iPod Content	x	
Chapter Quizzes	x	

- **Study Guide:**

  The Study Guide enables students to learn and apply marketing principles instead of simply memorizing facts for an examination. The Study Guide includes chapter outlines for student note-taking, sample tests, critical thinking questions, and flash cards.

- **Student Editions with Video DVD:**

  This package includes *Marketing*, 9/e and the DVD containing Video Cases. Requiring this package encourages student learning in an interactive multimedia experience.

- **iPod Content:**

  This additional student supplement can be purchased on the OLC. The 9th edition of *Marketing* is the first to include the multimedia addition of iPod content. With narrated PowerPoint slides and case videos, students can be studying and learning while they are on the go with their MP3 player.

- **Student Online Learning Center (OLC):**

  This rich book-specific Online Learning Center website contains multiple choice review quizzes, chapter objectives, key term flashcards, and chapter in review. This is also the location for purchasing access to the iPod content.

Acknowledgments

To ensure continuous improvement of our textbook and supplements we have utilized an extensive review and development process for each of our past editions. Building on that history, the *Marketing,* ninth edition development process included several phases of evaluation and a variety of stakeholder audiences (e.g., students, instructors, etc.).

- In the first phase of the review process the authors visited instructors and students at a variety of campuses to discuss the use and effectiveness of the text and supplements.

- The second phase of the review process asked users and non-users to suggest improvements to the text and supplements through a detailed review of each component while used in the classroom.

- In the third phase a group of experienced marketing instructors provided feedback through user and nonuser symposia. These sessions provided feedback about the text, supplements, and online resources.

- Finally, a group of instructors provided evaluations of revised materials and tested new technologies related to the ninth edition supplements

Reviewers who were vital in the changes that were made to this edition include:

Ismet Anitsal
Tennessee Tech University

David J. Burns
Xavier University

Larry Carter
Old Dominion University

Melissa Clark
University of North Alabama

Paul Clark
Indiana State University-Terre Haute

Brent Cunningham
Jacksonville State University

Bob Dahlstrom
University of Kentucky

Neel Das
Appalachian State University

Joseph Defilippe
Suffolk Community College-Brentwood

Irene J. Dickey
University of Dayton

Elizabeth R. Flynn
Florida State University-Tallahassee

Judy Foxman
Southern Methodist University

Jennifer Friestad
Anoka-Ramsey Community College

Stephen Garrott
Troy University-Ecampus

Rajesh Iyer
Valdosta State University

David Jamison
South Carolina State University

Wesley Johnston
Georgia State University

Janice Karlen
LaGuardia Community College

Rajiv Kashyap
William Patterson University

Anand Kumar
University of South Florida

Jane Lang
East Carolina University

J. Ford Laumer
Auburn University

Marilyn Lavin
University of Wisconsin-Whitewater

Eldon L. Little
Indiana University, Southeast

James G. Lollar
Radford University

Richard Lutz
University of Florida

Carolyn Massiah
University of Central Florida

Michael Mayo
Kent State University

Kristy McManus
University of Tennessee at Chattanooga

Samuel E. McNeely
Murray State University

Herbert A. Miller
University of Texas-Austin

Chip E. Miller
Drake University

Steven Moff
Pennsylvania College of Technology

James A. Muncy
Valdosta State University

David Terry Paul
Ohio State

Renee Pfeifer-Luckett
University of Wisconsin-Whitewater

Priyali Rajagopal
Southern Methodist University

Rosemary Ramsey
Wright State University-Dayton

Linda Rochford
University of Minnesota

Tom Rossi
Broome Community College

Vicki D. Rostedt
University of Akron

Lisa M. Sciulli
Indiana University of Pennsylvania

Susan Sieloff
Northeastern University

Kimberly D. Smith
County College of Morris

Sandra Smith
University of Minnesota

Tom H. Stevenson
University of North Carolina at Charlotte

Rick Sweeney
University of Cincinnati

Ruth A. Taylor
Texas State University

Bronis J. Verhage
Georgia State University

Michelle Wetherbee
Piedmont College

Poh-Lin Yeoh
Bentley College

Sandra Young
University of Denver

Gail M. Zank
Texas State University-San Marcos

The preceding section demonstrates the amount of feedback and developmental input that went into this project, and we are deeply grateful to the numerous people who have shared their ideas with us. Reviewing a book or supplement takes an incredible amount of energy and attention. We are glad so many of our colleagues took the time to do it. Their comments have inspired us to do our best. Reviewers who contributed to the first eight editions of this book include:

James Lollar
Paul Londrigan
Lynn Loudenback
Ann Lucht
Mike Luckett
Robert Luke
Michael R. Luthy
Richard J. Lutz
Marton L. Macchiete
Rhonda Mack
Patricia Manninen
Kenneth Maricle
Tom Marshall
Elena Martinez
Tamara Masters
Charla Mathwick
James McAlexander
Peter J. McClure
Phyllis McGinnis
Jim McHugh
Gary F. McKinnon
Ed McLaughlin
Jo Ann McManamy
Bob McMillen
Lee Meadow
James Meszaros
George Miaoulis
Soon Hong Min
Ronald Michaels
Stephen W. Miller
William G. Mitchell
Kim Montney
Melissa Moore
Linda Morable
Fred Morgan
Gordon Mosley
William Motz
Donald F. Mulvihill
Jeanne Munger
Linda Munilla
Bill Murphy
Janet Murray
Keith Murray
Joseph Myslivec
Sunder Narayanan
Bob Newberry
Donald G. Norris

Carl Obermiller
Dave Olson
James Olver
Ben Oumlil
Notis Pagiavlas
Allan Palmer
Dennis Pappas
June E. Parr
Philip Parron
Richard Penn
John Penrose
William Pertula
Michael Peters
Susan Peterson
William S. Piper
Stephen Pirog
Gary Poorman
Vonda Powell
Joe Puzi
Edna Ragins
Daniel Rajaratnam
James P. Rakowski
Barbara Ribbens
Cathie Rich-Duval
Joe Ricks
Heikki Rinne
William Rodgers
Jean Romeo
Teri Root
Vicki Rostedt
Heidi Rottier
Larry Rottmeyer
Robert W. Ruekert
Maria Sanella
Charles Schewe
Starr F. Schlobohm
Roberta Schultz
Stan Scott
Eberhard Seheuling
Harold S. Sekiguchi
Doris M. Shaw
Eric Shaw
Ken Shaw
Dan Sherrel
Bob E. Smiley
Allen Smith
Ruth Ann Smith

Norman Smothers
James V. Spiers
Craig Stacey
Miriam B. Stamps
Joe Stasio
Tom Stevenson
Kathleen Stuenkel
Scott Swan
Michael Swenson
Robert Swerdlow
Vincent P. Taiani
Clint Tankersley
Ruth Taylor
Andrew Thacker
Tom Thompson
Dan Toy
Fred Trawick
Thomas L. Trittipo
Sue Umashankar
Ottilia Voegtli
Jeff von Freymann
Gerald Waddle
Randall E. Wade
Blaise Waguespack, Jr.
Harlan Wallingford
Mark Weber
Don Weinrauch
Robert S. Welsh
Ron Weston
Sheila Wexler
Max White
James Wilkins
Erin Wilkinson
Janice Williams
Kaylene Williams
Robert Williams
Jerry W. Wilson
Joseph Wisenblit
Robert Witherspoon
Van R. Wood
Wendy Wood
Lauren Wright
William R. Wynd
Mark Young
Leon Zurawicki

Thanks are also due to many faculty members who contributed to the text chapters and cases. They include: Linda Rochford of the University of Minnesota-Duluth; Kevin Upton of the University of Minnesota-Twin Cities; Nancy Nentl of Metropolitan State University; David Brennan of St. Thomas University; and Leigh McAlister of the University of Texas at Austin. Michael Vessey provided cases, research assistance, many special images, and led our efforts on the Instructor's Manual, In-Class Activities, and Instructor's Survival Kit. Rick Armstrong of Armstrong Photography,

Nick Kaufman and Michelle Morgan of NKP Media, Bruce McLean of World Class Communication Technologies, Paul Fagan of Fagan Productions, Dan Hundley and George Heck of Token Media, Martin Walter of White Room Digital, Scott Bolin of Bolin Marketing, and Dan Stephenson of the Philadelphis Phillies produced the videos. William Carner of Columbia College provided the study guide. Carol Johnson of the University of Denver was responsible for the revision of the text bank.

Many businesspeople also provided substantial assistance by making available information that appears in the text, videos, and supplements—much of it for the first time in college materials. Thanks are due to David Ford, Don Rylander, Lauretta Logan and Chris Quam of Ford Consulting Group; Mark Rehborg of Tony's Pizza, Ann Hand and Kathy Seegebrecht of BP; Kimberly Mosford and Ryan Schroeder of Business Incentives; Vivian Callaway, Sandy Proctor, and Anna Stoesz of General Mills; David Windorski of 3M; Nicholas Skally, Jeremy Stonier, and Joe Olivas of Rollerblade; Stan Jacot of ConAgra Snack Foods; Sandra Smith of Smith Communications; Erin Patton of the MasterMind Group, LLC; Kim Nagele of JCPenney, Inc.; Charles Besio of the Sewell Automotive Group, Inc.; and Kate Hodebeck of Cadbury Schweppes America's Beverages, Inc.; Beverly Roberts of U.S. Census Bureau; Jennifer Gebert of Ghirardelli Chocolate Company; Michael Kuhl of 3M Sports and Leisure; Barbara Davis of Ken Davis Products, Inc.; Stan Jacot of ConAgra Snack Foods; Kerry Barnett of Valassis Communications; and Leslie Herman and Jeff Gerst of Bolin Marketing working with Carma Laboratories (Carmex). We also acknowledge the special help of a team that worked with us on the Fallon Worldwide video case: Fred Senn, Bruce Blister, Kevin Flat, Ginny Grossman, Kim Knutson, Julie Smith, Erin Taut, and Rob White.

Staff support from the Southern Methodist University, the University of Denver, and the University of Minnesota was essential. We gratefully acknowledge the help of Wanda Hanson, Jeanne Milazzo, Gloria Valdez and Dedre Henderson for their many contributions.

Checking countless details related to layout, graphics, clear writing, and last-minute changes to ensure timely examples is essential for a sound and accurate textbook. This also involves coordinating activities of authors, designers, editors, compositors, and production specialists. Christine Vaughan of McGraw-Hill/Irwin's production staff and editorial consultant Gina Huck Siegert of Imaginative Solutions, Inc., provided the necessary oversight and hand-holding for us, while retaining a refreshing sense of humor, often under tight deadlines. Thank you again.

Finally, we acknowledge the professional efforts of the McGraw-Hill/Irwin staff. Completion of our book and its many supplements required the attention and commitment of many editorial, production, marketing, and research personnel. Our Burr Ridge-based team included Paul Ducham, Doug Hughes, Colleen Honan, Kelly Pekelder, Carol Bielski, Matthew Baldwin, Jeremy Cheshareck, Sue Lombardi, Lynn Bluhm, Krista Bettino, Nicky Miller, and many others. In addition we relied on Michael Hruby for constant attention regarding photo elements of the text. Handling the countless details of our text, supplement, and support technologies has become an incredibly complex challenge. We thank all these people for their efforts!

Roger A. Kerin
Steven W. Hartley
William Rudelius

BRIEF CONTENTS

DETAILED CONTENTS

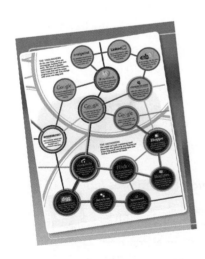

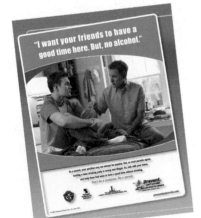

Part 2   Understanding Buyers and Markets

Part 3   Targeting Marketing Opportunities

Part 4   Satisfying Marketing Opportunities

18 INTEGRATED MARKETING COMMUNICATIONS AND DIRECT MARKETING   463

19 ADVERTISING, SALES PROMOTION, AND PUBLIC RELATIONS   489

20 PERSONAL SELLING AND SALES MANAGEMENT 521

Part 5

Managing the Marketing Process

MARKETING

1

Creating Customer Relationships and Value through Marketing

LEARNING OBJECTIVES

After reading this chapter you should be able to:

LO1 Define marketing and identify the requirements for marketing to occur.

LO2 Explain how marketing discovers and satisfies consumer needs.

LO3 Distinguish between marketing mix elements and environmental forces.

LO4 Explain how organizations build strong customer relationships and customer value through marketing.

LO5 Describe how today's customer relationship era differs from prior eras oriented to production and selling.

LO6 Explain how marketing creates utilities for consumers.

HOW DO COLLEGE STUDENTS STUDY? A NEW PRODUCT CHALLENGE FOR 3M!

How does today's college student read books, take notes, prepare for exams—actually study?

Answering that question was only part of the curious challenge 3M inventor David Windorski and others faced awhile back. True, he needed useful details on how college students do their day-to-day studying, including preparing for exams. But he also wanted to identify ways to convert his knowledge about student study habits into a product that would improve their studying and that could use 3M's technology and be manufactured and marketed by 3M.

Sound simple? Perhaps! But David Windorski spent several years of his life moving his idea of a new product into an actual commercial version.[1]

After a quick look at how the original Post-it® Notes came to be, let's follow Windorski's winding path through the marketing research, technical research and development, manufacturing, and marketing that resulted in his innovative Post-it® brand products.

The Legend: The Product Nobody Seemed to Want

The world leader in adhesive technology, 3M manufactures and markets hundreds of adhesive products from Scotch® brand Magic™ Tape to Nexcare™ Tattoo™ Waterproof Bandages for kids. In a surprising, oft-told success story, more than 30 years ago, 3M inventor, Spencer Silver discovered a curious adhesive in his laboratory. It was an adhesive that would stick temporarily with finger pressure, unstick with a simple tug without leaving a mark, and restick when wanted.

Several years later, Silver's colleague Art Fry put the "restickable" adhesive to work. He applied it to paper notes he used to mark hymns while singing with his church choir. But 3M still needed to figure out:

1. Who might use the restickable notes.

2. How, when, and where they might be used.

Finally, 3M got the idea to mail some of these notes to executive assistants of chief executive officers of the 500 largest corporations in the United States to see if they wanted and could use them. The resounding "Yes, we love them" answers paved the way for 3M's Post-it® Notes—the product we see today.

 +  =

3M's Post-it® Notes
or Post-it® Flags

Felt Tip Highlighters

3M product that will
combine Post-it® Notes
or Post-it® Flags and
highlighters

For the creative way a
student project helped
lead to a new product for
college students using 3M's
technology, see the text.

David Windorski, 3M inventor,
holds some of his early
clay models that combined
Post-it® brand products and
highlighters.

3M Company
www.mmm.com

Discovering Student Studying Needs

Fast-forward to David Windorski's challenge. As an inventor of Post-it® brand products, Windorski was seeking ways to design new products for college students. He had some creative "thinking time" under 3M's "15% Rule" in which inventors can use up to 15 percent of their time to do initially unfunded research that might lead to marketable 3M products. Working with a team of four college students, Windorski and the team observed and questioned dozens of students about how they studied—how they used their textbooks, how they wrote and used their lecture notes, how they did research and wrote papers, how they reviewed for exams, and so on.

Windorski describes what college students were telling him about their studying habits that might lead to a new Post-it® product:

> The basic idea for the product comes from students' studying behavior. What they often do is highlight a page in their book or their notes and then they can't find the important page after they highlighted it. So it's kind of natural behavior to highlight a passage and then mark the page with a Post-it® Note or Post-it® Flag of some kind. So it's reasonable to put Post-it® products together with a highlighter to have two functions in one.

Satisfying Student Studying Needs

How do you enhance a highlighter to be useful for students in their studying? This is exactly the question David Windorski had to solve with his inventive mind.

Designing a marketable product for students was not done overnight. It took Windorski a few years of creativity, hard work, and attention to countless details. He started by trying to attach a pad of small Post-it® Flags to the top of a highlighter. This design combined the two products but had a giant drawback: The combination was awkward and the Post-it® Flags would probably tear off when bouncing around in students' backpacks.

So Windorski went back to his drawing board—or more literally, to wood blocks and modeling clay. Some of his early models appear in the photo. A wooden mock-up—a nonworking model—showed Windorski how the 2-in-1 product would feel. Then he modeled the product in clay, which featured two revolutionary ideas: (1) using *small* Post-it® Flags rather than the larger Post-it® Notes and (2) putting the Post-it® Flags *inside* the barrel of the highlighter.

4

Besides the college student segment, can 3M use its technology to reach the office segment? Marketing programs for these two segments appear later in the chapter.

Was this the finished product? Not at all! Windorski's search for the 2-in-1 highlighter plus Post-it® Flags encountered many more breakthroughs and dead ends before he had a product that students could actually use in studying. And he had a lot more work to produce a few hundred prototypes that students could actually try and tell him about the product.

Windorski had taken some giant steps in trying not only to discover students' needs for his product but also to satisfy those needs for a practical, useful product. He was also starting to wonder if his ideas might be extended to apply to a possible product for office workers. Later in the chapter we'll see what products resulted from his innovative thinking and 3M's initial marketing plan that launched his products into the hands of students and other consumers.

WHAT IS MARKETING?

Here's some good news: In many respects you are a marketing expert already because you do many marketing activities every day. For example, would you sell more high-definition 42-inch plasma Panasonic TVs for $3,999 or $999?[2] You answered $999, right? And because of your good experiences with your past Panasonic TVs, you'd seriously consider the plasma Panasonic TV. Or knowing prices for plasma TVs are falling rapidly, you might wait six months to buy.

Your experience in shopping for products already gives you great insights into the world of marketing. As a consumer, you've been involved in thousands of marketing decisions—but mainly on the buying, not the selling, side. To test your expertise, try the "marketing expert" questions in Figure 1–1. You'll find the answers in the next few pages.

The bad news is, good marketing isn't always easy. In 3M's case, it's easy to talk about finding new applications for 3M's technologies but not so simple to do. One of 3M's strategies is to market Post-it® brand products designed for the special needs of different groups, or segments, of users. What special features might 3M build into a Post-it® product for (1) the college student segment and (2) the office worker segment? Give some thought to this. We'll analyze 3M's strategies for these two segments later in the chapter.

FIGURE 1–1

The see-if-you're-really-a-marketing-expert test

Answer the questions below. The correct answers are given later in the chapter.

1. True or false. You can now buy a robotic floor washer that scrubs your hard-surface floor even when you're not there and better than you can mop it.
2. Among the 91 percent of college seniors owning credit cards, what percent has four or more? (*a*) 5%, (*b*) 20%, (*c*) 35%, (*d*) over 50%.
3. True or false. The 60-year lifetime value of a loyal Kleenex customer is $994.
4. To be socially responsible, 3M puts what recycled material into its very successful ScotchBrite® Never Rust™ Soap Pads? (*a*) aluminum cans, (*b*) steel-belted tires, (*c*) plastic bottles, (*d*) computer screens.

3M's Technology, Marketing, and You

What strategy did the Post-it® brand marketing team use to launch its new products? By the end of this chapter, you will know the answer.

One key to how well 3M succeeds lies in the subject of this book: marketing. In this chapter and in the rest of the book we'll introduce you to many of the people, organizations, ideas, and activities in marketing that have spawned the products and services that have been towering successes, shattering failures, or something in between.

Marketing and Your Career

Marketing affects all individuals, all organizations, all industries, and all countries. This book seeks to teach you marketing concepts, often by having you actually "do marketing"—by putting you in the shoes of a marketing manager facing actual marketing opportunities and problems. The book also shows marketing's many applications and how it affects our lives. This knowledge should make you a better consumer, help you in your career, and enable you to be a more informed citizen.

In this chapter and those that follow, you will feel the excitement of marketing. You will be introduced to the dynamic changes that will affect all of us in the future. You will also meet many men and women whose marketing creativity sometimes achieved brilliant, extraordinary results. And who knows? Somewhere in these pages you may find a career. Career planning ideas related to marketing appear in Appendix C of this book.

Perhaps your future may involve doing sales and marketing for a large organization. Working for a well-known company—Dell, General Electric, Target, eBay—can be personally satisfying and financially rewarding, and you may gain special respect from your friends.

But there's a downside. The job security that existed three decades ago in these kinds of organizations is largely gone because of increasing global competition, changing technology, huge distribution efficiencies, and other factors.

Small businesses also offer marketing careers. Small businesses are the source of the majority of new U.S. jobs. So you might become your own boss by being an entrepreneur and starting your own business. American entrepreneurship is known throughout the world because of people like Meg Whitman of eBay and Steve Jobs of Apple who took great risks but converted innovative ideas into thriving, successful businesses that provide thousands of jobs today.

The Marketing Matters box describes the revolutionary impact three entrepreneurs in their 20s have had on the Internet—and perhaps on how you spend your free time.[3] Not every start-up business achieves their spectacular success. In fact, more than half of new businesses fail within five years of their launch.

Does small business sound like fun? We'll visit many small businesses and their marketing challenges later in the book to introduce you to both the excitement and dangers of being your own small business boss.

What wild idea are these three 20-somethings hatching in their garage? For the idea, who they are, and the spectacular new business they launched, see the Marketing Matters box.

Marketing: Delivering Benefits to the Organization, Its Stakeholders, and Society

The American Marketing Association represents marketing professionals. Combining its 2004 and 2007 definitions, "**marketing** is the activity for creating, communicating, delivering and exchanging offerings that benefit the organization, its stakeholders and society at large."[4]

Marketing Matters > > > > entrepreneurship

Payoff for the Joys (!) and Sleepless Nights (?) of Starting Your Own Small Business: YouTube!!!!

What happens when you drop Mentos into a Diet Coke? Don't know the answer?

Then you're not a serious YouTube viewer! If you need an answer, ask the student sitting next to you in class. And don't try it at home.

In one 12-month period, a single website—YouTube.com—revolutionized the Internet's world of videos and was named *Time* magazine's Invention of the Year for 2006. The number of new videos uploaded every day is exploding—about 70,000 a day in January 2007. In that month viewers watched 100 million videos a day, up from 10 million a day a year earlier.

The minds behind YouTube are three 20-somethings: Steve Chen, Chad Hurley, and Jawed Karim. Even the three entrepreneurs are astounded at their success. *Time* says the reason for YouTube's success is its rare combination of being both "edgy and easy" for users.

The three men met at PayPal, now the Internet's leading online payment service. The three moved out and worked together on a new concept—a website where anyone could upload content that others could view. That was radical because until then only those who owned the website would provide the content.

Google bought YouTube in October 2006 for $1.65 billion, only 21 months after its founding. Hurley (standing) and Chen (sitting) in the left photo are now Google employees addressing issues such as making YouTube.com profitable through its advertising and avoiding potential lawsuits resulting from uploaded content that is copyrighted. Karim left the company and is doing graduate work in computer science at Stan-

ford University (in the right photo).

Where will this end? Go to YouTube.com and see for yourself!

Many people incorrectly believe that marketing is the same thing as advertising or personal selling; this definition shows marketing to be a far broader activity. It stresses the importance of delivering genuine benefits in the offerings of goods, services, and ideas marketed to customers. Also, note that the organization doing the marketing, the stakeholders affected (such as customers, employees, suppliers, and shareholders), and society should all benefit.

To serve both buyers and sellers, marketing seeks (1) to discover the needs and wants of prospective customers and (2) to satisfy them. These prospective customers include both individuals, buying for themselves and their households, and organizations that buy for their own use (such as manufacturers) or for resale (such as wholesalers and retailers). The key to achieving these two objectives is the idea of **exchange**, which is the trade of things of value between buyer and seller so that each is better off after the trade.

The Diverse Factors Influencing Marketing Activities

Although an organization's marketing activity focuses on assessing and satisfying consumer needs, countless other people, groups, and forces interact to shape the nature of its activities (Figure 1–2 on the next page). Foremost is the organization

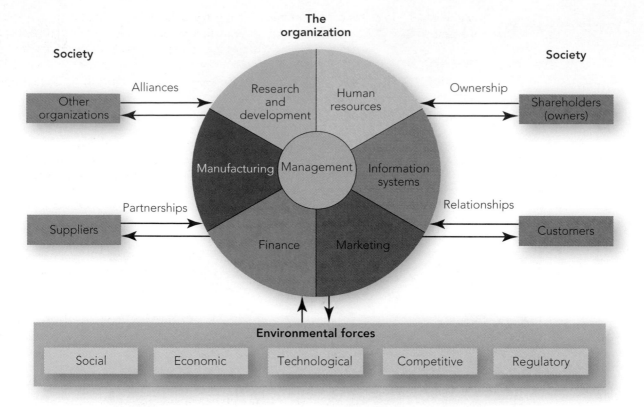

FIGURE 1–2

A marketing department relates to many people, organizations, and forces. Note that the marketing department both *shapes* and *is shaped by* its relationship with these external groups.

itself, whose mission and objectives determine what business it is in and what goals it seeks. Within the organization, management is responsible for establishing these goals. The marketing department works closely with a network of other departments and employees to help provide the customer-satisfying products required for the organization to survive and prosper.

Figure 1–2 also shows the key people, groups, and forces outside the organization that influence marketing activities. The marketing department is responsible for facilitating relationships, partnerships, and alliances with the organization's customers, its shareholders (or often representatives of groups served by a non-profit organization), its suppliers, and other organizations. Environmental forces such as social, economic, technological, competitive, and regulatory factors also shape an organization's marketing activities. Finally, an organization's marketing decisions are affected by and, in turn, often have an important impact on society as a whole.

The organization must strike a balance among the sometimes differing interests of these individuals and groups. For example, it is not possible to simultaneously provide the lowest-priced and highest-quality products to customers and pay the highest prices to suppliers, highest wages to employees, and maximum dividends to shareholders.

Requirements for Marketing to Occur

For marketing to occur, at least four factors are required: (1) two or more parties (individuals or organizations) with unsatisfied needs, (2) a desire and ability on their part to be satisfied, (3) a way for the parties to communicate, and (4) something to exchange.

Two or More Parties with Unsatisfied Needs Suppose you've developed an unmet need—a desire for information about how computer and telecommunications are interacting to reshape the workplace—but you didn't yet know that *ComputerWorld* magazine existed. Also unknown to you was that several copies of *ComputerWorld* were sitting on the magazine rack at your nearest bookstore, waiting to be purchased. This is an example of two parties with unmet needs: you, with a need for technology-related information, and your bookstore owner, needing someone to buy a copy of *ComputerWorld*.

Desire and Ability to Satisfy These Needs   Both you and the bookstore owner want to satisfy these unmet needs. Furthermore, you have the money to buy the item and the time to get to the bookstore. The store's owner has not only the desire to sell *ComputerWorld* but also the ability to do so since it's stocked on the shelves.

A Way for the Parties to Communicate   The marketing transaction of buying a copy of *ComputerWorld* will never occur unless you know the product exists and its location. Similarly, the store owner won't stock the magazine unless there's a market of potential buyers nearby. When you receive a free sample in the mail or see the magazine on display in the bookstore, this communications barrier between you (the buyer) and your bookstore (the seller) is overcome.

Something to Exchange   Marketing occurs when the transaction takes place and both the buyer and seller exchange something of value. In this case, you exchange your money for the bookstore's magazine. Both you and the bookstore have gained something and also given up something, but you are both better off because you have each satisfied your unmet needs. You have the opportunity to read *ComputerWorld*, but you gave up some money; the store gave up the magazine but received money, which enables it to remain in business. This exchange process and, of course, the ethical and legal foundations of exchange are central to marketing.[5]

---

learning review

1. What is marketing?

2. Marketing focuses on _____ and _____ consumer needs.

3. What four factors are needed for marketing to occur?

HOW MARKETING DISCOVERS AND SATISFIES CONSUMER NEEDS

The importance of discovering and satisfying consumer needs is so critical to understanding marketing that we look at each of these two steps in detail next.

Discovering Consumer Needs

The first objective in marketing is discovering the needs of prospective consumers. This is far more difficult than it sounds.

Discovering consumer needs may look easy, but when you get down to the specifics of developing new products, problems crop up. For one thing, consumers may not always know or be able to describe what they need and want. When Apple built its first Apple II personal computer and started a new industry, consumers didn't really know what the benefits would be. So they had to be educated and to learn how to use personal computers. Also, Bell, a U.S. bicycle helmet maker, has listened to its customers, collected hundreds of their ideas, and put several into its new products.[6] This is where effective marketing research, the topic of Chapter 8, can help.

For these four products, identify (1) what benefits the product provides buyers and (2) what "showstoppers" might kill the product in the marketplace. Answers are discussed in the text.

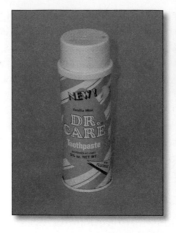

Vanilla-mint-flavored toothpaste in an aerosol container

Meat-and-cheese microwavable sandwiches

Robotic floor washer

Reduced-carbohydrate cola with some sugar

The Challenge: Meeting Consumer Needs with New Products

New-product experts generally estimate that up to 94 percent of the more than 33,000 new consumable products (food, beverage, health, beauty, and other household and pet products) introduced in the United States annually "don't succeed in the long run."[7] Robert M. McMath, who has studied more than 70,000 of these new-product launches, has two key suggestions: (1) focus on what the customer benefit is, and (2) learn from the past.[8]

The solution to preventing such product failures seems embarrassingly obvious. First, find out what consumers need and want. Second, produce what they need and want, and don't produce what they don't need and want. This is far more difficult than it sounds. The four products shown above illustrate just how hard it is to achieve new-product success, a topic covered in more detail in Chapter 10.

Without reading further, think about the potential benefits to customers and possible "showstoppers"—factors that might doom the product—for each of the four products pictured. Some of the products may come out of your past, and others may be on your horizon. Here's a quick analysis of the four products, sometimes with comments adapted from McMath:

- *Dr. Care toothpaste.* As a result of extensive research, Dr. Care family toothpaste in its aerosol container was introduced more than two decades ago. The vanilla-mint-flavored product's benefits were advertised as being easy to use and sanitary. Pretend for a minute that you are five years old and left alone in the bathroom to brush your teeth using your Dr. Care toothpaste. Hmm! Apparently, surprised parents were not enthusiastic about the bathroom wall paintings by their future Rembrandts—a showstopper that doomed this creative product.[9]
- *Hot Pockets.* Introduced in 1983, these convenient meat-and-cheese microwavable sandwiches are a favorite brand among students. More than 20 varieties have been introduced, from Hot Pockets Pizza Snacks to Hot Pockets Subs. A none-too-serious potential showstopper: Excessive ice crystals can form on the product due to variations in freezer temperatures; if this happens and the sandwich is thawed before eaten, it may not taste as good.[10]
- *IRobot's Scooba™ robotic floor washer.* Introduced during the 2005 holiday season, the Scooba robotic floor washer vacuums, washes, scrubs, and dries a hard-surface floor in a single operation (question 1, Figure 1–1). At $259.99 the Scooba does a better job than a mop, which just spreads the dirt around according to reviews. The thousands sold seem to refute the potential showstopper that Scooba can't get into corners.[11]
- *Coca-Cola's C2.* In summer 2003, Coca-Cola spent $50 million to launch C2, a reduced-carb cola that still contained some sugar to add taste. The company's biggest new product since Diet Coke two decades earlier, C2 was targeted to 20- to 40-year-olds wanting some sugar in their cola while also watching the calories. C2 was sometimes priced 60 percent higher at retail than Coke, a devastating concern to buyers. But the big showstopper: Many cola drinkers were disappointed in C2's taste, complaining it was flat or had an unpleasant aftertaste.[12]

Firms spend billions of dollars annually on marketing and technical research that significantly reduces, but doesn't eliminate, new-product failure. So meeting the changing needs of consumers is a continuing challenge for firms around the world.

Consumer Needs and Consumer Wants   Should marketing try to satisfy consumer needs or consumer wants? The answer is both. Heated debates rage over this question, fueled by the definitions of needs and wants and the amount of freedom given to prospective customers to make their own buying decisions.

A *need* occurs when a person feels deprived of basic necessities such as food, clothing, and shelter. A *want* is a need that is shaped by a person's knowledge, culture, and personality. So if you feel hungry, you have developed a basic need and desire to eat something. Let's say you then want to eat an apple or a candy bar because, based on your past experience and personality, you know these will satisfy your hunger need. Effective marketing, in the form of creating an awareness of good products at convenient locations, can clearly shape a person's wants.

Does marketing persuade people to buy the "wrong" things—say, a candy bar rather than an apple to satisfy hunger pangs—or too many things—such as college students who have too many credit cards or use them unwisely. Of increasing concern, as described in the Making Responsible Decisions box on the next page is whether college students are overwhelmed with credit card debt.[13] Among college seniors owning credit cards, over half (question 2, Figure 1–1) have four or more with an average balance over $2,800.

Certainly, marketing tries to influence what we buy. A question then arises: At what point do we want government and society to step in to protect consumers?

Student Credit Cards—What Is the Real Price?

Thousands of college students across the United States are drowning in credit card debt.

In 2005, 91 percent of college seniors had at least one credit card, and more than half had four or more credit cards. These seniors carried an average balance of $2,864. About one-fourth used credit cards to pay tuition, often to get extra airline frequent-flyer miles.

The complete picture is even more bleak: Only one in five college students pays off the credit card balance each month. Often the average annual interest rate companies charge is 18 percent, far higher than a student with a good credit rating would pay for loans at a local bank. And even scarier—the interest rate goes up for a missed monthly payment, a 10 percent increase being common! Let's suppose that you've found a good interest rate and that at graduation your credit card company is charging 13 percent annual interest on your $2,000 balance. Paying this balance off at 2 percent a month will require 18 years and seven months of payments with $1,996.75 in interest—about the amount of the original balance!

The nonfinancial price for students may be even higher. College health services that offer psychological counseling report that many students suffer from depression because of their credit card debt. Other students drop out of college to go to work to clear their credit card debt. And a bad record on paying credit card balances will lead to a poor credit rating, which is essential later when obtaining loans for large purchases such as cars or computers.

Financial experts advise students using credit cards to:

- Pay off the balance monthly—and on time.
- Find a card with a low interest rate, especially when *not* paying off the monthly balance. Compare credit card features you want at www.creditcards.com.
- Make purchases with cash whenever possible because that forces serious thinking that is skipped by bringing out that plastic card.

Also, Nellie Mae, the nation's leading educational lender, provides students with debt-management tools and help at www.nelliemae.com.

What should be done to help students address their credit card debt problems? Require them to take personal finance training? Restrict the number of cards they own? Lower the maximum credit line? Have Congress pass laws to rein in credit card companies? What do you think?

Most consumers would say they want government to protect us from harmful drugs and unsafe cars but not from candy bars and soft drinks. To protect college students, should government restrict their use of credit cards? Such questions have no clear-cut answers, which is why legal and social issues are central to marketing. Because even psychologists and economists still debate the exact meanings of *need* and *want,* we shall use the terms interchangeably throughout the book.

As shown in the left side of Figure 1–3, discovering needs involves looking carefully at prospective customers, whether they are children buying M&Ms candy, college students buying Rollerblade in-line skates, or firms buying Xerox photocopying machines. A principal activity of a firm's marketing department is to scrutinize its consumers to understand what they need and want and the trends and factors that shape them.

What a Market Is   Potential consumers make up a **market**, which is people with both the desire and the ability to buy a specific product. All markets ultimately are people. Even when we say a firm bought a Xerox copier, we mean one or several people in the firm decided to buy it. People who are aware of their unmet needs may have the desire to buy the product, but that alone isn't sufficient. People must also have the ability to buy, such as the authority, time, and money. People may even "buy" an idea that results in an action, such as having their blood pressure checked annually or turning down their thermostat to save energy.

FIGURE 1–3

Marketing seeks first to discover consumer needs through extensive research. It then seeks to satisfy those needs by successfully implementing a marketing program possessing the right combination of the marketing mix—the four Ps.

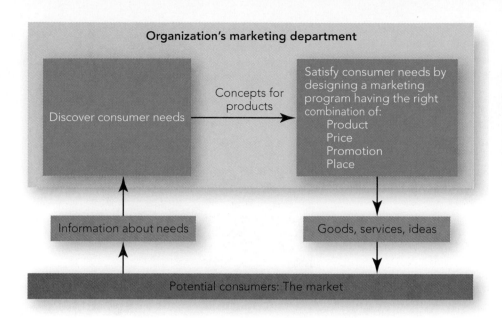

Organization's marketing department

Discover consumer needs

Concepts for products

Satisfy consumer needs by designing a marketing program having the right combination of:
Product
Price
Promotion
Place

Information about needs

Goods, services, ideas

Potential consumers: The market

Satisfying Consumer Needs

Marketing doesn't stop with the discovery of consumer needs. Because the organization obviously can't satisfy all consumer needs, it must concentrate its efforts on certain needs of a specific group of potential consumers. This is the **target market**—one or more specific groups of potential consumers toward which an organization directs its marketing program.

LO3

The Four Ps: Controllable Marketing Mix Factors   Having selected its target market consumers, the firm must take steps to satisfy their needs, as shown in the right side of Figure 1–3. Someone in the organization's marketing department, often the marketing manager, must develop a complete marketing program to reach consumers by using a combination of four tools, often called the four Ps—a useful shorthand reference to them first published by Professor E. Jerome McCarthy:[14]

- *Product.* A good, service, or idea to satisfy the consumer's needs.
- *Price.* What is exchanged for the product.
- *Promotion.* A means of communication between the seller and buyer.
- *Place.* A means of getting the product to the consumer.

We'll define each of the four Ps more carefully later in the book, but for now it's important to remember that they are the elements of the **marketing mix**, the marketing manager's controllable factors—product, price, promotion, and place—that can be used to solve a marketing problem. For example, when a company puts a product on sale, it is changing one element of the marketing mix—namely, the price. The marketing mix elements are called controllable factors because they are under the control of the marketing department in an organization.

The Uncontrollable, Environmental Forces   While marketers can control their marketing mix factors, other factors are mostly beyond their control (see Figure 1–2). These are the **environmental forces** in a marketing decision, the uncontrollable factors involving social, economic, technological, competitive, and regulatory forces. Examples are what consumers themselves want and need, changing technology, the state of the economy in terms of whether it is expanding or

contracting, actions that competitors take, and government restrictions. These five forces may serve as accelerators or brakes on marketing, sometimes expanding an organization's marketing opportunities and other times restricting them. These five environmental forces are covered in Chapter 3.

Traditionally, many marketing executives have treated these environmental forces as rigid, absolute constraints that are entirely outside their influence. However, recent studies and marketing successes have shown that a forward-looking, action-oriented firm can often affect some environmental factors, for example, by achieving technological or competitive breakthroughs.

THE MARKETING PROGRAM: HOW CUSTOMER RELATIONSHIPS ARE BUILT

A firm's marketing program connects the firm to its customers. To clarify this link, we first discuss the critically important concepts of customer value, customer relationships, and relationship marketing, and then illustrate these concepts with 3M's marketing program for its new product for students.

Customer Value and Customer Relationships

Intense competition in today's fast-paced domestic and global markets has caused massive restructuring of many American industries and businesses. American managers are seeking ways to achieve success in this new, more intense level of global competition.

This has prompted many successful U.S. firms to focus on "customer value." That firms gain loyal customers by providing unique value is the essence of successful marketing. What is new, however, is a more careful attempt at understanding how a firm's customers perceive value and then actually creating and delivering that value.[15] For our purposes, **customer value** is the unique combination of benefits received by targeted buyers that includes quality, convenience, on-time delivery, and both before-sale and after-sale service at a specific price. Loyal, satisfied customers are likely to repurchase more and therefore be more profitable.[16] Firms now actually try to place a dollar value on a loyal, satisfied customer. For example, loyal Kleenex customers average 6.7 boxes a year, about $994 over 60 years in today's dollars (question 3, Figure 1–1).[17]

Research suggests that firms cannot succeed by being all things to all people. Instead, firms must find ways to build long-term customer relationships to provide unique value that they alone can deliver to targeted markets. Many successful firms have chosen to deliver outstanding customer value with one of three value strategies: best price, best product, or best service.

Companies such as Wal-Mart, Southwest Airlines, Costco, and Dell Computer have all been successful offering consumers the best price. Other companies such as Starbucks, Nike, Microsoft, and Johnson & Johnson claim to provide the best products on the market. Finally, companies such as Lands' End and Home Depot deliver value by providing exceptional service.

But changing tastes can devastate once-successful marketing strategies. Lands' End, now part of Sears, must focus on strategies to defeat new groups of competitors: boutique specialty stores, catalog retailers, and Internet sellers (see Chapter 2).

Relationship Marketing

Meaningful customer relationships are achieved by a firm identifying creative ways to connect closely to its customers through specific marketing mix actions implemented in its marketing program.

Relationship Marketing: Easy to Understand The hallmark of developing and maintaining effective customer relationships is today called **relationship marketing**, linking the organization to its individual customers, employees, suppliers, and other partners for their mutual long-term benefits. Note that these mutual long-term benefits between the organization and its customers require links to other vital stakeholders, including suppliers, employees, and "partners" such as wholesalers or retailers in a manufacturer's channel of distribution. In many settings, relationship marketing is more effective when there is personal ongoing communication between individuals—both in the selling and buying organizations.[18]

Relationship Marketing: Hard to Do Huge manufacturers find the rigorous standards of relationship marketing difficult to achieve. But today's information technology, along with cutting-edge manufacturing and marketing processes, have led to tailoring goods or services to the tastes of individual customers in high volumes at a relatively low cost. Thus, you can place an Internet order for all the components of a Dell or Apple computer and have it delivered in four or five days—in a configuration tailored to your unique wants.

But other forces are working against these kinds of personal relationships between company and customer. Researchers Fournier, Dobscha, and Mick observe that "the number of one-on-one relationships that companies ask consumers to maintain is untenable,"[19] as evidenced by the dozens of credit card and financing offers a typical consumer gets in a year. A decade ago you might have gone to a small store to buy a book or music record, being helped in your buying decision by a salesclerk or the store owner. With today's Internet purchases, you will probably have difficulty achieving the same personal, tender-loving-care connection that you once had with your own special book or music store.

The Marketing Program

Effective relationship marketing strategies help marketing managers discover what prospective customers need. They must translate this information into some concepts for products the firm might develop (Figure 1–3). These concepts must then be converted into a tangible **marketing program**—a plan that integrates the marketing mix to provide a good, service, or idea to prospective buyers. These prospects then react to the offering favorably (by buying) or unfavorably (by not buying), and the process is repeated. As shown in Figure 1–3, in an effective organization this process is continuous: Consumer needs trigger product concepts that are translated into actual products that stimulate further discovery of consumer needs.

A 3M Product and Marketing Program to Help Students Study

To see some specifics of an actual marketing program, let's return to our earlier example of 3M inventor David Windorski and his search for a way to combine felt-tip highlighters and 3M's Post-it® Notes or Post-it® Flags to help college students in their studying. We will look at how Windorski worked with 3M: (1) to move his invention from ideas and mock-ups to a commercial highlighter product, (2) to add a new product that extends the product line, and (3) to undertake an actual marketing program to introduce the resulting products.

After much research and trials, David Windorski's wood and clay models led to Post-it® Flag Highlighters in many colors.

Moving from Ideas to a Marketable Highlighter Product   After working on 15 or 20 wood and clay models, Windorski concluded he had to build a highlighter product that would dispense Post-it® Flags because the Post-it® Notes were simply too large to put inside the barrel of a highlighter.

   Hundreds of the initial highlighter prototypes with Post-it® Flags inside were produced and given to students—and also office workers—to get their reactions. Two suggestions from users quickly emerged:

- Because of the abuse the product will take in students' pockets and backpacks, the product needs a convenient, reliable cover to protect the Post-it® Flags when it isn't being used.
- Package the highlighter two ways—as a single yellow highlighter and as a three-pack in the favorite student colors of yellow, pink, and blue.

   This customer feedback, while very useful, also caused special technical challenges for Windorski. For example, he soon discovered that to make the highlighter rugged enough for students, he had to design a rotating cover that would enclose the Post-it® Flags but not pinch them when rotated. Also, Windorski's design required that each injection-molded component of the highlighter meet tolerances less than the thickness of a piece of paper. And he worked closely with the final assembly team to ensure the highlighter achieved 3M's tight quality standards.

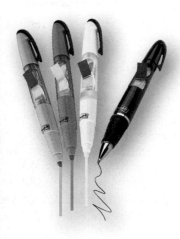

3M's product line of Post-it® Flag Highlighters and Post-it® Flag pens includes variations in color and line widths.

Extending the Product Line   Most of David Windorski's initial design energies under 3M's 15% Rule had gone into his Post-it® Flag Highlighter research and development. But Windorski also considered other related products. Many people in offices need immediate access to Post-it® Flags while writing with pens. Students are a potential market for this product, too, but probably a smaller market segment than office workers.

   Marketing research among North American office workers refined the design and showed the existence of a sizable market for a Post-it® Flag Pen. Even here, however, Windorski encountered surprises: Consumers in one country may prefer blue ink while those in the country next door prefer black ink. The same is true of the width of line the pen produces.

A Marketing Program for the Post-it® Flag Highlighter and Pen
After several years of research, development, and production engineering to make sure the products could be manufactured at reasonable cost, 3M introduced its new products. Figure 1–4 outlines the strategies for each of the four marketing mix elements in 3M's program to market its Post-it® Flag Highlighters and Post-it® Flag Pens. Though similar, we can compare the marketing program for each of the two products:

MARKETING MIX ELEMENT	COLLEGE STUDENT SEGMENT	OFFICE WORKER SEGMENT	RATIONALE FOR MARKETING PROGRAM ACTIVITY
 Product strategy	Offer Post-it® Flag Highlighter to help college students in their studying	Offer Post-it® Flag Pen to help office workers in their day-to-day work activities	Listen carefully to the needs and wants of potential customer segments to use 3M technology to introduce a useful, innovative product
 Price strategy	Seek retail price of about $3.99 to $4.99 for single Post-it® Flag Highlighter or $5.99 to $7.99 for a three-pack	Seek retail price of about $3.99 to $4.99 for a single Post-it® Flag Pen; wholesale prices are less	Set prices that provide genuine value to the customer segment that is targeted
 Promotion strategy	Run limited promotion with a TV ad and some ads in college newspapers and then rely on student word-of-mouth messages to inform other students	Run limited promotion among distributors to get them to stock the product and then rely on word-of-mouth messages to inform other users	Increase awareness of potential users in both customer segments who have never heard of this new, innovative 3M product
 Place strategy	Distribute Post-it® Flag Highlighters through college and university bookstores, office supply stores, and mass merchandisers	Distribute Post-it® Flag Pens through office wholesalers and retailers and mass merchandisers; must reach organizations' purchasing departments	Make it easy for prospective buyers to buy at convenient retail outlets (both products) or to get at work (Post-it® Flag Pens only)

FIGURE 1–4

Marketing programs for the initial introduction of two new Post-it® brand products targeted at two distinctly different customer segments: college students and office workers.

- *Post-it® Flag Highlighter.* The target market is mainly college students, so 3M's initial challenge was to build student awareness of a product that they didn't know existed and had never seen. The company used a mix of print ads in college newspapers and TV ads, and then relied on student word-of-mouth advertising—one student telling his or her roommate how great the product is. Gaining distribution in bookstores and having attractive packaging was also critical. Plus, 3M charged a price to distributors that it hoped would result in a reasonable retail price to students and also provide 3M and its distributors with an acceptable profit.
- *Post-it® Flag Pen.* The primary target market is people working in offices. However, as with the Post-it® Flag Highlighter, the market segments overlap, so 3M gained distribution in some college bookstores of Post-it® Flag Pens, too. But as shown in Figure 1–4, the Post-it® Flag Highlighter is primarily purchased by ultimate consumers—mostly students. In contrast, the Post-it® Flag Pens are mainly business products—bought by the purchasing department in an organization and stocked as office supplies for employees to use. So the marketing program in Figure 1–4 reflects the different distribution or "place" strategies for the two products.

How did these new products do for 3M? They did so well that 3M bestowed a prestigious award on Windorski and his team. Their success has also led to new marketing actions for the products discussed in the case at the end of the chapter. A good investment for 3M in encouraging David Windorski to think creatively under the company's 15% Rule!

4. An organization can't satisfy the needs of all consumers, so it must focus on one or more subgroups, which are its _____.

5. What are the four marketing mix elements that make up the organization's marketing program?

6. What are environmental forces?

HOW MARKETING BECAME SO IMPORTANT

To understand why marketing is a driving force in the modern global economy, let us look at the (1) evolution of the market orientation, (2) ethics and social responsibility in marketing, and (3) breadth and depth of marketing activities.

Evolution of the Market Orientation

Many market-oriented manufacturing organizations have experienced four distinct stages in the life of their firms.[20] We can use Pillsbury, now part of General Mills, and General Electric as examples.

Production Era Goods were scarce in the early years of the United States, so buyers were willing to accept virtually any goods that were produced and make do with them as best they could. The central notion was that products would sell themselves, so the major concern of business firms was production, not marketing. Robert Keith, a Pillsbury president, described his company at this stage: "We are professional flour millers. . . . Our basic function is to mill quality flour."[21] As shown in Figure 1–5, this production era generally continued in America through the 1920s.

Sales Era About that time, many firms discovered that they could produce more goods than their regular buyers could consume. Competition grew. The usual solution was to hire more salespeople to find new buyers. Pillsbury's philosophy at this stage was summed up simply by Keith: "We must hire salespersons to sell it [the flour] just as we hire accountants to keep our books." The role of the Pillsbury salesforce was simply to find consumers for the goods that the firm could produce best. This sales era continued into the 1950s for Pillsbury and into the 1960s for many other American firms (see Figure 1–5).

The Marketing Concept Era In the 1960s, marketing became the motivating force among many American firms. Then the policy became, "we are in the business of satisfying needs and wants of consumers." This is really a brief statement of what has come to be known as the **marketing concept**, the idea that an organization should (1) strive to satisfy the needs of consumers (2) while also trying to achieve the organization's goals.

The statement of a firm's commitment to satisfying consumer wants and needs that probably launched the marketing concept appeared in a 1952 annual report of General Electric: "The concept introduces . . . marketing . . . at the beginning rather than the end of the production cycle and integrates marketing into each phase of the business."[22] This statement emphasizes that marketing ideas are fed into the production cycle *before* an item is designed, rather than *after* it is produced. Clearly, the marketing concept is a focus on the consumer. Unfortunately, many companies found that actually implementing the concept was very difficult.

The Customer Relationship Era Firms such as General Electric, Marriott, and Toyota have achieved great success by putting huge effort into implementing the marketing concept, giving their firms what has been called a *market orientation*.

18

FIGURE 1–5

Four different orientations in the history of American business. Today's customer relationship era focuses on satisfying the high expectations of customers.

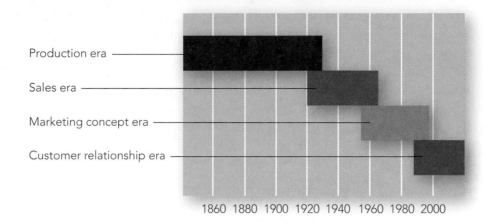

Production era

Sales era

Marketing concept era

Customer relationship era

1860 1880 1900 1920 1940 1960 1980 2000

An organization that has a **market orientation** focuses its efforts on (1) continuously collecting information about customers' needs, (2) sharing this information across departments, and (3) using it to create customer value.[23] The result is today's "customer relationship era," in which firms seek continuously to satisfy the high expectations of customers.

An important outgrowth of this focus on the customer is the recent attention placed on **customer relationship management (CRM)**, the process of identifying prospective buyers, understanding them intimately, and developing favorable long-term perceptions of the organization and its offerings so that buyers will choose them in the marketplace.[24] This process requires the involvement and commitment of managers and employees throughout the organization[25] and a growing application of information, communication, and Internet technology, as will be described throughout this book. Unfortunately, many expensive CRM computer systems have not provided the expected benefits because they failed to identify exactly which customer segments the company wanted to reach.

The foundation of customer relationship management is really **customer experience**, which is the internal response that customers have to all aspects of an organization and its offering. This internal response includes both the direct and indirect contacts of the customer with the company. Direct contacts include the customer's contacts with the seller through buying, using, and obtaining service. Indirect contacts most often involve unplanned "touches" with the company through word-of-mouth comments from other customers, reviewers, and news reports.

The disconnect between what companies *think they are providing* versus what customers *say they are receiving* shows how important customer experience is. A recent survey of 362 companies showed only 8 percent of them described the experience they received as customers as "superior," but 80 percent actually believed their own companies were supplying "superior" customer experience.[26]

Ethics and Social Responsibility: Balancing the Interests of Different Groups

As organizations have changed their orientation, society's expectations of marketers have also changed. Today, the standards of marketing practice have shifted from an emphasis on producers' interests to consumers' interests. In addition, organizations are increasingly encouraged to consider the social and environmental consequences of their actions for all parties. Guidelines for ethical and socially responsible behavior can help managers balance consumer, organizational, and societal interests.

Ethics   Many marketing issues are not specifically addressed by existing laws and regulations. Should information about a firm's customers be sold to other organizations? Should advertising by professional service providers, such as accountants and attorneys, be restricted? Should consumers be on their own to assess the safety of a product? These questions raise difficult ethical issues. Many companies, industries, and professional associations have developed codes of ethics to assist managers.

Social Responsibility   While many ethical issues involve only the buyer and seller, others involve society as a whole. For example, suppose you change the oil in your old Chevy yourself and dump the used oil in a corner of your backyard. Is this just a transaction between you and the oil manufacturer? Not quite! The used oil will contaminate the soil, so society will bear a portion of the cost of your behavior. This example illustrates the issue of social responsibility, the idea that organizations are accountable to a larger society.

The well-being of society at large should also be recognized in an organization's marketing decisions. In fact, some marketing experts stress the **societal marketing concept**, the view that organizations should satisfy the needs of consumers in a way that provides for society's well-being.[27] For example, ScotchBrite® Never Rust™ soap pads from 3M—which are made from recycled plastic bottles—are more expensive than competitors (SOS and Brillo) but superior because they don't rust or scratch (question 4, Figure 1–2).

The societal marketing concept is directly related to *macromarketing,* which is the study of the aggregate flow of a nation's goods and services to benefit society.[28] Macromarketing addresses broad issues such as whether marketing costs too much, whether advertising is wasteful, and what resource scarcities and pollution side effects result from the marketing system. While macromarketing issues are addressed briefly in this book, the book's main focus is on how an individual organization directs its marketing activities and allocates its resources to benefit its customers, or *micromarketing.* Because of the importance of ethical and social responsibility issues in marketing today, Chapter 4 focuses on them, but they are touched on throughout the book.

The Breadth and Depth of Marketing

LO6

Marketing today affects every person and organization. To understand this, let's analyze (1) who markets, (2) what they market, (3) who buys and uses what is marketed, (4) who benefits from these marketing activities, and (5) how they benefit.

In this ad, the Nature Conservancy markets its cause—protecting the environment—by superimposing a 1912 photo on the same location today.

Who Markets?   Every organization markets. It's obvious that business firms involved in manufacturing (Tommy Hilfiger, Heinz), retailing (Abercrombie & Fitch, Target), and providing services (America Online, Chicago Cubs) market their offerings. Today, many other types of marketing are also popular. Nonprofit organizations (San Francisco Opera, your local hospital) also engage in marketing.[29] Your college or university, for example, probably has a marketing program to attract students, faculty members, and donations.

Places (cities, states, countries) often use marketing efforts to attract tourists, conventions, and new investment to provide local jobs. While the *Arizona Highways* magazine helps market its state, entire countries, such as Norway and China, market themselves as tourist attractions.[30] Special events or causes use marketing to inform and influence a target audience. These marketing activities range from government agencies discouraging smoking to private groups promoting social causes such as literacy, health, or the environment. Finally, individuals such as political candidates often use marketing to gain attention and preference.

Russia's State Hermitage Museum uses an Internet "virtual tour" to help market itself to potential visitors from around the world.

What Is Marketed?   Goods, services, and ideas are marketed. *Goods* are physical objects, such as toothpaste, cameras, or computers, that satisfy consumer needs. *Services* are intangible items such as airline trips, financial advice, or art museums. *Ideas* are intangibles involving thoughts about actions or causes.

Financial pressures have caused art museums to embark on creative activities to market their unique services—the viewing of art works by visitors—to increase revenues. This often involves levels of rare creativity unthinkable several decades ago. For example, New York's Guggenheim Museum challenged the concept of what an art museum is with its exhibition on "The Art of the Motorcycle."[31] The search for new revenues spurred the Dallas Museum of Art to stay open for 100 consecutive hours to celebrate its centennial, and Chicago's Field Museum now offers a licensing program featuring Sue, its Tyrannosaurus rex skeleton.[32]

Recently Russia's world-class State Hermitage Museum sought ways to show its art exhibits to potential visitors from around the globe. The answer: Use today's technology, partner with IBM, and develop a "virtual tour" of its 1,000-room museum founded by Catherine the Great. To be a "virtual tourist," go to www.hermitagemuseum.org, and click on the "Virtual Visit" link. The Hermitage Museum hopes "virtual visits" from people like you will encourage actual personal visits some time in the future.[33]

Who Benefits?   In our free-enterprise society, three specific groups benefit from effective marketing: consumers who buy, organizations that sell, and society as a whole. True competition between products and services in the marketplace ensures that we consumers can find value from the best products, the lowest prices, or exceptional service. Providing choices leads to the consumer satisfaction and quality of life that we have come to expect from our economic system.

Who Buys and Uses What Is Marketed?   Both individuals and organizations buy and use goods and services that are marketed. **Ultimate consumers** are the people who use the goods and services purchased for a household. In contrast, **organizational buyers** are those manufacturers, wholesalers, retailers, and government

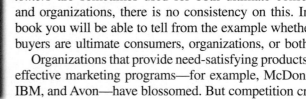

agencies that buy goods and services for their own use or for resale. Although the terms *consumers, buyers,* and *customers* are sometimes used for both ultimate consumers and organizations, there is no consistency on this. In this book you will be able to tell from the example whether the buyers are ultimate consumers, organizations, or both.

Organizations that provide need-satisfying products with effective marketing programs—for example, McDonald's, IBM, and Avon—have blossomed. But competition creates problems for ineffective competitors, such as eToys and hundreds of other dot-com businesses that failed in the last few years.[34]

Finally, effective marketing benefits society. It enhances competition, which, in turn, improves both the quality of products and services and lowers their prices. This makes countries more competitive in world markets and provides jobs and a higher standard of living for their citizens.

How Do Consumers Benefit? Marketing creates **utility**, the benefits or customer value received by users of the product. This utility is the result of the marketing exchange process and the way society benefits from marketing.[35] There are four different utilities: form, place, time, and possession. The value to consumers that comes from the production or alteration of a good or service constitutes *form utility.* *Place utility* is the value to consumers of having a good or service available where needed, whereas *time utility* is the value to consumers of having a good or service available when needed. *Possession utility* is the value to consumers of making an item easy to purchase so consumers can use it.

Thus, marketing provides consumers with place, time, and possession utilities by making the good or service available at the right place and right time for the right consumer. Although form utility usually arises in manufacturing activity and could be seen as outside the scope of marketing, an organization's marketing activities influence the product features and packaging. Marketing creates its utilities by bridging space (place utility) and hours (time utility) to provide products (form utility) for consumers to own and use (possession utility).

learning review

7. Like Pillsbury and General Electric, many firms have gone through four distinct orientations for their business: starting with the _____ era and ending with today's _____ era.

8. What are the two key characteristics of the marketing concept?

LEARNING OBJECTIVES REVIEW

LO1 *Define marketing and identify the requirements for marketing to occur.*
Marketing is an organizational function and a set of processes for creating, communicating, and delivering value to customers and for managing customer relationships in ways that benefit the organization and its stakeholders. This definition relates to two primary goals of marketing: (*a*) assessing the needs of consumers and (*b*) satisfying them. For marketing to occur, it is necessary to have (*a*) two or more parties with unmet needs, (*b*) a desire and ability to satisfy them, (*c*) communication between the parties, and (*d*) something to exchange.

LO2 *Explain how marketing discovers and satisfies consumer needs.*
The first objective in marketing is discovering the needs of prospective consumers. This is not an easy task because consumers may not always know or be able to describe what they need and want. A need occurs when a person feels physiologically deprived of basic necessities such as food, clothing, and shelter. A want is a felt need that is shaped by a person's knowledge, culture, and personality. Effective marketing can clearly shape a person's wants and tries to influence what we buy. The second objective in mar-

keting is satisfying the needs of targeted consumers. Because an organization obviously can't satisfy all consumer needs, it must concentrate its efforts on certain needs of a specific group of potential consumers or target market—one or more specific groups of potential consumers toward which an organization directs its marketing program. Having selected its target market consumers, the organization then takes action to satisfy their needs by developing a unique marketing program to reach them.

LO3 *Distinguish between marketing mix elements and environmental forces.*
Four elements in a marketing program designed to satisfy customer needs are product, price, promotion, and place. These elements are called the marketing mix, the four Ps, or the controllable variables because they are under the general control of the marketing department. Environmental forces, also called uncontrollable variables, are largely beyond the organization's control. These include social, economic, technological, competitive, and regulatory forces.

LO4 *Explain how organizations build strong customer relationships and customer value through marketing.*
The essence of successful marketing is to provide sufficient value to gain loyal, long-term customers. Customer value is the unique

combination of benefits received by targeted buyers that usually includes quality, price, convenience, on-time delivery, and both before-sale and after-sale service. Marketers do this by using one of three value strategies: best price, best product, or best service.

LO5 *Describe how today's customer relationship era differs from prior eras oriented to production and selling.*
U.S. business history is divided into four periods: the production era, the sales era, the marketing concept era, and the current customer relationship era. The production era covers the period to the 1920s when buyers were willing to accept virtually any goods that were available. The central notion was that products would sell themselves. The sales era lasted from the 1920s to the 1960s. Manufacturers found they could produce more goods than buyers could consume, and competition grew, so the solu-

tion was to hire more salespeople to find new buyers. In the 1960s, the marketing concept era dawned, when organizations began to integrate marketing into each phase of the business. In today's customer relationship era, organizations focus their efforts on (*a*) continuously collecting information about customers' needs, (*b*) sharing this information across departments, and (*c*) using it to create customer value.

LO6 *Explain how marketing creates utilities for consumers.*
Marketing creates utility, which consists of the benefits or customer value received by users of the product and is the result of the exchange process. Marketing provides four types of utilities that are designed to get the right product or service to consumers (form utility) where (place utility) and when (time utility) they need it so they can ultimately use or consume it (possession utility).

FOCUSING ON KEY TERMS

customer experience p. 19
customer relationship management (CRM) p. 19
customer value p. 14
environmental forces p. 13
exchange p. 7

market p. 12
market orientation p. 19
marketing p. 6
marketing concept p. 18
marketing mix p. 13
marketing program p. 15

organizational buyers p. 21
relationship marketing p. 15
societal marketing concept p. 20
target market p. 13
ultimate consumers p. 21
utility p. 22

APPLYING MARKETING KNOWLEDGE

1 What consumer wants (or benefits) are met by the following products or services? (*a*) Carnation Instant Breakfast, (*b*) Adidas running shoes, (*c*) Hertz Rent-A-Car, and (*d*) television home shopping programs.

2 Each of the four products, services, or programs in question 1 has substitutes. Respective examples are (*a*) a ham and egg breakfast, (*b*) regular tennis shoes, (*c*) taking a bus, and (*d*) a department store. What consumer benefits might these substitutes have in each case that some consumers might value more highly than those mentioned in question 1?

3 What are the characteristics (e.g., age, income, education) of the target market customers for the following products or services? (*a*) *National Geographic* magazine, (*b*) *Wired* magazine, (*c*) New York Giants football team, and (*d*) the U.S. Open tennis tournament.

4 A college in a metropolitan area wishes to increase its evening-school offerings of business-related courses such as marketing, accounting, finance, and management. Who are the target market customers (students) for these courses?

5 What actions involving the four marketing mix elements might be used to reach the target market in question 4?

6 What environmental factors (uncontrollable variables) must the college in question 4 consider in designing its marketing program?

7 The 3M company is now trying to sell its Post-it® Notes globally. What are the advantages and disadvantages of trying to reach new global markets?

8 Does a firm have the right to "create" wants and try to persuade consumers to buy goods and services they didn't know about earlier? What are examples of "good" and "bad" want creation? Who should decide what is good and bad?

building your marketing plan

If your instructor assigns a marketing plan for your class, don't make a face and complain about the work—for two special reasons. First, you will get insights into trying to actually "do marketing" that often go beyond what you can get by simply reading the textbook. Second, thousands of graduating students every year get their first job by showing prospective employers a "portfolio" of samples of their written work from col-

lege—often a marketing plan if they have one. This can work for you.

This "Building Your Marketing Plan" section at the end of each chapter suggests ways to improve and focus your marketing plan. You will use the sample marketing plan in Appendix A (following Chapter 2) as a guide, and this section after each chapter will help you apply those Appendix A ideas to your own marketing plan.

The first step in writing a good marketing plan is to have a business or product that enthuses you and for which you can get detailed information, so you can avoid glittering generalities. We offer these additional bits of advice in selecting a topic:

- *Do* pick a topic that has personal interest for you—a family business, a business or product you or a friend might want to launch, or a student organization needing marketing help.
- *Do not* pick a topic that is so large it can't be covered adequately or so abstract it will lack specifics.

1 Now to get you started on your marketing plan, list four or five possible topics and compare these with the criteria your instructor suggests and those shown above. Think hard, because your decision will be with you all term and may influence the quality of the resulting marketing plan you show to a prospective employer.

2 When you have selected your marketing plan topic, whether the plan is for an actual business, a possible business, or a student organization, write the "company description" in your plan, as shown in Appendix A.

---

video case 1   3M's Post-it® Flag Highlighter: Extending the Concept!

"I didn't go out to students and ask, 'What are your needs, or what are your wants?'" 3M inventor David Windorski explains to a class of college students. "And even if I did ask, they probably wouldn't say, 'Put flags inside a highlighter.'"

So Windorski turned the classic textbook approach to marketing on its head.

That classic approach—as you saw earlier in Chapter 1—says to start with needs and wants of potential customers and then develop the product. But sometimes new-product development runs in the opposite direction: Start with a new product idea—such as personal computers—and then see if there is a market. This is really what Windorski did, using a lot of marketing research along the way after he developed the concept of the Post-it® Flag Highlighter.

EARLY MARKETING RESEARCH

David Windorski initially talked to a team of local college students to try to understand how they study, take notes and prepare for exams. He then spent several years working with clay and wood models, a sawed-in-half highlighter, and finally a computer-generated model using the latest laser technology.

During this new-product development process, Windorski and 3M did a lot of marketing research on students. Some was unconventional, while other research was quite traditional. For example, students were asked to dump the contents of their backpacks on the table and to explain what they carried around and then to react to some early highlighter models. Also, several times six or seven students were interviewed together and observed by 3M researchers from behind a one-way mirror—the focus group technique discussed later in Chapter 8. Other students were interviewed individually. And when early working models of the Post-it® Flag Highlighter finally existed, several hundred were produced and given to students to use for a month. Their reactions were captured on a questionnaire.

THE NEW PRODUCT LAUNCH

After the initial marketing research and dozens of technical tests in 3M laboratories, David Windorski's new 3M highlighter product was ready to be manufactured and marketed. Figure 1-4 in the chapter only skims the surface of the many research and development, manufacturing, and marketing issues needed to be overcome to introduce the new 3M product.

Here's a snapshot of the pre-launch issues that were solved before the product could be introduced:

- Technical issues. Can we generate a computer-aided database for injection molded parts? What tolerances do we need? The 3M highlighter is really a technological marvel. For the snap fits and other parts on the highlighter to work, tolerances must be several thousandths of an inch—less than the thickness of a paper.
- Manufacturing issues. Where should the product be manufactured? 3M chose a company outside the U.S., which necessitated precise translations of critical technical specifications. Windorski spent time in the factory working with engineers and manufacturing specialists there to ensure that 3M's precise production standards would be achieved.
- Product issues. What should the brand name be for the new highlighter product? Marketing research and many meetings gave the answer: "The Post-it® Flag Highlighter." How many to a package? What color(s)? What should the packaging look like that (1) can display the product well at retail and (2) communicate its points of difference effectively?
- Price issues. With many competing highlighters, what should the price be for 3M's premium highlighter that will provide 3M adequate profit? Should the suggested retail price be the same in college bookstores, mass merchandisers (Wal-Mart, Target), and office supply stores (Office Max, Office Depot)?

- Promotion issues. How can 3M tell students the product exists? Might office workers want it and use it? Should there be print ads, TV ads, and point-of-sale displays explaining the product?
- Place (distribution) issues. With the limited shelf space in college bookstores and other outlets, how can 3M convince retailers to stock its new product?

THE MARKETING PROGRAM TODAY AND TOMORROW

3M has discovered that its highlighter has turned out to be more popular than it expected. 3M often hears from end users how much they like the product.

So what can 3M do for an encore to build on the initial success? This involves taking great care to introduce new product extensions to attract new customers while still retaining its solid foundation of loyal existing customers. Also, 3M's products have to appeal not only to the ultimate consumers but also to retailers who want new items to display in high-traffic areas.

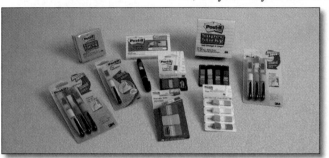

Product and packaging decisions for the Post-it® Flag Highlighter reflect this innovative focus. 3M recently introduced a broader array of colors in a two-pack with a new 'Samba' Latin color palette of green and purple with metallic sparkle for a fall back-to-college promotion. This expanded the existing 3M line of yellow, blue, and pink highlighter colors. As to packaging, it's critical that it (1) communicate the 2-products-in-1 idea, (2) be attractive, and (3) achieve both goals with the fewest words.

David Windorski also invented another product for students based on adhesive technology: restickable 3 inch by 5 inch note cards. Their point of difference: They stick to surfaces for brainstorming sessions or notebooks when you want them to and slide across each other *without sticking* when you want them to do that. Asked by students how it's possible, Windorski just smiles.

At 3M, promotion budgets are limited because it relies heavily on its technology for a competitive advantage. This also applies to the Post-it® Flag Highlighter. So you probably have never seen a print or TV ad for it. Yet potential student buyers, the product's main target market,

must be made aware that it exists. So 3M searches continually for simple, effective promotions to alert students about this product.

Great technology is meaningless unless the product is available where potential buyers can purchase it. Unlike college bookstores that exist largely to serve students, mass merchandisers and office supply stores track, measure, and seek to maximize the profit of every square foot of selling space. So 3M must convince these retail chains that selling space devoted to its highlighter line will be more profitable than alternative uses. The challenge for 3M: Finding ways to make the Post-it® Flag Highlighter prominent on shelves of college bookstores and retail chains.

If the Post-it® Flag Highlighter is doing well in the U.S., why not try to sell it around the world? But even here 3M faces critical questions: Which countries will be the best markets? What highlighter colors and packaging works best in each country? How do we physically get the product to these markets in a timely and cost-efficient basis?

Questions

1 (a) How did 3M's David Windorski get ideas from college students to help him in designing the final commercial version of the Post-it® Flag Highlighter? (b) How were these ideas important to the success of the products?

2 What (a) special advantages and (b) potential problems did 3M have in introducing a new highlighter-with-flags product for college students in 2004?

3 Visit your college bookstore before you answer. (a) Where would you display the Post-it® Flag Highlighter in a college bookstore, and (b) how can the display increase student awareness of the product?

4 In what ways might 3M try to promote its Post-it® Flag Highlighter and make students more aware of the product?

5 What are (a) the special opportunities and (b) potential challenges for 3M in taking its Post-it® Flag Highlighter into international markets? (c) On which countries should 3M focus its marketing efforts?

BEN&JERRY'S HOME | **OUR COMPANY** | **OUR PRODUCTS** | **SCOOP SHOPS** | **FUN STUFF** | **GIFT SHOP**

Our Company

- About Us
- Our Mission
- Contact Us
- Factory Tours
- International
- Press Center
- Jobs at Ben & Jerry's
- FAQ's
- Research Library

Our Mission Statement

Ben & Jerry's is founded on and dedicated to a sustainable corporate concept of linked prosperity. Our mission consists of 3 interrelated parts::

Product Mission
To make, distribute & sell the finest quality all natural ice cream & euphoric concoctions with a continued commitment to incorporating wholesome, natural ingredients and promoting business practices that respect the Earth and the Environment.

Economic Mission
To operate the Company on a sustainable financial basis of profitable growth, increasing value for our stakeholders & expanding opportunities for development and career growth for our employees.

Social Mission
To operate the company in a way that actively recognizes the central role that business plays in society by initiating innovative ways to improve the quality of life locally, nationally & internationally.

Central To The Mission Of Ben & Jerry's is the belief that all three parts must thrive equally in a manner that commands deep respect for individuals in and outside the company and supports the communities of which they are a part.

Leading with Progressive Values Across Our Business

We have a progressive, nonpartisan social mission that seeks to meet human needs and eliminate injustices in our local, national and international communities by integrating these concerns into our day-to-day business activities. Our focus is on children and families, the environment and sustainable agriculture on family farms.

- Capitalism and the wealth it produces do not create opportunity for everyone equally. We recognize that the gap between the rich and the poor is wider than at anytime since the 1920's. We strive to create economic opportunities for those who have been denied them and to advance new models of economic justice that are sustainable and replicable.

- By definition, the manufacturing of products creates waste. We strive to minimize our negative impact on the environment.

- The growing of food is overly reliant on the use of toxic chemicals and other methods that are unsustainable. We support sustainable and safe methods of food production that reduce environmental degradation, maintain the productivity of the land over time, and support the economic viability of family farms and rural communities.

- We seek and support nonviolent ways to achieve peace and justice. We believe government resources are more productively used in meeting human needs than in building and maintaining weapons systems.

- We strive to show a deep respect for human beings inside and outside our company and for the communities in which they live.

Learn more! check out our Social Mission News or Our Environment

2

Developing Successful Marketing and Organizational Strategies

LEARNING OBJECTIVES

After reading this chapter you should be able to:

LO1 Describe the kinds of organizations that exist and the three levels of strategy in them.

LO2 Describe how core values, mission, organizational culture, business, and goals are important to organizations.

LO3 Explain how organizations set strategic directions by assessing where they are now and seek to be in the future.

LO4 Describe the strategic marketing process and its three key phases: planning, implementation, and evaluation.

LO5 Explain how the marketing mix elements are blended into a cohesive marketing program.

AN "A" IN AN ICE CREAM MAKING COURSE! CAN THIS *REALLY* BECOME A BUSINESS?

The two entrepreneurs who aced their college course in ice cream making aren't your typical Tom, Dick, or Harry! Here's what the organization they founded is doing today:

- It buys all of its milk and cream from one dairy cooperative whose members guarantee the supplies are bovine growth-hormone free.

- It launched several Fair Trade Certified™ flavors to support small-scale family farms and their workers in the developing world through fair prices and eco-friendly farming practices.

- Its PartnerShop, Scoopers Making Change, and Cones 2 Career programs help nonprofit organizations give jobs to and train at-risk youth.

- Its new product line includes Body & Soul "low carb/low fat" ice cream flavors, milk shakes, frozen yogurts, sorbets, waffle cones, and ice cream sandwiches.

It also sponsors the "Do Us a Flavor Contest" that allows customers to submit a new "euphoric" ice cream flavor. A recent "Flavor Guru" winner was Puttin' on the Ritz, a swirl of vanilla ice cream, caramel, Ritz crackers, and chunks of chocolate.

This creative, funky approach to business at Ben & Jerry's Homemade, Inc., links its mission, core values, and prosperity to social causes designed to improve humanity, as shown on its website.[1]

Ben & Jerry's proves the American dream still lives. In 1978, longtime friends Ben Cohen and Jerry Greenfield headed north to Vermont to start an ice cream parlor in a renovated gas station.[2] Buoyed with enthusiasm, $12,000 in borrowed and saved money, and ideas from a $5 Penn State correspondence course in ice cream making (with perfect scores on their open book tests!), Ben and Jerry were off and running.[3] Today, Ben & Jerry's is owned by Unilever and earns about $240 million in annual sales worldwide, mainly from selling its incredibly rich premium ice cream.[4] While customers love Cherry Garcia and its other ice cream flavors, many want to support Ben & Jerry's social mission, too.

Chapter 2 describes how organizations such as Ben & Jerry's, Medtronic, and Kodak set goals to give an overall direction that is linked to their organizational and marketing strategies. For the marketing department, these strategies are converted into plans that must be implemented. The results are then evaluated to assess the degree to which they accomplish the company's goals, consistent with its core values and mission.

TODAY'S ORGANIZATIONS

In today's global competition, it is important to recognize (1) the kinds of organizations that exist, (2) what strategy is, and (3) how this strategy relates to the three levels found in many large organizations.

Kinds of Organizations

An *organization* is a legal entity of people who share a common mission. This motivates them to develop *offerings* (products, services, or ideas) that create value for both the organization and its customers by satisfying their needs and wants.[5] Today's organizations can be divided into business firms and nonprofit organizations.

A *business firm* is a privately owned organization that serves its customers in order to earn a profit so that it can survive.[6] **Profit** is the money left after a business firm's total expenses are subtracted from its total revenues and is the reward for the risk it undertakes in marketing its offerings.

In contrast, a *nonprofit organization* is a nongovernmental organization that serves its customers but does not have profit as an organizational goal. Instead, its goals may be operational efficiency or client satisfaction. Regardless, it also must receive sufficient funds to continue operations. Charities and farm cooperatives affiliated with Ben & Jerry's are examples of this kind of organization. For simplicity in the rest of the book, the terms *firm, company, corporation,* and *organization* are used interchangeably to cover both business and nonprofit operations.

Organizations that develop similar offerings, when grouped together, create an *industry,* such as the computer industry or the automobile industry.[7] As a result, organizations make strategic decisions that reflect the dynamics of the industry to create a compelling and sustainable advantage for their offerings relative to those of competitors to achieve a superior level of performance.[8] The foundation of much of an organization's marketing strategy is having a clear understanding of the industry within which it competes.

What Is Strategy?

An organization has limited human, financial, technological, and other resources available to produce and market its offerings—it can't be all things to all people!

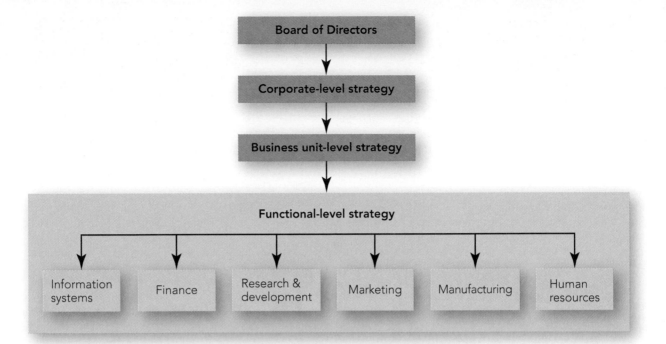

FIGURE 2–1

The board of directors oversees the three levels of strategy in organizations: corporate, business unit, and functional.

Every organization must develop strategies to help focus and direct its efforts to accomplish its goals. However, the definition of strategy has been the subject of debate among management and marketing theorists.[9] For our purpose, **strategy** is an organization's long-term course of action designed to deliver a unique customer experience while achieving its goals.[10] Whether explicit or implicit, all organizations set a strategic direction. And marketing helps not only to set this direction but also to move the organization there.

Structure of Today's Organizations

Large organizations such as Medtronic and Kodak are extremely complex. They usually consist of three organizational levels whose strategy is linked to marketing, as shown in Figure 2–1.

Corporate Level The **corporate level** is where top management directs overall strategy for the entire organization. "Top management" usually means the board of directors, individuals both inside and outside the organization with a variety of skills and experiences that are invaluable in establishing overall strategy.

The chief executive officer (CEO) is the highest ranking officer in the organization and is usually a member of its board of directors. This person must possess leadership skills and expertise ranging from overseeing the organization's daily operations to spearheading strategy planning efforts that may determine its very survival.

In recent years many large firms have changed the title of the head of marketing from vice president of marketing to chief marketing officer (CMO). The Marketing Matters box on the next page describes the breadth of responsibilities three key marketing executives—with various titles—in widely different firms have in creating, communicating, and delivering value to their organization's customers. But whatever their titles, the head of marketing in today's organizations not only frame marketing strategy but also see that it is implemented to achieve critical marketing goals.[11]

Strategic Business Unit Level Some multimarket, multiproduct firms, such as General Electric or Johnson & Johnson, really manage a portfolio of businesses called strategic business units (SBUs).[12] The term **strategic business unit (SBU)** refers to a subsidiary, division, or unit of an organization that markets a set of related offerings to a clearly defined group of customers. At the **strategic business unit level**, managers set a more specific strategic direction for their businesses to exploit value-creating opportunities. For less complex firms with a single business focus, such as Ben & Jerry's, the corporate and business unit levels may merge.

Functional Level Each strategic business unit has a **functional level**, where groups of specialists actually create value for the organization. The term *department* generally refers to these specialized functions such as marketing and finance (Figure 2–1). At the functional level, the organization's strategic direction becomes its most specific and focused. Just as there is a hierarchy of levels within an organization, there is a hierarchy of strategic directions set by managers at each level.

A key role of the marketing department is to look outward, keeping the organization focused on creating value both for it and for customers. This is accomplished by listening to customers, developing and producing offerings, and implementing marketing program activities. In large organizations, marketing may be called on to assist managers at higher levels to assess environmental trends or aid in their strategic planning efforts.

When developing marketing programs for new offerings or for improving existing ones, an organization's senior management may form **cross-functional teams**. These consist of a small number of people from different departments who are mutually accountable to accomplish a task or a common set of performance goals. Sometimes these teams will have representatives from outside the organization, such as suppliers or customers, to assist them.

> ### learning review
>
> 1. What is the difference between a business firm and a nonprofit organization?
> 2. What are examples of a functional level in an organization?

STRATEGY IN VISIONARY ORGANIZATIONS

LO2

Management experts stress that to be successful, today's organizations must be visionary—must both anticipate future events and respond quickly and effectively. This requires a visionary organization to specify its foundation (why), set a direction (what), and formulate strategies (how) as shown in Figure 2–2.[13] An organization's foundation is its philosophical reason for being—why it exists. So its senior managers must identify its core values and describe its mission and organizational culture—its purpose for being. Next, these managers can set the direction for the organization by defining its business and specifying its long-term and short-term goals.

Recently, the "organizational foundation" box in Figure 2–2 and the three elements inside it have taken on greater importance because of the failure of Enron. The organizational culture in Enron lost touch with its core values. Key Enron executives were convicted of crimes, the company was liquidated, and employees and shareholders lost billions of dollars. The result: Many organizations today are reinforcing their foundation elements.

Organizational Foundation

An organization's foundation or ideology says, "This is what we are; this is what we stand for." It rarely changes, regardless of the environment or latest strategy planning fad.[14] Successful visionary organizations use this foundation to provide guidance and inspiration to its employees through three elements: core values, mission, and organizational culture.

Core Values An organization's **core values** are the fundamental, passionate, and enduring principles that guide its conduct over time.[15] An example of core values is Hewlett-Packard's the "HP Way." These core values of Hewlett-Packard (HP) originated with William Hewlett and David Packard, who co-founded the company in a garage in 1939. When their fledgling company was struggling in the 1940s, the two men composed the core values that came to be known as the "HP Way." These core values include "a deep respect for the individual, a dedication to affordable quality and reliability, a commitment to community responsibility, and a view that the company exists to

FIGURE 2–2
Today's visionary organization uses key elements to (1) establish a foundation and (2) set a direction using (3) its strategies that enable it to develop and market its offerings successfully.

Organizational foundation (why)		Organizational direction (what)		Organizational strategies (how)

• Core values
• Mission
• Organizational culture
	+	• Business
		• Goals (objectives)
		  ○ Long-term
		  ○ Short-term
			=	• By level
				  ○ Corporate
				  ○ SBU
				  ○ Functional
				• By offering (product, service, idea)

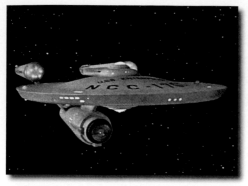

To discover what is probably the best known mission statement in America for this starship, which has stimulated astronauts and inventors, see the text.

make technical contributions for the advancement and welfare of humanity."[16] The current "HP Way" at www.hp.com derives from Hewlett and Packard's 1940s statement and guides future decisions of the company.

Let's analyze this core values idea. First, core values are developed by an organization's founders or senior management and are consistent with their essential beliefs and character.[17] Second, core values capture the collective heart and soul of the organization. They should inspire and motivate employees to take productive action. Third, core values are timeless; they should not change due to short-term financial, operational, or strategic concerns. Last, core values guide the organization's conduct. They shape its mission, establish the norms of its organizational culture, and influence its strategy.

To be effective, an organization's core values must be supported by the chief executive officer and board of directors. They also must be communicated to employees and other *stakeholders,* the people who are affected by what the company does and how well it performs. This group includes employees, shareholders, and board members, as well as suppliers, distributors, creditors, unions, government, local communities, and, of course, customers. If the values are not communicated and supported, they are hollow words—one of the reasons for Enron's failure.[18]

Mission By understanding its core values, an organization can take steps to define its **mission**, a statement of the organization's function in society, often identifying its customers, markets, products, and technologies. Today, often used interchangeably with *vision,* a *mission statement* should be clear, concise, meaningful, inspirational, and long-term.[19]

Here is perhaps the best known mission statement in America:

> To explore strange new worlds, to seek out new life and new civilizations, to boldly go where no one has gone before.

This mission for the Starship *Enterprise* as Gene Roddenberry wrote it for the *Star Trek* adventure series is inspirational for many NASA astronauts. This 40-year-old television series has had tremendous impact on American society: Inventors of many of today's taken-for-granted technologies (personal computers, cellular phones, magnetic resonance imaging) claim they were inspired by technical devices they saw in the TV program.[20]

This inspiration and focus appears in the mission of many organizations, including:

- American Red Cross: "To provide relief to victims of disaster and help prevent, prepare for, and respond to emergencies."
- Southwest Airlines: To be dedicated "to the highest quality of Customer Service delivered with a sense of warmth, friendliness, individual pride, and Company Spirit."
- Medtronic: "To contribute to human welfare by application of biomedical engineering in the research, design, manufacture, and sale of instruments or appliances that alleviate pain, restore health, and extend life."

Each statement exhibits the qualities of a good mission: a clear, challenging, and compelling picture of an envisioned future.

Recently, organizations have added a social element to their mission statements to reflect an ideal that is morally right and worthwhile.[21] This is what Ben & Jerry's social mission statement is all about, as shown in the chapter opening. Stakeholders, particularly customers, employees, and now society, are asking organizations to be exceptional citizens by providing long-term value while solving society's problems.[22]

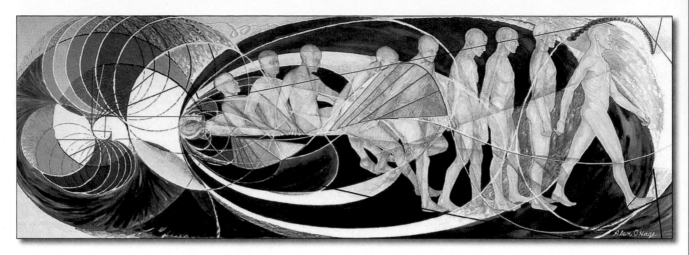

People see this "rising figure" mural in the headquarters of a world-class corporation. What does it signify? What does it say to employees? To others? For some insights and why it is important, see the text.

Medtronic
www.medtronic.com

Organizational Culture An organization must be connected with all of its stakeholders. So an important corporate-level marketing function is communicating its core values and mission. Some organizations print these statements on cards or placards. Others take a more dramatic approach—like the "rising figure" wall mural at Medtronic's headquarters, which powerfully communicates the inspiration and focus of its mission to its employees, doctors, and patients alike.[23] These activities shape an organizational culture.

Whether at the corporate, strategic business unit, or functional level, an **organizational culture** exists, which is a set of values, ideas, attitudes, and norms of behavior that is learned and shared among the members of an organization. At Medtronic, a corporate officer presents each new employee with a medallion depicting a "rising figure" on one side and the company's mission on the other. Each December, five or six patients, accompanied by their physicians, describe to a large employee holiday celebration how Medtronic products have changed their lives. These activities send clear messages to employees and other stakeholders about Medtronic's cohesive organizational culture.

When corporations merge or are acquired, organizational cultures can collide, often resulting from conflicts in missions and goals. However, when Unilever acquired Ben & Jerry's in April 2000, it allowed the firm to keep and even expand its social mission, as described earlier in this chapter.

Organizational Direction

As shown in Figure 2–2, the organization's foundation enables it to set a direction, in terms of (1) the "business it is in" and (2) its specific goals.

In the first half of the 20th century, what "business" did railroads believe they were in? The text reveals their disastrous error.

Business A **business** describes the clear, broad, underlying industry category or market sector of an organization's offering. To help define its business, an organization can start by looking at the set of organizations that sell similar offerings—those that are in direct competition with each other, such as "the automobile business" or "the personal computer business." So, the organization can begin to answer the questions, "What do we do?" or "What business are we in?"

To help us, professor Theodore Levitt argues in his now-famous "Marketing Myopia" article that American railroads in the first half of the 20th century had a narrow, production-oriented statement of their business. They proclaimed, "We are in the railroad business!" This narrow business definition lost sight of who their customers were and what these needs were. Railroads saw only other railroads as competitors and failed to develop strategies to compete with airlines, barges, pipelines, trucks, bus lines, and cars—offerings that carried both goods and people. As a result, many railroads eventually merged or went bankrupt. Railroads would probably have fared better over the past century by recognizing they were in "the transportation business."[24]

Disney is not in the movie and theme park business; rather it *is* in the entertainment business, creating fun and fantasy for its customers. Similarly, Medtronic is the world leader in developing, producing, and marketing heart pacemakers and other implantable medical devices. Yet Medtronic *is not* in the medical device business. It *is* in the business of alleviating pain, restoring health, and extending life.

Goals **Goals** or **objectives** (terms used interchangeably in this textbook) are statements of an accomplishment of a task to be achieved, often by a specific time. For example, Kodak may have the goal of being the top seller of digital cameras by 2010 (currently, it is third). Goals and objectives convert the organization's mission and business into performance targets to measure how well it is doing.

As shown in Figure 2–2, goals get converted into organizational strategies at the corporate, strategic business unit, and functional levels. All lower-level goals must contribute to achieving goals at the next, higher level.

Later in the chapter we'll look into "marketing dashboards" as an aid in evaluation, the final step in the strategic marketing process. Marketing dashboards and the evaluation step require specific goals against which actual results can be compared. Useful criteria for writing effective goals are given by the acronym SMART:

- **S**pecific: Be a precise description of what is to be achieved
- **M**easurable: Be a quantitative value to show attainment
- **A**ttainable: Be achievable, but challenging
- **R**elevant: Be pertinent to the organization's mission
- **T**ime-based: Have a deadline for completion

Business firms can pursue several different types of goals:

- *Profit.* Classic economic theory assumes a firm seeks to maximize profits—to get as high a financial return on its investments (ROI) as possible.
- *Sales* (in terms of dollars or units). If profits are acceptable, a firm may elect to maintain or increase its sales level even though profitability may not be maximized.
- *Market share.* **Market share** is the ratio of sales revenue of the firm to the total sales revenue of all firms in the industry, including the firm itself. A firm may choose to maintain or increase its market share, sometimes at the expense of greater profits if industry status or prestige is at stake.
- *Quality.* A firm may target the highest quality, as Medtronic does with its implantable medical devices.
- *Customer satisfaction.* Customers are the reason the organization exists, so their perceptions and actions are of vital importance. Their satisfaction can be measured directly with surveys or tracked with proxy measures such as number of customer complaints or percentage of orders shipped within 24 hours of receipt.
- *Employee welfare.* An organization may recognize the critical importance of its employees by having an explicit goal stating its commitment to good employment opportunities and working conditions for them.
- *Social responsibility.* A firm may seek to balance conflicting goals of consumers, employees, and stockholders to promote overall welfare of all these groups, even at the expense of profits. U.S. firms manufacturing products abroad increasingly seek to be good global citizens by engaging in sustainable development practices: paying reasonable wages and reducing pollution. For example, as described in the Making Responsible Decisions box, 3M has an environmental goal of reducing its solid waste generated from its operations by 20 percent by 2010.[25]

Nonprofit organizations (such as museums, symphony orchestras, and hospitals) also have goals such as to strive to serve consumers as efficiently as possible. Similarly, in seeking to serve the public good, government agencies also set performance goals.

Making Responsible Decisions > > > > sustainability

The Global Dilemma: How to Achieve Sustainable Development

Corporate executives and world leaders are increasingly asked to address the issue of "sustainable development." This term was formally defined in a 1987 United Nations report as meeting present needs "without compromising the ability of future generations to meet their own needs." What often happens is the achievement of profits for a firm and economic development for a country by adding jobs in highly polluting industries, thereby pushing cleanup actions into the future.

Eastern Europe and the nations of the former Soviet Union provide an example. Tragically, poisoned air and dead rivers are the legacies of seven decades of Communist rule. With more than a third of the households of many of these nations below the poverty level, should the immediate goal be a cleaner environment or more food, clothing, housing, and consumer goods? What should the heads of these govern-

ments do? What should Western firms trying to enter these new, growing markets do? What will be the impact on future generations?

The 3M Company developed an innovative program called Pollution Prevention Pays (3P) to reduce harmful environmental impacts, while making a profit doing so. The company estimates that the 3P program in the last quarter century has cut its pollution by 1.6 billion pounds while saving almost $900 million in raw materials and avoiding fines. The company's current environmental goals are to improve energy efficiency per pound of product by 20 percent while reducing waste per pound by 25 percent.

Should the environment or economic growth come first? What are the societal trade-offs? Will profit-making firms adopt and implement a 3P kind of program?

---

learning review

3. What is the meaning of an organization's mission?

4. What is the difference between an organization's "business" and its "goals"?

SETTING STRATEGIC DIRECTIONS

Setting strategic directions involves answering two difficult questions: (1) Where are we now? and (2) Where do we want to go?

A Look Around: Where Are We Now?

Asking an organization where it is at the present time involves identifying its competencies, customers, and competitors. More detailed approaches to assessing where the company is now include SWOT analysis, discussed later in this chapter, and environmental scanning (Chapter 3).

Competencies Senior managers of an organization must ask a critical question: What do we do best? The answer involves a frank assessment of the organization's core **competencies**, which are its special capabilities, including skills, technologies, and resources that distinguish it from other organizations and that provide value to its customers. Exploiting these competencies can lead to success, particularly if other organizations cannot copy them.[26] Medtronic's competencies include world-class technology plus training, service, and marketing activities that respond to life-threatening medical needs and wants. *BusinessWeek* magazine calls Medtronic "the standard setter for quality."[27]

Competencies should be distinctive enough to provide a **competitive advantage**, a unique strength relative to competitors, often based on quality, time, cost, or innovation.[28] For example, if 3M's goal of generating a specific portion of its sales from new products is to be a competitive advantage, then it must have a supporting competency in research and development, new-product innovation, and marketing.

Hewlett-Packard has developed a competitive advantage with its *fast cycle time,* which allows it to bring innovative products to markets rapidly in large volumes.[29]

Many firms seek a competence in total quality management (TQM). *Quality* involves improving those features and characteristics of an offering that influence its ability to satisfy customer needs. Firms often try to improve quality or shorten new product cycles through *benchmarking*—discovering the best practices of organizations in its own and other industries and then imitating them to leapfrog its competitors. Benchmarking often involves studying operations of best-of-class organizations in completely different businesses. When General Mills sought ideas on how to reduce the time to convert its production lines from one cereal to another, it sent a team to observe the pit crews at the Indianapolis 500 race. The result: General Mills cut its plant changeover time by more than half.

Customers Ben & Jerry's customers are primarily ice cream and frozen yogurt eaters. But these customers have different form, flavor, fat, and convenience preferences. Medtronic's customers are cardiologists and heart surgeons who serve patients. An organization that has a clear customer focus is Lands' End. Its stores and website communicate a remarkable statement about its commitments to customer experience and product quality with these unconditional words:

Guaranteed. Period.®

The Lands' End guarantee has always been an unconditional one. Its website reads: "If you're not satisfied with any item, simply return it to us at any time for an exchange or refund of its purchase price." But to get the message across more clearly to its customers, it created the two-word guarantee above. However, Lands' End (now part of Sears) minimizes returns because many of its customers (a quarter of them are new) order their clothes based on their exact measurements. The crucial point: Strategy must provide genuine value and benefits to present and prospective customers to ensure they have a satisfying customer experience, which is the central goal of marketing today.[30]

Competitors In today's global competition, the distinctions among competitors are increasingly blurred. Take Lands' End. It started in the catalog retailing industry, but identifying its competitors today simply as other catalog retailers would be a huge oversimplification. Now Lands' End competes not only with other clothing catalog retailers but also with traditional department stores, mass merchandisers, and specialty shops. Even well-known clothing brands such as Liz Claiborne now have their own chain stores.

Although only some of the clothing in any of these stores may compete directly with Lands' End offerings, all these outlets have websites to sell over the Internet. This means there's a lot of competition out there! Now part of the merged Sears–Kmart operations, Lands' End also operates departments within Sears stores, almost competing with itself. Successful firms such as Lands' End must continuously assess who their competitors are and how they change in order to develop their own unique strategies.

Growth Strategies: Where Do We Want to Go?

Knowing where the organization is at the present time enables managers to set a direction for the firm and start to allocate resources to move in that direction. Two techniques to aid in these decisions are (1) business portfolio analysis and (2) hedgehog and blue ocean strategies.

Business Portfolio Analysis   The Boston Consulting Group (BCG), a nationally known management consulting firm, uses *business portfolio analysis* to quantify performance measures and growth targets to analyze its clients' SBUs as though they were a collection of separate investments.[31] The purpose of the tool is to determine the appeal of each SBU or offering and then determine the amount of cash, if any, each should receive. The BCG analysis can also be applied at the offering, product, or brand level. More than 75 percent of the largest U.S. firms have used this analytical tool.

The BCG business portfolio analysis requires an organization to locate the position of each of its SBUs on a growth-share matrix (see Figure 2–3 on the next page). The vertical axis is the *market growth rate*, which is the annual rate of growth of the SBU's industry. The horizontal axis is the *relative market share*, defined as the sales of the

Kodak today must make a series of difficult marketing decisions. From what you know about cameras and photos, assess Kodak's sales opportunities for the four products shown here. For some possible answers and a way to show these opportunities graphically, see the text and Figure 2–3.

Kodak

www.kodak.com

Kodak digital cameras

Kodak ink-jet printers and cartridges to print photos at home

Kodak film

Kodak self-service kiosks in retail outlets

②

Kodak digital cameras

①

Kodak film sales in the U.S., Canada, and Western Europe

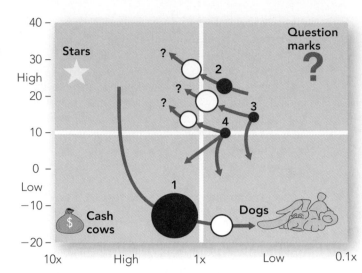

③

Kodak ink-jet printers and cartridges to print photos at home

④

Kodak self-service kiosks in retail outlets

Relative market share
(share relative to largest competitor)

FIGURE 2–3

Boston Consulting Group business portfolio analysis for Kodak's consumer-related SBUs as they appeared in 2003 (solid circle) and might appear in 2010 (hollow circle).

SBU divided by the sales of the largest firm in the industry. A relative market share of 10× (at the left end of the scale) means that the SBU has 10 times the share of its largest competitor, whereas a share of 0.1× (at the right end of the scale) means it has only 10 percent of the share of its largest competitor.

BCG has given specific names and descriptions to the four resulting quadrants in its growth-share matrix based on the amount of cash they generate for or require from the organization:

- *Cash cows* are SBUs that generate large amounts of cash, far more than they can invest profitably in themselves. They have dominant shares of slow-growth markets and provide cash to cover the organization's overhead and to invest in other SBUs.
- *Stars* are SBUs with a high share of high-growth markets that may need extra cash to finance their own rapid future growth. When their growth slows, they are likely to become cash cows.
- *Question marks or problem children* are SBUs with a low share of high-growth markets. They require large injections of cash just to maintain their market share, much less increase it. The names imply management's dilemma for these SBUs: choosing the right ones to invest in and phasing out the rest.
- *Dogs* are SBUs with low shares of slow-growth markets. Although they may generate enough cash to sustain themselves, they do not hold the promise of ever becoming real winners for the organization. Dropping SBUs that are dogs may be required, except when relationships with other SBUs, competitive considerations, or potential strategic alliances exist.[32] Some new offerings may start out as dogs, and as the market grows, they can become a question mark, a star, or even a cash cow.

In its business portfolio analysis, an organization's SBUs often start as question marks and proceed counterclockwise around Figure 2–3 to become stars, then cash cows, and finally dogs. Because an organization has limited influence on market growth rate, its main alternative is to try to change its relative market share. To accomplish this, management decides what role each SBU should have in the future and either injects or removes cash from it.

Nicknamed "Big Yellow" for the color of its film packages, Kodak relied until about 2000 not on its cameras but on its film for the bulk of its revenues and profits because of the billions of photos taken every year. Called the "razor and blades" strategy, the company made money on the repeat business from the lower-cost disposables

Antonio Perez is betting that Kodak's new high-tech ink-jet printers can reenergize the company's sales revenues.

(the "blades" or film), *not* on the product with which they are used (the "razor" or film camera). The appearance of digital cameras changed Kodak's business forever because of disappearing film sales.

Shortly after Antonio M. Perez became Kodak's president in 2003, he peered into a microscope in one of Kodak's labs. Perez was astounded to see droplets of a new ink invented by Kodak scientists that could produce vivid colors lasting 100 years—not the 15 years of many current color prints. "It was the holy grail of ink-jet printing, and they had it here," he remembers.[33]

So he launched Kodak's super-secret "Goya" project to convert the technology into real products. These ink-jet droplets were a key element in Kodak's shift of its strategic priorities from film to digital technology. Our analysis here focuses on consumer-related product lines and SBUs, but the Goya ink-jet technology is also expected to revolutionize the commercial offset printing of four-color magazines and catalogs.[34]

Four Kodak SBUs in solid circles in Figure 2–3 are shown as they might have appeared to Antonio Perez in 2003 and can serve as an example of BCG analysis. The area of each circle in Figure 2–3 is roughly proportional to the corresponding SBU's 2003 sales revenue. In a more complete analysis, its other SBUs would be included. This Kodak example also shows the agonizing strategic decisions that must be made by executives in firms in an industry facing revolutionary change—the situation Kodak confronts with the arrival of digital technology.

The success of Kodak's new digital strategy and its product lines shown in Figure 2–3 depends on how millions of consumers take photos and convert them into printed images over the next decade. Here is a snapshot of the sales opportunities and threats Perez might have envisioned in 2003 and looks to in 2010 (in the hollow circles) for the four consumer product lines, reflected in the comments of industry analysts:

1. *Kodak film.* An $8 billion *cash cow* in 2003, Kodak film sales are still the company's biggest single source of revenue. But now in a free fall because of digital cameras, Kodak film sales are expected to decline 10 to 15 percent per year indefinitely.
2. *Kodak digital cameras.* Perez saw sales of Kodak's popular line of EasyShare digital cameras double to $2 billion from 2003 to 2006. Kodak clearly expects its digital cameras to be a *star* soon. The challenge: In 2007 it is third in market share behind Canon and Sony in the United States with new rivals emerging, such as cell phones with digital cameras.[35]
3. *Kodak ink-jet printers and cartridges to print digital photos at home.* In 2007 about 56 percent of digital camera owners printed their images at home. In that year Kodak launched a line of multipurpose machines to print high-quality photos, make copies, and send faxes. It's a "razor and blade" strategy again with high-quality ink cartridges that will make photos at half the cost of Hewlett-Packard's (HP) printers. Perez counts on this printer-and-cartridge combination becoming a *star* in the Kodak portfolio. But HP is the entrenched 300-pound gorilla in this market. So the future of this *question mark* could range from being a *star* to a *dog*.[36]

4. *Kodak self-service kiosks in retail outlets.* These self-service printers initially were too much of a hassle for many consumers. But new easy-to-use Kodak machines won many consumers' hearts. By 2007, 80,000 photo kiosks were in retail stores around the world. A potential *star?* Maybe. But in early 2007 Xerox announced a venture with Kodak's archrival Fuji to put self-service kiosks in retailers![37]

Are these BCG projections valid? Your use of digital cameras and how you make your prints hold the answer. Some industry experts believe this may determine Kodak's ability to survive.

The primary strength of business portfolio analysis lies in forcing a firm to place each of its SBUs in the growth-share matrix, which in turn suggests which SBUs will be cash producers and cash users in the future. Weaknesses of this analysis arise from the difficulty in (1) getting the needed information and (2) incorporating competitive information into business portfolio analysis.[38]

Hedgehog and Blue Ocean Analyses   Today an organization needs to differentiate itself from its competitors to succeed in this highly competitive marketplace. It must be unique. Two recent ideas can help an organization go from "good to great" by either (1) becoming the best in its industry or (2) going outside of it.

Can we be the best in our industry and become a hedgehog? Jim Collins, author of *Good to Great,* believes that an excellent organization must employ the "Hedgehog Concept."[39] The Greek parable of the hedgehog and the fox says that "the fox knows many things but the hedgehog knows one big thing." An organization using the Hedgehog Concept develops a simple, excellent offering that captures the imagination of its employees and its customers. Top managers at Walgreens might give these answers to Collins' three basic questions in developing a compelling offering:

- What can we be the best at in the world? For example, Walgreens can become the best at offering great customer service in the most convenient drugstores in any geographic market.
- What drives our economic engine? For Walgreens, it can be customer profit per visit—a very measurable goal that can be tracked using a dashboard.
- What are we deeply passionate about? Walgreens is passionate about providing the best possible customer experience at the most convenient locations.

Can we go outside our industry and swim into Blue Oceans?   W. Chan Kim and Renée Mauborgne, co-authors of *Blue Ocean Strategy*, believe that an organization must swim out of the "red ocean of bloody competition" and into a "blue ocean having less competition."[40] We can use the strategy of Southwest Airlines to see both oceans:

- *Red oceans.* These represent an organization's existing industry—such as airlines—whose boundaries are well defined and accepted by its sellers and buyers. Here, an organization, such as American Airlines, competes for market share. Over time, the number of competitors increases and they begin to look alike so that their offerings and brands become commodities—barely distinguishable to consumers. So the ocean (market) becomes blood red as competitors (sharks) eat each other up battling for market share. For the airlines, the result has been a wave of mergers and bankruptcies.
- *Blue oceans.* These denote all industries (1) not yet in existence or (2) that are created by expanding industry boundaries. An organization that follows a blue ocean strategy reduces or eliminates some factors an industry competes on while raising and creating value to buyers on other factors. This creates a leap in value for both the organization and its customers.[41]

Southwest Airlines reached a blue ocean by providing a unique customer experience. This expanded existing industry boundaries through coupling friendly service

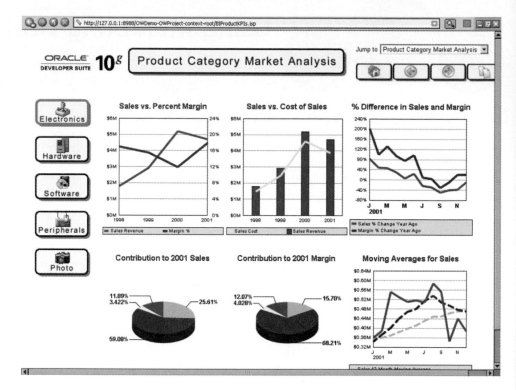

and high-speed transportation with a flexible schedule and low price. This allowed Southwest to differentiate itself from its competitors such as American Airlines.[42] Southwest's blue ocean strategy has been hard to imitate because (1) it generates economies of scale—attracting large numbers of customers quickly while reducing operating costs—and (2) competitors have difficulty changing their offerings to compete due to corporate inertia.[43]

Tracking Strategic Directions with Marketing Dashboards

Although marketing managers can set strategic directions for their organizations, how do they know if they are making progress in getting there? One answer is increasingly common: By using marketing dashboards.

Car Dashboards and Marketing Dashboards
A **marketing dashboard** is the visual display on a single computer screen of the essential information related to achieving a marketing objective.[44] Often it is an Internet-based display with real-time information, and active hyperlinks to provide further detail. An example is when a chief marketing officer wants to see hourly what the effect of a new TV advertising campaign is on a product's sales.

The idea of a marketing dashboard really comes from that of a car's dashboard. On a car's dashboard we glance at the fuel gauge and take action when our gas is getting low. With a marketing dashboard, a marketing manager glances at a graph or table and makes a decision whether or not to take action, or often to do more analysis to understand the problem better.[45]

Marketing Metrics and Graphics in Designing Marketing Dashboards
Oracle's marketing dashboard in Figure 2–4 shows graphic displays of key measures of a product category's performance, such as sales, cost of sales, and percent margin.[46] Each performance variable is a **marketing metric**, a measure of the quantitative value or trend of a marketing activity or result.[47]

The choice of which marketing metrics to display is critical for a busy manager, who can be overwhelmed with too much information. So, as with the Oracle

Using Marketing Dashboards

Which States Are Underperforming?

As a marketer, before stepping on the gas in your business, you ask "how fast is my business going?" It is now January 2010. Three years ago, you started your own company to sell a snack that includes a top-secret ingredient you discovered while volunteering in the Amazon after graduation. The snack is really delicious and adds IQ and strength with every bite!

Your Challenge The snack is sold in all 50 states. Your goal is 10 percent growth annually. You want to get 2010 off to a fast start. You want to act quickly to solve any sales problems. You know that pockets of sales stagnation or decline (0 percent or negative growth) are offset by growth markets with greater than 10 percent growth.

Studying a table of the sales and percent change versus a year ago in each of the 50 states would work but be very time consuming. A good graphic is better. You choose the following marketing metric, where "sales" is measured in units:

Annual % Sales Change

$$= \frac{(2009 \text{ Sales} - 2008 \text{ Sales}) \times 100}{2008 \text{ Sales}}$$

You want to act quickly to improve sales. In your map growth that is greater than 10 percent is GREEN, 0 to 10 percent growth is ORANGE, and decline is RED. Notice that you (1) picked a metric, and (2) made your own rules that GREEN is good, ORANGE is bad, and RED is very bad.

Your Findings At a glance you see that sales growth in the Northeastern states is weaker than the 10 percent target, and sales are actually declining in many of the states.

Your Action Marketing is often about grappling with sales shortfalls. You'll need to start by trying to identify and correct the problems in the largest volume states that are underperforming—in this case in the Northeastern U.S.

You'll want to do the marketing research to see if the problem starts with (1) an external factor like changing consumer tastes or (2) an internal factor like a breakdown in your distribution system.

Annual Percentage Change in Unit Volume, by State

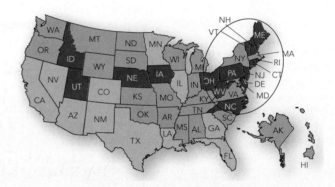

marketing dashboard, often only six or seven marketing metrics are shown on the marketing dashboard computer screen to be checked throughout the day. Dashboard designers also take great care to show graphs and tables in easy-to-understand formats to enable clear interpretation at a glance.[48]

Often a manager's glance at a marketing dashboard is a decision to "drill down" into the company's databases to understand the problem better. The Using Marketing Dashboards box is an example. In running your own company, you want to track your snack's sales. So you choose to drill down into your databases to analyze sales by state—and then decide on an action.

The three-step "challenge-findings-action" format in the box is one used in the Using Marketing Dashboards boxes throughout the textbook. The format stresses the importance of using marketing dashboards and data as a means to taking effective actions.

Most organizations tie the marketing metrics they track in their marketing dashboards to the qualitative objectives established in their **marketing plan**, which is a road map for the marketing activities of an organization for a specified future time period, such as one year or five years. Appendix A at the end of this chapter

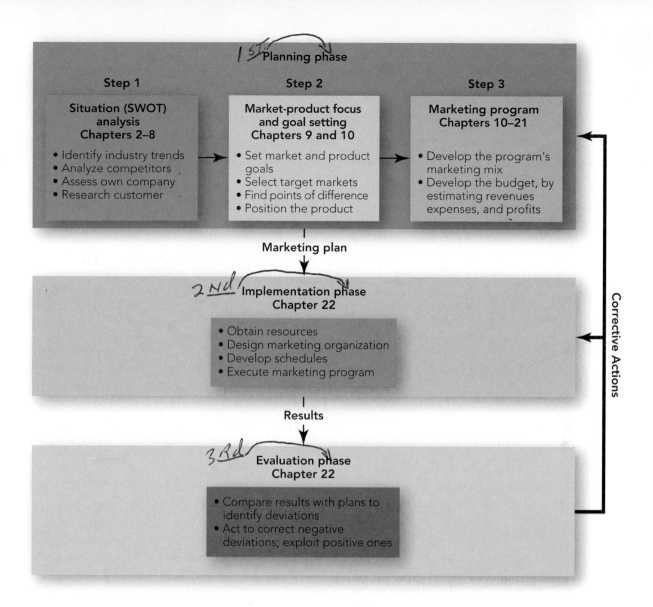

FIGURE 2–5

The strategic marketing process has three vital phases: planning, implementation, and evaluation. The figure also shows where these phases are discussed in the text.

provides guidelines for writing a marketing plan and also presents a sample marketing plan for Paradise Kitchens,® Inc., a firm that produces and distributes a line of spicy chilies under the Howlin' Coyote® brand name. Appendix A also links each section of the marketing plan to the relevant textbook chapter to assist students who are writing marketing plans.

The sequence of activities in the strategic marketing process shown in Figure 2–5 also parallels the elements of the marketing plan that appear in Appendix A. The strategic marketing process is covered in detail in the next section.

---

learning review

5. What is business portfolio analysis?

6. What is the difference between a hedgehog strategy and a blue ocean strategy?

7. What are marketing dashboards and why are they important?

THE STRATEGIC MARKETING PROCESS

After the organization assesses where it's at and where it wants to go, other questions emerge, such as:

1. How do we allocate our resources to get where we want to go?
2. How do we convert our plans to actions?
3. How do our results compare with our plans, and do deviations require new plans?

To answer these questions, an organization uses the **strategic marketing process**, whereby an organization allocates its marketing mix resources to reach its target markets. This process is divided into three phases: planning, implementation, and evaluation (Figure 2–5).

Strategic Marketing Process: The Planning Phase

As shown in Figure 2–5, the planning phase of the strategic marketing process consists of the three steps shown at the top of the figure: (1) situation analysis, (2) market-product focus and goal setting, and (3) the marketing program. Let's use the recent marketing planning experiences of several companies to look at each of these steps.

Figure 2–5 also shows how the strategic marketing process integrates the chapters in this book. Chapters 2 through 8 provide the information for the situation (SWOT) analysis, step 1 of the planning phase. Step 2, developing a market-product focus and goals for the product, is covered in Chapters 9 and 10. The elements of the marketing program in step 3—the 4Ps—are discussed in Chapters 10 through 21. The book concludes with Chapter 22, which ties together the planning, implementation, and evaluation phases of the strategic marketing process.

Step 1: Situation (SWOT) Analysis The essence of **situation analysis** is taking stock of where the firm or product has been recently, where it is now, and where it is headed in terms of the organization's plans and the external factors and trends affecting it. The situation analysis box in Figure 2–5 is the first of the three steps in the planning phase.

An effective shorthand summary of the situation analysis is a **SWOT analysis**, an acronym describing an organization's appraisal of its internal **S**trengths and **W**eaknesses and its external **O**pportunities and **T**hreats. Both the situation and SWOT analyses can be done at the level of the entire organization, the business unit, the product line, or the specific product. As an analysis moves from the level of the entire organization to the specific product, it, of course, gets far more detailed. For small firms or those with basically a single product line, an analysis at the firm or product level is really the same thing.

How can Ben & Jerry's develop new products and social responsibility programs that contribute to its mission? The text describes how the strategic marketing process and its SWOT analysis can help.

Ben & Jerry's
www.benjerry.com

FIGURE 2–6

Ben & Jerry's: a SWOT analysis to keep it growing. The picture painted in this SWOT analysis is the basis for management actions.

Location of Factor	TYPE OF FACTOR	
	Favorable	Unfavorable
Internal	**Strengths** • Prestigious, well-known brand name among U.S. consumers • Large share of the U.S. super premium ice cream market • Complements Unilever's other ice cream brands (Breyers, Good Humor) • Widely recognized for its social mission, values, and actions	**Weaknesses** • Danger that B&J's social responsibility actions may add costs, reduce focus on core business, and alienate some customers • Need for experienced managers to help growth • Modest sales growth and profits in recent years
External	**Opportunities** • Growing demand for quality ice cream in overseas markets • Increasing U.S. demand for frozen yogurt, sorbet, and other low-fat, low-carb desserts • Success of many U.S. firms in extending successful brand from one product category to others	**Threats** • Consumer concern with sugary and fatty desserts; B&J customers are the type who read new government-ordered nutritional labels • Competes with General Mills' Häagen-Dazs and Nestlé's Dreyer's brands • International downturns increase the risks for B&J in European and Asian markets

The SWOT analysis is based on an exhaustive study of the four areas shown in step 1 of the planning phase of the strategic marketing process (Figure 2–5). Knowledge of these areas forms the foundation on which the firm builds its marketing program:

- Identify trends in the organization's industry.
- Analyze the organization's competitors.
- Assess the organization itself.
- Research the organization's present and prospective customers.

Let's assume you are the Unilever vice president responsible for integrating Ben & Jerry's into Unilever's business. You might do the SWOT analysis shown in Figure 2–6. Note that your SWOT table has four cells formed by the combination of internal versus external factors (the rows) and favorable versus unfavorable factors (the columns) that summarize Ben & Jerry's strengths, weaknesses, opportunities, and threats.

A SWOT analysis helps identify the strategy-related factors in these four cells that can have a major effect on the firm. The goal is not simply to develop the SWOT analysis but to translate the results of the analysis into specific actions to help the firm grow and succeed. The ultimate goal is to identify the *critical* factors affecting the firm and then build on vital strengths, correct glaring weaknesses, exploit significant opportunities, and avoid disaster-laden threats. That is a big order.

The Ben and Jerry's SWOT analysis in Figure 2–6 can be the basis for these kinds of specific actions. An action in each of the four cells might be:

- *Build on a strength.* Find specific efficiencies in distribution with Unilever's existing ice cream brands.
- *Correct a weakness.* Recruit experienced managers from other consumer product firms to help stimulate growth.
- *Exploit an opportunity.* Develop a new line of low-fat, low-carb frozen yogurts and sorbets to respond to consumer health concerns.
- *Avoid a disaster-laden threat.* Focus on less risky international markets, such as Canada and Mexico.

Examples of more in-depth study in these four areas appear in the SWOT analysis in Figure A–1 in the marketing plan in Appendix A and the chapters in this textbook cited in that plan.

Step 2: Market-Product Focus and Goal Setting   Determining which products will be directed toward which customers (step 2 of the planning phase in Figure 2–5) is essential for developing an effective marketing program (step 3). This decision is often based on **market segmentation**, which involves aggregating prospective buyers into groups, or segments, that (1) have common needs and (2) will respond similarly to a marketing action. This enables an organization to identify the segments on which it will focus its efforts—its target market segments—and develop specific marketing programs to reach them.

As always, understanding the customer is essential. In the case of Medtronic, executives researched a potential new market in Asia by talking extensively with doctors in India and China. They learned that these doctors saw some of the current state-of-the-art features of heart pacemakers as less essential and too expensive. Instead, they wanted an affordable pacemaker that was reliable and easy to implant. This information led Medtronic to develop and market a new product, the Champion heart pacemaker, directed at the needs of this Asian market segment.

Goal setting involves setting measurable marketing objectives to be achieved. Such objectives would be different depending on the level of marketing involved. For a specific market, the goal may be to introduce a new product, such as Medtronic's Champion pacemaker in Asia or Toyota's launch of its hybrid car, the Prius. For a specific brand or product, the goal may be to create a promotional campaign or pricing strategy that will get more consumers to purchase. For an entire marketing program, the objective is often a series of actions to be implemented over several years.

Using the strategic marketing process shown in Figure 2–5, let's examine Medtronic's five-year plan to reach the "affordable and reliable" segment of the pacemaker market:[49]

- *Set marketing and product goals.* The chances of new-product success are increased by specifying both market and product goals. Based on their market research showing the need for a reliable yet affordable pacemaker, Medtronic executives set the following as their goal: Design and market such a pacemaker in the next three years that could be manufactured in China for the Asian market.
- *Select target markets.* The Champion pacemaker will be targeted at cardiologists and medical clinics performing heart surgery in India, China, and other Asian countries.
- *Find points of difference.* **Points of difference** are those characteristics of a product that make it superior to competitive substitutes. Just as a competitive advantage is a unique strength of an entire organization compared to its competitors, points of difference are unique characteristics of one of its products that make it superior to competitive products it faces in the marketplace. For the Champion pacemaker, the key points of difference are *not* the state-of-the-art features that drive up production costs and are important to only a minority of patients. Instead, they are high quality, long life, reliability, ease of use, and low cost.
- *Position the product.* The pacemaker will be "positioned" in cardiologists' and patients' minds as a medical device that is high quality and reliable with a long, nine-year life. The name Champion is selected after testing acceptable names among doctors in India, China, Pakistan, Singapore, and Malaysia.

Details in these four elements of step 2 provide a solid foundation to use in developing the marketing program, step 3 in the planning phase of the strategic marketing process.

LO5

Step 3: Marketing Program   Activities in step 2 tell the marketing manager which customers to target and which customer needs the firm's product offerings

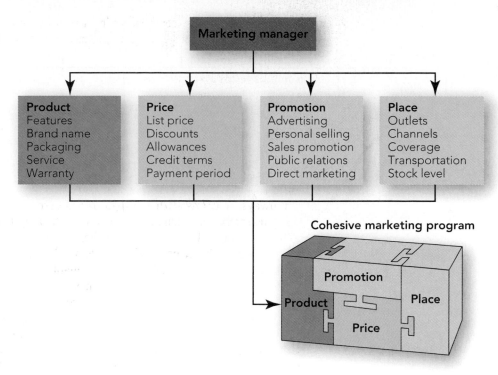

can satisfy—the *who* and *what* aspects of the strategic marketing process. The *how* aspect—step 3 in the planning phase—involves developing the program's marketing mix and its budget.

Figure 2–7 shows components of each marketing mix element that are combined to provide a cohesive marketing program. For the five-year marketing plan of Medtronic, these marketing mix activities include the following:

- *Product strategy.* Offer a Champion brand heart pacemaker with features needed by Asian patients.
- *Price strategy.* Manufacture the Champion to control costs so that it can be priced below $1,000 (in U.S. dollars)—an affordable price for Asian markets.
- *Promotion strategy.* Feature demonstrations at cardiologist and medical conventions across Asia to introduce the Champion and highlight the device's features and application.
- *Place (distribution) strategy.* Search out, utilize, and train reputable medical distributors across Asia to call on cardiologists and medical clinics.

Putting this marketing program into effect requires that the firm commit time and money to it in the form of a sales forecast (see Chapter 9) and budget that must be approved by top management.

learning review

8. What is the difference between a strength and an opportunity in a SWOT analysis?
9. What is market segmentation?
10. What are points of difference and why are they important?

Strategic Marketing Process: The Implementation Phase

As shown in Figure 2–5, the result of the tens or hundreds of hours spent in the planning phase of the strategic marketing process is the firm's marketing plan. Implementation,

President/Chief Executive Officer

| Vice President Information Systems Department | Vice President Research and Development Department | Vice President Manufacturing Department | Vice President* Marketing Department | Vice President Accounting and Finance Department | Vice President Human Resources Department |

Manager Product Planning

Manager Marketing Research

Manager Sales

Manager Advertising and Promotion

Sales Regions and Representatives

*Called chief marketing officer (CMO) in many corporations

FIGURE 2–8

Organization of a typical manufacturing firm, showing a breakdown of the marketing department.

Dubbed "Queen of the Geeks" by her employees, Susan H. Tousi set exacting quality standards in leading Kodak's ink-jet research and development.

the second phase of the strategic marketing process, involves carrying out the marketing plan that emerges from the planning phase. If the firm cannot put the marketing plan into effect—in the implementation phase—the planning phase was a waste of time. Figure 2–5 also shows the four components of the implementation phase: (1) obtaining resources, (2) designing the marketing organization, (3) developing schedules, and (4) actually executing the marketing program designed in the planning phase. Kodak provides a case example.

Obtaining Resources   In late 2003, Kodak announced its bold plan (discussed earlier) to reenergize the film manufacturer for the new age of digital cameras and prints. Antonio Perez needed money to implement the plan. So Perez in 2007 sold Kodak's medical imaging unit for $2.5 billion and announced continuing painful employment cuts to 28,000 by the end of the year, down from its 145,000 peak in 1984.[50]

Designing the Marketing Organization   A marketing program needs a marketing organization to implement it. Figure 2–8 shows the organization chart of a typical manufacturing firm, giving some details of the marketing department's structure. Four managers of marketing activities are shown to report to the vice president of marketing. Several regional sales managers and an international sales manager may report to the manager of sales. This marketing organization is responsible for converting marketing plans to reality as part of the corporate team.

Developing Schedules   Effective implementation requires goals, deadlines, and schedules. To implement his plan to focus on Kodak's digital business opportunities, Kodak and Perez set a key goal in 2003:[51]

- Boost sales from $13 billion in 2003 to $16 billion in 2006.
- Boost sales from $16 billion in 2006 to $20 billion in 2010.

48

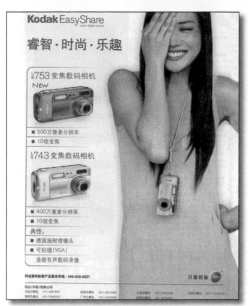

To help fill in its planning gap, Kodak is pursuing opportunities for sales of digital cameras in China.

Achieving Kodak's 2010 goal of $20 billion in annual sales is especially difficult because actual annual sales revenues have declined slightly since 2003. To help achieve this aggressive sales target, Perez picked Susan H. Tousi to run Kodak's ink-jet research and development—project "Goya," which must succeed to reach the 2010 goal. Spraying ink through 3,840 nozzles at 24,000 drops per second to yield vibrant, long-lasting color prints required the latest chemistry and nanotechnology. Getting the ink formula right required 24-hour marathons. Tousi repeatedly sent researchers back to their labs because results didn't meet her standards. And Kodak's new line of ink-jet printers was launched in February 2007. For her exacting quality standards, Tousi's employees named her "Queen of the Geeks!"[52]

To achieve these goals, Perez also worked with key Kodak executives to schedule the acquisition of and partnering with firms having digital expertise.

Executing the Marketing Program Marketing plans are meaningless pieces of paper without effective execution of those plans. This effective execution requires attention to detail for both marketing strategies and marketing tactics. A **marketing strategy** is the means by which a marketing goal is to be achieved, usually characterized by a specified target market and a marketing program to reach it. The term implies both the end sought (target market) and the means to achieve it (marketing program). At this marketing strategy level, Kodak will seek to increase sales of digital cameras and ink-jet printers for consumers and products for commercial printers.

To implement a marketing program successfully, hundreds of detailed decisions are often required. These decisions, called **marketing tactics**, are detailed day-to-day operational decisions essential to the overall success of marketing strategies. At Kodak, writing ads and setting prices for its new lines of digital cameras are examples of marketing tactics.

Marketing strategies and marketing tactics blend into each other. Effective marketing program implementation requires excruciating concern for both.

Strategic Marketing Process: The Evaluation Phase

The evaluation phase of the strategic marketing process seeks to keep the marketing program moving in the direction set for it (see Figure 2–4). Accomplishing this requires the marketing manager to (1) compare the results of the marketing program with the goals in the written plans to identify deviations and (2) act on these deviations—correcting negative deviations and exploiting positive ones.

Comparing Results with Plans to Identify Deviations In late 2003, as Antonio Perez looked at Kodak's sales revenues from 1998 through 2003, he didn't like what he saw: the very flat trend, or AB in Figure 2–9 on the next page. Extending the 1998–2003 trend to 2010 along BC shows declining sales revenues, a totally unacceptable, no-growth strategy.

Kodak's growth target of 5 to 6 percent annually, the line BD in Figure 2–9, would give sales revenues of $16 billion in 2006 and $20 billion in 2010. This reveals a wedge-shaped shaded gap in the figure. Planners call this the *planning gap,* the difference between the projection of the path to reach a new goal (line BD) and the projection of the path of the results of a plan already in place (line BC).

The ultimate purpose of the firm's marketing program is to "fill in" this planning gap—in Kodak's case, to move its future sales revenue line from the no-growth line BC up to the challenging target of line BD. But poor performance can result in actual sales revenues being far less than the targeted levels. This is the essence of evaluation: comparing actual results with goals set.

FIGURE 2–9

The evaluation phase of the strategic marketing process requires that the organization compare actual results with goals to identify and act on deviations to fill in its "planning gap." The text describes how Kodak hopes to fill in its planning gap by 2010.

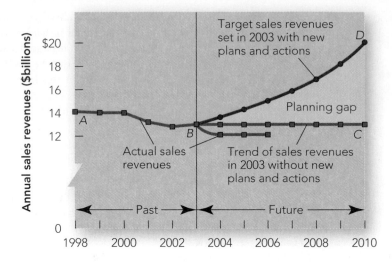

Acting on Deviations   When evaluation shows that actual performance fails to meet expectations, managers need to take corrective actions. And when actual results are far better than the plan called for, creative managers find ways to exploit the situation. Two possible Kodak midcourse corrections for both positive and negative deviations from targets illustrate these management actions:

- *Exploiting a positive deviation.* If Kodak's innovative "Goya" ink-jet printers sell better than expected, Kodak might try to move quickly to offer these to international customers.
- *Correcting a negative deviation.* However, if the Xerox-Fuji joint venture to market self-service kiosks in retail outlets is effective, Kodak might launch a new aggressive marketing program to reach this segment.

The strategic marketing process is discussed in greater detail again in Chapter 22.

learning review

11. What is the implementation phase of the strategic marketing process?

12. How do the goals set for a marketing program in the planning phase relate to the evaluation phase of the strategic marketing process?

LEARNING OBJECTIVES REVIEW

LO1   *Describe the kinds of organizations that exist and the three organizational levels of strategy.*

An organization is a legal entity of people who share a common mission. There are two kinds. One is a business firm that is a privately owned organization that serves its customers in order to earn a profit so that it can survive. The other is a nonprofit organization that is a nongovernmental organization that serves its customers but does not have profit as an organizational goal. Most large business firms and nonprofit organizations are divided into three levels of strategy: (a) the corporate level, where top management directs overall strategy for the entire organization; (b) the strategic business unit level, where managers set a more specific strategic direction for their businesses to set value-creating opportunities; and (c) the functional level, where groups of specialists actually create value for the organization.

LO2   *Describe how core values, mission, organizational culture, business, and goals are important to organizations.*

Organizations exist to accomplish something for someone. To give organizations direction and focus, they continuously assess their core values, mission, organizational culture, business, and goals. Today's organizations specify their foundation, set a direction, and formulate strategies—'why,' 'what,' and 'how' factors, respectively. Core values are the organization's fundamental, passionate, and enduring principles that guide its conduct over time—what Enron forgot when it lost sight of its responsibilities to its stakeholders. The organization's mission is a statement of its function in society, often identifying its customers, markets, products, and technologies. Organizational culture is a set of values, ideas, attitudes, and norms of behavior that is learned and shared among the members of an organization. To answer the question, 'What business are we in?' an organization defines its "business"—the clear, broad, underlying industry category or market sector of its offering. Finally, the organization's goals (or objectives) are statements of an accomplishment of a task to be achieved, often by a specific time.

LO3 *Explain how organizations set strategic directions by assessing where they are now and seek to be in the future.*

Managers of an organization ask two key questions to set a strategic direction. The first question, Where are we now? requires an organization to (a) reevaluate its competencies to ensure that its special capabilities still provide a competitive advantage; (b) assess its present and prospective customers to ensure they have a satisfying customer experience—the central goal of marketing today; and (c) analyze its current and potential competitors from a global perspective to determine whether it needs to redefine its business. The second question, Where do we want to go? requires an organization to set a specific direction and allocate resources to move it in that direction. Business portfolio, hedgehog, and blue ocean analyses help do this.

LO4 *Describe the strategic marketing process and its three key phases: planning, implementation, and evaluation.*

An organization uses the strategic marketing process to allocate its marketing mix resources to reach its target markets. This process consists of three phases, which are usually formalized in a marketing plan. The planning phase consists of (a) a situation (SWOT) analysis of the organization's strengths, weaknesses, opportunities, and threats; (b) a market-product focus through market segmentation, points of difference analysis, and goal setting; and (c) a marketing program that specifies the budget and activities (marketing strategies and tactics) for each marketing mix element. The implementation phase carries out the marketing plan that emerges from the planning phase. It has four key elements: obtaining resources, designing the marketing organization, developing schedules, and executing the marketing program. The evaluation phase compares the results from the implemented marketing program with the marketing plan's goals to identify the "planning gaps" and take actions to exploit positive deviations or correct negative ones.

LO5 *Explain how the marketing mix elements are blended into a cohesive marketing program.*

A marketing manager uses information obtained during the SWOT analysis, market-product focus, and goal-setting steps in the planning process to develop marketing strategies and marketing tactics for each marketing mix element for a given product, which are then implemented, as specified in the marketing plan, as a marketing program.

FOCUSING ON KEY TERMS

business p. 33
competencies p. 35
competitive advantage p. 35
core values p. 31
corporate level p. 29
cross-functional teams p. 30
functional level p. 30
goals p. 34
market segmentation p. 46

market share p. 34
marketing dashboard p. 41
marketing metric p. 41
marketing plan p. 42
marketing strategy p. 49
marketing tactics p. 49
mission p. 32
objectives p. 34
organizational culture p. 33

points of difference p. 46
profit p. 28
situation analysis p. 44
strategic business unit (SBU) p. 30
strategic business unit level p. 30
strategic marketing process p. 44
strategy p. 29
SWOT analysis p. 44

APPLYING MARKETING KNOWLEDGE

1 Using Medtronic as an example, (a) explain how a mission statement gives a strategic direction to its organization. (b) Create a mission statement for your own career.

2 What competencies best describe (a) your college or university and (b) your favorite restaurant?

3 Why does a product often start as a question mark and then move counterclockwise around BCG's growth-share matrix shown in Figure 2–3?

4 What is the main result of each of the three phases of the strategic marketing process? (a) planning, (b) implementation, and (c) evaluation.

5 Select one strength, one weakness, one opportunity, and one threat from the SWOT analysis for Ben & Jerry's, shown in Figure 2–6. Suggest a single action that Unilever might take to address each one.

6 The goal-setting step in the planning phase of the strategic marketing process sets quantified objectives for use in the evaluation phase. What does a manager do if measured results are below objectives? Above objectives?

building your marketing plan

1 Read Appendix A, "Building an Effective Marketing Plan." Then write a 600-word executive summary for the Paradise Kitchens marketing plan using the numbered headings shown in the plan. When you have completed the draft of your own marketing plan, use what you learned in writing an executive summary for Paradise Kitchens to write a 600-word executive summary to go in the front of your own marketing plan.

2 Using Chapter 2 and Appendix A as guides, give focus to your marketing plan by (a) writing your mission statement in 25 words or less, (b) listing three nonfinancial goals and three financial goals, (c) writing your competitive advantage in 35 words or less, and (d) doing a SWOT analysis table.

"We want to get people to drive an extra block or cut across an extra lane of traffic to choose BP over its competitors," claims Ann Hand, Senior Vice President—Global Brand Marketing and Innovation.[53] BP, formerly known as British Petroleum, is one of the world's largest producers and marketers of petroleum products. Through innovative marketing and with a focus on the environment, BP has recently been transforming itself into a consumer-centric provider of energy products and services that are broader than just oil and gas.

KEY ELEMENTS IN BP'S "BEYOND PETROLEUM" TRANSFORMATION

Increased energy demand due to the growing economies of both the developed and developing countries as well as supply constraints have caused oil prices to rise sharply during the past few decades. This, along with the heightened awareness of global climate change in the late 1990s, created an opportunity for BP to transform its mission statement to the following:

"Our business is about finding, producing, and marketing the natural energy resources on which the modern world depends."

BP then reorganized itself primarily into two strategic performance (i.e. business) units to support its mission. These "SPUs" consist of activities related to the (1) discovery and production of oil and natural gas and (2) refining and marketing of petroleum products.

BP also identified and evaluated many opportunities to increase its sales and profits. One strategy was through acquisitions. During the late 1990s, BP invested $120 billion to add competitors Amoco, ARCO, and Castrol to its business portfolio. BP now produces about three percent of the planet's oil and gas, operates in over 100 countries around the world, and serves 13 million customers per day at 24,600 retail sites, including 12,300 stations in the United States. The benefits to its stakeholders: BP global sales now exceed $250 billion.

In 2000, BP introduced a new brand identity to reflect the integrated company it had become. The BP shield and Amoco torch were replaced by a new Helios logo that more appropriately reflects BP's corporate and retail brand image as a green, environmentally-friendly company. Because a brand image communicates the brand's essence—an emotional tie between the company and its customers—it provides confidence to customers: they know they can get high-quality gas, conveniently purchase food and beverages, and travel onwards refreshed. Thus, BP is not just about gasoline—it goes "beyond petroleum."

Within its refining and marketing SPU, BP sells gasoline at its branded retail gas stations, which include the BP, Amoco Ultimate, Wild Bean Café and BP Connect brands (eastern U.S.) and the ARCO and *am/pm* brands (western U.S.). In the near term, BP's retail strategy will focus on high-growth metropolitan areas in the U.S. through new and franchised service stations. In the long-term, BP plans to transform the retail gasoline landscape with its new Helios House and Helios Power strategies (see below).

BP'S FOUR CORE VALUES

BP specifies four core values to express the way the organization does business and help translate the mission into practical action:

- *Progressive:* BP is always looking for new and better ways to conduct business. It has developed a relationship with Ford to build hydrogen vehicles and fueling stations in California, Michigan, and elsewhere. BP also has reformulated its BP Amoco Ultimate fuel to reduce air pollutants.
- *Innovative:* Through the creative approaches of employees, and the development and application of cutting-edge drilling technology, BP seeks breakthrough solutions for its customers.
- *Green:* BP is committed to environmental leadership—the proactive and responsible treatment of the planet's natural resources and developing lower carbon emission energy sources. As a result, BP now stores its gasoline in double-skinned tanks to prevent spills and leaks.
- *Performance-driven:* BP sets the global standards of performance on financial and environmental dimensions, as well as safety, growth, and customer and employee satisfaction.

HELIOS HOUSE: TRANSFORMING BP'S GASOLINE RETAILING

Since 1977, the percentage of gasoline stations in the United States that also contain a convenience store has gone from 5 percent to more than 50 percent. To support the demand for convenience store offerings, BP developed a very successful convenience store concept called *am/pm*. This branded offering was created and tested on ARCO sites in the western U.S.; in the future, *am/pm* will partner with the BP retail brand and penetrate the eastern U.S.

Currently, the *am/pm* stores sell both fuel and over 2,000 convenience items (snacks, beverages, necessities, etc.). Sales from the over 1,000 *am/pm* stores now exceed $6 billion; both the number and sales revenues are expected to grow significantly during the next several years as BP transforms many of its existing gas stations into *am/pm* stores.

In early 2007, BP launched a two-part strategy to change the way consumers think about its gas stations. One part was Helios House, a new-look gasoline station located in Los Angeles that will serve as a living laboratory to test ideas in a real environment. Ann Hand, who manages BP's $280 million global marketing programs, was instrumental in the planning and implementation of Helios House. Becoming operational during April 2007, Helios House was designed to be eco-friendly from the top down. The building itself was constructed from recycled, sustainable, and non-toxic materials. Moreover, its canopy has 90 solar panels to generate its own electricity. The roof is covered with grass to reduce the building's heating and cooling needs and has rain collectors to irrigate the surrounding drought-tolerant landscape. The facility also has energy-efficient lighting, using just one-fifth less energy compared to a traditional gas station. As a result of these and other design features, Helios House became the first gas station to be certified as green by the U.S. Green Building Council.

Helios House also offers customers (1) clean, well-maintained restrooms, (2) friendly "green team" employees who will not only greet customers with a smile but also check their cars' tire pressure to ensure proper inflation—which boosts gas mileage, and (3) tips on creating a green lifestyle through its www.thegreencurve.com website. According to Kathy Seegebrecht, BP's U.S. Advertising Manager, "Helios House will serve as a place where BP can have a conversation with its customers about green ideas and how its gas station can play a part in creating a better environment. It was designed to serve as a beacon to inspire the employees and franchisees through the U.S."

Helios House is *not* a prototype of BP's station of the future. However, it will be an incubator of green ideas that can be implemented among its existing and new stations. It is just too costly to replace 25,000 existing stations throughout the world. Seegebrecht concludes, "Helios House is showing us that in a more brand-conscious world, where we all want the best of everything, people might actually want a better gas station." How successful has the Helios House been? "The site has nearly doubled its fuel volumes."

HELIOS POWER: BP'S PROMOTION OF ITS GASOLINE RETAILING

The second part of BP's strategy was a promotional campaign to transform BP's retail brand image at its locations in the U.S. Buying gasoline is a low involvement purchase and consumers have low expectations regarding their purchase experiences. Armed with that consumer insight, BP created and executed the $45 million Helios Power advertising and brand building campaign, which is an extension of BP's

"Beyond Petroleum" corporate campaign that began in the early 2000s. The Helios Power campaign consisted of the following marketing tactics:

- *"A little better" tagline.* BP customers can expect to receive "a little better" experience at its service stations and other retail outlets compared to those of its competitors. Hand elaborates, "In this market, a little better means a lot. People see refueling as a necessary and unpleasant chore. However, BP can be cleaner and friendlier, and that's why people will choose us rather than our competitors." And this choice will be made on an emotional basis because customers "like what we stand for."[54]
- *Animated TV ads.* These feature a family of characters (the Lighthouse family, the Babies, and the Beeps) and a catchy tune designed to reinforce the emotional appeal of the BP brand. The TV ads aired during some of the top U.S. TV shows (*American Idol, Ugly Betty*) and also had exposure on YouTube. The purposes of the ads were to generate awareness of and an emotional connection to the BP brand and its offerings.
- *In-store give-aways.* At the launch in April 2007, environmentally-friendly paper bags, T-shirts with a fun new look from the campaign, kids activity books and trading cards featuring the campaign characters, and sunflower seed packets were handed out to customers throughout the entire network of BP stations.
- *Unique website.* The www.alittlebettergasstation.com website features the "Gas Mania" interactive game, selected animations, ringtones, screensavers, a sweepstakes, and the TV ads.
- *Street teams.* BP and Ford teamed up to promote the use of BP's Ultimate gasoline in Ford's new Edge automobile. Videos featuring groups of college-aged students were created to showcase the BP brand in Florida and the ARCO brand in California.

Questions

1 (*a*) What is BP's "Helios" strategy? (*b*) How does this strategy relate to BP's mission and core values?

2 Conduct a SWOT (strengths, weaknesses, opportunities, and threats) analysis for BP's "Helios" initiative—looking forward globally to the next three years.

3 What are some ways BP could use to effectively communicate its "Helios" strategy to consumers?

4 What are the long-term benefits to (*a*) society and (*b*) BP of its "Helios" initiative?

5 Looking at BP's Helios Power marketing strategy and its "street team" marketing tactic: (*a*) What objectives would you set for this tactic? (*b*) How would you propose BP measure the results?

A BUILDING AN EFFECTIVE MARKETING PLAN

"New ideas are a dime a dozen," observes Arthur R. Kydd, "and so are new products and new technologies." Kydd should know. As chief executive officer of St. Croix Venture Partners, he and his firm have provided the seed money and venture capital to launch more than 60 start-up firms in the last 25 years. Today, those firms have more than 5,000 employees. Kydd explains:

> I get 200 to 300 marketing and business plans a year to look at, and St. Croix provides start-up financing for only two or three. What sets a potentially successful idea, product, or technology apart from all the rest is markets and marketing. If you have a real product with a distinctive point of difference that satisfies the needs of customers, you may have a winner. And you get a real feel for this in a well-written marketing or business plan.[1]

This appendix (1) describes what marketing and business plans are, including the purposes and guidelines in writing effective plans, and (2) provides a sample marketing plan.

MARKETING PLANS AND BUSINESS PLANS

After explaining the meanings, purposes, and audiences of marketing plans and business plans, this section describes some writing guidelines for them and what external funders often look for in successful plans.

Meanings, Purposes, and Audiences

A marketing plan is a road map for the marketing activities of an organization for a specified future period of time, such as one year or five years.[2] It is important to note that no single "generic" marketing plan applies to all organizations and all situations. Rather, the specific format for a marketing plan for an organization depends on the following:

- *The target audience and purpose.* Elements included in a particular marketing plan depend heavily on (1) who the audience is and (2) what its purpose is. A marketing plan for an internal audience seeks to point the direction for future marketing activities and is sent to all individuals in the organization who must implement the plan or who will be affected by it. If the plan is directed to an external audience, such as friends, banks, venture capitalists, or potential investors, for the purpose of raising capital, it has the additional function of being an important sales document. In this case, it contains elements such as the strategic plan/focus, organization, structure, and biographies of key personnel that would rarely appear in an internal marketing plan. Also, the financial information is far more detailed when the plan is used to raise outside capital. The elements of a marketing plan for each of these two audiences are compared in Figure A–1.
- *The kind and complexity of the organization.* A small neighborhood restaurant has a somewhat different marketing plan than Nestlé, which serves international markets. The restaurant's plan would be relatively simple and directed at serving customers in a local market. In Nestlé's case, because there is a hierarchy of marketing plans, various levels of detail would be used—such as the entire organization, the strategic business unit, or the product/product line.
- *The industry.* Both the restaurant serving a local market and Medtronic, selling heart pacemakers globally, analyze competition. Not only are their geographic thrusts far different, but also the complexities of their offerings and, hence, the time periods likely to be covered by their plans differ. A one-year marketing plan may be adequate for the restaurant, but Medtronic may need a five-year planning horizon because product-development cycles for complex, new medical devices may be three or four years.

In contrast to a marketing plan, a **business plan** is a road map for the entire organization for a specified future period of time, such as one year or five years.[3] A key difference between a marketing plan and a business plan is that the business plan contains details on the research and development (R&D)/operations/manufacturing activities of the organization. Even for a manufacturing business, the marketing plan

Element of the plan	Marketing plan		Business plan	
	For internal audience (to direct the firm)	For external audience (to raise capital)	For internal audience (to direct the firm)	For external audience (to raise capital)
1. Executive summary	✓	✓	✓	✓
2. Description of company		✓		✓
3. Strategic plan/focus		✓		✓
4. Situation analysis	✓	✓	✓	✓
5. Market-product focus	✓	✓	✓	✓
6. Marketing program strategy and tactics	✓	✓	✓	✓
7. R&D and operations program			✓	✓
8. Financial projections	✓	✓	✓	✓
9. Organization structure		✓		✓
10. Implementation plan	✓	✓	✓	✓
11. Evaluation and control		✓		✓
Appendix A: Biographies of key personnel		✓		✓
Appendix B, etc.: Details on other topics	✓	✓	✓	✓

FIGURE A–1

Elements in typical marketing and business plans targeted at different audiences

is probably 60 or 70 percent of the entire business plan. For businesses like a small restaurant or an auto repair shop, their marketing and business plans are virtually identical. The elements of a business plan typically targeted at internal and external audiences appear in the two right-hand columns in Figure A–1.

The Most-Asked Questions by Outside Audiences

Lenders and prospective investors reading a business or marketing plan that is used to seek new capital are probably the toughest audiences to satisfy. Their most-asked questions include the following:

1. Is the business or marketing idea valid?
2. Is there something unique or distinctive about the product or service that separates it from substitutes and competitors?
3. Is there a clear market for the product or service?
4. Are the financial projections realistic and healthy?
5. Are the key management and technical personnel capable, and do they have a track record in the industry in which they must compete?
6. Does the plan clearly describe how those providing capital will get their money back and make a profit?

Rhonda Abrams, author of *The Successful Business Plan*, observes, "Although you may spend five months preparing your plan, the cold, hard fact is that an investor or lender can dismiss it in less than five minutes."[4] While her comments apply to plans seeking to raise capital, the first five questions just listed apply equally well to plans for internal audiences.

Writing and Style Suggestions

There are no magic one-size-fits-all guidelines for writing successful marketing and business plans. Still, the following writing and style guidelines generally apply:[5]

- Use a direct, professional writing style. Use appropriate business terms without jargon. Present and future tenses with active voice ("I will write an effective marketing plan.") are generally better than past tense and passive voice ("An effective marketing plan was written by me.").

- Be positive and specific to convey potential success. At the same time, avoid superlatives ("terrific," "wonderful"). Specifics are better than glittering generalities. Use numbers for impact, justifying projections with reasonable quantitative assumptions, where possible.
- Use bullet points for succinctness and emphasis. As with the list you are reading, bullets enable key points to be highlighted effectively.
- Use A-level (the first level) and B-level (the second level) headings under the numbered section headings to help readers make easy transitions from one topic to another. This also forces the writer to organize the plan more carefully. Use these headings liberally, at least one every 200 to 300 words.
- Use visuals where appropriate. Photos, illustrations, graphs, and charts enable massive amounts of information to be presented succinctly.
- Shoot for a plan 15 to 35 pages in length, not including financial projections and appendixes. An uncomplicated small business may require only 15 pages, while a high-technology start-up may require more than 35 pages.
- Use care in layout, design, and presentation. Laser printers give a more professional look than ink-jet printers do. Use 11- or 12-point type (you are now reading 10.5-point type) in the text. Use a serif type (with "feet," like that you are reading now) in the text because it is easier to read, and sans serif (without "feet") in graphs and charts like Figure A–1. A bound report with a nice cover and clear title page adds professionalism.

These guidelines are used, where possible, in the sample marketing plan that follows.

SAMPLE FIVE-YEAR MARKETING PLAN FOR PARADISE KITCHENS,® INC.

To help interpret the marketing plan for Paradise Kitchens, Inc., that follows, we will describe the company and suggest some guidelines in interpreting the plan.

Background on Paradise Kitchens, Inc.

With a degree in chemical engineering, Randall F. Peters spent 15 years working for General Foods and Pillsbury with a number of diverse responsibilities: plant operations, R&D, restaurant operations, and new business development. His wife, Leah, with degrees in both molecular cellular biology and food science, held various Pillsbury executive positions in new category development and packaged goods, and restaurant R&D. In the company's start-up years, Paradise Kitchens survived on the savings of Randy and Leah, the cofounders. With their backgrounds, they decided Randy should serve as president and CEO of Paradise Kitchens, and Leah should focus on R&D and corporate strategy.

Interpreting the Marketing Plan

The marketing plan on the next pages, based on an actual Paradise Kitchens plan, is directed at an external audience (see Figure A–1). To protect proprietary information about the company, some details and dates have been altered, but the basic logic of the plan has been kept.

Notes in the margins next to the Paradise Kitchens plan fall into two categories:

1. *Substantive notes* are in blue boxes. These notes elaborate on the significance of an element in the marketing plan and are keyed to chapter references in this textbook.
2. *Writing style, format, and layout notes* are in red boxes and explain the editorial or visual rationale for the element.

A word of encouragement: Writing an effective marketing plan is hard, but challenging and satisfying, work. Dozens of the authors' students have used effective marketing plans they wrote for class in their interviewing portfolio to show prospective employers what they could do and to help them get their first job.

Color-coding Legend

Blue boxes explain significance of marketing plan elements.

Red boxes give writing style, format, and layout guidelines.

The Table of Contents provides quick access to the topics in the plan, usually organized by section and subsection headings.

Seen by many experts as the single most important element in the plan, the two-page Executive Summary "sells" the plan to readers through its clarity and brevity. For space reasons, it is not shown here, but the Building Your Marketing Plan exercise at the end of Chapter 2 asks the reader to write an Executive Summary for this plan.

The Company Description highlights the recent history and recent successes of the organization.

The Strategic Focus and Plan sets the strategic direction for the entire organization, a direction with which proposed actions of the marketing plan must be consistent. This section is not included in all marketing plans. See Chapter 2.

The qualitative Mission statement focuses the activities of Paradise Kitchens for the stakeholder groups to be served. See Chapter 2.

FIVE-YEAR MARKETING PLAN
Paradise Kitchens,® Inc.

Table of Contents

1. Executive Summary

2. Company Description

Paradise Kitchens®, Inc., was started by cofounders Randall F. Peters and Leah E. Peters to develop and market Howlin' Coyote® Chili, a unique line of single serve and microwavable Southwestern/Mexican style frozen chili products. The Howlin' Coyote line of chili was first introduced into the Minneapolis–St. Paul market and expanded to Denver two years later and Phoenix two years after that.

To the Company's knowledge, Howlin' Coyote is the only premium-quality, authentic Southwestern/Mexican style, frozen chili sold in U.S. grocery stores. Its high quality has gained fast, widespread acceptance in these markets. In fact, same-store sales doubled in the last year for which data are available. The Company believes the Howlin' Coyote brand can be extended to other categories of Southwestern/Mexican food products, such as tacos, enchiladas, and burritos.

Paradise Kitchens believes its high-quality, high-price strategy has proven successful. This marketing plan outlines how the Company will extend its geographic coverage from 3 markets to 20 markets by the year 2013.

3. Strategic Focus and Plan

This section covers three aspects of corporate strategy that influence the marketing plan: (1) the mission, (2) goals, and (3) core competence/sustainable competitive advantage of Paradise Kitchens.

Mission

The mission of Paradise Kitchens is to market lines of high-quality Southwestern/Mexican food products at premium prices that satisfy consumers in this fast-growing food segment while providing challenging career opportunities for employees and above-average returns to stockholders.

Goals

For the coming five years Paradise Kitchens seeks to achieve the following goals:

- Nonfinancial goals
    1. To retain its present image as the highest-quality line of Southwestern/ Mexican products in the food categories in which it competes.
    2. To enter 17 new metropolitan markets.
    3. To achieve national distribution in two convenience store or supermarket chains by 2008 and five by 2009.
    4. To add a new product line every third year.
    5. To be among the top five chili lines—regardless of packaging (frozen or canned)—in one-third of the metro markets in which it competes by 2009 and two-thirds by 2011.
- Financial goals
    1. To obtain a real (inflation-adjusted) growth in earnings per share of 8 percent per year over time.
    2. To obtain a return on equity of at least 20 percent.
    3. To have a public stock offering by the year 2009.

Core Competency and Sustainable Competitive Advantage

In terms of core competency, Paradise Kitchens seeks to achieve a unique ability to (1) provide distinctive, high-quality chilies and related products using Southwestern/Mexican recipes that appeal to and excite contemporary tastes for these products and (2) deliver these products to the customer's table using effective manufacturing and distribution systems that maintain the Company's quality standards.

To translate these core competencies into a sustainable competitive advantage, the Company will work closely with key suppliers and distributors to build the relationships and alliances necessary to satisfy the high taste standards of our customers.

In keeping with the goal of achieving national distribution through chains, Paradise Kitchens recently obtained distribution through a convenience store chain where it uses this point-of-purchase ad that adheres statically to the glass door of the freezer case.

4. Situation Analysis

This situation analysis starts with a snapshot of the current environment in which Paradise Kitchens finds itself by providing a brief SWOT (strengths, weaknesses, opportunities, threats) analysis. After this overview, the analysis probes ever-finer levels of detail: industry, competitors, company, and consumers.

SWOT Analysis

Figure 1 shows the internal and external factors affecting the market opportunities for Paradise Kitchens. Stated briefly, this SWOT analysis highlights the great strides taken by the company since its products first appeared on grocers' shelves.

Figure 1.   SWOT Analysis for Paradise Kitchens

Internal Factors	Strengths	Weaknesses
Management	Experienced and entrepreneurial management and board	Small size can restrict options
Offerings	Unique, high-quality, high-price products	Many lower-quality, lower-price competitors
Marketing	Distribution in three markets with excellent acceptance	No national awareness or distribution; restricted shelf space in the freezer section
Personnel	Good workforce, though small; little turnover	Big gap if key employee leaves
Finance	Excellent growth in sales revenues	Limited resources may restrict growth opportunities when compared to giant competitors
Manufacturing	Sole supplier ensures high quality	Lack economies of scale of huge competitors
R&D	Continuing efforts to ensure quality in delivered products	Lack of canning and microwavable food processing expertise

External Factors	Opportunities	Threats
Consumer/Social	Upscale market, likely to be stable; Southwestern/Mexican food category is fast-growing segment due to growth in Hispanic American population and desire for spicier foods	Premium price may limit access to mass markets; consumers value a strong brand name
Competitive	Distinctive name and packaging in its markets	Not patentable; competitors can attempt to duplicate product; others better able to pay slotting fees
Technological	Technical breakthroughs enable smaller food producers to achieve many economies available to large competitors	Competitors have gained economies in canning and microwavable food processing
Economic	Consumer income is high; convenience important to U.S. households	More households "eating out," and bringing prepared take-out into home
Legal/Regulatory	High U.S. Food & Drug Administration standards eliminate fly-by-night competitors	Mergers among large competitors being approved by government

In the Company's favor internally are its strengths of an experienced management team and board of directors, excellent acceptance of its lines in the three metropolitan markets in which it competes, and a strong manufacturing and distribution system to serve these limited markets. Favorable external factors (opportunities) include the increasing appeal of Southwestern/Mexican foods, the strength of the upscale market for the Company's products, and food-processing technological breakthroughs that make it easier for smaller food producers to compete.

Among unfavorable factors, the main weakness is the limited size of Paradise Kitchens relative to its competitors in terms of the depth of the management team, available financial resources, and national awareness and distribution of product lines. Threats include the danger that the Company's premium prices may limit access to mass markets and competition from the "eating-out" and "take-out" markets.

Industry Analysis: Trends in Frozen and Mexican Foods

Frozen Foods. According to Grocery Headquarters, consumers are flocking to the frozen food section of grocery retailers. The reasons: hectic lifestyles demanding increased convenience and an abundance of new, tastier, and nutritious products.[6] By 2007, total sales of frozen food in supermarkets, drugstores, and mass merchandisers, such as Target and Costco (excluding Wal-Mart) reached $29 billion. Prepared frozen meals, which are defined as meals or entrees that are frozen and require minimal preparation, accounted for $8.1 billion, or 26 percent of the total frozen food market.

Sales of Mexican entrees totaled $506 million.[7] Heavy consumers of frozen meals, those who eat five or more meals every two weeks, tend to be kids, teens, and young adults 35–44 years old.[8]

Mexican Foods. Currently, Mexican foods such as burritos, enchiladas, and tacos are used in two-thirds of American households. These trends reflect a generally more favorable attitude on the part of all Americans toward spicy foods that include red chili peppers. The growing Hispanic population in the U.S., about 44 million and almost $798 billion in purchasing power in 2007, partly explains the increasing demand for Mexican food. This Hispanic purchasing power is projected to be $1.2 trillion in 2011.[9]

Competitors in the Chili Market

The chili market represents over $500 million in annual sales. On average, consumers buy five to six servings annually, according to the NPD Group. The products fall primarily into two groups: canned chili (75 percent of sales) and dry chili (25 percent of sales).

This page uses a "block" style and does *not* indent each paragraph, although an extra space separates each paragraph. Compare this page with page 60, which has indented paragraphs. Most readers find indented paragraphs in marketing plans and long reports are easier to follow.

The Company Analysis provides details of the company's strengths and marketing strategies that will enable it to achieve the mission and goals identified earlier. See Chapters 2, 8, and 22.

The higher-level "A heading" of Customer Analysis has a more dominant typeface and position than the lower-level "B heading" of Customer Characteristics. These headings introduce the reader to the sequence and level of topics covered. The organization of this textbook uses this kind of structure and headings.

Satisfying customers and providing genuine value to them is why organizations exist in a market economy. This section addresses the question of "Who are the customers for Paradise Kitchens' products?" See Chapters 5, 6, 7, 8, and 9.

Bluntly put, the major disadvantage of the segment's dominant product, canned chili, is that it does not taste very good. A taste test described in an issue of *Consumer Reports* magazine ranked 26 canned chili products "poor" to "fair" in overall sensory quality. The study concluded, "Chili doesn't have to be hot to be good. But really good chili, hot or mild, doesn't come out of a can."

Company Analysis

The husband-and-wife team that cofounded Paradise Kitchens, Inc., has 44 years of experience between them in the food-processing business. Both have played key roles in the management of the Pillsbury Company. They are being advised by a highly seasoned group of business professionals, who have extensive understanding of the requirements for new-product development.

The Company now uses a single outside producer with which it works closely to maintain the consistently high quality required in its products. The greater volume has increased production efficiencies, resulting in a steady decrease in the cost of goods sold.

Customer Analysis

In terms of customer analysis, this section describes (1) the characteristics of customers expected to buy Howlin' Coyote products and (2) health and nutrition concerns of Americans today.

Customer Characteristics. Demographically, chili products in general are purchased by consumers representing a broad range of socioeconomic backgrounds. Howlin' Coyote chili is purchased chiefly by consumers who have achieved higher levels of education and whose income is $50,000 and higher. These consumers represent 50 percent of canned and dry mix chili users.

The household buying Howlin' Coyote has one to three people in it. Among married couples, Howlin' Coyote is predominantly bought by households in which both spouses work. While women are a majority of the buyers, single men represent a significant segment.

Because the chili offers a quick way to make a tasty meal, the product's biggest users tend to be those most pressed for time. Howlin' Coyote's premium pricing also means that its purchasers are skewed toward the higher end of the income range. Buyers range in age from 25 to 54 and often live in the western United States, where spicy foods are more readily eaten.

The five Howlin' Coyote entrees offer a quick, tasty meal with high-quality ingredients.

This section demonstrates the company's insights into a major trend that has a potentially large impact.

Size of headings should give a professional look to the report and not overwhelm the reader. These two headings are too large.

As noted in Chapter 10, the chances of success for a new product are significantly increased if objectives are set for the product itself and if target market segments are identified for it. This section makes these explicit for Paradise Kitchens. The objectives also serve as the planned targets against which marketing activities are measured in program implementation and control.

Health and Nutrition Concerns. Coverage of food issues in the U.S. media is often erratic and occasionally alarmist. Because Americans are concerned about their diets, studies from organizations of widely varying credibility frequently receive significant attention from the major news organizations. For instance, a study of fat levels of movie popcorn was reported in all the major media. Similarly, studies on the healthfulness of Mexican food have received prominent play in print and broadcast reports. The high caloric levels of much Mexican and Southwestern-style food have been widely reported and often exaggerated. Some Mexican frozen-food competitors, such as Don Miguel, Mission Foods, Ruiz Foods, and Jose Ole, plan to offer or have recently offered more "carb-friendly" and "fat-friendly" products in response to this concern.

Howlin' Coyote is already lower in calories, fat, and sodium than its competitors, and those qualities are not currently being stressed in its promotions. Instead, in the space and time available for promotions, Howlin' Coyote's taste, convenience, and flexibility are stressed.

5. Market-Product Focus

This section describes the five-year marketing and product objectives for Paradise Kitchens and the target markets, points of difference, and positioning of its lines of Howlin' Coyote chilies.

Marketing and Product Objectives

Howlin' Coyote's marketing intent is to take full advantage of its brand potential while building a base from which other revenue sources can be mined—both in and out of the retail grocery business. These are detailed in four areas below:

- Current markets. Current markets will be grown by expanding brand and flavor distribution at the retail level. In addition, same-store sales will be grown by increasing consumer awareness and repeat purchases, thereby leading to the more efficient broker/warehouse distribution channel.

- New markets. By the end of Year 5, the chili, salsa, burrito, and enchilada business will be expanded to a total of 20 metropolitan areas. This will represent 70 percent of U.S. food store sales.

- Food service. Food service sales will include chili products and smothering sauces. Sales are expected to reach $693,000 by the end of Year 3 and $1.5 million by the end of Year 5.

- New products. Howlin' Coyote's brand presence will be expanded at the retail

A heading should be spaced closer to the text that follows (and that it describes) than the preceding section to avoid confusion for the reader. This rule is not followed for the Target Markets heading, which now unfortunately appears to "float" between the preceding and following paragraphs.

This section identifies the specific niches or target markets toward which the company's products are directed. When appropriate and when space permits, this section often includes a market-product grid. See Chapter 9.

An organization cannot grow by offering only "me-too products." The greatest single factor in a new product's failure is the lack of significant "points of difference" that sets it apart from competitors' substitutes. This section makes these points of difference explicit. See Chapter 10.

A positioning strategy helps communicate the company's unique points of difference of its products to prospective customers in a simple, clear way. This section describes this positioning. See Chapters 9 and 10.

level through the addition of new products in the frozen-foods section. This will be accomplished through new-product concept screening in Year 1 to identify new potential products. These products will be brought to market in Years 2 and 3.

Target Markets

The primary target market for Howlin' Coyote products is households with one to three people, where often both adults work, with individual income typically above $50,000 per year. These households contain more experienced, adventurous consumers of Southwestern/ Mexican food and want premium quality products.

To help buyers see the many different uses for Howlin' Coyote chili, recipes are even printed on the *inside* of the packages.

Points of Difference

The "points of difference"—characteristics that make Howlin' Coyote chilies unique relative to competitors—fall into three important areas:

- Unique taste and convenience. No known competitor offers a high-quality, "authentic" frozen chili in a range of flavors. And no existing chili has the same combination of quick preparation and home-style taste that Howlin' Coyote does.
- Taste trends. The American palate is increasingly intrigued by hot spices. In response to this trend, Howlin' Coyote brands offer more "kick" than most other prepared chilies.
- Premium packaging. Howlin' Coyote's packaging graphics convey the unique, high-quality product contained inside and the product's nontraditional positioning.

Positioning

In the past chili products have been either convenient or tasty, but not both. Howlin' Coyote pairs these two desirable characteristics to obtain a positioning in consumers' minds as very high-quality "authentic Southwestern/Mexican tasting" chilies that can be prepared easily and quickly.

6. Marketing Program

The four marketing mix elements of the Howlin' Coyote chili marketing program are detailed below. Note that "chile" is the vegetable and "chili" is the dish.

Product Strategy

After first summarizing the product line, the approach to product quality and packaging are covered.

Product Line. Howlin' Coyote chili, retailing for $3.99 for an 11-ounce serving, is available in five flavors. The five are Green Chile Chili, Red Chile Chili, Beef and Black Bean Chili, Chicken Chunk Chili, and Mean Bean Chili.

Unique Product Quality. The flavoring systems of the Howlin' Coyote chilies are proprietary. The products' tastiness is due to extra care lavished upon the ingredients during production. The ingredients used are of unusually high quality. Meats are low-fat cuts and are fresh, not frozen, to preserve cell structure and moistness. Chilies are fire-roasted for fresher taste. Tomatoes and vegetables are select quality. No preservatives or artificial flavors are used.

Packaging. Reflecting the "cutting edge" marketing strategy of its producers, Howlin' Coyote bucks conventional wisdom in packaging. It avoids placing predict-able photographs of the product on its contain-ers. Instead, Howlin' Coyote's package shows a Southwestern motif that communicates the product's out-of-the-ordinary positioning.

The Southwestern motif makes Howlin' Coyote's packages stand out in a supermarket's freezer case.

Price Strategy

Howlin' Coyote Chili is, at $3.99 for an 11-ounce package, priced comparably to the other frozen offerings and higher than the canned and dried chili varieties. However, the significant taste advantages it has over canned chilies and the convenience advantages over dried chilies justify this pricing strategy.

Promotion Strategy

Key promotion programs feature in-store demonstrations, recipes, and cents-off coupons.

Elements of the Promotion Strategy are highlighted in terms of the three key promotional activities the company is emphasizing: in-store demonstrations, recipes, and cents-off coupons. For space reasons the company's online strategies are not shown in the plan. See Chapters 18, 19, 20, and 21.

Another bulleted list adds many details for the reader, including methods of gaining customer awareness, trial, and repeat purchases as Howlin' Coyote enters new metropolitan areas.

The Place Strategy is described here in terms of both (1) the present method and (2) the new one to be used when the increased sales volume makes it feasible. See Chapters 15, 16, and 17.

All the marketing mix decisions covered in the just-described marketing program have both revenue and expense effects. These are summarized in this section of the marketing plan.

Note that this section contains no introductory overview sentence. While the sentence is not essential, many readers prefer to see it to avoid the abrupt start with Past Sales Revenues.

In-Store Demonstrations. In-store demonstrations enable consumers to try Howlin' Coyote products and discover their unique qualities. Demos will be conducted regularly in all markets to increase awareness and trial purchases.

Recipes. Because the products' flexibility of use is a key selling point, recipes are offered to consumers to stimulate use. The recipes are given at all in-store demonstrations, on the back of packages, through a mail-in recipe book offer, and in coupons sent by direct-mail or freestanding inserts.

Cents-Off Coupons. To generate trial and repeat-purchase of Howlin' Coyote products, coupons are distributed in four ways:

- In Sunday newspaper inserts. These inserts are widely read and help generate awareness.

- In-pack coupons. Each box of Howlin' Coyote chili will contain coupons for $1 off two more packages of the chili. These coupons will be included for the first three months the product is shipped to a new market. Doing so encourages repeat purchases by new users.

- Direct-mail chili coupons. Those households that fit the Howlin' Coyote demographics described previously will be mailed coupons.

- In-store demonstrations. Coupons will be passed out at in-store demonstrations to give an additional incentive to purchase.

Place (Distribution) Strategy

Howlin' Coyote is distributed in its present markets through a food distributor. The distributor buys the product, warehouses it, and then resells and delivers it to grocery retailers on a store-by-store basis. As sales grow, we will shift to a more efficient system using a broker who sells the products to retail chains and grocery wholesalers.

Sunday newspaper inserts encourage consumer trial and provide recipes to show how Howlin' Coyote chili can be used in summer meals.

7. Financial Data and Projections

Past Sales Revenues

Historically, Howlin' Coyote has had a steady increase in sales revenues since its introduction in 1999. In 2003, sales jumped spectacularly, due largely to new promotion strategies. Sales have continued to rise, but at a less dramatic rate. The trend in sales revenues appears in Figure 2.

Five-Year Projections

Five-year financial projections for Paradise Kitchens appear below. These projections reflect the continuing growth in number of cases sold (with eight packages of Howlin' Coyote chili per case) and increasing production and distribution economies.

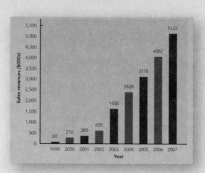

Figure 2.   Sales Revenues for Paradise Kitchens, Inc.

| | | | Projections | | | | |
Financial Element	Units	Actual 2007	Year 1 2008	Year 2 2009	Year 3 2010	Year 4 2011	Year 5 2012
Cases sold	1,000	353	684	889	1,249	1,499	1,799
Net sales	$1,000	5,123	9,913	12,884	18,111	21,733	26,080
Gross profit	$1,000	2,545	4,820	6,527	8,831	10,597	12,717
Operating profit (loss)	$1,000	339	985	2,906	2,805	3,366	4,039

8. Organization

Paradise Kitchens' present organization appears in Figure 3. It shows the four people reporting to the President. Below this level are both the full-time and part-time employees of the Company.

Figure 3.   The Paradise Kitchens Organization

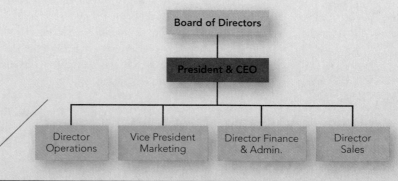

The Implementation Plan shows how the company will turn plans into results. Gantt charts are often used to set deadlines and assign responsibilities for the many tactical marketing decisions needed to enter a new market.

The essence of Evaluation and Control is comparing actual sales with the targeted values set in the plan and taking appropriate actions. Note that the section briefly describes a contingency plan for alternative actions, depending on how successful the entry into a new market turns out to be.

Various appendixes may appear at the end of the plan, depending on the purpose and audience for them. For example, resumes of key personnel or detailed financial spreadsheets often appear in appendixes. For space reasons these are not shown here.

At present Paradise Kitchens operates with full-time employees in only essential positions. It now augments its full-time staff with key advisors, consultants, and subcontractors. As the firm grows, people with special expertise will be added to the staff.

9. Implementation Plan

Introducing Howlin' Coyote chilies to 17 new metropolitan areas is a complex task and requires that creative promotional activities gain consumer awareness and initial trial among the target market households identified earlier. The anticipated rollout schedule to enter these metropolitan markets appears in Figure 4.

Figure 4.   Rollout Schedule to Enter New U.S. Markets

Year	New Markets Added	Cumulative Markets	Cumulative Percentage of U.S. Markets
Today (2007)	2	5	16
Year 1 (2008)	3	8	21
Year 2 (2009)	4	12	29
Year 3 (2010)	2	14	37
Year 4 (2011)	3	17	45
Year 5 (2012)	3	20	53

The diverse regional tastes in chili will be monitored carefully to assess whether minor modifications may be required in the chili recipes. As the rollout to new metropolitan areas continues, Paradise Kitchens will assess manufacturing and distribution trade-offs. This is important in determining whether to start new production with selected high-quality regional contract packers.

10. Evaluation and Control

Monthly sales targets in cases have been set for Howlin' Coyote chili for each metropolitan area. Actual case sales will be compared with these targets and tactical marketing programs modified to reflect the unique sets of factors in each metropolitan area. The speed of the roll-out program will increase or decrease, depending on Paradise Kitchens' performance in the successive metropolitan markets it enters.

Appendix A. Biographical Sketches of Key Personnel

Appendix B. Detailed Financial Projections

THE TOOLMAKERS

On the new Web, users are increasingly building their own tools. The result is greater customization and convenience, from maps that can be easily programmed to ads that change with every new blog post

craigslist
The classified-ad service has 23 employees but receives more traffic than all but seven other sites

Linked in
Social networking for suits. It brings together an élite clientele of global executives

ebaY
At the auction site, the users are the police: customer ratings weed out the bad eggs

Google
The search empire built itself around a social function: counting links between websites

WIKIPEDIA
The ultimate crowdsourcing model, it showed that the masses are as smart as the experts

myspace.com
a place for friends
With 120 million users, it's a whole new society, with features that maximize individuality

Google
AdSense
Provides free ads relevant to your website, then pays you if people click on them

Google
Maps
Users can add their own points of interest to create mashups like www.beerhunter.ca

amazon.com
With customer reviews and recommendations, book buying is now a communal experience

THE GATHERERS

The crowd isn't just expressing itself more; it's also gathering and filtering all those blog posts and photographs and finding an audience for them

Blogger
The popular blogging-software service makes every would-be pundit a publisher

iStockphoto
This photo store taps an army of amateurs, who can sell their shots for as little as $1

flickr
The photo-scrapbook site helped popularize tagging as a way to organize information

Bloglines
Lets users subscribe to various sites then receive updates from each one on a single page

digg
The crowd as news editor: readers "digg" stories they like and "bury" ones they don't

del.icio.us
Allows users to share their Web-browser bookmarks, all organized by tags users provide

Technorati

Its search and ranking functions reveal the topics that are burning up the blogosphere

3

Scanning the Marketing Environment

LEARNING OBJECTIVES
After reading this chapter you should be able to:

LO1 Explain how environmental scanning provides information about social, economic, technological, competitive, and regulatory forces.

LO2 Describe how social forces such as demographics and culture can have an impact on marketing strategy.

LO3 Discuss how economic forces such as macroeconomic conditions and consumer income affect marketing.

LO4 Describe how technological changes can affect marketing.

LO5 Discuss the forms of competition that exist in a market and key components of competition.

LO6 Explain the major legislation that ensures competition and regulates the elements of the marketing mix.

WEB 2.0 IS ALL ABOUT YOU!

The Web is changing at an extraordinary pace and each new change provides more customization and convenience for you. If you use Myspace.com, Del.icio.us, Secondlife, or any one of hundreds of new products on the Web you are already part of the new world of the Web!

Not long ago the Web simply provided a modern channel for traditional businesses. Music led the way with file-sharing services such as Napster and eventually online stores such as iTunes. The entire entertainment industry followed by offering books, movies, television, radio, and photography on the Web. The digital revolution allowed all of these businesses to benefit from the technical aspects of the Web.

Now the term *Web 2.0* is used to describe the changes in the World Wide Web that reflect the growing interest in collaboration, open sharing of information, and customer control. Many products and services such as podcasts, weblogs, videologs, social networking, bookmarking, wikis, folksonomy, and RSS feeds are already available, and many more are in development.

As the focus moves from providing a new channel for existing businesses to empowering individual consumers with customized products, suddenly the Web is all about you! You can create your own video and post it on YouTube, sell your photos on iStockphoto, build a social networking site on Ning, and publish your ideas at Blogger. How did this happen? The marketing environment changed!

First, technologies such as high-speed Internet, high-resolution displays, and file-transfer software were developed. Second, the regulatory environment changed to allow the exchange and sale of copyrighted materials such as songs and movies. Third, competitive forces by companies such as Apple, Google, eBay, Microsoft, and Amazon gave the Web worldwide exposure. Finally, consumers changed. They are making it clear that they want "a tool for bringing together the small contributions of millions of people and making them matter." The future promises to be even more exciting. Some experts are already talking about Web 3.0![1]

Many businesses operate in environments where important forces change. Anticipating and responding to changes such as those taking place on the Web often means the difference between marketing success and failure. This chapter describes how the marketing environment has changed in the past and how it is likely to change in the future.

ENVIRONMENTAL SCANNING

LO1

Changes in the marketing environment are a source of opportunities and threats to be managed. The process of continually acquiring information on events occurring outside the organization to identify and interpret potential trends is called **environmental scanning**.

Tracking Environmental Trends

Environmental trends typically arise from five sources: social, economic, technological, competitive, and regulatory forces. As shown in Figure 3–1 and described later in this chapter, these forces affect the marketing activities of a firm in numerous ways. To illustrate how environmental scanning is used, consider the following trend:[2]

> Coffee industry marketers have observed that the percentage of adults who drink coffee declined from 75 percent in 1962 to 49 percent in 2004 and then increased to 57 percent in 2007. Age-specific analysis indicates that the percentage of 18- to 24-year-olds who drink coffee has risen from 16 percent in 2003 to 37 percent today.

What types of businesses are likely to be influenced by these trends? What future would you predict for coffee?

You may have concluded that the change from a declining trend to an increase in coffee consumption is likely to influence coffee manufacturers, coffee shops, and supermarkets. If so, you are correct—manufacturers have responded by offering new flavors and seasonal blends, coffee shops are automating to prepare drinks faster, and supermarkets have added coffee boutiques and gourmet brands. Predicting the future requires assumptions about the number of years the trends will continue and the rate of increase or decline in various age groups. Did you consider these issues in your analysis? Because experts make different assumptions, their forecasts range from decline, to no growth, to a 7 percent annual increase through 2010, a range that probably includes your forecast.

Environmental scanning also involves explaining trends. Why did coffee consumption decline for many years and increase recently? One explanation for the decline is that consumers switched from coffee to other beverages such as soft drinks, juices, and bottled water. Another explanation is that preferences shifted to more expensive types of

FIGURE 3–1

Environmental forces affect the organization, as well as its suppliers and customers.

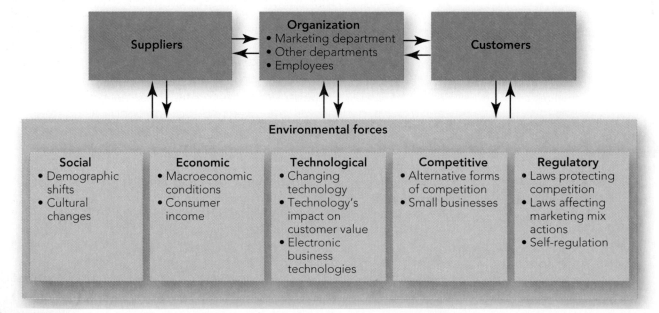

ENVIRONMENTAL FORCE	TREND IDENTIFIED BY AN ENVIRONMENTAL SCAN
Social	• Expanding use of social networks and collaborative web services • Increasing mobility and diversity of the population • Growing concern over global warming and climate change
Economic	• Shift to a global economy and the growing importance of China and India • Baby boomers begin turning sixty and spending retirement funds • Virtual online communities developing their own economies
Technological	• Increasing popularity of Mobile TV • Advances in biometrics as a security solution • Growing demand for portable, renewable power sources
Competitive	• Dramatic increase in customer-generated content about competitive options • New metrics for assessment increase performance comparisons • Development and growth of competitive intelligence departments
Regulatory	• Increasing legislation requiring digital storage of corporate records • Greater concern for privacy and personal information collection • New regulations to respond to fear of terrorism

FIGURE 3–2

An environmental scan of today's marketplace shows the many important trends that influence marketing.

coffee, and consumers reduced their use to maintain the same level of expenditure. The recent increases may be the result of new coffee products distributed in supermarkets and vending machines, and gourmet single-serving products for homes and offices. Identifying and interpreting trends such as the decline and increase in coffee consumption, and developing explanations such as those offered in this paragraph, are essential to successful environmental scanning.[3]

An Environmental Scan of Today's Marketplace

What other trends might affect marketing in the future? A firm conducting an environmental scan of the marketplace might uncover key trends such as those listed in Figure 3–2 for each of the five environmental forces.[4] Although the list of trends is far from complete, it reveals the breadth of an environmental scan—from the increasing diversity of the U.S. population, to the growing economic impact of China and India, to the dramatic growth of customer-generated content. These trends affect consumers and the businesses and organizations that serve them. Trends such as these are described in the following discussions of the five environmental forces.

SOCIAL FORCES

The **social forces** of the environment include the demographic characteristics of the population and its values. Changes in these forces can have a dramatic impact on marketing strategy.

Demographics

Describing a population according to selected characteristics such as age, gender, ethnicity, income, and occupation is referred to as **demographics**. Several organizations

World Population by Region, 1950, 2005 and 2050

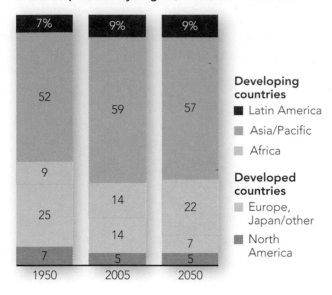

World Population by Age Groups, 1950–2050

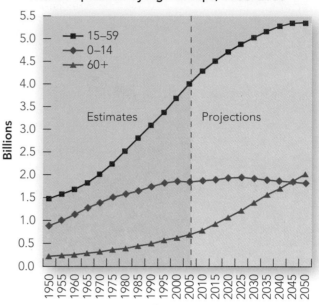

FIGURE 3–3

The distribution of the world population is changing. Africa is growing and the population is getting older.

such as the Population Reference Bureau and the United Nations monitor the world population profile, while many other organizations such as the U.S. Census Bureau provide information about the American population.

The World Population at a Glance The most recent estimates indicate there are 6.7 billion people in the world today, and the population is likely to grow to 9.2 billion by 2050. While this growth has led to the term *population explosion,* the increases have not occurred worldwide; they are primarily in the developing countries of Africa, Asia, and Latin America. In fact, India is predicted to have the world's largest population in 2050 with 1.6 billion people, and China will be a close second with 1.4 billion people. Figure 3–3 shows the declining proportion of the world's population in North America, Europe, Australia, and Japan.[5]

Another important global trend is the shifting age structure of the world population. The number of people older than 60 is expected to more than triple in the coming decades and reach 2 billion by 2050. Again, the magnitude of this trend varies by region, and developed countries such as the United States are expected to face the highest growth rates of the elderly age group. Global income levels and living standards have also been increasing, although the averages across countries are very different. Per capita income, for example, ranges from $43,000 in Luxembourg, to $24,000 in Canada, to $800 in Afghanistan.

For marketers, global trends such as these have many implications. Obviously, the relative size of countries such as India and China will mean they represent huge markets for many product categories. Elderly populations in developed countries are likely to save less and begin spending their funds on health care, travel, and other retirement-related products and services. Economic progress in developing countries will lead to growth in entrepreneurship, new markets for infrastructure related to manufacturing, communication, and distribution, and the growth of exports.[6]

The U.S. Population Studies of the demographic characteristics of the U.S. population suggest several important trends. Generally, the population is becoming larger, older, and more diverse. In 2008, the U.S. population was estimated to be 303 million people. If current trends in life expectancy, birthrates, and immigration continue, by 2030 the U.S. population will exceed 360 million people. This growth suggests that niche markets based on age, life stage, family structure, geographic location, and ethnicity will become increasingly important. The global trend toward an older population is particularly true in the United States. Today, there are approximately 35 million people 65 and older. By 2030, this age group will include more than 70 million people, or 20 percent of the population. You may have noticed companies trying to attract older consumers. Mobile phone manufacturer LG, for example, recently introduced a phone with large easy-to-read buttons for seniors. Finally, the term *minority* as it is currently used is likely to become obsolete as the size of most ethnic groups will double during the next two decades.[7]

Generational Cohorts A major reason for the graying of America is that the **baby boomers**—the generation of children born between 1946 and 1964—are growing older. As the 78 million boomers have aged, their participation in the workforce and their earnings have increased, making them an important consumer market. This group accounts for an estimated 56 to 58 percent of the purchases in most consumer product and service categories. In the future, boomers' interests will reflect concern for their children and grandchildren, their own health, and their retirement, and companies will need to position products to respond to these interests. Generally, baby boomers are receptive to anything that makes them feel younger. Olay's Total Effects product line, for example, includes anti-aging moisturizers, cleansing cloths, and restoration treatments designed for this age group.

The baby boom cohort is followed by **Generation X**, which includes the 15 percent of the population born between 1965 and 1976. This period is also known as the baby bust, because the number of children born each year was declining. This is a generation of consumers who are self-reliant, supportive of racial and ethnic diversity, and better educated than any previous generation. They are not prone to extravagance and are likely to pursue lifestyles that are a blend of caution, pragmatism, and traditionalism. In terms of net worth, Generation X is the first generation to have less than the previous generation. As baby boomers move toward retirement, however, Generation X is becoming a dominant force in many markets. Generation X, for example, is replacing baby boomers as the largest segment of business travelers. In response, hotel companies are creating new concepts that appeal to the younger market. Surveys of Generation X travelers indicate they want casual, tech-friendly lodging with 24-hour access to food and drinks, so Hyatt Corporation is building 400 new Hyatt Place all-suite hotels featuring control panels for MP3 players and computers, plasma-screen TVs, and a coffee and wine bar.[8]

Which generational cohorts are these three advertisers trying to reach?

Generation Y Is Becoming a Generation of Entrepreneurs!

Generation Y is known as a savvy and demanding group of consumers who feel personally responsible for making a difference in the world. They also have an extraordinary optimism about their potential for fame and fortune. Rather than pursue traditional "corporate" jobs, however, many millennials are becoming entrepreneurs.

Many Generation Y children grew up in families where their parents found it difficult to create a work–life balance. To avoid that conflict, this generation is attracted to new ventures where they can be their own boss. As management consultant Bruce Tulgan explains, "They want to create a custom life and create the kind of career that fits around the kind of life they want."

Ben Kaufman is a typical example of the Gen Y entrepreneur. As a 20-year-old college student he started a company named Mophie that makes cases, armbands, and belt clips as iPod accessories. The success of the company has attracted $1.5 million in venture capital, but more importantly for Kaufman, it allows him to have a job that he likes. Similarly, Sheena Lindahl used her interest in creating her own career to start a business called Extreme Entrepreneurship Education, a business designed to help and inspire college students.

The Bureau of Labor Statistics predicts that the future will bring many more entrepreneurs like Kaufman. There are currently 370,000 entrepreneurs in the 16 to 24 age category, and the historical growth rate is expected to double through 2014. Are you a future Gen Y entrepreneur?

The generational cohort labeled **Generation Y** includes the 72 million Americans born between 1977 and 1994. This was a period of increasing births, which resulted from baby boomers having children, and it is often referred to as the echo-boom or baby boomlet. Generation Y exerts influence on music, sports, computers, video games, and especially cell phones. Generation Y views wireless communication as a lifeline to friends and family and has been the first to use Web-enabled mobile phones to stream video, send and receive text messages, play games, and access e-mail. This is also a group that is attracted to purposeful work where they have control. The accompanying Marketing Matters box describes the entrepreneurial spirit of Generation Y.[9] The term *millennials* is also used, with inconsistent definitions, to refer to younger members of Generation Y and sometimes to Americans born since 1994.

Because the members of each generation are distinctive in their attitudes and consumer behavior, marketers have been studying the many groups or cohorts that make up the marketplace and have developed *generational marketing* programs for them. In addition, global marketers have discovered that many of the American generational differences also exist outside of the United States.[10]

The American Household As the population age profile has changed, so has the structure of the American household. In 1960, 75 percent of all households consisted of married couples. Today, that type of household is just 50 percent of the population. Only 25 percent of households are married couples with children, and 10 percent are households with working fathers and stay-at-home moms. Some of the fastest-growing types of households are those with a single person, those with a single parent, and those with unmarried partners. Businesses are trying to develop products and services that reflect the changing structure of households. Ocean Village, for example, noticed a 26 percent increase in the number of single parents traveling with children, so it added three-berth cabins on its cruise ships to cater to the trend.[11]

The increase in cohabitation (households with unmarried partners) may be one reason that the divorce rate has declined slightly in recent years. Even so, the likelihood that a couple will divorce exceeds 40 percent and the total number of divorced people is 21.6 million. The majority of divorced people eventually remarry, which has given rise to the **blended family**, one formed by merging two previously separated units into a single household. Today, one of every three Americans is a stepparent, stepchild, stepsibling, or some other member of a blended family. Hallmark Cards, Inc., now has specially designed cards and verses for blended families.[12]

Population Shifts   A major regional shift in the U.S. population toward western and southern states is under way. From 2005 to 2006, Arizona, Nevada, Idaho, Georgia, and Texas grew at the fastest rates. Three states—California, Texas, and Florida—will account for 45 percent of the population change in the United States through 2025, gaining more than 6 million people in each state.[13]

Populations are also shifting within states. In the early 1900s, the population shifted from rural areas to cities. From the 1930s through the 1980s, the population shifted from the cities to suburbs. During the 1990s and 2000s, the population began to shift again, from suburbs to more remote suburbs called *exurbs* and to smaller towns called *penturbia*. Today, 30 percent of all Americans live in central cities, 50 percent live in suburbs, and 20 percent live in rural locations.[14]

To assist marketers in gathering data on the population, the Census Bureau has developed a classification system to describe the varying locations of the population. The system consists of two types of *statistical areas*:

- A *metropolitan statistical area* has at least one urbanized area of 50,000 or more people and adjacent territory that has a high degree of social and economic integration.
- A *micropolitan statistical area* has at least one urban cluster of at least 10,000 but less than 50,000 people and adjacent territory that has a high degree of social and economic integration.

If a metropolitan statistical area contains a population of 2.5 million or more, it may be subdivided into smaller areas called *metropolitan divisions*. In addition, adjacent metropolitan statistical areas and micropolitan statistical areas may be grouped into *combined statistical areas*.[15]

There are currently 362 metropolitan statistical areas, which include 83 percent of the population, and 573 micropolitan areas, which include 10 percent of the population.

Racial and Ethnic Diversity   A notable trend is the changing racial and ethnic composition of the U.S. population. Approximately one in four U.S. residents is African American, American Indian, Asian, Pacific Islander, or a representative of another racial or ethnic group. Diversity is further evident in the variety of peoples that make up these groups. For example, Asians consist of Asian Indians, Chinese, Filipinos, Japanese, Koreans, and Vietnamese. For the first time, the 2000 Census allowed respondents to choose more than one of the six race options, and more than 6 million reported more than one race. Hispanics, who may be from any race, currently make up 12 percent of the U.S. population and are represented by Mexicans, Puerto Ricans, Cubans, and others of Central and South American ancestry. While the United States is becoming more diverse, Figure 3–4 on the next page suggests that the minority racial and ethnic groups tend to be concentrated in geographic regions.[16]

The racial and ethnic composition of the United States is expected to change even more by 2025. Between 2005 and 2025, the Hispanic population will grow from 42 million to more than 68 million, or almost 20 percent of the total population. The number of Asian Americans in the United States will also double to 24 million, or 7 percent of the population, and the African American population will be approximately 45 million, or 13 percent of the population. The new Census category, *multiracials,* currently makes up 2.4 percent of the population, but because of the limited information about this group, growth forecasts are difficult to make. Overall,

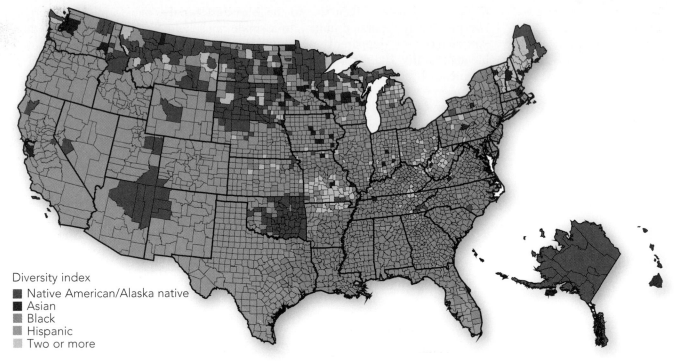

Diversity index
■ Native American/Alaska native
■ Asian
■ Black
■ Hispanic
☐ Two or more

FIGURE 3–4

Racial and ethnic groups (excluding Caucasians) are concentrated in geographic regions of the United States.

the trends in the composition of the population suggest that the U.S. market will no longer be dominated by one group and that non-Hispanic Caucasians will be a declining majority over the next two decades.

While the growing size of these groups has been identified through new Census data, their economic impact on the marketplace is also very noticeable. By 2010, Hispanics, African Americans, and Asians will spend $1.09 trillion, $1.02 trillion, and $578 billion each year, respectively. To adapt to this new marketplace, many companies are developing **multicultural marketing** programs, which are combinations of the marketing mix that reflect the unique attitudes, ancestry, communication preferences, and lifestyles of different races. Because businesses must now market their products to a consumer base with many racial and ethnic identities, in-depth marketing research that allows an accurate understanding of each culture is essential.[17]

Additional analysis of population demographic data, such as the information shown in Figure 3–4, suggests that racial and ethnic groups tend to be concentrated in geographic regions. This information allows companies to combine their multicultural marketing efforts with regional marketing activities. Consider, for example, that 48 percent of Asian Americans live in Los Angeles, New York City, and San Francisco, and that two-thirds of Hispanics live in Florida, Texas, and California. Saturn combined multicultural and regional marketing by running a Spanish-language advertising campaign in geographic areas with Spanish-speaking consumers. Similarly, a Home Depot TV ad shows a native of Mexico with his Venezuelan wife and their American-born daughter to reflect some of the differences in the Spanish language.[18] In Chapter 9 you will learn more about this approach to the market referred to as geographic segmentation.

Culture

A second social force, **culture**, incorporates the set of values, ideas, and attitudes that are learned and shared among the members of a group. Because many of the

Saturn combined ethnic and regional marketing by using Spanish-language promotions like this one in some states.

La Chica Que Siempre Llega Tarde.

El ION Red Line De Saturn Con 205 Caballos De Fuerza.

La gente primero.

elements of culture influence consumer buying patterns, monitoring national and global cultural trends is important for marketing. Cross-cultural analysis needed for global marketing is discussed in Chapter 7.

The Changing Attitudes and Roles of Men and Women

One of the most notable cultural changes in the United States in the past 30 years has been in the attitudes and roles of men and women in the marketplace. In fact, some experts predict that as this trend continues, there will eventually be very few differences in the buying patterns of men and women.

Your mothers and grandmothers probably remember advertising targeted at them that focused on the characteristics of household products—like laundry detergent that got clothes "whiter than white." In the 1970s and 1980s, ads began to create a bridge between genders with messages such as Secret's "strong enough for a man, but made for a woman." In the 1990s, marketing to women focused on their challenge of balancing family and career interests. Since then, women and men have encouraged the slow movement toward equality in the marketplace. As a result, today's Generation Y represents the first generation of women who have no collective memory of the dramatic changes we have undergone. As one expert explains, "Feminism today is like fluoride; we scarcely notice that we have it."

Several factors have contributed to the shift in attitudes. First, many young women had career mothers who provided a reference point for lifestyle choices. Second, increased participation in organized sports eliminated one of the most visible inequalities in opportunities for women. And finally, the Internet has provided exposure to the marketplace through a mechanism that makes gender, race, and ethnicity invisible. Most of the 35 million Generation Y women view themselves as confident, strong, and feminine. In addition, research suggests that the majority of adults today believe men and women should equally share most responsibilities.[19]

Many companies that had a consumer base that was primarily men or primarily women in the past are preparing for growth from the other gender. Grocery stores, car dealers, investment services, and many others hope to appeal to both groups in the future. Ugg Australia, for example, built a strong reputation among women with its distinctive boots and is now trying to attract men with new products and advertising. Similarly, Liz Claiborne developed Claiborne for Men, and Cole Haan expanded its line of shoes to include products for women. Some industries have been slower to eliminate stereotypes and gender roles in their business and marketing approaches. A recent study reported that 68 percent of women say they "can't identify with women used in advertising." The financial services industry, for example, has focused on male customers in the past, using campaign messages that worked for men but not for women. To better serve the specific investment needs of women, Merrill Lynch created a women-specific marketing department that uses research about women's buying process to design its products and marketing activities.[20]

Changing Values Culture also includes values, which vary with age but tend to be very similar for men and women. All age groups, for example, rank "protecting the family" and "honesty" as the most important values. Consumers under 20 years old rank "friendship" third, while the 20-to-29 and 30-to-39 age groups rank "self-esteem" and "health and fitness" as their third most important values, respectively.

An increasingly important value for consumers is preserving the environment and other health issues. These values are reflected in the growth of products that consumers believe are consistent with their values. Dannon Co., for example, has developed probiotic yogurts such as Light & Fit Crave Control yogurt and immunity-boosting DanActive for health-conscious consumers. Concern for the environment is one reason consumers are buying hybrid gas-electric automobiles such as the Toyota Prius and energy-efficient lightbulbs such as General Electric's Energy Smart fluorescent bulbs. Companies are also changing their business practices to respond to trends in consumer values. Wal-Mart has set ambitious goals to cut energy use, switch to renewable power, and reduce packaging on the products it carries.[21]

A change in consumption orientation is also apparent. Today, and for the foreseeable future, **value consciousness**—or the concern for obtaining the best quality, features, and performance of a product or service for a given price—will drive consumption behavior. For many consumers this means bargaining for better price, not just when they are buying a car or a house, but in almost any purchasing situation. Innovative marketers have responded to this new orientation in numerous ways. Some retailers are now authorizing employees to respond to consumers who bargain by giving discounts off of advertised rates. Some companies have created new outlets for value-conscious consumers. Holiday Inn Worldwide, for example, has opened Holiday Inn Express hotels, designed to offer comfortable accommodations with room rates lower than Holiday Inns. Similarly, Nordstrom offers 50 to 75 percent discounts through its Nordstrom Rack Stores.[22]

---

learning review

1. Describe three generational cohorts.

2. Why are many companies developing multicultural marketing programs?

3. How are important values such as health and fitness reflected in the marketplace today?

ECONOMIC FORCES

The second component of the environmental scan, the **economy**, pertains to the income, expenditures, and resources that affect the cost of running a business and household. We'll consider two aspects of these economic forces: a macroeconomic view of the marketplace and a microeconomic perspective of consumer income.

Macroeconomic Conditions

Of particular concern at the macroeconomic level is the inflationary or recessionary state of the economy, whether actual or perceived by consumers or businesses. In an inflationary economy, the cost to produce and buy products and services escalates as prices

FIGURE 3–5

The Vehicle Buying Attitudes component of the Index of Consumer Sentiment (ICS) is a good predictor of vehicle sales.

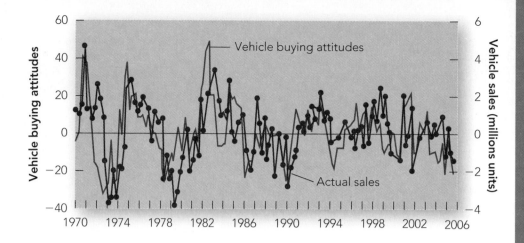

increase. From a marketing standpoint, if prices rise faster than consumer incomes, the number of items consumers can buy decreases. This relationship is evident in the cost of a college education. The price of attending college has increased 29 percent during the past 10 years while median family income rose 3 percent during the same period.[23]

Whereas inflation is a period of price increases, recession is a time of slow economic activity. Businesses decrease production, unemployment rises, and many consumers have less money to spend. The U.S. economy experienced recessions in the early 1970s, early 1980s, and early 1990s. The economy again entered a recessionary period from 2001 through 2003, and then began a period of growth.[24]

Consumer expectations of an inflationary and recessionary U.S. economy are an important element of environmental scanning. Consumer spending, which accounts for two-thirds of the U.S. economic activity, is affected by expectations of the future. The two most popular surveys of consumer expectations are the Consumer Confidence Index, conducted by a nonprofit business research organization called the Conference Board, and the Index of Consumer Sentiment, conducted by the Survey Research Center at the University of Michigan. The surveys track the responses of consumers to specific questions about their expectations, and the results are reported once each month. For example, the Index of Consumer Sentiment asks, "Looking ahead, do you think that a year from now you will be better off financially, worse off or just about the same as now?" The answers to the questions are used to construct an index. The higher the index, the more favorable are consumer expectations. Figure 3–5 shows the fluctuation in the Vehicle Buying Attitudes component of the Index of Consumer Sentiment and its close relationship to vehicle sales. The consumer expectations surveys are closely monitored by many companies, particularly manufacturers and retailers of cars, furniture, and major appliances. Chrysler, for example, uses the surveys to plan its automobile production and avoid producing too many or too few cars.[25]

Consumer Income

The microeconomic trends in terms of consumer income are also important issues for marketers. Having a product that meets the needs of consumers may be of little value if they are unable to purchase it. A consumer's ability to buy is related to income, which consists of gross, disposable, and discretionary components.

Gross Income   The total amount of money made in one year by a person, household, or family unit is referred to as **gross income** (or "money income" at the Census Bureau). While the typical U.S. household earned only about $8,700 of income in 1970, it earned about $48,201 in 2006. When gross income is adjusted for inflation, however, income of that typical U.S. household was relatively stable. In fact,

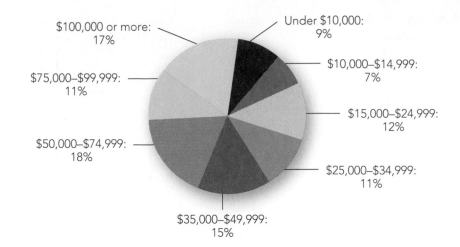

inflation-adjusted income has only varied between $40,187 and $49,244 since 1977. Figure 3–6 shows the distribution of annual income among U.S. households.[26] Are you from a typical household? Read the accompanying Going Online box to learn how you can determine the median household income in your hometown.

Disposable Income   The second income component, **disposable income**, is the money a consumer has left after paying taxes to use for food, shelter, clothing, and transportation. Thus, if taxes rise at a faster rate than does income, consumers must economize. In recent years, consumers' allocation of income has shifted. As the marketplace has become more efficient, producing products that are more durable and use less energy, consumers have increased their disposable income. Car maintenance costs, for example, have declined 28 percent since 1985, because automobile quality has improved. Much of the money is being spent on new categories of "necessities" such as vitamins and supplements; antibacterial body washes, lotions, and deodorants; antiwrinkle creams; and children's shampoos, toothpaste, and bath products.[27]

As consumers' discretionary income increases, so does the opportunity to indulge in the luxurious leisure travel marketed by Cunard.

Cunard
www.cunard.com

Discretionary Income   The third component of income is **discretionary income**, the money that remains after paying for taxes and necessities. Discretionary income is used for luxury items such as a cruise on the *Queen Mary 2*. An obvious problem in defining discretionary versus disposable income is determining what is a luxury and what is a necessity.

The Department of Labor monitors consumer expenditures through its annual Consumer Expenditure Survey. In 2005, consumers spent approximately 13 percent of their income on food, 33 percent on housing, and 4 percent on clothes. While an additional 35 percent is often spent on transportation, health care, and insurance, the remainder is generally viewed as discretionary. The percentage of income spent on food and housing typically declines as income increases, which can provide an increase in discretionary income. Discretionary expenditures can also be increased by reducing savings. The Bureau of Labor Statistics has observed that the percentage of income put into savings has been steadily declining and is expected to be only 2.7 percent in 2012, compared with 3.7 percent today.[28]

TECHNOLOGICAL FORCES

Our society is in a period of dramatic technological change. **Technology**, the third environmental force, refers to inventions or innovations from applied science or engineering research. Each new wave of technological innovation can replace existing products and companies. Do you recognize the items pictured here and what they may replace?

Technology of Tomorrow

Technological change is the result of research, so it is difficult to predict. Some of the most dramatic technological changes occurring now, however, include the following:

- Internet TV and mobile TV will become simple and available for most consumers.
- Advances in nanotechnology, the science of unimaginably small electronics, will lead to smaller microprocessors, efficient fuel cells, and cancer-detection sensors.
- Touch-screen and gesture-based navigation technology will change how we interface with computers, phones, and most electronics.

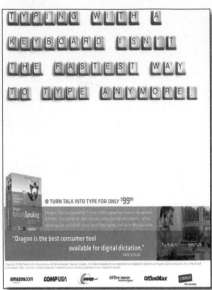

Technological change leads to new products. What products might be replaced by these innovations?

- Companies will begin building software databases so that lines of code can be reused, and open software will allow users to customize products to their specific interests and applications.

These trends in technology are already seen in today's marketplace. Samsung has developed new phones that will utilize the next-generation networks (WiMAX) to allow users to surf the Web and watch TV. Nintendo uses motion-sensing chips in its Wii game system, and the social networking site, MySpace, allows users to change the software code to customize their profile layout. Other technologies such as high-definition disc players, speech recognition software, and customized music services are likely to replace or substitute for existing products and services such as DVD players, keyboards, and radio.[29]

Technology's Impact on Customer Value

Advances in technology are having important effects on marketing. First, the cost of technology is plummeting, causing the customer value assessment of technology-based products to focus on other dimensions such as quality, service, and relationships. When Plaxo introduced its address book software, it gave the product away at no charge, reasoning that satisfied customers would later buy upgrades and related products. A similar approach is now used by many cellular telephone vendors, who charge little for the telephone if the purchase leads to a telephone service contract.[30]

Technology also provides value through the development of new products. Many automobile manufacturers now offer customers a navigation system that uses satellite signals to help the driver reach any destination. Under development are radarlike collision avoidance systems that disengage cruise control, reduce the engine speed, and even apply the brakes.[31] Other new products likely to be available soon include a "smart ski" with an embedded microprocessor that will adjust the flexibility of the ski to snow conditions; injectable health monitors that will send glucose, oxygen, and other clinical information to a wristwatch-like monitor; and electronic books that will allow you to download any volume and view it on pages coated with electronic "ink" and embedded electrodes.[32]

Technology can also change existing products and the ways they are produced. Many companies are using technological developments to allow *recycling* products through the manufacturing cycle several times. The National Association for Plastic Container Recovery, for example, estimates that 50 percent of all plastic bottles are now recycled, usually to make polyester fibers that are spun into everything from sweaters to upholstery.

RePlanet offers recycling through its kiosks and centers, and Wisk precycles by reducing the size of its packaging.

In Southern California, Tomra Systems has launched a chain of 250 rePlanet recycling kiosks that it hopes to spread across the United States. Consumers receive between 2.5 and 10 cents per recycled container. Another approach is *precycling*—efforts by manufacturers to reduce waste by decreasing the amount of packaging they use. The development of new packaging materials, for example, has allowed DuPont to produce a collapsible pouch as an alternative to milk cartons in school lunch programs.[33]

Electronic Business Technologies

The transformative power of technology may be best illustrated by the rapid growth of the **marketspace**, an information- and communication-based electronic exchange environment mostly occupied by sophisticated computer and telecommunication technologies and digitized offerings. Any activity that uses some form of electronic communication in the inventory, exchange, advertisement, distribution, and payment of goods and services is often called **electronic commerce**. Network technologies are now used for everything from filing expense reports, to monitoring daily sales, to sharing information with employees, to communicating instantly with suppliers.

Many companies have adapted Internet-based technology internally to support their electronic business strategies. An **intranet**, for example, is an Internet-based network used within the boundaries of an organization. It is a private network that may or may not be connected to the public Internet. **Extranets**, which use Internet-based technologies, permit communication between a company and its supplier, distributors, and other partners (such as advertising agencies).

COMPETITIVE FORCES

The fourth component of the environmental scan, **competition**, refers to the alternative firms that could provide a product to satisfy a specific market's needs. There are various forms of competition, and each company must consider its present and potential competitors in designing its marketing strategy.

Alternative Forms of Competition

LO5

Four basic forms of competition form a continuum from pure competition to monopolistic competition to oligopoly to pure monopoly. Chapter 13 contains further discussions on pricing practices under these four forms of competition.

At one end of the continuum is *pure competition,* in which every company has a similar product. Companies that deal in commodities common to agribusiness (for example, wheat, rice, and grain) often are in a pure competition position in which distribution (in the sense of shipping products) is important but other elements of marketing have little impact.

In the second point on the continuum, *monopolistic competition,* the many sellers compete with their products on a substitutable basis. For example, if the price of coffee rises too much, consumers may switch to tea. Coupons or sales are frequently used marketing tactics.

Oligopoly, a common industry structure, occurs when a few companies control the majority of industry sales. For example, AT&T, MCI, Verizon, and Sprint control approximately 80 percent of the $16 billion international long-distance telephone service market. Similarly, the entertainment industry in the United States is dominated by Viacom, Disney, and Time Warner, and the major firms in the U.S. defense contractor industry are Boeing, United Technologies, and Lockheed Martin. Critics of oligopolies suggest that because there are few sellers, price competition among firms is not desirable because it leads to reduced profits for all producers.[34]

The final point on the continuum, *pure monopoly,* occurs when only one firm sells the product. Monopolies are common for producers of goods considered essential to a community: water, electricity, and telephone service. Typically, marketing plays a small role in a monopolistic setting because it is regulated by the state or federal government. Government control usually seeks to ensure price protection for the buyer, although deregulation in recent years has encouraged price competition in the electricity market.[35] Concern that Microsoft's 86 percent share of the PC operating system market is a monopoly has led to lawsuits and consent decrees from the U.S. Justice Department and fines from the European Union.[36]

Components of Competition

In developing a marketing program, companies must consider the factors that drive competition: entry, bargaining power of buyers and suppliers, existing rivalries, and substitution possibilities.[37] Scanning the environment requires a look at all of them. These factors relate to a firm's marketing mix decisions and may be used to create a barrier to entry, increase brand awareness, or intensify a fight for market share. Read the accompanying Using Marketing Dashboards box for ideas about assessing the components of competition.[38]

Entry In considering the competition, a firm must assess the likelihood of new entrants. Additional producers increase industry capacity and tend to lower prices. A company scanning its environment must consider the possible **barriers to entry** for other firms, which are business practices or conditions that make it difficult for new firms to enter the market. Barriers to entry can be in the form of capital requirements, advertising expenditures, product identity, distribution access, or the cost to customers of switching suppliers. The higher the expense of the barrier, the more likely it will deter new entrants. For example, Lucent Technologies is one of the major suppliers of phone network equipment in the world, and its past customers find it less expensive to upgrade their equipment than switch to another supplier.[39]

Power of Buyers and Suppliers A competitive analysis must consider the power of buyers and suppliers. Powerful buyers exist when they are few in number, there are low switching costs, or the product represents a significant share of the buyer's total costs. This last factor leads the buyer to exert significant pressure for price competition. A supplier gains power when the product is critical to the buyer and when it has built up the switching costs.

Using Marketing Dashboards

Assessing Competition Is a Key to Success

To include competition in your marketing dashboard, you need to assess the components of competition. For example, the probability of a new competitor entering a market can be assessed on a scale from 0% to 100%. The power or influence of a buyer or supplier declines as the number of buyers and suppliers in the same product category increases. As the number of similar firms or substitute products increases the competitiveness of an industry increases. The combination of these measurements will allow you to make an overall assessment of competitors and their likely actions.

Your Challenge You are responsible for price recommendations for an existing product that has been very successful during the past year. In general, you believe that there is a strong relationship between price and sales, and that a reduction in price would lead to an increase in sales. That is:

Sales Increase (%) =
Price Reduction(%) × Ratio of Sales Increase to Price Reduction

Your goal is to increase sales by ten percent.

Your Findings After studying the prices of similar products and their sales you estimate that a 1 percent decrease in price will lead to a 4 percent increase in sales. This calculation, however, ignores the likely reaction of competitors. That is, when a firm lowers its price, competitors may reduce price also, changing the ratio of sales increase to price reduction for the product. Based on your assessment of the components of competition you estimate that competitors will meet half of your price reduction.

Your Action The information about competition allows you to adjust your estimates. Since competitors will meet half of your price reduction, the increase in sales will probably be about half of your original estimate. So, the ratio of sales increase to price reduction will change from 4-to-1 to 2-to-1. To achieve the 10 percent increase in sales you estimate that a 5 percent price reduction is needed (5% × 2/1).

This use of marketing metrics shows how assessment of competition can allow higher precision in the actions taken by marketing managers.

Note: The ratio of the unit amount of increase in sales for each unit decrease in price is often referred to as price elasticity, and is discussed in Chapter 13.

Existing Competitors and Substitutes Competitive pressures among existing firms depend on the rate of industry growth. In slow-growth settings, competition is more heated for any possible gains in market share. High fixed costs also create competitive pressures for firms to fill production capacity. For example, airlines offer discounts for making early reservations and charge penalties for changes or cancellations in an effort to fill seats, which represent a high fixed cost.

Small Businesses as Competitors

While large companies provide familiar examples of the forms and components of competition, small businesses make up the majority of the competitive landscape for most businesses. Consider that there are approximately 23 million small businesses in the United States, which employ half of all private sector employees. In addition, small businesses generate 60 to 80 percent of all new jobs annually and 50 percent of the gross domestic product (GDP). Research has shown a strong correlation between national economic growth and the level of new small business activity in the previous years.[40]

learning review

4. What is the difference between a consumer's disposable and discretionary income?

5. How does technology impact customer value?

6. In pure competition there are a _____ number of sellers.

REGULATORY FORCES

For any organization, the marketing and broader business decisions are constrained, directed, and influenced by regulatory forces. **Regulation** consists of restrictions state and federal laws place on business with regard to the conduct of its activities. Regulation exists to protect companies as well as consumers. Much of the regulation from the federal and state levels is the result of an active political process and has been passed to ensure competition and fair business practices. For consumers, the focus of legislation is to protect them from unfair trade practices and ensure their safety.

Protecting Competition

Major federal legislation has been passed to encourage competition, which is deemed desirable because it permits the consumer to determine which competitor will succeed and which will fail. The first such law was the *Sherman Antitrust Act* (1890). Lobbying by farmers in the Midwest against fixed railroad shipping prices led to the passage of this act, which forbids (1) contracts, combinations, or conspiracies in restraint of trade and (2) actual monopolies or attempts to monopolize any part of trade or commerce. Because of vague wording and government inactivity, however, there was only one successful case against a company in the nine years after the act became law, and the Sherman Act was supplemented with the *Clayton Act* (1914). This act forbids certain actions that are likely to lessen competition, although no actual harm has yet occurred.

In the 1930s, the federal government had to act again to ensure fair competition. During that time, large chain stores appeared, such as the Great Atlantic & Pacific Tea Company (A&P). Small businesses were threatened, and they lobbied for the *Robinson-Patman Act* (1936). This act makes it unlawful to discriminate in prices charged to different purchasers of the same product, where the effect may substantially lessen competition or help to create a monopoly.

Product-Related Legislation

Various federal laws in existence specifically address the product component of the marketing mix. Some are aimed at protecting the company, some at protecting the consumer, and at least one at protecting both.

Company Protection A company can protect its competitive position in new and novel products under the patent law, which gives inventors the right to exclude others from making, using, or selling products that infringe the patented invention. The federal copyright law is another way for a company to protect its competitive position in a product. The copyright law gives the author of a literary, dramatic, musical, or artistic work the exclusive right to print, perform, or otherwise copy that work. Copyright is secured automatically when the work is created. However, the published work should bear an appropriate copyright notice, including the copyright symbol, the first year of publication, and the name of the copyright owner, and it must be registered under the federal copyright law. Digital technology has necessitated new copyright legislation, called the *Digital Millenium Copyright Act* (1998), to improve protection of copyrighted digital products. In addition, producers of DVD movies, music recordings, and software want protection from devices designed to circumvent antipiracy elements of their products.[41]

These products are identified by protected trademarks. Are any of these trademarks in danger of becoming generic?

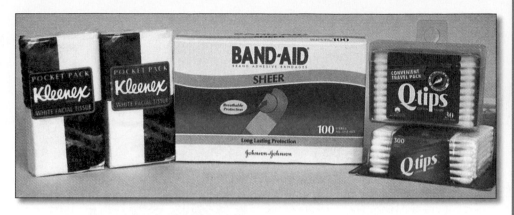

Consumer Protection There are many consumer-oriented federal laws regarding products. The various laws include more than 30 amendments and separate laws relating to food, drugs, and cosmetics, such as the *Infant Formula Act* (1980), the *Nutritional Labeling and Education Act* (1990), new labeling requirements for dietary supplements (1997), and proposed labeling guidelines for trans fats (2006).[42] Various other consumer protection laws have a broader scope, such as the *Fair Packaging and Labeling Act* (1966), the *Child Protection Act* (1966), and the *Consumer Product Safety Act* (1972), which established the Consumer Product Safety Commission to monitor product safety and establish uniform product safety standards. Many of these laws came about because of **consumerism**, a grassroots movement started in the 1960s to increase the influence, power, and rights of consumers in dealing with institutions. This movement continues and is reflected in growing consumer demands for ecologically safe products and ethical and socially responsible business practices. One hotly debated issue concerns liability for environmental abuse.

Both Company and Consumer Protection Trademarks are intended to protect both the firm selling a trademarked product and the consumer buying it. A Senate report states:

> The purposes underlying any trademark statute [are] twofold. One is to protect the public so that it may be confident that, in purchasing a product bearing a particular trademark which it favorably knows, it will get the product which it asks for and wants to get. Secondly, where the owner of a trademark has spent energy, time, and money in presenting to the public the product, he is protected in this investment from misappropriation in pirates and cheats.

This statement was made in connection with another product-related law, the *Lanham Act* (1946), which provides for registration of a company's trademarks. Historically, the first user of a trademark in commerce had the exclusive right to use that particular word, name, or symbol in its business. Registration under the Lanham Act provides important advantages to a trademark owner that has used the trademark in interstate or foreign commerce, but it does not confer ownership. A company can lose its trademark if it becomes generic, which means that it has primarily come to be merely a common descriptive word for the product. Coca-Cola, Whopper, and Xerox are registered trademarks, and competitors cannot use these names. Aspirin and escalator are former trademarks that are now generic terms in the United States and can be used by anyone.

In 1988, the *Trademark Law Revision Act* resulted in a major change to the Lanham Act, allowing a company to secure rights to a name before actual use by declaring an intent to use the name.[43] In 2003, the United States agreed to participate in the *Madrid Protocol*, which is a treaty that facilitates the protection of U.S. trademark rights throughout the world.[44] See the Making Responsible Decisions box on the next page to learn about a use (or misuse) of trademarks called Doppelgangers.[45]

Are Doppelgangers a First Amendment Right?

Have you seen an ad or a logo that looked like a familiar brand but was slightly different? Some examples you might be familiar with include a commercial for Chevy Tahoe saying "global warming is here," and Starbucks logos that read "Evil Empire" or "Frankenbucks Coffee." These parodies—sometimes called Doppelgangers—are a growing form of citizen protest called culture jamming. The purpose of the parodies is to undermine the integrity of existing brand marketing. Companies currently have different responses to Doppel-

gangers. Some companies ignore them, others try to monitor the parodies for insight about consumer perceptions of the company, and others try to fight back. Starbucks, for example, has used cease and desist letters, injunctions, and trademark infringement litigation to try to stop the creation and distribution of Doppelgangers. Do you think consumers have the right to use this form of culture jamming? Should companies try to stop the practice? What is your opinion?

One of the most recent changes in trademark law is the U.S. Supreme Court's ruling that companies may obtain trademarks for colors associated with their products. Over time, consumers may begin to associate a particular color with a specific brand. Examples of products that may benefit from the new law include NutraSweet's sugar substitute in pastel blue packages and Owens-Corning Fiberglas Corporation's pink insulation.[46] Another recent addition to trademark law is the *Federal Dilution Act* (1995), which is used to prevent someone from using a trademark on a noncompeting product (e.g., "Cadillac" brushes).[47]

Pricing-Related Legislation

The pricing component of the marketing mix is the focus of regulation from two perspectives: price fixing and price discounting. Although the Sherman Act did not outlaw price fixing, the courts view this behavior as *per se illegal* (*per se* means "through or of itself"), which means the courts see price fixing itself as illegal.

Certain forms of price discounting are allowed. Quantity discounts are acceptable; that is, buyers can be charged different prices for a product provided there are differences in manufacturing or delivery costs. Promotional allowances or services may be given to buyers on an equal basis proportionate to volume purchased. Also, a firm can meet a competitor's price "in good faith." Legal and regulatory aspects of pricing are covered in more detail in Chapter 14.

Distribution-Related Legislation

The government has four concerns with regard to distribution—earlier referred to as "place" actions in the marketing mix—and the maintenance of competition. The first, *exclusive dealing,* is an arrangement a manufacturer makes with a reseller to handle only its products and not those of competitors. This practice is only illegal under the Clayton Act when it substantially lessens competition.

Requirement contracts require a buyer to purchase all or part of its needs for a product from one seller for a period of time. These contracts are not always illegal but depend on the court's interpretation of their impact on distribution.

Exclusive territorial distributorships are a third distribution issue often under regulatory scrutiny. In this situation, a manufacturer grants a distributor the sole rights to sell a product in a specific geographical area. The courts have found few violations with these arrangements.

The fourth distribution strategy is a *tying arrangement,* whereby a seller requires the purchaser of one product to also buy another item in the line. These contracts may be illegal when the seller has such economic power in the tying product that the seller can restrain trade in the tied product. Legal aspects of distribution are reviewed in greater detail in Chapter 15.

Advertising- and Promotion-Related Legislation

Promotion and advertising are aspects of marketing closely monitored by the Federal Trade Commission (FTC), which was established by the *FTC Act of 1914.* The FTC has been concerned with deceptive or misleading advertising and unfair business practices and has the power to (1) issue cease and desist orders and (2) order corrective advertising. In issuing a *cease and desist order,* the FTC orders a company to stop practices it considers unfair. With *corrective advertising,* the FTC can require a company to spend money on advertising to correct previous misleading ads. The enforcement powers of the FTC are so significant that often just an indication of concern from the commission can cause companies to revise their promotion.

A landmark legal battle regarding deceptive advertising involved the Federal Trade Commission and Campbell Soup Co. It had been Campbell's practice to insert clear glass marbles into the bottom of soup containers used in print advertisements to bring the soup ingredients (e.g., noodles or chicken) to the surface. The FTC ruled that the advertising was deceptive because it misrepresented the amount of solid ingredients in the soup, and it issued a cease and desist order. Campbell and its advertising agency agreed to discontinue the practice. Future ads used a ladle to show the ingredients.[48]

Other laws have been introduced to regulate promotion practices. The *Deceptive Mail Prevention and Enforcement Act* (1999), for example, provides specifications for direct-mail sweepstakes, such as the requirement that the statement "No purchase is necessary to enter" is displaycd in the mailing, in the rules, and on the entry form. Similarly, the *Telephone Consumer Protection Act* (1991) provides requirements for telemarketing promotions, including fax promotions. Telemarketing is also subject to a law that created the *National Do Not Call Registry,* which is a list of consumer phone numbers of people who do not want to receive unsolicited telemarketing calls. Finally, new laws such as the *Children's Online Privacy Protection Act* (1998) and the *Controlling the Assault of Non-Solicited Pornography and Marketing (CAN-SPAM) Act* (2004) are designed to restrict information collection and unsolicited e-mail promotions on the Internet.[49]

Control through Self-Regulation

The government has provided much legislation to create a competitive business climate and protect the consumer. An alternative to government control is **self-regulation**, where an industry attempts to police itself. The major television networks, for example, have used self-regulation to set their own guidelines for TV ads for children's toys. These guidelines have generally worked well. There are two problems with self-regulation, however: noncompliance by members and enforcement. In addition, if attempts at self-regulation are too strong, they may violate the Robinson-Patman Act. The best-known self-regulatory group is the Better Business Bureau (BBB). This agency is a voluntary alliance of companies whose goal is to help maintain fair practices. Although the BBB has no legal power, it does try to use "moral suasion" to get members to comply with its ruling. The BBB recently developed a reliability assurance program, called BBB Online, to provide objective consumer protection for Internet shoppers. Before they display the BBB Online logo on their website, participating companies must be members of their local Better Business Bureau, have been in business for at least one year,

Companies must meet certain requirements before they can display this logo on their websites.

www.bbbonline.com

have agreed to abide by BBB standards of truth in advertising, and have committed to work with the BBB to resolve consumer disputes that arise over goods or services promoted or advertised on their site.[50]

learning review

7. The _____ Act was punitive toward monopolies, whereas the _____ Act was preventive.

8. Describe some of the recent changes in trademark law.

9. How does the Better Business Bureau encourage companies to follow its standards for commerce?

LEARNING OBJECTIVES REVIEW

LO1 *Explain how environmental scanning provides information about social, economic, technological, competitive, and regulatory forces.*
Many businesses operate in environments where important forces change. Environmental scanning is the process of acquiring information about these changes to allow marketers to identify and interpret trends. There are five environmental forces businesses must monitor: social, economic, technological, competitive, and regulatory. By identifying trends related to each of these forces, businesses can develop and maintain successful marketing programs. Several trends that most businesses are monitoring include the increasing diversity of the U.S. population, the growing economic impact of China and India, and the dramatic growth of customer-generated content.

LO2 *Describe how social forces such as demographics and culture can have an impact on marketing strategy.*
Demographic information describes the world population; the U.S. population; the generational cohorts such as baby boomers, Generation X, and Generation Y; the structure of the American household; the geographic shifts of the population; and the racial and ethnic diversity of the population that has led to multicultural marketing programs. Cultural factors include the trend toward fewer differences in male and female consumer behavior and the impact of values such as "health and fitness" on consumer preferences.

LO3 *Discuss how economic forces such as macroeconomic conditions and consumer income affect marketing.*
Economic forces include the strong relationship between consumers' expectations about the economy and their spending. Gross income has remained stable for more than 30 years although the rate of saving has been declining.

LO4 *Describe how technological changes can affect marketing.*
Technological innovations can replace existing products and services. Changes in technology can also have an impact on customer value by reducing the cost of products, improving the quality of products, and providing new products that were not previously feasible. Electronic commerce is transforming how companies do business.

LO5 *Discuss the forms of competition that exist in a market and key components of competition.*
There are four forms of competition: pure competition, monopolistic competition, oligopoly, and monopoly. The key components of competition include the likelihood of new competitors, the power of buyers and suppliers, and the presence of competitors and possible substitutes. While large companies are often used as examples of marketplace competitors, there are 23 million small businesses in the United States, which have a significant impact on the economy.

LO6 *Explain the major legislation that ensures competition and regulates the elements of the marketing mix.*
Regulation exists to protect companies and consumers. Legislation that ensures a competitive marketplace includes the Sherman Antitrust Act. Product-related legislation includes copyright and trademark laws that protect companies and packaging and labeling laws that protect consumers. Pricing- and distribution-related laws are designed to create a competitive marketplace with fair prices and availability. Regulation related to promotion and advertising reduces deceptive practices and provides enforcement through the Federal Trade Commission. Self-regulation through organizations such as the Better Business Bureau provides an alternative to federal and state regulation.

FOCUSING ON KEY TERMS

baby boomers p. 73
barriers to entry p. 84
blended family p. 75
competition p. 83
consumerism p. 87
culture p. 76
demographics p. 71
discretionary income p. 81

disposable income p. 80
economy p. 78
electronic commerce p. 83
environmental scanning p. 70
extranets p. 83
Generation X p. 73
Generation Y p. 74
gross income p. 79

intranet p. 83
marketspace p. 83
multicultural marketing p. 76
regulation p. 86
self-regulation p. 89
social forces p. 71
technology p. 81
value consciousness p. 78

APPLYING MARKETING KNOWLEDGE

1 For many years Gerber has manufactured baby food in small, single-sized containers. In conducting an environmental scan, identify three trends or factors that might significantly affect this company's future business, and then propose how Gerber might respond to these changes.

2 Describe the new features you would add to an automobile designed for consumers in the 55+ age group. In what magazines would you advertise to appeal to this target market?

3 The population shift from suburbs to exurbs and penturbia was discussed in this chapter. What businesses and industries are likely to benefit from this trend? How will retailers need to change to accommodate these consumers?

4 New technologies are continuously improving and replacing existing products. Although technological change is often difficult to predict, suggest how the following companies and products might be affected by the Internet and digital technologies: (*a*) Kodak cameras

and film, (*b*) American Airlines, and (*c*) the Metropolitan Museum of Art.

5 In recent years in the brewing industry, a couple of large firms that have historically had most of the beer sales (Anheuser-Busch and Miller) have faced competition from many small "micro" brands. In terms of the continuum of competition, how would you explain this change?

6 The Johnson Company manufactures buttons and pins with slogans and designs. These pins are inexpensive to produce and are sold in retail outlets such as discount stores, hobby shops, and bookstores. Little equipment is needed for a new competitor to enter the market. What strategies should Johnson consider to create effective barriers to entry?

7 Why would Xerox be concerned about its name becoming generic?

8 Develop a "Code of Business Practices" for a new online vitamin store. Does your code address advertising? Privacy? Use by children? Why is self-regulation important?

building your marketing plan

Your marketing plan will include a situation analysis based on internal and external factors that are likely to affect your marketing program.

1 To summarize information about external factors, create a table similar to Figure 3–2 and identify three trends related to each of the five forces (social, economic, tech-

nological, competitive, and regulatory) that relate to your product or service.

2 When your table is completed, describe how each of the trends represents an opportunity or a threat for your business.

video case 3 Geek Squad: A New Business for a New Environment

"As long as there's innovation there is going to be new kinds of chaos," explains Robert Stephens, founder of the technology support company Geek Squad. The chaos Stephens is referring to is the difficulty we have all experienced trying to keep up with the many changes in our environment, particularly those related to computers, technology, software, communication, and entertainment. Generally, consumers have found it difficult to install, operate, and use many of the electronic products available today. "It takes time to read the manuals," continues Stephens. "I'm going to save you that time because I stay home on Saturday nights and read them for you!"

THE COMPANY

The Geek Squad story begins when Stephens, a native of Chicago, passed up an Art Institute scholarship to pursue

a degree in computer science. While Stephens was a computer science student he took a job fixing computers for a research laboratory, and he also started consulting. He could repair televisions, computers, and a variety of other items, although he decided to focus on computers. His experiences as a consultant led him to realize that most people needed help with technology and that they saw value in a service whose employees would show up at a specified time, be friendly, use understandable language, and solve the problem. So, with just $200, Stephens formed Geek Squad in 1994.

Geek Squad set out to provide timely and effective help with all computing needs regardless of the make, model, or place of purchase. Geek Squad employees were called "agents" and wore uniforms consisting of black pants or skirts, black shoes, white shirts, black clip-on ties, a badge, and a black jacket with a Geek Squad logo to create a "humble" attitude that was not threatening to

televisions, products with Internet interfaces, and a general trend toward computers, phones, entertainment systems, and even appliances being interconnected are just a few examples of new products and applications for consumers to learn about. There are also technology-related problems such as viruses, spyware, lost data, and "crashed" or inoperable computers. New technologies have also created a demand for new types of maintenance such as password management, operating system updates, disk cleanup, and 'defragging.'

Another environmental change that contributes to the popularity of Geek Squad is the change in social factors such as demographics and culture. In the past many electronics manufacturers and retailers focused primarily on men. Women, however, are becoming increasingly interested in personal computing and home entertainment, and, according to the Consumer Electronics Association, are likely to outspend men in the near future. Best Buy's consumer research indicates that women expect personal service during the purchase and installation after the purchase–exactly the service Geek Squad is designed to provide. Our culture is also embracing the Geek Squad concept. If you follow television programming you may have noticed the series *Chuck* where one of the characters works for the "Nerd Herd" at "Buy More" and drives a car like a Geekmobile on service calls!

Competition, economics, and the regulatory environment have also had a big influence on Geek Squad. As discount stores such as Wal-Mart and PC makers such as Dell began to compete with Best Buy, Circuit City, and CompUSA, new services such as in-home installation were needed to create value for customers. Now, just as changes in competition created an opportunity for Geek Squad, it is also leading to another level of competition as Circuit City has introduced its own computer support service called Firedog, Dell has introduced Dell-On-Call, and cable companies are offering their own services. The economic situation for electronics continues to improve as

customers. Agents drove black-and-white Volkswagen Beetles, or Geekmobiles, with a logo on the door, and charged fixed prices for services, regardless of how much time was required to provide the service. The "house call" services ranged from installing networks, to debugging a computer, to setting up an entertainment system, and cost from \$100 to \$300. "We're like 'Dragnet;' we show up at people's homes and help," offers Stephens. "We're also like 'Ghostbusters,' and there's a pseudogovernment feel to it like 'Men in Black.'"

In 2002, Geek Squad was purchased by leading consumer electronics retailer Best Buy for about \$3 million. Best Buy had observed very high return rates for most of its complex products. Shoppers would be excited about new products, purchase them and take them home, get frustrated trying to make them actually work, and then return them to the store demanding a refund. In fact, Best Buy research revealed that consumers were beginning to see service as a critical element of the purchase. The partnership was an excellent match. Best Buy consumers welcomed the help. Stephens became Geek Squad's chief inspector and a Best Buy vice president and began putting a Geek Squad "precinct" in every Best Buy store, creating some stand-alone Geek Squad Stores, and providing 24-hour telephone support. There are now more than 2,000 agents in the United States, Canada, the United Kingdom, and China, and return rates have declined by 25-35 percent. Geek Squad customer materials now suggest that the service is "Saving the World One Computer at a Time. 24 Hours a Day. Your Place or Ours!"

THE CHANGING ENVIRONMENT

Many changes in the environment occurred to create the need for Geek Squad's services. Future changes are also likely to change the way Geek Squad operates. An environmental scan helps understand the changes.

The most obvious changes may be related to technology. Wireless broadband technology, high-definition

prices decline and median income in the U.S., particularly for women, is increasing. In 2007, consumers purchased 16 million high-definition televisions, but household penetration is still below 40 percent. Finally, the regulatory environment continues to change with respect to electronic transfer of copyrighted materials such as music and movies and software. Geek Squad must monitor the changes to ensure that its services comply with relevant laws.

THE FUTURE FOR GEEK SQUAD

The combination of many positive environmental factors helps explain the extraordinary success of Geek Squad. Today, it repairs more than 3,000 PCs a day and generates more than $1 billion in revenue. Since Geek Squad services have a high-profit margin they contribute to the overall performance of Best Buy, and they help generate traffic in the store and create store loyalty. To continue to grow, however, Geek Squad will need to continue to scan the environment and try new approaches to creating customer value.

One possible new approach is to find additional locations that are convenient to consumers. For example, Geek Squad locations are being tested in some FedEx/Kinko stores and in some Office Depot stores. Another possible approach is to create new houses that are designed for the newest consumer electronics products. To test this idea Best Buy has created partnerships with home builders to wire new houses with high-speed cables and networking equipment that Geek Squad agents can use to create ideal computer and entertainment systems. Geek Squad is also using new technology to improve. Agents now use a smart phone to access updated schedules, log in their hours, and run diagnostics tests on client's equipment. Finally, to attract the best possible employees, Geek Squad and Best Buy are trying a "results-only work environment" that has no fixed schedules and no mandatory meetings. By encouraging employees to make their own work-life decisions the Geek Squad hopes to keep morale and productivity high.

Other changes and opportunities are certain to appear soon. Despite the success of the Geek Squad, and the potential for additional growth, however, Robert Stephens is modest and claims, "Geeks may inherit the Earth, but they have no desire to rule it!"

Questions

1 What are the key environmental factors that created an opportunity for Robert Stephens to start the Geek Squad?

2 What changes in the purchasing patterns of (a) all consumers, and (b) women made the acquisition of Geek Squad particularly important for Best Buy?

3 Based on the case information and what you know about consumer electronics, conduct an environmental scan for Geek Squad to identify key trends. For each of the five environmental forces (social, economic, technological, competitive, and regulatory), identify trends likely to influence Geek Squad in the near future.

4 What promotional activities would you recommend to encourage consumers who use independent installers to switch to Geek Squad?

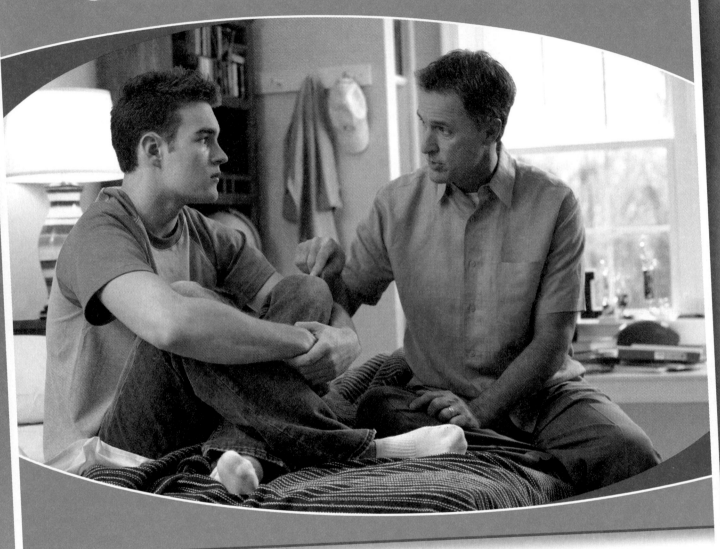

"I want your friends to have a good time here. But, no alcohol."

As a parent, your position may not always be popular. But, as most parents agree, hosting a teen drinking party is wrong and illegal. So, talk with your teens, and help them find ways to have a good time without drinking.

Don't be a pushover. Be a parent.

  National Fatherhood Initiative®  **THE ASSOCIATION OF JUNIOR LEAGUES INTERNATIONAL INC.**  **prevent.** don't provide alcohol to minors ANHEUSER-BUSCH, INC.

preventdontprovide.com

4

Ethical and Social Responsibility in Marketing

LEARNING OBJECTIVES

After reading this chapter you should be able to:

LO1 Explain the differences between legal and ethical behavior in marketing.

LO2 Identify factors that influence ethical and unethical marketing decisions.

LO3 Describe the different concepts of social responsibility.

LO4 Recognize unethical and socially irresponsible consumer behavior.

THERE IS MORE TO ANHEUSER-BUSCH THAN MEETS THE PALATE

Why would a company spend more than a half-billion dollars since 1982 trying to convince people not to abuse its products and millions of dollars more to decrease litter and solid waste? Ask Anheuser-Busch, the world's largest brewer.

Anheuser-Busch has been an advocate for responsible drinking for more than two decades. The company began an aggressive campaign to fight alcohol abuse and underage drinking with its landmark "Know When to Say When" campaign in 1982. In 1989, a Consumer Awareness and Education Department was established within the company. This department was charged with developing and implementing programs, advertising, and partnerships that promote responsible drinking; helping prevent alcohol abuse; and helping stop underage drinking before it starts. For example, about 6 million copies of the company's *Family Talk about Drinking* guidebook have been distributed free to parents and educators in the past decade.

The brewer recently began a new chapter in its awareness and education efforts with the launch of its "Responsibility Matters" campaign. This effort emphasizes and implements effective education and awareness programs that promote responsibility and responsible behaviors, such as parents talking with their children about underage drinking, adults being designated drivers, retailers checking IDs to prevent sales to minors, and more. Anheuser-Busch believes these efforts are partly responsible for the sizable decline in drunk-driving accidents, underage drinking, and other forms of alcohol abuse since 1982.

Responsibility at Anheuser-Busch is broader than its successful alcohol awareness and education initiatives. The company is an advocate and sponsor of numerous efforts to preserve the natural environment. A notable example is its massive recycling effort through Anheuser-Busch Recycling Corporation (ABRC). ABRC is the world's largest recycler of aluminum cans. ABRC recycles over 800 million pounds of aluminum annually, the equivalent of about 130 percent of the beer cans Anheuser-Busch ships worldwide. The rationale for founding ABRC was simple: Voluntary recycling reduces litter and solid waste while conserving natural resources.

Anheuser-Busch acts on what it views as an ethical obligation to its customers and the general public with its alcohol awareness and education programs. At the same time, the company's efforts to protect the environment reflect its broader social responsibility. Not surprisingly, Anheuser-Busch is one of "The World's Most Admired Companies" according to *Fortune* magazine.[1]

NATURE AND SIGNIFICANCE OF MARKETING ETHICS

Ethics are the moral principles and values that govern the actions and decisions of an individual or group.[2] They serve as guidelines on how to act rightly and justly when faced with moral dilemmas.

Ethical/Legal Framework in Marketing

A good starting point for understanding the nature and significance of ethics is the distinction between legality and ethicality of marketing decisions. Figure 4–1 helps visualize the relationship between laws and ethics.[3] Whereas ethics deal with personal moral principles and values, **laws** are society's values and standards that are enforceable in the courts. This distinction can sometimes lead to the rationalization that if a behavior is within reasonable ethical and legal limits, then it is not really illegal or unethical. When a recent survey asked the question, "Is it OK to get around the law if you don't actually break it?" about 61 percent of businesspeople who took part responded 'yes.'[4] How would you answer this question?

There are numerous situations in which judgment plays a large role in defining ethical and legal boundaries. Consider the following situations. After reading each, assign it to the cell in Figure 4–1 that you think best fits the situation along the ethical–legal continuum.[5]

1. More than 70 percent of the physicians in the Maricopa County (Arizona) Medical Society agreed to establish a maximum fee schedule for health services to curb rising medical costs. All physicians were required to adhere to this schedule as a condition for membership in the society. The U.S. Supreme Court ruled that this agreement to set prices violated the Sherman Act and represented price fixing, which is illegal. Was the society's action ethical?

2. A company in California sells a computer program to auto dealers showing that car buyers should finance their purchase rather than paying cash. The program omits the effect of income taxes and misstates the interest earned on savings over the loan period. The finance option always provides a net benefit over the cash option. Company employees agree that the program does mislead buyers, but say

FIGURE 4–1

Four ways to classify marketing decisions according to ethical and legal relationships

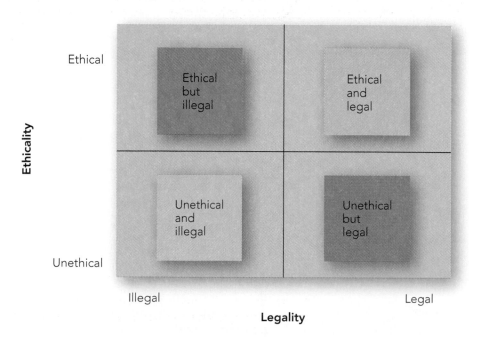

the company will "provide what [car dealers] want as long as it is not against the law." Is this practice ethical?

3. China is the world's largest tobacco-producing country and has 300 million smokers. Approximately 700,000 Chinese die annually from smoking-related illnesses. This figure is expected to rise to more than 2 million by 2025. China legally restricts tobacco imports. U.S. trade negotiators advocate free trade, thus allowing U.S. tobacco companies to market their products in China. Is the Chinese trade position ethical?

4. A group of college students recorded movies at a local theater and then uploaded the movies to the Internet. Federal statutes state that the unauthorized reproduction, distribution, or exhibition of copyrighted motion pictures is illegal. The students then directed friends and family to a peer-to-peer Internet network that allowed them to download the movies for free. Are the students ethical? Are the students' friends and family ethical?

Did these situations fit neatly into Figure 4–1 as clearly ethical and legal or unethical and illegal? Probably not. As you read further in this chapter, you will be asked to consider other ethical dilemmas.

Current Perceptions of Ethical Behavior

There has been a public outcry about the ethical practices of businesspeople.[6] Public opinion surveys show that 58 percent of U.S. adults rate the ethical standards of business executives as only "fair" or "poor;" 90 percent think white-collar crime is "very common" or "somewhat common;" 76 percent say the lack of ethics in businesspeople contributes to tumbling societal moral standards; only the U.S. government is viewed as less trustworthy than corporations among institutions in the United States; and advertising practitioners, telemarketers, and car salespeople are thought to be among the least ethical occupations. Surveys of corporate employees generally confirm this public perception. When asked if they were aware of ethical problems in their companies, 52 percent say, "yes."

There are at least four possible reasons the state of perceived ethical business conduct is at its present level. First, there is increased pressure on businesspeople to make decisions in a society characterized by diverse value systems. Second, there is a growing tendency for business decisions to be judged publicly by groups with different values and interests. Third, the public's expectations of ethical business behavior has increased. Finally, and most disturbing, ethical business conduct may have declined.

learning review

1. What are ethics?

2. What are four possible reasons for the present state of ethical conduct in the United States?

UNDERSTANDING ETHICAL MARKETING BEHAVIOR

LO2

Researchers have identified numerous factors that influence ethical marketing behavior.[7] Figure 4–2 on the next page presents a framework that shows these factors and their relationships.

Societal Culture and Norms

As described in Chapter 3, *culture* refers to the set of values, ideas, and attitudes that are learned and shared among the members of a group. Culture also serves

FIGURE 4–2

A framework for understanding
ethical behavior. Each of these
influences will have an effect
on ethical marketing behavior.

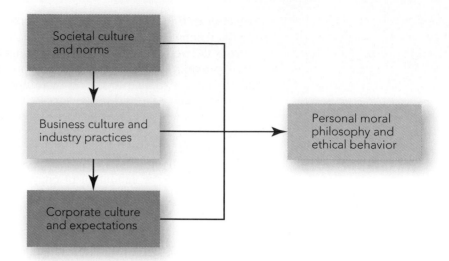

as a socializing force that dictates what is morally right and just. This means
that moral standards are relative to particular societies.[8] These standards often
reflect the laws and regulations that affect social and economic behavior, which
can create moral dilemmas. For example, Levi Strauss decided to end much of its
business dealings in China because of what the company called "pervasive human
rights abuses." According to its vice president for corporate marketing: "There
are wonderful commercial opportunities in China. But when ethical issues collide
with commercial appeal, we try to ensure ethics as the trump card. For us, ethical
issues precede all others."[9]

Societal values and attitudes also affect ethical and legal relationships among
individuals, groups, and business institutions and organizations. Consider the copying of another's copyright, trademark, or patent. These are viewed as intellectual property. Unauthorized use, reproduction, or distribution of intellectual property is illegal in the United States and most countries, which can result in fines
and prison terms for perpetrators. The owners of intellectual property also lose.
For example, annual lost sales from the theft of intellectual property amount to
$5 billion in the music industry, $6 billion in the movie industry, and $33 billion
in the software industry.[10] Lost sales, in turn, result in lost jobs, royalties, wages,
and tax revenue. But what about a person downloading copyrighted music, movies,
and software over the Internet or from peer-to-peer file-sharing programs, without
paying the owner of this property? Is this an ethical or unethical act? It depends on
who you ask. Surveys of the U.S. public indicate that the majority consider these
acts unethical. However, only a third of U.S. college students say such practices
are unethical.[11]

Business Culture and Industry Practices

Societal culture provides a foundation for understanding moral behavior in business
activities. *Business cultures* "comprise the effective rules of the game, the boundaries
between competitive and unethical behavior, [and] the codes of conduct in business
dealings."[12] Consumers have witnessed numerous instances where business cultures
in the brokerage (inside trading), insurance (deceptive sales practices), and defense
(bribery) industries went awry. Business culture affects ethical conduct both in the
exchange relationship between sellers and buyers and in the competitive behavior
among sellers.

The Federal Trade Commission plays an active role in educating consumers and businesses about the importance of personal information privacy on the Internet. FTC initiatives are detailed on its website.

Federal Trade Commission
www.ftc.gov

Ethics of Exchange   The exchange process is central to the marketing concept. Ethical exchanges between sellers and buyers should result in both parties being better off after a transaction.

Before the 1960s, the legal concept of **caveat emptor**—let the buyer beware—was pervasive in the American business culture. In 1962, President John F. Kennedy outlined a **Consumer Bill of Rights** that codified the ethics of exchange between buyers and sellers. These were the right (1) to safety, (2) to be informed, (3) to choose, and (4) to be heard. Consumers expect and often demand that these rights be protected, as have American businesses.

The right to safety manifests itself in industry and federal safety standards for most products sold in the United States. In fact, the U.S. Consumer Product Safety Commission routinely monitors the safety of 15,000 consumer products. However, even the most vigilant efforts to ensure safe products cannot foresee every possibility. In fact, personal claims and property damage from consumer product safety incidents cost companies more than $700 billion annually. Consider the case of batteries used in laptop and notebook computers. Dell Inc. learned that the lithium-ion batteries in its notebook computers, made by Sony Energy Devices Corporation of Japan, posed a fire hazard to consumers. The company recalled 2.7 million batteries and gave consumers a replacement before any personal injuries resulted.[13]

The right to be informed means that marketers have an obligation to give consumers complete and accurate information about products and services, but this is not always the case. For example, three U.S. advertising agencies recently agreed to settle Federal Trade Commission (FTC) claims that they failed to disclose the actual costs of car leases and credit transactions in their advertising for three Japanese carmakers.[14] This right also applies to the solicitation of personal information over the Internet and its subsequent use by marketers.[15] A FTC survey of websites indicated that 92 percent collect personal information such as consumer e-mail addresses, telephone numbers, shopping habits, and financial data. Yet, only two-thirds of websites inform consumers of what is done with this information once obtained. The FTC wants more than posted privacy notices that merely inform consumers of a company's data-use policy, which critics say are often vague, confusing, or too legalistic to be understood. This view is shared by two-thirds of consumers who worry about protecting their personal information online. The consumer right to be informed has spawned much federal legislation, such as the *Children's Online Privacy Protection Act* (1998), and self-regulation initiatives restricting disclosure of personal information.

Relating to the right to choose, today many supermarket chains demand "slotting allowances" from manufacturers, in the form of cash or free goods, to stock new products.[16] This practice could limit the number of new products available to consumers and interfere with their right to choose. One critic of this practice remarked, "If we had had slotting allowances a few years ago, we might not have had granola, herbal tea, or yogurt."

Finally, the right to be heard means that consumers should have access to public-policy makers regarding complaints about products and services. This right is illustrated in limitations put on telemarketing practices. Consumer complaints about late-night and repeated calls resulted in the *Telephone Consumer Protection Act of 1991*. The FTC established the Do Not Call Registry in 2003 for consumers who

Making Responsible Decisions > > > > > > > ethics

Corporate Conscience in the Cola War

Suppose you are a senior executive at Pepsi-Cola and that a Coca-Cola employee offers to sell you the marketing plan and sample for a new Coke product at a modest price? Would you buy it knowing Pepsi-Cola could gain a significant competitive edge in the cola war?

When this question was posed in an online survey of marketing and advertising executives, 67 percent said they would buy the plan and product sample if there were no repercussions. What did Pepsi-Cola do when this offer actually occurred? The company immediately contacted Coca-Cola, which contacted the FBI. An undercover FBI agent paid the employee $30,000 in cash stuffed in a Girl Scout cookie box as a down payment and later arrested the employee and accomplices. When asked about the inci-

dent, a Pepsi-Cola spokesperson said: "We only did what any responsible company would do. Competition must be tough, but must always be fair and legal."

Why did the 33 percent of respondents in the online survey say they would decline the offer? Most said they would prefer competing ethically so they could sleep at night. According to a senior advertising agency executive who would decline the offer: "Repercussions go beyond potential espionage charges. As long as we have a conscience, there are repercussions."

So what happened to the Coca-Cola employee? She was sentenced to eight years in prison and ordered to pay $40,000 in restitution. Her accomplices were sentenced to five years in prison.

---

do not want to receive unsolicited telemarketing calls. Today, 76 percent of U.S. adults have their telephone numbers listed in the registry, which is managed by the FTC. A telemarketer can be fined $11,000 for each call made to a telephone number posted on the registry.

Ethics of Competition   Business culture also affects ethical behavior in competition. Two kinds of unethical behavior are most common: (1) economic espionage and (2) bribery.

Economic espionage is the clandestine collection of trade secrets or proprietary information about a company's competitors. This practice is illegal and unethical and carries serious criminal penalties for the offending individual or business. Espionage activities include illegal trespassing, theft, fraud, misrepresentation, wiretapping, the search of a competitor's trash, and violations of written and implicit employment agreements with noncompete clauses. More than half of the largest firms in the United States have uncovered espionage in some form, costing them $300 billion annually in lost sales.[17]

Economic espionage is most prevalent in high-technology industries, such as electronics, specialty chemicals, industrial equipment, aerospace, and pharmaceuticals, where technical know-how and trade secrets separate industry leaders from followers. But espionage can occur anywhere—even in the soft drink industry! Read the accompanying Making Responsible Decisions box to learn how Pepsi-Cola responded to an offer to obtain confidential information in its archrival's marketing plans.[18]

The second form of unethical competitive behavior is giving and receiving bribes and kickbacks. Bribes and kickbacks are often disguised as gifts, consultant fees,

and favors. This practice is more common in business-to-business and government marketing than in consumer marketing. For example, two American Honda Motor Company executives were fined and sentenced to prison for extracting $15 million in kickbacks from Honda dealers and advertising agencies, and a series of highly publicized trials uncovered widespread bribery in the U.S. Defense Department's awarding of $160 billion in military contracts.[19]

In general, bribery is most evident in industries experiencing intense competition and in countries in the earlier stages of economic development. According to a recent U.N. study, 15 percent of all companies in industrialized countries have to pay bribes to win or retain business. In Asia, this figure is 40 percent. In Eastern Europe, 60 percent of all companies must pay bribes to do business. A recent poll of senior executives engaged in global marketing revealed that Bangladesh and Chad were the most likely countries to evidence bribery to win or retain business. Iceland and Finland were the least likely.[20] Bribery on a worldwide scale is monitored by Transparency International. Visit its website described in the accompanying Going Online box, and view the most recent country rankings on this practice.

The prevalence of economic espionage and bribery in international marketing has prompted laws to curb these practices. Two significant laws, the *Economic Espionage Act* (1996) and the *Foreign Corrupt Practices Act* (1977), address these practices in the United States. Both are detailed in Chapter 7.

Corporate Culture and Expectations

A third influence on ethical practices is corporate culture. *Corporate culture* is the set of values, ideas, and attitudes that is learned and shared among the members of an organization. The culture of a company demonstrates itself in the dress ("We don't wear ties"), sayings ("The IBM Way"), and manner of work (team efforts) of employees. Culture is also apparent in the expectations for ethical behavior present in formal codes of ethics and the ethical actions of top management and co-workers.

Codes of Ethics A **code of ethics** is a formal statement of ethical principles and rules of conduct. It is estimated that 86 percent of U.S. companies have some sort of ethics code and one of every four large companies has corporate ethics officers. At United Technologies, for example, 160 corporate ethics officers distribute

AMERICAN MARKETING ASSOCIATION STATEMENT OF ETHICS

Preamble

The American Marketing Association commits itself to promoting the highest standard of professional ethical norms and values for its members. Norms are established standards of conduct that are expected and maintained by society and/or professional organizations. Values represent the collective conception of what people find desirable, important and morally proper. Values serve as the criteria for evaluating the actions of others. Marketing practitioners must recognize that they not only serve their enterprises but also act as stewards of society in creating, facilitating and executing the efficient and effective transactions that are part of the greater economy. In this role, marketers should embrace the highest ethical *norms* of practicing professionals and the ethical *values* implied by their responsibility toward stakeholders (e.g., customers, employees, investors, channel members, regulators and the host community).

General Norms

1. Marketers must do no harm. This means doing work for which they are appropriately trained or experienced so that they can actively add value to their organizations and customers. It also means adhering to all applicable laws and regulations and embodying high ethical standards in the choices they make.
2. Marketers must foster trust in the marketing system. This means that products are appropriate for their intended and promoted uses. It requires that marketing communications about goods and services are not intentionally deceptive or misleading. It suggests building relationships that provide for the equitable adjustment and/or redress of customer grievances. It implies striving for good faith and fair dealing so as to contribute toward the efficacy of the exchange process.
3. Marketers must embrace, communicate and practice the fundamental ethical values that will improve consumer confidence in the integrity of the marketing exchange system. These basic *values* are intentionally aspirational and include honesty, responsibility, fairness, respect, openness and citizenship.

Ethical Values

Honesty—to be truthful and forthright in our dealings with customers and stakeholders.

- We will tell the truth in all situations and at all times.
- We will offer products of value that do what we claim in our communications.
- We will stand behind our products if they fail to deliver their claimed benfits.
- We will honor our explicit and implicit commitments and promises.

Responsibility—to accept the consequences of our marketing decisions and strategies.

- We will make strenuous efforts to serve the needs of our customers.
- We will avoid using coercion with all stakeholders.
- We will acknowledge the social obligations to stakeholders that come with increased marketing and economic power.
- We will recognize our special commitments to economically vulnerable segments of the market such as children, the elderly and

FIGURE 4–3

American Marketing Association Statement of Ethics

American Marketing Association

www.marketingpower.com

the company's ethics code, translated into 24 languages, to employees who work for this defense and engineering giant around the world.[21] Ethics codes and committees typically address contributions to government officials and political parties, relations with customers and suppliers, conflicts of interest, and accurate record-keeping. For example, General Mills provides guidelines for dealing with suppliers, competitors, and customers, and recruits new employees who share these views.

However, an ethics code is rarely enough to ensure ethical behavior. Coca-Cola has an ethics code and emphasizes that its employees be ethical in their behavior. But that did not stop some Coca-Cola employees from rigging the results of a test market for a frozen soft drink to win Burger King's business. Coca-Cola subsequently agreed to pay Burger King and its operators more than $20 million to settle the matter.[22]

Lack of specificity is a major reason for the violation of ethics codes. Employees must often judge whether a specific behavior is unethical. The American

FIGURE 4-3
(Continued)

others who may be substantially disadvantaged.

Fairness—to try to balance justly the needs of the buyer with the interests of the seller.

- We will represent our products in a clear way in selling, advertising and other forms of communication; this includes the avoidance of false, misleading and deceptive promotion.
- We will reject manipulations and sales tactics that harm customer trust.
- We will not engage in price fixing, predatory pricing, price gouging or "bait-and-switch" tactics.
- We will not knowingly participate in material conflicts of interest.

Respect—to acknowledge the basic human dignity of all stakeholders.

- We will value individual differences even as we avoid stereotyping customers or depicting demographic groups (e.g., gender, race, sexual orientation) in a negative or dehumanizing way in our promotions.
- We will listen to the needs of our customers and make all reasonable efforts to monitor and improve their satisfaction on an ongoing basis.
- We will make a special effort to understand suppliers, intermediaries and distributors from other cultures.
- We will appropriately acknowledge the contributions of others, such as consultants, employees and coworkers, to our marketing endeavors.

Openness—to create transparency in our marketing operations.

- We will strive to communicate clearly with all our constituencies.
- We will accept constructive criticism from our customers and other stakeholders.
- We will explain significant product or service risks, component substitutions or other foreseeable eventualities that could affect customers or their perception of the purchase decision.
- We will fully disclose list prices and terms of financing as well as available price deals and adjustments.

Citizenship—to fulfill the economic, legal, philanthropic and societal responsibilities that serve stakeholders in a strategic manner.

- We will strive to protect the natural environment in the execution of marketing campaigns.
- We will give back to the community through volunteerism and charitable donations.
- We will work to contribute to the overall betterment of marketing and its reputation.
- We will encourage supply chain members to ensure that trade is fair for all participants, including producers in developing countries.

Implementation

Finally, we recognize that every industry sector and marketing subdiscipline (e.g., marketing research, e-commerce, direct selling, direct marketing, advertising) has its own specific ethical issues that require policies and commentary. An array of such codes can be accessed through links on the AMA website. We encourage all such groups to develop and/or refine their industry and discipline-specific codes of ethics to supplement these general norms and values.

Marketing Association has addressed this issue by providing a detailed statement of ethics, which all members agree to follow. This statement is shown in Figure 4–3.

Ethical Behavior of Top Management and Co-Workers A second reason for violating ethics codes rests in the perceived behavior of top management and co-workers.[23] Observing peers and top management and gauging responses to unethical behavior play an important role in individual actions. A study of business executives reported that 40 percent had been implicitly or explicitly rewarded for engaging in ethically troubling behavior. Moreover, 31 percent of those who refused to engage in unethical behavior were penalized, either through outright punishment or a diminished status in the company.[24] Clearly, ethical dilemmas often bring personal and professional conflict. For this reason, numerous states have laws protecting **whistle-blowers**, employees who report unethical or illegal

What does 3M's Scotchgard have to do with ethics, social responsibility, and a $200 million loss in annual sales? Read the text to find out.

actions of their employers. Some firms, such as General Dynamics and Dun & Bradstreet, have appointed ethics officers responsible for safeguarding these individuals from recrimination.

Your Personal Moral Philosophy and Ethical Behavior

Ultimately, ethical choices are based on the personal moral philosophy of the decision maker. Moral philosophy is learned through the process of socialization with friends and family and by formal education. It is also influenced by the societal, business, and corporate culture in which a person finds him- or herself. Two prominent personal moral philosophies have direct bearing on marketing practice: (1) moral idealism and (2) utilitarianism.[25]

Moral Idealism   **Moral idealism** is a personal moral philosophy that considers certain individual rights or duties as universal, regardless of the outcome. This philosophy exists in the Consumer Bill of Rights and is favored by moral philosophers and consumer interest groups. For example, the right to know applies to probable defects in an automobile that relate to safety.

This philosophy also applies to ethical duties. A fundamental ethical duty is to do no harm. Adherence to this duty prompted the recent decision by 3M executives to phase out production of a chemical 3M had manufactured for nearly 40 years. The substance, used in far-ranging products from pet food bags, candy wrappers, carpeting, and 3M's popular Scotchgard fabric protector, had no known harmful health or environmental effect. However, the company discovered that the chemical appeared in minuscule amounts in humans and animals around the world and accumulated in tissue. Believing that the substance could be possibly harmful in large doses, 3M voluntarily stopped its production, resulting in a $200 million loss in annual sales.[26]

Utilitarianism   An alternative perspective on moral philosophy is **utilitarianism**, which is a personal moral philosophy that focuses on "the greatest good for the greatest number" by assessing the costs and benefits of the consequences of ethical behavior. If the benefits exceed the costs, then the behavior is ethical. If not, then the behavior is unethical. This philosophy underlies the economic tenets of capitalism and, not surprisingly, is embraced by many business executives and students.[27]

Utilitarian reasoning was apparent in Nestlé Food Corporation's marketing of Good Start infant formula, sold by Nestlé's Carnation Company. The formula, promoted as hypoallergenic, was designed to prevent or reduce colic caused by an infant's allergic reaction to cow's milk, a condition suffered by 2 percent of babies. However, some severely milk-allergic infants experienced serious side effects after using Good Start, including convulsive vomiting. Physicians and parents charged that the hypoallergenic claim was misleading, and the Food and Drug Administration investigated the matter. A Nestlé vice president defended the claim and product, saying, "I don't understand why our product should work in 100 percent of cases. If we wanted to say it was foolproof, we would have called it allergy-free. We call it hypo-, or less, allergenic."[28] Nestlé officials seemingly believed that most allergic infants would benefit from Good Start—"the greatest good for the greatest number." However, other views prevailed, and the claim was dropped from the product label.

An appreciation for the nature of ethics, coupled with a basic understanding of why unethical behavior arises, alerts a person to when and how ethical issues exist in marketing decisions. Ultimately, ethical behavior rests with the individual, but the consequences affect many.

UNDERSTANDING SOCIAL RESPONSIBILITY IN MARKETING

LO3

As we saw in Chapter 1, the societal marketing concept stresses marketing's social responsibility by not only satisfying the needs of consumers but also providing for society's welfare. **Social responsibility** means that organizations are part of a larger society and are accountable to that society for their actions. Like ethics, agreement on the nature and scope of social responsibility is often difficult to come by, given the diversity of values present in different societal, business, and corporate cultures.

Three Concepts of Social Responsibility

Figure 4–4 shows three concepts of social responsibility: (1) profit responsibility, (2) stakeholder responsibility, and (3) societal responsibility.

Profit Responsibility *Profit responsibility* holds that companies have a simple duty: to maximize profits for their owners or stockholders. This view is expressed by Nobel Laureate Milton Friedman, who said, "There is one and only one social responsibility of business—to use its resources and engage in activities designed to increase

FIGURE 4–4
Three concepts of social responsibility. Each concept of social responsibility relates to particular constituencies. There is often conflict in satisfying all constituencies at the same time.

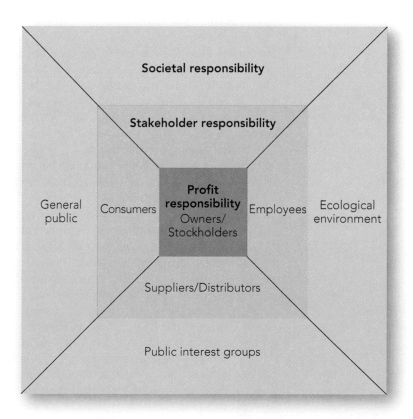

its profits so long as it stays within the rules of the game, which is to say, engages in open and free competition without deception or fraud."[29] Genzyme, the maker of Cerezyme, a drug that treats a genetic illness called Gaucher's disease that affects 20,000 people worldwide, has been criticized for apparently adopting this view in its pricing practices. Genzyme charges up to $170,000 for a year's worth of Cerezyme. A Genzyme spokesperson responded saying the company spends about $150 million annually to manufacture Cerezyme and freely gives the drug to patients without insurance. Also, the company invested considerable dollars in research over several years to develop Cerezyme, and the drug's profits are reinvested in ongoing R&D programs. [30]

Stakeholder Responsibility Criticism of the profit view has led to a broader concept of social responsibility. *Stakeholder responsibility* focuses on the obligations an organization has to those who can affect achievement of its objectives. These constituencies include consumers, employees, suppliers, and distributors. Source Perrier S.A., the supplier of Perrier bottled water, exercised this responsibility when it recalled 160 million bottles of water in 120 countries after traces of a toxic chemical were found in 13 bottles. The recall cost the company $35 million, and $40 million more in lost sales. Even though the chemical level was not harmful to humans, Source Perrier's president believed he acted in the best interests of the firm's consumers, distributors, and employees by removing "the least doubt, as minimal as it might be, to weigh on the image of the quality and purity of our product"—which it did.[31]

Failure to consider a company's broader constituencies can have negative consequences. For example, Bridgestone/Firestone, Inc., executives were widely criticized for how they responded to complaints about the safety of selected Firestone-brand tires. These tires had been linked to crashes that killed at least 174 people and injured more than 700 in the United States. The company recalled 6.5 million tires under pressure from the National Highway Traffic Safety Administration. After the recall, Firestone tire sales fell by nearly one-half, which affected Firestone employees, suppliers, and distributors as well. Ford Motor Company, a large buyer of Firestone tires, ended its exclusive contract with the tire producer.[32]

Societal Responsibility An even broader concept of social responsibility has emerged in recent years. *Societal responsibility* refers to obligations that organizations have (1) to the preservation of the ecological environment and (2) to the general public. Concerns about the environment and public welfare are represented by interest and advocacy groups such as Greenpeace, an international environmental organization.

Chapter 3 detailed the importance of ecological issues in marketing. Companies have responded to this concern through what is termed **green marketing**—marketing efforts to produce, promote, and reclaim environmentally sensitive products.

Green marketing takes many forms.[33] At 3M, product development opportunities emanate both from consumer research and its "Pollution Prevention Pays" program. This program solicits employee suggestions on how to reduce pollution and recycle materials. Since 1975, this program has generated over 6,000 ideas that eliminated more than 2.5 billion pounds of air, water, and solid-waste pollutants from the environment. Xerox's "Design for the Environment" program focuses on ways to make its equipment recyclable and remanufacturable. Today, 90 percent of Xerox-designed products are remanufacturable. This effort has kept more than 1.6 billion pounds of equipment from being discarded in U.S. landfills since 1991. Boise Cascade, a leading North American timber manufacturer, and Lowe's and Home Depot, two home-and-garden center retail chains, have discontinued the sale of wood products from the world's endangered forests. Wal-Mart has instituted buying practices that encourage its suppliers to use containers and packaging made from corn, not oil-based resins. The company expects this initiative

Avon Products, Inc., successfully employs cause marketing programs in the fight against breast cancer.

Avon Products, Inc.
www.avon.com

will save 800,000 barrels of oil annually. These voluntary responses to environmental issues have been implemented with little or no additional cost to consumers and resulted in cost savings to companies.

A global undertaking to further green marketing efforts is the ISO 14000 initiative developed by the International Standards Organization (ISO) in Geneva, Switzerland. **ISO 14000** consists of worldwide standards for environmental quality and green marketing practices. These standards are embraced by 157 countries, including the United States, members of the European Union, and many Pacific Rim nations. More than 125,000 companies have met ISO 14000 standards for environmental quality and green marketing. About 21 percent of all ISO 14000 certified companies are Japanese firms, making Japan a world leader in environmental protection.[34]

Socially responsible efforts on behalf of the general public are becoming more common. A formal practice is **cause marketing**, which occurs when the charitable contributions of a firm are tied directly to the customer revenues produced through the promotion of one of its products.[35] This definition distinguishes cause marketing from a firm's standard charitable contributions, which are outright donations. For example, Procter & Gamble raises funds for the Special Olympics when consumers purchase selected company products, and MasterCard International links usage of its card with fund-raising for institutions that combat cancer, heart disease, child abuse, drug abuse, and muscular dystrophy. Barnes & Noble promotes literacy, and Coca-Cola sponsors local Boys and Girls Clubs. Avon Products, Inc., focuses on different issues in different countries. These include breast cancer, domestic violence, disaster relief among many others. Cause marketing programs incorporate all three concepts of social responsibility by addressing public concerns and satisfying customer needs. They can also enhance corporate sales and profits as described in the Marketing Matters box on the next page.[36]

The Social Audit: Doing Well by Doing Good

Converting socially responsible ideas into actions involves careful planning and monitoring of programs. Many companies develop, implement, and evaluate their social responsibility efforts by means of a **social audit**, which is a systematic assessment of a firm's objectives, strategies, and performance in terms of social responsibility. Frequently, marketing and social responsibility programs are

Marketing and social responsibility programs are often integrated, as is the case with McDonald's. Its concern for ill children worldwide is apparent in the opening of another Ronald McDonald House for children and their families. This time in China.

McDonald's
www.mcdonalds.com

Will Consumers Switch Brands for a Cause? Yes, If ...

American Express Company pioneered cause marketing when it sponsored the renovation of the Statue of Liberty. This effort raised $1.7 million for the renovation, increased card usage among cardholders, and attracted new cardholders. In 2001, U.S. companies raised more than $5 billion for causes they champion. It is estimated that cause marketing will raise over $10 billion in 2010.

Cause marketing benefits companies as well as causes. Research indicates that 92 percent of U.S. consumers say they have a more favorable opinion of companies that support causes. Also, 89 percent of consumers under 25 years old say they will switch to a brand or retailer that supports a good cause if the price and quality of brands or retailers are equal. In short, cause marketing may be a valued point of difference for brands and companies, all other things being equal.

For more information, including news, links, and case studies, visit the Cause Marketing Forum website at www. causemarketingforum.com.

integrated, as is the case with McDonald's. The company's concern for the needs of families with children who are chronically or terminally ill was converted into over 245 Ronald McDonald Houses around the world. These facilities, located near treatment centers, enable families to stay together during the child's care. In this case, McDonald's is contributing to the welfare of a portion of its target market.

A social audit consists of five steps:[37]

1. Recognition of a firm's social expectations and the rationale for engaging in social responsibility endeavors.
2. Identification of social responsibility causes or programs consistent with the company's mission.
3. Determination of organizational objectives and priorities for programs and activities it will undertake.
4. Specification of the type and amount of resources necessary to achieve social responsibility objectives.
5. Evaluation of social responsibility programs and activities undertaken and assessment of future involvement.

Corporate attention to social audits will increase as companies seek to achieve sustainable development and improve the quality of life in a global economy. **Sustainable development** involves conducting business in a way that protects the natural environment while making economic progress. Ecologically responsible initiatives such as green marketing represent one such initiative. Recent initiatives related to working conditions at offshore manufacturing sites that produce goods for U.S. companies focus on quality-of-life issues. Public opinion surveys show that 90 percent of U.S. citizens are concerned about working conditions under which products are made in Asia and Latin America. Companies such as Reebok, Nike, Liz Claiborne, Levi Strauss, and Mattel have responded by imposing codes of conduct to reduce harsh or abusive working conditions at offshore manufacturing facilities.[38] Reebok, for example, now monitors production of its sporting apparel and equipment to ensure that no child labor is used in making its products.

Companies that evidence societal responsibility have been rewarded for their efforts. Research has shown that these companies (1) benefit from favorable word of mouth among consumers and (2) typically outperform less responsible companies on financial performance.[39]

Turning the Table: Consumer Ethics and Social Responsibility

Consumers also have an obligation to act ethically and responsibly in the exchange process and in the use and disposition of products. Unfortunately, consumer behavior is spotty on both counts.

Unethical practices of consumers are a serious concern to marketers.[40] These practices include: filing warranty claims after the claim period; misredeeming coupons; making fraudulent returns of merchandise; providing inaccurate information on credit applications; tampering with utility meters; tapping cable TV lines; pirating music, movies, and software from the Internet; and submitting phony insurance claims.

Consumers also act unethically toward each other. According to the FBI, consumer complaints about online auction fraud, in which consumers misrepresent their goods to others, outnumbers all reports of online crime. The cost to marketers of such behavior in lost sales and prevention expenses is huge. For example, consumers who redeem coupons for unpurchased products or use coupons for other products cost manufacturers $1 billion each year. Fraudulent automobile insurance claims cost insurance companies more than $10 billion annually. In addition, retailers lose about $30 billion yearly from shoplifting and $9.6 billion annually from fraudulent returns of merchandise.

Research on unethical consumer behavior indicates that these acts are rarely motivated by economic need. This behavior appears to be influenced by (1) a belief that a consumer can get away with the act and it is worth doing and (2) the rationalization that the act is justified or driven by forces outside the individual—"everybody does it." These reasons were vividly expressed by a 24-year-old who pirated a movie, was sentenced to six months of house arrest, three years of probation, and a $7,000 fine. He said, "I didn't like paying for movies," and added, "so many people do it, you never think you're going to get caught."[41]

Consumer purchase, use, and disposition of environmentally sensitive products relate to consumer social responsibility. Research indicates that consumers are sensitive to

Reebok has been a leader in improving workplace conditions in Asian factories that produce its sporting apparel and equipment.

Reebok
www.reebok.com

ecological issues.[42] However, research also shows that consumers (1) may be unwilling to sacrifice convenience and pay potentially higher prices to protect the environment and (2) lack the knowledge to make informed decisions dealing with the purchase, use, and disposition of products.

Consumer confusion over which products are environmentally safe is also apparent, given marketers' rush to produce "green products." For example, few consumers realize that nonaerosol "pump" hairsprays are the second-largest cause of air pollution, after drying paint. In California alone, 27 tons of noxious hairspray fumes are expelled every day. And "biodegradable" claims on a variety of products, including trash bags, have not proven to be accurate, thus leading to buyer confusion. The FTC has drafted guidelines that describe the circumstances when environmental claims can be made and would not constitute misleading information. For example, an advertisement or product label touting a package as "50 percent more recycled content than before" could be misleading if the recycled content has increased from 2 percent to 3 percent.[43]

Ultimately, marketers and consumers are accountable for ethical and socially responsible behavior. The twenty-first century will prove to be a testing period for both.

learning review

6. What is meant by social responsibility?

7. Marketing efforts to produce, promote, and reclaim environmentally sensitive products are called _____.

8. What is a social audit?

LEARNING OBJECTIVES REVIEW

LO1 *Explain the differences between legal and ethical behavior in marketing.*

A good starting point for understanding the nature and significance of ethics is the distinction between legality and ethicality of marketing decisions. Whereas ethics deal with personal moral principles and values, laws are society's values and standards that are enforceable in the courts. This distinction can lead to the rationalization that if a behavior is within reasonable ethical and legal limits, then it is not really illegal or unethical. Judgment plays a large role in defining ethical and legal boundaries in marketing. Ethical dilemmas arise when acts or situations are not clearly ethical and legal or unethical and illegal.

LO2 *Identify factors that influence ethical and unethical marketing decisions.*

Four factors influence ethical marketing behavior. First, societal culture and norms serve as socializing forces that dictate what is morally right and just. Second, business culture and industry practices affect ethical conduct both in the exchange relationships between buyers and sellers and the competitive behavior among sellers. Third, corporate culture and expectations are often defined by corporate ethics codes and the ethical behavior of top management and co-workers. Finally, an individual's personal moral philosophy, such as moral idealism or utilitarianism, will dictate ethical choices. Ultimately, ethical behavior rests with the individual, but the consequences affect many.

LO3 *Describe the different concepts of social responsibility.*

Social responsibility means that organizations are part of a larger society and are accountable to that society for their actions. There are three concepts of social responsibility. First, profit responsibility holds that companies have a simple duty: to maximize profits for their owners or stockholders. Second, stakeholder responsibility focuses on the obligations an organization has to those who can affect achievement of its objectives. Those constituencies include consumers, employees, suppliers, and distributors. Finally, societal responsibility focuses on obligations that organizations have to the preservation of the ecological environment and the general public. Companies are placing greater emphasis on societal responsibility today and are reaping the rewards of positive word of mouth from their consumers and favorable financial performance.

LO4 *Recognize unethical and socially irresponsible consumer behavior.*

Consumers, like marketers, have an obligation to act ethically and responsibly in the exchange process and in the use and disposition of products. Unfortunately, consumer behavior is spotty on both counts. Unethical consumer behavior includes filing warranty claims after the claim period, misredeeming coupons, pirating music, movies, and software from the Internet, and submitting phony insurance claims, among other behaviors. Unethical behavior is rarely motivated by economic need. Rather, research indicates that this behavior is influenced by (*a*) a belief that a consumer can get away with the act and it is worth doing and (*b*) the rationalization that such acts are justified or driven by forces outside the individual—"everybody does it." Consumer purchase, use, and disposition of environmentally sensitive products relate to consumer social responsibility. Even though consumers are sensitive to ecological issues they (*a*) may be unwilling to sacrifice convictions and pay potentially higher prices to protect the environment and (*b*) lack the knowledge to make informed decisions dealing with the purchase, use, and disposition of products.

FOCUSING ON KEY TERMS

cause marketing p. 107
caveat emptor p. 99
code of ethics p. 101
Consumer Bill of Rights p. 99
economic espionage p. 100

ethics p. 96
green marketing p. 106
ISO 14000 p. 107
laws p. 96
moral idealism p. 104

social audit p. 107
social responsibility p. 105
sustainable development p. 108
utilitarianism p. 104
whistle-blowers p. 103

APPLYING MARKETING KNOWLEDGE

1 What concepts of moral philosophy and social responsibility are applicable to the practices of Anheuser-Busch described in the introduction to this chapter? Why?

2 Five ethical situations were presented in this chapter: (*a*) a medical society's decision to set fee schedules, (*b*) the use of a computer program by auto dealers to arrange financing, (*c*) smoking in China, (*d*) downloading movies, and (*e*) the pricing of Cerezyme for the treatment of a rare genetic illness. Where would each of these situations fit in Figure 4–1?

3 The American Marketing Association Statement of Ethics shown in Figure 4–3 details the rights and duties of parties in the marketing exchange process. How do these rights and duties compare with the Consumer Bill of Rights?

4 Compare and contrast moral idealism and utilitarianism as alternative personal moral philosophies.

5 How would you evaluate Milton Friedman's view of the social responsibility of a firm?

6 The text lists several unethical practices of consumers. Can you name others? Why do you think consumers engage in unethical conduct?

7 Cause marketing programs have become popular. Describe two such programs with which you are familiar.

building your marketing plan

Consider these potential stakeholders that may be affected in some way by the marketing plan on which you are working: shareholders (if any), suppliers, employees, customers, and society in general. For each group of stakeholders,

1 Identify what, if any, ethical and social responsibility issues might arise.

2 Describe, in one or two sentences, how your marketing plan addresses each potential issue.

video case 4   Starbucks Corporation: Serving More than Coffee

 Wake up and smell the coffee—Starbucks is everywhere! As the world's No. 1 specialty coffee retailer, Starbucks serves more than 25 million customers in its stores every week. The concept of Starbucks goes far beyond being a coffeehouse or coffee brand. It represents the dream of its founder, Howard Schultz, who wanted to take the experience of an Italian—specifically, Milan—espresso bar to every corner of every city block in the world. So what is the *Starbucks experience?* According to the company,

> You get more than the finest coffee when you visit Starbucks. You get great people, first-rate music, a comfortable and upbeat meeting place, and sound advice on brewing excellent coffee at home. At home you're part of a family. At work you're part of a company. And somewhere in between there's a place where you can sit back and be yourself. That's what a Starbucks store is to many of its customers—a kind of "third place" where they can escape, reflect, read, chat, or listen.

But there is more. Starbucks has embraced corporate social responsibility like few other companies. A recent Starbucks Corporate Social Responsibility Annual Report described the company's views on social responsibility:

> Starbucks defines corporate social responsibility as conducting our business in ways that produce social, environmental, and economic benefits to the communities in which we operate. In the end, it means being responsible to our stakeholders.

There is a growing recognition of the need for corporate accountability. Consumers are demanding more than "product" from their favorite brands. Employees are choosing to work for companies with strong values. Shareholders are more inclined to invest in business with outstanding corporate reputations. Quite simply, being socially responsible is not only the right thing to do; it can distinguish a company from its industry peers.

Starbucks not only recognizes the central role that social responsibility plays in its business. It also takes constructive action to be socially responsible.

THE COMPANY

Starbucks is the leading retailer, roaster, and brand of specialty coffee in the world with more than 7,500 retail locations in North America, Latin America, Europe, the Middle East, and the Pacific Rim. Beginning in 1971 with a single retail location in Seattle, Washington, Starbucks became a Fortune 500 company in 2003 with annual sales exceeding $4 billion. In addition, Starbucks is ranked as one of the "Ten Most Admired Companies in America" and one of the "100 Best Companies to Work For" by *Fortune* magazine. It has been recognized as one of the "Most Trusted Brands" by *Ad Week* magazine. *Business Ethics* magazine placed Starbucks 21st in its list of the "100 Best Citizens" in 2003. Starbucks' performance can be attributed to a passionate pursuit of its mission and adherence to six guiding principles. Both appear in Figure 1.

COMMITMENT TO CORPORATE SOCIAL RESPONSIBILITY

Starbucks continually emphasizes its commitment to corporate social responsibility. Speaking at the annual shareholders meeting in March 2004, Howard Schultz said,

> From the beginning, Starbucks has built a company that balances profitability with a social conscience. Starbucks busi-

ness practices are even more relevant today as consumers take a cultural audit of the goods and services they use. Starbucks is known not only for serving the highest quality coffee, but for enriching the daily lives of its people, customers, and coffee farmers. This is the key to Starbucks' ongoing success and we are pleased to report our positive results to shareholders and partners (employees).

Each year, Starbucks makes public a comprehensive report on its corporate social responsibility initiatives. A central feature of this annual report is the alignment of the company's social responsibility decisions and actions with Starbucks Mission Statement and Guiding Principles. The Starbucks 2003 Corporate Social Responsibility Report, titled "Living Our Values," focused on six topical areas: (*a*) partners, (*b*) diversity, (*c*) coffee, (*d*) customers, (*e*) community and environment, and (*f*) profitability.

Partners

Starbucks employs some 74,000 people around the world. The company considers its employees as partners following the creation of Starbucks' stock option plan in 1991, called "Bean Stock." The company believes that giving eligible full- and part-time employees an ownership in the company and sharing the rewards of Starbucks' financial success has made the sense of partnership real. In addition, the company has one of the most competitive employee benefits and compensation packages in the retail industry. Ongoing training, career advancement opportunities, partner recognition programs, and diligent efforts to ensure a healthy and safe work environment have all contributed to the fact that Starbucks has one of the lowest employee turnover rates within the restaurant and fast-food industry.

Diversity

Starbucks strives to mirror the customers and communities it serves. On a quarterly basis, the company monitors the demographics of its workforce to determine whether

FIGURE 1

Starbucks Mission Statement and Guiding Principles

Establish Starbucks as the premier purveyor of the finest coffee in the world while maintaining our uncompromising principles as we grow.

The following six principles will help us measure the appropriateness of our decisions:

1. Provide a great work environment and treat each other with respect and dignity.
2. Embrace diversity as an essential component in the way we do business.
3. Apply the highest standards of excellence to the purchasing, roasting, and fresh delivery of our coffee.
4. Develop enthusiastically satisfied customers all the time.
5. Contribute positively to our communities and our environment.
6. Recognize that profitability is essential to our future success.

they reflect the communities in which Starbucks operates. In 2003, Starbucks' U.S. workforce was comprised of 63 percent women and 24 percent people of color. The company also is engaged in a joint venture called Urban Coffee Opportunities (UCO) created to bring Starbucks stores to diverse neighborhoods. There were 52 UCO locations employing almost 1,000 Starbucks partners at the end of 2003.

Supplier diversity is also emphasized. To do business with Starbucks as a diverse supplier, that company must be 51 percent owned, operated, and managed by women, minorities, or socially disadvantaged individuals and meet Starbucks requirements of quality, service, value, stability, and sound business practice. The company spent $80 million with diverse suppliers in 2003 and expected to spend $95 million with diverse suppliers in 2004.

Coffee

Starbucks' attention to quality coffee extends to its coffee growers located in more than 20 countries. Sustainable development is emphasized. This means that Starbucks pays coffee farmers a fair price for the beans; that the coffee is grown in an ecologically sound manner; and that Starbucks invests in the farming communities where its coffees are produced.

One long-standing initiative is Starbucks' partnership with Conservation International, a nonprofit organization dedicated to protecting soil, water, energy, and biological diversity worldwide. Starbucks is particularly focused on environmental protection and helping local farmers earn more for their crops. In 2003, Starbucks invested more than $1 million in social programs, notably health and education projects, that benefited farming communities in nine countries, from Columbia to Indonesia.

Customers

Starbucks serves customers in 32 countries. The company and its partners are committed to providing each customer the optimal Starbucks experience every time they visit a store. For very loyal Starbucks customers, that translates into 18 visits per month on average.

Making a connection with customers at each store and building the relationship a customer has with Starbucks *baristas,* or coffee brewers, is important in creating the Starbucks experience. Each barista receives 24 hours of training in customer service and basic retail skills, as well as "Coffee Knowledge" and "Brewing the Perfect Cup" classes. Baristas are taught to anticipate the customers' needs and to make eye contact while carefully explaining the various coffee flavors and blends. Starbucks also enhances the customer relationship by soliciting feedback and responding to patrons' experiences and concerns. Starbucks Customer Relations reviews and responds to every inquiry or comment, often within 24 hours for telephone calls and e-mails.

Community and Environment

Efforts to contribute positively to the communities it serves and the environments in which it operates are emphasized in Starbucks' guiding principles. "We aren't in the coffee business, serving people. We are in the people business, serving coffee," says Howard Schultz. Starbucks and its partners have been recognized for volunteer support and financial contributions to a wide variety of local, national, and international social, economic, and environmental initiatives. For example, the "Make Your Mark" program rewards partners' gifts of time for volunteer work with charitable donations from Starbucks. In addition, Starbucks is a supporter of CARE International, a nonprofit organization dedicated to fighting global poverty.

Starbucks is also committed to environmental responsibility. Starbucks has a longtime involvement with Earth Day activities. It has instituted companywide energy and water conservation programs and waste reduction, recycling, and reuse initiatives proposed by partner *Green Teams.*

Profitability

At Starbucks, profitability is viewed as essential to its future success. When Starbucks' guiding principles were conceived, profitability was included but intentionally placed last on the list. This was done not because profitability was the least important. Instead, it was believed that adherence to the five other principles would ultimately lead to good financial performance. In fact, it has.

Questions

1 How does Starbucks' approach to social responsibility relate to the three concepts of social responsibility described in the text?
2 What role does sustainable development play in Starbucks' approach to social responsibility?

PERFORMED BETTER. After *Car and Driver* readers put Camry, Accord and the all-wheel-drive Ford Fusion to the test in Washington, D.C., *Road & Track* invited enthusiasts to do the same in Los Angeles. Once again, for styling, handling and performance, drivers said Fusion kicked the competition. Visit a Ford Dealer or go to fordchallenge.com. Bold Moves.

Ford FUSION

5 Understanding Consumer Behavior

LEARNING OBJECTIVES
After reading this chapter you should be able to:

 LO1 Describe the stages in the consumer purchase decision process.

 LO2 Distinguish among three variations of the consumer purchase decision process: routine, limited, and extended problem solving.

 LO3 Identify major psychological influences on consumer behavior.

 LO4 Identify the major sociocultural influences on consumer behavior.

WHO'S REALLY BUYING THAT NEW CAR? JUST ASK HER!

Who buys 68 percent of new cars? Who influences 85 percent of new-car-buying decisions? Women. Yes, women.

Women are a driving force in the U.S. automotive industry. Enlightened carmakers have hired women designers, engineers, and marketing executives to better understand and satisfy this valuable car-buying consumer and influencer. What have they learned? Women and men think and feel differently about key elements of the new-car-buying decision process and experience.

- *The sense of styling.* Women and men care about styling. For men, styling is more about a car's exterior lines and accents. Women are more interested in interior design and finishes. Designs that fit their proportions, provide good visibility, offer ample storage space, and make for effortless parking are particularly important.

- *The need for speed.* Both sexes want speed, but for different reasons. Men think about how many seconds it takes to get from zero to 60 miles per hour. Women want to feel secure that the car has enough acceleration to outrun an 18-wheeler trying to pass them on a freeway entrance ramp.

- *The substance of safety.* Safety for men is about features that help avoid an accident, such as antilock brakes and responsive steering. For women, safety is about features that help to survive an accident, including passenger airbags and reinforced side panels.

- *The shopping experience.* The new-car-buying experience differs between men and women. Generally, men decide upfront what car they want and set out alone to find it. By contrast, women approach it as an intelligence-gathering expedition. They actively seek information and postpone a purchase decision until all options have been evaluated. Women frequently visit auto-buying websites, read car-comparison articles, and scan car advertisements. Still, recommendations of friends and relatives matter most. Women typically shop three dealerships before making a purchase decision—one more than men. While only a third of women say that price is the most influential when they shop for a new car, 71 percent say price determines the final decision.

Carmakers have learned that women, more than men, dislike the car-buying experience. In particular, women dread the price negotiations that is often involved in buying a new car. Not surprisingly, 76 percent of women car buyers take a man with them to finalize the terms of sale.[1]

This chapter examines **consumer behavior**, the actions a person takes in purchasing and using products and services, including the mental and social processes that come before and after these actions. This chapter shows how the behavioral sciences help answer questions such as why people choose one product or brand over another, how they make these choices, and how companies use this knowledge to provide value to consumers.

CONSUMER PURCHASE DECISION PROCESS AND EXPERIENCE

Behind the visible act of making a purchase lies an important decision process and consumer experience that must be investigated. The stages a buyer passes through in making choices about which products and services to buy is the **purchase decision process**. This process has the five stages shown in Figure 5–1: (1) problem recognition, (2) information search, (3) alternative evaluation, (4) purchase decision, and (5) postpurchase behavior.

Problem Recognition: Perceiving a Need

Problem recognition, the initial step in the purchase decision, is perceiving a difference between a person's ideal and actual situations big enough to trigger a decision.[2] This can be as simple as finding an empty milk carton in the refrigerator; noting, as a first-year college student, that your high school clothes are not in the style that other students are wearing; or realizing that your laptop computer may not be working properly.

In marketing, advertisements or salespeople can activate a consumer's decision process by showing the shortcomings of competing (or currently owned) products. For instance, an advertisement for a flash-memory MP3 player could stimulate problem recognition because it emphasizes "maximum music from one device."

Information Search: Seeking Value

After recognizing a problem, a consumer begins to search for information, the next stage in the purchase decision process. First, you may scan your memory for previous experiences with products or brands.[3] This action is called *internal search*. For frequently purchased products such as shampoo and conditioner, this may be enough.

Or a consumer may undertake an *external search* for information.[4] This is needed when past experience or knowledge is insufficient, the risk of making a wrong purchase decision is high, and the cost of gathering information is low. The primary sources of external information are: (1) *personal sources,* such as relatives and friends whom the consumer trusts; (2) *public sources,* including various product-rating organizations such as *Consumer Reports,* government agencies, and TV "consumer programs;" and (3) *marketer-dominated sources,* such as information from sellers including advertising, company websites, salespeople, and point-of-purchase displays in stores.

Suppose you consider buying a flash-memory MP3 player. You will probably tap several of these information sources: friends and relatives, advertisements, brand and company websites, and stores carrying these players (for demonstrations). You might study the comparative evaluation of flash-memory MP3 players appearing in *Consumer Reports,* a portion of which appears in Figure 5–2.[5]

FIGURE 5–1

The purchase decision process consists of five stages.

BRAND	MODEL	RETAIL PRICE	EASE OF USE	HEADPHONE QUALITY	AUDIO QUALITY	PICTURE QUALITY	AUDIO PLAYBACK TIME (HOURS)
Cowon	iAudio U3	$180	Very Good	Very Good	Excellent	Very Good	18
Samsung	YP-T87	175	Very Good	Good	Excellent	Good	17
Apple	iPod Nano	200	Very Good	Very Good	Excellent	Good	15
iRiver	U10	200	Very Good	Very Good	Excellent	Very Good	28
RCA	Lyra RD 2217	125	Good	Good	Excellent	NA	39
Creative	Zen Nano Plus	70	Good	Good	Fair	NA	13
Philips	SA 178	100	Good	Good	Excellent	NA	13
Sony	Network Walkman	95	Good	Good	Excellent	NA	41

Rating: ● Excellent ◓ Very Good ○ Good ◒ Fair ● Poor

FIGURE 5–2

Consumer Reports' evaluation of flash-memory MP3 players (abridged)

Consumer Reports

www.consumerreports.org

Alternative Evaluation: Assessing Value

The information search stage clarifies the problem for the consumer by (1) suggesting criteria to use for the purchase, (2) yielding brand names that might meet the criteria, and (3) developing consumer value perceptions. Given only the information shown in Figure 5–2, what selection criteria would you use in buying a flash-memory MP3 player? Would you use price, audio quality, ease of use, or some other combination of these and other criteria?

For some of you, the information provided may be inadequate because it does not contain all the factors you might consider when evaluating flash-memory MP3 players. These factors are a consumer's **evaluative criteria**, which represent both the objective attributes of a brand (such as audio playback time) and the subjective ones (such as prestige) you use to compare different products and brands.[6] Firms try to identify and capitalize on both types of criteria to create the best value for the money sought by you and other consumers. These criteria are often displayed in advertisements.

Consumers often have several criteria for evaluating brands. (Didn't you in the preceding exercise?) Knowing this, companies seek to identify the most important evaluative criteria that consumers use when judging brands. For example, among the evaluative criteria shown in the columns of Figure 5–2, suppose you use three in considering flash-memory MP3 players: (1) a list price under $200, (2) audio quality, and (3) audio playback time of at least 15 hours. These criteria establish the brands in your **consideration set**—the group of brands that a consumer would consider acceptable from among all the brands in the product class of which he or she is aware.[7] Your evaluative criteria result in four models and four brands (Cowon, Samsung, RCA, and Sony) in your consideration set. If these alternatives don't satisfy you, you can change your evaluative criteria to create a different consideration set of models and brands. For example, ease of use might join the list of evaluative criteria if this is the first MP3 player you have purchased.

Purchase Decision: Buying Value

Having examined the alternatives in the consideration set, you are almost ready to make a purchase decision. Two choices remain: (1) from whom to buy and (2) when to buy. For a product like a flash-memory MP3 player, the information search process probably involved visiting retail stores, seeing different brands in catalogs, and viewing a flash-memory MP3 player on a seller's website. The choice of which seller to buy from will depend on such considerations as the terms of sale, your past experience buying from the seller, and the return policy. Often a purchase decision involves a simultaneous evaluation of both product attributes and seller characteristics. For example, you might choose the second-most preferred flash-memory MP3 brand at a store or website with a liberal refund and return policy versus the most preferred brand at a store or website with more conservative policies.

Deciding when to buy is determined by a number of factors. For instance, you might buy sooner if one of your preferred brands is on sale or its manufacturer offers a rebate. Other factors such as the store atmosphere, pleasantness or _ease_ of the shopping experience, salesperson assistance, time pressure, and financial circumstances could also affect whether a purchase decision is made or postponed.[8]

Use of the Internet to gather information, evaluate alternatives, and make buying decisions adds a technological dimension to the consumer purchase decision process and buying experience. Consumer benefits and costs associated with this technology and its marketing implications are detailed in Chapter 21.

Postpurchase Behavior: Value in Consumption or Use

After buying a product, the consumer compares it with his or her expectations and is either satisfied or dissatisfied. If the consumer is dissatisfied, marketers must determine whether the product was deficient or consumer expectations too high. Product deficiency may require a design change. If expectations are too high, perhaps the company's advertising or the salesperson oversold the product's features and benefits.

Sensitivity to a customer's consumption or use experience is extremely important in a consumer's value perception. For example, research on telephone services provided by Sprint and AT&T indicates that satisfaction or dissatisfaction affects consumer value perceptions.[9] Studies show that satisfaction or dissatisfaction affects consumer communications and repeat-purchase behavior. Satisfied buyers tell three other people about their experience. Dissatisfied buyers complain to nine people.[10] Satisfied buyers also tend to buy from the same seller each time a purchase occasion arises. The financial impact of repeat-purchase behavior is significant, as described in the accompanying Marketing Matters box.[11]

Firms such as General Electric (GE), Johnson & Johnson, Coca-Cola, and British Airways focus attention on postpurchase behavior to maximize customer satisfaction and retention. These firms, among many others, now provide toll-free telephone numbers, offer liberalized return and refund policies, and engage in extensive staff training to handle complaints, answer questions, record suggestions, and solve consumer problems. For example, GE has a database that stores 750,000 answers about 8,500 of its models in 120 product lines to handle 3 million calls annually. Such efforts produce positive postpurchase communications among consumers and foster relationship building between sellers and buyers.

Often a consumer is faced with two or more highly attractive alternatives, such as a Cowon or Samsung flash-memory MP3 player. If you choose Cowon, you may think, "Should I have purchased the Samsung?" This feeling of post-purchase psychological tension or anxiety is called **cognitive dissonance**. To alleviate it, consumers often attempt to applaud themselves

A satisfactory or unsatisfactory consumption or use experience is an important factor in postpurchase behavior. Marketer attention to this stage can pay huge dividends as described in the text.

Marketing Matters > > > > > customer value

The Value of a Satisfied Customer to the Company

Customer satisfaction and experience underlie the marketing concept. But how much is a satisfied customer worth?

This question has prompted firms to calculate the financial value of a satisfied customer over time. Frito-Lay, for example, estimates that the average loyal consumer in the southwestern United States eats 21 pounds of salty snack chips a year. At a price of $2.50 a pound, this customer spends $52.50 annually on the company's salty snacks such as Lays and Ruffles potato chips, Doritos and Tostitos tortilla chips, and Fritos corn chips. Exxon estimates that a loyal customer will spend $500 annually for its branded gasoline, not including candy, snacks, oil, or repair services purchased at its gasoline stations. Kimberly-Clark reports that a loyal customer will buy 6.7 boxes of its Kleenex tissues each year and will spend $994 on facial tissues over 60 years, in today's dollars.

These calculations have focused marketer attention on the buying experience, customer satisfaction, and retention. Ford Motor Company has set a target of increasing customer retention—the percentage of Ford owners whose next car is also a Ford—from 60 percent to 80 percent. Why? Ford executives say that each additional percentage point is worth a staggering $100 million in profits.

This calculation is not unique to Ford. Research shows that a 5 percent improvement in customer retention can increase a company's profits by 70 to 80 percent.

1 bottle of "prima donna pink"
+10 perfect piggies
———————————
pure joy

Wiggle your toes with delight at the super soft feel of Kleenex® tissues.
Now softer than ever. **thank goodness for Kleenex** tissue.

for making the right choice. So after your purchase, you may seek information to confirm your choice by asking friends questions like, "Don't you like my new MP3 player?" or by reading ads of the brand you chose. You might even look for negative features about the brand you didn't buy and decide that the Samsung headphones didn't feel right. Firms often use ads or follow-up calls from salespeople in this postpurchase stage to comfort buyers that they made the right decision. For many years, Buick ran an advertising campaign with the message, "Aren't you really glad you bought a Buick?"

Consumer Involvement and Problem-Solving Variations

LO2

Sometimes consumers don't engage in the five-stage purchase decision process. Instead, they skip or minimize one or more stages depending on the level of **involvement**, the personal, social, and economic significance of the purchase to the consumer.[12] High-involvement purchase occasions typically have at least one of three characteristics: The item to be purchased (1) is expensive, (2) can have serious personal consequences, or (3) could reflect on one's social image. For these occasions, consumers engage in extensive information search, consider many product attributes and brands,

品质，特征

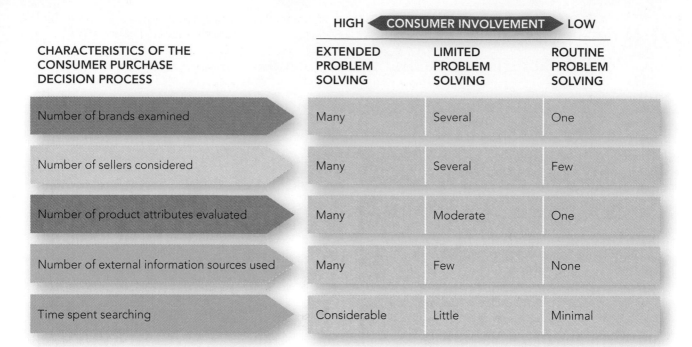

CHARACTERISTICS OF THE CONSUMER PURCHASE DECISION PROCESS	EXTENDED PROBLEM SOLVING	LIMITED PROBLEM SOLVING	ROUTINE PROBLEM SOLVING
Number of brands examined	Many	Several	One
Number of sellers considered	Many	Several	Few
Number of product attributes evaluated	Many	Moderate	One
Number of external information sources used	Many	Few	None
Time spent searching	Considerable	Little	Minimal

FIGURE 5–3

Comparison of problem-solving variations: Extended problem solving, Limited problem solving, and Routine problem solving

form attitudes, and participate in word-of-mouth communication. Low-involvement purchases, such as toothpaste and soap, barely involve most of us, but audio and video systems and automobiles are very involving.

There are three general variations in the consumer purchase decision process based on consumer involvement and product knowledge. Figure 5–3 shows some of the important differences between the three problem-solving variations.

Extended Problem Solving In extended problem solving, each of the five stages of the consumer purchase decision process is used in the purchase, including considerable time and effort on external information search and in identifying and evaluating alternatives. Several brands are in the consideration set, and these are evaluated on many attributes. Extended problem solving exists in high-involvement purchase situations for items such as automobiles and elaborate audio systems.

Limited Problem Solving In limited problem solving, consumers typically seek some information or rely on a friend to help them evaluate alternatives. In general, several brands might be evaluated using a moderate number of different attributes. You might use limited problem solving in choosing a toaster, a restaurant for lunch, and other purchase situations in which you have little time or effort to spend.

Routine Problem Solving For products such as table salt and milk, consumers recognize a problem, make a decision, and spend little effort seeking external information and evaluating alternatives. The purchase process for such items is virtually a habit and typifies low-involvement decision making. Routine problem solving is typically the case for low-priced, frequently purchased products.

Involvement and Marketing Strategy Low and high consumer involvement has important implications for marketing strategy. If a company markets a low-

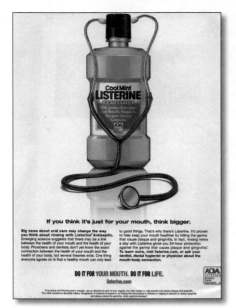

What does this ad for CoolMint Listerine have to do with consumer involvement? Read the text to find out.

involvement product and its brand is a market leader, attention is placed on (1) maintaining product quality, (2) avoiding stockout situations so that buyers don't substitute a competing brand, and (3) advertising messages that reinforce a consumer's knowledge or assures buyers they made the right choice. Market challengers have a different task. They must break buying habits and use free samples, coupons, and rebates to encourage trial of their brand. Advertising messages will focus on getting their brand into a consumer's consideration set. For example, Campbell's V8 vegetable juice advertising message—"I could have had a V8!"—is targeted at consumers who routinely purchase fruit juices and soft drinks. Marketers can also link their brand attributes with high-involvement issues. Listerine does this by linking regular use of its mouthwash with oral care and good health.

Marketers of high-involvement products recognize that their consumers constantly seek and process information about objective and subjective brand attributes, form evaluative criteria, rate product attributes in various brands, and combine these ratings for an overall brand evaluation—like that described in the flash-memory MP3 player purchase decision. Market leaders freely ply consumers with product information through advertising and personal selling and create chat rooms and communities on their company or brand websites. Market challengers capitalize on this behavior through comparative advertising that focuses on existing product attributes and often introduce novel evaluative criteria for judging competing brands. Challengers also benefit from Internet search engines such as MSN Search and Google that assist buyers of high-involvement products.

Situational Influences

Often the purchase situation will affect the purchase decision process. Five **situational influences** have an impact on your purchase decision process: (1) the purchase task, (2) social surroundings, (3) physical surroundings, (4) temporal effects, and (5) antecedent states.[13] The purchase task is the reason for engaging in the decision in the first place. Information searching and evaluating alternatives may differ depending on whether the purchase is a gift, which often involves social visibility, or for the buyer's own use. Social surroundings, including the other people present when a purchase decision is made, may also affect what is purchased. Physical surroundings such as decor, music, and crowding in retail stores may alter how purchase decisions are made. Temporal effects such as time of day or the amount of time available will influence where consumers have breakfast and lunch and what is ordered. Finally, antecedent states, which include the consumer's mood or the amount of cash on hand, can influence purchase behavior and choice.

Figure 5–4 on the next page shows the many influences that affect the consumer purchase decision process. The decision to buy a product also involves important psychological and sociocultural influences. These two influences are covered in the remainder of this chapter. Marketing mix influences are described in Chapters 10 through 20.

learning review

1. What is the first stage in the consumer purchase decision process?

2. The brands a consumer considers buying out of the set of brands in a product class of which the consumer is aware is called the _____ .

3. What is the term for postpurchase anxiety?

FIGURE 5–4
Influences on the consumer
purchase decision process
come from both internal and
external sources.

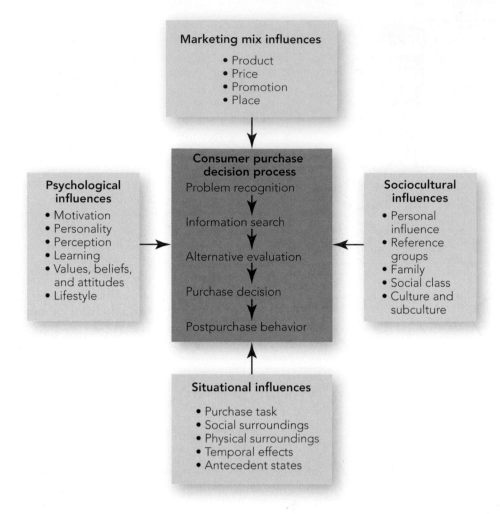

PSYCHOLOGICAL INFLUENCES ON CONSUMER BEHAVIOR

Psychology helps marketers understand why and how consumers behave as they do. In particular, psychological concepts such as motivation and personality; perception; learning; values, beliefs, and attitudes; and lifestyle are useful for interpreting buying processes and directing marketing efforts.

Motivation and Personality

Motivation and personality are two familiar psychological concepts that have specific meanings and marketing implications. These concepts are closely related and are used to explain why people do some things and not others.

Motivation   **Motivation** is the energizing force that stimulates behavior to satisfy a need. Because consumer needs are the focus of the marketing concept, marketers try to arouse these needs.

An individual's needs are boundless. People possess physiological needs for basics such as water, shelter, and food. They also have learned needs, including self-esteem, achievement, and affection. Psychologists point out that these needs may be hierarchical; that is, once physiological needs are met, people seek to satisfy their learned needs.

Figure 5–5 shows one need hierarchy and classification scheme that contains five need classes.[14] *Physiological needs* are basic to survival and must be satisfied first.

FIGURE 5–5

Hierarchy of needs. The hierarchy of needs is based on the idea that motivation comes from a need. If a need is met, it's no longer a motivator, so a higher-level need becomes the motivator. Higher-level needs demand support of lower-level needs.

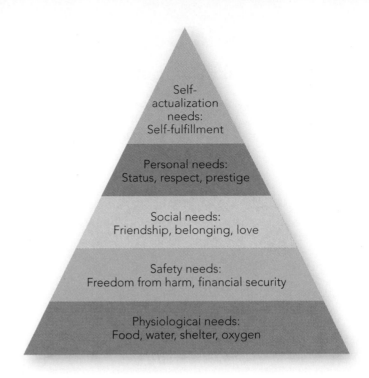

A Red Lobster advertisement featuring a seafood salad attempts to activate the need for food. *Safety needs* involve self-preservation as well as physical and financial well-being. Smoke detector and burglar alarm manufacturers focus on these needs, as do insurance companies and retirement plan advisors. *Social needs* are concerned with love and friendship. Dating services, such as Match.com and eHarmony, and fragrance companies try to arouse these needs. *Personal needs* include the need for achievement, status, prestige, and self-respect. The American Express Platinum Card and Brooks Brothers Clothiers appeal to these needs. Sometimes firms try to arouse multiple needs to stimulate problem recognition. Michelin combined safety with parental love to promote tire replacement for automobiles. *Self-actualization needs* involve personal fulfillment. For example, a long-running U.S. Army recruiting program invited enlistees to "Be all you can be."

Personality   While motivation is the energizing force that makes consumer behavior purposeful, a consumer's personality guides and directs behavior. **Personality** refers to a person's consistent behaviors or responses to recurring situations.

Although many personality theories exist, most identify key *traits*—enduring characteristics within a person or in his or her relationship with others. Such traits include assertiveness, extroversion, compliance, dominance, and aggression, among others. These traits are inherited or formed at an early age and change little over the years. Research suggests that compliant people prefer known brand names and use more mouthwash and toilet soaps. Aggressive types use razors, not electric shavers, apply more cologne and aftershave lotions, and purchase signature goods such as Gucci, Yves St. Laurent, and Donna Karan as an indicator of status.[15]

Cross-cultural analysis also suggests that residents of different countries have a *national character,* or a distinct set of personality characteristics common among people of a country or society.[16] For example, North Americans and Germans are relatively more assertive than Russians and the English.

These personality characteristics are often revealed in a person's **self-concept**, which is the way people see themselves and the way they believe others see them. Marketers recognize that people have an actual self-concept and an ideal self-concept. The actual self refers to how people actually see themselves. The ideal self describes how

The Ethics of Subliminal Messages

For about 50 years, the topic of subliminal perception and the presence of subliminal messages and images embedded in commercial communications have sparked heated debate.

The Federal Communications Commission has denounced subliminal messages as deceptive. Still, consumers spend $50 million a year for audiotapes with subliminal messages designed to help them raise their self-esteem, quit smoking, or lose weight. Almost two-thirds of U.S. consumers think subliminal messages are present in commercial communications; about half are convinced that this practice can cause them to buy things they don't want.

Subliminal messages are not illegal in the United States, however, and marketers are often criticized for pursuing opportunities to create these messages in both electronic and print media. A book by August Bullock, *The Secret Sales Pitch: An Overview of Subliminal Advertising,* is devoted to this topic. Bullock identifies images and advertisements that he claims contain subliminal messages and describes techniques that can be used for conveying these messages.

Do you believe that attempts to implant subliminal messages in electronic and print media are a deceptive practice and unethical, regardless of their intent?

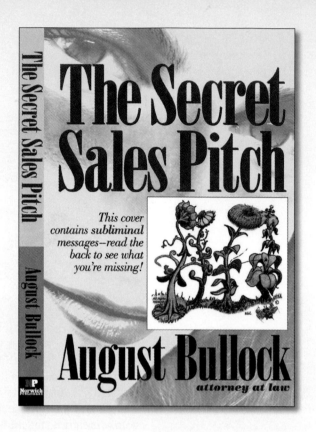

people would like to see themselves. These two self-images are reflected in the products and brands a person buys, including automobiles, home appliances and furnishings, magazines, clothing, grooming and leisure products, and frequently, the stores a person shops. The importance of self-concept is summed up by a senior executive at Barnes & Noble: "People buy books for what the purchase says about them—their taste, their cultivation, their trendiness."[17]

Perception

One person sees a Cadillac as a mark of achievement; another sees it as ostentatious. This is the result of **perception**—the process by which an individual selects, organizes, and interprets information to create a meaningful picture of the world.

Selective Perception   Because the average consumer operates in a complex environment, the human brain attempts to organize and interpret information with a process called *selective perception,* a filtering of exposure, comprehension, and retention. *Selective exposure* occurs when people pay attention to messages that are consistent with their attitudes and beliefs and ignore messages that are inconsistent. Selective exposure often occurs in the postpurchase stage of the consumer decision process, when consumers read advertisements for the brand they just bought. It also occurs when a need exists—you are more likely to "see" a McDonald's advertisement when you are hungry rather than after you have eaten a pizza.

Why does the Good Housekeeping seal for Clorox's Fresh Step Crystals cat litter appear in the ad? Why does Mary Kay, Inc., offer a free sample of its Velocity brand fragrance through its website? The answers appear in the text.

The Clorox Company
www.freshstep.com

Mary Kay, Inc.
www.marykay.com

Selective comprehension involves interpreting information so that it is consistent with your attitudes and beliefs. A marketer's failure to understand this can have disastrous results. For example, Toro introduced a small, lightweight snowblower called the Snow Pup. Even though the product worked, sales failed to meet expectations. Why? Toro later found out that consumers perceived the name to mean that Snow Pup was a toy or too light to do any serious snow removal. When the product was renamed Snow Master, sales increased sharply.[18]

Selective retention means that consumers do not remember all the information they see, read, or hear, even minutes after exposure to it. This affects the internal and external information search stage of the purchase decision process. This is why furniture and automobile retailers often give consumers product brochures to take home when they leave the showroom.

Because perception plays an important role in consumer behavior, it is not surprising that the topic of subliminal perception is a popular item for discussion. **Subliminal perception** means that you see or hear messages without being aware of them. The presence and effect of subliminal perception on behavior is a hotly debated issue, with more popular appeal than scientific support. Indeed, evidence suggests that such messages have limited effects on behavior.[19] If these messages did influence behavior, would their use be an ethical practice? (See the accompanying Making Responsible Decisions box on the previous page.)[20]

Perceived Risk Perception plays a major role in the perceived risk in purchasing a product or service. **Perceived risk** represents the anxieties felt because the consumer cannot anticipate the outcomes of a purchase but believes there may be negative consequences. Examples of possible negative consequences are the size of the financial outlay required to buy the product (Can I afford $500 for those skis?), the risk of physical harm (Is bungee jumping safe?), and the performance of the product (Will the whitening toothpaste work?). A more abstract form is psychosocial (What will my friends say if I get a tatto?). Perceived risk affects information search, because the greater the perceived risk, the more extensive the external search stage is likely to be.

Recognizing the importance of perceived risk, companies develop strategies to reduce the consumer's risk and encourage purchases. These strategies and examples of firms using them include the following:

- *Obtaining seals of approval:* The Good Housekeeping seal for Fresh Step Crystals cat litter.
- *Securing endorsements from influential people:* The National Fluid Milk Processor Promotion Board "Got Milk" advertising campaign.
- *Providing free trials of the product:* Samples of Mary Kay's Velocity fragrance.
- *Giving extensive usage instructions:* Clairol hair coloring.
- *Providing warranties and guarantees:* Cadillac's four-year, 50,000-mile, bumper-to-bumper warranty.

Learning

Much consumer behavior is learned. Consumers learn which information sources to consult for information about products and services, which evaluative criteria to use when assessing alternatives, and, more generally, how to make purchase decisions. **Learning** refers to those behaviors that result from (1) repeated experience and (2) reasoning.

Behavioral Learning *Behavioral learning* is the process of developing automatic responses to a situation built up through repeated exposure to it. Four variables are central to how consumers learn from repeated experience: drive, cue, response, and reinforcement. A *drive* is a need that moves an individual to action. Drives, such as hunger, might be represented by motives. A *cue* is a stimulus or symbol perceived by consumers. A *response* is the action taken by a consumer to satisfy the drive, whereas a *reinforcement* is the reward. Being hungry (drive), a consumer sees a cue (a billboard), takes action (buys a sandwich), and receives a reward (it tastes great!).

Marketers use two concepts from behavioral learning theory. *Stimulus generalization* occurs when a response elicited by one stimulus (cue) is generalized to another stimulus. Using the same brand name for different products is an application of this concept, such as Tylenol Cold & Flu and Tylenol P.M. *Stimulus discrimination* refers to a person's ability to perceive differences in stimuli. Consumers' tendency to perceive all light beers as being alike led to Budweiser Light commercials that distinguished between many types of "lights" and Bud Light.

Cognitive Learning Consumers also learn through thinking, reasoning, and mental problem solving without direct experience. This type of learning, called *cognitive learning,* involves making connections between two or more ideas or simply observing the outcomes of others' behaviors and adjusting your own accordingly. Firms also influence this type of learning. Through repetition in advertising, messages such as "Advil is a headache remedy" attempt to link a brand (Advil) and an idea (headache remedy) by showing someone using the brand and finding relief.

Brand Loyalty Learning is also important to marketers because it relates to habit formation—the basis of routine problem solving. Furthermore, there is a close link between habits and **brand loyalty**, which is a favorable attitude toward and consistent purchase of a single brand over time. Brand loyalty results from the positive reinforcement of previous actions. So a consumer reduces risk and saves time by consistently purchasing the same brand of shampoo and has favorable results—healthy, shining hair. There is evidence of brand loyalty in many commonly purchased products in the United States and the global marketplace. However, the incidence of brand loyalty appears to be declining in North America, Mexico, Western European nations, and Japan.[21]

Attitudes toward Colgate Total toothpaste and Extra Strength Bayer aspirin were successfully changed by these ads. How? Read the text to find out how marketers can change consumer attitudes toward products and brands.

Colgate-Palmolive
www.colgate.com

Bayer Corporation
www.bayerus.com

Values, Beliefs, and Attitudes

Values, beliefs, and attitudes play a central role in consumer decision making and related marketing actions.

Attitude Formation   An **attitude** is a "learned predisposition to respond to an object or class of objects in a consistently favorable or unfavorable way."[22] Attitudes are shaped by our values and beliefs, which are learned. Values vary by level of specificity. We speak of American core values, including material well-being and humanitarianism. We also have personal values, such as thriftiness and ambition. Marketers are concerned with both but focus mostly on personal values. Personal values affect attitudes by influencing the importance assigned to specific product attributes. Suppose thriftiness is one of your personal values. When you evaluate cars, fuel economy (a product attribute) becomes important. If you believe a specific car brand has this attribute, you are likely to have a favorable attitude toward it.

Beliefs also play a part in attitude formation. **Beliefs** are a consumer's subjective perception of how a product or brand performs on different attributes. Beliefs are based on personal experience, advertising, and discussions with other people. Beliefs about product attributes are important because, along with personal values, they create the favorable or unfavorable attitude the consumer has toward certain products, services, and brands.

Attitude Change   Marketers use three approaches to try to change consumer attitudes toward products and brands, as shown in the following examples.[23]

1. *Changing beliefs about the extent to which a brand has certain attributes.* To allay consumer concern that aspirin use causes an upset stomach, Bayer Corporation successfully promoted the gentleness of its Extra Strength Bayer Plus aspirin.

2. *Changing the perceived importance of attributes.* Pepsi-Cola made freshness an important product attribute when it stamped freshness dates on its cans. Before doing so, few consumers considered cola freshness an issue. After Pepsi spent about $25 million on advertising and promotion, a consumer survey found that 61 percent of cola drinkers believed freshness dating was an important attribute.

3. *Adding new attributes to the product.* Colgate-Palmolive included a new antibacterial ingredient, tricloson, in its Colgate Total toothpaste and spent $100 million marketing the brand. The result? Colgate replaced Crest as the market leader for the first time in 25 years.

Consumer Lifestyle

Lifestyle is a mode of living that is identified by how people spend their time and resources, what they consider important in their environment, and what they think of themselves and the world around them. The analysis of consumer lifestyles, called *psychographics,* provides insights into consumer needs and wants. Lifestyle analysis has proven useful in segmenting and targeting consumers for new and existing products and services (see Chapter 9).

Psychographics, the practice of combining psychology, lifestyle, and demographics, is often used to uncover consumer motivations for buying and using products and services. A prominent psychographic system is VALS from SRI Consulting Business Intelligence (SRIC-BI).[24] The VALS system identifies eight consumer segments based on (1) their primary motivation for buying and having certain products and services and (2) their resources.

According to SRIC-BI researchers, consumers are motivated to buy products and services and seek experiences that give shape, substance, and satisfaction to their lives. But not all consumers are alike. Consumers are inspired by one of three primary motivations—ideals, achievement, and self-expression—that give meaning to their self or the world and govern their activities. The different levels of resources enhance or constrain a person's expression of his or her primary motivation. A person's resources include psychological, physical, demographic, and material capacities such as income, self-confidence, and risk-taking. Before reading further, visit the VALS website shown in the accompanying Going Online box. Complete the short survey to learn which segment best describes you.

The VALS system seeks to explain why and how consumers make purchase decisions.

- *Ideals-motivated groups.* Consumers motivated by ideals are guided by knowledge and principle. These consumers divide into two segments. *Thinkers* are mature,

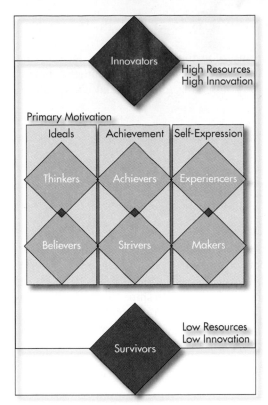

The VALS classification system places consumers with abundant resources—psychological, physical, and material means and capacities—near the top of the chart and those with minimal resources near the bottom. The chart segments consumers by their basis for decision making: ideals, achievement, or self-expression. The boxes intersect to indicate that some categories may be considered together. For instance, a marketer may categorize Thinkers and Believers together.

reflective, and well-educated people who value order, knowledge, and responsibility. They are practical consumers, deliberate information-seekers, who value durability and functionality in products over styling and newness. *Believers,* with fewer resources, are conservative, conventional people with concrete beliefs based on traditional, established codes: family, religion, community, and the nation. They choose familiar products and brands, favor American-made products, and are generally brand loyal.

- *Achievement-motivated groups.* Consumers motivated by achievement look for products and services that demonstrate success to their peers or to a peer group they aspire to. These consumers include *Achievers,* who have a busy, goal-directed lifestyle and a deep commitment to career and family. Image is important to them. They favor established, prestige products and services and are interested in time-saving devices given their hectic schedules. *Strivers* are trendy, fun-loving, and less self-confident than Achievers. They also have lower levels of education and household income. Money defines success for them. They favor stylish products and are as impulsive as their financial circumstances permit.

- *Self-expression-motivated groups.* Consumers motivated by self-expression desire social or physical activity, variety, and risk. *Experiencers* are young, enthusiastic, and impulsive consumers who become excited about new possibilities but are equally quick to cool. They savor the new, the offbeat, and the risky. Their energy finds an outlet in exercise, sports, outdoor recreation, and social activities. Much of their income is spent on fashion items, entertainment, and socializing and particularly on looking good and having the latest things. *Makers,* with fewer resources, express themselves and experience the world by working on it—building a house, raising children, or fixing a car. They are practical people who have constructive skills, value self-sufficiency, and are unimpressed by material possessions except those with a practical or functional purpose.

- *High- and low-resource groups.* Two segments stand apart. *Innovators* are successful, sophisticated, take-charge people with high self-esteem and abundant resources of all kinds. Image is important to them, not as evidence of power or status, but as an expression of cultivated tastes, independence, and character. They are receptive to new ideas and technologies. Their lives are characterized by variety. *Survivors,* with the least resources of any segment, focus on meeting basic needs (safety and security) rather than fulfilling desires. They represent a modest market for most products and services and are loyal to favorite brands, especially if they can be purchased at a discount.

Each of these segments exhibits unique media preferences. Experiencers and Strivers are the most likely to visit Internet chat rooms. Innovators, Thinkers, and Achievers tend to read business and news magazines such as *Fortune* and *Time.* Experiencers read sports magazines, whereas Makers read automotive magazines. Believers are the heaviest readers of *Reader's Digest.*

learning review

4. The problem with the Toro Snow Pup was an example of selective _____.

5. What three attitude-change approaches are most common?

6. What does *lifestyle* mean?

SOCIOCULTURAL INFLUENCES ON CONSUMER BEHAVIOR

Sociocultural influences, which evolve from a consumer's formal and informal relationships with other people, also exert a significant impact on consumer behavior. These involve personal influence, reference groups, the family, social class, culture, and subculture.

Personal Influence

A consumer's purchases are often influenced by the views, opinions, or behaviors of others. Two aspects of personal influence are very important to marketing: opinion leadership and word-of-mouth activity.

Opinion Leadership   Individuals who exert direct or indirect social influence over others are called **opinion leaders**. Opinion leaders are considered to be knowledgeable about or users of particular products and services, so their opinions influences others' choices. Opinion leadership is widespread in the purchase of cars and trucks, entertainment, clothing and accessories, club membership, consumer electronics, vacation locations, food, and financial investments. A study by *Popular Mechanics* magazine identified 18 million opinion leaders who influence the purchases of some 85 million consumers for do-it-yourself products.

About 10 percent of U.S. adults are opinion leaders.[25] Identifying, reaching, and influencing opinion leaders is a major challenge for companies. Some firms use sports figures or celebrities as spokespersons to represent their products, such as actor Uma Thurman and NASCAR driver Jeff Gordon for TAG Heuer watches. Others promote their products in media believed to reach opinion leaders. Still others use more direct approaches. For example, Chrysler Corporation invited influential community leaders and business executives to test-drive its new models. Some 6,000 accepted the offer, and 98 percent said they would recommend their tested car. The company estimated that the number of favorable recommendations totaled 32,000.

Firms use actors or athletes as spokespersons to represent their products, such as Uma Thurman and Jeff Gordon for TAG Heuer watches, in the hope that they are opinion leaders.

TAG Heuer
www.tagheuer.com

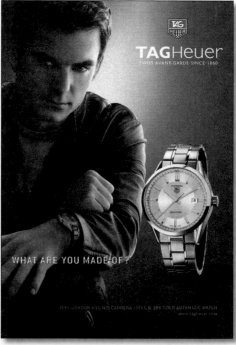

Marketing Matters > > > > > customer value

BzzAgent—The Buzz Experience

Have you recently heard about a new product, movie, website, book, or restaurant from someone you know . . . or a complete stranger? If so, you may have had a buzz experience.

Marketers recognize the power of word of mouth. The challenge has been to harness that power. BzzAgent Inc. does just that. Its nationwide volunteer army of over 350,000 natural-born talkers channel their chatter toward products and services they deem authentically worth talking about. "Our goal is to capture honest word of mouth," says David Balter, BzzAgent's founder, "and to build a network that turns passionate customers into brand evangelists."

BzzAgent's method is simple. Once a client signs on with Bzz-Agent, the company searches its "agent" database for those who match the demographic and psychographic profile of the target market for a client's offering. Agents then can sign up for a buzz campaign and receive a sample product and a training manual for buzz-creating strategies. Each time an agent completes an activity, he or she is expected to file an online

report describing the nature of the buzz and its effectiveness. BzzAgent coaches respond with encouragement and feedback on additional techniques.

Agents keep the products they promote. They also earn points redeemable for books, CDs, and other items by filing detailed reports. Who are the agents? About 65 percent are older than 25, 70 percent are women, and two are Fortune 500 CEOs. All are gregarious and genuinely like the product or service, otherwise they wouldn't participate in the buzz campaign.

Estée Lauder, Monster.com, Anheuser-Busch, Penguin Books, Lee jeans, Arby's, Nestlé, Hershey Foods, and Volkswagen have used BzzAgent. But BzzAgent's buzz isn't cheap, and not everything is buzz worthy. Deploying 1,000 agents on a 12-week campaign can cost a company $95,000, exclusive of product samples. BzzAgent researches a product or service before committing to a campaign and rejects about 80 percent of the companies that seek its service. It also refuses campaigns for politicians, religious groups, and certain products, such as firearms. Interested in Bzz-Agent? Visit its website at www.bzzagent.com.

Word of Mouth The influencing of people during conversations is called **word of mouth**. Word of mouth is the most powerful and authentic information source for consumers because it typically involves friends viewed as trustworthy. According to a recent study, 67 percent of U.S. consumer product sales are directly based on word-of-mouth activity among friends, family, and colleagues.[26]

The power of personal influence has prompted firms to promote positive and retard negative word of mouth. For instance, "teaser" advertising campaigns are run in advance of new-product introductions to stimulate conversations. Other techniques such as advertising slogans, music, and humor also heighten positive word of mouth. Many commercials shown during the Super Bowl are created expressly to initiate conversations about the advertisements and featured product or service the next day. Increasingly, companies recruit and deploy people to produce *buzz*—popularity created by consumer word of mouth. Read the accompanying Marketing Matters box to learn how this is done by BzzAgent.[27]

On the other hand, rumors about Kmart (snake eggs in clothing), McDonald's (worms in hamburgers), Corona Extra beer (contaminated beer), and Snickers candy bars in Russia (a cause of diabetes) have resulted in negative word of mouth, none of which was based on fact. Overcoming or neutalizing negative word of mouth is difficult and costly. Marketers have found that supplying factual information, providing toll-free numbers for consumers to call the company, and giving appropriate product demonstrations have proven helpful.

The power of word of mouth has been magnified by the Internet through online forums, chat rooms, blogs, bulletin boards, and websites. In fact, Ford uses special software to monitor online messages and find out what consumers are saying about its vehicles. Chapter 21 describes how marketers track, initiate, and manage word of mouth in an online environment.

Reference Groups

Reference groups are people to whom an individual looks as a basis for self-appraisal or as a source of personal standards. Reference groups affect consumer purchases because they influence the information, attitudes, and aspiration levels that help set a consumer's standards. For example, one of the first questions one asks others when planning to attend a social occasion is, "What are you going to wear?" Reference groups have an important influence on the purchase of luxury products but not of necessities—reference groups exert a strong influence on the brand chosen when its use or consumption is highly visible to others.

Consumers have many reference groups, but three groups have clear marketing implications. A *membership group* is one to which a person actually belongs, including fraternities and sororities, social clubs, and the family. Such groups are easily identifiable and are targeted by firms selling insurance, insignia products, and charter vacations. An *aspiration group* is one that a person wishes to be a member of or wishes to be identified with, such as a professional society. Firms frequently rely on spokespeople or settings associated with their target market's aspiration group in their advertising. A *dissociative group* is one that a person wishes to maintain a distance from because of differences in values or behaviors.

Family Influence

Family influences on consumer behavior result from three sources: consumer socialization, passage through the family life cycle, and decision making within the family or household.

Consumer Socialization The process by which people acquire the skills, knowledge, and attitudes necessary to function as consumers is **consumer socialization**.[28] Children learn how to purchase (1) by interacting with adults in purchase situations and (2) through their own purchasing and product usage experiences. Research shows that children evidence brand preferences at age two, and these preferences often last a lifetime. This knowledge prompted the licensing of the well-known Craftsman brand name to MGA Entertainment for its children's line of My First Craftsman power tools; Time, Inc. to launch *Sports Illustrated for Kids*; and Yahoo! and America Online to offer special areas where young audiences can view their children's menu—Yahoo! Kids and Kids Only, respectively.

Family Life Cycle Consumers act and purchase differently as they go through life. The **family life cycle** concept describes the distinct phases that a family progresses through from formation to retirement, each phase bringing with it identifiable purchasing behaviors.[29] Figure 5–6 illustrates the traditional progression as well as contemporary variations of the family life cycle. Today, the *traditional family*— married couples with children younger than 18 years—constitute just 22 percent of all U.S. households. The remaining 78 percent of U.S. households include single parents, unmarried couples, divorced, never-married, or widowed individuals, and older married couples whose children no longer live at home.

Young singles' buying preferences are for nondurable items, including prepared foods, clothing, personal care products, and entertainment. They represent a target market for recreational travel, automobile, and consumer electronics firms. Young

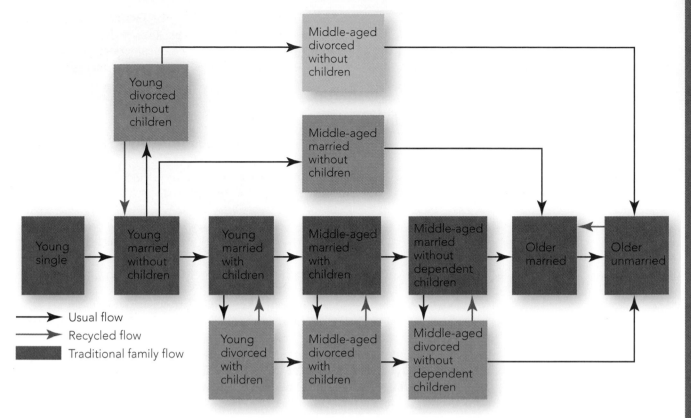

FIGURE 5–6

Modern family life cycle stages and flows. Can you identify people you know in different stages? Do they follow the purchase patterns described in the text?

married couples without children are typically more affluent than young singles because usually both spouses are employed. These couples exhibit preferences for furniture, housewares, and gift items for each other. Young marrieds with children are driven by the needs of their children. They make up a sizable market for life insurance, various children's products, and home furnishings. Single parents with children are the least financially secure of households with children. Their buying preferences are often affected by a limited economic status and tend toward convenience foods, child care services, and personal care items.

Middle-aged married couples with children are typically better off financially than their younger counterparts. They are a significant market for leisure products and home improvement items. Middle-aged couples without children typically have a large amount of discretionary income. These couples buy better home furnishings, status automobiles, and financial services. Persons in the last two phases—older married and older unmarried—make up a sizable market for prescription drugs, medical services, vacation trips, and gifts for younger relatives.

Family Decision Making   A third influence in the decision-making process occurs within the family.[30] Two decision-making styles exist: spouse-dominant and joint decision making. With a joint decision-making style, most decisions are made by both husband and wife. Spouse-dominant decisions are those for which either the husband or the wife is mostly responsible. Research indicates that wives tend to have more say when purchasing groceries, children's toys, clothing, and medicines. Husbands tend to be more influential in home and car maintenance purchases. Joint decision making is common for cars, vacations, houses, home appliances and electronics, and medical care. As a rule, joint decision making increases with the education of the spouses.

Roles of individual family members in the purchase process are another element of family decision making. Five roles exist: (1) information gatherer, (2) influencer, (3) decision maker, (4) purchaser, and (5) user. Family members assume different

In the **female** the ability to match colors comes at an early age. In the **male** it comes when he marries a female.

The City Casuals three-button, crepe jacket. 100% cotton, French-yarn shirt, Bedford cord pants, and a touch of color.

HAGGAR
Stuff you can work with.

roles for different products and services. This knowledge is important to firms. For example, 89 percent of wives either influence or make outright purchases of men's clothing. Knowing this, Haggar Clothing, a menswear marketer, now advertises in women's magazines such as *Vanity Fair* and *Redbook*. Even though women are often the grocery decision maker, they are not necessarily the purchaser. More than 40 percent of all food-shopping dollars are spent by male customers.

Increasingly, preteens and teenagers are the information gatherers, influencers, decision makers, and purchasers of products and services for the family, given the prevalence of working parents and single-parent households. Children under 12 directly influence more than $325 billion in annual family purchases. Teenagers influence another $600 billion and spend another $190 million of their own money annually. These figures help explain why, for example, Nabisco, Johnson & Johnson, Hewlett-Packard, Apple, Kellogg, P&G, Sony, and Oscar Mayer, among countless other companies, spend more than $40 billion annually in electronic and print media that reach preteens and teens.

Social Class

A more subtle influence on consumer behavior than direct contact with others is the social class to which people belong. **Social class** may be defined as the relatively permanent, homogeneous divisions in a society into which people sharing similar values, interests, and behavior can be grouped. A person's occupation, source of income (not level of income), and education determine his or her social class. Generally speaking, three major social class categories exist—upper, middle, and lower—with subcategories within each. This structure has been observed in the United States, Great Britain, Western Europe, and Latin America.[31]

To some degree, persons within social classes exhibit common values, attitudes, beliefs, lifestyles, and buying behaviors. Compared with the middle classes, people in the lower classes have a more short-term time orientation, are more emotional than rational in their reasoning, think in concrete rather than abstract terms, and see fewer personal opportunities. Members of the upper classes focus on achievements and the future and think in abstract or symbolic terms.

Companies use social class as a basis for identifying and reaching particularly good prospects for their products and services. For instance, JCPenney has historically appealed to the middle classes. *New Yorker* magazine reaches the upper classes.

In general, people in the upper classes are targeted by companies for items such as financial investments, expensive cars, and formal evening wear. The middle classes represent a target market for home improvement centers, automobile parts stores, and personal hygiene products. Firms also recognize differences in media preferences among classes: lower and working classes prefer tabloid magazines; middle classes read fashion, romance, and celebrity (*People*) magazines; and upper classes tend to subscribe to literary, travel, and news magazines.

Culture and Subculture

As described in Chapter 3, *culture* refers to the set of values, ideas, and attitudes that are learned and shared among the members of a group. Thus, we often refer to the American culture, the Latin American culture, or the Japanese culture. Cultural underpinnings of American buying patterns were described in Chapter 3; Chapter 7 will explore the role of culture in global marketing.

Subgroups within the larger, or national, culture with unique values, ideas, and attitudes are referred to as **subcultures**. Various subcultures exist within the American culture. The three largest racial/ethnic subcultures in the United States are Hispanics, African Americans, and Asian Americans. Collectively, they are expected to spend about $3 trillion for goods and services in 2011.[32] Each group exhibits sophisticated social and cultural behaviors that affect buying patterns, which provides the basis for multicultural marketing programs described in Chapter 3.

Hispanic Buying Patterns Hispanics represent the largest racial/ethnic subculture in the United States in terms of population and spending power. About 50 percent of Hispanics in the United States are immigrants, and the majority are under the age of 25. One-third of Hispanics are younger than 18.

Research on Hispanic buying practices has uncovered several consistent patterns:[33]

1. Hispanics are quality and brand conscious. They are willing to pay a premium price for premium quality and are often brand loyal.
2. Hispanics prefer buying American-made products, especially those offered by firms that cater to Hispanic needs.
3. Hispanic buying preferences are strongly influenced by family and peers.
4. Hispanics consider advertising a credible product information source, and U.S. firms spend more than $4 billion annually on advertising to Hispanics.
5. Convenience is not an important product attribute to Hispanic homemakers with respect to food preparation or consumption, nor is low caffeine in coffee and soft drinks, low fat in dairy products, and low cholesterol in packaged foods.

Despite some consistent buying patterns, marketing to Hispanics has proven to be a challenge for two reasons. First, the Hispanic subculture is diverse and composed of Mexicans, Puerto Ricans, Cubans, and others of Central and South American ancestry. Cultural differences among these nationalities often affect product preferences. For example, Campbell Soup Company sells its Casera line of soups, beans, and sauces using different recipes to appeal to Puerto Ricans on the East Coast and Mexicans in the Southwest. Second, a language barrier exists, and commercial messages are frequently misinterpreted when translated into Spanish. Volkswagen learned this lesson when the Spanish translation of its "Driver's Wanted" slogan suggested "chauffeurs wanted." The Spanish slogan was changed to "*Agarra calle*", a slang expression that can be loosely translated as "let's hit the road".

Sensitivity to the unique needs of Hispanics by firms has paid huge dividends. For example, Metropolitan Life Insurance is the largest insurer of Hispanics. Goya Foods dominates the market for ethnic food products sold to

The Hershey Company recently launched a successful line of candy items tailored to Hispanic taste preferences.

The Hershey Company
www.thehersheycompany.com

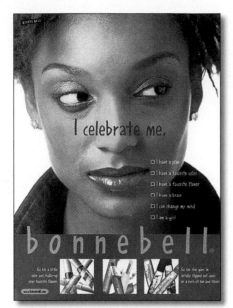

African American women represent a large market for health and beauty products. Cosmetic companies such as Bonne Bell Cosmetics, Inc., actively seek to serve this market.

Bonne Bell Cosmetics, Inc.
www.bonnebell.com

Hispanics. Best Foods' Mazola Corn Oil captures two-thirds of the Hispanic market for this product category. Time, Inc., has more than 750,000 subscribers to its *People en Espanol*.

African American Buying Patterns　African Americans have the second-largest spending power of the three racial/ethnic subcultures in the United States. Consumer research on African American buying patterns has focused on similarities and differences with Caucasians. When socioeconomic status differences between African Americans and Caucasians are removed, there are more similarities than points of difference. Differences in buying patterns are greater within the African American subculture, due to levels of socioeconomic status, than between African Americans and Caucasians of similar status.

Even though similarities outweigh differences, there are consumption patterns that do differ between African Americans and Caucasians.[34] For example, African Americans spend far more than Caucasians on boy's clothing, rental goods, and audio equipment. Adult African Americans are twice as likely to own a pager and spend twice as much for online services, on a per capita basis, than Caucasians. African American women spend three times more on health and beauty products than Caucasian women. Furthermore, the typical African American family is five years younger than the typical Caucasian family. This factor alone accounts for some of the observed differences in preferences for clothing, music, shelter, cars, and many other products, services, and activities. Finally, it must be emphasized that, historically, African Americans have been deprived of employment and educational opportunities in the United States. Both factors have resulted in income disparities between African Americans and Caucasians, which influence purchase behavior.

Recent research indicates that while African Americans are price conscious, they are strongly motivated by quality and choice. They respond more to products such as apparel and cosmetics and advertising that appeal to their African American pride and heritage as well as address their ethnic features and needs regardless of socioeconomic status.

Asian American Buying Patterns　About 70 percent of Asian Americans are immigrants. Most are under the age of 30.

The Asian subculture is composed of Chinese, Japanese, Filipinos, Koreans, Asian Indians, people from Southeast Asia, and Pacific Islanders. The diversity of the Asian subculture is so great that generalizations about buying patterns of this group are difficult to make.[35] Consumer research on Asian Americans suggests that individuals and families divide into two groups. *Assimilated* Asian Americans are conversant in English, highly educated, hold professional and managerial positions, and exhibit buying patterns very much like the typical American consumer. *Non-assimilated* Asian Americans are recent immigrants who still cling to their native languages and customs.

The diversity of Asian Americans evident in language, customs, and tastes requires marketers to be sensitive to different Asian nationalities. For example, Anheuser-Busch's agricultural products division sells eight varieties of California-grown rice, each with a different Asian label to cover a range of nationalities and tastes. The company's advertising also addresses the preferences of Chinese, Japanese, and Koreans for different kinds of rice bowls. McDonald's actively markets to Asian Americans. According to a company executive, "We recognize diversity in this market. We try to make our messages in the language they prefer to see them." Recently McDonald's launched an advertising campaign that emphasized the company's Chicken Select product for Chinese, Vietnamese, and Korean consumers.

This advertisement featured Chinese basketball star Yao Ming and ran in Asian-language print publications nationwide, focusing on Korean Americans.

McDonald's Corporation
www.mcdonald's.com

Studies show that the Asian American subculture as a whole is characterized by hard work, strong family ties, appreciation for education, and median family incomes exceeding those of any other ethnic group. This subculture is also the most entrepreneurial in the United States, as evidenced by the number of Asian-owned businesses. These qualities led Metropolitan Life Insurance to identify Asian Americans as a target for insurance following the company's success in marketing to Hispanics.

learning review

7. What are the two primary forms of personal influence?

8. Marketers are concerned with which types of reference groups?

9. What two challenges must marketers overcome when marketing to Hispanics?

LEARNING OBJECTIVES REVIEW

LO1 *Describe the stages in the consumer purchase decision process.*

The consumer purchase decision process consists of five stages. They are problem recognition, information search, alternative evaluation, purchase decision, and postpurchase behavior. Problem recognition is perceiving a difference between a person's ideal and actual situation big enough to trigger a decision. Information search involves remembering previous purchase experiences (internal search) and external search behavior such as seeking information from other sources. Alternative evaluation clarifies the problem for the consumer by (*a*) suggesting the evaluative criteria to use for the purchase, (*b*) yielding brand names that might meet the criteria, and (*c*) developing consumer value perceptions. The purchase decision involves the choice of an alternative, including from whom to buy and when to buy. Postpurchase behavior involves the comparison of the chosen alternative with a consumer's expectations, which leads to satisfaction or dissatisfaction and subsequent purchase behavior.

LO2 *Distinguish among three variations of the consumer purchase decision process: routine, limited, and extended problem solving.*

Consumers don't always engage in the five-stage purchase decision process. Instead, they skip or minimize one or more stages depending on the level of involvement—the personal, social, and economic significance of the purchase. For low-involvement purchase occasions, consumers engage in routine problem solving. They recognize a problem, make a decision, and spend little effort seeking external information and evaluating alternatives. For high-involvement purchase occasions, each of the five stages of the consumer purchase decision process is used, including considerable time and effort on external information search and in identifying and evaluating alternatives. With limited problem solving, consumers typically seek some information or rely on a friend to help them evaluate alternatives.

LO3 *Identify major psychological influences on consumer behavior.*

Psychology helps marketers understand why and how consumers behave as they do. In particular, psychological concepts such as motivation and personality; perception; learning; values, beliefs, and attitudes; and lifestyle are useful for interpreting buying processes. Motivation is the energizing force that stimulates behavior to satisfy a need. Personality refers to a person's consistent behaviors or responses to recurring situations. Perception is the process by which an individual selects, organizes, and interprets information to create a meaningful picture of the world. Consumers filter information through selective exposure, comprehension, and retention.

Much consumer behavior is learned. Learning refers to those behaviors that result from (a) repeated experience and (b) reasoning. Brand loyalty results from learning. Values, beliefs, and attitudes are also learned and influence how consumers evaluate products, services, and brands. A more general concept is lifestyle. Lifestyle, also called psychographics, combines psychology and demographics and focuses on how people spend their time and resources, what they consider important in their environment, and what they think of themselves and the world around them.

LO4 *Identify the major sociocultural influences on consumer behavior.*

Sociocultural influences, which evolve from a consumer's formal and informal relationships with other people, also affect consumer behavior. These involve personal influence, reference groups, the family, social class, culture, and subculture. Opinion leadership and word-of-mouth behavior are two major sources of personal influence on consumer behavior. Reference groups are people to whom an individual looks as a basis for self-approval or as a source of personal standards. Family influences on consumer behavior result from three sources: consumer socialization; passage through the family life cycle; and decision making within the family or household. A more subtle influence on consumer behavior than direct contact with others is the social class to which people belong. Persons within social classes tend to exhibit common values, attitudes, beliefs, lifestyles, and buying behaviors. Finally, a person's culture and subculture have been shown to influence product preferences and buying patterns.

FOCUSING ON KEY TERMS

attitude p. 127
beliefs p. 127
brand loyalty p. 126
cognitive dissonance p. 118
consideration set p. 117
consumer behavior p. 116
consumer socialization p. 132
evaluative criteria p. 117
family life cycle p. 132

involvement p. 119
learning p. 126
lifestyle p. 128
motivation p. 122
opinion leaders p. 130
perceived risk p. 125
perception p. 124
personality p. 123

purchase decision process p. 116
reference groups p. 132
self-concept p. 123
situational influences p. 121
social class p. 134
subcultures p. 135
subliminal perception p. 125
word of mouth p. 131

APPLYING MARKETING KNOWLEDGE

1 Review Figure 5–2 in the text, which shows the flash-memory MP3 player attributes identified by *Consumer Reports*. Which attributes are important to you? What other attributes might you consider? Which brand would you prefer?

2 Suppose research at Panasonic reveals that prospective buyers are anxious about buying high-definition television sets. What strategies might you recommend to the company to reduce consumer anxiety?

3 A Porsche salesperson was taking orders on new cars because he was unable to satisfy the demand with the limited number of cars in the showroom and lot.

Several persons had backed out of the contract within two weeks of signing the order. What explanation can you give for this behavior, and what remedies would you recommend?

4 Which social class would you associate with each of the following items or actions: (*a*) tennis club membership, (*b*) an arrangement of plastic flowers in the kitchen, (*c*) *True Romance* magazine, (*d*) *Smithsonian* magazine, (*e*) formally dressing for dinner frequently, and (*f*) being a member of a bowling team.

5 Assign one or more levels of the hierarchy of needs and the motives described in Figure 5–5 to the following products: (*a*) life insurance, (*b*) cosmetics, (*c*) *The Wall Street Journal,* and (*d*) hamburgers.

6 With which stage in the family life cycle would the purchase of the following products and services be most closely identified: (*a*) bedroom furniture, (*b*) life insurance, (*c*) a Caribbean cruise, (*d*) a house mortgage, and (*e*) children's toys?

7 "The greater the perceived risk in a purchase situation, the more likely that cognitive dissonance will result." Does this statement have any basis given the discussion in the text? Why?

building your marketing plan

To do a consumer analysis for the product—the good, service, or idea—in your marketing plan:

1 Identify the consumers who are most likely to buy your product—the primary target market—in terms of (*a*) their demographic characteristics and (*b*) any other kind of characteristics you believe are important.

2 Describe (*a*) the main points of difference of your product for this group and (*b*) what problem they help solve for the consumer, in terms of the first stage in the consumer purchase decision process in Figure 5–1.

3 Identify the one or two key influences for each of the four outside boxes in Figure 5–4: (*a*) marketing mix, (*b*) psychological, (*c*) sociocultural, and (*d*) situational influences.

This consumer analysis will provide the foundation for the marketing mix actions you develop later in your plan.

video case 5 Best Buy: Using Customer Centricity to Connect with Customers

"So much of our business success comes down to understanding consumer behavior," explains Joe Brandt, a store service manager at one of Best Buy's newest stores. "What we do is we try to keep our ear to the railroad tracks. In essence, we listen to the customer to be able to change on a dime when a customer wants us to tailor that experience a certain way and provide certain shopping experiences and certain services."

"Consumers look at a lot of different things," Joe added. "They look at brands, shopability of the store, how easy it is to navigate the store, how pleasant the employees are, price, and how we take care of the customer." Overall there are many factors that "customers look at when they're making a purchase decision."

THE COMPANY

Best Buy is the world's largest consumer electronics retailer with 1,172 stores, 140,000 employees, and $35.9 billion in revenue. Its U.S. and Canadian market share is almost 20 percent, far ahead of rivals Circuit City, Wal-Mart and Costco.

Best Buy operates superstores which provide a limited number of product categories with great depth within the categories. The retailer sells consumer electronics, home office products, appliances, entertainment software and related services. In addition to its U.S. and Canadian stores, Best Buy has recently opened stores in China and has announced plans to open stores in Puerto Rico, Mex-

ico and Turkey. Best Buy also offers its products online through bestbuy.com, and design and installation services through Geek Squad and Magnolia Audio and Video.

Best Buy began as The Sound of Music, a small specialty audio retailer, in 1966. A tornado severely damaged one of its stores in 1981. Instead of closing the store for repairs, Dick Schulze, the owner, had a tornado sale in which more goods were brought in from its other stores and prices were slashed. The sale was so successful that it was repeated the following two years. "When the tornado hit, we decided to market to the community as a whole, and get electronics out there to everybody. We geared ourselves up to win by understanding what consumers want in technology," said Joe Brandt. In 1983, The Sound of Music changed its name to Best Buy and opened its first superstore.

The company continued to grow as the consumer electronics category exploded in the 1980s and 1990s. Based on consumer feedback, Best Buy moved away from the traditional sales approach in 1989 by eliminating commissioned sales representatives. This move was embraced by customers, but questioned by some suppliers and Wall Street analysts who thought it would reduce sales and profits. Best Buy's approach was successful at generating growth in stores and revenues. However, company expenses increased and profits declined. When growth of the consumer electronics market slowed and mass marketers like Wal-Mart, Target, Costco, and Sam's Club became competitors, Best Buy considered changes to its approach.

Best Buy began to differentiate itself from the mass marketers by offering more services, delivery, and installation. Instead of selling individual products, it concentrated on selling entire systems. The acquisition of the Geek Squad to provide in-store, home and office computer services and Magnolia Audio and Video to provide complete audio and home theater systems reflect these changes. These additions significantly increased profit and insulated the company from discount store competition. Responding to customer needs and competitive changes was an important part of Best Buy's strategy.

ADOPTING "CUSTOMER CENTRICITY" AT BEST BUY

When Dick Schulze stepped down as CEO, his successor, Brad Anderson, began looking for new ideas to continue the company's growth. He invited Larry Seldon of Columbia University to present his theory of "customer centricity." Seldon's theory suggested that some customers account for a disproportionate amount of a firm's sales and profits. Anderson adapted the theory to try to understand the needs and behaviors of specific types of customers, or segments. Initial research identified five segments which included:

- **Barry:** The affluent professional who wants the best technology and entertainment, and who demands excellent service.
- **Jill:** The prototypical "soccer mom" who is a busy suburban mom who wants to enrich her children's lives with technology and entertainment.
- **Carrie and Buzz:** The "early adopter," active, younger customer who wants the latest technology and entertainment.
- **Ray:** The "practical adopter" who is a family man who wants technology that improves his life through technology and entertainment.
- **Small business:** The customer who runs his or her own business and has specific needs relating to growing sales and increasing the profitability of the business.

Best Buy used "lab" stores to test product offerings, store designs, and service offerings targeted at each segment. Successful offerings and designs were then expanded to a larger number of pilot stores which would undergo significant physical changes and require substantial new training of sales associates. The cost of applying customer centricity to a store was often as much as $600,000. Early results were impressive as customer centricity stores reported sales much higher than the chain average. As Best Buy began rapid conversion of hundreds of Best Buy stores to the centricity formats, however, expenses increased and profit declined.

THE ISSUES

The impact of Best Buy's new approach on profitability led the company to continue to adapt its ideas about customers. One consideration, for example, was that the "Jill" segment should be broadened to include all females. Research showed that women spend $68 billion on consumer electronics each year and influence 89 percent of all purchases. Unfortunately, females did not embrace the Best Buy experience, largely because its stores were male-oriented in merchandise, appearance, and staffing. "Men and women shop very differently," observes Brandt. Men "typically love the technology" and they like to "play with it" while women are "looking for a knowledgeable person who can answer their questions in a simple manner." To address this problem Best Buy began to implement many changes that would make Best Buy *the* place for women to shop (and work!).

Today, Best Buy is trying a variety of new approaches. Its stores, for example, are being changed to be more appealing to women. Store layout has been changed to include larger aisles, softer colors, less noise, and reduced visibility of boxes and extra stock. In addition, Best Buy now offers women, and all customers, a personal shopping assistant who will walk a customer through the store, demonstrate how the products function, and arrange for delivery and installation after the sale. Best Buy has also created rooms that resemble a home in the store to show customers exactly how the products will look when they are installed. According to Brandt, "we try to personalize the experience as much as possible, and we really try to build a relationship. Once we do that we have the opportunity to really listen and answer questions that customers have." Best Buy is undertaking other initiatives as well. It created the Women's Leadership Forum (WOLF) to develop female leaders within the company. Early results have yielded an increase in applications and a decline in turnover. Overall, these changes appear to be working. Best Buy has observed an increase in its female market share in consumer electronics!

In the future Best Buy's customer centricity efforts will continue to focus on understanding consumer behavior and improving the customer experience. Brandt explains: "Customer centricity, in simple terms, is listening to the customer, putting the customer at the forefront of everything we do. That is, whatever shopping experience that they are looking for, we gear our company and our structure to satisfy that need as much as possible."

Questions

1 How has an understanding of consumer behavior helped Best Buy grow from a small specialty audio retailer to the world's largest consumer electronics retailer?

2 What were the advantages and disadvantages of using "customer centricity" to create five segments of Best Buy customers?

3 How are men and women different in their consumer behavior when they are shopping in a Best Buy store?

4 What are two or three (*a*) objective evaluative criteria and (*b*) subjective evaluative criteria female consumers use when shopping for electronics at Best Buy?

5 What challenges does Best Buy face in the future?

Every Day Matters™

JCPenney®

$5

fall & winter catalog 2007
1.800.222.6161 | jcp.com

6

Understanding Organizations as Customers

LEARNING OBJECTIVES

After reading this chapter you should be able to:

 LO1 Distinguish among industrial, reseller, and government organizational markets.

 LO2 Describe the key characteristics of organizational buying that make it different from consumer buying.

 LO3 Explain how buying centers and buying situations influence organizational purchasing.

 LO4 Recognize the importance and nature of online buying in industrial, reseller, and government organizational markets.

BUYING PAPER IS A GLOBAL BUSINESS DECISION AT JCPENNEY

Kim Nagele views paper differently than most people do. As the senior procurement agent at JCPMedia, he and a team of purchasing professionals buy more than 260,000 tons of paper annually at a cost of hundreds of millions of dollars.

JCPMedia is the print and paper purchasing arm for JCPenney, the fifth-largest retailer in the United States and the largest catalog merchant of general merchandise in the Western Hemisphere. Paper is serious business at JCPMedia, which buys paper for JCPenney catalogs, newspaper inserts, and direct-mail pieces. Some 10 companies from around the world including International Paper in the United States, Catalyst Paper Inc., in Canada, Stora-Enso in Sweden, and UPM-Kymmene, Inc., in Finland, supply paper to JCPMedia.

The choice of paper and suppliers is also a significant business decision given the sizable revenue and expense consequences. Therefore, JCPMedia paper buyers work closely with JCPenney marketing personnel and within budget constraints to assure that the right quality and quantity of paper is purchased at the right price point for merchandise featured in the millions of catalogs, newspaper inserts, and direct-mail pieces distributed every year.

In addition to paper quality and price, buyers formally evaluate supplier capabilities. These include a supplier's capacity to deliver selected grades of paper from specialty items to magazine papers, the availability of specific types of paper to meet printing deadlines, and ongoing environmental programs. For example, a supplier's forestry management and environmental practices are considered in the JCPMedia buying process.[1]

The next time you thumb through a JCPenney catalog, newspaper insert, or direct-mail piece, take a moment to notice the paper. Considerable effort and attention was given to its selection and purchase by Kim Nagele and JCPMedia paper buyers.

Purchasing paper for JCPMedia is one example of organizational buying. This chapter examines the different types of organizational buyers; key characteristics of organizational buying, including online buying; buying situations; unique aspects of the organizational buying process; and some typical buying procedures and decisions in today's organizational markets.

THE NATURE AND SIZE OF ORGANIZATIONAL MARKETS

LO1

Understanding organizational markets and buying behavior is a necessary prerequisite for effective business marketing. **Business marketing** is the marketing of goods and services to companies, governments, or not-for-profit organizations for use in the creation of goods and services that they can produce and market to others. Because over half of all U.S. business school graduates take jobs in firms that engage in business marketing, it is important to understand the characteristics of organizational buyers and their buying behavior.

Organizational buyers are those manufacturers, wholesalers, retailers, and government agencies that buy goods and services for their own use or for resale. For example, these organizations buy computers and telephone services for their own use. However, manufacturers buy raw materials and parts that they reprocess into the finished goods they sell. Wholesalers and retailers resell the goods they buy without reprocessing them. Organizational buyers include all buyers in a nation except ultimate consumers. These organizational buyers purchase and lease large volumes of capital equipment, raw materials, manufactured parts, supplies, and business services. In fact, because they often buy raw materials and parts, process them, and sell the upgraded product several times before it is purchased by the final organizational buyer or ultimate consumer, the total annual purchases of organizational buyers are far greater than those of ultimate consumers. IBM alone buys nearly $40 billion in goods and services each year for its own use or resale.[2]

Organizational buyers are divided into three different markets: (1) industrial, (2) reseller, and (3) government markets.[3] Each market is described next.

Industrial Markets

There are about 12 million firms in the industrial, or business, market. These *industrial firms* in some way reprocess a product or service they buy before selling it again to the next buyer. This is certainly true of Corning, Inc., which transforms an exotic blend of materials to create optical fiber capable of carrying much of the telephone traffic in the United States on a single strand. It is also true (if you stretch your imagination) of a firm selling services, such as a bank that takes money from its depositors, reprocesses it, and "sells" it as loans to borrowers.

The importance of services in the United States today is emphasized by the composition of industrial markets. Companies that primarily sell physical goods (manufacturers; mining; construction; and farms, timber, and fisheries) represent 26 percent of all the industrial firms. The services market sells diverse services such as legal advice, auto repair, and dry cleaning. Along with finance, insurance, and real estate businesses, and transportation, communication, public utility firms, and not-for-profit organizations, service companies represent about 74 percent of all industrial firms. Because of the size and importance of service companies and not-for-profit organizations (such as the American Red Cross), services marketing is discussed in detail in Chapter 12.

Reseller Markets

Wholesalers and retailers that buy physical products and resell them again without any reprocessing are *resellers*. In the United States there are almost 3 million retailers and 860,000 wholesalers. In Chapters 15 through 17 we shall see how manufacturers use wholesalers and retailers in their distribution ("place") strategies as channels through which their products reach ultimate consumers. In this chapter we look at these resellers mainly as organizational buyers in terms of (1) how they make their own buying decisions and (2) which products they choose to carry.

Government Markets

Government units are the federal, state, and local agencies that buy goods and services for the constituents they serve. There are about 88,000 of these government units in

The Orion lunar spacecraft to be designed, developed, tested, and evaluated by Lockheed Martin Corp. is an example of a purchase by a government unit, namely the National Aeronautics and Space Administration (NASA). Read the text to find out how much NASA will pay for the Orion lunar spacecraft.

Lockheed Martin Corporation
www.lockheedmartin.com

the United States. These purchases include the $3.9 billion the National Aeronautics and Space Administration (NASA) intends to pay to Lockheed Martin to develop and produce the Orion lunar spacecraft scheduled for launch in 2014 as well as lesser amounts spent by local school and sanitation districts.[4]

Global Organizational Markets

Industrial, reseller, and government markets also exist on a global scale. International trade statistics indicate that the largest exporting industries in the United States focus on organizational buyers, not ultimate consumers. In fact, capital equipment (such as construction equipment, computers, and telecommunications) and industrial supplies (such as machine parts) account for about 46 percent of all U.S. exports of products and services.

The majority of world trade involves exchange relationships that span the globe.[5] For example, Volvo Aero of Sweden, Ishikawajima-Harima Heavy Industries of Japan, and Chemical Automatics Design Bureau of Russia provide key components used in the high-performance liquid-hydrogen-fueled rocket engine made for space exploration by U.S.-based Pratt & Whitney. This engine is deployed in the Atlas, Titan, and Delta launch vehicles made by Lockheed Martin and Boeing, which are sold to space agencies of many countries for use in deploying communication and weather satellites. Additional examples of business marketing in the global arena appear in Chapter 7.

MEASURING DOMESTIC AND GLOBAL INDUSTRIAL, RESELLER, AND GOVERNMENT MARKETS

The measurement of industrial, reseller, and government markets is an important first step for a firm interested in gauging the size of one, two, or all three of these markets in the United States and around the world. This task has been made easier with the **North American Industry Classification System (NAICS)**.[6] The NAICS provides common industry definitions for Canada, Mexico, and the United States, which

makes it easier to measure economic activity in the three member countries of the North American Free Trade Agreement (NAFTA). The NAICS replaced the Standard Industrial Classification (SIC) system, a version of which has been in place for more than 50 years in the three NAFTA member countries. The SIC neither permitted comparability across countries nor accurately measured new or emerging industries. Furthermore, the NAICS is consistent with the International Standard Industrial Classification of All Economic Activities, published by the United Nations, to facilitate measurement of global economic activity.

The NAICS groups economic activity to permit studies of market share, demand for goods and services, import competition in domestic markets, and similar studies. It designates industries with a numerical code in a defined structure. A six-digit coding system is used. The first two digits designate a sector of the economy, the third digit designates a subsector, and the fourth digit represents an industry group. The fifth digit designates a specific industry and is the most detailed level at which comparable data is available for Canada, Mexico, and the United States. The sixth digit designates individual country-level national industries. Figure 6–1 presents an abbreviated breakdown within the information industries sector (code 51) to illustrate the classification scheme.

The NAICS permits a firm to find the NAICS codes of its present customers and then obtain NAICS-coded lists for similar firms. Also, it is possible to monitor NAICS categories to determine the growth in various sectors and industries to identify promising marketing opportunities. However, the NAICS has an important limitation. Five-digit national industry codes are not available for all three countries because the respective governments will not reveal data when too few organizations exist in a category.

A further refinement in the measurement of organizational markets is the *North American Product Classification System* (NAPCS).[7] The NAPCS provides a classification system for products and services that is consistent across Canada, Mexico, and the United States and international classification systems, such as the Central Product Classification System of the United Nations. The NAICS and NAPCS represent the continued effort toward economic integration in North America and the world.

FIGURE 6–1

NAICS breakdown for information industries sector: NAICS code 51 (abbreviated)

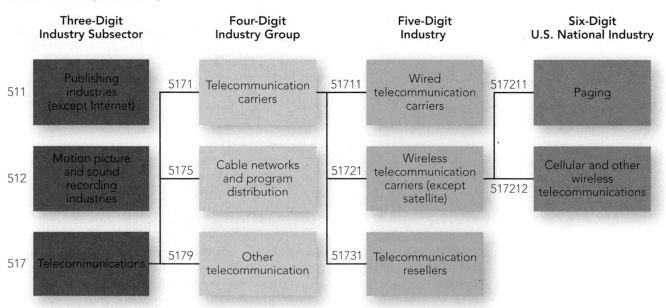

learning review

1. What are the three main types of organizational buyers?

2. What is the North American Industry Classification System (NAICS)?

CHARACTERISTICS OF ORGANIZATIONAL BUYING

LO2

Organizations are different from individuals, so buying for an organization is different from buying for yourself or your family. True, in both cases the objective in making the purchase is to solve the buyer's problem—to satisfy a need or want. But unique objectives and policies of an organization put special constraints on how it makes buying decisions. Understanding the characteristics of organizational buying is essential in designing effective marketing programs to reach these buyers. Key characteristics of organizational buying are listed in Figure 6–2 and discussed next.[8]

Demand Characteristics

Consumer demand for products and services is affected by their price and availability and by consumers' personal tastes and discretionary income. By comparison, industrial demand is derived. **Derived demand** means that the demand for industrial products and services is driven by, or derived from, demand for consumer products and services. For example, the demand for Weyerhaeuser's pulp and paper products is based on consumer demand for newspapers, Domino's "keep warm" pizza-to-go boxes, FedEx packages, and disposable diapers. Derived

FIGURE 6–2

Key characteristics and dimensions of organizational buying behavior

CHARACTERISTICS   **DIMENSIONS**

Market characteristics	• Demand for industrial products and services is derived. • Few customers typically exist, and their purchase orders are large.
Product or service characteristics	• Products or services are technical in nature and purchased on the basis of specifications. • Many of goods purchased are raw and semifinished. • Heavy emphasis is placed on delivery time, technical assistance, and post-sale service.
Buying process characteristics	• Technically qualified and professional buyers follow established purchasing policies and procedures. • Buying objectives and criteria are typically spelled out, as are procedures for evaluating sellers and their products or services. • There are multiple buying influences, and multiple parties participate in purchase decisions. • There are reciprocal arrangements, and negotiation between buyers and sellers is commonplace. • Online buying over the Internet is widespread.
Marketing mix characteristics	• Direct selling to organizational buyers is the rule, and distribution is very important. • Advertising and other forms of promotion are technical in nature. • Price is often negotiated, evaluated as part of broader seller and product or service qualities, and frequently affected by quantity discounts.

demand is based on expectations of future consumer demand. For instance, Whirlpool buys parts for its washers and dryers in anticipation of consumer demand, which is affected by the replacement cycle for these products and by consumer income.

Size of the Order or Purchase

The size of the purchase involved in organizational buying is typically much larger than that in consumer buying. The dollar value of a single purchase made by an organization often runs into thousands or millions of dollars. For example, Siemens Energy & Automation's Airport Logistics Division was recently awarded a $28 million contract to build a baggage handling and security sytem for JetBlue Airways' new terminal at John F. Kennedy International Airport.[9] With so much money at stake, most organizations place constraints on their buyers in the form of purchasing policies or procedures. Buyers must often get competitive bids from at least three prospective suppliers when the order is above a specific amount, such as $5,000. When the order is above an even higher amount, such as $50,000, it may require the review and approval of a vice president or even the president of the company. Knowing how the size of the order affects buying practices is important in determining who participates in the purchase decision and makes the final decision, and also the length of time required to arrive at a purchase agreement.

Number of Potential Buyers

Firms selling consumer products or services often try to reach thousands or millions of individuals or households. For example, your local supermarket or bank probably serves thousands of people, and Kellogg tries to reach 80 million North American households with its breakfast cereals and probably succeeds in selling to a third or half of these in any given year. In contrast, firms selling to organizations are often restricted to far fewer buyers. Gulfstream Aerospace Corporation can sell its business jets to a few thousand organizations throughout the world, and B. F. Goodrich sells its original equipment tires to fewer than 10 car manufacturers.

Organizational Buying Objectives

Organizations buy products and services for one main reason: to help them achieve their objectives. For business firms the buying objective is usually to increase profits through reducing costs or increasing revenues. For example, 7-Eleven buys automated inventory systems to increase the number of products that can be sold through its convenience stores and to keep them fresh. Nissan Motor Company switched its advertising agency because it expects the new agency to devise a more effective ad campaign to help it sell more cars and increase revenues. To improve executive decision making, many firms buy advanced computer systems to process data. The objectives of nonprofit firms and government agencies are usually to meet the needs of the groups they serve. Thus, a hospital buys a high-technology diagnostic device to serve its patients better. Recognizing the high costs of energy, Sylvania promotes to prospective buyers cost savings and increased profits made possible by its fluorescent and halogen lights.

Many companies today have broadened their buying objectives to include an emphasis on buying from minority- and women-owned suppliers and vendors. Companies such as Pitney Bowes, PepsiCo, Coors, and JCPenney report that sales, profits, and customer satisfaction have increased because of their minority- and women-owned supplier and vendor initiatives.[10] You can learn about Procter

Supplier Diversity Is a Fundamental Business Strategy at Procter & Gamble

"Supplier diversity is no longer an issue of social conscience," says A. G. Lafley, chairman of the board, president, and chief executive officer at Procter & Gamble, Inc. "It is a fundamental business strategy." At P&G, purchases from minority- and women-owned suppliers are targeted to reach $2.5 billion by 2010 . . . and for good reason.

Minority- and women-owned suppliers deliver a competitive advantage to P&G. They (1) provide innovative and new ways to help P&G deliver greater value to its con-

sumers; (2) help P&G achieve greater cost efficiencies; and (3) assist P&G in finding new ways to market its brands to consumers.

To learn more about P&G's supplier diversity initiatives and hear from many of its minority- and women-owned suppliers, visit the P&G website at www.pg.com/supplier_diversity and watch the video titled, "Economic Inclusion: A Corporate Commitment."

& Gamble's commitment to and success of its supplier diversity efforts in the accompanying Going Online box.[11] Other companies include environmental initiatives. For example, Lowe's and Home Depot, two home-and-garden center chains, no longer purchase lumber from companies that harvest timber from the world's endangered forests.[12] Successful business marketers recognize that understanding buying objectives is a necessary first step in marketing to organizations.

Organizational Buying Criteria

In making a purchase, the buying organization must weigh key buying criteria that apply to the potential supplier and what it wants to sell. **Organizational buying criteria** are the objective attributes of the supplier's products and services and the capabilities of the supplier itself. These criteria serve the same purpose as the evaluative criteria used by consumers and described in Chapter 5. Seven of the most commonly used criteria are: (1) price, (2) ability to meet the quality specifications required for the item, (3) ability to meet required delivery schedules, (4) technical capability, (5) warranties and claim policies in the event of poor performance, (6) past performance on previous contracts, and (7) production facilities and capacity.[13] Suppliers that meet or exceed these criteria create customer value.

Organizational buyers who purchase products and services in the global marketplace often supplement their buying criteria with supplier ISO 9000 standards certification. **ISO 9000** standards, developed by the International Standards Organization (ISO) in Geneva, Switzerland, refer to standards for registration and certification of a manufacturer's quality management and assurance system based on an on-site audit of practices and procedure. The 3M Co., which buys and markets its products globally, has over 80 percent of its manufacturing and service facilities ISO 9000 certified. According to the company's director of quality control, certification also gives 3M confidence in the consistent quality of its suppliers' manufacturing systems and products.[14]

Many organizational buyers today are transforming their buying criteria into specific requirements that are communicated to prospective suppliers. This practice, called **supplier development**, involves the deliberate effort by organizational buyers to build relationships that shape suppliers' products, services, and capabilities to fit a buyer's needs and those of its customers. For example, consider Deere &

Company, the maker of John Deere farm, construction, and lawn-care equipment. Deere employs 94 supplier-development engineers who work full-time with the company's suppliers to improve their efficiency and quality and reduce their costs. According to a Deere senior executive, "Their quality, delivery, and costs are, after all, our quality, delivery, and costs."[15] Read the accompanying Marketing Matters box to learn how Harley-Davidson emphasizes supplier collaboration in its product design.[16]

With many U.S. manufacturers using a *just-in-time* (JIT) inventory system that reduces the inventory of production parts to those to be used within hours or days, on-time delivery is becoming an even more important buying criterion and, in some instances, a requirement. Caterpillar trains its key suppliers in JIT inventory system and conducts supplier seminars on how to diagnose, correct, and implement continuous quality improvement programs. The just-in-time inventory system is discussed further in Chapter 16.

Buyer–Seller Relationships and Supply Partnerships

Another distinction between organizational and consumer buying behavior lies in the nature of the relationship between organizational buyers and suppliers. Specifically, organizational buying is more likely to involve complex negotiations concerning delivery schedules, price, technical specifications, warranties, and claim policies. These negotiations also can last for an extended period of time. This was the case when the Lawrence Livermore National Laboratory acquired two IBM supercomputers—each with capacity to perform 360 trillion mathematical operations per second—at a cost of $290 million.[17]

Making Responsible Decisions > > > > > > > ethics

Scratching Each Other's Back—The Ethics of Reciprocity in Organizational Buying

Reciprocity, the buying practice in which two organizations agree to purchase each other's products and services, is frowned upon by the U.S. Justice Department because it restricts the normal operation of the free market. Reciprocal buying practices do exist, however, in a variety of forms, including certain types of trade arrangements in international marketing. Furthermore, the extent to which reciprocity is viewed as an ethical issue varies across cultures. In many Asian countries, for instance, reciprocity is often a positive and widespread practice.

Reciprocity is occasionally addressed in the ethics codes of companies or their purchasing policies. For instance, IBM describes its reciprocity policy in the company's Global Procurement Principles and Practices Statement:

> IBM's goal is to buy goods and services which have the best prices, quality, delivery, and technology. IBM has a policy against reciprocal buying arrangements because those arrangements can interfere with this goal.

Do you think reciprocal buying is unethical?

Reciprocal arrangements also exist in organizational buying. **Reciprocity** is an industrial buying practice in which two organizations agree to purchase each other's products and services. The U.S. Justice Department disapproves of reciprocal buying because it restricts the normal operation of the free market. However, the practice exists and can limit the flexibility of organizational buyers in choosing alternative suppliers. Regardless of the legality of reciprocal buying, do you believe this practice is ethical? See the Making Responsible Decisions box.[18]

Long-term contracts are also prevalent.[19] As an example, Kraft Foods, Inc., recently announced it intends to spend $1.7 billion over seven years for global information technology services provided by Electronic Data Systems. Hewlett-Packard is engaged in a 10-year, $3 billion contract to manage Procter & Gamble's information technology in 160 countries.

In some cases, buyer–seller relationships evolve into supply partnerships.[20] A **supply partnership** exists when a buyer and its supplier adopt mutually beneficial objectives, policies, and procedures for the purpose of lowering the cost or increasing the value of products and services delivered to the ultimate consumer. Intel, the world's largest manufacturer of microprocessors and the "computer inside" most personal computers, is a case in point. Intel supports its suppliers by offering them quality management programs and by investing in supplier equipment that produces fewer product defects and boosts supplier productivity. Suppliers, in turn, provide Intel with consistent high-quality products at a lower cost for its customers, the makers of personal computers, and finally you, the ultimate customer. Retailers, too, have forged partnerships with their suppliers. Wal-Mart has such a relationship with Procter & Gamble for ordering and replenishing P&G's products in its stores. By using computerized cash register scanning equipment and direct electronic linkages to P&G, Wal-Mart can tell P&G what merchandise is needed, along with how much, when, and to which store to deliver it on a daily basis. Because supply partnerships, also involve the physical distribution of goods, they are again discussed in Chapter 16 in the context of supply chains.

The Buying Center: A Cross-Functional Group

LO3

For routine purchases with a small dollar value, a single buyer or purchasing manager often makes the purchase decision alone. In many instances, however, several people in the organization participate in the buying process. The individuals in this group, called a **buying center**, share common goals, risks, and knowledge important to a purchase decision. For most large multistore chain resellers, such as Sears, 7-Eleven convenience stores, Target, or Safeway, the buying center is highly formalized and is called a *buying committee.* However, most industrial firms or government units use informal groups of people or call meetings to arrive at buying decisions.

The importance of the buying center requires that a firm marketing to many industrial firms and government units understand the structure, technical and business functions represented, and behavior of these groups.[21] Four questions provide guidance in understanding the buying center in these organizations: Which individuals are in the buying center for the product or service? What is the relative influence of each member of the group? What are the buying criteria of each member? How does each member of the group perceive our firm, our products and services, and our salespeople?

Answers to these questions are difficult to come by, particularly when dealing with industrial firms, resellers, and governments outside the United States. For example, U.S. firms are often frustrated by the fact that Japanese buyers "ask a thousand questions" but give few answers, sometimes rely on third-party individuals to convey views on proposals, are prone to not "talk business," and often say yes to be courteous when they mean no. U.S. firms in the global chemical industry recognize that prodution engineering personnel have a great deal of influence in Hungarian buying groups, whereas purchasing agents in the Canadian chemical industry have relatively more influence in buying decisions.

People in the Buying Center The compostion of the buying center in a given organization depends on the specific item being bought. Although a buyer or purchasing manager is almost always a member of the buying center, individuals from other functional areas are included, depending on what is to be purchased. In buying a million-dollar machine tool, the president (because of the size of the purchase) and the production vice president or manager would probably be members. For key components to be included in a final manufactured product, a cross-functional group of individuals from research and development (R&D), engineering, and quality control are likely to be added. For new word-processing equipment, experienced secretaries who will use the equipment would be members. Still, a major question in penetrating the buying center is finding and reaching the people who will initiate, influence, and actually make the buying decision.

Roles in the Buying Center Researchers have identified five specific roles that an individual in a buying center can play.[22] In some purchases the same person may perform two or more of these roles.

Effective marketing to organizations requires an understanding of buying centers and their role in purchase decisions.

- *Users* are the people in the organization who actually use the product or service, such as a secretary who will use a new word processor.
- *Influencers* affect the buying decision, usually by helping define the specifications for what is bought. The information systems manager would be a key influencer in the purchase of a new mainframe computer.
- *Buyers* have formal authority and responsibility to select the supplier and negotiate the terms of the contract. Kim Nagele performs this role as senior procurement agent at JCPMedia as described in the chapter opening example.
- *Deciders* have the formal or informal power to select or approve the supplier that receives the contract. Whereas in routine orders the decider is usually the buyer or purchasing manager, in important technical purchases it is more likely to be someone from R&D, engineering, or quality control. The decider for a key component being incorporated in a final manufactured product might be any of these three people.
- *Gatekeepers* control the flow of information in the buying center. Purchasing personnel, technical experts, and secretaries can all keep salespeople or information from reaching people performing the other four roles.

Buying Situations and the Buying Center The number of people in the buying center largely depends on the specific buying situation. Researchers who have studied organizational buying identify three types of buying situations, called **buy classes**. These buy classes vary from the routine reorder, or *straight rebuy,* to the completely new purchase, termed *new buy.* In between these extremes is the *modified rebuy.* Some examples will clarify the differences.[23]

- *Straight rebuy.* Here the buyer or purchasing manager reorders an existing product or service from the list of acceptable suppliers, probably without even checking with users or influencers from the engineering, production, or quality control departments. Office supplies and maintenance services are usually obtained as straight rebuys.
- *Modified rebuy.* In this buying situation the users, influencers, or deciders in the buying center want to change the product specifications, price, delivery schedule, or supplier. Although the item purchased is largely the same as with the straight rebuy, the changes usually necessitate enlarging the buying center to include people outside the purchasing department.
- *New buy.* Here the organization is a first-time buyer of the product or service. This involves greater potential risks in the purchase, so the buying center is enlarged to include all those who have a stake in the new buy. Procter & Gamble's purchase of a multimillion-dollar fiber-optic network from Corning, Inc., for its corporate offices in Cincinnati, represented a new buy.[24]

Figure 6–3 summarizes how buy classes affect buying center tendencies in different ways.[25]

The marketing and sales strategies of the sellers facing each of these three buying situations can vary greatly because the importance of personnel from functional areas such as purchasing, engineering, production, and R&D often varies with (1) the type of buying situation and (2) the stage of the purchasing process.[26] If it is a new buy for the manufacturer, you should be prepared to act as a consultant to the buyer, work with technical personnel, and expect a long time for a buying decision to be reached. However, if the manufacturer has bought the item from you before (a straight or

FIGURE 6–3

The buying situation affects buying center behavior in different ways. Understanding these differences can pay huge dividends.

BUYING CENTER DIMENSION	BUY-CLASS SITUATION		
	NEW BUY	STRAIGHT REBUY	MODIFIED REBUY
People involved	Many	One	Two to three
Decision time	Long	Short	Moderate
Problem definition	Uncertain	Well-defined	Minor modifications
Buying objective	Good solution	Low-priced supplier	Low-priced supplier
Suppliers considered	New/present	Present	Present
Buying influence	Technical/operating personnel	Purchasing agent	Purchasing agent and others

modified rebuy), you might emphasize a competitive price and a reliable supply in meetings with the purchasing agent.

learning review

3. What one department is almost always represented by a person in the buying center?

4. What are the three types of buying situations or buy classes?

CHARTING THE ORGANIZATIONAL BUYING PROCESS

Organizational buyers, like consumers, engage in a decision process when selecting products and services. **Organizational buying behavior** is the decision-making process that organizations use to establish the need for products and services and identify, evaluate, and choose among alternative brands and suppliers. There are important similarities and differences between the two decision-making processes. To better understand the nature of organizational buying behavior, we first compare it with consumer buying behavior and then describe an actual organizational purchase in detail.

Stages in the Organizational Buying Process

As shown in Figure 6–4 (and covered in Chapter 5), the five stages a student might use in buying a flash-memory MP3 player also apply to organizational purchases. However, comparing the two right-hand columns in Figure 6–4 reveals some key differences. For example, when a flash-memory MP3 player manufacturer buys earphones for its units from a supplier, more individuals are involved, supplier capability becomes more important, and the postpurchase evaluation behavior is more formalized.

The earphone-buying decision process is typical of the steps made by organizational buyers. Let's now examine in detail the decision-making process for a more complex product—machine vision systems.

Buying a Machine Vision System

Machine vision is widely regarded as one of the keys to the factory of the future. The chief elements of a machine vision system are its optics, light source, camera, video processor, and computer software. Vision systems are mainly used for product inspection. They are also becoming important as one of the chief elements in the information feedback loop of systems that control manufacturing processes. Vision systems, selling in the price range of $25,000 to $250,000, are mostly sold to original equipment manufacturers (OEMs) who incorporate them in still larger industrial automation systems, which sell for millions of dollars. Companies worldwide are expected to spend more than $10 billion for machine vision systems in 2010.[27]

Finding productive applications for machine vision involves the constant search for technology and designs that satisfy user needs. The buying process for machine vision components and assemblies is frequently a new buy because many machine vision systems contain elements that require some custom design. Let's track five purchasing stages that a company such as the Industrial Automation Division of Siemens, a large German industrial firm, would follow when purchasing components and assemblies for the machine vision systems it produces and installs.

Problem Recognition   Sales engineers constantly canvass industrial automation equipment users such as American National Can, Ford Motor Company, Grumman Aircraft, and many Asian and European firms for leads on upcoming industrial automation projects. They also keep these firms current on Siemens' technology, products,

STAGE IN THE BUYING DECISION PROCESS	CONSUMER PURCHASE: FLASH-MEMORY MP3 PLAYER FOR A STUDENT	ORGANIZATIONAL PURCHASE: EARPHONES FOR A FLASH-MEMORY MP3 PLAYER
Problem recognition	Student doesn't like the features of the MP3 player now owned and desires a new one.	Marketing research and sales departments observe that competitors are improving the earphones on their MP3 players. The firm decides to improve the earphones on its own new models, which will be purchased from an outside supplier.
Information search	Student uses past experience, that of friends, ads, the Internet, and *Consumer Reports* to collect information and uncover alternatives.	Design and production engineers draft specifications for earphones. The purchasing department identifies suppliers of MP3 player earphones.
Alternative evaluation	Alternative flash-memory MP3 players are evaluated on the basis of important attributes desired in a player, and several stores are visited.	Purchasing and engineering personnel visit with suppliers and assess (1) facilities, (2) capacity, (3) quality control, and (4) financial status. They drop any suppliers not satisfactory on these factors.
Purchase decision	A specific brand of flash-memory MP3 player is selected, the price is paid, and the student leaves the store.	They use (1) quality, (2) price, (3) delivery, and (4) technical capability as key buying criteria to select a supplier. Then they negotiate terms and award a contract.
Postpurchase behavior	Student reevaluates the purchase decision, may return the player to the store if it is unsatisfactory.	They evaluate suppliers using a formal vendor rating system and notify a supplier if earphones do not meet their quality standard. If the problem is not corrected, they drop the firm as a future supplier.

FIGURE 6–4

Comparing the stages in a consumer and organizational purchase decision process.

and services. When a firm needing a machine vision capability identifies a project that would benefit from Siemens' expertise, company engineers typically work with the firm to determine the kind of system required to meet the customer's need.

After a contract is won, project personnel must often make a **make-buy decision**—an evaluation of whether components and assemblies will be purchased from outside suppliers or built by the company itself. (Siemens produces many components and assemblies.) When these items are to be purchased from outside suppliers, the company engages in a thorough supplier search and evaluation process.

Information Search   Companies such as Siemens employ a sophisticated process for identifying outside suppliers of components and assemblies. For standard items such as connectors, printed circuit boards, and components such as resistors and capacitors, the purchasing agent consults the company's purchasing databank, which contains information on hundreds of suppliers and thousands of products. All products in the databank have been prenegotiated as to price, quality, and delivery time, and many have been assessed using **value analysis**—a systematic appraisal of the design, quality, and performance of a product to reduce purchasing costs.

For one-of-a-kind components or assemblies such as new optics, cameras, and light sources, the company relies on its engineers to keep current on new developments in product technology. This information is often found in technical journals and industry magazines or at international trade shows where suppliers display their most recent

An optic component in a larger machine vision system for soft drinks

Percentage of machine vision buyers citing individual selection criteria

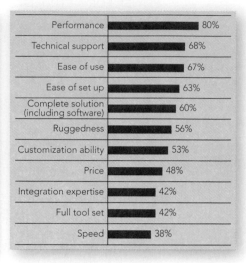

Criteria	Percentage
Performance	80%
Technical support	68%
Ease of use	67%
Ease of set up	63%
Complete solution (including software)	60%
Ruggedness	56%
Customization ability	53%
Price	48%
Integration expertise	42%
Full tool set	42%
Speed	38%

FIGURE 6–5

Product and supplier selection criteria for buying machine vision equipment emphasize factors other than price.

innovations. In some instances, supplier representatives might be asked to make presentations to the buying center at Siemens. Such a group often consists of a project engineer; several design, system, and manufacturing engineers; and a purchasing agent.

Alternative Evaluation   The main buying criteria used to select machine vision suppliers and products are displayed in Figure 6–5.[28] Product performance, a supplier's technical support, and ease of use are the three most frequently mentioned buying criteria for machine vision suppliers and products. Interestingly, price is among the least frequently mentioned. Typically, two or three suppliers for each standard component and assembly are identified from a **bidder's list**—a list of firms believed to be qualified to supply a given item. This list is generated from the company's purchasing databank as well as from engineering inputs. Specific items that are unique or one-of-a-kind may be obtained from a single supplier after careful evaluation by the buying center.

Firms selected from the bidder's list are sent a quotation request from the purchasing agent, describing the desired quantity, delivery date(s), and specifications of the components or assemblies. Suppliers are expected to respond within 30 days.

Purchase Decision   Unlike the short purchase stage in a consumer purchase, the period from supplier selection to order placement to product delivery can take several weeks or even months. Even after bids for components and assemblies are submitted, further negotiation concerning price, performance, and delivery terms is likely. Sometimes conditions related to warranties, indemnities, and payment schedules have to be agreed on. The purchase decision is further complicated by the fact that two or more suppliers of the same item might be awarded contracts. This practice can occur when large orders are requested. Furthermore, suppliers who are not chosen are informed why their bids were not selected.

Postpurchase Behavior   As in the consumer purchase decision process, postpurchase evaluation occurs in the industrial purchase decision process, but it is formalized and often more sophisticated. All items purchased are examined in a formal product acceptance process. The performance of the supplier is also monitored and recorded. Performance on past contracts determines a supplier's chances of being asked to bid on future purchases, and poor performance may result in a supplier's name being dropped from the bidder's list.

This example of an organizational purchase suggests four lessons for marketers who want to increase their chances of selling products and services to organizations. Firms selling to organizations must: (1) understand the organization's needs, (2) get on the right bidder's list, (3) find the right people in the buying center, and (4) provide value to organizational buyers.

learning review

5. What is a make-buy decision?

6. What is a bidder's list?

ONLINE BUYING IN ORGANIZATIONAL MARKETS

LO4

Organizational buying behavior and business marketing continues to evolve with the application of Internet technology. Organizations dwarf consumers in terms of online transactions made, average transaction size, and overall purchase volume. In fact, organizational buyers account for about 80 percent of the global dollar value of all online transactions.[29] Online organizational buyers around the world will purchase between $8 trillion and $10 trillion worth of products and services by 2010. Organizational buyers in the United States will account for about 60 percent of these purchases.

Prominence of Online Buying in Organizational Markets

Online buying in organizational markets is prominent for three major reasons.[30] First, organizational buyers depend heavily on timely supplier information that describes product availability, technical specifications, application uses, price, and delivery schedules. This information can be conveyed quickly via Internet technology. Second, this technology has been shown to substantially reduce buyer order processing costs. At General Electric, online buying has cut the cost of a transaction from $50 to $100 per purchase to about $5. Third, business marketers have found that Internet technology can reduce marketing costs, particularly sales and advertising expense, and broaden their potential customer base for many types of products and services.

For these reasons, online buying is popular in all three kinds of organizational markets. For example, airlines electronically order over $400 million in spare parts from the Boeing Company each year. Customers of W. W. Grainger, a large U.S. wholesaler of maintenance, repair, and operating supplies, buy more than $425 million worth of these products annually online. Supply and service purchases totaling $650 million each year are made online by the Los Angeles County government.

Online buying can assume many forms. Organizational buyers can purchase directly from suppliers. For instance, a buyer might acquire a dozen desktop photocopiers from Xerox.com. This same buyer might purchase office furniture and supplies through a reseller such as Office Depot at www.officedepot.com. Increasingly, organizational buyers and business marketers are using e-marketplaces and online auctions to purchase and sell products and services.

E-Marketplaces: Virtual Organizational Markets

A significant development in organizational buying has been the creation of online trading communities, called **e-marketplaces**, that bring together buyers and supplier organizations. These online communities go by a variety of names, including B2B exchanges and e-hubs, and make possible the real-time exchange of information, money, products, and services.

Marketing Matters > > > > entrepreneurship

eBay Means Business for Entrepreneurs

San Jose, California-based eBay, Inc., is a true Internet phenomenon. By any measure, it is the predominant person-to-person trading community in the world. But there is more.

eBayBusiness offers a trading platform for 23 million small businesses in the United States and even greater numbers around the world. Transactions on eBayBusiness exceed sales of $20 billion annually.

The eBayBusiness platform has proven to be a boon for small businesses. According to an eBay-commissioned survey conducted by ACNielsen, 82 percent of small businesses using eBayBusiness report that it helped their business grow and expand, 78 percent say it helped to reduce their costs, and 79 percent say their business had become more profitable. Additionally, eBayBusiness promotes entrepreneurship. According to the general manager of eBayBusiness, "Many of our sellers started their businesses specifically as a result of the ability to use eBay as their e-commerce platform."

Today, more than 724,000 Americans report that eBay is their primary or secondary source of income—up 68 percent from 2003 when 430,000 Americans were making some or all of their income selling on eBay. According to a spokesperson from the American Enterprise Institute for Public Policy Research, "The potential for entrepreneurs to realize success through eBay is significant."

E-marketplaces can be independent trading communities or private exchanges.[31] Independent e-marketplaces act as a neutral third party and provide an Internet technology trading platform and a centralized market that enable exchanges between buyers and sellers. They charge a fee for their service and exist in settings that have one or more of the following features: (1) thousands of geographically dispersed buyers and sellers, (2) volatile prices caused by demand and supply fluctuations, (3) time sensitivity due to perishable offerings and changing technologies, and (4) easily comparable offerings between a variety of sellers.

Examples of independent e-marketplaces include PlasticsNet (plastics), Hospital Network.com (healthcare supplies and equipment), and Textile Web (garment and apparel products). Small business buyers and sellers, in particular, benefit from independent e-marketplaces. These e-marketplaces offer them an economical way to expand their customer base and reduce the cost of products and services. To serve entrepreneurs and the small business market in the United States, eBay launched eBayBusiness. Read the accompanying Marketing Matters box to learn more about this independent trading community.[32]

Large companies tend to favor private exchanges that link them with their network of qualified suppliers and customers. Private exchanges focus on streamlining a company's purchase transactions with its suppliers and customers. Like independent e-marketplaces, they provide a technology trading platform and central market for buyer–seller interactions. They are not a neutral third party, however, but represent the interests of their owners. For example, Agentrics is an international business-to-business exchange that serves the e-marketplace. It connects more than 250 retail

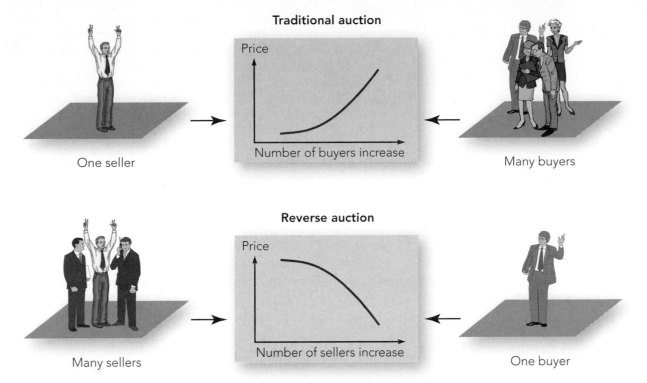

Traditional auction

Price

Number of buyers increase

One seller

Many buyers

Reverse auction

Price

Number of sellers increase

Many sellers

One buyer

FIGURE 6–6

How buyer and seller participants and price behavior differ by type of online auction. As an organizational buyer, would you prefer to participate in a traditional auction or a reverse auction?

customers with 80,000 suppliers. Its members include Best Buy, Campbell Soup, Costco, Radio Shack, Safeway, Target, Tesco, and Walgreens.[33] The Global Health-care Exchange engages in the buying and selling of health care products for some 1,400 hospitals and more than 100 health care suppliers, such as Abbott Laboratories, GE Medical Systems, Johnson & Johnson, Medtronic USA, and McKesson Corporation.[34] Each of these private exchanges has saved their members over $2 billion since 2000 due to efficiencies in purchase transactions.

Online Auctions in Organizational Markets

Online auctions have grown in popularity among organizational buyers and business marketers. Many e-marketplaces offer this service. Two general types of auctions are common: (1) a traditional auction and (2) a reverse auction.[35] Figure 6–6 shows how buyer and seller participants and price behavior differ by type of auction. Let's look at each auction type more closely to understand the implications of each for buyers and sellers.

In a **traditional auction** a seller puts an item up for sale and would-be buyers are invited to bid in competition with each other. As more would-be buyers become involved, there is an upward pressure on bid prices. Why? Bidding is sequential. Prospective buyers observe the bids of others and decide whether or not to increase the bid price. The auction ends when a single bidder remains and "wins" the item with its highest price. Traditional auctions are often used to dispose of excess merchandise. For example, Dell, Inc., sells surplus, refurbished, or closeout computer merchandise at its dellauction.com website.

A reverse auction works in the opposite direction from a traditional auction. In a **reverse auction**, a buyer communicates a need for a product or service and would-be suppliers are invited to bid in competition with each other. As more would-be suppliers become involved, there is a downward pressure on bid prices for the buyer's business. Why? Like traditional auctions, bidding is sequential and prospective suppliers observe the bids of others and decide whether or not to decrease the bid price. The auction ends when a single bidder remains and "wins" the business with its lowest price. Reverse auctions benefit organizational buyers by reducing the cost of their purchases. As an example, United Technologies Corp., estimates that it has saved $600 million on the purchase of $6 billion in supplies using online reverse auctions.[36]

Clearly, buyers welcome the lower prices generated by reverse auctions. Suppliers often favor reverse auctions because they give them a chance to capture business that they might not have otherwise had because of a long-standing purchase relationship between the buyer and another supplier. On the other hand, suppliers say that reverse auctions put too much emphasis on prices, discourage consideration of other important buying criteria, and may threaten supply partnership opportunities.[37]

learning review

7. What are e-marketplaces?

8. In general, which type of online auction creates upward pressure on bid prices and which type creates downward pressure on bid prices?

LEARNING OBJECTIVES REVIEW

LO1 *Distinguish among industrial, reseller, and government organizational markets.*

There are three different organizational markets: industrial, reseller, and government. Industrial firms in some way reprocess a product or service they buy before selling it to the next buyer. Resellers—wholesalers and retailers—buy physical products and resell them again without any reprocessing. Government agencies, at the federal, state, and local levels, buy goods and services for the constituents they serve. The North American Industry Classification System (NAICS) provides common industry definitions for Canada, Mexico, and the United States, which facilitates the measurement of economic activity for these three organizational markets.

LO2 *Describe the key characteristics of organizational buying that make it different from consumer buying.*

Seven major characteristics of organizational buying make it different from consumer buying. These include demand characteristics, size of the order or purchase, number of potential buyers, buying objectives, buying criteria, buyer–seller relationships and supply partnerships, and multiple buying influences within organizations. The organizational buying process itself is more formalized, more individuals are involved, supplier capability is more important, and the postpurchase evaluation behavior often includes performance of the supplier and the item purchased. Figure 6–4 details how the purchase of an MP3 player differs between a consumer and organizational purchase. The case example describing the purchase of machine vision systems by an industrial firm illustrates this process in greater depth.

LO3 *Explain how buying centers and buying situations influence organizational purchasing.*

Buying centers and buying situations have an important influence on organizational purchasing. A buying center consists of a group of individuals who share common goals, risks, and knowledge important to a purchase decision. A buyer or purchasing manager is almost always a member of a buying center. However, other individuals may affect organizational purchasing due to their unique roles in a purchase decision. Five specific roles that a person may play in a buying center include users, influencers, buyers, deciders, and gatekeepers. The specific buying situation will influence the number of people in and the different roles played in a buying center. For a routine reorder of an item—a straight rebuy situation—a purchasing manager or buyer will typically act alone in making a purchasing decision. When an organization is a first-time purchaser of a product or service—a new buy situation—a buying center is enlarged and all five roles in a buying center often emerge. A modified rebuy buying situation lies between these two extremes. Figure 6–3 offers additional insights into how buying centers and buying situations influence organization purchasing.

LO4 *Recognize the importance and nature of online buying in industrial, reseller, and government organizational markets.*

Organizations dwarf consumers in terms of online transactions made and purchase volume. Online buying in organizational markets is popular for three reasons. First, organizational buyers depend on timely supplier information that describes product availability, technical specifications, application uses, price, and delivery schedules. This information can be conveyed quickly via Internet technology. Second, this technology substantially reduces buyer order processing costs. Third, business marketers have found that Internet technology can reduce marketing costs, particularly sales and advertising expense, and broaden their customer base. Two developments in online buying have been the creation of e-marketplaces and online auctions. E-marketplaces provide a technology trading platform and a centralized market for buyer–seller transactions and make possible the real-time exchange of information, money, products, and services. These e-marketplaces can be independent trading communities, such as PlasticsNet, or private exchanges such as the Global Healthcare Exchange. Online traditional and reverse auctions represent a second major development. With traditional auctions, the highest-priced bidder "wins." Conversely, the lowest-priced bidder "wins" with reverse auctions.

FOCUSING ON KEY TERMS

bidder's list p. 156
business marketing p. 144
buy classes p. 153
buying center p. 151
derived demand p. 147
e-marketplaces p. 157
ISO 9000 p. 149

make-buy decision p. 155
North American Industry Classification
System (NAICS) p. 145
organizational buyers p. 144
organizational buying behavior p. 154
organizational buying criteria p. 149

reciprocity p. 151
reverse auction p. 159
supplier development p. 149
supply partnership p. 151
traditional auction p. 159
value analysis p. 155

APPLYING MARKETING KNOWLEDGE

1 Describe the major differences among industrial firms, resellers, and government units in the United States.

2 Explain how the North American Industry Classification System (NAICS) might be helpful in understanding industrial, reseller, and government markets, and discuss the limitations inherent in this system.

3 List and discuss the key characteristics of organizational buying that make it different from consumer buying.

4 What is a buying center? Describe the roles assumed by people in a buying center and what useful questions should be raised to guide any analysis of the structure and behavior of a buying center.

5 Effective marketing is of increasing importance in today's competitive environment. How can firms more effectively market to organizations?

6 A firm that is marketing multimillion-dollar wastewater treatment systems to cities has been unable to sell a new type of system. This setback has occurred even though the firm's systems are cheaper than competitive systems and meet U.S. Environmental Protection Agency (EPA) specifications. To date, the firm's marketing efforts have been directed to city purchasing departments and the various state EPAs to get on approved bidder's lists. Talks with city-employed personnel have indicated that the new system is very different from current systems and therefore city sanitary and sewer department engineers, directors of these two departments, and city council members are unfamiliar with the workings of the system. Consulting engineers, hired by cities to work on the engineering and design features of these systems and paid on a percentage of system cost, are also reluctant to favor the new system. (*a*) What roles do the various individuals play in the purchase process for a wastewater treatment system? (*b*) How could the firm improve the marketing effort behind the new system?

building your marketing plan

Your marketing plan may need an estimate of the size of the market potential or industry potential (see Chapter 9) for a particular product-market in which you compete. Use these steps:

1 Define the product-market precisely, such as ice cream.
2 Visit the NAICS website at www.census.gov.

3 Click "NAICS" and enter a keyword that describes your product-market (e.g., ice cream).
4 Follow the instructions to the specific NAICS code and economic census data that details the dollar sales and provides the estimate of market or industry potential.

video case 6   Lands' End: Where Buyers Rule

Organizational buying is a part of the marketing effort that influences every aspect of business at Lands' End. As senior vice president of operations Phil Schaecher explains, "When we talk about purchasing at Lands' End, most people think of the purchase of merchandise for resale, but we buy many other things aside from merchandise, everything from the simplest office supply to the most sophisticated piece of material-handling equipment." As a result, Lands' End has developed a sophisticated approach to organizational buying, which is one of the keys to its incredible success.

THE COMPANY

The company started by selling sailboat equipment, duffle bags, rainsuits, and sweaters from a basement location in Chicago's old tannery district. In its first catalog, the company name was printed with a typing error—the apostrophe in the wrong place—but the fledgling company couldn't afford to correct and reprint it. So ever since, the company name has been Lands' End—with the misplaced apostrophe.

When the company outgrew its Chicago location, founder Gary Comer relocated it to Dodgeville, Wisconsin, where he had fallen in love with the rolling hills and changing seasons. The original business ideas were simple: "Sell only things we believe in, ship every order the day it arrives, and unconditionally guarantee everything." Over time, the company developed eight principles of doing business:

- Never reduce the quality of a product to make it cheaper.
- Price products fairly and honestly.
- Accept any return for any reason.
- Ship items in stock the day after the order is received.
- What is best for the customer is best for Lands' End.
- Place contracts with manufacturers who are cost-conscious and efficient.
- Operate efficiently.
- Encourage customers to shop in whatever way they find most convenient.

These principles became the guidelines for the company's dedicated local employees and helped create extraordinary expectations from Lands' End customers.

Today, Lands' End is one of the world's largest direct merchants of traditionally styled clothing for the family, soft luggage, and products for the home. The products are offered through catalogs, on the Internet, and in retail stores. Last year, Lands' End distributed more than 200 million catalogs designed for specific segments, including *The Lands' End Catalog, Lands' End Men, Lands' End Plus Size Collection, Lands' End Kids, Lands' End for School Uniforms, Lands' End Home,* and *Lands' End Business Outfitters.* In a typical day, catalog shoppers place more than 40,000 telephone calls to the company. The Lands' End website (www.landsend.com) also offers every Lands' End product and a wide variety of Internet shopping innovations such as a 3-D model customized to each customer (called My Virtual Model™); individually tailored clothes (called Lands' End Custom™); and a feature that allows customers to "chat" online directly with a customer service representative (called Lands' End Live™). Lands' End also operates stores in the United States, the United Kingdom, Germany, and Japan. Selected Lands' End merchandise is also sold in Sears stores, following the purchase of Lands' End by Sears in 2002.

The company's goal is to please customers with the highest levels of quality and service in the industry. Lands' End maintains the high quality of its products through several important activities. For example, the company works directly with mills and manufacturers to retain control of quality and design. "The biggest difference between Lands' End and some other retailers or catalog businesses is that we actually design all the product here and we do all the specifications. Therefore, the manufacturer is building that product directly to our specs, we are not buying off of somebody else's line,"

explains Joan Mudget, vice president of quality assurance. In addition, Lands' End tests its products for comfort and fit by paying real people (local residents and children) to "wear-test" and "fit-test" all types of garments.

Service has also become an important part of the Lands' End reputation. Customers expect prompt, professional service at every step—initiating the order, making selections, shipping, and follow-up (if necessary). Some of the ways Lands' End meets these expectations include offering the simplest guarantee in the industry—"Guaranteed. Period."—toll-free telephone lines open 24 hours a day, 364 days a year, continuous product training for telephone representatives, and two-day shipping. Lands' End operators even send personal responses to all e-mail messages, approximately 230,000 per year.

ORGANIZATIONAL BUYING AT LANDS' END

The sixth Lands' End business principle (described above) is accomplished through the company's organizational buying process. First, its buyers specify fabric quality, construction, and sizing standards, which typically exceed industry standards, for current and potential Lands' End products. Then the buyers literally search around the world for the best possible source of fabrics and products. Once a potential supplier is identified, one of the company's 150 quality assurance personnel makes an information-gathering visit. The purpose of the visit is to understand the supplier's values, to assess four criteria (economic, quality, service, and vendor), and to determine if the Lands' End standards can be achieved.

Lands' End evaluations of potential suppliers lead to the selection of what the company hopes will become long-term partners. As Mudget explains, "When we're looking for new manufacturers we are looking for the long term. I think one of the most interesting things is we're not out there looking for new vendors every year to fill the same products." In fact, Lands' End believes that the term *supplier* does not adequately describe the importance the company places on the relationships. Lands' End suppliers are viewed as allies, supporters, associates, colleagues, and stakeholders in the future of the company. Once an alliance is formed the product specifications and the performance on those specifications are regularly evaluated.

Lands' End buyers face a variety of buying situations. Straight rebuys involve reordering an existing product—such as shipping boxes—without evaluating or changing specifications. Modified rebuys involve changing some aspect of a previously ordered product—such as the collar of a knit shirt—based on input from consumers, retailers, or other people involved in the purchase decision. Finally, new buys involve first-time purchases—such as Lands' End addition of men's suits to its product line. The complexity of the process can vary with the type of purchase. Schaecher explains, "As you get more complicated in the purchase there are more things you look at to decide on a vendor."

FUTURE CHALLENGES FOR LANDS' END

Lands' End faces several challenges as it pursues improvements in its organizational buying process. First, new technologies offer opportunities for fast, efficient, and accurate communication with suppliers. Ed Smidebush, general inventory manager, describes a new system at Lands' End: "Our quick response system is a computerized system where we transmit electronically to our vendors each Sunday night, forecast information as well as stock positions and purchase order information so that on Monday morning this information will be incorporated directly into their manufacturing reports so that they can prioritize their production." Occasionally Lands' End must work with its suppliers to improve their technology and information system capabilities.

Another challenge for Lands' End is to anticipate changes in consumer interests. While it has many years of experience with retail consumers, preferences for colors, fabrics, and styles change frequently, requiring buyers to constantly monitor the marketplace. In addition, Lands' End's more recent offerings to corporate customers require constant attention "because business customers' wants and incentives, and the environment in which they're shopping, are very different from consumers at home," explains marketing manager Hilary Kleese.

Finally, Lands' End must anticipate the quantities of each of its products consumers are likely to order. To do this, historical information is used to develop forecasts. One of the best tests of their forecast accuracy is the holiday season, when Lands' End receives more than 100,000

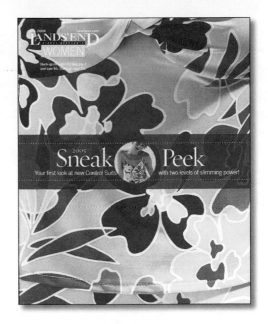

calls each day. Having the right products available is important because, as every employee knows from Principle 4, every order must be shipped the day after it is received.

Questions

1 (*a*) Who is likely to comprise the buying center in the decision to select a new supplier for Lands' End? (*b*) Which of the buying center members are likely to play the roles of users, influencers, buyers, deciders, and gatekeepers?

2 (*a*) Which stages of the organizational buying decision process does Lands' End follow when it selects a new supplier? (*b*) What selection criteria does the company utilize in the process?

3 Describe purchases Lands' End buyers typically face in each of the three buying situations: straight rebuy, modified rebuy, new buy.

COVERGIRL

封面女郎

7

Understanding and Reaching Global Consumers and Markets

PROCTER & GAMBLE IS CHANGING THE FACE OF CHINA

The face of China is changing thanks to Procter & Gamble. P&G is the largest consumer products company in China due in large measure to the popularity of its skin care and cosmetic brands among Chinese women, including Olay whitening skin creams, SK-11 skin care products, and Cover Girl and Max Factor cosmetics. P&G's success in China results from a passionate effort to meet the beauty needs of Chinese women since 1988.

P&G cosmetics have been adapted to Chinese skin tones and fashion trends. So too, the company's marketing practices have been changed. Consider the Cover Girl brand—the best-selling mass market cosmetic brand in the United States. Only after two years of painstaking R&D and market analysis, did P&G launch the Cover Girl brand in China in 2005.

Why didn't P&G simply export Cover Girl products from the United States to China? "You can't just import cosmetics here," says Daisy Ching, the regional account director at Cover Girl's advertising agency in China, Grey Global Group. "Companies have to understand what beauty means to Chinese women and what they look for, and product offerings and communications have to be adjusted accordingly."

For Cover Girl, that meant starting from scratch. "We needed to tailor-make everything for this market—the products, the brand proposition, the packaging. Everything is different. You can say the only thing that didn't change is the Cover Girl brand name," recalled Tasai Hsin-Hsin, P&G's associate marketing director for cosmetics in Greater China.[1]

This chapter describes today's complex and dynamic global marketing environment. It begins with an overview of world trade and the emergence of a borderless economic world. Attention is then focused on prominent cultural, economic, and political-regulatory factors that present both an opportunity and challenge for global marketers. Four major global market entry strategies are then detailed. Finally, the task of designing, implementing, and evaluating worldwide marketing programs for companies and products, such as Procter & Gamble and Cover Girl cosmetics, is described.

DYNAMICS OF WORLD TRADE

LO1

The dollar value of world trade has more than doubled in the past decade and will exceed $12 trillion in 2010. Manufactured goods and commodities account for 74 percent of world trade. Service industries, including telecommunications, transportation, insurance, education, banking, and tourism, represent the other 26 percent of world trade.

World Trade Flows

All nations and regions of the world do not participate equally in world trade. World trade flows reflect interdependencies among industries, countries, and regions and manifest themselves in country, company, industry, and regional exports and imports.

Global Perspective   Figure 7–1 shows the estimated dollar value of exports and imports among North American countries, Europe, Asian/Pacific Rim countries, and the rest of the world, including intraregional trade flows.[2] The United States, Europe, Canada, China, and Japan together account for more than two-thirds of world trade.

Not all trade involves the exchange of money for goods or services. In a world where 70 percent of all countries do not have convertible currencies or where government-owned enterprises lack sufficient cash or credit for imports, other means of payment are used. An estimated 15 to 20 percent of world trade involves **countertrade**, the practice of using barter rather than money for making global sales.[3]

FIGURE 7–1

Illustrative world trade flows for manufactured goods and commodities within and between geographic regions (billions of U.S. dollars)

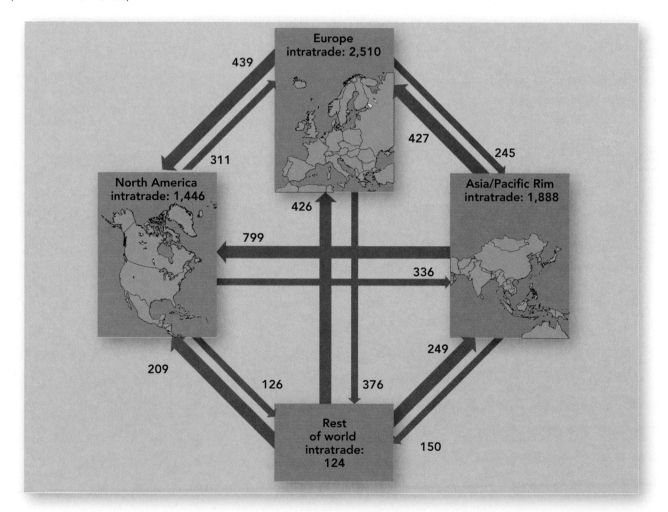

Countertrade is popular with many Eastern European nations, Russia, and Asian countries. For example, the Malaysian government recently exchanged 20,000 tons of rice for an equivalent amount of Philippine corn. Volvo of North America delivered automobiles to the Siberian police force when Siberia had no cash to pay for them. It accepted payment in oil, which it then sold for cash to pay for media advertising in the United States.[4]

A global perspective on world trade views exports and imports as complementary economic flows: A country's imports affect its exports and exports affect its imports. Every nation's imports arise from the exports of other nations. As the exports of one country increase, its national output and income rise, which in turn leads to an increase in the demand for imports. This nation's greater demand for imports stimulates the exports of other countries. Increased demand for exports of other nations energizes their economic activity, resulting in higher national income, which stimulates their demand for imports. In short, imports affect exports and vice versa. This phenomenon is called the *trade feedback effect* and is one argument for free trade among nations.

United States Perspective   The United States is the world's perennial leader in terms of **gross domestic product** (GDP), which is the monetary value of all goods and services produced in a country during one year. The United States is also among the world's leaders in exports due in large part to its global prominence in the aerospace, chemical, office equipment, information technology, pharmaceutical, telecommunications, and professional service industries. However, the U.S. percentage share of world exports has shifted downward over the past 30 years, whereas its percentage share of world imports has increased. Therefore, the relative position of the United States as a supplier to the world has diminished despite an absolute growth in exports. At the same time, its relative role as a marketplace for the world has increased, particularly for automobile, oil, textile, apparel, and consumer electronics products.

The difference between the monetary value of a nation's exports and imports is called the **balance of trade**. When a country's exports exceed its imports, it incurs a surplus in its balance of trade. When imports exceed exports, a deficit results. World trade trends in U.S. exports and imports are reflected in the U.S. balance of trade. Since 1975, two important things have happened in U.S. exports and imports. First, imports have significantly exceeded exports each year, indicating that the United States has a continuing balance of trade deficit. Second, the volume of both exports and imports has increased dramatically since the mid-1970s, showing why almost every American is significantly affected. The effect varies from the products they buy (Samsung DVD players from South Korea, Waterford crystal from Ireland, Louis Vuitton luggage from France) to those they sell (Cisco Systems' Internet technology to Europe, Du Pont's chemicals to the Far East, Merck pharmaceuticals to Africa) and the jobs and improved standard of living that result.

World trade flows to and from the United States reflect demand and supply interdependencies for goods and services among nations and industries. The four largest importers of U.S. goods and services are Canada, China, Mexico, and Japan. These countries purchase approximately 67 percent of U.S. exports. The four largest exporters to the United States are Canada, China, Mexico, and Japan.

The United States is Asia's largest export market, buying about one-third of the exports of Japan, Taiwan, South Korea, and China, a quarter of Hong Kong's exports, and 40 percent of the Philippines's exports. The trade imbalance between the United States and Asia is illustrated by the fact that Japan, South Korea, and China combine for about 80 percent of the total U.S. balance of trade deficit.

Competitive Advantage of Nations

As companies in many industries find themselves competing against foreign competitors at home and abroad, government policy makers around the world are increasingly asking why some companies and industries in a country succeed globally while others lose

FIGURE 7–2
Porter's diamond of national
competitive advantage
contains four key elements
that explain why some
industries and firms in
different countries become
world leaders.

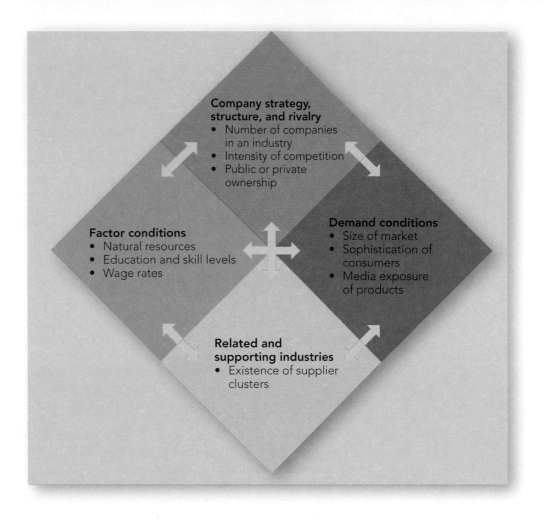

ground or fail. Harvard Business School professor Michael Porter suggests a "diamond" to explain a nation's competitive advantage and why some industries and firms become world leaders.[5] He identified four key elements, which appear in Figure 7–2:

1. *Factor conditions.* These reflect a nation's ability to turn its natural resources, education, and infrastructure into a competitive advantage. Consider Holland, which exports 58 percent of the world's cut flowers. The Dutch lead the world in the cut-flower industry because of their research in flower cultivation, packaging, and shipping—not because of their weather.

2. *Demand conditions.* These include both the number and sophistication of domestic customers for an industry's product. Japan's sophisticated consumers demand quality in their consumer electronics, thereby making Japan's producers such as Sony, Sanyo, Sharp, Pioneer, JVC, Matsushita, and Hitachi among the world leaders in the electronics industry.

3. *Related and supporting industries.* Firms and industries seeking leadership in global markets need clusters of world-class suppliers that accelerate innovation. Swiss companies are leaders in the global watch market, in part, because of high quality supporting watch-movement makers.

4. *Company strategy, structure, and rivalry.* These factors include the conditions governing the way a nation's businesses are organized and managed, along with the intensity of domestic competition. The Italian shoe industry has become a world leader because of intense domestic competition among firms such as MAB, Bruno Magli, and Rossimoda, which has made shoes for Christian Dior and Anne Klein Couture.

Sharp and Bruno Magli have succeeded in the global marketplace as well as in their domestic markets.

Sharp
www.sharpusa.com

Bruno Magli
www.brunomagli.it

In Porter's study, case histories of firms in more than 100 industries were analyzed. While the strategies used by successful global competitors differed in many respects, a common theme emerged: A firm that succeeds in global markets has first succeeded in intense domestic competition. Hence, competitive advantage for global firms grows out of continuous improvement, innovation, and change.

However, pursuit of a country's competitive advantage in global markets has a dark side—economic espionage.[6] *Economic espionage* is the clandestine collection of trade secrets or proprietary information about competitors. This practice is common in high-technology industries such as electronics, specialty chemicals, industrial equipment, aerospace, and pharmaceuticals, where technical know-how and trade secrets separate global industry leaders from followers. It is estimated that economic espionage costs U.S. firms $250 billion a year. The intelligence services of some 23 nations routinely target U.S. firms for information about research and development efforts, manufacturing and marketing plans, and customer lists. To counteract this threat, the **Economic Espionage Act (1996)** makes the theft of trade secrets by foreign entities a federal crime in the United States. This act prescribes prison sentences of up to 15 years and fines up to $500,000 for individuals. Agents of foreign governments found guilty of economic espionage face a 25-year prison sentence and a $10 million fine.

---

learning review

1. What is the trade feedback effect?

2. What variables influence why some companies and industries in a country succeed globally while others lose ground or fail?

MARKETING IN A BORDERLESS ECONOMIC WORLD

LO2

Global marketing has and continues to be affected by a growing borderless economic world. Four trends in the past decade have significantly influenced the landscape of global marketing:

Trend 1: Gradual decline of economic protectionism by individual countries.

Trend 2: Formal economic integration and free trade among nations.

Trend 3: Global competition among global companies for global customers.

Trend 4: Emergence of a networked global marketspace.

Decline of Economic Protectionism

Protectionism is the practice of shielding one or more industries within a country's economy from foreign competition through the use of tariffs or quotas. The economic argument for protectionism is that it limits the outsourcing of jobs, protects a nation's political security, discourages economic dependency on other countries, and encourages the development of domestic industries. Read the accompanying Making Responsible Decisions box and ask yourself if protectionism has an ethical dimension.[7]

Tariffs and quotas discourage world trade as depicted in Figure 7–3. **Tariffs**, which are a government tax on goods or services entering a country, primarily serve to raise prices on imports. The average tariff on manufactured goods in industrialized countries is 4 percent. However, wide differences exist across nations. For example, European Union countries have a 10 percent tariff on cars imported from Japan, which is about four times higher than the tariff imposed by the United States on Japanese cars.

The effect of tariffs on world trade and consumer prices is substantial. Consider U.S. rice exports to Japan. The U.S. Rice Millers' Association claims that if the Japanese rice market were opened to imports by lowering tariffs, lower prices would save Japanese consumers $6 billion annually, and the United States would gain a large share of the Japanese rice market. Similarly, tariffs imposed on bananas by European Union countries cost consumers $2 billion a year.

FIGURE 7–3

How does protectionism affect world trade? Protectionism hinders world trade through tariff and quota policies of individual countries. Tariffs increase prices and quotas limit supply.

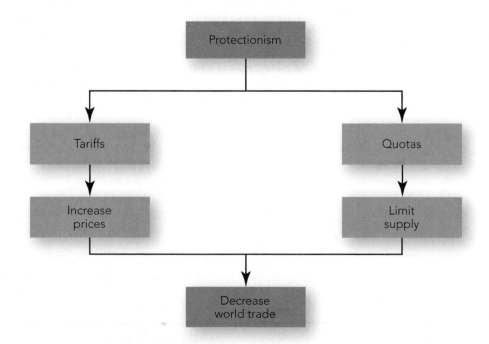

Making Responsible Decisions > > > > > > > > ethics

Global Ethics and Global Economics—The Case of Protectionism

World trade benefits from free and fair trade among nations. Nevertheless, governments of many countries continue to use tariffs and quotas to protect their various domestic industries. Why? Protectionism earns profits for domestic producers and tariff revenue for the government. There is a cost, however. Protectionist policies cost Japanese consumers between $75 billion and $110 billion annually. U.S. consumers pay about $70 billion each year in higher prices because of tariffs and other protective restrictions.

Sugar and textile import quotas in the United States, automobile and ba-

nana import tariffs in European countries, beer import tariffs in Canada, and rice import tariffs in Japan protect domestic industries but also interfere with world trade for these products. Regional trade agreements, such as those found in the provisions of the European Union and the North American Free Trade Agreement, may also pose a situation whereby member nations can obtain preferential treatment in quotas and tariffs but nonmember nations cannot.

Protectionism, in its many forms, raises an interesting global ethical question. Is protectionism, no matter how applied, an ethical practice?

A **quota** is a restriction placed on the amount of a product allowed to enter or leave a country. Quotas can be mandated or voluntary and may be legislated or negotiated by governments. Import quotas seek to guarantee domestic industries access to a certain percentage of their domestic market. For example, there is a limit on imported television sets to Great Britain and Italian quotas on Japanese motorcycles. The United States also imposes quotas. For instance, U.S. sugar import quotas have existed for more than 50 years and preserve about half of the U.S. sugar market for domestic producers. American consumers pay $1.5 billion annually in extra food costs because of this quota. Import quotas on textiles and apparel from Asian countries cost U.S. consumers almost $20 billion per year in higher prices.

Every country engages in some form of protectionism. However, protectionism has declined over the past 50 years due in large part to the *General Agreement on Tariffs and Trade (GATT)*. This international treaty was intended to limit trade barriers and promote world trade through the reduction of tariffs, which it did. However, GATT did not explicitly address nontariff trade barriers, such as quotas and world trade in services, which often sparked heated trade disputes between nations.

World Trade Organization
www.wto.org

As a consequence, the major industrialized nations of the world formed the **World Trade Organization** (WTO) in 1995 to address a broad array of world trade issues.[8] There are 150 WTO member countries, including the United States, which account for more than 90 percent of world trade. The WTO is a permanent institution that sets rules governing trade between its members through panels of trade experts who decide on trade disputes between members and issue binding decisions. The WTO reviews more than 200 disputes annually. For instance, the WTO denied Kodak's multimillion-dollar damage claim that the Japanese government protected Fuji Photo from import competition. In another decision, the WTO allowed Britain, Ireland, and the European Union to reclassify U.S.-produced local area network (LAN) computer equipment as telecommunications gear. The new classification effectively doubled the import tariff on these U.S. goods.

FIGURE 7–4

The European Union in 2007 consists of 27 countries with more than 500 million consumers.

European Union

www.europa.eu.int

Rise of Economic Integration

In recent years, a number of countries with similar economic goals have formed transnational trade groups or signed trade agreements for the purpose of promoting free trade among member nations and enhancing their individual economies. Three of the best-known examples are the European Union (or simply EU), the North American Free Trade Agreement (NAFTA), and Asian Free Trade Areas.

European Union   The European Union consists of 27 member countries that have eliminated most barriers to the free flow of goods, services, capital, and labor across their borders (see Figure 7–4).[9] This single market houses more than 500 million consumers with a combined gross domestic product larger than that of the United States. In addition, 14 countries have adopted a common currency called the *euro*. Adoption of the euro has been a boon to electronic commerce in the EU by eliminating the need to continually monitor currency exchange rates.

The EU creates abundant marketing opportunities because firms do not need to market their products and services on a nation-by-nation basis. Rather, pan-European marketing strategies are possible due to greater uniformity in product and packaging standards; fewer regulatory restrictions on transportation, advertising, and promotion imposed by countries; and removal of most tariffs that affect pricing practices. For example, Colgate-Palmolive Company now markets its Colgate toothpaste with one formula and package across EU countries at one price. Black & Decker—the maker of electrical hand tools, appliances, and other consumer products—now produces 8, not 20, motor sizes for the European market, resulting in production and marketing cost savings. These practices were previously impossible because of different government and trade regulations. Europeanwide distribution from fewer locations is also feasible given open borders. French tire maker Michelin closed 180 of its European distribution centers and now uses just 20 to serve all EU countries.

North American Free Trade Agreement The North American Free Trade Agreement lifted many trade barriers between Canada, Mexico, and the United States and created a marketplace with more than 450 million consumers.[10] NAFTA has stimulated trade flows among member nations as well as cross-border retailing, manufacturing, and investment. For example, NAFTA paved the way for Wal-Mart to move to Mexico and Mexican supermarket giant, Gigante, to move into the United States. Whirlpool Corporation's Canadian subsidiary stopped making washing machines in Canada and moved that operation to Ohio. Whirlpool then shifted the production of kitchen ranges and compact dryers to Canada. Ford invested $60 million in its Mexico City manufacturing plant to produce smaller cars and light trucks for global sales.

In 2006, a comprehensive free trade agreement among Costa Rica, the Dominican Republic, El Salvador, Guatemala, Honduras, Nicaragua, and the United States extended many NAFTA benefits to Central American countries and the Dominican Republic. Called CAFTA-DR, this agreement is viewed as a step toward a 34-country Free Trade Area of the Americas for the Western Hemisphere.

Asian Free Trade Agreements Efforts to liberalize trade in East Asia—from Japan and the four "Little Dragons" (Hong Kong, Singapore, South Korea, and Taiwan) through Thailand, Malaysia, and Indonesia—are also growing. Although the trade agreements are less formal than those underlying the EU and NAFTA, they have reduced tariffs among countries and promoted trade.

A New Reality: Global Competition among Global Companies for Global Consumers

The emergence of a largely borderless economic world has created a new reality for marketers of all shapes and sizes. Today, world trade is driven by global competition among global companies for global consumers.

Global Competition **Global competition** exists when firms originate, produce, and market their products and services worldwide. The automobile, pharmaceutical, apparel, electronics, aerospace, and telecommunication fields represent well-known industries with sellers and buyers on every continent. Other industries that are increasingly global in scope include soft drinks, cosmetics, ready-to-eat cereals, snack chips, and retailing.

Global competition broadens the competitive landscape for marketers. The familiar "cola war" waged by Pepsi-Cola and Coca-Cola in the United States has been repeated around the world, including India, China, and Argentina. Procter & Gamble's Pampers and Kimberly-Clark's Huggies have taken their disposable diaper rivalry from the United States to Western Europe. Boeing and Europe's Airbus vie for lucrative commercial aircraft contracts on virtually every continent.

Collaborative relationships also are becoming a common way to meet the demands of global competition. Global **strategic alliances** are agreements among two or more independent firms to cooperate for the purpose of achieving common goals such as a competitive advantage or customer value creation. For example, General Mills and Nestlé of Switzerland created Cereal Partners Worldwide to fine-tune Nestlé's European cereal marketing and distribute General Mills cereals worldwide. Today this global alliance produces almost $2 billion in annual sales in more than 130 countries.

Pepsi-Cola, now available in more than 190 countries and territories, accounts for a quarter of all soft drinks sold internationally. This Brazilian ad—"How to make jeans last 10 years"—features the popular Diet Pepsi brand targeted at weight-conscious consumers.

PepsiCo, Inc.
www.pepsico.com

Global Companies Three types of companies populate and compete in the global marketplace: (1) international firms, (2) multinational firms, and (3) transnational firms.[11] All three employ people in different countries, and many have administrative, marketing, and manufacturing operations (often called *divisions* or *subsidiaries*) around the world. However, a firm's orientation toward and strategy for global markets and marketing defines the type of company it is or attempts to be.

An *international firm* engages in trade and marketing in different countries as an extension of the marketing strategy in its home country. Generally speaking, these firms market their existing products and services in other countries the same way they do in their home country. Avon, for example, successfully distributes its product line through direct selling in Asia, Europe, and South America, employing virtually the same marketing strategy used in the United States.

A *multinational firm* views the world as consisting of unique parts and markets to each part differently. Multinationals use a **multidomestic marketing strategy**, which means that they have as many different product variations, brand names, and advertising programs as countries in which they do business. For example, Lever Europe, a division of Unilever, markets its fabric softener known as Snuggle in the United States in 10 European countries under seven brand names, including Kuschelweich in Germany, Coccolino in Italy, and Mimosin in France. These products have different packages, different advertising programs, and occasionally different formulas. Procter & Gamble markets Mr. Clean, its popular multipurpose cleaner, in North America and Asia. But you won't necessarily find the Mr. Clean brand in other parts of the world. In many Latin American countries, Mr. Clean is Mastro Limpio. Mr. Clean is Mr. Proper in most parts of Europe, Africa, and the Middle East.

A *transnational firm* views the world as one market and emphasizes cultural similarities across countries or universal consumer needs and wants more than differences. Transnational marketers employ a **global marketing strategy**—the practice of standardizing marketing activities when there are cultural similarities and adapting them when cultures differ. This approach benefits marketers by allowing them to realize economies of scale from their production and marketing activities.

Global marketing strategies are popular among many business-to-business marketers such as Caterpillar and Komatsu (heavy construction equipment) and Texas Instruments,

Marketing Matters > > > > > customer value

The Global Teenager—A Market of 500 Million Voracious Consumers with $100 Billion to Spend

The "global teenager" market consists of 500 million 13- to 19-year-olds in Europe, North and South America, and industrialized nations of Asia and the Pacific Rim who have experienced intense exposure to television (MTV broadcasts in 169 countries in 28 languages), movies, travel, the Internet, and global advertising by companies such as Apple, Sony, Nike, and Coca-Cola. The similarities among teens across these countries are greater than their differences. For example, a global study of middle-class teenagers' rooms in 25 industrialized countries indicated it was difficult, if not impossible, to tell whether the rooms were in Los Angeles, Mexico City, Tokyo, Rio de Janeiro, Sidney, or Paris. Why? Teens spend $100 billion annually for a common gallery of products: Sony video games, Tommy Hilfiger apparel,

Levi's blue jeans, Nike athletic shoes, Swatch watches, Apple iPods, Diesel apparel and accessories, and Procter & Gamble Clearasil facial medicine.

Teenagers around the world appreciate fashion and music, and desire novelty and trendier designs and images. They also acknowledge an Americanization of fashion and culture based on another study of 6,500 teens in 26 countries. When asked what country had the most influence on their attitudes and purchase behavior, 54 percent of teens from the United States, 87 percent of those from Latin America, 80 percent of the Europeans, and 80 percent of those from Asia named the United States. This phenomenon has not gone unnoticed by parents. As one parent in India said, "Now the youngsters dress, talk, and eat like Americans."

Intel, Hitachi, and Motorola (semiconductors). Consumer goods marketers such as Timex, Seiko, and Swatch (watches), Coca-Cola and Pepsi-Cola (cola soft drinks), Mattel and Lego (children's toys), Gillette (personal care products), L'Oréal and Shiseido (cosmetics), and McDonald's (quick-service restaurants) successfully execute this strategy.

Each of these companies markets a **global brand**—a brand marketed under the same name in multiple countries with similar and centrally coordinated marketing programs.[12] Global brands have the same product formulation or service concept, deliver the same benefits to consumers, and use consistent advertising across multiple countries and cultures. This isn't to say that global brands are not sometimes tailored to specific cultures or countries. However, adaptation is only used when necessary to better connect the brand to consumers in different markets. Consider McDonald's.[13] This global marketer has adapted its proven formula of "food, fun, and families" across 119 countries. Although the Golden Arches and Ronald McDonald appear worldwide, McDonald's tailors other aspects of its marketing program. It serves beer in Germany, wine in France, and coconut, mango, and tropical mint shakes in Hong Kong. Hamburgers are made with different meat and spices in Japan, Thailand, India, and the Philippines. But McDonald's world-famous French fry is standardized. Its French fry in Beijing, China, tastes like the one in Paris, France, which tastes like the one in your neighborhood.

Global Consumers Global competition among global companies often focuses on the identification and pursuit of global consumers as described in the accompanying Marketing Matters box.[14] **Global consumers** consist of consumer

Sweden's IKEA is capitalizing on the home-improvement trend sweeping through China. The home-furnishings retailer is courting young Chinese consumers who are eagerly updating their housing with modern, colorful but inexpensive furniture. IKEA entered China in 1998. The company expects to have at least 10 stores open in China by 2010.

IKEA
www.ikea.com

groups living in many countries or regions of the world who have similar needs or seek similar features and benefits from products or services. Evidence suggests the presence of a global middle-income class, a youth market, and an elite segment, each consuming or using a common assortment of products and services, regardless of geographic location. A variety of companies have capitalized on the global consumer. Whirlpool, Sony, and IKEA have benefited from the growing global middle-income class desire for kitchen appliances, consumer electronics, and home furnishings, respectively. Levi's, Nike, Coca-Cola, and Apple have tapped the global youth market. DeBeers, Chanel, Gucci, Rolls-Royce, and Sotheby's and Christie's, the world's largest fine art and antique auction houses, cater to the elite segment for luxury goods worldwide.

Emergence of a Networked Global Marketspace

The use of Internet technology as a tool for exchanging goods, services, and information on a global scale is the fourth trend affecting world trade. Over 1 billion businesses, educational institutions, government agencies, and households worldwide are expected to have Internet access by 2010. The broad reach of this technology suggests that its potential for promoting world trade is huge.

The promise of a networked global marketspace is that it enables the exchange of goods, services, and information from companies *anywhere* to customers *anywhere* at *any time* and at a lower cost. This promise has become a reality for buyers and sellers in industrialized countries that possess the telecommunications infrastructure necessary to support Internet technology. In particular, companies engaged in business-to-business marketing have spurred the growth of global electronic commerce.[15] Ninety percent of global electronic commerce revenue arises from business-to-business transactions among a dozen countries in North America, Western Europe, and the Asia/Pacific Rim region. Industries that have benefited from this technology include industrial chemicals and controls; maintenance, repair, and operating supplies; computer and electronic equipment and components; aerospace parts; and agricultural and energy products. The United States, Canada, United Kingdom, Germany, Sweden, Japan, India, China, and Taiwan are among the most active participants in worldwide business-to-business electronic commerce.

Marketers recognize that the networked global marketspace offers unprecedented access to prospective buyers on every continent. Companies that have successfully capitalized on this access manage multiple country and language websites that customize content and communicate with consumers in their native tongue. Nestlé, the world's largest packaged food manufacturer, coffee roaster, and chocolate maker, is a case in point. The company operates 65 individual country websites in more than 20 languages that span five continents.

learning review

3. What is protectionism?

4. The North American Free Trade Agreement was designed to promote free trade among which countries?

5. What is the difference between a multidomestic marketing strategy and a global marketing strategy?

A GLOBAL ENVIRONMENTAL SCAN

Global companies conduct continuing environmental scans of the five sets of environmental factors described earlier in Figure 3–1 (social, economic, technological, competitive, and regulatory forces). This section focuses on three kinds of uncontrollable environmental variables—cultural, economic, and political-regulatory—that affect global marketing practices in strikingly different ways than those in domestic markets.

Cultural Diversity

Marketers must be sensitive to the cultural underpinnings of different societies if they are to initiate and consummate mutually beneficial exchange relationships with global consumers. A necessary step in this process is **cross-cultural analysis**, which involves the study of similarities and differences among consumers in two or more nations or societies.[16] A thorough cross-cultural analysis involves an understanding of and an appreciation for the values, customs, symbols, and language of other societies.

Values A society's **values** represent personally or socially preferable modes of conduct or states of existence that tend to persist over time. Understanding and working with these aspects of a society are important factors in global marketing. For example,

- McDonald's does not sell beef hamburgers in its restaurants in India because the cow is considered sacred by almost 85 percent of the population. Instead, McDonald's sells the Maharaja Mac: two all-mutton patties, special sauce, lettuce, cheese, pickles, onions on a sesame-seed bun.
- Germans have not been overly receptive to the use of credit cards such as Visa or MasterCard and installment debt to purchase goods and services. Indeed, the German word for debt, *Schuld,* is the same as the German word for guilt.

These examples illustrate how cultural values can influence behavior in different societies. Cultural values become apparent in the personal values of individuals that affect their attitudes and beliefs and the importance assigned to specific behaviors and attributes of goods and services. These personal values affect consumption-specific values, such as the use of installment debt by Germans, and product-specific values, such as the importance assigned to credit card interest rates.

Customs **Customs** are what is considered normal and expected about the way people do things in a specific country. Clearly customs can vary significantly from country to country. For example, 3M Company executives were perplexed when the company's Scotch-Brite floor-cleaning product initially produced lukewarm sales in the Philippines. When a Filipino employee explained that consumers there customarily clean floors by pushing coconut shells around with their feet, 3M changed the shape of the pad to a foot and sales soared. Some other customs may seem unusual to Americans. Consider, for example, that in France, men wear more than twice the number of cosmetics that women do and that Japanese women give Japanese men chocolates on Valentine's Day.

Cultural symbols evoke deep feelings. What cultural lesson did Coca-Cola executives learn when they used the Eiffel Tower and the Parthenon in a global advertising campaign? Read the text to find the answer.

The custom of giving token business gifts is popular in many countries where they are expected and accepted.[17] However, bribes, kickbacks, and payoffs offered to entice someone to commit an illegal or improper act on behalf of the giver for economic gain is considered corrupt in any culture. The prevalence of bribery in global marketing has led to an agreement among the world's major exporting nations to make bribery of foreign government officials a criminal offense. This agreement is patterned after the **Foreign Corrupt Practices Act (1977)**, as amended by the *International Anti-Dumping and Fair Competition Act* (1998). These acts make it a crime for U.S. corporations to bribe an official of a foreign government or political party to obtain or retain business in a foreign country. Bribery paid to foreign companies is another matter. In France and Greece, bribes paid to foreign companies are a tax-deductible expense!

Customs also relate to nonverbal behavior of individuals in different cultural settings. The story is told of U.S. executives negotiating a purchase agreement with their Japanese counterparts. The chief American negotiator made a proposal that was met with silence by the Japanese head negotiator. The American assumed the offer was not acceptable and raised the offer, which again was met with silence. A third offer was made, and an agreement was struck. Unknown to the American, the silence of the Japanese head negotiator meant that the offer was being considered, not rejected. The Japanese negotiator obtained several concessions from the American because of a misreading of silence. Unlike U.S. businesspeople, who tend to express opinions early in meetings and negotiations, Japanese executives prefer to wait and listen. The higher their position, such as chief negotiator, the more they listen.[18]

Cultural Symbols   **Cultural symbols** are things that represent ideas and concepts. Symbols and symbolism play an important role in cross-cultural analysis because different cultures attach different meanings to things. So important is the role of symbols that a field of study, called **semiotics**, has emerged that examines the correspondence between symbols and their role in the assignment of meaning for people. By adroitly using cultural symbols, global marketers can tie positive symbolism to their products, services, and brands to enhance their attractiveness to consumers. However, improper use of symbols can spell disaster. A culturally sensitive global marketer will know that[19]

- North Americans are superstitious about the number 13, and Japanese feel the same way about the number 4. *Shi,* the Japanese word for four, is also the word for death. Knowing this, Tiffany & Company sells its fine glassware and china in sets of five, not four, in Japan.
- "Thumbs-up" is a positive sign in the United States. However, in Russia and Poland, this gesture has an offensive meaning when the palm of the hand is

In Canada, all packages and labels must be printed in both English and French, and most major companies also run their ads in both languages. Here are both the English and French versions of a service ad for Hewlett-Packard. The company's website is multilingual too.

Hewlett-Packard
www.hp.com

shown, as AT&T learned. The company reversed the gesture depicted in ads, showing the back of the hand, not the palm.

Cultural symbols evoke deep feelings. Consider how executives at Coca-Cola Company's Italian office learned this lesson. In a series of advertisements directed at Italian vacationers, the Eiffel Tower, Empire State Building, and the Tower of Pisa were turned into the familiar Coca-Cola bottle. However, when the white marble columns in the Parthenon that crowns the Acropolis in Athens were turned into Coca-Cola bottles, the Greeks were outraged. Greeks refer to the Acropolis as the "holy rock," and a government official said the Parthenon is an "international symbol of excellence" and that "whoever insults the Parthenon insults international culture." Coca-Cola apologized for the ad.[20]

Global marketers are also sensitive to the fact that the country of origin or manufacture of products and services can symbolize superior or poor quality in some countries. For example, Russian consumers believe products made in Japan and Germany are superior in quality to products from the United States and the United Kingdom. Japanese consumers believe Japanese products are superior to those made in Europe and the United States. About half of Americans say the quality of products from Asia is not as good as products made in the United States.[21]

Language Global marketers should not only know the native tongues of countries in which they market their products and services but also the nuances and idioms of a language. Even though about 100 official languages exist in the world, anthropologists estimate that at least 3,000 different languages are spoken. There are 20 official languages spoken in the European Union, and Canada has two official languages (English and French). Seventeen major languages are spoken in India alone.

English, French, and Spanish are the principal languages used in global diplomacy and commerce. However, the best language to communicate with consumers is their own, as any seasoned global marketer will attest to. Unintended meanings of brand names and messages have ranged from the absurd to the obscene:

- When the advertising agency responsible for launching Procter & Gamble's successful Pert shampoo in Canada realized that the name means "lost" in French, it substituted the brand name Pret, which means "ready."

What does the Nestlé Kit Kat bar have to do with academic achievement in Japan? Read the text to find out.

Nestlé Company
www.nestle.com

- In Italy, Cadbury Schweppes, the world's third-largest soft-drink manufacturer, realized that its Schweppes Tonic Water brand had to be renamed Schweppes Tonica because "il water" turned out to be the idiom for a bathroom.
- The Vicks brand name common in the United States is German slang for sexual intimacy; therefore, Vicks is called Wicks in Germany.

Experienced global marketers use **back translation**, where a translated word or phrase is retranslated into the original language by a different interpreter to catch errors. For example, IBM's first Japanese translation of its "Solution for a small planet" advertising message yielded "Answers that make people smaller." The error was caught and corrected. Nevertheless, unintended translations can produce favorable results. Consider Kit Kat bars marketed by Nestlé worldwide. Kit Kat is pronounced "kitto katsu" in Japanese, which roughly translates to "I hope you win." Japanese teens eat Kit Kat bars for good luck, particularly when taking crucial school exams.[22]

The importance of language in global marketing is assuming greater importance in an increasingly networked and borderless economic world. For example, Oracle Corporation, a leading worldwide supplier of software, markets its products by language groups instead of through 145 country-specific efforts. The French group markets to France, Belgium, Switzerland, and Canada. A Spanish-language group oversees Spain and Latin America. Eight other language groups—English, Japanese, Korean, Chinese, Portuguese, Italian, Dutch, and German—cover Oracle's top revenue-producing countries.[23]

Cultural Ethnocentricity   The tendency for people to view their own values, customs, symbols, and language favorably is well-known. However, the belief that aspects of one's culture are superior to another's is called *cultural ethnocentricity* and is a sure impediment to successful global marketing.

An outgrowth of cultural ethnocentricity exists in the purchase and use of goods and services produced outside of a country. Global marketers are acutely aware that certain groups within countries disfavor imported products, not on the basis of price, features, or performance, but purely because of their foreign origin. **Consumer ethnocentrism** is the tendency to believe that it is inappropriate, indeed immoral, to purchase foreign-made products.[24] Ethnocentric consumers believe that buying imported products is wrong because such purchases are unpatriotic, harm domestic industries, and cause domestic unemployment. Consumer ethnocentrism has been observed among a segment of the population in the United States, France, Japan, Korea, and Germany as well as other parts of Europe and Asia. The prevalence of consumer ethnocentrism makes the job of global marketers more difficult.[25]

Economic Considerations

Global marketing is also affected by economic considerations. Therefore, a scan of the global marketplace should include (1) a comparative analysis of the economic development in different countries, (2) an assessment of the economic infrastructure in these countries, (3) measurement of consumer income in different countries, and (4) recognition of a country's currency exchange rates.

Stage of Economic Development   There are about 260 countries in the world today, each of which is at a slightly different point in terms of its stage of economic development. However, they can be classified into two major groupings that will help the global marketer better understand their needs:

- *Developed* countries have somewhat mixed economies. Private enterprise dominates, although they have substantial public sectors as well. The United States, Canada, Japan, and most of Western Europe can be considered developed.
- *Developing* countries are in the process of moving from an agricultural to an industrial economy. There are two subgroups within the developing category: (1) those that have already made the move and (2) those that remain locked

in a preindustrial economy. Countries such as Brazil, Poland, Hungary, India, China, Slovenia, Australia, Israel, Venezuela, and South Africa fall into the first group. In the second group are Afghanistan, Sri Lanka, Ethiopia, Tanzania, and Chad, where living standards are low and improvement will be slow.

About 86 percent of the world's population of roughly 6.8 billion people reside in developing countries on one-fifth of total world income. Four billion of these people live on less than $2 per day. In global marketing terms, they are viewed as being at the **bottom of the pyramid**, which is the largest, but poorest socioeconomic group of people in the world.[26]

Today, global companies are choosing to serve people at the bottom of the pyramid by being responsive to their conditions and needs. Motorola is an example. The company developed a low-cost cell phone with battery life as long as 500 hours for rural villagers without regular electricity and an extra-loud volume for use in noisy markets. Motorola's cell phone, a no-frills design priced at $40, has a standby time of two weeks and conforms to local languages and customs. Motorola has been successful selling this cell phone design in rural areas across China, India, and Turkey. Still, the task facing global marketers is not easy. A country's stage of economic development affects and is affected by other economic factors, as described next.

Economic Infrastructure   The *economic infrastructure*—a country's communications, transportation, financial, and distribution systems—is a critical consideration in determining whether to try to market to a country's consumers and organizations. Parts of the infrastructure that North Americans or Western Europeans take for granted can be huge problems elsewhere—not only in developing nations but even in Eastern Europe, the Indian subcontinent, and China where such an infrastructure is assumed to be in place.[27] Two-lane roads outside major urban centers that limit average speeds to 35 to 40 miles per hour are commonplace and a nightmare for firms requiring prompt truck delivery in these countries. In China, the bicycle is the preferred mode of transportation. This is understandable because China has few navigable roads outside its major cities where 80 percent of the population lives. In India, Coca-Cola uses large tricycles to distribute cases of Coke along narrow streets in many cities. Wholesale and retail institutions tend to be small, and a majority are operated by new owner–managers in many of these countries who are still learning the ways of a free market system.

The communication infrastructures in these countries also differ. This infrastructure includes telecommunication systems and networks in use, such as telephones, cable

The Coca-Cola Company has made a huge financial investment in bottling and distribution facilities in Russia.

The Coca-Cola Company
www.thecoca-colacompany.com

television, broadcast radio and television, computer, satellite, and wireless telephone. In general, the communication infrastructure in many developing countries is limited or antiquated compared with that of developed countries.

Even the financial and legal system can cause problems. Formal operating procedures among financial institutions and the notion of private property is still limited. As a consequence, for example, it is estimated that two-thirds of the commercial transactions in Russia involve nonmonetary forms of payment. The legal red tape involved in obtaining titles to buildings and land for manufacturing, wholesaling, and retailing operations also has been a huge problem. Nevertheless, the Coca-Cola Company invested $750 million from 1991 through 1998 to build bottling and distribution facilities in Russia, Frito-Lay spent $60 million to build a plant to make Lay's potato chips, and Mars opened a $200 million candy factory outside Moscow.

Consumer Income and Purchasing Power A global marketer selling consumer goods must also consider what the average per capita or household income is among a country's consumers and how the income is distributed to determine a nation's purchasing power. Per capita income varies greatly between nations. Average yearly per capita income in EU countries is about $30,000 and is less than $150 in some developing countries such as Liberia. A country's income distribution is important because it gives a more reliable picture of a country's purchasing power. Generally, as the proportion of middle-income households in a country increases, the greater a nation's purchasing power tends to be.

Figure 7–5 shows the worldwide disparity in the percentage distribution of households by level of purchasing power. In established market economies such as those in North America and Western Europe, 65 percent of households have an annual

FIGURE 7–5

Purchasing power differs around the world. Clear differences exist in household purchasing power around the world. This figure shows that 65 percent of households in established market economies, such as those in North America and Western Europe, have an annual purchasing power of $20,000 or more. By comparison, 75 percent of households in South Asia and Sub-Saharan Africa have a purchasing power less than $5,000.

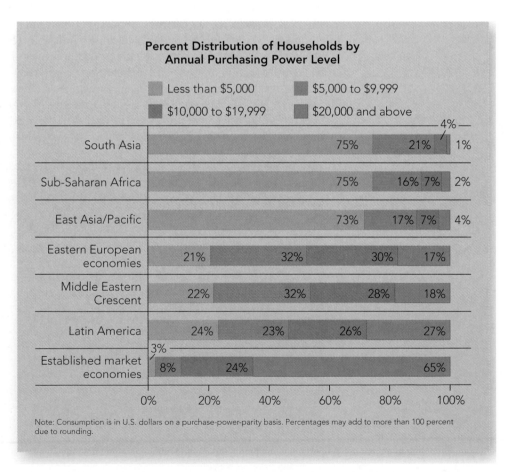

Note: Consumption is in U.S. dollars on a purchase-power-parity basis. Percentages may add to more than 100 percent due to rounding.

purchasing capability of $20,000 or more. In comparison, 75 percent of households in the developing countries of Sub-Saharan Africa have an annual purchasing power of less than $5,000.[28]

Seasoned global marketers recognize that people in developing countries often have government subsidies for food, housing, and health care that supplement their income. So people with seemingly low incomes are actually promising customers for a variety of products. For instance, a consumer in South Asia earning the equivalent of $250 per year can afford Gillette razors. When that consumer's income rises to $1,000, a Sony television becomes affordable, and a new Volkswagen or Nissan can be bought with an annual income of $10,000. In developing countries of Eastern Europe, a $1,000 annual income makes a refrigerator affordable, and $2,000 brings an automatic washer within reach—good news for Whirlpool, the world's leading manufacturer and marketer of major home appliances.

Efforts to raise household incomes in developing countries is evident in the growing popularity of microfinance. **Microfinance** is the practice of offering small, collateral-free loans to individuals who otherwise would not have access to the capital necessary to begin small businesses or other income-generating activities. An example of microfinance is found in Hindustan Lever's initiative in India. The company realized it could not sell to the rural poor in India unless it found ways to distribute its products such as soap, shampoos, and laundry detergents. Lever provided start-up loans to women to buy stocks of products to sell to local villagers. Today, about 1,300 poor women sell Lever products in 50,000 villages in India and account for about 15 percent of the company's rural sales in that country. Equally important, these women now have a source of income, whereas before they had nothing.[29]

Income growth in developing countries of Asia, Latin America, and Eastern Europe is expected to stimulate world trade well into the 21st century. The number of consumers in these countries earning the equivalent of $10,000 per year is expected to surpass the number of consumers in the United States, Japan, and Western Europe combined by 2015. For this reason, developing countries represent a prominent marketing opportunity for global companies.

Currency Exchange Rates   Fluctuations in exchange rates among the world's currencies are of critical importance in global marketing. Such fluctuations affect everyone, from international tourists to global companies.

A **currency exchange rate** is the price of one country's currency expressed in terms of another country's currency, such as the U.S. dollar expressed in Brazilian reals, Japanese yen, or Swiss francs. Failure to consider exchange rates when pricing products for global markets can have dire consequences. Mattel learned this lesson the hard way. The company was recently unable to sell its popular Holiday Barbie doll and accessories in some international markets because they were too expensive. Why? Barbie prices, expressed in U.S. dollars, were set without regard for how they would translate into foreign currencies and were too high for many buyers.[30]

Exchange rate fluctuations have a direct impact on the sales and profits made by global companies. When foreign currencies can buy more U.S. dollars, for example, U.S. products are less expensive for the foreign customer. This has been the case in recent years, and U.S. exports grew accordingly. Short-term fluctuations, however, can have a significant effect on the profits of global companies.[31] Hewlett-Packard recently gained nearly a half million dollars of additional profit through exchange rate fluctuation in one year. On the other hand, Honda recently lost $408 million on its European operations alone because of currency swings in the Japanese yen compared with the euro and British pound. Severe and protracted fluctuations in a country's currency can affect trade as well. For example, Procter & Gamble briefly suspended product shipments to Turkey, one of its largest export markets, because of instability of the Turkish currency.

Political-Regulatory Climate

The political and regulatory climate for marketing in a country or region of the world lies not only in identifying the current climate but in determining how long a favorable or unfavorable climate will last. An assessment of a country or regional political-regulatory climate includes an analysis of its political stability and trade regulations.

Political Stability Trade among nations or regions depends on political stability. Billions of dollars have been lost in the Middle East and Africa as a result of internal political strife, terrorism, and war. Losses such as these encourage careful selection of politically stable countries and regions of the world for trade.

Political stability in a country is affected by numerous factors, including a government's orientation toward foreign companies and trade with other countries. These factors combine to create a political climate that is favorable or unfavorable for marketing and financial investment in a country or region of the world. Marketing managers monitor political stability using a variety of measures and often track country risk ratings supplied by agencies such as the PRS Group. Visit the PRS Group website shown in the accompanying Going Online box to see political risk ratings for 140 countries. Expect to be surprised by the ranking of countries.

Trade Regulations Countries have a variety of rules that govern business practices within their borders. These rules often serve as trade barriers.[32] For example, Japan has some 11,000 trade regulations. Japanese car safety rules effectively require all automobile replacement parts to be Japanese and not American or European; public health rules make it illegal to sell aspirin or cold medicine without a pharmacist present. The Malaysian government has advertising regulations stating that "advertisements must not project or promote an excessively aspirational lifestyle," Greece bans toy advertising, Sweden outlaws all advertisements to children, and Saudi Arabia bans Mattel's Barbie dolls because they are a symbol of Western decadence.

Trade regulations also appear in free trade agreements among countries. EU nations abide by some 10,000 rules that specify how goods are to be made and marketed. For instance, the rules for a washing machine's electrical system are detailed on more than 100 typed pages. Regulations related to contacting consumers via telephone, fax, and e-mail without their prior consent also exist. The European Union's ISO 9000 quality standards, though not a trade regulation, have the same effect on business practice. These standards, described in Chapter 6, involve registration and certification of a manufacturer's quality management and quality assurance system. Many European companies require suppliers to be ISO 9000 certified as a condition of doing business with them. Certified companies have undergone an on-site audit that includes an inspection of its facilities to ensure that documented quality control procedures are in place and that all employees understand and follow them.

---

learning review

6. Semiotics involves the study of _____.

7. When foreign currencies can buy more U.S. dollars, are U.S. products more or less expensive for a foreign consumer?

COMPARING GLOBAL MARKET-ENTRY STRATEGIES

Once a company has decided to enter the global marketplace, it must select a means of market entry. Four general options exist: (1) exporting, (2) licensing, (3) joint venture, and (4) direct investment.[33] As Figure 7–6 demonstrates, the amount of financial commitment, risk, marketing control, and profit potential increases as the firm moves from exporting to direct investment.

Exporting

Exporting is producing goods in one country and selling them in another country. This entry option allows a company to make the least number of changes in terms of its product, its organization, and even its corporate goals. Host countries usually do not like this practice because it provides less local employment than under alternative means of entry.

FIGURE 7–6

A firm's profit potential and control over marketing activities increases as it moves from exporting to direct investment as a global market-entry strategy. But so does the firm's financial commitment and risk. Firms often engage in exporting, licensing, and joint ventures before pursuing a direct investment strategy.

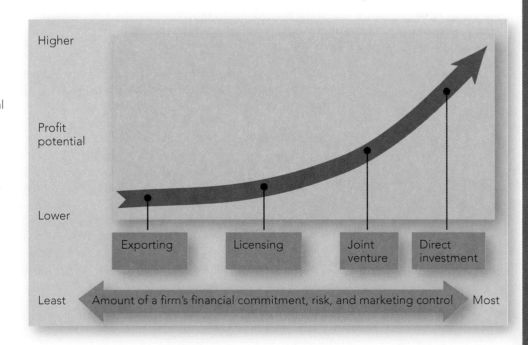

Marketing Matters > > > > entrepreneurship

Creative Cosmetics and Creative Export Marketing in Japan

How does a medium-sized U.S. cosmetics firm sell 1.5 million tubes of lipstick in Japan annually? Fran Wilson Creative Cosmetics can attribute its success to a top-quality product, effective advertising, and a novel export marketing program. The firm's Moodmatcher lip coloring comes in green, orange, silver, black, and six other hues that change to a shade of pink, coral, or red, depending on a woman's chemistry when it's applied.

The company does not sell to department stores. According to a company spokesperson, "Shiseido and Kanebo (two large Japanese cosmetics firms) keep all the other Japanese or import brands out of the major department stores." Rather, the company sells its Moodmatcher lipstick through a network of Japanese distributors that reach Japan's 40,000 beauty salons.

The result? The company, with its savvy Japanese distributors, accounts for 20 percent of the lipsticks exported annually to Japan by U.S. cosmetic companies.

Indirect exporting is when a firm sells its domestically produced goods in a foreign country through an intermediary. It has the least amount of commitment and risk but will probably return the least profit. Indirect exporting is ideal for a company that has no overseas contacts but wants to market abroad. The intermediary is often a distributer that has the marketing know-how and resources necessary for the effort to succeed. Fran Wilson Creative Cosmetics of New York uses an indirect exporting approach to sell its products in Japan. Read the accompanying Marketing Matters box to find out how this innovative marketer and its Japanese distributors sell 20 percent of the lipsticks exported to Japan by U.S. cosmetic companies.[34]

Direct exporting is when a firm sells its domestically produced goods in a foreign country without intermediaries. Most companies become involved in direct exporting when they believe their volume of sales will be sufficiently large and easy to obtain so that they do not require intermediaries. For example, the exporter may be approached by foreign buyers that are willing to contract for a large volume of purchases. Direct exporting involves more risk than indirect exporting for the company but also opens the door to increased profits. The Boeing Company applies a direct exporting approach. Boeing is the world's largest aerospace company and the largest U.S. exporter.

Even though exporting is commonly employed by large firms, it is the prominent global market-entry strategy among small- and medium-sized companies. For example, 60 percent of U.S. firms exporting products have fewer than 100 employees. These firms account for about 26 percent of total U.S. merchandise exports.[35]

Licensing

Under licensing, a company offers the right to a trademark, patent, trade secret, or other similarly valued items of intellectual property in return for a royalty or a fee.

McDonald's uses franchising as a market-entry strategy, and about 70 percent of the company's sales come from non-U.S. operations. Note that the golden arches appear prominently—one aspect of its global brand promise.

McDonald's
www.mcdonalds.com

Elite Food is a joint venture owned equally by Elite Industries Ltd. and PepsiCo. Elite Food markets Frito-Lay's Cheetos, Ruffles, and Doritos and other snacks in Israel.

Elite Food
www.elite.co.il

The advantages to the company granting the license are low risk and a capital-free entry into a foreign country. The licensee gains information that allows it to start with a competitive advantage, and the foreign country gains employment by having the product manufactured locally. For instance, Yoplait yogurt is licensed from Sodima, a French cooperative, by General Mills for sales in the United States.

There are some serious drawbacks to this mode of entry, however. The licensor forgoes control of its product and reduces the potential profits gained from it. In addition, while the relationship lasts, the licensor may be creating its own competition. Some licensees are able to modify the product somehow and enter the market with product and marketing knowledge gained at the expense of the company that got them started. To offset this disadvantage, many companies strive to stay innovative so that the licensee remains dependent on them for improvements and successful operation. Finally, should the licensee prove to be a poor choice, the name or reputation of the company may be harmed.

Two variations of licensing, *contract manufacturing* and *contract assembly,* represent alternative ways to produce a product within the foreign country. With contract manufacturing, a U.S. company may contract with a foreign firm to manufacture products according to stated specifications. The product is then sold in the foreign country or exported back to the United States. With contract assembly, the U.S. company may contract with a foreign firm to assemble (not manufacture) parts and components that have been shipped to that country. In both cases, the advantage to the foreign country is the employment of its people, and the U.S. firm benefits from the lower wage rates in the foreign country.

Contract manufacturing and assembly in developing countries has sparked controversy in the toy, textile, and apparel industries where poor working conditions, low pay, and child labor practices have been documented. However, this practice has been an economic boon to Taiwan where 55 percent of the world's notebook computers are made. In a typical year, U.S. companies such as Dell will have Taiwanese firms supply more than half of their notebook computer needs.[36]

A third variation of licensing is *franchising.* Franchising is one of the fastest-growing market-entry strategies. More than 75,000 franchises of U.S. firms are located in countries throughout the world. Franchises include soft-drink, motel, retailing, fast-food, and car rental operations and a variety of business services. McDonald's is a premier global franchiser. With some 23,000 units outside the United States, about 70 percent of McDonald's sales come from non-U.S. operations.[37]

Joint Venture

When a foreign company and a local firm invest together to create a local business, it is called a **joint venture**. These two companies share ownership, control, and profits of the new company. For example, Elite Food is a joint venture between Elite Industries and PepsiCo created to market Frito-Lay's Cheetos, Ruffles, and Doritos and other snacks in Israel.[38]

The advantages of this option are twofold. First, one company may not have the necessary financial, physical, or managerial resources to enter a foreign market alone. The joint venture between Ericsson, a Swedish telecommunications firm, and CGCT, a French switch maker, enabled them together to beat out AT&T for a $100 million French contract. Ericsson's

Nestlé has made a sizable direct investment in ice cream manufacturing in China to produce its global brands such as Drumstick. Nestlé operates 26 factories in China.

money and technology combined with CGCT's knowledge of the French market helped them to win the contract that neither of them could have won alone. Similarly, Ford and Volkswagen formed a joint venture to make four-wheel-drive vehicles in Portugal. Second, a government may require or strongly encourage a joint venture before it allows a foreign company to enter its market. This is the case in China. Today, more than 50,000 Chinese-foreign joint ventures operate in China.[39]

The disadvantages arise when the two companies disagree about policies or courses of action for their joint venture or when governmental bureaucracy bogs down the effort. For example, U.S. firms often prefer to reinvest earnings gained, whereas some foreign companies may want to spend those earnings. Or a U.S. firm may want to return profits earned to the United States, while the local firm or its government may oppose this—the problem faced by many potential joint ventures in Eastern Europe, Russia, Latin America, and South Asia.

Direct Investment

The biggest commitment a company can make when entering the global market is **direct investment**, which entails a domestic firm actually investing in and owning a foreign subsidiary or division. Examples of direct investment are Nissan's Smyrna, Tennessee, plant that produces pickup trucks and the Mercedes-Benz factory in Vance, Alabama, that makes the M-class sports utility vehicle. Many U.S.-based global companies also use this mode of entry. Reebok entered Russia by creating a subsidiary known as Reebok Russia.

For many companies, direct investment often follows one of the other three market-entry strategies.[40] For example, both FedEx and UPS entered China through joint ventures with Chinese companies. Each subsequently purchased the interests of its partner and converted the Chinese operations into a division. Following on the success of its European and Asian exporting strategy, Harley-Davidson now operates wholly owned marketing and sales subsidiaries in Germany, Italy, the United Kingdom, and Japan, among other countries.

The advantages to direct investment include cost savings, better understanding of local market conditions, and fewer local restrictions. Firms entering foreign markets using direct investment believe that these advantages outweigh the financial commitments and risks involved.

8. What mode of entry could a company follow if it has no previous experience in global marketing?

9. How does licensing differ from a joint venture?

CRAFTING A WORLDWIDE MARKETING PROGRAM

LO5

The choice of a market-entry strategy is a necessary first step for a marketer when joining the community of global companies. The next step involves the challenging task of designing, implementing, and controlling marketing programs worldwide.

Successful global marketers standardize global marketing programs whenever possible and customize them wherever necessary. The extent of standardization and customization is often rooted in a careful global environment scan supplemented with judgment based on experience and marketing research.

Product and Promotion Strategies

Global companies have five strategies for matching products and their promotion efforts to global markets. As Figure 7–7 shows, the strategies focus on whether a company extends or adapts its product and promotion message for consumers in different countries and cultures.

A product may be sold globally in one of three ways: (1) in the same form as in its home market, (2) with some adaptations, or (3) as a totally new product:[41]

1. *Product extension.* Selling virtually the same product in other countries is a product extension strategy. It works well for products such as Coca-Cola, Gillette razors, Wrigley's gum, Levi's jeans, Sony consumer electronics, Harley-Davidson motorcycles, Nike apparel and shoes, and Nokia cell phones. As a general rule, product extension seems to work best when the consumer market target for the product is alike across countries and cultures—that is, consumers share the same desires, needs, and uses for the product.
2. *Product adaptation.* Changing a product in some way to make it more appropriate for a country's climate or consumer preferences is a product adaptation strategy. Exxon sells different gasoline blends based on each country's

FIGURE 7–7

Five product and promotion strategies for global marketing exist based on whether a company extends or adapts its product and promotion message for consumers in different countries and cultures.

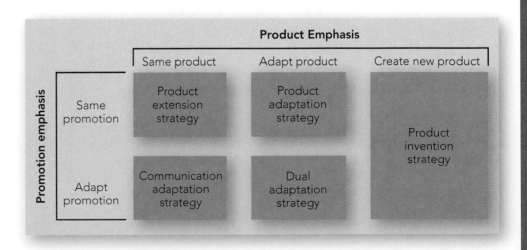

climate. Frito-Lay produces and markets its potato chips in Russia, but don't expect them to taste like the chips eaten in North America. Russians prefer dairy, meat, and seafood-flavored potato chips. Likewise, Gerber baby food comes in different varieties in different countries. Vegetable and rabbit meat is a favorite food in Poland. Freeze-dried sardines and rice is popular in Japan. Maybelline's makeup is formulaically adapted to local skin types and weather across the globe, including an Asia-specific mascara that doesn't run during the rainy season.

3. *Product invention.* Alternatively, companies can invent totally new products designed to satisfy common needs across countries. Black & Decker did this with its Snake Light Flexible Flashlight. Created to address a global need for portable lighting, the product became a best-seller in North America, Europe, Latin America, and Australia and is the most successful new product developed by Black & Decker. Similarly, Whirlpool developed a compact, automatic clothes washer specifically for households in developing countries with annual household incomes of $2,000. Called Ideale, the washer features bright colors because washers are often placed in home living areas, not hid in laundry rooms (which don't exist in many homes in developing countries). Demand for this product exceeded forecasts when it was introduced in Brazil, China, and India.

An identical promotion message is used for the product extension and product adaptation strategies around the world. Gillette uses the same global message for its men's toiletries: "Gillette, the Best a Man Can Get." Even though Exxon adapts its gasoline blends for different countries based on climate, the promotion message is unchanged: "Put a Tiger in Your Tank."

Global companies may also adapt their promotion message. For instance, the same product may be sold in many countries but advertised differently. As an example, L'Oréal, a French health and beauty products marketer, introduced its Golden Beauty brand of sun care products through its Helena Rubenstein subsidiary in Western Europe with a communication adaptation strategy. Recognizing that cultural and buying motive differences related to skin care and tanning exist, Golden Beauty advertising features dark tanning for northern Europeans, skin protection to avoid wrinkles among Latin Europeans, and beautiful skin for Europeans living along the Mediterranean Sea, even though the products are the same.

Gillette delivers the same global message whenever possible, as shown in the Gillette for Women Venus ads from Greece, Germany, and the United States.

The Gillette Company
www.gillette.com

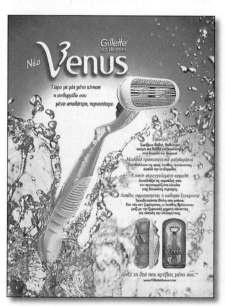
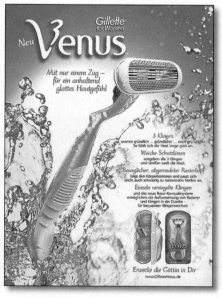
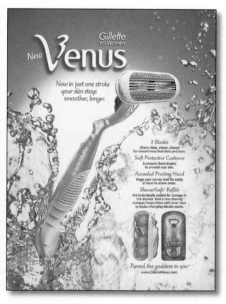

FIGURE 7–8

Channels of distribution in global marketing are often long and complex.

Other companies use a dual adaptation strategy by modifying both their products and promotion messages. Nestlé does this with Nescafé coffee. Nescafé is marketed using different coffee blends and promotional campaigns to match consumer preferences in different countries. For example, Nescafé, the world's largest brand of coffee, generally emphasizes the taste, aroma, and warmth of shared moments in its advertising around the world. However, Nescafé is advertised in Thailand as a way to relax from the pressures of daily life.

These examples illustrate the simple rule applied by global companies: Standardize product and promotion strategies whenever possible and customize them wherever necessary. This is the art of global marketing.[42]

Distribution Strategy

Distribution is of critical importance in global marketing. The availability and quality of retailers and wholesalers as well as transportation, communication, and warehousing facilities are often determined by a country's stage of economic development. Figure 7–8 outlines the channel through which a product manufactured in one country must travel to reach its destination in another country. The first step involves the seller; its headquarters is the starting point and is responsible for the successful distribution to the ultimate consumer.

The next step is the channel between two nations, moving the product from one country to another. Intermediaries that can handle this responsibility include resident buyers in a foreign country, independent merchant wholesalers who buy and sell the product, or agents who bring buyers and sellers together.

Once the product is in the foreign nation, that country's distribution channels take over.[43] These channels can be very long or surprisingly short, depending on the product line. In Japan, fresh fish go through three intermediaries before getting to a retail outlet. Conversely, shoes only go through one intermediary. In other cases, the channel does not even involve the host country. Procter & Gamble sells its soap door to door in the Philippines because there are no other alternatives in many parts of that country. The sophistication of a country's distribution channels increases as its economic infrastructure develops. Supermarkets facilitate selling products in many nations, but they are not popular or available in many others where culture and lack of refrigeration dictate shopping on a daily rather than a weekly basis. When Coke and Pepsi entered China, both had to create direct-distribution channels, investing in refrigerator units for small retailers.

Pricing Strategy

Global companies also face many challenges in determining a pricing strategy as part of their worldwide marketing effort. Individual countries, even those with free trade agreements, may impose considerable competitive, political, and legal constraints on the pricing latitude of global companies. For example, antitrust authorities in Germany limited Wal-Mart from selling some items below cost to lure shoppers.

Without the practice, Wal-Mart was unable to compete against German discount stores. This, and other factors, led Wal-Mart to leave Germany in 2006 following eight years without a profit.[44] Of course, economic factors such as the costs of production, selling, and tariffs, plus transportation and storage costs, also affect global pricing decisions.

Pricing too low or too high can have dire consequences. When prices appear too low in one country, companies can be charged with dumping, a practice subject to severe penalties and fines. **Dumping** is when a firm sells a product in a foreign country below its domestic price or below its actual cost. This is often done to build a company's share of the market by pricing at a competitive level. Another reason is that the products being sold may be surplus or cannot be sold domestically and, therefore, are already a burden to the company. The firm may be glad to sell them at almost any price. A recent trade dispute involving U.S. apple growers and Mexico is a case in point. Mexican trade officials claimed that U.S. growers were selling their red and golden delicious apples in Mexico below the actual cost of production. They imposed a 101 percent tariff on U.S. apples, and a severe drop in U.S. apple exports to Mexico resulted. Subsequent negotiations set a price floor on the price of U.S. apples sold to Mexico.[45]

When companies price their products very high in some countries but competitively in others, they face a gray market problem. A **gray market**, also called *parallel importing,* is a situation where products are sold through unauthorized channels of distribution.[46] A gray market comes about when individuals buy products in a lower-priced country from a manufacturer's authorized retailer, ship them to higher-priced countries, and then sell them below the manufacturer's suggested retail price through unauthorized retailers. Many well-known products have been sold through gray markets, including Olympus cameras, Seiko watches, Chanel perfume, and Mercedes-Benz cars. Parallel importing is legal in the United States. It is illegal in the European Union.

---

learning review

10. Products may be sold globally in three ways. What are they?

11. What is dumping?

LEARNING OBJECTIVES REVIEW

LO1 *Describe the nature and scope of world trade from a global perspective and its implications for the United States.*
A global perspective on world trade views exports and imports as complementary economic flows: A country's imports affect its exports and exports affect its imports. World trade flows to and from the United States reflect demand and supply interdependencies for goods among nations and industries. The four largest importers of U.S. goods and services are Canada, China, Mexico, and Japan. The four largest exporters to the United States are Canada, China, Mexico, and Japan. The United States imports more goods than it exports.

LO2 *Identify the major trends that have influenced the landscape of global marketing in the past decade.*
Four major trends have influenced the landscape of global marketing in the past decade. First, there has been a gradual decline of economic protectionism by individual countries, leading to a reduction in tariffs and quotas. Second, there is growing economic integration and free trade among nations, reflected in the creation of the European Union and the North American Free Trade Agreement. Third, there exists global competition among global companies for global consumers, resulting in firms adopting global marketing strategies and promoting global brands. And finally, a networked global marketspace has emerged using Internet technology as a tool for exchanging goods, services, and information on a global scale.

LO3 *Identify the environmental factors that shape global marketing efforts.*
Three major environmental factors shape global marketing efforts. First, there are cultural factors, including values, customs, cultural symbols, and language. Economic factors also shape global marketing efforts. These include a country's stage of economic development and economic infrastructure, consumer income and purchasing power, and currency exchange rates. Finally, political-regulatory factors in a country or region of the world create a favorable or unfavorable climate for global marketing efforts.

LO4 *Name and describe the alternative approaches companies use to enter global markets.*

Companies have four alternative approaches for entering global markets. These are exporting, licensing, joint venture, and direct investment. Exporting involves producing goods in one country and selling them in another country. Under licensing, a company offers the right to a trademark, patent, trade secret, or similarly valued items of intellectual property in return for a royalty or fee. In a joint venture, a foreign company and a local firm invest together to create a local business. Direct investment entails a domestic firm actually investing in and owning a foreign subsidiary or division.

LO5 *Explain the distinction between standardization and customization when companies craft worldwide marketing programs.*

Companies distinguish between standardization and customization when crafting worldwide marketing programs. Standardization means that all elements of the marketing program are the same across countries and cultures. Customization means that one or more elements of the marketing program are adapted to meet the needs or preferences of consumers in a particular country or culture. Global marketers apply a simple rule when crafting worldwide marketing programs: Standardize marketing programs whenever possible and customize them wherever necessary.

FOCUSING ON KEY TERMS

back translation p. 180
balance of trade p. 167
bottom of the pyramid p. 181
consumer ethnocentrism p. 180
countertrade p. 166
cross-cultural analysis p. 177
cultural symbols p. 178
currency exchange rate p. 183
customs p. 177
direct investment p. 188
dumping p. 192

Economic Espionage Act (1996) p. 169
exporting p. 185
Foreign Corrupt Practices Act (1977) p. 178
global brand p. 175
global competition p. 173
global consumers p. 175
global marketing strategy p. 174
gray market p. 192
gross domestic product p. 167
joint venture p. 187

microfinance p. 183
multidomestic marketing strategy p. 174
protectionism p. 170
quota p. 171
semiotics p. 178
strategic alliances p. 173
tariffs p. 170
values p. 177
World Trade Organization p. 171

APPLYING MARKETING KNOWLEDGE

1 What is meant by this statement: "Quotas are a hidden tax on consumers, whereas tariffs are a more obvious one"?

2 Is the trade feedback effect described in the text a long-run or short-run view on world trade flows? Explain your answer.

3 The United States is considered to be a global leader in the development and marketing of pharmaceutical products, and Merck & Co. of New Jersey is a world leader in prescription drug sales. What explanation can you give for this situation based on the text discussion concerning the competitive advantage of nations?

4 How successful would a television commercial in Japan be if it featured a husband surprising his wife in her dressing area on Valentine's Day with a small box of chocolates containing four candies? Why?

5 As a novice in global marketing, which alternative for global market-entry strategy would you be likely to start with? Why? What other alternatives do you have for a global market entry?

6 Coca-Cola is sold worldwide. In some countries, Coca-Cola owns the bottling facilities; in others, it has signed contracts with licensees or relies on joint ventures. When selecting a licensee in each country, what factors should Coca-Cola consider?

building your marketing plan

Does your marketing plan involve reaching global customers outside the United States? If the answer is no, read no further and do not include a global element in your plan.

If the answer is yes, try to identify:

1 What features of your product are especially important to potential customers.

2 In which countries these potential customers live.

3 Special marketing issues that are involved in trying to reach them.

Answers to these questions will help in developing more detailed marketing mix strategies described in later chapters.

"It's naive to treat 'international' as one big market—particularly within OTC," explains Marti Morfitt, president and CEO of CNS, the company that manufactures Breathe Right® nasal strips. "There are many discrete, unique markets, and local expertise is needed to understand the dynamics within each and address them effectively."

"OTC" refers to over-the-counter medical products like aspirin or cough syrup that customers can buy without a doctor's prescription. Breathe Right nasal strips qualify as an OTC product. But that doesn't mean there isn't a lot of technology and medical science behind it.

Breathe Right nasal strips are innovative adhesive strips with patented dual flex bars inside. When attached to the nose, they gently lift and hold open nasal passages, making it easier to breathe. Breathe Right strips are used for a variety of reasons, all to help breathe better through the nose: athletes hoping to play their best (particularly when wearing mouth guards); snorers (and their spouses) hoping for a quiet night's sleep; and allergy, sinusitis, and cold sufferers looking for drug-free relief from nasal congestion.

HOW IT ALL BEGAN

Breathe Right strips were invented by Bruce Johnson, a chronic nasal congestion sufferer. At times Johnson put straws or paper clips in his nose at night to keep his nasal passages open. He eventually came up with a prototype for Breathe Right strips. He brought his invention to CNS, Inc., which recognized its market potential. CNS took the strips to the Food and Drug Administration for approval of claims for relief of snoring and nasal congestion.

CNS, a small company, had a limited marketing budget. However, it got a big public relations break when Jerry Rice, the wide receiver for the San Francisco 49ers, wore a Breathe Right strip on national TV and scored two touchdowns during the 49ers' 1995 Super Bowl victory. Demand for the strips soared.

"What really helped sales of Breathe Right strips was that CNS had done a very effective job of getting press kits in the hands of news and sports media," says Morfitt. "When people on television asked, 'What is that funny looking thing on his nose?' the reporters could talk about how the strip was an effective consumer product for everyone. And a $1.4 million business turned into a $45 million business in just one year," she explains.

THE DECISION TO GO GLOBAL

As awareness and trial in the United States was building, CNS began to get inquiries from people in other countries asking where they could buy strips. In 1995 CNS decided to take advantage of global interest and introduce Breathe Right strips internationally.

What countries did CNS choose to enter with its Breathe Right strips? "Countries we focus on are those with a large OTC market, high per-capita spending in the OTC market, and future prospects for growth," says Kevin McKenna, vice president for international at CNS. All these factors relate to market size. "But the real key to success in a market is a local partner that is entrepreneurial and has an ability to execute in terms of achieving distribution and sales."

IMPORTANCE OF LOCAL PARTNERS

Dynamic world market changes in the last 30 years have influenced opportunities for global sales of Breathe Right strips. Key trends include increased availability of OTC products formerly available only by prescription; and a global push toward self-care, spurred by the increasing cost of health and medical care. Additionally, OTC products have extended beyond the traditional boundary of the pharmacy and into grocery and other channels; and the role of the pharmacist has expanded from that of medical professional to one that includes selling and marketing OTC products to consumers.

At the same time, changes were taking place within CNS. When Morfitt joined CNS in 1998, she began pulling together a new management group with extensive experience in marketing consumer packaged goods, both in the United States and abroad. CNS began seeking "hungry" international partners who would bring greater localized market expertise and direct-selling capabilities than past partners. Morfitt also wanted partners with demonstrated entrepreneurial spirit to match that of the new management team.

The company's partner in Italy, BluFarm Group, uses its local knowledge and direct-selling skills to partner with pharmacists to teach them how to increase sales of Breathe Right strips in their stores. In Italy, as throughout much of Europe, OTC products such as antacids, aspirin, and nasal strips are typically placed behind pharmacy counters and therefore not visible to customers. The only way to sell a product is for a customer to ask for it by name. BluFarm Group recognized the importance of in-store advertising and sales execution to build awareness and created point-of-sale materials such as window and counter displays to let customers know that Breathe Right strips were available in the store. "BluFarm's ability to capture consumers' awareness of Breathe Right strips as they walk in the retailer's door has beneficial results for CNS, BluFarm, pharmacists, and consumers," says McKenna.

"Working with an experienced local partner helps overcome surprises in global markets," says Nick Naumann, senior marketing communications manager at CNS. One surprise: universal product codes (UPC) on packaging aren't "universal"—they are used only in the United States and Canada. "Different forms of those codes in other countries can take a few weeks to six months or more of government review to obtain," he says.

Even the same packaging colors don't work around the globe. Research with U.S. consumers revealed they wanted darker packaging to suggest the strips' use at night by snorers and those with stuffed noses. "'Too grim and negative' Asian and European consumers told us," says Naumann. Breathe Right strips in those countries have a lighter, airier look than in the United States to convey the open feeling one gets from the nasal strips.

MANAGING GLOBAL GROWTH

Today, Breathe Right strips are sold in more than 25 countries. To ensure the Breathe Right brand continues to meet growth expectations, CNS now uses a three-stage approach to penetrate and develop new markets:

- Stage 1: Explore/test the concept.
  —Use screening criteria to identify high-potential markets.

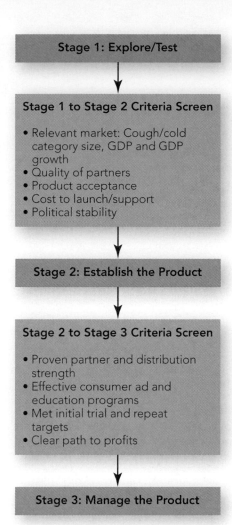

- —Identify potential partners.
- —Validate concept with research.
- —Develop strategy and launch test market.
- Stage 2: Establish the product.
  —Penetrate the marketplace.
  —Refine messages for local market.
  —Evaluate partnership and marketing strategies.
- Stage 3: Manage the product.
  —Achieve sustainability/ profitability.
  —Exploit new product and new use opportunities.

Overall, this approach starts with what works in the United States and extends it into new markets, paying close attention to local needs and customs. Throughout the three stages CNS conducts market research and makes financial projections.

As shown in the figure, at each stage of the market development process, performance must be met for the product to enter the next stage. Once success with Breathe Right nasal strips is established in a country, the groundwork is laid and international partners have the ability to introduce other Breathe Right products.

LOOKING FORWARD

"We believe the Breathe Right brand has great potential, both domestically and around the world," says Morfitt. "Growth will come both from further expansion of Breathe Right nasal strips and from other drug-free, better-breathing line extensions," says Morfitt.

Questions

1 What are the advantages and disadvantages for CNS taking Breathe Right strips into international markets?

2 What are the advantages to CNS of (a) using its three-stage process to enter new global markets and (b) having specific criteria to move through the stages?

3 Using the CNS criteria, with what you know, which countries should have highest priority for CNS?

4 Which single segment of potential Breathe Right strip users would you target to enter new markets?

5 Which marketing mix variables should CNS emphasize the most to succeed in a global arena? Why?

8

Marketing Research: From Customer Insights to Actions

TEST SCREENINGS: LISTENING TO CONSUMERS TO REDUCE MOVIE RISKS

Spider-Man 3. Pirates of the Caribbean: At World's End. Shrek The Third. Harry Potter and the Order of the Phoenix. Ocean's Thirteen. For studios engaged in the fiercely competitive world of filmmaking, these blockbuster movies premiered in 2007—the year of the sequel.[1]

What's in a Movie Name?

Consider *Shoeless Joe* and *Rope Burns*, two original, stand-alone movies of the recent past that were hugely successful. Don't remember these two movies? Well, test screenings—a form of marketing research—found that moviegoers like you had problems with these titles. Here's what happened:

- *Shoeless Joe* became *Field of Dreams* because audiences thought Kevin Costner might be playing a homeless person.

- *Rope Burns* became *Million Dollar Baby* because audiences didn't like the original name. The movie won the 2005 Academy Award™ for Best Picture and starred Hilary Swank as a woman boxer and Clint Eastwood as her trainer.

Filmmakers want movie titles that are concise, grab attention, capture the essence of the film, and have no legal restrictions to reduce risk to both the studio and audiences—the same factors that make a good brand name.[2]

The Risks in Today's Blockbuster Movies

Bad titles, poor scripts, temperamental stars who stomp off the set, costly special effects, and several blockbuster movies released at the same time are just some of the nightmares faced by movie producers. Today's films average more than $100 million to produce and market.[3] To recoup these staggering costs, movies must (1) appeal to both U.S. and international audiences, which now account for the majority of a movie's gross ticket sales, and (2) generate a significant portion of their revenues from DVD sales or rentals (via Blockbuster or Netflix) and digital downloads (from Apple's iTunes Store).[4]

So some studios try to reduce their new-movie gambles by creating a multiple-episode film series, such as *Spider-Man*, *Pirates*, *Shrek*, *Harry Potter*, and the most anticipated adventure sequel in 20 years: *Indiana Jones*. And some, like the producers of *Shrek*, now stagger the global release dates to coincide with school holidays in local countries instead of premiering their movies on the same day as the U.S. launch.[5]

REVENGE IS A FUNNY THING

GEORGE CLOONEY / BRAD PITT / MATT DAMON / ANDY GARCIA / DON CHEADLE / BERNIE MAC / ELLEN BARKIN AND AL PACINO

OCEAN'S THIRTEEN

COMING SOON

A look at movie risks! Shooting a sequel doesn't guarantee a movie's success. For a look at both the benefits and dangers of movie sequels, see the text.

But there are hidden dangers. For example, will the key actors be available if the studio wants to produce an Ocean's Fourteen? Or as Harry Potter or Indiana Jones age, will their characters still be sufficiently credible that moviegoers will buy tickets or DVDs? Daniel Radcliffe, who plays Harry Potter, will be 21 years old when the final *Harry Potter and the Deathly Hallows* goes into production in 2010, while 65-years-"young" Harrison Ford, who reprises his role as archeologist Dr. Indiana Jones, "will perform only those actions suitable to his age" in his 2007 sequel.[6] Also, shooting two or more sequels at a time may save production costs but increase marketing risk. For example, much of *Pirates 3* was shot simultaneously with *Pirates 2*.[7] However, if audiences hadn't liked *Pirates 2*, then *Pirates 3* could have been a financial disaster for the studio.

The mega-million-dollar question is: Will the studios recoup the estimated $200+ million production and marketing costs for the recent (and future?) sequels of *Spider-Man* and *Pirates*?[8] They hope so, given that the second sequels of both movies grossed over $750 million worldwide and are presently among the top 20 movies of all time—that is, until the sales of their third and other future sequels, such as *Indiana Jones* and *Harry Potter*, are finally tallied.[9]

Using Marketing Research to Reduce Movie Risk

Is research on movie titles and content expensive? Very! But the greater expense is selecting a bad title that can kill a movie and cost the studio millions of dollars. So movie studios use market research to reduce their risk of losses by hiring firms such as the National Research Group to conduct test screenings and tracking studies.

For test screenings, 300 to 400 prospective moviegoers are recruited to attend a "sneak preview" of a film before its release. After viewing the movie, the audience fills out an exhaustive survey to critique the title, plot, characters, music, and ending as well as the marketing program (posters, trailers, etc.) to identify improvements to make in the final edit of the movie.[10]

Without reading ahead, think about the answers to these questions:

- Whom would you recruit for movie test screenings?

- What questions would you ask to help you edit or modify the title or other aspects of a film?

Virtually every major U.S. movie produced today uses test screenings to obtain the key reactions of consumers likely to be in the target audience. Test screenings resulted in *Fatal Attraction* having probably the most commercially successful "ending-switch" of all time. In its sneak previews, audiences liked everything but the ending, which had Alex (Glenn Close) committing suicide and managing to frame Dan (Michael Douglas) as her murderer by leaving his fingerprints on the knife she used. The studio shot $1.3 million of new scenes for the ending that audiences eventually saw.[11]

Figure 8–1 summarizes some key questions used in these test screenings, both to select the people for the screenings and to obtain key reactions of those sitting in the screenings. Note how specific the studio's action is for each question asked, like change the title or ending. This is an example of effective, action-oriented marketing research.

The switch in endings for *Fatal Attraction* that resulted from test screenings reduced the studio's risk and undoubtedly contributed to the movie's

POINT WHEN ASKED	KEY QUESTIONS	ACTION AND USE OF QUESTION
Before the test screening	• How old are you? • How frequently do you pay to see movies?	• Find people who fit profile of target audience for movie. • Find people who frequently attend movies.
After the test screening	• What do you think of the title? What title would you suggest? • Were there any characters too distasteful? Who? How? • Did you like the ending? If not, how would you change it? • Would you recommend the movie to a friend?	• Change movie title. • Change aspects of some characters. • Change or clarify ending. • Overall indicator of liking and/or satisfaction with movie.

FIGURE 8–1

Marketing research questions asked in test screenings of movies. Note each kind of question leads to a specific action—a characteristic of effective marketing research.

box-office success. But even good marketing research can't guarantee success. Test screenings caused the studio to shoot a new ending for Jennifer Lopez and Ben Affleck in *Gigli*. Audiences hated that Ben Affleck's character died in the original ending, which they felt was too dark and inconsistent with the rest of the movie. The reshoot wasn't enough. Besides being a disaster at the box office, *Gigli* was nominated for "worst picture" and eight other "Razzies," the highest-profile bad-movie anti-Oscars given by voters of the Golden Raspberry Awards.[12]

Movie studios also use tracking studies, in which prospective moviegoers in the target audience are asked three key questions about an upcoming film release:[13]

- Are you aware of a particular film?

- Are you interested in seeing it?

- Would it be your first choice on a certain weekend?

Studios then use the data collected to forecast the movie's opening weekend box office sales; if necessary, they run last-minute ads to increase its awareness and interest—the "buzz" or word of mouth for the film. In some cases, a studio may postpone or advance a movie's release date, depending on the results for other movies scheduled for release at that time.

These examples show how marketing research is the link between marketing strategy and decisive actions, the main topic of this chapter. Also, marketing research is often used to help a firm develop sales forecasts, a topic in Chapter 9.

THE ROLE OF MARKETING RESEARCH

To place marketing research in perspective, we will describe (1) what it is, (2) some of the difficulties in conducting it, and (3) the five steps marketing executives can use in conducting marketing research.

What Is Marketing Research?

Marketing research is the process of defining a marketing problem and opportunity, systematically collecting and analyzing information, and recommending actions.[14] The broad goal of marketing research is to identify and define both

marketing problems and opportunities and to generate and improve marketing actions. Although marketing research isn't perfect, it seeks to reduce risk and uncertainty to improve decisions made by marketing managers.

Why Good Marketing Research Is Difficult

Ask a moviegoer if she liked the title for a film she just saw and you'll probably get a straightforward answer. But often marketing researchers face difficulties in asking consumers questions about new, unknown products. For example,

- Suppose your company is developing a brand new product, never before seen by consumers. Would consumers really know whether they are likely to buy a particular product that they probably have never thought about before?
- Imagine if you, as a consumer, were asked about your personal hygiene habits. Even though you knew the answer, would you reveal it? When personal or status questions are involved, will people give honest answers?
- Will consumers' actual purchase behavior be the same as their stated interest or intentions? Will they buy the same brand they say they will?

How can Fisher-Price do marketing research on young children who can't even fill out a questionnaire? For the answer, see the text.

Fisher-Price
www.fisherprice.com

A task of marketing research is to overcome these difficulties and to obtain the information needed to make reasonable estimates about what consumers will or won't buy.

Five-Step Marketing Research Approach to Making Better Decisions

A **decision** is a conscious choice from among two or more alternatives. All of us make many such decisions daily. At work we choose from alternative ways to accomplish an assigned task. At college we choose from alternative courses. As consumers we choose from alternative brands. No magic formula guarantees correct decisions.

Managers and researchers have tried to improve the outcomes of decisions by using more formal, structured approaches to *decision making,* the act of consciously choosing from alternatives. The systematic marketing research approach used to collect information to improve marketing decisions and actions described in this chapter uses five steps and is shown in Figure 8–2. Although the five-step approach described here focuses on marketing decisions, it provides a systematic checklist for making both business and personal decisions.

STEP 1: DEFINE THE PROBLEM

Children across the globe love to play with toys. Toys allow them to learn about themselves—their own abilities as well as their culture's social norms—how to interact with others, while having fun. So toy designers, such as those at Fisher-Price and Hasbro, conduct marketing research to discover how children play, how they learn, and what they like to play with.[15]

Fisher-Price, as part of its marketing research, gets children to play at its state-licensed nursery school in East Aurora, New York. From behind one-way mirrors,

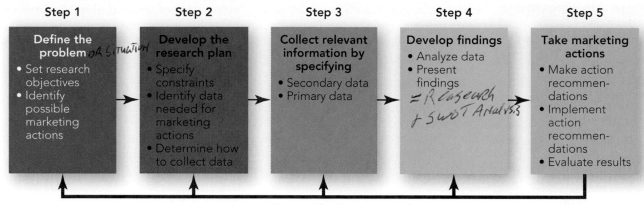

Step 1	Step 2	Step 3	Step 4	Step 5
Define the problem *OR SITUATION* • Set research objectives • Identify possible marketing actions	**Develop the research plan** • Specify constraints • Identify data needed for marketing actions • Determine how to collect data	**Collect relevant information by specifying** • Secondary data • Primary data	**Develop findings** • Analyze data • Present findings *= Research + SWOT Analysis*	**Take marketing actions** • Make action recommendations • Implement action recommendations • Evaluate results

Lessons learned for future research

FIGURE 8–2

Five-step marketing research approach leading to marketing actions. Lessons learned from past research mistakes are fed back to improve each of the steps.

Fisher-Price designers and marketing researchers watch the children use, and abuse, the toys and this helps the company develop better products.

The original model of a classic Fisher-Price toy, the Chatter Telephone™, was simply a wooden phone with a dial that rang a bell. Observers noted, however, that the children kept grabbing the receiver like a handle to pull the phone along behind them, so a designer added wheels, a noisemaker, and eyes that bobbed up and down.

A careful look at Fisher-Price's toy testing shows how to define the problem and its two key elements: setting the research objectives and identifying possible marketing actions suggested by the research.

Set the Research Objectives

The wheels, noisemaker, and bobbing eyes on Fisher-Price's hugely successful Chatter Telephone resulted from turning careful marketing research into major design improvements.

Research objectives are specific, measurable goals the decision maker—in this case, an executive at Fisher-Price—seeks to achieve in conducting the marketing research. For Fisher-Price, the immediate research objective was to decide whether to market the old or new telephone design.

In setting these research objectives, marketers have to be clear on the purpose of research they are about to do that leads to marketing actions. The three main types of marketing research, with examples explained in more detail later in the chapter, are:[16]

1. *Exploratory research* provides ideas about a relatively vague problem. General Mills discovered that the initial version of its Hamburger Helper wasn't satisfactory for many consumers, so it interviewed them to get ideas to improve the product.
2. *Descriptive research* generally involves trying to find the frequency that something occurs or the extent of a relationship between two factors. So when General Mills wants to study how loyal consumers are to its Wheaties, it can obtain data on the number of households buying Wheaties and competitive products.
3. *Causal research,* the most sophisticated, tries to determine the extent to which the change in one factor changes another one. In the Fisher-Price example discussed next, changing the toy designs is related to changes in the amount of time children play with the toy. Experiments and test markets, discussed later, are examples of causal research.

Identify Possible Marketing Actions

Effective decision makers develop specific **measures of success**, which are criteria or standards used in evaluating proposed solutions to the problem.

Marketing research isn't a perfect science. Recently it correctly identified Cybertron Transformers as a "hot toy" . . .

Different research outcomes—based on the measure of success—lead to different marketing actions. For the Fisher-Price problem, if a measure of success were the total time children spent playing with each of the two telephone designs, the results of observing them would lead to clear-cut actions as follows:

Measure of Success: Playtime	Possible Marketing Action
• Children spent more time playing with old design.	• Continue with old design; don't introduce new design.
• Children spent more time playing with new design.	• Introduce new design; drop old design.

One test of whether marketing research should be done is if different outcomes will lead to different marketing actions. If all the research outcomes lead to the same action—such as top management sticking with the older design regardless of what the observed children liked—the research is useless and a waste of money. In this causal research study, results showed that kids liked the new design, so Fisher-Price introduced its noisemaking pull-toy Chatter Telephone, which became a toy classic and has sold millions.

Digital Research, Inc., a marketing research firm, evaluates about 500 new toys annually from almost 150 toy manufacturers to select *Family Fun* magazine's Toy of the Year award. More than 1,300 children "toy testers" are involved.[17] Over the years, they've been right on the money in selecting Barney the TV dinosaur, Tickle Me Elmo, and Fisher-Price's Love to Dance Bear™ as hot toys—ones that jumped off retailers' shelves. But as shown with the toys in the margin, even careful marketing research can sometimes overlook hot toys. Forecasting which toys are hot and will sell well is critical for retailers, which must place orders to manufacturers 8 to 10 months before holiday shoppers walk into their stores. Bad forecasts can lead to lost sales for under-stocks and severe losses for overstocks.

Marketing researchers know that defining a problem is an incredibly difficult task. For example, if the objectives are too broad, the problem may not be researchable. If they are too narrow, the value of the research results may be seriously lessened. This is why marketing researchers spend so much time in defining a marketing problem precisely and writing a formal proposal that describes the research to be done.[18]

---

learning review

1. What is marketing research?

2. What are the three main purposes of marketing research that help lead to marketing actions?

STEP 2: DEVELOP THE RESEARCH PLAN

The second step in the marketing research process involves (1) specifying the constraints on the marketing research activity, (2) identifying the data needed for marketing decisions, and (3) determining how to collect the data.

Specify Constraints

The **constraints** in a decision are the restrictions placed on potential solutions to a problem. Common constraints in marketing problems are limitations on the time and money available to solve the problem. Thus, Fisher-Price might set two constraints on its decision to select either the old or new version of the Chatter Telephone: The decision must be made in 10 weeks and no research budget is available beyond that needed for collecting data in its nursery school.

. . . but missed on Hasbro's FurReal Friends Butterscotch Pony and Fisher-Price's TMX™ Elmo.

Identify Data Needed for Marketing Actions

Often marketing research studies wind up collecting a lot of data that are interesting but irrelevant for marketing decisions that result in marketing actions. In the Fisher-Price Chatter Telephone case, it might be nice to know the children's favorite colors, whether they like wood or plastic toys better, and so on. In fact, knowing answers to these questions might result in later modifications of the toy, but right now the problem is to select one of two toy designs. So this study must focus on collecting data that help managers make a clear choice between the two telephone designs.

Determine How to Collect Data

Determining how to collect useful marketing research data is often as important as actually collecting the data—step 3 in the process, which is discussed later. Two key elements in deciding how to collect the data are (1) concepts and (2) methods.

Concepts In the world of marketing, *concepts* are ideas about products or services. To find out about consumer reaction to a potential new product, marketing researchers frequently develop a *new-product concept,* that is, a picture or verbal description of a product or service the firm might offer for sale. For example, with the Chatter Telephone, Fisher-Price managers developed a new-product concept that involved adding a noisemaker, wheels, and eyes to the basic design, which would make the toy more fun for children and increase sales.

Methods *Methods* are the approaches that can be used to collect data to solve all or part of a problem. For example, if you are the marketing researcher at Fisher-Price responsible for the Chatter Telephone, you face a number of methods issues in developing your research plan, including the following:

- Can we actually ask three- or four-year-olds meaningful questions they can answer about their liking or disliking of the two designs?
- Are we better off not asking them questions but simply observing their behavior?
- If we simply observe the children's behavior, how can we do this in a way to get the best information without biasing the results?

Millions of other people have asked similar questions about millions of other products and services. How can you find and use the methodologies that other marketing researchers have found successful? Information on useful methods is available in trade-books, textbooks, and handbooks that relate to marketing and marketing research. Some periodicals and technical journals, such as the *Journal of Marketing* and the *Journal of Marketing Research* published by the American Marketing Association, summarize methods and techniques valuable in addressing marketing problems. Special methods vital to marketing are (1) sampling and (2) statistical inference.

Marketing researchers often select a group of distributors, customers, or prospects, ask them questions, and treat their answers as typical of all those in whom they are interested. There are two ways of **sampling**, or selecting representative elements from a population: probability and nonprobability sampling. **Probability sampling** involves using precise rules to select the sample such that each element of the population has a specific known chance of being selected. For example, if a college wants to know how last year's 1,000 graduates are doing, it can put their names in a bowl and randomly select 50 names to contact. The chance of being selected—50/1,000, or 0.05—is known in advance, and all graduates have an equal chance of being contacted. This procedure helps select a sample (the 50 graduates) that is representative of the entire population (the 1,000 graduates) and allows conclusions to be drawn about the entire population.

When time and budget are limited, researchers may opt for **nonprobability sampling** and use arbitrary judgments to select the sample so that the chance of selecting a particular element may be unknown or 0. If the college decides to select the 50 graduates from last year's class who live closest to the college, many members of the class have been arbitrarily excluded. This has introduced a bias that makes it dangerous to draw conclusions about the population from this geographically restricted sample.

The method of **statistical inference** involves drawing conclusions about a *population* (the "universe" of all people, stores, or salespeople about which researchers wish to generalize) from a *sample* (some elements of the universe) taken from that population. To draw accurate inferences about the population, the sample elements should be representative of that universe. If the sample is not typical, bias can be introduced, resulting in bad marketing decisions.

STEP 3: COLLECT RELEVANT INFORMATION

LO3

Collecting enough relevant information to make a rational, informed marketing decision sometimes simply means using your knowledge to decide immediately. At other times it entails collecting an enormous amount of information at great expense.

Figure 8–3 shows how the different kinds of marketing information fit together. **Data**, the facts and figures related to the problem, are divided into two main parts: secondary data and primary data. **Secondary data** are facts and figures that have already been recorded before the project at hand, whereas **primary data** are facts and figures that are newly collected for the project.

Secondary Data: Internal

Secondary data divide into two parts—internal and external secondary data—depending on whether the data come from inside or outside the organization needing the research.

FIGURE 8–3
Types of marketing information. Researchers must choose carefully among these to get the best results, considering time and cost constraints.

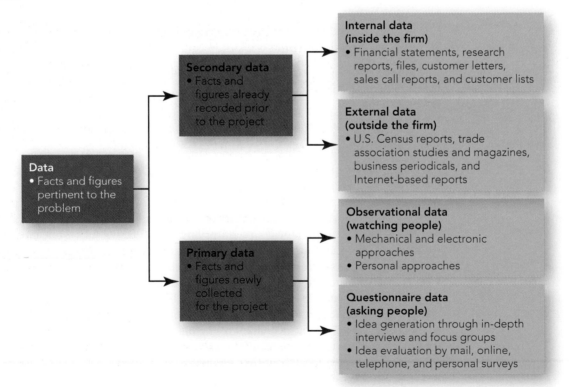

Examples of internal secondary data include detailed sales breakdowns by product line, by region, by customer, and by sales representative, as well as customer inquiries and complaints. So internal secondary data are often the starting point for a new marketing research study because using this information can result in huge time and cost savings.

Secondary Data: External

Published data from outside the organization are external secondary data. The U.S. Census Bureau publishes a variety of useful reports. Best known is the Census 2000, which is a count of the U.S. population that occurs every 10 years. Recently, the Census Bureau began collecting data annually from a smaller number of people through the American Community Survey. Both surveys contain detailed information on American households, such as the number of people per household and their age, sex, race/ethnic background, income, occupation, and education. Marketers use these data to identify characteristics and trends of ultimate consumers.

The Census Bureau also publishes the Economic Census, which is conducted every five years. These reports are vital to business firms selling products and services to organizations. The 2002 Economic Census contains data on the number and size of establishments in the United States that produce a good or service on the basis of its geography (states, counties, zip codes, etc.), industry sector (Manufacturing, Retail Trade, etc.), and North American Industry Classification System (NAICS). The Current Industrial Reports are periodic studies that provide data on the production quantity and shipment value of selected products. Finally, trade associations, universities, and business periodicals provide detailed data of value to market researchers and planners. These data are now available online via the Internet and can be identified and located using a search engine such as Google. The accompanying Going Online box provides examples.

A variety of marketing research organizations serves the needs of marketers. Specialized syndicated services provide a standard set of data on a regular basis, such as the Nielsen Media Research's TV ratings or J. D. Powers with its automotive quality and customer satisfaction research. Other market research suppliers contract with clients to conduct complete marketing research projects.

Several data services provide comprehensive information on household demographics and lifestyle, product purchases, TV viewing behavior, and responses to coupon and free-sample promotions. Their principal advantage is the ability of one service to collect, analyze, interrelate, and present all this information. For consumer product firms such as Procter & Gamble, sales data from various channels are critical to allocate scarce marketing resources. As a result, they use firms such as Information Resources' InfoScan and ACNielsen's ScanTrack to collect product sales and coupon/free-sample redemptions that have been scanned at the checkout counters of supermarket, drug, convenience, and mass merchandise retailers in the United States and other international markets.

Advantages and Disadvantages of Secondary Data

A general rule among marketing people is to obtain secondary data first and then collect primary data. Two important advantages of secondary data are (1) the tremendous time savings if the data have already been collected and published or exist internally and (2) the low cost, such as free or inexpensive census reports. Furthermore, a greater level of detail is often available through secondary data, especially U.S. Census Bureau data.

However, these advantages must be weighed against some significant disadvantages. First, the secondary data may be out of date, especially if they are U.S. Census data collected only every 5 or 10 years. Second, the definitions or categories might not be quite right for your project. For example, the age groupings might be wrong for your project. Finally, because the data are collected for another purpose, they may not be specific enough for your project. In such cases it may be necessary to collect primary data.

Going Online

Online Databases and Internet Resources Useful to Marketers

Information contained in online databases available via the Internet consists of indexes to articles in periodicals and statistical or financial data on markets, products, and organizations that are accessed either directly or via Internet search engines or portals through keyword searches.

Online databases of indexes, abstracts, and full-text information from periodicals include:

- LexisNexis™ Academic (www.lexisnexis.com), which provides full-text documents from over 6,000 news, business, legal, and reference publications.
- ProQuest databases (www.proquest.com), which provide summaries of management, marketing, and other business articles from more than 4,000 journals.

Statistical and financial data on markets, products, and organizations include:

- *The Wall Street Journal* (www.wsj.com), CNBC (www.cnbc.com), Bloomberg (www.bloomberg.com), and *Investor's*

Business Daily (www.investors.com) all provide up-to-the-minute business news and security prices plus research reports on companies, industries, and countries.

- STAT-USA (www.stat-usa.gov) of the U.S. Department of Commerce provides information on U.S. business, economic, and trade activity collected by the federal government.

Portals and search engines include:

- USA.gov (www.usa.gov), the portal to all U.S. government websites. Users click on links to browse by topic or enter keywords for specific searches.
- Google (www.google.com), the most popular portal to the entire Internet. Users click on links to browse by topic or enter keywords for specific searches.

Some of these websites are accessible only if your educational institution has paid a subscription fee. To see if you can access these sites for free, check with your institution's website.

---

learning review

3. What are constraints, as they apply to developing a research plan?
4. What is the difference between secondary and primary data?

Primary Data: Observing Behavior

The two principal ways to collect new or primary data for a marketing study are by (1) observing people and (2) asking them questions. These observational data, in turn, can be collected either by mechanical (including electronic) means or by personal observation.

Mechanical Observation Facts and figures obtained by watching, either mechanically or in person, how people actually behave is the way marketing researchers collect **observational data**. National TV ratings, such as those of Nielsen Media Research shown in Figure 8–4, are an example of mechanical observational data collected by a "people meter." The people meter is a box that (1) is attached to TV sets, VCRs, cable boxes, and satellite dishes in more than 9,000 homes across the country; (2) has a remote that operates the meter when a viewer begins and finishes watching a TV program; and (3) stores and then transmits the viewing information each night to Nielsen Media Research.[19]

Nielsen Media Research is developing this "Solo Meter" to measure TV viewing by those using personal video devices such as video iPods and cell phones. The device is part of Nielsen's A2/M2 Initiative discussed in the text.

Currently, Nielsen employs separate local samples in each of 210 local markets. Ten of the nation's largest markets that reach 30 percent of TV viewing households use the people meter technology to provide viewing information daily. In the rest of the markets, TV viewing is measured using less sophisticated meters or TV diaries or booklets (a paper-pencil manual measurement system). Markets without people meters use this measurement in February, May, July, and November, which are known as "the sweeps."[20]

However, by 2011, Nielsen will implement a new measurement program dubbed the *Anytime Anywhere Media Measurement (A2/M2) Initiative*. The purpose of A2/M2 is

FIGURE 8–4

Nielsen Television Index Ranking Report for network TV primetime households, week of September 24–30, 2007. The difference of a few share points in Nielsen TV ratings affects the cost of a TV ad on a show and even whether the show remains on the air.

Source: Copyright 2007 Nielsen Media Research.

RANK	PROGRAM	NETWORK	RATING	SHARE
1	Dancing with the Stars	ABC	12.8	19
2	CSI	CBS	12.4	19
3	Grey's Anatomy	ABC	12.3	19
4	Desperate Housewives	ABC	11.8	18
5	60 Minutes	CBS	11.3	17
6	House	FOX	10.8	16
7	Dancing with the Stars Results	ABC	10.7	16
8	NCIS	CBS	10.4	17
9	CSI: Miami	CBS	9.6	15
10	Criminal Minds	CBS	9.3	14

to "follow the video" of twenty-first century viewers. New "active/passive" people meter technology will measure all types of TV viewing behavior from a variety of devices and sources: DVR (digital video recorders), VOD (video on demand), Internet-delivered TV shows on computers via iTunes, streaming media, mobile media devices (cell phones, iPods, etc.), as well as outside the home in bars, fitness clubs, airports, etc. By 2008, Nielsen also planned to expand the people meter service to include the top 25 markets, which account for 50 percent of TV households. For smaller markets Nielsen will use improved people meters and paper-based viewing logs until a better technology, such as personal RFID (radio frequency ID) tags, can be developed.[21]

On the basis of all these observational data, Nielsen Media Research then calculates the rating and share of each TV program. With 110.2 million TV households in the United States, based on the 2000 U.S. Census, a single ratings point equals 1 percent, or 1,102,000 TV households.[22] For TV viewing, a share point is the percentage of TV sets in use tuned to a particular program. Because TV networks and cable sell almost $70 billion annually in advertising[23] and set advertising rates to advertisers on the basis of those data, precision in the Nielsen data is critical. Thus, a change of one percentage point in a rating can mean gaining or losing up to $70 million in advertising revenue because advertisers pay rates on the basis of the size of the audience for a TV program. So as Figure 8–4 shows, we might expect to pay more for a 30-second TV ad on *Grey's Anatomy* than one on *CSI: Miami*. Broadcast and cable networks may change the time slot or even cancel a TV program if its ratings are consistently poor and advertisers are unwilling to pay a rate based on a higher guaranteed rating.

But TV advertisers today have a special problem: With about three out of four TV viewers skipping ads with TiVo or channel surfing during commercials, how many people are actually seeing the TV ad? Now services such as Nielsen Media Research and Media Check offer advertisers minute-by-minute measurement of how many viewers stay tuned during commercials. The viewership data in Figure 8–4 includes not only live TV but also programs taped on digital video recorders (DVRs). With these more precise measures of who is likely to see a TV ad, buying TV ads is becoming a lot more scientific.[24]

What determines if *American Idol* stays on the air? For the importance of the TV "ratings game," see the text.

RANK	BRAND	UNIQUE AUDIENCE (000s)	ACTIVE REACH (%)	HOURS AND MINUTES PER PERSON PER WEEK
1	Google	112,245	71.3	1:06
2	Yahoo!	108,130	68.7	3:09
3	MSN/Windows Live	94,463	60.0	1:48
4	Microsoft	92,869	59.0	0:42
5	AOL Media Network	88,483	56.2	4:04
6	Fox Interactive Media	63,587	40.4	2:00
7	eBay	58,943	37.4	1:55
8	YouTube	54,501	34.6	0:57
9	Wikipedia	47,529	30.2	0:16
10	Apple	44,291	28.1	1:00

Nielsen Online Ratings also uses an electronic meter to record Internet user behavior. These data are collected via a meter installed on computers by tracking the actual mouse clicks made by a large sample of individuals in 13 countries as they surf the Internet. Nielsen Online Ratings identifies the top websites—or "brands"—that have the largest unique audiences and "active reach," which is the percent of total home and office users that visited the website. Figure 8–5, showing the top 10 Internet websites, gives interesting comparisons about Internet usage in terms of time spent at the website per person each week. For example, while Google reaches more people than eBay, the typical eBay user spends almost 50 minutes more per visit than a Google user does. Also, sophisticated software programs are now available to help Internet advertisers allocate these promotional dollars better.[25]

Is this *really* marketing research? A *mystery shopper* at work.

Personal Observation Observational data can take some strange twists. Jennifer Voitle, a laid-off investment bank employee with four advanced degrees, responded to an Internet ad and found a new career: *mystery shopper.* Companies pay her to check on the quality of their products and services and write a detailed report on what she finds. She gets paid to travel to Mexican and Hawaiian hotels, eat at restaurants, play golf, test-drive new cars at auto dealerships, shop for groceries and clothes, and play arcade games. But her role posing as a customer gives her client unique marketing research information that can be obtained in no other way. Says Jennifer, "Can you believe they call this work?"[26]

Watching consumers in person and videotaping them are other observational approaches. For example, Procter & Gamble watched women do their laundry, clean the floor, put on makeup, and so on because 80 percent of the customers who buy its products are women! Gillette marketing researchers actually videotaped consumers brushing

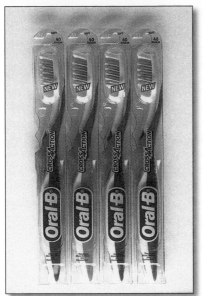

How do you do marketing research on something like toothbrushes? For a creative answer, see the text.

their teeth in their own bathrooms to see how they really brush—not just how they say they brush. The new-product result: Gillette's new Oral-B CrossAction toothbrush that's supposed to do a better job, at $4.99 each.[27]

A specialized observational approach is *ethnographic research,* in which anthropologists and other trained observers seek to discover subtle emotional reactions as consumers encounter products in their "natural use environment," such as in their home, car, or hotel. For example, Office Max used this anthropological method to observe how its shoppers interacted with its stores. The result: Office Max moved products that consumers bought in tandem closer together, thus increasing sales. Kraft recently launched Deli Creations, which are sandwiches made with its Oscar Mayer meats, Kraft cheeses, and Grey Poupon mustard, after spending several months with consumers in their kitchens. Kraft discovered that consumers wanted complete, ready-to-serve meals that are easy to prepare—and it had the products to create them.[28]

Personal observation is both useful and flexible, but it can be costly and unreliable when different observers report different conclusions in watching the same event. Also, although observation can reveal what people do, it cannot easily determine why they do it, such as why they are buying or not buying a product. This is the principal reason for using questionnaires.

Primary Data: Questioning Consumers

How many dozens of times have you filled out some kind of a questionnaire? Maybe at school to find out what kind of outside activities you might like. Or at the store where you shop to see if you are pleased with the kind of help and service you receive. Or by telephone or e-mail to get some ideas about your clothing preferences.

These are examples of the second principal way of gathering information from past, present, or potential consumers—which is by asking them questions and recording their answers. We can divide these questioning techniques into (1) idea generation methods and (2) idea evaluation methods, although the dividing line between them is often fuzzy and there are a number of special kinds of techniques in each category.[29] But all these questioning methods result in valuable **questionnaire data,** which are facts and figures obtained by asking people about their attitudes, awareness, intentions, and behaviors.

Mforma gets design ideas from teenagers—today's cutting-edge cell phone users.

Idea Generation Methods—Coming Up with Ideas "Oh, Dad, you *so* don't get it," is the kind of marketing research feedback Daniel Kranzler often gets when he conducts his *individual interviews* (a single researcher asking questions of one respondent). His company, Mforma, makes games and ring tones for cell phones. With

teenagers' ideas often driving the leading-edge designs and features in cell phones, Kranzler wants to connect with their latest thoughts. So for *very direct* input he turns to his 18-year-old daughter, Kat, who tells it like she sees it.[30]

General Mills sought ideas about why Hamburger Helper didn't fare well when introduced. Initial instructions called for cooking a half pound of hamburger separately from the noodles or potatoes, which were later mixed with the hamburger. So General Mills researchers used a special kind of individual interview called *depth interviews* in which researchers ask lengthy, freeflowing kinds of questions to probe for underlying ideas and feelings. These depth interviews showed that consumers (1) didn't think it contained enough meat and (2) didn't want the hassle of cooking in two different pots. So the Hamburger Helper product manager changed

Marketing research by Teenage Research Unlimited involves having teenagers complete a drawing describing themselves.

Listening carefully in focus groups to student and instructor suggestions benefits this text. Focus groups provide many creative ideas, which we authors try to use in the text, including easier-to-understand headings and answers to the Learning Review questions.

the recipe to call for a full pound of meat and to allow users to prepare it in one dish; this converted a potential failure into a success.[31]

Focus groups are informal sessions of 6 to 10 past, present, or prospective customers in which a discussion leader, or moderator, asks their opinions about the firm's and its competitors' products, how they use these products, and special needs they have that these products don't address. Often video-recorded and conducted in special interviewing rooms with a one-way mirror, these groups enable marketing researchers and managers to hear and watch consumer reactions. The informality and peer support in an effective focus group uncover ideas that are often difficult to obtain with individual interviews. For example, 3M ran eight focus groups around the United States and heard consumers complain that standard steel wool pads scratched their expensive cookware. These interviews led to 3M's internationally successful Scotch-Brite® Never Scratch soap pad.[32]

Finding "the next big thing" for consumers has become the obsession not only for consumer product firms but also for firms in many other industries. The result is that marketing researchers have come to rely on other—many would say bizarre— techniques than more traditional individual or focus group interviews. These "fuzzy front end" methods attempt to identify elusive consumer tastes or trends far before typical consumers have recognized them themselves. Examples of unusual ways to collect consumer data and their results include:

- Having consumers take a photo of themselves every time they snack. This resulted in General Mills' Homestyle Pop Secret popcorn, which delivers the real butter and bursts of salt in microwave popcorn that consumers thought they could only get from the stovetop variety.[33]
- Having teenagers complete a drawing. This is used by researchers at Teenage Research Unlimited (TRU) to help discover what teenagers like, wear, listen to, read, and watch. TRU surveys 2,000 teens twice a year to identify their lifestyles, attitudes, trends, and behaviors. With its Coolest Brand Meter™, TRU asks teens to specify the coolest brands within specific product categories, such as sneakers and clothing.[34]
- Hiring "cool hunters," people with tastes far ahead of the curve. This is used to identify the next big things likely to sweep popular teen culture. Many marketers consult Look-Look, a marketing research firm that can call on up to 20,000 "field correspondents" who specialize in hunting for "trendsetters" for ideas, products, and fashions that are deemed to be "cool" in large cities around the world. Look-Look provides these teenage field correspondents with digital cameras to send back uploaded images from parties, concerts, and sporting events.[35] For example, Wet Seal uses this method to anticipate teenage girls' fashions while Skechers uses it to spot footwear trends.

Marketing Matters > > > > > customer value

When Less Is More—Deleting Features to Open Up Huge Markets

New products! To invent them the natural thing is to add more features, new technologies, more glitz. Many new-product successes do just that.

But good marketing research can open huge new markets by taking features away and simplifying the product. Here are some less-is-more new-product breakthroughs that revolutionized national or global markets:

1. *Canon's tabletop copiers.* Canon's marketing research found it couldn't sell its little copiers to big companies, which were happy with their large Xerox machines. So Canon sold its little machines by the zillions to little companies with limited copying needs.
2. *Palm Computing's PalmPilot PDA.* Apple Computer's Newton personal digital assistant (PDA) was a great idea but was too complicated for users. Enter: PalmPilot inventors Donna Dubinsky and Jeff Hawkins, who deleted features to achieve the market breakthrough.

3. *Intuit's QuickBooks accounting software.* Competitors offered complex accounting software containing every feature professional accountants might possibly want. Intuit then introduced QuickBooks, a smaller, cheaper program with less functionality that won 70 percent of the huge market for small-business accounting software within two years.
4. *Swatch watches.* In 1983, a slim plastic watch with only 51 components appeared on the global market. That simplicity—plus top quality, affordable price, and creative designs—is the reason that more than 250 million Swatch watches have been sold.

Sometimes much less is much, much more!

One surprise: Innovation research shows that firms using disruptive innovation and creating newness by simplifying the product are often *not* the industry leaders selling the more sophisticated high-end products with more features.

  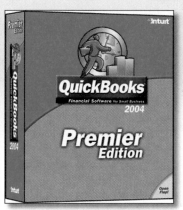 

Idea Evaluation Methods—Testing an Idea In idea evaluation, the marketing researcher tries to test ideas discovered earlier to help the marketing manager recommend marketing actions.

Marketing research to evaluate new-product ideas is especially difficult because potential buyers can't see or touch what they are asked to comment on. But a huge amount of marketing research is also done to ask users to evaluate and improve existing products. A surprising result is that many products in the marketplace have so many features they overwhelm the users. So effective marketing research often improves products by simplifying them—less is really more—which can greatly expand their products' markets, as discussed in the Marketing Matters box.[36] Chapter 10 on new-product development explores this problem of "feature bloat" in greater depth.

Idea evaluation methods often involve conventional questionnaires using personal, mail, telephone, e-mail, fax, or Internet surveys of a large sample of past, present, or prospective consumers. In choosing between these alternatives, the marketing researcher must balance cost against the expected quality of information obtained. Personal interview surveys have a major advantage of enabling the interviewer to be flexible in asking probing questions or getting reactions to visual materials, but they are very costly to conduct.

1. What things are most important to you when you decide to eat out and go to a fast-food restaurant?

   _____

   _____

   _____

2. Have you eaten at a fast-food restaurant in the past month?

   ☐ Yes   ☐ No

3. If you answered yes to question 2, how often do you eat fast food?

   ☐ Once a week   ☐ 2 to 3 times a month   ☐ Once a month or less

4. How important is it to you that a fast-food restaurant satisfies you on the following characteristics? [Check the box that describes your feelings for each item listed]

CHARACTERISTIC	VERY IMPORTANT	SOMEWHAT IMPORTANT	IMPORTANT	UNIMPORTANT	SOMEWHAT UNIMPORTANT	VERY UNIMPORTANT
• Taste of food	☐	☐	☐	☐	☐	☐
• Cleanliness	☐	☐	☐	☐	☐	☐
• Price	☐	☐	☐	☐	☐	☐
• Variety of menu	☐	☐	☐	☐	☐	☐

5. For each of the characteristics listed below, check the space on the scale that describes how you feel about Wendy's. Mark an X on only **one** of the five spaces listed for each item listed.

CHARACTERISTIC	CHECK THE SPACE THAT DESCRIBES THE DEGREE TO WHICH WENDY'S IS . . .						
• Taste of food	Tasty	_____	_____	_____	_____	_____	Not tasty
• Cleanliness	Clean	_____	_____	_____	_____	_____	Dirty
• Price	Inexpensive	_____	_____	_____	_____	_____	Expensive
• Variety of menu	Broad	_____	_____	_____	_____	_____	Narrow

FIGURE 8–6

To obtain the most valuable information from consumers, the Wendy's survey utilizes five different kinds of questions discussed in the text.

Mail surveys are usually biased because those most likely to respond have had especially positive or negative experiences with the product or brand. While telephone interviews allow flexibility, unhappy respondents may hang up on the interviewer, even with the efficiency of computer-assisted telephone interviewing (CATI). E-mail, fax, and Internet surveys are restricted to respondents having the technologies but are expanding rapidly.

The high cost of reaching respondents in their homes using personal interviews has led to a dramatic increase in the use of *mall intercept interviews,* which are personal interviews of consumers visiting shopping centers. These face-to-face interviews reduce the cost of personal visits to consumers in their homes while providing the flexibility to show respondents visual cues such as ads or actual product samples. However, a critical disadvantage of mall intercept interviews is that the people selected for the interviews may not be representative of the consumers targeted, giving a biased result.

Figure 8–6 shows a number of different formats for questions taken from a Wendy's survey that assessed fast-food restaurant preferences among present and prospective consumers. Question 1 is an example of an *open-ended question,* which allows respondents

6. Check one box that describes your agreement or disagreement with each statement listed below:

STATEMENT	STRONGLY AGREE	AGREE	DON'T KNOW	DISAGREE	STRONGLY DISAGREE
• Adults like to take their families to fast-food restaurants	☐	☐	☐	☐	☐
• Our children have a say in where the family chooses to eat	☐	☐	☐	☐	☐

7. How important are each of the following sources of information to you when selecting a fast-food restaurant to eat at? [Check one box for each source listed]

SOURCE OF INFORMATION	VERY IMPORTANT	SOMEWHAT IMPORTANT	NOT AT ALL IMPORTANT
• Television	☐	☐	☐
• Newspapers	☐	☐	☐
• Radio	☐	☐	☐
• Billboards	☐	☐	☐
• Flyers	☐	☐	☐

8. How often do you eat out at each of the following fast-food restaurants? [Check one box for each source listed]

RESTAURANT	ONCE A WEEK OR MORE	2 TO 3 TIMES A MONTH	ONCE A MONTH OR LESS
• Burger King	☐	☐	☐
• McDonald's	☐	☐	☐
• Wendy's	☐	☐	☐

9. Please answer the following questions about you and your household. [Check only one for each item]

a. What is your gender? ☐ Male ☐ Female

b. What is your marital status? ☐ Single ☐ Married ☐ Other (widowed, divorced, etc.)

c. How many children under age 18 live in your home? ☐ 0 ☐ 1 ☐ 2 ☐ 3 or more

d. What is your age? ☐ Under 25 ☐ 25–44 ☐ 45 or older

e. What is your total annual individual or household income?
☐ <$15,000 ☐ $15,000–49,000 ☐ $50,000 or more

FIGURE 8–6
(Continued)

to express opinions, ideas, or behaviors in their own words without being forced to choose among alternatives that have been predetermined by a marketing researcher. This information is invaluable to marketers because it captures the "voice" of respondents, which is useful in understanding consumer behavior, identifying product benefits, or developing advertising messages. In contrast, *closed-end* or *fixed alternative questions* require respondents to select one or more response options from a set of predetermined choices. Question 2 is an example of a *dichotomous question,* the simplest form of a fixed alternative question that allows only a "yes" or "no" response.

A fixed alternative question with three or more choices uses a *scale.* Question 5 is an example of a question that uses a *semantic differential scale,* a five-point scale in which the opposite ends have one- or two-word adjectives that have opposite meanings. For example, depending on how clean the respondent feels that Wendy's is, he or she would check the left-hand space on the scale, the right-hand space, or one of the five intervening points. Question 6 uses a *Likert scale,* in which the respondent indicates the extent to which he or she agrees or disagrees with a statement.

Wendy's does marketing research continuously to discover changing customer wants, while keeping its "Fresh, hot'n juicy®" image.

Wendy's Restaurant
www.wendys.com

How might Wal-Mart have done early marketing research to help develop its supercenters, which have achieved international success? For its unusual research, see the text.

The questionnaire in Figure 8–6 is an excerpt of a precisely worded survey that provides valuable information to the marketing researcher at Wendy's.[37] Questions 1 to 8 inform him or her about the likes and dislikes in eating out, frequency of eating out at fast-food restaurants generally and at Wendy's specifically, and sources of information used in making decisions about fast-food restaurants. Question 9 gives details about the personal or household characteristics, which can be used in trying to segment the fast-food market, a topic discussed in Chapter 9.

Electronic technology has revolutionized traditional concepts of interviews or surveys. Today, respondents can walk up to a kiosk in a shopping center, read questions off a screen, and key their answers into a computer on a touch screen. Even fully automated telephone interviews exist: An automated voice questions respondents over the telephone, who then key their replies on a touch-tone telephone.

Primary Data: Panels and Experiments

Panels   Two special ways that observations and questionnaires are sometimes used are panels and experiments.

Marketing researchers often want to know if consumers change their behavior over time, and so they take successive measurements of the same people. A *panel* is a sample of consumers or stores from which researchers take a series of measurements. For example, the NPD Group collects data about consumer purchases such as apparel, food, and electronics from its Online Panel, which consists of more than 2.5 million individuals worldwide. So a firm like General Mills can use descriptive research—counting the frequency of consumer purchases—to measure switching behavior from one brand of its breakfast cereal (Wheaties) to another (Cheerios) or to a competitor's (Kellogg's Special K). A disadvantage of panels is that the marketing research firm needs to recruit new members continually to replace those who drop out. These new recruits must match the characteristics of those they replace to keep the panel representative of the marketplace.

Experiments   An *experiment* involves obtaining data by manipulating factors under tightly controlled conditions to test cause and effect, an example of causal research. The interest is in whether changing one of the independent variables (a cause) will change the behavior of the dependent variable that is studied (the result). In marketing experiments, the independent variables of interest—sometimes called the marketing *drivers*—are often one or more of the marketing mix elements, such as a product's features, price, or promotion (like advertising messages or coupons). The ideal dependent variable usually is a change in purchases (incremental unit or dollar sales) of individuals, households, or organizations. For example, food companies often use *test*

markets, which is offering a product for sale on a limited basis in a defined area to help decide the likely effectiveness of potential marketing actions. So a test market is really a kind of marketing experiment to reduce risks. In 1988, Wal-Mart opened three experimental stand-alone supercenters to gauge consumer acceptance before deciding to open others. Today, Wal-Mart operates over 1,000 supercenters around the world.[38]

A potential difficulty with experiments is that outside factors (such as actions of competitors) can distort the results of an experiment and affect the dependent variable (such as sales). A researcher's task is to identify the effect of the marketing variable of interest on the dependent variable when the effects of outside factors in an experiment might hide it.

Using Marketing Dashboards
Making Sense of Syndicated Consumer Data

You've decided to undertake advertising and promotions that will grow sales of your Super Snack Bar. You can use a syndicated data source of household purchases to make wise choices.

Your Challenge The immediate question: Do you pursue new buyers or try to get existing customers to buy more?

Your dashboard chart uses the marketing metrics of U.S. Household penetration and buying rate to help you answer the question of new vs. existing buyers. It is based on household purchase data from a syndicated data source. Let's say there are 100 million households (abbreviated "HH" on the chart) in the U.S. Your product Super Snack Bar was purchased by 40 million of these households last year.

$$\text{U.S. HH Penetration} = (40 \text{ MM}/100 \text{ MM}) \times 100$$
$$= 40\% \text{ of HH.}$$

These 40 million households bought 120 million bars. The average bars purchased per household is called the buying rate.

$$\text{Buying rate} = (120\text{MM}/40\text{MM})$$
$$= 3 \text{ bars per HH.}$$

The dashboard chart shows how your Super Snack Bar compares with competitors, represented by the capital letters.

Your Findings What do we learn when we contrast our penetration and buying rate to our competitors?

The circled brands are the largest volume brands. They have the most penetration, and highest buying rates, so they have the highest sales.

How do you compare to other snack bar competition? Your buying rate is close to the top of all the bars shown but household penetration is lower than competitors A and E.

Your Action To reduce the penetration gap to these two competitors, you focus your marketing plan and volume goals on attracting new customers next year while maintaining the buying rate where it is! To attract new customers, you decide to reduce the risk of trial and offer free samples at grocery stores, college sporting events, and health clubs. You also have set aside funds to run a new advertising campaign.

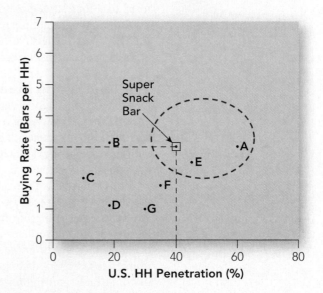

Advantages and Disadvantages of Primary Data

Compared with secondary data, primary data have the advantage of being more specific to the problem being studied. The main disadvantages are that primary data are usually far more costly and time consuming to collect than secondary data.

learning review

5. What is the difference between observational and questionnaire data?

6. Which survey provides the greatest flexibility for asking probing questions: mail, telephone, or personal interview?

7. What is the difference between a panel and an experiment?

Marketing Dashboards and Syndicated Panel Data

The Using Marketing Dashboards box shows how marketing managers convert syndicated panel data into actions. A number of market research companies pay households (and businesses) to record all their purchases using a paper or electronic diary, which are the data underlying many marketing dashboards. Such syndicated panel data economically answers questions that require consistent data collection over time, such as how many times do our customers buy our product in a year? How does that compare to last year and the year before?

For example, one syndicated sample has almost 100,000 households. Each household is given an electronic wand to scan the bar-codes on purchases that it makes. Last week's purchases are uploaded every week! This year-versus-year comparison, or asking 100,000 representative households to record all that they buy, is made affordable when lots of companies share the cost of one, syndicated sample. The sample is then used to project statistically the purchase behaviors of all households in the country. The Using Marketing Dashboards box shows how syndicated panel data helps a manager choose between efforts to attract new buyers or to try to get existing ones to buy more.

Using Information Technology to Trigger Marketing Actions

LO5

Today's marketing managers can be drowned in such an ocean of data that they need to adopt strategies for dealing with complex, changing views of the competition, the market, and the consumer. The Internet and the PC power of today provide a gateway to exhaustive data sources that vary from well-organized and correct to disorganized and incorrect.

The Marketing Manager's View of Sales Drivers

Figure 8–7 shows a marketing manager's view of the product or brand "drivers," the factors that influence buying decisions of a household or organization and, hence, sales. These drivers include both the controllable marketing mix factors like product and distribution as well as uncontrollable factors like competition and the changing tastes of households or organizational buyers.

Understanding these drivers involves managing this ocean of data. Sometimes hundreds of thousands of bits of data are created each week. Sources feeding this database ocean range from internal data about sales and customers to external data from syndication services and TV ratings. The marketer's task is to convert this data ocean into useful information on which to base informed decisions. In practice, some market researchers distinguish *data*—the facts and figures—from *information*—the distilled facts and figures whose interpretation leads to marketing actions.

FIGURE 8–7

Sales drivers: factors that influence product or brand sales. All these drivers must be considered in designing an effective marketing program.

SOURCE: Ford Consulting Group, Inc.

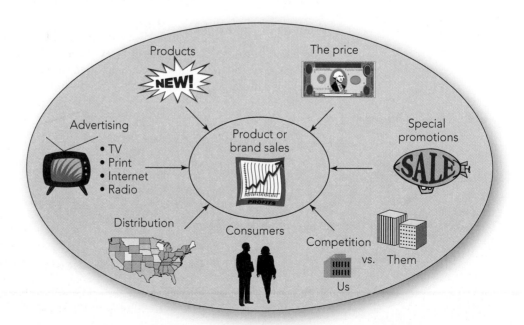

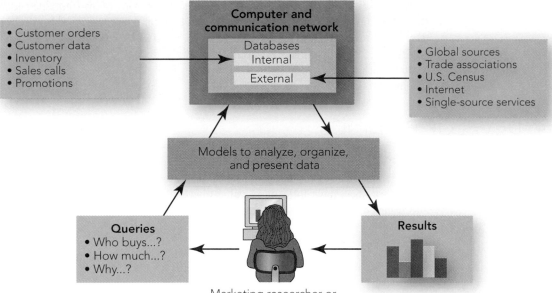

Computer and communication network

Databases
Internal
External

- Customer orders
- Customer data
- Inventory
- Sales calls
- Promotions

- Global sources
- Trade associations
- U.S. Census
- Internet
- Single-source services

Models to analyze, organize, and present data

Queries
- Who buys...?
- How much...?
- Why...?

Results

Marketing researcher or manager at desktop computer

FIGURE 8–8

How marketing researchers and managers use information technology to turn information into action

At 10 P.M. what is this man likely to buy besides these diapers? For the curious answer data mining gives, see the text.

Current information about products, competitors, and customers is almost always accessed and analyzed by computer. So today, these activities fall under the broader term of **information technology**, which involves operating computer networks that collect, store, and process data.

Key Elements of an Information System Figure 8–8 shows how marketing researchers and managers use information technology to frame questions that provide answers leading to marketing actions. At the bottom of Figure 8–8 the marketer queries the databases in the information system with marketing questions needing answers. These questions go through statistical models that analyze the relationships that exist among the data. The databases form the core, or *data warehouse,* where the ocean of data is collected and stored. After the search of this data warehouse, the models select and link the pertinent data, often presenting them in tables and graphics for easy interpretation. Marketers can also use *sensitivity analysis* to query the database with "what if" questions to determine how a hypothetical change in a driver like advertising can affect sales.

Data Mining: A New Approach to Searching the Data Ocean Traditional marketing research typically involves identifying possible drivers and then collecting data: Increasing couponing (the driver) during spring will increase trial by first-time buyers (the result). Marketing researchers then try to collect information to attempt to verify the truth of the relationship.

In contrast, **data mining** is the extraction of hidden predictive information from large databases. The focus is on finding statistical links about consumer purchasing patterns that suggest marketing actions.

Some of these purchase patterns are common sense: You may not need a computer to suspect that peanut butter and grape jelly purchases are linked and that it might be a good idea sometime to run a joint promotion between Skippy peanut butter and Welch's grape jelly. But would you have expected that men buying diapers in the evening sometimes buy a six-pack of beer as well? This is exactly what supermarkets discovered when they mined checkout data from scanners. So they placed diapers and beer near each other, then placed potato chips between them—and increased sales on all three items! On the near horizon: radio-frequency identification (RFID) technology using a "smart tag" microchip on the diapers and beer to tell whether they wind up in the same shopping bag—at 10 in the evening.[39]

Still, the success in data mining ultimately depends on humans—the judgments of the marketing managers and researchers in how to select, analyze, and interpret the information.

STEP 4: DEVELOP FINDINGS

Mark Twain once observed, "Collecting data is like collecting garbage. You've got to know what you're going to do with the stuff before you collect it." Thus, marketing data and information have little more value than garbage unless they are analyzed carefully and translated into logical findings, step 4 in the marketing research approach.[40]

Analyze the Data

Let's consider the case of Tony's Pizza and Teré Carral, the marketing manager responsible for the Tony's brand. We will use hypothetical data to protect Tony's proprietary information.

Teré is concerned about the limited growth in the Tony's brand over the past four years. She hires a consultant to collect and analyze data to explain what's going on with her brand and to recommend ways to improve its growth. Teré asks the consultant to put together a proposal that includes the answers to two key questions:

1. How are Tony's sales doing on a household basis? For example, are fewer households buying Tony's pizzas, or is each household buying fewer Tony's? Or both?
2. What factors might be contributing to Tony's very flat sales over the past four years?

Facts uncovered by the consultant are vital. For example, is the average household consuming more or less Tony's pizza than in previous years? Is Tony's flat sales performance related to a specific factor? With answers to these questions Teré can identify actions in her marketing plan and implement them over the coming year.

How are sales doing? To see how marketers at Tony's Pizza assessed this question and the reasons they came up with this ad, read the text.

Present the Findings

Findings should be clear and understandable from the way the data are presented. Managers are responsible for *actions*. Often it means delivering the results in clear pictures and, if possible, in a single page.

The consultant gives Teré the answers to her questions using the marketing dashboards in Figure 8–9, a creative way to present findings graphically. Let's look over the shoulders of Teré and the consultant while they interpret these findings:

- Figure 8–9A, the chart showing Annual Sales. This shows the annual growth of the Tony's Pizza brand is stable but virtually flat from 2005 through 2008.
- Figure 8–9B, the chart showing Average Annual Sales per Household. Look closely at this graph. At first glance, it may seem like sales in 2008 are *half* what they were in 2005, right? But be careful to read the numbers on the vertical axis. They show that household purchases of Tony's have been steadily declining over the past four years, from an average of 3.4 pizzas per household in 2005 to 3.1 pizzas per household in 2008. (Significant, but hardly a 50 percent drop.) Now the question is, if Tony's annual sales are stable, yet the average individual household is buying fewer Tony's pizzas, what's going on? The answer is, more households are buying

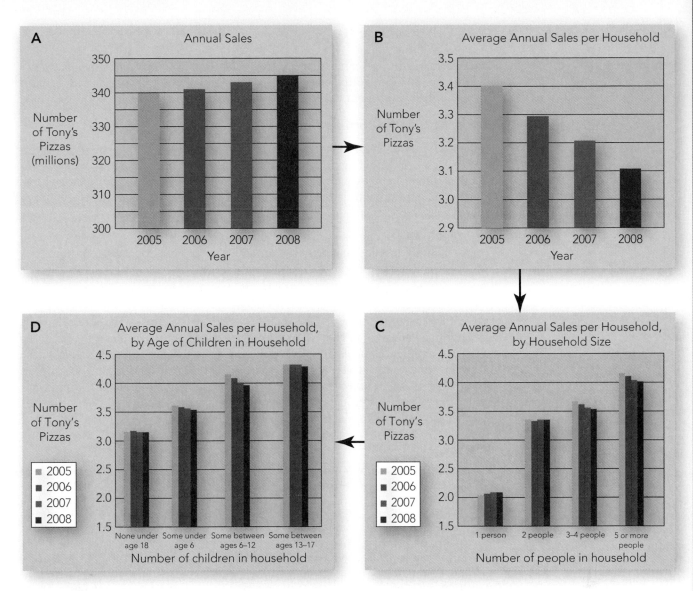

FIGURE 8–9

These marketing dashboards present findings to Tony's marketing manager that lead to recommendations and actions.

Source: Teré Carral, Tony's Pizza.

pizzas—it's just that each household is buying fewer Tony's pizzas. That households aren't choosing Tony's is a genuine source of concern. But again, here's a classic example of a marketing problem representing a marketing opportunity. The number of households buying pizza is *growing,* and that's good news for Tony's.

- Figure 8–9C, the chart showing Average Annual Sales per Household, by Household Size. This chart starts to show a source of the problem: Even though average sales of pizza to households with only one or two people is stable, households with three or four people and those with five or more are declining in average annual pizza consumption. Which households tend to have more than two people? Answer: Households *with children.* Therefore, we should look more closely at the pizza-buying behavior of households with children.

- Figure 8–9D, the chart showing Average Annual Sales per Household, by Age of Children in the Household. The picture is becoming very clear now: The real problem is in the serious decline in average consumption in the households with younger children, especially in households with children in the 6-to-12-year-old age group.

Identifying a sales problem in households with children 6 to 12 years old is an important discovery, as Tony's sales are declining in a market segment that is known to be one of the heaviest in buying pizzas.

STEP 5: TAKE MARKETING ACTIONS

Effective marketing research doesn't stop with findings and recommendations—someone has to identify the marketing actions, put them into effect, and monitor how the decisions turn out, which is the essence of step 5.

Make Action Recommendations

Teré Carral, the marketing manager for Tony's Pizza, met with her team to convert the market research findings into specific marketing recommendations with a clear objective: Target families with children ages 6 to 12 to reverse the trend among this segment and gain strength in one of the most important segments in the frozen pizza category. Her recommendation is to develop:

- An advertising campaign that will target children 6 to 12.
- A monthly promotion calendar with this 6-to-12 age group target in mind.
- A special event program reaching children 6 to 12.

Implement the Action Recommendations

As her first marketing action, Teré undertakes advertising research to develop ads that appeal to children in the 6-to-12 age group and their families. The research shows that children like colorful ads with funny, friendly characters. She gives these research results to her advertising agency, which develops several sample ads for her review. Teré selects three that are tested on children to try to identify the most appealing one. The one that gets the best results appears on page 218. Teré uses this ad in her next advertising campaign for Tony's Pizza.

Evaluate the Results

Evaluating results is a continuing way of life for effective marketing managers. There are really two aspects of this evaluation process:

- *Evaluating the decision itself.* This involves monitoring the marketplace to determine if action is necessary in the future. For Teré, is her new ad successful in appealing to 6-to-12-year-olds and their families? Are sales increasing to this target segment? The success of this strategy suggests Teré add more follow-up ads with colorful, funny, friendly characters.
- *Evaluating the decision process used.* Was the marketing research and analysis used to develop the recommendations effective? Was it flawed? Could it be improved for similar situations in the future? Teré and her marketing team must be vigilant for ways to improve the analysis and results—to learn lessons that might apply to future marketing research efforts at Tony's.

Again, systematic analysis does not guarantee success. But, as in the case of Tony's Pizza, it can improve a firm's success rate for its marketing decisions.

---

learning review

8. What does a marketing manager mean when she talks about a sales driver?

9. How does data mining differ from traditional marketing research?

10. In the marketing research for Tony's Pizza, what is an example of (*a*) a finding and (*b*) a marketing action?

LEARNING OBJECTIVES REVIEW

LO1 *Identify the reason for conducting marketing research.*
To be successful, an organization's offerings and its respective marketing programs must meet the wants and needs of potential customers. Marketing research reduces risk to the organization by providing its marketing managers with the vital information necessary to understand these wants and needs and deliver a

meaningful customer experience. They then translate this information into specific marketing actions.

LO2 *Describe the five-step marketing research approach that leads to marketing actions.*

Marketing researchers and managers engage in a five-step decision-making process about which information to collect to improve their marketing decisions. The first step of the five-step marketing research approach is to define the problem, which requires setting the research objectives and identifying possible marketing actions. The second step is to develop the research plan, which involves specifying the constraints, identifying data needed for marketing decisions, and determining how to collect the data. The third step is to collect the relevant information, which includes considering pertinent secondary data (both internal and external) and primary data (by observing and questioning consumers) as well as using information technology and data mining to trigger marketing actions. The fourth step is to develop findings from the marketing research data collected. This involves analyzing the data and presenting the findings of the research. The fifth and last step of the marketing research process is to take marketing actions, which involves making and implementing the action recommendations and then evaluating the results.

LO3 *Explain how secondary and primary data are used in marketing.*

Secondary data have already been recorded before the start of the project and consist of two parts: (a) internal secondary data, which originate from within the organization, such as sales reports and customer comments, and (b) external secondary data, which are created by other organizations, such as the U.S. Census Bureau (provides data on the country's population, manufacturers, retailers, and so on) or business and trade publications (provide data on industry trends, market size, etc.). Primary data are collected specifically for the project and are obtained by either observing or questioning people.

LO4 *Discuss the uses of observations, questionnaires, panels, and experiments.*

Marketing researchers observe people in various ways, such as electronically using Nielsen people meters to measure TV viewing and Internet habits or personally using mystery shoppers or ethnographic techniques. Questionnaires involve asking people questions (a) in person using interviews or focus groups or (b) via a questionnaire using a telephone, fax, print, e-mail, or an Internet survey. Panels involve a sample of consumers or stores that are repeatedly measured through time to see if their behaviors change. Experiments, such as test markets, involve measuring the effect of marketing variables such as price or advertising on sales.

LO5 *Explain how information technology and data mining link massive amounts of marketing information to meaningful marketing actions.*

Today's marketing managers are often overloaded with data—from internal sales and customer data to external data on TV viewing habits or grocery purchases from the scanner data at checkout counters. This can involve millions of bits of new information generated and obtained each day regarding an organization's sales drivers. Information technology enables this massive amount of marketing data to be stored, accessed, and processed. The resulting databases can be queried using data mining to find statistical relationships useful for marketing decisions and actions.

FOCUSING ON KEY TERMS

constraints p. 202
data p. 204
data mining p. 217
decision p. 200
information technology p. 217

marketing research p. 199
measures of success p. 201
nonprobability sampling p. 204
observational data p. 206
primary data p. 204

probability sampling p. 203
questionnaire data p. 209
sampling p. 203
secondary data p. 204
statistical inference p. 204

APPLYING MARKETING KNOWLEDGE

1 Look at Figure 8–1. (*a*) What kind of questions are these? (*b*) What difficulties might you have in tabulating answers to the questions about the movie title? (*c*) How might you address these problems?

2 (*a*) Why might a marketing researcher prefer to use secondary data rather than primary data in a study? (*b*) Why might the reverse be true?

3 Suppose your dean of admissions is considering surveying high school seniors about their perceptions of your school to design better informational brochures for them. What are the advantages and disadvantages of doing (*a*) telephone interviews and (*b*) an Internet survey of seniors who have requested information on the school?

4 Nielsen Media Research obtains ratings of local TV stations in small markets by having households fill out diary questionnaires. These give information on (*a*) who is watching TV and (*b*) what program. What are the limitations of this questionnaire method?

5 The format in which information is presented is often vital. (*a*) If you were a harried marketing manager and queried your information system, would you rather see the results in tables or charts and graphs? (*b*) What are one or two strengths and weaknesses of each format?

6 Wisk detergent decides to run a test market to see the effect of coupons and in-store advertising on sales. The index of sales is as follows:

Element in Test Market	Weeks Before Coupon	Week of Coupon	Week after Coupon
Without in-store ads	100	144	108
With in-store ads	100	268	203

What are your conclusions and recommendations?

7 Suppose Fisher-Price wants to run a simple experiment to evaluate a proposed chatter telephone design. It has two different groups of children on which to run its experiment for one week each. The first group has the old toy telephone, whereas the second group is exposed to the newly designed pull toy with wheels, a noisemaker, and bobbing eyes. The dependent variable is the average number of minutes during the two-hour play period that one of the children is playing with the toy, and the results are as follows:

Element in Experiment	First Group	Second Group
Independent variable	Old design	New design
Dependent variable	13 minutes	62 minutes

Should Fisher-Price introduce the new design? Why?

building your marketing plan

To help you collect the most useful data for your marketing plan, develop a three-column table:

1 In column 1, list the information you would ideally like to have to fill holes in your marketing plan.
2 In column 2, identify the source for each bit of information in column 1, such as a Web search, talking to prospective customers, looking at internal data, and so forth.
3 In column 3, set a priority on information you will have time to spend collecting by ranking them: 1 = most important; 2 = next most important, and so forth.

video case 8   Ford Consulting Group, Inc.: From Data to Actions

"The fast pace of working as a marketing professional isn't getting any easier," agrees David Ford, as he talks with Mark Rehborg, Tony's Pizza brand manager. "The speed of communication, the availability of real-time market information, and the responsibility for a brand's profit make marketing one of the most challenging professional jobs today."

Mark responds, "Ten years ago, we could reach 80 percent of our target market with 3 television spots—but today, to reach the same 80 percent, we would have to buy 97 spots. We haven't the luxury to be complacent—our core consumer, the 6- to 12-year-old 'big kid,' is part of a savvy, wired culture that is changing rapidly."

DASHBOARDS: DATA INTO ACTIONS

David Ford, president of Ford Consulting Group (FCG), prepares business analysis, often in the form of a dashboard, to assist clients such as Tony's in translating the market and sales information into marketing actions. David works with Mark to grow Tony's sales and profit performance. Mark uses information to choose where to spend his funds to promote his products. Many times, the sales force requests additional promotion funds to help them hit their sales targets.

The information used most often for sales and promotion analysis comes from places like ACNielsen's Scan-Track and Information Resources' InfoScan (IRI) that summarize sales data from grocery stores and other outlets that scan purchases at the checkout.

FCG's helps clients make sense of their existing information, *not* in helping clients collect more information.

The project that follows is typical of the work Ford Consulting Group (www.fordconsultinggroup.com) undertakes for a client. The data are hypothetical, but the situation is a very typical one in the grocery products industry. Here's a snapshot of some of the terms in the case:

- "You" have just come on the job, as the new marketing person.
- "NE" is the Northeastern sales region of Tony's.
- "SW, NW, SW" are the other sales regions.

PART 1: A TYPICAL QUESTION, ON A TYPICAL DAY

Let's dive into the background of a typical question you might face, on a typical day. On the opposite page are some memos you are given (one from Mark to you) as background.

You dig into data files and develop Table 1 that shows how Tony's is doing in the company's four sales regions and the entire United States on key marketing dimensions. Without reading further, take a deep breath and try to answer question 1 below.

PART 2: UNCOVERING THE TRUTH

Let's assume your analysis (question 1) shows NE is a problem, so we need to understand what's going on in the NE. Further effort enables you to develop Table 2. It shows the situation for the four largest supermarket chains in the Northeast sales region that carry Tony's. Now answer question 2.

Questions

1 Study Table 1. (*a*) How does the situation in the Northeast compare with the other regions in the United States? (*b*) What appears to be the reason(s) that sales are soft? (*c*) Write a 150-word e-mail with attachments to Mark Rehborg, your boss, giving your answers to *b*.

2 Study Table 2. (*a*) What do you conclude from this information? (*b*) Summarize your conclusions in a 150-word e-mail with attachments to Mark, who needs them for a meeting tomorrow with Margaret, the Northeast sales region manager. (*c*) What marketing actions might your memo suggest?

TO: Mark Rehborg, Tony's Brand Manager
FROM: Steve Quam, Tony's Field Sales
CC: Margaret Loiaza, NE Sales Region Manager

RE: Feedback on Sales Call at Food-Fast

Hi Mark—

Our sales call at Food-Fast wasn't so great. They don't see how our Tony's is going to sell well enough to justify the additional shelf-space. I also talked to Margaret and she said that second quarter may be weaker than planned across all the NE, and I should give you a heads-up. (She's on vacation this week, Aruba!) She's planning to schedule some time with you to talk about additional promotion money to do catch-up in the third quarter. She'll be there next week.

Steve

TO: You, the New Marketing Person
FROM: Mark Rehborg, Tony's Brand Manager (Your Boss)

RE: Small Project due Friday

Hi You,

Can you help out here? I've got a meeting with Margaret on Friday afternoon, and she's concerned that Food-Fast and the whole NE is going to need some additional promotion dollars.

Lauretta started the analysis and was hurt in a kickboxing accident yesterday and won't be back to work for a week. Her files are attached. Can you look through her files and summarize what's going on in the NE and the rest of the U.S.? Does Margaret need more promotion money?

Let's discuss Friday AM.

Mark

TABLE 1. COMPARISON OF TONY'S PERFORMANCE, BY REGION

Region	Quarterly Change in Volume (%)	Distribution[a] (%)	Price ($)	Price Gap[b] ($)	Promotion Support[c] (%)	Promotion Volume[d] (%)
NE	3%	93%	$1.29	+8	7%	14%
SE	5	95	1.11	−1	9	16
NW	8	98	1.19	+1	8	15
SW	6	96	1.25	0	8	15
U.S.	6	97	1.19	0	8	15

[a]% of outlets carrying Tony's.
[b]Price gap = (Our price) − (Competitor's price).
[c]Promotion support = % of the time brand was promoted.
[d]Promotion volume = % of the volume sold on promotion.

TABLE 2. COMPARISON OF MAJOR SUPERMARKET CHAINS IN THE NORTHEAST

Super-Market Chain	Quarterly Change In Volume (%)	Distribution[a] (%)	Price ($)	Price Gap[b] ($)	Promotion Support[c] (%)	Promotion Volume[d] (%)
Save-a-lot	5%	95%	$1.39	+10	10%	19%
Food-Fast	0	90	1.28	−1	3	4
Get-Fresh	0	90	1.30	+1	3	4
Dollars-Off	7	97	1.34	+5	7	14

NEED IT BY CHRISTMAS? Order by 11:59 PM PST December 19, 2006 with FREE STANDARD SHIPPING for guaranteed X-Mas delivery!
Shopping Cart | My Account | My Favorites | Help
1.800.927.7671
Zappos.com
Shoes
Handbags
Brands
Search
On Sale
Search by Size
Women's
Men's
Kids'
Gift Ideas
Accessories
New Styles
Why Shop at Zappos.com?
Visit Our Holiday Clearance & Save 25% off or more! click here...
Need it by Christmas?
Order by 11:59PM PST December 19, 2006 with Free Standard Shipping for Guaranteed Christmas Delivery!
FREE Shipping BOTH WAYS!
110% Price Protection
365-Day Return Policy
HACKER SAFE
TESTED DAILY 14-DEC
Shop for Latest Styles!
We are a Service Company that happens to sell...
Shoes
Handbags
Apparel
Accessories
FREE Shipping BOTH Ways
365-Day Return Policy
24/7 Customer Service: 1.800.927.7671
Free Shoe Giveaway!
Congratulations to this week's winner,
Karen K. from Jamaica Plain, MA!
Win Free Shoes!
SHOP ZAPPOS COUTURE
Click here to leave Zappos.com & visit Zappos Couture
TRENDS
BOOTS
HANDBAGS
APPAREL
Boots
Sandals
Men's Bags
Juniors
Kids
Search
Go!
Search
Search by Size
Go!
Narrow Shoes
Wide Shoes
Find shoes from over 500 brands!
Brand List | Designer Collection
Women's Athletic, Dress, Casual, Sale
Men's Athletic, Dress, Casual, Sale
SLIPPERS & BOOTS
Home
Brand List
Latest Styles
Apparel
Handbags
Diaper Bags
Holiday Clearance
UGG
Shop by Lifestyle
RODEO DRIVE
The Office
Shoes by Departmen
Men's Dress Shoes:
Dress Boots, Dress Comfort Shoes,
Lace-Up/Oxford, Dress Slip On, more.
Zappos

9

Segmenting, Positioning, and Forecasting Markets

LEARNING OBJECTIVES
After reading this chapter you should be able to:

LO1 Explain what market segmentation is and when to use it.

LO2 Identify the five steps involved in segmenting and targeting markets.

LO3 Recognize the factors used to segment consumer and organizational markets.

LO4 Develop a market-product grid to identify a target market and recommend resulting actions.

LO5 Explain how marketing managers position products in the marketplace.

LO6 Describe three approaches to developing a sales forecast for an organization.

ZAPPOS.COM: "THE SERVICE COMPANY THAT JUST HAPPENS TO SELL SHOES . . ."

Signs of being an entrepreneur can show up early in life. Take the case of Tony Hsieh (opposite page), now chief executive officer (CEO) of shoe retailer Zappos.com. The company name is derived from the Spanish word *zapatos* meaning *shoes*.

At age 12 Hsieh brought in several hundred dollars a month in his button-making business. In college Hsieh ran a business selling pizzas out of his dorm room. Fellow entrepreneur Alfred Lin bought whole pizzas from Hsieh and then sold them by the slice to other students.[1]

And where is pizza-slice marketer Alfred Lin today? He's Tony Hsieh's chief financial officer at Zappos.com.

A Clear Market Segmentation Strategy
Hsieh, Lin, and founder Nick Swinmurn have given Zappos a clear, specific market segmentation strategy: Sell a huge selection of shoes to people who will buy them online. This focus on the market segment of online buyers generated $597 million in 2006 sales, with a projected 30 percent increase for 2007.[2]

"With Zappos, the shoe store comes to you," says Pamela Leo, a New Jersey customer. "I can try the shoes in the comfort of my own home. . . . It's fabulous."[3] Besides the in-home convenience, Zappos offers free shipping both ways, 110 percent price protection, and a 365-day return policy.

The shoe choices for its online customers are staggering. A recent Zappos home page described "Today at Zappos" as: 1,146 brands, 913,210 UPCs (Universal Product Codes), 2,995,104 total products.

A Boring, Lightning-Fast Home Page
Here's what *CEO Insight* says about Zappos.com's home page:

- Not exactly an example of whiz-bang technology in action.

- Nothing moves, there are no ads, it's a little bland.

But the home page is also "fast as lightning." In fact, in late 2006 it was fastest of the top 50 Internet retailers to load on your computer: 0.879 seconds.[4]

On the practical, customer-friendly front, the Zappos 1-800 number is displayed prominently on every page of its website. The design of the website lets customers easily search by shoe size. And the Zappos call center is never closed.

Blue-Ribbon Customer Service

Asked about details of the Zappos website, Tony Hsieh almost yawns and says, "We try to spend most of our time on stuff that will improve customer-service levels."[5] As shown on its home page, Zappos positions itself as "a service company that happens to sell . . . shoes, handbags, apparel, and accessories."

This focus on customer service for the Zappos niche of online customers is something the company lives, breathes, and implements. Some examples:

- Customer service and loyalty is so critical both the Zappos call center and headquarters are in the same place—Las Vegas.

- Customer service employees don't use scripts and don't try to keep calls short.

- Every new employee in Las Vegas spends four weeks on the phone as a customer service representative and a week in its Kentucky warehouse.

- Operating the warehouse 24/7 lets customers order shoes as late as 11 p.m. and still get their shoes the next day.

The tender loving care of customers carries over to Zappos employees: All Zappos call center employees are invited to its Las Vegas vendor appreciation party held before the annual trade show.

The Zappos strategy illustrates successful market segmentation and targeting, the first topics in Chapter 9. The chapter ends with two related topics—positioning the organization, product, or brand and forecasting expected sales.

WHY SEGMENT MARKETS?

A business firm segments its markets so it can respond more effectively to the wants of groups of potential buyers and thus increase its sales and profits. Not-for-profit organizations also segment the clients they serve to satisfy client needs more effectively while achieving the organization's goals. Let's describe (1) what market segmentation is and (2) when it is necessary to segment markets, sometimes using the Zappos strategy as an example.

What Market Segmentation Means

People have different needs and wants, even though it would be easier for marketers if they didn't. **Market segmentation** involves aggregating prospective buyers into groups that (1) have common needs and (2) will respond similarly to a marketing action. **Market segments** are the relatively homogeneous groups of prospective buyers that result from the market segmentation process. Each market segment consists of people who are relatively similar to each other in terms of their consumption behavior.

The existence of different market segments has caused firms to use a marketing strategy of **product differentiation**. This strategy involves a firm using different marketing mix activities, such as product features and advertising, to help consumers perceive the product as being different and better than competing products. The perceived differences may involve physical features or nonphysical ones, such as image or price.

Segmentation: Linking Needs to Actions The process of segmenting a market and selecting specific segments as targets is the link between the various buyers' needs and the organization's marketing program, as shown in Figure 9–1. Market

226

FIGURE 9–1

Market segmentation links market needs to an organization's marketing program—specific marketing mix actions to satisfy those needs.

Identify market needs	Link needs to actions	Execute marketing program actions
Benefits in terms of • Product features • Expense • Quality • Savings in time and convenience	Take steps to segment and target markets	A marketing mix in terms of • Product • Price • Promotion • Place

segmentation is only a means to an end: to lead to tangible marketing actions that can increase sales and profitability.

The foundation of effective market segmentation is (1) forming meaningful groupings and (2) developing specific marketing mix actions. People or organizations should be grouped into a market segment according to the similarity of their needs and the benefits they look for in making a purchase. For example, the Zappos target customer segment is typically those who want a wide selection of shoes, want to be able to shop online conveniently in their own home, and want to receive the guarantee of quick delivery and free returns.

Also, the market segments must be related to specific marketing actions the organization can take. These actions may involve separate products or other aspects of the marketing mix such as price, promotion, or distribution strategies. Zappos' actions include offering a huge inventory of shoes, using an online selling strategy, and providing overnight distribution. So Zappos is not simply selling shoes but also the other service elements that lead to a positive customer experience and repeat purchases.

The Zappos Segmentation Strategy: Past, Present, and Future   In 1999 Zappos founder Nick Swinmurn spent an hour in several shoe stores in a mall and went home empty-handed because he couldn't find a pair of shoes with both the right size and right style. So Swinmurn quit his day job and decided to start Zappos—an online retailer that offered the absolute best selection of shoes and absolute best service.

Today, online sales account for $3 billion of the annual $40 billion U.S. shoe market. In 2007 Zappos' sales reached $840 million. In terms of market segments served, on any given day about 65 percent of Zappos shoppers are repeat customers, about 40 percent of them male.

What about the future? Zappos executives believe that the speed with which a customer receives an online purchase plays a big role in gaining repeat customers. So the company will continue to stress this point of difference, made possible by stocking in its warehouse every item it sells. Zappos' vision for the future:[6]

- One day, 30 percent of all retail transactions in the United States will be online.
- People will buy from the company with the best service and the best selection.
- Zappos will be that company.

And if customers associate Zappos with the absolute best service among online sellers, it can expand from shoes into handbags . . . into apparel . . . into . . . ?

When and How to Segment Markets

The one-size-fits-all mass markets—like that for Tide laundry detergent of 30 to 40 years ago—no longer exist. The global marketing officer at Procter & Gamble, which markets Tide, says, "Every one of our brands is targeted." Welcome to today's era of market segmentation and target marketing.[7]

A business firm goes to the trouble and expense of segmenting its markets when it expects that this will increase its sales, profit, and return on investment. When expenses are greater than the potentially increased sales from segmentation, a firm

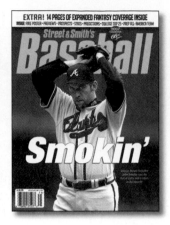
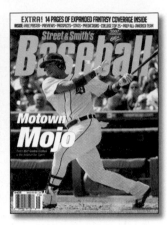
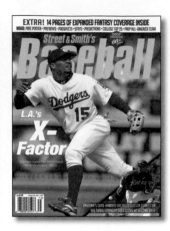

These *different* covers for the *same* magazine issue show a very effective market segmentation strategy. For which specific one it is and why it works, see the text.

Does Harry Potter appeal only to the kids' segment? See the text for the answer to this amazing publishing success.

should not attempt to segment its market. Three specific segmentation strategies that illustrate this point are: (1) one product and multiple market segments, (2) multiple products and multiple market segments, and (3) "segments of one," or mass customization.

One Product and Multiple Market Segments

When an organization produces only a single product or service and attempts to sell it to two or more market segments, it avoids the extra costs of developing and producing additional versions of the product, which often entail extremely high research, engineering, and manufacturing expenses. In this case, the incremental costs of taking the product into new market segments are typically those of a separate promotional campaign or a new channel of distribution. Although these expenses can be high, they are rarely as large as those for developing an entirely new product.

Movies, magazines, and books are single products frequently directed to two or more distinct market segments. Movie companies often run different TV commercials or magazine ads featuring different aspects of a newly released film (love, or drama, or spectacular scenery) that are targeted to different market segments. *Street & Smith's Baseball* annual issue uses different covers for its 14 regions of the United States, featuring a baseball star from that region.

Harry Potter's phenomenal seven-book success is based both on author J. K. Rowling's fiction-writing wizardry and her publisher's creativity in marketing to preteen, teen, and adult segments of readers around the world. By 2007, more than 350 million Harry Potter books had been sold globally in 64 languages. In the United States, the books were often at the top of *The New York Times* fiction bestseller list—for adults. *Harry Potter and the Deathly Hallows*, the seventh and final book in the series, had a record-shattering initial press run of 12 million copies in the United States. Although multiple TV commercials for movies and separate covers for magazines or separate advertisements for books are expensive, they are minor compared with the costs of producing an entirely new movie, magazine, or book for another market segment.

Multiple Products and Multiple Market Segments

Ford's different lines of cars, SUVs, and pickup trucks are each targeted at a different type of customer—examples of multiple products aimed at multiple market segments. Producing these different vehicles is clearly more expensive than producing only a single vehicle but is effective if it meets customers' needs better, doesn't reduce quality or increase price, and adds to Ford's sales revenues and profits.

Ann Taylor Stores Corp.'s Loft chain tries to reach trendy, casual customers while its flagship Ann Taylor chain targets a more sophisticated woman. Do these store fronts convey this difference? For the potential dangers of this two-segment strategy, see the text.

Marketing experts increasingly emphasize the two-tier marketing strategies—what some call "Tiffany/Wal-Mart strategies." Many firms are now offering different variations of the same basic product or service to high-end and low-end segments. Gap's Banana Republic chain sells blue jeans for $58, whereas its Old Navy stores sell a slightly different version for $22. The Walt Disney Company carefully markets two distinct Winnie-the-Poohs—such as the original line-drawn figures on fine china sold at Nordstrom and a cartoon-like Pooh on polyester bedsheets sold at Wal-Mart. The lines between customer segments often blur, however, leading to problems as shown with the Ann Taylor flagship store competing with its Loft outlets.

Segments of One: Mass Customization American marketers are rediscovering today what their ancestors running the corner general store knew a century ago: Each customer has unique needs and wants, and desires special tender loving care—the essence of *customer relationship management* (CRM). Economies of scale in manufacturing and marketing during the past century made mass-produced goods so affordable that most customers were willing to compromise their individual tastes and settle for standardized products. Today's Internet ordering and flexible manufacturing and marketing processes have made *mass customization* possible, which means tailoring goods or services to the tastes of individual customers on a high-volume scale.

Mass customization is the next step beyond *build-to-order* (BTO), manufacturing a product only when there is an order from a customer. Dell uses BTO systems that trim work-in-progress inventories and shorten delivery times to customers. Dell's three-day deliveries are made possible by restricting its computer manufacturing line to only a few basic modules and stocking a variety of each. This gives customers a good choice with quick delivery—Dell PCs can be assembled in four minutes. Most of Dell's customization comes from spending 90 minutes loading the unique software each customer selects. But even this system falls a bit short of total mass customization with virtually unlimited specification of features by customers.[8]

The Segmentation Trade-Off: CRM versus Synergies The key to successful product differentiation and market segmentation strategies is finding the ideal balance between satisfying a customer's individual wants and achieving organizational **synergy**, the increased customer value achieved through performing organizational functions like marketing or manufacturing more efficiently. The "increased customer value" can take many forms: more products, improved quality on existing products, lower prices, easier access to products through improved distribution, and so on. So the ultimate criterion for an organization's marketing success in customer relationship management is that customers should be better off as a result of the increased synergies.

The organization should also achieve increased revenues and profits from the product differentiation and market segmentation strategies it uses. When the increased customer value involves adding new products or a new chain of stores, the product differentiation–market segmentation trade-off raises a critical issue: Are the new products or new chain simply stealing customers and sales from the older, existing ones? This is known as cannibalization.

Ann Taylor Stores is an example of a specialty retailer struggling with how to keep the original chain of stores fresh without having the newcomer chain cannibalize sales from the original.[9] The flagship Ann Taylor chain targets a segment of polished, sophisticated women while its sister Ann Taylor Loft chain seeks to reach women wanting moderately priced, trendy, casual clothes they can wear to the office. The potential nightmare: Recently annual sales revenues of the Loft stores doubled and passed those of the Ann Taylor flagship chain, which was struggling to reach its target customers.

---

learning review

1. Market segmentation involves aggregating prospective buyers into groups that have two key characteristics. What are they?

2. In terms of market segments and products, what are the three market segmentation strategies?

STEPS IN SEGMENTING AND TARGETING MARKETS

Figure 9–2 identifies the five-step process used to segment a market and select the target segments on which it wants to focus. Segmenting a market requires both detailed analysis and large doses of common sense and managerial judgment. So market segmentation is both science and art!

Let's have you put on your marketing hat to use market segmentation to choose target markets and take useful marketing actions for your older sister's Wendy's restaurant. She wants to see if you learned something useful in your marketing class that can help her. If so, she'll make you a partner in her restaurant.

Her Wendy's is located next to a large urban university, one that offers both day and evening classes. Her restaurant offers the basic Wendy's fare: hamburgers, chicken and deli sandwiches, salads, fries, and Frosty desserts. Even though she is part of a chain and has some restrictions on menu and décor, she is free to set her hours of business and to develop local advertising. How can market segmentation help?

FIGURE 9–2

The five key steps in segmenting and targeting markets link market needs of customers to the organization's marketing program.

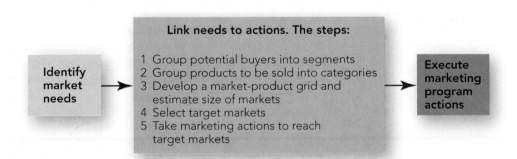

Step 1: Group Potential Buyers into Segments

It's not always a good idea to segment a market. Grouping potential buyers into meaningful segments involves meeting some specific criteria that answer the questions, "Would segmentation be worth doing and is it possible?" If so, a marketer must find specific variables that can be used to create these various segments.

Criteria to Use in Forming the Segments A marketing manager should develop segments for a market that meet five essential criteria:[10]

- *Simplicity and cost-effectiveness of assigning potential buyers to segments.* A marketing manager must be able to put a market segmentation plan into effect. This means identifying the characteristics of potential buyers in a market and then cost-effectively assigning them to a segment.
- *Potential for increased profit.* The best segmentation approach is the one that maximizes the opportunity for future profit and ROI. If this potential is maximized without segmentation, don't segment. For nonprofit organizations, the criterion is the potential for serving client users more effectively.
- *Similarity of needs of potential buyers within a segment.* Potential buyers within a segment should be similar in terms of a marketing action, such as product features sought or advertising media used.
- *Difference of needs of buyers among segments.* If the needs of the various segments aren't very different, combine them into fewer segments. A different segment usually requires a different marketing action that, in turn, means greater costs. If increased sales don't offset extra costs, combine segments and reduce the number of marketing actions.
- *Potential of a marketing action to reach a segment.* Reaching a segment requires a simple but effective marketing action. If no such action exists, don't segment.

Ways to Segment Consumer Markets Figure 9–3 on the next page shows four general bases of segmentation and the typical variables that can be used to segment U.S. consumer markets. Many are based on those from the 2000 U.S. Census. These four segmentation bases are: (1) *geographic segmentation*, which is based on where prospective customers live or work (region, city size); (2) *demographic segmentation*, which is based on some *objective* physical (gender, race), measurable (age, income), or other classification attribute (birth era, occupation) of prospective customers; (3) *psychographic segmentation*, which is based on some subjective mental or emotional attributes (personality), aspirations (lifestyle), or needs of prospective customers; and (4) *behavioral segmentation*, which is based on some observable actions or attitudes by prospective customers—such as where they buy, what benefits they seek, how frequently they buy, and why they buy. Some examples are:

- *Geographic segmentation: Region.* Campbell's found that its canned nacho cheese sauce, which could be heated and poured directly onto nacho chips, was too hot for Americans in the East and not hot enough for those in the West and Southwest. The result: Today, Campbell's plants in Texas and California produce a hotter nacho cheese sauce than that produced in the other plants to serve their regions better.
- *Demographic segmentation: Household size.* More than half of all U.S. households are made up of only one or two persons, so Campbell's packages meals with only one or two servings—from Great Starts breakfasts to L'Orient dinners.

What special benefit does a MicroFridge offer, and to which market segment might this appeal? The answer appears in the text.

Mac-Gray Corporation
www.microfridge.com

- *Psychographic segmentation: Lifestyle.* Claritas' lifestyle segmentation is based on the belief that "birds of a feather flock together." Thus, people of similar lifestyles tend to live near one another, have similar interests, and buy similar offerings. This is of great value to marketers. Claritas' PRIZM NE classifies every household in the United States into one of 66 unique market segments. See the Going Online box for a profile of where you live.
- *Behavioral segmentation: Product features.* Understanding what features are important to different customers is a useful way to segment markets because it can lead directly to specific marketing actions, such as a new product, an ad campaign, or a distribution system. For example, college dorm residents frequently want to keep and prepare their own food to save money or have a late-night snack. However, their dorm rooms are often woefully short of space. MicroFridge understands this and markets a combination microwave, refrigerator, and freezer targeted to these students.
- *Behavioral segmentation: Usage rate.* **Usage rate** is the quantity consumed or patronage—store visits—during a specific period. It varies significantly among different customer groups. Airlines have developed frequent-flier programs to encourage passengers to use the same airline repeatedly to create loyal customers. This technique, sometimes called *frequency marketing*, is a strategy that focuses on usage rate. One key conclusion emerges about usage: In market segmentation studies, some measure of usage by, or sales obtained from, various segments is central to the analysis.

FIGURE 9–3

Segmentation bases, variables, and breakdowns for U.S. consumer markets. In selecting a segmentation variable, a marketing manager needs it to lead to a marketing action.

Basis of Segmentation	Segmentation Variables	Typical Breakdowns
Geographic	Region	Northeast; Midwest; South; West; etc.
	City size	Under 10,000; 10,000–24,999; 25,000–49,999; 50,000–99,999; etc.
	Statistical area	Metropolitan and micropolitan statistical areas; Census tract; etc.
	Media-television	210 designated market areas (DMA) in the U.S. (Nielsen)
	Density	Urban; suburban; small town; rural
Demographic	Gender	Male; female
	Age	Under 6 yrs; 6–11 yrs; 12–17 yrs; 18–24 yrs; 25–34 yrs; etc.
	Race/ethnicity	African American; Asian; Hispanic; White/Caucasian; etc.
	Life stage	Infant; preschool; child; youth; collegiate; adult; senior
	Birth era	Baby boomer (1946–1964); Generation X (1965–1976); etc.
	Household size	1; 2; 3–4; 5 or more
	Marital status	Never married; married; separated; divorced; widowed; domestic partner
	Income	Under $15,000; $15,000–$24,999; $25,000–$34,999; etc.
	Education	Some high school or less; high school graduate (or GED); etc.
	Occupation	Managerial & professional; technical, sales; farming; etc.
Psychographic	Personality	Gregarious; compulsive; extroverted; aggressive; ambitious; etc.
	Values (VALS2)	Innovators; Thinkers; Achievers; Experiencers; Believers; Strivers; etc.
	Lifestyle (Claritas PRIZM NE)	Blue Blood Estates; Single City Blues; etc. 66 total neighborhood clusters
	Needs	Quality; service; price/value; health; convenience; etc.
Behavioral	Outlet type	Department; specialty; outlet; convenience; mass merchandiser; etc.
	Direct	Mail order/catalog; door-to-door; direct response; Internet
	Product features	Situation-specific; general
	Usage rate	Light user; medium user; heavy user
	User status	Nonuser; ex-user; prospect; first-time user; regular user
	Awareness/intentions	Unaware; aware; interested; intending to buy; purchaser; rejection

Going Online

What "Flock" Do You Belong to?

Who are your target customers? What are they like? Where do they live? How can you reach them? These questions are answered by Claritas, whose PRIZM NE classifies every household into one of 66 demographically and behaviorally distinct neighborhood segments to identify their lifestyles and purchase behavior within a defined geographic market area, such as zip code.

Want to know what your neighborhood is like? Go to claritas.com/MyBestSegments/Default.jsp and click the "You Are Where You Live" image. Then, type in your zip code (and security code) to find out what the most common segments are in your neighborhood. For a description of these segments, click the "Segment Main Links" tab. Is this your "flock?"

To obtain usage rate data for more than 450 consumer product categories, the Simmons Market Research Bureau semiannually surveys about 25,000 adults. The purpose is to discover how the products and services they buy and the media they watch relate to their behavioral, psychographic, and demographic characteristics. Figure 9–4 shows the results of a question Simmons asked about adult respondents' frequency of use (or patronage) of fast-food restaurants.[11]

As shown in the right column of Figure 9–4, the importance of the segment increases as we move up the table. Among nonusers of these restaurants, prospects (who might become users) are more important than nonprospects (who are never likely to become users). Moving up the rows to users, it seems logical that light users of these restaurants (0 to 5 times per month) are important but less so than medium users (6 to 13 times per month), who, in turn, are a less important segment than the critical group: heavy users (14 or more times per

FIGURE 9–4

Patronage of fast-food restaurants by adults 18 years and older. The table shows the critical importance of attracting heavy users and medium users to a fast-food restaurant.

User or Nonuser	Specific Segment	Number (1,000s)	Percentage	Actual Consumption (%)	Usage Index Per Person	Importance of Segment
Users	Heavy users (14+ per month)	32,189	15.0%	34.6%	400	High
	Medium users (6–13 per month)	54,511	25.3	39.8	271	
	Light users (0–5 per month)	95,295	44.3	25.6	100	
Total users		181,995	84.6	100.0	204	
Nonusers	Prospects	3,558	1.7	—	—	
	Nonprospects	29,568	13.7	—	—	
Total nonusers		33,126	15.4	—	—	Low
Total	Users and nonusers	215,121	100.0	—	—	

Source: Simmons Market Research Bureau, NCS/NHCS, Spring 2007, Adult Full-Year Choices System Crosstabulation Report based on visits within the past 30 days.

FIGURE 9-5

Comparison of various kinds of users and nonusers for Wendy's, Burger King, and McDonald's fast-food restaurants. This table gives a Wendy's restaurant a snapshot of its customers compared to those of its major competitors.

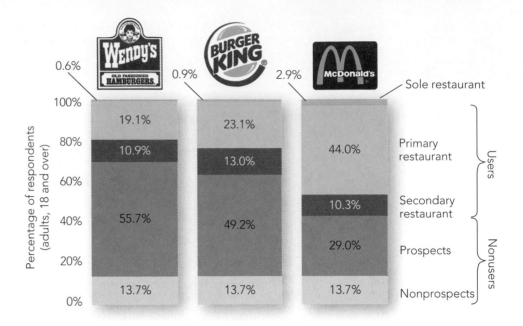

Source: Simmons Market Research Bureau NCS/NHCS Spring 2007 Adult Full-Year Choices System Crosstabulation Report based on visits within the past 30 days.

month). The Actual Consumption column in Figure 9–4 shows how much of the total monthly usage of these restaurants are accounted for by heavy, medium, and light users.

Usage rate is sometimes referred to in terms of the **80/20 rule**, a concept that suggests 80 percent of a firm's sales are obtained from 20 percent of its customers. The percentages in the 80/20 rule are not really fixed at exactly 80 percent and 20 percent but suggest that a small fraction of customers provides a large fraction of a firm's sales. For example, Figure 9–4 shows that the 15.0 percent of the U.S. population who are heavy users of fast-food restaurants provide 34.6 percent of the consumption volume.

The Usage Index per Person column in Figure 9–4 emphasizes the importance of the heavy-user group even more. Giving the light users (0 to 5 restaurant visits per month) an index of 100, the heavy users have an index of 400. In other words, for every $1.00 spent by a light user in one of these restaurants in a month, each heavy user spends $4.00. This is the reason for the emphasis in almost all marketing strategies on effective ways to reach these heavy users. As a Wendy's restaurant owner, you want to keep the heavy-user segment constantly in mind and focus most of your marketing efforts on reaching them.

As part of the Simmons fast-food survey, adult restaurant patrons were asked if each restaurant was (1) the sole or only restaurant they went to, (2) the primary one, or (3) one of several secondary ones. This national information, shown in Figure 9–5, might give you, as a Wendy's owner, some ideas in developing your local strategy. The Wendy's bar in Figure 9–5 shows that your sole (0.6 percent), primary (19.1 percent), and secondary (10.9 percent) user segments are somewhat behind Burger King and far behind McDonald's, so a natural strategy is to look at these two competitors and devise a marketing program to win customers from them.

The nonusers part of the Wendy's bar in Figure 9–5 also provides ideas. It shows that 13.7 percent of adult Americans don't go to fast-food restaurants in a typical month (also shown in Figure 9–4) and are really nonprospects—unlikely to ever patronize your restaurant. But the 55.7 percent of the Wendy's bar shown as prospects may be worth detailed thought. These

What variables might Xerox use to segment organizational markets for its answer to color copying problems? For the possible answer and related marketing actions, see the text.

234

adults use the product category (fast food) but do not go to Wendy's. New menu items or promotional strategies may succeed in converting these prospects into users that patronize Wendy's.

Variables to Use in Forming Segments   To help your sister analyze her Wendy's customers, you need to identify which variables to use to segment them. Because the restaurant is located near a large urban university, the most logical starting point for segmentation is really behavioral: Are the prospective customers students or nonstudents?

To segment the students, you could try a variety of (1) geographic variables, such as city or zip code, (2) demographic variables, such as gender, age, year in school, or college major, or (3) psychographic variables, such as personality or needs. But none of these variables really meets the five criteria listed previously—particularly, the fifth criterion about leading to a doable marketing action to reach the various segments. However, the behavioral variable of "students" versus "nonstudents" does meet these criteria. Broken down, the "students" variable includes:

- Students living in dormitories (university residence halls, sororities, fraternities).
- Students living near the university in apartments.
- Day commuter students living outside the area.
- Night commuter students living outside the area.

These segmentation variables are a combination of where the student lives and the time he or she is on campus (and near your restaurant). Broken down, the "nonstudents" variable includes:

- Faculty and staff members who work at the university.
- People who live in the area but aren't connected with the university.
- People who work in the area but aren't connected with the university.

People in each of these segments aren't quite as similar as those in the student segments, which makes them harder to reach with a marketing program or action. Think about (1) whether the needs of all these segments are different and (2) how various advertising media can be used to reach these groups effectively.

Ways to Segment Organizational Markets   A number of variables can be used to segment organizational markets (see Figure 9–6). For example, a product

FIGURE 9–6
Segmentation bases, variables, and breakdowns for U.S. organizational markets. These variables are used in business-to-business marketing.

Basis of Segmentation	Segmentation Variables	Typical Breakdowns
Geographic	Global region or country Statistical area Density	European Union, South America, etc.; U.S., Japan, India, etc. Metropolitan and micropolitan statistical areas; Census tract; etc. Urban; suburban; small town; rural
Demographic	NAICS code NAICS sector Number of employees Annual Sales	2 digit: Sector; 3 digit: subsector; 4 digit: industry group; etc. Agriculture, forestry (11); mining (21); utilities (22); etc. 1–99; 100–499; 500–999; 1,000–4,999; 5,000 + Under $1 million; $1 million–$9.9 million; $10 million–$49.9 million; etc.
	Number of locations	1–9; 10–49; 50–99; 100–499; 500–999; 1,000+
Behavioral	Kind Where used Application Purchase location Who buys Type of buy	Product; service Installation; component; supplies; etc. Office; production; etc. Centralized; decentralized Individual buyer; group of buyers New buy; modified rebuy; straight rebuy

manager at Xerox responsible for its new line of color printers might use these segmentation bases and corresponding variables:

- *Geographic segmentation: Statistical area.* Firms located in a metropolitan statistical area might receive a personal sales call, whereas those in a micropolitan statistical area might be contacted by telephone.
- *Demographic segmentation: NAICS code.* Firms categorized by the North American Industry Classification System code as manufacturers that deal with customers throughout the world might have different document printing needs than do retailers or lawyers serving local customers.
- *Demographic segmentation: Number of employees.* The size of the firm is related to the volume of digital documents produced, so firms with varying numbers of employees might be specific target markets for different Xerox systems.
- *Behavioral segmentation: Usage rate.* Similar to this segmentation variable for consumer markets, features are often of major importance in organizational markets. So Xerox can target organizations needing fast printing, copying, and scanning in color—the benefits and features emphasized in the ad for its new Xerox WorkCentre 7655 Color MFP system.

learning review

3. The process of segmenting and targeting markets is a bridge between what two marketing activities?

4. What is the difference between the demographic and behavioral bases of market segmentation?

Step 2: Group Products to Be Sold into Categories

What is "your"—assuming you become a partner—Wendy's restaurant selling? Of course you are selling individual products such as Frostys, hamburgers, and fries. But for marketing purposes you're really selling combinations of individual products that become a "meal." This distinction is critical, so let's discuss both (1) individual Wendy's products and (2) groupings of Wendy's products.

Individual Wendy's Products When Dave Thomas founded Wendy's in 1969, he offered only four basic items: "hot 'n juicy" hamburgers, Frosty Dairy Desserts (Frostys), French fries, and soft drinks. Since then, Wendy's has introduced many new products and innovations to compete for customers' fast-food dollars. Some of these are shown in Figure 9–7. New products include baked potatoes, salads, and low trans fat chicken sandwiches. But there are also nonproduct innovations to increase consumer convenience like drive-thru meals and ePay (to enable credit card purchases).

Figure 9–7 also shows that each product or innovation is not targeted equally to all market segments based on gender, needs, or university affiliation. The cells in Figure 9–7 labeled "P" represent Wendy's primary target market segments when it introduced each product or innovation. The boxes labeled "S" represent the secondary target market segments that also bought these products or used these innovations. In some cases, Wendy's discovered that large numbers of people in a segment not originally targeted for a particular product or innovation bought it anyway.

Groupings of Wendy's Products: Meals Finding a means of grouping the products a firm sells into meaningful categories is as important as grouping customers into segments. If the firm has only one product or service, this isn't a problem, but when it has dozens or hundreds, these must be grouped in some way so buyers can

MARKET SEGMENT		PRODUCT OR INNOVATION								
GENERAL	GROUP WITH NEED	HOT 'N JUICY HAMBURGER (1969)	DRIVE-THRU (1970)	99¢ SUPER VALUE MEALS (1989)	SALAD SENSATIONS (2002)	E-PAY (2003)	ADULT COMBO MEALS (2004)	LOW TRANS FAT CHICKEN SANDWICHES (2006)	FRESCATA DELI SANDWICHES (2006)	BREAKFAST SANDWICHES (2007)
GENDER	Male	P	P	P	S	P	P	S	P	P
	Female			P	P	S	P	P	P	
NEEDS	Price/Value			P	S		P			
	Health-Conscious				P			P	P	
	Convenience	S	P		S	P	S			P
	Meat Lovers	P		S			P	S	S	
UNIVERSITY AFFILIATION	Affiliated (Students, Faculty, Staff)	P	S	S	S	P	S	S	P	S
	Non Affiliated (Residents, Workers)	S	P	S	S	S	P	S	S	P

Key: P = Primary market   S = Secondary market

FIGURE 9–7
Wendy's new products and other innovations target specific market segments based on a customer's gender, needs, or university affiliation.

relate to them. This is why department stores and supermarkets are organized into product groups, with the departments or aisles containing related merchandise. Likewise, manufacturers have product lines that are the groupings they use in the catalogs sent to customers.

What are the product groupings for your Wendy's restaurant? It could be the item purchased, such as, hamburgers, salads, a Frosty, and French fries. This is where judgment—the qualitative aspect of marketing—comes in. Customers really buy an eating experience, or a meal occasion that satisfies a need at a particular time of day, so the product grouping that makes the most marketing sense is by meal or time of day: Breakfast, lunch, between-meal snack, dinner, and after-dinner snack. These groupings are more closely related to the way purchases are actually made and permit you to market the entire meal, not just your French fries or hamburgers.

Step 3: Develop a Market-Product Grid and Estimate the Size of Markets

A **market-product grid** is a framework to relate the market segments of potential buyers to products offered or potential marketing actions by an organization. In a complete market-product grid analysis, each cell in the grid can show the estimated market size of a given product sold to a specific market segment. Let's first look at forming a market-product grid for your Wendy's restaurant and then at estimating market sizes.

Forming a Market-Product Grid Developing a market-product grid means identifying and labeling the markets (or horizontal rows) and product groupings (or vertical columns), as shown in Figure 9–8 on the next page. From our earlier discussion we've chosen to divide the row market segments as students versus nonstudents,

FIGURE 9–8
Selecting a target market
for your Wendy's fast-food
restaurant next to an urban
university. The numbers show
the estimated size of market
in that cell, which leads to
selecting the shaded target
market.

Market Segments	Break-fast	Lunch	Between-Meal Snack	Dinner	After-Dinner Snack
PRODUCTS: MEALS					
Student					
Dormitory	0	1	3	0	3
Apartment	1	3	3	1	1
Day commuter	0	3	2	1	0
Night commuter	0	0	1	3	2
Nonstudent		*GAid*			
Faculty or staff	0	3	1	1	0
Live in area	0	1	2	2	1
Work in area	1	3	0	1	0

Key: 3 = Large market; 2 = Medium market; 1 = Small market; 0 = No market.

with subdivisions of each. The columns—or "products"—are really the meals (or eating occasions) customers enjoy at the restaurant.

Estimating Market Sizes Now the size of the market in each cell (the unique market-product combination) of the market-product grid must be estimated. For your Wendy's restaurant, this involves estimating the sales of each kind of meal expected to be sold to each student and nonstudent market segment.

The market size estimates in Figure 9–8 vary from a large market ("3") to no market at all ("0") for each cell in the market-product grid. These may be simple guesstimates if you don't have the time or money to conduct formal marketing research (as discussed in Chapter 8). But even such crude estimates of the size of specific markets using a market-product grid are helpful in determining which target market segments to select and which product groupings to offer.

Step 4: Select Target Markets

A firm must take care to choose its target market segments carefully. If it picks too narrow a set of segments, it may fail to reach the volume of sales and profits it needs. If it selects too broad a set of segments, it may spread its marketing efforts so thin that the extra expense exceeds the increased sales and profits.

Criteria to Use in Selecting the Target Segments There are two different kinds of criteria in the market segmentation process: those used to (1) divide the market into segments (discussed earlier) and (2) actually pick the target segments. Even experienced marketing executives often confuse these two different sets of criteria. Five criteria can be used to select the target segments for your Wendy's restaurant:

- *Market size.* The estimated size of the market in the segment is an important factor in deciding whether it's worth going after. There is really no market for breakfasts among dormitory students (Figure 9–8), so why devote any marketing effort toward reaching a small or nonexistent segment? However,

Going Online

Zestimates from Zillow

Want to know what your parents' home is worth? What about the current value of your home in your old neighborhood? Go to Zillow (www.zillow.com), which provides "zillions" of data for the place(s) where your "pillow" is located (zillion + pillow = Zillow!). Zillow is an online real estate service that answers the most important question, "How much is my home really worth?"

It calculates a Zestimate™ based on publicly available information (recently sold home prices, tax assessments, etc.) to arrive at a home's estimated market value. Zillow also provides the values and a "bird's eye" aerial view of your home and others in the neighborhood and allows realtors and even homeowners to adjust the Zestimate, upload a picture of the property, or post the home for sale—for free! So, go to Zillow, type in the address, and check out what your home is worth—you may NOT want to tell your parents about what you found out!

suppose you want to reach families in a particular income segment and believe the value of their home is a good indicator. Then you might do some research on Zillow.com, as described in the Going Online box.

- *Expected growth.* Although the size of the market in the segment may be small now, perhaps it is growing significantly or is expected to grow in the future. Sales of fast-food meals eaten outside the restaurants are projected to exceed those eaten inside. And Wendy's is the fast-food leader in average time to serve a drive-thru order—it is 16.7 seconds faster than McDonald's. This speed and convenience is potentially very important to night commuters in adult education programs.[12]

- *Competitive position.* Is there a lot of competition in the segment now or is there likely to be in the future? The less the competition, the more attractive the segment is. For example, if the college dormitories announce a new policy of "no meals on weekends," this segment is suddenly more promising for your restaurant. Wendy's recently introduced E-Pay pay-by-credit-card service at its restaurants to keep up with McDonald's.

- *Cost of reaching the segment.* A segment that is inaccessible to a firm's marketing actions should not be pursued. For example, the few nonstudents who live in the area may not be reachable with ads in newspapers or other media. As a result, do not waste money trying to advertise to them.

- *Compatibility with the organization's objectives and resources.* If your Wendy's restaurant doesn't yet have the cooking equipment to make breakfasts and has a policy against spending more money on restaurant equipment, then don't try to reach the breakfast segment. As is often the case in marketing decisions, a particular segment may appear attractive according to some criteria and very unattractive according to others.

Choose the Segments Ultimately, a marketing executive has to use these criteria to choose the segments for special marketing efforts. As shown in Figure 9–8, let's assume you've written off the breakfast product grouping for two reasons: it's too small a market and it's incompatible with your objectives and resources. In terms of competitive position and cost of reaching the segment, you choose to focus on the four student segments and *not* the three nonstudent segments (although

A late night oasis
on the highway of hunger.

Wendy's Late Night Pick-up Window
is open 'til midnight or later.
So, you can get a
hot 'n juicy Classic Single,
Classic Double with cheese
or Classic Triple with cheese,
and eat great, even late.

How can Wendy's target different market segments like night customers or commuting college students with different advertising programs? For the answer, see the text and Figure 9–9.

you're certainly not going to turn away business from the nonstudent segments!). This combination of market-product segments—your target market—is shaded in Figure 9–8.

Step 5: Take Marketing Actions to Reach Target Markets

The purpose of developing a market-product grid is to trigger marketing actions to increase sales and profits. This means that someone must develop and execute an action plan in the form of a marketing program.

Your Immediate Wendy's Segmentation Strategy
With your Wendy's restaurant you've already reached one significant decision: There is a limited market for breakfast, so you won't open for business until 10:30 a.m. In fact, Wendy's first attempt at a breakfast menu was a disaster and was discontinued in 1986. Wendy's evaluates possible new menu items continuously to compete not only with McDonald's and Burger King but also with a complex array of convenience stores and gas stations that sell reheatable packaged foods as well as new "easy-lunch" products.

Another essential decision is where and what meals to advertise to reach specific market segments. An ad in the student newspaper could reach all the student segments, but you might consider this approach too expensive and want a more focused effort to reach smaller segments. If you choose three segments for special actions (Figure 9–9), advertising actions to reach them might include:

- *Day commuters* (an entire market segment). Run ads inside commuter buses and put flyers under the windshield wipers of cars in parking lots used by

FIGURE 9–9
Advertising actions to reach specific student segments. These actions can vary from trying to reach an entire market segment or customers for a specific meal to a narrow niche (dinners for night commuters).

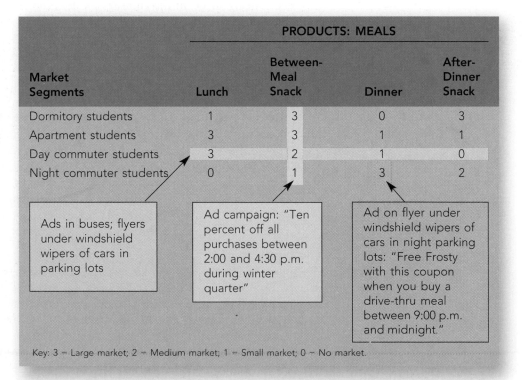

Market Segments	PRODUCTS: MEALS			
	Lunch	Between-Meal Snack	Dinner	After-Dinner Snack
Dormitory students	1	3	0	3
Apartment students	3	3	1	1
Day commuter students	3	2	1	0
Night commuter students	0	1	3	2

Ads in buses; flyers under windshield wipers of cars in parking lots

Ad campaign: "Ten percent off all purchases between 2:00 and 4:30 p.m. during winter quarter"

Ad on flyer under windshield wipers of cars in night parking lots: "Free Frosty with this coupon when you buy a drive-thru meal between 9:00 p.m. and midnight."

Key: 3 = Large market; 2 = Medium market; 1 = Small market; 0 = No market.

day commuters. These ads and flyers promote all the meals at your restaurant to a single segment of students, a horizontal cut through the market-product grid.

- *Between-meal snacks* (directed to all four student markets). To promote eating during this downtime for your restaurant, offer "Ten percent off all purchases between 2:00 and 4:30 p.m. during winter quarter." This ad promotes a single meal to all four student segments, a vertical cut through the market-product grid.
- *Dinners to night commuters.* The most focused of all three campaigns, this ad promotes a single meal to the single segment of night commuter students. The campaign might consist of a windshield flyer offering a free Frosty with the coupon when the person buys a drive-thru meal between 9:00 p.m. and midnight.

Depending on how your advertising actions work, you can repeat, modify, or drop them and design new campaigns for other segments you feel are worth the effort. This example of advertising your Wendy's restaurant is just a small piece of a complete marketing program using all the elements of the marketing mix. In 2006, Wendy's introduced new menu items to appeal to segments in the various nutritional concerns: low-trans-fat chicken and fries and its Frescata deli sandwiches with focaccia bread. And a special success is Wendy's focus on the after-dinner snack column in Figure 9–9: As shown in Wendy's ad, its late-night pickup window is open until midnight or later, even though most of its restaurants close their doors to customers at 10:00 p.m.

Future Strategies for Your Wendy's Restaurant Changing customer tastes and competition mean your sister and you must alter your strategies when necessary. This involves looking at both (1) what Wendy's headquarters is doing and (2) what might be changing in the area around your restaurant.

New Wendy's President and CEO Kerrii B. Anderson plans to continue the company's focus on high-quality hamburgers, salads, and vegetables. And she will continue to position Wendy's to be the preferred restaurant for lunch, between-meal snacks, dinner, and late night.[13] Some other innovations now coming off corporate Wendy's drawing boards:[14]

- Promotions to target younger, 16-to 34-year-old customers.
- A new vanilla-flavored Frosty, launched after considering over 100 different varieties of vanilla flavoring.
- Breakfasts, with new quick-to-serve menu items to lure commuting breakfast eaters—and overcome the too-slow-to-cook 1980s breakfast disaster.

With these corporate plans, maybe you'd better rethink your market segmentation decisions on hours of operation and breakfasts. Also, if new businesses have moved into your area, what about a new strategy to reach people that work in the area? Or a new promotion for the night owls and early birds—the 8 p.m. to 5 a.m. customers—that now generate one-sixth of revenues at some McDonald's restaurants?[15]

Apple's Ever-Changing Segmentation Strategy Steve Jobs and Steve Wozniak didn't realize they were developing today's multibillion-dollar PC industry when they invented the Apple I in a garage on April Fool's Day in 1976. Hobbyists, the initial target market, were not interested in the product. However, when the Apple II was displayed at a computer trade show in 1977, consumers loved it and Apple Computer was born. Typical of young companies, Apple focused on its products and had little concern for its markets. Its creative, young engineers were often likened to "Boy Scouts without adult supervision."[16]

What should Wendy's do nationally to compete with McDonald's and other fast-food restaurants? Wendy's president and CEO Kerrii B. Anderson has some strategies that are discussed in the text.

Steve Jobs left Apple in 1985, the company languished, and it constantly altered its market-product strategies. When Steve Jobs returned in 1997, he detailed his vision for a reincarnated Apple by describing a new market segmentation strategy that he called the "Apple Product Matrix." This strategy consisted of developing two general types of computers (desktops and portables) targeted at two general kinds of market segments—the consumer and professional sectors.

Today Jobs believes that the personal computer has entered the age of the digital lifestyle involving countless digital devices—such as MP3 players, cell phones, digital cameras, and so on. Jobs enthusiastically proclaims, "The Mac can become the digital hub of this new digital lifestyle." With "killer apps," such as iTunes, iLife, and iWork, and revolutionary products such as the iPhone and iPod, Jobs believes consumers can exploit the new digital lifestyle era.[17]

In most segmentation situations, a single product does not fit into an exclusive market niche. Rather, product lines and market segments overlap. So Apple's market segmentation strategy enables it to offer different products to meet the needs of different market segments, as shown in the Marketing Matters box. Stay tuned to see if Steve Jobs and these market-product strategies for his vision of the digital lifestyle era are on target. He's betting the company on it!

Market-Product Synergies: A Balancing Act

Recognizing opportunities for key synergies—that is, efficiencies—is vital to success in selecting target market segments and making marketing decisions. Market-product grids illustrate where such synergies can be found. How? Let's consider Apple's market-product grid in the accompanying Marketing Matters box and examine the difference between marketing synergies and product synergies shown there.

- *Marketing synergies.* Running horizontally across the grid, each row represents an opportunity for efficiency in terms of a market segment. Were Apple to focus on just one group of consumers, such as the medium/large business segment, its marketing efforts could be streamlined. Time would not have to be spent learning about the buying habits of students or college faculty. So it could probably do a single ad to reach the medium/large business target segment (the yellow row), highlighting the only products they'd need to worry about developing: the Mac Pro, the MacBook Pro, and the iMac. Although clearly this is not Apple's strategy today, focusing on a single customer segment is a common marketing strategy for new companies.
- *Product synergies.* Running vertically down the market-product grid, each column represents an opportunity for efficiency in research and development (R&D) and production. If Apple wanted to simplify its product line, reduce R&D and production expenses, and manufacture only one computer, which might it choose? Based on the market-product grid, Apple might do well to focus on the iMac (the orange column), since every segment purchases it.

A choice to take advantage of marketing synergies can often come at the expense of production ones because a single customer segment will likely require a variety of products, each of which will have to be designed and manufactured. The company saves money on marketing but spends more in production. Conversely, if product synergies are emphasized, marketing will have to address the concerns of a wide variety of consumers, which costs more time and money. Marketing managers responsible for developing a company's product line must

How has Apple moved from its 1977 Apple II to today's Mac Pro? The Marketing Matters box and text discussion provide insights into Apple's current market segmentation strategy.

Apple, Inc.
www.apple.com

Marketing Matters > > > > > > > technology

Apple's Segmentation Strategy—Camp Runamok No Longer

Camp Runamok was the nickname given to Apple in the early 1980s because the innovative company had no coherent series of product lines directed at identifiable market segments. Today, Apple has targeted its various lines of Macintosh computers at specific market segments, as shown in the market-product grid below. Because the market-product grid shifts as a firm's strategy changes, the one below is based on Apple's product lines in late 2007. The grid suggests the market segmentation strategy Steve Jobs is using to compete in what he sees as the age of the digital lifestyle, as described in the text.

MARKETS		HARDWARE PRODUCTS				
Sector	Segment	 Mac Pro	 MacBook Pro	 iMac	 MacBook	 Mac Mini
Consumer	Individuals	✓	✓	✓	✓	✓
	Small/home office	✓	✓	✓	✓	
	Students			✓	✓	✓
	Teachers	✓	✓	✓		
Professional	Medium/large business	✓	✓	✓		
	Creative	✓	✓	✓		
	College faculty	✓	✓	✓		
	College staff			✓	✓	

balance both product and marketing synergies as they try to increase the company's profits.

---

learning review

5. What are some criteria used to decide which segments to choose for targets?

6. In a market-product grid, what factor is estimated or measured for each of the cells?

7. What is the difference between marketing synergies and product synergies in a market-product grid?

POSITIONING THE PRODUCT

LO5

When a company introduces a new product, a decision critical to its long-term success is how prospective buyers view it in relation to those products offered by its competitors. **Product positioning** refers to the place an offering occupies in consumers' minds on important attributes relative to competitive products. By understanding where consumers

More "zip" for chocolate milk? The text and figure describe how American dairies have been successfully repositioning chocolate milk to appeal to American adults.

FIGURE 9–10

A perceptual map of the location of beverages in the minds of American adults. Toward which letter would you try to move the perception of chocolate milk to make it more appealing to these adults?

see a company's product or brand today, a marketing manager can seek to change its future position in their minds. This requires **product repositioning**, *changing* the place an offering occupies in a consumer's mind relative to competitive products.

Two Approaches to Product Positioning

There are two main approaches to positioning a new product in the market. *Head-to-head positioning* involves competing directly with competitors on similar product attributes in the same target market. Using this strategy, Dollar competes directly with Avis and Hertz.

Differentiation positioning involves seeking a less-competitive, smaller market niche in which to locate a brand. McDonald's tried to appeal to the health-conscious segment when it introduced the low-fat McLean Deluxe hamburger to avoid competing directly with Wendy's and Burger King. However, it was eventually dropped from the menu. Companies also follow a differentiation positioning strategy among brands within their own product line to minimize the cannibalization of a brand's sales or market shares.

Writing a Positioning Statement

Marketing managers often convert their positioning ideas for the offering into a succinct written positioning statement. The positioning statement not only is used internally within the marketing department but also for others, outside it, such as research and development engineers or advertising agencies.[18] Here is the Volvo positioning statement for the North American market:

> For upscale American families who desire a carefree driving experience, Volvo is a premium-priced automobile that offers the utmost in safety and dependability.

This focuses Volvo's North American marketing strategy and has led to adding side-door airbags for its cars. Also, Volvo advertising almost always mention safety and dependability—as seen in its "Volvo for life" campaigns.

Product Positioning Using Perceptual Maps

A key to positioning a product or brand effectively is the perceptions of customers. In determining its position and the preferences of customers, companies obtain three types of data from consumers:

1. Identification of the important attributes for a product class.
2. Judgments of existing products or brands with respect to these attributes.
3. Ratings of an "ideal" product's or brand's attributes.

The firm can then develop market strategies to move its product or brand to an ideal position. From these data, it is possible to develop a **perceptual map**, a means of displaying or graphing in two dimensions the location of products or brands in the minds of consumers to enable a manager to see how consumers perceive competing products or brands and then take marketing actions. Look at Figure 9–10 and develop a positioning strategy to make chocolate milk more appealing to adults.

High nutrition

Regular milk ○

○ Orange juice

Ⓑ

Chocolate milk ○

○ Milk shakes Ⓓ

○ Nutritionally designed diet drinks

○ Tea

Ⓒ

○ Sports drinks

Children's drinks

Adult drinks

Ⓔ

Mineral water

○ Skinny latte

○ Fruit-flavored drinks

○ Coffee

Ⓕ

○ Sugared soft drinks

Ⓐ

Low nutrition

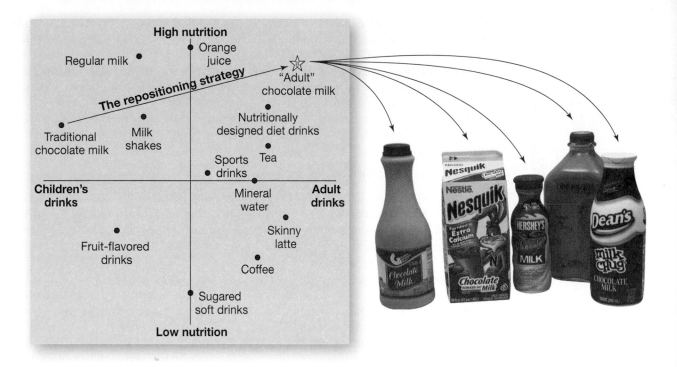

FIGURE 9–11

The strategy American dairies are using to reposition chocolate milk to reach adults: Have adults view chocolate milk both as more nutritional and "more adult."

Repositioning Chocolate Milk for Adults Figure 9–10 shows the positions that consumer beverages might occupy in the minds of Americans adults. Note that even these positions vary from one consumer to another. But for simplicity, let's assume these are the typical positions on the beverage perceptual map of adult Americans.

U.S. dairies, struggling to increase milk sales, hit on a wild idea: Target adults by positioning chocolate milk to the location of the star shown in the perceptual map in Figure 9–11, the position of letter "B" in Figure 9–10. Their arguments are nutritionally powerful. For women, chocolate milk provides calcium, critically important in female diets. And dieters get a more filling, nutritious beverage than with a soft drink for about the same calories.[19] The result: Chocolate milk sales increased dramatically, much of it because of adult consumption.[20] Part of this is due to giving chocolate milk "nutritional respectability" for adults, but another part is due to the innovative packaging that enables many new chocolate milk containers to fit in a car's cup holders.

SALES FORECASTING TECHNIQUES

Forecasting or estimating potential sales is often a key goal in a marketing research and market segmentation studies. Good sales forecasts are important for a firm as it schedules production.[21]

The term **market potential**, or **industry potential**, refers to the maximum total sales of a product by all firms to a segment during a specified time period under specified environmental conditions and marketing efforts of the firms. For example, the market potential for cake mix sales to U.S. consumers in 2008 might be 12 million cases—what Betty Crocker, Pinnacle Foods Group (Duncan Hines brand), and other cake mix producers would sell to American consumers under the assumptions that (1) past patterns of dessert consumption continue and (2) the same level of promotional effort continues relative to other desserts. The term **sales forecast**, or **company forecast**, refers to the total sales of a product that a firm expects to sell during a specified time period under specified environmental conditions and its own marketing efforts. For example, Betty Crocker might develop a sales forecast of 4 million cases of cake mix for U.S. consumers in 2008, assuming consumers' dessert preferences remain constant and competitors don't change prices.

Three main sales forecasting techniques are often used: (1) judgments of the decision maker, (2) surveys of knowledgeable groups, and (3) statistical methods.

Judgments of the Decision Maker

Probably 99 percent of all sales forecasts are simply the judgment of the person who must act on the results of the forecast—the individual decision maker. A **direct forecast** involves estimating the value to be forecast without any intervening steps. Examples appear daily: How many quarts of milk should I buy? How much money should I get out of the ATM?

You probably get the same cash withdrawal most times you use the ATM. But if you need to withdraw more than the usual amount, you would probably make some intervening steps (such as counting the cash in your pocket or estimating what you'll need for special events this week) to obtain your direct forecast.

A **lost-horse forecast** involves making a forecast using the last known value and modifying it according to positive or negative factors expected in the future. The technique gets its name from how you'd find a lost horse: Go to where it was last seen, put yourself in its shoes, consider those factors that could affect where you might go (to the pond if you're thirsty, the hayfield if you're hungry, and so on), and go there. For example, a product manager for Wilson's tennis rackets in 2008 who needed to make a sales forecast through 2010 would start with the known value of 2007 sales and list the positive factors (more tennis courts, more TV publicity) and the negative ones (competition from other sports, high prices of graphite and ceramic rackets) to arrive at the final series of annual sales forecasts.

Surveys of Knowledgeable Groups

If you wonder what your firm's sales will be next year, ask people who are likely to know something about future sales. Two common groups that are surveyed to develop sales forecasts are prospective buyers and the firm's salesforce.

A **survey of buyers' intentions forecast** involves asking prospective customers if they are likely to buy the product during some future time period. For industrial products with few prospective buyers, this can be effective. There are only a few hundred customers in the entire world for Boeing's largest airplanes, so Boeing surveys them to develop its sales forecasts and production schedules.

A **salesforce survey forecast** involves asking the firm's salespeople to estimate sales during a coming period. Because these people are in contact with customers and are likely to know what customers like and dislike, there is logic to this approach. However, salespeople can be unreliable forecasters—painting too rosy a picture if they are enthusiastic about a new product and too grim a forecast if their sales quota and future compensation are based on it.

Statistical Methods

The best-known statistical method of forecasting is **trend extrapolation**, which involves extending a pattern observed in past data into the future. When the pattern is described with a straight line, it is **linear trend extrapolation**. Suppose that in

How might a marketing manager at Wilson forecast tennis rackets sales through 2010? Use a lost-horse forecast, as described in the text.

FIGURE 9–12

Linear trend extrapolation of sales revenues at Xerox, made at the start of 2000

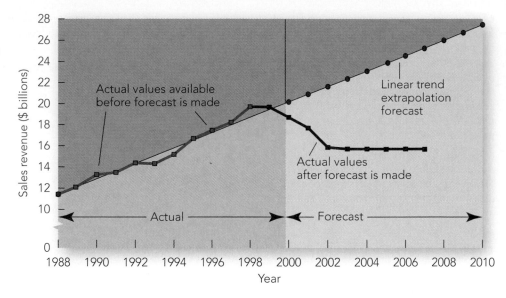

early 2000 you were a sales forecaster for the Xerox Corporation and had actual sales running from 1988 to 1999 (Figure 9–12). Using linear trend extrapolation, you draw a line to fit the past data and project it into the future to give the forecast values shown for 2000 to 2010.[22]

If in 2008 you want to compare your forecasts with actual results, you are in for a surprise—illustrating the strength and weakness of trend extrapolation. Trend extrapolation assumes that the underlying relationships in the past will continue into the future, which is the basis of the method's key strength: simplicity. If this assumption proves correct, you have an accurate forecast. However, if this proves wrong, the forecast is likely to be wrong. In this case, your forecasts from 2001 through 2007 were too high, as shown in Figure 9–12, largely because of fierce competition in the photocopying industry.

---

learning review

8. What is product positioning?

9. What are the three kinds of sales forecasting techniques?

LEARNING OBJECTIVES REVIEW

LO1 *Explain what market segmentation is and when to use it.*

Market segmentation involves aggregating prospective buyers into groups that (*a*) have common needs and (*b*) will respond similarly to a marketing action. Organizations go to the expense of segmenting their markets when it increases their sales, profits, and ability to serve customers better.

LO2 *Identify the five steps involved in segmenting and targeting markets.*

Step 1 is to group potential buyers into segments. Buyers within a segment should have similar characteristics to each other and respond similarly to marketing actions like a new product or a lower price. Step 2 involves putting related prod-

ucts to be sold into groups. In step 3, organizations develop a market-product grid with estimated size of markets in each of the market-product cells of the resulting table. Step 4 involves selecting the target market segments on which the organization should focus. Step 5 involves taking marketing mix actions—often in the form of a marketing program—to reach the target market segments.

LO3 *Recognize the factors used to segment consumer and organizational markets.*

Factors used to segment consumer markets include geographic, demographic, psychographic, and behavioral variables. Organizational markets use related variables except for psychographic ones.

LO4 *Develop a market-product grid to identify a target market and recommend resulting actions.*

Organizations use five key criteria to segment markets, whose groupings appear in the rows of the market-product grid. Groups of related products appear in the columns. After estimating the size of market in each cell in the grid, they select the target market segments on which to focus. They then identify marketing mix actions—often in a marketing program—to reach the target market most efficiently.

LO5 *Explain how marketing managers position products in the marketplace.*

Marketing managers often locate competing products on two-dimensional perceptual maps to visualize the products in the minds of consumers. They then try to position new products or reposition existing products in this space to attain the maximum sales and profits.

LO6 *Describe three approaches to developing a sales forecast for an organization.*

One approach uses subjective judgments of the decision maker, such as direct or lost-horse forecasts. Surveys of knowledgeable groups is a second method. It involves obtaining information such as the intentions of potential buyers or estimates of the salesforce. Statistical methods involving extending a pattern observed in past data into the future is a third example. The best-known example is linear trend extrapolation.

FOCUSING ON KEY TERMS

80/20 rule p. 234
company forecast p. 246
direct forecast p. 246
industry potential p. 245
linear trend extrapolation p. 246
lost-horse forecast p. 246
market potential p. 245

market-product grid p. 237
market segmentation p. 226
market segments p. 226
perceptual map p. 244
product differentiation p. 226
product positioning p. 243
product repositioning p. 244

sales forecast p. 246
salesforce survey forecast p. 246
survey of buyers' intentions forecast p. 246
synergy p. 229
trend extrapolation p. 246
usage rate p. 232

APPLYING MARKETING KNOWLEDGE

1 What variables might be used to segment these consumer markets? (*a*) lawn mowers, (*b*) frozen dinners, (*c*) dry breakfast cereals, and (*d*) soft drinks.

2 What variables might be used to segment these industrial markets? (*a*) industrial sweepers, (*b*) photocopiers, (*c*) computerized production control systems, and (*d*) car rental agencies.

3 In Figure 9–8, the dormitory market segment includes students living in college-owned residence halls, sororities, and fraternities. What market needs are common to these students that justify combining them into a single segment in studying the market for your Wendy's restaurant?

4 You may disagree with the estimates of market size given for the rows in the market-product grid in Figure 9–8. Estimate the market size, and give a brief justification for these market segments: (*a*) dormitory students, (*b*) day commuters, and (*c*) people who work in the area.

5 Suppose you want to increase revenues for your fast-food restaurant even further. Referring to Figure 9–9, what advertising actions might you take to increase revenues from (*a*) dormitory students, (*b*) dinners, and (*c*) after-dinner snacks from night commuters?

6 Which of the following variables would linear trend extrapolation be more accurate for? (*a*) Annual population of the United States or (*b*) annual sales of cars produced in the United States by General Motors. Why?

building your marketing plan

Your marketing plan needs (*a*) a market-product grid to focus your marketing efforts and also (*b*) leads to a forecast of sales for the company. Use these steps:

1 Define the market segments (the rows in your grid) using the factors in Figures 9–3 and 9–6.

2 Define the groupings of related products (the columns in your grid).

3 Form your grid and estimate the size of market in each market-product cell.

4 Select the target market segments on which to focus your efforts with your marketing program.

5 Use the information and the lost-horse forecasting technique to make a sales forecast (company forecast).

4D, TRS, TFS . . . and PLS! Does this look like a spoonful of alphabet soup?

Perhaps. But it really refers to Rollerblade's technologies, programs, and commitment to providing in-line skaters with the best quality of skates and skating experiences possible. Or "by providing benefits beyond what people are expecting to have," as Jeremy Stonier (left in photo), Rollerblade's vice president and general manager, describes it. In fact, more than 265 patents cover Rollerblade's leading-edge technology with more on the way, such as the new adjustable Crossfire™ and Activa™ in-line skates.

WHAT'S THE NEXT ACT AFTER LAUNCHING AN INDUSTRY?

What do you do for the next act, for your encore, when you create an entire industry?

That's the challenge facing Rollerblade,® which launched the in-line skate industry over two decades ago. But such success attracts lots of competitors. So what does the company do to grow the sport of in-line skating by providing exciting new products to build and maintain continuing, loyal customer relationships? Let's look at the quarter-century from Rollerblade's launch to its customer-oriented strategy today, which is embodied by Rollerblade's new tagline, "Go Where You Want to Go."

In the early 1700s, a Dutch inventor trying to simulate ice skating in the summer created the first roller skates by attaching spools in a single row to his shoes. His "in-line" arrangement was the standard design until 1863 when the first skates with rollers set as two pairs appeared. This two-pair design became the new standard, and in-line skates virtually disappeared from the market.

In 1980, two Minnesota hockey-playing brothers found an old pair of in-line skates while browsing through a sporting goods store. Working in their garage, they modified the design to add hard plastic wheels, a molded boot shell, and a toe brake. They sold their product, which they dubbed "Rollerblade skates," out of the back of their truck to off-season hockey players and skiers.

In the mid-1980s, Rollerblade marketing executive Mary Horwath concluded that the firm had to market its in-line skates to a broader range of customers. Conversations with in-line skaters convinced Horwath that using Rollerblade skates:

- Was incredible fun.
- Was a great aerobic workout and made the skater stronger and healthier.
- Was quite different from traditional roller skating, which was practiced alone, mostly inside, and mostly by young girls.
- Would appeal to more than just off-season ice hockey skaters and skiers.

Horwath set out to reposition Rollerblade, to change the image in people's minds from in-line skating as off-season training to in-line skating as a new kind of fun exercise that anyone could do. It worked. Horwath and the company succeeded in popularizing in-line skating and actually launched an entirely new industry that by 1997 had more than 27 million U.S. inline skaters.

The marketing problems of Rollerblade today are far different than those it faced in the late 1980s. Rollerblade's success in launching a new industry brought its own dangers: major competition in terms of not only more than 30 other skate manufacturers but also competing sports like skateboarding, biking, and snowboarding.

Yet Rollerblade still has 35 percent of the industry sales, with no other competitor having more than 10 percent. Still, the number of in-line skaters in the U.S. has declined from its 1997 peak, a concern for Rollerblade. If this declining trend continues, Rollerblade can only grow by increasing its share of the number of in-line skates sold annually, requiring innovation and creative marketing strategies to meet customer needs.

ROLLERBLADE'S KEY SEGMENTS

From the outset in-line skaters have been united by a common experience: the thrill and fun of the speed and freedom that comes from almost frictionless wheels on

DT4 in-line skate for the Urban/Street Segment

Crossfire 4D in-line skate for the Fitness/Recreation Segment

their feet. "As the market has matured, it has settled into four core groups of users," says Stonier. Each requires a number of unique skate features.

"The trickiest segment we sell to is probably the Urban/Street skaters—the 14- to 22-year-old in your neighborhood who is doing tricks you might see on ESPN's X Games," says Stonier. Members of Team Rollerblade, a skating group that gives demonstrations around the country, suggest and test new technologies that find their way first into skates for this segment. The Team Rollerblade Series (or TRS) DT4 in-line skate is designed for this segment, contains a "walkable" boot and Training Fit foot liner to keep the skater's feet cool, dry, and comfortable.

Skate buyers overlap somewhat in the Fitness/Recreation segment. The Fitness subgroup skates two or three times a week, at high speeds, and may even aspire to skate in an in-line marathon. As a result, Rollerblade developed the Crossfire 4D skate for men and the Activa 4D skate for women. "No other skate in the industry combines this level of form, function, fit, and aesthetics," exclaims Ronnie Kuliecza, director of product development. The 4D™ (D=drive) refers to an innovative, adjustable aluminum frame that when shorter allows for tighter turns and when longer permits more speed. These skates incorporate the new Crossfire Shell for stability and control for turning and 90mm wheels for speed. The skates also use the revolutionary TFS (Total Fit System) Power lacing closure mechanism. Pulling on the TFS disc provides an effortless, quick, and customized fit. Finally, the skates have the PLS (Power Lateral Support) to secure the heel and Air Power, inflatable chambers that secure the ankle.

Since most adult skaters are Recreation skaters, Rollerblade designed the new Astro (men) and Wing (women) skates for this larger subsegment. With these skates, both beginner and intermediate skaters get the comfort, reliability, and safety they want.

With the Junior segment, parents are always concerned about having to buy their children new shoes or skates as their feet grow. Not only does the Micro 500 X extendable skate adjust four sizes with a push of a button, but it also has the new TFS Micro closure system. With a simple push of a button and a turn of a dial, a thin cable provides quick closure.

The Race segment is just what the name implies—expert speed skaters wanting the maximum in technical features. The Race Machine Rosso skate has a hyper magnesium frame that holds four 100mm high performance wheels as well as a high tech boot for maximum performance.

The segments don't stop there. While the flagship Rollerblade brand is marketed in sporting goods and skate specialty stores, Rollerblade has a lower-priced Bladerunner line that is sold through mass merchandise (such as Wal-Mart and Target) and sporting goods chain stores. Finally, the global market has enormous potential. With China and South Korea showing high growth today, who knows what new segments could be next?

A FOCUS ON EACH CONSUMER

"One of the big differences between marketing today and in the future is that we will be able to reach each person, such as designing your own personal workout program," says Nicholas Skally (right in photo on previous page), Rollerblade's manager of marketing. Rollerblade's website (www.rollerblade.com) is a step in that direction. "An important benefit of the website is our ability to acquire marketing research data on individual consumers inexpensively," says Skally. This enables Rollerblade to get feedback and ideas directly from its end users.

Micro 500 X extendable in-line skate for the Junior Segment   Race Machine Rosso in-line skate for the Race Segment

Website topics include everything from helping you choose which skate is right for you (Product Selector) to helping you brush up on your braking technique though its Animated Skate Lesson. The website's "Skating for Fitness" link provides information on the benefits of in-line skating as well as a workout plan. It also has a Games section targeted for each segment so that "online" skaters can see how fast they can traverse a course or stop without skating into an object! The website allows interested users to subscribe to its newsletter. Finally, Rollerblade developed two "webmercials" designed as viral marketing tools (see Chapter 5) that can be viewed and shared on YouTube.

In the past, Rollerblade often sent out millions of direct-mail pieces or bought commercials on national TV networks. Today, Skally points out that Rollerblade now focuses more narrowly by selecting magazines that link directly to the user segments. Rollerblade also offers programs like its (1) Free Skate Lesson program, a coalition of skate schools providing free in-line skating lessons on Free Skate Lesson Day, held each May in major cities across America and (2) Camp Rollerblade, which occurs on Saturdays in selected cities during the spring-fall season.

ROLLERBLADE'S FIRSTS

"If you're going to buy a pair of in-line skates, it only make sense to buy from us," says Stonier, "because we're the ones who started it, perfected it, and continue to push the innovation." As evidence of Rollerblade's innovation, he points to a number of firsts, such as the use of polyurethane boots and wheels, high-tech closure systems, metal frames, dual bearings, and heel brakes. Other firsts include breathable liners, push-button adjustable children's skates, and more importantly, skates designed specifically for women *by women*. Rollerblade employed an engineering team composed of women to develop in-line skates with specially designed lines, cuffs, and footbeds that meets the unique needs of women.

In 2003, Rollerblade was sold to Tecnica of Italy, whose holdings include the Nordica brand of ski equipment. This acquisition provided both firms with huge technology synergies, allowing them to combine their state-of-the-art R&D and manufacturing resources.

Questions

1 What trends in the environmental forces (social, economic, technological, competitive, and regulatory) (*a*) work for and (*b*) work against Rollerblade's potential growth in the twenty-first century?
2 Compare the likely marketing goals for Rollerblade (*a*) in 1986 when Rollerblade was launched and (*b*) today.
3 What kind of focused communication and promotion actions might Rollerblade take to reach the (*a*) Fitness/ Recreation and (*b*) Junior market segments? For some starting ideas, visit www.rollerblade.com.
4 In searching for global markets to enter, (*a*) what are some criteria that Rollerblade should use to select countries to enter, and (*b*) what three or four countries meet these criteria best and are the most likely candidates?

10

Developing New Products and Services

we will go over all these

LEARNING OBJECTIVES

After reading this chapter you should be able to:

 LO1 Recognize the various terms that pertain to products and services.

 LO2 Identify the ways in which consumer and business goods can be classified.

 LO3 Explain the significance of "newness" in new products and services as it relates to the degree of consumer learning involved.

 LO4 Describe the factors contributing to a new product's or service's success or failure.

 LO5 Explain the purposes of each step of the new-product process.

NEW-PRODUCT REVOLUTIONS: APPLE, INC., AND ITS INNOVATION MACHINE

The stage in front of the huge auditorium is empty except for a podium and a huge screen.

Then in walks a legend ready for his annual magic show in his standard uniform—black turtleneck, jeans, and gray sneakers.

Apple's Innovation Machine

The legend is Steve Jobs, co-founder and now chief executive officer of Apple, Inc., rated *BusinessWeek's* most innovative company on the globe in 2006. The magic show is really the annual *Macworld* conference in Las Vegas where Jobs and his Apple colleagues present their latest innovations. A sample of Apple's new product revolutions:

- Apple II—the first personal computer.

- Macintosh—the first look at a mouse and a graphical user interface.

- iPod—the first really portable digital music player.

And the next one—Apple's iPhone—seems equally revolutionary.

To gain insights into new-product development, let's look briefly at (1) how the iPhone came about and (2) what the iPhone can do that makes it so innovative.[1]

How the iPhone Came About

"Everybody hates their phone," says Steve Jobs, "and that's not a good thing." Sample problems: Groping through your voice-mails by ear or finding the right text when they're all jumbled together. Which makes most of us feel frustrated—or stupid.

Enter Steve Jobs. Several years ago he saw competitors putting a lot of energy into developing "tablet PCs"—portable computers that use a touch screen rather than a mouse and keyboard. Jobs put some Apple engineers to work researching touch screens and got results. Any other company might have come up with a better tablet PC but not Jobs and Apple. His bigger-fish-to-fry vision: Use Apple's ideas, its technology, and the 200 new patents in its iPhone. Then enter the cell phone market that has almost a billion units in annual sales, even though Apple had never been in this market before.

What the iPhone Can Do

Today's "digital convergence" has led to multipurpose cell phones that can do everything from calling and text messaging to taking photos and Web browsing. To build the iPhone, Apple sheared off the front of a video iPod and replaced it with a bright, vivid—you guessed it!—touch

The iPhone's innovative touch screen emerged after Apple engineers studied tablet PCs, portable computers using . . . touch screens.

screen Jobs had his engineers study a few years back. The screen serves up the "buttons" you need at exactly the time you need them, giving you:

• Music—The screen lets you choose your music by album cover.

• Menu—The touch-screen icons let you scroll among phone, e-mail, Internet, iPod, and other applications.

• Messaging—Text messages are not clumped together but organized by conversation in elongated bubbles.

• E-mail—This is handled like a desktop computer, along with images.

• Internet—Tapping the screen with your finger lets you zoom in on part of a page.

Did you have to answer an iPhone call while reading this? Steve Jobs and Apple hope so because they plan to sell 10 million iPhones by the end of 2008—18 months after its June 2007 launch.[2]

LO1

The essence of marketing is in developing products such as Apple's new, technologically advanced iPhone to meet buyer needs. A **product** is a good, service, or idea consisting of a bundle of tangible and intangible attributes that satisfies consumers and is received in exchange for money or some other unit of value. Tangible attributes include physical characteristics such as color or sweetness, and intangible attributes include becoming healthier or wealthier. Hence, a product may be the breakfast cereal you eat, the accountant who fills out your tax return, or quitting smoking.

The life of a company often depends on how it conceives, produces, and markets new products, the topic of this chapter. This chapter covers decisions involved in developing and marketing new products and services. Chapters 11 and 12 discuss the process of managing existing products and services, respectively.

THE VARIATIONS OF PRODUCTS

A product varies in terms of whether it is a consumer or business good. For most organizations the product decision is not made in isolation because companies often offer a range of products. To better appreciate the product decision, let's first define some terms pertaining to products.

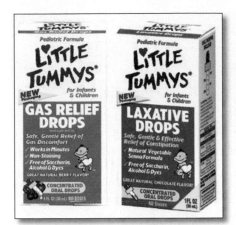

An extensive product line can benefit both consumers and retailers. To discover how Little Remedies' product line helps achieve this, see the text.

Product Line and Product Mix

A **product line** is a group of products that are closely related because they satisfy a class of needs, are used together, are sold to the same customer group, are distributed through the same type of outlets, or fall within a given price range. Nike's product lines include shoes and clothing, whereas the Mayo Clinic's product lines consist of inpatient hospital care, outpatient physician services, and medical research. Each product line has its own marketing strategy.

The product line for the Little Remedies® Products consists of more than a dozen nonprescription medicines for infants and children six years old and younger. An important benefit of having a broad product line like that for Little Remedies is it enables both consumers and retailers to simplify their buying decisions. For example, a family that has a good experience with one Little Remedies product might buy another one. Also, its extensive product line enables it to obtain distribution in retail chains like Babies "Я" Us and Wal-Mart, avoiding their need to deal with many different suppliers.

Within each product line is the *product item,* a specific product as noted by a unique brand, size, or price. For example, Ultra Downy softener for clothes comes in five different sizes; each size is considered a separate item or *stock keeping unit* (SKU), which is a unique identification number that defines an item for ordering or inventory purposes.

The third way to look at products is by the **product mix**, or the number of product lines offered by a company. Cray, Inc., has a small product mix of four supercomputer lines that are sold mostly to governments and large businesses. Fortune Brands, however, has a large product mix that includes many product lines such as sporting equipment (Titleist golf balls) and plumbing products (Moen faucets).

Classifying Products

Both the federal government and companies classify products, but for different purposes. The government's classification method helps it collect information on industrial activity. Companies classify products to help develop similar marketing strategies for the wide range of products offered. Two major ways to classify products are by type of user and degree of product tangibility.

Type of User   The first major type of product classification is according to the user. **Consumer goods** are products purchased by the ultimate consumer, whereas **business goods** (also called *B2B goods, industrial goods,* or *organizational goods*) are products that assist directly or indirectly in providing products for resale.

There are difficulties, however, with this classification because some products can be considered both consumer and business items. An Apple computer can be sold to consumers for personal use or to business firms for office use. Each classification results in different marketing actions. Viewed as a consumer product, the Apple computer would be sold through computer stores or directly from the company website. As a business product, the HP Compaq computer might be sold by a salesperson offering discounts for multiple purchases.

Degree of Tangibility   Classification by degree of tangibility divides products into one of three categories. First is a *nondurable* good, an item consumed in one or a few uses, such as food products and fuel. A *durable* good is one that usually lasts over an extended number of uses, such as appliances, automobiles, and stereo equipment. *Services* are defined as activities, benefits, or satisfactions offered for sale, such as marketing research, health care, and education. According to this classification, government data indicate that the United States is becoming a service economy, which is the reason for a separate chapter (Chapter 12) on the topic.

A visit to watch an Atlanta Braves baseball game is often a lot more than the game itself. As described in the text, it may involve a meal at the Chophouse (above) or many other services.

This classification method also provides direction for marketing actions. For nondurable products like Wrigley's gum, inexpensive and purchased frequently, consumer advertising and wide distribution in retail outlets is essential. Durable products such as cars, however, generally cost more than nondurable goods and last longer, so personal selling is an important marketing activity in answering consumer questions and concerns. Because services are intangible, special marketing effort is usually needed to communicate their benefits to potential buyers.

Services and New-Product Development "New-product" development in services like buying a stock or airline ticket or watching a Major League Baseball game occurs but, being intangible, is often difficult to observe step by step. Nevertheless, service innovations can have a huge impact on our lives. For example, online brokerage firms such as E*TRADE have revolutionized the financial services industry, as have travel reservation firms like Expedia.

Even today's visit to a Major League Baseball park is a study in new-product innovation. Visit Turner Field, home of the Atlanta Braves, and you may be in for a shock about what's going on besides baseball on the field. There's not only the members-only 755 club—honoring Hank Aaron's home run total—but there's also the Chophouse bar and grill for 20-somethings and a big playground sponsored by Cartoon Network. So appealing to different segments of Major League Baseball customers has become almost as important as fielding a winning team.[3]

CLASSIFYING CONSUMER AND BUSINESS GOODS

LO2

Because the buyer is the key to marketing, consumer and business product classifications are discussed in greater detail.

Specialty goods like Rolex watches require distinct marketing programs to reach narrow target markets.

Rolex
www.Rolex.com

Classification of Consumer Goods

Convenience, shopping, specialty, and unsought products are the four types of consumer goods. They differ in terms of (1) effort the consumer spends on the decision, (2) attributes used in purchase, and (3) frequency of purchase.

Convenience goods are items that the consumer purchases frequently, conveniently, and with a minimum of shopping effort. **Shopping goods** are items for which the consumer compares several alternatives on criteria, such as price, quality, or style. **Specialty goods** are items, such as Rolex watches, that a consumer makes a special effort to search out and buy. **Unsought goods** are items that the consumer either does not know about or knows about but docs not initially want. Figurc 10–1 on the next page shows how the classification of a consumer product into one of these four types results in different aspects of the marketing mix being stressed. Different degrees of brand loyalty and amounts of shopping effort by the consumer are displayed for sample products in each of the four types of consumer goods.

The manner in which a consumer good is classified depends on the individual. One person may view a camera as a shopping good and visit several stores before deciding on a brand, whereas a friend may view cameras as a specialty good and will buy only a Nikon.

Classification of Business Goods

A major characteristic of business goods is that their sales are often the result of *derived demand;* that is, sales of business and industrial goods frequently result (or are derived) from the sale of consumer goods. For example, if consumer demand for Ford cars (a consumer product) increases, the company may increase its demand for paint spraying equipment (a business product). Business goods may be classified as production or support goods.

Production Goods Items used in the manufacturing process that become part of the final product are **production goods**. These include raw materials such as grain or lumber, as well as component parts. For example, a company that manufactures door hinges used by Ford in its car doors is producing a component part. As noted in Chapter 6, the marketing of production goods is based on factors such as price, quality, delivery, and service. Marketers of these products tend to sell directly to industrial users.

Support Goods The second class of business goods is **support goods**, which are items used to assist in producing other goods and services. Support goods include installations, accessory equipment, supplies, and services.

- *Installations* consist of buildings and fixed equipment. Because a significant amount of capital is required to purchase installations, the industrial buyer deals directly with construction companies and manufacturers through sales representatives. The pricing of installations is often by competitive bidding.
- *Accessory equipment* includes tools and office equipment and is usually purchased in small-order sizes by buyers. As a result, instead of dealing directly with buyers, sellers of industrial accessories use distributors to contact a large number of buyers.
- *Supplies* are similar to consumer convenience goods and consist of products such as stationery, paper clips, and brooms. These are purchased with little

BASIS OF COMPARISON	CONVENIENCE	SHOPPING	SPECIALTY	UNSOUGHT
Product	Toothpaste, cake mix, hand soap, laundry detergent	Cameras, TVs, briefcases, clothing	Rolls-Royce cars, Rolex watches	Burial insurance, thesaurus
Price	Relatively inexpensive	Fairly expensive	Usually very expensive	Varies
Place (distribution)	Widespread; many outlets	Large number of selective outlets	Very limited	Often limited
Promotion	Price, availability, and awareness stressed	Differentiation from competitors stressed	Uniqueness of brand and status stressed	Awareness is essential
Brand loyalty of consumers	Aware of brand but will accept substitutes	Prefer specific brands but will accept substitutes	Very brand loyal; will not accept substitutes	Will accept substitutes
Purchase behavior of consumers	Frequent purchases; little time and effort spent shopping	Infrequent purchases; needs much comparison shopping time	Infrequent purchases; needs extensive search and decision time	Very infrequent purchases; some comparison shopping

WaS mentioned in class

FIGURE 10–1
How a consumer good is classified significantly affects what products consumers buy and the marketing strategies used.

effort, using the straight rebuy decision sequence discussed in Chapter 6. Price and delivery are key factors considered by the buyers of supplies.

- *Industrial services* are intangible activities to assist the industrial buyer. This category can include maintenance and repair services and advisory services such as tax or legal counsel, where the seller's reputation is critical.

learning review

1. Explain the difference between product mix and product line.

2. What are the four main types of consumer goods?

3. To which type of good (business or consumer) does the term *derived demand* generally apply?

NEW PRODUCTS AND WHY THEY SUCCEED OR FAIL

New products are the lifeblood of a company and keep it growing, but the financial risks are large. Before discussing how new products reach the market, we'll begin by looking at *what* a new product is.

What Is a New Product?

The term *new* is difficult to define. Is Sony's PlayStation 3 *new* when there was a PlayStation 2? Is Nintendo's Wii *new* when its GameCube launch goes back to 2001?

As you read the discussion about what "new" means in new-product development, think about how it affects the marketing strategies of Sony and Nintendo in their *new* video-game launches.

Sony Corporation
www.sony.com

Nintendo
www.nintendo.com

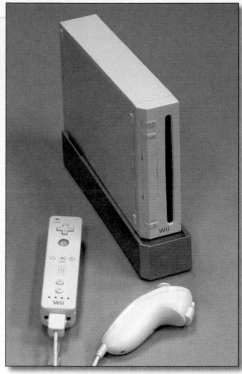

Got a complicated computer problem? Maybe your answer is a Geek Squad visit, as described in the text and Marketing Matters box.

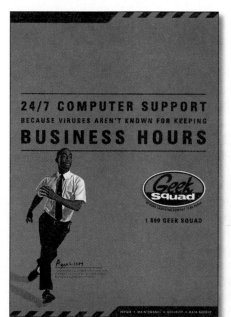

What does *new* mean for new-product marketing? Newness from several points of view and some marketing implications of this newness are discussed next.

Newness Compared with Existing Products   If a product is functionally different from existing products, it can be defined as new. Sometimes this newness is revolutionary and creates a whole new industry, as in the case of the Apple II computer. At other times additional features are added to an existing product to try to make it appeal to more customers. And as microprocessors now appear not only in computers and cell phones but also in countless applications in vehicles and appliances, consumers' lives get far more complicated. This proliferation of extra features—sometimes called "feature bloat"—overwhelms many consumers. The Marketing Matters box on the next page describes how founder Richard Stephens and his Geek Squad are working to address the rise of feature bloat.[4]

Newness in Legal Terms   The U.S. Federal Trade Commission (FTC) advises that the term *new* be limited to use with a product up to six months after it enters regular distribution. The difficulty with this suggestion is in the interpretation of the term *regular distribution*.

Newness from the Organization's Perspective   Successful organizations are starting to view newness and innovation in their products at three levels. At the lowest level, which usually involves the least risk, is a product line extension. This is an incremental improvement of an existing product for the company, such as Cheerios Crunch or Diet Coke Plus—extensions of the basic Cheerios or Diet Coke, respectively. At the next level is a significant jump in the innovation or technology, such as from a regular land-line telephone to a cell phone. The third level is true innovation, a truly revolutionary new product, like the first Apple computer in 1976. Effective new-product programs in large firms deal at all three levels.

Newness from the Consumer's Perspective   A fourth way to define new products is in terms of their effects on consumption. This approach

Marketing Matters > > > > > > > technology

You Bought a Combination Computer, Lawn Mower, and Dishwasher? Better Call the Geek Squad!

Adding more features to a product to satisfy more consumers seems like a no-brainer strategy.

Feature Bloat

In fact, most marketing research with potential buyers of a product done *before* they buy shows they say they *do want* more features in the product. It's when the new product gets home that the "feature bloat" problems occur—often overwhelming the consumer with mind-boggling complexity.

Home computers pose a special problem because there's no in-house technical assistance like that existing in large organizations. Also, to drive down prices of home computers, usually little customer support service is available. Call the manufacturers toll-free "help" line? One survey showed that 29 percent of the help-line callers wound up swearing at the customer service representative and 21 percent just screamed.

The Geek Squad to the Rescue

Computer feature bloat has given rise to what TV's *60 Minutes* says is "the multibillion-dollar service industry populated by the very people who used to be shunned in the high-school cafeteria: Geeks like Robert Stephens!"

What makes Stephens different is that a dozen years ago he turned his geekiness into the Geek Squad—a group

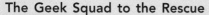

of technically savvy people who can fix almost any computer problem. "There's usually some frantic customer at the door pointing to some device in the corner that will not obey," Stephens explains.

"The biggest complaint about tech support people is rude, egotistical behavior," says Stephens. So he launched the Geek Squad to show some friendly humility by having team members work their wizardry while:

1. Showing genuine concern to customers.
2. Dressing in geeky white shirts, black clip-on ties and white socks, a "uniform" borrowed from NASA engineers.
3. Driving to customer calls in black-and-white VW "geekmobiles."

Do customers appreciate the 6,000-person Geek Squad, now owned by Best Buy? Robert Stephens answers by explaining, "People will say, 'They saved me . . . they saved my data.'" This includes countless college students working on their paper or thesis with data lost somewhere in their computer—"data they promised themselves they'd back up next week."

Later in the chapter we'll see examples of "less-is-more" successes, where taking features *out* of a product can lead to success.

For how the kind of innovation present in this ketchup bottle affects marketing strategy, see the text.

classifies new products according to the degree of learning required by the consumer, as shown in Figure 10–2.

With <u>*continuous innovation*</u>, no new behaviors must be learned. Toothpaste manufacturers can add new attributes or features like "whitens teeth" or "removes plaque," as when they introduce a new or improved product. But the extra features in the new toothpaste do not require buyers to learn new tooth-brushing behaviors, so it is a continuous innovation. The benefit of this simple innovation is that effective marketing mainly depends on generating awareness and not completely reeducating customers.

With <u>*dynamically continuous innovation*</u>, only minor changes in behavior are required. Heinz launched its EZ Squirt Ketchup in 2000 in an array of unlikely hues—from green and orange to pink and teal—with kid-friendly squeeze bottles and nozzles.[5] Encouraging kids to write their names on hot dogs or draw dinosaurs on burgers as they use this new product requires only minor behavioral changes. So the marketing strategy is to educate prospective buyers on the product's benefits, advantages, and proper use.

A <u>*discontinuous innovation*</u> involves making the consumer learn entirely new consumption patterns in order to use the product. So last month you bought a wireless router for your computer? Congratulations if you installed it yourself!

BASIS OF COMPARISON	CONTINUOUS INNOVATION	DYNAMICALLY CONTINUOUS INNOVATION	DISCONTINUOUS INNOVATION
Definition	Requires no new learning by consumers	Disrupts consumer's normal routine but does not require totally new learning	Requires new learning and consumption patterns by consumers
Examples	New improved shaver or detergent	Electric toothbrush, compact disc player, and automatic flash unit for cameras	VCR, digital video recorder, electric car
Marketing emphasis	Gain consumer awareness and wide distribution	Advertise points of difference and benefits to consumers	Educate consumers through product trial and personal selling

FIGURE 10–2

The degree of "newness" in a new product affects the amount of learning effort consumers must exert to use the product.

Recently, one-third of those bought at Best Buy were returned because they were too complicated to set up—the problem with a discontinuous innovation.[6] So marketing efforts for discontinuous innovations usually involve not only gaining initial consumer awareness but also educating consumers on both the benefits and proper use of the innovative product, activities that can cost millions of dollars.

Why Products Succeed or Fail

LO4

We all know the giant product successes—such as Microsoft Windows, Swatch watches, CNN. Yet the thousands of failures every year that slide quietly into oblivion cost American businesses billions of dollars. Research suggests that it takes about 3,000 raw unwritten ideas to produce a single commercially successful new product.[7] To learn marketing lessons and convert potential failures to successes, we can analyze why new products fail and then study several failures in detail. As we go through the new-product process later in the chapter, we can identify ways such failures might have been avoided—admitting that hindsight is clearer than foresight.

Marketing Reasons for New-Product Failures   Both marketing and nonmarketing factors contribute to new-product failures, as shown in the Marketing Matters box on the next page. Using the research results from several studies[8] on new-product success and failure and also those described in the Marketing Matters box, we can identify critical marketing factors—sometimes overlapping—that often separate new-product winners and losers:

1. *Insignificant point of difference.* Shown as the most important factor in the Marketing Matters box, a distinctive point of difference is essential for a new product to defeat competitive ones—through having superior characteristics that deliver unique benefits to the user. In the mid-1990s, General Mills introduced Fingos, a sweetened cereal flake about the size of a corn chip. Consumers were supposed to snack on them dry, but they didn't.[9] The point of difference was not important enough to get consumers to give up eating competing snacks such as popcorn, potato chips, or Cheerios from the box late at night.
2. *Incomplete market and product definition before product development starts.* Ideally, a new product needs a precise **protocol**, a statement that, before product development begins, identifies: (1) a well-defined target market; (2) specific customers' needs, wants, and preferences; and (3) what the product will be and

Marketing Matters > > > > > customer value

What Separates New-Product Winners and Losers?

What makes some products winners and others losers? Knowing this answer is a key to a new-product strategy. R. G. Cooper and E. J. Kleinschmidt studied 203 new industrial products to find the answers shown below.

The researchers defined the "product success rate" of new products as the percentage of products that reached the company's own profitability criteria. Product "winners" are the best 20 percent of performers and "losers" are

the worst 20 percent. For example, for the first factor in the table below, 98 percent of the winners had a major point of difference compared with only 18 percent of the losers.

The table below includes only marketing-related factors. Most of these marketing factors tie directly to the reasons cited in the text for new-product success and failure that are taken from a number of research studies.

Factor Affecting Product Success Rate	Product "Winners" (Best 20%)	–	Product "Losers" (Worst 20%)	=	% Difference (Winners – Losers)
• Point of difference, or uniquely superior product	98%	–	18%	=	80%
• Well-defined product before actual development starts	85	–	26	=	59
• Quality of execution of activities before actual development starts	75	–	31	=	44
• Synergy, or fit, with marketing mix activities	71	–	31	=	40
• Quality of execution of marketing mix activities	71	–	32	=	39
• Market attractiveness, ones with large markets, high growth	74	–	43	=	31

do. Without this precision, loads of money disappear as research and development (R&D) tries to design a vague product for a phantom market. Apple's early hand-sized Newton personal digital assistant (PDA) fizzled badly because no clear protocol existed and the device became too complicated.

3. *Too little market attractiveness.* Market attractiveness refers to the ideal situation every new-product manager looks for: a large target market with high growth and real buyer need. But often, when looking for ideal market niches, the target market is too small and competitive to warrant the R&D, production, and marketing expenses necessary to reach it. In the early 1990s, Kodak discontinued its Ultralife lithium battery with its 10-year shelf life because its 9-volt size accounted for less than 10 percent of the U.S. battery market.

4. *Poor execution of the marketing mix: name, package, price, promotion, distribution.* Coca-Cola thought its Minute Maid Squeeze-Fresh frozen orange juice concentrate in a squeeze bottle was a hit. The idea was that consumers could make one glass of juice at a time, and the concentrate stayed fresh in the refrigerator for over a month. After two test markets, the product was finished. Consumers loved the idea, but the product was messy to use, and the advertising and packaging didn't educate them effectively on how much concentrate to mix.

5. *Poor product quality or sensitivity to customer needs on critical factors.* Overlapping somewhat with point 1, this factor stresses that problems on one or two critical factors can kill the product, even though the general quality is high.

New-product success or failure? For the special problems these two products face, see the text.

For example, the Japanese, like the British, drive on the left side of the road. Until 1996, U.S. carmakers sent Japan few right-drive cars—unlike German carmakers who exported right-drive models in a number of their brands.[10]

6. _Bad timing._ The product is introduced too soon, too late, or at a time when consumer tastes are shifting dramatically. Bad timing gives new-product managers nightmares. Microsoft, for example, introduced its Zune player a few years after Apple launched its iPod, and other competitors offered new MP3 players.

7. _No economical access to buyers._ Grocery products provide an example. Today's mega-supermarkets carry more than 30,000 different SKUs. With about 40,000 new packaged goods products (food, beverage, health and beauty aids, household, and pet items) introduced each year, the fight for exposure is tremendous in terms of costs for advertising, distribution, and shelf space.[11] Because shelf space is judged in terms of sales per square foot, Thirsty Dog! (a zesty beef-flavored, vitamin-enriched, mineral-loaded, lightly carbonated bottled water for your dog) must displace an existing product on the supermarket shelves, a difficult task with the precise measures of revenues per square foot these stores use.

A Look at Some Failures Before reading the next two paragraphs, study the product failures described in Figure 10–3. Then think for several minutes to try to identify which of the seven reasons listed in the text is the most likely explanation for their failure. The two examples are discussed next.

FIGURE 10–3
Why did these two new products fail?

As explained in detail in the text, new products often fail because of one or a combination of seven reasons. Look at the two products described below, and try to identify which reason explains why they failed in the marketplace.

- Kimberly Clark's Avert Virucidal tissues that contained vitamin C derivatives scientifically designed to kill cold and flu germs when users sneezed, coughed, or blew their nose into them.
- OUT! International's Hey! There's A Monster In My Room spray that was designed to rid scary creatures from kids' rooms and had a bubble-gum fragrance.

Compare your insights with those in the text.

The text describes some new-product lessons this iRobot co-founder learned the hard way.

Kimberly Clark's Avert Virucidal tissues lasted 10 months in a test market in upstate New York before being pulled from the shelves. People didn't believe the claims and were frightened by the "-cidal" in the name, which they connected to events like "suicidal." So the tissue probably failed because of not having a clear point of difference and a bad name, and, hence, bad marketing mix execution—probably reasons 1 and 4 in the list in the text.

OUT! International's Hey! There's A Monster In My Room spray was creative and cute when introduced in 1993. But the name probably kept the kids awake at night more than their fear of the monsters because it suggested the monster was still hiding in the room. Question: Wouldn't calling it the Monster-Buster Spray—the secondary name shown at the bottom of the package—have licked the name problem? It looks like the spray was never really defined well in a protocol (reason 2) and definitely had poor name execution (reason 4).[12]

Simple marketing research on consumers should have revealed the problems. Developing successful new products may sometimes involve luck, but more often it involves having a product that really meets a need and has significant points of difference over competitive products.

What _Were_ They Thinking? Organizational Problems in New-Product Failure Besides the marketing reasons for new-product success and failure given above, a number of other organizational problems can cause disasters. Key ones—some that overlap—include:

1. _Not really listening to the "voice of the consumer."_ Product managers may believe they "know better" than their customers or feel they "can't afford" the valuable marketing research that could uncover problems.
2. _Skipping steps in the new-product process._ Though details may vary, the seven-step new-product process discussed in the next section is a sequence used in some form by most large organizations. Skipping a step often leads to disaster, the reason that many firms have a "gate" or "milestone" to ensure that one step is completed satisfactorily before going on to the next step.[13]
3. _Pushing a poorly conceived product into the market to generate quick revenue._ Today's marketing managers are under incredible pressure from top management to meet quarterly revenue targets. Often this focus on speed also results in overlooking the network of services needed to support the physical product.[14]
4. _"Groupthink" in task force and committee meetings._ Someone in the new-product planning meeting knows or suspects the product concept is a dumb idea. But that person is afraid to speak up for fear of being cast as a "negative thinker" and "not a team player" and then being ostracized from real participation in the group. And a strong public commitment to a new product by its key advocate may make it difficult to kill the product even when new negative information comes to light.[15]
5. _Not learning critical takeaway lessons from past failures._ The easiest lessons are from "intelligent failures"—ones that happen early in the new-product process so they are less expensive and that immediately give better understanding of customers' wants and needs.[16]

Helen Greiner, co-founder and chairman of iRobot, talks about lessons she learned from a key product failure. iRobot manufactures a variety of robots—from the Scooba floor washer mentioned in Chapter 1 to the PackBot bomb-disposal robot. Her lessons came from the Ariel, an amphibious mine-clearing robot that was the most advanced walking robot in the world at the time. Helen Greiner notes Ariel didn't satisfy the user's needs because "it couldn't walk far enough, it couldn't carry the payload it would need to carry, and it was too complex." The result: The failure shifted iRobot's focus from "innovation for innovation's sake" to "building practical and affordable robots that help people."[17]

Using Marketing Dashboards
Monitoring Your New-Product Launch

The goal of new-product introductions is to increase sales. Because sales expectations for new products are usually optimistic, they often are monitored on a month-by-month basis.

Your Challenge As the CEO, you carefully track the results of new-product launches. The dashboard figures show actual monthly results (blue line) matched up to goals (red line).

Let's say there are 100 million (MM) households in the United States. In terms of new households buying, your new Super Snack Bar is purchased by 5 million households (HH) in the first month, 4 million in the second month, and 3 million in the third month.

Triers = ((5MM+4MM+3MM)/100MM)*100 = 12% of HH have tried the new bar in the first 3 months.

Repeaters in first month: (1MM/5MM) = 20% of triers repeated. In the second month a total of 2MM HH bought again. This is divided into the triers in the first two months (5MM+4MM).

Repeat = [2MM bought again/All who bought to date (5MM + 4MM)] × 100 = 22%

Your Findings The top figure shows the number of households trying the new flavor (blue line), which is far below the red goal line. To make matters worse, consumers are not repeating to the level of the goal set in the bottom figure. Do you get the sense that this might be a sales train wreck?

Your Action There could be three different problems. (1) Why are fewer people trying the flavor than expected? This will trace to a marketing, sales, and communication issue. (2) Why are those who bought it not buying it again? This could be a distribution problem (it's not in stock) or it could be a product or packaging problem. (3) Lastly, it is possible that the product is doing fine, and the goals are unrealistic. You decide to tackle the third issue first. You ask the marketing research team for the details on other new-product introductions and make a careful comparison of the assumptions behind the red goals for your new product vs. the actual performance of your past new-product launches.

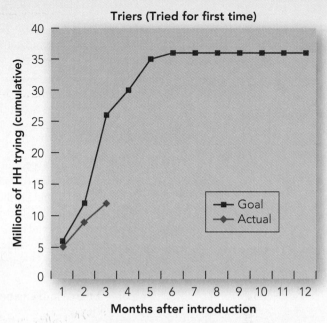

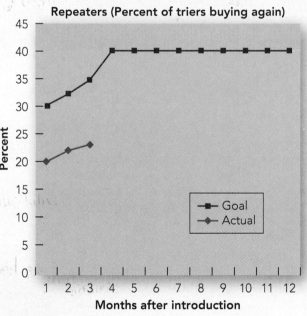

How Marketing Dashboards Can Reduce New-Product Failures

The Using Marketing Dashboards box shows how marketers measure actual-market performance versus the goals set in new-product planning. A new-product success in the marketplace is hardly guaranteed by it being ready to ship from the factory loading dock. The marketing manager responsible tracks its sales and acceptance in the marketplace to see what's working and what's not in the marketing mix actions for the product. Is the product getting on the retailers' shelves OK? Is the price right? Is the advertising effective?

learning review

4. From a consumer's viewpoint, what kind of innovation would an improved electric toothbrush be?

5. What does "insignificant point of difference" mean as a reason for new-product failure?

THE NEW-PRODUCT PROCESS

Innovation and new products are the lifeblood of most business firms. This is why many firms set goals for sales revenues derived from new products, as discussed in the Using Marketing Dashboards box. To develop new products efficiently, companies such as General Electric, Sony, and 3M take a specific sequence of steps before their products are ready for market. Figure 10–4 shows the seven stages of the **new-product process**, the stages a firm goes through to identify business opportunities and convert them to a salable good or service.

New-Product Strategy Development

For companies, **new-product strategy development** is the stage of the new-product process that defines the role for a new product in terms of the firm's overall corporate objectives. This step in the new-product process has been added by many companies recently to provide a needed focus for ideas and concepts developed in later stages.

Objectives of the Stage: Identify Markets and Strategic Roles During this new-product strategy development stage the company uses SWOT analysis (Chapter 2) and environmental scanning (Chapter 3) to identify factors to exploit. A key goal in new-product strategy development is to define the vital "protocol" explained earlier.

Improving Innovation: Cross-Functional Teams Ford's Taurus is often credited for breaking the mold in how U.S. manufacturers designed and built cars in

FIGURE 10–4

Stages in the new-product process

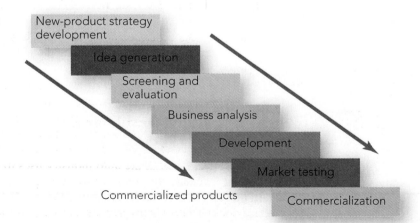

the early 1980s. Until then designers passed off their ideas to engineers who turned them into blueprints used by manufacturing to produce the cars marketing was supposed to sell. These groups rarely talked to each other in this sequential process.[18] Instead, Ford got all the departments working on the Taurus to talk together at the same time using cross-functional teams, which are vital in the new-product process. Unfortunately Ford's focus on SUVs caused Taurus to lose direction and it disappeared from the marketplace in 2007.

In 3M these teams enable individuals from R&D, manufacturing, marketing, and sales to work together simultaneously to focus on new product and market opportunities. Like Ford, 3M and other firms in the past often utilized these department people in sequence—sometimes resulting in R&D designing new products that the manufacturing department couldn't produce economically and that the marketing department couldn't sell.[19]

Idea Generation

The stage of the new-product process that involves developing a pool of concepts as candidates for new products, or **idea generation**, must build on the previous stage's results. The idea should be made as concrete as possible before moving to the next stage of the new-product process.[20] New-product ideas are generated by customers, suppliers, employees, basic R&D, and competitors. Also, there are other "outsiders": universities, investors, and small technology firms.

Customer and Supplier Suggestions Companies talk to customers and suppliers to discover new-product opportunities. So involving a company's salespeople in idea generation is very valuable because of their direct contacts with customers.[21] Whirlpool, trying to reduce costs by cutting the number of different product platforms in half, gets ideas from customers on ways to standardize components.[22] Business researchers now emphasize that firms must actively involve customers and suppliers in the product development process.[23] This often means focusing on what the new product will actually *do* for them rather than simply *what they want.*[24]

A. G. Lafley, the chief executive officer of Procter & Gamble (P&G), gives his executives a *revolutionary* thought: "Look outside the company for solutions to problems, rather than insisting P&G knows best." An example from his days running P&G's laundry detergent business: While consumers said P&G's laundry boxes were "easy to open," cameras they agreed to have installed in their laundry rooms showed they were opening the boxes with *screwdrivers.* His fix: Redesign the laundry boxes so they are easy to open![25]

Employee and Co-Worker Suggestions Employees may be encouraged to suggest new-product ideas through suggestion boxes or contests. The idea for Nature Valley Granola Bars from General Mills came when one of its marketing managers observed co-workers bringing granola to work in plastic bags.

As described at the start of Chapter 5, auto industry studies show that women buy about two-thirds of all vehicles and also influence about 85 percent of all sales. However, many auto manufacturers get ideas on new-car features by doing marketing research on gear-head guys who love cars. That's *exactly opposite* to what Volvo did recently in trying to bridge the gender gap. Volvo first obtained ideas on new-car features from all-female focus groups drawn from its Swedish workforce. It then named a five-woman team of Volvo managers to design a "concept car"—what the auto industry uses to test new designs, technical innovations, and consumer reactions.

Some features of Volvo's YCC (Your Concept Car) that appeared in auto shows include pressing a button on the car key and having the

Would women *really* help design this car? For how Volvo said "yes," see the text.

The Apple mouse. The Palm V PDA. The Crest Neat Squeeze toothpaste dispenser. The Steelecase Leap adjustable office chair. These are just some of the thousands of new products designed by an innovation lab you've probably never heard of but benefit from everyday. For David Kelley, co-founder of IDEO, product design includes both artistic and functional elements. And to foster this creativity, IDEO allows its designers and engineers much freedom—its offices look like schoolrooms; employees can hang their bicycles from the ceiling; there are rubber-band fights; and on Monday mornings, there are show-and-tell sessions.

Visit IDEO's website (www.ideo.com) to view its recent inventions and innovations for clients such as McDonald's self-ordering kiosk, the Zyliss' Mandolin fruit and vegetable slicer, LifePort's kidney transporter, Pepsi's High Visibility vending machine, and Nike's all-terrain sunglasses.

gull-wing doors pop open and the steering wheel pull in to make getting into the car easier, automatically parking the car in that parallel parking space, and customized seat covers that can be removed and washed. You *will* see many of these women-designed features on future Volvos, testimony to the importance of listening to employees and consumers in developing new products.[26]

Research and Development Breakthroughs Another source of new products is a firm's own research and development laboratories. Apple is a world leader in new-product development in computers and electronics. But even Apple sometimes goes outside its own labs—for example, when it found its original "mouse."

Professional R&D laboratories, sometimes called "innovation labs," that are outside the walls of large corporations also provide new-product ideas.[27] Labs at Arthur D. Little helped put the crunch in Cap'n Crunch cereal and the flavor in Carnation Instant Breakfast. As described in the Going Online box, IDEO is a world-class new-product development firm, having designed more than 4,000 of them.

Brainstorming sessions run at IDEO can generate 100 new ideas in an hour. Its "shop-a-long" visits with managers of client firms let the managers experience first-hand what one of its customers does. A sample recommendation from a shop-a-long with managers from a large U.S. health maintenance organization who actually could play the part of a patient: Make examining rooms larger to enable the nervous patient to have a friend or relative in the room while waiting for the doctor.[28]

Competitive Products New-product ideas can also be found by analyzing the competition. A six-person intelligence team from the Marriott Corporation spent six months traveling around the country staying at economy hotels. The team assessed the competition's strengths and weaknesses on everything from the soundproof qualities of the rooms to the softness of the towels. Marriott then budgeted $500 million for a new economy hotel chain, Fairfield Inns.

Universities, Inventors, and Small Technology Firms Texas Instruments (TI) manager Gene Franz spends his time looking for visionaries—a lot of them outside his company—with ideas TI could turn into products. Some examples:

- *Universities.* Their technology transfer centers often partner with firms like TI to commercialize inventions of their faculty.
- *Inventors.* Even today lone inventors and entrepreneurs exist with brilliant ideas—like the Israeli entrepreneur who invented a device a bit like the "tricoder" you saw on Star Trek: Point it at a patient and see his vital signs.[29]

- *Small technology firms.* Hewlett-Packard, Google, and The Geek Squad were tiny start-up businesses until a venture capital firm or large corporation found them, invested money in them, and helped them grow.

Great ideas can come from almost anywhere—if one can only recognize them.

Screening and Evaluation

Screening and evaluation is the stage of the new-product process that involves internal and external evaluations of the new-product ideas to eliminate those that warrant no further effort.

Internal Approach   Internally, the firm evaluates the technical feasibility of the proposal and whether the idea meets the objectives defined in the new-product strategy development step. The recent experience of 3M's George Dierberger illustrates this internal approach. Dierberger looks into technologies that have been developed in 3M's world-class adhesive laboratories. He found its microreplication technology that has 3,000 tiny gripping fingers per square inch. Internal evalution in 3M showed it could be incorporated into golf gloves to improve the players' grip. Details on how the 3M golf glove came to market appear in the video case at the end of the chapter.

External Approach   *Concept tests* are external evaluations that consist of preliminary testing of the new-product idea (rather than the actual product) with consumers. Generally, these tests are more useful with minor modifications of existing products than with really new, innovative products not familiar to consumers.[30] Concept tests usually rely on written descriptions of the product but may be augmented with sketches, mockups, or promotional literature. Several key questions are asked during concept testing: How does the customer perceive the product? Who would use it? How would it be used?

Frito-Lay spent a year interviewing 10,000 consumers about the concept of a multigrain snack chip before introducing its highly successful Sun Chips.

But consumers are changing, now concerned about healthy snacks, low-carb foods, trans fats, and so on—topics few Americans even thought about a couple of years ago. Frito-Lay started focusing efforts on a critical research issue: healthy snacks that taste good. This led to more concept tests and R&D that in 2004 eliminated trans fats from its Doritos, Tostitos, Fritos, and Cheetos by cooking in corn oil. Then in 2006, it shifted from cottonseed oil to sunflower oil in its Lay's and Ruffles chips to reduce saturated fats by 66 percent. The potential danger: Consumers may not like the taste of the new chips as well as they did the old ones, which have made Frito-Lay's line of potato chips the world's best-selling snack foods.[31]

learning review	6. What step in the new-product process has been added in recent years?
	7. What are the main sources of new-product ideas?
	8. What is the difference between internal and external screening and evaluation approaches used by a firm in the new-product process?

Business Analysis

Business analysis is the stage of the new-product process that involves specifying the product features and marketing strategy and making necessary financial projections

How do you print ink-jet images on Pringles chips safely and inexpensively? The text describes how a global search found the critical technology.

needed to commercialize a product. This is the last checkpoint before significant capital is invested in creating a *prototype,* a full-scale operating model of the product under development. Economic analysis, marketing strategy review, and legal examination of the proposed product are conducted at this stage.

The marketing strategy review studies the new-product idea in relation to the marketing program to support it. The proposed product is assessed to determine whether it will help or hurt sales of existing products. Likewise, the product is examined to assess whether it can be sold through existing channels or if new outlets will be needed. Profit projections involve estimating the number of units expected to be sold but also the costs of R&D, production, and marketing and whether it can be protected with a patent or copyright.

Development

Product ideas that survive the business analysis proceed to actual **development**, the stage of the new-product process that involves turning the idea on paper into a prototype. This results in a demonstrable, producible product in hand, which involves not only manufacturing the product but also performing laboratory and consumer tests to ensure that it meets the standards set.

The new product must be able to be manufactured at reasonable cost with the required quality. A 2002 brainstorming session at Procter & Gamble produced the idea of printing pop culture images on Pringles chips. So P&G often partners with movie or game companies for timely special promotions—like the appearance of *Spiderman 3.* But how do you print sharp images using edible dyes on thousands and thousands of chips each minute? Internal development would take too long and cost too much. P&G circulated the description of its unusual printing need globally. It discovered a university professor in Bologna, Italy, who had invented an ink-jet method for printing edible images on cakes and cookies. In less than a year P&G adapted the process and launched its new "Pringle Prints"—at a fraction of the time and cost internal development would have taken.[32] So an increasing new-product challenge—from physical products to computer software—is to manage a global development process that operates 24 hours a day.[33]

Some new products can be so important and costly that the company is betting its very existence on success. And creative, out-of-the-box thinking can be critical. In the pharmaceutical industry, no more than one out of every 5,000 to 10,000 new compounds developed in the labs emerges as an approved drug.[34] With the success rate on new drug compounds so low, pharmaceutical giant Eli Lilly has initiated "failure parties" to recognize excellent scientific work that unfortunately resulted in products that failed anyway. These parties result in Lilly's naming a team to learn the specific reasons for the failure. This "failure analysis" has resulted in Lilly sometimes finding ways to make the compound succeed in addressing the original disease for which it was designed.

During development, laboratory tests like this one on Barbie result in safer dolls and toys for children.

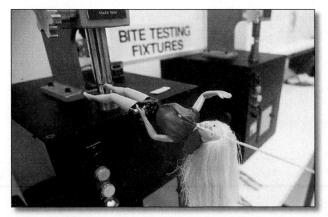

More surprisingly, a number of successful Lilly drugs trace their origins back to trials that demonstrated the drug was a flop for the initial medical problem it was intended to address but works well to treat a different disease. Some of these breakthroughs come from researchers using a Lilly "blue sky" fund that enables them to spend up to a day a week on projects with no clear immediate commercial value.[35] Google, too, stimulates creativity by letting its engineers spend a day a week to develop their own pet projects—a strategy that led to Google News.[36]

Lilly's drug prototypes go through exhaustive lab and clinical tests to see if they meet design criteria set for them

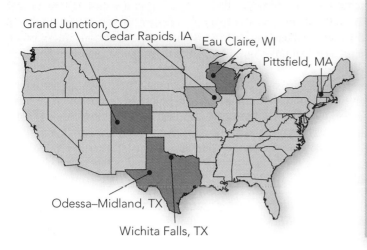

Demographic Characteristic	USA	Wichita Falls, TX
2000 population	281.4 mil.	140,518
Median age (years)	35.3	33.6
% of family households with children under 18	32.8%	33.8%
% Hispanic or Latino of any race	12.5%	11.8%
% African American	12.3%	9.6%
% Asian American	3.6%	1.7%
% Native American	1.5%	1.7%

FIGURE 10–5

Six important U.S. test markets and the "demographics winner": Wichita Falls, Texas, metropolitan statistical area

if used the way intended. But safety tests are also critical for when the product isn't used as planned. To make sure seven-year-olds can't bite Barbie's head off and choke, Mattel clamps her foot in steel jaws in a test stand and then pulls on her head with a wire. Similarly, car manufacturers have done extensive safety tests by crashing their cars into concrete walls.

Market Testing

Market testing is the stage of the new-product process that involves exposing actual products to prospective consumers under realistic purchase conditions to see if they will buy. Often a product is developed, tested, refined, and then tested again to get consumer reactions through either test marketing or simulated test markets.

Test Marketing   *Test marketing* involves offering a product for sale on a limited basis in a defined area. This test is done to determine whether consumers will actually buy the product and to try different ways of marketing it. Only about a third of the products test marketed do well enough to go on to the next phase. These market tests are usually conducted in cities that are viewed as being representative of U.S. consumers like the six shown in Figure 10–5. Of these cities, Wichita Falls, Texas, most closely matches the U.S. average found in the 2000 Census. Other criteria used in selecting test market cities include cable systems to deliver different ads to different homes, and tracking systems like those of AC Nielsen to measure sales resulting from different advertising campaigns.[37]

This gives the company an indication of potential sales volume and market share in the test area. Market tests are also used to check other elements of the marketing mix besides the product itself such as price, level of advertising support, and distribution. Because these market tests also are so time consuming and expensive and can alert competitors to a firm's plans, some firms skip test markets or use simulated test markets.

Simulated Test Markets   Because of the time, cost, and confidentiality problems of test markets, consumer packaged goods companies often turn to *simulated* (or *laboratory*) *test markets* (*STM*), a technique that simulates a full-scale test market but in a limited fashion. STMs are often run in shopping malls, where consumers are questioned to identify who uses the product class being tested. Willing participants are questioned on usage, reasons for purchase, and important product attributes. Qualified persons are then shown TV commercials or print ads for the test product along with competitors' advertising and are given money to make a decision to buy or not buy the firm's product—or the competitors' product—from a real or simulated store environment.

Commercializing a new french fry: To learn how Burger King's improved french fries confronted McDonald's fries, see the text.

When Test Markets Don't Work   Test marketing is a valuable step in the new-product process, but not all products can use it. Testing a service beyond the concept level is very difficult because the service is intangible and consumers can't see what they are buying. For example, how do you test market a new building for an art museum?

Similarly, test markets for expensive consumer products such as cars or costly industrial products such as jet engines are impractical. For these products, reactions of potential buyers to mockup designs or one-of-a-kind prototypes are all that is feasible. Carmakers test new style designs on early adopters (discussed in Chapter 11) who are more willing than the average customer to buy new designs or products.[38]

Commercialization

Finally, the product is brought to the point of **commercialization**—the stage of the new-product process that involves positioning and launching a new product in full-scale production and sales. Companies proceed very carefully at the commercialization stage because this is the most expensive stage for most new products. If competitors introduce a product that leapfrogs the firm's own new product or if cannibalization of its own existing products looks significant, the firm may halt the new-product launch permanently.

Countless other questions arise.[39] Should we make an advance announcement of the new-product introduction to stimulate interest and potential sales?[40] Do we need to add new salespeople?[41] Do the salespeople need extra training?

Large companies use *regional rollouts,* introducing the product sequentially into geographical areas of the United States, to allow production levels and marketing activities to build up gradually to minimize the risk of new-product failure. Grocery product manufacturers and some telephone service providers are two examples of firms that use this strategy.

Figure 10–6 identifies the purpose of each stage of the new-product process and the kinds of marketing information and methods used. The third column of the figure also suggests information that might help avoid some new-product failures. Although using the new-product process does not guarantee successful products, it does increase a firm's success rate.

Effective cross-functional teams at Hewlett-Packard have reduced new-product development times significantly.

Burger King's French Fries: The Complexities of Commercialization

Burger King's "improved french fries" are an example of what can go wrong at the commercialization stage. In the fast-food industry, McDonald's french fries are the gold standard against which all other fries are measured. In 1996, Burger King decided to take on McDonald's fries and spent millions of R&D dollars developing a starch-coated fry designed to retain heat longer and add crispiness. This crispiness was even defined:

"An audible crunch that should be present for seven or more chews!"

A 100-person team set to work and developed the starch-coated fry that beat McDonald's fries in taste tests, 57 percent to 35 percent, with 8 percent having no opinion. After "certifrying" 300,000 managers and employees on the new frying procedures, the fries were launched in early 1998 with a $70 million marketing budget. The launch turned into disaster. The reason: The new fry proved too complicated to get right day after day in Burger King restaurants, except under ideal conditions.[42]

By summer 2000, Burger King realized something had to be done. Solution: Launch a "new," coated fry in early 2001 that is easier for its kitchens to prepare. A commercialization stage success? You be the judge.

The Risks and Uncertainties of the Commercialization Stage

As the Burger King french fries show, the job is far from over when the new product gets to the commercialization stage. Despite brilliant technologies, the hundreds of dot-com failures in 2000 and 2001 show the difficulty of launching successful new products.

STAGE OF PROCESS	PURPOSE OF STAGE	MARKETING INFORMATION AND METHODS USED
New-product strategy development	Identify new-product niches to reach in light of company objectives	Company objectives; assessment of firm's current strengths and weaknesses in terms of market and product
Idea generation	Develop concepts for possible products	Ideas from employees and co-workers, consumers, R&D, and competitors; methods of brainstorming and focus groups
Screening and evaluation	Separate good product ideas from bad ones inexpensively	Screening criteria, concept tests, and weighted point systems
Business analysis	Identify the product's features and its marketing strategy, and make financial projections	Product's key features, anticipated marketing mix strategy; economic, marketing, production, legal, and profitability analyses
Development	Create the prototype product, and test it in the laboratory and on consumers	Laboratory and consumer tests on product prototypes
Market testing	Test product and marketing strategy in the marketplace on a limited scale	Test markets, simulated test markets (STMs)
Commercialization	Position and offer product in the marketplace	Perceptual maps, product positioning, regional rollouts

FIGURE 10–6

Marketing information and methods used in each stage of the new-product process

Grocery products pose special commercialization problems. Because shelf space is so limited, many supermarkets require a **slotting fee** for new products, a payment a manufacturer makes to place a new item on a retailer's shelf. This can run to several million dollars for a single product. But there's even another potential expense. If a new grocery product does not achieve a predetermined sales target, some retailers require a **failure fee**, a penalty payment a manufacturer makes to compensate a retailer for sales its valuable shelf space failed to make. These costly slotting fees and failure fees are further examples of why large grocery product manufacturers use regional rollouts.

Speed as a Factor in New-Product Success   In recent years, companies have discovered that speed or *time to market* (TtM) is often vital in introducing a new product. Recent studies have shown that high-tech products coming to market on time are far more profitable than those arriving late. So some companies—such as Sony, BMW, 3M, and Hewlett-Packard—have overlapped the sequence of stages described in this chapter.

With this approach, termed *parallel development,* cross-functional team members who conduct the simultaneous development of both the product and the production process stay with the product from conception to production. This has enabled Hewlett-Packard (HP) to reduce the development time for notebook computers from 12 months to 7.[43] In software development, *fast prototyping* used a "do it, try it, fix it" approach—encouraging continuing improvement even after the initial design. To speed up time to market many large companies are building "fences" around their new product teams to keep them from getting bogged down in red tape.[44]

Hewlett-Packard's new-product success can be traced to its founders' innovative management style that shunned the traditional rigid hierarchical structure. Instead, HP uses a decentralized system where the brainpower of its employees is freed to let them talk to whoever is needed to get the job done. This HP system is often referred to as the "birthplace of Silicon Valley."[45]

learning review

9. How does the development stage of the new-product process involve testing the product inside and outside the firm?

10. What is a test market?

11. What is commercialization of a new product?

LEARNING OBJECTIVES REVIEW

LO1 *Recognize the various terms that pertain to products and services.*

A product is a good, service, or idea consisting of a bundle of tangible and intangible attributes that satisfies consumers and is received in exchange for money or some other unit of value. Firms can offer a range of products, which involve decisions regarding the product item, product line, and product mix.

LO2 *Identify the ways in which consumer and business goods can be classified.*

Products can be classified by type of user and tangibility. By user, the major distinctions are consumer goods, which are products purchased by the ultimate consumer, and business goods, which are products that assist in providing other products for resale. By degree of tangibility, products may be classified as (*a*) nondurable goods, which are consumed in one or a few uses, (*b*) durable goods, which are items that usually last over an extended number of uses, or (*c*) services, which are activities, benefits, or satisfactions offered for sale.

Consumer goods can further be broken down based on the effort involved in the purchase decision process, marketing mix attributes used in the purchase, and the frequency of purchase: (*a*) convenience goods are items that consumers purchase frequently and with a minimum of shopping effort, (*b*) shopping goods are items for which consumers compare several alternatives on selected criteria, (*c*) specialty goods are items that consumers make special efforts to seek out and buy, and (*d*) unsought goods are items that consumers do not either know about or initially want.

Business goods can further be broken down into (*a*) production goods, which are items used in the manufacturing process that become part of the final product, such as raw materials or component parts, and (*b*) support goods, which are items used to assist in producing other goods and services and include installations, accessory equipment, supplies, and services.

LO3 *Explain the significance of "newness" in new products and services as it relates to the degree of consumer learning involved.*

From the important perspective of the consumer, "newness" is often seen as the degree of learning that a consumer must engage in to use the product. With a continuous innovation, no new behaviors must be learned. With a dynamically continuous innovation, only minor behavioral changes are needed. With a discontinuous innovation, consumers must learn entirely new consumption patterns.

LO4 *Describe the factors contributing to a new product's or service's success or failure.*

A new product or service often fails for these marketing reasons: (*a*) insignificant points of difference, (*b*) incomplete market and product definition before product development begins, (*c*) too little market attractiveness, (*d*) poor execution of the marketing mix, (*e*) poor product quality on critical factors, (*f*) bad timing, and (*g*) no economical access to buyers.

LO5 *Explain the purposes of each step of the new-product process.*

The new-product process consists of seven stages a firm uses to develop a salable good or service: (1) New-product strategy development involves defining the role for the new product within the firm's overall objectives. (2) Idea generation involves developing a pool of concepts from consumers, employees, basic R&D, and competitors to serve as candidates for new products. (3) Screening and evaluation involves evaluating new product ideas to eliminate those that are not feasible from a technical or consumer perspective. (4) Business analysis involves defining the features of the new product, developing the marketing strategy and marketing program to introduce it, and making a financial forecast. (5) Development involves not only producing a prototype product but also testing it in the lab and on consumers to see that it meets the standards set for it. (6) Market testing involves exposing actual products to prospective consumers under realistic purchasing conditions to see if they will buy the product. (7) Commercialization involves positioning and launching a product in full-scale production and sales with a specific marketing program.

FOCUSING ON KEY TERMS

business analysis p. 269
business goods p. 255

commercialization p. 272
consumer goods p. 255

convenience goods p. 257
development p. 270

APPLYING MARKETING KNOWLEDGE

1 Products can be classified as either consumer or business goods. How would you classify the following products? (*a*) Johnson's baby shampoo, (*b*) a Black & Decker two-speed drill, and (*c*) an arc welder.

2 Are products such as Nature Valley Granola bars and Eddie Bauer hiking boots convenience, shopping, specialty, or unsought goods?

3 Based on your answer to question 2, how would the marketing actions differ for each product and the classification to which you assigned it?

4 In terms of the behavioral effect on consumers, how would a PC, such as an Apple iMac, be classified? In light of this classification, what actions would you suggest to the manufacturers of these products to increase their sales in the market?

5 Several alternative definitions were presented for a new product. How would a company's marketing strategy be affected if it used (*a*) the legal definition or (*b*) a behavioral definition?

6 What methods would you suggest to assess the potential commercial success for the following new products? (*a*) a new, improved ketchup, (*b*) a three-dimensional television system that took the company 10 years to develop, and (*c*) a new children's toy on which the company holds a patent.

7 Concept testing is an important step in the new-product process. Outline the concept tests for (*a*) an electrically powered car and (*b*) a new loan payment system for automobiles that is based on a variable interest rate. What are the differences in developing concept tests for products as opposed to services?

building your marketing plan

In fine-tuning the product strategy for your marketing plan, do these two things:

1 Develop a simple three-column table in which (*a*) market segments of potential customers are in the first column and (*b*) the one or two key points of differences

of the product to satisfy the segment's needs are in the second column.

2 In the third column of your table, write ideas for specific new products for your business in each of the rows in your table.

video case 10   3M Greptile™ Grip Golf Glove: Great Gripping!

"Marketing is not brain surgery," says Dr. George Dierberger, Marketing and International Manager of 3M's Sports and Leisure Products Project. "We tend to make it a lot more difficult than it is. 3M wins with its technology. We're not in the 'me-too' business and in marketing we've got to remember that."

3M'S MICROREPLICATION TECHNOLOGY AND ITS GREPTILE GOLF GLOVE

The 3M Company is a $23 billion global, diversified technology business. Among its well-known brands are Post-it® Notes™, Scotch® tape, Scotch Brite® scouring pads, and Nexcare bandages. The key to 3M's market-

ing successes is its commitment to innovation. For more than a century, 3M's management has given its employees the freedom to try new ideas. This "culture of creativity" has led to the commercialization of more than 50,000 products.

The Sports and Leisure Products Project is a business unit managed by Dierberger and his marketing staff. Recently, Dierberger and his staff changed the conventional thinking about golfing. Using 3M's proprietary "microreplication" technology, and applying it to a golf glove, the new Greptile™ gripping material consists of thousands of tiny "gripping fingers" sewn into the upper palm and lower fingers of a golf glove. According to Dierberger, "It is the only glove on the market that actively improves a golfer's hold on the club by allowing a more relaxed grip, leading to greater driving distance with less grip pressure, even under wet conditions." Laboratory tests found that the Greptile material offers 610 percent greater gripping power than leather and 340 percent greater than tackified (sticky) grips. The result: On drives, the golf ball travels an average 10.5 feet farther!

Introduced in 2004, the new 3M Greptile Grip golf glove is made primarily of high-quality Cabretta sheep leather to give it a soft feel. Initially, 3M sold the Greptile Grip golf glove through Wal-Mart and other mass merchandisers for a suggested retail price of $12.95. And now it's also being stocked by golf retailers across the country like Golfsmith, Austad's, and Golf Galaxy. The golf glove was introduced in both men's and women's left-hand versions and in small, medium, medium/large, large, and extra-large hand sizes. A right-hand version for both genders appeared in 2005. The company projected first-year sales of $1 million in the United States.

THE GOLF MARKET

Several socioeconomic and demographic trends impact the golf glove market favorably. First, the huge baby boomer population (those born between 1946 and 1964) has matured, reaching its prime earning potential. This allows for greater discretionary spending on leisure activities, such as golf. According to the National Golf Foundation (NGF), most spending on golf equipment (clubs, bags, balls, shoes, gloves, etc.) is by consumers 50 and older—today's baby boomers. Second, according to the U.S. Census, the U.S. population has shifted regionally from the East and North to the South and West, where golfing is popular year-round due to the temperate weather. Third, the number of U.S. golf courses has been growing, totaling about 17,000 at the end of 2006.

Finally, golf is becoming an increasingly popular leisure activity for all age groups and ethnic backgrounds. According to the NGF, golf participants in the United States totaled 28.7 million in 2006. Female golfers now account for about 25 percent of all golfers while minority participation has increased to over 10 percent. According to the National Sporting Goods Association, sales of golf equipment was $3.2 billion in 2005, an increase of 3 percent from 2004.

THE GOLF GLOVE MARKET

The global market for golf gloves is estimated at $300 million, with the United States at $180 million or 60 per-

cent of worldwide sales. Historically, about 80 percent of golf gloves are sold through public and private on- and off-course golf pro specialty shops, golf superstores, and sporting good superstores. However, mass merchandisers have recently increased their shares due to the typically lower prices offered by these retailers. FootJoy and Titleist, both owned by Acushnet, are the top two golf glove market share leaders. Nike, which entered the golf equipment market with Tiger Woods as its spokesperson, has a measurable share of the golf glove market. Golf glove marketers focus on technology and comfort to create points of difference from their competitors.

3M'S NEW PRODUCT PROCESS

Since about half of 3M's products are less than five years old, the process used by 3M to develop new-product innovations is critical to its success and continued growth. Every innovation must meet 3M's new product criteria: (1) be a patentable or trademarked technology; (2) offer a superior value proposition to consumers; and (3) change the basis of competition by achieving a significant point of difference.

When developing a new product innovation such as the 3M Greptile Grip golf glove, 3M uses a rigorous seven-step process: (1) ideas, (2) concept, (3) feasibility, (4) development, (5) scale-up, (6) launch, and (7) post-launch. "But innovation is not a linear path—not just A, then B, then C," says Dierberger. "It's the adjustments you make after you've developed the product that determines your success. And it's learning lessons from testing on real customers to make the final tweaks—changing the price points, improving the benefits statement on the packaging, and sharpening the advertising appeals."

In the case of the 3M Greptile Grip golf glove, countless other examples of these adjustments appeared. Mike Kuhl, marketing coordinator at 3M, points out, "Consumer testing labs said the information on the back of our package was incomplete so we had dozens of golfers hit drives using our glove and competitive gloves to compare driving distance." And says 3M packaging engineer Travis Strom, "Our first glove package 'pillowed'—bulked up—on the shelf, had hard-to-read text, and wasn't appealing to golfers, so we had to redesign it. After all, you only have a few seconds to capture the customer's attention with the package and make a sale."

THE FUTURE OF 3M GOLF AND GREPTILE

In 2005, 3M Golf launched a premium golf glove consisting of the highest quality Cabretta leather and selling for a suggested retail price of $16.95 to $19.95. On the drawing board are some other 3M Greptile Grip products that may be in retail stores when you read this. In 2006, 3M launched versions of its Greptile Grip golf gloves in Japan and Europe, the second and third largest golf markets behind the United States.

Questions

1 What are the characteristics of the target market for the 3M Greptile Grip golf glove?

2 What are the key points of difference of the 3M Greptile Grip golf glove when compared to competitors' products, such as FootJoy and Nike? Substitute products, such as golf grips?

3 How does the Greptile Grip golf glove meet 3M's three criteria for new products?

4 Since 3M has no prior products for the golf market, what special promotion and distribution problems might 3M have?

5 How would you rate the 3M Greptile Grip golf glove on the following reasons for success and failure: (*a*) significant points of difference; (*b*) size and growth of the golf market; (*c*) product quality; (*d*) market timing; (*e*) execution of the marketing mix; (*f*) synergy or fit with 3M's R&D, manufacturing, or marketing capabilities; and (*g*) access to consumers.

11

Managing Products and Brands

LEARNING OBJECTIVES

After reading this chapter you should be able to:

 LO1 Explain the product life-cycle concept.

 LO2 Identify ways that marketing executives manage a product's life cycle.

 LO3 Recognize the importance of branding and alternative branding strategies.

 LO4 Describe the role of packaging, labeling, and warranties in the marketing of a product.

GATORADE: SATISFYING THE UNQUENCHABLE THIRST

The thirst for Gatorade is unquenchable. This brand powerhouse has posted yearly sales gains over four decades and commands about 82 percent of the sports beverage market in the United States.

Like Kleenex in the tissue market, Jello among gelatin desserts, and iPod for digital music players, Gatorade has become synonymous with sports beverages. Concocted in 1965 at the University of Florida as a rehydration beverage for the school's football team, the drink was coined "Gatorade" by an opposing team's coach after watching his team lose to the Florida Gators in the Orange Bowl. The name stuck, and a new beverage product class was born.

Stokely-Van Camp Inc. bought the Gatorade formula in 1967 and commercialized the product. The original Gatorade was a liquid with a lemon-lime flavor. An orange flavor was introduced in 1971 and a fruit punch flavor in 1983. Instant Gatorade arrived in 1979.

The Quaker Oats Company acquired Stokely-Van Camp in 1983. Quaker Oats executives quickly grew sales through a variety of means. More flavors were added and multiple package sizes were offered using different containers—glass and plastic bottles and aluminum cans. Distribution coverage expanded from convenience stores and supermarkets to vending machines, fountain service, and mass merchandisers such as Wal-Mart. Consistent advertising and promotion effectively conveyed the product's unique benefits and links to athletic competition. International opportunities were vigorously pursued. Today, Gatorade is sold in more than 90 countries in North America, Europe, Latin America, the Middle East, Africa, Asia, and Australia and has become a global brand.

Brand development spurred Gatorade's success. Gatorade Frost was introduced in 1997, with a "lighter, crisper" taste aimed at expanding the brand's reach beyond organized sports to other usage occasions. Gatorade Fierce with a "bolder" taste appeared in 1999. In the same year, Gatorade entered the bottled-water category with Propel Fitness Water, a lightly flavored water fortified with vitamins. The Gatorade Performance Series was introduced in 2001, featuring a Gatorade Energy Bar, Gatorade Energy Drink, and Gatorade Nutritional Shake.

Brand development accelerated after PepsiCo, Inc., purchased Quaker Oats and the Gatorade brand in 2001. Gatorade All Stars, designed for teens, and Gatorade Xtremo, developed for Latino consumers with an exotic blend of flavors and a bilingual label, were introduced in 2002. Gatorade X-Factor followed in 2003 with three flavors. In 2005, Gatorade Endurance Formula was introduced for serious runners, construction workers, and other people doing long, sweaty workouts. Gatorade Rain, a lighter tasting version of regular Gatorade,

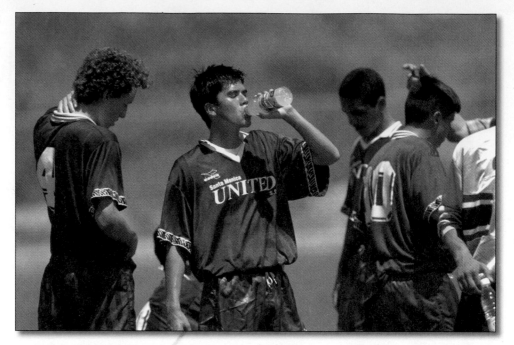

arrived in 2006 with berry, lime, and tangerine flavors. In 2007, Gatorade A.M. debuted for the morning workout consumer with three morning-friendly flavors and no caffeine. A low-calorie Gatorade drink called G2 was launched in 2008 as well as Gatorade Tiger, named for Tiger Woods. Today, Gatorade is available in over 30 flavors in the United States and more than 50 flavors internationally. Some 45 years after its creation, Gatorade remains a vibrant, multibillion-dollar growth brand with seemingly unlimited potential.[1]

The marketing of Gatorade illustrates effective product and brand management in a dynamic marketplace. This chapter shows how the actions taken by Gatorade executives are typical of those made by successful marketers.

THE PRODUCT LIFE CYCLE

Products, like people, are viewed as having a life cycle. The concept of the **product life cycle** describes the stages a new product goes through in the marketplace: introduction, growth, maturity, and decline (Figure 11–1).[2] The two curves shown in this figure, total industry sales revenue and total industry profit, represent the sum of sales revenue and profit of all firms producing the product. The reasons for the changes in each curve and the marketing decisions involved are detailed in the following pages.

Introduction Stage

The introduction stage of the product life cycle occurs when a product is introduced to its intended target market. During this period, sales grow slowly, and profit is minimal. The lack of profit is often the result of large investment costs in product development, such as the millions of dollars spent by Gillette to develop the Gillette Fusion razor shaving system. The marketing objective for the company at this stage is to create consumer awareness and stimulate *trial*—the initial purchase of a product by a consumer.

Companies often spend heavily on advertising and other promotion tools to build awareness and stimulate product trial among consumers in the introduction stage. For example, Gillette budgeted $200 million in advertising alone to introduce the Fusion shaving system to male shavers. The result? Over 60 percent of male shavers became aware of the new razor within six months and 26 percent tried the product.[3]

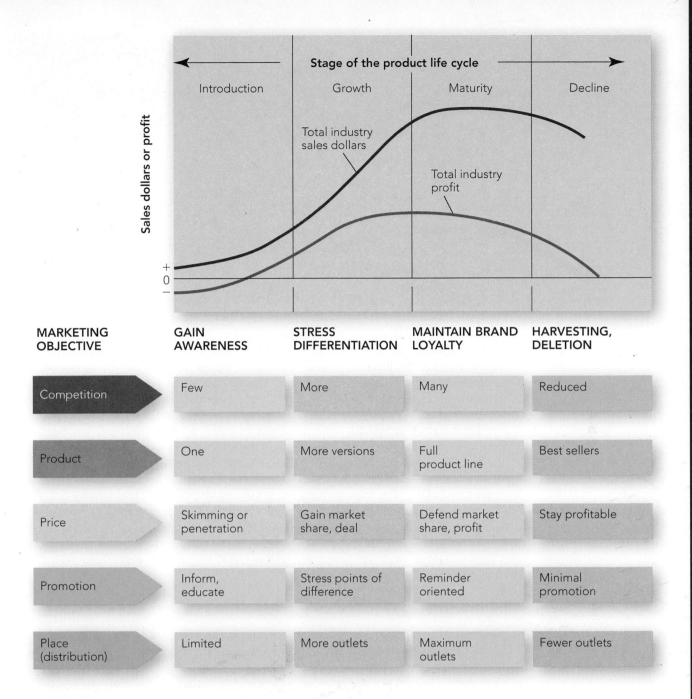

FIGURE 11–1

How stages of the product life cycle relate to a firm's marketing objectives and marketing mix actions

Advertising and promotion expenditures in the introduction stage are often made to stimulate *primary demand,* the desire for the product class rather than for a specific brand, since there are few competitors with the same product. As more competitors launch their own products and the product progresses along its life cycle, company attention is focused on creating *selective demand,* the preference for a specific brand.

Other marketing mix variables also are important at this stage. Gaining distribution can be a challenge because channel intermediaries may be hesitant to carry a new product. Also, a company often restricts the number of variations of the product to ensure control of product quality. Remember that the original Gatorade came in only one flavor—lemon-lime.

During introduction, pricing can be either high or low. A high initial price may be used as part of a *skimming* strategy to help the company recover the costs of development as well as capitalize on the price insensitivity of early buyers. A master of

FIGURE 11–2

Product life cycle for the stand-alone fax machine for business use: 1970–2010. All four product life-cycle stages appear: introduction, growth, maturity, and decline.

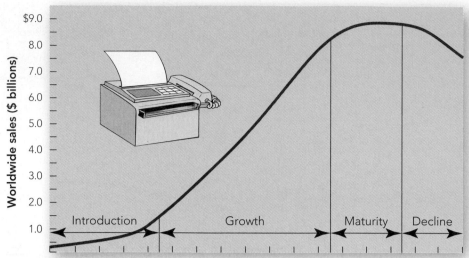

this strategy is 3M. According to a 3M manager, "We hit fast, price high, and get the heck out when the me-too products pour in."[4] High prices tend to attract competitors eager to enter the market because they see the opportunity for profit. To discourage competitive entry, a company can price low, referred to as *penetration pricing*. This pricing strategy helps build unit volume, but a company must closely monitor costs. These and other pricing techniques are covered in Chapter 14.

Figure 11–2 charts the stand-alone fax machine product life cycle for business use in the United States from the early 1970s to 2010.[5] As shown, sales grew slowly in the 1970s and early 1980s after Xerox pioneered the first portable fax machine. Fax machines were first sold direct to businesses by company salespeople and were premium priced. The average price for a fax machine in 1980 was a hefty $12,700. By today's standards, those fax machines were primitive. They contained mechanical parts, not electronic circuitry, and offered few features seen in today's models.

Several product classes are in the introductory stage of the product life cycle. These include high-definition television (HDTV) and "hybrid" (gasoline- and electric-powered) automobiles.

Growth Stage

The growth stage of the product life cycle is characterized by rapid increases in sales. It is in this stage that competitors appear. For example, Figure 11–2 shows the dramatic increase in sales of fax machines from 1986 to 1998. The number of companies selling fax machines also increased, from one in the early 1970s to four in the late 1970s to seven manufacturers in 1983, which sold nine brands. By 1998 there were some 25 manufacturers and 60 brands from which to choose.

The result of more competitors and more aggressive pricing is that profit usually peaks during the growth stage. For instance, the average price for a fax machine plummeted from $3,300 in 1985 to $500 in 1995. At this stage, the emphasis of advertising shifts to stimulating selective demand, in which product benefits are compared with those of competitors' offerings for the purpose of gaining market share.

Product sales in the growth stage grow at an increasing rate because of new people trying or using the product and a growing proportion of *repeat purchasers*—people who tried the product, were satisfied, and bought again. For the Gillette Fusion razor, over 60 percent of men who tried the razor adopted the product permanently. For successful products, the ratio of repeat to trial purchases grows as the product moves through the life cycle. Durable fax machines meant that replacement purchases were rare. However, it became common for more than one machine to populate a business

Hybrid automobiles made by Honda are in the introductory stage of the product life cycle. Digital cameras produced by Panasonic are in the growth stage. Each product and company faces unique challenges based on its product life-cycle stage.

Honda Motor Company
www.honda.com

Panasonic Corporation
www.panasonic.com

as their use became more widespread. In 1998, there was one fax machine for every eight people in a business in the United States.

Changes appear in the product in the growth stage. To help differentiate a company's brand from competitors, an improved version or new features are added to the original design, and product proliferation occurs. Changes in fax machines included: (1) models with built-in telephones; (2) models that used plain, rather than thermal, paper for copies; (3) models that integrated electronic mail; and (4) models that permitted confidential transmissions.

In the growth stage it is important to gain as much distribution for the product as possible. In the retail store, for example, this often means that competing companies fight for display and shelf space. Expanded distribution in the fax industry is an example. Early in the growth stage, just 11 percent of office machine dealers carried this equipment. By the mid-1990s, over 70 percent of these dealers sold fax equipment, and distribution was expanded to other stores selling electronic equipment.

Numerous product classes or industries are in the growth stage of the product life cycle. Examples include digital music players and digital cameras.

Maturity Stage

The maturity stage is characterized by a slowing of total industry sales or product class revenue. Also, marginal competitors begin to leave the market. Most consumers who would buy the product are either repeat purchasers of the item or have tried and abandoned it. Sales increase at a decreasing rate in the maturity stage as fewer new buyers enter the market. Profit declines due to fierce price competition among many sellers, and the cost of gaining new buyers at this stage rises.

Marketing attention in the maturity stage is often directed toward holding market share through further product differentiation and finding new buyers. Fax machine manufacturers developed Internet-enabled multifunctional models with new features

Will E-mail Spell Extinction for Fax Machines?

Technological substitution that creates value for customers often causes the decline stage in the product life cycle. Will e-mail replace fax machines?

This question has been debated for years. Even though e-mail continues to grow with broadening Internet access, millions of fax machines are still sold each years. Industry analysts estimate that the number of e-mail mailboxes worldwide will grow to 2.5 billion in 2010. However, the phenomenal popularity of e-mail has not brought fax machines to extinction. Why? The two technologies do not directly compete for the same messaging applications.

E-mail is used for text messages, and faxing is predominately used for communicating formatted documents by business users. Fax usage is expected to increase through 2009, even though unit sales of fax machines have declined on a worldwide basis. Internet technology and e-mail may eventually replace facsimile technology and paper, but not in the immediate future.

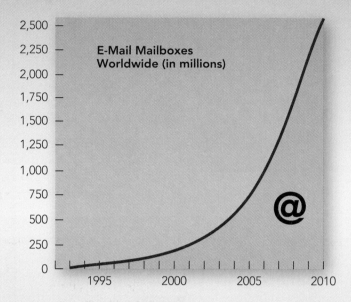

such as scanning, copying, and color reproduction. They also designed fax machines suitable for small and home businesses, which today represent a substantial portion of orders by sales. Still, a major consideration in a company's strategy in this stage is to control overall marketing cost by improving promotional and distribution efficiency.

Fax machines entered the maturity stage in the late 1990s. At the time, about 90 percent of industry sales were captured by five producers (Hewlett-Packard, Brother, Sharp, Lexmark, and Samsung), reflecting the departure of marginal competitors. By 2004, 200 million stand-alone fax machines were installed throughout the world, sending more than 120 billion faxes annually.

Numerous product classes and industries are in the maturity stage of their product life cycle. These include soft drinks, DVD players, and conventional TVs.

Decline Stage

The decline stage occurs when sales drop. Fax machines for business use moved to this stage in early 2005 and the average price for a fax machine had sunk below $100. Frequently, a product enters this stage not because of any wrong strategy on the part of companies, but because of environmental changes. The word-processing capability of personal computers pushed typewriters into decline. Digital music players are doing the same to compact discs in the recorded music industry. Will Internet technology and e-mail make fax machines extinct any time soon? The accompanying Marketing Matters box offers one perspective on this question.[6]

Products in the decline stage tend to consume a disproportionate share of management and financial resources relative to their future worth. A company will follow one of two strategies to handle a declining product: deletion or harvesting.

Deletion Product *deletion,* or dropping the product from the company's product line, is the most drastic strategy. Because a residual core of consumers still consume or use a product even in the decline stage, product elimination decisions are not taken lightly. For example, Sanford continues to sell its Liquid Paper correction fluid for use with typewriters in the era of word-processing equipment.

Harvesting   A second strategy, *harvesting,* is when a company retains the product but reduces marketing costs. The product continues to be offered, but salespeople do not allocate time in selling nor are advertising dollars spent. The purpose of harvesting is to maintain the ability to meet customer requests. Coca-Cola, for instance, still sells Tab, its first diet cola, to a small group of die-hard fans. According to Coke's CEO, "It shows you care. We want to make sure those who want Tab, get Tab."[7]

Some Dimensions of the Product Life Cycle

Some important aspects of product life cycles are (1) their length, (2) the shape of their sales curves, (3) how they vary with different levels of products, and (4) the rate at which consumers adopt products.

Length of the Product Life Cycle   There is no exact time that a product takes to move through its life cycle. As a rule, consumer products have shorter life cycles than business products. For example, many new consumer food products such as Frito-Lay's Baked Lay's potato chips move from the introduction stage to maturity in 18 months. The availability of mass communication vehicles informs consumers quickly and shortens life cycles. Also, technological change tends to shorten product life cycles as new-product innovation replaces existing products.

Shape of the Product Life Cycle   The product life-cycle sales curve shown in Figure 11–1 is the *generalized life cycle,* but not all products have the same shape to their curve. In fact, there are several different life-cycle curves, each type suggesting different marketing strategies. Figure 11–3 shows the shape of life-cycle sales curves for four different types of products: high-learning, low-learning, fashion, and fad products.

A *high-learning product* is one for which significant customer education is required and there is an extended introductory period (Figure 11–3A). It may surprise you, but personal computers had this life-cycle curve. Consumers in the 1980s had to learn the benefits of owning the product or be educated in a new way of performing familiar tasks. Convection ovens for home use required consumers to learn a new way of cooking and alter familiar recipes used with conventional ovens. As a result, these ovens spent years in the introductory period.

FIGURE 11–3

Alternative product life-cycle curves based on product types. Note the long introduction stage for a high-learning product compared with a low-learning product. Read the text for an explanation of different product life-cycle curves.

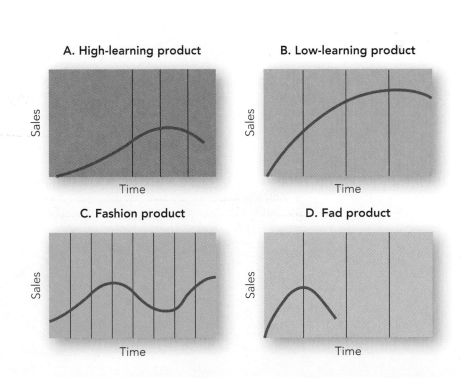

A. High-learning product

B. Low-learning product

C. Fashion product

D. Fad product

In contrast, for a *low-learning product* sales begin immediately because little learning is required by the consumer, and the benefits of purchase are readily understood (Figure 11–3B). This product often can be easily imitated by competitors, so the marketing strategy is to broaden distribution quickly. In this way, as competitors rapidly enter, most retail outlets already have the innovator's product. It is also important to have the manufacturing capacity to meet demand. An example of a successful low-learning product is Gillette's Fusion razor. This product achieved $1 billion in worldwide sales in less than three years.[8]

A *fashion product* (Figure 11–3C) is a style of the times. Life cycles for fashion products frequently appear in women's and men's apparel. Fashion products are introduced, decline, and then seem to return. The length of the cycles may be months, years, or decades. Consider women's hosiery. Product sales have been declining for years. Women consider it more fashionable to not wear hosiery—bad news for Hanesbrands, the leading marketer of women's sheer hosiery. According to an authority on fashion, "Companies might as well let the fashion cycle take its course and wait for the inevitable return of pantyhose."[9]

A *fad* experiences rapid sales on introduction and then an equally rapid decline (Figure 11–3D). These products are typically novelties and have a short life cycle. They include car tattoos sold in southern California and described as the first removable and reusable graphics for automobiles, and vinyl dresses and fleece bikinis made by a Minnesota clothing company.[10]

The Product Level: Class and Form   The product life cycle shown in Figure 11–1 is a total industry or product class sales curve. Yet, in managing a product it is important to often distinguish among the multiple life cycles (class and form) that may exist. **Product class** refers to the entire product category or industry, such as prerecorded music. **Product form** pertains to variations within the product class. For prerecorded music, product form exists in the technology used to provide the music such as cassette tapes, compact discs, and digital music players. Figure 11–4 shows the life cycles for these three product forms.[11]

The Life Cycle and Consumers   The life cycle of a product depends on sales to consumers. Not all consumers rush to buy a product in the introductory

FIGURE 11–4

Prerecorded music product life cycles by product form illustrate the effect of technology on sales. Do you remember the cassette tape?

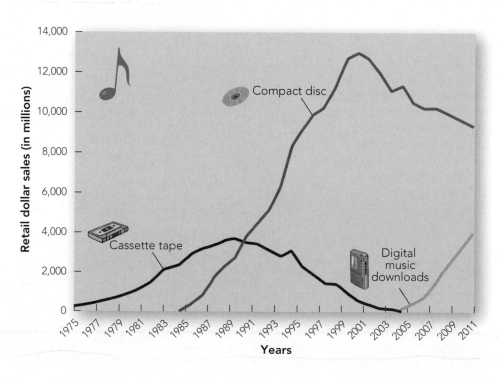

FIGURE 11–5

Five categories and profiles of product adopters. For a product to be successful, it must be purchased by innovators and early adopters.

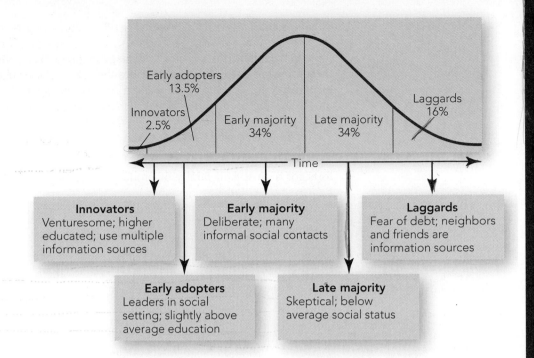

stage, and the shapes of the life-cycle curves indicate that most sales occur after the product has been on the market for some time. In essence, a product diffuses, or spreads, through the population, a concept called the *diffusion of innovation.*[12]

Some people are attracted to a product early. Others buy it only after they see their friends or opinion leaders with the item. Figure 11–5 shows the consumer population divided into five categories of product adopters based on when they adopt a new product. Brief profiles accompany each category. For any product to be successful, it must be purchased by innovators and early adopters. This is why manufacturers of new pharmaceuticals try to gain adoption by respected hospitals, clinics, and physicians. Once accepted by innovators and early adopters, the adoption of new products moves on to the early majority, late majority, and laggard categories.

Several factors affect whether a consumer will adopt a new product or not. Common reasons for resisting a product in the introduction stage are usage barriers (the product is not compatible with existing habits), value barriers (the product provides no incentive to change), risk barriers (physical, economic, or social), and psychological barriers (cultural differences or image).[13]

Companies attempt to overcome these barriers in numerous ways. They provide warranties, money-back guarantees, extensive usage instructions, demonstrations, and free samples to stimulate initial trial of new products. For example, software developers offer demonstrations downloaded from the Internet. Maybelline allows consumers to browse through the Cover Girl Color Match system on its website to find out how certain makeup products will look. Free samples are one of the most popular means to gain consumer trial. In fact, 71 percent of consumers consider a sample to be the best way to evaluate a new product.[14]

learning review

1. Advertising plays a major role in the _____ stage of the product life cycle, and _____ plays a major role in maturity.

2. How do high-learning and low-learning products differ?

3. What are the five categories of product adopters?

MANAGING THE PRODUCT LIFE CYCLE

An important task for a firm is to manage its products through the successive stages of their life cycles. This section describes the role of the product manager who is usually responsible for this and presents three ways to manage a product through its life cycle: modifying the product, modifying the market, and repositioning the product.

Role of a Product Manager

[handwritten: ≠ same as MARKETING manager]

The product manager, sometimes called *brand manager,* manages the marketing efforts for a close-knit family of products or brands. Introduced by Procter & Gamble in 1928, the product manager style of marketing organization is used by consumer goods firms, including General Mills and PepsiCo, and by industrial firms such as Intel and Hewlett-Packard. The U.S. Postal Service employs product managers as well.

All product managers are responsible for managing existing products through the stages of the life cycle. Some are also responsible for developing new products. Product managers' marketing responsibilities include developing and executing a marketing program for the product line described in an annual marketing plan and approving ad copy, media selection, and package design.

Product managers also engage in extensive data analysis related to their products and brands. Sales, market share, and profit trends are closely monitored. Managers often supplement these data with two measures: (1) a category development index (CDI) and (2) a brand development index (BDI). These indexes help to identify strong and weak market segments (usually demographic or geographic segments) for specific consumer products and brands and provide direction for marketing efforts. The calculation, visual display, and interpretation of these two indexes for Hawaiian Punch are described in the Using Marketing Dashboards box.

Harley-Davidson redesigned some of its motorcycle models to feature smaller hand grips, a lower seat, and an easier-to-pull clutch lever to create a more comfortable ride for women. According to Genevieve Schmitt, founding editor of WomenRidersNow.com, "They realize they are an up-and-coming segment and that they need to accommodate them."

Harley-Davidson, Inc.
www.harley-davidson.com

Modifying the Product

Product modification involves altering a product's characteristic, such as its quality, performance, or appearance, to increase the product's value to customers and increase sales. Wrinkle-free and stain-resistant clothing made possible by nanotechnology has revolutionized the men's and women's apparel business and stimulated industry sales of casual pants, shirts, and blouses. Nokia's global leadership position among cell phone handset manufacturers is due to continuous product modification. For example, Nokia offers a cell phone handset that plays music, shoots high-quality video, surfs the Internet, and holds a 2.4-inch screen for watching TV and playing videogames. Nokia's effort is called *product bundling*—the sale of two or more separate products in one package. In this case, the Nokia handset integrates six separate products: telephone, video camera, computer, video game player, television, and MP-3 player in one handset package.[15]

New features, packages, or scents can be used to change a product's characteristics and give the sense of a revised product. Procter & Gamble revamped Pantene shampoo and conditioner with a new vitamin formula and relaunched the brand with a multimillion-dollar advertising and promotion campaign. The result? Pantene, a brand first introduced in the 1940s, is now the top-selling shampoo and conditioner in the United States in an industry with more than 1,000 competitors.

Nokia Corporation
www.nokia.com

Modifying the Market

With **market modification** strategies, a company tries to find new customers, increase a product's use among existing customers, or create new use situations.

Using Marketing Dashboards
Knowing Your CDI and BDI

Where are sales for my product category and brand strongest and weakest? Data related to this question are often displayed in a marketing dashboard using two indexes: (1) category development index and (2) brand development index.

Your Challenge You have joined the marketing team for Hawaiian Punch, the number 1 fruit punch drink sold in the U.S. The brand has been marketed to mothers with children under 12 years old. The majority of Hawaiian Punch sales are in gallon and 2-liter bottles. Your assignment is to examine the brand's performance and identify growth opportunities for the Hawaiian Punch brand among households that consume prepared fruit drinks (the product category).

Your marketing dashboard displays a category development index and a brand development index provided by a syndicated marketing research firm. Each index is based on the calculations below:

Category Development Index (CDI) =
$$\frac{\text{Percent of a Product Category's Total U.S. Sales in a Market Segment}}{\text{Percent of the Total U.S. Population in a Market Segment}} \times 100$$

Brand Development Index (BDI) =
$$\frac{\text{Percent of a Brand's Total U.S. Sales in a Market Segment}}{\text{Percent of the Total U.S. Population in a Market Segment}} \times 100$$

A CDI over 100 indicates above-average product category purchases by a market segment. A number under 100 indicates below-average purchases. A BDI over 100 indicates a strong brand position in a segment; a number under 100 indicates a weak brand position.

You are interested in CDI and BDI displays for four household segments that consume prepared fruit drinks: (1) households without children; (2) households with children under 6; (3) households with children aged 7 to 12; and (4) households with children aged 13 to 18.

Your Findings The BDI and CDI measures displayed below show that Hawaiian Punch is consumed by households with children, and particularly households with children under age 12. The Hawaiian Punch BDI is over 100 for both segments—not surprising since the brand is marketed to these segments. Households with children 13 to 18 years old evidence high fruit drink consumption with a CDI over 100. But Hawaiian Punch is relatively weak in this segment with a BDI under 100.

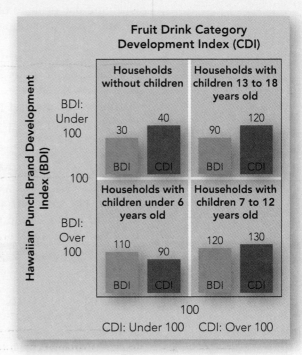

Your Action An opportunity for Hawaiian Punch exists among households with children 13 to 18 years old—teenagers. You might propose that Hawaiian Punch be repositioned for teens. In addition, you might recommend that Hawaiian Punch be packaged in single-serve cans or bottles to attract this segment, much like soft drinks. Teens might also be targeted for advertising and promotions.

Finding New Customers Produce companies have begun marketing and packaging prunes as dried plums to attract younger buyers. Harley-Davidson has tailored a marketing program to encourage women to take up cycling, thus doubling the number of potential customers for its motorcycles.[16]

Increasing a Product's Use Promoting more frequent usage has been a strategy of Campbell Soup Company. Because soup consumption rises in the winter and declines during the summer, the company now advertises more heavily in warm months to encourage consumers to think of soup as more than a cold-weather food. Similarly, the Florida Orange Growers Association advocates drinking orange juice throughout the day rather than for breakfast only.

Creating a New Use Situation

Finding new uses for an existing product has been the strategy behind Dockers, the U.S. market leader in casual pants. Originally intended as a single pant for every situation, Dockers now promotes different looks for different usage situations: work, weekend, dress, and golf.[17] The Milk Processor Education Program suggests new use situations by substituting milk for water or other ingredients when preparing food.

Repositioning the Product

Often a company decides to reposition its product or product line in an attempt to bolster sales. _Product repositioning_ changes the place a product occupies in a consumer's mind relative to competitive products. A firm can reposition a product by changing one or more of the four marketing mix elements. Four factors that trigger the need for a repositioning action are discussed next.

Reacting to a Competitor's Position

One reason to reposition a product is because a competitor's entrenched position is adversely affecting sales and market share. New Balance, Inc., successfully repositioned its athletic shoes to focus on fit, durability, and comfort rather than competing head-on against Nike and Reebok on fashion and professional sports. The company offers an expansive range of shoes and it networks with podiatrists, not sport celebrities.[18]

Reaching a New Market

When Unilever introduced iced tea in Britain in the mid-1990s, sales were disappointing. British consumers viewed it as leftover hot tea, not suitable for drinking. The company made its tea carbonated and repositioned it as a cold soft drink to compete as a carbonated beverage and sales improved. Johnson & Johnson effectively repositioned St. Joseph Aspirin from one for infants to an adult low-strength aspirin to reduce the risk of heart problems or strokes.[19]

Catching a Rising Trend

Changing consumer trends also lead to repositioning. Growing consumer interest in foods that offer health and dietary benefits is an example. Many products have been repositioned to capitalize on this trend. Quaker Oats makes the FDA-approved claim that oatmeal, as part of a low-saturated-fat, low-cholesterol diet, may reduce the risk of heart disease. Calcium-enriched

The Milk Processor Education Program (MilkPEP) promotes the use of milk rather than water or other ingredients in preparing food. According to a MilkPEP executive, "If every household one day a week added milk rather than water to instant coffee and made a caffe latte, it would add [up to] $100 million to the bottom line of the milk industry."

The Milk Processor Education Program
www.whymilk.com

Consumer Economics of Downsizing—Get Less, Pay More

For more than 30 years, Starkist put 6.5 ounces of tuna into its regular-sized can. Today, Starkist puts 6.125 ounces of tuna into its can, but charges the same price. Frito-Lay (Doritos and Lay's snack chips), Procter & Gamble (Pampers and Luvs disposable diapers), Nestlé (Poland Spring and Calistoga bottled waters) have whittled away at package contents 5 to 10 percent while maintaining their products' package size, dimensions, and prices. Kimberly-Clark cut its retail price on its jumbo pack of Huggies diapers from $13.50 to $12.50, but reduced the number of diapers per pack from 48 to 42. Georgia-Pacific reduced the content of its Brawny paper towel six-roll pack by 20 percent without lowering the price.

Consumer advocates charge that downsizing the content of packages while maintaining prices is a subtle and unannounced way of taking advantage of consumer buying habits. They also say downsizing is a price increase in disguise and deceptive, but legal. Manufacturers argue that this prac-

tice is a way of keeping prices from rising beyond psychological barriers for their products.

Is downsizing an unethical practice if manufacturers do not inform consumers that the package contents are less than they were previously?

---

products, such as Kraft American cheese and Uncle Ben's Calcium Plus rice, emphasize healthy bone structure for children and adults. Weight-conscious consumers have embraced low-fat and low-calorie diets in growing numbers. Today, most food and beverage companies offer reduced-fat and low-calorie versions of their products.

Changing the Value Offered In repositioning a product, a company can decide to change the value it offers buyers and trade up or down. **Trading up** involves adding value to the product (or line) through additional features or higher-quality materials. Michelin and Goodyear have done this with a "run-flat" tire that can travel up to 50 miles at 55 miles per hour after suffering total air loss. Dog food manufacturers, such as Ralston Purina, also have traded up by offering superpremium foods based on "life-stage nutrition." Mass merchandisers, such as Target and JCPenney, can trade up by adding a designer clothes section to their stores.

Trading down involves reducing the number of features, quality, or price. For example, some airlines have added more seats, thus reducing legroom, and limited snack service. Trading down exists when companies engage in *downsizing*—reducing the package content without changing package size and maintaining or increasing the package price. Firms are criticized for this practice, as described in the accompanying Making Responsible Decisions box.[20]

---

learning review

4. How does a product manager help manage a product's life cycle?

5. What does "creating a new use situation" mean in managing a product's life cycle?

6. Explain the difference between trading up and trading down in repositioning.

BRANDING AND BRAND MANAGEMENT

LO3

A basic decision in marketing products is **branding**, in which an organization uses a name, phrase, design, symbols, or combination of these to identify its products and distinguish them from those of competitors. A **brand name** is any word, device (design, sound, shape, or color), or combination of these used to distinguish a seller's goods or services. Some brand names can be spoken, such as a Gatorade or Rollerblade. Other brand names cannot be spoken, such as the rainbow-colored apple (the *logotype* or *logo*) that Apple originally put on its machines and in its ads. A **trade name** is a commercial, legal name under which a company does business. The Coca-Cola Company is the trade name of that firm.

A **trademark** identifies that a firm has legally registered its brand name or trade name so the firm has its exclusive use, thereby preventing others from using it. In the United States, trademarks are registered with the U.S. Patent and Trademark Office and protected under the Lanham Act. A well-known trademark can help a company advertise its offerings to customers and develop their brand loyalty.

Because a good trademark can help sell a product, *product counterfeiting,* which involves low-cost copies of popular brands not manufactured by the original producer, is a serious problem. Counterfeit products can steal sales from the original manufacturer or harm the company's reputation. U.S. companies lose between $200 billion and $250 billion each year to counterfeit products. To counteract counterfeiting, the U.S. government passed the *Stop Counterfeiting in Manufactured Goods Act* (2006), which makes counterfeiters subject to 20-year prison sentences and $15 million in fines.

Consumers may benefit most from branding. Recognizing competing products by distinct trademarks allows them to be more efficient shoppers. Consumers can recognize and avoid products with which they are dissatisfied, while becoming loyal to other, more satisfying brands. As discussed in Chapter 5, brand loyalty often eases consumers' decision making by eliminating the need for an external search.

Can you describe the brand personality traits for these two brands?

got2b
www.got2b.com

Mambo
www.lizclaiborne.com/mambo

Brand Personality and Brand Equity

Product managers recognize that brands offer more than product identification and a means to distinguish their products from competitors.[21] Successful and established brands take on a **brand personality**, a set of human characteristics associated with a brand name. Research shows that consumers often assign personality traits to products—traditional, romantic, rugged, sophisticated, rebellious—and choose brands that are consistent with their own or desired self-image. Marketers can and do imbue a brand with a personality through advertising that depicts a certain user or usage situation and conveys certain emotions or feelings to be associated with the brand. For example, the personality traits associated with Coca-Cola are all-American and real; with Pepsi, young and exciting; and with Dr Pepper, nonconforming and unique. The traits linked to Harley-Davidson are masculinity, defiance, and rugged individualism.

Brand name importance to a company has led to a concept called **brand equity**, the added value a brand name gives to a product beyond the functional benefits provided. This value has two distinct advantages. First, brand equity provides a competitive advantage. The Sunkist brand implies quality fruit, and the Disney name defines children's entertainment. A second advantage is that consumers are often willing to pay a higher price for a product with brand equity. Brand equity, in this instance, is represented by the premium a consumer will pay for one brand over another when the functional benefits provided are identical. Gillette razors and blades, Bose audio systems, Duracell batteries, Microsoft computer software, and Louis Vuitton luggage all enjoy a price premium arising from brand equity.

Creating Brand Equity   Brand equity doesn't just happen. It is carefully crafted and nurtured by marketing programs that forge strong, favorable, and unique customer associations and experiences with a brand. Brand equity resides in the minds of consumers and results from what they have learned, felt, seen, and heard about a brand over time. Marketers recognize that brand equity is not easily or quickly achieved. Rather, it arises from a sequential building process consisting of four steps (Figure 11–6 on the next page).[22]

- The first step is to develop positive brand awareness and an association of the brand in consumers' minds with a product class or need to give the brand an identity. Gatorade and Kleenex have achieved this in the sports drink and facial tissue product classes, respectively.
- Next, a marketer must establish a brand's meaning in the minds of consumers. Meaning arises from what a brand stands for and has two dimensions—a functional, performance-related dimension and an abstract, imagery-related dimension. Nike has done this through continuous product development and improvement and its links to peak athletic performance in its integrated marketing communications program.
- The third step is to elicit the proper consumer responses to a brand's identity and meaning. Here attention is placed on how consumers think and feel about a brand. Thinking focuses on a brand's perceived quality, credibility, and superiority relative to other brands. Feeling relates to the consumer's emotional reaction to a brand. Michelin elicits both responses for its tires. Not only is Michelin thought of as a credible and superior-quality brand, but consumers also acknowledge a warm and secure feeling of safety, comfort, and self-assurance without worry or concern about the brand.
- The final, and most difficult, step is to create a consumer-brand connection evident in an intense, active loyalty relationship between consumers and the brand. A deep psychological bond characterizes a consumer-brand connection and the personal identification customers have with the brand. Brands that have achieved this status include Harley-Davidson, Apple, and eBay.

FIGURE 11–6

The customer-based brand equity pyramid shows the four-step building process that forges strong, favorable, and unique customer associations with a brand.

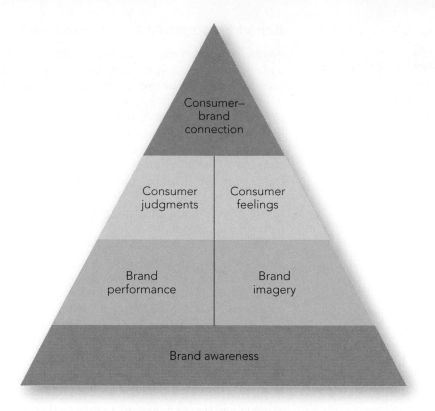

Valuing Brand Equity   Brand equity also provides a financial advantage for the brand owner.[23] Successful, established brand names, such as Gillette, Nike, Gatorade, and Nokia, have an economic value in the sense that they are intangible assets. The recognition that brands are assets is apparent in the decision to buy and sell brands. For example, Triarc Companies bought the Snapple brand from Quaker Oats in 1997 for $300 million and sold it to Cadbury Schweppes in 2000 for $900 million. This example illustrates that brands, unlike physical assets that depreciate with time and use, can appreciate in value when effectively marketed. However, brands can lose value when they are not managed properly. Consider the purchase and sale of Lender's Bagels. Kellogg bought the brand for $466 million only to sell it to Aurora Foods for $275 million three years later following deteriorating sales and profits.

Financially lucrative brand licensing opportunities arise from brand equity. **Brand licensing** is a contractual agreement whereby one company (licensor) allows its brand name(s) or trademark(s) to be used with products or services offered by another company (licensee) for a royalty or fee. For example, Playboy earns more than $260 million licensing its name and logo for merchandise. Disney makes billions of dollars each year licensing its characters for children's toys, apparel, and games. Licensing fees for Winnie the Pooh alone exceed $3 billion annually. General Motors sells more than $2 billion in licensed products each year.[24]

Successful brand licensing requires careful marketing analysis to assure a proper match between the licensor's brand and the licensee's products. World-renowned designer Ralph Lauren earns over $140 million each year by licensing his Ralph Lauren, Polo, and Chaps brands for dozens of products, including paint by Glidden, furniture by Henredon, footwear by Rockport, and fragrances by L'Oreal. Mistakes, such as Kleenex diapers, Bic perfume, and Domino's fruit-flavored bubble gum, represent a few examples of poor matches and licensing failures.

Picking a Good Brand Name

We take brand names such as Red Bull, iPod, and Adidas for granted, but it is often a difficult and expensive process to pick a good name. Companies will spend

General Motors is the worldwide leader in licensed product sales among automakers. A licensing arrangement is for HUMMER® Footwear made by Roper Footwear & Apparel.

General Motors
www.HUMMER.com

IT IS RECOMMENDED THAT YOU CHANGE YOUR SOCKS EVERY 3,000 MILES.

Introducing the only full line of footwear tough enough to be called HUMMER. Now you can sell your customers comfort, style, and performance that's like nothing else.

HUMMER FOOTWEAR • LIKE NOTHING ELSE.

between $25,000 and $100,000 to identify and test a new brand name. Five criteria are mentioned most often when selecting a good brand name.[25]

- *The name should suggest the product benefits.* For example, Accutron (watches), Easy Off (oven cleaner), Glass Plus (glass cleaner), Cling-Free (antistatic cloth for drying clothes), PowerBook (laptop computer), and Tidy Bowl (toilet bowl cleaner) all clearly describe the benefits of purchasing the product.
- *The name should be memorable, distinctive, and positive.* In the auto industry, when a competitor has a memorable name, others quickly imitate. When Ford named a car the Mustang, Pintos, Colts, and Broncos soon followed. The Thunderbird name led to the Phoenix, Eagle, Sunbird, and Firebird.
- *The name should fit the company or product image.* Sharp is a name that can apply to audio and video equipment. Bufferin, Excedrin, Anacin, and Nuprin are scientific-sounding names, good for analgesics. Eveready, Duracell, and DieHard suggest reliability and longevity—two qualities consumers want in a battery.
- *The name should have no legal or regulatory restrictions.* Legal restrictions produce trademark infringement suits, and regulatory restrictions arise through improper use of words. For example, the U.S. Food and Drug Administration discourages the use of the word *heart* in food brand names. This restriction led to changing the name of Kellogg's Heartwise cereal to Fiberwise, and Clorox's Hidden Valley Ranch Take Heart Salad Dressing had to be modified to Hidden Valley Ranch Low-Fat Salad Dressing. Increasingly, brand names need a corresponding address on the Internet. This further complicates name selection because about 140 million domain names are already registered.
- *Finally, the name should be simple* (such as Bold laundry detergent, Axe deodorant and body spray, and Bic pens) *and should be emotional* (such as Joy and Obsession perfumes). In the development of names for international use, having a nonmeaningful brand name has been considered a benefit. A name such as Exxon does not have any prior impressions or undesirable images among a diverse world population of different languages and cultures. The 7Up name is another matter. In Shanghai, China, the phrase means "death through drinking" in the local dialect. Sales have suffered as a result.

Do you have an idea for a brand name? If you do, check to see if the name has been already registered with the U.S. Patent and Trademark Office by visiting its website described in the accompanying Going Online box.

Branding Strategies

Companies can employ several different branding strategies, including multiproduct branding, multibranding, private branding, or mixed branding (Figure 11–7).

Multiproduct Branding Strategy With **multiproduct branding**, a company uses one name for all its products in a product class. This approach is sometimes called *family branding,* or *corporate branding* when the company's trade name is used. For example, General Electric, Samsung, Gerber, and Sony engage in corporate branding—the company's trade name and brand name are identical. Church & Dwight uses the Arm & Hammer family brand name for all its products featuring baking soda as the primary ingredient.

There are several advantages to multiproduct branding. Capitalizing again on brand equity, consumers who have a good experience with the product will transfer this favorable attitude to other items in the product class with the same name. Therefore, this brand strategy makes possible *line extensions,* the practice of using a current brand name to enter a new market segment in its product class. Campbell Soup Company employs a multiproduct branding strategy with soup line extensions. It offers regular Campbell soup, home-cooking style, and chunky varieties and more than 100 soup flavors. This strategy can result in lower advertising and promotion costs because the same name is used on all products, thus raising the level of brand

FIGURE 11–7
Alternative branding strategies are available to marketers. Each has advantages and disadvantages described in the text.

Branding strategy			
Multiproduct branding strategy	**Multibranding strategy**	**Private branding strategy**	**Mixed branding strategy**
Toro makes: Toro snowblowers Toro lawn mowers Toro garden hoses Toro sprinkler systems	Procter & Gamble makes: Tide Cheer Ivory Snow Bold	Sears has: Kenmore appliances Craftsman tools DieHard batteries	Michelin makes: Michelin tires Sears tires Epson makes: Epson printers IBM printers

Kimberly-Clark was able to leverage the strong Huggies brand equity among mothers when it introduced a full line of baby and toddler toiletries first in the United States and then globally. The success of this brand extension strategy is evident in the $500 million in annual sales generated globally.

Kimberly-Clark Corporation
www.kimberly-clark.com

awareness. A risk with line extension is that sales of an extension may come at the expense of other items in the company's product line. Line extensions work best when they provide incremental company revenue by taking sales away from competing brands or attracting new buyers.[26]

Some multiproduct branding companies employ *subbranding,* which combines a corporate or family brand with a new brand, to distinguish a part of its product line from others. Gatorade successfully used subbranding with the introduction of Gatorade Frost, Gatorade Rain, and Gatorade A.M. as examples. Similarly, Porsche successfully markets its higher-end Porsche Carrera and its lower-end Porsche Boxster.

A strong brand equity also allows for *brand extension,* the practice of using a current brand name to enter a completely different product class. For instance, equity in the Huggies family brand name has allowed Kimberly-Clark to successfully extend its name to a full line of baby and toddler toiletries. Honda's established name for motor vehicles has extended easily to snowblowers, lawn mowers, marine engines, and snowmobiles.

However, there is a risk with brand extensions. Too many uses for one brand name can dilute the meaning of a brand for consumers. Marketing experts claim this has happened to the Arm & Hammer brand given its use for toothpaste, laundry detergent, gum, cat litter, air freshener, carpet deodorizer, and antiperspirant.[27]

A variation on brand extensions is the practice of *co-branding;* the pairing of two brand names of two manufacturers on a single product.[28] For example, Hershey Foods has teamed with General Mills to offer a co-branded breakfast cereal called Reese's Peanut Butter Puffs and with Nabisco to provide Chips Ahoy! cookies using Hershey's chocolate morsels. Co-branding benefits firms by allowing them to enter new product classes and capitalize on an already established brand name in that product class.

Multibranding Strategy Alternately, a company can engage in **multibranding**, which involves giving each product a distinct name. Multibranding is a useful strategy when each brand is intended for a different market segment. P&G makes Camay soap for those concerned with soft skin and Safeguard for those who want deodorant protection. Black & Decker markets its line of tools for the household do-it-yourselfer segment with the Black & Decker name but uses the DeWalt name for its professional tool line. Disney uses the Miramax and Touchstone Pictures names for films directed at adults and its Disney name for children's films.

Multibranding is applied in a variety of ways. Some companies array their brands on the basis of price-quality segments.[29] Marriott International offers 14 hotel and resort brands, each suited for a particular traveler experience and budget. To illustrate, Marriott Marquis hotels and Vacation Clubs offer luxury amenities at a premium price. Marriott and Renaissance hotels offer medium- to high-priced accommodations. Courtyard hotels and Town Place Suites appeal to economy-minded travelers, whereas the Fairfield Inn is for those on a very low travel budget.

Other multibrand companies introduce new product brands as defensive moves to counteract competition. Called *fighting brands,* their chief purpose is to confront competitor brands. For instance, Frito-Lay introduced Santitas brand tortilla chip to go head-to-head against regional tortilla chip brands that were biting into sales of its flagship Doritos and Tostitos brand tortilla chips. Mattel launched its Flava brand of hip-hop fashion dolls in response to the popularity of Bratz brand dolls sold by MGA Entertainment, which were attracting the 8-to-12-year-old girl segment of Barbie brand sales.

Black & Decker uses a multibranding strategy to reach different market segments. Black & Decker markets its line of tools for the do-it-yourselfer market with the Black & Decker name but uses the DeWalt name for its professional tool line.

Black & Decker
www.blackanddecker.com

Compared with the multiproduct strategy, advertising and promotion costs tend to be higher with multibranding. The company must generate awareness among consumers and retailers for each new brand name without the benefit of any previous impressions. The advantages of this strategy are that each brand is unique to each market segment and there is no risk that a product failure will affect other products in the line. Still, some large multibrand firms have found that the complexity and expense of implementing this strategy can outweigh the benefits. For example, Unilever recently pruned its brands from some 1,600 to 400 through product deletion and sales to other companies.[30]

Private Branding Strategy   A company uses **private branding**, often called *private labeling* or *reseller branding,* when it manufactures products but sells them under the brand name of a wholesaler or retailer. Rayovac, Paragon Trade Brands, and Ralcorp Holdings are major suppliers of private label alkaline batteries, diapers, and grocery products, respectively. Radio Shack, Costco, Sears, Wal-Mart, and Kroger are large retailers that have their own brand names. Private branding is popular because it typically produces high profits for manufacturers and resellers. Consumers also buy them. It is estimated that one of every five items purchased at U.S. supermarkets, drugstores, and mass merchandisers bears a private brand.[31]

Mixed Branding Strategy   A fourth branding strategy is **mixed branding**, where a firm markets products under its own name(s) and that of a reseller because the segment attracted to the reseller is different from its own market. Beauty and fragrance marketer Elizabeth Arden is an example. The company sells its Elizabeth Arden brand through department stores and a line of skin care products at Wal-Mart with the "skinsimple" brand name. Companies such as Del Monte, Whirlpool, and Dial produce private brands of pet foods, home appliances, and soap, respectively, for resellers.

Marketing Matters > > > > > customer value

Creating Customer Value through Packaging—Pez Heads Dispense More Than Candy

Customer value can assume numerous forms. For Pez Candy, Inc. (www.pez.com), customer value manifests itself in some 450 Pez character candy dispensers. Each refillable dispenser ejects tasty candy tablets in a variety of flavors that delight preteens and teens alike in more than 60 countries.

Pez was formulated in 1927 by Austrian food mogul Edward Haas III and successfully sold in Europe as an adult breath mint. Pez, which comes from the German word for peppermint, *pfefferminz*, was originally packaged in a hygienic, headless plastic dispenser. Pez first appeared in the United States in 1953 with a headless dispenser, marketed to adults. After conducting extensive marketing research, Pez was repositioned with fruit flavors, repackaged with licensed character heads on top of the dispenser, and remarketed as a children's product in the mid-1950s. Since then, most top-level licensed characters and hundreds of other characters have become Pez heads. Consumers eat more than 3 billion Pez tablets annually in the United States alone, and company sales growth exceeds that of the candy industry as a whole.

The unique Pez package dispenses a "use experience" for its customers beyond the candy itself, namely, fun. And

fun translates into a 98 percent awareness level for Pez among teenagers and 89 percent among mothers with children. Pez has not advertised its product for years. With that kind of awareness, who needs advertising?

PACKAGING AND LABELING PRODUCTS

LO4

The **packaging** component of a product refers to any container in which it is offered for sale and on which label information is conveyed. A **label** is an integral part of the package and typically identifies the product or brand, who made it, where and when it was made, how it is to be used, and package contents and ingredients. To a great extent, the customer's first exposure to a product is the package and label and both are an expensive and important part of marketing strategy. For Pez Candy, Inc., the character head-on-a-stick plastic container that dispenses a miniature tablet candy is the central element of its marketing strategy as described in the accompanying Marketing Matters box.[32]

Creating Customer Value and Competitive Advantage through Packaging and Labeling

Packaging and labeling cost U.S. companies more than $120 billion annually and account for about 15 cents of every dollar spent by consumers for products.[33] Despite the cost, packaging and labeling are essential because both provide important benefits for the manufacturer, retailer, and ultimate consumer. Packaging and labeling also can provide a competitive advantage.

Communication Benefits A major benefit of packaging is the label information on it conveyed to the consumer, such as directions on how, where, and when to use the product and the source and composition of the product, which is needed to satisfy legal requirements of product disclosure. For example, the labeling system for packaged and processed foods in the United States provide a uniform format for nutritional and dietary information. Many packaged foods contain informative recipes

Quick. Name a soft drink.

Can you name this soft-drink brand? If you can, then the package has fulfilled its purpose.

to promote usage of the product. Campbell Soup estimates that the green bean casserole recipe on its cream of mushroom soup can accounts for $20 million in soup sales each year![34] Other information consists of seals and symbols, either government required or commercial seals of approval (such as the Good Housekeeping seal).

Functional Benefits Packaging often plays a functional role, such as storage, convenience, protection, or product quality. Storing food containers is one example, and beverage companies have developed lighter and easier ways to stack products on shelves and in refrigerators. Examples include Coca-Cola beverage packs designed to fit neatly onto refrigerator shelves and Ocean Spray Cranberries' rectangular juice bottles that allow 10 units per package versus 8 of its former round bottles.

The convenience dimension of packaging is increasingly important. Kraft Miracle Whip salad dressing, Heinz ketchup, and Skippy Squeez'It peanut butter are sold in squeeze bottles; microwave popcorn has been a major market success; and Chicken of the Sea tuna and Folgers coffee are packaged in single-serving portions. Nabisco offers portion-control package sizes for the convenience of weight-conscious consumers. It offers 100-calorie packs of Oreos, Cheese Nips, and other products in individual pouches.

Consumer protection is another important function of packaging, including the development of tamper-resistant containers. Today, companies commonly use safety seals or pop-tops that reveal previous opening. But, no package is truly tamper resistant. U.S. law now provides for maximum penalties of life imprisonment and $250,000 fines for package tampering. Consumer protection through labeling exists in "open dating," which states the expected shelf life of the product.

Functional features of packaging also can affect product quality. Procter & Gamble's Pringles, with its cylindrical packaging, offers uniform chips, minimal breakage, and for some consumers, better value for the money than flex-bag packages for chips. Not to be outdone, Frito-Lay, the world's leading producer of snack chips, decided to "stand up" to Pringles with its own line of Lay's Stax potato crisps. Consumers will be the final judge of which chip stacks up better.

Which chip stacks up better? Frito-Lay's launch of Lay's Stax potato crisps to compete against Procter & Gamble's Pringles illustrates the role of packaging in product and brand management.

Perceptual Benefits A third component of packaging and labeling is the perception created in the consumer's mind. Package and label shape, color, and graphics distinguish one brand from another, convey a brand's positioning, and build brand equity. According to the director of marketing for L'eggs hosiery, "Packaging is important to the positioning and equity of the L'eggs brand."[35] Why? Packaging and labeling have been shown to enhance brand recognition and facilitate the formation of strong, favorable, and unique brand associations.[36] This logic applies to Celestial Seasonings' packaging and labeling, which uses delicate illustrations, soft and warm colors, and quotations about life to reinforce the brand's positioning as a New Age, natural herbal tea.

Successful marketers recognize that changes in packages and labels can update and uphold a brand's image in the customer's mind. Just Born, Inc., a candy manufacturer of

The distinctive design of Celestial Seasonings' tea boxes reinforces the brand's positioning as a New Age, natural herbal tea.

such brands as Jelly Joes and Mike and Ike Treats is a case in point. For many years these brands were sold in old-fashioned black-and-white packages. However, when the packaging was updated to four color, with animated grape and cherry characters, sales jumped 25 percent. Pepsi-Cola has embarked on a packaging change to uphold its image among teens and young adults. Beginning in 2007, Pepsi-Cola debuted new graphics on its cans and bottles every three or four weeks to reflect the "fun, optimistic, and youthful spirit" of the brand to its customers.[37]

Because labels list a product's source, brands competing in the global marketplace can benefit from "country of origin or manufacture" perceptions as described in Chapter 7. Consumers tend to have stereotypes about country-product pairings that they judge "best"—English tea, French perfume, Italian leather, and Japanese electronics—which can affect a brand's image. Increasingly, Chinese firms are adopting the English language and Roman letters for their brand labels. This is being done because of a common perception in many Asian countries that "things Western are good."[38]

Contemporary Packaging and Labeling Challenges

Package and label designers face four challenges. They are: (1) the continuing need to connect with customers; (2) environmental concerns; (3) health, safety, and security issues; and (4) cost reduction.

Connecting with Customers Packages and labels must be continually updated to connect with customers. The challenge lies in creating aesthetic and functional design features that attract customer attention and deliver customer value in their use. If done right, the rewards can be huge.[39]

For example, the marketing team responsible for Kleenex tissues converted its standard rectangular box into an oval shape with colorful seasonal graphics. Sales soared with this aesthetic change in packaging. After months of in-home research, Kraft product managers discovered that consumers often transferred Chips Ahoy! cookies to jars for easy access and to avoid staleness. The company solved both problems by creating a patented resealable opening on the top of the bag. The result? Sales of the new package doubled that of the old package with the addition of this functional feature.

Environmental Concerns Because of widespread worldwide concern about the growth of solid waste and the shortage of viable landfill sites, the amount, composition, and disposal of packaging material continues to receive much attention. Recycling packaging material is a major thrust.[40] Procter & Gamble now uses recycled cardboard in over 70 percent of its paper packaging and is packaging Tide, Cheer, Era, and Dash detergents in jugs that contain 25 percent recycled plastic. Spic and Span liquid cleaner is packaged in 100 percent recycled material. Other firms, such as Wal-Mart, are emphasizing the use of less packaging material. In 2008, the company began working with its 600,000 global suppliers to reduce overall packaging and shipping material by 5 percent by 2013.

European countries have been trendsetters concerning packaging guidelines and environmental sensitivity. Many of these guidelines now exist in provisions governing trade to and within the European Union. In Germany, 80 percent of packaging material must be collected, and 80 percent of this amount must be recycled or reused to reduce solid waste in landfills. U.S. firms marketing in Europe have responded to these guidelines and ultimately benefited U.S. consumers.

Health, Safety, and Security Issues A third challenge involves the growing health, safety, and security concerns of packaging materials. Today, most U.S. and European consumers believe companies should make sure products and their packages are safe and secure, regardless of the cost, and companies are responding in numerous ways. Most butane lighters sold today, like those made by Scripto, contain a child-resistant safety latch to prevent misuse and accidental fire. Child-proof caps on pharmaceutical products and household cleaners and sealed lids on food packages are now common. New packaging technology and materials that extend a product's *shelf life* (the time a product can be stored) and prevent spoilage continue to be developed with special applications for developing countries.

Cost Reduction About 80 percent of packaging material used in the world consists of paper, plastics, and glass. As the cost of these materials rise, companies are constantly challenged to find innovative ways to cut packaging costs while delivering value to their customers. As an example, Hewlett-Packard reduced the size and weight of its Photosmart product package and shipping container. Through design and material changes, packaging material costs fell by more than 50 percent. Shipping costs per unit dropped 41 percent.[41]

PRODUCT WARRANTY

A final component for product consideration is the **warranty**, which is a statement indicating the liability of the manufacturer for product deficiencies. There are various types of product warranties with different implications for manufacturers and customers.

General Motors proudly advertises its 100,000-mile, five-year powertrain limited warranty for its automobiles.

General Motors Corporation
www.gm.com

Some companies offer *express warranties,* which are written statements of liabilities. In recent years, the FTC has required greater disclosure on express warranties to indicate whether the warranty is a limited-coverage or full-coverage alternative. A *limited-coverage warranty* specifically states the bounds of coverage and, more important, areas of noncoverage. A *full warranty* has no limits of noncoverage. The *Magnuson-Moss Warranty/FTC Improvement Act* (1975) regulates the content of consumer warranties and so has strengthened consumer rights with regard to warranties. Increasingly, manufacturers are being held to *implied warranties,* which assign responsibility for product deficiencies to the manufacturer. Studies show that the type of warranty can affect a consumer's product evaluation. Brands with limited warranties tend to receive less positive evaluations compared with full-warranty items.[42]

Warranties are also important in light of product liability claims. In the early part of the twentieth century, the courts protected companies. The trend now is toward "strict liability" rulings, where a manufacturer is liable for any product defect, whether it followed reasonable research standards or not. This issue remains hotly contested between companies and consumer advocates.

Warranties represent much more to the buyer than just protection from negative consequences—they offer a significant marketing advantage for the producer. Sears has built a strong reputation for its Craftsman tool line with a simple warranty: If you break a tool, it's replaced with no questions asked. Zippo has an equally simple warranty: "If it ever fails, we'll fix it free."

learning review

7. What are the five criteria mentioned most often when selecting a good brand name?

8. What are the three major benefits of packaging and labeling?

9. What is the difference between an expressed and an implied warranty?

LEARNING OBJECTIVES REVIEW

LO1 *Explain the product life-cycle concept.*

The product life cycle describes the stages a new product goes through in the marketplace: introduction, growth, maturity, and decline. Product sales growth and profitability differ at each stage, and marketing managers have marketing objectives and marketing mix strategies unique to each stage based on consumer behavior and competitive factors. In the introductory stage, the need is to establish primary demand, whereas the growth stage requires selective demand strategies. In the maturity stage, the need is to maintain market share; the decline stage necessitates a deletion or harvesting strategy. Some important aspects of product life cycles are (*a*) their length, (*b*) the shape of the sales curve, (*c*) how they vary by product classes and forms, and (*d*) the rate at which consumers adopt products.

LO2 *Identify ways that marketing executives manage a product's life cycle.*

Marketing executives manage a product's life cycle three ways. First, they can modify the product itself by altering its characteristics, such as product quality, performance, or appearance. Second, they can modify the market by finding new customers for the product, increasing a product's use among existing customers, or creating new use situations for the product. Finally, they can reposition the product using any one or a combination of marketing mix elements. Four factors trigger a repositioning action. They include reacting to a competitor's position, reaching a new market, catching a rising trend, and changing the value offered to consumers.

LO3 *Recognize the importance of branding and alternative branding strategies.*

A basic decision in marketing products is branding, in which an organization uses a name, phrase, design, symbols, or a combination of these to identify its products and distinguish them from those of its competitors. Product managers recognize that brands offer more than product identification and a means to distinguish their products from competitors. Successful and established brands take on a brand personality and acquire brand equity—the added value a given brand name gives to a product beyond the functional benefits provided—that is crafted and nurtured by marketing programs that forge strong, favorable, and unique consumer associations with a brand. A good brand name should suggest the product benefits, be memorable, fit the company or product image, be free of legal restrictions, and be simple and emotional. Companies can and do employ several different branding strategies. With multiproduct branding, a company uses one name for all its products in a product class. A multibranding strategy involves giving each product a distinct name. A company uses private branding when it manufactures products but sells them under the brand name of a wholesaler or retailer. Finally, a company can employ mixed branding, where it markets products under its own name(s) and that of a reseller.

LO4 *Describe the role of packaging, labeling, and warranties in the marketing of a product.*

Packaging, labeling, and warranties play numerous roles in the marketing of a product. The packaging component of a product refers to any container in which it is offered for sale and on which label information is conveyed. Manufacturers, retailers, and consumers acknowledge that packaging and labeling provide communication, functional, and perceptual benefits. Contemporary packaging and labeling challenges include (*a*) the continuing need to connect with customers, (*b*) environmental concerns, (*c*) health, safety, and security issues, and (*d*) cost reduction. Warranties indicate the liability of the manufacturer for product deficiencies and are an important element of product and brand management.

FOCUSING ON KEY TERMS

brand equity p. 293
brand licensing p. 294
brand name p. 292
brand personality p. 293
branding p. 292
label p. 299
market modification p. 288

mixed branding p. 298
multibranding p. 297
multiproduct branding p. 296
packaging p. 299
private branding p. 298
product class p. 286
product form p. 286

product life cycle p. 280
product modification p. 288
trade name p. 292
trademark p. 292
trading down p. 291
trading up p. 291
warranty p. 302

APPLYING MARKETING KNOWLEDGE

1 Listed here are three different products in various stages of the product life cycle. What marketing strategies would you suggest to these companies? (*a*) Canon digital cameras—growth stage, (*b*) Panasonic high-definition television—introductory stage, and (*c*) handheld manual can openers—decline stage.

2 It has often been suggested that products are intentionally made to break down or wear out. Is this strategy a planned product modification approach?

3 The product manager of GE is reviewing the penetration of trash compactors in American homes. After more than two decades in existence, this product is in relatively few homes. What problems can account for this poor acceptance? What is the shape of the trash compactor life cycle?

4 For years, Ferrari has been known as the manufacturer of expensive luxury automobiles. The company plans to attract the major segment of the car-buying market who purchase medium-priced automobiles. As Ferrari considers this trading-down strategy, what branding strategy would you recommend? What are the trade-offs to consider with your strategy?

5 The nature of product warranties has changed as the federal court system reassesses the meaning of warranties. How does the regulatory trend toward warranties affect product development?

building your marketing plan

For the product offering in your marketing plan,

1 Identify (*a*) its stage in the product life cycle and (*b*) key marketing mix actions that might be appropriate, as shown in Figure 11–1.

2 Develop (*a*) branding and (*b*) packaging strategies, if appropriate for your offering.

video case 11   BMW: "Newness" and the Product Life Cycle

"We're fortunate right now at BMW in that all of our products are new and competitive," says Jim McDowell, vice president of marketing at BMW, as he explains BMW's product life cycle. "Now, how do you do that? You have to introduce new models over time. You have to logically plan out the introductions over time, so you're not changing a whole model range at the same time you're changing another model range."

BMW's strategy is to keep its products in the introduction and growth stages by periodically introducing new models in each of its product lines. In fact, in contrast to many auto manufacturers that launch a new model and then leave it unchanged, BMW works continually to improve its existing products. Explains McDowell, "Anyone can sell a lot of cars the first year, when a car is new. It is our challenge to constantly improve the car and to continuously find new innovative ways to market it."

BMW—THE COMPANY AND ITS PRODUCTS

BMW started in 1916 as a manufacturer of airplane engines. "When you look at our roundel, the BMW symbol, it is a blue-and-white circle," says McDowell, "that is meant to represent the spinning propeller on a plane, to remind us of our heritage." Since then the company has added motorcycle and automobile production. Today, BMW is one of the preeminent luxury car manufacturers in Europe, North America, and the world.

BMW produces several lines of cars including the 1, 3, 5, 6, and 7 series, the Z line of roadsters, the X line of "sport activity vehicles," and the M line of "motor sport" sedans. Currently, the U.S., Germany, and the United Kingdom are BMW's largest markets. BMW recently introduced its 1 series—a compact car designed to compete with the Volkswagen Golf in Europe and the Rabbit in the U.S.—to attract a new younger audience. In addition BMW owns

the MINI and Rolls-Royce brands. Combined sales of BMW, MINI, and Rolls-Royce exceed $59 billion and are expected to increase 40% by 2020. Reasons for the growing popularity of BMW include high-performance products, unique advertising, an award-winning website, innovations such as "smart" electronics that "learn" what the driver prefers, and new vehicles such as the V-series which will compete with popular minivans.

PRODUCT LIFE CYCLE

BMW cars typically have a product life cycle of seven years. To keep products in the introductory and growth stages, BMW regularly introduces new models for each of its series to keep the entire series "new." For instance, with the 3 series, it will introduce the new sedan model one year, the new coupe the next year, then the convertible, then the station wagon, and then the sport hatchback. That's a new product introduction for five of the seven years of the product life cycle. McDowell explains, "So, even though we have seven-year life cycles, we constantly try to make the cars meaningfully different and new about every three years. And that involves adding features and other capabilities to the cars as well." How well does this strategy work? BMW often sees its best sales numbers in either the sixth or seventh year after the product introduction.

As global sales have increased, BMW has become aware of some international product life cycle differences. For example, it has discovered that some competitive products have life cycles that are shorter or longer than seven years. In Sweden and Britain, automotive product life cycles are eight years, while in Japan they are typically only four years long.

BMW uses a system of "product advocates" to manage the marketing efforts of its product lines. McDowell explains that a series advocate would actually use and drive that series and would constantly be thinking "How can I better serve my customer?" In addition to modifying each model throughout the product life cycle, BMW modifies the markets it serves. For example, during the past 10 years BMW has expanded its market by appealing to a much larger percentage of women, African Americans, Asians, and Hispanics. BMW's positioning strategy is the same worldwide and that is to offer high-performance, luxury vehicles to individuals. "You won't find it as a taxi or a fleet car," says McDowell. Generally, once a model is positioned and introduced, BMW avoids trying to reposition it.

BRANDING

"BMW is fortunate—we don't have too much of a dilemma as to what we're going to call our cars." McDowell is referring to BMW's trademark naming system that consists of the product line number and the motor type. For example, the designation "328" tells you the car is in the 3 series and the engine is 2.8 liters in size. BMW has found this naming system to be clear and logical and can be easily understood around the world.

The Z, X, and M series don't quite fit in with this system. BMW had a tradition of building experimental, open-air cars and calling them Z's, so when one of them was selected for production, BMW decided to continue with the Z name. For the sport activity vehicles BMW also used a letter name—the X series—since the four-wheel-drive vehicle didn't fit with the sedan-oriented 1, 3, 5, 6, and 7 series. The M series has a 20-year history with BMW as the line with the luxury and racing-level performance. The lettered series now includes the Z4, X3, X5, M3, M5, and M6. Compared to the evocative

names many car manufacturers choose to garner excitement for their new models, the BMW numbers and letters are viewed as a simple and effective branding strategy.

In the past BMW has built a brand personality for its vehicles with high-visibility product placements. BMW products, for example, have been featured in four James Bond films. Similarly, BMW hired master directors to create a series of Internet-based mini-movies called "The Hire"–which featured "the ultimate driving machine" and edgy actors. The movies were so successful and attracted so much attention from consumers and industry experts that the movies have been placed into the Museum of Modern Art. Other marketing programs that contribute to the BMW brand personality include the BMW Art Car Collection, created by internationally acclaimed artists, sponsorship of America's Cup and Formula 1 Series racing teams, and events such as the BMW Golf Club International tournament.

MANAGING THE PRODUCT THROUGH THE WEB—THE WAVE OF THE FUTURE

One of the ways BMW is improving its product offerings even further is through its innovative website (www.bmwusa.com). At the site, customers can learn about the particular models, e-mail questions, and request literature or test-drives from their local BMW dealership. What really sets BMW's website apart from other car manufacturers, though, is the ability for customers to configure a car to their own specifications (interior choices, exterior choices, engine, packages, and options) and then transfer that information to their local dealer. As Carol Burrows, product communications manager for BMW, explains, "The BMW website is an integrated part of the overall marketing strategy for BMW. The full range of products can be seen and interacted with online. We offer pricing options online. Customers can go to their local dealership via the website to further discuss costs for purchase of a car. And it is a distribution channel for information that allows people access to the information 24 hours a day at their convenience." The ultimate extravagance in buying a car is having everything customized to the owner's preferences. Today, 80 percent of European buyers and 30 percent of U.S. buyers use the BMW website to choose from 350 model variations, 500 options, 90 exterior colors, and 170 interior trims to create their perfect vehicle!

Questions

1 Compare the product life cycle described by BMW for its cars to the product life cycle shown in Figure 11–1. How are they (*a*) similar and (*b*) dissimilar?

2 Based on BMW's typical product life cycle, what marketing strategies are appropriate for the 3 series? The X5?

3 Which of the three ways to manage the product life cycle does BMW utilize with its products—modifying the product, modifying the market, or repositioning the product?

4 How would you describe BMW's branding strategy (manufacturer branding, private branding, or mixed branding)? Why?

5 Go to the BMW website (www.bmwusa.com) and design a car to your own specifications. How does this enable you as a customer to evaluate the product differently than would be otherwise possible?

12

Managing Services

LEARNING OBJECTIVES

After reading this chapter you should be able to:

 LO1 Describe four unique elements of services.

 LO2 Recognize how services differ and how they can be classified.

 LO3 Explain how consumers purchase and evaluate services.

 LO4 Develop a customer contact audit to identify service advantages.

 LO5 Discuss the important roles of internal marketing and customer experience management in service organizations.

 LO6 Explain the role of the four Ps in the services marketing mix.

SPACE TOURISM TAKES OFF!

If you have ever wanted to visit the Space Station, float in zero gravity, or view the planet from an altitude of 60 miles, there are new services available just for you. Space tourism has been a topic of discussion among *Star Trek* and *Star Wars* enthusiasts for years, but today commercial space travel is a reality. The prices and experiences vary, but now you can buy a ticket to space just like you buy an airline ticket!

Five people have already paid about $25 million for a ride on a Russian Soyuz rocket to visit the International Space Station. They train with cosmonauts, help conduct experiments, and live aboard the Space Station for 7 to 10 days. If you can't get a week off of work or school, however, you can book a three-hour space flight on Virgin Galactic for about $200,000. You'll have to get in line though because 200 people have already purchased tickets from the "spaceline" founded by businessman Richard Branson. "Virgin Galactic will be run as a business . . . with the sole purpose of making space travel more and more affordable," says Branson. Other space tourism services will be available soon. Amazon. com founder Jeff Bezos is building a spaceport in Texas, and another company called DreamSpace will offer trips to space for $10,000 to $39,000.

While the actual time in space may be short, there are many other elements to the experience. One of the pilots of the Virgin Galactic vehicles explained: "If you want to be an astronaut, you have to dress like one. So we're going to have the coolest, sexiest pressure suits you've ever seen in your life." Some people are even predicting that there will soon be a hotel in orbit![1]

There are also many traditional service organizations competing for customers by offering enjoyable, memorable experiences. Walt Disney was one of the first to recognize the importance of sights, sounds, tastes, aromas, and textures to provide a unique experience when he created Disneyland. Hard Rock Cafes and Planet Hollywood restaurants use a similar approach to sell dining experiences that include food, music, entertainment, and a fun environment. Companies that sell goods with a service element are also offering experiences. Nike, for example, offers fun activities and promotional events in its Niketown stores, and Steinway provides a free concert including a pianist, invitations, and hors d'oeuvres in its customers' homes. These businesses are increasing the value of their offering to customers by engaging them in the experiential element of their service.[2]

Some experts believe we are on the verge of a new economic era driven by an *experience economy*.[3] Coffee can be purchased as a commodity in a grocery store and brewed at home at a cost of about 10 cents per cup. Coffee can also be purchased from 7-Eleven, where consumers pay for the convenience of the service, for a cost of about 75 cents per cup. But most of us have paid about $3 per cup at a Starbucks where the look of the shop, the jazz music, and the barrista's knowledge of the beans creates a "coffee experience" that is still a good value. ESPN Zone, Home Depot, Apple (stores), and many other companies are also responding to consumers' preferences for compelling experiences.

As the actions of Virgin Galactic, Hard Rock Cafe, Starbucks and the other examples above illustrate, the marketing of services is dynamic and challenging. In this chapter, we discuss how services differ from traditional products (goods), how consumers make purchase decisions, and the ways in which the marketing mix is used.

THE UNIQUENESS OF SERVICES

Services are intangible activities or benefits that an organization provides to consumers (such as airline trips, financial advice, or automobile repair) in exchange for money or something else of value.

Services have become a significant component of the global economy and one of the most important components of the U.S. economy. The World Trade Organization estimates that all countries exported merchandise valued at $10.1 trillion and commercial services valued at $2.4 trillion. In the United States, more than 41 percent of the gross domestic product (GDP) now comes from services. As shown in Figure 12–1, services accounted for $5.5 trillion in 2006, which is an increase of more than 80 percent since 1990. Projections indicate that by 2012, goods-producing firms will employ 23.3 million people and service firms will employ more than 129 million. Services also represent a large export business—the $431 billion of services exports in 2006 is one of the few areas in which the United States has a trade surplus.[4]

FIGURE 12–1

Services are now a larger part of the U.S. gross domestic product (GDP) than goods.

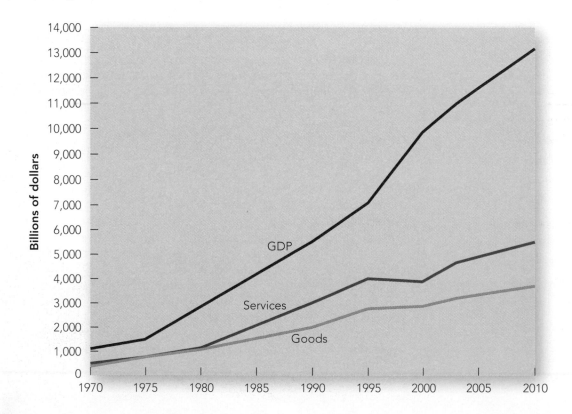

The growth of this sector is the result of increased demand for services that have been available in the past and the increasing interest in new services. Concierge services, for example, have been popular in hotels such as the Breakers in Palm Beach, Florida, which has a staff of 11 concierges who serve the hotel's guests. Outside the hotel industry, Northwest Airlines recently announced a partnership with White Tie, an international-luxury concierge service, which will be available to the airline's frequent flyers. Concierge services are even available for individual consumers and households. Concierge Couture, for example, will get you tickets to the Super Bowl, a private island vacation, a pet sitter, or even pick up your groceries! Other new services include Luggage Free, which will pick up your luggage at your home and deliver it to your destination to help you avoid lines at the airport; HealthCheckUSA, which now offers an online medical testing service; and zillow.com, which will help you determine the price of almost any home in the United States. These firms and many others like them are examples of the imaginative services that will play a role in our economy in the future.[5]

The Four I's of Services

There are four unique elements to services: *intangibility, inconsistency, inseparability,* and *inventory.* These four elements are referred to as the **four I's of services**.

Intangibility   Services are intangible; that is, they can't be held, touched, or seen before the purchase decision. In contrast, before purchasing a traditional product, a consumer can touch a box of laundry detergent, kick the tire of an automobile, or sample a new breakfast cereal. Because services tend to be a performance rather than an object, they are much more difficult for consumers to evaluate. To help consumers assess and compare services, marketers try to make them tangible or show the benefits of using the service.

The Lufthansa and Singapore Airlines ads show travelers in the airlines' new seats and also emphasize broadband Internet connections, comfortable sleeping, and other tangible benefits. American Express also provides tangible benefits by offering cardholders points and cash through its bonus rewards program.

Why do many services emphasize their tangible benefits? The answer appears in the text.

Lufthansa
www.lufthansa-usa.com

Singapore Airlines
www.singaporeair.com

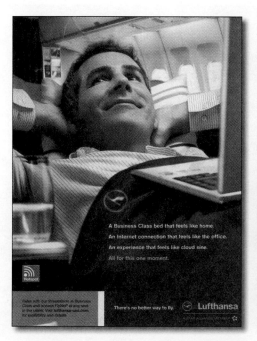

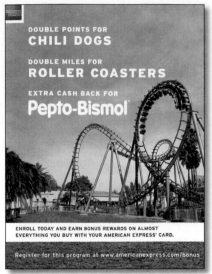

American Express provides tangible benefits through its reward program.

American Express Co.
www.americanexpress.com

Inconsistency Developing, pricing, promoting, and delivering services is challenging because the quality of a service is often inconsistent. Because services depend on the people who provide them, their quality varies with each person's capabilities and day-to-day job performance. Inconsistency is much more of a problem in services than it is with tangible goods. Tangible products can be good or bad in terms of quality, but with modern production lines the quality will at least be consistent. On the other hand, one day the Philadelphia Phillies baseball team may have great hitting and pitching and look like a pennant winner and the next day lose by 10 runs. Or a soprano at New York's Metropolitan Opera may have a bad cold and give a less-than-perfect performance. Whether the service involves tax assistance at H&R Block or guest relations at the Ritz-Carlton, organizations attempt to reduce inconsistency through standardization and training.[6]

Inseparability A third difference between services and goods, and related to problems of consistency, is inseparability. In most cases, the consumer cannot (and does not) separate the deliverer of the service from the service itself. For example, to receive an education, a person may attend a university. The quality of the education may be high, but if the student has difficulty interacting with instructors, finds counseling services poor, or does not receive adequate library or computer assistance, he or she may not be satisfied with the educational experience. Students' evaluations of their education will be influenced primarily by their perceptions of instructors, counselors, librarians, and other people at the university. Allstate's reminder that "You're in good hands" emphasizes the importance of its agents.

The amount of interaction between the consumer and the service provider depends on the extent to which the consumer must be physically present to receive the service. Some services such as haircuts, golf lessons, medical diagnoses, and food service require the customer to participate in the delivery of the services. Other services such as car repair, dry cleaning, and waste disposal process tangible objects with less involvement from the customer. Finally, services such as banking, consulting, and insurance can now be delivered electronically, often requiring no face-to-face customer interaction.[7]

People play an important role in the delivery of many services.

Allstate
www.allstate.com

LOW COST	Cost of inventory	HIGH COST

Real estate agency Hair salon	Insurance company	Dry cleaner	Auto repair center	Restaurant	Hotel	Amusement park	Airline Hospital

FIGURE 12–2

Inventory carrying costs of services depend on the cost of employees and equipment.

Inventory   Inventory of services is different from that of goods. Inventory problems exist with goods because many items are perishable and because there are costs associated with handling inventory. With services, inventory carrying costs are more subjective and are related to **idle production capacity**, which is when the service provider is available but there is no demand. The inventory cost of a service is the cost of paying the person used to provide the service along with any needed equipment. If a physician is paid to see patients but no one schedules an appointment, the fixed cost of the idle physician's salary is a high inventory carrying cost. In some service businesses, however, the provider of the service is on commission (a Merrill Lynch stockbroker) or is a part-time employee (a clerk at Sears). In these businesses, inventory carrying costs can be significantly lower or nonexistent because the idle production capacity can be cut back by reducing hours or having no salary to pay because of the commission compensation system. Figure 12–2 shows a scale of inventory carrying costs represented on the low end by real estate agencies and hair salons and on the high end by airlines and hospitals. The inventory carrying costs of airlines is high because of high-salaried pilots and very expensive equipment. In contrast, real estate agencies and hair salons have employees who work on commission and need little expensive equipment to conduct business. One reason service providers must maintain production capacity is because of the importance of time to today's customers. People don't want to wait long at the emergency room!

The Service Continuum

The four I's differentiate services from goods in most cases, but many companies are not clearly service-based or good-based organizations. Is Hewlett-Packard a computer company or service business? Although Hewlett-Packard manufactures computers, printers, and other goods, many of the company's employees work in its services division providing systems integration, networking, consulting, education, and product support.[8] As companies look at what they bring to the market, there is a range from the tangible to the intangible or good-dominant to service-dominant offerings referred to as the **service continuum** (Figure 12–3 on the next page).

Teaching, nursing, and the theater are intangible, service-dominant activities, and intangibility, inconsistency, inseparability, and inventory are major concerns in their marketing. Salt, neckties, and dog food are tangible goods, and the problems represented by the four I's are not relevant in their marketing. However, some businesses are a mix of intangible service and tangible good factors. A clothing tailor provides a service but also a good, the finished suit. How pleasant, courteous, and attentive the tailor is to the customer is an important component of the service, and how well the clothes fit is an important part of the product. As shown in Figure 12–3, a fast-food restaurant is about half tangible goods (the food) and half intangible services (courtesy, cleanliness, speed, and convenience).

FIGURE 12–3

The service continuum shows
how offerings can vary in
their balance of goods and
services.

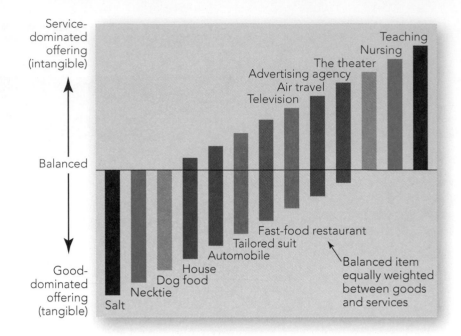

For many businesses today it is useful to distinguish between their core product—
either a good or a service—and supplementary services. A core service offering such
as a bank account, for example, also has supplementary services such as deposit assistance, parking or drive-through availability, ATMs, and monthly statements. Supplementary services often allow service providers to differentiate their offering from
competitors, and they may add value for consumers. While there are many potential
supplementary services, key categories of supplementary services include consultation,
finance, order taking, billing, and upgrades.[9]

Classifying Services

Throughout this book, marketing organizations, techniques, and concepts are classified
to show the differences and similarities in an organized framework. Services can also
be classified in several ways, according to whether (1) they are delivered by people or
equipment, (2) they are profit or nonprofit, or (3) they are government sponsored.

Delivery by People or Equipment As seen in Figure 12–4, many companies offer services. Professional services include management consulting firms
such as Booz, Allen & Hamilton or Accenture. Skilled labor is required to offer
services such as Sears appliance repair or Sheraton catering service. Unskilled
labor such as that used by Brinks store-security forces is also a service provided
by people.

Equipment-based services do not have the marketing concerns of inconsistency
because people are removed from the provision of the service. Electric utilities,
for example, can provide service without frequent personal contact with customers. Motion picture theaters have projector operators that consumers never see. A
growing number of customers use self-service technologies such as Home Depot's
self checkout, Southwest Airlines self check-in, and Schwab's online stock trading
without interacting with any service employees.[10]

Profit or Nonprofit Organizations Many organizations involved in services also distinguish themselves by their tax status as profit or nonprofit organizations.
In contrast to *profit organizations, nonprofit organizations'* excesses in revenue over
expenses are not taxed or distributed to shareholders. When excess revenue exists, the

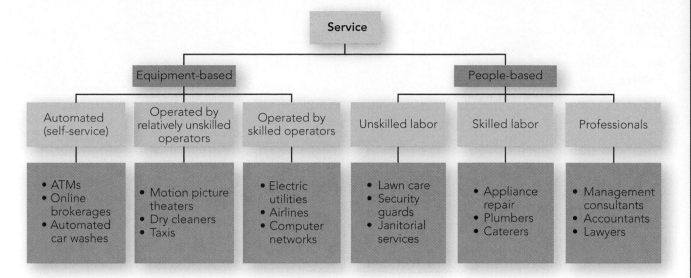

	Service				
Equipment-based			**People-based**		
Automated (self-service)	Operated by relatively unskilled operators	Operated by skilled operators	Unskilled labor	Skilled labor	Professionals
• ATMs • Online brokerages • Automated car washes	• Motion picture theaters • Dry cleaners • Taxis	• Electric utilities • Airlines • Computer networks	• Lawn care • Security guards • Janitorial services	• Appliance repair • Plumbers • Caterers	• Management consultants • Accountants • Lawyers

FIGURE 12–4

Services can be classified as equipment-based or people-based.

money goes back into the organization's treasury to allow continuation of the service. Based on the corporate structure of the nonprofit organization, it may pay tax on revenue-generating holdings not directly related to its core mission. Nonprofit organizations in the United States now have expenditures of $1 trillion and employ 10 percent of the workforce.[11]

The United Way, Greenpeace, Outward Bound, The Salvation Army, and The Nature Conservancy are examples of nonprofit organizations. Historically, misconceptions have limited the use of marketing practices by such organizations.[12] In recent years, however, nonprofit organizations have turned to marketing to help achieve their goals. The American Red Cross is a good example. To increase the organization's blood donor base it recently hired an advertising agency to develop a campaign that includes advertising, direct marketing, public relations, and customer relationship

Nonprofit and government-sponsored services often advertise.

Red Cross
www.redcross.org

United States Postal Service
www.usps.com

Marketing Matters > > > > > customer value

Marketing Is a Must for 1.5 Million Nonprofits!

For many years "the M-word was not considered a good thing," explains Tom Peterson, the vice president for marketing at anti-poverty nonprofit Heifer International. As the 1.5 million charitable causes, universities, foundations, hospitals, and other nonprofits began to compete for members and donations, however, the need for marketing became apparent. The *Susan G. Komen for the Cure* organization has been one of the most successful to adapt. Its walks and races and partnerships with companies such as American Airlines, Ford, and Microsoft now generate more than $180 million annually and have allowed it to invest nearly $1 billion in cancer research and community outreach programs.

Nonprofit organizations should follow many of the same principles businesses use. First, they should create a specific and realistic mission statement. The Chicago Children's Museum's mission statement, for example, is "to create a community where play and learning connect." Second, the organizations should have a unique selling proposition that will help consumers understand what the organization will do for sponsors or members or others. St. Jude Children's

Research Hospital emphasizes that it is "Finding cures. Saving children." Nonprofits should also use common branding practices to select a name, logo, or tag line. The Museum of Modern Art's acronym "MoMA," the Komen pink ribbon logo, and the American Heart Association's tagline "Learn and Live" are all successful examples.

In the past many nonprofit organizations relied solely on free public service announcements for their communication. Now successful nonprofit budgets include advertising and Web-based tools to facilitate awareness and engagement. For example, the American Heart Association allocated $12 million to its advertising activities, which led to $40 million in contributions. Similarly the March of Dimes created an online forum where people can share stories, and it now has an average of 8,100 posts each month.

Businesses are responding also. Some become sponsors of events or encourage employees to make donations. They can also become members of nonprofit organizations. The 1% for the Planet organization has 450 member companies that donate 1 percent of their sales to approved nonprofit groups such as the Surfrider Foundation, Amazon Watch, and Rainforest Relief.

---

management. In addition, to help raise public awareness of Red Cross services, it is also continuing its annual National Celebrity Cabinet, which currently includes Forest Whitaker, Jamie Lee Curtis, Heidi Klum, Julianne Moore, and Tim McGraw.[13] See the accompanying Marketing Matters box to learn about essential marketing activities for nonprofit organizations.[14]

Government Sponsored   A third way to classify services is based on whether they are government sponsored. Although there is no direct ownership and they are nonprofit organizations, governments at the federal, state, and local levels provide a broad range of services. The United States Postal Service, for example, has adopted many marketing activities. First-class postage revenue has declined as postal service customers have increased their use of the Internet to send e-mail, pay bills, and file taxes. Rather than fight the trend, however, the Postal Service is embracing the Internet. Its website, www.usps.com, allows consumers to buy stamps, arrange deliveries, and manage mailing lists online. In addition, new post office boxes are designed in a shoebox size to better meet the needs of consumers who shop for clothing and shoes online. Businesses can even buy stamps with their company brand and logo on them now. The Postal Service's "Easy Come. Easy Go" campaign is designed to allow it to compete with UPS, FedEx, DHL, and foreign postal services for global package delivery business. Finally, you may have noticed that many post offices are now also retail outlets that sell collector stamps, Pony Express sweatshirts, and even neckties![15]

1. What are the four I's of services?

2. Would inventory carrying costs for an accounting firm with certified public accountants be (*a*) high, (*b*) low, or (*c*) nonexistent?

3. To eliminate service inconsistencies, companies rely on _____ and _____.

HOW CONSUMERS PURCHASE SERVICES

Colleges, hospitals, hotels, and even charities are facing an increasingly competitive environment. Successful service organizations, like successful product-oriented firms, must understand how the consumer makes a service purchase decision and quality evaluation and in what ways a company can present a differential advantage relative to competing offerings.

The Purchase Process

Many aspects of services affect the consumer's evaluation of the purchase. Because services cannot be displayed, demonstrated, or illustrated, consumers cannot make a prepurchase evaluation of all the characteristics of services.[16] Similarly, because service providers may vary in their delivery of a service, an evaluation of a service may change with each purchase. Figure 12–5 portrays how different types of goods and services are evaluated by consumers. Tangible goods such as clothing, jewelry, and furniture have *search* properties, such as color, size, and style, which can be determined before purchase. Services such as restaurants and child care have *experience* properties, which can only be discerned after purchase or during consumption. Finally, services provided by specialized professionals such as medical diagnoses and legal services have *credence* properties, or characteristics that the consumer may find impossible to evaluate even after purchase and consumption.[17] To reduce the uncertainty created by these properties, service consumers turn to personal sources of information such as early adopters, opinion leaders, and reference group members during the purchase decision process.[18] The Mayo Clinic uses an organized, explicit

FIGURE 12–5
Consumers use search, experience, and credence properties to evaluate services.

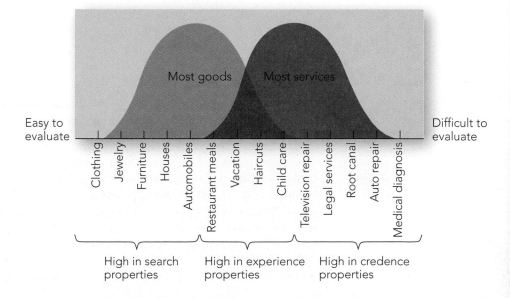

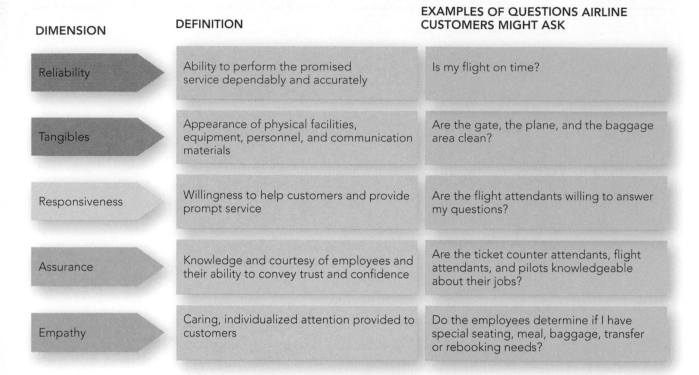

DIMENSION	DEFINITION	EXAMPLES OF QUESTIONS AIRLINE CUSTOMERS MIGHT ASK
Reliability	Ability to perform the promised service dependably and accurately	Is my flight on time?
Tangibles	Appearance of physical facilities, equipment, personnel, and communication materials	Are the gate, the plane, and the baggage area clean?
Responsiveness	Willingness to help customers and provide prompt service	Are the flight attendants willing to answer my questions?
Assurance	Knowledge and courtesy of employees and their ability to convey trust and confidence	Are the ticket counter attendants, flight attendants, and pilots knowledgeable about their jobs?
Empathy	Caring, individualized attention provided to customers	Do the employees determine if I have special seating, meal, baggage, transfer or rebooking needs?

FIGURE 12–6

There are five dimensions of service quality.

approach called "evidence management" to present customers with concrete and convincing evidence of its strengths.[19]

Assessing Service Quality

Once a consumer tries a service, how is it evaluated? Primarily by comparing expectations about a service offering to the actual experience a consumer has with the service.[20] Differences between the consumer's expectations and experience are identified through **gap analysis**. This type of analysis asks consumers to assess their expectations and experiences on dimensions of service quality such as those described in Figure 12–6.[21] Expectations are influenced by word-of-mouth communications, personal needs, past experiences, and promotional activities, while actual experiences are determined by the way an organization delivers its service.[22] The relative importance of the various dimensions of service quality varies by the type of service.[23] What if someone is dissatisfied and complains? Recent studies suggest that customers who experience a "service failure" will increase their satisfaction if the service makes a satisfactory service recovery effort, but not if there is a second failure.[24] See the Going Online box for ideas about monitoring service failures.[25]

Customer Contact and Relationship Marketing

Consumers judge services on the entire sequence of steps that make up the service process. To focus on these steps, or "service encounters," a firm can develop a **customer contact audit**—a flowchart of the points of interaction between consumer and service provider.[26] This is particularly important in high-contact services such as hotels, educational institutions, and automobile rental agencies. Figure 12–7 is a consumer contact audit for renting a car from Hertz. The interactions identified in a customer contact audit often serve as the basis for developing relationships with customers. Recent research suggests that authenticity and sincerity of the interactions affect the success of the relationships.[27]

Going Online

How Can You Monitor Service Failure? Blog Watching!

Only 5 to 10 percent of dissatisfied customers choose to complain—the rest switch companies or make negative comments to other people. Increasingly the forum for personal comments is on the Web through weblogs, or blogs. Companies can monitor the postings on blogs for insights into service failures. Try using www.blogsearch.google.com or

www.technorati.com to find blog entries about a service you know. There are also Web services such as www.buzzlogic.com and www.reputationdefender.com available to monitor blogs. Most public relations experts agree that it is best to respond to, rather than ignore, comments on the Web. Try creating your own blog now!

A Customer's Car Rental Activities   A customer decides to rent a car and (1) contacts the rental company (see Figure 12–7). A customer service representative receives the information (2) and checks the availability of the car at the desired location. When the customer arrives at the rental site (3), the reservation system is again accessed, and the customer provides information regarding payment, address, and driver's license (4). A car is assigned to the customer (5), who proceeds by bus to the car pickup (6). On return to the rental location (7), the customer checks in (8), a customer service representative collects information on mileage, gas consumption, and damages (9), and a bill is printed (10).

Each of the steps numbered 1 to 10 is a customer contact point where the tangible aspects of Hertz service are seen by the customer. Figure 12–7, however, also shows

FIGURE 12–7

Customer contact audit for a car rental (green shaded boxes indicate customer activity)

The Hertz Corporation
www.hertz.com

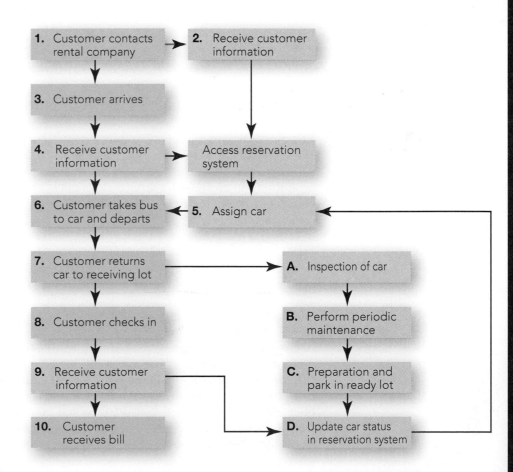

a series of steps lettered A to D that involve an inspection, maintenance, preparation for the next customer, and an update of the reservation system. These steps are essential in providing a clean, well-maintained car, but they are not points of customer interaction. To create a service advantage, Hertz must create a competitive advantage in the sequence of interactions with the customer. For example, Hertz has attempted to eliminate step 4 for some customers with its Hertz #1 Club—these customers simply show their drivers license and pick up the car's keys.

Relationship Marketing The contact between a service provider and a customer represents a service encounter that is likely to influence the customer's assessment of the purchase. The number of encounters in a service experience may vary. Disney, for example, estimates that a park visitor will have 74 encounters with Disney employees in a single visit. These encounters represent opportunities to develop social bonds, or relationships, with customers. The relationship may also be developed through loyalty incentives such as airline frequent flyer programs. Relationship marketing provides several benefits for service customers including the continuity of a single provider, customized service delivery, reduced stress due to a repetitive purchase process, and an absence of switching costs. Recent surveys of consumers have indicated that while customers of many services are interested in being "relationship customers," they require that the relationship be balanced in terms of loyalty, benefits, and respect for privacy,[28] and that there is a higher expectation of future use of the service.[29]

MANAGING THE MARKETING OF SERVICES

LO5

Just as the unique aspects of services necessitate changes in the consumer's purchase process, the marketing management process requires special adaptation.[30] As emphasized earlier in the chapter, in services marketing the employee plays a central role in creating the service experience, and in building and maintaining relationships with customers.[31] This aspect of services marketing has led to a concept called internal marketing.[32]

Internal marketing is based on the notion that a service organization must focus on its employees, or internal market, before successful programs can be directed at customers.[33] Services need to ensure that employees have the attitude, skills, and commitment needed to meet customer expectations and sustain customer loyalty. This idea suggests that employee development through recruitment, training, communication, coaching, management, and leadership are critical to the success of service organizations.[34]

Once internal marketing programs have prepared employees for their interactions with customers, organizations can better manage the services they provide. **Customer experience management (CEM)** is the process of managing the entire customer experience with the company. CEM experts suggest that the process should be intentional and planned, consistent so that every experience is similar, differentiated from other service offerings, and relevant and valuable to the target market. Companies such as Disney, Southwest Airlines, the Ritz-Carlton, and Starbucks all manage the experience they offer customers. They integrate their activities to connect with customers at each contact point to move beyond customer relationships to customer loyalty.[35]

Let's use the four Ps framework for discussing the marketing mix for services.

Product (Service)

LO6

The concepts of the product component of the marketing mix discussed in Chapters 10 and 11 apply equally well to Cheerios (a good) and to American Express (a service). Yet there are three aspects of the product/service element of the marketing mix that warrant special attention: exclusivity, brand name, and capacity management.

Exclusivity Chapter 10 pointed out that one favorable dimension in a new product is its ability to be patented. A patent gives the manufacturer of a product exclusive rights to its production for 17 years. A major difference between products and services is that services cannot be patented. Hence, the creator of a successful fast-food hamburger chain could quickly discover the concept being copied by others. Domino's Pizza, for example, has seen many competitors copy the quick delivery advantage that propelled the company to success. Many businesses today try to distinguish their core product with new or improved supplementary services through outsourcing: Hotels outsource concierge services, airlines outsource maintenance, and banks outsource the mailing of monthly statements.[36]

Branding An important aspect in marketing goods is the branding strategy used. However, because services are intangible and, therefore, more difficult to describe, the brand name or identifying logo of the service organization is particularly important in consumer decisions.[37] The financial services industry, for example, has failed to use branding to distinguish what consumers perceive to be similar offerings by banks, mutual fund companies, brokerage firms, and insurance companies. UPS, however, recently changed its logo after 42 years, to communicate the addition of supply chain management services to its package delivery service.[38] Take a look at the logos to determine how successful some companies have been in branding their service with a name and symbol.

Logos create service identities.

Capacity Management Most services have a limited capacity due to the inseparability of the service from the service provider and the perishable nature of the service. For example, to "buy" an appendectomy, a patient must be in the hospital at the same time as the surgeon and only one patient can be helped at that time. Similarly, no additional surgery can be conducted tomorrow because of an unused operating room or an available surgeon today—the service capacity is lost if it is not used. So the service component of the marketing mix must be integrated with efforts to influence consumer demand.[39] This is referred to as **capacity management**.

Service organizations must manage the availability of the offering so that (1) demand matches capacity over the duration of the demand cycle (for example, one day, week, month, or year), and (2) the organization's assets are used in ways that will maximize the return on investment (ROI).[40] Figure 12–8 on the next page shows how a hotel tries to manage its capacity during the high and low seasons. Differing price structures are assigned to each segment of consumers to help moderate or adjust demand for the service. Airline contracts fill a fixed number of rooms throughout the year. In the low season, when more rooms are available, tour packages at appealing prices are used to attract groups or conventions, such as an offer for seven nights in Orlando at a reduced price. Weekend packages are also offered to vacationers. In the high-demand season, groups are less desirable because guests who will pay high

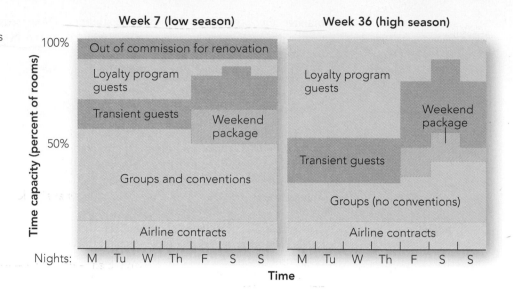

prices travel to Florida on their own. The accompanying Using Marketing Dashboards box demonstrates how JetBlue Airways uses a capacity management measure called *load factor* to assess its profitability.

Price

In the service industries, *price* is referred to in various ways. Hospitals refer to charges; consultants, lawyers, physicians, and accountants to fees; airlines to fares; and hotels to rates. Regardless of the term used, price plays two essential roles: (1) to affect consumer perceptions and (2) to be used in capacity management. Because of the intangible nature of services, price can indicate the quality of the service. Would you wonder about the quality of a $100 surgery? Studies have shown that when there are few well-known cues by which to judge a product, consumers use price.[41] Look at the accompanying ad for eye surgery. Would you have concerns about the offer or think it's a good value for the money?

The capacity management role of price is also important to movie theaters, airlines, restaurants, and hotels. Many service businesses use **off-peak pricing**, which consists of charging different prices during different times of the day or days of the week to reflect variations in demand for the service. Airlines offer discounts for weekend travel, and movie theaters offer matinee prices. Cellular telephone pricing plans typically offer peak (sometimes called "anytime") minutes for calls made during the day and off-peak minutes for calls made at night or on weekends. The different prices reflect the cell phone company's effort to shift demand to low-volume time periods.[42]

Place (Distribution)

Place or distribution is a major factor in developing a service marketing strategy because of the inseparability of services from the producer. Historically in services marketing, little attention has been paid to distribution. But as competition grows, the value of convenient distribution, or access, is being recognized. Hairstyling chains such

Price influences perceptions of services.

Using Marketing Dashboards
Are JetBlue's Flights Profitably Loaded?

Capacity management is critical in the marketing of many services. For example, having the right number of airline seats or hotel rooms available at the right time, price, and place can spell the difference between a profitable or unprofitable service operation.

Airlines feature *load factor* as a capacity management measure on their marketing dashboards, along with two other measures; namely the *operating cost* per available seat flown one mile and the revenue generated by each seat flown one mile called *yield*. Load factor is the percentage of available seats flown one mile occupied by a paying customer.

These three measures combine to show airline operating income or loss per available seat flown one mile:

Operating income (loss) per available seat flown one mile
= [Yield × Load factor] − Operating expense

Your Challenge As a marketing analyst for New York City-based JetBlue Airways, you have been asked to determine the operating income or loss per available seat flown one mile for the first six months of 2007. In addition, you have been asked to determine what load factor JetBlue must reach to breakeven assuming its current yield and operating expense will not change in the immediate future.

Your Findings JetBlue's yield, load factor, and operating expense marketing dashboard displays are shown below.

You can conclude from these measures that JetBlue Airways posted about a 0.21¢ loss per available seat flown one mile in the first six months of 2007:

Operating loss per available seat flown one mile
= [9.83¢ × 82.1%] − 8.28¢ = −.2096¢

Assuming JetBlue's yield and operating expense will not change and using a little algebra, the airline's load factor will have to increase from 82.1% to 84.23% to breakeven:

Operating income (loss) per available seat flown one mile
= [9.83¢ × Load factor] − 8.28¢ = 0¢
Load factor = 84.23%

Your Action Assuming yield and operating expenses will not change, you should recommend that JetBlue consider revising its flight schedules to better accommodate traveler needs and advertise these changes. Consideration might be also given to how JetBlue utilizes its existing airplane fleet to serve its customers and produce a profit.

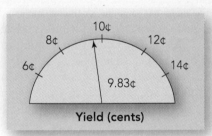

Yield (cents)

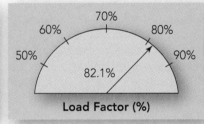

Load Factor (%)

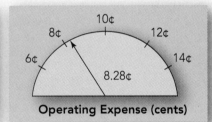

Operating Expense (cents)

as Cost Cutters Family Hair Care, tax preparation offices such as H&R Block, and accounting firms such as Deloitte Touche Tohmatsu all use multiple locations for the distribution of services. In the banking industry, customers of participating banks using the Cirrus system can access any one of thousands of automatic teller systems throughout the United States. The availability of electronic distribution through the Internet now provides global coverage for travel services, banking, entertainment, insurance services, stock trading, and many other information-based services.[43]

Promotion

The value of promotion, specifically advertising, for many services is to show the benefits of purchasing the service. It is valuable to stress availability, location, consistent

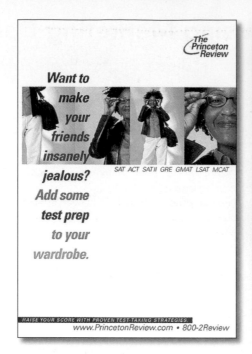

quality, and efficient, courteous service.[44] The *Princeton Review* ad above, for example, describes the benefits available to its customers—higher test scores. In addition, services must be concerned with their image. Promotional efforts, such as Accenture's "High performance. Delivered." campaign or Merrill Lynch's use of the bull in its ads, contribute to image and positioning strategies.[45] In most cases promotional concerns of services are similar to those of products.

Another form of promotion, *publicity,* has played a major role in the promotional strategy of nonprofit services and some professional organizations. Nonprofit organizations such as public school districts, the Chicago Symphony Orchestra, religious organizations, and hospitals have used publicity to disseminate their messages. Because of the heavy reliance on publicity, many services use *public service announcements* (PSAs), and because PSAs are free, nonprofit groups have tended to rely on them as the foundation of their media plan.[46] However, as discussed in Chapter 19, the timing and location of a PSA are under the control of the medium, not the organization. So the nonprofit service group cannot control who sees the message or when the message is given.

SERVICES IN THE FUTURE

What can we expect from the services industry in the future? New and better services, of course, and an unprecedented variety of choices. Many of the changes will be the result of two factors: technological development and an expanding scope in the global economy.

Technogical advances are rapidly changing the service industry. In fact, many of the likely changes in the United States are already taking place in Europe and Asia where new generations of technology have leapfrogged North America. The key elements of future services include mobility, convergence, personalization, and collaboration. Mobility will be provided by new generations of networks that will allow TV, GPS, high-speed data transfer, and audio programming on portable digital devices. Products such as the Apple iPhone are indications of the coming convergence of voice, video, and data in a single product. Personalization is also underway at services such as Amazon.com where past transactions are analyzed to customize information seen by customers. Smart cards, already in use in Europe, will soon be viable in the United States. Finally, collaboration services that allow Web-conferencing, dating and matchmaking, and even remote involvement of friends when someone is shopping are coming![47]

An expanding scope of influence in the global economy is also changing the service industry. While the past decade has seen services grow to become the dominant part of the economy in the United States, the future is likely to see more emphasis on the global marketing of services and increasing attention to cross-cultural implications for services. Recent studies indicate that consumers in countries such as Australia, China, Germany, India, and the United States place varying emphasis on service quality and underscore the need to "think global and act local." Finally, some experts predict that the dominant view of economic exchange will shift from its current focus on goods and tangible resources to services and intangible attributes.[48]

---

learning review

6. Matching demand with capacity is the focus of _____ management.

7. How does a movie theater use off-peak pricing?

8. What factors will influence future changes in services?

LEARNING OBJECTIVES REVIEW

LO1 *Describe four unique elements of services.*
The four unique elements of services—the four I's—are intangibility, inconsistency, inseparability, and inventory. Intangibility refers to the tendency of services to be a performance that cannot be held or touched, rather than an object. Inconsistency is a characteristic of services because they depend on people to deliver them, and people vary in their capabilities and in their day-to-day performance. Inseparability refers to the difficulty of separating the deliverer of the service (hair stylist) from the service itself (hair salon). Inventory refers to the need to have service production capability when there is service demand.

LO2 *Recognize how services differ and how they can be classified.*
Services differ in terms of the balance of the part of the offering that is based on goods and the part of the offering that is based on service. Services can be delivered by people or equipment, they can be provided by profit or nonprofit organizations, and they can be government sponsored.

LO3 *Explain how consumers purchase and evaluate services.*
Because services are intangible, prepurchase evaluation is difficult for consumers. To choose a service consumers use search, experience, and credence qualities to evaluate the good and service elements of an offering. Once a consumer tries a service, it is evaluated by comparing expectations with the actual experience on five dimensions of quality—reliability, tangibles, responsiveness, assurance, and empathy. Differences between expectations and experience are identified through gap analysis.

LO4 *Develop a customer contact audit to identify service advantages.*
A customer contact audit is a flowchart of the points of interaction between a consumer and a service provider. The interactions identified in a customer contact audit often serve as the basis for developing relationships with customers.

LO5 *Discuss the important roles of internal marketing and customer experience management in service organizations.*
Because the employee plays a central role in creating the service experience, and in building and maintaining relationships with customers, services have adopted a concept called internal marketing. This concept suggests that services need to ensure that employees (the internal market) have the attitude, skills, and commitment needed to meet customer expectations. Customer experience management is the process of managing the entire customer experience with the company to ensure customer loyalty.

LO6 *Explain the role of the four Ps in the services marketing mix.*
Each of the four Ps can be applied to services marketing. Important aspects of the product element include exclusivity, the use of services to distinguish an offering; branding, the use of a brand name or logo to help consumer identify the service; and capacity management, the efforts designed to influence the timing of consumer demand. Pricing is reflected in charges, fees, fares, and rates and can be used to influence perceptions of the quality of a service and to manage capacity. Place (or distribution) is used to provide access and convenience. Promotional tools such as advertising and publicity are a means of communicating the benefits of a service.

APPLYING MARKETING KNOWLEDGE

1 Explain how the four I's of services would apply to a Marriott Hotel.

2 Idle production capacity may be related to inventory or capacity management. How would the pricing component of the marketing mix reduce idle production capacity for (*a*) a car wash, (*b*) a stage theater group, and (*c*) a university?

3 Look back at the service continuum in Figure 12–3. Explain how the following points in the continuum differ in terms of consistency: (*a*) salt, (*b*) automobile, (*c*) advertising agency, and (*d*) teaching.

4 What are the search, experience, and credence properties of an airline for the business traveler and pleasure traveler? What properties are most important to each group?

5 Outline the customer contact audit for the typical deposit you make at your neighborhood bank.

6 The text suggests that internal marketing is necessary before a successful marketing program can be directed at consumers. Why is this particularly true for service organizations?

7 Outline the capacity management strategies that an airline must consider.

8 How does off-peak pricing influence demand for services?

9 Draw the channel of distribution for the following services: (*a*) a restaurant, (*b*) a hospital, and (*c*) a hotel.

10 In recent years, many service businesses have begun to provide their employees with uniforms. Explain the rationale behind this strategy in terms of the concepts discussed in this chapter.

building your marketing plan

In this section of your marketing plan you should distinguish between your core product—a good or a service—and supplementary services.

1 Develop an internal marketing program that will ensure that employees are prepared to deliver the core and supplementary services.

2 Conduct a customer contact audit and create a flowchart similar to Figure 12–7 to identify specific points of interaction with customers.

3 Describe marketing activities that will (*a*) address each of the four I's as they relate to your service and (*b*) encourage the development of relationships with your customers.

Add this as an appendix to your marketing plan and use the results in developing your marketing mix strategy.

video case 12 Philadelphia Phillies, Inc.: Sports Marketing 101

"Bring everyone in closer. Have fans feel 'I'm not alone here; lots of others are in the seats. This is a *happening*!'" chuckles David Montgomery, president and chief executive officer of the Philadelphia Phillies, Inc.

He continues, "Old Veterans Stadium had too big an inventory of seats for baseball. The new facility and the fact that it's a game played in summer out in the open air really takes you to a much broader audience. Our challenge is to appeal to all the segments in that audience." What Montgomery is referring to is the Phillies' new world-class Citizens Bank Park baseball stadium that opened in 2004. It is a baseball-only ballpark, seating 43,500 fans, where every seat is angled toward home plate to give fans the best view of the action. This contrasts with the 62,000-seat Veterans Stadium that both the Phillies and the Philadelphia Eagles football team shared from 1971 to 2003 where sight lines were always a compromise for the two sports.

The new fan-friendly Phillies stadium is just one element in today's complex strategy to effectively market the Philadelphia Phillies to several different segments of fans—a far different challenge than in the past. A century ago Major League Baseball was pretty simple. You built a stadium. You hired the ballplayers. You printed tickets—hoping and praying a winning team would bring in fans and sell those tickets. And your advertising consisted of printing the team's home schedule in the local newspaper.

THE PHILLIES TODAY: APPEALS, SEGMENTS, AND ACTIVITIES

Baseball, like other sports, is a service whose primary benefit is entertainment. Marketing a Major League Baseball team is far different today.

"How do you market a product that is all over the board?" asks David Buck, the Phillies' vice president of marketing. He first gives a general answer to his question: "The ballpark experience is the key. As long as you project an image of a fun ballpark experience in everything you do, you're going to be in good shape. Our best advertising is word of mouth from happy fans." Next come the specifics. Marketing the appeal of a fun ballpark experience to all segments of fans is critical because the Phillies can't promise a winning baseball team. Every team, even the New York Yankees, has its ups and downs. The Phillies are no different.

Reaching the different segments of fans is a special challenge because each segment attends a game for different reasons and therefore will respond to different special promotions:

- The diehards. Intense baseball fans who are there to watch the strategy and see the Phillies win.

- Kids 14 years and under. At the game with their families, to get bat or bobble-head doll premiums, and have a "run-the-bases" day.
- Women and men 15 years and older. Special "days out," such as Mother's Day or Father's Day.
- Seniors, 60 years and over. A "stroll-the-bases" day.
- 20- and 30-somethings. Meet friends at the ballpark and restaurants for a fun night out.
- Corporate and community groups. At the game to have fun but also to get to know members of their respective organizations better.

It's clear that not all fans are there for exactly the same "fun ballpark experience."

The segments don't stop there. Marisol Lezeano, the Phillies' community outreach coordinator, says, "In the Philadelphia area, we've got a lot of different ethnic groups and we want to make all of them Phillies fans." So she plans special nights for these groups: the Goya Latino Family Celebration night with a Latino Legends poster of Phillies Hispanic players; Asia Pacific night with a giant cloth dragon dancing its way across the outfield; and The Sound of Philadelphia night honoring Black Music Month featuring various African-American music groups. "We want all communities to come to the ballpark. We're all fans. It's great. Please be with us," she emphasizes.

The "fun ballpark experience" today also goes beyond simply watching the Phillies play a baseball game. Fans at Citizens Bank Park can also:

- Buy souvenirs at the Phanatic Attic, within the Majestic Clubhouse Store.
- Romp in the Phanatic Phun Zone, the largest soft-play area for kids in Major League Baseball and scale a giant, inflatable baseball rock-climbing wall.

- Test their skills in a pitching game.
- Play the giant Ballpark Pinball game.
- Stroll through Ashburn Alley (named for a famous Phillie), an outdoor food and entertainment area to see the All-Star Walk and the Wall of Fame.
- Eat at McFadden's Restaurant and Saloon year round or Harry the K's Bar & Grill.
- View one of the largest digital video scoreboards in baseball.
- Purchase a luxury suite to experience enhanced amenities.

PROMOTIONAL ACTIVITIES

The range of the Phillies' promotional activities today is mind numbing. Before and during the season, the Phillies run a series of TV ads to generate and/or maintain fan interest. A recent ad campaign targeted kids by showing that the Phillies' players themselves are just like them. The tagline: "There's a little fan in all of us."

The Phillies also use "special promotion days," which typically increase fan attendance by 30 to 35 percent for

a game, according to David Buck. These days often generate first-time visits by people who have never seen a Major League Baseball game. They generally fall into three categories: (1) theme nights, (2) event days, and (2) premium gift days.

Theme nights are devoted to special community groups or other fan segments. Examples include College Nights (fellow classmates, alumni, and faculty), dates for families of the military and law enforcement, Rooftop Thursdays (having a luau with friends on the stadium rooftop), and others. Event days can involve camera days where fans can take players' photos—three FUJIFILM Fridays each season for the Phillies. Or they can involve fireworks, an old-timers' game, or running or strolling the bases. Some events are especially memorable. Phillies fans still talk about the ostrich race in which a terrified Phillies' broadcaster wound up in the first row of stands when the ostrich pulling him and his cart panicked due to crowd noise.

"Our premiums or giveaways are directed at specific groups," says Scott Brandreth, the Phillies' merchandising manager. "During the year, we probably have two or three for all fans, six or seven for children 14 years or younger, and maybe one for women over 15, and one for men over 15—often for Mother's Day and Father's Day." These giveaways range from bobble-head dolls and nesting dolls to baseball caps, rally towels, and Louisville Slugger bats. To control expenses, the Phillies try to keep the cost of the premiums in the range of $1 to $3.

Other promotional activities fall in both the traditional and nontraditional categories. Personal appearances at public and charity events by Phillies' players and their wives, radio and TV ads, and special events paid for by sponsors have been used by baseball teams for decades. But newer, more nontraditional promotions include the $95 million naming rights for the Citizens Bank Park, Phillies Phantasy Camp (where you can "play ball" with Phillies' legends for a week in January in Florida), special "infield club seats," the Phillies Grand Slam Sweepstakes, where fans can win tickets for a luxury suite, and Phillies youth baseball clubs and leagues. Fans also can now get Phillies updates and order tickets on its website (www.phillies.com).

Probably the best-known mascot in professional sports, the Phillie Phanatic is a Philadelphia legend. This oversized, green furry mascot has been around for over 25 years. It not only appears in the ballpark at all Phillies' home games, but also makes appearances at charity and public events year round. Or rather the *three* Phanatics do so, because the demand is too great for a single Phanatic. "The Phanatic is a great character because he doesn't carry wins or losses," says David Montgomery. "Fans young and old can relate to him . . . he makes you smile, makes you laugh, and adds to the enjoyment of the game."

BOTTOM LINE: REVENUES AND EXPENSES

"We're a private business that serves the public," David Montgomery points out. "And we've got to make sure our revenues more than cover our expenses." He identifies five key sources of revenues and the approximate annual percentages for each:

Sources of Revenue	Approx. %
1. Ticket sales (home and away games)	52%
2. National media (network TV and radio)	13
3. Local media (over-the-air TV, pay TV, radio)	13
4. Advertising (publications, co-sponsorship promotions)	12
5. Concessions (food, souvenirs, restaurants)	10
Total	100

Balanced against these revenues are some major expenses that include players' salaries (about $90 million in 2007)[49] and salaries of more than 150 full-time employees. Other expenses are those for scouting and drafting 40 to 60 new players per year, operating six minor-league farm clubs, and managing a labor force of 400 persons for each of the Phillies' 81 regular season home games at Citizens Bank Park.

David Montgomery never gets bored. "When I finished business school, I had to choose between a marketing research job at a large paper products company or marketing the Philadelphia Phillies," explains Montgomery, who started with the Phillies by selling season and group tickets. "And it was no real decision because there never has been one day on this job that wasn't different and exciting," he says.

Questions

1 (*a*) What is the "product" that the Phillies market? (*b*) What "products" are the Phillies careful not to market?

2 How does the "quality" dimension in marketing the Philadelphia Phillies as an entertainment service differ from that in marketing a consumer product such as a breakfast cereal?

3 When David Montgomery talks about reducing the "inventory of seats" in the new versus old stadium, what does he recognize as (*a*) advantages and (*b*) disadvantages?

4 Considering all five elements of the promotional mix (advertising, personal selling, public relations, sales promotion, and direct marketing), what specific promotional activities should the Phillies use? Which should be used off-season? During the season?

5 What kind of special promotion gift days (with premiums) and event days (no premiums) can the Phillies use to increase attendance by targeting these fan segments: (*a*) 14 and under, (*b*) 15 and over, (*c*) other special fan segments, and (*d*) all fans?

Sports
MLB Baseball
NFL Football
NCAA Football
NBA Basketball
NHL Hockey
MLS Soccer
NASCAR
WWE
Ultimate Fighting
US Open Tennis
David Beckham
All Other Sports

Concerts
Hannah Montana
Van Halen
Dave Matthews Band
Stevie Wonder
Jimmy Buffett
Eagles and Dixie Chicks
Kenny Chesney
Bon Jovi
Genesis
Jennifer Lopez and Marc Anthony
Rush
Aerosmith
Projekt Revolution
Def Leppard
The Police
The Cure
Rascal Flatts
Toby Keith
Justin Timberlake
Maroon 5

Rock The Bells
Family Values Tour
Virgin Music Festival
All Other Concerts

Theater
Broadway Shows
Comedy Shows
Cirque Du Soleil
Classical Music & Opera

Welcome to **StubHub!** Where Fans Buy & Sell Tickets™

MLB.com
Official Ticket Marketplace of MLB.com

StubHub!
Buy/Sell Tickets

This Week's Top Tickets   **US Open Tennis, NFL Opening Week**

MLB: Yankees, Red Sox, Cubs, Tigers, Angels, Mets, Phillies, Giants, Cards
NFL: Chargers, Bears, Skins, Cowboys, 49ers, Eagles, Giants, Bengals, Colts
Jaguars, Patriots, Seahawks, Packers, Steelers, Jets, Broncos, Texans
NCAA FB: USC, Michigan, Penn St, Notre Dame, Cal, LSU, Texas, Alabama, Ohio St
Concerts: Beyonce Premium Packages, Dave Matthews Band, Stevie Wonder
Theater: Wicked, Jersey Boys, Grease, Young Frankenstein, Spring Awakening

Gift**Finder**

1. What do they like?
[Pick a category ▾]

2. Where do they live?
[Choose a location ▾]

3. How many tickets?
[# of tickets ▾]

4. What's your budget?
[Price per ticket ▾]

[Find]

Gift Certificates >

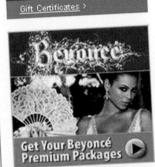
Get Your Beyoncé Premium Packages ▶

US Open

All Tickets

Concert Tickets
Artists A - C
Artists D - G
Artists H - K
Artists L - O
Artists P - S
Artists T - Z
Upcoming Concert Tours

Sports Tickets
Baseball Tickets
Basketball Tickets
Bodybuilding Tickets
Extreme Sports Tickets
Fight Tickets (Boxing, UFC)
Football Tickets
Golf Tickets
Hockey Tickets
Horse Racing Tickets
Lacrosse Tickets
Motorsports Tickets
Rodeo Tickets
Roller Derby Tickets
Rugby Tickets
Soccer Tickets
Tennis Tickets
Track and Field Tickets
Volleyball Tickets
Wrestling Tickets

StubHub! Exclusives
Exclusive Events and All-Inclusive Packages

Theater Tickets and Arts Tickets
Broadway Tickets and National Tours Tickets
Burning Man Tickets

13

Building the Price Foundation

LEARNING OBJECTIVES
All OF These

After reading this chapter you should be able to:

 LO1 Identify the elements that make up a price.

 LO2 Recognize the objectives a firm has in setting prices and the constraints that restrict the range of prices a firm can charge.

 LO3 Explain what a demand curve is and the role of revenues in pricing decisions.

 LO4 Describe what price elasticity of demand means to a manager facing a pricing decision.

 LO5 Explain the role of costs in pricing decisions.

 LO6 Describe how various combinations of price, fixed cost, and unit variable cost affect a firm's break-even point.

WHEN MOTHER MAY <u>NOT</u> KNOW BEST: THE LAUNCH OF STUBHUB.COM!

"It was definitely something that my mother was *not* thrilled about," recalls Jeff Fluhr.[1]

The "it" Fluhr's mother was concerned about was him dropping out of the Stanford University MBA program his first year there.

Plan for the Start-up

Fluhr and his classmate, Eric Baker, had entered a class competition for the best business plan. Their idea: "Need A Ticket.com," a centralized website where people owning tickets to sporting events or concerts could auction them off. The idea seemed so great that Fluhr dropped out of graduate school to start the new business. But, as with most marketing or business plans for start-ups, actually turning the plan into reality wasn't as easy as the two entrepreneurs expected.

Fluhr and Baker launched their ticket-selling business in late 2000, right after the dot-com crash, so they had trouble raising money from investors. Then the 9/11 terrorist attacks caused many fans to stop attending entertainment events involving large crowds. StubHub worked its way to profitability when people started buying tickets for these events and when it changed its basic marketing approach. Over the years it has raised $15 million from new venture investors.[2]

The original business plan focused on selling tickets on other websites such as Microsoft's MSN and then having StubHub split the revenues from the resold tickets. In 2003, the approach changed to what it is today: Direct buyers and sellers to the StubHub website that lets sellers sell their tickets at a fixed price, a price that declines as the date of the event approaches, or by auction.

How StubHub Works Now

The StubHub pricing formula is very straightforward. Suppose you want to sell a ticket for $100. The buyer pays $110 for the ticket, the extra $10 being the 10 percent commission to StubHub. It, in turn, pays you $85 for the ticket you sold, factoring in its $15 or 15 percent commission to you, the seller.[3] So StubHub makes $25 on the sale.

Internet websites have revolutionized pricing and efficiently connecting buyers and sellers—from eBay and Amazon.com to travel sites like Priceline.com and Expedia. In the ticket reselling business, StubHub competes with giants like eBay (a former partner and its biggest competitor), Ticketmaster, and smaller competitors such as Craigslist,

TicketsNow, and Razor Gator. It is estimated that today more than half of all tickets to major events are purchased online and about one-fourth of all seats to events like rock concerts are resold.[4]

Apparently by January 2007, eBay had seen enough of StubHub's competition and bought it for $310 million. Meanwhile, founder Eric Baker had left StubHub after several years—only to raise funding to launch a similar company, Viagogo, to go after the European ticket reselling market.[5]

StubHub: Who Benefits and How?

StubHub benefits from the revenues it obtains from both the sellers and buyers of the tickets it handles. The benefits to people selling and buying tickets to popular events from StubHub are also quite clear: By connecting sellers and buyers, each is able to benefit from the transaction—either by gaining money or the ticket.

But what about the benefits to the sports team, concert, or theater involved? For tickets that are resold, the sponsors of these events get no extra revenue because the tickets have already been sold to the initial buyer. But with over half of tickets to major events sold online, StubHub's website can help generate *extra ticket sales* for the original sponsors. This is why Stub-Hub now has formal relationships not only with National Football League and National Basketball Association teams but also with many sports programs at major universities such as Alabama, Southern California, Stanford, Kansas State, and Purdue.[6]

Pricing decisions involve carefully assessing consumer demand, revenues, fixed costs, and variable costs before setting a final price. If the answers were easy, hundreds of failed dot-com firms with brilliant ideas, technologies, and marketing plans would still be going strong today. Before reading further, take the price quiz in Figure 13–1 and then compare your answers to those given throughout the chapter.

Among all marketing and operations factors in a business firm, price is unique. It is the place where all other business decisions come together. The price must be "right"—in the sense that customers must be willing to pay it and it must generate enough sales dollars to pay for the cost of developing, producing, and marketing the product *and* earn a profit for the company. Small changes in price can have big effects on both the number of units sold and company profit. In fact, among 1,000 large U.S. companies, research

FIGURE 13–1

Quick-take quiz on price: Answers that are part numbers, part good judgment

Answer the questions below. The correct answers are given later in the chapter.

1. What do Airbus and Boeing forecast the total market to be for commercial jetliners seating at least 100 passengers over the next two decades? (*a*) $950 million. (*b*) $10.8 billion, (*c*) $378 billion, (*d*) $2.7 trillion.
2. Which of these products has a U.S. demand that is least sensitive to price increases? (*a*) clothing, (*b*) gasoline, (*c*) vacation airline tickets, (*d*) cars.
3. In automating a manufacturing plant, which of these would definitely increase in the short run? (*a*) price, (*b*) fixed cost, (*c*) total revenue, (*d*) variable cost.

shows that a 1 percent price increase translates to a 12 percent increase in profitability, other factors remaining the same.[7]

Welcome to the fascinating—and intense—world of pricing, where many forces come together in the price buyers are asked to pay. This chapter covers important factors used in setting prices.

NATURE AND IMPORTANCE OF PRICE

The price paid for goods and services goes by many names. You pay *tuition* for your education, *rent* for an apartment, *interest* on a bank credit card, and a *premium* for car insurance. Your dentist or physician charges you a *fee*, a professional or social organization charges *dues*, and airlines charge a *fare*. In business, an executive is given a *salary*, a salesperson receives a *commission*, and a worker is paid a *wage*. And what you pay for clothes or a haircut is termed a *price*.

What Is a Price?

LO1

These examples highlight the many varied ways that price plays a part in our daily lives. From a marketing viewpoint, **price** is the money or other considerations (including other goods and services) exchanged for the ownership or use of a good or service. Recently, Wilkinson Sword exchanged some of its knives for advertising used to promote its razor blades. This practice of exchanging goods and services for other goods and services rather than for money is called **barter**. These transactions account for billions of dollars annually in domestic and international trade.

For most products, money is exchanged. However, the amount paid is not always the same as the list, or quoted, price because of discounts, allowances, and extra fees. While discounts, allowances, and rebates make the effective price lower, other marketing tactics raise the real price. One new 21st century pricing tactic is to use "special fees" and "surcharges." This practice is driven by consumers' zeal for low prices combined with the ease of making price comparisons on the Internet. Buyers are more willing to pay extra fees than a higher list price, so sellers use add-on charges as a way of having the consumer pay more without raising the list price.[8]

All these factors that increase or decrease the price are put together in a "price equation," which is shown for several different products in Figure 13–2 on the next page. They are a key consideration when you buy your next car. As an extreme example, suppose you decide you want to buy a 2007 Bugatti Veyron, the world's fastest production car, that can move you from 0 to 62 mph in 2.5 seconds with a top speed of 253 mph. The Veyron has a list price of $1.4 million, and only 300 are expected to be crafted. However, if you put $500,000 down now and finance the balance over the next year, you will receive a rebate of $100,000 off the list price. For your 2000 Honda Civic DX four-door sedan that has 80,000 miles and is in fair condition, you are given a trade-in allowance of $4,350, which is the *Kelley Blue Book* (www.kbb.com) trade-in value of your car.

In addition, you will have to pay sales tax of $98,350 (7 percent), auto registration fees of $1,000 to the state, and a $5,000 destination charge to ship the car from Europe. Finally, your total finance charge is $41,974 based on an annual interest rate of 8.5 percent.

In deciding whether to buy a new $1.4 million Bugatti Veyron, consider incentives, allowances, and extra fees—as well as the original list price!

ITEM PURCHASED	PRICE EQUATION			
	PRICE	= LIST PRICE	INCENTIVES AND – ALLOWANCES	+ EXTRA FEES
New car bought by an individual	Final price	= List price	– Rebate Cash discount Old car trade-in	+ Financing charges Special accessories Destination charges
Term in college bought by a student	Tuition	= Published tuition	– Scholarship Other financial aid Discounts for number of credits taken	+ Special activity fees
Merchandise bought from a wholesaler by a retailer	Invoice price	= List price	– Quantity discount Cash discount Seasonal discount Functional or trade discount	+ Penalty for late payment

FIGURE 13–2

The "price" a buyer pays can take different names, depending on what is purchased.

Applying the price equation (as shown in Figure 13–2) to your purchase, your final price is:

Final price = List price − (Incentives + Allowances) + Extra fees

= $1,400,000 − ($100,000 + $4,350) + ($98,350 + $1,000 + $5,000 + $41,974)

= $1,441,974

Your monthly payment for the one-year loan of $900,000 is $78,498.[9] Are you still interested? Perhaps not. But for the next car you buy, pay attention to the factors beyond the "list price."

Price as an Indicator of Value

From a consumer's standpoint, price is often used to indicate value when it is compared with the perceived benefits such as quality, durability, and so on of a product or service. Specifically, **value** is the ratio of perceived benefits to price, or[10]

$$\text{Value} = \frac{\text{Perceived benefits}}{\text{Price}}$$

This relationship shows that for a given price, as perceived benefits increase, value increases. For example, if you're used to paying $9.99 for a medium pizza, wouldn't a large pizza at the same price be more valuable? Conversely, for a given price, value decreases when perceived benefits decrease.

Creative marketers engage in **value-pricing**, the practice of simultaneously increasing product and service benefits while maintaining or decreasing price. For some products, price influences consumers' perception of overall quality and ultimately its value to consumers.[11] In a survey of home furnishing buyers, 84 percent agreed with the statement: "The higher the price, the higher the quality."[12] For example, Kohler introduced a walk-in bathtub that is safer for children and the elderly. Although priced higher than conventional step-in bathtubs, it has proven very successful because buyers are willing to pay more for what they perceive as the value of the extra safety.

Here "value" involves the judgment by a consumer of the worth and desirability of a product or service relative to substitutes that satisfy the same need.

For how a McDonald's "Value Meal" is an example of applying a "value pricing" strategy, see the text.

In this instance a "reference value" emerges, which involves comparing the costs and benefits of substitute items. The value of "supersizing" at fast-food restaurants comes from getting more bang for your buck—generally, a larger quantity for the same or a lower price. For example, if you order a "Value Meal" at McDonald's, the price you pay is less than if you bought each item in the meal separately.

Price in the Marketing Mix

Pricing is a critical decision made by a marketing executive because price has a direct effect on a firm's profits. This is apparent from a firm's **profit equation**:

$$Profit = Total\ revenue - Total\ cost$$
$$= (Unit\ price \times Quantity\ sold) - (Fixed\ cost + Variable\ cost)$$

What makes this relationship even more complicated is that price affects the quantity sold, as illustrated with demand curves later in this chapter. Furthermore, since the quantity sold usually affects a firm's costs because of efficiency of production, price also indirectly affects costs. Thus, pricing decisions influence both total revenue (sales) and total cost, which makes pricing one of the most important decisions marketing executives face.

The importance of price in the marketing mix necessitates an understanding of six major steps in the process organizations go through in setting prices (Figure 13–3):

1. Identify pricing objectives and constraints.
2. Estimate demand and revenue.
3. Determine cost, volume, and profit relationships.
4. Select an approximate price level.
5. Set list or quoted price.
6. Make special adjustments to list or quoted price.

The first three steps are covered in this chapter and the last three in Chapter 14.

FIGURE 13–3

The six steps in setting price. The first three steps are covered in this chapter and the last three steps in Chapter 14.

Step 1	Step 2	Step 3	Step 4	Step 5	Step 6
Identify pricing objectives and constraints • Objectives like profit, market share, and survival • Constraints like demand for product class and brand, newness, costs, and competition	**Estimate demand and revenue** • Demand estimation • Sales revenue estimation • Price elasticity estimation	**Determine cost, volume, and profit relationships** • Cost estimation • Marginal analysis, in relation to profit • Break-even analysis, in relation to profit	Select an approximate price level	Set list or quoted price	Make special adjustments to list or quoted price

← Chapter 13 →   ← Chapter 14 →

STEP 1: IDENTIFY PRICING OBJECTIVES AND CONSTRAINTS

With such a variety of alternative pricing strategies available, a marketing manager must consider the pricing objectives and constraints that will narrow the range of choices. While pricing objectives frequently reflect corporate goals, pricing constraints often relate to conditions existing in the marketplace.

Identifying Pricing Objectives

Pricing objectives involve specifying the role of price in an organization's marketing and strategic plans. To the extent possible, these pricing objectives are carried to lower levels in the organization, such as in setting objectives for marketing managers responsible for an individual brand. These objectives may change depending on the financial position of the company as a whole, the success of its products, or the segments in which it is doing business. H. J. Heinz, for example, has specific pricing objectives for its Heinz Ketchup brand that vary by country. Chapter 2 discussed seven broad objectives that an organization may pursue, which tie in directly to the organization's pricing policies.

Profit   Three different objectives relate to a firm's profit, which is often measured in terms of return on investment (ROI) or return on assets (ROA). These objectives have different implications for pricing strategy. One objective is *managing for long-run profits,* in which a company—such as many Japanese car or TV set manufacturers—gives up immediate profit in exchange for achieving a higher market share by developing quality products to penetrate competitive markets over the long term. Products are priced relatively low compared to their cost to develop, but the firm expects to make greater profits later because of its high market share.

A *maximizing current profit* objective, such as for a quarter or year, is common in many firms because the targets can be set and performance measured quickly. American firms are sometimes criticized for this short-run orientation. As noted earlier, a *target return* objective occurs when a firm sets a profit goal (such as 20 percent for pretax ROI), usually determined by its board of directors.

A couple does some furniture shopping in an IKEA store in China. For what "Flattening the World" is coming to mean for global firms like Sweden's IKEA, see the text and Marketing Matters box.

Marketing Matters > > > > > > > > technology

How Flattening the World Affects Both Revenues and Costs: Infosys Technologies, Ltd., Intel, China Mobile, IKEA . . . and You!

The New York Times writer Tom Friedman says he got the idea for the title of his award-winning book *The World Is Flat* on a trip to Bangalore, India, a place he describes as "India's Silicon Valley."

Columbus sailed *west* from Europe to try to find India and the sources of wealth in his day—precious metals, silks, and spices. Friedman was flying *east* to India from New York to try to learn more about the key sources of wealth of our day—computer software algorithms, information technology, call centers, and efficient manufacturing.

In visiting Infosys Technologies, Ltd., 40 minutes from Bangalore, Friedman found himself on a park-like campus with manicured lawns and many glass-and-steel buildings. Nandan Nilekani, chief executive officer of Infosys, told Freidman that outsourcing was just one dimension of fundamental changes in world business. Nilekani went on to explain that broadband connectivity, the explosion of software and search engines, and lower-priced computers have made it easy for anyone to do remote development. These elements today have created a platform where intellectual work can be delivered from anywhere, which often lowers costs.

Nilekani looked at Friedman and summed up his comments with, "Tom, the playing field is being leveled."

Hundreds of global companies are looking to developing economies not only as sources of trained personnel in information technology and outsourced manufacturing, but also to generate new revenues from sales of their products and services. Some examples:

- Intel has trained more than 600,000 teachers in India and 700,000 in China and placed PCs in 6,000 villages in India.
- China Mobile Ltd. with over 300 million customers is the world's largest cell phone system and is adding 5 million new customers a month.
- Swedish retailer IKEA, which has sold 32 million Billy bookcases since 1978, now carries its contemporary designs in 226 stores in Europe, Asia, the United States, and Australia and uses suppliers from around the world.

Maybe—just maybe—the world *is* flattening! And students reading these words must prepare themselves for future jobs on this leveled playing field.

To generate profits in today's global marketplace, international firms look around the world to find both new markets to increase revenues and suppliers whose efficiencies and lower hourly wages can reduce manufacturing and other costs. The Marketing Matters box describes how the "world is flattening," or how the global "playing field is being leveled," as the chief executive officer of India's Infosys Technologies, Ltd., says.[13]

IKEA, the huge Swedish retailer, understands this. It is *both* opening new stores *and* contracting with furniture manufacturers around the world. To compete in China, IKEA has slashed prices to appeal to consumers in the country's growing middle class. The strategy seems to be working: IKEA'S new store in Beijing—opened in 2006—has floor space the size of eight football fields and forecasts 6 million visitors annually.

Sales Given that a firm's profit is high enough for it to remain in business, an objective may be to increase sales revenue, which will in turn lead to increases in market share and profit. Objectives related to sales revenue or unit sales have the advantage of being translated more easily into meaningful targets for marketing managers responsible for a product line or brand than profit objectives. However, cutting price on one product in a firm's line may increase its sales revenue but reduce those of related products.

Market Share Market share is the ratio of the firm's sales revenues or unit sales to those of the industry (competitors plus the firm itself). Companies often pursue a market share objective when industry sales are relatively flat or declining. In the late 1990s, Boeing cut prices drastically to try to maintain its 60 percent market share and encountered huge losses. Although increased market share is a primary goal of some firms, others see it as a means to other ends: increasing sales and profits.

Unit Volume Many firms use *unit volume,* the quantity produced or sold, as a pricing objective. These firms often sell multiple products at very different prices and need to match the unit volume demanded by customers with price and production capacity. Using unit volume as an objective can be counterproductive if a volume objective is achieved, say, by drastic price cutting that drives down profit.

Survival In some instances, profits, sales, and market share are less important objectives of the firm than mere survival. Specialty-toy retailers increasingly are facing survival problems because they can't match price cuts by big discount retailers like Wal-Mart and Target, the reason FAO Schwartz filed for bankruptcy.

Social Responsibility A firm may forgo higher profit on sales and follow a pricing objective that recognizes its obligations to customers and society in general. Medtronics followed this pricing policy when it introduced the world's first heart pacemaker. A critical social responsibility issue today is drug pricing—setting a price low enough to make the drug affordable by consumers needing it but high enough for drug companies to cover research costs and make a profit.[14]

Identifying Pricing Constraints

Factors that limit the range of prices a firm may set are **pricing constraints**. Consumer demand for the product clearly affects the price that can be charged. Other constraints on price vary from factors within the organization to competitive factors outside the organization. Legal and regulatory constraints on pricing are discussed in Chapter 14.

Demand for the Product Class, Product, and Brand The number of potential buyers for the product class (cars), product (sports cars), and brand (Bugatti Veyron) clearly affects the price a seller can charge. So does whether the item is a luxury—like a Veyron—or a necessity—like bread and a roof over your head. Generally, the greater the demand for a product, the higher the price that can be set. The nature of demand is discussed later in the chapter.

Newness of the Product: Stage in the Product Life Cycle The newer a product and the earlier it is in its life cycle, the higher is the price that can usually be charged. Willing to spend up to $10,000 for a new high definition (HD) Panasonic plasma TV? The high initial price is possible because of patents and limited competition early in its product life cycle. By the time you read this, the price will probably be much lower.

Sometimes—when nostalgia or fad factors come into play—prices may rise later in the product's life cycle. As described in the Going Online box, collectibles such as a 1952 Mickey Mantle baseball card or old sneakers can experience skyrocketing

The text describes factors that affect a product's price. And you can check the Going Online box to see if those old Beanie Babies in your attic or a recent Ichiro Suzuki bobble-head doll have value.

prices.[15] But they can take a nosedive too. Publishing competitive prices on the Internet for the same or similar brands of products has revolutionized access to price comparisons for both collectors and buyers of more traditional products.[16]

Single Product versus a Product Line   When Sony introduced its Walkman CD player, it was not only unique and in the introductory stage of its product life cycle but also the *only* CD player Sony sold, so the firm had great latitude in setting a price. Now, with a wide range of Sony CD products and technologies, the price of individual models has to be consistent with the others based on features provided, and meaningful price differentials must communicate value to consumers.

Cost of Producing and Marketing the Product   In the long run, a firm's price must cover all the costs of producing and marketing a product. If the price doesn't cover these costs, the firm will fail; so in the long run, a firm's costs set a floor under its price. In the 1990s, no-frills airlines like Southwest, JetBlue, and AirTran set low airfares, forcing large competing U.S. airlines to cut costs and lower ticket prices. But times change. So in 2006, rising fuel costs and introducing more high-end perks like their upscale competitors offered caused these same no-frills airlines to raise ticket prices.[17]

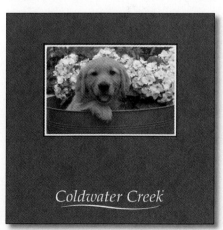

Setting hundreds of prices that will be valid for the life of a catalog involves many risky decisions.

Cost of Changing Prices and Time Period They Apply   If Scandinavian Airlines asks General Electric (GE) to provide spare jet engines to power the new Boeing 737 it just bought, GE can easily set a new price for the engines to reflect its latest information since only one buyer has to be informed. But if Coldwater Creek decides that sweater prices are too low in its catalogs after thousands of catalogs have been mailed to customers, it has a big problem, so it must consider the cost of changing prices and the time period for which they apply in developing the price list for its catalog items. A recent study of four supermarket chains found the average annual cost of these price changes was $105,887, which represents 0.70 percent of revenues and an astounding 35.2 percent of net margins.[18] In actual practice, research indicates that most firms change the prices of their major products once a year. But on a website, prices can change from minute to minute.[19]

Type of Competitive Market The seller's price is constrained by the type of market in which it competes. Economists generally delineate four types of competitive markets. From most competitive to least competitive, these are pure competition, monopolistic competition, oligopoly, and pure monopoly. Figure 13–4 shows that the type of competition dramatically influences the range of price competition and, in turn, the nature of product differentiation and extent of advertising. A firm must recognize the general type of competitive market it is in to understand the range of both its price and nonprice strategies. Examples of how prices can be affected by the four competitive situations:

- *Pure competition.* Hundreds of local grain elevators sell corn whose price per bushel is set by the marketplace. Within strains, the corn is identical, so advertising only informs buyers that the seller's corn is available.
- *Monopolistic competition.* Dozens of regional, private brands of peanut butter compete with national brands like Skippy and Jif. Both price competition (regional, private brands being lower than national brands) and nonprice competition (product features and advertising) exist.
- *Oligopoly.* The few sellers of aluminum (Reynolds, Alcoa) or large jetliners (Boeing, Airbus) try to avoid price competition because it can lead to disastrous price wars in which all lose money. Yet firms in such industries stay aware of a competitor's price cuts or increases and may follow suit. The products can be undifferentiated (aluminum) or differentiated (large jetliners), and informative advertising that avoids head-to-head price competition is used.[20] In video games the Microsoft Xbox 360's oligopolistic competition with Sony and Nintendo is so severe that it was losing $126 on every unit sold at its $399 introductory price.[21]
- *Pure monopoly.* In 1994, Johnson & Johnson (J&J) revolutionized the treatment of coronary heart diseases by introducing the stent—a tiny mesh tube "spring" that props open clogged arteries. Initially a monopoly, J&J stuck with its early $1,595 price and achieved $1 billion in sales and 91 percent market share by the end of 1996. But its reluctance to give price reductions for large-volume purchases to hospitals antagonized them. When competitors introduced an improved stent

FIGURE 13–4

Pricing, product, and advertising strategies available to firms in four types of competitive markets

TYPE OF COMPETITIVE MARKET

STRATEGIES AVAILABLE	PURE COMPETITION (Many sellers who follow the market price for identical, commodity products)	MONOPOLISTIC COMPETITION (Many sellers who compete on nonprice factors)	OLIGOPOLY (Few sellers who are sensitive to each other's prices)	PURE MONOPOLY (One seller who sets the price for a unique product)
Extent of price competition	Almost none: market sets price	Some: compete over range of prices	Some: price leader or follower of competitors	None: sole seller sets price
Extent of product differentiation	None: products are identical	Some: differentiate products from competitors	Various: depends on industry	None: no other producers
Extent of advertising	Little: purpose is to inform prospects that seller's products are available	Much: purpose is to differentiate firm's products from competitors	Some: purpose is to inform but avoid price competition	Little: purpose is to increase demand for product class

at lower prices, J&J's market share plummeted to 8 percent two years later.[22] Microsoft is another example. Its competitors and customers have argued in court that it engaged in illegal acts that reduced competition and increased prices.[23]

Competitors' Prices A firm must know or anticipate what specific price its present and potential competitors are charging now or will charge. In 2006, U.S. auto manufacturers wanted to raise prices but seldom did because of competitors' price "deals," such as thousands of dollars of cash rebates or up to $6,000 in "free gas."[24]

---

learning review

1. What factors impact the list price to determine the final price?

2. What is the difference between pricing objectives and pricing constraints?

3. How does the type of competitive market a firm is in affect its range in setting price?

STEP 2: ESTIMATE DEMAND AND REVENUE

Basic to setting a product's price is the extent of customer demand for it. Marketing executives must also translate this estimate of customer demand into estimates of revenues the firm expects to receive.

Fundamentals of Estimating Demand

How much money would you pay for your favorite magazine? If the price kept going up, at some point you would probably quit buying it. Conversely, if the price kept going down, you might eventually decide not only to keep buying your magazine but also to get your friend a subscription too. The lower the price, the higher the demand. The publisher wants to sell more magazines, but will it sell enough additional copies to make up for the lower price per copy? Here's how one firm decided to find out.

For the results of a creative pricing experiment run by *Newsweek* magazine, see the text.

Newsweek conducted a pricing experiment at newsstands in 11 cities throughout the United States. At that time, Houston newsstand buyers paid $2.25, while in Fort Worth, New York, Los Angeles, and Atlanta they paid the regular $2.00 price. In San Diego, the price was $1.50, while in Minneapolis–St. Paul, New Orleans, and Detroit it was only $1.00. By comparison, the regular newsstand price for *Time* and *U.S. News & World Report*, *Newsweek*'s competitors, was $1.95. Why did *Newsweek* conduct the experiment? According to a *Newsweek* executive, "We want to figure out what the demand curve for our magazine at the newsstand is."[25]

The Demand Curve A **demand curve** is a graph relating the quantity sold and price, which shows the maximum number of units that will be sold at a given price. Demand curve D_1 in Figure 13–5A on the next page. shows the newsstand demand for *Newsweek* under the existing conditions. Note that as price falls, more people decide to buy and unit sales increase. But price is not the complete story in estimating demand. Economists emphasize three other key factors:

1. *Consumer tastes.* As we saw in Chapter 3, these depend on many factors such as demographics, culture, and technology. Because consumer tastes can change quickly, up-to-date marketing research is essential.

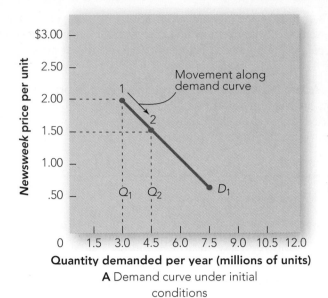

A Demand curve under initial conditions

B Shift the demand curve with more favorable conditions

FIGURE 13–5

Demand curves for *Newsweek* showing the effect on annual sales (quantity demanded per year) by a change in price caused by (A) a movement along the demand curve and (B) a shift of the demand curve.

2. *Price and availability of similar products.* The laws of demand work for one's competitors, too. If the price of *Time* magazine falls, more people will buy it. That then means fewer people will buy *Newsweek. Time* is considered by economists to be a substitute for *Newsweek.* Online magazines are also a substitute, one whose availability has increased tremendously in recent years. The point to remember is, as the price of substitutes falls or their availability increases, the demand for a product (*Newsweek,* in this case) will fall.

3. *Consumer income.* In general, as real consumer income (allowing for inflation) increases, demand for a product also increases.

The first two factors influence what consumers *want* to buy, and the third affects what they *can* buy. Along with price, these are often called **demand factors,** or factors that determine consumers' willingness and ability to pay for goods and services. As discussed earlier in Chapters 8 and 10, it is often very difficult to estimate demand for new products, especially because consumer likes and dislikes are often so difficult to read clearly. For example, Campbell Soup spent seven years and $55 million on a supersecret project to produce a line of Intelligent Quisine (IQ) food products. The company expected that its line of 41 breakfasts, lunches, dinners, and snacks would be the first foods "scientifically proven to lower high levels of cholesterol, blood sugar, and blood pressure."[26] After 15 months in an Ohio test market, Campbell Soup yanked the entire IQ line when it fell far short of expectations because customers found the line too pricey and lacking in variety.

Movement Along versus Shift of a Demand Curve Demand curve D_1 in Figure 13–5A shows that as the price of *Newsweek* is lowered from $2.00 to $1.50 an issue, the quantity demanded increases from 3.0 million (Q_1) to 4.5 million (Q_2) units per year. This is an example of a *movement along a demand curve* and assumes that other factors (consumer tastes, price and availability of substitutes, and consumer income) remain unchanged.

What if some of these factors do change? For example, if advertising causes more people to want *Newsweek,* newsstand distribution is increased; or if consumer incomes rise, then the demand for all magazines, including *Newsweek,* increases. Now the initial demand curve, D_1 (the blue line in Figure 13–5B), no longer represents the demand; instead, a new curve, D_2, must be drawn. D_2 (the red line in Figure 13–5B) represents the new demand for *Newsweek.* Economists call this a *shift in the demand curve*—in this case, a shift to the right, from D_1 to D_2. This increased

FIGURE 13–6

Fundamental concepts about "revenues," which are the monies received from selling the product: Total revenue, average revenue, and marginal revenue.

Total revenue (TR) is the total money received from the sale of a product. If

$\quad$ TR = Total revenue
$\quad\ $ P = Unit price of the product
$\quad\ $ Q = Quantity of the product sold

Then

$\quad$ TR = P $\times$ Q

Average revenue (AR) is the average amount of money received for selling one unit of a product, or simply the price of that unit. Average revenue is the total revenue divided by the quantity sold:

$$AR = \frac{TR}{Q} = P$$

Marginal revenue (MR) is the change in total revenue that results from producing and marketing one additional unit:

$$MR = \frac{\text{Change in TR}}{\text{1 unit increase in Q}} = \frac{\Delta TR}{\Delta Q} = \text{slope of TR curve}$$

demand means that more *Newsweek* magazines are wanted for a given price: At a price of $2.00, the demand is 6 million units per year (Q_3) on D_2 rather than 3 million units per year (Q_1) on D_1.

Fundamentals of Estimating Revenue

While economists may talk about "demand curves," marketing executives are more likely to speak in terms of "revenues generated," which are the monies received by the firm for selling its products. Demand curves lead directly to three related revenue concepts critical to pricing decisions: **total revenue (TR), average revenue (AR),** and **marginal revenue (MR)** (Figure 13–6).

Demand Curves and Revenue Figure 13–7A on the next page again shows the demand curve for *Newsweek,* but it is now extended to intersect both the price and quantity axes. The demand curve shows that as price is changed, the quantity of *Newsweek* magazines sold throughout the United States changes. This relationship holds whether the price is increased from $2.50 to $3.00 on the demand curve or is reduced from $1 to $0 on the curve. In the former case the market demands no *Newsweek* magazines, whereas in the latter case 9 million could be given away at $0 per unit.

It is likely that if *Newsweek* was given away, more than 9 million would be demanded. This fact illustrates two important points. First, it can be dangerous to extend a demand curve beyond the range of prices for which it really applies. Second, most demand curves are rounded (or convex) to the origin, thereby avoiding an unrealistic picture of what demand looks like when a straight-line curve intersects either the price axis or the quantity axis.

Figure 13–7B shows the total revenue curve for *Newsweek* calculated from the demand curve shown in Figure 13–7A. The total revenue curve is developed by simply multiplying the unit price times the quantity for each of the points on the demand curve. Total revenue starts at $0 (point A), reaches a maximum of $6,750,000 at point D, and returns to $0 at point G. This shows that as price is reduced in the A-to-D segment of the curve, total revenue is increased. However, cutting price in the D-to-G segment results in a decline in total revenue.

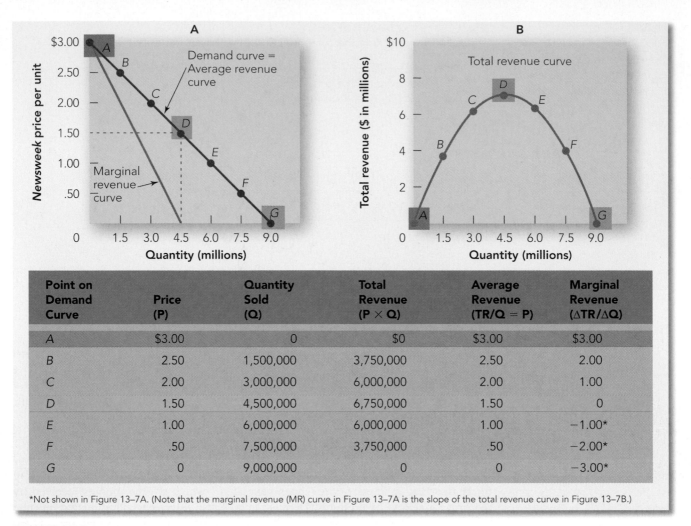

Point on Demand Curve	Price (P)	Quantity Sold (Q)	Total Revenue (P × Q)	Average Revenue (TR/Q = P)	Marginal Revenue (ΔTR/ΔQ)
A	$3.00	0	$0	$3.00	$3.00
B	2.50	1,500,000	3,750,000	2.50	2.00
C	2.00	3,000,000	6,000,000	2.00	1.00
D	1.50	4,500,000	6,750,000	1.50	0
E	1.00	6,000,000	6,000,000	1.00	−1.00*
F	.50	7,500,000	3,750,000	.50	−2.00*
G	0	9,000,000	0	0	−3.00*

*Not shown in Figure 13–7A. (Note that the marginal revenue (MR) curve in Figure 13–7A is the slope of the total revenue curve in Figure 13–7B.)

FIGURE 13–7

How *Newsweek*'s downward-sloping demand curve affects its total, average, and marginal revenues.

Marginal revenue, which is the slope of the total revenue curve, is positive but decreasing when the price lies in the range from $3 to above $1.50 per unit. Below $1.50 per unit, though, marginal revenue is actually negative, so the extra quantity of magazines sold is more than offset by the decrease in the price per unit.

For any downward-sloping, straight-line demand curve, the marginal revenue curve always falls at a rate twice as fast as the demand curve. As shown in Figure 13–7A, the marginal revenue becomes $0 per unit at a quantity sold of 4.5 million units—the very point at which total revenue is maximum (see Figure 13–7B). A rational marketing manager would never operate in the region of the demand curve in which marginal revenue is negative. This means that in Figure 13–7A this manager would set prices only in the *A*-to-*D* segment of the demand curve. Also, when market share falls, the easy answer is to cut price, often with devastating results: A 1 percent price cut in the food and drug industry results in a 24 percent decline in profits, other factors being equal.[27]

What price did *Newsweek* select after conducting its experiment? It kept the price at $2.00. However, through expanded newsstand distribution and more aggressive advertising, *Newsweek* was later able to shift its demand curve to the right and charge a price of $2.50 without affecting its newsstand volume.

Does forecasting future demand and revenue sound easy? Study the accompanying Marketing Matters box to understand the special difficulties that Airbus and Boeing face trying to forecast the demand and revenue for their state-of-the-art commercial jetliners years before they roll off the production line.[28]

The Airbus versus Boeing Face-Off—How Many Can We Sell and at What Price . . . in a $2.7 Trillion Market?

Boeing and Airbus—fierce competitors and the only manufacturers of huge commercial jetliners today—rarely agree. Their aircraft have different designs, different appeals. But they do agree on one thing.

They agree that the size of the market for commercial jetliners over the next two decades will be $2.7 trillion! That's trillion—as in 1,000 billion (See question 1, Figure 13–1)—and represents about 25,000 new aircraft seating 100 or more passengers!

The Products

Their main entrants to capture shares of this huge market are Boeing's 787 Dreamliner (see photo) and Airbus's A350XWB. Boeing's jetliner will seat 210 to 330 passengers with the Airbus design seating 275 to 350. Each will fly about 8,500 nautical miles slightly under the speed of sound with quiet, fuel-efficient engines. The Boeing Dreamliner starts flying in 2008; the Airbus A350XWB in 2013.

Marketing and Pricing

To help airline customers simplify their buying decisions, both Airbus and Boeing have huge showrooms. Here potential customers can consider different seats, carpeting, entertainment options, and electronically controlled windows. This also discourages airlines from "over-customization," which can add extra costs and even delay deliveries as much as two years because of special wiring needs.

And the prices? About $300 million each—plus or minus a few million—depending on customization decisions and special quantity discounts.

Demand

How many will be sold? By late 2007 Boeing had 710 orders for its 787 Dreamliner and Airbus had 228 orders for its A350XWB, only a fraction of what they need to break even. Time will tell whether Boeing or Airbus read their customers' needs better.

LO4

Price Elasticity of Demand With a downward-sloping demand curve, marketing managers are especially interested in how sensitive consumer demand and the firm's revenues are to changes in the product's price. This can be conveniently measured by **price elasticity of demand**, or the percentage change in quantity demanded relative to a percentage change in price. Price elasticity of demand (E) is expressed as follows:

$$\text{Price elasticity of demand} = E = \frac{\text{Percentage change in quantity demanded}}{\text{Percentage change in price}}$$

Because quantity demanded usually decreases as price increases, price elasticity of demand is usually a negative number. However, for the sake of simplicity and by convention, elasticity figures are shown as positive numbers. Finally, price elasticity of demand assumes three forms: elastic demand, inelastic demand, and unitary demand.

Elastic demand exists when a 1 percent decrease in price produces more than a 1 percent increase in quantity demanded, thereby actually increasing sales revenue. This results in a price elasticity that is greater than 1 with elastic demand. In other words, a product with elastic demand is one in which a slight decrease in price results in a relatively large increase in demand or units sold. The reverse is also true; with elastic demand, a slight increase in price results in a relatively large decrease in demand. So marketers may cut price to increase consumer demand, the units sold, and total revenue for one of these products, depending on what competitors' prices are.

Inelastic demand exists when a 1 percent decrease in price produces less than a 1 percent increase in quantity demanded, thereby actually decreasing sales revenue.

Is clothing or gasoline more sensitive to price changes? For the answer, see the text and its discussion of price elasticity of demand.

This results in a price elasticity that is less than 1 with inelastic demand. So a product with inelastic demand means that slight increases or decreases in price will not significantly affect the demand, or units sold, for the product. The concern for marketers is that while lowering price will increase the quantity sold, revenues will actually fall. *Unitary demand* exists when the percentage change in price is identical to the percentage change in quantity demanded so that sales revenue remains the same. In this instance, price elasticity is equal to 1.

Price elasticity is important to marketing managers because of its relationship to total revenue, so it is important that marketing managers recognize that price elasticity of demand is not the same over all possible prices of a product. Figure 13–7B illustrates this point using the *Newsweek* demand curve shown in Figure 13–7A. As the price decreases from $2.50 to $2.00, total revenue increases, indicating an elastic demand. However, when the price decreases from $1.00 to 50 cents, total revenue declines, indicating an inelastic demand. Unitary demand elasticity exists at a price of $1.50.

Decisions Involving Price Elasticity The price elasticity of CDs is the reason that Vivendi Universal in 2003 ran a series of test markets across the United States to find what it calls the maximum pricing "sweet spot" among shoppers. The ideal retail price for CDs was found to be $12.98. To implement this pricing structure, Vivendi cut the top wholesale price it charges retailers from $12.02 to $9.09, which should lead to retail price reductions up to 32 percent. Two other factors probably influenced Vivendi's pricing decision: (1) the widespread online music piracy and (2) the price cuts in DVDs several years earlier, which caused people to start buying DVDs rather than renting them and to discover they are sometimes cheaper than buying CDs.[29]

Price elasticity of demand is determined by a number of factors. First, the more substitutes a product or service has, the more likely it is to be price elastic. For example, a new sweater, shirt, or blouse has many possible substitutes and is price elastic, but gasoline has almost no substitutes and is price inelastic. In fact, with the American love affair with cars and driving, we are surprisingly insensitive to a price increase in gasoline: A recent study showed a 10 percent increase in price results in only a 0.6 percent decrease in gasoline consumption (question 2, Figure 13–1).[30]

Second, products and services considered to be necessities are price inelastic, so open-heart surgery is price inelastic, whereas airline tickets for a vacation are price elastic.

Third, items that require a large cash outlay compared with a person's disposable income are price elastic. Accordingly, cars and yachts are price elastic; books tend to be price inelastic.

Because 12- to 17-year-olds often have limited "spending money," this group is very price elastic in its demand for cigarettes. As a result, many legislators recommend far higher excise taxes on cigarettes to increase their prices significantly with the goal of reducing teenage smoking. Thus, price elasticity is not only a relevant concept for marketing managers, but is also important for public policy affecting pricing practices.[31]

learning review

4. What is the difference between a movement along and a shift of a demand curve?

5. What is total revenue and how is it calculated?

6. What does it mean if a product has a price elasticity of demand that is greater than 1?

STEP 3: DETERMINE COST, VOLUME, AND PROFIT RELATIONSHIPS

Why is Pets.com only a memory while its sock puppet has found new life? For the answers, see the text and the Marketing Matters box.

LO5

While revenues are the monies received by the firm from selling its products or services to customers, costs or expenses are the monies the firm pays out to its employees and suppliers. Marketing managers often use marginal analysis and break-even analysis to relate revenues and costs, topics covered in this section.

The Importance of Controlling Costs

Understanding the role and behavior of costs is critical for all marketing decisions, particularly pricing decisions. Five cost concepts are important in pricing decisions: **total cost (TC), fixed cost (FC), variable cost (VC), unit variable cost (UVC)**, and **marginal cost (MC)** (Figure 13–8).

Many firms go bankrupt because their costs get out of control, causing their total costs to exceed their total revenues over an extended period. This is why sophisticated marketing managers make pricing decisions that balance both their revenues and costs. Ford has this very problem with its costs. In early 2007 Ford's fixed costs in producing its vehicles were $57 billion, about $2 billion more than those of General Motors. And its variable costs per vehicle posed an even more serious issue: $15,000 per vehicle compared to $12,000 per vehicle at General Motors.[32]

As described in the Marketing Matters box on the next page, travel dot-com firms have been more successful than their brick-and-mortar counterparts at least partly because of far lower fixed costs.[33] But the high fixed costs tied up in an airline's planes is the reason an airline is delighted to sell last-day tickets for half of the full fare because the revenue obtained by filling the seat far exceeds the low unit variable cost of the passenger's snack and baggage handling.

FIGURE 13–8

Fundamental concepts about "costs," which are the monies the firm pays out to its employees and suppliers: Total cost, fixed cost, variable cost, unit variable cost, and marginal cost.

Total cost (TC) is the total expense incurred by a firm in producing and marketing a product. Total cost is the sum of fixed cost and variable cost.

Fixed cost (FC) is the sum of the expenses of the firm that are stable and do not change with the quantity of a product that is produced and sold. Examples of fixed costs are rent on the building, executive salaries, and insurance.

Variable cost (VC) is the sum of the expenses of the firm that vary directly with the quantity of a product that is produced and sold. For example, as the quantity sold doubles, the variable cost doubles. Examples are the direct labor and direct materials used in producing the product and the sales commissions that are tied directly to the quantity sold. As mentioned above:

$$TC = FC + VC$$

Variable cost expressed on a per unit basis is called **unit variable cost (UVC),** or:

$$UVC = \frac{VC}{Q}$$

Marginal cost (MC) is the change in total cost that results from producing and marketing one additional unit of a product:

$$MC = \frac{\text{Change in TC}}{1 \text{ unit increase in Q}} = \frac{\Delta TC}{\Delta Q} = \text{slope of TC curve}$$

Marginal Analysis and Profit Maximization

A basic idea in business, economics, and indeed everyday life is **marginal analysis**, which is a continuing, concise trade-off of incremental costs against incremental revenues. In personal terms, marginal analysis means that people will continue to do something as long as the incremental return exceeds the incremental cost. This same idea holds true in marketing and pricing decisions. In this setting, marginal analysis means that as long as revenue received from the sale of an additional product (marginal revenue) is greater than the additional cost of producing and selling it (marginal cost), a firm will expand its output of that product.

Break-Even Analysis

LO6

Marketing managers often employ an approach that considers cost, volume, and profit relationships based on the profit equation. **Break-even analysis** is a technique that analyzes the relationship between total revenue and total cost to determine profitability at various levels of output. The **break-even point (BEP)** is the quantity at which total revenue and total cost are equal. Profit then comes from all units sold beyond the BEP. In terms of the definitions in Figure 13–8,

$$\text{BEP}_{\text{Quantity}} = \frac{\text{Fixed cost}}{\text{Unit price} - \text{Unit variable cost}} = \frac{\text{FC}}{\text{P} - \text{UVC}}$$

Calculating a Break-Even Point Consider a picture frame store. Suppose you wish to identify how many pictures you must sell to cover your fixed cost at a given price. Let's assume demand for your framed pictures is strong so the average price customers are willing to pay for each picture is $120. Also, suppose your fixed cost (FC) is $32,000 (for real estate taxes, interest on a bank loan, and other fixed expenses) and unit variable cost (UVC) for a picture is now $40 (for labor, glass, frame, and matting). Your break-even quantity ($BEP_{Quantity}$) is 400 pictures, as follows:

$$BEP_{Quantity} = \frac{\text{Fixed cost}}{\text{Unit price} - \text{Unit variable cost}} = \frac{FC}{P - UVC}$$
$$= \frac{\$32,000}{\$120 - \$40}$$
$$= 400 \text{ pictures}$$

Marginal analysis is central to the concept of maximizing profits. In Figure 13–9A, marginal revenue and marginal cost are graphed. Marginal cost starts out high at lower quantity levels, decreases to a minimum through production and marketing efficiencies, and then rises again due to the inefficiencies of overworked labor and equipment. Marginal revenue follows a downward slope. In Figure 13–9B, total cost and total revenue curves corresponding to the marginal cost and marginal revenue curves are graphed. Total cost initially rises as quantity increases but increases at the slowest rate at the quantity where marginal cost is lowest. The total revenue curve increases to a maximum and then starts to decline, as shown in Figure 13–9B.

The message of marginal analysis, then, is to operate up to the quantity and price level where marginal revenue equals marginal cost (MR = MC). Up to the output quantity at which MR = MC, each increase in total revenue resulting from selling one additional unit exceeds the increase in the total cost of producing and marketing that unit. Beyond the point at which MR = MC, however, the increase in total revenue from selling one more unit is less than the cost of producing and marketing that unit. At the quantity at which MR = MC, the total revenue curve lies farthest above the total cost curve because they are parallel, and profit is a maximum.

FIGURE 13–9

Profit is a maximum at the quantity at which marginal revenue and marginal cost are equal.

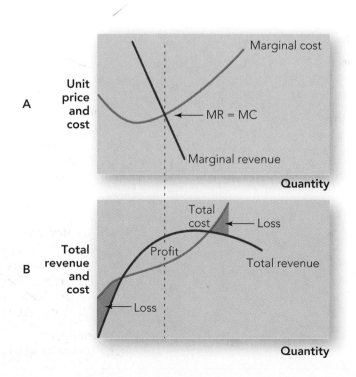

Quantity of Pictures Sold (Q)	Price Per Picture (P)	Total Revenue (TR) = (P × Q)	Unit Variable Cost (UVC)	Total Variable Cost (VC) = (UVC × Q)	Fixed Cost (FC)	Total Cost (TC) = (FC + VC)	Profit = (TR − TC)
0	$120	$0	$40	$0	$32,000	$32,000	−$32,000
200	120	24,000	40	8,000	32,000	40,000	−16,000
400	120	48,000	40	16,000	32,000	48,000	0
600	120	72,000	40	24,000	32,000	56,000	16,000
800	120	96,000	40	32,000	32,000	64,000	32,000
1,000	120	120,000	40	40,000	32,000	72,000	48,000
1,200	120	144,000	40	48,000	32,000	80,000	64,000

FIGURE 13–10

Calculating a break-even point for the picture frame store in the text example shows its profit starts at 400 framed pictures per year.

The row shaded in orange in Figure 13–10 shows that your break-even quantity at a price of $120 per picture is 400 pictures. At less than 400 pictures, your picture frame store incurs a loss, and at more than 400 pictures it makes a profit. Figure 13–10 also shows that if you could increase your annual picture sales to 1,000, your store would make a profit of $48,000—the row shaded in green in the figure.

Figure 13–11 shows a graphic presentation of the break-even analysis, called a **break-even chart**. It shows that total revenue and total cost intersect and are equal at a quantity of 400 pictures sold, which is the break-even point at which profit is exactly $0. You want to do better? If your frame store could increase the quantity sold annually to 1,000 pictures, the graph in Figure 13–11 shows you can earn an annual profit of $48,000, just as shown by the row shaded in green in Figure 13–10. Other financial aspects of a picture frame store appear in Appendix B.

FIGURE 13–11

Break-even analysis chart for a picture frame store shows the break-even point at 400 pictures.

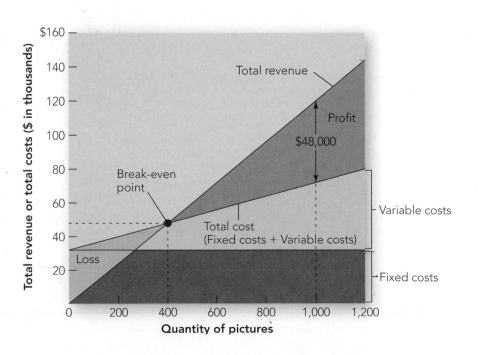

FIGURE 13–12

The cost trade-off: fixed versus variable costs

Executives in virtually every mass-production industry—from locomotives and cars to electronic calculators and breakfast cereals—are searching for ways to increase quality and reduce production costs to remain competitive in world markets. Increasingly they are substituting robots, automation, and computer-controlled manufacturing systems for blue- and white-collar workers.

To understand the implications of this on the break-even point (BEP) and profit, consider this example of an electronic calculator manufacturer:

Before Automation	After Automation
$P = \$10$ per unit	$P = \$10$ per unit
$FC = \$1,000,000$	$FC = \$4,000,000$
$UVC = \$7$ per unit	$UVC = \$2$ per unit
$BEP_{Quantity} = \dfrac{FC}{P - UVC}$	$BEP_{Quantity} = \dfrac{FC}{P - UVC}$
$= \dfrac{\$1,000,000}{\$10 - \$7}$	$= \dfrac{\$4,000,000}{\$10 - \$2}$
$= 333,333$ units	$= 500,000$ units

The automation increases the fixed cost and increases the break-even quantity from 333,333 to 500,000 units per year. So if annual sales fall within this range, the calculator manufacturer will incur a loss with the automated plant, whereas it would have made a profit if it had not automated.

But what about its potential profit if it sells 1 million units a year? Look carefully at the two break-even charts below, and see the text to check your conclusions.

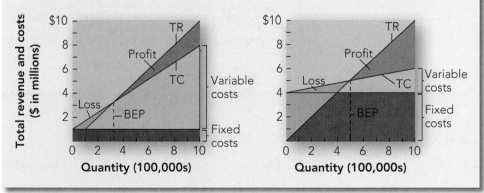

Applications of Break-Even Analysis Because of its simplicity, break-even analysis is used extensively in marketing, most frequently to study the impact on profit of changes in price, fixed cost, and variable cost. The mechanics of break-even analysis are the basis of the widely used electronic spreadsheets offered by computer programs such as Microsoft Excel that permit managers to answer hypothetical "what if" questions about the effect of changes in prices and costs on their profit.

The power of break-even analysis is shown in Figure 13–12. If an electronic calculator manufacturer automates its production, thereby increasing fixed cost and reducing variable cost by substituting machines for workers, this increases the break-even point from 333,333 to 500,000 units per year. Note in this example that only the fixed costs increase immediately (question 3, Figure 13–1). The manufacturer hopes these fixed costs will be offset in the longer run by reduced unit variable costs.

But what about the impact of the higher level of fixed costs on profit? Remember, profit at any output quantity is given by:

Profit = Total revenue − Total cost

$$= (P \times Q) - [FC + (UVC \times Q)]$$

Before automation, profit at 1 million units of sales is:

$$
\begin{aligned}
\text{Profit} &= (P \times Q) - [FC + (UVC \times Q)] \\
&= (\$10 \times 1{,}000{,}000) - [\$1{,}000{,}000 + (\$7 \times 1{,}000{,}000)] \\
&= \$10{,}000{,}000 - \$8{,}000{,}000 \\
&= \$2{,}000{,}000
\end{aligned}
$$

After automation, profit at 1 million units of sales is:

$$
\begin{aligned}
\text{Profit} &= (P \times Q) - [FC + (UVC \times Q)] \\
&= (\$10 \times 1{,}000{,}000) - [\$4{,}000{,}000 + (\$2 \times 1{,}000{,}000)] \\
&= \$10{,}000{,}000 - \$6{,}000{,}000 \\
&= \$4{,}000{,}000
\end{aligned}
$$

Automation, by adding to fixed costs, increases profit by $2 million at 1 million units of sales. Thus, as the quantity sold increases for the automated plant, the potential increase in profit can be huge. This is shown by comparing the orange wedges in Figure 13–12 break-even charts before and after automation. So with large production and sales volumes, automated plants for Ford cars or Texas Instruments calculators produce large profits. Also, firms in other industries, such as airline, railroad, and hotel and motel industries, that require high fixed costs can reap large profits when they go even slightly beyond the break-even point.

---

learning review

7. What is the difference between fixed costs and variable costs?

8. What is a break-even point?

LEARNING OBJECTIVES REVIEW

LO1 *Identify the elements that make up a price.*
Price is the money or other considerations (such as barter) exchanged for the ownership or use of a good or service. Although price typically involves money, the amount exchanged is often different from the list or quoted price because of incentives (rebates, discounts, etc.), allowances (trade), and extra fees (finance charges, surcharges, etc.).

LO2 *Recognize the objectives a firm has in setting prices and the constraints that restrict the range of prices a firm can charge.*
Pricing objectives specify the role of price in a firm's marketing strategy and may include profit, sales revenue, market share, unit volume, survival, or some socially responsible price level. Pricing constraints that restrict a firm's pricing flexibility include demand, product newness, other products sold by the firm, production and marketing costs, cost of price changes, type of competitive market, and the prices of competitive substitutes.

LO3 *Explain what a demand curve is and the role of revenues in pricing decisions.*
A demand curve is a graph relating the quantity sold and price, which shows the maximum number of units that will be sold at a given price. Three demand factors affect price: (*a*) consumer tastes, (*b*) price and availability of substitute products, and (*c*) consumer income. These demand factors determine consumers' willingness and ability to pay for goods and services. Assuming these demand factors remain unchanged, if the price of a product is lowered or raised, then the quantity demanded for it will increase or decrease, respectively.

Three important forms of revenues impact a firm's pricing decisions: (*a*) total revenue, which is the total money received from the sale of a product; (*b*) average revenue, which is the average amount of money received for selling one unit of a product (which is simply the price of the unit); and (*c*) marginal revenue, which is the change in total revenue that results from producing and marketing one additional unit.

LO4 *Describe what price elasticity of demand means to a manager facing a pricing decision.*

Price elasticity of demand measures the responsiveness of units of a product sold to a change in price, which is expressed as the percentage change in the quantity of a product demanded divided by the percentage change in price. Price elasticity is important to marketing managers because a change in price usually has an important effect on the number of units of the product sold and on total revenue.

LO5 *Explain the role of costs in pricing decisions.*

Five important costs impact a firm's pricing decisions: (*a*) total cost, or total expenses, the sum of fixed cost and variable cost incurred by a firm in producing and marketing a product; (*b*) fixed cost, the sum of expenses of the firm that are stable and do not change with the quantity of a product that is produced and sold; (*c*) variable cost, the sum of expenses of the firm that vary directly with the quantity of a product that is produced and sold; (*d*) unit variable cost, variable cost expressed on a per unit basis; and (*e*) marginal cost, the change in total cost that results from producing and marketing one additional unit of the product.

LO6 *Describe how various combinations of price, fixed cost, and unit variable cost affect a firm's break-even point.*

Break-even analysis is a technique that analyzes the relationship between total revenue and total cost to determine profitability at various levels of output. The break-even point is the quantity at which total revenue and total cost are equal. Assuming no change in price, if the costs of a firm's product increase due to higher fixed costs (manufacturing or advertising) or variable costs (direct labor or materials), then its break-even point will be higher. And if total cost is unchanged, an increase in price will reduce the break-even point.

FOCUSING ON KEY TERMS

average revenue (AR) p. 341
barter p. 331
break-even analysis p. 346
break-even chart p. 348
break-even point (BEP) p. 346
demand curve p. 339
demand factors p. 340
fixed cost (FC) p. 345

marginal analysis p. 346
marginal cost (MC) p. 345
marginal revenue (MR) p. 341
price (P) p. 331
price elasticity of demand p. 343
pricing constraints p. 336
pricing objectives p. 334
profit equation p. 333

total cost (TC) p. 345
total revenue (TR) p. 341
unit variable cost (UVC) p. 345
value p. 332
value-pricing p. 332
variable cost (VC) p. 345

APPLYING MARKETING KNOWLEDGE

1 How would the price equation apply to the purchase price of (*a*) gasoline, (*b*) an airline ticket, and (*c*) a checking account?

2 What would be your response to the statement, "Profit maximization is the only legitimate pricing objective for the firm"?

3 How is a downward-sloping demand curve related to total revenue and marginal revenue?

4 A marketing executive once said, "If the price elasticity of demand for your product is inelastic, then your price is probably too low." What is this executive saying in terms of the economic principles discussed in this chapter?

5 A marketing manager reduced the price on a brand of cereal by 10 percent and observed a 25 percent increase in quantity sold. The manager then thought that if the price were reduced by another 20 percent, a 50 percent increase in quantity sold would occur. What would be your response to the marketing manager's reasoning?

6 A student theater group at a university has developed a demand schedule that shows the relationship between ticket prices and demand based on a student survey, as follows:

(*a*) Graph the demand curve and the total revenue curve based on these data. What ticket price might be set based on this analysis? (*b*) What other factors should be considered before the final price is set?

Ticket Price	Number of Students Who Would Buy
$1	300
2	250
3	200
4	150
5	100

7 Touché Toiletries, Inc., has developed an addition to its Lizardman Cologne line tentatively branded Ode d'Toade Cologne. Unit variable costs are 45 cents for a three-ounce bottle, and heavy advertising expenditures in the first year would result in total fixed costs of $900,000. Ode d'Toade Cologne is priced at $7.50 for a three-ounce bottle. How many bottles of Ode d'Toade must be sold to break even?

8 Suppose that marketing executives for Touché Toiletries reduced the price to $6.50 for a three-ounce bottle of Ode d'Toade and the fixed costs were $1,100,000. Suppose further that the unit variable cost remained at 45 cents for a three-ounce bottle. (*a*) How many bottles must be sold to break even? (*b*) What dollar profit level would Ode d'Toade achieve if 200,000 bottles were sold?

9 Executives of Random Recordings, Inc., produced an album entitled *Sunshine/Moonshine* by the Starshine Sisters Band. (*a*) Using the price and cost information in the table, prepare a chart like that in Figure 13–10 showing total cost, fixed cost, and total revenue for album quantity sold levels starting at 10,000 albums through 100,000 albums at 10,000 album intervals, that is, 10,000; 20,000; 30,000; and so on. (*b*) What is the break-even point for the album?

Selling price	$7.00 per album
Album cover	$1.00 per album
Songwriter's royalties	$0.30 per album
Recording artists' royalties	$0.70 per album
Direct material and labor costs to produce the album	$1.00 per album
Fixed cost of producing an album (advertising, studio fee, etc.)	$100,000

building your marketing plan

In starting to set a final price:

1 List two pricing objectives and three pricing constraints.
2 Think about your customers and competitors and set three possible prices.

3 Assume a fixed cost and unit variable cost and (*a*) calculate the break-even points and (*b*) plot a break-even chart for the three prices specified in step 2.

video case 13 Washburn Guitars: Using Break-Even Points to Make Pricing Decisions

"We offer a guitar at every price point for every skill level," explains Kevin Lello, vice president of marketing at Washburn Guitars. Washburn is one of the most prestigious guitar manufacturers in the world, offering instruments that range from one-of-a-kind, custom-made acoustic and electric guitars and basses to less-expensive, mass-produced guitars. Lello has responsibility for marketing Washburn's products and ensuring that the price of each product matches the company's objectives related to sales, profit, and market share. "We do pay attention to break-even points," adds Lello. "We need to know exactly how much a guitar costs us, and how much the overhead is for each guitar."

THE COMPANY

The modern Washburn Guitars company started in 1977 when a small Chicago firm bought the century-old Washburn brand name and a small inventory of guitars, parts, and promotional supplies. At that time, annual company sales of about 2,500 guitars generated revenues of $300,000. Washburn's first catalog, appearing in 1978, told a frightening truth:

> Our designs are translated by Japan's most experienced craftsmen, assuring the consistent quality and craftsmanship for which they are known.

At that time, the American guitar-making craft was at an all-time low. Guitars made by Japanese firms, such as Ibane and Yamaha, were in use by an increasing number of professionals.

Times have changed for Washburn. Today, the company sells about 50,000 guitars each year and annual revenues exceed $40 million. All this resulted from Washburn's aggressive marketing strategies to develop product lines with different price points targeted at musicians in distinctly different market segments.

THE PRODUCTS AND MARKET SEGMENTS

One of Washburn's early successes was the trendsetting Festival Series of cutaway, thin-bodied flattops, with built-in bridge pickups and controls. This guitar became the standard for live performances as its popularity with rock and country stars increased. Over the years several generations of musicians have used Washburn guitars. Early artists included Bob Dylan, Dolly Parton, Greg Allman, and the late George Harrison of the Beatles. In recent years, Mike Kennerty of the All American Rejects, Rick Savage of Def Leppard, and Hugh McDonald of Bon Jovi have been among the many musicians who use Washburn products.

Until 1991, all Washburn guitars were manufactured in Asia. That year Washburn started building its high-end guitars in the United States. Today, Washburn marketing executives divide its product line into four categories to appeal to different market segments. From high end to low end these are:

- One-of-a-kind, custom instruments
- Batch-custom instruments

- Mass-customized instruments
- Mass-produced instruments

The one-of-a-kind custom products appeal to the many stars who use Washburn instruments as well as collectors. The batch-custom products appeal to professional musicians. The mass-customized products appeal to musicians with intermediate skill levels who may not yet be professionals. Finally, the mass-produced units are targeted at first-time buyers and are still manufactured in Asian factories.

PRICING ISSUES

Setting prices for its various lines presents a continuing challenge for Washburn. Not only do the prices have to reflect the changing tastes of its various segments of musicians, but the prices must also be competitive with the prices of other guitars manufactured and marketed globally. The price elasticity of demand, or price sensitivity, for Washburn's products varies between its segments. To reduce the price sensitivity for some of its products Washburn uses endorsements by internationally known musicians who play its instruments and lend their names to lines of Washburn signature guitars. Stars playing Washburn guitars such as Nuno Bettencourt, formerly of Extreme and Population 1; Paul Stanley of KISS; Scott Ian of Anthrax; and Dan Donegan of Disturbed have their own lines of signature guitars—the "batch-custom" units mentioned earlier. These guitars receive excellent reviews. *Total Guitar* magazine, for example, recently said, "If you want a truly original axe that has been built with great attention to detail . . . then the Washburn Maya Pro DD75 could be the one."

Bill Abel, Washburn's vice president of sales, is responsible for reviewing and approving prices for the company's lines of guitars. Setting a sales target of 2,000 units for a new line of guitars, he is considering a suggested retail price of $349 per unit for customers at one of the hundreds of retail outlets carrying the Washburn line. For planning purposes, Abel estimates half of the final retail price will be the price Washburn nets when it sells its guitar to the wholesalers and dealers in its channel of distribution.

Looking at Washburn's financial data for its present plant, Abel estimates that this line of guitars must bear these fixed costs:

Rent and taxes	= $14,000
Depreciation of equipment	= $ 4,000
Management and quality control program	= $20,000

In addition, he estimates the variable costs for each unit to be:

Direct materials = $25/unit

Direct labor = 15 hours/unit @ $8/hour

Carefully kept production records at Washburn's plant make Abel believe that these are reasonable estimates. He explains, "Before we begin a production run, we have a good feel for what our costs will be. The U.S.-built N-4, for example, simply costs more than one of our foreign-produced electrics."

Caught in the global competition for guitar sales, Washburn continually searches for ways to reduce and control costs. For example, Washburn recently purchased Parker Guitar, another guitar manufacturer that designed products for professionals and collectors, and will combine the two production facilities in a new location. Washburn expects the acquisition to lower its fixed and variable costs. Specifically, Washburn projects that its new factory location will reduce its rent and taxes expense by 40 percent, and the new skilled employees will reduce the hours of work needed for each unit by 15 percent.

By managing the prices of its products, Washburn also helps its dealers and retailers. In fact, Abel believes it is another reason for Washburn's success: "We have excellent relationships with the independent retailers. They're our lifeblood, and our outlet to sell our product. We sell through chains and online dealers, but it's the independent dealer that sells the guitars. So we take a smaller margin from them because they have to do more work. They appreciate it, and they go the extra mile for us."

Questions

1 What factors are most likely to affect the demand for the lines of Washburn guitars (*a*) bought by a first-time guitar buyer and (*b*) bought by a sophisticated musician who wants a signature model?

2 For Washburn, what are examples of (*a*) shifting the demand curve to the right to get a higher price for a guitar line (movement of the demand curve) and (*b*) pricing decisions involving moving along a demand curve?

3 In Washburn's factory, what is the break-even point for the new line of guitars if the retail price is (*a*) $349, (*b*) $389, and (*c*) $309? Also, (*d*) if Washburn achieves the sales target of 2,000 units at the $349 retail price, what will its profit be?

4 Assume that the merger with Parker leads to the cost reductions projected in the case. Then, what will be the (*a*) new break-even point at a $349 retail price for this line of guitars and (*b*) new profit if it sells 2,000 units?

5 If for competitive reasons, Washburn eventually has to move all its production back to Asia, (*a*) which specific fixed and variable costs might be lowered and (*b*) what additional fixed and variable costs might it expect to incur?

14

Arriving at the Final Price

STANDING TALL IN STARBURY SIGNATURE SNEAKERS

How much would you expect to pay for a pair of signature sneakers endorsed by a well-known professional basketball player? $150? $200? How about $14.98?

Stephon Marbury has set about to dismiss the notion that affordable sneakers cannot be a status shoe. How? In 2006, he endorsed the Starbury Collection of basketball shoes priced at $14.98. Within months, *BusinessWeek* featured Starbury shoes as one of the best new products in 2006. *Footwear News* heralded the product as its "Launch of the Year."

But why would a 10-year NBA veteran and New York Knicks point guard with a multiyear, multimillion-dollar contract endorse a $14.98 sneaker? "Kids shouldn't have to feel the pressure to spend so much to feel good about the way they look," Marbury says. "It is very important to me that the Starbury Collection have a strong social component for kids and parents, especially in urban areas." On his website, he declares the Starbury brand is "for the people" and a "movement" that is "bigger than basketball." Marbury added, "The big picture is not having a $200 pair of sneakers when your mother's income is $15,000."

Starbury sneakers were designed in collaboration with Steve & Barry's University Sportswear, which began as a collegiate apparel store at the University of Pennsylvania in 1985. Steve & Barry's operates nearly 200 stores in 33 states with the aim of providing top-quality merchandise at low prices. This aim, coupled with Stephon Marbury's philosophy, led to a professionally designed sneaker with features comparable to shoes endorsed by celebrity athletes priced 10 times higher or more. In Marbury's words, "If you take my shoe and you take a $150 shoe, cut it down in half, and it does the same thing."

So why were Starbury sneakers priced at $14.98 and not a higher price? "It certainly doesn't cost $150 to make a high-performance basketball shoe. The cost of the good is a lot closer to $14.98," said Erin Patton, former architect of Nike's Jordan Brand and principal of TMG, the New York-based brand management consulting firm, who spearheaded the Starbury launch. "When consumers spend $150 for a sneaker, they pay for expensive advertising and promotion, and athlete endorsement contracts. These costs are included in the manufacturer's price of the shoe *before* the retailer markup, which often doubles the retail price to consumers. Steve and Barry's developed an innovative, cost-driven business over a 20-year period to manufacture and sell product exclusively in its stores at rock-bottom prices without passing unnecessary costs on

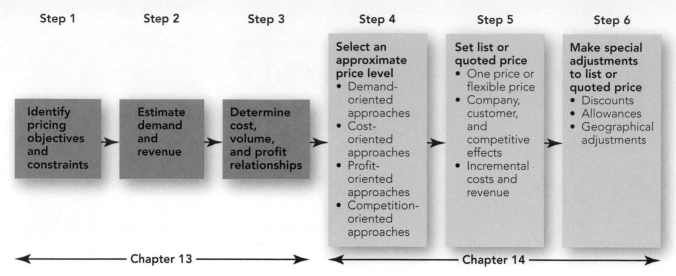

| | | | Select an approximate price level • Demand-oriented approaches • Cost-oriented approaches • Profit-oriented approaches • Competition-oriented approaches | Set list or quoted price • One price or flexible price • Company, customer, and competitive effects • Incremental costs and revenue | Make special adjustments to list or quoted price • Discounts • Allowances • Geographical adjustments |
| Identify pricing objectives and constraints | Estimate demand and revenue | Determine cost, volume, and profit relationships | | | |

← ———— Chapter 13 ———— →   ← ———— Chapter 14 ———— →

FIGURE 14–1

The six steps in setting price. The first three steps were covered in Chapter 13. The last three steps are covered in this chapter.

to consumers. That price-value proposition for the masses has always been at the core of the company's philosophy, but partnering with Stephon Marbury placed lightning in the bottle."

Did the $14.98 retail price resonate with consumers? Over 3 million Starbury sneakers were sold within eight months of the product's launch![1]

This chapter describes how companies like Starbury and Steve & Barry's set an approximate price level for their offerings, highlights important considerations in setting a list or quoted price, and identifies various price adjustments that can be made to prices set by a company—the last three steps involved in setting prices (Figure 14–1). In addition, legal and regulatory aspects of pricing are described.

STEP 4: SELECT AN APPROXIMATE PRICE LEVEL

A key for a marketing manager setting a final price for a product is to find an approximate price level to use as a reasonable starting point. Four common approaches to helping find this approximate price level are (1) demand-oriented, (2) cost-oriented, (3) profit-oriented, and (4) competition-oriented approaches (Figure 14–2). Although these approaches are discussed separately below, some of them overlap, and a seasoned marketing manager will consider several in selecting an approximate price level.

Demand-Oriented Pricing Approaches

Demand-oriented approaches weigh factors underlying expected customer tastes and preferences more heavily than such factors as cost, profit, and competition when selecting a price level.

Skimming Pricing A firm introducing a new or innovative product can use **skimming pricing**, setting the highest initial price that customers really desiring the product are willing to pay. These customers are not very price sensitive because they weigh the new product's price, quality, and ability to satisfy their needs against the same characteristics of substitutes. As the demand of these customers is satisfied, the firm lowers the price to attract another, more price-sensitive segment. Thus, skimming pricing gets its name from skimming successive layers of "cream," or customer segments, as prices are lowered in a series of steps.

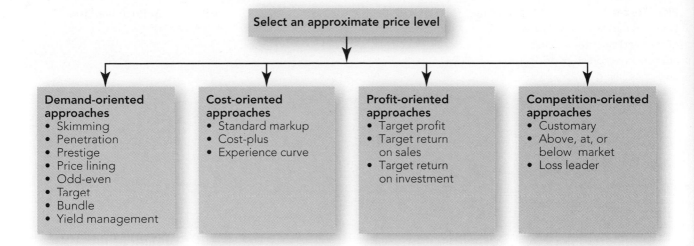

FIGURE 14–2

Four approaches for selecting an approximate price level

Skimming pricing is an effective strategy when: (1) enough prospective customers are willing to buy the product immediately at the high initial price to make these sales profitable, (2) the high initial price will not attract competitors, (3) lowering price has only a minor effect on increasing the sales volume and reducing the unit costs, and (4) customers interpret the high price as signifying high quality. These four conditions are most likely to exist when the new product is protected by patents or copyrights or its uniqueness is understood and valued by consumers. Gillette, for example, adopted a skimming strategy for its five-blade Fusion brand shaving system since many of these conditions applied. The Gillette Fusion shaving system has 70 patents that protect its product technology.

Penetration Pricing Setting a low initial price on a new product to appeal immediately to the mass market is **penetration pricing**, the exact opposite of skimming pricing. Nintendo consciously chose a penetration strategy when it introduced the Nintendo Wii, its newest generation video game console.

The conditions favoring penetration pricing are the reverse of those supporting skimming pricing: (1) many segments of the market are price sensitive, (2) a low initial price discourages competitors from entering the market, and (3) unit production and marketing costs fall dramatically as production volumes increase. A firm using penetration pricing may (1) maintain the initial price for a time to gain profit lost from its low introductory level or (2) lower the price further, counting on the new volume to generate the necessary profit.

In some situations, penetration pricing may follow skimming pricing. A company might initially price a product high to attract price-insensitive consumers and recoup initial research and development costs and introductory promotional expenditures. Once this is done, penetration pricing is used to appeal to a broader segment of the population and increase market share.[2]

Prestige Pricing As noted in Chapter 13, consumers may use price as a measure of the quality or prestige of an item so that as price is lowered beyond some point, demand for the item actually falls. **Prestige pricing** involves setting a high price so that quality- or status-conscious consumers will be attracted to the product and buy it (see Figure 14–3A on the next page). The demand curve slopes downward and to the right between points A and B but turns back to the left between points B and C because demand is actually reduced between points B and C. From A to B buyers see the lowering of price as a bargain and buy more; from B to C they become dubious about the quality and prestige and buy less. A marketing manager's pricing strategy here is to stay above price P_0 (the initial price).

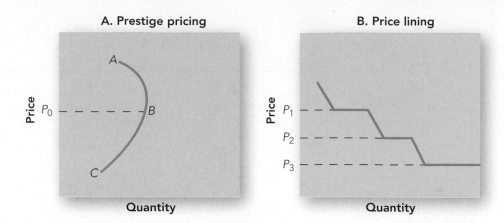

FIGURE 14-3
Demand curves for two types of demand-oriented pricing approaches—prestige pricing and price lining—apply to different kinds of products.

A. Prestige pricing

Price

P_0

A

B

C

Quantity

B. Price lining

Price

P_1

P_2

P_3

Quantity

Rolls-Royce cars, Chanel perfume, Cartier jewelry, Lalique crystal, and Swiss watches have an element of prestige pricing in them and may sell worse at lower prices than at higher ones.[3] The recent success of Swiss watchmaker TAG Heuer is an example. The company raised the average price of its watches from $250 to $1,000, and its sales volume jumped sevenfold.[4] Recently, Energizer learned that buyers of high-performance alkaline batteries tend to link a lower price with lower quality. The accompanying Marketing Matters box describes the pricing lesson learned by Energizer.[5]

Price Lining Often a firm that is selling not just a single product but a line of products may price them at a number of different specific pricing points, which is called **price lining**. For example, a department store manager may price a line of women's casual slacks at $59, $79, and $99. As shown in Figure 14–3B, this assumes that demand is elastic at each of these price points but inelastic between these price points. In some instances, all the items might be purchased for the same cost and then marked up at different percentages to achieve these price points based on color, style, and expected demand. In other instances, manufacturers design products for different price points, and retailers apply approximately the same markup percentages to achieve the three or four different price points offered to consumers. Sellers often feel that a limited number (such as three or four) of price points is preferable to 8 or 10 different ones, which may only confuse prospective buyers.[6]

Odd-Even Pricing Sears offers a Craftsman radial saw for $499.99, the suggested retail price for the Gillette Fusion shaving system is $11.99, and Kmart sells Windex glass cleaner on sale for 99 cents. Why not simply price these items at $500, $12, and $1, respectively? These firms are using **odd-even pricing**, which involves setting prices a few dollars or cents under an even number. The presumption is that consumers see the Sears radial saw as priced at "something over $400" rather than "about $500." In theory, demand increases if the price drops from $500 to $499.99. There is some evidence to suggest this does happen. However, research suggests that overuse of odd-ending prices tends to mute its effect on demand.[7]

Target Pricing Manufacturers will sometimes estimate the price that the ultimate consumer would be willing to pay for a product. They then work backward through markups taken by retailers and wholesalers to determine what price they can charge wholesalers for the product. This practice, called **target pricing**, results in the manufacturer deliberately adjusting the composition and features of a product to achieve the target price to consumers. Canon uses this practice for pricing its cameras, as does Heinz for its complete line of pet foods.[8]

Energizer's Lesson in Price Perception—Value Lies in the Eye of the Beholder

Battery manufacturers are as tireless as a certain drum-thumping bunny in their efforts to create products that perform better, last longer, and not incidentally, outsell the competition. The commercialization of new alkaline battery technology at a price that creates value for consumers is not always obvious or easy. Just ask the marketing executives at Energizer about their experience with pricing Energizer Advanced Formula and Energizer e^2 AA alkaline batteries.

When Duracell launched its high-performance Ultra brand AA alkaline battery with a 25 percent price premium over standard Duracell batteries, Energizer quickly countered with its own high-performance battery—Energizer Advanced Formula. Believing that consumers would not pay the premium price, Energizer priced its Advanced Formula brand at the same price as its standard AA alkaline battery, expecting to gain market share from Duracell. It did not happen. Why? According to industry analysts, consumers associated Energizer's low price with inferior quality in the high-performance segment. Instead of gaining market share, Energizer lost market share to Duracell and Rayovac, the number three battery manufacturer.

Having learned its lesson, Energizer subsequently released its e^2 high-performance battery, this time priced 4 percent higher than Duracell Ultra and about 50 percent higher than Advanced Formula. The result? Energizer recovered lost sales and market share. The lesson learned? Value lies in the eye of the beholder.

Bundle Pricing A frequently used demand-oriented pricing practice is **bundle pricing**—the marketing of two or more products in a single package price. For example, Delta Air Lines offers vacation packages that include airfare, car rental, and lodging. Bundle pricing is based on the idea that consumers value the package more than the individual items. This is due to benefits received from not having to make separate purchases and enhanced satisfaction from one item given the presence of another. Moreover, bundle pricing often provides a lower total cost to buyers and lower marketing costs to sellers.[9]

Yield Management Pricing Have you noticed seats on airline flights are priced differently within coach class? What you observed is **yield management pricing**—the charging of different prices to maximize revenue for a set amount of capacity at any given time.[10] As described in Chapter 12, service businesses engage in capacity management, and an effective way to do this is by varying prices by time, day, week, or season. Yield management pricing is a complex approach that continually matches demand and supply to customize the price for a service. Airlines, hotels, cruise ships, and car rental companies frequently use it. American Airlines estimates that yield management pricing produces an annual revenue that exceeds $500 million.[11]

learning review

1. What are the circumstances in pricing a new product that might support skimming or penetration pricing?

2. What is odd-even pricing?

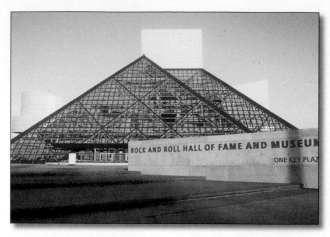

How was the price of the Rock and Roll Hall of Fame and Museum determined? Read the text to find out.

Rock and Roll Hall of Fame and Museum
www.rockhall.com

Cost-Oriented Pricing Approaches

With cost-oriented approaches a price setter stresses the cost side of the pricing problem, not the demand side. Price is set by looking at the production and marketing costs and then adding enough to cover direct expenses, overhead, and profit.

Standard Markup Pricing Managers of supermarkets and other retail stores have such a large number of products that estimating the demand for each product as a means of setting price is impossible. Therefore, they use **standard markup pricing**, which entails adding a fixed percentage to the cost of all items in a specific product class. This percentage markup varies depending on the type of retail store (such as furniture, clothing, or grocery) and on the product involved. High-volume products usually have smaller markups than do low-volume products. Supermarkets such as Kroger, Safeway, and Jewel have different markups for staple items and discretionary items. The markup on staple items like sugar, flour, and dairy products varies from 10 percent to 23 percent, whereas markups on discretionary items like snack foods and candy ranges from 27 percent to 47 percent. These markups must cover all expenses of the store, pay for overhead costs, and contribute something to profits. For supermarkets these markups, which may appear very large, result in only a 1 percent profit on sales revenue if the store is operating efficiently.

By comparison, consider the markups on snacks and beverages purchased at your local movie theater. The markup is 87 percent on soft drinks, 65 percent on candy bars, and 90 percent on popcorn. An explanation of how to compute a markup, along with operating statement data and other ratios, is given in Appendix B to this chapter.

Cost-Plus Pricing Many manufacturing, professional services, and construction firms use a variation of standard markup pricing. **Cost-plus pricing** involves summing the total unit cost of providing a product or service and adding a specific amount to the cost to arrive at a price. Cost-plus pricing generally assumes two forms. With *cost-plus percentage-of-cost pricing,* a fixed percentage is added to the total unit cost. This is often used to price one- or few-of-a-kind items, as when an architectural firm charges a percentage of the construction costs of, say, the $92 million Rock and Roll Hall of Fame and Museum in Cleveland, Ohio.

In buying highly technical, few-of-a-kind products such as hydroelectric power plants or space satellites, country governments have found that general contractors are reluctant to specify a formal, fixed price for the procurement. Therefore, they use *cost-plus fixed-fee pricing,* which means that a supplier is reimbursed for all costs, regardless of what they turn out to be, but is allowed only a fixed fee as profit that is independent of the final cost of the project. For example, suppose that the National Aeronautics and Space Administration agreed to pay Boeing $1.2 billion as the cost of a space shuttle and agreed to a $100 million fee for providing that space shuttle. Even if Boeing's cost increased to $2 billion for the space shuttle, its fee would remain $100 million.

Cost-plus pricing is the most commonly used method to set prices for business products.[12] Increasingly, however, this method is finding favor among business-to-business marketers in the service sector. For example, the rising cost of legal fees has prompted some law firms to adopt a cost-plus pricing approach. Rather than billing business clients on an hourly basis, lawyers and their clients agree on a fixed fee based on expected costs plus a profit for the law firm. Many advertising

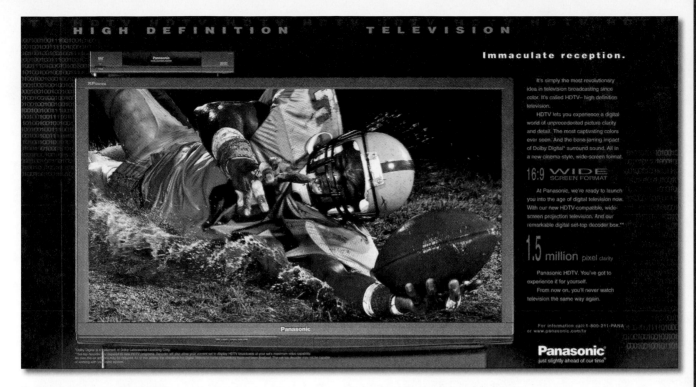

Panasonic is a leader in the successful commercialization of flat-panel HDTV. It, like its competitors, will rely on experience curve pricing to drive down prices.

Panasonic
www.panasonic.com

agencies now use this approach. Here, the client agrees to pay the agency a fee based on the cost of its work plus some agreed-on profit, which is often a percentage of total cost.[13]

Experience Curve Pricing The method of **experience curve pricing** is based on the learning effect, which holds that the unit cost of many products and services declines by 10 percent to 30 percent each time a firm's experience at producing and selling them doubles. This reduction is regular or predictable enough that the average cost per unit can be mathematically estimated. For example, if the firm estimates that costs will fall by 15 percent each time volume doubles, then the cost of the 100th unit produced and sold will be about 85 percent of the cost of the 50th unit, and the 200th unit will be 85 percent of the 100th unit. Therefore, if the cost of the 50th unit is $100, the 100th unit would cost $85, the 200th unit would be $72.25, and so on. Because prices often follow costs with experience curve pricing, a rapid decline in price is possible.

Japanese, Korean, and U.S. firms in the electronics industry often adopt this pricing approach. This cost-based pricing approach complements the demand-based pricing strategy of skimming followed by penetration pricing. For example, DVD player prices have decreased from $900 to less than $100, fax machine prices have declined from $1,000 to under $100, and cellular telephones that once sold for $4,000 are now priced below $99. Panasonic, Sony, Samsung, LG, Philips, and other television manufacturers use experience curve pricing for flat panel, high-definition television (HDTV) sets. Consumers benefit because prices will decline as cumulative sales volume grows.

Profit-Oriented Pricing Approaches

A price setter may choose to balance both revenues and costs to set price using profit-oriented approaches. These might either involve a target of a specific dollar volume of profit or express this target profit as a percentage of sales or investment.

Target Profit Pricing   A firm may set an annual target of a specific dollar volume of profit, which is called **target profit pricing**. Suppose a picture framing store owner wishes to use target profit pricing to establish a price for a typical framed picture and assumes the following:

- Variable cost is a constant $22 per unit.
- Fixed cost is a constant $26,000.
- Demand is insensitive to price up to $60 per unit.
- A target profit of $7,000 is sought at an annual volume of 1,000 units (framed pictures).

The price can be calculated as follows:

$$\text{Profit} = \text{Total revenue} - \text{Total cost}$$
$$\text{Profit} = (P \times Q) - [FC + (UVC \times Q)]$$
$$\$7,000 = (P \times 1,000) - [\$26,000 + (\$22 \times 1,000)]$$
$$\$7,000 = 1,000P - (\$26,000 + \$22,000)$$
$$1,000P = \$7,000 + \$48,000$$
$$P = \$55$$

Note that a critical assumption is that this higher average price of a framed picture will not cause the demand to fall.

Target Return-on-Sales Pricing   A shortcoming with target profit pricing is that although it is simple and the target involves only a specific dollar volume, there is no benchmark of sales or investment used to show how much of the firm's effort is needed to achieve the target. Firms such as supermarket chains often use **target return-on-sales pricing** to set typical prices that will give them a profit that is a specified percentage, say, 1 percent, of the sales volume. Suppose the owner decides to use target return-on-sales pricing for the frame shop and makes the same first three assumptions shown previously. The owner now sets a target of 20 percent return on sales at an annual volume of 1,250 units. This results in the following price:

$$\text{Target return on sales} = \frac{\text{Target profit}}{\text{Total revenue}}$$
$$20\% = \frac{TR - TC}{TR}$$
$$0.20 = \frac{P \times Q - [FC + (UVC \times Q)]}{TR}$$
$$0.20 = \frac{P \times 1,250 - [\$26,000 + (\$22 \times 1,250)]}{P \times 1,250}$$
$$P = \$53.50$$

So at a price of $53.50 per unit and an annual quantity of 1,250 frames,

$$TR = P \times Q = \$53.50 \times 1,250 = \$66,875$$

$$TC = FC + (UVC \times Q) = \$26,000 + (\$22 \times 1,250) = \$53,500$$

$$\text{Profit} = TR - TC = \$66,875 - \$53,500 = \$13,375$$

As a check,

$$\text{Target return on sales} = \frac{\text{Target profit}}{\text{Total revenue}} = \frac{\$13,375}{\$66,875} = 20\%$$

Target Return-on-Investment Pricing   Firms such as General Motors and many public utilities set annual return-on-investment (ROI) targets such as ROI of

Assumptions or Results	Financial Element	Last Year	SIMULATION A	B	C	D
ASSUMPTIONS	Price per unit (P)	$50	$54	$54	$58	$58
	Units sold (Q)	1,000	1,200	1,100	1,100	1,000
	Change in unit variable cost (UVC)	0%	+10%	+10%	+20%	+20%
	Unit variable cost	$22.00	$24.20	$24.20	$26.20	$26.40
	Total expenses	$8,000	Same	Same	Same	Same
	Owner's salary	$18,000	Same	Same	Same	Same
	Investment	$20,000	Same	Same	Same	Same
	State and federal taxes	50%	Same	Same	Same	Same
SPREADSHEET SIMULATION	Net sales (P × Q)	$50,000	$64,800	$59,400	$63,800	$58,000
	Less: COGS (Q × UVC)	22,000	29,040	26,620	29,040	26,400
	Gross margin	$28,000	$35,760	$32,780	$34,760	$31,600
	Less: total expenses	8,000	8,000	8,000	8,000	8,000
	Less: owner's salary	18,000	18,000	18,000	18,000	18,000
	Net profit before taxes	$2,000	$9,760	$6,780	$8,760	$5,600
	Less: taxes	1,000	4,880	3,390	4,380	2,800
	Net profit after taxes	$1,000	$4,880	$3,390	$4,380	$2,800
	Investment	$20,000	$20,000	$20,000	$20,000	$20,000
	Return on investment	5.0%	24.4%	17.0%	21.9%	14.0%

FIGURE 14–4

Results of a computer spreadsheet simulation to select a price to achieve a target return on investment

20 percent. **Target return-on-investment pricing** is a method of setting prices to achieve this target.

Suppose the store owner sets a target ROI of 10 percent, which is twice that achieved the previous year. She considers raising the average price of a framed picture to $54 or $58—up from last year's average of $50. To do this, she might improve product quality by offering better frames and higher-quality matting, which will increase the cost but will probably offset the decreased revenue from the lower number of units that can be sold next year.

To handle this wide variety of assumptions, today's managers use computerized spreadsheets to project operating statements based on a diverse set of assumptions. Figure 14–4 shows the results of a computerized spreadsheet simulation, with assumptions shown at the top and the projected results at the bottom. A previous year's operating statement results are shown in the column headed "Last Year," and the assumptions and spreadsheet results for four different sets of assumptions are shown in columns A, B, C, and D.

In choosing a price or another action using spreadsheet results, the manager must (1) study the results of the computer simulation projections and (2) assess the realism of the assumptions underlying each set of projections. For example, the store owner sees from the bottom row of Figure 14–4 that all four spreadsheet simulations exceed the after-tax target ROI of 10 percent. But after more thought, she judges it to be more realistic to set an average price of $58 per unit, allow the unit variable cost to increase by 20 percent to account for more expensive framing and matting, and settle for the same unit sales as the 1,000 units sold last year. She selects simulation D in this computerized spreadsheet approach to target ROI pricing and has a goal of 14 percent after-tax ROI.

Competition-Oriented Pricing Approaches

Rather than emphasize demand, cost, or profit factors, a price setter can stress what competitors or "the market" is doing.

Customary Pricing   For some products where tradition, a standardized channel of distribution, or other competitive factors dictate the price, **customary pricing** is used. Tradition prevails in the pricing of Swatch watches. The $40 customary price for the basic model changed little in 10 years. Candy bars offered through standard vending machines have a customary price of 75 cents, and a significant departure from this price may result in a loss of sales for the manufacturer. Hershey changes the amount of chocolate in its candy bars depending on the price of raw chocolate rather than vary its customary retail price so that it can continue selling through vending machines.

Above-, At-, or Below-Market Pricing   For most products, it is difficult to identify a specific market price for a product or product class. Still, marketing managers often have a subjective feel for the competitors' price or market price. Using this benchmark, they then may deliberately choose a strategy of **above-, at-, or below-market pricing**. 3 C's

Among watch manufacturers, Rolex takes pride in emphasizing that it makes one of the most expensive watches you can buy, a clear example of above-market pricing. Manufacturers of national brands of clothing such as Hart Schaffner & Marx and Christian Dior and retailers such as Neiman-Marcus deliberately set premium prices for their products.

Large department store chains such as JCPenney generally use at-market pricing. These chains often establish the going market price in the minds of their competitors. Similarly, Revlon cosmetics and Arrow brand shirts are generally priced "at market." They also provide a reference price for competitors that use above- and below-market pricing.

In contrast, a number of firms use below-market pricing. Manufacturers and retailers that offer private brands of products ranging from peanut butter to shampoo deliberately set prices for these products about 8 percent to 10 percent below the prices of nationally branded competitive products such as Skippy peanut butter and Vidal Sassoon shampoo. Below-market pricing also exists in business-to-business marketing. Hewlett-Packard, for instance, initially priced its office personal computers below competitors to promote a value image among corporate buyers.[14]

Companies use a "price premium" to assess whether its products and brands are above, at, or below the market. An illustration of how the price premium measure is calculated, displayed, and interpreted appears in the Using Marketing Dashboards box.

Loss-Leader Pricing   For a special promotion retail stores deliberately sell a product below its customary price to attract attention to it. The purpose of this **loss-leader pricing** is not to increase sales but to attract customers in hopes they will buy other products as well, particularly the discretionary items with large markups. For example, Best Buy, Target, and Wal-Mart sell CDs at about half of music companies' suggested retail price to attract customers to their stores.[15]

learning review

3. What is standard markup pricing?

4. What profit-based pricing approach should a manager use if he or she wants to reflect the percentage of the firm's resources used in obtaining the profit?

5. What is the purpose of loss-leader pricing when used by a retail firm?

Using Marketing Dashboards

Are Cracker Jack Prices Above, At, or Below the Market?

How would you determine whether a firm's retail prices are above, at, or below the market? You might visit retail stores and record what prices retailers are charging for products or brands. This laborious activity can be simplified by combining two consumer market share measures to create a "price premium" display on your marketing dashboard.

Your Challenge Frito-Lay is considering whether to buy the Cracker Jack brand of caramel popcorn from Borden, Inc. Frito-Lay research shows that Cracker Jack has a strong brand equity. But, Cracker Jack's dollar sales market share and pound volume market share declined recently and trailed the Crunch 'n Munch brand as shown in the table.

Borden's management used an above-market, premium pricing strategy for Cracker Jack. Specifically, Cracker Jack's suggested retail price was set to yield an average price premium per pound of 28 percent relative to Crunch 'n Munch. As a Frito-Lay marketer studying Cracker Jack, your challenge is to calculate and display Cracker Jack's actual price premium relative to Crunch 'n Munch. A price premium is the percentage by which the actual price charged for a specific brand exceeds (or falls short of) a benchmark established for a similar product or basket of products. This premium can be calculated as follows:

Price Premium (%)

$$= \frac{\text{Dollar Sales Market Share for a Brand}}{\text{Unit Volume Market Share for a Brand}} - 1$$

Brand	Dollar Sales Market Share	Pound Volume Market Share
Crunch 'n Munch	32%	32%
Cracker Jack	26	19
Fiddle Faddle	7	8
Private Brands	4	8
Seasonal, Specialty, and Regional (S,S,R) Brands	31 / 100%	33 / 100%

Your Findings Using caramel popcorn brand market share data, the Cracker Jack price premium is 1.368, or 36.8 percent, calculated as follows: (26 percent ÷ 19 percent) − 1 = .368. By comparison, Crunch 'n Munch enjoys no price premium. Its dollar sales market share and unit (pound) market share are equal: (32 percent ÷ 32 percent) − 1 = 0, or zero percent. The price premium, or lack thereof, of other brands can be displayed in a marketing dashboard as shown below.

Your Action Cracker Jack's price premium clearly exceeds the 28 percent Borden benchmark relative to Crunch 'n Munch. Cracker Jack's price premium may have overreached its brand equity. Consideration might be given to assessing Cracker Jack's price premium relative to its market position should Frito-Lay purchase the brand.

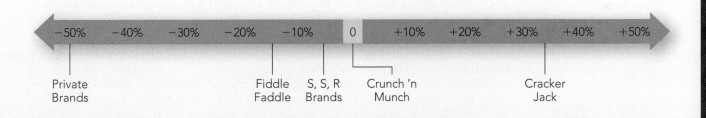

| −50% | −40% | −30% | −20% | −10% | 0 | +10% | +20% | +30% | +40% | +50% |

Private Brands · Fiddle Faddle · S, S, R Brands · Crunch 'n Munch · Cracker Jack

STEP 5: SET THE LIST OR QUOTED PRICE

LO2

The first four steps in setting price covered in Chapter 13 and this chapter result in an approximate price level for the product that appears reasonable. But it still remains for the manager to set a specific list or quoted price in light of all relevant factors.

What price policy does Family Dollar Stores use? Read the text to find the answer.

Choosing a Price Policy

Choosing a price policy is important in setting a list or quoted price. Two options are common—a one-price policy or a flexible-price policy.

One-Price Policy A **one-price policy**, also called *fixed pricing,* is setting one price for all buyers of a product or service. For example, when you buy a Wilson (K) factor tennis racket from a sporting goods store, you are offered the product at a single price. You can buy it or not, but there is no variation in the price under the seller's one-price policy. Saturn Corporation and CarMax use this approach in their stores and features a "no haggle, one price" price for cars. Some retailers have married this policy with a below-market approach. Dollar Valley Stores and 99¢ Only Stores sell everything in their stores for $1 or less. Family Dollar Stores sell everything for $2.

Flexible-Price Policy In contrast, a **flexible-price policy**, also called *dynamic pricing,* involves setting different prices for products and services depending on individual buyers and purchase situations. A flexible-price policy gives sellers considerable discretion in setting the final price in light of demand, cost, and competitive factors. Yield management pricing is a form of flexible pricing because prices vary by an individual buyer's purchase situation, company cost considerations, and competitive conditions. Dell Inc. uses flexible pricing. It continually adjusts prices in response to changes in its own costs, competitive pressures, and demand from customers, from one segment of the personal computer market to another. "Our flexibility allows us to be [priced] different even within a day," says a Dell spokesperson.[16]

Most companies use a one-price policy. However, flexible pricing has grown in popularity because of increasingly sophisticated information technology. Today, many marketers have the ability to customize a price for an individual on the basis of his or her purchasing patterns, product preferences, and price-sensitivity, all of which are stored in company data warehouses. For example, online marketers routinely adjust prices in response to purchase situations and past purchase behaviors of online buyers. Some online marketers monitor an online shopper's *clickstream*—the way that person navigates through the website. If the visitor behaves like a price-sensitive shopper—perhaps by comparing many different products and prices—that person may be offered a lower price.[17]

Flexible pricing means that some customers pay more and others less for the same product or service. And flexible pricing is not without its critics because of this discriminatory potential. For example, car dealers have traditionally used flexible pricing on the basis of buyer–seller negotiations to agree on a final sales price. However, flexible pricing may result in discriminatory practices in car buying as detailed in the Making Responsible Decisions box.[18] There are also legal issues associated with flexible pricing. As noted later in this chapter, constraints under the Robinson-Patman Act prevent carrying a flexible-price policy to the extreme of price discrimination.

Company, Customer, and Competitive Effects on Pricing

As the final list or quoted price is set, the effects on the company, customers, and competitors must be assessed.

Making Responsible Decisions > > > > > > > ethics

Flexible Pricing—Is There Race and Gender Discrimination in Bargaining for a New Car?

What do 60 percent of prospective buyers dread when looking for a new car? That's right! They dread negotiating the price. Price bargaining demonstrates shortcomings of flexible pricing when purchasing a new car: the potential for minority price discrimination.

A National Bureau of Economic Research study of 750,000 car purchases indicated that Blacks, Hispanics, and women, on average, paid roughly $423, $483, and $105 more, respectively, for a new car in the $21,000 range than the typical purchaser. Smaller price premiums remained after adjusting for income, education, and other factors that may affect price negotiations.

Company Effects For a firm with more than one product, a decision on the price of a single product must consider the price of other items in its product line or related product lines in its product mix. Within a product line or mix there are usually some products that are substitutes for one another and some that complement each other.[19] Frito-Lay recognizes that its tortilla chip product line consisting of Baked Tostitos, Tostitos, and Doritos brands are partial substitutes for one another and its bean and cheese chip-dip line and salsa sauces complement the tortilla chip line.

A manager's challenge when marketing multiple products is **product-line pricing**, the setting of prices for all items in a product line. When setting prices, the manager seeks to cover the total cost and produce a profit for the complete line, not necessarily for each item. For example, the penetration price for Nintendo's Wii video game console was likely at or below its cost, but the price of its video games (complementary products) was set high enough to cover the loss and deliver a handsome profit for the Nintendo product line.

Product-line pricing involves determining (1) the lowest-priced product and price, (2) the highest-priced product and price, and (3) price differentials for all other products in the line.[20] The lowest- and highest-priced items in the product line play important roles. The highest-priced item is typically positioned as the premium item in quality and features. The lowest-priced item is the traffic builder designed to capture the attention of the hesitant or first-time buyer. Price differentials between items in the line should make sense to customers and reflect differences in their perceived value of the products offered. Behavioral research also suggests that the price differentials should get larger as one moves up the product line.

Customer Effects In setting price, marketers weigh factors heavily that satisfy the perceptions or expectations of ultimate consumers, such as the customary prices for a variety of consumer products. Retailers have found that they should not price their store brands 20 to 25 percent below manufacturers' brands.[21] When they do, consumers often view the lower price as signaling lower quality and don't buy.

Manufacturers and wholesalers must choose prices that result in profit for resellers in the channel to gain their cooperation and support. Toro failed to do this on its lines of lawn mowers and snow throwers. It decided to augment its traditional hardware outlet distribution by also selling through mass merchandisers such as Target. To do so, it set mass merchandiser prices far below those for its traditional hardware outlets. Unhappy hardware stores abandoned Toro products in favor of mowers and snow throwers from competitors.

Competitive Effects   A manager's pricing decision is immediately apparent to most competitors, who may retaliate with price changes of their own. Therefore, a manager who sets a final list or quoted price must anticipate potential price responses from competitors. Regardless of whether a firm is a price leader or follower, it wants to avoid cutthroat price wars in which no firm in the industry makes a satisfactory profit.

A **price war** involves successive price cutting by competitors to increase or maintain their unit sales or market share. Price wars erupt in a variety of industries, from consumer electronics to disposable diapers, from soft drinks to airlines, and from grocery retailing to telephone services. Managers expecting that a lower price will result in a larger market share, higher unit sales, and greater profit for their company often initiate them. This may occur. But, if competitors match the lower price, other things being equal, the expected market share, sales, and profit gain are lost. According to an analysis of large U.S. companies, a 1 percent price cut—assuming no change in unit volume or costs—lowers a company's net profit by an average of 8 percent.[22]

Marketers are advised to consider price cutting only when one or more conditions exist: (1) the company has a cost or technological advantage over its competitors, (2) primary demand for a product class will grow if prices are lowered, and (3) the price cut is confined to specific products or customers (as with airline tickets), and not across the board.[23]

Balancing Incremental Costs and Revenues

When a price is changed or new advertising or selling programs are planned, their effect on the quantity sold must be considered. This assessment, called *marginal*

FIGURE 14-5

Expected incremental revenue from pricing and other marketing actions must more than offset incremental costs to achieve an incremental profit.

Suppose the owner of a picture framing store is considering buying a series of magazine ads to reach her upscale target market. The cost of the ads is $1,000, the average price of a framed picture is $50, and the unit variable cost (materials plus labor) is $30.

This is a direct application of marginal analysis that an astute manager uses to estimate the incremental revenue or incremental number of units that must be obtained to at least cover the incremental cost. In this example, the number of extra picture frames that must be sold is obtained as follows:

$$\text{Incremental number of frames} = \frac{\text{Extra fixed cost}}{\text{Price} - \text{Unit variable cost}}$$

$$= \frac{\$1,000 \text{ of advertising}}{\$50 - \$30}$$

$$= 50 \text{ frames}$$

So unless there are other benefits of the ads, such as long-term goodwill, she should buy the ads only if she expects they will increase frame sales by at least 50 units.

analysis (Chapter 13), involves a continuing, concise trade-off of incremental costs against incremental revenues.

Do marketing and business managers really use marginal analysis? Yes, they do, but they often don't use phrases such as *marginal revenue, marginal cost,* and *elasticity of demand.*

Think about these managerial questions:

• How many extra units do we have to sell to pay for that $1,000 advertisement?
• Should we hire three more salespeople or not?

These questions are a form of marginal or incremental analysis, even though these exact words are not used.

Figure 14–5 shows the power, and some limitations, of marginal analysis applied to a marketing decision. Note that the frame store owner must either conclude that a simple advertising campaign will more than pay for itself in additional sales or not undertake the campaign. The decision could also have been made to increase the average price of a framed picture to cover the cost of the campaign, but the principle still applies: Expected incremental revenues from pricing and other marketing actions must more than offset incremental costs.

The example in Figure 14–5 shows both the main advantage and difficulty of marginal analysis. The advantage is its commonsense usefulness, and the difficulty is obtaining the necessary data to make decisions. The owner can measure the cost quite easily, but the incremental revenue generated by the ads is difficult to measure. She could partly solve this problem by offering $2 off the purchase price with use of a coupon printed in the ad to see which sales resulted from the ad.

STEP 6: MAKE SPECIAL ADJUSTMENTS TO THE LIST OR QUOTED PRICE

LO3

When you pay 75 cents for a bag of M&Ms in a vending machine or receive a quoted price of $10,000 from a contractor to renovate a kitchen, the pricing sequence ends with the last step just described: setting the list or quoted price. But when you are a manufacturer of M&M candies or gas grills and sell your product to dozens or hundreds of wholesalers and retailers in your marketing channel, you may need to make special adjustments to the list or quoted price. Wholesalers adjust list or quoted

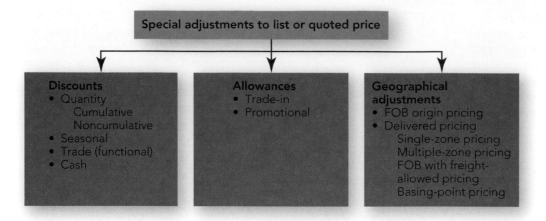

Special adjustments to list or quoted price

Discounts
- Quantity
    Cumulative
    Noncumulative
- Seasonal
- Trade (functional)
- Cash

Allowances
- Trade-in
- Promotional

Geographical adjustments
- FOB origin pricing
- Delivered pricing
    Single-zone pricing
    Multiple-zone pricing
    FOB with freight-allowed pricing
    Basing-point pricing

FIGURE 14–6

Three special adjustments to list or quoted price include discounts, allowances, and geographical adjustments. Each can substantially change the final price.

prices they set for retailers. Retailers, in turn, do the same for consumers. Three special adjustments to the list or quoted price are (1) discounts, (2) allowances, and (3) geographical adjustments (Figure 14–6).

Discounts

Discounts are reductions from the list price that a seller gives a buyer as a reward for some activity of the buyer that is favorable to the seller. Four kinds of discounts are especially important in marketing strategy: (1) quantity, (2) seasonal, (3) trade (functional), and (4) cash.[24]

Quantity Discounts To encourage customers to buy larger quantities of a product, firms at all levels in the marketing channel offer **quantity discounts**, which are reductions in unit costs for a larger order. For example, a photocopying service such as AlphaGraphics might set a price of 10 cents a copy for 1 to 25 copies, 9 cents a copy for 26 to 100, and 8 cents a copy for 101 or more. Because the photocopying service gets more of the buyer's business and has longer production runs that reduce its order-handling costs, it is willing to pass on some of the cost savings in the form of quantity discounts to the buyer.

Quantity discounts are of two general kinds: noncumulative and cumulative. *Noncumulative quantity discounts* are based on the size of an individual purchase order. They encourage large individual purchase orders, not a series of orders. This discount is used by FedEx to encourage companies to ship a large number of packages at one time. *Cumulative quantity discounts* apply to the accumulation of purchases of a product over a given time period, typically a year. Cumulative quantity discounts encourage repeat buying by a single customer to a far greater degree than do noncumulative quantity discounts.

Seasonal Discounts To encourage buyers to stock inventory earlier than their normal demand would require, manufacturers often use seasonal discounts. A firm such as Toro that manufactures lawn mowers and snow throwers offers seasonal discounts to encourage wholesalers and retailers to stock up on lawn mowers in January and February and on snow throwers in July and August—five or six months before the seasonal demand by ultimate consumers. This enables Toro to smooth out seasonal manufacturing peaks and troughs, thereby contributing to more efficient production. It also rewards wholesalers and retailers for the risk they accept in assuming increased inventory carrying costs and having supplies in stock at the time they are wanted by customers.

Trade (Functional) Discounts To reward wholesalers and retailers for marketing functions they will perform in the future, a manufacturer often gives *trade*, or *functional, discounts*. These reductions off the list or base price are offered to

Marketers provide a variety of discounts to marketing channel members who in turn often pass them along to consumers. Toro uses seasonal discounts to stimulate consumer demand and smooth out seasonal manufacturing peaks and troughs. Promotional discounts are used by retailers such as Payless to offer items at sale prices.

The Toro Company
www.toro.com

Payless Shoe Source
www.payless.com

resellers in the marketing channel on the basis of (1) where they are in the channel and (2) the marketing activities they are expected to perform in the future.

Suppose a manufacturer quotes price in the following form: list price—$100 less 30/10/5. The first number in the percentage sequence always refers to the retail end of the channel. The last number always refers to the wholesaler or jobber closest to the manufacturer in the channel. The trade discounts are simply subtracted one at a time. This price quote shows $100 is the manufacturer's suggested retail price; 30 percent of the suggested retail price is available to the retailer to cover costs and provide a profit of $30 ($100 × 0.3 = $30); wholesalers closest to the retailer in the channel get 10 percent of their selling price ($70 × 0.1 = $7); and the final group of wholesalers in the channel (probably jobbers) that are closest to the manufacturer get 5 percent of their selling price ($63 × 0.05 = $3.15). Thus, starting with the manufacturer's suggested retail price and subtracting the three trade discounts shows that the manufacturer's selling price to the wholesaler or jobber closest to it is $59.85 (Figure 14–7).

Traditional trade discounts have been established in various product lines such as hardware, food, and pharmaceutical items. Although the manufacturer may suggest the trade discounts shown in the example just cited, the sellers are free to alter the discount schedule depending on their competitive situation.

FIGURE 14–7

The structure of trade discounts affects the manufacturer's selling price and margins made by resellers in a marketing channel.

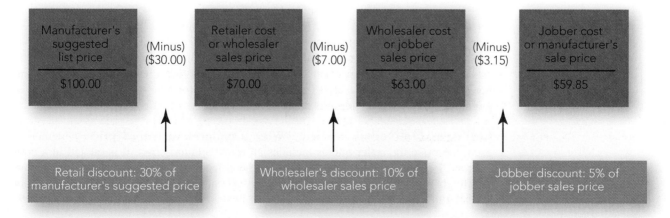

Cash Discounts To encourage retailers to pay their bills quickly, manufacturers offer them *cash discounts*. Suppose a retailer receives a bill quoted at $1,000, 2/10 net 30. This means that the bill for the product is $1,000, but the retailer can take a 2 percent discount ($1,000 × 0.02 = $20) if payment is made within 10 days and send a check for $980. If the payment cannot be made within 10 days, the total amount of $1,000 is due within 30 days. It is usually understood by the buyer that an interest charge will be added after the first 30 days of free credit.

Retailers provide cash discounts to consumers as well to eliminate the cost of credit granted to consumers. These discounts take the form of discount-for-cash policies.

Allowances

Allowances, like discounts, are reductions from list or quoted prices to buyers for performing some activity. They include trade-in and promotional allowances.

Trade-in Allowances A new-car dealer can offer a substantial reduction in the list price of that new Toyota Camry by offering you a trade-in allowance of $1,000 for your Chevrolet Cavalier. A *trade-in allowance* is a price reduction given when a used product is part of the payment on a new product. Trade-ins are an effective way to lower the price a buyer has to pay without formally reducing the list price.

Promotional Allowances Sellers in the marketing channel can qualify for **promotional allowances** for undertaking certain advertising or selling activities to promote a product. Various types of allowances include an actual cash payment or an extra amount of "free goods" (as with a free case of frozen pizzas to a retailer for every dozen cases purchased). Frequently, a portion of these savings is passed on to the consumer by retailers.

Some companies, such as Procter & Gamble, have chosen to reduce promotional allowances for retailers by using everyday low pricing. **Everyday low pricing** (EDLP) is the practice of replacing promotional allowances with lower manufacturer list prices. EDLP promises to reduce the average price to consumers while minimizing promotional allowances that cost manufacturers billions of dollars every year. However, EDLP does not necessarily benefit supermarkets as described in the Marketing Matters box.[25]

Geographical Adjustments

Geographical adjustments are made by manufacturers or even wholesalers to list or quoted prices to reflect the cost of transportation of the products from seller to buyer. The two general methods for quoting prices related to transportation costs are (1) FOB origin pricing and (2) uniform delivered pricing.

FOB Origin Pricing FOB means "free on board" some vehicle at some location, which means the seller pays the cost of loading the product onto the vehicle that is used (such as a barge, railroad car, or truck). **FOB origin pricing** usually involves the seller's naming the location of this loading as the seller's factory or warehouse (such as "FOB Detroit" or "FOB factory"). The title to the goods passes to the buyer at the point of loading, so the buyer becomes responsible for picking the specific mode of transportation, for all the transportation costs, and for subsequent handling of the product. Buyers farthest from the seller face the big disadvantage of paying the higher transportation costs.

Uniform Delivered Pricing When a **uniform delivered pricing** method is used, the price the seller quotes includes all transportation costs. It is quoted in a contract as "FOB buyer's location," and the seller selects the mode of transportation, pays the freight charges, and is responsible for any damage that may occur because the seller retains title to the goods until delivered to the buyer. Although they go by various names,

Marketing Matters > > > > > customer value

Everyday Low Prices at the Supermarket = Everyday Low Profits—Creating Customer Value at a Cost

Who wouldn't welcome low retail prices every day? The answer is supermarket chains—76 percent of U.S. grocery stores have not adopted this practice. Supermarkets prefer Hi-Lo pricing based on frequent specials where prices are temporarily lowered then raised again. Hi-Lo pricing reflects allowances that manufacturers give supermarkets to push their product. Consider a New York City supermarket whose advertisement is shown here. It regularly pays $1.15 for a can of Bumble Bee white tuna ($55.43 ÷ 48 = $1.15), but the allowances reduce the cost to 96 cents. A price special of 99 cents still provides a 3 cent retail markup ($0.99 retail price in ad − $0.96 cost). When the price on tuna returns to its regular level, the store's gross margin on tuna increases substantially on those cans that were bought with the allowance but not sold during the price special promotion.

Everyday low pricing (EDLP) eliminates manufacturer allowances and can reduce average retail prices by up to 10 percent. While EDLP provides lower average prices than Hi-Lo pricing, EDLP does not allow for deeply discounted price specials. EDLP can create everyday customer value and modestly increase supermarket sales—but at a cost. Already slim supermarket chain profits can slip by 18 percent with EDLP without the benefit of allowances as described

earlier. Also, some argue that EDLP without price specials is boring for many grocery shoppers who welcome price specials. EDLP has been hailed as "value pricing" by manufacturers, but supermarkets view it differently. For them, EDLP means "Everyday Low Profits!"

---

there are four kinds of delivered pricing methods: (1) single-zone pricing, (2) multiple-zone pricing, (3) FOB with freight-allowed pricing, and (4) basing-point pricing.

In *single-zone pricing* all buyers pay the same delivered price for the products, regardless of their distance from the seller. So, although a retail store offering free delivery in a metropolitan area has lower transportation costs for goods shipped to customers nearer the store than for those shipped to distant ones, customers pay the same delivered price.

In *multiple-zone pricing* a firm divides its selling territory into geographic areas or zones. The delivered price to all buyers within any one zone is the same, but prices across zones vary depending on the transportation cost to the zone and the level of competition and demand within the zone. The U.S. Postal Service uses multiple-zone pricing for mailing certain packages.

With *FOB with freight-allowed pricing,* also called *freight absorption pricing,* the price is quoted by the seller as "FOB plant—freight allowed." The buyer is allowed to deduct freight expenses from the list price of the goods, so the seller agrees to pay, or "absorb," the transportation costs.

Basing-point pricing involves selecting one or more geographical locations (basing point) from which the list price for products plus freight expenses are charged to the buyer. For example, a company might designate St. Louis as the basing point and charge all buyers a list price of $100 plus freight from St. Louis to their location. Basing-point pricing methods have been used in the steel, cement, and lumber industries where freight expenses are a significant part of the total cost to the buyer and products are largely undifferentiated.

Legal and Regulatory Aspects of Pricing

Arriving at a final price is clearly a complex process. The task is further complicated by legal and regulatory restrictions. Five pricing practices have received the most scrutiny: (1) price fixing, (2) price discrimination, (3) deceptive pricing, (4) geographical pricing, and (5) predatory pricing[26] (Figure 14–8).

Price Fixing A conspiracy among firms to set prices for a product is termed **price fixing**. Price fixing is illegal per se under the Sherman Act (*per se* means in and of itself). When two or more competitors explicitly or implicitly set prices, this practice is called *horizontal price fixing*. For example, six foreign vitamin companies pled guilty to price fixing in the human and animal vitamin industry and paid the largest fine in U.S. history, a hefty $335 million.[27]

Vertical price fixing involves controlling agreements between independent buyers and sellers (a manufacturer and a retailer) whereby sellers are required to not sell products below a minimum retail price. This practice, called *resale price maintenance*, was declared illegal per se in 1975 under provisions of the *Consumer Goods Pricing Act*. Nevertheless, this practice is not uncommon. Shoe supplier Nine West recently agreed to settle government charges that the company restricted competition by coercing retailers to adhere to its resale prices. Nine West agreed to pay $34 million in the settlement.[28] However, manufacturers and wholesalers can fix the maximum retail price for their products provided the price agreement does not create an "unreasonable restraint of trade" or is anticompetitive.

It is important to recognize that a "manufacturer's suggested retail price," or MSRP, is not illegal per se. The issue of legality only arises when manufacturers enforce such a practice by coercion. Furthermore, there appears to be a movement toward a "*rule of reason*" in horizontal and vertical price fixing cases.[29] This rule holds that circumstances surrounding a practice must be considered before making a judgment about its legality. The rule of reason perspective is the direct opposite of the per se rule.

Price Discrimination The Clayton Act as amended by the Robinson-Patman Act prohibits **price discrimination**—the practice of charging different prices to different buyers for goods of like grade and quality. However, not all price differences are illegal; only those that substantially lessen competition or create a monopoly are deemed unlawful. Moreover, "goods" is narrowly defined and does not include discrimination in services.

FIGURE 14–8
Several pricing practices are affected by legal and regulatory restrictions. These restrictions seek to benefit both consumers and companies.

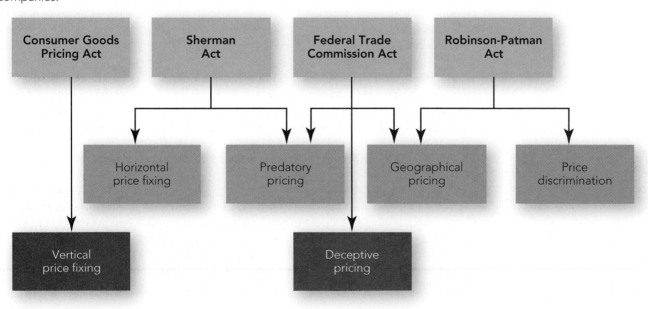

The offer of "free" merchandise or service is a promotional device often used to attract customers. The Federal Trade Commission (FTC) acknowledges that such offers are a useful and valuable marketing practice. However, the FTC also recognizes that such offers must be made with extreme care so as to avoid any possibility that consumers will be misled or deceived.

The FTC has issued its "Guide Concerning Use of the Word 'Free' and Similar Representations" at www.ftc.gov/bcp/guides/free. This guide illustrates that the term *free* has multiple dimensions. Suppose a marketer substitutes similar words for *free*, such as *gift, given without charge*, or *bonus*. What is the FTC's position on this practice?

BUY ONE, GET ONE FREE

A unique feature of the Robinson-Patman Act is that it allows for price differentials to different customers under the following conditions:

1. When price differences charged to different customers do not exceed the differences in the cost of manufacture, sale, or delivery resulting from differing methods or quantities in which such goods are sold or delivered to buyers. This condition is called the cost justification defense.
2. When price differences result from changing market conditions, avoiding obsolescence of seasonal merchandise, including perishables, or closing out sales.
3. When price differences are quoted to selected buyers in good faith to meet competitors' prices and are not intended to injure competition. This condition is called the meet-the-competition defense.

The Robinson-Patman Act also covers promotional allowances. To legally offer promotional allowances to buyers, the seller must do so on a proportionally equal basis to all buyers distributing the seller's products. In general, the rule of reason applies frequently in price discrimination cases and is often applied to cases involving flexible pricing practices of firms.

Deceptive Pricing   Price deals that mislead consumers fall into the category of *deceptive pricing*. Deceptive pricing is outlawed by the Federal Trade Commission Act. The FTC monitors such practices and has published a regulation titled "Guides against Deceptive Pricing" to help businesspeople avoid a charge of deception. The five most common deceptive pricing practices are described in Figure 14–9 on the next page. As you read about these practices it should be clear that laws cannot be passed and enforced to protect consumers and competitors against all of these practices, so it is essential to rely on the ethical standards of those making and publicizing pricing decisions. An often used pricing practice is to promote products and services for free—a great price! It would seem that the meaning of "free" is obvious. Think again. Visit the FTC website described in the Going Online box to learn what *free* means.

Geographical Pricing   FOB origin pricing is legal, as are FOB freight-allowed pricing practices, providing no conspiracy to set prices exists. Basing-point pricing can be viewed as illegal under the Robinson-Patman Act and the Federal Trade Commission Act if there is clear-cut evidence of a conspiracy to set prices. In general, geographical pricing practices have been immune from legal and regulatory restrictions, except in those instances in which a conspiracy to lessen competition exists under the Sherman Act or price discrimination exists under the Robinson-Patman Act.

DECEPTIVE PRICING PRACTICE	DESCRIPTION
Bait and switch	A deceptive practice exists when a firm offers a very low price on a product (the bait) to attract customers to a store. Once in the store, the customer is persuaded to purchase a higher-priced item (the switch) using a variety of tricks, including (1) downgrading the promoted item, (2) not having the item in stock, or (3) refusing to take orders for the item.
Bargains conditional on other purchases	This practice may exist when a buyer is offered "1-Cent Sales," "Buy 1, Get 1 Free," and "Get 2 for the Price of 1." Such pricing is legal only if the first items are sold at the regular price, not a price inflated for the offer. Substituting lower-quality items on either the first or second purchase is also considered deceptive.
Comparable value comparisons	Advertising such as "Retail Value $100.00, Our Price $85.00" is deceptive if a verified and substantial number of stores in the market area did not price the item at $100.
Comparisons with suggested prices	A claim that a price is below a manufacturer's suggested or list price may be deceptive if few or no sales occur at that price in a retailer's market area.
Former price comparisons	When a seller represents a price as reduced, the item must have been offered in good faith at a higher price for a substantial previous period. Setting a high price for the purpose of establishing a reference for a price reduction is deceptive.

FIGURE 14–9

Five most common deceptive pricing practices

Predatory Pricing **Predatory pricing** is the practice of charging a very low price for a product with the intent of driving competitors out of business. Once competitors have been driven out, the firm raises its prices. This practice is illegal under the Sherman Act and the Federal Trade Commission Act. Proving the presence of this practice has been difficult and expensive because it must be shown that the predator explicitly attempted to destroy a competitor and the predatory price was below the defendant's average cost.

---

learning review

6. Why would a seller choose a flexible-price policy over a one-price policy?

7. If a firm wished to encourage repeat purchases by a buyer throughout a year, would a cumulative or noncumulative quantity discount be a better strategy?

8. Which pricing practices are covered by the Sherman Act?

LEARNING OBJECTIVES REVIEW

LO1 *Describe how to establish the "approximate price level" using demand-oriented, cost-oriented, profit-oriented, and competition-oriented approaches.*

Demand, cost, profit, and competition influence the initial consideration of the approximate price level for a product or service. Demand-oriented pricing approaches stress consumer demand and revenue implications of pricing and include eight types: skimming, penetration, prestige, price lining, odd-even, target, bundle, and yield management. Cost-oriented pricing approaches emphasize the cost aspects of pricing and include three types:

standard markup, cost-plus, and experience curve pricing. Profit-oriented pricing approaches focus on a balance between revenues and costs to set a price and include three types: target profit, target return-on-sales, and target return-on-investment pricing. And finally, competition-oriented pricing approaches stress what competitors or the marketplace are doing and include three types: customary; above-, at-, or below-market; and loss-leader pricing. Although these approaches are described separately, some of them overlap, and an effective marketing manager will consider several in searching for an approximate price level.

LO2 *Recognize the major factors considered in deriving a final list or quoted price from the approximate price level.*

Given an approximate price level for a product or service, a manager sets a list or quoted price by considering three additional factors. First, a manager must decide whether to follow a one-price versus a flexible-price policy. Second, the manager should consider the effects of the proposed price on the company, customer, and competitors. Finally, consideration should be given to balancing incremental costs and revenues, particularly when price and cost changes are planned.

LO3 *Identify the adjustments made to the approximate price level on the basis of discounts, allowances, and geography.*

Numerous adjustments can be made to the approximate price level. Discounts are reductions from the list or quoted price that a seller gives a buyer as a reward for some activity of the buyer that is favorable to the seller. These include quantity, seasonal, trade (functional), and cash discounts. Allowances offered to buyers also reduce list or quoted prices. Trade-in allowances and promotional allowances are most common. Finally, geographical adjustments are made to list or quoted prices to reflect transportation costs from sellers to buyers. The two general methods for quoting prices related to transportation costs are FOB origin pricing and uniform delivered pricing.

LO4 *Name the principal laws and regulations affecting specific pricing practices.*

There are four principal laws that affect six major pricing practices. The Sherman Act specifically prohibits horizontal price fixing and predatory pricing. The Consumer Goods Pricing Act makes it illegal for companies to engage in vertical price fixing or resale price maintenance agreements. The Federal Trade Commission Act outlaws deceptive pricing. Provisions in this act also address aspects of predatory pricing and geographical pricing. Finally, the Robinson-Patman Act prohibits price discrimination for goods of like grade and quality, covers the use of promotional allowances, and addresses certain aspects of geographical pricing.

FOCUSING ON KEY TERMS

above-, at-, or below-market pricing p. 364
basing-point pricing p. 373
bundle pricing p. 359
cost-plus pricing p. 360
customary pricing p. 364
everyday low pricing p. 372
experience curve pricing p. 361
flexible-price policy p. 366
FOB origin pricing p. 372
loss-leader pricing p. 364

odd-even pricing p. 358
one-price policy p. 366
penetration pricing p. 357
predatory pricing p. 376
prestige pricing p. 357
price discrimination p. 374
price fixing p. 374
price lining p. 358
price war p. 368
product-line pricing p. 367
promotional allowances p. 372

quantity discounts p. 370
skimming pricing p. 356
standard markup pricing p. 360
target pricing p. 358
target profit pricing p. 362
target return-on-investment pricing p. 363
target return-on-sales pricing p. 362
uniform delivered pricing p. 372
yield management pricing p. 359

APPLYING MARKETING KNOWLEDGE

1 Under what conditions would a digital camera manufacturer adopt a skimming price approach for a new product? A penetration approach?

2 What are some similarities and differences between skimming pricing, prestige pricing, and above-market pricing?

3 A producer of microwave ovens has adopted an experience curve pricing approach for its new model. The firm believes it can reduce the cost of producing the model by 20 percent each time volume doubles. The cost to produce the first unit was $1,000. What would be the approximate cost of the 4,096th unit?

4 The Hesper Corporation is a leading manufacturer of high-quality upholstered sofas. Current plans call for an increase of $600,000 in the advertising budget. If the firm sells its sofas for an average price of $850 and the unit variable costs are $550, then what dollar sales increase will be necessary to cover the additional advertising?

5 Suppose executives estimate that the unit variable cost for their VCR is $100, the fixed cost related to the product is $10 million annually, and the target volume for next year is 100,000 recorders. What sales price will be necessary to achieve a target profit of $1 million?

6 A manufacturer of motor oil has a trade discount policy whereby the manufacturer's suggested retail price is $30 per case with the terms of 40/20/10. The manufacturer sells its products through jobbers, who sell to wholesalers, who sell to gasoline stations. What will the manufacturer's sale price be?

7 Suppose a manufacturer of exercise equipment sets a suggested price to the consumer of $395 for a particular piece of equipment to be competitive with similar equipment. The manufacturer sells its equipment to a sporting goods wholesaler who receives 25 percent of the selling price and a retailer who receives 50 percent of the selling price. What demand-oriented pricing approach is being used, and at what price will the manufacturer sell the equipment to the wholesaler?

8 Is there any truth in the statement, "Geographical pricing schemes will always be unfair to some buyers"? Why or why not?

To arrive at the final price(s) for your offering(s):

1 Modify the three prices from your Chapter 13 analysis in light of (*a*) pricing considerations for demand-, cost-, profit-, and competition-oriented Chapter 14 approaches and (*b*) possibilities for discounts, allowances, and geographic adjustments.

2 Do a break-even analysis for each of these three new prices.

3 Choose the final price(s).

video case 14 The Starbury Collection: Setting a Price. Making a Difference.

Why would Stephon Marbury, a 10-year NBA veteran and New York Knicks point guard with a multiyear, multimillion-dollar contract, put his seal of approval on a $14.98 basketball sneaker without a lucrative endorsement guarantee?

Why would Steve & Barry's University Sportswear sell a $14.98 sneaker and forgo a meaty retail margin when other stores charge as much as $150 for a pair of signature sneakers?

More to the point, in a world where the average basketball sneaker is priced at $100 and signature shoes are priced much higher, could the Stephon Marbury and Steve & Barry's partnership market $14.98 signature sneakers in a cost-efficient and profitable manner? In a word, yes.

STEPHON MARBURY + STEVE & BARRY'S = THE STARBURY COLLECTION

In 2005, Stephon Marbury approached executives at Steve & Barry's with a revolutionary idea—market an inexpensive quality basketball sneaker and apparel line with his endorsement and call it the Starbury Collection. Why did Stephon Marbury do this? "Things are crazy out there," Marbury said. "There's kids who are shot over shoes for $150, $100. There's poor mothers out there who bury their child for a basketball sneaker. We're talking about clothes." He added, "It was very important to me that the Starbury Collection have a strong social component for kids and parents, especially in urban areas."

Steve & Barry's executives enthusiastically embraced Marbury's idea given the retailer's aim of providing top-quality merchandise at low prices at its nearly 200 stores in 33 states. In short order, Steve & Barry's contacted Rocketfish, the athletic gear design firm best known for providing high-performance basketball sneaker concepts to Nike, Reebok, and Converse. It then contracted with a supplier to produce the shoe to tight specifications. Rocketfish worked closely with Marbury and Steve & Barry's to create the Starbury One, a sneaker that delivered all the comfort and stability required for professional basketball players and recreational ballers alike. The retail price—$14.98. In an independent and extensive test conducted at the Parsons School of Design in New York City, Starbury One sneakers were found to be no different in the quality of design and materials from a major sneaker brand that retailed for $150.

BRINGING THE STARBURY COLLECTION TO MARKET: ENTER ERIN PATTON

With a great product at a great price, Steve & Barry's president, Andy Todd, turned to Erin Patton to prepare the Starbury Collection launch and build the brand. Patton was no stranger to brand building. He spent five years as the marketing director for the Air Jordan brand at Nike. According to Patton, "Stephon Marbury understood the difficulty parents and kids face keeping pace with the exorbitant price of sneakers. He knows what it means for inner-city kids and the extreme measures that are sometimes used to get these products." Patton viewed Marbury's initiative as "an industry changing event"—and one he too wanted to happen. Marking it happen was another matter.

With a limited marketing budget, Patton realized that an unconventional launch for the Starbury Collection was

Flava of the year.

All-new Starbury styles. In stores April 1st.
Only $14.98, all day, every day. No joke.

What's YOUR flava?

starbury
BY STEPHON MARBURY

Exclusively at Steve & Barry's. The movement is at www.starbury.com

necessary. The Starbury Collection was launched on August 17, 2006, followed by a 40-city, 17-day tour of Steve & Barry's stores with Stephon Marbury in the lead. The launch and tour were timed to send a message to parents from lower-income families as they were doing their back-to-school shopping: You can afford to have your kids look and feel like an NBA basketball player. Starbury Collection ads appeared in exclusively urban publications such as *Slam and Dime* and a website (starbury.com) featuring urban phrases, such as "you feel me," which means you understand what I'm saying.

THE RESULT

The result? Over 3 million Starbury sneakers were sold within eight months of the August 2006 launch. In 2007, the Starbury Collection line expanded from 50 products to more than 200. The line includes the Starbury Two sneaker, polo shirts, skateboard shoes, and other lifestyle products; all under $15. "The Starbury Collection is about Steph's vision to eliminate the pressure that parents and kids feel to spend top dollar on the latest sneakers and clothing," said Todd. By setting the right price, the Starbury Collection at Steve & Barry's University Sportswear seeks to make a difference.

Questions

1 What broad pricing objective is most apparent in Stephon Marbury's offer to endorse a signature sneaker for $14.98?

2 In what ways are the demand factors of (*a*) consumer tastes, (*b*) price and availability of substitute products, and (*c*) consumer income important in influencing consumer demand for the Starbury Collection of sneakers and apparel?

3 For analysis purposes only, assume that (*a*) a pair of Starbury One sneakers is delivered to Steve & Barry's from its supplier at a price of $10.00, (*b*) the launch program cost $500,000 including the tour expenses, website development, and print advertising production and placement, and (*c*) these were the only relevant costs. How many pairs of Starbury One sneakers must Steve & Barry's sell to break even given these launch costs? Has Steve & Barry's achieved a 15 percent return on sales given that 3 million pairs of Starbury One sneakers have been sold?

B FINANCIAL ASPECTS OF MARKETING

Basic concepts from accounting and finance provide valuable tools for marketing executives. This appendix describes an actual company's use of accounting and financial concepts and illustrates how they assist the owner in making marketing decisions.

THE CAPLOW COMPANY

An accomplished artist and calligrapher, Jane Westerlund decided to apply some of her experience to the picture framing business in Minneapolis. She bought an existing retail frame store, The Caplow Company, from a friend who owned the business and wanted to retire. She avoided the do-it-yourself end of the framing business and chose three kinds of business activities: (1) cutting the frame, mats, and glass for customers who brought in their own pictures or prints to be framed; (2) selling prints and posters that she had purchased from wholesalers; and (3) restoring high-quality frames and paintings.

To understand how accounting, finance, and marketing relate to each other, let's analyze (1) the operating statement for her frame shop, (2) some general ratios of interest that are derived from the operating statement, and (3) some ratios that pertain specifically to her pricing decisions.

The Operating Statement

The *operating statement* (also called an *income statement* or *profit-and-loss statement*) summarizes the profitability of a business firm for a specific time period, usually a month, quarter, or year. The title of the operating statement for The Caplow Company shows it is for a one-year period (Figure B–1). The purpose of an operating statement is to show the profit of the firm and the revenues and expenses that led to that profit. This information tells the owner or manager what has happened in the past and suggests actions to improve future profitability.

The left side of Figure B–1 shows that there are three key elements to all operating statements: (1) sales of the firm's goods and services, (2) costs incurred in making and selling the goods and services, and (3) profit or loss, which is the difference between sales and costs.

Sales Elements The sales element of Figure B–1 has four terms that need explanation:

- *Gross sales* are the total amount billed to customers. Dissatisfied customers or errors may reduce the gross sales through returns or allowances.
- *Returns* occur when a customer gives the item purchased back to the seller, who either refunds the purchase price or allows the customer a credit on subsequent purchases. In any event, the seller now owns the item again.
- *Allowances* are given when a customer is dissatisfied with the item purchased and the seller reduces the original purchase price. Unlike returns, in the case of allowances the buyer owns the item.
- *Net sales* are simply gross sales minus returns and allowances.

The operating statement for The Caplow Company shows that

Gross sales	$80,500
Less: Returns and allowances	500
Net sales	$80,000

The low level of returns and allowances shows the shop generally has done a good job in satisfying customers, which is essential in building the repeat business necessary for success.

Cost Elements The *cost of goods sold* (COGS) is the total cost of the products sold during the period. This item

THE CAPLOW COMPANY

Operating Statement

For the Year Ending December 31, 2007

Sales	Gross sales			$80,500
	Less: Returns and allowances			500
	Net sales			$80,000
Costs	Cost of goods sold:			
	Beginning inventory at cost		$ 6,000	
	Purchases at billed cost	$21,000		
	Less: Purchase discounts	300		
	Purchases at net cost	20,700		
	Plus: freight-in	100		
	Net cost of delivered purchases		20,800	
	Direct labor (framing)		14,200	
	Cost of goods available for sale		41,000	
	Less: Ending inventory at cost		5,000	
	Cost of goods sold			36,000
	Gross margin (gross profit)			$44,000
	Expenses:			
	Selling expenses:			
	Sales salaries	2,000		
	Advertising expense	3,000		
	Total selling expense		5,000	
	Administrative expenses:			
	Owner's salary	18,000		
	Bookkeeper's salary	1,200		
	Office supplies	300		
	Total administrative expense		19,500	
	General expenses:			
	Depreciation expense	1,000		
	Interest expense	500		
	Rent expense	2,100		
	Utility expenses (heat, electricity)	3,000		
	Repairs and maintenance	2,300		
	Insurance	2,000		
	Social security taxes	2,200		
	Total general expense		13,100	
	Total expenses			37,600
Profit or loss	Profit before taxes			$ 6,400

varies according to the kind of business. A retail store purchases finished goods and resells them to customers without reworking them in any way. In contrast, a manufacturing firm combines raw and semifinished materials and parts, uses labor and overhead to rework these into finished goods, and then sells them to customers. All these activities are reflected in the cost of goods sold item on a manufacturer's operating statement. Note that the frame shop has some features of a pure retailer (prints and posters it buys that are resold without alteration) and a pure manufacturer (assembling the raw materials of molding, matting, and glass to form a completed frame).

Some terms that relate to cost of goods sold need clarification:

• *Inventory* is the physical material that is purchased from suppliers, may or may not be reworked, and is available for sale to customers. In the frame shop, inventory includes molding, matting, glass, prints, and posters.

- *Purchase discounts* are reductions in the original billed price for reasons such as prompt payment of the bill or the quantity bought.
- *Direct labor* is the cost of the labor used in producing the finished product. For the frame shop, this is the cost of producing the completed frames from the molding, matting, and glass.
- *Gross margin (gross profit)* is the money remaining to manage the business, sell the products or services, and give some profit. Gross margin is net sales minus cost of goods sold.

The two right-hand columns in Figure B–1 between "Net sales" and "Gross margin" calculate the cost of goods sold:

Net sales		$80,000
Cost of goods sold		
Beginning inventory at cost	$ 6,000	
Net cost of delivered purchases	20,800	
Direct labor (framing)	14,200	
Cost of goods available for sale	41,000	
Less: ending inventory at cost	5,000	
Cost of goods sold		36,000
Gross margin (gross profit)		$44,000

This section considers the beginning and ending inventories, the net cost of purchases delivered during the year, and the cost of the direct labor going into making the frames. Subtracting the $36,000 cost of goods sold from the $80,000 net sales gives the $44,000 gross margin.

Jane Westerlund (left) and an assistant assess the restoration of a gold frame for regilding.

Three major categories of expenses are shown in Figure B–1 below the gross margin:

- *Selling expenses* are the costs of selling the product or service produced by the firm. For The Caplow Company there are two such selling expenses: sales salaries of part-time employees waiting on customers and the advertising expense of simple newspaper ads and direct-mail ads sent to customers.
- *Administrative expenses* are the costs of managing the business, and for The Caplow Company include three expenses: the owner's salary, a part-time bookkeeper's salary, and office supplies expense.
- *General expenses* are miscellaneous costs not covered elsewhere; for the frame shop these include seven items: depreciation expense (on equipment), interest expense, rent expense, utility expenses, repairs and maintenance expense, insurance expense, and social security taxes.

As shown in Figure B–1, selling, administrative, and general expenses total $37,600 for The Caplow Company.

Profit Element   What the company has earned, the *profit before taxes,* is found by subtracting cost of goods sold and expenses from net sales. For The Caplow Company, Figure B–1 shows that profit before taxes is $6,400.

General Operating Ratios to Analyze Operations

Looking only at the elements of Caplow's operating statement that extend to the right-hand column highlights the firm's performance on some important dimensions. Using operating ratios such as *expense-to-sales ratios* for expressing basic expense or profit elements as a percentage of net sales gives further insights:

Element in Operating Statement	Dollar Value	Percentage of Net Sales
Gross sales	$80,500	
Less: Returns and allowances	500	
Net sales	80,000	100%
Less: Cost of goods sold	36,000	45
Gross margin	44,000	55
Less: Total expenses	37,600	47
Profit (or loss) before taxes	$ 6,400	8%

Westerlund can use this information to compare her firm's performance from one time period to the next. To do so, it is especially important that she keep the same definitions for each element of her operating statement, also a significant factor in using the electronic spreadsheets discussed in Chapter 14. Performance comparisons between periods are more difficult if she changes definitions for the accounting elements in the operating statement.

She can use either the dollar values or the operating ratios (the value of the element of the operating statement divided by net sales) to analyze the firm's performance. However, the operating ratios are more valuable than the dollar values for two reasons: (1) the simplicity of working with percentages rather than dollars and (2) the availability of operating ratios of typical firms in the same industry, which are published by Dun & Bradstreet and trade associations. Thus, Westerlund can compare her firm's performance not only with that of *other* frame shops but also with that of *small* frame shops that have annual net sales, for example, under $100,000. In this way, she can identify where her operations are better or worse than other similar firms. For example, if trade association data showed a typical frame shop of her size had a ratio of cost of goods sold to net sales of 37 percent, compared with her 45 percent, she might consider steps to reduce this cost through purchase discounts, reducing inbound freight charges, finding lower-cost suppliers, and so on.

Ratios to Use in Setting and Evaluating Price

Using The Caplow Company as an example, we can study four ratios that relate closely to setting a price: (1) markup, (2) markdown, (3) stockturns, and (4) return on investment. These terms are defined in Figure B–2 and explained below.

Markup Both *markup* and gross margin refer to the amount added to the cost of goods sold to arrive at the selling price, and they may be expressed either in dollar or percentage terms. However, the term *markup* is more commonly used in setting retail prices. Suppose the average price Westerlund charges for a framed picture is $80. Then in terms of the first two definitions in Figure B–2 and the earlier information from the operating statement,

Element of Price	Dollar Value
Cost of goods sold	$36
Markup (or gross margin)	44
Selling price	$80

The third definition in Figure B–2 gives the percentage markup on selling price:

$$\text{Markup on selling price } (\%) = \frac{\text{Markup}}{\text{Selling price}} \times 100$$

$$= \frac{44}{80} \times 100 = 55\%$$

FIGURE B–2

How to calculate selling price, markups, markdown, stockturn rate, and return on investment

Name of Financial Element or Ratio	What It Measures	Equation
Selling price ($)	Price customer sees	Cost of goods sold (COGS) + Markup
Markup ($)	Dollars added to COGS to arrive at selling price	Selling price − COGS
Markup on selling price (%)	Relates markup to selling price	$\dfrac{\text{Markup}}{\text{Selling price}} \times 100 = \dfrac{\text{Selling price} - \text{COGS}}{\text{Selling price}} \times 100$
Markup on cost (%)	Relates markup to cost	$\dfrac{\text{Markup}}{\text{COGS}} \times 100 = \dfrac{\text{Selling price} - \text{COGS}}{\text{COGS}} \times 100$
Markdown (%)	Ability of firm to sell its products at initial selling price	$\dfrac{\text{Markdowns}}{\text{Net sales}} \times 100$
Stockturn rate	Ability of firm to move its inventory quickly	$\dfrac{\text{COGS}}{\text{Average inventory at cost}}$ or $\dfrac{\text{Net sales}}{\text{Average inventory at selling price}}$
Return on investment (%)	Profit performance of firm compared with money invested in it	$\dfrac{\text{Net profit after taxes}}{\text{Investment}} \times 100$

And the percentage markup on cost is obtained as follows:

$$\text{Markup on cost (\%)} = \frac{\text{Markup}}{\text{Cost of goods sold}} \times 100$$

$$= \frac{44}{36} \times 100 = 122.2\%$$

Inexperienced retail clerks sometimes fail to distinguish between the two definitions of markup, which (as the preceding calculations show) can represent a tremendous difference, so it is essential to know whether the base is cost or selling price. Marketers generally use selling price as the base for talking about markups unless they specifically state that they are using cost as a base.

Retailers and wholesalers that rely heavily on markup pricing (discussed in Chapter 14) often use standardized tables that convert markup on selling price to markup on cost, and vice versa. The two equations below show how to convert one to the other:

$$\text{Markup on selling price (\%)} = \frac{\text{Markup on cost (\%)}}{100\% + \text{Markup on cost (\%)}} \times 100$$

$$\text{Markup on cost (\%)} = \frac{\text{Markup on selling price (\%)}}{100\% - \text{Markup on selling price (\%)}}$$

Using the data from The Caplow Company gives:

$$\text{Markup on selling price (\%)} = \frac{\text{Markup on cost (\%)}}{100\% + \text{Markup on cost (\%)}} \times 100$$

$$= \frac{122.2}{100 + 122.2} \times 100 = 55\%$$

$$\text{Markup on cost (\%)} = \frac{\text{Markup on selling price (\%)}}{100\% - \text{Markup on selling price (\%)}} \times 100$$

$$= \frac{55}{100 - 55} \times 100 = 122.2\%$$

The use of an incorrect markup base is shown in Westerlund's business. A markup of 122.2 percent on her cost of goods sold for a typical frame she sells gives 122.2% × $36 = $44 of markup. Added to the $36 cost of goods sold, this gives her a selling price of $80 for the framed picture. However, a new clerk working for her who erroneously priced the framed picture at 55 percent of cost of goods sold set the final price at $55.80 ($36 of cost of goods sold plus 55% × $36 = $19.80). The error, if repeated, can be disastrous: frames would be accidentally sold at $55.80, or $24.20 below the intended selling price of $80.

Markdown A *markdown* is a reduction in a retail price that is necessary if the item will not sell at the full selling price to which it has been marked up. The item might not sell for a variety of reasons: the selling price was set too high or the item is out of style or has become soiled or damaged. The seller "takes a markdown" by lowering the price to sell it, thereby converting it to cash to buy future inventory that will sell faster.

The markdown percentage cannot be calculated directly from the operating statement. As shown in the fifth item of Figure B–2, the numerator of the markdown percentage is the total dollar markdowns. Markdowns are reductions in the prices of goods that are purchased by customers. The denominator is net sales.

Suppose The Caplow Company had a total of $700 in markdowns on the prints and posters that are stocked and available for sale. Since the frames are custom made for individual customers, there is little reason for a markdown there. Caplow's markdown percent is then:

A customer discusses choices of framing and matting for her print with Jane Westerlund.

$$\text{Markdown (\%)} = \frac{\text{Markdowns}}{\text{Net sales}} \times 100$$

$$= \frac{\$700}{\$80,000} \times 100$$

$$= 0.875\%$$

Other kinds of retailers often have markdown ratios several times this amount. For example, women's dress stores have markdowns of about 25 percent, and menswear stores have markdowns of about 2 percent.

Stockturn Rate   A business firm is eager to have its inventory move quickly, or "turn over." *Stockturn rate,* or simply stockturns, measures this inventory movement. For a retailer a slow stockturn rate may show it is buying merchandise customers don't want, so this is a critical measure of performance. When a firm sells only a single product, one convenient way to measure stockturn rate is simply to divide its cost of goods sold by average inventory at cost. The sixth item in Figure B–2 shows how to calculate stockturn rate using information in the operating statement:

$$\text{Stockturn rate} = \frac{\text{Cost of goods sold}}{\text{Average inventory at cost}}$$

The dollar amount of average inventory at cost is calculated by adding the beginning and ending inventories for the year and dividing by 2 to get the average. From Caplow's operating statement, we have:

$$\text{Stockturn rate} = \frac{\text{Cost of goods sold}}{\text{Average inventory at cost}}$$

$$= \frac{\text{Cost of goods sold}}{\dfrac{\text{Beginning inventory} + \text{Ending inventory}}{2}}$$

$$= \frac{\$36,000}{\dfrac{\$6,000 + \$5,000}{2}}$$

$$= \frac{\$36,000}{\$5,500}$$

$$= 6.5 \text{ stockturns per year}$$

What is considered a "good stockturn" varies by the kind of industry. For example, supermarkets have limited shelf space for thousands of new products from manufacturers each year, so they watch stockturn carefully by product line. The stockturn rate in supermarkets for breakfast foods is about 17 times per year, for pet food about 22 times per year, and for paper products about 25 times per year.

Return on Investment A better measure of the performance of a firm than the amount of profit it makes in a year is its *return on investment* (ROI), which is the ratio of net income to the investment used to earn that net income. To calculate ROI, it is necessary to subtract income taxes from profit before taxes to obtain net income, then divide this figure by the investment that can be found on a firm's balance sheet (which is another accounting statement that shows the firm's assets, liabilities, and net worth). While financial and accounting experts have many definitions for *investment,* an often-used definition is "total assets."

For our purposes, let's assume that Westerlund has total assets (investment) of $20,000 in The Caplow Company, which covers inventory, store fixtures, and framing equipment. If she pays $1,000 in income taxes, her store's net income is $5,400, so her ROI is given by the seventh item in Figure B–2:

$$\text{Return on investment} = \text{Net income/Investment} \times 100$$

$$= \$5,400/\$20,000 \times 100$$

$$= 27\%$$

If Westerlund wants to improve her ROI next year, the strategies she might take are found in this alternative equation for ROI:

$$\text{ROI} = \text{Net sales/Investment} \times \text{Net income/Net sales}$$

$$= \text{Investment turnover} \times \text{Profit margin}$$

This equation suggests that The Caplow Company's ROI can be improved by raising investment turnover or increasing profit margin. Increasing stockturns will accomplish the former, whereas lowering cost of goods sold to net sales will cause the latter.

15

Managing Marketing Channels and Wholesaling

LEARNING OBJECTIVES

going through all OBJectives

After reading this chapter you should be able to:

LO1 Explain what is meant by a marketing channel of distribution and why intermediaries are needed.

LO2 Distinguish among traditional marketing channels, electronic marketing channels, and different types of vertical marketing systems.

LO3 Describe the factors and considerations that affect a company's choice and management of a marketing channel.

LO4 Recognize how conflict, cooperation, and legal considerations affect marketing channel relationships.

APPLE STORES: CREATING A HIGH-TOUCH CUSTOMER EXPERIENCE IN A HIGH-TECH MARKETING CHANNEL

Apple thrives on innovation . . . in retailing. Yes, retailing! In a short seven-year span, Apple stores have become the gold standard for delivering an unparalleled customer experience. So how did Apple do it?

The vision behind Apple stores was to develop an atmosphere where consumers can experience the thrill of owning and using Apple's complete line of Macintosh computers and an array of digital cameras, camcorders, the entire iPod product family, and more with the assistance of a knowledgeable and customer-friendly staff. In the words of Apple CEO Steven Jobs, Apple stores were to deliver "A buying experience as good as our products." And so it has.

"Apple has changed people's expectations of what retail should be about," says Candace Corlett, a retailing consultant. Product assortments are arranged by customer interests, not product type. Apple products are easily accessible to encourage a customer to "test-drive" them in a shopping environment where clutter is conspicuously absent. Each store's interior design is ultra-modern with a pristine layout and inviting displays. In newer stores, checkout counters have been replaced with Easy Pay, an Apple system that allows salespeople to wander the store with a wireless credit card reader and ask, "Would you like to pay for that?"

But there is more. The customer experience is enhanced with two novel in-store features. Stores contain a Genius Bar where customers can obtain product information and service on all Apple products from genial technical experts. The Genius Bar is complemented by the Studio in another part of the store. The Studio is staffed by "Creatives" who offer one-to-one training on everything from preparing an iMovie to how to deejay a friend's wedding.

Has the focus on an innovative customer experience paid off? Apple stores achieved $1 billion in sales faster than any retail business in history, taking just three years to reach that mark. Equally important, the 220 (and counting) company-owned stores are profitable.[1]

This chapter focuses on marketing channels of distribution and why they are an important component in the marketing mix. It then shows how such channels benefit consumers and the sequence of firms that make up a marketing channel. Finally, it describes factors that influence the choice and management of marketing channels, including channel conflict, cooperation, and legal restrictions.

NATURE AND IMPORTANCE OF MARKETING CHANNELS

Reaching prospective buyers, either directly or indirectly, is a prerequisite for successful marketing. At the same time, buyers benefit from distribution systems used by companies.

What Is a Marketing Channel of Distribution?

You see the results of distribution every day. You may have purchased Lay's Potato Chips at a 7-Eleven store, a book through Amazon.com, and Levi's jeans at Sears. Each of these items was brought to you by a marketing channel of distribution, or simply a **marketing channel**, which consists of individuals and firms involved in the process of making a product or service available for use or consumption by consumers or industrial users.

Marketing channels can be compared with a pipeline through which water flows from a source to terminus. Marketing channels make possible the flow of goods from a producer, through intermediaries, to a buyer. Intermediaries go by various names (Figure 15–1) and perform various functions. Some intermediaries actually purchase items from the seller, store them, and resell them to buyers. For example, Celestial Seasonings produce specialty teas and sell them to food wholesalers. The wholesalers then sell these teas to supermarkets and grocery stores, which, in turn, sell them to consumers. Other intermediaries such as brokers and agents represent sellers but do not actually take title to products—their role is to bring a seller and buyer together. Century 21 real estate agents are examples of this type of intermediary. The importance of intermediaries is made even clearer when we consider the functions they perform and the value they create for buyers.

Value Is Created by Intermediaries

Few consumers appreciate the value created by intermediaries; however, producers recognize that intermediaries make selling goods and services more efficient because they minimize the number of sales contacts necessary to reach a target market.

FIGURE 15–1

A variety of terms is used for marketing intermediaries. They vary in specificity and use in consumer and business markets.

TERM	DESCRIPTION
Middleman	Any intermediary between manufacturer and end-user markets
Agent or broker	Any intermediary with legal authority to act on behalf of the manufacturer
Wholesaler	An intermediary who sells to other intermediaries, usually to retailers; term usually applies to consumer markets
Retailer	An intermediary who sells to consumers
Distributor	An imprecise term, usually used to describe intermediaries who perform a variety of distribution functions, including selling, maintaining inventories, extending credit, and so on; a more common term in business markets but may also be used to refer to wholesalers
Dealer	A more imprecise term than *distributor* that can mean the same as distributor, retailer, wholesaler, and so forth

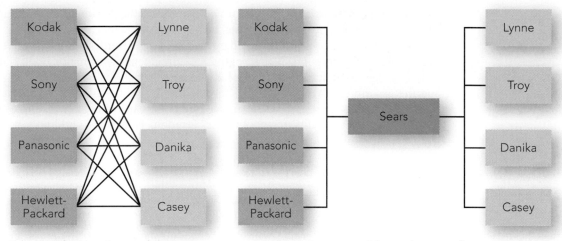

Contacts with no intermediaries
4 producers x 4 buyers = 16 contacts

Contacts with one intermediary
4 producers + 4 buyers = 8 contacts

FIGURE 15–2

Intermediaries minimize transactions and the cost of distribution for producers and customers.

Figure 15–2 shows a simple example of how this comes about in the digital camera industry. Without a retail intermediary (such as Sears), Kodak, Sony, Panasonic, and Hewlett-Packard would each have to make four contacts to reach the four buyers shown who are in the target market. However, each producer has to make only one contact when Sears acts as an intermediary. Equally important from a macromarketing perspective, the total number of industry transactions is reduced from 16 to 8, which reduces producer cost and hence benefits the customer.

Important Functions Performed by Intermediaries Intermediaries make possible the flow of products from producers to buyers by performing three basic functions (Figure 15–3). Intermediaries perform a *transactional function* that involves buying, selling, and risk taking because they stock merchandise in anticipation of sales. Intermediaries perform a *logistical function* evident in the gathering, storing, and dispersing of products (see Chapter 16 on supply chain and logistics management). Finally, intermediaries perform *facilitating functions,* which assist producers in making goods and services more attractive to buyers.

FIGURE 15–3

Marketing channel intermediaries perform three fundamental functions, each of which consists of different activities.

TYPE OF FUNCTION	ACTIVITIES RELATED TO FUNCTION
Transactional function	• *Buying*: Purchasing products for resale or as an agent for supply of a product • *Selling*: Contacting potential customers, promoting products, and seeking orders • *Risk taking*: Assuming business risks in the ownership of inventory that can become obsolete or deteriorate
Logistical function	• *Assorting*: Creating product assortments from several sources to serve customers • *Storing*: Assembling and protecting products at a convenient location to offer better customer service • *Sorting*: Purchasing in large quantities and breaking into smaller amounts desired by customers • *Transporting*: Physically moving a product to customers
Facilitating function	• *Financing*: Extending credit to customers • *Grading*: Inspecting, testing, or judging products, and assigning them quality grades • *Marketing information and research*: Providing information to customers and suppliers, including competitive conditions and trends

All three functions must be performed in a marketing channel, even though each channel member may not participate in all three. Channel members often negotiate about which specific functions they will perform. Borders, a leading U.S. book retailer, is a case in point. It has negotiated agreements with major book publishers whereby they assume responsibility for choosing books for Borders to buy, displaying the assortment of books on its shelves, and providing information on new titles and consumer reading preferences in specific book categories. For example, Harper-Collins has responsibility for cookbooks, Random House for children's books, and Pearson for computer books.[2]

Consumers Also Benefit from Intermediaries   Consumers also benefit from intermediaries. Having the goods and services you want, when you want them, where you want them, and in the form you want them is the ideal result of marketing channels.

In more specific terms, marketing channels help create value for consumers through the four utilities described in Chapter 1: time, place, form, and possession. Time utility refers to having a product or service when you want it. For example, FedEx provides next-morning delivery. Place utility means having a product or service available where consumers want it, such as having a Texaco gas station located on a long stretch of lonely highway. Form utility involves enhancing a product or service to make it more appealing to buyers. Consider the importance of bottlers in the soft-drink industry. Coca-Cola and Pepsi-Cola manufacture the flavor concentrate (cola, lemon-lime) and sell it to bottlers—intermediaries—which then add sweetener and the concentrate to carbonated water and package the beverage in bottles and cans, which are then sold to retailers. Possession utility entails efforts by intermediaries to help buyers take possession of a product or service, such as having airline tickets delivered by a travel agency.

learning review	1. What is meant by a marketing channel?
	2. What are the three basic functions performed by intermediaries?

CHANNEL STRUCTURE AND ORGANIZATION

A product can take many routes on its journey from a producer to buyers. Marketers continually search for the most efficient route from the many alternatives available. As you'll see, there are some important differences between the marketing channels for consumer goods and those for business goods.

Marketing Channels for Consumer Goods and Services

Figure 15–4 shows the four most common marketing channels for consumer goods and services. It also shows the number of levels in each marketing channel, as evidenced by the number of intermediaries between a producer and ultimate buyers. As the number of intermediaries between a producer and buyer increases, the channel is viewed as increasing in length. Thus, the producer → wholesaler → retailer → consumer channel is longer than the producer → consumer channel.

Direct Channel   Channel A represents a *direct channel* because a producer and ultimate consumers deal directly with each other. Many products and services are distributed this way. A number of insurance companies sell their financial services using a direct channel and branch sales offices. The Schwan Food Company of Marshall,

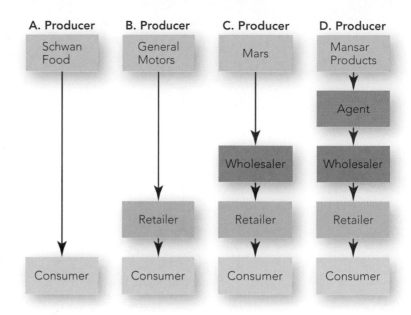

Minnesota, markets a full line of frozen foods in the United States using about 6,500 route salespeople who sell from refrigerated trucks. Because there are no intermediaries with a direct channel, the producer must perform all channel functions.

Indirect Channel   The remaining three channel forms are *indirect channels* because intermediaries are inserted between the producer and consumers and perform numerous channel functions. Channel B, with a retailer added, is most common when a retailer is large and can buy in large quantities from a producer or when the cost of inventory makes it too expensive to use a wholesaler. Automobile manufacturers such as General Motors, Ford, and Toyota use this channel, and a local car dealer acts as a retailer. Why is there no wholesaler? So many variations exist in the product that it would be impossible for a wholesaler to stock all the models required to satisfy buyers; in addition, the cost of maintaining an inventory would be too high. However, large retailers such as Sears, 7-Eleven, Staples, Safeway, and Home Depot buy in sufficient quantities to make it cost effective for a producer to deal with only a retail intermediary.

Adding a wholesaler in Channel C is most common for low-cost, low-unit value items that are frequently purchased by consumers, such as candy, confectionary items, and magazines. For example, Mars sells its line of candies to wholesalers in case quantities, who then break down (sort) the cases so that individual retailers can order in boxes or much smaller quantities.

Channel D, the most indirect channel, is employed when there are many small manufacturers and many small retailers, and an agent is used to help coordinate a large supply of the product. Mansar Products, Ltd., is a Belgian producer of specialty jewelry that uses agents to sell to wholesalers in the United States, which then sell to many small independent jewelry retailers.

Marketing Channels for Business Goods and Services

The four most common channels for business goods and services are shown in Figure 15–5 on the next page. In contrast with channels for consumer products, business channels typically are shorter and rely on one intermediary or none at all because business users are fewer in number, tend to be more concentrated geographically, and buy in larger quantities (see Chapter 6).

Direct Channel   Channel A, represented by IBM's large, mainframe computer business, is a direct channel. Firms using this channel maintain their own salesforce

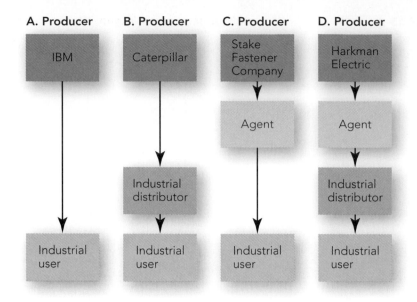

FIGURE 15–5

Common marketing channels for business goods and services differ by the kind and number of intermediaries.

and perform all channel functions. This channel is employed when buyers are large and well defined, the sales effort requires extensive negotiations, and the products are of high unit value and require hands-on expertise in terms of installation or use.

Indirect Channel   Channels B, C, and D are indirect channels with one or more intermediaries to reach industrial users. In Channel B an **industrial distributor** performs a variety of marketing channel functions, including selling, stocking, delivering a full product assortment, and financing. In many ways, industrial distributors are like wholesalers in consumer channels. Caterpillar uses industrial distributors to sell its construction and mining equipment in over 200 countries. In addition to selling, Caterpillar distributors stock 40,000 to 50,000 parts and service equipment using highly trained technicians.

Channel C introduces a second intermediary, an *agent,* who serves primarily as the independent selling arm of producers and represents a producer to industrial users. For example, Stake Fastener Company, a producer of industrial fasteners, has an agent call on industrial users rather than employing its own salesforce.

Channel D is the longest channel and includes both agents and distributors. For instance, Harkman Electric, a producer of electric products, uses agents to call on electrical distributors who sell to industrial users.

Electronic Marketing Channels

These common marketing channels for consumer and business goods and services are not the only routes to the marketplace. Advances in electronic commerce have opened new avenues for reaching buyers and creating customer value.

Interactive electronic technology has made possible **electronic marketing channels**, which employ the Internet to make goods and services available for consumption or use by consumers or business buyers. A unique feature of these channels is that they combine electronic and traditional intermediaries to create time, place, form, and possession utility for buyers.[3]

Figure 15–6 shows the electronic marketing channels for books (Amazon.com), automobiles (Autobytel.com), reservation services (Orbitz.com), and personal computers (Dell.com). Are you surprised that they look a lot like common marketing channels? An important reason for the similarity resides in channel functions detailed in Figure 15–3. Electronic intermediaries can and do perform transactional and facilitating functions effectively and at a relatively lower cost than traditional

FIGURE 15–6

Consumer electronic marketing channels look much like those for consumer goods and services. Read the text to learn why.

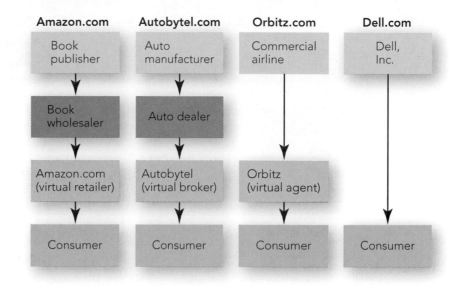

intermediaries because of efficiencies made possible by information technology. However, electronic intermediaries are incapable of performing elements of the logistical function, particularly for products such as books and automobiles. This function remains with traditional intermediaries or with the producer, as evident with Dell, Inc., and its direct channel.

Many services can be distributed through electronic marketing channels, such as car rental reservations, marketed by Alamo.com, financial securities by Schwab. com, and insurance by MetLife.com. Software too can be marketed this way. However, many other services such as health care and auto repair still involve traditional intermediaries.

Direct and Multichannel Marketing

Many firms also use direct and multichannel marketing to reach buyers. **Direct marketing channels** allow consumers to buy products by interacting with various advertising media without a face-to-face meeting with a salesperson. Direct marketing channels include mail-order selling, direct-mail sales, catalog sales, telemarketing, interactive media, and televised home shopping (for example, the Home Shopping Network). Some firms sell products almost entirely through direct marketing. These firms include L.L. Bean (apparel), Sharper Image (expensive gifts and novelties), and Newegg.com (consumer electronics). Manufacturers such as Nestlé and Sunkist, in addition to using traditional channels composed of wholesalers and retailers, employ direct marketing through catalogs and telemarketing to reach more buyers. Direct marketing is covered in greater depth in Chapter 18.

Multichannel marketing is the *blending* of different communication and delivery channels that are *mutually reinforcing* in attracting, retaining, and building relationships with consumers who shop and buy in traditional intermediaries and online. Multichannel marketing seeks to integrate a firm's electronic and delivery channels. At Eddie Bauer, for example, every effort is made to make the apparel shopping and purchase experience for its customers the same in its retail stores, with its catalog, and at its website. According to an Eddie Bauer marketing manager, "We don't distinguish between channels because it's all Eddie Bauer to our customers."[4]

Multichannel marketing also can leverage the value-adding capabilities of different channels. For example, retail stores can leverage their physical presence by allowing customers to pick up their online orders at a nearby store or return or exchange nonstore purchases if they wish. Catalogs can serve as shopping tools

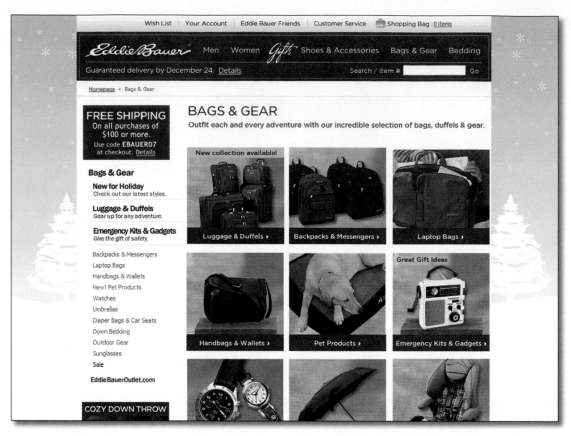

Eddie Bauer engages in multichannel marketing through its 431 retail and outlet stores in North America, Japan, and Germany, its website, and catalog.

Eddie Bauer
www.eddiebauer.com

for online purchasing, as they do for store purchasing. Websites can help consumers do their homework before visiting a store. Office Depot has leveraged its store, catalog, and website channels with impressive results. The company does more than $4.5 billion in online retail sales annually. Multichannel marketing is discussed further in Chapter 21 on interactive marketing.

Dual Distribution and Strategic Channel Alliances

In some situations producers use **dual distribution**, an arrangement whereby a firm reaches different buyers by employing two or more different types of channels for the same basic product. For example, GE sells its large appliances directly to home and apartment builders but uses retail stores, including Lowe's home centers, to sell to consumers. In some instances, firms pair multiple channels with a multibrand strategy (see Chapter 11). This is done to minimize cannibalization of the firm's family brand and differentiate the channels. For example, Hallmark sells its Hallmark greeting cards through Hallmark stores and select department stores, and its Ambassador brand of cards through discount and drugstore chains.

In other instances, a firm will distribute modified products through different channels. Zoecon Corporation sells its insect control chemicals to professional pest-control operators such as Orkin and Terminex. A modified compound is sold to Boyle-Midway for use in its Black-Flag Roach Ender brand.

A recent innovation in marketing channels is the use of **strategic channel alliances**, whereby one firm's marketing channel is used to sell another firm's products. An alliance between Kraft Foods and Starbucks is a case in point. Kraft distributes Starbucks coffee in U.S. supermarkets and internationally. Strategic alliances are popular in global marketing, where the creation of marketing channel relationships is expensive and time consuming. For example, General Motors distributes the

Nestlé and General Mills—Cereal Partners Worldwide

Can you say Nestlé Cheerios *miel amandes*? Millions of French start their day with this European equivalent of General Mills' Honey Nut Cheerios, made possible by Cereal Partners Worldwide (CPW). CPW is a strategic alliance designed from the start to be a global business. It joined the cereal manufacturing and marketing capability of U.S.-based General Mills with the worldwide distribution clout of Swiss-based Nestlé.

From its headquarters in Switzerland, CPW first launched General Mills cereals under the Nestlé label in France, the United Kingdom, Spain, and Portugal in 1991. Today, CPW competes in 130 international markets.

The General Mills–Nestlé strategic channel alliance also increased the ready-to-eat cereal worldwide market share of these companies, which are already rated as the two best-managed firms in the world. CPW currently accounts for over 25 percent of global cereal sales with about $2 billion in annual revenue.

Swedish Saab through its Saturn dealers in Canada. General Mills and Nestlé have an extensive alliance that spans 130 international markets from Mexico to China. Read the accompanying Marketing Matters box so you won't be surprised when you are served Nestlé (not General Mills) Cheerios when traveling outside North America.[5]

A Closer Look at Channel Intermediaries

Channel structures for consumer and business products assume various forms based on the number and type of intermediaries. Knowledge of the roles played by these intermediaries is important for understanding how channels operate in practice.

The terms *wholesaler, agent,* and *retailer* have been used in a general fashion consistent with the meanings given in Figure 15–1. However, on closer inspection, a variety of specific types of intermediaries emerges. These intermediaries engage in wholesaling activities—those activities involved in selling products and services to those who are buying for the purposes of resale or business use. Intermediaries engaged in retailing activities are discussed in detail in Chapter 17. Figure 15–7 on the next page describes the functions performed by major types of independent wholesalers.[6]

Merchant Wholesalers **Merchant wholesalers** are independently owned firms that take title to the merchandise they handle. They go by various names, including industrial distributor (described earlier). Over 80 percent of the firms engaged in wholesaling activities are merchant wholesalers.

Merchant wholesalers are classified as either full-service or limited-service wholesalers, depending on the number of functions performed. Two major types of full-service wholesalers exist. *General merchandise* (or *full-line*) *wholesalers* carry a broad assortment of merchandise and perform all channel functions. This type of wholesaler is most prevalent in the hardware, drug, and clothing industries. However,

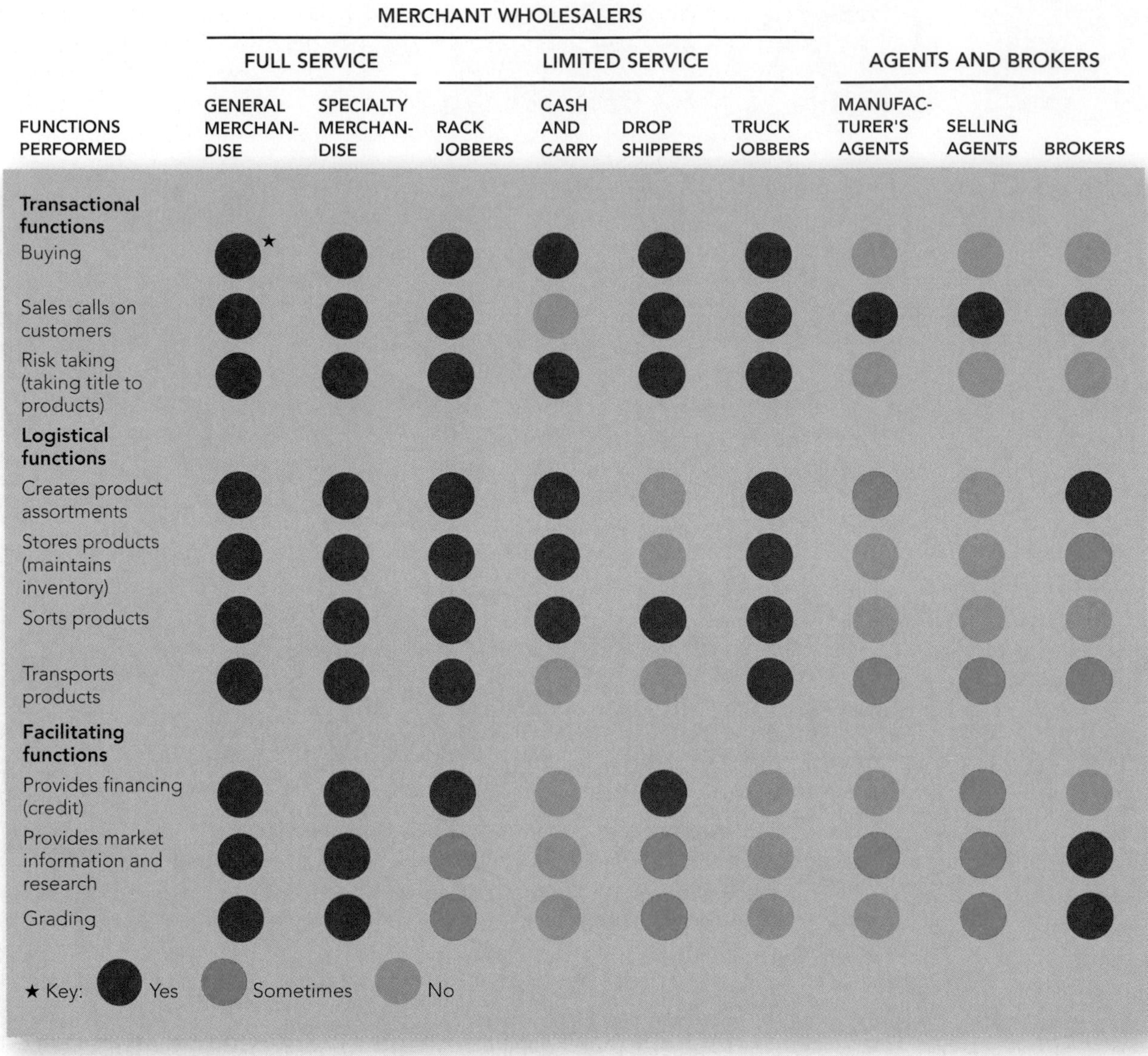

FIGURE 15–7

Functions performed by independent wholesaler types vary. Only full-service wholesalers perform all channel functions.

FUNCTIONS PERFORMED	FULL SERVICE		LIMITED SERVICE				AGENTS AND BROKERS		
	GENERAL MERCHAN-DISE	SPECIALTY MERCHAN-DISE	RACK JOBBERS	CASH AND CARRY	DROP SHIPPERS	TRUCK JOBBERS	MANUFAC-TURER'S AGENTS	SELLING AGENTS	BROKERS
Transactional functions									
Buying	Yes ★	Yes	Yes	Yes	Yes	Yes	Sometimes	Sometimes	Sometimes
Sales calls on customers	Yes	Yes	Yes	No	Yes	Yes	Yes	Yes	Yes
Risk taking (taking title to products)	Yes	Yes	Yes	Yes	Yes	Yes	No	No	No
Logistical functions									
Creates product assortments	Yes	Yes	Yes	Yes	Sometimes	Yes	Sometimes	Sometimes	Yes
Stores products (maintains inventory)	Yes	Yes	Yes	Yes	No	Yes	Sometimes	Sometimes	No
Sorts products	Yes	Yes	Yes	Yes	Yes	Yes	No	No	No
Transports products	Yes	Yes	Sometimes	No	No	Yes	No	No	No
Facilitating functions									
Provides financing (credit)	Yes	Yes	Yes	No	Yes	No	No	Sometimes	No
Provides market information and research	Yes	Yes	Sometimes	No	Sometimes	Sometimes	Yes	Yes	Yes
Grading	Yes	Yes	Sometimes	Sometimes	Sometimes	Sometimes	No	No	Yes

★ Key: ● Yes ● Sometimes ○ No

these wholesalers do not maintain much depth of assortment within specific product lines. *Specialty merchandise* (or *limited-line*) *wholesalers* offer a relatively narrow range of products but have an extensive assortment within the product lines carried. They perform all channel functions and are found in the health foods, automotive parts, and seafood industries.

Four major types of limited-service wholesalers exist. *Rack jobbers* furnish the racks or shelves that display merchandise in retail stores, perform all channel functions, and sell on consignment to retailers, which means they retain the title to the products displayed and bill retailers only for the merchandise sold. Familiar products such as hosiery, toys, housewares, and health and beauty items are sold by rack jobbers. *Cash and carry wholesalers* take title to merchandise but sell only to buyers who call on them, pay cash for merchandise, and furnish their own transportation for merchandise. They carry a limited product assortment and do not make deliveries, extend credit, or supply market information. This wholesaler is common in electric supplies, office supplies, hardware products, and groceries.

Drop shippers, or desk jobbers, are wholesalers that own the merchandise they sell but do not physically handle, stock, or deliver it. They simply solicit orders from retailers and other wholesalers and have the merchandise shipped directly from a producer to a buyer. Drop shippers are used for bulky products such as coal, lumber, and chemicals, which are sold in extremely large quantities. *Truck jobbers* are small wholesalers that have a small warehouse from which they stock their trucks for distribution to retailers. They usually handle limited assortments of fast-moving or perishable items that are sold for cash directly from trucks in their original packages. Truck jobbers handle products such as bakery items, dairy products, and meat.

Agents and Brokers Unlike merchant wholesalers, agents and brokers do not take title to merchandise and typically perform fewer channel functions. They make their profit from commissions or fees paid for their services, whereas merchant wholesalers make their profit from the sale of the merchandise they own.

Manufacturer's agents and selling agents are the two major types of agents used by producers. **Manufacturer's agents**, or *manufacturer's representatives*, work for several producers and carry noncompetitive, complementary merchandise in an exclusive territory. Manufacturer's agents act as a producer's sales arm in a territory and are principally responsible for the transactional channel functions, primarily selling. They are used extensively in the automotive supply, footwear, and fabricated steel industries.

By comparison, **selling agents** represent a single producer and are responsible for the entire marketing function of that producer. They design promotional plans, set prices, determine distribution policies, and make recommendations on product strategy. Selling agents are used by small producers in the textile, apparel, food, and home furnishing industries.

Brokers are independent firms or individuals whose principal function is to bring buyers and sellers together to make sales. Brokers, unlike agents, usually have no continuous relationship with the buyer or seller but negotiate a contract between two parties and then move on to another task. Brokers are used extensively by producers of seasonal products (such as fruits and vegetables) and in the real estate industry.

A unique broker that acts in many ways like a manufacturer's agent is a food broker, representing buyers and sellers in the grocery industry. Food brokers differ from conventional brokers because they act on behalf of producers on a permanent basis and receive a commission for their services. For example, Nabisco uses food brokers to sell its candies, margarine, and Planters peanuts, but it sells its line of cookies and crackers directly to retail stores.

Manufacturer's Branches and Offices Unlike merchant wholesalers, agents, and brokers, manufacturer's branches and sales offices are wholly owned extensions of the producer that perform wholesaling activities. Producers assume wholesaling functions when there are no intermediaries to perform these activities, customers are few in number and geographically concentrated, or orders are large or require significant attention. A *manufacturer's branch office* carries a producer's inventory and performs the functions of a full-service wholesaler. A *manufacturer's sales office* does not carry inventory, typically performs only a sales function, and serves as an alternative to agents and brokers.

Vertical Marketing Systems and Channel Partnerships

The traditional marketing channels described so far represent a loosely knit network of independent producers and intermediaries brought together to distribute goods and services. However, other channel arrangements exist for the purpose of improving efficiency in performing channel functions and achieving greater marketing effectiveness. These arrangements are called vertical marketing systems and channel partnerships. **Vertical marketing systems** are professionally managed and centrally coordinated marketing channels designed to achieve channel economies and maximum marketing impact.[7] Figure 15–8 on the next page depicts the major types of vertical marketing systems: corporate, contractual, and administered.

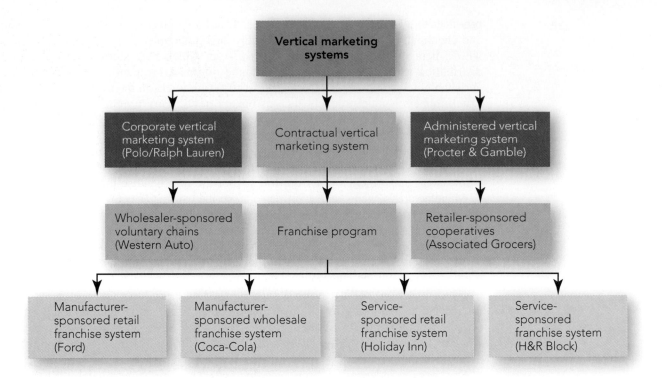

FIGURE 15–8

There are three major types of vertical marketing systems—corporate, contractual, and administered. Contractual systems are the most popular.

Corporate Systems The combination of successive stages of production and distribution under a single ownership is a *corporate vertical marketing system*. For example, a producer might own the intermediary at the next level down in the channel. This practice, called *forward integration*, is exemplified by Polo/Ralph Lauren, which manufactures clothing and also owns apparel shops. Other examples of forward integration include Goodyear, Apple, and Sherwin-Williams. Alternatively, a retailer might own a manufacturing operation, a practice called *backward integration*. For example, Kroger supermarkets operate 42 manufacturing facilities that produce everything from aspirin to cottage cheese, for sale under the Kroger label. Tiffany & Co., the exclusive jewelry retailer, manufactures about half of the fine jewelry items for sale through its 150 stores and boutiques worldwide.

Companies seeking to reduce distribution costs and gain greater control over supply sources or resale of their products pursue forward and backward integration. However, both types of integration increase a company's capital investment and fixed costs. For this reason, many companies favor contractual vertical marketing systems to achieve channel efficiencies and marketing effectiveness.

Contractual Systems Under a *contractual vertical marketing system*, independent production and distribution firms integrate their efforts on a contractual basis to obtain greater functional economies and marketing impact than they could achieve alone. Contractual systems are the most popular among the three types of vertical marketing systems.

Three variations of contractual systems exist. *Wholesaler-sponsored voluntary chains* involve a wholesaler that develops a contractual relationship with small, independent retailers to standardize and coordinate buying practices, merchandising programs, and inventory management efforts. With the organization of a large number of independent retailers, economies of scale and volume discounts can be achieved to compete with chain stores. IGA and Ben Franklin variety and craft stores represent wholesaler-sponsored voluntary chains. *Retailer-sponsored cooperatives* exist when small, independent retailers form an organization that operates a wholesale facility cooperatively. Member retailers then concentrate their buying power through the

Tiffany & Co. and H&R Block represent two different types of vertical marketing systems. Read the text to find out how they differ.

Tiffany & Co.
www.tiffany.com

H&R Block
www.hrblock.com

wholesaler and plan collaborative promotional and pricing activities. Examples of retailer-sponsored cooperatives include Associated Grocers and Ace Hardware.

The most visible variation of contractual systems is franchising. **Franchising** is a contractual arrangement between a parent company (a franchisor) and an individual or firm (a franchisee) that allows the franchisee to operate a certain type of business under an established name and according to specific rules. Franchises generate $1.5 trillion in sales through 770,000 outlets annually in the United States.[8]

Four types of franchise arrangements are most popular. *Manufacturer-sponsored retail franchise systems* are prominent in the automobile industry, where a manufacturer such as Ford licenses dealers to sell its cars subject to various sales and service conditions. *Manufacturer-sponsored wholesale systems* exist in the soft-drink industry, where Pepsi-Cola licenses wholesalers (bottlers) that purchase concentrate from Pepsi-Cola and then carbonate, bottle, promote, and distribute its products to supermarkets and restaurants. *Service-sponsored retail franchise systems* are provided by firms that have designed a unique approach for performing a service and wish to profit by selling the franchise to others. Holiday Inn, Avis, and McDonald's represent this franchising approach. *Service-sponsored franchise systems* exist when franchisors license individuals or firms to dispense a service under a trade name and specific guidelines. Examples include Snelling and Snelling, Inc., employment services and H&R Block tax services. Franchising is discussed further in Chapter 17.

Administered Systems In comparison, *administered vertical marketing systems* achieve coordination at successive stages of production and distribution by the size and influence of one channel member rather than through ownership. Procter & Gamble, given its broad product assortment ranging from disposable diapers to detergents, is able to obtain cooperation from supermarkets in displaying, promoting, and pricing its products. Wal-Mart can obtain cooperation from manufacturers in terms of product specifications, price levels, and promotional support, given its position as the world's largest retailer.

Channel Partnerships Increasingly, channel members are forging channel partnerships akin to supply partnerships described in Chapter 6. A **channel partnership** consists of agreements and procedures among channel members for ordering and physically distributing a producer's products through the channel to the ultimate consumer.[9] A central feature of channel partnerships is the collaborative use of information and communication technology to better serve customers and reduce the time and cost of performing channel functions. Channel partnerships are elaborated upon in Chapter 16 on supply chain and logistics management.

learning review

3. What is the difference between a direct and an indirect channel?

4. Why are channels for business products typically shorter than channels for consumer products?

5. What is the principal distinction between a corporate vertical marketing system and an administered vertical marketing system?

CHANNEL CHOICE AND MANAGEMENT

Marketing channels not only link a producer to its buyers but also provide the means through which a firm implements various elements of its marketing strategy. Therefore, choosing a marketing channel is a critical decision.

Factors Affecting Channel Choice and Management

The final choice of a marketing channel by a producer depends on a number of factors that often interact with each other.

Environmental Factors Environmental factors described in Chapter 3 have an important effect on the choice and management of a marketing channel. For example, Tupperware Corporation, a name synonymous with kitchen utensils and plastic storage containers sold in the home at Tupperware parties, now uses shopping mall kiosks and an online catalog to sell its wares. Changing family lifestyles with high employment among women prompted this action. Advances in the technology of growing, transporting, and storing perishable cut flowers has allowed Kroger to eliminate flower wholesalers and buy direct from flower growers around the world. Kroger's annual cut flower sales exceed $100 million, making it the largest flower retailer in the world. The Internet has created new marketing channel opportunities for a variety of products, including consumer electronics, books, music, video, and clothing and accessory items.

Regulatory factors also influence channel choice, notably in global markets. Read the accompanying Marketing Matters box to learn how Avon responded to China's ban on direct selling in 1998 and subsequent lifting of the ban in 2005.[10]

Consumer Factors Consumer characteristics have a direct bearing on the choice and management of a marketing channel. Determining which channel is most appropriate is based on answers to fundamental questions such as: Who are potential customers? Where do they buy? When do they buy? How do they buy? What do they buy? These answers also indicate the type of intermediary best suited to reaching target buyers.

For example, Ricoh Company, Ltd., studied the serious (as opposed to recreational) camera user and concluded that a change in marketing channels was necessary. The company terminated its contract with a wholesaler that sold to mass merchandise stores and began using manufacturer's agents who sold to photo specialty stores. These stores agreed to stock and display Ricoh's full line and promote it prominently. Sales volume tripled within 18 months. Recognizing that car buyers now comparison shop on the Internet, automakers now promote their own websites to provide price and model information as well as dealer locations.

Marketing Matters > > > > > entrepreneurship

Avon Is Calling Again in China

What do you do when your marketing channel is banned by a government? Just ask executives at Avon, Inc., the world's largest cosmetic and beauty products direct selling company.

Avon pioneered direct selling in China in 1990. By 1998, the company had about 75,000 active independent representatives successfully selling its product line in China. The entrepreneurial spirit among Chinese women had proven to fit well with Avon's direct selling channel. Then, in April 1998, the Chinese State Council issued an order banning all forms of direct selling in China.

In response, Avon established a retail distribution network that grew to include some 6,300 independent beauty

boutiques and over 1,000 cosmetic parlors in department stores across China by 2005. Then, in December 2005, direct selling was permitted in China provided companies met specific operating and licensing requirements. Avon was the first company to meet these standards and began recruiting representatives. By 2008, Avon had over 200,000 active representatives in China. Avon's retail network has been retained to offer after-sales services—including order pick-ups and product returns—and sell Avon products.

Andrea Jung, Avon's chairwoman and CEO, says the market in China could soon add $1 billion to the company's annual profit.

Product Factors In general, highly sophisticated products such as large, scientific computers, unstandardized products such as custom-built machinery, and products of high unit value are distributed directly to buyers. Unsophisticated, standardized products with low unit value, such as table salt, are typically distributed through indirect channels. A product's stage in the life cycle also affects marketing channels. This was shown in the description of the fax machine product life cycle in Chapter 11.

Company Factors A firm's financial, human, or technological capabilities affect channel choice. For example, firms that are unable to employ a salesforce might use manufacturer's agents or selling agents to reach wholesalers or buyers. If a firm has multiple products for a particular target market, it might use a direct channel. Firms with a limited product line might use intermediaries to reach buyers.

Company factors also apply to intermediaries. For example, personal computer hardware and software producers wishing to reach business users might look to value-added resellers such as Bell Microproducts, which has its own salesforce and service staff that calls on businesses.

Channel Choice Considerations

Recognizing that numerous routes to buyers exist and also recognizing the factors just described, marketing executives typically consider three questions when choosing a marketing channel and intermediaries:

1. Which channel and intermediaries will provide the best coverage of the target market?
2. Which channel and intermediaries will best satisfy the buying requirements of the target market?
3. Which channel and intermediaries will be the most profitable?

Target Market Coverage Achieving the best coverage of the target market requires attention to the density—that is, the number of stores in a geographical

Read the text to learn which buying requirements are satisfied by Jiffy Lube and PETCO.

Jiffy Lube International
www.jiffylube.com

PETCO Animal Supplies
www.petco.com

area—and type of intermediaries to be used at the retail level of distribution.[11] Three degrees of distribution density exist: intensive, exclusive, and selective.

Intensive distribution means that a firm tries to place its products and services in as many outlets as possible. Intensive distribution is usually chosen for convenience products or services such as candy, fast food, newspapers, and soft drinks. For example, Coca-Cola's retail distribution objective is to place its products "within an arm's reach of desire." Cash, yes cash, is distributed intensively by Visa. It operates over 1 million automatic teller machines in more than 170 countries.

Exclusive distribution is the extreme opposite of intensive distribution because only one retail outlet in a specified geographical area carries the firm's products. Exclusive distribution is typically chosen for specialty products or services such as automobiles, some women's fragrances, men's and women's apparel and accessories, and yachts. Gucci, one of the world's leading luxury goods companies, uses exclusive distribution in the marketing of its Yves Saint Laurent, Sergio Rossi, Boucheron, Opium, and Gucci brands. Sometimes retailers sign exclusive distribution agreements with manufacturers and suppliers. For instance, Radio Shack sells only Acer, Compaq, and Hewlett-Packard desktop computers in its 6,000 stores.

Selective distribution lies between these two extremes and means that a firm selects a few retail outlets in a specific geographical area to carry its products. Selective distribution weds some of the market coverage benefits of intensive distribution to the control over resale evident with exclusive distribution. For this reason, selective distribution is the most common form of distribution intensity. It is usually associated with shopping goods or services such as Rolex watches, Ben Hogan golf clubs, and Henredon furniture.

Satisfying Buyer Requirements A second consideration in channel choice is gaining access to channels and intermediaries that satisfy at least some of the interests buyers might want fulfilled when they purchase a firm's products or services. These interests fall into four broad categories: (1) information, (2) convenience, (3) variety, and (4) pre- or postsale services. Each relates to customer experience.

Information is an important requirement when buyers have limited knowledge or desire specific data about a product or service. Properly chosen intermediaries communicate with buyers through in-store displays, demonstrations, and personal selling. Consumer electronics manufacturers such as Sony and Apple have opened their own retail outlets staffed with highly trained personnel, to inform buyers how their products can better satisfy each customer's needs.

Going Online

Visit an Apple Store to See What All the Excitement Is About

Interested in visiting an Apple store to see what all the excitement is about? Is a store situated near you? If you answered yes to the first question and no to the second, then log on to www.ifoapplestore.com. Here you will find exterior and interior photographs and video tours of various Apple stores, including a walking tour led by Steven Jobs himself. If you are interested in learning whether or not an Apple store is planned for your area, visit this website to find announcements of grand openings.

Convenience has multiple meanings for buyers, such as proximity or driving time to a retail outlet. For example, 7-Eleven stores, with more than 30,000 outlets worldwide, many of which are open 24 hours a day, satisfy this interest for buyers. Candy and snack-food firms benefit by gaining display space in these stores. For other consumers, convenience means a minimum of time and hassle. Jiffy Lube, which promises to change engine oil and filters quickly, appeals to this aspect of convenience. For those who shop on the Internet, convenience means that websites must be easy to locate and navigate, and image downloads must be fast. A commonly held view among website developers is the "eight second rule": Consumers will abandon their efforts to enter or navigate a website if download time exceeds eight seconds.[12]

Variety reflects buyers' interest in having numerous competing and complementary items from which to choose. Variety is evident in the breadth and depth of products and brands carried by intermediaries, which enhances their attraction to buyers. Thus, manufacturers of pet food and supplies seek distribution through pet superstores such as PETCO and PetSmart, which offer a wide array of pet products.

Pre- or postsale services provided by intermediaries are an important buying requirement for products such as large household appliances that require delivery, installation, and credit. Therefore, Whirlpool seeks dealers that provide such services.

Steven Jobs' decision to distribute Apple products through company-owned stores was motivated by the failure of retailers to deliver on these four consumer interests for Apple. "I started to get scared," said Jobs, "we had to innovate here."[13] Visit the website in the Going Online box to learn more about Apple stores.

Profitability The third consideration in choosing a channel is profitability, which is determined by the margins earned (revenue minus cost) for each channel member and for the channel as a whole. Channel cost is the critical dimension of profitability. These costs include distribution, advertising, and selling expenses associated with different types of marketing channels. The extent to which channel members share these costs determines the margins received by each member and by the channel as a whole.

Companies routinely monitor the performance of their marketing channels. Read the Using Marketing Dashboards box on the next page to see how Charlesburg Furniture views the sales and profit performance of its marketing channels.

Global Dimensions of Marketing Channels

Marketing channels around the world reflect traditions, customs, geography, and the economic history of individual countries and societies. Even so, the basic marketing

Using Marketing Dashboards

Channel Sales and Profit at Charlesburg Furniture

Charlesburg Furniture is one of 1,000 wood furniture manufacturers in the United States. The company sells its furniture through furniture store chains, independent furniture stores, and department store chains in the southern United States. The company has traditionally allocated its marketing funds for cooperative advertising, in-store displays, and retail sales support on the basis of dollar sales by channel.

Your Challenge As the Vice President of Sales & Marketing at Charlesburg Furniture, you have been asked to review the company's sales and profit in its three channels and recommend a course of action. The question: Should Charlesburg Furniture continue to allocate its marketing funds on the basis of channel dollar sales or profit?

Your Findings Charlesburg Furniture tracks the sales and profit from each channel (and individual customer) and sales trends on its marketing dashboard. This information is displayed in the marketing dashboard below.

Several findings stand out. Furniture store chains and independent furniture stores account for 85.2 percent of

Charlesburg Furniture sales and 93 percent of company profit. These two channels also evidence growth as measured by annual percentage change in sales. By comparison, department store chains annual percentage sales growth has declined and recorded negative growth in 2007. This channel accounts for 14.8 percent of company sales and 7 percent of company profit.

Your Action Charlesburg Furniture should consider abandoning the practice of allocating marketing funds solely on the basis of channel sales volume. The importance of independent furniture stores to Charlesburg's profitability warrants further spending, particularly given this channel's favorable sales trend. Doubling the percentage allocation for marketing funds for this channel may be too extreme, however. Rather, an objective-task promotional budgeting method should be adopted (see Chapter 18). Charlesburg Furniture might also consider the longer term role of department store chains as a marketing channel.

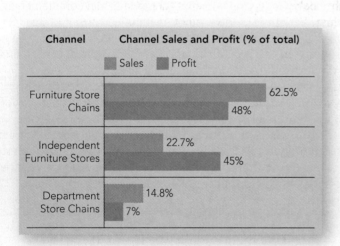

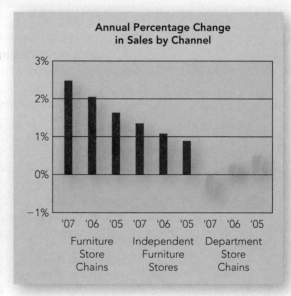

channel functions must be performed. But differences do exist and are illustrated by marketing channels in Japan, one of the world's largest economies and a major U.S. trade partner.

Intermediaries outside Western Europe and North America tend to be small, numerous, and often owner operated as described in Chapter 7. Japan, for example, has less than one-half of the population and a land mass less than 5 percent of the United States.

For the answer to how Schick became a razor and blade market share leader in Japan read the text.

Schick
www.schick.com

LO4

However, Japan and the United States have about the same number of wholesalers and retailers. Why? Japanese marketing channels tend to include many intermediaries based on tradition and lack of storage space. As many as five intermediaries are involved in the distribution of soap in Japan compared with one or two in the United States.

Understanding marketing channels in global markets is often a prerequisite to successful marketing. For example, Gillette attempted to sell its razors and blades through company salespeople in Japan as it does in the United States, thus eliminating wholesalers traditionally involved in marketing toiletries. However, Schick sold its razors and blades through the traditional Japanese channel involving wholesalers. The result? Schick achieved a commanding lead over Gillette in the Japanese razor and blade market.[14]

Channel relationships also must be considered. In Japan, the distribution *keiretsu* (translated as "alignments") bonds producers and intermediaries together. The bond, through vertical integration and social and economic ties, ensures that each channel member benefits from the distribution alignment. The dominant member of the distribution *keiretsu*, which is typically a producer, has considerable influence over channel member behavior, including which competing products are sold by other channel members. Well-known Japanese companies such as Matsushita (electronics), Nissan and Toyota (automotive products), and Kirin (and other brewers and distillers) employ the distribution *keiretsu* extensively. Shiseido and Kanebo, for instance, influence the distribution of cosmetics through Japanese department stores.

Channel Relationships: Conflict, Cooperation, and Law

Unfortunately, because channels consist of independent individuals and firms, there is always potential for disagreements concerning who performs which channel functions, how profits are allocated, which products and services will be provided by whom, and who makes critical channel-related decisions. These channel conflicts necessitate measures for dealing with them. Sometimes they result in legal action.

Sources of Conflict in Marketing Channels **Channel conflict** arises when one channel member believes another channel member is engaged in behavior that prevents it from achieving its goals. Two types of conflict occur in marketing channels: vertical conflict and horizontal conflict.

Vertical conflict occurs between different levels in a marketing channel—for example, between a manufacturer and a wholesaler or retailer or between a wholesaler and a retailer. Three sources of vertical conflict are most common.[15] First, conflict arises when a channel member bypasses another member and sells or buys products direct, a practice called **disintermediation**. This conflict emerged when Jenn-Air, a producer of kitchen appliances, decided to terminate its distributors and sell directly to retailers. Second, disagreements over how profit margins are distributed among channel members produce conflict. This happened when the world's biggest music company, Universal Music Group, adopted a pricing policy for CDs that squeezed the profit margins for specialty music retailers. A third conflict situation arises when manufacturers believe wholesalers or retailers are not giving their products adequate attention. For example, Nike stopped shipping popular sneakers such as Nike Shox NZ to Foot Locker in retaliation for the retailer's decision to give more shelf space to shoes costing under $120.

Horizontal conflict occurs between intermediaries at the same level in a marketing channel, such as between two or more retailers (Target and Kmart) or two or more wholesalers that handle the same manufacturer's brands. Two sources of horizontal conflict are common.[16] First, horizontal conflict arises when a manufacturer increases its distribution coverage in a geographical area. For example, a franchised Saturn dealer in Chicago might complain to General Motors that another franchised Saturn dealer has located too close to its dealership. Second, dual distribution causes conflict when different types of retailers carry the same brands. For instance, Goodyear tire dealers became irate when Goodyear Tire Company decided to sell its brands through Sears, Wal-Mart, and Sam's Clubs. Many switched to competing tire makers.

Channel conflict is sometimes visible to consumers. Read the text to learn what antagonized independent Goodyear tire dealers.

Goodyear Tire and Rubber Company
www.goodyear.com

Securing Cooperation in Marketing Channels Conflict can have destructive effects on the workings of a marketing channel so it is necessary to secure cooperation among channel members.

Channel Captain One means is through a **channel captain**, a channel member that coordinates, directs, and supports other channel members. Channel captains can be producers, wholesalers, or retailers. P&G assumes this role because it has a strong consumer following in brands such as Crest, Tide, and Pampers. Therefore, it can set policies or terms that supermarkets will follow. McKesson, a pharmaceutical drug wholesaler, is a channel captain because it coordinates and supports the product flow from numerous small drug manufacturers to drugstores and hospitals nationwide. Wal-Mart and Office Depot are retail channel captains because of their strong consumer image, number of outlets, and purchasing volume.

Channel Influence A firm becomes a channel captain because it is the channel member with the ability to influence the behavior of other members.[17] Influence can take four forms. First, economic influence arises from the ability of a firm to reward other members given its strong financial position or customer franchise. Microsoft Corporation and Wal-Mart have such influence. Expertise is a second source of influence. For example, American Hospital Supply helps its customers (hospitals) manage inventory and streamline order processing for hundreds of medical supplies. Third, identification with a particular channel member can create influence for that channel member. For instance, retailers may compete to carry the Ralph Lauren line, or clothing manufacturers may compete to be carried by Neiman-Marcus, Nordstrom, or Bloomingdale's. In both instances, the desire to be identified with a channel member gives that firm influence over others. Finally, influence can arise from the legitimate right of one channel member to direct the behavior of other members. This situation would occur under contractual vertical marketing systems where a franchisor can legitimately direct how a franchisee behaves. Other means for securing cooperation in marketing channels rest in the different variations of vertical marketing systems.

Channel influence can be used to gain concessions from other channel members. For instance, some large supermarket chains expect manufacturers to pay allowances, in the form of cash or free goods, to stock and display their products. Some manufacturers call these allowances "extortion" as described in the Making Responsible Decisions box.[18]

Legal Considerations Conflict in marketing channels is typically resolved through negotiation or the exercise of influence by channel members. Sometimes conflict produces legal action. Therefore, knowledge of legal restrictions affecting channel strategies and practices is important. Some restrictions were described in Chapter 14, namely vertical price fixing and price discrimination. However, other legal considerations unique to marketing channels warrant attention.[19]

In general, suppliers can select whomever they want as channel intermediaries and may refuse to deal with whomever they choose. However, the Federal Trade Commission and the Justice Department monitor channel practices that restrain competition, create monopolies, or otherwise represent unfair methods of competition under the Sherman Act (1890) and the Clayton Act (1914). Six channel practices have received the most attention (Figure 15–9).

Dual distribution, although not illegal, can be viewed as anticompetitive in some situations. The most common situation arises when a manufacturer distributes through

The Ethics of Slotting Allowances

Have you ever wondered why your favorite cookies are no longer to be found at your local supermarket? Or that delicious tortilla chip you like to serve at parties is missing from the shelf and replaced by another brand?

Blame it on slotting allowances. Some large supermarket chains demand slotting allowances from food manufacturers, paid in the form of money or free goods to stock and display products. These allowances, which can run up to $25,000 per item for a supermarket chain, cost U.S. food makers about $1 billion annually. Not surprisingly, slotting allowances have been labeled "ransom," "extortional allowances," and "commercial bribery" by manufacturers because they already pay supermarkets $25 billion a year in "trade dollars" to promote and discount their products. Small food manufacturers, in particular, view slotting allowances as an economic barrier to distribution for their products. Supermarket operators see these allowances as a reasonable cost of handling business for manufacturers.

Is the practice of charging slotting allowances unethical behavior?

its own vertically integrated channel in competition with independent wholesalers and retailers that also sell its products. If the manufacturer's behavior is viewed as an attempt to lessen competition by eliminating wholesalers or retailers, then such action would violate both the Sherman and Clayton Acts.

Vertical integration is viewed in a similar light. Although not illegal, this practice is sometimes subject to legal action under the Clayton Act if it has the potential to lessen competition or foster monopoly.

The Clayton Act specifically prohibits exclusive dealing and tying arrangements when they lessen competition or create monopolies. *Exclusive dealing* exists when a supplier requires channel members to sell only its products or restricts distributors from selling directly competitive products. *Tying arrangements* occur when a supplier requires a distributor purchasing some products to buy others from the supplier. These arrangements often arise in franchising. They are illegal if the tied products could be purchased at fair market values from other suppliers at desired quality standards of the franchiser. Full-line forcing is a special kind of tying arrangement. This practice involves a supplier requiring that a channel member carry its full line of products in order to sell a specific item in the supplier's line.

Even though a supplier has a legal right to choose intermediaries to carry and represent its products, a *refusal to deal* with existing channel members may be illegal under the Clayton Act. *Resale restrictions* refer to a supplier's attempt to stipulate to whom distributors may resell the supplier's products and in what specific geographical areas or territories they may be sold. These practices have been prosecuted under the Sherman Act. Today, however, the courts apply the "rule of reason" in such cases and consider whether such restrictions have a "demonstrable economic effect."

FIGURE 15–9

Channel strategies and practices are affected by legal restrictions. The Clayton Act and the Sherman Act place restrictions on specific strategies and practices.

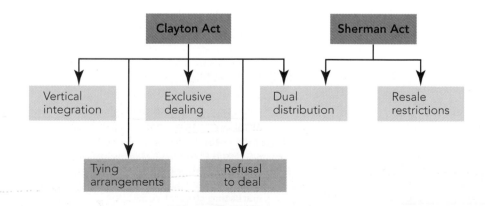

6. What are the three degrees of distribution density?

7. What are the three questions marketing executives consider when choosing a marketing channel and intermediaries?

8. What is meant by *exclusive dealing*?

LEARNING OBJECTIVES REVIEW

LO1 *Explain what is meant by a marketing channel of distribution and why intermediaries are needed.*
A marketing channel of distribution, or simply a marketing channel, consists of individuals and firms involved in the process of making a product or service available for use or consumption by consumers or industrial users. Intermediaries make possible the flow of products from producers to buyers by performing three basic functions. The transactional function involves buying, selling, and risk taking because intermediaries stock merchandise in anticipation of sales. The logistical function involves the gathering, storing, and dispensing of products. The facilitating function assists producers in making goods and services more attractive to buyers. The performance of these functions by intermediaries creates time, place, form, and possession utility for consumers.

LO2 *Distinguish among traditional marketing channels, electronic marketing channels, and different types of vertical marketing systems.*
Traditional marketing channels describe the route taken by products and services from producers to buyers. This route can range from a direct channel with no intermediaries, because a producer and ultimate consumers deal directly with each other, to indirect channels where intermediaries (agents, wholesalers, distributors, or retailers) are inserted between a producer and consumer and perform numerous channel functions. Electronic marketing channels employ the Internet to make goods and services available for consumption or use by consumer or business buyers. Vertical marketing systems are professionally managed and centrally coordinated marketing channels designed to achieve channel economics and maximum marketing impact. There are three major types of vertical marketing systems (VMS). A corporate VMS combines successive stages of production and distribution under a single ownership. A contractual VMS exists when independent production and distribution firms integrate their efforts on a contractual basis to obtain greater functional economies and marketing impact than they could achieve alone. An administered VMS achieves coordination at successive stages of production and distribution by the size and influence of one channel member rather than through ownership.

LO3 *Describe the factors and considerations that affect a company's choice and management of a marketing channel.*
Four factors affect a company's choice and management of a marketing channel. These are environmental factors, consumer factors, product factors, and company factors, all of which interact with each other. Recognizing that numerous routes to buyers exist and also recognizing the factors just described, marketers consider three questions when choosing and managing a marketing channel and intermediaries. First, which channel and intermediaries will provide the best coverage of the target market? Marketers typically choose one of three levels of market coverage: intensive, selective, or exclusive distribution. Second, which channel and intermediaries will best satisfy the buying requirements of the target market? These buying requirements fall into four categories: information, convenience, variety, and attendant services. Finally, which channel and intermediaries will be the most profitable? Here marketers look at the margins earned (revenues minus cost) for each channel member and for the channel as a whole.

LO4 *Recognize how conflict, cooperation, and legal considerations affect marketing channel relationships.*
Because marketing channels consist of independent individuals and firms, there is always potential for conflict which sometimes results in legal action. So channel members try to find ways to cooperate for their mutual benefit. Two types of conflict occur in marketing channels. Vertical conflict occurs between different levels in a marketing channel, for example, between a manufacturer and a wholesaler or retailer, or between a wholesaler and a retailer. Horizontal conflict occurs between intermediaries at the same level in a marketing channel, such as between two retailers or two or more wholesalers that handle the same manufacturer's brands. Because conflict can have destructive effects on the workings of a marketing channel, channel members seek ways to cooperate. One way is through a channel captain—a channel member that coordinates, directs, and supports other channel members. A firm becomes a channel captain because of its ability to influence the behavior of other channel members. Nevertheless, channel conflict can result in legal action. The most common legal actions arise from channel practices that restrain competition, create monopolies, or represent unfair methods of competition.

FOCUSING ON KEY TERMS

brokers p. 399
channel captain p. 408
channel conflict p. 407
channel partnership p. 401
direct marketing channels p. 395
disintermediation p. 407
dual distribution p. 396

electronic marketing channels p. 394
exclusive distribution p. 404
franchising p. 401
industrial distributor p. 394
intensive distribution p. 404
manufacturer's agents p. 399
marketing channel p. 390

merchant wholesalers p. 397
multichannel marketing p. 395
selective distribution p. 404
selling agents p. 399
strategic channel alliances p. 396
vertical marketing systems p. 399

APPLYING MARKETING KNOWLEDGE

1 A distributor for Celanese Chemical Company stores large quantities of chemicals, blends these chemicals to satisfy requests of customers, and delivers the blends to a customer's warehouse within 24 hours of receiving an order. What utilities does this distributor provide?

2 Suppose the president of a carpet manufacturing firm has asked you to look into the possibility of bypassing the firm's wholesalers (who sell to carpet, department, and furniture stores) and selling direct to these stores. What caution would you voice on this matter, and what type of information would you gather before making this decision?

3 What type of channel conflict is likely to be caused by dual distribution, and what type of conflict can be reduced by direct distribution? Why?

4 How does the channel captain idea differ among corporate, administered, and contractual vertical marketing systems with particular reference to the use of the different forms of influence available to firms?

5 Comment on this statement: "The only distinction among merchant wholesalers and agents and brokers is that merchant wholesalers take title to the products they sell."

6 How do specialty, shopping, and convenience goods generally relate to intensive, selective, and exclusive distribution? Give a brand name that is an example of each goods-distribution matchup.

7 How would you respond to the statement: "Marketing channels with the highest sales always produce the highest profit."

building your marketing plan

Does your marketing plan involve selecting channels and intermediaries? If the answer is no, read no further and do not include this element in your plan. If the answer is yes:

1 Identify which channel and intermediaries will provide the best coverage of the target market for your product or service.

2 Specify which channel and intermediaries will best satisfy the important buying requirements of the target market.

3 Determine which channel and intermediaries will be the most profitable.

4 Select your channel(s) and intermediary(ies).

video case 15   Golden Valley Microwave Foods: The Surprising Channel

"We developed the technology that launched the microwave popcorn business and helped make ACT II the number one brand in the world," says Jack McKeon, president of Golden Valley Microwave Foods, a division of ConAgra Foods, Inc. "But we were also lucky along the way, as we backed into what has become one of the biggest distribution channels in the industry today, one that no one ever saw coming."

Founded in 1978, today Golden Valley is the global leader in producing and marketing microwave popcorn. Its ACT II brand is tops in the industry. But it hasn't always been easy.

THE LAUNCH: THE IDEA AND THE TECHNOLOGY

In the mid-1980s only about 15 percent of U.S. households had microwave ovens, so launching a microwave foods business was risky. Golden Valley's initial marketing research turned up two key points of difference or benefits that people wanted in their microwave popcorn: (1) fewer unpopped kernels and (2) good popping results in all types of microwave ovens, even low-powered ovens—the kind that many households with microwaves had at the time. Golden Valley's research and development (R&D) staff successfully addressed these wants by developing a microwave popcorn bag utilizing a thin strip of material laminated between layers of paper, which focused the microwave energy to produce high-quality popped corn, regardless of an oven's power. This breakthrough significantly increased the size of the microwave popcorn market (and is still used in all microwave popcorn bags today). Using its revolutionary package, Golden Valley introduced ACT II in 1984.

THE LUCKY DAY: BOTH CAPITAL AND MASS MERCHANDISERS

From its founding in 1978 until a public offering of its stock in September 1986, Golden Valley was privately owned and, like most start-ups, was severely undercapitalized. Due to the cost of developing and introducing ACT II, Golden Valley needed a partner to help develop the business. Its solution was to enter into a licensing agreement to share its technology for packaging microwave popcorn with one of the largest food manufacturers in the industry. The licensing partner would sell the popcorn under its own brand name in grocery stores and supermarkets. In turn, Golden Valley agreed it would not distribute its ACT II brand in U.S. grocery stores or supermarkets for 10 years. This meant that Golden Valley had to find other channels of distribution in which to sell its microwave popcorn.

For the next 10 years the company developed many new channels. ACT II products were sold through vending machines, video stores (e.g., Blockbuster), institutions (e.g., movie theaters, colleges, military bases), drugstores (e.g., Walgreen's, Rite-Aid, Eckerd Drugs), club stores (e.g., Sam's, Costco, and BJ's), and convenience stores. "But the huge opportunity we discovered and developed was the mass merchandiser channel through chains like Wal-Mart and Target," says McKeon. "ACT II microwave popcorn was the first item of any kind to sell a million units in a week for Target, and that happened in 1987. Wal-Mart, too, was on the front end of this market and today is the top seller of microwave popcorn in any channel, selling far more popcorn than the leading grocery chains. Mass merchandisers now account for over a third of all the microwave popcorn sold in the U.S. They created the ACT II business as we know it today, and it was accomplished without a dime of conventional consumer promotions. That's one of the really unique parts of the ACT II story."

THE SITUATION TODAY

In the United States today, over 90 percent of households own microwave ovens, and more than 60 percent of households are microwave popcorn consumers who spend more than $688 million on the product each year. "Our marketing research shows ACT II is especially strong in young families with kids," says Frank Lynch, vice president of marketing at Golden Valley. This conjures up an image of Mom and Dad watching a movie on TV with the kids and eating ACT II popcorn, a picture close to reality. "ACT II has good market penetration in almost all age, income, urban versus rural, and ethnic segments," he continues.

"From the beginning, Golden Valley has been the leader in the microwave popcorn industry," says McKeon, "and we plan to continue that record." As evidence, he cites a number of Golden Valley's "firsts":

- First mass-marketed microwave popcorn.
- First flavored microwave popcorn.
- First microwave popcorn tub.
- First fat-free microwave popcorn.
- First extra-butter microwave popcorn.
- First one-step sweetened microwave popcorn.

This list highlights a curious market segmentation phenomenon that has emerged in the last five years—the no-butter versus plenty-of-butter consumers. Originally popcorn was seen as junk food. Later studies by nutritionists pointed out its health benefits: low calories and high fiber. This caused Golden Valley to introduce its low-fat popcorn to appeal to the health-conscious segment of consumers. When it comes to eating popcorn while watching a movie at home on TV, however, the more butter on their popcorn, the better. Recently, much of the growth in popcorn sales has been in the spoil-yourself-with-a lot-of-butter-on-your-popcorn segment.

Because of these diverse consumer tastes in popcorn, Golden Valley has developed a variety of popcorn products around its ACT II brand. Besides the low-fat and extra butter versions, these include the original flavors (natural and butter), sweet glazed products, popcorn in tubs, and Kettle Corn. In 2004, ACT II Big Boy was introduced to appeal to the economy segment. It also has a line of ACT II non-popcorn snacks such as soft pretzels and snack mixes.

Golden Valley positions ACT II as unpretentious, fun, and youthful—a great product at a reasonable price. By stressing the value aspect of ACT II, Golden Valley has positioned the brand to appeal to today's growing value consciousness of consumers seeking quality products at reasonable prices. In terms of market share, these strategies have enabled ACT II to become the leader in the microwave popcorn market.

OPPORTUNITIES FOR FUTURE GROWTH

For many years the growth of the microwave popcorn industry closely followed the growth of household ownership of microwave ovens—from under 20 percent to over 90 percent. But now, with a microwave oven in virtually every U.S. home, Golden Valley is trying to identify new market segments, new products, and innovative ways to appeal to all the major marketing channels.

In the United States, Golden Valley's strategy must include finding creative ways to continue to work with existing channels where it has special strength, such as the mass merchandiser channel. It also needs to further develop opportunities in the grocery store and supermarket channel. Now that the 10-year restriction on sales in grocery stores and supermarkets has expired, distribution through wholesalers that reach grocery stores and supermarkets is possible.

Global markets, too, present opportunities. Golden Valley has followed the penetration of microwave ovens in countries around the world, and used brokers to help gain distribution in those markets. Currently, Golden Valley has sales in more than 32 countries and the leading share in most of those markets. However, foreign markets represent foreign tastes, something that does not always lend itself to standardized products. United Kingdom consumers, for example, think of popcorn as a candy or child's food rather than the salty snack it is in the United States. Even in the Disney Park in Paris, American-style popcorn is absent, as French consumers sprinkle sugar on their popcorn. Swedes like theirs very buttery while many Mexicans like jalapeno-flavored popcorn.

Questions

1 Visit ACT II's website at www.ACTII.com and examine the assortment of products offered today. Are (*a*) the assortment or (*b*) the packaging related to Golden Valley's distribution channels or the segments they serve?

2 Use Figure 15–4 to create a description of the channels of distribution being used by Golden Valley today.

3 Compared to selling through the non-grocery channels, what kind of product, price, and promotion strategies might Golden Valley use to reach the grocery channel more effectively?

4 What special marketing issues does Golden Valley face as it pursues growth in global markets?

Supply Chain:
Managing Logistics
For the 21st Century

16

Customer-Driven Supply Chain and Logistics Management

SNAP! CRACK! POP! EVEN WORLD-CLASS COMPANIES LIKE NIKE CAN FEEL THE BULLWHIP'S STING

Bad things can happen to great companies. Just ask Nike about the bullwhip's sting.

What is the bullwhip, and why does its sting hurt so bad? Companies define the *bullwhip* as too much or too little inventory to satisfy customer needs, missed production schedules, and ineffective transportation or delivery caused by miscommunication among material suppliers, manufacturers, and resellers of consumer and industrial goods. Its sting is poor customer service and lost revenue and profit opportunities.

So what does the bullwhip have to do with Nike, well known for consistently delivering the right athletic shoes, at the right time, place, and quantity to satisfy the fashion and functional needs of its buyers? Nike mistakenly sent double orders to its overseas factories, resulting in an oversupply of shoes. Meanwhile, production of its hot-selling shoes did not keep pace with customer demand. To offset shipping delays for its popular shoes, Nike transported them by plane at $4 to $8 a pair from Asia, compared with about 75 cents a pair by boat. Customers were displeased and company sales and profitability suffered.[1]

Welcome to the critical world of customer-driven supply chain and logistics management. The essence of the problem is simple: It makes no sense to have brilliant marketing programs to sell world-class products if the products aren't available at the right time, at the right place, and in the right form and condition that customers want them. It's finding the continuing solutions through time that's always the challenge.

This chapter describes the significance of supply chains and logistics management to the practice of marketing. In particular, attention is placed on the necessary alignment between supply chain management and marketing strategy, the trade-offs managers make between total distribution costs and customer service, and the increased application of information in managing the physical flow of goods to the final customer. Finally, the importance of reclaiming recyclable and reusable materials from customers for repair, remanufacturing, redistribution, or disposal is addressed in the context of reverse logistics.

SIGNIFICANCE OF SUPPLY CHAIN
AND LOGISTICS MANAGEMENT

We often hear or use the term *distribution* but seldom appreciate its significance in marketing. U.S. companies spend $560 billion transporting raw materials and finished goods each year, another $332 billion on material handling, warehousing, storage, and holding inventory, and $40 billion managing the distribution process, including the cost of information technology. Worldwide, these activities and investments cost companies about $3.4 trillion each year.[2] In this section, we highlight contemporary perspectives on distribution, including supply chains and logistics, and describe the linkage between supply chain management and marketing strategy.

Relating Marketing Channels, Logistics, and Supply Chain Management

A marketing channel relies on logistics to make products available to consumers and industrial users, a point emphasized in Chapter 15. **Logistics** involves those activities that focus on getting the right amount of the right products to the right place at the right time at the lowest possible cost. The performance of these activities is **logistics management**, the practice of organizing the *cost-effective flow* of raw materials, in-process inventory, finished goods, and related information from point of origin to point of consumption to satisfy *customer requirements*.

Three elements of this definition deserve emphasis. First, logistics deals with decisions needed to move a product from the source of raw materials to consumption, or the *flow* of the product. Second, those decisions have to be made in a *cost-effective* manner. While it is important to drive down logistics costs, there is a limit—the third point of emphasis. A firm needs to drive down logistics costs as long as it can deliver expected *customer service,* which means satisfying customer requirements. The role of management is to see that customer needs are satisfied in the most cost-effective manner. When properly done, the results can be spectacular.

Procter & Gamble is a case in point. The company set out to meet the needs of consumers more effectively by collaborating and partnering with its suppliers and retailers to ensure that the right products reached store shelves at the right time and at a lower cost. The effort was judged a success when, during a recent 18-month period, P&G's retail customers recorded a $65 million savings in logistics costs while customer service increased.[3]

The Procter & Gamble experience is not an isolated incident. Today, logistics management is embedded in a broader view of distribution, consistent with the emphasis on supply and channel partnering described in Chapters 6 and 15. Companies now recognize that getting the right items needed for consumption or production to the right place at the right time in the right condition at the right cost is often beyond their individual capabilities and control. Instead, collaboration, coordination, and information sharing among manufacturers, suppliers, and distributors are necessary to create a seamless flow of goods and services to customers. This perspective is represented in the concept of a supply chain and the practice of customer-driven supply chain management.

Supply Chains versus Marketing Channels

A **supply chain** is a sequence of firms that perform activities required to create and deliver a good or service to consumers or industrial users. It differs from a marketing channel in terms of membership. A supply chain includes suppliers that provide raw material inputs to a manufacturer as well as the wholesalers and retailers that deliver finished goods to you. The management process is also different.

Supply chain management is the integration and organization of information and logistics activities *across firms* in a supply chain for the purpose of creating and

FIGURE 16–1

Relating logistics management and supply chain management to supplier networks and marketing channels

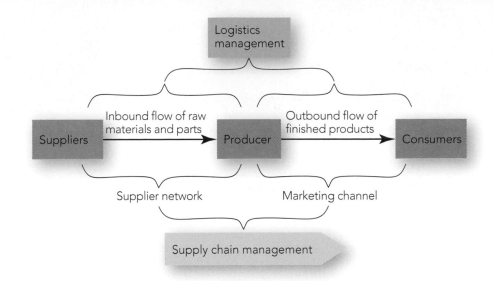

delivering goods and services that provide value to consumers. The relation among marketing channels, logistics management, and supply chain management is shown in Figure 16–1. An important feature of customer-driven supply chain management is its application of sophisticated information technology that allows companies to share and operate systems for order processing, transportation scheduling, and inventory and facility management.

Sourcing, Assembling, and Delivering a New Car: The Automotive Supply Chain

All companies are members of one or more supply chains. A supply chain is essentially a sequence of linked suppliers and customers in which every customer is, in turn, a supplier to another customer until a finished product reaches the final consumer. Even a simplified supply chain diagram for carmakers shown in Figure 16–2 illustrates how complex a supply chain can be.[4] A carmaker's supplier network includes thousands of firms that provide the 5,000 or so parts in a typical automobile. They provide items ranging from raw materials such as steel and rubber to components, including transmissions, tires, brakes, and seats, to complex subassemblies and assemblies evident in chassis and suspension systems that make for a smooth, stable ride. Coordinating and scheduling material and component flows for their assembly into actual automobiles by carmakers is dependent on logistical activities, including transportation, order processing, inventory control, materials handling, and information technology.

A central link is the carmaker supply chain manager, who is responsible for translating customer requirements into actual orders and arranging for delivery dates and financial arrangements for car dealers. This is not an easy task given different consumer preferences

FIGURE 16–2

The automotive supply chain includes thousands of firms that provide the 5,000 or so parts in a typical car.

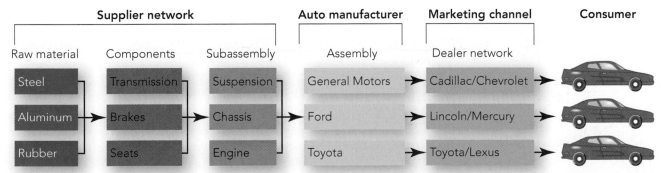

417

and how much consumers are willing to pay. To appreciate the challenge facing supply chain managers, visit the Volkswagen website described in the accompanying Going Online box, and assemble your own Jetta based on your preferences and price.

Logistical aspects of the automobile marketing channel are also an integral part of the supply chain. Major responsibilities include transportation (which involves the selection and oversight of external carriers—trucking, airline, railroad, and shipping companies—for cars and parts to dealers), the operation of distribution centers, the management of finished goods inventories, and order processing for sales. Supply chain managers also play an important role in the marketing channel. They work with car dealers to ensure that the right automobiles are delivered to different locations. In addition, they make sure that spare and service parts are available so that dealers can meet the car maintenance and repair needs of consumers. All of this is done with the help of information technology that links the entire automotive supply chain. What does all of this cost? Logistics costs represent 25 percent to 30 percent of the retail price of a typical new car.

Supply Chain Management and Marketing Strategy

The automotive supply chain illustration shows how information and logistics activities are integrated and organized across firms to create and deliver a car for you. What's missing from this illustration is the linkage between a specific company's supply chain and its marketing strategy. Just as companies have different marketing strategies, they also designs and manage supply chains differently. The goals to be achieved by a firm's marketing strategy determine whether its supply chain needs to be more responsive or efficient in meeting customer requirements.

Aligning a Supply Chain with Marketing Strategy There are a variety of supply chain configurations, each of which is designated to perform different tasks well. Marketers today recognize that the choice of a supply chain follows from a clearly defined marketing strategy and involves three steps:[5]

1. *Understand the customer.* To understand the customer, a company must identify the needs of the customer segment being served. These needs, such as a desire for a low price or convenience of purchase, help a company define the relative importance of efficiency and responsiveness in meeting customer requirements.

Marketing Matters > > > >> customer value

IBM's Integrated Supply Chain—Delivering a Total Solution for Its Customers

IBM is one of the world's great business success stories because of its ability to reinvent itself to satisfy shifting customer needs in a dynamic global marketplace. The company's transformation of its supply chain is a case in point.

Beginning in 2001, IBM set about to build a single integrated supply chain that would handle raw material procurement, manufacturing, logistics, customer support, order entry, and customer fulfillment across all of IBM—something that had never been done before. Why would IBM undertake this task? According to IBM's CEO, Samuel J. Palmisano, "You cannot hope to thrive in the IT industry if you are a high-cost, slow-moving company. Supply chain is one of the new competitive battlegrounds. We are committed to being the most efficient and productive player in our industry."

The task wasn't easy. With factories in 10 countries, IBM buys 2 billion parts a year from 33,000 suppliers, offers 78,000 products available in 3 million possible variations, moves over 2 billion pounds of machines and parts annually, processes 1.7 million customer orders annually in North America alone, and operates in 150 countries. Yet with surprising efficiency, IBM overhauled its supply chain from raw material sourcing to postsales support.

Today, IBM is uniquely poised to configure and deliver a tailored mix of hardware, software, and service to provide a total solution for its customers. Not surprisingly, IBM's integrated supply chain is now heralded as one of the best in the world!

---

2. *Understand the supply chain*. Second, a company must understand what a supply chain is designed to do well. Supply chains range from those that emphasize being responsive to customer requirements and demand to those that emphasize efficiency with a goal of supplying products at the lowest possible delivered cost.

3. *Harmonize the supply chain with the marketing strategy*. Finally, a company needs to ensure that what the supply chain is capable of doing well is consistent with the targeted customer's needs and its marketing strategy. If a mismatch exists between what the supply chain does particularly well and a company's marketing strategy, the company will either need to redesign the supply chain to support the marketing strategy or change the marketing strategy. Read the accompanying Marketing Matters box to learn how IBM overhauled its complete supply chain to support its marketing strategy.[6]

How are these steps applied and how are efficiency and responsive considerations built into a supply chain? Let's look at how two well-known companies—Dell and Wal-Mart—have harmonized their supply chain and marketing strategy.[7]

Dell: A Responsive Supply Chain   The Dell marketing strategy primarily targets customers who desire having the most up-to-date computer systems customized to their needs. These customers are also willing to: (1) wait to have their customized computer system delivered in a few days, rather than picking out a model at a retail store, and (2) pay a reasonable, though not the lowest price in the marketplace. Given Dell's customer segment, the company has the option of adopting an efficient or responsive supply chain.

An efficient supply chain may use inexpensive, but slower, modes of transportation, emphasize economies of scale in its production process by reducing the variety of system configurations offered, and limit its assembly and inventory storage facilities to a single location, say Austin, Texas, where the company is headquartered. If Dell opted only for efficiency in its supply chain, it would be difficult if not impossible to

Dell and Wal-Mart emphasize responsiveness and efficiency in their supply chains, respectively. The text details how they do this.

Dell, Inc.
www.dell.com

Wal-Mart, Inc.
www.walmartstores.com

satisfy its target customer's desire for rapid delivery and a wide variety of customizable products. Dell instead has opted for a responsive supply chain. It relies on more expensive express transportation for receipt of components from suppliers and delivery of finished products to customers. The company achieves product variety and manufacturing efficiency by designing common platforms across several products and using common components. Dell operates manufacturing facilities in Texas, North Carolina, Tennessee, Brazil, Ireland, Malaysia, and China to assure rapid delivery. Moreover, Dell has invested heavily in information technology to link itself with suppliers and customers.

Wal-Mart: An Efficient Supply Chain Now let's consider Wal-Mart. Wal-Mart's marketing strategy is to be a reliable, lower-price retailer for a wide variety of mass consumption consumer goods. This strategy favors an efficient supply chain designed to deliver products to consumers at the lowest possible cost. Efficiency is achieved in a variety of ways. For instance, Wal-Mart keeps relatively low inventory levels, and most is stocked in stores available for sale, not in warehouses gathering dust. The low inventory arises from Wal-Mart's innovative use of *cross-docking*—a practice that involves unloading products from suppliers, sorting products for individual stores, and quickly reloading products onto its trucks for a particular store. No warehousing or storing of products occurs, except for a few hours or, at most, a day. Cross-docking allows Wal-Mart to operate only a small number of distribution centers to service its vast network of Wal-Mart Stores, Supercenters, Neighborhood Markets, and Sam's Clubs which contributes to efficiency. On the other hand, the company runs its own fleet of trucks to service its stores. This does increase cost and investment, but the benefits in terms of responsiveness justify the cost in Wal-Mart's case.

Wal-Mart has invested much more than its competitors in information technology to operate its supply chain. The company feeds information about customer requirements and demand from its stores back to its suppliers, which manufacture only what is being demanded. This large investment has improved the efficiency of Wal-Mart's supply chain and made it responsive to customer needs.

Three lessons can be learned from these two examples. First, there is no one best supply chain for every company. Second, the best supply chain is the one that is consistent with the needs of the customer segment being served and complements a company's marketing strategy. And finally, supply chain managers are often called upon to make trade-offs between efficiency and responsiveness on various elements of a company's supply chain.

learning review

1. What is the principal difference between a marketing channel and a supply chain?

2. The choice of a supply chain involves what three steps?

OBJECTIVE OF INFORMATION AND LOGISTICS MANAGEMENT IN A CUSTOMER-DRIVEN SUPPLY CHAIN

LO3

The objective of information and logistics management in a customer-driven supply chain is to minimize logistics costs while delivering maximum customer service. The Dell and Wal-Mart examples highlighted how two market leaders have realized this objective by different means. An important similarity between these two companies is that both use information to leverage logistics activities, reduce logistics costs, and improve customer service.

Information's Role in Supply Chain Responsiveness and Efficiency

Information consists of data and analysis regarding inventory, transportation, distribution facilities, and customers throughout the supply chain.[8] Continuing advances in information technology make it possible to track logistics activities and customer service variables and manage them for efficiency and responsiveness. For example, information on customer demand patterns allows pharmaceutical companies such as Eli Lilly and GlaxoSmithKline to produce and stock drugs in anticipation of customer needs. This improves supply chain responsiveness because customers will find the drugs when and where they want them. Demand information improves supply chain efficiency because pharmaceutical firms are better able to meet customer needs and produce, transport, and store the required amount of inventory.

A variety of technologies are used to transmit and manage information in a supply chain. **Electronic data interchanges (EDIs)** combine proprietary computer and telecommunication technologies to exchange electronic invoices, payments, and

Hewlett-Packard is a leader in the application of information technology to supply chain management.

Hewlett-Packard
www.hp.com

How to light up a supply chain.

Advance Transformer, a leading component manufacturer for lighting systems, had legacy IT systems that no longer kept up with production demands. They turned to HP to help them better manage their supply chain. Now, with a unified management of the whole infrastructure, their systems automatically solve problems as they occur. All this has reduced production time from 28 to 5 days, cut inventory levels by 50% and revealed the bright side of change. www.hp.com/adapt

Solutions for the adaptive enterprise.

information among suppliers, manufacturers, and retailers. When linked with store scanning equipment and systems, EDI provides a seamless electronic link from a retail checkout counter to suppliers and manufacturers. EDI is commonly used in retail, apparel, transportation, pharmaceutical, grocery, health care, and insurance industries, as well as by local, state, and federal government agencies. About 95 percent of the companies listed in the Fortune 1000 use EDI. At Hewlett-Packard, for example, 1 million EDI transactions are made every month.

Another technology is the *extranet,* which is an Internet-based network that permits secure business-to-business communication between a manufacturer and its suppliers, distributors, and sometimes other partners (such as advertising agencies). Extranets are less expensive and more flexible to operate than EDI because of their connection to the public Internet. This technology is prominent in private electronic exchanges described in Chapter 6. For example, WhirlpoolWebWorld.com allows Whirlpool to fulfill retailer orders quickly and inexpensively and better match appliance demand and supply.

Whereas EDI and extranets transmit information, other technologies help manage information in a supply chain. Enterprise resource planning (ERP) technology and supply chain management software track logistics cost and customer service variables, both of which are described next.

Total Logistics Cost Concept

For our purposes, **total logistics cost** includes expenses associated with transportation, materials handling and warehousing, inventory, stockouts (being out of inventory), order processing, and return goods handling. Note that many of these costs are interrelated so that changes in one will impact the others. For example, as the firm attempts to minimize its transportation costs by shipping in larger quantities, it will also experience an increase in inventory levels. Larger inventory levels will not only increase inventory costs but should also reduce stockouts. It is important, therefore, to study the impact on all of the logistics decision areas when considering a change.

Figure 16–3 provides a graphic example. An oft-used supply chain strategy is for a firm to have a number of warehouses, which receive shipments in large quantities and then redistribute smaller shipments to local customers. As the number of warehouses increases, inventory costs rise and transportation costs fall. That is, more inventory is warehoused, but it is transported in volume closer to customers. The net effect is to minimize the total costs of logistics shown in Figure 16–3 by having 10 warehouses. This means the total cost curve is minimized at a point where neither of the two individual cost elements is at a minimum but the overall system is.

Studying its total logistics cost has had revolutionary consequences for National Semiconductor, which produces computer chips. In two years it cut its standard delivery time 47 percent, reduced distribution costs 2.5 percent, and increased sales 34 percent by shutting down six warehouses around the world and air-freighting its microchips from its huge distribution center in Singapore. It does this even though

FIGURE 16–3

How total logistics cost varies with the number of warehouses used based on inventory costs and transportation costs. The goal is to minimize total logistics cost.

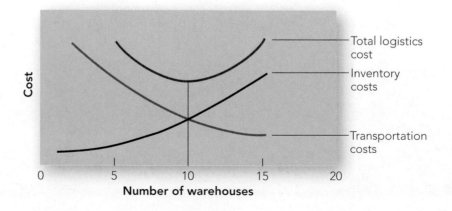

it has six factories in Israel, Britain, and the United States. National also discovered that a lot of its chips were actually profit-losers, and it cut the number of products it sells by 45 percent, thereby simplifying logistics and increasing profits.[9]

Customer Service Concept

If a supply chain is a *flow,* the end of it—or *output*—is the service delivered to customers. However, service can be expensive. One company found that to increase on-time delivery from a 95 percent rate to a 100 percent rate tripled total logistics costs. Higher levels of service require tactics such as more inventory to reduce stockouts, more expensive transportation to improve speed and lessen damage, and double or triple checking of orders to ensure correctness. A firm's goal should be to provide superior customer service while controlling logistics costs. Customer service is now seen not merely as an expense but as a means to increase customer satisfaction and sales. For example, a 3M survey about customer service among 18,000 European customers in 16 countries revealed surprising agreement in all countries about the importance of customer service. Respondents stressed factors such as condition of product delivered, on-time delivery, quick delivery after order placement, and effective handling of problems.[10]

Within the context of a supply chain, **customer service** is the ability of logistics management to satisfy users in terms of time, dependability, communication, and convenience. As suggested by Figure 16–4, a supply chain manager's key task is to balance these four customer service factors against total logistics cost factors.

Time   In a supply chain setting, time refers to **lead time** for an item, which means the lag from ordering an item until it is received and ready for use or sale. This is also referred to as *order cycle time* or *replenishment time* and may be more important to retailers or wholesalers than consumers. The various elements that make up the typical order cycle include recognition of the need to order, order transmittal, order processing, documentation, and transportation. A current emphasis in supply chain management is to reduce lead time so that the inventory levels of customers may be minimized. Another emphasis is to make the process of reordering and receiving products as simple as possible, often through electronic data and inventory systems called **quick response** or **efficient consumer response** delivery systems. These inventory management systems are designed to reduce the retailer's lead time for receiving merchandise, thereby lowering a retailer's inventory investment, improving customer service levels, and reducing logistics expense (see the Marketing Matters box on the next page).[11] The order processing portion of lead time will be discussed later in this chapter.

FIGURE 16–4

Supply chain managers balance total logistics cost factors against customer service factors.

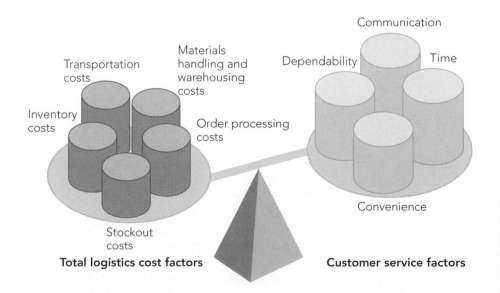

Marketing Matters > > > > >> >> technology

For Fashion and Food Merchandising, Haste Is as Important as Taste

Fashion and food have a lot in common. Both depend a lot on taste and both require timely merchandising. By its nature, fashion dictates that suppliers and retailers be able to adjust to new styles, colors, and different seasons. Fashion retailers need to identify what's hot, so it can be ordered quickly, and what's not, to avoid markdowns. Saks Fifth Avenue has employed a *quick response* delivery system for fashion merchandise since the mid-1990s. Saks' point-of-sale scanner system records each day's sales. When stock falls below a minimum level, the system automatically generates a replenishment order. Vendors of fashion merchandise, such as Donna Karan

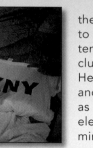

(DKNY), receive an electronic order, which is processed within 48 hours.

Food marketers and retailers use the term *efficient consumer response* to describe their replenishment systems. All major food companies, including General Mills, Del Monte, Heinz, Nestlé, and Beatrice Foods, and many supermarket chains such as Kroger, Safeway, and A&P rely on electronic replenishment systems to minimize stockouts of popular items and overstocks of slow-moving items. Lowered retailer inventories and efficient logistics practices have been projected to save U.S. grocery shoppers $30 billion a year.

Dependability Dependability is the consistency of replenishment. This is important to all firms in a supply chain and to consumers. It can be broken into three elements: consistent lead time, safe delivery, and complete delivery. Consistent service allows planning (such as appropriate inventory levels), whereas inconsistencies create surprises. Intermediaries may be willing to accept longer lead times if they know about them in advance and can thus make plans. While surprise delays may shut down a production line, early deliveries will be almost as troublesome because of the problems of storing the extra inventory. Dependability is essential for the just-in-time inventory strategies discussed at the end of the chapter.

Communication Communication is a two-way link between buyer and seller that helps in monitoring service and anticipating future needs. Status reports on orders are a typical example of improved communication between buyer and seller. The increased communication capability of transportation carriers has enhanced the accuracy of such tracing information and improved the ability of buyers to schedule shipments. Note, however, that such information is still reactive and is not a substitute for consistent on-time deliveries. Therefore, some firms have partnered with firms specializing in logistics in an effort to institutionalize a more proactive flow of useful information. Unisys, a major technology firm, relies on DHL's global service parts logistics system to enable monitoring, management, and inventory level reporting across regions of the world. This system provides timely information into the status of orders throughout the Unisys supply chain from multiple suppliers.[12]

Convenience The concept of convenience for a supply chain manager means that there should be a minimum of effort on the part of the buyer in doing business with the seller. Is it easy for the customer to order? Are the products available from many outlets? Does the buyer have to buy huge quantities of the product? Will the seller arrange all necessary details, such as transportation? The seller must concentrate on removing unnecessary barriers to customer convenience. This customer service factor has promoted the use of vendor-managed inventory practices discussed later in the chapter.

Customer Service Standards

Firms that operate effective supply chains usually develop a set of written customer service standards. These serve as objectives and provide a benchmark against which results can be measured for control purposes. In developing these standards, information is collected on customers' needs. It is also necessary to know what competitors offer as well as the willingness of customers to pay a bit more for better service. After these and similar questions are answered, realistic standards are set and an on-going monitoring program is established. The examples below suggest that customer service standards will differ by type of firm.

Type of Firm	Customer Service Standard
Wholesaler	At least 98 percent of orders filled accurately
Manufacturer	Order cycle time of no more than five days
Retailer	Returns accepted within 30 days
Airline	At least 90 percent of arrivals on time
Trucker	A maximum of 5 percent loss and damage per year
Restaurant	Lunch served within five minutes of order

Effective customer service can yield substantial returns. The head of IBM's integrated supply chain group estimates that a 1 percent increase in customer service satisfaction translates into $2 billion to $3 billion of additional revenue to his company.[13]

Companies rely on marketing dashboards to monitor customer service standards. Read the Using Marketing Dashboards box on the next page to see one application and interpretation of the link between out-of-stocks and on-time delivery.

---

learning review

3. The objective of information and logistics management in a supply chain is to _____.

4. How does consumer demand information increase supply chain responsiveness and efficiency?

5. What is the relationship between the number of warehouses a company operates, its inventory costs, and its transportation costs?

KEY LOGISTICS FUNCTIONS IN A SUPPLY CHAIN

The four key logistic functions in a supply chain include (1) transportation, (2) warehousing and materials handling, (3) order processing, and (4) inventory management. These functions have become so complex and interrelated that many companies have outsourced them to third-party logistics providers.

Third-party logistics providers are firms that perform most or all of the logistics functions that manufacturers, suppliers, and distributors would normally perform themselves.[14] Today, 82 percent of manufacturers listed in the Fortune 500 outsource one or more logistics functions, at least on a limited basis. Ryder Systems, UPS Supply Chain Solutions, FedEx Supply Chain Services, DHL, and Penske Logistics are just a few of the companies that specialize in handling logistics functions for their clients. For example, Ryder manages the four key logistics functions for the Snapple Beverage Corporation.

The four major logistics functions and the involvement of third-party logistics providers are described in detail next.

Using Marketing Dashboards
Diagnosing Out-of-Stocks and On-Time Delivery for Organic Produce

Supply chain managers recognize that out-of-stocks means lost sales. And poor on-time delivery is often the culprit. These measures are routinely compared on a weekly or monthly basis against a numerical standard and each other.

Your Challenge You have just joined Superior Supermarkets as a distribution analyst. Superior Supermarkets is a 150-store chain that serves small cities and towns in the south central United States through its own distribution center. During your first meeting with the Vice President of Distribution, the topic of produce out-of-stocks arose. Specifically, organic produce (fresh fruits and vegetables) out-of-stocks had increased. Out-of-stocks are calculated as follows:

$$\text{Out-of-Stocks (\%)} = \frac{\text{Number of outlets where a brand or product is listed but unavailable}}{\text{Total number of outlets where a brand or product is listed}}$$

Poor on-time delivery of produce was the suspected reason for the rise in out-of-stocks. On-time delivery is calculated as follows:

$$\text{On-Time Delivery (\%)} = \frac{\text{Number of deliveries achieved in the timeframe promised}}{\text{Total number of deliveries initiated in a time period}}$$

Your challenge is to examine whether on-time delivery performance might be the reason for the organic produce out-of-stocks situation at Superior Supermarkets.

Your Findings Superior Supermarkets monitor out-of-stocks and on-time delivery on a monthly basis. A 3 percent out-of-stock standard and a 98 percent on-time delivery standard have been set by the company. Monthly results for organic produce are displayed on the company's marketing dashboard shown below.

Clearly, the downward trend in on-time delivery corresponds with the upward trend in out-of-stocks for organic produce.

Your Action As a distribution analyst, you might recommend that the transportation department needs to improve its performance. However, the issue might reach deeper into the order cycle time for organic produce. Recall that order cycle time includes the recognition of the need to place, transmit, process, document, and transport the order. The actual *cause* of out-of-stocks might reside in the four prior elements of order cycle time and not just transportation.

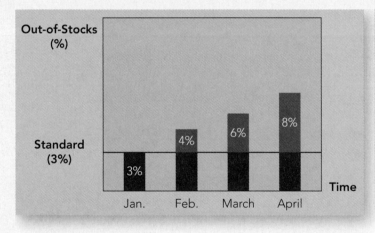

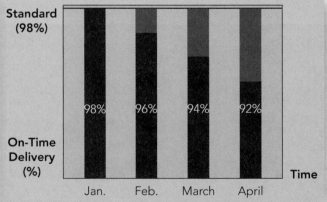

Transportation

Transportation provides the movement of goods necessary in a supply chain. There are five basic modes of transportation: railroads, motor carriers, air carriers, pipelines, and water carriers, and modal combinations involving two or more modes, such as truck trailers on a rail flatcar.

All transportation modes can be evaluated on six basic service criteria:

- *Cost.* Charges for transportation.
- *Time.* Speed of transit.

UPS Supply Chain Solutions and Ryder Systems are two third-party logistics providers that perform most or all of the logistics functions that manufacturers, suppliers, and distributors would normally perform.

UPS Supply Chain Solutions
www.ups.com/supply_chain

Ryder Systems
www.ryder.com

- *Capability.* What can be realistically carried with this mode.
- *Dependability.* Reliability of service regarding time, loss, and damage.
- *Accessibility.* Convenience of the mode's routes (such as pipeline availability).
- *Frequency.* Scheduling.

Figure 16–5 on the next page summarizes the relative service advantages and disadvantages of five modes of transportation available.[15]

Railroads Railroads typically carry heavy, bulky items over long distances. Of the commodities tracked by the rail industry, coal, farm products, chemicals, and nonmetallic minerals represent about 70 percent of the total tonnage. Railroads can carry larger shipments than trucks (in terms of total weight per vehicle), but their routes are less extensive. Service innovations include unit trains and intermodal service. A *unit train* is dedicated to one commodity (often coal), using permanently coupled cars that run a continuous loop from a single origin to a single destination and back. Even though the train returns empty, the process captures enough operating efficiencies to make it one of the lowest-cost transportation alternatives available. Unit trains keep to a specific schedule so that the customers can plan on reliable delivery and usually carry products that can be loaded and unloaded quickly and automatically.

Railroads also apply the unit train concept to *intermodal transportation,* which involves combining different transportation modes to get the best features of each. The result is a service that attracts high-valued freight, which would normally go by truck. The most popular combination is truck-rail, called *piggyback* or *trailer on flatcar (TOFC).* The other popular use of an intermodal combination is associated with export/ import traffic and uses containers in place of trailers. These containers can be loaded on ships, trains, and truck trailers, so in terms of the on-land segment of international shipments, a container is handled the same way as a trailer. Containers are used in international trade because they use less space on oceangoing vessels.

TRANSPORTATION MODE	RELATIVE ADVANTAGES	RELATIVE DISADVANTAGES
Rail	• Full capability • Extensive routes • Low cost	• Some reliability, damage problems • Not always complete pickup and delivery • Sometimes slow
Truck	• Complete pickup and delivery • Extensive routes • Fairly fast	• Size and weight restrictions • Higher cost • More weather sensitive
Air	• Fast • Low damage • Frequent departures	• High cost • Limited capabilities
Pipeline	• Low cost • Very reliable • Frequent departures	• Limited routes (accessibility) • Slow
Water	• Low cost • Huge capacities	• Slow • Limited routes and schedules • More weather sensitive

FIGURE 16–5
Advantages and disadvantages of five modes of transportation

Motor Carriers In contrast to the railroad industry, the for-hire motor carrier industry is composed of many small firms, including as many as 500,000 independent truckers and firms that own their own trucks for transporting their own products.

The greatest advantage of motor carriers is the complete door-to-door service. Trucks can go almost anywhere there is a road, and with the design of specialized equipment, they can carry a variety of products. Their physical limitations are size and weight restrictions enforced by the states. Trucks have the reputation for maintaining a better record than rail for loss and damage and providing faster, more reliable service, especially for shorter distances. As a result, trucks carry higher-valued goods that are time-sensitive and expensive to carry in inventory. The trade-off is that truck rates are substantially higher than rail rates.

Air Carriers and Express Companies Air freight is costly, but its speed may create savings in lower inventory. The items that can be carried are limited by space constraints and are usually valuable, time-sensitive, and lightweight, such as perishable flowers, clothing, and electronic parts. Specialized firms provide ground support in terms of collecting shipments and delivering them to the air terminal. When air freight is handled by major airlines—such as American, United, Delta, or Northwest—it is often carried as cargo using the excess luggage space of scheduled passenger flights.

Freight Forwarders *Freight forwarders* are firms that accumulate small shipments into larger lots and then hire a carrier to move them, usually at reduced rates. Recall that transportation companies provide rate incentives for larger quantities. Forwarders collect many small shipments consigned to a common destination and pay the carrier the lower rate based on larger volume, so they often convert shipments that are less-than-truckload (LTL) into full truckloads, thereby receiving better shipping rates. The rates charged by the forwarder to the individual shippers, in turn, are somewhat less than the small quantity rate, and the difference is the forwarder's margin. In general, the shipment receives improved service at lower cost.

Air freight forwarders are an example of specialization in one transportation mode. In some cases, airlines will subcontract excess space to *air freight forwarders or express companies,* which are firms that market air express services to the general public. Where

BAX Global is a worldwide supply chain and transportation company with some 500 facilities in 133 countries. This advertisement shows how BAX Global supplies Dell Inc. with products from locations around the world.

BAX Global
www.baxglobal.com

markets are large enough, major airlines have responded with pure air freight service between specific airports, often involving international destinations.

Warehousing and Materials Handling

Warehouses may be classified in one of two ways: (1) storage warehouses and (2) distribution centers. In *storage warehouses* the goods are intended to come to rest for some period of time, as in the aging of products or in storing household goods. *Distribution centers,* on the other hand, are designed to facilitate the timely movement of goods and represent a very important part of a supply chain. They represent the second most significant cost in a supply chain after transportation.

Distribution centers not only allow firms to hold their stock in decentralized locations but are also used to facilitate sorting and consolidating products from different manufacturing plants or suppliers. For example, a distribution center operated by ODW Logistics, Inc., a third-party logistics provider, provides these services. Pioneer Electronics, Inc., relies on ODW not just for warehousing and distribution, but for basic assembly as well. ODW employees put plasma television sets and stereo speakers delivered separately from China in a single box with receivers from Thailand, other smaller parts from around the world, and installation instructions. The boxes are then shipped to the home-theater sections of Wal-Mart stores, Best Buy, and Circuit City.[16] Some physical transformation can also take place in distribution centers such as mixing or blending different ingredients, labeling, and repackaging. Paint companies such as Sherwin-Williams and Benjamin Moore use distribution centers for this purpose. In addition, distribution centers may serve as manufacturers' sales offices, described in Chapter 15, and order processing centers.

Materials handling, which involves moving goods over short distances into, within, and out of warehouses and manufacturing plants, is a key part of warehouse operations. The two major problems with this activity are high labor costs and high rates of loss and damage. Every time an item is handled, there is a chance for loss or damage. Common materials handling equipment includes forklifts, cranes, and conveyors. Today, materials handling in warehouses is automated by using computers and robots to reduce the cost of holding, moving, and recording inventories.

Order Processing

There are several stages in the processing of an order, and a failure at any one of them can cause a problem with the customer. The process starts with transmitting the order by a variety of means such as the Internet, an extranet, or electronic data interchange. This is followed by entering the order in the appropriate databases and sending the information to those needing it. For example, a regional warehouse is notified to prepare an order. After checking inventory, a new quantity may need to be reordered from the production line, or purchasing may be requested to reorder from a vendor. If the item is currently out of stock, a *backorder* is created, and the whole process of keeping track of a small part of the original order must be managed. In addition, credit may have to be checked for some customers, all documentation for the order must be prepared, transportation must be arranged, and an order confirmation must be sent. Order processing systems are evaluated in terms of speed and accuracy.

United Airlines Cargo provides fast, global delivery, often utilizing containers.

United Airlines

Electronic order processing has replaced manual processing for most large companies.[17] For example, 96 percent of IBM's purchase transactions with suppliers are conducted on the Internet. Kiwi Brands, the Douglassville, Pennsylvania, marketer of Kiwi shoe polish, Endust, and Behold, receives 75 percent of its retailers' purchase orders via EDI. The company has also implemented financial EDI, sending invoices to retailers and receiving payment order/remittance advice documents and electronic funds transfer (EFT) payments. Shippers as well are linked to the system, allowing Kiwi to receive shipment status messages electronically.

Inventory Management

Inventory management is one of the primary responsibilities of the supply chain manager. The major problem is maintaining the delicate balance between too little and too much. Too little inventory may result in poor service, stockouts, brand switching, and loss of market share; too much leads to higher costs because of the money tied up in inventory and the chance that it may become obsolete. Remember the sting of the bullwhip described at the beginning of the chapter?

Reasons for Inventory Traditionally, carrying inventory has been justified on several grounds: (1) to offer a buffer against variations in supply and demand, often caused by uncertainty in forecasting demand; (2) to provide better service for those customers who wish to be served on demand; (3) to promote production efficiencies; (4) to provide a hedge against price increases by suppliers; (5) to promote purchasing and transportation discounts; and (6) to protect the firm from contingencies such as strikes and shortages.

However, companies today view inventory as something to be moved, not stored, and more of a liability than an asset. The traditional justification for inventory has resulted in excessive inventories that have proven costly to maintain. Consider the U.S. automobile industry. Despite efforts to streamline its supply chain, industry analysts estimate that $230 billion worth of excess inventory piles up annually in the form of unused raw materials, parts waiting to be delivered, and vehicles sitting on dealers' lots.[18]

Inventory Costs Specific inventory costs are often hard to detect because they are difficult to measure and occur in many different parts of the firm. A classification of inventory costs includes the following:

- *Capital costs.* The opportunity costs resulting from tying up funds in inventory instead of using them in other, more profitable investments; these are related to interest rates.

Did you know Microsoft Corporation is also involved in supply chain management? This advertisement features Microsoft Dynamics and its just-in-time solution for supply chain management.

Microsoft Dynamics
www.microsoft.com/dynamics

- *Inventory service costs.* Items such as insurance and taxes that are present in many states.
- *Storage costs.* Warehousing space and materials handling.
- *Risk costs.* Possible loss, damage, pilferage, perishability, and obsolescence.

Storage costs, risk costs, and some inventory service costs vary according to the characteristics of the item inventoried. For example, perishable products or highly seasonal items have higher risk costs than a commodity type product such as lumber. Capital costs are always present and are proportional to the *values* of the item and prevailing interest rates. The costs of carrying inventory vary with the particular circumstances but quite easily could range from 10 to 35 percent for different firms.

Supply Chain Inventory Strategies   Conventional wisdom a decade ago was that a firm should protect itself against uncertainty by maintaining a reserve inventory at each of its production and stocking points. This has been described as a "just-in-case" philosophy of inventory management and led to unnecessary high levels of inventory. In contrast is the **just-in-time (JIT) concept**, which is an inventory supply system that operates with very low inventories and requires fast, on-time delivery. When parts are needed for production, they arrive from suppliers "just in time," which means neither before nor after they are needed. Note that JIT is used in situations where demand forecasting is reliable, such as when supplying an automobile production line, and is not suitable for inventories that are to be stored over significant periods of time.

Saturn's manufacturing operation in Spring Hill, Tennessee, uses a sophisticated JIT system.[19] A central computerized system directs trucks to deliver preinspected parts at specific times 21 hours a day, six days a week to one of the plant's 56 receiving docks. Incredibly, the JIT system must coordinate Saturn's 300 suppliers located in the United States, Canada, and Mexico. Does the JIT system work for Saturn? The answer

Reverse Logistics and Green Marketing Go Together at Hewlett-Packard: Recycling e-waste

Between 20 and 50 million tons of electronic waste find their way to landfills around the world annually. Americans alone are expected to discard 550 million analog TV sets and computer monitors and Japanese consumers will trash 610 million cell phones in 2010. The result? Landfills are seeping lead, chromium, mercury, and other toxins, prevalent in digital debris, into the environment.

Fortunately, Hewlett-Packard has taken it upon itself to act responsibly and address this issue through its highly regarded reverse logistics program. Hewlett-Packard has recycled computer and printer hardware since 1987 and is an industry leader in this practice. The company's

recycling service is available today in more than 40 countries, regions, and territories. By 2010, Hewlett-Packard will have recycled over 1 billion pounds of used products to be refurbished for resale or donation or for recovery of materials.

The recycling effort at Hewlett-Packard is also part of the company's Design for Supply Chain program. Among other initiatives in this program, emphasis is placed on product and packaging changes to reduce reverse supply chain and environmental costs. For example, design changes have increased the recycling of its popular ink-jet supplies by 25 percent.

---

is a resounding yes. The Saturn production line has been shut down only once—for 18 minutes!—because the right part was not delivered at the right place and time.

Electronic data interchange and electronic messaging technology coupled with the constant pressure for faster response time in replenishing inventory have also changed the way suppliers and customers do business in a supply chain. The approach, called **vendor-managed inventory (VMI)**, is an inventory-management system whereby the *supplier* determines the product amount and assortment a customer (such as a retailer) needs and automatically delivers the appropriate items.

Campbell Soup's system illustrates how VMI works.[20] Campbell first establishes EDI links with retailers. Every morning, retailers electronically inform the company of their demand for all Campbell products and the inventory levels in their distribution centers. Campbell uses that information to forecast future demand and determine which products need replenishment based on upper and lower inventory limits established with each retailer. Trucks leave the Campbell shipping plant that afternoon and arrive at the retailer's distribution centers with the required replenishments the same day.

CLOSING THE LOOP: REVERSE LOGISTICS

The flow of goods in a supply chain does not end with the consumer or industrial user. Companies today recognize that a supply chain can work in reverse. **Reverse logistics** is a process of reclaiming recyclable and reusable materials, returns, and reworks from the point of consumption or use for repair, remanufacturing, redistribution, or disposal. The effect of reverse logistics can be seen in the reduced waste in landfills and lowered operating costs for companies. The accompanying Making Responsible Decisions box describes the successful reverse logistics initiative at Hewlett-Packard.[21]

Companies such as Kodak (reusable cameras), Motorola and Sony Ericsson Mobile Communications (return and reuse of cell phones), and Caterpillar, Xerox, and IBM (remanufacturing and recycling) have implemented acclaimed reverse logistics programs.[22] Other firms have enlisted third-party logistics providers to handle this process along with other supply chain functions. GNB Technologies, Inc., a manufacturer of lead-acid batteries for automobiles and boats, has outsourced much of its supply chain activity to UPS Supply Chain Services.[23] The company contracts with UPS to manage its shipments between plants, distribution centers, recycling centers, and retailers. This includes movement of both new batteries and used products destined for recycling and covers both truck and railroad shipments. This partnership along with the initiatives of other battery makers has paid economic and ecological dividends. By recycling 90 percent of the lead from used batteries, manufacturers have kept the demand for new lead in check, thereby holding down costs to consumers. Also, solid waste management costs and the environmental impact of lead in landfills are reduced.

learning review

6. What are the basic trade-offs between the five modes of transportation?

7. What types of inventory should use storage warehouses and which type should use distribution centers?

8. What are the strengths and weaknesses of a just-in-time system?

LEARNING OBJECTIVES REVIEW

LO1 *Recognize the relationship between marketing channels, logistics, and supply chain management.*
A marketing channel relies on logistics to make products available to consumers and industrial users. Logistics involves those activities that focus on getting the right amount of the right products to the right place at the right time at the lowest possible cost. The performance of these activities is logistics management—the practice of organizing the cost-effective flow of raw materials, in-process inventory, finished goods, and related information from point of origin to point of consumption to satisfy customer requirements.

A supply chain is a sequence of firms that perform activities required to create and deliver a good or service to consumers or industrial users. It differs from a marketing channel in terms of membership. A supply chain includes suppliers that provide raw material inputs to a manufacturer as well as the wholesalers and retailers that deliver goods. The management process is also different. Supply chain management is the integration and organization of information and logistics activities across firms in a supply chain for the purpose of creating and delivering goods and services that provide value to consumers.

LO2 *Describe how a company's supply chain aligns with its marketing strategy.*
A company's supply chain follows from a clearly defined marketing strategy. The alignment of a company's supply chain with its marketing strategy involves three steps. First, a supply chain must reflect the needs of the customer segment being served. Second, a company must understand what a supply chain is designed to do well. Supply chains range from those that emphasize being responsive to customer requirements and demands to those that emphasize efficiency with the goal of supplying products at the lowest possible delivered cost. Finally, a supply chain must be consistent with the targeted customer's needs and the company's marketing strategy. The Dell and Wal-Mart examples in the chapter illustrate how this alignment is achieved by two well-known companies.

LO3 *Identify the major logistics cost and customer service factors that managers consider when making supply chain decisions.*
Companies strive to provide superior customer service while controlling logistics cost. The major customer service factors include the length of time between orders and deliveries, dependability in replenishing inventory, communication between buyers and sellers, and convenience in buying from the seller. Logistics cost factors include transportation, materials handling and warehousing, order processing, inventory, and stockouts.

LO4 *Describe the key logistics functions in a supply chain.*
The four key logistics functions in a supply chain include transportation, warehousing and materials handling, order processing, and inventory management. Transportation provides the movement of goods necessary in a supply chain. The five major transportation modes are railroads, motor carriers, air carriers, pipelines, and water carriers. Warehousing and materials handling include the storing, sorting, and handling of products at storage warehouses or distribution centers. Order processing includes order receipt, delivery, invoicing, and collection from customers. Inventory management involves minimizing inventory-carrying costs while maintaining sufficient stocks of products to satisfy anticipated customer needs. Two popular inventory management practices are just-in-time (JIT) and vendor-managed inventory (VMI) systems.

FOCUSING ON KEY TERMS

customer service p. 423
efficient consumer response p. 423
electronic data interchange (EDI) p. 421
just-in-time (JIT) concept p. 431
lead time p. 423

logistics p. 416
logistics management p. 416
quick response p. 423
reverse logistics p. 432
supply chain p. 416
supply chain management p. 416

third-party logistics providers p. 425
total logistics cost p. 422
vendor-managed inventory (VMI) p. 432

APPLYING MARKETING KNOWLEDGE

1 List several companies to which logistical activities might be unimportant. Also list several whose focus is only on the inbound or outbound side.

2 What are some types of businesses in which order processing may be among the paramount success factors?

3 List the customer service factors that would be vital to buyers in the following types of companies: (*a*) manufacturing, (*b*) retailing, (*c*) hospitals, and (*d*) construction.

4 Name some cases when extremely high service levels (e.g., 99 percent) would be warranted.

5 Name the mode of transportation that would be the best for the following products: (*a*) farm machinery, (*b*) cut flowers, (*c*) frozen meat, and (*d*) coal.

6 The auto industry is a heavy user of the just-in-time concept. Why? What other industries would be good candidates for its application? What do they have in common?

7 Look again at Figure 16–3. Explain why as the number of warehouses increases, (*a*) inventory costs rise and (*b*) transportation costs fall.

8 What relationship would you expect to see between a company's on-time delivery percentage and its out-of-stock percentage?

building your marketing plan

Does your marketing plan involve a product? If the answer is no, read no further and do not include this element in your plan. If the answer is yes:

1 If inventory is involved, (*a*) identify the three or four major kinds of inventory needed for your organization (retail stock, finished goods, raw materials, supplies, and so on), and (*b*) suggest ways to reduce their costs.

2 (*a*) Rank the four customer service factors (time, dependability, communication, and convenience) from most important to least important from your customers' point of view, and (*b*) identify actions for the one or two most important to serve customers better.

video case 16   Amazon: Delivering the Goods . . . Millions of Times a Day

 "The new economy means that the balance of power has shifted toward the consumer," explains Jeff Bezos, CEO of Amazon.com, Inc. The global online retailer is a pioneer of fast, convenient, low-cost virtual shopping that has attracted millions of consumers. Of course, while Amazon has changed the way many people shop, the company still faces the traditional and daunting task of creating a seamless flow of deliveries to its customers—often millions of times each day.

THE COMPANY

Bezos started Amazon.com with a simple idea: to use the Internet to transform book buying into the fastest, easiest, and most enjoyable shopping experience possible. The company was incorporated in 1994 and opened its virtual doors in July 1995. At the forefront of a huge growth of dot-com businesses, Amazon pursued a get-big-fast business strategy. Sales grew rapidly and Amazon began adding products and services other than books. In fact, Amazon soon set its goal on being the world's most customer-centric company, where custom-

ers can find and discover anything they might want to buy online!

Today Amazon claims to have the "Earth's Biggest Selection™" of products and services, including books, CDs, videos, toys and games, electronics, kitchenware, computers, free electronic greeting cards, and auctions. Other services allow customers to:

- Search for books, music, and videos with any word from the title or any part of the artist's name.
- Browse hundreds of product categories.
- Receive personalized recommendations, based on past purchases, through e-mail or when they log on.

These products and services have attracted millions of people in more than 220 countries and made Amazon.com, along with its international sites in Canada, the United Kingdom, Germany, Japan, France, and China, the leading online retailer.

Despite its incredible success with consumers and continuing growth in sales, Amazon.com found it difficult to be profitable. Many industry observers questioned the viability of online retailing and Amazon's business model. Then, in 2002, Amazon shocked many people by becoming profitable. The Company has remained profitable and its sales now exceed $14 billion annually. There are a variety of explanations for the turnaround. Generally, Bezos suggests that "efficiencies allow for lower prices, spurring sales growth across the board, which can be handled by existing facilities without much additional cost." More specifically, the facilities Bezos is referring to are the elements of its supply chain, which are one of the most complex and expensive aspects of the company's business.

it is taped and labeled. A network of trucks and regional postal hubs then conclude the process with delivery of the order.

The success of Amazon's logistics and supply chain management activities may be most evident during the year-end holiday shopping season. Amazon received orders for 37.9 million items between November 9 and December 21 one year, including orders for 450,000 Harry Potter books and products, and orders for 36,000 items placed just before the holiday delivery deadline. Well over 99 percent of the orders were shipped and delivered on time.

SUPPLY CHAIN AND LOGISTICS MANAGEMENT AT AMAZON.COM

What happens after an order is submitted on Amazon's website but before it arrives at the customer's door? A lot. Amazon.com maintains huge distribution, or "fulfillment," centers where it keeps inventory of more than 2.7 million products. This is one of the key differences between Amazon.com and some of its competitors—it actually stocks products. So Amazon must manage the flow of products from its suppliers to its distribution centers and the flow of customer orders from the distribution centers to individuals' homes or offices.

The process begins with the suppliers. "Amazon's goal is to collaborate with our suppliers to increase efficiencies and improve inventory turnover," explains Jim Miller, vice president of supply chain at Amazon.com. "We want to bring to suppliers the kind of interactive relationship that has inspired customers to shop with us," he adds. For example, Amazon is using software to more accurately forecast purchasing patterns by region, which allows it to give its suppliers better information about delivery dates and volumes. Before the development of this software, 12 percent of incoming inventory was sent to the wrong location, leading to lost time and delayed orders. Now only 4 percent of the incoming inventory is mishandled.

At the same time, Amazon has been improving the part of the process that sorts the products into the individual orders. Jeffrey Wilke, Amazon's senior vice president of operations, says, "We spent the whole year really focused on increasing productivity." Again, technology has been essential. "The speed at which telecommunications networks allow us to pass information back and forth has enabled us to do the real-time work that we keep talking about. In the past, it would have taken too long to get this many items through a system," explains Wilke. Once the order is in the system, computers ensure that all items are included in the box before

AMAZON'S CHALLENGES

Despite all of Amazon's recent improvements, logistics experts estimate that the company's distribution centers are operating at approximately 40 percent of their capacity. This situation suggests that Amazon must reduce its capacity or increase its sales.

Several sales growth options are possible. First, Amazon can continue to pursue growth through sales of books, CDs, and videos. Expanded lists of books, music, and movies from throughout the world and convenient selection services may appeal to current and potential customers. Second, Amazon can continue its expansion into new product and service categories. This approach would prevent Amazon from becoming a niche merchant of books, music, and movies, and position it as an online department store. Finally, Amazon can pursue a strategy of providing access to its existing operations to other retailers. For example, Amazon shoppers can purchase products from Target and Office Depot, and visit web sites of Amazon partners such as Shutterfly, Tire Rack, and WeightWatchers.

Amazon.com has come a long way toward proving that online retailing can work. As the company strives to maintain profitability and continue its growth, its future success is likely to depend on the success of its logistics and supply chain management activities.

Questions

1 How do Amazon.com's logistics and supply chain management activities help the company create value for its customers?
2 What systems did Amazon develop to improve the flow of products from suppliers to Amazon distribution centers? What systems improved the flow of orders from the distribution centers to customers?
3 Why will logistics and supply chain management play an important role in the future success of Amazon.com?

17

Retailing

RETAILERS ARE REINVENTING THEIR STORES TO MATCH THE WAY YOU WANT TO SHOP!

Retailers are undergoing a transformation that is designed to make the shopping experience better for you. They are adding bars and restaurants, using technology to allow customers to send images and messages to friends from the fitting rooms, and even building new stores with "open" designs. The combination of being at the mall, interacting with friends who are there, and engaging your personal network online just like you would with MySpace or Facebook will soon be part of the new "social retailing^SM."

For many years luxury department stores such as Barneys New York, Bergdorf Goodman, Neiman Marcus, Nordstrom, and Saks Fifth Avenue have used the same approach—offer expensive, well-known designer clothing in an elegant setting. Young consumers, however, are often looking for a different experience. To adapt to the new preferences many retailers are making changes to their existing stores. Bergdorf Goodman, for example, has added a deejay who will download music onto iPods, Saks has an upscale restaurant for shoppers, and Nordstrom offers live piano music. Some stores are offering "girlfriends" fitting rooms, which have space for as many as five friends, while others are trying fitting rooms with Privalite glass walls that allow privacy when shoppers are trying something on, but become transparent with the touch of a switch!

If friends can't actually be at the store to critique purchases, however, they will soon be able to participate in the shopping through online connections. New interactive fitting-room mirrors at Bloomingdale's allow shoppers to send images to anyone through online, mobile, and live video communication tools and then receive comments back from them. Other new technologies include "virtual" mirrors that project shoes onto customer's feet, and body scanners that collect 200,000 data points to determine exact sizes.

Some retailers are also creating new stores to attract young customers. Neiman Marcus, for example, is opening new stores, called Cusp, that feature "edgy" labels in an open floor plan with exposed ductwork and concrete floors. Sales associates are called "stylists" and a blog (www.blogonthecusp.com) takes the place of advertising. Similarly, Barneys is expanding its Co-op stores, which carry merchandise targeted at those in their 20s and 30s.[1]

Increasing social elements is just one example of the many exciting changes occurring in retailing today. This chapter examines the critical role of retailing in the marketplace and the challenging decisions retailers face as they strive to create value for customers.

What types of products will consumers buy through catalogs, television, the Internet, or by telephone? In what type of store will consumers look for products they don't buy directly? How important is the location of the store? Will customers expect services such as alterations, delivery, installation, or repair? What price should be charged for each product? These are difficult and important questions that are an integral part of retailing. In the channel of distribution, retailing is where the customer meets the product. It is through retailing that exchange (a central aspect of marketing) occurs. **Retailing** includes all activities involved in selling, renting, and providing goods and services to ultimate customers for personal, family, or household use.

THE VALUE OF RETAILING

LO1

Retailing is an important marketing activity. Not only do producers and consumers meet through retailing actions, but retailing also creates customer value and has a significant impact on the economy. To consumers, the value of retailing is in the form of utilities provided (Figure 17–1). Retailing's economic value is represented by the people employed in retailing as well as by the total amount of money exchanged in retail sales (Figure 17–2).

Consumer Utilities Offered by Retailing

The utilities provided by retailers create value for consumers. Time, place, form, and possession utilities are offered by most retailers in varying degrees, but one utility is often emphasized more than others. Look at Figure 17–1 to see how well you can match the retailer with the utility being emphasized in the description.

FIGURE 17–1

Which retailer best provides which utilities?

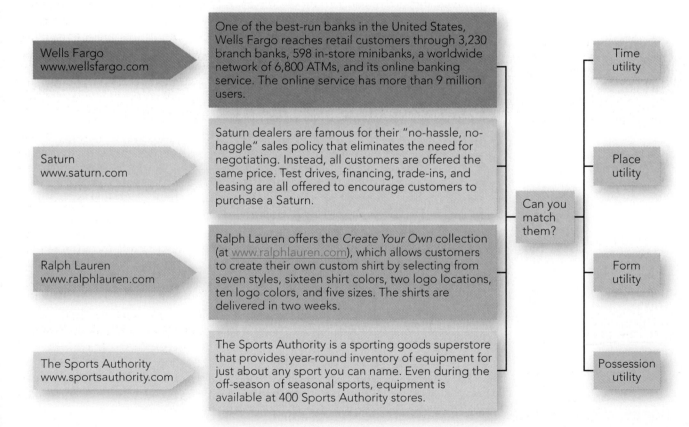

438

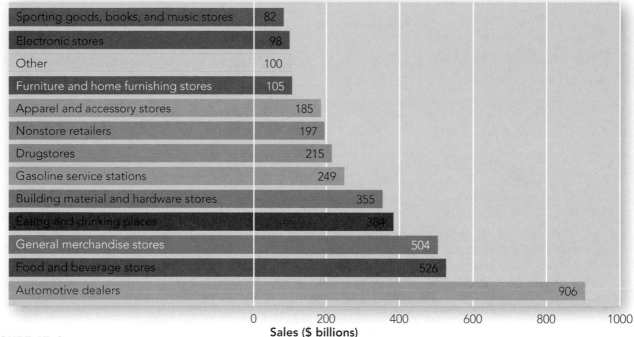

Type of retailer	Sales ($ billions)
Sporting goods, books, and music stores	82
Electronic stores	98
Other	100
Furniture and home furnishing stores	105
Apparel and accessory stores	185
Nonstore retailers	197
Drugstores	215
Gasoline service stations	249
Building material and hardware stores	355
Eating and drinking places	384
General merchandise stores	504
Food and beverage stores	526
Automotive dealers	906

FIGURE 17–2

Are you surprised by the relative size of different types of retailers?

Karstadt is one of the largest retailers outside the U.S.

Providing minibanks in supermarkets, as Wells Fargo does, puts the bank's products and services close to the consumer, providing place utility. By providing financing or leasing and taking used cars as trade-ins, Saturn makes the purchase easier and provides possession utility. Form utility—production or alteration of a product—is offered by Polo Ralph Lauren through its online *Create Your Own* program, which offers shirts that meet each customer's specifications. Finding the right sporting equipment during the off-season is the time utility provided by the Sports Authority. Many retailers offer a combination of the four basic utilities. Some supermarkets, for example, offer convenient locations (place utility) and are open 24 hours (time utility). In addition, consumers may seek additional utilities such as entertainment, recreation, or information.[2]

The Global Economic Impact of Retailing

Retailing is important to the U.S. and global economies. Three of the 15 largest businesses in the United States are retailers (Wal-Mart, Home Depot, and Costco).[3] Wal-Mart's $351 billion of sales in 2006 surpassed the gross domestic product of all but 23 countries for that same year. Wal-Mart, Home Depot, and Costco together have more than 2.3 million employees—more than the combined populations of Austin, Texas; Spokane, Washington; and Columbus, Ohio. Figure 17–2 shows that many other retailers, including food stores, automobile dealers, and general merchandise outlets, are also significant contributors to the U.S. economy.[4]

Outside the United States large retailers include Daiei in Japan, Carrefour in France, KarstadtQuell in Germany, and Marks & Spencer in Britain.[5] In emerging economies such as China and Mexico, a combination of local and global retailers is evolving. Wal-Mart, for example, has 2,909 stores outside the United States, including stores in Brazil, China, Japan, Mexico, and the United Kingdom.

learning review

1. When Polo makes shirts to a customer's exact preferences, what utility is provided?

2. Two measures of the impact of retailing in the global economy are _____ and _____.

CLASSIFYING RETAIL OUTLETS

For manufacturers, consumers, and the economy, retailing is an important component of marketing that has several variations. Because of the large number of alternative forms of retailing, it is easier to understand the differences among retail institutions by recognizing that outlets can be classified in several ways. First, **form of ownership** distinguishes retail outlets based on whether individuals, corporate chains, or contractual systems own the outlet. Second, **level of service** is used to describe the degree of service provided to the customer. Three levels of service are provided by self-, limited-, and full-service retailers. Finally, the type of **merchandise line** describes how many different types of products a store carries and in what assortment. The alternative types of outlets are discussed in greater detail in the following pages.

Form of Ownership

There are three general forms of retail ownership—individual, corporate chain, and contractual system.

Independent Retailer One of the most common forms of retail ownership is the independent business, owned by an individual. Small retailers account for most of the 1.5 million retail establishments in the United States and include hardware stores, bakeries, clothing stores, and restaurants. In addition, there are 29,000 jewelry stores, 22,000 florists, and 43,000 sporting good and hobby stores. The advantage of this form of ownership for the owner is that he or she can be his or her own boss.[6] The accompanying Marketing Matters box discusses some of the skills needed to be a successful retailing entrepreneur.[7] For customers, the independent store can offer convenience, quality personal service, and lifestyle compatibility.

Corporate Chain A second form of ownership, the corporate chain, involves multiple outlets under common ownership. Many of the department store names you may know—Bon Marche, Lazurus, Burdines, Famous Barr, Filenes, Foleys, and Marshall Field's—are now one of 866 Macy's stores nationwide. Macy's Inc. also owns 40 Bloomingdale's, which compete with other chains such as Saks Fifth Avenue and Neiman Marcus.

In a chain operation, centralization in decision making and purchasing is common. Chain stores have advantages in dealing with manufacturers, particularly as the size of the chain grows. A large chain can bargain with a manufacturer to obtain good service or volume discounts on orders. Target's large volume makes it a strong negotiator with manufacturers of most products. The buying power of chains is seen when consumers compare chain store prices with other types of stores. Consumers also benefit in dealing with chains because there are multiple outlets with similar merchandise and consistent management policies.

Retailing has become a high-tech business for many large chains. Wal-Mart, for example, has developed a sophisticated inventory management and cost control system that allows rapid price changes for each product in every store. In addition, stores such as Wal-Mart and Target are implementing pioneering new technologies such as radio frequency identification (RFID) tags to improve the quality of information available about products.

Marketing Matters > > > > > entrepreneurship

Are You a Future Retailing Entrepreneur?

Many marketing students consider careers in retailing. Are you one of them? Do you think you could start and run your own retail business? Jim Sinegal, the entrepreneur who started Costco, suggests that to be successful in retailing you need the ability to know what products or services would sell best to different types of customers—an ability he calls "merchandising savvy." Of course, other qualities are important also. *Entrepreneur* magazine suggests that you need good people skills, general business skills, access to start-up capital, and partners who are equally passionate as you about an idea.

Where can you get new retailing ideas? Watch other retailers for new approaches, such as Whole Foods' new approach to supermarkets. Or use a website such as www.springwise.com where new retailing trends and ideas are monitored in the "idea database." Is it too soon for you to start developing your new retailing idea? Probably not. Sinegal was just 18 years old when he took his first retail job—unloading mattresses!

Contractual Systems Contractual systems involve independently owned stores that band together to act like a chain. The three kinds described in Chapter 15 are retailer-sponsored cooperatives, wholesaler-sponsored voluntary chains, and franchises. One retailer-sponsored cooperative is the Associated Grocers, which consists of neighborhood grocers that all agree with several other independent grocers to buy their meat from the same wholesaler. In this way, members can take advantage of volume discounts commonly available to chains and also give the impression of being a large chain, which may be viewed more favorably by some consumers. Wholesaler-sponsored voluntary chains such as Independent Grocers' Alliance (IGA) try to achieve similar benefits.

As noted in Chapter 15, in a franchise system an individual or firm (the franchisee) contracts with a parent company (the franchisor) to set up a business or retail outlet. The franchisor usually assists in selecting the location, setting up the store or facility, advertising, and training personnel. The franchisee usually pays a onetime franchise fee and an annual royalty, usually tied to franchise's sales. There are two general types of franchises: *business-format franchises,* such as McDonald's, Radio Shack, and Blockbuster, and *product-distribution franchises,* such as a Ford dealership or a Coca-Cola distributor. In business-format franchising, the franchisor provides step-by-step procedures for most aspects of the business and guidelines for the most likely decisions a franchisee will face.

Franchising is attractive because it offers an opportunity for people to enter a well-known, established business for which managerial advice is provided. Also, the franchise fee may be less than the cost of setting up an independent business. The International Franchise Association recently reported that there are 760,000 franchised

Subway is a popular business-format franchisor.

Franchise	Type of Business	Total Start-up Cost	Number of Franchises
Subway	Sandwich Restaurant	$75,000–222,000	26,100
Dunkin donuts	Bakery	$179,000–1,600,000	7,400
Jackson Hewitt Tax Service	Income Tax Preparation	$49,000–92,000	6,500
7-Eleven	Convenience Store	$65,000–227,000	31,600
UPS Store	Business Support Center	$154,000–267,000	5,700

FIGURE 17–3

The top five franchises in the United States vary from sandwich restaurants to tax preparation services.

businesses in the United States, which generate $1.53 trillion in annual sales and employ more than 9.7 million people. Franchising is popular in international markets also—more than half of all U.S. franchisors have operations in other countries. What is the fastest-growing franchise? For the past year it has been Subway, which now has 26,000 locations, including 4,000 stores outside of the United States.[8]

Franchise fees paid to the franchisor can range from $15,000 for a Subway franchise to $45,000 for a McDonald's restaurant franchise. When the fees are combined with other costs such as real estate and equipment, however, the total investment can be much higher. Franchisees also pay an ongoing royalty fee that ranges from 5 percent for a UPS Store to 15 percent for a Jackson Hewitt franchise. Figure 17–3 shows the top five franchises, as rated by *Entrepreneur* magazine, based on factors such as size, financial strength, stability, years in business, and costs. By selling franchises, an organization reduces the cost of expansion but loses some control. A good franchisor, however, will maintain strong control of the outlets in terms of delivery and presentation of merchandise and try to enhance recognition of the franchise name.[9]

Level of Service

Even though most customers perceive little variation in retail outlets by form of ownership, differences among retailers are more obvious in terms of level of service. In some department stores, such as Loehman's, very few services are provided. Some grocery stores, such as the Cub Foods chain, require customers to bag the food themselves. Other outlets, such as Neiman Marcus, provide a wide range of customer services from gift wrapping to wardrobe consultation.

Self-Service Self-service requires that the customers perform many functions and little is provided by the outlet. Warehouse clubs such as Costco, for example, are usually self-service, with all nonessential customer services eliminated. Similarly most gas stations today are self-service. New forms of self-service are being developed in grocery stores, airlines, camera/photo stores, and hotels. US Airways has installed more than 600 self-service kiosks in all 107 of its U.S. and Caribbean terminals to allow passengers to find a seat and print out a boarding pass without the help of an attendant. Hilton Hotels has self-service kiosks in 170 of its Embassy Suites hotels and all of its domestic Hilton properties. Guests swipe a credit card, select from room options, and receive their room keys. Throughout the United States more than 600,000 self-service kiosks are in use today. In general, the trend is toward retailing experiences that make customers co-creators of the value they receive.[10]

Limited Service Limited-service outlets provide some services, such as credit and merchandise return, but not others, such as clothing alterations. General merchandise stores such as Wal-Mart, Kmart, and Target are usually considered limited service outlets. Customers are responsible for most shopping activities, although salespeople are available in departments such as consumer electronics, jewelry, and lawn and garden.

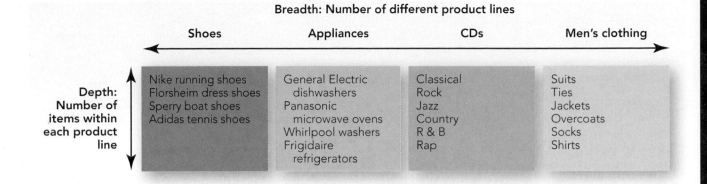

Shoes	Appliances	CDs	Men's clothing
Nike running shoes Florsheim dress shoes Sperry boat shoes Adidas tennis shoes	General Electric dishwashers Panasonic microwave ovens Whirlpool washers Frigidaire refrigerators	Classical Rock Jazz Country R & B Rap	Suits Ties Jackets Overcoats Socks Shirts

Depth: Number of items within each product line

FIGURE 17–4

Stores vary in terms of the breadth and depth of their merchandise lines.

Full-Service

Full-service retailers, which include most specialty stores and department stores, provide many services to their customers. Neiman Marcus, Nordstrom, and Saks Fifth Avenue, for example, all rely on better service to sell more distinctive, higher-margin goods and to retain their customers. Nordstrom offers a wide variety of services, including free exchanges, easy returns, credit cards through Nordstrom bank, a live help line, an online gift finder, catalogs, a four-level loyalty program called Nordstrom Fashion Rewards, and a beauty hotline. Some Nordstrom stores also offer a "Personal Touch" department, which provides shopping assistants for consumers who need help with style, color, and size selection, and a concierge service for assistance with anything else. Nordstrom stores typically have 50 percent more salespeople on the floor than similarly sized stores, and the salespeople are renowned for their professional and personalized attention to customers. Nordstrom also offers RSS feeds to notify customers when new merchandise is available.[11]

Type of Merchandise Line

Retail outlets also vary by their merchandise lines, the key distinction being the breadth and depth of the items offered to customers (Figure 17–4). **Depth of product line** means that the store carries a large assortment of each item, such as a shoe store that offers running shoes, dress shoes, and children's shoes. **Breadth of product line** refers to the variety of different items a store carries, such as appliances and CDs.

Depth of Line Stores that carry a considerable assortment (depth) of a related line of items are limited-line stores. Oshman's sporting goods stores carry considerable depth in sports equipment ranging from weight-lifting accessories to running shoes. Stores that carry tremendous depth in one primary line of merchandise are single-line stores. Victoria's Secret, a nationwide chain, carries great depth in women's lingerie. Both limited- and single-line stores are often referred to as *specialty outlets.*

Specialty discount outlets focus on one type of product, such as electronics (Best Buy), office supplies (Staples), or books (Barnes and Noble) at very competitive prices. These outlets are referred to in the trade as *category killers* because they often dominate the market. Best Buy, for example, controls 17 percent of the consumer electronics market, and Staples is the leader in office supplies.[12]

Staples is the category killer in office supplies.

Breadth of Line Stores that carry a broad product line, with limited depth, are referred to as *general merchandise stores.* For example, large department stores such as Dillard's, Macy's, and Neiman Marcus carry a wide range of different types of products but not unusual sizes. The breadth and depth of merchandise lines are important decisions for a retailer. Traditionally, outlets carried related lines of goods. Today, however, **scrambled merchandising,** offering several

	Hypermarket		Supercenter	
Region of Popularity	Europe		United States	
Average size	200–300,000 sq. ft.		100–220,000 sq. ft.	
Number of products	50,000		40,000	
Annual revenue	$100,000,000 per store		$60,000,000 per store	

FIGURE 17–5

Hypermarkets are popular in Europe.

unrelated product lines in a single store, is common. The modern drugstore carries food, camera equipment, magazines, paper products, toys, small hardware items, and pharmaceuticals. Supermarkets rent videos, print photos, and sell flowers.

A form of scrambled merchandising, the **hypermarket**, has been successful in Europe. These hypermarkets are large stores (more than 200,000 square feet) based on a simple concept: Offer consumers everything in a single outlet, eliminating the need to stop at more than one location. The stores provide variety, quality, and low price for food and groceries and general merchandise. In France, the concept is so successful that hypermarkets maintain a 51 percent share of the grocery market. Carrefour, one of the largest hypermarket retailers, has 218 hypermarkets in France, 408 additional stores in the rest of Europe and is expanding in China where it has 97 new hypermarkets.[13]

In the United States, retailers discovered that shoppers were uncomfortable with the huge size of hypermarkets. They developed a variation of the hypermarket called the *supercenter,* which combines a typical merchandise store (approximately 70,000 square feet) with a full-size grocery. Wal-Mart, Kmart, and Target are now using the concept very successfully. Wal-Mart currently operates 2,300 supercenters and is the nation's largest grocer and third-largest pharmacy. The concept is so successful that Wal-Mart plans to open an additional 4,000 supercenters in the United States during the next five years.[14] Figure 17–5 shows the differences between the supercenter and hypermarket concepts.

Scrambled merchandising is convenient for consumers because it eliminates the number of stops required in a shopping trip. However, for the retailer this merchandising policy means there is competition between very dissimilar types of retail outlets, or **intertype competition**. A local bakery may compete with a department store, discount outlet, or even a local gas station. Scrambled merchandising and intertype competition make it more difficult to be a retailer.

learning review

3. Centralized decision making and purchasing are an advantage of _____ ownership.

4. What are some examples of new forms of self-service retailers?

5. Would a shop for big men's clothes carrying pants in sizes 40 to 60 have a broad or deep product line?

NONSTORE RETAILING

Most of the retailing examples discussed earlier in the chapter, such as corporate chains, department stores, and limited- and single-line specialty stores, involve store retailing. Many retailing activities today, however, are not limited to sales in a store. Nonstore retailing occurs outside a retail outlet through activities that involve varying levels of customer and retailer involvement. Figure 17–6 shows six forms of nonstore retailing: automatic vending, direct mail and catalogs, television home shopping, online retailing, telemarketing, and direct selling.

FIGURE 17–6
Many types of retailers do not have stores.

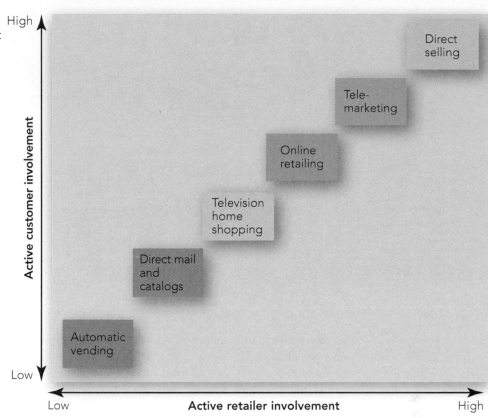

Automatic Vending

Nonstore retailing includes vending machines, which make it possible to serve customers when and where stores cannot. Machine maintenance, operating costs, and location leases can add to the cost of the products, so prices in vending machines tend to be higher than those in stores. About 29 percent of the products sold from vending machines are cold beverages, another 19 percent are candy and snacks, and 36 percent is food. Many other products are quickly becoming available in vending machines. Zoom Systems is putting machines with MP3 players, skin cream, cell phones, and cameras in shopping malls, hotels, and airports across the country. The 5.6 million vending machines currently in use in the United States generate more than $21 billion in annual sales.[15]

Improved technology is making vending machines easier to use by reducing the need for cash. Many machines already accept credit cards, and some machines in Japan allow cashless purchases using cell phones. Japan's largest mobile phone company, DoCoMo, has introduced cell phones equipped with an electronic cash system that will allow consumers to charge vending machine purchases to their cell phone accounts. Another improvement in vending machines is the use of wireless technology to notify vendors when their machines are empty. Nestlé, for example, is installing hundreds of ice cream vending machines in France and England that send wireless messages to drivers of supply trucks. Finally, one of the biggest developments in vending is the trend toward fully automated stores. Get and Go Express stores now open in Florida feature 16 vending machines that offer many of the products typically found in a convenience store, and Moviebank USA recently opened a completely automated video rental store in Reno, Nevada.[16]

Vending machines offer many products found in convenience stores.

Specialty catalogs appeal to market niches.

Direct Mail and Catalogs

Direct-mail and catalog retailing is attractive because it eliminates the cost of a store and clerks. For example, it costs a traditional retail store $34 to acquire a new customer, whereas catalog customers are acquired for approximately $14. In addition, direct mail and catalogs improve marketing efficiency through segmentation and targeting, and they create customer value by providing a fast and convenient means of making a purchase. The average U.S. household now receives 18 direct mail items or catalogs each week, and research indicates that 85 percent of the households read some or all of their mail. The Direct Marketing Association estimates that direct mail and catalog retailing creates 1.7 million jobs and $1.9 trillion in sales. Direct mail and catalog retail is popular outside of the United State also. Furniture retailer IKEA delivered 160 million copies of its catalog in 25 languages last year.[17]

One reason for the growth in catalog sales is that traditional retailers such as Crate and Barrel and OfficeMax are adding catalog operations. As consumer's direct-mail purchases have increased, the number of catalogs and the number of products sold through catalogs have increased. The competition, combined with increases in postal rates, however, have caused catalog retailers to focus on proven customers rather than prospective customers. Another successful approach used by many catalog retailers is to send specialty catalogs to market niches identified in their databases. L. L. Bean, a long-standing catalog retailer, has developed an individual catalog for fly-fishing enthusiasts. Similarly, Lillian Vernon Corporation sends a specialty catalog called "Lilly's Kids" to customers with children or grandchildren, and JCPenney sends a catalog called "Big & Tall" to customers who have purchased large-size clothing.[18]

Creative forms of catalog retailing are also being developed. Victoria's Secret mails as many as 45 catalogs each year to its customers to generate mail-order, telephone-order and online business and to increase traffic in its 900 stores. JCPenney is also an example of a retailer using catalogs, the Internet, and its stores as complementary channels serving its customers. Each year *Multichannel Merchant* magazine evaluates hundreds of entries to select the winners of the Multichannel Merchant Awards in 18 categories of catalogs and websites. Recent winners might be catalogs you have received—the L.L. Bean catalog, the Orvis Company catalog, and the American Girl catalog.[19]

Television Home Shopping

Television home shopping is possible when consumers watch a shopping channel on which products are displayed; orders are then placed over the telephone or the Internet. Currently, the three largest programs are QVC, HSN, and ShopNBC. QVC ("quality,

Television home shopping programs serve millions of customers each year.

value, convenience") broadcasts live 24 hours each day, 364 days a year and reaches 151 million households in the United States, United Kingdom, Germany, and Japan. The company generates sales of more than $6.5 billion from its 42 million customers by offering 250 new products each week and shipping more than 100 million packages each year. The television home shopping channels offer apparel, jewelry, cooking, home improvement products, electronics, toys, and even food products. Of all of these products, the best-selling item ever was a Dell personal computer![20]

In the past, television home shopping programs have attracted mostly 40- to 60-year-old women. To begin to attract a younger audience QVC has invited celebrities onto the show. For example, *American Idol* judge Paula Abdul, supermodel Heidi Klum, and singer Carly Simon have all been on the show selling jewelry and CDs. New partnerships, such as QVC's agreement to be the NFL's "official television retailer," also help attract new customers. The shopping programs are also using other forms of retailing. QVC now has three types of retail stores: a studio store at its headquarters, QVC @ the Mall in the Mall of America in Minnesota, and five outlet stores. Similarly, the Home Shopping Network has added catalogs to its online and television offerings. Finally, several television shopping programs are testing interactive technology that allows viewers to place orders with their remote control rather than the telephone.[21]

Online Retailing

Online retailing allows consumers to search for, evaluate, and order products through the Internet. For many consumers the advantages of this form of retailing are the 24-hour access, the ability to comparison shop, in-home privacy, and variety. Studies of online shoppers indicated that men were initially more likely than women to buy something online. As the number of online households increased, however, the profile of online shoppers changed to include all shoppers. In addition, the number of online retailers grew rapidly for several years and then declined as many stand-alone, Internet-only businesses failed or consolidated. Today, there has been a melding of traditional and online retailers—"bricks and clicks"—that are using experiences from both approaches to create better value and experiences for customers. Wal-Mart (www.walmart.com) and JCPenney (www.jcp.com) have recently introduced "site-to-store" service that allows customers to order online and pick up the order without a shipping fee at the store of their choice. Experts predict that online sales will reach $328 billion by 2010.[22]

Online retail purchases can be the result of several very different approaches. First, consumers can pay dues to become a member of an online discount service such as www.netMarket.com. The service offers tens of thousands of products and more than 1,200 brand names at very low prices to its 25 million subscribers. Another approach to online retailing is to use a shopping "bot" such as www.mysimon.com. This site searches the Internet for a product specified by the consumer and provides a report on the locations of the best prices available. Consumers can also use the Internet to go directly to online malls (www.fashionmall.com), apparel retailers (www.gap.com), bookstores (www.amazon.com), computer manufacturers (www.dell.com), grocery stores (www.peapod.com), music and video stores (www.cdnow.com), and travel agencies (www.travelocity.com). A final approach to online retailing is the online auction, such as www.ebay.com, where consumers bid on more than 1,000 categories of products.[23] See the Going Online box on the next page for a description of a new form of "reverse" auction.[24]

One of the biggest problems online retailers face is that nearly two-thirds of online shoppers make it to "checkout" and then leave the website

Shopping "bots" find the best prices for products consumers specify.

to compare shipping costs and prices on other sites. Of the shoppers who leave, 70 percent do not return. One way online retailers are addressing this issue is to offer consumers a comparison of competitors' offerings. At Booksamillion.com, for example, consumers can use a "comparison engine" to compare prices with Amazon.com, Barnesandnoble.com, and Borders.com.[25] Experts suggest that online retailers should think of their websites as dynamic billboards if they are to attract and retain customers.[26]

Online retailers are also trying to improve the online retailing experience by adding experiential or interactive activities to their websites. Similarly, car manufacturers such as BMW, Mercedes, and Jaguar encourage website visitors to "build" a vehicle by selecting interior and exterior colors, packages, and options and then view the customized virtual car. In addition, the merger of television home shopping and online retailing will be possible through TV-based Internet platforms such as Microsoft's MSN TV, which uses an Internet appliance attached to a television to connect to the Internet. Owning a television or a computer isn't a necessity for online retailing, however, as many hotels, bars, libraries, airports, and other public locations offer Internet kiosks. In China consumers can shop online in more than 110,000 Internet cafes.[27]

Telemarketing

Another form of nonstore retailing, called **telemarketing**, involves using the telephone to interact with and sell directly to consumers. Compared with direct mail, telemarketing is often viewed as a more efficient means of targeting consumers. Insurance companies, brokerage firms, and newspapers have often used this form of retailing as a way to cut costs but still maintain access to their customers. According to the Direct Marketing Association, annual telemarketing sales exceed $500 billion.[28]

The telemarketing industry has recently gone through dramatic changes as a result of new legislation related to telephone solicitations. Issues such as consumer privacy, industry standards, and ethical guidelines have encouraged discussion among consumers, Congress, the Federal Trade Commission, and businesses. The result was legislation that created the National Do-Not-Call registry (www.donotcall.gov) for consumers who do not want to receive telephone calls related to company sales

Consumers can easily access the Internet in many locations today.

efforts. Recent surveys indicate that 76 percent of U.S. adults have signed up for the registry. Companies that use telemarketing have already adapted by adding compliance software to ensure that numbers on the list are not called. In addition, some firms are considering shifting their telemarketing budgets to direct-mail and door-to-door techniques.[29]

Direct Selling

Direct selling, sometimes called door-to-door retailing, involves direct sales of goods and services to consumers through personal interactions and demonstrations in their home or office. A variety of companies, including familiar names such as Avon, Fuller Brush, Mary Kay Cosmetics, and World Book, have created an industry with more than $22 billion in sales by providing consumers with personalized service and convenience. In the United States, there are more than 14 million direct salespeople working full-time and part-time in 70 product categories.[30]

Growth in the direct selling industry is the result of two trends. First, many direct selling retailers are expanding into markets outside of the United States. Avon, for example, has 5 million sales representatives in 114 countries and is hiring an additional 399,000 new salespeople in China alone. More than 70 percent of Amway's $8 billion in sales now comes from outside the United States.[31] Similarly, other retailers such as Herbalife and Electrolux are rapidly expanding into new markets. Direct selling is likely to continue to grow in markets where the lack of effective distribution channels increases the importance of door-to-door convenience and where the lack of consumer knowledge about products and brands will increase the need for a person-to-person approach.

The second trend is the growing number of companies that are using direct selling to reach consumers who prefer one-on-one customer service and a social shopping experience rather than online shopping or big discount stores. The Direct Selling Association reports that the number of companies using direct selling has increased by 30 percent in the past five years. Companies such as Pampered Chef, Crayola, Jockey, and the Body Shop have all recently started using direct selling to broaden their customer base.[32]

learning review

6. Successful catalog retailers often send _____ catalogs to _____ markets identified in their databases.

7. How are retailers increasing consumer interest and involvement in online retailing?

8. Where are direct selling retail sales growing? Why?

RETAILING STRATEGY

This section describes how a retailer develops and implements a retailing strategy by positioning the store and taking specific retailing mix actions. Figure 17–7 identifies the relationship between positioning and the retailing mix.

Positioning a Retail Store

LO4

The classification alternatives presented in the previous sections help determine one store's position relative to its competitors. The **retail positioning matrix** is a matrix developed by the MAC Group, Inc., a management consulting firm.[33] This matrix positions retail outlets on two dimensions: breadth of product line and value added. As defined previously, *breadth of product line* is the range of products sold through each outlet. The second dimension, *value added,* includes elements such as location (as with 7-Eleven stores), product reliability (as with Holiday Inn or McDonald's), or prestige (as with Saks Fifth Avenue or Brooks Brothers).

The retail positioning matrix in Figure 17–8 shows four possible positions. An organization can be successful in any position, but unique strategies are required within each quadrant. Consider the four stores shown in the matrix:

1. Bloomingdale's has high value added and a broad product line. Retailers in this quadrant pay great attention to store design and product lines. Merchandise often has a high margin of profit and is of high quality. The stores in this position typically provide high levels of service.
2. Wal-Mart has low value added and a broad line. Wal-Mart and similar firms typically trade a lower price for increased volume in sales. Retailers in this position focus on price with low service levels and an image of being a place for good buys.
3. Tiffany & Co. has high value added and a narrow line. Retailers of this type typically sell a very restricted range of products that are of high-status quality. Customers are also provided with high levels of service.
4. Payless ShoeSource has low value added and a narrow line. Such retailers are specialty mass merchandisers. Payless ShoeSource, for example, carries athletic shoes at a discount.[34] These outlets appeal to value-conscious consumers. Economies of scale are achieved through centralized advertising, merchandising, buying, and distribution. Stores are usually the same in design, layout, and merchandise; hence they are often referred to as "cookie-cutter" stores.

FIGURE 17–7

Elements of a retailing strategy

450

FIGURE 17–8
There are four positioning
strategies for retailers.

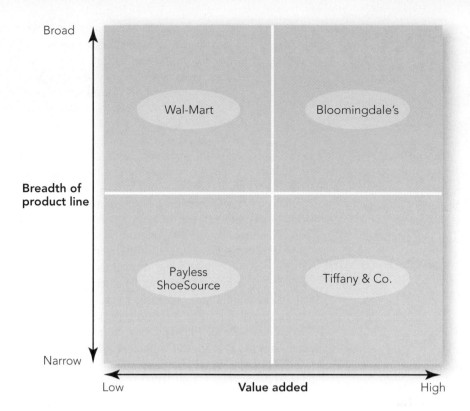

Retailing Mix

In developing retailing strategy, managers work with the **retailing mix**, which includes activities related to managing the store and the merchandise in the store. The retailing mix is similar to the marketing mix and includes retail pricing, store location, retail communication, and merchandise.

Retail Pricing In setting prices for merchandise, retailers must decide on the markup, markdown, and timing for markdowns. As mentioned in the appendix to Chapter 14 (Appendix B), the *markup* refers to how much should be added to the cost the retailer paid for a product to reach the final selling price. Retailers decide on the *original markup,* but by the time the product is sold, they end up with a *maintained markup.* The original markup is the difference between retailer cost and initial selling price. When products do not sell as quickly as anticipated, their price is reduced. The difference between the final selling price and retailer cost is the maintained markup, which is also called the *gross margin.*

Discounting a product, or taking a *markdown,* occurs when the product does not sell at the original price and an adjustment is necessary. Often new models or styles force the price of existing models to be marked down. Discounts may also be used to increase demand for complementary products.[35] For example, retailers might take a markdown on CD players to increase sales of CDs or reduce the price of cake mix to generate frosting purchases. The *timing* of a markdown can be important. Many retailers take a markdown as soon as sales fall off to free up valuable selling space and cash. However, other stores delay markdowns to discourage bargain hunters and maintain an image of quality. There is no clear answer, but retailers must consider how the timing might affect future sales. Recent research indicates that frequent promotions increase consumers' ability to remember regular prices.[36]

Although most retailers plan markdowns, many retailers use price discounts as a part of their regular merchandising policy. Wal-Mart and Home Depot, for example, emphasize consistently low prices and eliminate most markdowns with a strategy often called *everyday low pricing.*[37] Because consumers often use price as an indicator of product quality, however, the brand name of the product and the image of the store become important

T.J. Maxx is a popular off-price retailer.

decision factors in these situations.[38] Another strategy, *everyday fair pricing,* is advocated by retailers that may not offer the lowest price but try to create value for customers through service and the total buying experience.[39] Consumers often use the prices of *benchmark* or *signpost* items, such as a can of Coke, to form an overall impression of the store's prices.[40] In addition, price is the most likely to influence consumers' assessment of merchandise value.[41] When store prices are based on rebates, retailers must be careful to avoid negative consumer perceptions if the rebate processing time is long (e.g., six weeks).[42]

Off-price retailing is a retail pricing practice that is used by retailers such as T.J. Maxx, Burlington Coat Factory, and Ross Stores. **Off-price retailing** involves selling brand-name merchandise at lower than regular prices. The difference between the off-price retailer and a discount store is that off-price merchandise is bought by the retailer from manufacturers with excess inventory at prices below wholesale prices, while the discounter buys at full wholesale price (but takes less of a markup than do traditional department stores). Because of this difference in the way merchandise is purchased by the retailer, selection at an off-price retailer is unpredictable, and searching for bargains has become a popular activity for many consumers. "It's more like a sport than it is like ordinary shopping," says Christopher Boring of Columbus, Ohio's Retail Planning Associates.[43] Savings to the consumer at off-price retailers are reported as high as 70 percent off the prices of a traditional department store.

There are several variations of off-price retailing. One is the *warehouse club.* These large stores (more than 100,000 square feet) are rather stark outlets with no elaborate displays, customer service, or home delivery. They require an annual membership fee (ranging from $30 to $100) for the privilege of shopping there. While a typical Wal-Mart stocks 30,000 items, warehouse clubs carry about 3,500 items and usually stock just one brand of appliance or food product. Service is minimal, and customers usually must pay by cash or check. Customers are attracted by the ultralow prices and surprise deals on selected merchandise, although several of the clubs have recently started to add ancillary services such as optical shops and pharmacies to differentiate themselves from competitors. The major warehouse clubs in the United States include Wal-Mart's Sam's Club, BJ's Wholesale Club, and Costco's Warehouse Club. Sales of these off-price retailers have grown faster than the rest of the retail industry and exceeded $110 billion in 2006.[44]

A second variation is the *outlet store.* Factory outlets, such as Van Heusen Factory Store, Bass Shoe Outlet, and Oneida Factory Store, offer products for 25 to 30 percent off the suggested retail price. Manufacturers use the stores to clear excess merchandise and to reach consumers who focus on value shopping. Retail outlets such as Nordstrom Rack and Off 5th (Saks Fifth Avenue outlet) allow retailers to sell excess merchandise and still maintain an image of offering merchandise at full price in their primary store. The number of factory outlet centers has increased to 312, with sales of $11.2 billion. Some experts expect the next trend to combine the various types of off-price retailers in "value-retail centers."[45]

A third variation of off-price retailing is offered by single-price, or extreme value, retailers such as Family Dollar, Dollar General, and Dollar Tree. These stores average about 6,000 square feet in size and attract customers who want value and a "corner store" environment rather than a large supercenter experience. Some experts predict extraordinary growth of these types of retailers. Dollar General, for example, already has 8,000 stores and plans for 700 new stores.[46]

Store Location A second aspect of the retailing mix involves deciding where to locate the store and how many stores to have. Department stores, which started downtown in most cities, have followed customers to the suburbs, and in recent years more stores have been opened in large regional malls. Most stores today are near several others in one of five settings: the central business district, the regional center, the community shopping center, the strip, or the power center.

Off 5th provides an outlet for excess merchandise from Saks Fifth Avenue.

The **central business district** is the oldest retail setting, the community's downtown area. Until the regional outflow to suburbs, it was the major shopping area, but the suburban population has grown at the expense of the downtown shopping area. Consumers often view central business district shopping as less convenient because of lack of parking, higher crime rates, and exposure to the weather. Many cities such as Cincinnati, Denver, and San Antonio have implemented plans to revitalize shopping in central business districts by attracting new offices, entertainment, and residents to downtown locations.

Regional shopping centers consist of 50 to 150 stores that typically attract customers who live or work within a 5- to 10-mile range. These large shopping areas often contain two or three *anchor stores,* which are well-known national or regional stores such as Sears, Saks Fifth Avenue, and Bloomingdale's. The largest variation of a regional center is the West Edmonton Mall in Alberta, Canada. The shopping center is a conglomerate of 800 stores, nine amusement centers, 110 restaurants, and a 355-room Fantasyland hotel.[47]

A more limited approach to retail location is the **community shopping center**, which typically has one primary store (usually a department store branch) and often about 20 to 40 smaller outlets. Generally, these centers serve a population of consumers who are within a 10- to 20-minute drive.

Not every suburban store is located in a shopping mall. Many neighborhoods have clusters of stores, referred to as a **strip location**, to serve people who are within a 5- to 10-minute drive. Gas station, hardware, laundry, grocery, and pharmacy outlets are commonly found in a strip location. Unlike the larger shopping centers, the composition of these stores is usually unplanned. A variation of the strip shopping location is called the **power center**, which is a huge shopping strip with multiple anchor (or national) stores. Power centers are seen as having the convenient location found in many strip centers and the additional power of national stores. These large strips often have two to five anchor stores and often contain a supermarket, which brings the shopper to the power center on a weekly basis.[48]

Retail Communication A retailer's communication activities can play an important role in positioning a store and creating its image. While the traditional elements of communication and promotion are discussed in Chapter 19 on advertising and Chapter 20 on personal selling, the message communicated by the many other elements of the retailing mix are also important.

Deciding on the image of a retail outlet is an important retailing mix factor that has been widely recognized and studied since the late 1950s. Pierre Martineau described image as "the way in which the store is defined in the shopper's mind," partly by its functional qualities and partly by an aura of psychological attributes.[49] In this definition, *functional* refers to mix elements such as price ranges, store layouts, and breadth and depth of merchandise lines. The psychological attributes are the intangibles such as a sense of belonging, excitement, style, or warmth. Image has been found to include impressions of the corporation that operates the store, the category or type of store, the product categories in the store, the brands in each category, merchandise and service quality, and the marketing activities of the store.[50]

Closely related to the concept of image is the store's atmosphere or ambiance. Many retailers believe that sales are affected by layout, color, lighting, and music in the store as well as by how crowded it is. In addition, the physical surroundings that influence customers may affect the store's employees.[51] In creating the right image and atmosphere, a retail store tries to attract its target audience with what those consumers seek from the buying experience, so the store will fortify the beliefs and the emotional reactions buyers are seeking.[52] While store image perceptions can exist independently of shopping experiences, consumers' shopping experiences can also influence store perceptions.[53]

Merchandise A final element of the retailing mix is the merchandise offering. Managing the breadth and depth of the product line requires retail buyers who are familiar with the needs of the target market and the alternative products available from the many manufacturers that might be interested in having a product avail-

Using Marketing Dashboards
Why Apple Stores May Be the Best in the United States!

How effective is my retail format compared to other stores? How are my stores performing this year compared to last year? Information related to this question is often displayed in a marketing dashboard using two measures: (1) sales per square foot, and (2) same store sales growth.

Your Challenge You have been assigned to evaluate the Apple store retail format. The store's simple, inviting, open atmosphere has been the topic of discussion among many retailers. Apple, however, is new to the retailing business and many experts have been skeptical of the format. To allow an assessment of Apple stores, use *sales per square foot* as an indicator of how effectively retail space is used to generate revenue and *same store growth* to compare the increase in sales of stores that have been open for the same period of time. The calculations for these indicators are:

Sales per square foot
= Total sales/Selling area in square feet

Same store growth
= (Store sales in year 2 − Store sales in year 1)/
Store sales in year 1

Your Findings You decide to collect sales information for Saks, Neiman Marcus, Best Buy, Tiffany, and Apple stores to allow comparisons with other successful retailers. The information you collect allows the calculation of *sales per square foot* and *same store growth* for each store. The results are then easy to compare in the graphs below.

Your Action The results of your investigation indicate that Apple stores' sales per square foot are higher than any of the comparison stores at $4,000. In addition, Apple's same store growth rate of 45 percent is higher than all of the other stores. You conclude that the elements of Apple's format are very effective and even indicate that Apple may currently be the best retailer in the United States.

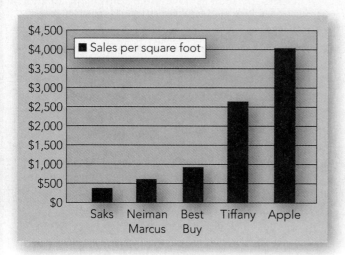

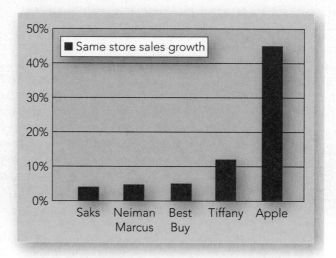

able in the store. A popular approach to managing the assortment of merchandise today is called **category management**. This approach assigns a manager with the responsibility for selecting all products that consumers in a market segment might view as substitutes for each other, with the objective of maximizing sales and profits in the category. For example, a category manager might be responsible for shoes in a department store or paper products in a grocery store.

Many retailers are developing an advanced form of category management called *consumer marketing at retail* (CMAR). Recent surveys show that, as part of their CMAR programs, retailers are conducting research, analyzing the data to identify shopper problems, translating the data into retailing mix actions, executing shopper-friendly in-store programs, and monitoring the performance of the merchandise. Wal-Mart, for example, has used the approach to test baby-product and dollar-product categories. Grocery stores such as Safeway and Kroger use the approach to determine the appropriate mix of brand name and private label products. Specialty retailer Barnes & Noble recently won a best practice award for its application of the approach to the selection, presentation, and promotion of magazines.[54]

Retailers have a variety of metrics that can be used to assess the effectiveness of a store or retail format. First, there are measures related to customers such as the number of transactions per customer, the average transaction size per customer, the number of customers per day or per hour, and the average length of a store visit. Second, there are measures related to products such as number of returns, inventory turnover, inventory carrying cost, and average number of items per transaction. Finally, there are financial measures, such as gross margin, sales per employee, return on sales, and markdown percentage.[55] The two most popular measures for retailers are *sales per square foot* and *same store growth rate.* The accompanying Using Marketing Dashboards box describes the calculation of these measures for Apple stores.[56]

learning review

9. What are the two dimensions of the retail positioning matrix?

10. How does original markup differ from maintained markup?

11. A huge shopping strip with multiple anchor stores is a _____ center.

THE CHANGING NATURE OF RETAILING

Retailing is the most dynamic aspect of a channel of distribution. New types of retailers are always entering the market, searching for a new position that will attract customers. The reason for this continual change is explained by two concepts: the wheel of retailing and the retail life cycle.

The Wheel of Retailing

The **wheel of retailing** describes how new forms of retail outlets enter the market.[57] Usually they enter as low-status, low-margin stores such as a drive-in hamburger stand with no indoor seating and a limited menu (Figure 17–9, box 1 on the next page). Gradually these outlets add fixtures and more embellishments to their stores (in-store seating, plants, and chicken sandwiches as well as hamburgers) to increase the attractiveness for customers. With these additions, prices and status rise (box 2). As time passes, these outlets add still more services and their prices and status increase even further (box 3). These retail outlets now face some new form of retail outlet that again appears as a low-status, low-margin operator (box 4), and the wheel of retailing turns as the cycle starts to repeat itself.

When Ray Kroc started the first McDonald's in 1955 it opened shortly before lunch and closed just after dinner, offering a limited menu for the two meals without any inside seating for customers. Over time, the wheel of retailing has led to new products and services. In 1975, McDonald's introduced the Egg McMuffin and turned breakfast into a fast-food meal. Today, McDonald's has an extensive menu, seating, and services such as wireless Internet connections. For the future, McDonald's is testing new products such as premium-blend coffee, frying oil without trans fats, and fruit smoothies; new formats such as its coffee, pastry, and sandwich outlets called McCafe, and seating "zones" for different types of customers; and 24/7 "always open" hours.

The wheel of retailing has come full circle for Taco Bell.

The changes are leaving room for new forms of outlets such as Checker Drive-In Restaurants. The chain opened fast-food stores that offered only basics—burgers, fries, and cola, a drive-through window and no inside seating—and now has more than 800 stores. The wheel is turning for other outlets too—Boston Market has added pick-up, delivery, and full-service catering to its original restaurant format, and it also provides Boston Market meal solutions through supermarket delis and Boston Market frozen meals in the frozen food sections. For still others, the wheel has come full circle. Taco Bell is now opening small,

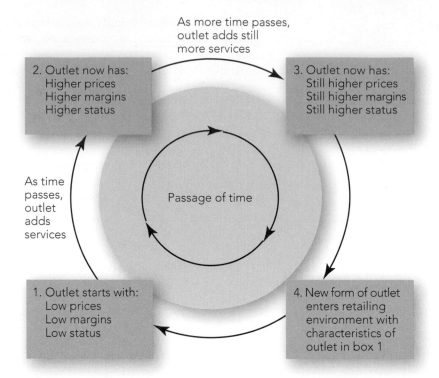

limited-offering outlets in gas stations, discount stores, or "wherever a burrito and a mouth might possibly intersect."[58]

Discount stores were a major new retailing form in the 1960s and priced their products below those of department stores. As prices in discount stores rose, in the 1980s they found themselves overpriced compared with a new form of retail outlet—the warehouse club. Today, off-price retailers and factory outlets are offering prices even lower than warehouses.

The Retail Life Cycle

The process of growth and decline that retail outlets, like products, experience is described by the **retail life cycle**.[59] Figure 17–10 shows the retail life cycle and the position of various current forms of retail outlets on it. Early growth is the stage of emergence of a retail outlet, with a sharp departure from existing competition. Market share rises gradually, although profits may be low because of start-up costs. In the next stage, accelerated development, both market share and profit achieve their greatest growth rates. Usually multiple outlets are established as companies focus on the distribution element of the retailing mix. In this stage, some later competitors may enter. Wendy's, for example, appeared on the hamburger chain scene almost 20 years after McDonald's had begun operation. The key goal for the retailer in this stage is to establish a dominant position in the fight for market share.

The battle for market share is usually fought before the maturity stage, and some competitors drop out of the market. In the wars among hamburger chains, Jack in the Box, Gino Marchetti's, and Burger Chef used to be more dominant outlets. New retail forms enter in the maturity stage, stores try to maintain their market share, and price discounting occurs.

The challenge facing retailers is to delay entering the decline stage in which market share and profit fall rapidly. Specialty apparel retailers, such as the Gap, Limited, Benetton, and Ann Taylor, have noticed a decline in market share after a decade of growth. To prevent further decline, these retailers will need to find ways of discouraging their customers from moving to low-margin, mass-volume outlets or high-price, high-service boutiques.[60]

FIGURE 17–10
The retail life cycle describes stages of growth and decline for retail outlets.

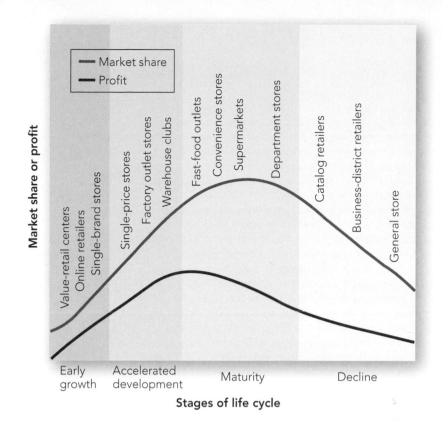

- Market share
- Profit

Market share or profit

Value-retail centers
Online retailers
Single-brand stores
Single-price stores
Factory outlet stores
Warehouse clubs
Fast-food outlets
Convenience stores
Supermarkets
Department stores
Catalog retailers
Business-district retailers
General store

Early growth | Accelerated development | Maturity | Decline

Stages of life cycle

FUTURE CHANGES IN RETAILING

Two exciting trends in retailing—the growth of multichannel retailing and the increasing focus on customer experience management—are likely to lead to many changes for retailers and consumers in the future.

Multichannel Retailing

The retailing formats described previously in this chapter represent an exciting menu of choices for creating customer value in the marketplace. Each format allows retailers to offer unique benefits and meet particular needs of various customer groups. While each format has many successful applications, retailers in the future are likely to combine many of the formats to offer a broader spectrum of benefits and experiences.[61] These **multichannel retailers** will utilize and integrate a combination of traditional store formats and nonstore formats such as catalogs, television, and online retailing.[62] Barnes & Noble, for example, created Barnesandnoble.com to compete with Amazon.com. Similarly, Office Depot has integrated its store, catalog, and Internet operations.

Integrated channels can make shopping simpler and more convenient. A consumer can research choices online or in a catalog and then make a purchase online, over the telephone, or at the closest store. In addition, the use of multiple channels allows retailers to reach a broader profile of customers. While online retailing may cannibalize catalog business to some degree, an online transaction costs about half as much to process as a catalog order. Multichannel retailers also benefit from the synergy of sharing information among the different channel operations. Online retailers, for example, have recognized that the Internet is more of a transactional medium than a relationship-building medium and are working to find ways to complement traditional customer interactions.[63] The benefits of multichannel marketing are also apparent in the spending behavior of consumers as described in the Marketing Matters box on the next page.[64]

The Multichannel Marketing Multiplier

Multichannel marketing is the blending of different communication and delivery channels that are mutually reinforcing in attracting, retaining, and building relationships with consumers who shop and buy in the traditional marketplace and marketspace. Industry analysts refer to the complementary role of different communication and delivery channels as an *influence effect*.

Retailers that integrate and leverage their stores, catalogs, and websites have seen a sizable lift in yearly sales recorded from individual customers. Eddie Bauer is a good example. Customers who shop only one of its channels spend $100 to $200 per year. Those who shop in two channels spend $300 to $500 annually. Customers who shop all these channels—store, catalog, and website—spend $800 to $1,000 per year. Moreover, multichannel customers have been found to be *three times* as profitable as single-channel customers.

JCPenney has seen similar results. The company is a leading multichannel retailer and reports that a JCPenney customer who shops in all three channels—store, catalog, and website—spends *four to eight times* as much as a customer who shops in only one channel, as shown in the chart.

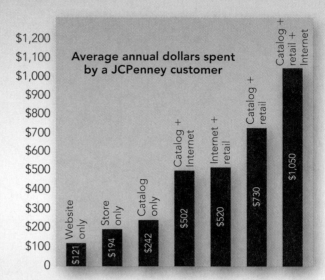

Average annual dollars spent by a JCPenney customer

Website only	$121
Store only	$194
Catalog only	$242
Catalog + Internet	$502
Internet + retail	$520
Catalog + retail	$730
Catalog + retail + Internet	$1,050

Managing the Customer Experience

The chapter opening example described how department stores are changing to create social retailing experiences. While many of those changes appeal to women and address the way women like to shop, retailers are also paying more attention to men and their shopping behavior. Men have typically been viewed as infrequent "mission shoppers" who go to a store only as a means of obtaining a product as efficiently as possible. Today's young men, however, are changing their shopping behavior. Recent research found that 84 percent of men said they purchase their own clothes, compared with just 65 percent four years ago. To appeal to men, many stores are creating standalone men's sections that combine clothes, accessories, and gadgets in one place. The new sections use "masculine" interior designs with simple colors, stainless-steel fixtures, and dark wood floors. Bloomingdale's in Manhattan has even added seating, sports magazines, and televisions to the men's areas. All of these changes are intended to create a better experience for male shoppers. As Jack Hruska, executive vice president at Bloomingdale's, explains, "We hope to make men feel more comfortable and at home by giving them a place to unwind while they are shopping."[65]

learning review

12. According to the wheel of retailing, when a new retail form appears, how would you characterize its image?

13. Market share is usually fought out before the _____ stage of the retail life cycle.

14. What is an influence effect?

LEARNING OBJECTIVES REVIEW

LO1 *Identify retailers in terms of the utilities they provide.*
Retailers provide time, place, form, and possession utilities. Time utility is provided by stores with convenient time-of-day (e.g., open 24 hours) or time-of-year (e.g., seasonal sports equipment available all year) availability. Place utility is provided by the number and location of the stores. Possession utility is provided by making a purchase possible (e.g., financing) or easier (e.g., delivery). Form utility is provided by producing or altering a product to meet the customer's specifications (e.g., custom-made shirts).

LO2 *Explain the alternative ways to classify retail outlets.*
Retail outlets can be classified by their form of ownership, level of service, and type of merchandise line. The forms of ownership include independent retailers, corporate chains, and contractual systems that include retailer-sponsored cooperatives, wholesaler-sponsored voluntary chains, and franchises. The levels of service include self-service, limited-service, and full-service outlets. Stores classified by their merchandise line include stores with depth, such as sporting good specialty stores, and stores with breadth, such as large department stores.

LO3 *Describe the many methods of nonstore retailing.*
Nonstore retailing includes automatic vending, direct mail and catalogs, television home shopping, online retailing, telemarketing, and direct selling. The methods of nonstore retailing vary by the level of involvement of the retailer and the level of involvement of the customer. Vending, for example, has low involvement, whereas both the consumer and the retailer have high involvement in direct selling.

LO4 *Classify retailers in terms of the retail positioning matrix, and specify retailing mix actions.*
The retail positioning matrix positions retail outlets on two dimensions: breadth of product line and value added. There are four possible positions in the matrix—broad product line/low value added (Wal-Mart), narrow product line/low value added (Payless Shoe Source), broad product line/high value added (Bloomingdale's), and narrow product line/high value added (Tiffany). Retailing mix actions are used to manage a retail store and the merchandise in a store. The mix variables include pricing, store location, communication activities, and merchandise. Two common forms of assessment for retailers are "sales per square foot" and "same store growth."

LO5 *Explain changes in retailing with the wheel of retailing and the retail life cycle concepts.*
The wheel of retailing concept explains how retail outlets typically enter the market as low-status, low-margin stores. Over time, stores gradually add new products and services, increasing their prices, status, and margins, and leaving an opening for new low-status, low-margin stores. The retail life cycle describes the process of growth and decline for retail outlets through four stages: early growth, accelerated development, maturity, and decline.

FOCUSING ON KEY TERMS

breadth of product line p. 443
category management p. 454
central business district p. 453
community shopping center p. 453
depth of product line p. 443
form of ownership p. 440
hypermarket p. 444
intertype competition p. 444

level of service p. 440
merchandise line p. 440
multichannel retailers p. 457
off-price retailing p. 452
power center p. 453
regional shopping centers p. 453
retail life cycle p. 456
retail positioning matrix p. 450

retailing p. 438
retailing mix p. 451
scrambled merchandising p. 443
strip location p. 453
telemarketing p. 448
wheel of retailing p. 455

APPLYING MARKETING KNOWLEDGE

1 Discuss the impact of the growing number of dual-income households on (*a*) nonstore retailing and (*b*) the retail mix.

2 How does value added affect a store's competitive position?

3 In retail pricing, retailers often have a maintained markup. Explain how this maintained markup differs from original markup and why it is so important.

4 What are the similarities and differences between the product and retail life cycles?

5 How would you classify Wal-Mart in terms of its position on the wheel of retailing versus that of an off-price retailer?

6 Develop a chart to highlight the role of each of the four main elements of the retailing mix across the four stages of the retail life cycle.

7 In Figure 17–8 Payless ShoeSource was placed on the retail positioning matrix. What strategies should Payless ShoeSource follow to move itself into the same position as Tiffany?

8 Breadth and depth are two important components in distinguishing among types of retailers. Discuss the breadth and depth implications of the following retailers discussed in this chapter: (*a*) Nordstrom, (*b*) Wal-Mart, (*c*) L. L. Bean, and (*d*) Best Buy.

9 According to the wheel of retailing and the retail life cycle, what will happen to factory outlet stores?

10 The text discusses the development of online retailing in the United States. How does the development of this retailing form agree with the implications of the retail life cycle?

building your marketing plan

Does your marketing plan involve using retailers? If the answer is no, read no further and do not include a retailing element in your plan. If the answer is yes:

1 Use Figure 17–7 to develop your retailing strategy by (*a*) selecting a position in the retail positioning matrix and (*b*) specifying the details of the retailing mix.

2 Develop a positioning statement describing the breadth of the product line (broad versus narrow) and value added (low versus high).

3 Describe an appropriate combination of retail pricing, store location, retail communication, and merchandise assortment.

video case 17 Mall of America: Shopping and a Whole Lot More

"If you build it, they will come" not only worked in the movie *Field of Dreams* but also applies—big time—to Mall of America.

Located in a suburb of Minneapolis, Mall of America (www.mallofamerica.com) is the largest completely enclosed retail and family-entertainment complex in the United States. "We're more than a mall, we're a destination," explains Maureen Cahill, an executive at Mall of America. More than 100,000 people each day—40 million visitors each year—visit the one-stop complex offering retail shopping, guest services, convenience, a huge variety of entertainment, and fun for all. "Guest services" include everything from high school and college classrooms to a doctor's office and a wedding chapel.

THE CONCEPT AND CHALLENGE

The idea for the Mall of America came from the West Edmonton Mall in Alberta, Canada. The Ghermezian Brothers, who developed that mall, sought to create a unique mall that would attract not only local families but also tourists from the Upper Midwest, the nation, and even from abroad.

The two challenges for Mall of America: How can it (1) attract and keep the large number of retail establishments needed to (2) continue to attract even more millions of visitors than today? A big part of the answer is in Mall of America's positioning—"There is a place for fun in your life!"

THE STAGGERING SIZE AND OFFERINGS

Opened August 1992 amid tremendous worldwide publicity, Mall of America faced skeptics who had their doubts because of its size, its unique retail-entertainment mix, and the nationwide recession. Despite these concerns, it opened with more than 80 percent of its space leased and attracted more than 1 million visitors its first week.

Mall of America is 4.2 million square feet, the equivalent of 88 football fields. This makes it three to four times the size of most other regional malls. It includes four anchor department stores: Nordstrom, Macy's, Bloomingdale's, and Sears. It also includes more than 520 specialty stores, from Brooks Brothers and Sharper Image to Marshall's and DSW Shoe Warehouse. Approximately 36 percent of Mall of America's space is devoted to anchors and 64 percent to specialty stores. This makes the space allocation the reverse of most regional malls.

The retail-entertainment mix of Mall of America is incredibly diverse. For example, there are more than 100 apparel and accessory stores, 18 jewelry stores, and 33 shoe stores. Two food courts with 27 restaurants plus more than 30 other restaurants scattered throughout the building meet most food preferences of visitors. Another surprise: Mall of America is home to many "concept stores," where retailers introduce a new type of store or design. Because of its incredible size, the mall has 194 stores not found at competing regional malls. In addition, it has an entrepreneurial program for people with an innovative retail idea and limited resources. They can open up a kiosk, wall unit, or small store for a specified time period or as a temporary seasonal tenant.

Unique features of Mall of America include:

- A seven-acre theme park with more than 50 attractions and rides, including a roller coaster, Ferris wheel, and games in a glass-enclosed, skylighted area with more than 400 trees.
- Underwater Adventures, where visitors are surrounded by sharks, stingrays, and sea turtles; can adventure among fish native to the north woods; and can discover what lurks at the bottom of the Mississippi River.
- Entertainment choices that include a 14-screen theater, A.C.E.S. Flight Simulation, NASCAR Silicon Motor Speedway, and Dinosaur Walk Museum.
- The LEGO Land Imagination Center, a 6,000-square-foot showplace with more than 30 full-sized models.

As a host to corporate events and private parties, Mall of America has a rotunda that opens to all four floors that facilitates presentations, demonstrations, and exhibits.

Organizations such as Pepsi, Visa-USA, and Chevrolet have used the facilities to gain shopper awareness. Mall of America is a rectangle with the anchor department stores at the corners and amusement park in the sky-lighted central area, making it easy for shoppers to understand and navigate. It has 12,550 free parking ramp spaces on site and another 7,000 spaces nearby during peak times.

THE MARKET

The Minneapolis–St. Paul metropolitan area is a market with more than 3 million people. A total of 30 million people live within a day's drive of Mall of America. A survey of its shoppers showed that 32 percent of the shoppers travel 150 miles or more and account for more than 50 percent of the sales revenues. Located three miles from the Minneapolis/St. Paul International Airport, Mall of America provides a shuttle bus from the airport every half hour. Light-rail service from the airport and downtown Minneapolis is also available.

Tourism accounts for four out of ten visits to Mall of America. About 6 percent of visitors come from outside the United States. Some come just to see and experience Mall of America, while others take advantage of the cost savings available on goods (Japan) or taxes (Canada and states with sales taxes on clothing).

THE FUTURE: FACING THE CHALLENGES

Where does Mall of America head in the future?

"We just did a brand study and found that Mall of America is one of the most recognized brands in the world," says Cahill. "They might not know where we are sometimes, but they've heard of Mall of America and they know they want to come."

"What we've learned since 1992 is to keep the Mall of America fresh and exciting," she explains. "We're constantly looking at what attracts people and adding to that. We're adding new stores, new attractions, and new events. We hold more than 350 events a year and with everyone from Garth Brooks to Sarah Ferguson to N Sync."

Mall of America recently announced a plan for a 5.6 million-square-foot expansion, the area of another 117 football fields, connected by pedestrian skyway to the present building. "The second phase will not be a duplicate of what we have," says Cahill. "We have plans for at least three hotels, a performing arts center, a business office complex, an art or history museum, and possibly even a television broadcast facility."

One of the first elements of the expansion includes a recently opened 306,000 square foot IKEA store. Other new elements will include a 13,000 square foot restaurant called Cantina Corona, a 6,000-seat performing arts auditorium created by AEG, a 300,000 square foot Bass Pro store, and a 200-room Kimpton Hotel. All of these new additions and the many offerings of the current mall reinforce that Mall of America is a shopping destination and a whole lot more!

Questions

1 Why has Mall of America been such a marketing success so far?

2 What (*a*) retail and (*b*) consumer trends have occurred since Mall of America was opened in 1992 that it should consider when making future plans?

3 (*a*) What criteria should Mall of America use in adding new facilities to its complex? (*b*) Evaluate (*i*) retail stores, (*ii*) entertainment offerings, and (*iii*) hotels on these criteria.

4 What specific marketing actions would you propose that Mall of America managers take to ensure its continuing success in attracting visitors (*a*) from the local metropolitan area and (*b*) from outside of it?

18 Integrated Marketing Communications and Direct Marketing

HOW DO MARKETERS FIGHT THE GAME CONSOLE WARS? WITH INTEGRATED MARKETING COMMUNICATIONS!

Chances are that sometime recently you've played, or seen others playing, one of the three popular video entertainment systems. Sony's PlayStation, Microsoft's Xbox, and Nintendo's Wii are all in a dog-fight for your gaming time and budget. The battle is being fought with complex integrated marketing communications campaigns that include almost every form of media. "All the media focus is on next-gen consoles and games," explains Erik Whiteford, marketing director at game software developer 2K Sports.

The stakes are high because so many worldwide consumers have one or more of the systems. Since 2000, Sony has shipped more than 110 million units of its PS2 model, which is now being replaced by the new PS3 and competing with the Xbox 360 and the Wii. Recently, the industry reached $7.4 billion in sales. Experts believe consumers will continue to purchase more than 6 million of each of the new systems each year, and by 2011 Sony will have about 44 percent of the market, compared to 40 percent for Xbox and 16 percent for Wii.

Sony's integrated campaign features a variety of components including television ads on broadcast and cable networks; print ads in monthly, weekly, and daily publications; online advertising on gaming, sports, and lifestyle websites; and billboard and bus shelter ads in metropolitan areas. The campaign also includes interactive elements at its Playbeyond.com website, 14,000 kiosks at retailers, and a huge truck called the "PlayStation Experience" that stops at concerts to let visitors play the Sony system and games on location. In Europe the launch campaign also includes short films shown in movie theaters.

Microsoft's Xbox campaign also integrates many communication elements. In addition to television ads and short online movies, Xbox has advertising with partner retailers including Target, Wal-Mart, and Sears. The Nintendo Wii campaign includes TV advertising; a promotion with Coca-Cola on the packaging of its Fanta, Sprite, and Dr Pepper brands; and live stunts by actors playing Wii tennis in front of a huge screen.

While the messages in the many forms of media may vary slightly, the campaigns are designed to emphasize a single theme. Sony is trying to communicate a message that the PS3 is "an experience 'beyond' games, harnessing the power of imagination." Microsoft's message for the Xbox 360 is "Jump In" and move to the next generation of gaming. Nintendo is positioning its Wii as a gaming system for the entire family.

What are some of the most innovative elements of these integrated campaigns? Sony included Blu-ray discs of *Talladega Nights: The Ballad of Ricky Bobby* in 500,000 PS3 boxes. Kellogg put Xbox 360 cartridges in 80 million cereal boxes in its highest-value promotion ever. At the Los Angeles launch of the Wii, videos of people singing songs about the Wii were posted on YouTube.com. Perhaps you've seen some of the promotions, and you are certain to see more in the future as the console wars continue.[1]

The many types of promotion used by Sony, Microsoft, and Nintendo demonstrate the opportunity for creativity in communicating with potential customers and the importance of integrating the various elements of a communication program. Promotion represents the fourth element in the marketing mix. The promotional element consists of communication tools, including advertising, personal selling, sales promotion, public relations, and direct marketing. The combination of one or more of these communication tools is called the **promotional mix**. All of these tools can be used to: (1) inform prospective buyers about the benefits of the product, (2) persuade them to try it, and (3) remind them later about the benefits they enjoyed by using the product. In the past, marketers often viewed the communication tools as separate and independent. The advertising department, for example, often designed and managed its activities without consulting departments or agencies that had responsibility for sales promotion or public relations. The result was often an overall communication effort that was uncoordinated and, in some cases, inconsistent. Today, the concept of designing marketing communications programs that coordinate all promotional activities—advertising, personal selling, sales promotion, public relations, and direct marketing—to provide a consistent message across all audiences is referred to as **integrated marketing communications (IMC)**. In addition, by taking consumer expectations into consideration, IMC is a key element in a company's customer experience management strategy.[2]

This chapter provides an overview of the communication process, a description of the promotional mix elements, several tools for integrating the promotional mix, and a process for developing a comprehensive promotion program. One of the promotional mix elements, direct marketing, is also discussed in this chapter. Chapter 19 covers advertising, sales promotion, and public relations, and Chapter 20 discusses personal selling.

THE COMMUNICATION PROCESS

Communication is the process of conveying a message to others and it requires six elements: a source, a message, a channel of communication, a receiver, and the processes of encoding and decoding[3] (Figure 18–1). The **source** may be a company or person who has information to convey. The information sent by a source, such as a description of a new cellular telephone, forms the **message**. The message is conveyed by means of a **channel of communication** such as a salesperson, advertising media, or public relations tools. Consumers who read, hear, or see the message are the **receivers**.

Encoding and Decoding

Encoding and decoding are essential to communication. **Encoding** is the process of having the sender transform an idea into a set of symbols. **Decoding** is the reverse, or the process of having the receiver take a set of symbols, the message, and transform the symbols back to an idea. Look at the accompanying automobile advertisement: Who is the source, and what is the message?

Decoding is performed by the receivers according to their own frame of reference: their attitudes, values, and beliefs.[4] HUMMER is the source and the advertisement

FIGURE 18–1
The communication process
consists of six key elements.

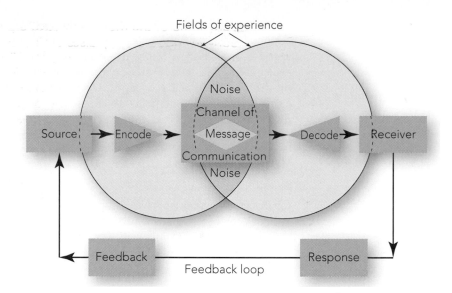

is the message, which appeared in *Wired* magazine (the channel). How would you interpret (decode) this advertisement? The picture and text in the advertisement show that the source's intention is to generate interest in a vehicle "Like Nothing Else"—a statement the source believes will appeal to the readers of the magazine.

The process of communication is not always a successful one. Errors in communication can happen in several ways. The source may not adequately transform the abstract idea into an effective set of symbols, a properly encoded message may be sent through the wrong channel and never make it to the receiver, the receiver may not properly transform the set of symbols into the correct abstract idea, or finally, feedback may be so delayed or distorted that it is of no use to the sender. Although communication appears easy to perform, truly effective communication can be very difficult.

How would you decode this ad?

HUMMER
www.HUMMER.com

For the message to be communicated effectively, the sender and receiver must have a mutually shared **field of experience**—a similar understanding and knowledge they apply to the message. Figure 18–1 shows two circles representing the fields of experience of the sender and receiver, which overlap in the message. Some of the better-known message problems have occurred when U.S. companies have taken their messages to cultures with different fields of experience. Many misinterpretations are merely the result of bad translations. For example, KFC made a mistake when its "finger-lickin' good" slogan was translated into Mandarin Chinese as "eat your fingers off!"[5]

Feedback

Figure 18–1 shows a line labeled *feedback loop,* which consists of a response and feedback. A **response** is the impact the message had on the receiver's knowledge, attitudes, or behaviors. **Feedback** is the sender's interpretation of the response and indicates whether the message was decoded and understood as intended. Chapter 19 reviews approaches called *pretesting* that ensure that messages are decoded properly.

Noise

Noise includes extraneous factors that can work against effective communication by distorting a message or the feedback received (Figure 18–1). Noise can be a simple error, such as a printing mistake that affects the meaning of a newspaper advertisement, or using words or pictures that fail to communicate the message clearly. Noise can also occur when a salesperson's message is misunderstood by a prospective buyer, such as when a salesperson's accent, use of slang terms, or communication style make hearing and understanding the message difficult.

---

learning review

1. What are the six elements required for communication to occur?

2. A difficulty for U.S. companies advertising in international markets is that the audience does not share the same _____.

3. A misprint in a newspaper ad is an example of _____.

THE PROMOTIONAL ELEMENTS

LO2

To communicate with consumers, a company can use one or more of five promotional alternatives: advertising, personal selling, public relations, sales promotion, and direct marketing. Figure 18–2 summarizes the distinctions among these five elements. Three of these elements—advertising, sales promotion, and public relations—are often said to use *mass selling* because they are used with groups of prospective buyers. In contrast, personal selling uses *customized interaction* between a seller and a prospective buyer. Personal selling activities include face-to-face, telephone, and interactive electronic communication. Direct marketing also uses messages customized for specific customers.

Advertising

Advertising is any paid form of nonpersonal communication about an organization, good, service, or idea by an identified sponsor. The *paid* aspect of this definition is important because the space for the advertising message normally must be bought. An occasional exception is the public service announcement, where the advertising time or space is donated. A full-page, four-color ad in *Time* magazine, for example, costs $241,350. The *nonpersonal* component of advertising is also important. Advertising involves mass media (such as TV, radio, and magazines), which are nonpersonal and do not have an immediate feedback loop as does personal selling. So before the message is

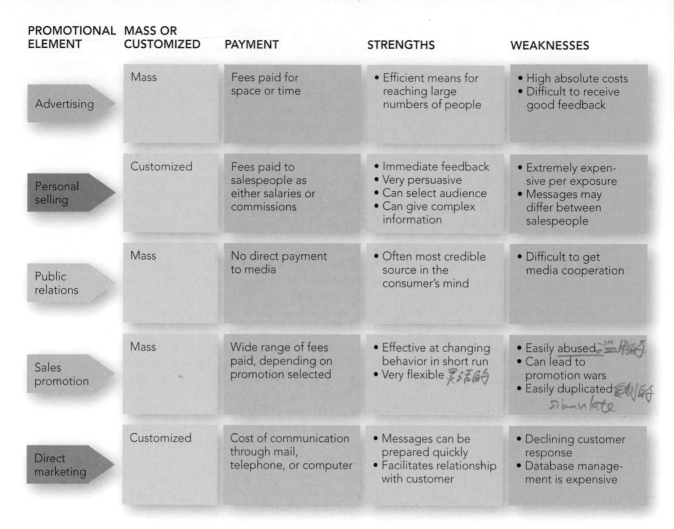

PROMOTIONAL ELEMENT	MASS OR CUSTOMIZED	PAYMENT	STRENGTHS	WEAKNESSES
Advertising	Mass	Fees paid for space or time	• Efficient means for reaching large numbers of people	• High absolute costs • Difficult to receive good feedback
Personal selling	Customized	Fees paid to salespeople as either salaries or commissions	• Immediate feedback • Very persuasive • Can select audience • Can give complex information	• Extremely expensive per exposure • Messages may differ between salespeople
Public relations	Mass	No direct payment to media	• Often most credible source in the consumer's mind	• Difficult to get media cooperation
Sales promotion	Mass	Wide range of fees paid, depending on promotion selected	• Effective at changing behavior in short run • Very flexible	• Easily abused • Can lead to promotion wars • Easily duplicated
Direct marketing	Customized	Cost of communication through mail, telephone, or computer	• Messages can be prepared quickly • Facilitates relationship with customer	• Declining customer response • Database management is expensive

FIGURE 18–2

The five elements of the promotional mix

sent, marketing research plays a valuable role; for example, it determines that the target market will actually see the medium chosen, and that the message will be understood.

There are several advantages to a firm using advertising in its promotional mix. It can be attention-getting—as with the Diet Coke ad shown on the next page—and also can communicate specific product benefits to prospective buyers. By paying for the advertising space, a company can control *what* it wants to say and, to some extent, to *whom* the message is sent. Advertising also allows the company to decide *when* to send its message (which includes how often). The nonpersonal aspect of advertising also has its advantages. Once the message is created, the same message is sent to all receivers in a market segment. If the pictorial, text, and brand elements of an advertisement are properly pretested, an advertiser can ensure the ad's ability to capture consumers' attention[6] and trust that the same message will be decoded by all receivers in the market segment.

Advertising has some disadvantages. As shown in Figure 18–2 and discussed in depth in Chapter 19, the costs to produce and place a message are significant, and the lack of direct feedback makes it difficult to know how well the message was received.

Personal Selling

The second major promotional alternative is **personal selling**, defined as the two-way flow of communication between a buyer and seller, designed to influence a person's or group's purchase decision. Unlike advertising, personal selling is usually face-to-face communication between the sender and receiver. Why do companies use personal selling?

There are important advantages to personal selling, as summarized in Figure 18–2. A salesperson can control to *whom* the presentation is made, reducing the amount of *wasted coverage,* or communication with consumers who are not in the target audience. The personal component of selling has another advantage in that the seller can see or hear the potential buyer's reaction to the message. If the feedback is unfavorable, the salesperson can modify the message.

The flexibility of personal selling can also be a disadvantage. Different salespeople can change the message so that no consistent communication is given to all customers. The high cost of personal selling is probably its major disadvantage. On a cost-per-contact basis, it is generally the most expensive of the five promotional elements.

Public Relations

Public relations is a form of communication management that seeks to influence the feelings, opinions, or beliefs held by customers, prospective customers, stockholders, suppliers, employees, and other publics about a company and its products or services.[7] Many tools such as special events, lobbying efforts, annual reports, press conferences,[8] RSS feeds, and image management may be used by a public relations department, although publicity often plays the most important role. **Publicity** is a nonpersonal, indirectly paid presentation of an organization, good, or service. It can take the form of a news story, editorial, or product announcement. A difference between publicity and both advertising and personal selling is the "indirectly paid" dimension. With publicity a company does not pay for space in a mass medium (such as television or radio) but attempts to get the medium to run a favorable story on the company. In this sense, there is an indirect payment for publicity in that a company must support a public relations staff.

An advantage of publicity is credibility. When you read a favorable story about a company's product (such as a glowing restaurant review), there is a tendency to believe it. Travelers throughout the world have relied on Frommer's guides such as *Australia from $60 a Day.* These books outline out-of-the-way, inexpensive restaurants and hotels, giving invaluable publicity to these establishments. Such businesses do not (nor can they) buy a mention in the guide.

The disadvantage of publicity relates to the lack of the user's control over it. A company can invite media to cover an interesting event such as a store opening or a new product release, but there is no guarantee that a story will result, if it will be positive, or who will be in the audience. Social media, such as blogs, have grown dramatically and allow uncontrollable public discussions of almost any company activity. Many public relations departments now focus on facilitating and responding to

Advertising, public relations, and sales promotion are three elements of the promotional mix.

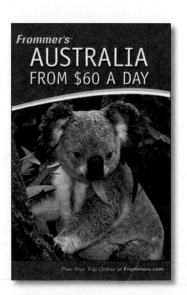

online discussions. McDonald's, for example, responds to comments about McDonald's products and promotions on the blog, *Open for Discussion*.[9] Generally, publicity is an important element of most promotional campaigns, although the lack of control means that it is rarely the primary element. Research related to the sequence of IMC elements, however, indicates that publicity followed by advertising with the same message increases the positive response to the message.[10]

Sales Promotion

A fourth promotional element is **sales promotion**, a short-term inducement of value offered to arouse interest in buying a good or service. Used in conjunction with advertising or personal selling, sales promotions are offered to intermediaries as well as to ultimate consumers. Coupons, rebates, samples, and contests such as Dairy Queen's "Freeze! Click! Win!" promotion are just a few examples of sales promotions discussed later in this chapter.[11]

The advantage of sales promotion is that the short-term nature of these programs (such as a coupon or sweepstakes with an expiration date) often stimulates sales for their duration. Offering value to the consumer in terms of a cents-off coupon or rebate may increase store traffic from consumers who are not store-loyal.[12]

Sales promotions cannot be the sole basis for a campaign because gains are often temporary and sales drop off when the deal ends.[13] Advertising support is needed to convert the customer who tried the product because of a sales promotion into a long-term buyer.[14] If sales promotions are conducted continuously, they lose their effectiveness. Customers begin to delay purchase until a coupon is offered, or they question the product's value. Some aspects of sales promotions also are regulated by the federal government. These issues are reviewed in detail in Chapter 19.

Direct Marketing

Another promotional alternative, **direct marketing**, uses direct communication with consumers to generate a response in the form of an order, a request for further information, or a visit to a retail outlet.[15] The communication can take many forms including face-to-face selling, direct mail, catalogs, telephone solicitations, direct response advertising (on television and radio and in print), and online marketing. Like personal selling, direct marketing often consists of interactive communication. It also has the advantage of being customized to match the needs of specific target markets. Messages can be developed and adapted quickly to facilitate one-to-one relationships with customers.

While direct marketing has been one of the fastest-growing forms of promotion, it has several disadvantages. First, most forms of direct marketing require a comprehensive and up-to-date database with information about the target market. Developing and maintaining the database can be expensive and time consuming. In addition, growing concern about privacy has led to a decline in response rates among some customer groups. Companies with successful direct marketing programs are sensitive to these issues and often use a combination of direct marketing alternatives together, or direct marketing combined with other promotional tools, to increase value for customers.

learning review

4. Explain the difference between advertising and publicity when both appear on television.

5. Which promotional element should be offered only on a short-term basis?

6. Cost per contact is high with the _____ element of the promotional mix.

INTEGRATED MARKETING COMMUNICATIONS—
DEVELOPING THE PROMOTIONAL MIX

A firm's promotional mix is the combination of one or more of the promotional tools it chooses to use. In putting together the promotional mix, a marketer must consider two issues. First, the balance of the elements must be determined. Should advertising be emphasized more than personal selling? Should a promotional rebate be offered? Would public relations activities be effective? Several factors affect such decisions: the target audience for the promotion,[16] the stage of the product's life cycle, characteristics of the product, decision stage of the buyer, and even the channel of distribution. Second, because the various promotional elements are often the responsibility of different departments, coordinating a consistent promotional effort is necessary. A promotional planning process designed to ensure integrated marketing communications can facilitate this goal.

Publications such as *Restaurant News* reach business buyers.

The Target Audience

Promotional programs are directed to the ultimate consumer, to an intermediary (retailer, wholesaler, or industrial distributor), or to both. Promotional programs directed to buyers of consumer products often use mass media because the number of potential buyers is large. Personal selling is used at the place of purchase, generally the retail store. Direct marketing may be used to encourage first-time or repeat purchases. Combinations of many media alternatives are a necessity for some target audiences today. The Marketing Matters box describes how Generation Y consumers can be reached through mobile marketing programs.[17]

Advertising directed to business buyers is used selectively in trade publications, such as *Restaurant News* magazine for buyers of restaurant equipment and supplies. Because business buyers often have specialized needs or technical questions, personal selling is particularly important. The salesperson can provide information and the necessary support after sales.

Intermediaries are often the focus of promotional efforts. As with business buyers, personal selling is the major promotional ingredient. The salespeople assist intermediaries in making a profit by coordinating promotional campaigns sponsored by the manufacturer and by providing marketing advice and expertise. Intermediaries' questions often pertain to the allowed markup, merchandising support, and return policies.

The Product Life Cycle

LO3

All products have a product life cycle (see Chapter 11), and the composition of the promotional mix changes over the four life-cycle stages, as shown for Purina Dog Chow in Figure 18–3.

Introduction Stage Informing consumers in an effort to increase their level of awareness is the primary promotional objective in the introduction stage of the product life cycle. In general, all the promotional mix elements are used at this time, although the use of specific mix elements during any stage depends on the product and situation. News releases about Purina's new nutritional product are sent to veterinary magazines, trial samples are sent to registered dog owners, advertisements are placed in *Dog World* magazine, and the salesforce begins to approach supermarkets to get orders. Advertising is particularly important as a means of reaching as many people as possible to build awareness and interest. Publicity may even begin slightly before the product is commercially available.

Growth Stage The primary promotional objective of the growth stage is to persuade the consumer to buy the product—Purina Dog Chow—rather than substitutes, so the marketing manager seeks to gain brand preference and solidify distribution. Sales promotion assumes less importance in this stage, and publicity is not a factor because it depends on novelty of the product. The primary promotional element is advertising, which stresses brand differences. Personal selling is

FIGURE 18–3

Promotional tools used over the product life cycle of Purina Dog Chow

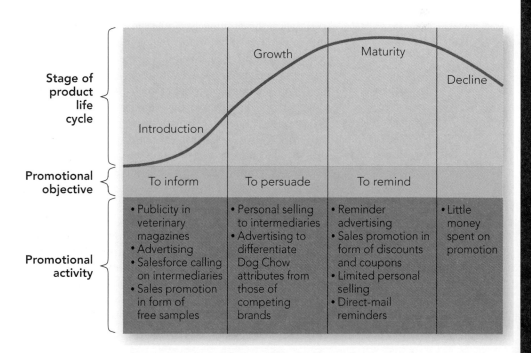

	Introduction	Growth	Maturity	Decline
Promotional objective	To inform	To persuade	To remind	
Promotional activity	• Publicity in veterinary magazines • Advertising • Salesforce calling on intermediaries • Sales promotion in form of free samples	• Personal selling to intermediaries • Advertising to differentiate Dog Chow attributes from those of competing brands	• Reminder advertising • Sales promotion in form of discounts and coupons • Limited personal selling • Direct-mail reminders	• Little money spent on promotion

Purina sponsors the Incredible Dog Challenge to maintain existing buyers.

used to solidify the channel of distribution. For consumer products such as dog food, the salesforce calls on the wholesalers and retailers in hopes of increasing inventory levels and gaining shelf space. For business products, the salesforce often tries to get contractual arrangements to be the sole source of supply for the buyer.

Maturity Stage In the maturity stage, the need is to maintain existing buyers, and advertising's role is to remind buyers of the product's existence. Sales promotion, in the form of discounts and coupons offered to both ultimate consumers and intermediaries, is important in maintaining loyal buyers. In a test of one mature consumer product, it was found that 80 percent of the product's sales at this stage resulted from sales promotions.[18] Sponsoring events can also help maintain loyalty. For the past 10 years, Purina has sponsored the Incredible Dog Challenge, which is now covered by ESPN and ESPN2.[19] Direct marketing actions such as direct mail are used to maintain involvement with existing customers and to encourage repeat purchases. Price cuts and discounts can also significantly increase a mature brand's sales. The salesforce at this stage seeks to satisfy intermediaries. An unsatisfied customer who switches brands is hard to replace.

Decline Stage The decline stage of the product life cycle is usually a period of phaseout for the product, and little money is spent in the promotional mix. The rate of decline can be rapid when a product is replaced by an improved or lower cost product, for example, or slow if there is a loyal group of customers.

Product Characteristics

The proper blend of elements in the promotional mix also depends on the type of product. Three specific characteristics should be considered: complexity, risk, and ancillary services. *Complexity* refers to the technical sophistication of the product and hence the amount of understanding required to use it. It's hard to provide much information in a one-page magazine ad or a 30-second television ad, so the more complex the product, the greater the emphasis on personal selling. Gulfstream asks potential customers to call their senior vice president in its ads. No information is provided for simple products such as Heinz ketchup.

A second element is the degree of risk represented by the product's purchase. *Risk* for the buyer can be assessed in terms of financial risk, social risk, and physical risk. A private jet, for example, might represent all three risks—it is expensive, employees and customers may see and evaluate the purchase, and safety and reliability are important. Although advertising helps, the greater the risk, the greater the need for personal selling. Consumers are unlikely to associate any of these risks with ketchup.

The level of ancillary services required by a product also affects the promotional strategy. *Ancillary services* pertain to the degree of service or support required after the sale. This characteristic is common to many industrial products and consumer purchases. Who will provide maintenance for the plane? Advertising's role is to establish the seller's reputation. Direct marketing can be used to describe how a product or service can be customized to individual needs. However, personal selling is essential to build buyer confidence and provide evidence of customer service.

How do Gulfstream aircraft and Heinz ketchup differ on complexity, risk, and ancillary services?

Gulfstream
www.gulfstreamvsp.com

Heinz
www.heinz.com

Stages of the Buying Decision

Knowing the customer's stage of decision making can also affect the promotional mix. Figure 18–4 shows how the importance of the promotional elements varies with the three stages in a consumer's purchase decision.

Prepurchase Stage   In the prepurchase stage, advertising is more helpful than personal selling because advertising informs the potential customer of the existence of the product and the seller. Sales promotion in the form of free samples also can play an important role to gain low-risk trial. When the salesperson calls on the customer after heavy advertising, there is some recognition of what the salesperson represents. This is particularly important in industrial settings in which sampling of the product is usually not possible.

FIGURE 18–4

How the importance of promotional elements varies during the stages of consumer's purchase decision

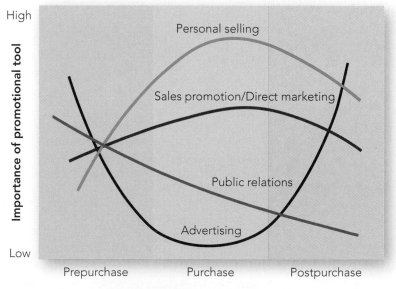

Purchase Stage At the purchase stage, the importance of personal selling is highest, whereas the impact of advertising is lowest. Sales promotion in the form of coupons, deals, point-of-purchase displays, and rebates can be very helpful in encouraging demand. In this stage, although advertising is not an active influence on the purchase, it is the means of delivering the coupons, deals, and rebates that are often important. Recent research indicates that direct marketing activities shorten the time consumers take to adopt a product or service.[20]

Postpurchase Stage In the postpurchase stage, the salesperson is still important. In fact, the more personal contact after the sale, the more the buyer is satisfied. Advertising is also important to assure the buyer that the right purchase was made. Advertising and personal selling help reduce the buyer's postpurchase anxiety.[21] Sales promotion in the form of coupons and direct marketing reminders can help encourage repeat purchases from satisfied first-time triers. Public relations plays a small role in the postpurchase stage.

Channel Strategies

Chapter 15 discussed the channel flow from a producer to intermediaries to consumers. Achieving control of the channel is often difficult for the manufacturer, and promotional strategies can assist in moving a product through the channel of distribution. This is where a manufacturer has to make an important decision about whether to use a push strategy, pull strategy, or both in its channel of distribution.[22]

Push Strategy Figure 18–5A shows how a manufacturer uses a **push strategy,** directing the promotional mix to channel members to gain their cooperation in ordering and stocking the product. In this approach, personal selling and sales promotions play major roles. Salespeople call on wholesalers to encourage orders and provide sales assistance. Sales promotions, such as case discount allowances (20 percent off the regular case price), are offered to stimulate demand. By pushing the product through the channel, the goal is to get channel members to push it to their customers.

Ford Motor Company, for example, provides support and incentives for its 4,200 Ford and Lincoln-Mercury dealers. Through a multi-level program, Ford provides incentives to reward dealers for meeting sales goals. Dealers receive an incentive when they are near a goal, another when they reach a goal, and a larger incentive if they exceed sales projections. Ford also offers some dealers special incentives for maintaining superior

FIGURE 18–5

A comparison of push and pull promotional strategies

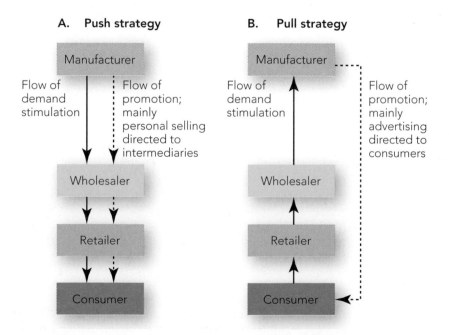

facilities or improving customer service. All of these actions are intended to encourage Fords dealers to "push" the Ford products through the channel to consumers.[23]

Pull Strategy   In some instances, manufacturers face resistance from channel members who do not want to order a new product or increase inventory levels of an existing brand. As shown in Figure 18–5B, a manufacturer may then elect to implement a **pull strategy** by directing its promotional mix at ultimate consumers to encourage them to ask the retailer for a product. Seeing demand from ultimate consumers, retailers order the product from wholesalers and thus the item is pulled through the intermediaries. Pharmaceutical companies, for example, now spend more than $4 billion annually on *direct-to-consumer* prescription drug advertising, to complement traditional personal selling and free samples directed only at doctors.[24] The strategy is designed to encourage consumers to ask their doctor for a specific drug by name—pulling it through the channel. Successful campaigns such as the adjacent print ad, which says "Ask your doctor about new Juvéderm," can have dramatic effects on the sales of a product.

---

learning review

7. Describe the promotional objective for each stage of the product life cycle.

8. At what stage of the consumer purchase decision is the importance of personal selling highest? Why?

9. Explain the differences between a push strategy and a pull strategy.

DEVELOPING AN IMC PROGRAM

LO4

Because media costs are high, promotion decisions must be made carefully, using a systematic approach. Paralleling the planning, implementation, and evaluation steps described in the strategic marketing process (Chapter 2), the promotion decision process is divided into (1) developing, (2) executing, and (3) assessing the promotion program (Figure 18–6). Development of the promotion program focuses on the four *W*s:

- *Who* is the target audience?
- *What* are (1) the promotion objectives, (2) the amounts of money that can be budgeted for the promotion program, and (3) the kinds of promotion to use?
- *Where* should the promotion be run?
- *When* should the promotion be run?

FIGURE 18–6

The promotion decision process includes planning, implementation, and evaluation.

Identifying the Target Audience

The first decision in developing the promotion program is identifying the *target audience*, the group of prospective buyers toward which a promotion program is

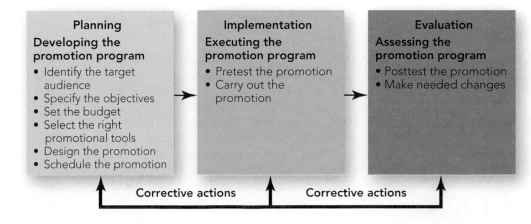

directed. To the extent that time and money permit, the target audience for the promotion program is the target market for the firm's product, which is identified from marketing research and market segmentation studies. The more a firm knows about its target audiences—including their lifestyle, attitudes, and values—the easier it is to develop a promotion program. If a firm wanted to reach you with television and magazine ads, for example, it would need to know what TV shows you watch and what magazines you read.

Specifying Promotion Objectives

After the target audience is identified, a decision must be reached on what the promotion should accomplish. Consumers can be said to respond in terms of a **hierarchy of effects**, which is the sequence of stages a prospective buyer goes through from initial awareness of a product to eventual action (either trial or adoption of the product).[25] The five stages are:

- *Awareness*—the consumer's ability to recognize and remember the product or brand name.
- *Interest*—an increase in the consumer's desire to learn about some of the features of the product or brand.
- *Evaluation*—the consumer's appraisal of the product or brand on important attributes.
- *Trial*—the consumer's actual first purchase and use of the product or brand.
- *Adoption*—through a favorable experience on the first trial, the consumer's repeated purchase and use of the product or brand.

For a totally new product, the sequence applies to the entire product category, but for a new brand competing in an established product category it applies to the brand itself. These steps can serve as guidelines for developing promotion objectives.

Although sometimes an objective for a promotion program involves several steps in the hierarchy of effects, it often focuses on a single stage. Regardless of what the specific objective might be, from building awareness to increasing repeat purchases,[26] promotion objectives should possess three important qualities. They should (1) be designed for a well-defined target audience, (2) be measurable, and (3) cover a specified time period.

Setting the Promotion Budget

From Figure 18–7 it is clear that the promotion expenditures needed to reach U.S. households are enormous. Note that four companies—Procter & Gamble, AT&T, General Motors, and Time Warner—each spend a total of more than $3 billion annually on promotion.[27]

After setting the promotion objectives, a company must decide how much to spend. Determining the ideal amount for the budget is difficult because there is no precise way to measure the exact results of spending promotion dollars. However, several methods can be used to set the promotion budget.[28]

Percentage of Sales   In the **percentage of sales budgeting** approach, funds are allocated to promotion as a percentage of past or anticipated sales, in terms of either dollars or units sold. A common budgeting method,[29] this approach is often stated in terms such as "Our promotion budget for this year is 3 percent of last year's gross sales." The advantage of this approach is obvious: It is simple and provides a financial safeguard by tying the promotion budget to sales. However, there is a major fallacy in this approach, which implies that sales cause promotion. Using this method, a company may reduce its promotion budget because of a downturn in past sales or an anticipated downturn in future sales—situations in which it may need

Rank	Company	Advertising (Millions)	+	All Other Promotion (Millions)	=	Total (Millions)
1	Procter & Gamble	$3,527		$1,371		$4,898
2	AT&T	2,341		1,003		3,344
3	General Motors	2,208		1,088		3,296
4	Time Warner	1,838		1,251		3,089
5	Verizon	1,947		875		2,822
6	Ford	1,701		876		2,577
7	GlaxoSmithKline	1,295		1,149		2,444
8	Disney	1,438		882		2,320
9	Johnson & Johnson	1,351		939		2,290
10	Unilever	848		1,250		2,098

FIGURE 18–7

U.S. promotion expenditures by companies in 2006

promotion the most. See the Using Marketing Dashboards box on the next page for an application of the promotion-to-sales ratio to the automotive industry.

Competitive Parity A second common approach, **competitive parity budgeting**, is matching the competitor's absolute level of spending or the proportion per point of market share. This approach has also been referred to as *matching competitors* or *share of market*. It is important to consider the competition in budgeting.[30] Consumer responses to promotion are affected by competing promotional activities, so if a competitor runs 30 radio ads each week, it may be difficult for a firm to get its message across with only five messages.[31] The competitor's budget level, however, should not be the only determinant in setting a company's budget. The competition might have very different promotional objectives, which require a different level of promotion expenditures.

All You Can Afford Common to many small businesses is **all-you-can-afford budgeting**, in which money is allocated to promotion only after all other budget items are covered. As one company executive said in reference to this budgeting process, "Why, it's simple. First, I go upstairs to the controller and ask how much they can afford to give us this year. She says a million and a half. Later, the boss comes to me and asks how much we should spend, and I say 'Oh, about a million and a half.' Then we have our promotion appropriation."[32]

Fiscally conservative, this approach has little else to offer. Using this budgeting philosophy, a company acts as though it doesn't know anything about a promotion-sales relationship or what its promotion objectives are.

Objective and Task The best approach to budgeting is **objective and task budgeting**, whereby the company (1) determines its promotion objectives, (2) outlines the tasks to accomplish these objectives, and (3) determines the promotion cost of performing these tasks.[33] This method takes into account what the company wants to accomplish and requires that the objectives be specified.[34] Strengths of the other budgeting methods are integrated into this approach because each previous method's strength is tied to the objectives. For example, if the costs are beyond what the company can afford, objectives are reworked and the tasks revised. The difficulty with this method is the judgment required to determine the tasks needed to accomplish objectives.

Selecting the Right Promotional Tools

Once a budget has been determined, the combination of the five basic IMC tools—advertising, personal selling, sales promotion, public relations, and direct marketing—can

Using Marketing Dashboards

How Much Should You Spend on IMC?

Integrated marketing communications programs coordinate a variety of promotion alternatives to provide a consistent message across audiences. The amount spent on the various promotional elements, or on the total campaign, may vary depending on the target audience, the type of product, where the product is in the product life cycle, and the channel strategy selected. Managers often use the promotion-to-sales ratio on their marketing dashboard to assess how effective the IMC program expenditures are at generating sales.

Your Challenge As a manager at General Motors you've been asked to assess the effectiveness of all promotion expenditures during the past year. The promotion-to-sales ratio can be used by managers to make year-to-year comparisons of their programs, to compare the effectiveness of their program with competitor's programs, or to make comparisons with industry averages. You decide to calculate the promotion-to-sales ratio for General Motors. In addition, to allow a comparison, you decide to make the same calculation for one of your competitors, Ford, and for the entire automobile industry. The ratio is calculated as follows:

Promotion-to-sales ratio =
Total promotion expenditures/Total sales

Your Findings The information needed for these calculations is readily available from trade publications and annual reports. The following graph shows the promotion-to-sales ratio for General Motors and Ford (two companies featured in Figure 18–7) and the automotive industry. General Motors spent $3.296 billion on its IMC program to generate $129 billion in U.S. sales for a ratio of 2.6 (percent). Ford's ratio was 3.2, and the industry average was 2.7.

Your Action General Motor's promotion-to-sales ratio is substantially lower than Ford's and slightly lower than the industry average. This suggests that the current mix of promotional activities and the level of expenditures are both creating an effective IMC program. In the future you will want to monitor the factors that may influence the ratio. The average ratio for the beverage industry has risen to 9 while the average for grocery stores is about 1.

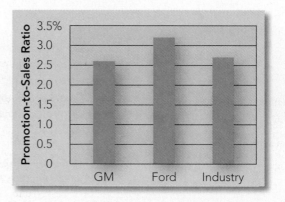

be specified. While many factors provide direction for selection of the appropriate mix, the large number of possible combinations of the promotional tools means that many combinations can achieve the same objective. Therefore, an analytical approach and experience are particularly important in this step of the promotion decision process. The specific mix can vary from a simple program using a single tool to a comprehensive program using all forms of promotion. The Olympics have become a very visible example of a comprehensive integrated communication program. Because the Games are repeated every two years, the promotion is almost continuous. Included in the program are advertising campaigns, personal selling efforts by the Olympic committee and organizers, sales promotion activities such as product tie-ins and sponsorships, public relations programs managed by the host cities, and direct marketing efforts targeted at a variety of audiences including governments, organizations, firms, athletes, and individuals.[35] At this stage, it is also important to assess the relative importance of the various tools. While it may be desirable to utilize and integrate several forms of promotion, one may deserve emphasis. The Olympics, for example, place exceptional importance on public relations and publicity.

The Olympics use a comprehensive IMC program.

Designing the Promotion

The central element of a promotion program is the promotion itself. Advertising consists of advertising copy and the artwork that the target audience is intended to see or hear.

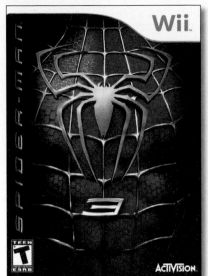

Video games based on movies are often released before the movie.

Personal selling efforts depend on the characteristics and skills of the salesperson. Sales promotion activities consist of the specific details of inducements such as coupons, samples, and sweepstakes. Public relations efforts are readily seen in tangible elements such as news releases, and direct marketing actions depend on written, verbal, and electronic forms of delivery. The design of the promotion will play a primary role in determining the message that is communicated to the audience. This design activity is frequently viewed as the step requiring the most creativity. In addition, successful designs are often the result of insight regarding consumer's interests and purchasing behavior. All of the promotion tools have many design alternatives. Advertising, for example, can utilize fear, humor, attractiveness, or other themes in its appeal.[36] Similarly, direct marketing can be designed for varying levels of personal or customized appeals. One of the challenges of IMC is to design each promotional activity to communicate the same message.

Scheduling the Promotion

Once the design of each of the promotional program elements is complete, it is important to determine the most effective timing of their use. The promotion schedule describes the order in which each promotional tool is introduced and the frequency of its use during the campaign. Movie studio Columbia TriStar, for example, uses a schedule of several promotional tools for its movies. To generate interest in a movie such as *Spider-Man 3,* a video game based on the movie characters was released before the movie. In addition, Columbia offered behind-the-scenes clips and character profiles on Comcast cable service and on a Spider-Man website. It also released a movie "trailer" that was shown on television and in theaters. Then movie-related products such as 3D beverage cups available at 7-Eleven convenience stores and action figure premiums available in Burger King Kids Meals were offered. After the movie was released, an online contest encouraged fans to build and submit their own mini Spider-Man videos to compete for the chance to include their video on the bonus disc that is part of the *Spider-Man* DVD package.[37]

Overall, the scheduling of the various promotions was designed to generate interest, bring consumers into theaters, and then encourage additional purchases after seeing the movie. Several factors such as seasonality and competitive promotion activity can also influence the promotion schedule. Businesses such as ski resorts, airlines, and professional sports teams are likely to reduce their promotional activity during the "off" season. Similarly, restaurants, retail stores, and health clubs are likely to increase their promotional activity when new competitors enter the market.

EXECUTING AND ASSESSING THE PROMOTION PROGRAM

Carrying out the promotion program can be expensive and time consuming. One researcher estimates that "an organization with sales less than $10 million can successfully implement an IMC program in one year, one with sales between $200 million and $500 million will need about three years, and one with sales between $2 billion and $5 billion will need five years." In addition, firms with a market orientation are more likely to implement an IMC program.[38] To facilitate the transition, there are approximately 200 integrated marketing communications agencies in operation. In addition, some of the largest agencies are adopting approaches that embrace "total communications solutions."

Starcom USA, which recently won *Advertising Age* magazine's Media Agency of the Year award, for example, is part of an integrated network of 5,800 global media professionals in 110 offices in 67 countries. The agency's services include media management, direct response media planning, Internet and digital communications, sports sponsorships, gaming, and multicultural, entertainment and event marketing. One of its integrated campaigns for Allstate insurance company created a partnership with Discovery Channel's *It Takes a Thief* series, and utilized sweepstakes, a website, and print advertising, in addition to its traditional personal selling by Allstate agents. While many agencies still have departments dedicated to promotion, direct marketing, and other specialties, the trend today is clearly toward a long-term perspective in which all forms of promotion are integrated. Starcom is organized into three areas—consumer insight, consumer activation, and measurement of effectiveness.[39]

An important factor in developing successful IMC programs is to create a process that facilitates their design and use. A tool used to evaluate a company's current process is the IMC audit. The audit analyzes the internal communication network of the company; identifies key audiences; evaluates customer databases; assesses messages in recent advertising, public relations releases, packaging, websites, and e-mail communication, signage, sales promotions, and direct mail; and determines the IMC expertise of company and agency personnel.[40] This process is becoming increasingly important as consumer-generated media such as blogs, RSS, podcasts, and social networks become more popular. Now, in addition to ensuring that traditional forms of communication are integrated, companies must be able to monitor consumer content, respond to inconsistent messages, and even answer questions from individual customers.[41]

As shown earlier in Figure 18–6, the ideal execution of a promotion program involves pretesting each design before it is actually used to allow for changes and modifications that improve its effectiveness. Similarly, posttests are recommended to evaluate the impact of each promotion and the contribution of the promotion toward achieving the program objectives. The most sophisticated pretest and posttest procedures have been developed for advertising and are discussed in Chapter 19. Testing procedures for sales promotion and direct marketing efforts currently focus on comparisons of different designs or responses of different segments. To fully benefit from IMC programs, companies must create and maintain a test-result database that allows comparisons of the relative impact of the promotional tools and their execution options in varying situations. Information from the database will allow informed design and execution decisions and provide support for IMC activities during internal reviews by financial or administrative personnel. The San Diego Padres baseball team, for example, developed a database of information relating attendance to its integrated campaign using a new logo, special events, merchandise sales, and a loyalty program.

Currently, about one-fourth of all businesses assess program effectiveness by measuring "most of their communication tactics."[42] For most organizations, the assessment focuses on trying to determine which element of promotion works better. In an integrated program, however, media advertising might be used to build awareness, sales promotion to generate an inquiry, direct mail to provide additional information to individual prospects, and a personal sales call to complete the transaction. The tools are used for different reasons, and their combined use creates a synergy that should be the focus of the assessment.[43] Another level of assessment is necessary when firms have international promotion programs.

---

learning review

10. What are the characteristics of good promotion objectives?

11. What is the weakness of the percentage of sales budgeting approach?

12. How have advertising agencies changed to facilitate the use of IMC programs?

DIRECT MARKETING

LO5

Direct marketing has many forms and utilizes a variety of media. Several forms of direct marketing—direct mail and catalogs, television, telemarketing, and direct selling—were discussed as methods of nonstore retailing in Chapter 17. In addition, although advertising is discussed in Chapter 19, a form of advertising—direct response advertising—is an important form of direct marketing. Finally, interactive or online marketing is discussed in detail in Chapter 21. In this section, the growth of direct marketing, its value for consumers and sellers, and key global, technological, and ethical issues are discussed.

The Growth of Direct Marketing

The increasing interest in customer relationship management is reflected in the dramatic growth of direct marketing. The ability to customize communication efforts and create one-to-one interactions is appealing to most marketers, particularly those with IMC programs. While many direct marketing methods are not new, the ability to design and use them has increased with the availability of customer information databases and new printing technologies. In recent years, direct marketing growth has outpaced total economic growth. Direct marketing expenditures of $166 billion are expected to grow at a rate of 6 percent. Similarly, 2007 revenues of $2.06 trillion are expected to grow to $2.63 trillion by 2011. The percentage of total U.S. revenues which are the result of direct marketing is currently 7 percent and growing! Figure 18–8 shows some of the most popular forms of direct marketing and their typical response rates. For example, direct mail is the most popular method. It is used by 69 percent of marketers and generates a 2.18 percent response rate.[44]

While direct mail is still the most common form of direct marketing, most campaigns use several methods. Xerox is one example of a company that has integrated its direct marketing activities. Consumers in Xerox's target market receive a personalized mailer that asks them to confirm receipt of the mailer on an Internet site. Once the consumers register at the site they can use the portal to find relevant information about their printing needs. Other forms of direct marketing such as catalogs, e-mail, and telephone calls can then be used to follow up on the initial contact with the customer. Many companies also integrate their direct marketing with other forms of promotion. State Farm insurance company used TV and print ads and direct mail to target 18- to 25-year-old customers with its "Now What?" campaign.[45]

Another component of the growth in direct marketing is the increasing popularity of the newest direct marketing channel—the Internet. As discussed in Chapter 21, total online sales have risen from close to nothing in 1996 to projections of $340 billion in 2011. Continued growth in the number of consumers with Internet access and the number of businesses with websites and electronic commerce offerings is likely to contribute to the future growth of direct marketing.

The Value of Direct Marketing

One of the most visible indicators of the value of direct marketing for consumers is the level of use of various forms of direct marketing. For example, 43 percent of

FIGURE 18–8

Business use and response rates of popular forms of direct marketing

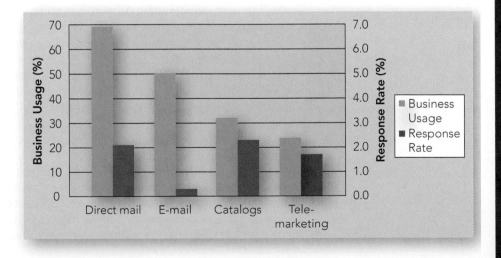

WELCOME HOME

FOUR SEASONS PRIVATE RESIDENCES DENVER.
A HOME THAT IS EXACTLY WHERE,
WHEN AND WHAT YOU WOULD LIKE IT TO BE.

FOUR SEASONS
PRIVATE RESIDENCES
Denver

Four Seasons uses direct mail to generate leads for its private residences.

the U.S. population has ordered merchandise or services by mail, phone, or Internet; more than 12 million adults have purchased items from a television offer; the average adult spends more than 30 hours per year accessing online services; and more than 21 percent of all adults make three to five purchases from a catalog each year. Consumers report many benefits, including the following: They don't have to go to a store, they can usually shop 24 hours a day, buying direct saves time, they avoid hassles with salespeople, they can save money, it's fun and entertaining, and direct marketing offers more privacy than in-store shopping. Many consumers also believe that direct marketing provides excellent customer service. Toll-free telephone numbers, customer service representatives with access to information regarding purchasing preferences, overnight delivery services, and unconditional guarantees all help create value for direct marketing customers. At Landsend.com, when customers need assistance they can click the "Lands' End Live" icon to receive help from a sales representative on the phone or online until the correct product is found. "It's like we were walking down the aisle in a store," says one Lands' End customer![46]

The value of direct marketing for sellers can be described in terms of the responses it generates.[47] **Direct orders** are the result of offers that contain all the information necessary for a prospective buyer to make a decision to purchase and complete the transaction. Priceline.com, for example, will send *PriceBreaker* e-mail alerts to people in its database. The messages offer discounted fares and rates to customers who can travel on very short notice. **Lead generation** is the result of an offer designed to generate interest in a product or service and a request for additional information. Four Seasons Hotels now sell private residences in several of their properties and send direct mail to prospective residents asking them to request additional information on the telephone or through a website. Finally, **traffic generation** is the outcome of an offer designed to motivate people to visit a business. General Motors recently mailed a sweepstakes to 5 million prospective car buyers inviting them to match a number on the mailing with a number on display in the dealer showrooms for a chance to win a new car. Nearly 400,000 customers visited GM dealers, and 40,000 of those purchased new cars![48]

Technological, Global, and Ethical Issues in Direct Marketing

The information technology and databases described in Chapter 8 are key elements in any direct marketing program. Databases are the result of organizations' efforts to collect demographic, media, and consumption profiles of customers so that direct marketing tools, such as catalogs, can be directed at specific customers. For example, Lillian Vernon started her very successful mail-order company four decades ago at her kitchen table by putting all her merchandise in a single catalog: Laundry baskets and men's slippers on one page might be followed by toys on the next. But in the last few years Lillian Vernon has shifted to a database approach with the 150 million catalogs mailed annually. There are now home-oriented, children's, and Christmas-ornament catalogs targeted at customers who have purchased these kinds of merchandise from the main catalog in the past.[49]

While most companies try to keep records of their customers' past purchases, many other types of data are needed to use direct marketing to develop one-to-one relationships with customers. Data, however, have little value by themselves. To translate data into information the data must be unbiased, timely, pertinent, accessible, and organized in a way that helps the marketing manager make decisions that lead to direct marketing actions. Some data, such as lifestyles, media use, and consumption behavior, must be collected in consumers' homes. Other types of data can be collected from the businesses where purchases are made. Technology such as optical scanners helps collect data with as little intrusion on the customer as possible. In addition, transactional websites and online search services can be sources of information. Google, for example, keeps search histories for 18 months to identify consumer tastes and interests.[50]

Making Responsible Decisions > > > > > > > > ethics

Is Spam Out of Control?

More than 1 billion e-mail messages are sent each day in the United States. Experts estimate that about three-fourths of them are direct marketing messages—personalized offers from companies such as Pepsi, Victoria's Secret, Toyota, and the Phoenix Suns. In fact, e-mail advertisers spend more than $2 billion on their campaigns each year. One reason is that e-mail offers one-to-one conversations with each prospective consumer. Another reason is that the average cost per e-mail message is less than $.01 compared to $0.75 to $2.00 for direct mail and $1 to $3 for telemarketing.

Some consumers have complained that they are inundated with unsolicited messages, sometimes called "spam," and ignore them, while marketers believe that better management of e-mail campaigns will improve the value of e-mail advertising for customers. Two general approaches to managing e-mail are being discussed. The "opt-out" system allows recipients to decline future messages after the first contact. The "opt-in" system requires advertisers to obtain e-mail addresses from registration questions on websites, business-reply cards, and even entry forms for contests or sweepstakes. Surveys indicate that about 77 percent of the unsolicited e-mails are deleted without being read, while only 2 percent of the e-mails received with the consumer's permission are deleted.

In the United States, the *Controlling the Assault of Non-Solicited Pornography and Marketing Act* (CAN-SPAM) requires e-mail be truthful and to provide an opt-out return e-mail address. In Japan, new regulations that require opt-in procedures are being discussed. What is your opinion? Why?

Direct marketing faces several challenges and opportunities in global markets today. Several countries such as Italy and Denmark, for example, have requirements for mandatory "opt-in"—that is, potential customers must give permission to include their name on a list for direct marketing solicitations. In addition, the availability of international mailing lists has declined because publications such as *Forbes* Global Edition and *BusinessWeek* European Edition have been discontinued. Replacing postal lists with e-mail lists is a potential solution although obtaining e-mail addresses is difficult also. In other countries, the mail, telephone, and Internet systems are not as well developed as they are in the United States. The need for improved reliability and security of the postal system in South Africa, for example, has slowed the growth of direct mail, while the dramatic growth of mobile phone penetration has created an opportunity for direct mobile marketing campaigns. Another issue for global direct marketers is payment. The availability of credit and credit cards varies throughout the world, creating the need for alternatives such as C.O.D., bank deposits, and online payment accounts.[51]

Global and domestic direct marketers both face challenging ethical issues today. Considerable attention has been given to some annoying direct marketing activities such as telephone solicitations during dinner and evening hours. Concerns about privacy, however, have led to various attempts to provide guidelines that balance consumer and business interests. The European Union passed a consumer privacy law, called the Data Protection Directive, after several years of discussion with the Federation of European Direct Marketing and the U.K.'s Direct Marketing Association. In the United States, the Federal Trade Commission and many state legislatures have also been concerned about privacy. Several bills that call for a do-not-mail registry similar to the do-not-call registry are being discussed.[52] Another issue, the proliferation of e-mail advertising, has received increasing attention from consumers and marketers recently. The Making Responsible Decisions box offers some details of the debate.[53]

---

learning review

13. The ability to design and use direct marketing programs has increased with the availability of _____ and _____.

14. What are the three types of responses generated by direct marketing activities?

LEARNING OBJECTIVES REVIEW

LO1 *Discuss integrated marketing communication and the communication process.*
Integrated marketing communication is the concept of designing marketing communications programs that coordinate all promotional activities—advertising, personal selling, sales promotion, public relations, and direct marketing—to provide a consistent message across all audiences. The communication process conveys messages with six elements: a source, a message, a channel of communication, a receiver, and encoding and decoding. The communication process also includes a feedback loop and can be distorted by noise.

LO2 *Describe the promotional mix and the uniqueness of each component.*
There are five promotional alternatives. Advertising, sales promotion, and public relations are mass selling approaches, whereas personal selling and direct marketing use customized messages. Advertising can have high absolute costs but reaches large numbers of people. Personal selling has a high cost per contact but provides immediate feedback. Public relations is often difficult to obtain but is very credible. Sales promotion influences short-term consumer behavior. Direct marketing can help develop customer relationships although maintaining a database can be very expensive.

LO3 *Select the promotional approach appropriate to a product's target audience, life-cycle stage, and characteristics, as well as stages of the buying decision and channel strategies.*
The promotional mix depends on the target audience. Programs for consumers, business buyers, and intermediaries might emphasize advertising, personal selling, and sales promotion, respectively. The promotional mix also changes over the product life-cycle stages. During the introduction stage, all promotional mix elements are used. During the growth stage advertising is emphasized, while the maturity stage utilizes sales promotion and direct marketing. Little promotion is used during the decline stage. Product characteristics also help determine the promotion mix. The level of complexity, risk, and ancillary services required will determine which element is needed. Knowing the customer's stage in the buying process can help select appropriate promotions. Advertising and public relations can create awareness in the prepurchase stage, personal selling and sales promotion can facilitate the purchase, and advertising can help reduce anxiety in the postpurchase stage. Finally, the promotional mix can depend on the channel strategy. Push strategies require personal selling and sales promotions directed at channel members, while pull strategies depend on advertising and sales promotion directed at consumers.

LO4 *Describe the elements of the promotion decision process.*
The promotional decision process consists of three steps: planning, implementation, and control. The planning step consists of six elements: identify the target audience, specify the objectives, set the budget, select the right promotional elements, design the promotion, and schedule the promotion. The implementation step includes pretesting. The control step includes posttesting.

LO5 *Explain the value of direct marketing for consumers and sellers.*
The value of direct marketing for consumers is indicated by its level of use. For example, 68 percent of them have made a purchase by phone or mail, and 12 million people have purchased items from a television offer. The value of direct marketing for sellers can be measured in terms of three types of responses: direct orders, lead generation, and traffic generation.

FOCUSING ON KEY TERMS

advertising p. 466
all-you-can-afford budgeting p. 477
channel of communication p. 464
communication p. 464
competitive parity budgeting p. 477
decoding p. 464
direct marketing p. 469
direct orders p. 482
encoding p. 464
feedback p. 466

field of experience p. 466
hierarchy of effects p. 476
integrated marketing communications (IMC) p. 464
lead generation p. 482
message p. 464
noise p. 466
objective and task budgeting p. 477
percentage of sales budgeting p. 476
personal selling p. 467

promotional mix p. 464
public relations p. 468
publicity p. 468
pull strategy p. 475
push strategy p. 474
receivers p. 464
response p. 466
sales promotion p. 469
source p. 464
traffic generation p. 482

APPLYING MARKETING KNOWLEDGE

1 After listening to a recent sales presentation, Mary Smith signed up for membership at the local health club. On arriving at the facility, she learned there was an additional fee for racquetball court rentals. "I don't remember that in the sales talk; I thought they said all facilities were included with the membership fee," complained Mary. Describe the problem in terms of the communication process.

2 Develop a matrix to compare the five elements of the promotional mix on three criteria—to *whom* you deliver the message, *what* you say, and *when* you say it.

3 Explain how the promotional tools used by an airline would differ if the target audience were (*a*) consumers who travel for pleasure and (*b*) corporate travel departments that select the airlines to be used by company employees.

4 Suppose you introduced a new consumer food product and invested heavily both in national advertising (pull strategy) and in training and motivating your field salesforce to sell the product to food stores (push strategy). What kinds of feedback would you receive from both the advertising and your salesforce? How could you increase both the quality and quantity of each?

5 Fisher-Price Company, long known as a manufacturer of children's toys, has introduced a line of clothing for children. Outline a promotional plan to get this product introduced in the marketplace.

6 Many insurance companies sell health insurance plans to companies. In these companies the employees pick the plan, but the set of offered plans is determined by the company. Recently Blue Cross–Blue Shield, a health insurance company, ran a television ad stating, "If your employer doesn't offer you Blue Cross–Blue Shield coverage, ask why." Explain the promotional strategy behind the advertisement.

7 Identify the sales promotion tools that might be useful for (*a*) Tastee Yogurt, a new brand introduction, (*b*) 3M self-sticking Post-it Notes, and (*c*) Wrigley's Spearmint Gum.

8 Design an integrated marketing communications program—using each of the five promotional elements—for Rhapsody, the online music service.

9 BMW recently introduced its first sport utility vehicle, the X5, to compete with other popular all-wheel-drive vehicles such as the Mercedes-Benz M-class and Jeep Grand Cherokee. Design a direct marketing program to generate (*a*) leads, (*b*) traffic in dealerships, and (*c*) direct orders.

10 Develop a privacy policy for database managers that provides a balance of consumer and seller perspectives. How would you encourage voluntary compliance with your policy? What methods of enforcement would you recommend?

building your marketing plan

To develop the promotion strategy for your marketing plan, follow the steps suggested in the planning phase of the promotion decision process described in Figure 18–6.

1 You should (*a*) identify the target audience, (*b*) specify the promotion objectives, (*c*) set the promotion budget, (*d*) select the right promotion tools, (*e*) design the promotion, and (*f*) schedule the promotion.

2 Also specify the pretesting and posttesting procedures needed in the implementation and control phases.

3 Finally, describe how each of your promotion tools are integrated to provide a consistent message.

video case 18   Las Vegas: Creating a Brand with IMC

"We made a decision collectively with the agency that we needed to go into the branding of Las Vegas," observes Rossi Ralenkotter, president and CEO of the Las Vegas Convention and Visitors Authority (LVCVA). The mission of LVCVA is to attract visitors to Las Vegas through its many promotional activities. Although Las Vegas has grown from its early days as a destination for southern California residents, branding provides an opportunity for additional growth. Now the LVCVA is undertaking the challenge of creating a campaign that utilizes all of its resources and delivers a consistent message. As Ralenkotter explained, "We need to have a fully integrated program."

A HISTORY OF LAS VEGAS

The first settlers to the area that is now Las Vegas arrived in 1855. The population grew and the city of Las Vegas was incorporated in 1911. To encourage tourism, gaming was legalized in 1931, and one of the first hotels, the Flamingo, opened in 1946. Other hotels soon followed, including the Sahara, the Sands, the New Frontier, the Royal Nevada, The Showboat, The Riviera, The Fremont, Binion's Horseshoe, and The Tropicana. Although gaming was the primary attraction, entertainment by the biggest stars of films and music like Elvis Presley, Frank Sinatra, Dean Martin, Abbott and Costello, Bing Crosby, and Carol Channing also became popular. By 1975 Nevada gaming revenues were $1 billion and growing.

Las Vegas entered a new era with the construction of large resort hotels. Each development became larger or more expensive than its predecessors, including the 3,000-room Mirage in 1989, the 5,000-room MGM Grand in 1993, the $1.7 billion Bellagio in 1998, and megaresort Wynn Las Vegas in 2005. The hotels developed elaborate casinos and competed for visitors with performances by entertainers. Wayne Newton, for example, eventually gave more than 25,000 Las Vegas performances and Sigfried and Roy gave 15,000. New forms of entertainment such as *Star Trek: The Experience* and *Cirque du Soleil* became popular. In an effort to become a place with more than gaming and live performances, Las Vegas built theme parks, roller coasters, and childrens' activities to position itself as a family-friendly destination. Generally, these marketing efforts were not successful and Las Vegas Convention and Visitors Authority decided to consider other approaches to attracting visitors.

In short order, the MGM Grand replaced its amusement park with night clubs, the Hard Rock Hotel began offering blackjack in its pools, and Treasure Island replaced its child-themed pirate show with a version targeted at adults. Dining experiences changed as "celebrity" chefs such as Emeril Lagasse, Charlie Palmer, and Wolfgang Puck opened sophisticated restaurants. Hotels added extravagant spas and designer shops and there is also the Guggenheim Hermitage Museum and a gallery of works from the Boston Museum of Fine Arts. Finally, traditional events such as automobile racing at the Las Vegas Motor Speedway, national events such as the NBA All-Star game, and relatively new events such as the Ultimate Fighting Championship became popular attractions. All of the activities proved to be incredibly popular. In fact, while gaming revenue reached $7 billion, shows, hotels, restaurants, clubs and shops generated another $23 billion!

THE LAS VEGAS CONVENTION AND VISITORS AUTHORITY

The Las Vegas Convention and Visitors Authority was created by the Nevada State Legislature to manage the cyclical nature of tourism. Officials noticed that the number of visitors to Las Vegas declined during weekdays, summer months, and holiday seasons. The marketing division of the LVCVA became responsible for increasing leisure travel visits, and convention and meeting attendance. The marketing division created three departments to be responsible for advertising, sports and sponsorships, and Internet marketing. The advertising department uses a variety of media to reach potential visitors. The sports and sponsorship department helps create the Las Vegas brand by communicating messages about local events to millions of participants and fans. The Internet marketing department is responsible for ensuring relevant and timely Web content, responding to website inquiries, and monitoring the performance of Web promotions. The marketing division serves as a liaison with the LVCVA's advertising and promotion agency. It also facilitates the correct and timely use of strategy and content in all promotional campaigns and branding efforts.

Ralenkotter asked advertising and promotion agency R&R Partners to identify a new campaign for Las Vegas. The agency had a philosophy of using marketing research to develop a deep understanding of customers, and of using innovative thinking to create effective solutions to marketing challenges. R&R Partners also believed that it was important to manage a consistent brand message across all audiences and all media. After their initial research, they initiated a discussion with the LVCVA to begin a shift from product advertising which emphasized specific features of the city and its hotels to a brand campaign that emphasized the emotions that visitors experience when they are in Las Vegas. Over time an idea emerged. "The idea 'What Happens Here, Stays Here' was two or three or four years in the making," explains Randy Snow, executive vice president and creative director at R&R Partners. He added, "We conducted a year-long

account planning exercise and discovered the emotional connection between Las Vegas and its customers." Ralenkotter agreed to the concept and authorized a $58 million, 20-month integrated marketing communications campaign.

THE LAS VEGAS IMC CAMPAIGN

The emotional element that the research had uncovered was the idea that people often feel free to do or see things in Las Vegas that they might not do or see anywhere else. R&R Partners continued to conduct research and many of the ideas for the campaign came from actual visitors. The agency was careful to include men and women, business and leisure travelers, and visitors from different parts of the United States. Additional findings from the research made it clear that the campaign would need to be fully integrated to include advertising, public relations, personal selling, and promotional efforts. First, the diversity of the visitors to Las Vegas meant that they used many different types of media in their travel decisions. Second, several of the segments that visited Las Vegas were "multitaskers" and used multiple sources of information at the same time. The agency also knew that an integrated marketing communication campaign would multiply the effectiveness of its budget.

Advertising

The initial "Vegas Stories" campaign ran television ads that told stories about enticing experiences a visitor might have in Las Vegas and concluded with "What Happens Here, Stays Here." Print ads with the same message also began running in magazines. The slogan became an instant hit, and soon became a pop-culture catchphrase. For example, flight attendants were heard welcoming airline travelers to Las Vegas and then saying "And remember folks, what happens here, stays here." Similarly, the tagline was used on Jay Leno's *Tonight Show*, newscasts, talk shows, and TV sitcoms. Billy Crystal even closed the Academy Awards by saying, "And remember. What happens at the Oscars, stays at the Oscars." By the end of the year the campaign was ranked as one of the top ten most likeable campaigns according to *USA Today*'s Ad Tracker.

Public Relations and Promotions

The public relations department was able to obtain coverage in newspapers and evening news programs when the NFL refused to run one of the new campaign ads during the Super Bowl. New television series programming such as *CSI* and *Las Vegas* became popular and added to the visibility of Las Vegas. Poker programs such as ESPN's *United States Poker Championship,* the Travel Channel's

World Poker Tour, and Fox Sports Net's *Poker Superstars Invitational Tournament* made the gaming experience easily accessible. R&R Partners also worked with *Time* magazine on an article that became a cover story.

Other promotional elements also contributed to the success of the campaign. Sweepstakes offered the chance to win special experiences such as New Year's Eve in Las Vegas, and the LVCVA also facilitated sports sponsorships, including many golf tournaments.

Online

Another element of the integrated campaign included Web offerings. The LVCVA created a tourism website (www.visitlasvegas.com) with information about hotels and activities, and links to special offers. The website also integrated the new campaign by providing interactive links such as "Be Anyone in Las Vegas." The humorous link allows visitors to create an identity that includes a name (e.g., Vinny) and a profession (e.g., Double Agent) and "everything you need to back up your story, including a brief history, a printable business card, a prerecorded 1-800 number, and a website." Another link allows potential visitors to send personalized video email messages to friends with the tagline, "What Happens Here, Stays Here." Banner ads and paid search engine advertising help generate more than 500,000 "hits" each month.

Personal Selling

In addition, a personal selling staff follows up on the awareness created by other elements of the campaign by calling on travel agents, corporate meeting planners, and trade show producers. Overall, each element of the campaign is designed to provide a message consistent with other elements.

FUTURE STRATEGY

How can the LVCVA and R&R Partners assess the success of their campaign? One important measure is the essence of the LVCVA mission—number of visitors. Other measures might include the revenue produced by visitors to Las Vegas, the amount of gaming revenue, the number of convention delegates, and the number of airline passengers arriving in Las Vegas. Table 1 shows information about each of these measures prior to the introduction of the campaign in 2003 (shown in black), and following the campaign (shown in pink). Each of the measures had a dramatic increase, suggesting that the campaign was a huge success!

So where does Ralenkotter go from here? A variation of the campaign will begin to focus on visitor stories that use Las Vegas experiences such as Broadway shows or extraordinary restaurants as an "alibi." Las Vegas is also likely to get bigger and better as new developments such as MGM Mirage's $7 billion Project CityCenter and Boyd Gaming's $4 billion Echelon Place are completed. Finally, Vegas is going global. American-run casinos such as the Mirage have announced plans to build casinos in China, and others are looking at Britain, Thailand, and even Singapore. The success of the campaign is likely to lead to other new ventures also. As Ralenkotter observes, "We are the talk of the travel industry!"

Questions

1 What information about consumers led the advertising agency to suggest a shift from product advertising to brand marketing? How are the two approaches different?

2 What characteristics of Las Vegas visitors suggested that an integrated marketing communications campaign would be necessary?

3 Which of the promotional elements described in Figure 18-2 were used by the Las Vegas Convention and Visitors Authority in the "What Happens Here, Stays Here" campaign? What measures indicate that the campaign was a success?

4 What are several new strategies Las Vegas might pursue as it continues its brand marketing activities? Will the program elements that worked in the U.S. also work in China and other countries?

	Number of Visitors	Revenue from Visitors	Gaming Revenue from Visitors	Number of Convention Delegates	Number of Airline Passengers
TABLE 1: LAS VEGAS VISITOR STATISTICS					
2000	35,859,691	31,462,337,364	7,671,252,000	3,853,363	36,865,866
2001	35,017,317	31,907,491,818	7,636,547,000	5,014,240	35,179,960
2002	35,071,505	31,613,937,641	7,630,562,000	5,105,450	35,009,011
2003	35,540,126	32,777,906,318	7,830,856,000	5,657,796	36,265,932
2004	37,388,781	33,724,467,453	8,711,426,000	5,724,864	41,441,531
2005	38,566,717	36,733,452,851	9,717,322,000	6,166,194	44,267,370
2006	38,914,889	39,419,205,580	10,643,206,000	6,307,961	46,193,329

19

Advertising, Sales Promotion, and Public Relations

LEARNING OBJECTIVES

After reading this chapter you should be able to:

LO1 Explain the differences between product advertising and institutional advertising and the variations within each type.

LO2 Describe the steps used to develop, execute, and evaluate an advertising program.

LO3 Explain the advantages and disadvantages of alternative advertising media.

LO4 Discuss the strengths and weaknesses of consumer-oriented and trade-oriented sales promotions.

LO5 Recognize public relations as an important form of communication.

ADVERTISERS HAVE ANOTHER LIFE ON SECOND LIFE!

Do you have a second life online? Do you have a Web ID? An avatar? If you do, you are one of many, and advertisers are eager to meet you in your virtual world.

The world of advertising has changed dramatically in just the past few years. First, there are many new forms of media, such as social networking sites, blogs, and podcasts, to compete with traditional media. Some experts have suggested that MySpace and YouTube may have been the most influential new media in decades. Second, consumers have changed their behavior to use more than one source of advertising at the same time. Gregg Hanno, a former magazine publisher, observed that watching TV, while listening to music, flipping through a magazine, and surfing the Internet is the new "normal." Finally, technology, such as digital video recorders and TiVo, that allows consumers to skip or "zap" commercials has put consumers in control.

So what is an advertiser to do? One answer has been to create a presence in a virtual world. Second Life is a game-like virtual world where users live as online versions of themselves while interacting with real-life brands. Wells Fargo was one of the first to use this media alternative when it launched a virtual environment called Stagecoach Island in Second Life to attract young, tech-savvy customers and teach them about banking. Since then many other companies such as Coca-Cola, Coldwell Banker, Adidas, and Reebok have created islands and stores on Second Life.

As advertisers and consumers have become more familiar with virtual worlds, many new approaches are being developed. Coca-Cola, for example, is also using a MySpace social-networking page, del.icio.us keyword tagging, a Flickr photo page, and a YouTube video clip. MTV was on Second Life but then decided to create its own online environments to accompany its TV series such as *Pimp My Ride.* Each site weaves the TV show story line into the digital world. Disney created its own Virtual Magic Kingdom that replicates Disney's amusement parks online. All of the options represent varying levels of security, customization, and control for the advertisers.

What's next? One possibility is adding more functionality to the interactivity of current sites. At Zwinky.com, for example, rapper 50 Cent created a fully functioning avatar that fans can customize and use as their own. Similarly, musician Avril Lavigne partnered with Stardoll, a site that creates virtual likenesses of celebrities, just before the release of a new album. Another site, Doppelganger, now hosts the Pussycat Dolls Music Lounge. Advertisers are also likely to try to improve traditional advertising. New research suggests that TiVo users are less likely to fast-forward through ads if they are very engaging and entertaining or if they ask for a direct response. To accommodate the fast pace and short attention of most consumers today, many advertisers are simply moving to shorter ads.[1]

Virtual advertising, and the use of new media, are just a few of the many exciting changes taking place in the field of advertising today. They also illustrate the importance of advertising as one of the five promotional mix elements in marketing communications programs. This chapter describes three of the promotional mix elements—advertising, sales promotion, and public relations. Direct marketing was covered in Chapter 18, and personal selling is covered in Chapter 20.

TYPES OF ADVERTISEMENTS

Chapter 18 described **advertising** as any paid form of nonpersonal communication about an organization, a good, a service, or an idea by an identified sponsor. As you look through any magazine, watch television, listen to the radio, or browse the Internet, the variety of advertisements you see or hear may give you the impression that they have few similarities. Advertisements are prepared for different purposes, but they basically consist of two types: product advertisements and institutional advertisements.

Product Advertisements

LO1

Focused on selling a good or service, **product advertisements** take three forms: (1) pioneering (or informational), (2) competitive (or persuasive), and (3) reminder. Look at the ads for Verizon, Sony, and M&Ms to determine the type and objective of each ad.

Used in the introductory stage of the product life cycle, *pioneering* advertisements tell people what a product is, what it can do, and where it can be found. The key objective of a pioneering advertisement (such as the ad for Verizon's new Blackberry World Edition) is to inform the target market. Informative ads have been found to be interesting, convincing, and effective.[2]

Advertising that promotes a specific brand's features and benefits is *competitive*. The objective of these messages is to persuade the target market to select the firm's brand rather than that of a competitor. An increasingly common form of competitive

Advertisements serve varying purposes. Which ad would be considered a (1) pioneering, (2) competitive, and (3) reminder ad?

advertising is *comparative* advertising, which shows one brand's strengths relative to those of competitors.[3] The Sony ad, for example, highlights the competitive advantage of the Sony camera over its primary competitors Canon and Nikon. Studies indicate that comparative ads attract more attention and increase the perceived quality of the advertiser's brand.[4] Firms that use comparative advertising need market research to provide legal support for their claims.[5]

Reminder advertising is used to reinforce previous knowledge of a product. The M&Ms ad shown reminds consumers about a special event, in this case, Valentine's Day. Reminder advertising is good for products that have achieved a well-recognized position and are in the mature phase of their product life cycle. Another type of reminder ad, *reinforcement,* is used to assure current users they made the right choice. One example: "Aren't you glad you use Dial. Don't you wish everybody did?"

Institutional Advertisements

The objective of **institutional advertisements** is to build goodwill or an image for an organization rather than promote a specific good or service. Institutional advertising has been used by companies such as Texaco, Pfizer, and IBM to build confidence in the company name.[6] Often this form of advertising is used to support the public relations plan or counter adverse publicity. Four alternative forms of institutional advertisements are often used:

1. *Advocacy* advertisements state the position of a company on an issue. Lorillard Tobacco Company places ads discouraging teenagers from smoking. Another form of advocacy advertisement is used when organizations make a request related to a particular action or behavior, such as a request by American Red Cross for blood donations.
2. *Pioneering institutional* advertisements, like the pioneering ads for products discussed earlier, are used for announcements about what a company is, what it can do, or where it is located. Recent Bayer ads, stating "We cure more headaches than you think," are intended to inform consumers that the company produces many products in addition to aspirin. When Travelers decided to begin using the umbrella logo again, and changed its stock symbol and official name, it ran pioneering institutional ads to inform consumers.

Lorillard uses an advocacy ad to communicate its position on tobacco use, and Travelers uses a pioneering ad to inform readers about its logo, stock symbol, and name.

A competitive institutional ad by dairy farmers tries to increase demand for milk, and a reminder ad by the U.S. Army tries to keep the attention of the target market.

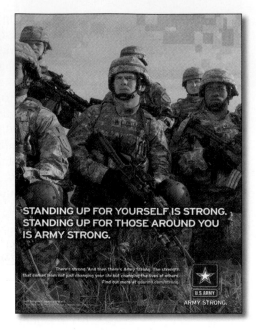

3. *Competitive institutional* advertisements promote the advantages of one product class over another and are used in markets where different product classes compete for the same buyers. America's milk processors and dairy farmers use their "Got Milk?" campaign to increase demand for milk as it competes against other beverages.

4. *Reminder institutional* advertisements, like the product form, simply bring the company's name to the attention of the target market again. The Army branch of the U.S. military sponsors a campaign to remind potential recruits of the opportunities in the Army.

---

learning review

1. What is the difference between pioneering and competitive ads?

2. What is the purpose of an institutional advertisement?

DEVELOPING THE ADVERTISING PROGRAM

LO2

The promotion decision process described in Chapter 18 can be applied to each of the promotional elements. Advertising, for example, can be managed by following the three steps (developing, executing, and evaluating) of the process.

Identifying the Target Audience

To develop an effective advertising program advertisers must identify the target audience. All aspects of an advertising program are likely to be influenced by the characteristics of the prospective consumer. Understanding the lifestyles, attitudes, and demographics of the target market is essential. When Under Armour began advertising to women, the ads did not have the same ending as the men's ads: "We must protect this house!" Women said they wanted similar ads so Under Armour introduced a new "hard-core athlete" campaign for women.[7] Similarly, the placement of ads depends on the audience. When HUMMER, the biggest and most expensive sport utility vehicle in the market, began its $3 million campaign targeted at "rugged individualists" with incomes above $200,000, it selected *Wired, Spin, Red Herring, BusinessWeek, Skiing,* and *Cigar Aficionado* to carry the ads.[8] Even scheduling can depend on the audience. Claritin, a popular allergy medication, schedules its use of brochures, in-store displays, coupons, and advertising to correspond to the allergy season, which varies by geographic region.[9] To eliminate possible bias that might result from subjective judgments about some population segments, the Federal Communications Commission suggests that advertising program decisions be based on market research about the target audience.[10]

Specifying Advertising Objectives

The guidelines for setting promotion objectives described in Chapter 18 also apply to setting advertising objectives. This step helps advertisers with other choices in the promotion decision process such as selecting media and evaluating a campaign. Advertising with an objective of creating awareness, for example, would be better matched with a magazine than a directory such as the Yellow Pages.[11] The Magazine Publishers of America believe objectives are so important that they offer a $100,000 prize each year to the campaign that best meets its objectives. The last winner, MINI USA, won with its "Covert" campaign, which increased online traffic 75 percent and surpassed goals by 200 percent.[12] Similarly, the Advertising Research Foundation is collecting information about the effectiveness of advertising, particularly new forms such as online advertising.[13] Experts believe that factors such as product category, brand, and consumer involvement in the purchase decision may change the importance—and, possibly, the sequence—of the stages of the hierarchy of effects. Snickers, for example, knew that its consumers were unlikely to engage in elaborate information processing when it designed a recent campaign. The result was ads with simple humorous messages rather than extensive factual information.[14]

Setting the Advertising Budget

During the 1990 Super Bowl, it cost companies $700,000 to place a 30-second ad. By 2007, the cost of placing a 30-second ad during Super Bowl XLI was $2.6 million (see Figure 19–1 on the next page). The reason for the escalating cost is the growing number of viewers: 45.9 million homes and 90.7 million people tune in. In addition, the audience is attractive to advertisers because research indicates that it is equally split between men and women and that before the game 54 percent of survey respondents were "looking forward" to watching the 59 spots. The ads are effective too: Movies promoted on the Super Bowl achieve 40 percent more revenue than movies not promoted on the Super Bowl. As a result, the Super Bowl attracts relatively new advertisers such as Van Heusen and Garmin and regular advertisers such as Anheuser-Busch and Chevrolet. Which ads were rated the highest? Diamond Emerald Nuts, Anheuser-Busch, Chevrolet, and Blockbuster.[15] To see your favorite Super Bowl ad again, read the Going Online box on the next page.

Do you remember this Sierra Mist ad from the Super Bowl?

While not all advertising options are as expensive as the Super Bowl, most alternatives still represent substantial financial commitments and require a formal budgeting process. In the automobile industry, for example, Chrysler and Honda have market shares of approximately 14.4 percent and 9.1 percent, and advertising and promotion budgets of $1.425 billion and $878 million, respectively. Using a competitive parity budgeting approach each company spends between $96 million and $98 million for each percent of market share. Using an objective and task approach, Coca-Cola allocated $50 million to introduce C2, its new 70-calorie, low-carb soft drink.[16]

If you missed some of the ads during the last Super Bowl, or if you liked some of them so much you want to see them again, you can review the ads at www.superbowl-ads.com. All ads for the past 10 Super Bowls and classics like the "1984" Apple Computer ad are available to view.

Which ads are your favorites? Compare the ads from different years. Do you notice any changes?

Designing the Advertisement

An advertising message usually focuses on the key benefits of the product that are important to a prospective buyer in making trial and adoption decisions. The message depends on the general form or appeal used in the ad and the actual words included in the ad.

Message Content   Most advertising messages are made up of both informational and persuasional elements. These two elements, in fact, are so intertwined that it is sometimes difficult to tell them apart. For example, basic information contained in many ads such as the product name, benefits, features, and price are presented in a way that tries to attract attention and encourage purchase. On the other hand, even

FIGURE 19–1

The Super Bowl delivers a huge audience, if you can afford the cost of placing an ad.

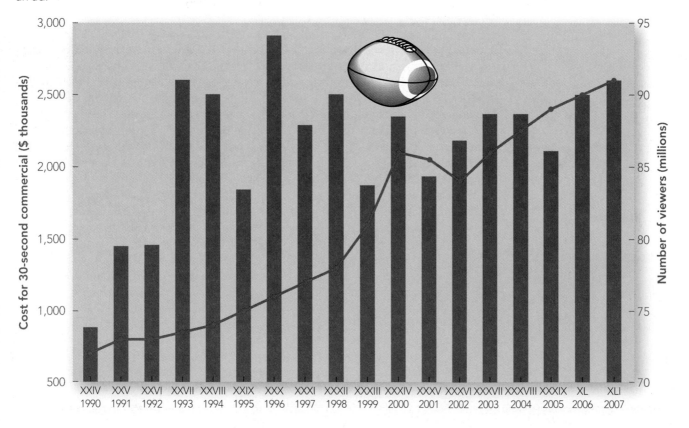

the most persuasive advertisements have to contain at least some basic information to be successful.

Information and persuasive content can be combined in the form of an appeal to provide a basic reason for the consumer to act. Although the marketer can use many different types of appeals, common advertising appeals include fear appeals,[17] sex appeals, and humorous appeals.

Fear appeals suggest to the consumer that he or she can avoid some negative experience through the purchase and use of a product or service, a change in behavior, or a reduction in the use of a product. Examples with which you may be familiar include: fire or smoke detector ads that depict a home burning; political candidate endorsements that warn against the rise of other, unpopular ideologies; or social cause ads warning of the serious consequences of drug and alcohol use or AIDS. Insurance companies often try to show the negative effects on the relatives of those who die prematurely without carrying enough life or mortgage insurance. Food producers encourage the purchase of low-carb, low-fat, and high-fiber products as a means of reducing weight, cholesterol levels, and the possibility of a heart attack.[18] The Partnership for a Drug-Free America recently ran an ad with a fear appeal: The headline reads "Sniffing can harm your nervous system." When using fear appeals, the advertiser must be sure that the appeal is strong enough get the audience's attention and concern but not so strong that it will lead them to tune out the message. In fact, recent research on antismoking ads indicates that stressing the severity of long-term health risks may actually enhance smoking's allure among youth.[19]

In contrast, *sex appeals* suggest to the audience that the product will increase the attractiveness of the user. Sex appeals can be found in almost any product category, from automobiles to toothpaste. The contemporary women's clothing store Bebe, for example, designs its advertising to "attract customers who are intrigued by the playfully sensual and evocative imagery of the Bebe lifestyle." Unfortunately, many commercials that use sex appeals are only successful at gaining the attention of the audience; they have little impact on how consumers think, feel, or act. Some advertising experts even argue that such appeals get in the way of successful communication by distracting the audience from the purpose of the ad.[20]

Humorous appeals imply either directly or subtly that the product is more fun or exciting than competitors' offerings. As with fear and sex appeals, the use of humor is widespread in advertising and can be found in many product categories. You may have smiled at the popular Geico "So easy a caveman can do it" campaign, which

These ads are examples of fear appeal, sex appeal, and humor appeal, respectively.

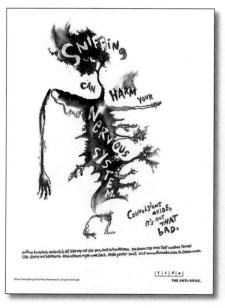

was designed to generate traffic to Geico's website. The ads have been so popular that people started asking Geico where the cavemen lived, what they liked to eat, and what their hobbies were. The consumer interest led Geico to introduce a website, www. cavemanscrib.com, where millions of visitors have learned more about the caveman and Geico.[21] You may have a favorite humorous ad character, such as the Energizer battery bunny, the AFLAC duck, or the Geico gecko. Unfortunately for the advertiser, humor tends to wear out quickly, eventually boring the consumer. Another problem with humorous appeals is that their effectiveness may vary across cultures if used in a global campaign.[22]

Creating the Actual Message   Advertising agency Berlin Cameron was recently designated as *Advertising Age* magazine's U.S. Agency of the Year for its "rare combination of new-business savvy, strategic insight, creative prowess, and big personality." Examples of the agency's approach include the "Treat yourself well. Everyday." campaign for Dasani bottled water, the "Imagine" campaign for Samsung consumer electronics and the "Real" campaign for Coca-Cola.[23]

Berlin Cameron and other agencies use many forms of advertising to create their messages. A very popular form of advertising today is the use of a celebrity spokesperson. Berlin Cameron's use of well-known personalities such as Courteney Cox and David Arquette in a Coca-Cola ad is an example. Many companies use athletes, movie and television stars, musicians, and other celebrities to talk to consumers through their ads. Advertisers who use a celebrity spokesperson believe that the ads are more likely to influence sales. The popular "Got Milk?" campaign reversed a steady decline in milk consumption with celebrities such as actress Angelina Jolie, author Dr. Phil McGraw, MTV star Carson Daly, supermodel Gisele Bundchen, Ronald McDonald, and many others. The two top celebrity spokespersons in recent years have been Tiger Woods, who appears in American Express, Nike, Titleist, and Buick ads, and Michael Jordan, who appears in Nike, Hanes, Rayovac, Gatorade, and Ballpark hotdog ads. Hershey Foods signed Jessica Simpson to endorse its new product Ice Breakers Liquid Ice. Thomas Hernquist, Hershey's chief marketing officer, says Jessica was selected because she "is energetic, fun, and sociable, so she's a perfect match for our new product."

The "Treat yourself well. Everyday." campaign for Dasani is one example of creative advertising that helped agency Berlin Cameron win the Agency of the Year award.

Samsung uses a strong visual component to create a message.

imagine a TV that fills the room with drama.

SAMSUNG

One potential shortcoming of this form of advertising is that the spokesperson's image may change to be inconsistent with the image of the company or brand. NBA star Kobe Bryant's court appearances caused many companies to probe the backgrounds of potential endorsers and to consider retired athletes and legacy (deceased) athletes who are low risk and still have lasting appeal in the marketplace.[24]

Another issue involved in creating the message is the complex process of translating the copywriter's ideas into an actual advertisement. Designing quality artwork, layout, and production for the advertisements is costly and time consuming. High-quality TV commercials typically cost about $335,000 to produce a 30-second ad, a task done by about 2,000 small commercial production companies across the United States. One reason for the high costs is that as companies have developed global campaigns, the need to shoot commercials in exotic locations has increased. Audi recently filmed commercials in Germany, Australia, and Morocco. Actors are expensive also. The Screen Actors Guild reports that an actor in a typical network TV car ad would earn between $12,000 and $15,000.[25]

learning review

3. What other decisions can advertising objectives influence?
4. What is a potential shortcoming of using a celebrity spokesperson?

Selecting the Right Media

Every advertiser must decide where to place its advertisements. The alternatives are the *advertising media,* the means by which the message is communicated to the target audience. Newspapers, magazines, radio, and TV are examples of advertising media. This decision on media selection is related to the target audience, type of product, nature of the message, campaign objectives, available budget, and the costs of the alternative media. Figure 19–2 on the next page shows the distribution of the $285 billion spent on advertising among the many media alternatives.[26]

FIGURE 19–2

Television, direct mail, and newspapers account for more than 60 percent of all advertising expenditures (in millions).

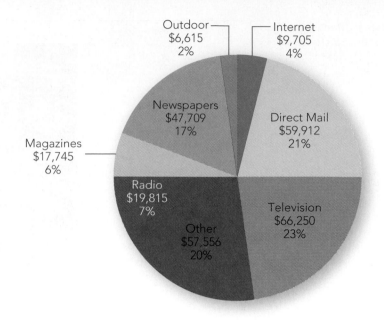

Choosing a Medium and a Vehicle within That Medium In deciding where to place advertisements, a company has several media to choose from and a number of alternatives, or vehicles, within each medium. Often advertisers use a mix of media forms and vehicles to maximize the exposure of the message to the target audience while at the same time minimizing costs. These two conflicting goals of (1) maximizing exposure and (2) minimizing costs are of central importance to media planning.

Basic Terms Media buyers speak a language of their own, so every advertiser involved in selecting the right media for their campaigns must be familiar with some common terms used in the advertising industry.

Because advertisers try to maximize the number of individuals in the target market exposed to the message, they must be concerned with reach. **Reach** is the number of different people or households exposed to an advertisement. The exact definition of reach sometimes varies among alternative media. Newspapers often use reach to describe their total circulation or the number of different households that buy the paper. Television and radio stations, in contrast, describe their reach using the term **rating**—the percentage of households in a market that are tuned to a particular TV show or radio station. In general, advertisers try to maximize reach in their target market at the lowest cost.

Although reach is important, advertisers are also interested in exposing their target audience to a message more than once. This is because consumers often do not pay close attention to advertising messages, some of which contain large amounts of relatively complex information. When advertisers want to reach the same audience more than once, they are concerned with **frequency**, the average number of times a person in the target audience is exposed to a message or advertisement. Like reach, greater frequency is generally viewed as desirable.[27] Studies indicate that with repeated exposure to advertisements consumers respond more favorably to brand extensions.[28]

When reach (expressed as a percentage of the total market) is multiplied by frequency, an advertiser will obtain a commonly used reference number called **gross rating points** (GRPs). To obtain the appropriate number of GRPs to achieve an advertising campaign's objectives, the media planner must balance reach and frequency. The balance will also be influenced by cost. **Cost per thousand** (CPM) refers to the cost of reaching 1,000 individuals or households with the advertising message in

Using Marketing Dashboards
What Is the Best Way to Reach 1,000 Customers?

Marketing managers must choose from many advertising options as they design a campaign to reach potential customers. Because there are so many media alternatives (television, radio, magazines, etc.) and multiple options within each of the media, it is important to monitor the efficiency of advertising expenditures on your marketing dashboard.

Your Challenge As the marketing manager for a company about to introduce a new soft drink into the U.S. market, you are preparing a presentation in which you must make recommendations for the advertising campaign. You have observed that competitors use magazine ads, newspaper ads, and even Super Bowl ads! To compare the cost of some of the alternatives you decide to use one of the most common measures in advertising: cost per thousand impressions (CPM). The CPM is calculated as follows:

Cost per thousand impressions =
    Advertising cost ($)/Impressions generated (in 1000s)

Your challenge is to determine the most efficient use of your advertising budget.

Your Findings Your research department helps you collect cost and audience size information for three options: full-page color ads in *Sports Illustrated* magazine and *USA Today* newspaper, and a 30-second television ad during the Super

Bowl. With this information you are able to calculate the cost per thousand impressions for each alternative.

Media Alternative	Cost of Ad	Audience Size	Cost per Thousand Impressions
USA Today (newspaper)	$411,500	2,524,965	$163
Sports Illustrated (magazine)	$302,680	3,150,000	$96
Super Bowl (television)	$2,600,000	91,000,000	$29

Your Action Based on the calculations for these options you see that there is a large variation in the cost of reaching 1,000 potential customers (CPM) and also in the absolute cost of the advertising. Although advertising on the Super Bowl has the lowest CPM, $29 for each 1,000 impressions, it also has the largest absolute cost! Your next step will be to consider other factors such as your total available budget, the profiles of the audiences each alternative reaches, and whether the type of message you want to deliver is better communicated in print or on television.

---

a given medium (*M* is the Roman numeral for 1,000). See the accompanying Using Marketing Dashboards box for an example of the use of CPM in media selection.

Different Media Alternatives

Figure 19–3 on the next page summarizes the advantages and disadvantages of the major advertising media, which are described in more detail below. Direct mail was discussed in Chapter 18.

LO3

It's not a sport, it's a passion.

Television Television is a valuable medium because it communicates with sight, sound, and motion. Print advertisements alone could never give you the sense of a sports car accelerating from a stop or cornering at high speed. In addition, network television is the only medium that can reach 95 percent of the homes in the United States.[29] *Out-of-home* TV also reaches millions of viewers in bars, hotels, offices, and college campuses each week.[30]

Television's major disadvantage is cost: The price of a prime-time, 30-second ad run on *Grey's Anatomy* is $419,000 and the average price for all prime-time programs is $127,990.[31] Because of these high charges, many advertisers choose less expensive "spot" ads, which run between programs in 10-, 15-, 30-, or 60-second lengths. Shorter ads reduce costs but severely restrict the amount of information and emotion that can be conveyed. Research indicates, however, that two different versions of a 15-second commercial, run back-to-back, will increase recall over long intervals.[32]

MEDIUM	ADVANTAGES	DISADVANTAGES
Television	Reaches extremely large audience; uses picture, print, sound, and motion for effect; can target specific audiences	High cost to prepare and run ads; short exposure time and perishable message; difficult to convey complex information
Radio	Low cost; can target specific local audiences; ads can be placed quickly; can use sound, humor, and intimacy effectively	No visual element; short exposure time and perishable message; difficult to convey complex information
Magazines	Can target specific audiences; high-quality color; long life of ad; ads can be clipped and saved; can convey complex information	Long time needed to place ad; relatively high cost; competes for attention with other magazine features
Newspapers	Excellent coverage of local markets; ads can be placed and changed quickly; ads can be saved; quick consumer response; low cost	Ads compete for attention with other newspaper features; short life span; poor color
Yellow Pages	Excellent coverage of geographic segments; long use period; available 24 hours/365 days	Proliferation of competitive directories in many markets; difficult to keep up-to-date
Internet	Video and audio capabilities; animation can capture attention; ads can be interactive and link to advertiser	Animation and interactivity require large files and more time to load; effectiveness is still uncertain
Outdoor	Low cost; local market focus; high visibility; opportunity for repeat exposures	Message must be short and simple; low selectivity of audience; criticized as a traffic hazard
Direct mail	High selectivity of audience; can contain complex information and personalized messages; high-quality graphics	High cost per contact; poor image (junk mail)

FIGURE 19–3

Advertisers must consider the advantages and disadvantages of the many media alternatives.

Another problem with television advertising is the likelihood of *wasted coverage*—having people outside the market for the product see the advertisement. The cost and wasted coverage problems of TV advertising can be reduced through the specialized cable and direct broadcast (satellite) channels. Advertising time is often less expensive on cable and direct broadcast channels than on the major networks. There are currently about 150 options—such as ESPN, MTV, Lifetime, Oxygen, the Speed Channel, the History Channel, the Science Channel, and the Food Network—that reach very narrowly defined audiences. Other forms of television are changing television advertising also. Pay-per-view and downloadable movie services and digital video recorders (DVRs), for example, offer the potential of commercial-free viewing. Many cable and satellite TV services now offer boxes with built-in DVRs and remotes with "30-second skip" buttons for ad-zapping.

Another popular form of television advertising is the infomercial. **Infomercials** are program-length (30-minute) advertisements that take an educational approach to communication with potential customers. Today, more than 90 percent of all TV stations air infomercials, and more than 25 percent of all consumers have purchased a product as a result of seeing an infomercial. Volvo, Club Med, General Motors,

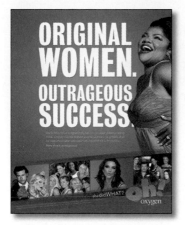

Oxygen is one of many specialized channels available to advertisers.

Bank of America, Mattel, Revlon, Texaco, and many other companies have used infomercials as a means of providing information that is relevant, useful, and entertaining to prospective customers. TiVo, the DVR manufacturer, for example, is using infomercials to show "how the DVR works, with vignettes on how it adds value to the TV-viewing experience."[33]

Radio There are seven times as many radio stations as television stations in the United States. The major advantage of radio is that it is a segmented medium. There are the Farm Radio Network, the Physicians' Network, all-talk shows, and hard rock stations, all listened to by different market segments. The average college student is a surprisingly heavy radio listener and spends more time during the day listening to radio than watching network television—2.2 hours versus 1.6 hours. Thus, advertisers with college students as their target market must consider radio.

The disadvantage of radio is that it has limited use for products that must be seen. Another problem is the ease with which consumers can tune out a commercial by switching stations. A new form of radio available through satellite services offers up to 200 digital-quality coast-to-coast radio channels to consumers for a monthly subscription fee. Sirius Satellite Radio and XM Satellite Radio offer commercial-free channels and channels with only about 6 minutes of advertising per hour compared with 15 to 20 minutes heard on "free" channels.[34] Radio is also a medium that competes for people's attention as they do other activities such as driving, working, or relaxing. Peak radio listening time is during the drive times (6 to 10 a.m. and 4 to 7 p.m.).

Magazines Magazines have become a very specialized medium, primarily because there are currently more than 19,419 magazines. New magazines are introduced each year, such as *Cookie,* a lifestyle-parenting magazine targeted at modern mothers; *All You,* a general topics magazine sold only through Wal-Mart; and *American Thunder,* a magazine about NASCAR racing for men.

Magazines such as *CosmoGirl* appeal to narrowly defined segments.

The marketing advantage of this medium is the great number of special-interest publications that appeal to narrowly defined segments. Runners read *Runner's World,* sailors buy *Yachting,* gardeners subscribe to *Garden Design,* and teenagers peruse *CosmoGirl.* More than 466 publications focus on computers and technology, 600 are dedicated to travel, and 361 magazine titles are related to music.[35] Each magazine's readers often represent a unique profile. Take the *Rolling Stone* reader, who tends to listen to music more than most people—so Sony knows an ad for its MP3 Walkman in *Rolling Stone* is reaching the desired target audience. In addition to the distinct audience profiles of magazines, good color production is an advantage that allows magazines to create strong images.[36]

The cost of advertising in national magazines is a disadvantage, but many national publications publish regional and even metro editions, which reduces the absolute cost and wasted coverage. *Time* publishes well over 400 different editions, including Latin American, Canadian, Asian, South Pacific, European, and U.S. editions. The U.S. editions include national, demographic, regional, state, and city options. In addition to cost, another limitation to magazines is their infrequency. At best, magazines are printed on a weekly basis, with many specialized publications appearing only monthly or less often. Although specialization can be an advantage of this medium, consumer interests can be difficult to translate into a magazine theme—a fact made clear by the hundreds of magazine failures during the past decade. *Jane, ElleGirl, Teen People, Virtual City, Business 2.0, Top Model, Life,* and *Esquire Sportsman,* for example, all failed to attract and keep a substantial number of readers or advertisers.[37] Which magazine has the highest circulation? It's *Parade* magazine with 32.7 million readers.

Newspapers Newspapers are an important local medium with excellent reach potential. Daily publication allows advertisements to focus on specific current events, such as a 24-hour sale. Local retailers often use newspapers as their sole advertising medium. Newspapers are rarely saved by the purchaser, however, so companies are generally limited to ads that call for an immediate customer response (although customers can clip and save ads they select). Companies also cannot depend on newspapers for color reproduction as good as that in most magazines.

National advertising campaigns rarely include this medium except in conjunction with local distributors of their products. In these instances, both parties often share the advertising costs using a cooperative advertising program, which is described later in this chapter. Another exception is the use of newspapers such as *The Wall Street Journal* and *USA Today*, each of which have national distribution of more than 2 million readers.

Print ads help attract readers to *The Wall Street Journal*.

www.wsj.com

Three trends are influencing newspapers today. The first is the dramatic increase in their cost of production and distribution. As printing and paper costs have increased, newspapers in cities such as Seattle and Denver have attempted to cut costs by merging their printing operations with another newspaper under a legal arrangement called a joint operating agreement (JOA). In cities such as Phoenix and Houston, population growth and suburban sprawl have increased the cost of distribution, requiring the newspapers to print outlying editions earlier, run multiple printing facilities, and use digital displays on the delivery vehicles to help control costs. The second trend is the growth in online newspapers. More than 60 newspapers, including the *Chicago Tribune, New York Times, Dallas Morning News, San Jose Mercury News,* and *Washington Post,* are online, and many others are expected. Finally, in many large cities free tabloid newspapers such as Boston's *Metro* and New York's *am NewYork* are targeting commuters and creating new competition for traditional paid-for newspapers.[38]

Yellow Pages Yellow pages represent an advertising media alternative comparable to radio and magazines in terms of expenditures—about $14 billion in the United States and $25 billion globally. According to the Yellow Pages Integrated Media Association, consumers turn to print yellow pages more than 15 billion times annually and online

Yellow Pages have many advantages including a long life span.

yellow pages an additional 1.6 billion times per year. One reason for this high level of use is that the 6,500 yellow pages directories reach almost all households with telephones. Yellow pages are a directional medium because they help consumers know where purchases can be made after other media have created awareness and demand.

The yellow pages have several other advantages. First, they are available 24 hours each day and 365 days each year. In addition, yellow pages have a long life span—directories are typically published once each year and provide advertisers with many advertisement size options. A disadvantage of yellow pages advertising is the proliferation of directories. In fact, many major cities are now covered by six or more directories, including directories for specific neighborhoods and ethnic groups. Another disadvantage is the lack of timeliness, because yellow pages can only be updated with new information once each year. Yellow pages are typically used for local advertising—85 percent of all yellow pages expenditures are local—because of the difficulty of coordinating a nationwide campaign in yellow pages directories.[39]

Internet The Internet represents a relatively new medium for advertisers although it has already attracted a wide variety of industries. Online advertising is similar to print advertising in that it offers a visual message. It has additional advantages, however, because it can also use the audio and video capabilities of the Internet. Sound and movement may simply attract more attention from viewers, or they may provide an element of entertainment to the message. Online advertising also has the unique feature of being interactive. Called *rich media,* these interactive ads have drop-down menus, built-in games, or search engines to engage viewers.[40] Although online advertising is relatively small compared to other traditional media, it offers an opportunity to reach younger consumers who have developed a preference for online communication.[41]

There are a variety of online advertising options. The most common—banner ads—represent approximately 50 percent of online ad expenditures, although their effectiveness has declined to a current click-through rate of 0.3 percent. One of the fastest-growing forms of Internet advertising is called search marketing. About 80 percent of all Internet traffic begins at a search engine such as Google or Yahoo! (see Figure 19–4). *Advertising Age* estimates that consumers conduct 9.8 billion searches each year. Now search engine agencies help firms add tags, wikis, and RSS to the content of a site to increase search rankings. Firms such as DoubleClick provide assessment of the effectiveness of a website.[42] Other forms of online advertising include skyscrapers, pop-ups, interstitials, and minisites that use streaming video and audio and are becoming similar to television advertising. Many advertisers are also adding entertainment elements.

FIGURE 19–4

Google and Yahoo! have the largest shares of Internet searches and offer opportunities for online advertising.

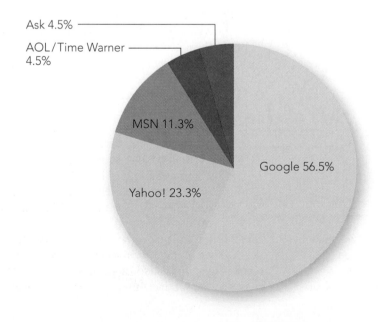

Ask 4.5%
AOL/Time Warner 4.5%
MSN 11.3%
Google 56.5%
Yahoo! 23.3%

Who Is Responsible for Click Fraud?

Spending on Internet advertising is expected to reach $29 billion in 2010 as many advertisers shift their budgets from print and TV to the Internet. For most advertisers one advantage of online advertising is that they only pay when someone clicks on their ad. Unfortunately, the growth of the medium has led to "click fraud," which is the deceptive clicking of ads solely to increase the amount advertisers must pay. There are several forms of click fraud. One method is the result of Paid-to-Read (PTR) websites that recruit and pay members to simply click on ads. Another method is the result of "clickbots," which are software programs that produce automatic clicks on ads. While the activity is difficult to detect and stop, experts estimate that up to 15% of clicks may be the result of fraud, and may be costing advertisers as much as $500 million each year!

Two of the largest portals for Internet advertising are Google and Yahoo! Both firms try to filter out illegitimate clicks although some advertisers claim that they are still being charged for PTR

and clickbot traffic. Although the laws that may govern click fraud are not very clear, Google and Yahoo! have each settled class action lawsuits and agreed to provide rebates or credits to advertisers who were charged for fraudulent clicks.

Investigations of the online advertising industry have discovered a related form of click fraud which occurs when legitimate website visitors click on ads without any intention of looking at the site. As one consumer explains, "I always try and remember to click on the ad banners once in a while to try and keep the sites free." Stephen Dubner calls this "webtipping"!

As the Internet advertising industry grows it will become increasingly important to resolve the issue of click fraud. Consumers, advertisers, websites that carry paid advertising, and the large web portals are all involved in a complicated technical, legal, and social situation. Who do you think is responsible for click fraud? Who should lead the way in the effort to find a solution?

DoubleClick's Dart Search service can provide an assessment of the effectiveness of a website.

One disadvantage of online advertising is that because the medium is relatively new, technical and administrative standards for the various formats are still evolving. This situation makes it difficult for advertisers to run national online campaigns across multiple sites. The Interactive Advertising Bureau provides some guidance for online advertising standards and makes recommendations for new formats. Another disadvantage to online advertising is the difficulty of measuring impact. Online advertising lags behind radio, TV, and print in offering advertisers proof of effectiveness. To address this issue several companies are testing methods of tracking where viewers go on their computer in the days and weeks after seeing an ad. Nielsen's Online rating service, for example, measures actual click-by-click behavior through meters installed on the computers of 225,000 individuals in 26 countries both at home and at work (see www.nielsen-online.com for recent ratings). The accompanying Making Responsible Decisions box describes how click fraud is increasing the necessity of assessing online advertising effectiveness.[43] Another suggestion being tested by Volvo and Unilever is *permission-based* advertising, where viewers agree to watch a commercial online in exchange for points, samples, or access to premium content, and advertisers only pay for completed views.[44]

Outdoor A very effective medium for reminding consumers about your product is outdoor advertising, such as the scoreboard at San Diego's Qualcomm Stadium. The most common form of outdoor advertising, called *billboards,* often results in good reach and frequency and has been shown to increase purchase rates.[45] The visibility of this medium is good supplemental reinforcement for well-known products, and it is a relatively low-cost, flexible alternative. A company can buy space just in the desired geographical market. A disadvantage to billboards, however, is that no opportunity exists for lengthy advertising copy. Also, a good billboard site depends on traffic patterns and sight lines. In many areas, environmental laws have limited the use of this medium.

Outdoor advertising can be an effective medium for reminding consumers about a product.

If you have ever lived in a metropolitan area, chances are you might have seen another form of outdoor advertising, *transit advertising.* This medium includes messages on the interior and exterior of buses, subway cars, and taxis. As use of mass transit grows, transit advertising may become increasingly important. Selectivity is available to advertisers, who can buy space by neighborhood or bus route. One disadvantage to this medium is that the heavy travel times, when the audiences are the largest, are not conducive to reading advertising copy. People are standing shoulder to shoulder on the subway, hoping not to miss their stop, and little attention is paid to the advertising.

The outdoor advertising industry has experienced a surge of growth recently. Lower costs, faster technology, and a lot of creativity have attracted large, national advertisers such as Sony, Microsoft, and America Online.[46] Orlando's Transportation Authority utilizes a wireless system to receive advertising for flat-screen monitors mounted in its 240 buses. Handmark and Nokia are developing a mobile advertising service that will reach millions of commuters with mobile phones and wireless handhelds (e.g., Blackberry, Palm, Apple, etc.).[47] Although outdoor advertising expenditures have grown to more than $6.6 billion, the industry must address environmental concerns through self-regulation or be restricted by legislation. For example, four states have banned billboards, and New York City's Metropolitan Transportation Authority has banned tobacco advertising on buses and subways.[48]

Other Media As traditional media have become more expensive and cluttered, advertisers have been attracted to a variety of nontraditional advertising options called out-of-home advertising, or *place-based media.* Messages are placed in locations that attract a specific target audience such as airports, doctors' offices, health clubs, theaters (where ads are played on the screen before the movies are shown), even bathrooms of bars, restaurants, and nightclubs.[49] Soon there will be advertising on video screens on gas pumps, ATMs, and in elevators, and increasingly it will be interactive. New York's La Guardia airport has started putting ads on baggage conveyors, and Beach 'n Billboard will even imprint ads in the sand on a beach.[50]

Out-of-home advertising is also becoming interactive.

Selection Criteria Choosing between these alternative media is difficult and depends on several factors. First, knowing the media habits of the target audience is essential to deciding among the alternatives. Second, occasionally product attributes necessitate that certain media be used. For example, if color is a major aspect of product appeal, radio is excluded. Newspapers allow advertising for quick actions to confront competitors, and magazines are more appropriate for complicated messages because the reader can spend more time reading the message. The final factor in selecting a medium is cost. When possible, alternative media are compared using a common denominator that reflects both reach and cost—a measure such as CPM.

Scheduling the Advertising

There is no correct schedule to advertise a product, but three factors must be considered. First is the issue of *buyer turnover,* which is how often new buyers enter the market to buy the product. The higher the buyer turnover, the greater is the amount of advertising required. A second issue in scheduling is the *purchase frequency;* the more frequently the product is purchased, the less repetition is required. Finally, companies must consider the *forgetting rate,* the speed with which buyers forget the brand if advertising is not seen.

Setting schedules requires an understanding of how the market behaves. Most companies tend to follow one of three basic approaches:

1. *Continuous (steady) schedule.* When seasonal factors are unimportant, advertising is run at a continuous or steady schedule throughout the year.
2. *Flighting (intermittent) schedule.* Periods of advertising are scheduled between periods of no advertising to reflect seasonal demand.
3. *Pulse (burst) schedule.* A flighting schedule is combined with a continuous schedule because of increases in demand, heavy periods of promotion, or introduction of a new product.

For example, products such as dry breakfast cereals have a stable demand throughout the year and would typically use a continuous schedule of advertising. In contrast, products such as snow skis and suntan lotions have seasonal demands and receive flighting-schedule advertising during the seasonal demand period. Some products such as toys or automobiles require pulse-schedule advertising to facilitate sales throughout the year and during special periods of increased demand (such as holidays or new car introductions). Some evidence suggests that pulsing schedules are superior to other advertising strategies.[51] In addition, recent research findings indicate that the effectiveness of a particular ad wears out quickly and, therefore, many alternative forms of a commercial may be more effective.[52]

---

learning review

5. You see the same ad in *Time* and *Fortune* magazines and on billboards and TV. Is this an example of reach or frequency?

6. Why has the Internet become a popular advertising medium?

7. What factors must be considered when choosing among alternative media?

EXECUTING THE ADVERTISING PROGRAM

Executing the advertising program involves pretesting the advertising copy and actually carrying out the advertising program. John Wanamaker, the founder of Wanamaker's Department Store in Philadelphia, remarked, "I know half my advertising is wasted, but I don't know what half." By evaluating advertising efforts, marketers can try to ensure that their advertising expenditures are not wasted.[53] Evaluation is done usually at two separate times: before and after the advertisements are run in the actual campaign. Several methods used in the evaluation process at the stages of idea formulation and copy development are discussed below.

Pretesting the Advertising

To determine whether the advertisement communicates the intended message or to select among alternative versions of the advertisement, **pretests** are conducted before the advertisements are placed in any medium.

Portfolio Tests   Portfolio tests are used to test copy alternatives. The test ad is placed in a portfolio with several other ads and stories, and consumers are asked to read through the portfolio. Afterward, subjects are asked for their impressions of the ads on several evaluative scales, such as from "very informative" to "not very informative."

Jury Tests   Jury tests involve showing the ad copy to a panel of consumers and having them rate how they liked it, how much it drew their attention, and how attractive they thought it was. This approach is similar to the portfolio test in that

FIGURE 19–5

Alternative structures of advertising agencies used to carry out the advertising program

TYPE OF AGENCY	SERVICES PROVIDED
Full-service agency	Does research, selects media, develops copy, and produces artwork; also coordinates integrated campaigns with all marketing efforts
Limited-service (specialty) agency	Specializes in one aspect of creative process; usually provides creative production work; buys previously unpurchased media space
In-house agency	Provides range of services, depending on company needs

consumer reactions are obtained. However, unlike the portfolio test, a test advertisement is not hidden within other ads.

Theater Tests   Theater testing is the most sophisticated form of pretesting. Consumers are invited to view new television shows or movies in which test commercials are also shown. Viewers register their feelings about the advertisements either on handheld electronic recording devices used during the viewing or on questionnaires afterward.

Carrying Out the Advertising Program

The responsibility for actually carrying out the advertising program can be handled in one of three ways, as shown in Figure 19–5. The **full-service agency** provides the most complete range of services, including market research, media selection, copy development, artwork, and production. Agencies that assist a client by both developing and placing advertisements have traditionally charged a commission of 15 percent of media costs. As corporations have introduced integrated marketing approaches, however, most (70 percent) advertisers have switched from paying commissions to incentives or fees based on performance. Brad Brinegar, former CEO of advertising agency Leo Burnett USA, says, "A lot of value we offer is in strategic thinking, and how to pay for that is very different from traditional media spending." The most common performance criteria used are sales, brand and ad awareness, market share, and copy test results. Procter & Gamble's switch to sales-based incentives actually turned out better for its agency than media commissions would have. Global marketing director Bob Wehling explains: "P&G's goal in changing compensation wasn't to cut costs, the goal was to increase sales and to support agencies in developing more comprehensive marketing plans that focus less exclusively on TV advertising and more on a broad array of reaching consumers."[54]

Limited-service agencies specialize in one aspect of the advertising process such as providing creative services to develop the advertising copy, buying previously unpurchased media (media agencies), or providing Internet services (Internet agencies). Limited-service agencies that deal in creative work are compensated by a contractual agreement for the services performed. Finally, **in-house agencies** made up of the company's own advertising staff may provide full services or a limited range of services.

ASSESSING THE ADVERTISING PROGRAM

The advertising decision process does not stop with executing the advertising program. The advertisements must be posttested to determine whether they are achieving their intended objectives, and results may indicate that changes must be made in the advertising program.

Posttesting the Advertising

An advertisement may go through **posttests** after it has been shown to the target audience to determine whether it accomplished its intended purpose. Five approaches common in posttesting are discussed here.[55]

Aided Recall After being shown an ad, respondents are asked whether their previous exposure to it was through reading, viewing, or listening. The Starch test shown in the accompanying photo uses aided recall to determine the percentage of those (1) who remember seeing a specific magazine ad (*noted*), (2) who saw or read any part of the ad identifying the product or brand (*seen-associated*), and (3) who read at least half of the ad (*read most*). Elements of the ad are then tagged with the results, as shown in the picture.

Starch scores an advertisement using aided recall.

Unaided Recall A question such as "What ads do you remember seeing yesterday?" is asked of respondents without any prompting to determine whether they saw or heard advertising messages.

Attitude Tests Respondents are asked questions to measure changes in their attitudes after an advertising campaign, such as whether they have a more favorable attitude toward the product advertised.[56]

Inquiry Tests Additional product information, product samples, or premiums are offered to an ad's readers or viewers. Ads generating the most inquiries are presumed to be the most effective.

Sales Tests Sales tests involve studies such as controlled experiments (e.g., using radio ads in one market and newspaper ads in another and comparing the results) and consumer purchase tests (measuring retail sales that result from a given advertising campaign). The most sophisticated experimental methods today allow a manufacturer, a distributor, or an advertising agency to manipulate an advertising variable (such as schedule or copy) through cable systems and observe subsequent sales effects by monitoring data collected from checkout scanners in supermarkets.[57]

Making Needed Changes

Results of posttesting the advertising copy are used to reach decisions about changes in the advertising program. If the posttest results show that an advertisement is doing poorly in terms of awareness or cost efficiency, it may be dropped and other ads run in its place in the future. On the other hand, sometimes an advertisement may be so successful it is run repeatedly or used as the basis of a larger advertising program.

> **learning review**
>
> 8. Explain the difference between pretesting and posttesting advertising copy.
>
> 9. What is the difference between aided and unaided recall posttests?

SALES PROMOTION

LO4

Sales promotion has become a key element of the promotional mix, which now accounts for more than $342 billion in annual expenditures. In a recent survey by *PROMO* magazine, marketing professionals reported that approximately 41 percent of their budgets were allocated to advertising, 28 percent to consumer promotion, 28 percent to trade promotion, and 3 percent to other marketing activities.[58] The allocation of marketing expenditures reflects the trend toward integrated promotion programs, which include a variety of promotion elements. Selection and integration of the many promotion techniques require a good understanding of the advantages and disadvantages of each kind of promotion.[59]

Consumer-Oriented Sales Promotions

Directed to ultimate consumers, **consumer-oriented sales promotions**, or simply *consumer promotions*, are sales tools used to support a company's advertising and personal selling. The alternative consumer-oriented sales promotion tools include coupons, deals, premiums, contests, sweepstakes, samples, loyalty programs, point-of-purchase displays, rebates, and product placement (see Figure 19–6 on the next page).

Coupons Coupons are sales promotions that usually offer a discounted price to the consumer, which encourages trial. Approximately 286 billion coupons are distributed in the United States each year. Coupon redemptions have been declining since 1992 and are now at 2.6 billion coupons, or approximately .9 percent. One explanation for the decline is that the average expiration period has been declining—to about three months—giving consumers less time to redeem coupons. The average face value of redeemed coupons is about 96 cents. Companies that have increased their use of coupons include Procter & Gamble, H.J. Heinz, Nestlé, ConAgra, and Kraft. In addition, the number of coupons generated at Internet sites (e.g., www.valpak.com and www.couponsonline.com) and over cell phones has been increasing. Coupons are often viewed as a key element of an integrated marketing program. When Duracell signed Jon Bon Jovi as a spokesperson, for example, coupons on Duracell battery packs offered $3 to $5 off Bon Jovi CDs and coupons on the CDs offered discounts on batteries.[60]

Do coupons help increase sales? Studies suggest that market share does increase during the period immediately after coupons are distributed.[61] There are also indications, however, that couponing can reduce gross revenues by lowering the price paid by already-loyal consumers.[62] Therefore, the 9,000 manufacturers who currently use coupons are particularly interested in coupon programs directed at potential first-time buyers. One means of focusing on these potential buyers is through electronic in-store coupon machines that match coupons to your most recent purchases. A recent survey suggests that 81 percent of Americans use coupons when grocery shopping.[63]

Coupons are often far more expensive than the face value of the coupon; a 25-cent coupon can cost three times that after paying for the advertisement to deliver it, dealer handling, clearinghouse costs, and redemption. In addition, misredemption, or paying the face value of the coupon even though the product was not purchased, should be added to the cost of the coupon. The Coupon Information Corporation estimates that companies pay out refunds of more than $500 million each year as a result of coupon fraud.[64]

Deals Deals are short-term price reductions, commonly used to increase trial among potential customers or to retaliate against a competitor's actions. For example, if a rival manufacturer introduces a new cake mix, the company responds with a "two packages for the price of one" deal. This short-term price reduction builds up the stock on the kitchen shelves of cake mix buyers and makes the competitor's introduction more difficult.

Coupons encourage trial by offering a discounted price.

KIND OF SALES PROMOTION	OBJECTIVES	ADVANTAGES	DISADVANTAGES
Coupons	Stimulate demand	Encourage retailer support	Consumers delay purchases
Deals	Increase trial; retaliate against competitor's actions	Reduce consumer risk	Consumers delay purchases; reduce perceived product value
Premiums	Build goodwill	Consumers like free or reduced-price merchandise	Consumers buy for premium, not product
Contests	Increase consumer purchases; build business inventory	Encourage consumer involvement with product	Require creative or analytical thinking
Sweepstakes	Encourage present customers to buy more; minimize brand switching	Get customer to use product and store more often	Sales drop after sweepstakes
Samples	Encourage new product trial	Low risk for consumer	High cost for company
Loyalty programs	Encourage repeat purchases	Help create loyalty	High cost for company
Point-of-purchase displays	Increase product trial; provide in-store support for other promotions	Provide good product visibility	Hard to get retailer to allocate high-traffic space
Rebates	Encourage customers to purchase; stop sales decline	Effective at stimulating demand	Easily copied; steal sales from future; reduce perceived product value
Product placement	Introduce new products; demonstrate product use	Positive message in a noncommercial setting	Little control over presentation of product

FIGURE 19–6

Sales promotions can be used to achieve many objectives.

Premiums A promotional tool often used with consumers is the premium, which consists of merchandise offered free or at a significant savings over its retail price. This latter type of premium is called *self-liquidating* because the cost charged to the consumer covers the cost of the item. McDonald's, for example, used a free premium in a promotional partnership with DreamWorks during the release of the movies *Shrek the Third* and *Bee Movie*. Collectible toys that portrayed movie characters were given away free with the purchase of a Happy Meal. Milk-Bone dog biscuits used a self-liquidating premium when it offered a ball toy for $8.99 and two proofs of purchase.[65] By offering a premium, companies encourage customers to return frequently or to use more of the product.

Contests A fourth sales promotion in Figure 19–6, the contest, is where consumers apply their skill or analytical or creative thinking to try to win a prize. This form of promotion has been growing as requests for videos, photos, and essays are a good match with the trend toward consumer-generated content. For example, Doritos sponsored the "Crash the Super Bowl" contest, asking people to create their own 30-second ad about Doritos. A panel of judges selected five finalists from the 1,070 entries, and the public voted online for its favorite. The ads were viewed more than 3 million times, and the top two ads aired on the Super Bowl.[66] If you like contests, you can even enter online now at websites such as www.playhere.com.

Sweepstakes *Reader's Digest* and Publisher's Clearing House are two well-known sweepstakes. These sales promotions require participants to submit some kind of entry but are purely games of chance requiring no analytical or creative effort by the consumer. The approach is very effective—*Time* magazine obtained 1.4 million new subscribers in one year through sweepstakes promotions.[67]

Two variations of sweepstakes are popular now. First is the sweepstake that offers products that consumers value. ConAgra Foods, for example, created the "Shrek's Quest for the Crown" instant-win promotion. The game offered a chance to win a $1,000 Visa gift card by entering UPC codes from ConAgra products tied to the *Shrek the Third* DVD release at a promotion website. Coca-Cola has a similar sweepstakes called "My Coke Rewards" which allows consumers to use codes from bottle caps to enter to win prizes or to collect points to be redeemed for rewards. The second is the sweepstake that offers an "experience" as the prize. For example, one of television's most popular series, *American Idol,* sponsors a 53-city live concert tour of the show's finalists. Concert attendees can enter a sweepstakes to win a trip for two to the season finale of *American Idol* in Los Angeles.[68] Federal laws, the Federal Trade Commission, and state legislatures have issued rules covering sweepstakes, contests, and games to regulate fairness, ensure that the chance for winning is represented honestly, and guarantee that the prizes are actually awarded.[69]

Samples Another common consumer sales promotion is sampling, which is offering the product free or at a greatly reduced price. Often used for new products, sampling puts the product in the consumer's hands. A trial size is generally offered that is smaller than the regular package size. If consumers like the sample, it is hoped they will remember and buy the product. When Mars changed its Milky Way Dark to Milky Way Midnight, it gave away more than 1 million samples to college students at night clubs, several hundred campuses, and popular spring break locations. Awareness of the candy bar rose to 60 percent, trial rose 166 percent, and sales rose 25 percent. Recent research indicates that 63 percent of college students who receive

Consumer-oriented promotions use sweepstakes to attract prospective customers and loyalty programs to reward repeat customers.

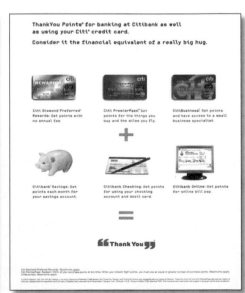

a sample will also purchase the product. Overall, companies invest more than $2 billion in sampling programs each year.[70]

Loyalty Programs Loyalty programs are a sales promotion tool used to encourage and reward repeat purchases by acknowledging each purchase made by a consumer and offering a premium as purchases accumulate. The most popular loyalty programs today are the frequent-flier and frequent-traveler programs used by airlines, hotels, and car rental services to reward loyal customers. American Airlines customers, for example, earn points for each mile they fly and can then redeem the accumulated points for free tickets or upgrades on the airline. American Airlines also offers a credit card that provides points for all charges made on it.

Loyalty programs are also becoming popular in other product categories. The Food Marketing Institute reports that 76 percent of all large grocery retailers offer a frequent-shopper program. American Express offers several levels of loyalty programs for its cardholders, including its First Collection program for Platinum card users. Another example is Best Buy, which began its Reward Zone program just a few years ago and already has 7 million members. How many people participate in loyalty programs? There are now more than 1.3 billion memberships, for an average of 12 for each adult in the United States.[71]

Point-of-purchase displays help increase consumers' attention in a store.

Point-of-Purchase Displays In a store aisle, you often encounter a sales promotion called a *point-of-purchase display*. These product displays take the form of advertising signs, which sometimes actually hold or display the product, and are often located in high-traffic areas near the cash register or the end of an aisle. The point-of-purchase display for Nabisco's annual back-to-school program is designed to maximize the consumer's attention to lunch box and after-school snacks, and to provide storage for the products. Annual expenditures on point-of-purchase promotions now exceed $19 billion and are expected to grow as point-of-purchase becomes integrated with all forms of promotion.[72]

Some studies estimate that two-thirds of a consumer's buying decisions are made in the store. This means that grocery product manufacturers want to get their message to you at the instant you are next to their brand in your supermarket aisle, perhaps through a point-of-purchase display. At a growing number of supermarkets this may be done with "floorgraphics"—floor displays with animation and sound—and "shelfscents"—displays that release a product's scent to potential consumers.[73] The advantage of these methods of promotion is that they do not rely on the consumers' ability to remember the message for long periods of time. Other in-store promotions such as interactive kiosks are also becoming popular.

Rebates Another consumer sales promotion in Figure 19–6, the cash rebate, offers the return of money based on proof of purchase. This tool has been used heavily by car manufacturers facing increased competition. For example, Ford offers recent college graduates a $500 rebate on many of its vehicles, as part of its College Graduate Purchase Program.[74]

When a rebate is offered on lower-priced items, the time and trouble of mailing in a proof of purchase to get the rebate check often means that many buyers never take advantage of it. However, this "slippage" is less likely to occur with frequent users of rebate promotions.[75] In addition, online consumers are more likely to take advantage of rebates.

Product Placement A final consumer promotion, **product placement**, involves the use of a brand-name product in a movie, television show, video, or commercial for another product. It was Steven Spielberg's placement of Hershey's Reese's Pieces in *E.T.* that first brought a lot of interest to the candy. Similarly, when Tom Cruise wore Bausch and Lomb's Ray-Ban sunglasses in *Risky Business* and its Aviator glasses in *Top Gun,* sales skyrocketed from 100,000 pairs to 7,000,000 pairs

in five years. After *Toy Story*, Etch-A-Sketch sales increased 4,500 percent and Mr. Potato Head sales increased 800 percent.

More recently, you might remember seeing the Aston Martin and the Range Rover, both Ford products, in *Casino Royale,* or the Dairy Queen brand in *Astronaut Farmer* and on episodes of *The Apprentice.* In the television show *Survivor,* participants often receive Doritos and Mountain Dew as rewards. If you listened closely you may have heard actor Hugh Grant say he had "Googled" Drew Barrymore's character in *Music and Lyrics.* Companies are usually eager to gain exposure for their products, and studios believe that product placements add authenticity to the film or program. The studios typically receive fees in exchange for the in-program exposure.[76]

A variation of this form of promotion, called *reverse product placement*, brings fictional products to the marketplace. Bertie Bott's Every Flavor Beans, for example, began as an imaginary brand in Harry Potter books. Similarly, the movie *Forrest Gump* led to the Bubba Gump Shrimp Company restaurant chain. Finally, 7-Eleven converted 12 of its stores into Kwik-E-Marts, the imaginary convenience stores in the television cartoon series, *The Simpsons*, to coincide with the release of *The Simpsons Movie*.[77]

Trade-Oriented Sales Promotions

Trade-oriented sales promotions, or simply *trade promotions,* are sales tools used to support a company's advertising and personal selling directed to wholesalers, retailers, or distributors. Some of the sales promotions just reviewed are used for this purpose, but there are three other common approaches targeted uniquely to these intermediaries: (1) allowances and discounts, (2) cooperative advertising, and (3) training of distributors' salesforces.

Allowances and Discounts Trade promotions often focus on maintaining or increasing inventory levels in the channel of distribution. An effective method for encouraging such increased purchases by intermediaries is the use of allowances and discounts. However, overuse of these price reductions can lead to retailers changing their ordering patterns in the expectation of such offerings. Although there are many variations that manufacturers can use with discounts and allowances, three common approaches are the merchandise allowance, the case allowance, and the finance allowance.[78]

Reimbursing a retailer for extra in-store support or special featuring of the brand is a *merchandise allowance.* Performance contracts between the manufacturer and trade member usually specify the activity to be performed, such as a picture of the product in a newspaper with a coupon good at only one store. The merchandise allowance then consists of a percentage deduction from the list case price ordered during the promotional period. Allowances are not paid by the manufacturer until it sees proof of performance (such as a copy of the ad placed by the retailer in the local newspaper).

A second common trade promotion, a *case allowance,* is a discount on each case ordered during a specific time period. These allowances are usually deducted from the invoice. A variation of the case allowance is the "free goods" approach, whereby retailers receive some amount of the product free based on the amount ordered, such as 1 case free for every 10 cases ordered.[79]

A final trade promotion, the *finance allowance,* involves paying retailers for financing costs or financial losses associated with consumer sales promotions. This trade promotion is regularly used and has several variations. One type is the floor stock protection program—manufacturers give retailers a case allowance price for products in their warehouse, which prevents shelf stock from running down during the promotional period. Also common are freight allowances, which compensate retailers that transport orders from the manufacturer's warehouse.

Cooperative Advertising   Resellers often perform the important function of promoting the manufacturer's products at the local level. One common sales promotional activity is to encourage both better quality and greater quantity in the local advertising efforts of resellers through **cooperative advertising**. These are programs by which a manufacturer pays a percentage of the retailer's local advertising expense for advertising the manufacturer's products.

Usually the manufacturer pays a percentage, often 50 percent, of the cost of advertising up to a certain dollar limit, which is based on the amount of the purchases the retailer makes of the manufacturer's products. In addition to paying for the advertising, the manufacturer often furnishes the retailer with a selection of different ad executions, sometimes suited for several different media. A manufacturer may provide, for example, several different print layouts as well as a few broadcast ads for the retailer to adapt and use.[80]

Training of Distributors' Salesforces   One of the many functions the intermediaries perform is customer contact and selling for the producers they represent. Both retailers and wholesalers employ and manage their own sales personnel. A manufacturer's success often rests on the ability of the reseller's salesforce to represent its products.

Thus, it is in the best interest of the manufacturer to help train the reseller's salesforce. Because the reseller's salesforce is often less sophisticated and knowledgeable about the products than the manufacturer might like, training can increase their sales performance. Training activities include producing manuals and brochures to educate the reseller's salesforce. The salesforce then uses these aids in selling situations. Other activities include national sales meetings sponsored by the manufacturer and field visits to the reseller's location to inform and motivate the salesperson to sell the products. Manufacturers also develop incentive and recognition programs to motivate reseller's salespeople to sell their products.

learning review

10. Which sales promotional tool is most common for new products?

11. What's the difference between a coupon and a deal?

12. Which trade promotion is used on an ongoing basis?

PUBLIC RELATIONS

As noted in Chapter 18, public relations is a form of communication management that seeks to influence the image of an organization and its products and services. Public relations efforts may utilize a variety of tools and may be directed at many distinct audiences. While public relations personnel usually focus on communicating positive aspects of the business, they may also be called on to minimize the negative impact of a problem or crisis. Firestone, for example, recalled 6.5 million tires when National Highway Traffic Safety Administration officials launched an investigation into consumer complaints about the tires. Debates with Ford Motor Company about the tire failures being due to overloading or underinflation created a difficult situation for the public relations department.[81] The most frequently used public relations tool is publicity.

Publicity Tools

In developing a public relations campaign, several methods of obtaining nonpersonal presentation of an organization, good, or service without direct cost—**publicity tools**—are available to the public relations director. Many companies frequently use the *news release,* consisting of an announcement regarding changes in the company or the product line. The objective of a news release is to inform a newspaper, radio station, or other medium of an idea for a story. A recent study found that more than 40 percent of all free mentions of a brand name occur during news programs.[82]

A second common publicity tool is the *news conference.* Representatives of the media are all invited to an informational meeting, and advance materials regarding the content are sent. This tool is often used when negative publicity—as in the cases of the options backdating scandals, the recalls of unsafe Chinese-made products, and the San Francisco Bay oil spill—requires a company response.[83]

Nonprofit organizations rely heavily on *public service announcements* (PSAs), which are free space or time donated by the media. For example, the charter of the American

Kid Rock uses publicity to promote his music.

Red Cross prohibits any local chapter from advertising, so to solicit blood donations local chapters often depend on PSAs on radio or television to announce their needs.

Finally, today many high-visibility individuals are used as publicity tools to create visibility for their companies, their products, and themselves. Richard Branson uses visibility to promote the Virgin Group, Kid Rock uses it to promote his music, and U.S. senators use it to promote themselves as political candidates. These publicity efforts are coordinated with news releases, conferences, advertising, donations to charities, volunteer activities, endorsements, and any other activities that may have an impact on public perceptions.[84]

INCREASING THE VALUE OF PROMOTION

Today's customers seek value from companies that provide leading-edge products, hassle-free transactions at competitive prices, and customer intimacy.[85] Promotion practices have changed dramatically to improve transactions and increase customer intimacy by (1) emphasizing long-term relationships and (2) increasing self-regulation.

Building Long-Term Relationships with Promotion

Many changes in promotional techniques have been driven by marketers' interest in developing long-term relationships with their customers. Promotion can contribute to brand and store loyalty by improving its ability to target individual preferences and by engaging customers in valuable and entertaining communication. New media such as the Internet and mobile telephones have provided immediate opportunities for personalized promotion activities such as e-mail advertising. In addition, technological developments have helped traditional media such as TV and radio focus on individual preferences through services such as TiVo and XM Satellite Radio. Although the future holds extraordinary promise for the personalization of promotion, the industry will need to manage and balance consumers' concerns about privacy as it proceeds.

Changes that help engage consumers have also been numerous. Marketers have attempted to utilize interactive technologies and to integrate new media and technologies into the overall creative process. Ad agencies are increasingly integrating public relations, direct marketing, advertising, and promotion into comprehensive campaigns. In fact, some experts predict that advertising agencies will soon become "communications consulting firms." Further, increasingly diverse and global audiences necessitate multimedia approaches and sensitivity communication techniques that engage the varied groups.[86] Overall, companies hope that these changes will build customer relationships for the long term—emphasizing a lifetime of purchases rather than a single transaction.

Self-Regulation

Unfortunately, over the years many consumers have been misled, or even deceived, by some promotions. Examples include sweepstakes in which the gifts were not awarded, rebate offers that were a terrible hassle, and advertisements whose promises were great, until the buyer read the small print. In one of the worst scandals in promotion history, McDonald's assisted an FBI investigation of the firm responsible for its sweepstakes, because the promotion agency security director was suspected of stealing winning game pieces.[87]

Promotions targeted at special groups such as children and the elderly also raise ethical concerns. For example, providing free samples to children in elementary schools or linking product lines to TV programs and movies have led to questions about the need for restrictions on promotions.[88] Although the Federal Trade Commission does provide some guidelines to protect consumers and special groups from misleading promotions, some observers believe more government regulation is needed.

To rely on formal regulation by federal, state, and local governments of all promotional activities would be very expensive. As a result, there are increasing efforts by advertising agencies, trade associations, and marketing organizations at *self-regulation*.[89] By imposing standards that reflect the values of society on their promotional activities, marketers can (1) facilitate the development of new promotional methods, (2) minimize regulatory constraints and restrictions, and (3) help consumers gain confidence in the communication efforts used to influence their purchases. As organizations strive for effective self-regulation, marketing executives will need to make sound ethical judgments about the use of existing and new promotional practices.

---

learning review

13. What is a news release?

14. What is the difference between government regulation and self-regulation?

LEARNING OBJECTIVES REVIEW

LO1 *Explain the differences between product advertising and institutional advertising and the variations within each type.*
Product advertisements focus on selling a good or service and take three forms: Pioneering advertisements tell people what a product is, what it can do, and where it can be found; competitive advertisements persuade the target market to select the firm's brand rather than a competitor's; and reminder advertisements reinforce previous knowledge of a product. Institutional advertisements are used to build goodwill or an image for an organization. They include advocacy advertisements, which state the position of a company on an issue, and pioneering, competitive, and reminder advertisements, which are similar to the product ads but focused on the institution.

LO2 *Describe the steps used to develop, execute, and evaluate an advertising program.*
The promotion decision process can be applied to each of the promotional elements. The steps to develop an advertising program include identify the target audience, specify the advertising objectives, set the advertising budget, design the advertisement, create the message, select the media, and schedule the advertising. Executing the program requires pretesting, and evaluating the program requires posttesting.

LO3 *Explain the advantages and disadvantages of alternative advertising media.*
Television advertising reaches large audiences and uses picture, print, sound, and motion; its disadvantages, however, are that it is expensive and perishable. Radio advertising is inexpensive and can be placed quickly, but it has no visual element and is perishable. Magazine advertising can target specific audiences and can convey complex information, but it takes a long time to place the ad and is relatively expensive. Newspapers provide excellent coverage of local markets and can be changed quickly, but they have a short life span and poor color. Yellow pages advertising has a long use period and is available 24 hours per day; its disadvantages, however, are that there is a proliferation of directories and they cannot be updated frequently. Internet advertising can be interactive, but its effectiveness is difficult to measure. Outdoor advertising provides repeat exposures, but its message must be very short and simple. Direct mail can be targeted at very selective audiences, but its cost per contact is high.

LO4 *Discuss the strengths and weaknesses of consumer-oriented and trade-oriented sales promotions.*
Coupons encourage retailer support but may delay consumer purchases. Deals reduce consumer risk but reduce perceived value.

Premiums offer consumers additional merchandise they want, but they may be purchasing only for the premium. Contests create involvement but require creative thinking. Sweepstakes encourage repeat purchases, but sales drop after the sweepstakes. Samples encourage product trial but are expensive. Loyalty programs help create loyalty but are expensive to run. Displays provide visibility but are difficult to place in retail space. Rebates stimulate demand but are easily copied. Product placement provides a positive message in a noncommercial setting but is difficult to control. Trade-oriented sales promotions include (*a*) allowances and discounts, which increase purchases but may change retailer ordering patterns, (*b*)

cooperative advertising, which encourages local advertising, and (*c*) salesforce training, which helps increase sales by providing the salespeople with product information and selling skills.

LO5 *Recognize public relations as an important form of communication.*

Public relations activities usually focus on communicating positive aspects of the business. A frequently used public relations tool is publicity. Publicity tools include new releases and news conferences. Nonprofit organization often use public service announcements.

FOCUSING ON KEY TERMS

advertising p. 490
consumer-oriented sales promotions
   p. 509
cooperative advertising p. 514
cost per thousand p. 498
frequency p. 498
full-service agency p. 507
gross rating points p. 498

infomercials p. 500
in-house agencies p. 507
institutional advertisements p. 491
limited-service agencies p. 507
posttests p. 508
pretests p. 506
product advertisements
   p. 490

product placement p. 512
publicity tools p. 515
rating p. 498
reach p. 498
trade-oriented sales promotions
   p. 513

APPLYING MARKETING KNOWLEDGE

1 How does competitive product advertising differ from competitive institutional advertising?

2 Suppose you are the advertising manager for a new line of children's fragrances. Which form of media would you use for this new product?

3 You have recently been promoted to be director of advertising for the Timkin Tool Company. In your first meeting with Mr. Timkin, he says, "Advertising is a waste! We've been advertising for six months now and sales haven't increased. Tell me why we should continue." Give your answer to Mr. Timkin.

4 A large life insurance company has decided to switch from using a strong fear appeal to a humorous approach. What are the strengths and weaknesses of such a change in message strategy?

5 Which medium has the lowest cost per thousand?

Medium	Cost	Audience
TV show	$5,000	25,000
Magazine	2,200	6,000
Newspaper	4,800	7,200
FM radio	420	1,600

6 Some national advertisers have found that they can have more impact with their advertising by running a large number of ads for a period and then running no ads at all for a period. Why might such a flighting schedule be more effective than a continuous schedule?

7 Each year managers at Bausch and Lomb evaluate the many advertising media alternatives available to them as they develop their advertising program for contact lenses. What advantages and disadvantages of each alternative should they consider? Which media would you recommend to them?

8 What are two advantages and two disadvantages of the advertising posttests described in the chapter?

9 Federated Banks is interested in consumer-oriented sales promotions that would encourage senior citizens to direct deposit their Social Security checks with the bank. Evaluate the sales promotion options, and recommend two of them to the bank.

10 How can public relations be used by Firestone and Ford following investigations into complaints about tire failures?

11 Describe a self-regulation guideline you believe would improve the value of (*a*) an existing form of promotion and (*b*) a new promotional practice.

building your marketing plan

To augment your promotion strategy from Chapter 18:

1 Use Figure 19–3 to select the advertising media you will include in your plan by analyzing how combinations of media (e.g., television and Internet advertising, radio and yellow pages advertising) can complement each other.

2 Use Figure 19–6 to select your consumer-oriented sales promotion activities.

3 Specify which trade-oriented sales promotions and public relations activities you will use.

"Most people think of Fallon as being in the advertising business, but we don't really think of ourselves that way," says Rob White, president of Fallon Worldwide. "We believe that we are a creativity company that happens to do some advertising," he continues. As an example, he points out that Fallon starts upstream of a firm's communication issues to identify the key business problem and uses creativity to help solve it. Sometimes this involves a heavy dose of advertising and other times almost none. But it always takes a very creative flair.

Founded in 1981, Fallon Worldwide—or simply Fallon—has won dozens of advertising awards. This includes two Agency of the Year awards given by *Advertising Age* magazine. "I think Fallon's success is due to two important things," says White. "One is the people and the other one is the culture that bonds the people together. When you create a special kind of culture with collaboration and teamwork from a very high level and people with different backgrounds, amazing things can happen," he explains.

Bruce Bildsten, Fallon creative group director, echoes this focus on creativity: "It's always a challenge as creative director to try to stay at the forefront and come up with something that people haven't seen. I desperately try not to look at other advertising for ideas. I always challenge our people to look at work from other parts of the world—film, novels, music—for inspiration."

A look at two promotional campaigns developed at Fallon show how creativity, teamwork, and not looking at traditional ads from other agencies come together to build award-winning campaigns. Both campaigns discussed below have been recognized for their creativity and their success at achieving the clients' objectives.

CITIBANK: ATTRACTING BALANCE SEEKERS

Citibank approached Fallon because it knew it had a problem. Citi had been successful in the past by being a low-cost provider, having great service, and by focusing on direct marketing. Suddenly that wasn't enough. Competition had increased significantly and customer perceptions of banks and credit card companies had changed. Laurel Flatt, Fallon account director on the Citibank account, describes the challenge: "New banks were springing up all over the place. There were new credit card companies. Consumers looked at financial services as simply a commodity. Your relationship with your bank, your credit card company was once a very, very special relationship." Now, however, consumers viewed one bank as being no different than another.

When Citibank came to Fallon, it said that it really wanted to be "un-banklike," it wanted to be different.

Fallon asked the question, "What is the right way to be un-banklike in a way that will generate results for the Citi brand?" Qualitative and quantitative research identified a segment of consumers that Fallon labeled "balance seekers." This group amounted to about 50 percent of the market for financial services. Balance seekers viewed financial services and money as a means to an end, something that helps them lead the life they live. This segment also shared an attitude that was receptive to the idea of an un-banklike message, though they had different income levels, assets, ages, and other demographic characteristics.

Fallon translated un-banklike to mean very friendly, human, and a little bit quirky—very different from the serious tone of traditional bank and financial services companies. In addition, Fallon wanted the Citi brand to represent a healthy approach to money. Finally, Fallon wanted to communicate that the credit card protects consumers and their purchases.

Fallon's ad executions were funny and engaging. One ad shows a middle-aged woman from Minnesota getting a tattoo. The tag line is "It didn't seem right to us, either" and talks about Citi's Fraud Early Warning system to identify unusual spending behavior. Another ad shows a truck driver from Iowa asleep under a hair dryer at La Petite Lily Day Spa with the same tag line and message about how Citi's identity theft solutions can help make things right. The Citi campaign utilized billboards and wall advertising, bus shelter kiosks, magazines, and television.

Fallon used brand-tracking to chart the degree of differentiation of the Citi brand. Over time, the differentiation climbed as more and more people perceived Citi as different from other banks yet relevant in their lives. Sales results were also positive. Card acquisition and card usage increased dramatically!

HOLIDAY INN EXPRESS: ATTRACTING "SMART" CONSUMERS

When Holiday Inn decided to enter the limited-service hotel segment with its Holiday Inn Express hotels, it hired Fallon Worldwide to develop the campaign. Holiday Inn had a long history with American consumers who remembered it as the hotel for family road trips. Most of the growth in the hotel industry, however, was related to business travel, and that segment already had two strong competitors—Courtyard by Marriott and Hampton Inns. Holiday Inn Express was starting with a budget that was much smaller than its competitors, so Fallon knew it needed to "outsmart rather than outspend" them.

The agency's first step was to identify the target market. It conducted extensive research to understand the psychological profile of users of that type of hotel and the motivations for their lodging choices. Fallon decided to focus on a specific group of travelers who seldom made reservations. "In this case it was males 25–54 that tend to travel by car when they do business, so they were true 'road warriors,'" explains Mike Buchner, chief operating officer and client services director at Fallon. The research revealed another insight about these travelers. They only wanted the necessities,

but they felt savvy for making a practical choice. This emotional benefit became the creative focus of the discussions at Fallon and resulted in the Holiday Inn Express "Stay Smart" campaign.

The campaign used television ads designed to create awareness and differentiate Holiday Inn Express by showing how Holiday Inn Express makes guests feel smart about their hotel selection. One ad, for example, shows a man giving advice to a tourist who is being confronted by a bear. When asked if he is a forest ranger, the man responds, "No, but I did stay in a Holiday Inn Express last night." A similar ad shows a man dressed as a clown giving advice to a bull rider at a rodeo. Then the man explains that he is not a rodeo clown but a children's birthday party clown, and the conclusion is the same: "But I did stay at a Holiday Inn Express last night." To create the greatest impact with the limited budget, Fallon only ran the ads on Sundays and Mondays—days that the target market typically did not travel. In addition, they only ran the ads on cable networks such as CNN, ESPN and Fox Sports—programs that research showed were very popular with road warriors.

The Stay Smart advertising theme eventually became the basis for an entire branding effort. Holiday Inn Express now offers SimplySmart bathroom designs, SimplySmart bedding collections, Smart Roast coffee, and even a webcast about activities in America called The Smart Show. The result has been very positive as the number of visitors, sales, and operating profits have increased. In fact, the campaign is so successful that Holiday Inn Express now has 1,583 hotels and is the fastest growing hotel brand in the United States, adding two new hotels each week!

PUSHING THE CREATIVE BARRIERS

How does Fallon keep the creative juices flowing—from developing new promotional campaigns to using new media? The founders of Fallon Worldwide, Pat Fallon and Fred Senn, explain how they do it in their new book titled *Juicing the Orange*. Generally, they emphasize the "need to build a culture of creativity." They believe that "only a campaign that makes a genuine human connection with the audience can invite the consumer to participate in your message." So, watch for the creativity that led Fallon to such success with Citibank and Holiday Inn Express to continue to develop award-winning commercials for its many other clients, including Sony, Garmin, NBC, Purina, Nordstrom, *Time* magazine, and Volkswagen!

Questions

1 Fallon Worldwide stresses its creativity, as shown by the comments from the Fallon people in the case. In what ways do the Citi and Holiday Inn Express campaigns reflect their creativity? What were the sources of the ideas in the two campaigns?

2 In the Citi and Holiday Inn Express campaigns what were (*a*) the target markets, and (*b*) each brand's positioning?

3 Compare the media used for the Citi and the Holiday Inn Express campaigns. Why were these media chosen? Do you expect the use of these media to change in the future?

4 How might Fallon and its clients measure the success of (*a*) the Citi, and (*b*) the Holiday Inn Express campaigns?

20

Personal Selling and Sales Management

LEARNING OBJECTIVES

After reading this chapter you should be able to:

LO1 Discuss the nature and scope of personal selling and sales management in marketing.

LO2 Identify the different types of personal selling.

LO3 Explain the stages in the personal selling process.

LO4 Describe the major functions of sales management.

XEROX DELIVERS AN EXCEPTIONAL CUSTOMER EXPERIENCE BY SELLING THE WAY CUSTOMERS WANT TO BUY

Anne Mulcahy has a challenging assignment. As the chairman of the board and chief executive officer at Xerox Corporation, she is in the midst of successfully managing one of the greatest feats in the annals of business history: restoring Xerox's legendary marketing and financial vitality.

Her success to date can be attributed to staying in sync with Xerox customers and employees. "I believe strongly that my success as a leader is driven by my commitment to understanding and meeting customers' requirements, as well as developing and nurturing a motivated and proud workforce," says Mulcahy.

Mulcahy is ideally suited to the task. She began her 32-year Xerox career as a field sales representative and assumed increasingly responsible management and executive positions. These included chief staff officer, president of Xerox's General Markets Operations, and president and chief operating officer of Xerox. As chairman and CEO, Mulcahy had to muster the knowledge and experience gained from this varied background. Not surprisingly, her field sales background played a pivotal role.

"We will win back market share one customer at a time, one sale at a time," Mulcahy says. "We'll do that by providing greater value than our competitors—and that means selling the way customers want to buy." She adds, "Doing what's right for the customer—that's our guiding principle." And attention to the customer buying experience has paid huge dividends. Xerox sales revenue and net income have soared during Mulcahy's tenure as chairman and CEO. Her dedicated customer focus and field sales experience bodes well for the continued success of Xerox.[1]

This chapter describes the scope and significance of personal selling and sales management in marketing and creating value for customers. It first highlights the many forms of personal selling. Next, the major steps in the selling process are outlined with an emphasis on building buyer-seller relationships. Attention is then focused on salesforce management and its critical role in achieving a company's broader marketing objectives. Three major salesforce management functions are then detailed. They are sales plan formulation, sales plan implementation, and salesforce evaluation. Finally, technology's persuasive influence on how selling is done and how salespeople are managed is described.

SCOPE AND SIGNIFICANCE OF PERSONAL SELLING AND SALES MANAGEMENT

Chapter 18 described personal selling and management of the sales effort as being part of the firm's promotional mix. Although it is important to recognize that personal selling is a useful vehicle for communicating with present and potential buyers, it is much more. Take a moment to answer the questions in the personal selling and sales management quiz in Figure 20–1. As you read on, compare your answers with those in the text.

Nature of Personal Selling and Sales Management

Personal selling involves the two-way flow of communication between a buyer and seller, often in a face-to-face encounter, designed to influence a person's or group's purchase decision. However, with advances in telecommunications, personal selling also takes place over the telephone, through video teleconferencing and Internet-enabled links between buyers and sellers.

Personal selling remains a highly human-intensive activity despite the use of technology. Accordingly, the people involved must be managed. **Sales management** involves planning the selling program and implementing and evaluating the personal selling effort of the firm. The tasks involved in managing personal selling include setting objectives; organizing the salesforce; recruiting, selecting, training, and compensating salespeople; and evaluating the performance of individual salespeople.

Selling Happens Almost Everywhere

"Everyone lives by selling something," wrote author Robert Louis Stevenson a century ago. His observation still holds true today. The Bureau of Labor Statistics reports that about 14 million people are employed in sales positions in the United States. Included in this number are manufacturing sales personnel, real estate brokers, stockbrokers, and salesclerks who work in retail stores. In reality, however, virtually every occupation that involves customer contact has an element of personal selling. For example, attorneys, accountants, bankers, and company personnel recruiters perform sales-related activities, whether or not they acknowledge it.

About 20 percent of chief executive officers in the largest U.S. corporations have significant sales experience in their work history like Anne Mulcahy at Xerox.[2] (What

---

FIGURE 20–1

Personal selling and sales management quiz. Check your answers as you read the chapter.

1. What percentage of chief executive officers in the largest U.S. companies has significant sales experience in their work history? (check one)

   10% _____   30% _____   50% _____

   20% _____   40% _____   60% _____

2. What percentage of an average field sales representative's time each work week is spent actually selling to customers? (check one)

   45% _____   55% _____   65% _____

3. "A salesperson's job is finished when a sale is made." True or false? (circle one)

   True   False

4. About what percentage of U.S. companies includes customer satisfaction as a measure of salesperson performance? (check one)

   10% _____   30% _____   50% _____

   20% _____   40% _____   60% _____

Could this be a salesperson in the operating room? Read the text to find why Medtronic salespeople visit hospital operating rooms.

Medtronic
www.medtronic.com

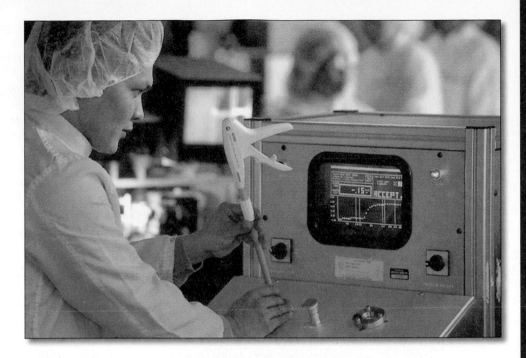

percentage did you check for question 1 in Figure 20–1?) Thus, selling often serves as a stepping-stone to top management, as well as being a career path itself.

Personal Selling in Marketing

Personal selling serves three major roles in a firm's overall marketing effort. First, salespeople are the critical link between the firm and its customers. This role requires that salespeople match company interests with customer needs to satisfy both parties in the exchange process. Second, salespeople *are* the company in a consumer's eyes. They represent what a company is or attempts to be and are often the only personal contact a customer has with the company. For example, the "look" projected by Gucci salespeople is an important factor in communicating the style of the company's apparel line. Third, personal selling may play a dominant role in a firm's marketing program. This situation typically arises when a firm uses a push marketing strategy, described in Chapter 18. Avon, for example, pays almost 40 percent of its total sales dollars for selling expenses. Pharmaceutical firms and office and educational equipment manufacturers also rely heavily on personal selling in the marketing of their products.

Creating Customer Solutions and Value through Salespeople: Relationship and Partnership Selling

As the critical link between the firm and its customers, salespeople can create customer value in many ways. For instance, by being close to the customer, salespeople can identify creative solutions to customer problems. Salespeople at Medtronic, Inc., the world leader in the heart pacemaker market, are in the operating room for more than 90 percent of the procedures performed with their product and are on call, wearing pagers, 24 hours a day. "It reflects the willingness to be there in every situation, just in case a problem arises—even though nine times out of ten the procedure goes just fine," notes a satisfied customer.[3] Salespeople can create value by easing the customer buying process. This happened at AMP, Inc., a producer of electrical products. Salespeople and customers had a difficult time getting product specifications and performance data on AMP's 70,000 products quickly and accurately. The company now records all information on CD-ROM disks that can be scanned instantly by salespeople and customers. Customer value is also created by salespeople who follow through after the sale. At Jefferson Smurfit Corporation, a multibillion-dollar supplier of packaging products, one of its salespeople juggled production from three of the company's plants to satisfy an unexpected demand for boxes from General Electric. This person's action led to the company being given GE's Distinguished Supplier Award.

Relationship Selling Customer value creation is made possible by **relationship selling**, the practice of building ties to customers based on a salesperson's attention and commitment to customer needs over time. Relationship selling involves mutual respect and trust among buyers and sellers. It focuses on creating long-term customers, not a onetime sale. A survey of 300 senior sales executives revealed that 96 percent consider "building long-term relationships with customers" to be the most important activity affecting sales performance. Companies such as Xerox, American Express, Electronic Data Systems, Motorola, and Owens-Corning have made relationship building a core focus of their sales effort.[4]

Partnership Selling Some companies have taken relationship selling a step further and forged partnerships between buyer and seller organizations. With **partnership selling**, sometimes called *enterprise selling,* buyers and sellers combine their expertise and resources to create customized solutions; commit to joint planning; and share customer, competitive, and company information for their mutual benefit, and ultimately the customer. As an approach to sales, partnership selling relies on cross-functional business specialists who apply their knowledge and expertise to achieve better customer solutions, lower cost, and greater customer value. Partnership selling complements supplier and channel partnering described in Chapters 6, 15, and 16. This practice is embraced by General Electric, Honeywell, DuPont, and IBM. For example, on any given day, IBM has 30 information technology hardware and software specialists, business consultants, and engineers working at Charles Schwab, a large brokerage firm, all under the direction of a senior IBM sales executive. Their job? Create and manage a complex state-of-the-art financial planning system that assists Schwab clients with their retirement planning.[5]

Relationship and partnership selling represent another dimension of customer relationship management. Both emphasize the importance of learning about customer needs and wants and tailoring solutions to customer problems as a means to customer value creation.

---

learning review

1. What is personal selling?

2. What is involved in sales management?

THE MANY FORMS OF PERSONAL SELLING

LO2

Personal selling assumes many forms based on the amount of selling done and the amount of creativity required to perform the sales task. Broadly speaking, three types of personal selling exist: order taking, order getting, and customer sales support activities. While some firms use only one of these types of personal selling, others use a combination of all three.

Order Taking

Typically, an **order taker** processes routine orders or reorders for products that were already sold by the company. The primary responsibility of order takers is to preserve 保持 an ongoing relationship with existing customers and maintain sales.

A Frito-Lay salesperson takes inventory of snacks for the store manager to sign. In this situation, the manager will make a straight rebuy decision.

Frito-Lay, Inc.
www.fritolay.com

Two types of order takers exist. *Outside order takers* visit customers and replenish inventory stocks of resellers, such as retailers or wholesalers. For example, Frito-Lay salespeople call on supermarkets, convenience stores, and other establishments to ensure that the company's line of snack products (such as Doritos and Tostitos tortilla chips) is in adequate supply. In addition, outside order takers often provide assistance in arranging displays.

Inside order takers, also called *order clerks* or *salesclerks,* typically answer simple questions, take orders, and complete transactions with customers. Many retail clerks are inside order takers. Inside order takers are often employed by companies that use *inbound telemarketing,* the use of toll-free telephone numbers that customers can call to obtain information about products or services and make purchases. In business-to-business settings, order taking arises in straight rebuy situations as described in Chapter 6.

Order takers generally do little selling in a conventional sense and engage in only modest problem solving with customers. They often represent products that have few options, such as magazine subscriptions and highly standardized industrial products. Inbound telemarketing is also an essential selling activity for more "customer service" driven firms, such as Dell Inc. At these companies, order takers undergo extensive training so that they can better assist callers with their purchase decisions.

Order Getting

An **order getter** sells in a conventional sense and identifies prospective customers, provides customers with information, persuades customers to buy, closes sales, and follows up on customers' use of a product or service. Like order takers, order getters can be inside (an automobile salesperson) or outside (a Xerox salesperson). Order getting involves a high degree of creativity and customer empathy and is typically required for selling complex or technical products with many options, so considerable product knowledge and sales training are necessary. In modified rebuy or new-buy purchase situations in business-to-business selling, an order getter acts as a problem solver who identifies how a particular product may satisfy a customer's need. Similarly, in the purchase of a service, such as insurance, a Metropolitan Life insurance agent can provide a mix of plans to satisfy a buyer's needs depending on income, stage of the family's life cycle, and investment objectives.

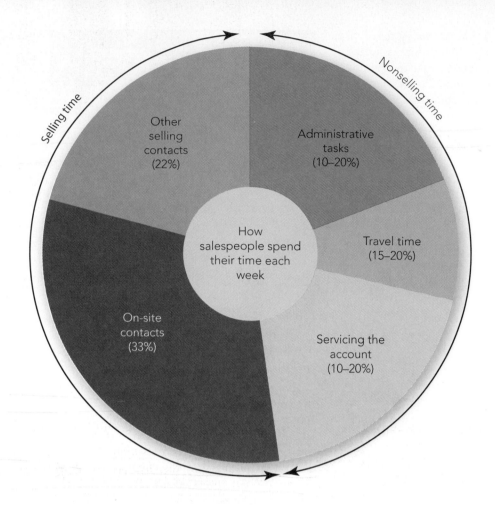

Order getting is not a 40-hour-per-week job. Industry research shows that outside order getters, or field service representatives, often work over 50 hours per week. As shown in Figure 20–2, 55 percent of their time is spent selling. What percent did you check for question 2 in Figure 20–1?) Another 10 to 20 percent is devoted to customer service calls. The remainder of their workweek is occupied by getting to customers and performing administrative tasks.[6]

Order getting by outside salespeople is also expensive. It is estimated that the average cost of a single field sales call on a business customer is about $350, factoring in salespeople compensation, benefits, and travel-and-entertainment expenses. This cost illustrates why outbound telemarketing is popular. *Outbound telemarketing* is the practice of using the telephone rather than personal visits to contact current and prospective customers. A much lower cost per sales call (from $20 to $25) and little or no field expense accounts for its widespread appeal. Over 100 million outbound telemarketing calls are made to homes and businesses each year in the United States.[7]

Customer Sales Support Personnel

Customer sales support personnel augment the selling effort of order getters by performing a variety of services. For example, *missionary salespeople* do not directly solicit orders but rather concentrate on performing promotional activities and introducing new products. They are used extensively in the pharmaceutical industry, where they persuade physicians to prescribe a firm's product. Actual sales are made through wholesalers or directly to pharmacists who fill prescriptions. A *sales engineer* is a salesperson who specializes in identifying, analyzing, and solving customer problems and brings know-how and technical expertise to the selling situation but

Marketing Matters > > > > > customer value

Creating and Sustaining Customer Value through Cross-Functional Team Selling

The day of the lone salesperson calling on a customer is rapidly becoming history. Today, 75 percent of companies employ cross-functional teams of professionals to work with customers to improve relationships, find better ways of doing things, and, of course, create and sustain value for their customers.

Xerox and IBM pioneered cross-functional team selling, but other firms were quick to follow as they spotted the potential to create and sustain value for their customers. Recognizing that corn growers needed a herbicide they could apply less often, a DuPont team of chemists, sales and marketing executives, and regulatory specialists created just the right product that recorded sales of $57 million in its first year. Procter & Gamble uses teams of marketing, sales, advertising, computer systems, and supply chain personnel to work with its major retailers, such as Wal-Mart, to identify ways to develop, promote, and deliver products. Pitney Bowes, Inc., which produces sophisticated computer systems that weigh, rate, and track packages for firms such as UPS and Federal Express, also uses sales teams to meet customer needs. These teams consist of sales personnel, "carrier management specialists," and engineering and administrative executives who continually find ways to improve the technology of shipping goods across town and around the world.

Efforts to create and sustain customer value through cross-functional team selling have become a necessity as customers seek greater value for their money. According to the vice president for procurement of a Fortune 500 company, "Today, it's not just getting the best price but getting the best value—and there are a lot of pieces to value."

often does not actually sell products and services. Sales engineers are popular in selling business products such as chemicals and heavy equipment.

In many situations firms engage in cross-functional **team selling**, the practice of using an entire team of professionals in selling to and servicing major customers.[8] Team selling is used when specialized knowledge is needed to satisfy the different interests of individuals in a customer's buying center. For example, a selling team might consist of a salesperson, a sales engineer, a service representative, and a financial executive, each of whom would deal with a counterpart in the customer's firm. Selling teams have grown in popularity due to partnering and take different forms.

In *conference selling*, a salesperson and other company resource people meet with buyers to discuss problems and opportunities. In *seminar selling*, a company team conducts an educational program for a customer's technical staff, describing state-of-the-art developments. IBM and Xerox pioneered cross-functional team selling in working with prospective buyers. Other firms have embraced this practice and created and sustained value for their customers, as described in the accompanying Marketing Matters box.[9]

learning review

3. What is the principal difference between an order taker and an order getter?

4. What is team selling?

THE PERSONAL SELLING PROCESS: BUILDING RELATIONSHIPS

Selling, and particularly order getting, is a complicated activity that involves building buyer–seller relationships. Although the salesperson–customer interaction is essential to personal selling, much of a salesperson's work occurs before this meeting and continues after the sale itself. The **personal selling process** consists of six stages: (1) prospecting, (2) preapproach, (3) approach, (4) presentation, (5) close, and (6) follow-up (see Figure 20–3).

Prospecting

Personal selling begins with the *prospecting* stage—the search for and qualification of potential customers. There are three types of prospects. A *lead* is the name of a person who may be a possible customer. A *prospect* is a customer who wants or needs the product. If an individual wants the product, can afford to buy it, and is the decision maker, this individual is a *qualified prospect*.

Leads and prospects are generated using several sources. For example, advertising may contain a coupon or a toll-free number to generate leads. Some companies use

FIGURE 20–3

Stages and objectives of the personal selling process. Each stage is critical for successful selling and building a relationship.

STAGE	OBJECTIVE	COMMENTS
1. Prospecting	Search for and qualify prospects	Start of the selling process; prospects produced through advertising, referrals, and cold canvassing
2. Preapproach	Gather information and decide how to approach the prospect	Information sources include personal observation, other customers, and own salespeople
3. Approach	Gain prospect's attention, stimulate interest, and make transition to the presentation	First impression is critical; gain attention and interest through reference to common acquaintances, a referral, or product demonstration
4. Presentation	Begin converting a prospect into a customer by creating a desire for the product or service	Different presentation formats are possible; however, involving the customer in the product or service through attention to particular needs is critical; important to deal professionally and ethically with prospect skepticism, indifference, or objections
5. Close	Obtain a purchase commitment from the prospect and create a customer	Salesperson asks for the purchase; different approaches include the trial close and assumptive close
6. Follow-up	Ensure that the customer is satisfied with the product or service	Resolve any problems faced by the customer to ensure customer satisfaction and future sales possibilities

Trade shows are a popular source for leads and prospects. Companies like TSCentral provide comprehensive trade show information.

TSCentral

www.tscentral.com

exhibits at trade shows, professional meetings, and conferences to generate leads or prospects. Staffed by salespeople, these exhibits are used to attract the attention of prospective buyers and disseminate information. Others utilize the Internet for generating leads and prospects. Today, salespeople are using websites, e-mail, bulletin boards, and newsgroups to connect to individuals and companies that may be interested in their products or services.

Another approach for generating leads is through *cold canvassing* or *cold calling,* either in person or by telephone. This approach simply means that a salesperson may open a directory, pick a name, and contact that individual or business. Even with a high refusal rate, cold canvassing can be successful.[10] For example, on one occasion, 41 brokers at Lehman Brothers identified 18,004 prospects, qualified 1,208 of them, made 659 sales presentations, and opened 40 new accounts in four working days. However, cold canvassing is frowned upon in most Asian and Latin American societies. Personal visits, based on referrals, are expected.

Cold canvassing is often criticized by U.S. consumers and is now regulated. A recent survey reported that 75 percent of U.S. consumers consider this practice an intrusion on their privacy, and 72 percent find it distasteful.[11] *The Telephone Consumer Protection Act* (1991) contains provisions to curb abuses such as early morning or late night calling. Additional federal regulations require more complete disclosure regarding solicitations, include provisions that allow consumers to avoid being called at any time through the Do Not Call Registry, and impose fines for violations. For example, satellite television provider DirecTV was fined $5.3 million for making thousands of calls to consumers who had put their telephone numbers on the Do Not Call Registry.[12]

Preapproach

Once a salesperson has identified a qualified prospect, preparation for the sale begins with the preapproach. The *preapproach* stage involves obtaining further information on the prospect and deciding on the best method of approach. Knowing how the prospect prefers to be approached, and what the prospect is looking for in a product or service, is essential regardless of cultural setting.

For instance, a Merrill Lynch stockbroker will need information on a prospect's discretionary income, investment objectives, and preference for discussing brokerage services over the telephone or in person. For business product companies such as Texas Instruments, the preapproach involves identifying the buying role of a prospect (for example, influencer or decision maker), important buying criteria, and the prospect's receptivity to a formal or informal presentation. Identifying the best time to contact a prospect is also important. Northwestern Mutual Life Insurance Company suggests the best times to call on people in different occupations: dentists before 9:30 a.m., lawyers between 11:00 a.m. and 2:00 p.m., and college professors between 7:00 and 8:00 p.m.

This stage is very important in international selling where customs dictate appropriate protocol. In many South American countries, for example, buyers expect salespeople to be punctual for appointments. However, prospective buyers are routinely 30 minutes late. South Americans take negotiating seriously and prefer straightforward presentations, but a hard-sell approach will not work.[13]

Successful salespeople recognize that the preapproach stage should never be shortchanged. Their experience coupled with research on customer complaints indicate that failure to learn as much as possible about the prospect is unprofessional and the ruin of a sales call.

Approach

The *approach* stage involves the initial meeting between the salesperson and prospect, where the objectives are to gain the prospect's attention, stimulate interest, and build the foundation for the sales presentation itself and the basis for a working relationship. The first impression is critical at this stage, and it is common for salespeople to begin the conversation with a reference to common acquaintances, a referral, or even the product or service itself. Which tactic is taken will depend on the information obtained in the prospecting and preapproach stages.

The approach stage is very important in international settings. In many societies outside the United States, considerable time is devoted to nonbusiness talk designed to establish a rapport between buyers and sellers. For instance, it is common for two or three meetings to occur before business matters are discussed in the Middle East and Asia. Gestures are also very important. The initial meeting between a salesperson and a prospect in the United States customarily begins with a firm handshake. Handshakes also apply in France, but they are gentle, not firm. Forget the handshake in Japan. An appropriate bow is expected. What about business cards? Business cards should be printed in English on one side and the language of the prospective customer on the other. Knowledgeable U.S. salespeople know that their business cards should be handed to Asian customers using both hands, with the name facing the receiver. In Asia, anything involving a person's name demands respect.

How business cards are exchanged with Asian customers is very important. Read the text to learn the appropriate protocol in the approach stage of the personal selling process.

Presentation

The *presentation* stage is at the core of the order-getting selling process, and its objective is to convert a prospect into a customer by creating a desire for the product or service. Three major presentation formats exist: (1) stimulus-response format, (2) formula selling format, and (3) need-satisfaction format.

Stimulus-Response Format The **stimulus-response presentation** format assumes that given the appropriate stimulus by a salesperson, the prospect will buy.

With this format the salesperson tries one appeal after another, hoping to hit the right button. A counter clerk at McDonald's is using this approach when he or she asks whether you'd like an order of french fries or a dessert with your meal. The counter clerk is engaging in what is called *suggestive selling*. Although useful in this setting, the stimulus-response format is not always appropriate, and for many products a more formalized format is necessary.

Formula Selling Format The **formula selling presentation** format is based on the view that a presentation consists of information that must be provided in an accurate, thorough, and step-by-step manner to inform the prospect. A popular version of this format is the *canned sales presentation,* which is a memorized, standardized message conveyed to every prospect. Used frequently by firms in telephone and door-to-door selling of consumer products (for example, Kirby vacuum cleaners), this approach treats every prospect the same, regardless of differences in needs or preference for certain kinds of information.

Canned sales presentations can be advantageous when the differences between prospects are unknown or with novice salespeople who are less knowledgeable about the product and selling process than experienced salespeople. Although it guarantees a thorough presentation, it often lacks flexibility and spontaneity and, more important, does not provide for feedback from the prospective buyer—a critical component in the communication process and the start of a relationship.

Need-Satisfaction Format The stimulus-response and formula selling formats share a common characteristic: The salesperson dominates the conversation. By comparison, the **need-satisfaction presentation** format emphasizes probing and listening by the salesperson to identify needs and interests of prospective buyers. Once these are identified, the salesperson tailors the presentation to the prospect and highlights product benefits that may be valued by the prospect. The need-satisfaction format, which emphasizes problem solving and customer solutions, is the most consistent with the marketing concept and relationship building.

Rockport sales representatives are adept at adaptive selling to retail buyers.

The Rockport Company
www.rockport.com

Two selling styles are common with this format.[14] **Adaptive selling** involves adjusting the presentation to fit the selling situation, such as knowing when to offer solutions and when to ask for more information. Sales research and practice show that knowledge of the customer and sales situation are key ingredients for adaptive selling. Many consumer service firms such as brokerage and insurance firms and consumer product firms like Rockport, AT&T, and Gillette effectively apply this selling style.

Consultative selling focuses on problem identification, where the salesperson serves as an expert on problem recognition and resolution. With consultative selling, problem solution options are not simply a matter of choosing from an array of existing products or services. Rather, novel solutions often arise, thereby creating unique value for the customer.

Consultative selling is prominent in business-to-business marketing. Johnson Controls' Automotive Systems Group, IBM's Global Services, and DHL Worldwide Express offer customer solutions through their consultative selling style, as does Xerox. According to a senior Xerox sales executive, "Our business is no longer about selling boxes. It's about selling digital, networked-based information management solutions, and this requires a highly customized and consultative selling process." But what does a customer solution really mean? The Marketing Matters box on the next page offers a unique answer.[15]

Handling Objections A critical concern in the presentation stage is handling objections. *Objections* are excuses for not making a purchase commitment or decision.

Some objections are valid and are based on the characteristics of the product or service or price. However, many objections reflect prospect skepticism or indifference. Whether valid or not, experienced salespeople know that objections do not put an end to the presentation. Rather, techniques can be used to deal with objections in a courteous, ethical, and professional manner. The following six techniques are the most common:[16]

1. *Acknowledge and convert the objection.* This technique involves using the objection as a reason for buying. For example, a prospect might say, "The price is too high." The reply: "Yes, the price is high because we use the finest materials. Let me show you. . . ."

2. *Postpone.* The postpone technique is used when the objection will be dealt with later in the presentation: "I'm going to address that point shortly. I think my answer would make better sense then."

3. *Agree and neutralize.* Here a salesperson agrees with the objection, then shows that it is unimportant. A salesperson would say, "That's true. Others have said the same. But, they thought that issue was outweighed by other benefits."

4. *Accept the objection.* Sometimes the objection is valid. Let the prospect express such views, probe for the reason behind it, and attempt to stimulate further discussion on the objection.

5. *Denial.* When a prospect's objection is based on misinformation and clearly untrue, it is wise to meet the objection head on with a firm denial.

6. *Ignore the objection.* This technique is used when it appears that the objection is a stalling mechanism or is clearly not important to the prospect.

Each of these techniques requires a calm, professional interaction with the prospect and is most effective when objections are anticipated in the preapproach stage. Handling objections is a skill requiring a sense of timing, appreciation for the prospect's state of mind, and adeptness in communication. Objections also should be handled ethically. Lying or misrepresenting product or service features are grossly unethical practices.

Close

The *closing* stage in the selling process involves obtaining a purchase commitment from the prospect. This stage is the most important and the most difficult because the salesperson must determine when the prospect is ready to buy. Telltale signals indicating a readiness to buy include body language (prospect reexamines the product or contract closely), statements ("This equipment should reduce our maintenance costs"), and questions ("When could we expect delivery?").

The close itself can take several forms. Three closing techniques are used when a salesperson believes a buyer is about ready to make a purchase: (1) trial close, (2) assumptive close, and (3) urgency close. A *trial close* involves asking the prospect to make a decision on some aspect of the purchase: "Would you prefer the blue or gray model?" An *assumptive close* entails asking the prospect to consider choices concerning delivery, warranty, or financing terms under the assumption that a sale has been finalized. An *urgency close* is used to commit the prospect quickly by making reference to the timeliness of the purchase: "The low interest financing ends next week," or "That is the last model we have in stock." Of course, these statements should be used only if they accurately reflect the situation; otherwise, such claims would be unethical. When a prospect is clearly ready to buy, the final close is used, and a salesperson asks for the order.

Follow-Up

The selling process does not end with the closing of a sale; rather, professional selling requires customer follow-up. One marketing authority equated the follow-up with courtship and marriage, by observing, "the sale merely consummates the courtship. Then the marriage begins. How good the marriage is depends on how well the relationship is managed."[17] The *follow-up* stage includes making certain the customer's purchase has been properly delivered and installed and difficulties experienced with the use of the item are addressed. Attention to this stage of the selling process solidifies the buyer–seller relationship. Research shows that the cost and effort to obtain repeat sales from a satisfied customer is roughly half of that necessary to gain a sale from a new customer.[18] In short, today's satisfied customers become tomorrow's qualified prospects or referrals. (What was your answer to question 3 in the quiz?)

---

learning review

5. What are the six stages in the personal selling process?

6. What is the distinction between a lead and a qualified prospect?

7. Which presentation format is most consistent with the marketing concept? Why?

THE SALES MANAGEMENT PROCESS

LO4

Selling must be managed if it is going to contribute to a firm's marketing objectives. Although firms differ in the specifics of how salespeople and the selling effort are managed, the sales management process is similar across firms. Sales management consists of three interrelated functions: (1) sales plan formulation, (2) sales plan implementation, and (3) salesforce evaluation (Figure 20–4 on the next page).

Sales Plan Formulation: Setting Direction

Formulating the sales plan is the most basic of the three sales management functions. According to the vice president of the Harris Corporation, a global communications

FIGURE 20–4

The sales management process involves sales plan formulation, sales plan implementation, and evaluation of the salesforce.

company, "If a company hopes to implement its marketing strategy, it really needs a detailed sales planning process."[19] The **sales plan** is a statement describing what is to be achieved and where and how the selling effort of salespeople is to be deployed. Sales plan formulation involves three tasks: (1) setting objectives, (2) organizing the salesforce, and (3) developing account management policies.

Setting Objectives Setting objectives is central to sales management because this task specifies what is to be achieved. In practice, objectives are set for the total salesforce and for each salesperson. Selling objectives can be output related and focus on dollar or unit sales volume, number of new customers added, and profit. Alternatively, they can be input related and emphasize the number of sales calls and selling expenses. Output- and input-related objectives are used for the salesforce as a whole and for each salesperson. A third type of objective that is behaviorally related is typically specific for each salesperson and includes his or her product knowledge, customer service, and selling and communication skills.

Increasingly, firms are also emphasizing knowledge of competition as an objective since salespeople are calling on customers and should see what competitors are doing. In fact, a recent survey indicated that 89 percent of companies encourage their salespeople to gather competitive intelligence.[20] But should salespeople explicitly ask their customers for information about competitors? Read the accompanying Making Responsible Decisions box to see how salespeople view this practice.[21]

Whatever objectives are set, they should be precise and measurable and specify the time period over which they are to be achieved. Once established, these objectives serve as performance standards for the evaluation of the salesforce, the third function of sales management.

Organizing the Salesforce Organizing a selling organization is the second task in formulating the sales plan. Three questions are related to organization. First, should the company use its own salesforce, or should it use independent agents such as manufacturer's representatives? Second, if the decision is made to employ company salespeople, then should they be organized according to geography, customer type, or product or service? Third, how many company salespeople should be employed?

The decision to use company salespeople or independent agents is made infrequently. The decision itself is based on an analysis of economic and behavioral factors. An economic analysis examines the costs of using both types of salespeople and is a form of break-even analysis.

Consider a situation in which independent agents would receive a 5 percent commission on sales, and company salespeople would receive a 3 percent commission, salaries, and benefits. In addition, with company salespeople, sales administration costs would be incurred for a total fixed cost of $500,000 per year. At what sales level would independent or company salespeople be less costly? This question can be answered by setting the costs of the two options equal to each other and solving for the sales level amount, as shown in the equation on the next page:

Making Responsible Decisions > > > > > > > ethics

The Ethics of Asking Customers about Competitors

Salespeople are a valuable source of information about what is happening in the marketplace. By working closely with customers and asking good questions, salespeople often have firsthand knowledge of customer problems and wants. They also are able to spot the activities of competitors. However, should salespeople explicitly ask customers about competitor strategies such as pricing practices, product development efforts, and trade and promotion programs?

Gaining knowledge about competitors by asking customers for

information is a ticklish ethical issue. Research indicates that 25 percent of U.S. salespeople engaged in business-to-business selling consider this practice unethical, and their companies have explicit guidelines for this practice. It is also noteworthy that Japanese salespeople consider this practice to be more unethical than do U.S. salespeople.

Do you believe that asking customers about competitor practices is unethical? Why or why not?

$$\text{Total cost of company salespeople} = \text{Total cost of independent agents}$$
$$[0.03(X) + \$500,000] = 0.05(X)$$

where X = sales volume. Solving for X, sales volume equals $25 million, indicating that below $25 million in sales independent agents would be cheaper, but above $25 million a company salesforce would be cheaper. This relationship is shown in Figure 20–5.

Economics alone does not answer this question, however. A behavioral analysis is also necessary and should focus on issues related to the control, flexibility, effort, and availability of independent and company salespeople.[22] An individual firm must weigh the pros and cons of the economic and behavioral considerations before making this decision.

If a company elects to employ its own salespeople, then it must choose an organizational structure based on (1) geography, (2) customer, or (3) product (Figure 20–6 on the next page). A geographical structure is the simplest organization, where the United States, or indeed the globe, is first divided into regions and each region is divided into districts or territories. Salespeople are assigned to each district with defined

FIGURE 20–5

A break-even chart for comparing independent agents and a company salesforce includes an analysis of selling costs and sales.

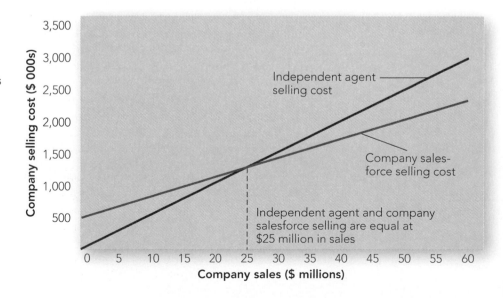

FIGURE 20–6
Organizing the salesforce
by customer, product, and
geography is common.
Read the text to learn why
companies use different
salesforce organizations.

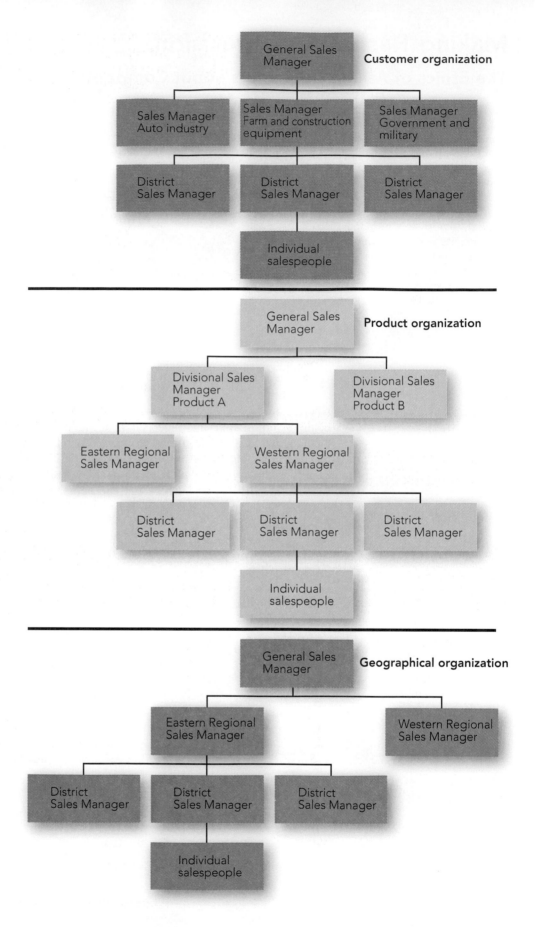

Customer organization

Product organization

Geographical organization

geographical boundaries and call on all customers and represent all products sold by the company. The principal advantage of this structure is that it can minimize travel time, expenses, and duplication of selling effort. However, if a firm's products or customers require specialized knowledge, then a geographical structure is unsuitable.

When different types of buyers have different needs, a customer sales organizational structure is used. In practice this means that a different salesforce calls on each separate type of buyer or marketing channel. For example, Kodak recently switched from a geographical to a marketing channel structure with different sales teams serving specific retail channels: mass merchandisers, photo specialty outlets, and food and drug stores. The rationale for this approach is that more effective, specialized customer support and knowledge are provided to buyers. However, this structure often leads to higher administrative costs and some duplication of selling effort, because two separate salesforces are used to represent the same products.

An important variation of the customer organizational structure is **key account management**—the practice of using team selling to focus on important customers so as to build mutually beneficial, long-term, cooperative relationships.[23] Key account management involves teams of sales, service, and often technical personnel who work with purchasing, manufacturing, engineering, logistics, and financial executives in customer organizations. This approach, which often assigns company personnel to a customer account, results in "customer specialists" who can provide exceptional service. Procter & Gamble uses this approach with Wal-Mart, as does Black & Decker with Home Depot.

When specific knowledge is required to sell certain types of products, then a product sales organization is used. For example, Lone Star Steel has a salesforce that sells drilling pipe to oil companies and another that sells specialty steel products to manufacturers. The primary advantage of this structure is that salespeople can develop expertise with technical characteristics, applications, and selling methods associated with a particular product or family of products. However, this structure produces high administrative costs and duplication of selling effort because two company salespeople may call on the same customer.

In short, there is no one best sales organization for all companies in all situations. Rather, the organization of the salesforce should reflect the marketing strategy of the firm. Each year about 10 percent of U.S. firms change their sales organizations to implement new marketing strategies.

The third question related to salesforce organization involves determining the size of the salesforce. For example, why do you think Frito-Lay has about 17,500 salespeople who call on supermarkets, convenience stores, and other establishments to sell snack foods? The answer lies in the number of accounts (customers) served, the frequency of calls on accounts, the length of an average call, and the amount of time a salesperson can devote to selling.

A common approach for determining the size of a salesforce is the **workload method**. This formula-based method integrates the number of customers served, call frequency, call length, and available selling time to arrive at a figure for the salesforce size. For example, Frito-Lay needs about 17,500 salespeople according to the following workload method formula:

Steel companies such as Lone Star Steel often organize their salesforce by product or product families to better serve customers.

Lone Star Steel
www.lonestarsteel.com

$$NS = \frac{NC \times CF \times CL}{AST}$$

where,

NS = Number of salespeople

NC = Number of customers

CF = Call frequency necessary to service a customer each year

CL = Length of an average call

AST = Average amount of selling time available per year

Frito-Lay sells its products to 350,000 supermarkets, convenience stores, and other establishments. Salespeople should call on these accounts at least once a week, or 52 times a year. The average sales call lasts an average of 81 minutes (1.35 hour). An average salesperson works 2,000 hours a year (50 weeks × 40 hours a week), but 12 hours a week are devoted to nonselling activities such as travel and administration, leaving 1,400 hours a year. Using these guidelines, Frito-Lay would need

$$NS = \frac{350,000 \times 52 \times 1.35}{1,400} = 17,550 \text{ salespeople}$$

The value of this formula is apparent in its flexibility; a change in any one of the variables will affect the number of salespeople needed. Changes are determined, in part, by the firm's account management policies.

Developing Account Management Policies   The third task in formulating a sales plan involves developing **account management policies** specifying whom salespeople should contact, what kinds of selling and customer service activities should be engaged in, and how these activities should be carried out. These policies might state which individuals in a buying organization should be contacted, the amount of sales and service effort that different customers should receive, and the kinds of information salespeople should collect before or during a sales call.

An example of an account management policy in Figure 20–7 shows how different accounts or customers can be grouped according to level of opportunity and the firm's competitive sales position.[24] When specific account names are placed in each cell, salespeople clearly see which accounts should be contacted, with what level of selling and service activity, and how to deal with them. Accounts in cells 1 and 2 might have high frequencies of personal sales calls and increased time spent on a call. Cell 3 accounts will have lower call frequencies, and cell 4 accounts might be contacted through telemarketing or direct mail rather than in person. For example, Union Pacific Railroad put its 20,000 smallest accounts on a telemarketing program. A subsequent survey of these accounts indicated that 84 percent rated Union Pacific's sales effort "very effective" compared with 67 percent before the switch.

FIGURE 20–7

An account management policy grid grouping customers according to the level of opportunity and a firm's competitive sales position

Competitive position of sales organization

	High	**Low**
High	**1** *Attractiveness:* Accounts offer a good opportunity because they have high potential and the sales organization has a strong position. *Account management policy:* Accounts should receive high level of sales calls and service to retain and possibly build accounts.	**3** *Attractiveness:* Accounts may offer a good opportunity if the sales organization can overcome its weak position. *Account management policy:* Emphasize a heavy sales organization position or shift resources to other accounts if a stronger sales organization position is impossible.
Low	**2** *Attractiveness:* Accounts are somewhat attractive because the sales organization has a strong position, but future opportunity is limited. *Account management policy:* Accounts should receive moderate level of sales and service to maintain current position of sales organization.	**4** *Attractiveness:* Accounts offer little opportunity, and the sales organization position is weak. *Account management policy:* Consider replacing personal calls with telephone sales or direct mail to service accounts. Consider dropping account if unprofitable.

Account opportunity

A person's success at work depends on many talents, including intelligence and technical skills. Recent research indicates that an individual's emotional intelligence is also important, if not more important! Emotional intelligence has five dimensions: (1) self-motivation skills; (2) self-awareness, or knowing one's own emotions; (3) the ability to manage one's emotions and impulses; (4) empathy, or the ability to sense how others are feeling; and (5) social skills, or the ability to handle the emotions of other people.

What is your emotional intelligence? Visit the website at www.ihhp.com/quiz.php. Answer 20 questions to learn what your emotional intelligence is and obtain additional insights.

Sales Plan Implementation: Putting the Plan into Action

The sales plan is put into practice through the tasks associated with sales plan implementation. Whereas sales plan formulation focuses on "doing the right things," implementation emphasizes "doing things right." The three major tasks involved in implementing a sales plan are: (1) salesforce recruitment and selection, (2) salesforce training, and (3) salesforce motivation and compensation.

Salesforce Recruitment and Selection Effective recruitment and selection of salespeople is one of the most crucial tasks of sales management. It entails finding people who match the type of sales position required by a firm. Recruitment and selection practices would differ greatly between order-taking and order-getting sales positions, given the differences in the demands of these two jobs. Therefore, recruitment and selection begin with a carefully crafted job analysis and job description followed by a statement of job qualifications.

A *job analysis* is a study of a particular sales position, including how the job is to be performed and the tasks that make up the job. Information from a job analysis is used to write a *job description,* a written document that describes job relationships and requirements that characterize each sales position. It explains: (1) to whom a salesperson reports, (2) how a salesperson interacts with other company personnel, (3) the customers to be called on, (4) the specific activities to be carried out, (5) the physical and mental demands of the job, and (6) the types of products and services to be sold.

The job description is then translated into a statement of job qualifications, including the aptitudes, knowledge, skills, and a variety of behavioral characteristics considered necessary to perform the job successfully. Qualifications for order-getting sales positions often mirror the expectations of buyers: (1) imagination and problem-solving ability, (2) honesty, (3) intimate product knowledge, and (4) attentiveness reflected in responsiveness to buyer needs and customer loyalty and follow-up.[25] Firms use a variety of methods for evaluating prospective salespeople. Personal interviews, reference checks, and background information provided on application forms are the most frequently used methods.

Successful selling also requires a high degree of emotional intelligence. **Emotional intelligence** is the ability to understand one's own emotions and the emotions of people with whom one interacts on a daily basis. These qualities are important for adaptive selling and may spell the difference between effective and ineffective order-getting salespeople.[26] Are you interested in what your emotional intelligence might be? Read the accompanying Going Online box and test yourself.

The search for qualified salespeople has produced an increasingly diverse salesforce in the United States. Women now represent almost half of all professional salespeople, and minority representation is growing. The fastest growth rate is among salespeople of Asian and Hispanic descent[27] (see Figure 20–8 on the next page).

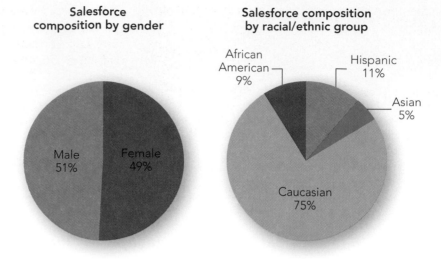

Salesforce composition by gender

Male 51%
Female 49%

Salesforce composition by racial/ethnic group

African American 9%
Hispanic 11%
Asian 5%
Caucasian 75%

Salesforce Training   Whereas recruitment and selection of salespeople is a onetime event, salesforce training is an ongoing process that affects both new and seasoned salespeople.[28] Sales training covers much more than selling practices. For example, IBM Global Services salespeople, who sell consulting and various information technology services, take at least two weeks of in-class and Internet-based training on both consultative selling and the technical aspects of business.

Training new salespeople is an expensive process. Salespeople in the United States receive employer-sponsored training annually at a cost of over $7 billion per year. On-the-job training is the most popular type of training, followed by individual instruction taught by experienced salespeople. Formal classes, seminars taught by sales trainers, and computer-based training are also popular.

Salesforce Motivation and Compensation   A sales plan cannot be successfully implemented without motivated salespeople. Research on salesperson motivation suggests that: (1) a clear job description, (2) effective sales management practices, (3) a personal need for achievement, and (4) proper compensation, incentives, or rewards will produce a motivated salesperson.[29]

The importance of compensation as a motivating factor means that close attention must be given to how salespeople are financially rewarded for their efforts. Salespeople are paid using one of three plans: (1) straight salary, (2) straight commission, or (3) a combination of salary and commission. Under a *straight salary compensation plan,* a salesperson is paid a fixed fee per week, month, or year. With a *straight commission compensation plan,* a salesperson's earnings are directly tied to the sales or profit generated. For example, an insurance agent might receive a 2 percent commission of $2,000 for selling a $100,000 life insurance policy. A *combination compensation plan* contains a specified salary plus a commission on sales or profit generated.

Each compensation plan has its advantages and disadvantages.[30] A straight salary plan is easy to administer and gives management a large measure of control over how salespeople allocate their efforts. However, it provides little incentive to expand sales volume. This plan is used when salespeople engage in many nonselling activities, such as account or customer servicing. A straight commission plan provides the maximum amount of selling incentive but can detract salespeople from providing customer service. This plan is common when nonselling activities are minimal. Combination plans are most preferred by salespeople and attempt to build on the advantages of salary and commission plans while reducing potential shortcomings of each. A majority of companies use combination plans today.

Why is Jill Moore, a successful Mary Kay Cosmetics national sales director, posing with a new pink Cadillac Escalade before the company's annual sales meeting? Read the text to learn how Mary Kay rewards its top sales performers.

Mary Kay Cosmetics, Inc.
www.marykay.com

Nonmonetary rewards are also given to salespeople for meeting or exceeding objectives. These rewards include trips, honor societies, distinguished salesperson awards, and letters of commendation. Some unconventional rewards include the new pink Cadillacs and Pontiacs, and jewelry given by Mary Kay Cosmetics to outstanding salespeople. Mary Kay, with 12,000 cars, has the largest fleet of General Motors cars in the world.[31]

Effective recruitment, selection, training, motivation, and compensation programs combine to create a productive salesforce. Ineffective practices often lead to costly salesforce turnover. The expense of replacing and training a new salesperson, including the cost of lost sales, can be high. Also, new recruits are often less productive than seasoned salespeople.

Salesforce Evaluation: Measuring Results

The final function in the sales management process involves evaluating the salesforce. It is at this point that salespeople are assessed as to whether sales objectives were met and account management policies were followed. Both quantitative and behavioral measures are used to tap different selling dimensions.

Quantitative Assessments Quantitative assessments are based on input- and output-related objectives set forth in the sales plan. Input-related measures focus on the actual activities performed by salespeople such as those involving sales calls, selling expenses, and account management policies. The number of sales calls made, selling expense related to sales made, and the number of reports submitted to superiors are frequently used input measures.

Output measures often appear in a sales quota. A **sales quota** contains specific goals assigned to a salesperson, sales team, branch sales office, or sales district for a stated time period. Dollar or unit sales volume, last year/current sales ratio, sales of specific products, new accounts generated, and profit achieved are typical goals. The time period can range from one month to one year.

Behavioral Evaluation Behavioral measures are also used to evaluate salespeople. These include assessments of a salesperson's attitude, attention to customers, product knowledge, selling and communication skills, appearance, and professional demeanor. Even though these assessments are sometimes subjective, they are frequently considered and, in fact, inevitable, in salesperson evaluation. Why? These factors are often important determinants of quantitative outcomes.

About 60 percent of U.S. companies now include customer satisfaction as a behavioral measure of salesperson performance. (What percentage did you check for question 4 in Figure 20–1?) The relentless focus on customer satisfaction by Eastman Chemical Company salespeople contributed to the company being named a recipient of the prestigious Malcolm Baldrige National Quality Award.[32] Eastman surveys its customers with multiple versions of its customer satisfaction questionnaire delivered in nine languages. Some 25 performance items are studied, including on-time and correct delivery, product quality, pricing practice, and sharing of market information. Salespeople review the results with customers. Eastman salespeople know that "the second most important thing they have to do is get their customer satisfaction surveys out to and back from customers," says Eastman's sales training director. "Number one, of course, is getting orders."

Increasingly, companies are using marketing dashboards to track salesperson performance for evaluation purposes. An illustration appears in the Using Marketing Dashboards box on the next page.

Using Marketing Dashboards
Tracking Salesperson Performance at Moore Chemical & Sanitation Supply, Inc.

Moore Chemical & Sanitation Supply, Inc. (MooreChem) is a large midwestern supplier of cleaning chemicals and sanitary products. MooreChem sells to janitorial companies that clean corporate and professional office buildings.

MooreChem recently installed a sales and account management planning software package that included a dashboard for each of its sales representatives. Salespeople had access to their dashboards as well. These dashboards included seven measures—sales revenue, gross margin, selling expense, profit, average order size, new customers, and customer satisfaction. Each measure was gauged to show actual salesperson performance relative to target goals.

Your Challenge As a newly promoted district sales manager at MooreChem, your responsibilities include tracking each salesperson's performance in your district. You are also responsible for directing the sales activities and practices of district salespeople.

In anticipation of a performance review with one of your salespeople, Brady Boyle, you review his dashboard for the previous quarter. Provide a constructive review of his performance.

Your Findings Brady Boyle's quarterly performance is displayed below. Boyle has exceeded targeted goals for sales revenue, selling expenses, and customer satisfaction. All of these measures show an upward trend. He has met his target for gaining new customers and average order size. But, Boyle's gross margin and profit are below targeted goals. These measures evidence a downward trend as well. Brady Boyle's mixed performance requires a constructive and positive correction.

Your Action Brady Boyle should already know how his performance compares with targeted goals. Remember, Boyle has access to his dashboard. Recall that he has exceeded his sales target, but is considerably under his profit target. Boyle's sales trend is up, but his profit trend is down.

You will need to focus attention on Boyle's gross margin and selling expense results and trend. Boyle, it seems, is spending time and money selling lower margin products that produce a targeted average order size. It may very well be that Boyle is actually expending effort selling more products to his customers. Unfortunately, the product mix yields lower gross margins, resulting in a lower profit.

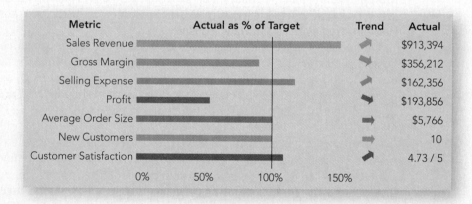

Metric	Actual as % of Target	Trend	Actual
Sales Revenue		↗	$913,394
Gross Margin		↘	$356,212
Selling Expense		↗	$162,356
Profit		↘	$193,856
Average Order Size		➡	$5,766
New Customers		➡	10
Customer Satisfaction		↗	4.73 / 5

Salesforce Automation and Customer Relationship Management

Personal selling and sales management have undergone a technological revolution with the integration of salesforce automation into customer relationship management processes. In fact, the convergence of computer, information, communication, and Internet technologies has transformed the sales function in many companies and made the promise of customer relationship management a reality. **Salesforce automation** (SFA) is the use of these technologies to make the sales function more effective and efficient. SFA applies to a wide range of activities, including each stage in the personal selling process and management of the salesforce itself.[33]

 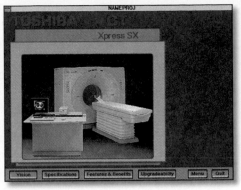

Toshiba America Medical System salespeople have found computer technology to be an effective sales presentation tool and training device.

Toshiba America Medical Systems
www.toshiba.com

Salesforce automation exists in many forms. Examples of SFA applications include computer hardware and software for account analysis, time management, order processing and follow-up, sales presentations, proposal generation, and product and sales training. Each application is designed to ease administrative tasks and free up time for salespeople to be with customers building relationships, designing solutions, and providing service.

Salesforce Technology Technology has become an integral part of field selling. Today, most companies supply their field salespeople with laptop computers. For example, salespeople for Godiva Chocolates use their laptop computers to process orders, plan time allocations, forecast sales, and communicate with Godiva personnel and customers. While in a department store candy buyer's office, such as Neiman Marcus, a salesperson can calculate the order cost (and discount), transmit the order, and obtain a delivery date within minutes from Godiva's order processing department.[34]

Toshiba America Medical System salespeople use laptop computers with built-in CD-ROM capabilities to provide interactive presentations for their computerized tomography (CT) and magnetic resonance imaging (MRI) scanners. In it the customer sees elaborate three-dimensional animations, high-resolution scans, and video clips of the company's products in operation as well as narrated testimonials from satisfied customers. Toshiba has found this application to be effective both for sales presentations and for training its salespeople.[35]

Salespeople rely upon multiple communication technologies to perform their selling and nonselling tasks today.

Salesforce Communication Technology has changed the way salespeople communicate with customers, other salespeople and sales support personnel, and management. Facsimile, electronic mail, and voice mail are common communication technologies used by salespeople today. Cellular (phone) technology, which now allows salespeople to exchange data, text, and voice transmissions, is also popular. Whether traveling or in a customer's office, these technologies provide information at the salesperson's fingertips to answer customer questions and solve problems.

Advances in communication and computer technologies have made possible the mobile and home sales office. Some salespeople now equip minivans with a fully functional desk, swivel chair, light, computer, printer, fax machine, cellular phone, and a satellite dish. Jeff Brown, an agent manager with U.S. Cellular, uses such a mobile office. He says, "If I arrive at a prospect's office and they can't see me right away, then I can go outside to work in my office until they're ready to see me."[36]

Home offices are now common. Hewlett-Packard is a case in point. The company shifted its U.S. salesforce into home offices, closed several regional sales offices, and saved millions of dollars in staff salaries and office rent. A fully equipped home office for each salesperson includes a notebook computer, fax/copier, cellular phone, two phone lines, and office furniture.

Perhaps the greatest impact on salesforce communication is the application of Internet technology. Today, salespeople are using their company's intranet for a variety of purposes. At EDS, a professional services firm, salespeople access its intranet to download client material, marketing content, account information, technical papers, and competitive profiles. In addition, EDS offers 7,000 training classes that salespeople can take anytime and anywhere.

Salesforce automation is clearly changing how selling is done and how salespeople are managed. Its numerous applications promise to boost selling productivity, improve customer relationships, and decrease selling cost.

---

learning review

8. What are the three types of selling objectives?

9. What three factors are used to structure sales organizations?

10. How does emotional intelligence tie to adaptive selling?

LEARNING OBJECTIVES REVIEW

LO1 *Discuss the nature and scope of personal selling and sales management in marketing.*
Personal selling involves the two-way flow of communication between a buyer and seller, often in a face-to-face encounter, designed to influence a person's or group's purchase decision. Sales management involves planning the selling program and implementing and controlling the personal selling effort of the firm. The scope of selling and sales management is apparent in three ways. First, virtually every occupation that involves customer contact has an element of personal selling. Second, selling plays a significant role in a company's overall marketing effort. Salespeople occupy a boundary position between buyers and sellers; they *are* the company to many buyers and account for a major cost of marketing in a variety of industries; and they can create value for customers. Finally, through relationship and partnership selling, salespeople play a central role in tailoring solutions to customer problems as a means to customer value creation.

LO2 *Identify the different types of personal selling.*
Three types of personal selling exist: (*a*) order taking, (*b*) order getting, and (*c*) customer sales support activities. Each type differs from the others in terms of actual selling done and the amount of creativity required to perform the sales task. Order takers process routine orders or reorders for products that were already sold by the company. They generally do little selling in a conventional sense and engage in only modest problem solving with customers. Order getters sell in a conventional sense and identify prospective customers, provide customers with information, persuade customers to buy, close sales, and follow up on customers' use of a product or service. Order getting involves a high degree of creativity and customer empathy and is typically required for selling complex or technical products with many options. Customer sales support personnel augment the sales effort of order getters by performing a variety of services. Sales support personnel are prominent in cross-functional team selling, the practice of using an entire team of professionals in selling to and servicing major customers.

LO3 *Explain the stages in the personal selling process.*
The personal selling process consists of six stages: (*a*) prospecting, (*b*) preapproach, (*c*) approach, (*d*) presentation, (*e*) close, and (*f*) follow-up. Prospecting involves the search for and qualification of potential customers. The preapproach stage involves obtaining further information on the prospect and deciding on the best method of approach. The approach stage involves the initial meeting between the salesperson and prospect. The presentation stage involves converting a prospect into a customer by creating a desire for the product or service. The close involves obtaining a purchase commitment from the prospect. The follow-up stage involves making certain that the customer's purchase has been properly delivered and installed and difficulties experienced with the use of the item are addressed.

LO4 *Describe the major functions of sales management.*
Sales management consists of three interrelated functions: (*a*) sales plan formulation, (*b*) sales plan implementation, and (*c*) evaluation of the salesforce. Sales plan formulation involves setting objectives, organizing the salesforce, and developing account management policies. Sales plan implementation involves salesforce recruitment, selection, training, motivation, and compensation. Finally, salesforce evaluation focuses on quantitative assessments of sales performance and behavioral measures such as customer satisfaction that are linked to selling objectives and account management policies.

APPLYING MARKETING KNOWLEDGE

1 Jane Dawson is a new sales representative for the Charles Schwab brokerage firm. In searching for clients, Jane purchased a mailing list of subscribers to *The Wall Street Journal* and called them all regarding their interest in discount brokerage services. She asked if they have any stocks and if they have a regular broker. Those people without a regular broker were asked their investment needs. Two days later, Jane called back with investment advice and asked if they would like to open an account. Identify each of Jane Dawson's actions in terms of the personal selling process.

2 For the first 50 years of business the Johnson Carpet Company produced carpets for residential use. The salesforce was structured geographically. In the past five years, a large percentage of carpet sales has been to industrial users, hospitals, schools, and architects. The company also has broadened its product line to include area rugs, Oriental carpets, and wall-to-wall carpeting. Is the present salesforce structure appropriate, or would you recommend an alternative?

3 Where would you place each of the following sales jobs on the order-taker/order-getter continuum shown below? (*a*) Burger King counter clerk, (*b*) automobile insurance salesperson, (*c*) Hewlett-Packard computer salesperson, (*d*) life insurance salesperson, and (*e*) shoe salesperson.

Order taker	Order getter

4 Listed here are two different firms. Which compensation plan would you recommend for each firm, and

what reasons would you give for your recommendations? (*a*) A newly formed company that sells lawn care equipment on a door-to-door basis directly to consumers; and (*b*) the Nabisco Company, which sells heavily advertised products in supermarkets by having the salesforce call on these stores and arrange shelves, set up displays, and make presentations to store buying committees.

5 The TDK tape company services 1,000 audio stores throughout the United States. Each store is called on 12 times a year, and the average sales call lasts 30 minutes. Assuming a salesperson works 40 hours a week, 50 weeks a year, and devotes 75 percent of the time to actual selling, how many salespeople does TDK need?

6 A furniture manufacturer is currently using manufacturer's representatives to sell its line of living room furniture. These representatives receive an 8 percent commission. The company is considering hiring its own salespeople and has estimated that the fixed cost of managing and paying their salaries would be $1 million annually. The salespeople would also receive a 4 percent commission on sales. The company has sales of $25 million dollars, and sales are expected to grow by 15 percent next year. Would you recommend that the company switch to its own salesforce? Why or why not?

7 Suppose someone said to you, "The only real measure of a salesperson is the amount of sales produced." How might you respond?

building your marketing plan

Does your marketing plan involve a personal selling activity? If the answer is no, read no further and do not include a personal selling element in your plan. If the answer is yes:

1 Identify the likely prospects for your product or service.

2 Determine what information you should obtain about the prospect.

3 Describe how you would approach the prospect.

4 Outline the presentation you would make to the prospect for your product or service.

5 Develop a sales plan, focusing on the organizational structure you would use for your salesforce (geography, product, or customer).

"I'm like the quarterback of the team. I manage 250 accounts, and anything from billing issues, to service issues, to selling the products. I'm really the face to the customer," says Alison Capossela, a Washington, D.C.-based Xerox sales representative.

As the primary company contact for Xerox customers, Alison is responsible for developing and maintaining customer relationships. To accomplish this she uses a sophisticated selling process which requires many activities from making presentations, to attending training sessions, to managing a team of Xerox personnel, to monitoring competitors' activities. The face-to-face interactions with customers, however, are the most rewarding for Capossela. "It's an amazing feeling; the more they challenge me the more I fight back. It's fun!" she explains.

THE COMPANY

Xerox Corporation's mission is to "help people find better ways to do great work by constantly leading in document technologies, products, and services that improve customers' work processes and business results." To accomplish this mission Xerox employs 53,700 people in 160 countries. With annual sales of $16 billion, Xerox is the world's leading document management enterprise and a Fortune 500 company. Xerox offers a wide range of products and services. These include printers, copiers and fax machines, multifunction and network devices, high-speed color presses, digital imaging and archiving products and services, and supplies such as toner, paper, and ink. The entire company is guided by customer-focused and employee-centered core values (e.g., "We succeed through satisfied customers") and a passion for innovation, speed, and adaptability.

Xerox was founded in 1906 as a manufacturer of photographic paper called The Haloid Company. In 1947, the company purchased the license to basic xerographic patents. The following year it received a trademark for the word "Xerox." By 1973 Xerox had introduced the automatic, plain-paper copier, opened offices in Japan, and its Palo Alto Research Center (PARC) had invented the world's first personal computer (the Alto), the "mouse," and graphical user interface software. In 1994, Xerox adopted "The Document Company" as its signature and the partially digitized red "X" as its corporate symbol. Despite this extraordinary history of success, Xerox was $19 billion in debt by 2000 and was losing business rapidly. Many experts predicted that the company would fail.

The Xerox board of directors knew a change was needed and it asked Anne M. Mulcahy to serve as the company's CEO. Mulcahy had begun her career as a sales representative at Xerox and observed that "we had lost our way in terms of delivering value to customers." Mulcahy reduced the size of the workforce by one-third and invested in new technologies, while keeping the Xerox culture and values. The changes, coupled with Mulcahy's commitment to a sales organization that focused on customer relationships, reversed Xerox's decline. As Kevin Warren, vice president of sales explains: "One of the reasons she has been so successful is that she absolutely resonates with all the people. I think [because of] the fact that she started out as a sales rep, people feel like she is one of them." The turnaround has been such an extraordinary success that Mulcahy was recently recognized by *Forbes* magazine as the fifth most powerful woman in the world!

THE SELLING PROCESS AT XEROX

When Mulcahy became CEO, Xerox began a shift to a consultative selling model that focused on helping customers solve their business problems rather than just placing more equipment in their office. The shift meant that sales reps needed to be less product-oriented and more relationship- and value-oriented. Xerox wanted to be a provider of total solutions. Today, Xerox has more than 8,000 sales professionals throughout the world who spend a large amount of their day developing customer relationships. Capossela explains: "Fifty percent of my day is spent with my customers, twenty-five percent is following up with phone calls or emails, and another twenty-five percent involves preparing proposals." The approach has helped Xerox attract new customers and keep existing customers.

The sales process at Xerox typically follows the six stages of the personal selling process identified in Figure 20–3: (1) Xerox identifies potential clients through responses to advertising, referrals, and telephone calls; (2) the salesforce prepares for a presentation by familiarizing themselves with the potential client and its document needs; (3) a Xerox sales representative approaches the prospect and suggests a meeting and presentation; (4) as the presentation begins, the salesperson summarizes relevant information about potential solutions Xerox can offer, states what he or she hopes to get out of the meeting, explains how the products and services work, and reinforces the benefits of working with Xerox; (5) the salesperson engages in an action close (gets a signed document or a firm confirmation of the sale); and then (6) continues to meet and communicate with the client to provide assistance and monitor the effectiveness of the installed solution.

Xerox sales representatives also use the selling process to maintain relationships with existing customers.

In today's competitive environment it is not unusual to have customers who have been approached by competitors or who are required to obtain more than one bid before renewing a contract. Xerox has teams of people who collect and analyze information about competitors and their products. The information is sent out to sales reps or offered to them through workshops and seminars. The most difficult competitors are the ones that have also invested in customer relationships. The selling process allows Xerox to continually react and respond to new information and take advantage of opportunities in the marketplace.

the new consultative selling approach. The components of the program consisted of interactive training sessions and distance-learning Webinars. Every new sales representative at Xerox receives eight weeks of training development in the field and at the Xerox Corporate University in Virginia. "The training program is phenomenal!" according to Capossela. The training and its focus on the customer is part of the Xerox culture outside of the sales organization also. Every senior executive at Xerox is responsible for working with at least one customer. They also spend a full day every month responding to incoming customer calls and inquiries.

THE SALES MANAGEMENT PROCESS AT XEROX

The Xerox salesforce is divided into four geographic organizations: North America, which includes the United States and Canada; Europe, which includes 17 countries; Global Accounts, which manages large accounts that operate in multiple locations; and Developing Markets, which includes all other geographic territories that may require Xerox products and services. Within each geographic area, the majority of Xerox products and services are typically sold through its direct salesforce. Xerox also utilizes a variety of other channels, including value-added resellers, independent agents, dealers, systems integrators, telephone, and Internet sales channels.

Motivation and compensation is an important aspect of any salesforce. At Xerox there is a passion for winning that provides a key incentive for sales reps. In addition, the compensation plan plays an important role. As Warren explains, "Our compensation plans are a combination of salary as well as an opportunity to leverage earnings through sales commissions and bonuses." Xerox also has a recognition program called the President's Club where the top performers are awarded a five-day trip to one of the top resorts in the world. The program has been a huge success and has now been offered for more than 30 years.

Perhaps the most well-known component of Xerox's sales management process is its sales representative training program. For example, Xerox developed the "Create and Win" program to help sales reps learn

WHAT IS IN THE FUTURE FOR THE XEROX SALESFORCE?

The recent growth and success at Xerox is creating many opportunities for the company and for its sales representatives. For example, Xerox is accelerating the development of its top salespeople. Mentors are used to provide advice for day-to-day issues and long-term career planning. In addition, globalization has become such an important initiative at Xerox that experienced and successful sales representatives are quickly given opportunities to manage large global accounts. Xerox is also moving toward an approach that empowers sales representatives to make decisions about how to handle accounts. The large number of Xerox customers means there are a variety of different corporate styles, and the sales reps are increasingly the best qualified to manage the relationship. This approach is just one more example of Xerox's commitment to customers and creating customer value.

Questions

1 Why was Anne Mulcahy's experience as a sales representative an important part of Xerox's growth in recent years?

2 How did the sales approach change after Mulcahy became the CEO of Xerox?

3 How does Xerox create customer value though its personal selling process? How does Alison Capossela provide solutions for Xerox customers?

4 Why is the Xerox training program so important to the company's success?

21

Implementing Interactive and Multichannel Marketing

LEARNING OBJECTIVES

After reading this chapter you should be able to:

LO1 Describe what interactive marketing is and how it creates customer value, customer relationships, and customer experiences.

LO2 Identify the demographic and lifestyle profile of online consumers.

LO3 Explain why certain types of products and services are particularly suited for interactive marketing.

LO4 Describe why consumers shop and buy online and how marketers influence online purchasing behavior.

LO5 Define cross-channel shoppers and the role of transactional and promotional websites in reaching these shoppers.

SEVEN CYCLES. ONE BIKE. YOURS.

"One bike: Yours" is the company motto for Seven Cycles, Inc., located in Watertown, Massachusetts. And for good reason.

Seven Cycles is the largest custom bicycle frame builder in the world. The company produces a huge range of road, mountain, cyclo-cross, triathlon, single-speed, and tandem bikes annually, and no two bikes are exactly alike. At Seven Cycles, attention is focused on each customer's unique cycling experience through the optimum fit, function, performance, and comfort of his or her very own bike. According to one satisfied customer, "Getting a Seven is more of a creation than a purchase."

The marketing success of Seven Cycles is due certainly to its state-of-the-art bicycle frames. But as Rob Vandermark, company founder and president, says, "Part of our success is that we are tied to a business model that includes the Internet."

Seven Cycles uses its multi-language (English, German, Chinese, Japanese, and Korean) website (www.sevencycles.com) to let customers get deeply involved in the frame-building process and the selection of wheels, drivetrain components, saddle, and handlebars to complete the bike. It enables customers to design their own bike using the company's Custom Kit™ fitting system that considers the rider's size and riding habits. Then, customers can track their custom bike all the way through the development and production process by clicking "Where's My Frame?" on the Seven Cycles website.

This customization process and continuous feedback makes for a collaborative relationship between Seven Cycles, its 230 authorized dealers and distributors, and customers in 40 countries. "It also results in a customer experience as unique as each bike made," says Jennifer Miller, director of marketing at Seven Cycles.[1]

This chapter describes how companies design and implement interactive marketing programs that capitalize on the unique value-creation capabilities of Internet technology. We begin by explaining how this technology can create customer value, build customer relationships, and produce customer experiences in novel ways. Next, we describe how Internet technology affects and is affected by consumer behavior and marketing practice. Finally, we show how marketers integrate and leverage their communication and delivery channels using Internet technology to implement multichannel marketing programs.

CREATING CUSTOMER VALUE, RELATIONSHIPS, AND EXPERIENCES IN MARKETSPACE

LO1

Consumers and companies populate two market environments today. One is the traditional *marketplace.* Here buyers and sellers engage in face-to-face exchange relationships in a material environment characterized by physical facilities (stores and offices) and mostly tangible objects. The other is the *marketspace,* an Internet-enabled digital environment characterized by face-to-screen exchange relationships and electronic images and offerings.

The existence of two market environments has been a boon for consumers. Today, consumers can shop for and purchase a wide variety of products and services in either market environment. Actually, many consumers now browse and buy in both market environments, and more are expected to do so in the future. Figure 21–1 shows the growth in online shoppers and estimated retail sales in the United States since 2000.[2] By 2011, 156 million individuals, or 80 percent of Internet users ages 14 and older, will shop online in the United States. They are projected to buy $340 billion worth of products and services in 2011.

Marketing in two market environments also poses significant challenges for companies. Companies with origins in the traditional marketplace, such as Procter & Gamble, Wal-Mart, and General Motors, are challenged to define the nature and scope of their marketspace presence. These companies continue to refine the role of Internet technology in attracting, retaining, and building consumer relationships to improve their competitive positions in the traditional marketplace while achieving a marketspace presence.

On the other hand, companies with marketspace origins, including Amazon.com, eBay, E*TRADE, and others, are challenged to continually refine, broaden, and deepen their marketspace presence, and consider what role, if any, the traditional marketplace will play in their future. Regardless of origin, a company's success in achieving a meaningful marketspace presence hinges largely on its ability to design and execute a marketing program that capitalizes on the unique value-creation and relationship-building capabilities of Internet technology in delivering a favorable customer experience.

Customer Value Creation in Marketspace

FIGURE 21–1

Trend in online shoppers and online retail sales revenue in the United States

Why has the marketspace captured the eye and imagination of marketers worldwide? Recall from Chapter 1 that marketing creates time, place, form, and possession

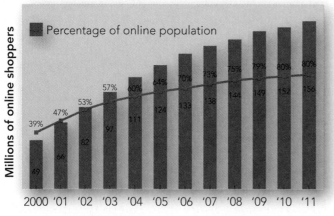

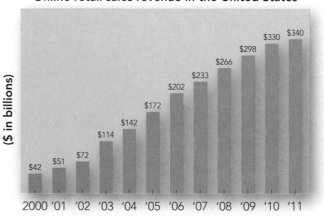

utilities, thereby providing value. Marketers believe that the possibilities for customer value creation are greater in the digital marketspace than in the physical marketplace.

In marketspace, the provision of direct, on-demand information is possible from marketers *anywhere* to customers *anywhere at any time.* Why? Operating hours and geographical constraints do not exist in marketspace. For example, Recreational Equipment (www.rei.com), an outdoor gear marketer, reports that 35 percent of its orders are placed between 10:00 p.m. and 7:00 a.m., long after and before retail stores are open for business. This isn't surprising. About 58 percent of Internet users prefer to shop and buy in their pajamas.[3] Similarly, a U.S. consumer from Chicago can access Marks & Spencer (www.marks-and-spencer.co.uk), the well-known British department store, to shop for clothing as easily as a person living near London's Piccadilly Square.

Possession utility—getting a product or service to consumers so they can own or use it—is accelerated. Airline, car rental, and lodging electronic reservation systems such as Orbitz (www.orbitz.com) allow comparison shopping for the lowest fares, rents, and rates and almost immediate access to and confirmation of travel arrangements and accommodations. Not surprisingly, Internet usage among people who travel on a regular basis is 20 percent higher than those who travel infrequently.[4]

The greatest marketspace opportunity for marketers, however, lies in its potential for creating form utility. Interactive two-way Internet-enabled communication capabilities in marketspace invite consumers to tell marketers specifically what

Seven Cycles creates form utility in the creation of customized bikes for its customers in 40 countries.

Seven Cycles, Inc.
www.sevencycles.com

Pavement. Dirt. **Whatever.**

No matter what form your two-wheeled passion takes. Whatever road, trail, or entirely improvised route you follow. There is a Seven for you. Expertly designed and handcrafted for who you are and the way you ride.

seven cycles

www.sevencycles.com   telephone 617.923.7774   email info@sevencycles.com   **One Bike. Yours.**

their requirements are, making customization of a product or service to fit the buyer's exact needs possible. For instance, at Godiva.com, customers can choose an assortment of their favorite chocolates from an online catalog for a gift or a delectable self-indulgent treat. Or, consumers can arrange for a custom-made mountain bike from Seven Cycles as described in the chapter opening example.

Interactivity, Individuality, and Customer Relationships in Marketspace

Marketers also benefit from two unique capabilities of Internet technology that promote and sustain customer relationships. One is *interactivity;* the other is *individuality*.[5] Both capabilities are important building blocks for buyer–seller relationships. For these relationships to occur, companies need to interact with their customers by listening and responding to their needs. Marketers must also treat customers as individuals and empower them to (1) influence the timing and extent of the buyer–seller interaction and (2) have a say in the kind of products and services they buy, the information they receive, and in some cases, the prices they pay.

Internet technology allows for interaction, individualization, and customer relationship building to be carried out on a scale never before available and makes interactive marketing possible. **Interactive marketing** involves two-way buyer–seller electronic communication in a computer-mediated environment in which the buyer controls the kind and amount of information received from the seller. Interactive marketing today is characterized by sophisticated choiceboard and personalization systems that transform information supplied by customers into customized responses to their individual needs.

Choiceboards A **choiceboard** is an interactive, Internet-enabled system that allows individual customers to design their own products and services by answering a few questions and choosing from a menu of product or service attributes (or components), prices, and delivery options.[6] Customers today can design their own computers with Dell's online configurator, style their own athletic shoe at NikeID.com, assemble their own investment portfolios with Schwab's mutual fund evaluator, build their own bicycle at SevenCycles.com, and create a diet and fitness program at ediet.com that fits their lifestyle. Because choiceboards collect precise information about preferences and behavior of individual buyers, a company becomes more knowledgeable about a customer and better able to anticipate and fulfill that customer's needs.

Most choiceboards are essentially transaction devices. However, companies such as Dell have expanded the functionality of choiceboards using collaborative filtering technology. **Collaborative filtering** is a process that automatically groups people with similar buying intentions, preferences, and behaviors and predicts future purchases.[7] For example, say two people who have never met buy a few of the same CDs over time. Collaborative filtering software is programmed to reason that these two buyers might have similar musical tastes: If one buyer likes a particular CD, then the other will like it as well. The outcome? Collaborative filtering gives marketers the ability to make a dead-on sales recommendation to a buyer in *real time*. You see collaborative filtering applied each time you view a selection at Amazon.com and see "Customers who bought this (item) also bought. . . ."

Choiceboards and collaborative filtering represent two important capabilities of Internet technology and have changed the way companies operate today.

Nike has effectively used choiceboard technology for customizing athletic shoes.

Nike
www.nikeID.com

According to an electronic commerce manager at IBM, "The business model of the past was make and sell. Now instead of make and sell, it's sense and respond."[8]

Personalization Choiceboards and collaborative filtering are marketer-initiated efforts to provide customized responses to the needs of individual buyers. Personalization systems are typically buyer-initiated efforts. **Personalization** is the consumer-initiated practice of generating content on a marketer's website that is custom tailored to an individual's specific needs and preferences. For example, Yahoo! (www.yahoo.com) allows users to create personalized MyYahoo pages. Users can add or delete a variety of types of information from their personal pages, including specific stock quotes, weather conditions in any city in the world, and local television schedules. In turn, Yahoo! can use the buyer profile data entered when users register at the site to tailor e-mail messages, advertising, and content to the individual—and even post a happy birthday greeting on the user's special day.

An aspect of personalization is a buyer's willingness to have tailored communications brought to his or her attention. Obtaining this approval is called **permission marketing**—the solicitation of a consumer's consent (called *opt-in*) to receive e-mail and advertising based on personal data supplied by the consumer. Permission marketing is a proven vehicle for building and maintaining customer relationships, provided it is properly used.

Companies that successfully employ permission marketing adhere to three rules.[9] First, they make sure opt-in customers only receive information that is relevant and meaningful to them. Second, their customers are given the option of *opting out,* or changing the kind, amount, or timing of information sent to them. Finally, their customers are assured that their name or buyer profile data will not be sold or shared with others. This assurance is important because nearly half of adult Internet users have expressed concern about the privacy of their personal information.[10]

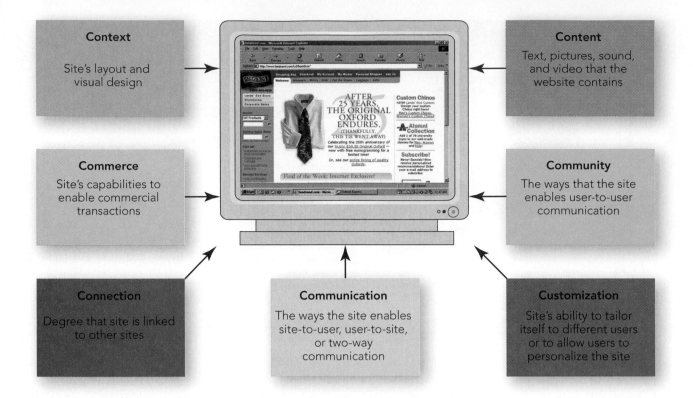

Context		Content
Site's layout and visual design		Text, pictures, sound, and video that the website contains

Commerce		Community
Site's capabilities to enable commercial transactions		The ways that the site enables user-to-user communication

Connection	Communication	Customization
Degree that site is linked to other sites	The ways the site enables site-to-user, user-to-site, or two-way communication	Site's ability to tailor itself to different users or to allow users to personalize the site

FIGURE 21–2

Seven website design elements that drive customer experience

Creating an Online Customer Experience

A continuing challenge for companies is the design and execution of marketing programs that capitalize on the unique and evolving customer value-creation capabilities of Internet technology. Companies now realize that applying Internet technology to create time, place, form, and possession utility is just a starting point for creating a meaningful marketspace presence. Today, the quality of the customer experience produced by a company is the standard by which a meaningful marketspace presence is measured.

From an interactive marketing perspective, *customer experience* is defined as the sum total of the interactions that a customer has with a company's website, from the initial look at a homepage through the entire purchase decision process.[11] Companies produce a customer experience through seven website design elements. These elements are context, content, community, customization, communication, connection, and commerce, each of which is summarized in Figure 21–2. A closer look at these elements illustrates how each contributes to customer experience.

Context refers to a website's aesthetic appeal and functional look and feel reflected in site layout and visual design. A functionally oriented website focuses largely on the company's offering, be it products, services, or information. For instance, travel websites, such as Travelocity.com, tend to be functionally oriented with an emphasis on destinations, scheduling, and prices. In contrast, beauty websites, such as Revlon.com, are more aesthetically oriented. As these examples suggest, context attempts to convey the core consumer benefit provided by the company's offerings. *Content* applies to all digital information on a website, including the presentation form—text, video, audio, and graphics. Content quality and presentation along with context dimensions combine to engage a website visitor and provide a platform for the five remaining design elements.

ENOUGH DREAMING. IT'S TIME TO RIDE.

Harley-Davidson pays close attention to creating a favorable customer experience by employing all seven website design elements.

Harley-Davidson
www.harley-davidson.com

Website *customization* is the ability of a site to modify itself to, or be modified by, each individual user. This design element is prominent in websites that offer personalized content, such as MyeBay and MyYahoo! The *connection* element in website design is the network of formal linkages between a company's site and other sites. These links are embedded in the website; appear as highlighted words, a picture, or graphic; and allow a user to effortlessly visit other sites with a mouse click. Connection is a major design element for informational websites such as *The New York Times.* For example, users of NYTimes.com can access the book review section and link to Barnes & Noble to order a book or browse related titles without ever visiting a store.

Communication refers to the dialogue that unfolds between the website and its users. Consumers—particularly those who have registered at a site—now expect that communication be interactive and individualized in real time much like a personal conversation. In fact, some websites now enable a user to talk directly with a customer representative while shopping the site. For example, two-thirds of the sales through Dell.com involve human sales representatives. In addition, an increasing number of company websites encourage user-to-user communications hosted by the company to create virtual communities, or simply, *community.* This design element is growing in popularity because it has been shown to enhance customer experience and build favorable buyer–seller relationships. Examples of communities range from the Huggies Baby Network hosted by Kimberly-Clark (www.huggies.com) to the Harley Owners Group (HOG) sponsored by Harley-Davidson (www.harley-davidson.com).

The seventh design element is *commerce*—the website's ability to conduct sales transactions for products and services. Online transactions are quick and simple in well-designed websites. Amazon.com has mastered this design element with "one-click shopping," a patented feature that allows users to place and order products with a single mouse click.

All websites do not include every design element. Although every website has context and content, they differ in the use of the remaining five elements. Why? Websites have different purposes. For example, only websites that emphasize the actual sale of products and services include the commerce element. Websites that are used primarily for advertising and promotion purposes emphasize the communication element. The difference between these two types of websites is discussed later in the chapter in the description of multichannel marketing.

Companies use a broad array of measures to assess website performance. Increasingly, the amount of time per month visitors spend on their website, or "stickiness,"

Using Marketing Dashboards

Sizing Up Site Stickiness at Sewell Automotive Companies

Automobile dealerships have invested significant time, effort, and money in their websites. Why? Car browsing and shopping on the Internet is now commonplace.

Dealerships commonly measure website performance by tracking visit, visitor traffic, and "stickiness"—the amount of time per month visitors spend on their website. Website design, easy navigation, involving content, and visual appeal combine to enhance the interactive customer experience and website stickiness.

To gauge stickiness, companies monitor the average time spent per unique visitor (in minutes) on their websites. This is done by tracking and displaying the average visits per monthly unique visitor and the average time spent per visit, in minutes, in their marketing dashboards. The relationship is as follows:

$$\begin{aligned}&\text{Average Time Spent} \\ &\text{Per Unique Visitor (minutes)}\end{aligned} =$$

$$\left(\begin{aligned}&\text{Average Visits per} \\ &\text{Monthly Unique Visitor}\end{aligned}\right) \times \left(\begin{aligned}&\text{Average Time Spent} \\ &\text{per Visit (minutes)}\end{aligned}\right)$$

Your Challenge As the manager responsible for Sewell.com, the Sewell Automotive Companies website, you have been asked to report on the effect recent improvements in the company's website have had on the amount of time per month visitors spend on the website.

Sewell ranks among the largest U.S. dealerships and is a recognized customer service leader in the automotive industry. Its website reflects the company's commitment to an unparalleled customer experience at its family of Cadillac, HUMMER, Saab, Lexus, Pontiac, Buick, GMC, and Infiniti dealerships.

Your Findings Examples of monthly marketing dashboard traffic and time measures are displayed below for June 2006, three months before the website improvements (green arrow), and June 2007, three months after the improvements were made (red arrow).

The average time spent per unique monthly visitor increased from 8.5 minutes in June 2006 to 11.9 minutes in June 2007—a sizeable jump. The increase is due primarily to the upturn in the average time spent per visit from 7.1 minutes to 8.5 minutes. The average number of visits also increased, but the percentage change was much less.

Your Action Improvements in the website have noticeably "moved the needle" on average time spent per unique visitor. Still, additional action may be required to increase average visits per monthly unique visitor. These actions might include an analysis of Sewell's Web advertising program, search engine initiatives with Google, links to automobile manufacturer corporate websites, and broader print and electronic media advertising.

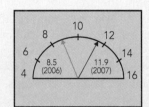

Average Time Spent
per Unique Visitor (minutes)

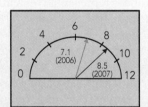

Average Time Spent
per Visit (minutes)

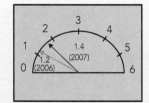

Average Visits per
Monthly Unique Visitor

is used to gauge customer experience. Read the Using Marketing Dashboards box to learn how stickiness is measured and interpreted at Sewell Automotive Companies.

learning review

1. The consumer-initiated practice of generating content on a marketer's website that is custom tailored to an individual's specific needs and preferences is called _____.

2. Companies produce a customer experience through what seven website design elements?

ONLINE CONSUMER BEHAVIOR AND MARKETING PRACTICE IN MARKETSPACE

Who are online consumers, and what do they buy? Why do they choose to shop and purchase products and services in the digital marketspace rather than or in addition to the traditional marketplace? Answers to these questions have a direct bearing on marketspace marketing practices.

Who Is the Online Consumer?

LO2

Many labels are given online consumers—cybershoppers, Netizens, and e-shoppers—suggesting they are a homogeneous segment of the population. They are not, but as a group, they do differ demographically from the general population.

Profiling the Online Consumer   Online consumers differ from the general population in one important respect. They own or have access to a computer or an Internet-enabled device, such as a wireless cellular telephone or personal digital assistant. Figure 21–3 profiles Internet usage by age, racial/ethnic group, education, and household income.[12]

Online consumers are the subsegment of all Internet users who employ this technology to research products and services and make purchases. Research indicates that about 90 percent of all adult Internet users have sought online product or service information at one time or another.[13] For example, some 70 percent of prospective travelers have researched travel information online, even though

FIGURE 21–3

Internet usage in the United States varies by age, racial/ethnic group, education, and household income.

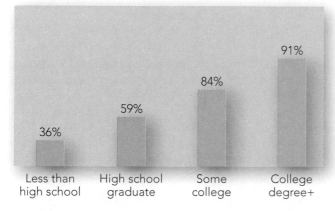

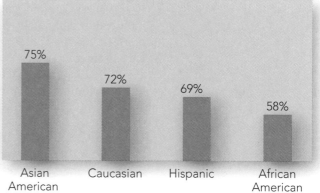

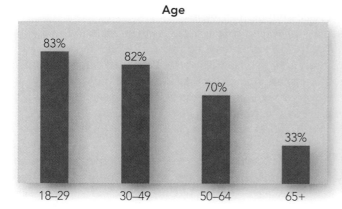

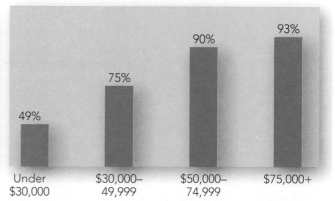

fewer than 25 percent have actually made online travel reservations. More than 60 percent have researched automobiles before making a purchase, but less than 5 percent of users actually bought a vehicle online. Almost 70 percent of adult Internet users have actually purchased a product or service online at one time or another.

As a group, online consumers, like Internet users, are more likely to be women than men and tend to be better educated, younger, and more affluent than the general U.S. population, which makes them an attractive market.[14] Even though online shopping and buying is growing in popularity, a small percentage of online consumers still account for a disproportionate share of online retail sales in the United States. It is estimated that 20 percent of online consumers who spend $1,000-plus per year online account for 87 percent of total consumer online sales.[15] Also, women tend to purchase more goods and services online than men.

In general, online consumers also tend to use a range of information and communication technology as a platform to express themselves online and engage the digital marketspace. Recent research sponsored by the Pew Internet & American Life Project has categorized information and communication technology users into 10 groups based on their use of devices to connect to the Internet, the activities they engage in, and their attitudes toward the marketspace.[16] To learn which group you fall into, take the quiz described in the accompanying Going Online box.

Online Consumer Lifestyle Segmentation Not all Internet users use the technology the same way, nor are they likely to be exclusive online consumers. Numerous marketing research firms have studied the lifestyles and shopping and spending habits of online consumers. A recurrent insight is that online consumers are diverse and represent different kinds of people seeking different kinds of online experiences. As an illustration, Harris Interactive, a large U.S. research firm, has identified six distinct online consumer lifestyle segments.[17]

The largest online consumer lifestyle segment, called *click-and-mortar*, consists of women who tend to browse retailer websites but actually buy products in traditional retail outlets. They make up 23 percent of online consumers and represent an important segment for multichannel retailers that also feature catalog and store operations, such as J. Crew and JCPenney.

Twenty percent of online consumers are *hunter-gatherers*—married couples with children at home who use the Internet like a consumer magazine to gather information and compare products and prices. They can be found visiting comparison shopping websites such as DealCatcher.com and mySimon.com on a regular basis. The accompanying Marketing Matters box provides an in-depth look at today's "Internet mom."[18]

Meet Today's Internet Mom—All 31 Million!

Do you have fond childhood memories of surfing the Internet with your mother? Today's children probably will.

Recent research indicates that 31 million mothers are online regularly. They're typically 38 years old and tend to be married, college educated, and working outside the home. A study conducted by C&R Research on behalf of Disney Online has identified four segments of mothers based on their Internet usage.

The *Yes Mom* segment represents 14 percent of online moms. They work outside the home, go online eight hours per week, and value the convenience of obtaining information about products and services. The *Mrs. Net Skeptic* segment accounts for 31 percent of online moms. They tend to be stay-at-home moms, are extremely family-oriented, and go online six hours per week for parenting and children's education information and food and cooking tips. The *Tech Nester* mom (32 percent of online moms) believes the Internet brings their family closer together. They average 10 hours per week online and prefer online shopping to in-store shopping. The fourth segment—*Passive Under Pressure* moms—tend to be Internet newbies and go online, but infrequently.

The first three segments, which account for 77 percent of online moms, agree that the Internet has simplified their lives. They also say that the Internet has been an invaluable information source for vacation travel, financial products, and automobiles and for useful ideas and suggestions on family-related topics. Online moms ranked weather, food and cooking, entertainment, news, health, and parenting as the most popular websites to visit.

Nineteen percent of online consumers are *brand loyalists* who regularly visit their favorite bookmarked websites and spend the most money online. They are better-educated and more affluent Internet users who effortlessly navigate familiar and trusted websites and enjoy the online browsing and buying experience.

Next there are *time-sensitive materialists* who regard the Internet as a convenience tool for buying music, books, and computer software and electronics. They account for 17 percent of online consumers and can be found visiting Amazon.com, Dell.com, and Sony.com.

The *hooked, online, and single* segment consists of young, affluent, and single online consumers who bank, play games, and spend more time online than any other segment. They make up 16 percent of online consumers, enjoy auction websites such as eBay, and visit game websites like Slingo.com, MSN Games, AOL Games, and Jigzone.com.

Five percent of online consumers are the *ebivalent newbies*—relative newcomers to the Internet who rarely spend money online but seek product information. Do any of these segments describe your online lifestyle and spending habits?

What Online Consumers Buy

Much still needs to be learned about online consumer purchase behavior. Although research has documented the most frequently purchased products and services bought

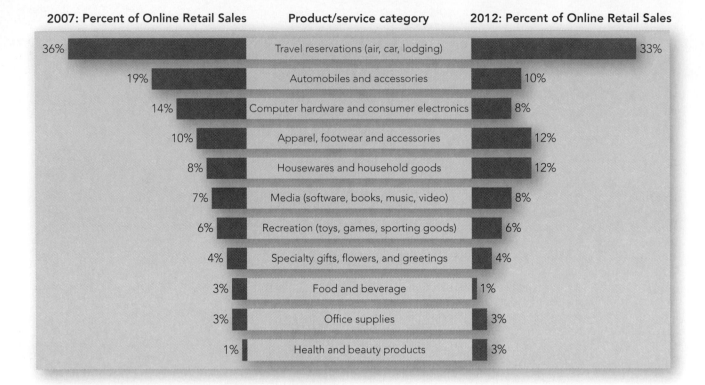

2007: Percent of Online Retail Sales	Product/service category	2012: Percent of Online Retail Sales
36%	Travel reservations (air, car, lodging)	33%
19%	Automobiles and accessories	10%
14%	Computer hardware and consumer electronics	8%
10%	Apparel, footwear and accessories	12%
8%	Housewares and household goods	12%
7%	Media (software, books, music, video)	8%
6%	Recreation (toys, games, sporting goods)	6%
4%	Specialty gifts, flowers, and greetings	4%
3%	Food and beverage	1%
3%	Office supplies	3%
1%	Health and beauty products	3%

FIGURE 21–4

Estimated percentage of online retail sales by product/service category: 2007 and 2012

online, marketers also need to know why these items are popular in the digital marketspace.

There are six general product and service categories that dominate online consumer buying today and for the foreseeable future as shown in Figure 21–4.[19] One category consists of items for which product information is an important part of the purchase decision, but prepurchase trial is not necessarily critical. Items such as computers, computer accessories, and consumer electronics sold by Dell.com fall into this category. So do books, which accounts for the sales growth of Amazon.com and Barnes & Noble (www.barnesandnoble.com). Both booksellers publish short reviews of new books that visitors to their websites can read before making a purchase decision.

A second category includes items for which audio or video demonstration is important. This category consists of CDs, videos, and DVDs sold by Columbia House.com. The third category contains items that can be delivered digitally, including computer software, travel and lodging reservations and confirmations, financial brokerage services, and electronic ticketing. Popular websites for these items include Travelocity.com, Ticketmaster.com, and Schwab.com.

Unique items, such as collectibles, specialty goods, and foods and gifts, represent a fourth category. Collectible auction houses (www.sothebys.com), food merchants (www.harryanddavid.com), and flower marketers (www.1800flowers.com) sell these products. A fifth category includes items that are regularly purchased and where convenience is very important. Many consumer-packaged goods, such as grocery products, fall into this category. A final category of items consists of highly standardized products and services for which information about price is important. Certain kinds of insurance (auto and homeowners), home improvement products, casual apparel, and toys make up this category.

Why Consumers Shop and Buy Online

Marketers emphasize the customer value-creation possibilities, the importance of interactivity, individuality and relationship building, and producing customer

FIGURE 21–5

Why do consumers shop and buy online? Read the text to learn how convenience, choice, customization, communication, cost, and control result in a favorable customer experience.

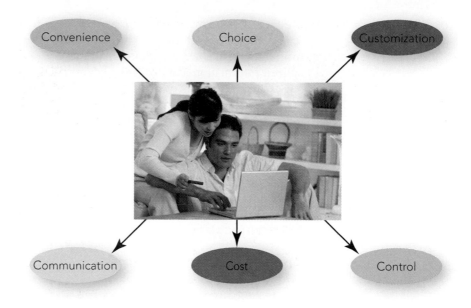

experience in the new marketspace. However, consumers typically refer to six reasons they shop and buy online: convenience, choice, customization, communication, cost, and control (Figure 21–5).

Convenience Online shopping and buying is *convenient.* Consumers can visit Wal-Mart at www.walmart.com to scan and order from among thousands of displayed products without fighting traffic, finding a parking space, walking through long aisles, and standing in store checkout lines. Alternatively, online consumers can use **bots**, electronic shopping agents or robots that comb websites to compare prices and product or service features. In either instance, an online consumer has never ventured from his or her computer monitor. However, for convenience to remain a source of customer value creation, websites must be easy to locate and navigate, and image downloads must be fast.

A commonly held view among online marketers is the **eight-second rule**: Customers will abandon their efforts to enter and navigate a website if download time exceeds eight seconds. Furthermore, the more clicks and pauses between clicks required to access information or make a purchase, the more likely it is a customer will exit a website.

Choice *Choice,* the second reason consumers shop and buy online, has two dimensions. First, choice exists in the product or service selection offered to consumers. Buyers desiring selection can avail themselves of numerous websites for almost anything they want. For instance, online buyers of consumer electronics can shop individual manufacturers such as Bose (www.bose.com), Sony (www.sony.com), and QVC.com, a general merchant that offers more than 100,000 products.

Choice assistance is the second dimension. Here, the interactive capabilities of Internet-enabled technologies invite customers to engage in an electronic dialogue with marketers for the purpose of making informed choices. Lands' End (www.landsend.com) provides choice assistance with its "My Virtual Model" apparel service. Men and women submit their body shape, skin color, hair style, height, weight, and other attributes. The model then "tries on" outfits identified by the customer. Like any good salesperson, the service recommends flattering outfits for purchase.

Customization Even with a broad selection and choice assistance, some customers prefer one-of-a-kind items that fit their specific needs. *Customization* arises from Internet-enabled capabilities that make possible a highly interactive and individualized information and exchange environment for shoppers and buyers. Remember the earlier NikeID, Schwab, Dell, and SevenCycles examples? To varying degrees, online consumers also benefit from **customerization**—the growing practice of not only customizing a product or service but also personalizing the marketing and overall shopping and buying interaction for each customer.[20] Customerization seeks to do more than offer consumers the right product, at the right time, at the right price. It combines choiceboard and personalization systems to expand the exchange environment beyond a transaction and makes shopping and buying an enjoyable, personal experience.

Communication Online consumers particularly welcome the *communication* capabilities of Internet-enabled technologies. This communication can take three forms: (1) marketer-to-consumer e-mail notification, (2) consumer-to-marketer buying and service requests, and (3) consumer-to-consumer chat rooms and instant messaging, plus social networking websites such as MySpace and Facebook.

Communication has proven to be a double-edged sword for online consumers. On the one hand, the interactive communication capabilities of Internet-enabled technologies increase consumer convenience, reduce information search costs, and make choice assistance and customization possible. Communication also promotes the development of company-hosted and independent **web communities**—websites that allow people to congregate online and exchange views on topics of common interest. For instance, Coca-Cola hosts MyCoke.com, and iVillage.com is an independent web community for women and includes topics such as career management, personal finances, parenting, relationships, beauty, and health.

Web logs, or blogs, are another form of communication. A **blog** is a web page that serves as a publicly accessible personal journal for an individual or organization. Blogs have grown in popularity because they provide online forums on a wide variety of subjects ranging from politics to car repair. It is estimated that the 5,000-plus comments a week on gmblogs.com is worth $100,000 in marketing research each week to General Motors.[21]

On the other hand, communications can take the form of electronic junk mail or unsolicited e-mail, called **spam**. The prevalence of spam has prompted many online services to institute policies and procedures to prevent spammers from spamming their subscribers, and several states have antispamming laws. In 2004, the *CAN-SPAM (Controlling the Assault of Non-Solicited Pornography and Marketing) Act* became effective and restricts information collection and unsolicited e-mail promotions on the Internet.

Internet-enabled communication capabilities also make possible *buzz,* a popular term for word-of-mouth behavior in marketspace. Chapter 5 described the importance of word of mouth in consumer behavior. Internet technology has magnified its significance. According to Jeff Bezos, president of Amazon.com, "If you have an unhappy customer on the Internet, he doesn't tell his six friends, he tells his 6,000 friends![22] Buzz is particularly influential for toys, cars, sporting goods, motion pictures, apparel, consumer electronics, pharmaceuticals, health and beauty products, and health care services. Some marketers have capitalized on this phenomenon by creating buzz through viral marketing.

Viral marketing is an Internet-enabled promotional strategy that encourages individuals to forward marketer-initiated messages to others via e-mail. There are three approaches to viral marketing. Marketers can embed a message in the product or service so that customers hardly realize they are passing it along. The classic example is Hotmail, which was one of the first companies to provide free,

De Beers effectively applies viral marketing at its custom ring website. How? Users of the custom ring feature can show what they have designed to friends and relatives.

De Beers
www.adiamondisforever.com

Internet-based e-mail. Each outgoing e-mail message has the tagline: "Get Your Private, Free Email from MSN Hotmail." Today, Hotmail has more than 100 million users.

Marketers can also make the website content so compelling that viewers want to share it with others. De Beers has done this at www.adiamondisforever.com, where users can design their own rings and show them to others. One out of five website visitors e-mail their ring design to friends and relatives who visit the site. Similarly, eBay reports that more than half its visitors are referred by other visitors. Finally, marketers can offer incentives (discounts, sweepstakes, or free merchandise) for referrals.

Cost   Consumer *cost* is a fifth reason for online shopping and buying. Many popular items bought online can be purchased at the same price or cheaper than in retail stores.[23] Lower prices also result from Internet-enabled software that permits **dynamic pricing**, the practice of changing prices for products and services in real time in response to supply and demand conditions. As described in Chapter 14, dynamic pricing is a form of flexible pricing and can often result in lower prices. It is typically used for pricing time-sensitive items like airline seats, scarce items found at art or collectible auctions, and out-of-date items such as last year's models of computer equipment and accessories. A consumer's cost of external information search, including time spent and often the hassle of shopping, is also reduced. Greater shopping convenience and lower external search costs are two major reasons for the popularity of online shopping and buying among women, and particularly for those who work outside the home.

Control   The sixth reason consumers prefer to buy online is the *control* it gives them over their shopping and purchase decision process. Online shoppers and buyers are empowered consumers. They deftly use Internet technology to seek information, evaluate alternatives, and make purchase decisions on their own time, terms, and conditions. For example, studies show that shoppers spend an average of five hours researching cars online before setting foot in a showroom.[24] The result of these activities is a more informed consumer and discerning shopper. In the words of one marketing consultant, "In the marketspace, the customer is in charge."[25]

Even though consumers have many reasons for shopping and buying online, a segment of Internet users refrain from making purchases for privacy and security reasons. These consumers are concerned about a rarely mentioned seventh

Let the E-Buyer Beware

Privacy and security are two key reasons consumers are leery of online shopping and buying. A recent Gartner Research poll reported that 46 percent of online consumers have privacy and security concerns about the Internet. Even more telling, many have stopped shopping a website or forgone an online purchase because of these concerns. Industry analysts estimate that about $913 million in e-commerce sales are lost annually because of security concerns among online shoppers. Another $1 billion is lost because of shoppers who refuse to shop on-line at all because of privacy and security concerns.

Consumer concerns are not without merit. According to the Federal Trade Commission, 46 percent of fraud complaints are Internet related. In addition, consumers lose millions of dollars each year due to identity theft resulting from breaches in company security systems. A percolating issue is whether the U.S. government should pass more stringent Internet privacy and security laws. About 70 percent of online consumers favor such action. Companies, however, favor self-regulation. For example, TRUSTe (www.truste.com) awards its trademark to company websites that comply with standards of privacy protection and disclosure. Still, consumers are ultimately responsible for using care and caution when engaging in online behavior, including e-commerce. Consumers have a choice of whether or not to divulge personal information and monitor how their information is being used.

What role should the U.S. government, company self-regulation, and consumer vigilance play in dealing with privacy and security issues in the digital marketspace?

C—cookies. **Cookies** are computer files that a marketer can download onto the computer of an online shopper who visits the marketer's website. Cookies allow the marketer's website to record a user's visit, track visits to other websites, and store and retrieve this information in the future. Cookies also contain visitor information such as expressed product preferences, personal data, passwords, and financial information, including credit card numbers. Clearly, cookies make possible customized and personalized content for online shoppers. The controversy surrounding cookies is summed up by an authority on the technology: "At best a cookie makes for a user-friendly Web world: like a doorman or salesclerk who knows who you are. At worst, cookies represent a potential loss of privacy."[26] Read the accompanying Making Responsible Decisions box to learn more about privacy and security issues in the digital marketplace.[27]

When and Where Online Consumers Shop and Buy

Shopping and buying also happen at different times in marketspace than in the traditional marketplace.[28] About 80 percent of online retail sales occur Monday through Friday. The busiest shopping day is Wednesday. By comparison, 35 percent of retail store sales are registered on the weekend. Saturday is the most popular shopping day. Monday through Friday online shopping and buying often occur during normal work hours—some 70 percent of online consumers say they visit websites from their place of work, which partially accounts for the sales level during the workweek. Favorite websites for workday shopping and buying include those featuring event tickets, auctions, online periodical subscriptions, flowers and gifts, consumer electronics, and travel. Websites offering health and beauty items, apparel and accessories, and music and video tend to be browsed and bought from a consumer's home.

<table>
<tr><td rowspan="3">learning review</td><td>3. What is the eight-second rule?</td></tr>
<tr><td>4. Which online consumer lifestyle segment spends the most money online and which spends the most time online?</td></tr>
<tr><td>5. What are the six reasons consumers prefer to shop and buy online?</td></tr>
</table>

CROSS-CHANNEL SHOPPERS AND MULTICHANNEL MARKETING

Consumers are more likely to browse than buy online. Consumer marektspace browsing and buying in the traditional marketplace has given rise to the cross-channel shopper and the importance of multichannel marketing.

Who Is the Cross-Channel Shopper?

A **cross-channel shopper** is an online consumer who researches products online and then purchases them at a retail store.[29] Recent research shows that 51 percent of U.S. online consumers are cross-channel shoppers. These shoppers represent both genders equally and are only slightly younger than online consumers. They tend to have a higher education, earn significantly more money, and are more likely to embrace technology in their lives than online consumers who don't cross-channel shop.

Cross-channel shoppers want the right product, at the best price, and they don't want to wait several days for delivery. The top reasons these shoppers research items online before buying in stores include: (1) the desire to compare products among different retailers; (2) the need for more information than is available in stores; and (3) the ease of comparing their options without having to trek to multiple retail locations.

Research shows that sales arising from cross-channel shoppers dwarf exclusive online retail sales. Retail sales revenue from cross-channel shoppers in 2011 is estimated to be $1 trillion—about three times greater than online retail sales.

Implementing Multichannel Marketing

The prominence of cross-channel shoppers has focused increased attention on multichannel marketing. Recall from Chapter 15 that multichannel marketing is the blending of different communication and delivery channels that are mutually reinforcing in attracting, retaining, and building relationships with consumers who shop and buy in the traditional marketplace and online—the cross-channel shopper.

The most common cross-channel shopping and buying path is to browse one or more websites and then purchase an item at a retail store. This shopping path might suggest that company websites for cross-channel shoppers should be similar. But they are not. Websites play a multifaceted role in multichannel marketing because they can serve as either a communication or delivery channel. Two general applications of websites exist based on their intended purpose: (1) transactional websites and (2) promotional websites.

Multichannel Marketing with Transactional Websites *Transactional websites* are essentially electronic storefronts. They focus principally on converting an online browser into an online, catalog, or in-store buyer using the website design elements described earlier. Transactional websites are most common among store and catalog retailers and direct selling companies, such as Tupperware. Retailers and direct selling firms have found that their websites, while cannibalizing sales volume from stores, catalogs, and sales representatives, attract new customers and influence sales. Consider Victoria's Secret, the well-known specialty retailer of intimate apparel for women ages 18 to 45. It reports that almost 60 percent of its website customers are men, most of whom generate new sales volume for the company.[30]

Transactional websites are used less frequently by manufacturers of consumer products. A recurring issue for manufacturers is the threat of *channel conflict,* described in Chapter 15, and the potential harm to trade relationships with their retailing intermediaries. Still, manufacturers do use transactional websites, often cooperating with retailers. For example, Callaway Golf Company markets its golf merchandise at www.callawaygolf.com but relies on a retailer close to the buyer to fill the order. The retailer ships the order to the buyer within 24 hours and its credited with the sale. The majority of retailers that sell Callaway merchandise participate in this relationship, including retail chains Golf Galaxy and Dick's Sporting Goods. According to Callaway's chief executive officer, "This arrangement allows us to satisfy the consumer but to do so in a way that didn't violate our relationship with our loyal trade partners—those 15,000 outlets that sell Callaway products."[31]

In addition, Callaway, like other manufacturers, lists stores on the website where merchandise can be shopped and bought. More often than not, however, manufacturers using multichannel marketing channels employ websites for advertising and promotion purposes.

Multichannel Marketing with Promotional Websites *Promotional websites* have a very different purpose than transactional sites. They advertise and promote a company's products and services and provide information on how items can be used and where they can be purchased. They often engage the visitor in an interactive experience involving games, contests, and quizzes with electronic coupons and other gifts as prizes. Procter & Gamble maintains separate websites for dozens of its leading brands, including Pringles potato chips (www.pringles.com), Vidal Sassoon hair products (www.vidalsassoon.com), Scope mouthwash (www.getclose.com), and Pampers diapers (www.pampers.com). Promotional sites are effective in generating interest in and trial of a company's products (see Figure 21–6).[32] General Motors reports that 80 percent of the people visiting a Saturn store first visited the brand's website (www.saturn.com) and 70 percent of Saturn leads come from its website.

Promotional websites also can be used to support a company's traditional marketing channel and build customer relationships. This is the objective of the Clinique Division of Estée Lauder, Inc., which markets cosmetics through department stores. Clinique reports that 80 percent of current customers who visit its website (www.clinique.com) later purchase a Clinique product at a department store; 37 percent of non-Clinique buyers make a Clinique purchase after visiting the company's website.

FIGURE 21–6

Implementing multichannel marketing with promotional websites is common today. Two successes are found at Saturn Corporation and the Clinique Division of Estée Lauder, Inc.

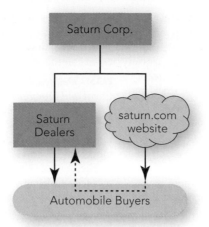

- 70% of Saturn leads come from its website.
- 80% of people visiting a Saturn dealer first visited its website.

- 80% of current Clinique buyers who visit its website later purchase a Clinique product at a store.
- 37% of non-Clinique buyers make a Clinique purchase after visiting its website.

The popularity of multichannel marketing is apparent in its growing impact on online retail sales.[33] Fully 70 percent of U.S. online retail sales in 2007 were made by companies that practiced multichannel marketing. Multichannel marketers are expected to register about 90 percent of U.S. online retail sales in 2012.

learning review

6. A cross-channel shopper is _____.

7. Channel conflict between manufacturers and retailers is likely to arise when manufacturers use _____ websites.

LEARNING OBJECTIVES REVIEW

LO1 *Describe what interactive marketing is and how it creates customer value, customer relationships, and customer experiences.*

Interactive marketing involves two-way buyer–seller electronic communication in a computer-mediated environment in which the buyer controls the kind and amount of information received from the seller. It creates customer value by providing time, place, form, and possession utility for consumers. Customer relationships are created and sustained through two unique capabilities of Internet technology: interactivity and individuality. From an interactive marketing perspective, customer experience represents the sum total of the interactions that a customer has with a company's website, from the initial look at a homepage through the entire purchase decision process. Companies produce a customer experience through seven website design elements. These elements are context, content, community, customization, communication, connection, and commerce.

LO2 *Identify the demographic and lifestyle profile of online consumers.*

As a group, online consumers are more likely to be women than men and tend to be better educated, younger, and more affluent than the general U.S. population. Women tend to purchase more goods and services online than men. The lifestyle profile of online consumers reflects the different kinds of online experiences they seek. Six lifestyle segments have been identified. The click-and-mortar segment consists of women who browse retailer websites but actually buy products at retail outlets. Hunter-gatherers use the Internet like a consumer magazine to gather information and compare products and services. Brand loyalists regularly visit their favorite bookmarked websites and spend the most money online. Time-sensitive materialists regard the Internet as a convenient tool for buying. The hooked, online, and single segment spends more time online than any segment. Ebivalent newbies are relative newcomers to the Internet who rarely spend money online, but seek product information.

LO3 *Explain why certain types of products and services are particularly suited for interactive marketing.*

Certain types of products and services seem to be particularly suited for interactive marketing. One category consists of items for which product information is an important part of the purchase decision, but prepurchase trial is not necessarily critical. A second category involves items for which audio or video demonstration is important. A third category contains items that can be digitally delivered. Unique items represent a fourth category. A fifth category includes items that are regularly purchased and where convenience is very important. A final category consists of highly standardized items for which information about price is important.

LO4 *Describe why consumers shop and buy online and how marketers influence online purchasing behavior.*
There are six reasons consumers shop and buy online. They are convenience, choice, customization, communication, cost, and control. Marketers have capitalized on these reasons through a variety of means. For example, they provide choice assistance using choiceboard and collaborative filtering technology, which also provides opportunities for customization. Company-hosted web communities and viral marketing practices capitalize on the communications dimensions of Internet-enabled technolo-gies. Dynamic pricing provides real-time responses to supply and demand conditions, often resulting in lower prices to consumers. Permission marketing is popular given consumer interest in control.

LO5 *Define cross-channel shoppers and the role of transactional and promotional websites in reaching these shoppers.*
A cross-channel shopper is an online consumer who researches products online and then purchases them at a retail store. These shoppers are reached through multichannel marketing. Websites play a multifaceted role in multichannel marketing because they can serve as either a delivery or communication channel. In this regard, transactional websites are essentially electronic storefronts. They focus principally on converting an online browser into an online, catalog, or in-store buyer using the website design elements described earlier. On the other hand, promotional websites serve to advertise and promote a company's products and services and provide information on how items can be used and where they can be purchased.

FOCUSING ON KEY TERMS

blog p. 562
bots p. 561
choiceboard p. 552
collaborative filtering p. 552
cookies p. 564
cross-channel shopper p. 565

customerization p. 562
dynamic pricing p. 563
eight-second rule p. 561
interactive marketing p. 552
online consumers p. 557

permission marketing p. 553
personalization p. 553
spam p. 562
viral marketing p. 562
web communities p. 562

APPLYING MARKETING KNOWLEDGE

1 About 70 percent of Internet users have actually purchased something online. Have you made an online purchase? If so, why do you think so many people who have access to the Internet are not also online buyers? If not, why are you reluctant to do so? Do you think that electronic commerce benefits consumers even if they don't make a purchase?

2 Like the traditional marketplace, marketspace offers marketers opportunities to create greater time, place, form, and possession utility. How do you think Internet-enabled technology rates in terms of creating these values? Take a shopping trip at a virtual retailer of your choice (don't buy anything unless you really want to). Then compare the time, place, form, and possession utility provided by the virtual retailer that you enjoyed during a nonelectronic experience shopping for the same product category.

3 Visit Amazon.com (www.amazon.com) or Barnes & Noble (www.barnesandnoble.com). As you tour the company's website, think about how shopping for books online compares with a trip to your university bookstore to buy books. Specifically, compare and contrast your shopping experiences with respect to convenience, choice, customization, communication, cost, and control.

4 Suppose you are planning to buy a new car so you visit www.edmunds.com. Based on your experience visiting that site, do you think you would enjoy more or less control in negotiating with the dealer when you actually purchase your vehicle?

5 Visit the website for your university or college. Based on your visit, would you conclude that the site is a transactional site or a promotional site? Why? How would you rate the site in terms of the six website design elements that affect customer experience?

building your marketing plan

Does your marketing plan involve a marketspace presence for your product or service? If the answer is no, read no further and do not include this element in your plan. If the answer is yes, then attention must be given to developing a website in your marketing plan. A useful starting point is to:

1 Describe how each website element—context, content, community, customization, communication, connection, and commerce—will be used to create a customer experience.

2 Identify a company's website that best reflects your website conceptualization.

---

video case 21　McFarlane Toys: The Best of Interactive Marketing

"All my life, I've been underwhelmed by the sports action figures sold in the toy aisles," says Todd McFarlane, founder of McFarlane Toys.

This assessment of the marketplace led McFarlane to create his own toy manufacturing company, an entirely new category of toys called "upscale figures," and an extraordinarily sophisticated marketing strategy based on traditional and interactive approaches. McFarlane Toys is now one of the world's largest toy companies. The company's products include action figures of professional athletes, rock stars, NASCAR drivers, and characters from movies such as *The Terminator*, *The Matrix*, and *Austin Powers*. Its marketing programs have used Internet contests, virtual showrooms, online catalogs, and a variety of other award-winning tools. Overall, McFarlane Toys has transformed a category that used to be just plastic replicas for children into an art collectible for adults. McFarlane explains, "It's about creating a toy that, if you had it on your shelf, somebody wouldn't say, 'Are you collecting toys? How old are you?'"

THE COMPANY

McFarlane started his career as an artist for Marvel/Epic Comics, working on issues of *Incredible Hulk*, *Amazing Spider-Man*, *Batman*, and *Coyote*. Eventually he formed Image Comics with six other Marvel artists and began work on his own comic book, *Spawn*. The first issue of *Spawn* sold a record-breaking 1.7 million copies. Since then the series has become a top-selling comic published in 16 languages and sold in more than 120 countries.

The success of *Spawn* soon generated licensing proposals from toy companies, movies studios, and television producers. When McFarlane met with each of the companies, however, he was concerned about his ability to have creative control over the toy production. As a result, he started his own toy company, McFarlane Toys, in order to guarantee his fans high quality, intricately detailed, and reasonably priced action figures. *Spawn* action figures quickly became one of the most successful toys on the market.

Following the introduction of the Spawn action figures, McFarlane began producing action figures of pop culture icons in film, music, gaming, and sports. The company also signed license agreements with the four major North American sports leagues—football, baseball, basketball, and hockey. In addition, McFarlane Toys produced toys for licensors such as the Beatles, *Shrek*, KISS, *The Simpsons*, *Alien*, AC/DC, Jimi Hendrix, and many others. The quality and the collectibility of the figures has given McFarlane Toys a worldwide reputation among retailers and consumers.

When he founded McFarlane Toys, McFarlane said, "I'm just going to do action figures. I'm going to be the king of Aisle 7." Other opportunities soon appeared, however, and he became involved in the production of feature films, music videos, electronic games, and animated television. Some of these projects have included the live-action film *Spawn* which grossed $50 million in just 19 days; the HBO series *Todd McFarlane's Spawn* which won an Emmy award; and the music video for Korn's *Freak on a Leash* which received a Grammy award. These activities have helped expand the growing number of McFarlane Toy fans.

Today McFarlane Toys is ranked among the top five makers of action figures. McFarlane manages the company as the "creative force" from its headquarters in Tempe, Arizona. The toy designers work in New Jersey and the toys are manufactured in China. Currently, it takes about 12 months for a product idea on paper to make its way through the rigorous process of becoming a toy on the shelf.

THE TOY INDUSTRY

Toys are big business. Worldwide toy sales exceed $60 billion. The United States is the largest toy market and accounts for 35 percent of worldwide industry sales. A child in the United States receives about $242 worth of toys per year on average. By comparison, the average annual expenditure per child outside the United States is $26. Dolls represent the largest single category of toys, although action figures account for $1.3 billion in sales. Figure 1 on the next page shows the dollar sales of individual toy categories in the United States.

Category	Sales ($ Billions)
Action Figures & Accessories	$ 1.3
Arts & Crafts	2.4
Building Sets	.7
Dolls	2.7
Games/Puzzles	2.4
Infant/Preschool	3.1
Learning & Exploration	.4
Outdoor & Sports Toys	2.7
Plush	1.3
Vehicles	1.8
All Other Toys	2.5
TOTAL	$21.3

FIGURE 1

Toy Category Sales in the United States
(Listed alphabetically)

U.S. mass merchants are the principal retailers of toys. General merchandise and discounters like Wal-Mart, Kmart, and Target register 54 percent of retail toy sales. Toy chains account for 20 percent of retail sales. Other retailers, such as catalog, toy, hobby and game stores, department stores, and food and drug stores, record 20 percent of sales. Online sales account for 6 percent of sales. Wal-Mart stores are the number one toy retailer in the United States.

The worldwide toy industry is dominated by two U.S. toy makers: Mattel and Hasbro. Japan's Bandai Company and Sanrio, and Denmark's LEGO Company are also major toy makers.

E-COMMERCE AND INTERACTIVE MARKETING AT MCFARLANE TOYS

Shortly after forming McFarlane Toys, McFarlane set up a booth in the annual industry trade show in New York called Toy Fair. Even though the new company didn't have any toys produced yet, an action figure buyer from a toy chain store saw photos of the proposed toys and agreed to place an order. Other traditional retailing opportunities in large discount stores such as Wal-Mart and small, local comic book stores such as Diamonds soon followed. McFarlane Toys also utilized traditional forms of marketing, including media interviews and public relations events, to reach buyers who represented toy stores. McFarland also recently opened its first retail store in Arizona, which showcases current products and prototypes of future releases of the various lines of action figures. Collectors

from around the world have visited the store to purchase products, attend artist autograph sessions, and to meet McFarlane!

Since the target market for McFarlane Toys products is older children and young adults—who make 30 to 40 percent of all action figure purchases—e-commerce and interactive marketing offered another opportunity to reach action figure consumers. The McFarlane Toys website (www.spawn.com) is a good example of the *convenience* online marketing can offer. The site provides a store for purchasing action figures in each of the lines (e.g., movie figures, music figures, baseball figures, comic book figures, etc.). High-quality images allow shoppers to view each figure before adding it to a "basket" and then placing the order. The site also offers visitors a *choice* for the location of their purchase. A "Where to Buy" link lists all retailers and other online "e-tailers" such as www.comicsplusonline.com and www.allstarfigures.com.

The website also provides a variety of opportunities for *communication*. Consumer-to-marketer communication is provided through the "Contact Us" link. In addition, marketer-to-consumer information is provided through the McFarlane newsletter, which is sent to visitors who register to receive the update. Finally, consumers can use the spawn.com message board to participate in discussions about action figures, movies, and comics, or to buy, sell, and trade McFarlane products. There are 54,400 registered users of the message board forums. A unique way that McFarlane provides *customization* of his offerings for his customers is through the Collector's Club, which offers exclusive, limited-edition action figures to members.

Online consumers are also typically concerned about *cost* and *control*. McFarlane tries to keep the cost of most of his toys under $15 by keeping production expenses low. Online shoppers also receive special offers when warehouse inventory is being reduced or eliminated. Of course, sales and discounts can often be found by utilizing the links to the many stores and online retailers that carry McFarlane Toys. Online users control their interaction with McFarlane by providing information only through "opt-in" solicitation for purchases, message board use, and newsletter e-mail delivery.

ISSUES FOR THE FUTURE

Of course, McFarlane's success has attracted attention from consumers, retailers, and competitors. New small firms such as Palisades Toys, Art Asylum, Playmates, and Mezco are now turning out action figures. Larger firms, such as Hasbro, are also trying to compete. As more companies enter the category, obtaining new licensing agreements is also becoming more difficult.

While McFarlane has been heard to comment, "It's just stuff," he is very committed to continuing to develop and grow the category he created. In the future, expect to see additional action figures, movies, music videos, and video games. McFarlane Toys is also working at maintaining the strong relationship with its loyal customers through online contests, customer polls about potential new products, and a new product idea link to company designers.

Questions

1 Describe the channels of distribution McFarlane Toys uses to reach its action figure customers.

2 Why have interactive marketing strategies been successful for McFarlane Toys? What unique elements are part of its online experience?

3 How does McFarlane Toys address each of the six C's consumers consider when shopping and buying online?

22

Pulling It All Together: The Strategic Marketing Process

MARKETING STRATEGY AT GENERAL MILLS: NOT JUST A CEREAL COMPANY ANYMORE!

When you were growing up on Cheerios®, General Mills—or "Big G" from its well-known logo—was known mainly for its breakfast cereals.

"But sometimes you have to break the rules at every level," says Vivian Milroy Callaway (photo at left). "Which is what we did when we acquired Pillsbury in 2001. After the acquisition, cereal went from being our number one business to being one of a big three that includes meals (Hamburger Helper and Green Giant) as well as desserts (Pillsbury and Betty Crocker).[1]"

As vice president of the Center for Learning & Experimentation at Big G, Callaway is responsible for helping uncover new product ideas for the company's product portfolio. Looking over her shoulder at General Mills reveals both how competitive today's cereal business is and a few of the company's creative initiatives outside the cereal industry.

Cereal Industry Facts of Life

A quick survey of the cereal industry shows:

- Only one out of four new brands "succeeds," defined as maintaining distribution for three to four years, in the $6 billion-a-year U.S. ready-to-eat (RTE) cereal market.[2] But that RTE market has had flat or slightly declining sales in recent years.[3]

- This decline in the ready-to-eat cereals market is caused by Americans following low-carbohydrate diets, munching breakfast bars, eating breakfast at fast-food restaurants, and buying lower-priced "bagged" or generic private label brands.[4]

- The launch of a new cereal typically costs up to $30 million and usually involves replacing one of more than 300 competing breakfast cereals already sitting somewhere on a supermarket shelf.

Callaway "broke the rules" in developing a new dessert concept: She looked at the concept *not alone* by itself—but in relation to *all* the other sweet treats people were eating. "One of my challenges," says Callaway, "is that consumers often say one thing in marketing research studies and then do something else when facing a supermarket shelf." To overcome this problem, Callaway and her team did a lot of "iterative experimentation" in the marketplace. These marketing experiments involved putting a prototype dessert in a store, measuring

You've eaten healthy all day and want something quick for your sweet tooth? Try Warm Delights microwaveable desserts—just add water and microwave in the container!

the results, improving the prototype, and repeating the process.[5]

Does Callaway's job sound easy?

Creative Initiatives Outside Cereals

In 2006 General Mills introduced more than 300 new food products around the world that responded to what consumers are asking for: ability to eat the product on the go, single portions, greater cooking convenience, and healthier eating.[6]

Sometimes it's possible to get all these features in the same new product and other times not. Examples of new noncereal products from General Mills include:[7]

- Eat-on-the-go products—Nature Valley Healthy Heart Chewy Granola Bars and Curves® Chewy Granola Bars.

- Single portions—Hamburger Helper Microwave Singles meals and Green Giant Just for One microwaveable vegetables.

- Healthier eating—Progresso® Light Soups with only 60 calories and 0 Weight Watchers Points® per serving.

- Greater cooking convenience—Betty Crocker® Warm Delights™ microwaveable desserts (simply add water and microwave in the container), and Pillsbury® Ready to Bake!™ cookies (refrigerated cookies already formed into cookie shapes).

Introducing these new products may sound simple, but even technology can be a problem. For example, when Callaway's marketing researchers discovered that consumers actually like to see the chocolate chips on top of their chocolate chip cookies, General Mills invested in new manufacturing equipment to make this a reality. Putting the chocolate chips on top increased sales 50 percent.

This chapter discusses issues and techniques related to the planning, implementation, and evaluation phases of the strategic marketing process, which were introduced in Chapter 2. Throughout the chapter, you'll obtain insights into the marketing strategies now emerging at General Mills and other firms. The video case at the end of the chapter describes how Vivian Callaway broke traditional rules to introduce the company's highly successful Warm Delights desserts.

MARKETING BASICS: DOING WHAT WORKS AND ALLOCATING RESOURCES

As noted in Chapter 2, corporate and marketing executives search continuously to find a competitive advantage—a unique strength relative to competitors. Having identified this competitive advantage, they must figure out how to exploit it.[8] This involves (1) finding and using what works for their organization and industry and (2) allocating resources effectively.

Finding and Using What Really Works

In a five-year study, researchers Nohria, Joyce, and Roberson conducted in-depth analysis of 160 companies and more than 200 management tools and techniques, such as supply chain management, customer relationship management (CRM), or use of an intranet. The result? Individual management tools and techniques had no direct relationship to superior business performance in the companies.[9]

What *does* matter? The researchers concluded that four basic business and management practices are what matter—"what really works," to use their phrase. These are: (1) strategy, (2) execution, (3) culture, and (4) structure. Firms with excellence in all four of these areas are likely to achieve superior business performance. And in terms of individual tools and techniques, the researchers concluded that which of these the firm chooses to use is less important than flawless execution of the ones it does use.

Industry leaders like Wal-Mart, Home Depot, and Dell do all four of the basic practices extremely well, not just two or three, and are vigilant to keep doing them well when conditions change. Coca-Cola and Kodak, superstars a decade ago, are struggling today to get these basics right and regain past success. Let's look at companies that stand out today in each of the four basics:

- *Strategy: Devise and maintain a clearly stated, focused strategy.* While Wal-Mart may be the unstoppable force in mass-merchandise retailing, in warehouse clubs its Sam's Club is not. The winner to date: Costco Wholesale, with 60 percent as many stores as Sam's Club but almost twice the sales revenue. A key reason is its focused strategy based on the knowledge that of all U.S. retail channels, warehouse clubs attract the largest proportion of affluent shoppers. Costco's strategy: Sell a limited selection of branded high-end merchandise at low prices.[10]
- *Execution: Develop and maintain flawless operational execution.* Toyota is generally acknowledged as the best in the world in revolutionizing the design and manufacture of autos. Toyota managers created the doctrine of *kaizen,* or continuous improvement. For example, by speeding up decisions, Toyota reduced the time to get one model from the drawing board to the showroom to 19 months, about half the industry average.[11]
- *Culture: Develop and maintain a performance-oriented culture.* Always near the top of *Fortune's* list of the 100 Best Companies to Work For is Smuckers— yes, the "With a name like Smuckers" company. Its straightforward culture is based on four key elements in its code of conduct: "Listen with your full attention, look for the good in others, have a sense of humor, and say thank you for a job well done." The performance result? Low employee turnover and large appreciation in the value of its stock.
- *Structure: Build and maintain a fast, flexible, flat organization.* Successful small organizations often grow into bureaucratic large ones with layers of managers and red tape that slow decision making. An exception and the unquestioned all-time leader in delivering world-class aircraft with only about 50 engineers and designers and 100 expert machinists: Lockheed's Skunk Works. Discussed later in the chapter, its first director set guidelines for organizational structure and implementation. Attempts have been made to try to apply these Skunk Works guidelines to U.S. auto industry projects and operations as far away as France and Russia. Key guidelines are (1) give the director the authority to

These companies achieve excellence in what really matters—a clear focused strategy for Costco and a performance-oriented culture for Smuckers.

make quick decisions and (2) use a small number of good people who can talk to anyone in the organization to solve a problem.[12]

Of course, in practice a firm cannot allocate unlimited resources to achieving each of these business basics. It must make choices on where its resources can give the greatest return, the topic of the next section.

Allocating Marketing Resources Using Sales Response Functions

A **sales response function** relates the expense of marketing effort to the marketing results obtained.[13] For simplicity in the examples that follow, only the effects of annual marketing effort on annual sales revenue will be analyzed, but the concept applies to other measures of marketing success—such as profit, units sold, or level of awareness—as well.

Maximizing Incremental Revenue Minus Incremental Cost   Economists give managers a specific guideline for optimal resource allocation: Allocate the firm's marketing, production, and financial resources to the markets and products where the excess of incremental revenues over incremental costs is greatest. This parallels the marginal revenue–marginal cost analysis of Chapter 13.

Figure 22–1 illustrates the resource allocation principle that is inherent in the sales response function. The firm's annual marketing effort, such as sales and advertising expenses, is plotted on the horizontal axis. As the annual marketing effort increases, so does the resulting annual sales revenue, which is plotted on the vertical axis. The relationship is assumed to be S-shaped, showing that an additional $1 million of marketing effort, from $3 million to $4 million, results in far greater increases of sales revenue in the midrange ($20 million) of the curve than at either end. An increase from $2 million to $3 million in spending yields an increase of $10 million in sales; an increase from $6 million to $7 million in spending leads to an increase of $5 million in sales.

A Numerical Example of Resource Allocation   Suppose Figure 22–1 shows the situation for a new General Mills product such as Fruity Cheerios®, an extension of the Cheerios brand targeted at health-conscious consumers. Each serving of Fruity Cheerios contains at least 23 grams of whole grain and 100 percent of an adult's daily needs of 12 key vitamins and minerals.

FIGURE 22–1

Sales response function shows the impact of various levels of marketing effort on annual sales revenue for two different years.

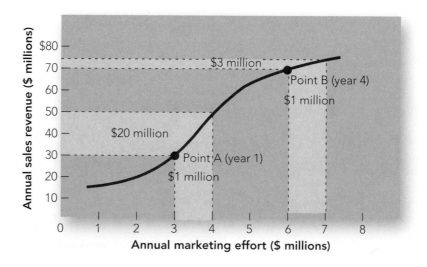

Recently introduced Fruity Cheerios reflects General Mills' increased emphasis on whole grains and nutrition in its breakfast cereals.

Also assume that the sales response function doesn't change through time as a result of changing consumer tastes and incomes. Point A shows the position of the firm in year 1, whereas Point B shows it three years later in year 4. Suppose General Mills decides to launch new advertising and sales promotions that, let's say, increase its marketing effort for the brand from $3 million to $6 million a year. If the relationship in Figure 22–1 holds true and is a good picture of consumer purchasing behavior, the sales revenues of Fruity Cheerios should increase from $30 million to $70 million a year.

Let's look at the major resource allocation question: What are the probable increases in sales revenue for Fruity Cheerios in year 1 and year 4 if General Mills were to spend an additional $1 million in marketing effort? As Figure 22–1 reveals,

Year 1

Increase in marketing effort from $3 million to $4 million = $1 million.

Increase in sales revenue from $30 million to $50 million = $20 million.

Ratio of incremental sales revenue to effort = $20,000,000:$1,000,000 = 20:1.

Year 4

Increase in marketing effort from $6 million to $7 million = $1 million.

Increase in sales revenue from $70 million to $73 million = $3 million.

Ratio of incremental sales revenue to effort = $3,000,000:$1,000,000 = 3:1.

Thus, in year 1 a dollar of extra marketing effort returned $20 in sales revenue, whereas in year 4 it returned only $3. If no other expenses are incurred, it might make sense to spend $1 million in year 4 to gain $3 million in incremental sales revenue. However, it may be far wiser for General Mills to invest the money in one of its other brands, such as its new line of Warm Delights microwaveable desserts.

The essence of resources allocation is simple: Put incremental resources where the incremental returns are greatest over the foreseeable future. For General Mills this means allocating its available resources efficiently among its broad portfolio of product lines, some of which are shown in the photo below. This portfolio includes many products marketed under its Big G brand, as well as ones offered under other brand names. Note in the photo the diversity of segmentation variables—from nutrition- or convenience-conscious segments to age and household-size segments.

Allocating Marketing Resources in Practice   General Mills, like many firms in these businesses, does extensive analysis using **share points**, or percentage points of market share, as the common basis of comparison to allocate marketing resources effectively for different product lines within the same firm. This allows it to

How can General Mills best allocate available resources among its portfolio of brands? Several frameworks within the strategic marketing process help answer the question.

seek answers to the question, "How much is it worth to us to try to increase our market share by another 1 (or 2, or 5, or 10) percentage point?"

This analysis enables higher-level managers to make resource allocation trade-offs among different kinds of business units owned by the company. To make these resource allocation decisions, marketing managers must estimate: (1) the market share for the product, (2) the revenues associated with each point of market share (a share point in breakfast cereals may be five times what it is in cake mixes), (3) the contribution to overhead and profit (or gross margin) of each share point, and (4) possible cannibalization effects on other products in the line (for example, new Fruity Cheerios might reduce sales of regular Cheerios).[14]

Planning phase

	Step 1	**Step 2**	**Step 3**	**Implementation phase**	**Evaluation phase**
Action	**Situation (SWOT) analysis** • Identify industry trends • Analyze competitors • Assess own company • Research customers	**Market-product focus and goal setting** • Set market and product goals • Select target markets • Find points of difference • Position the product	**Marketing program** • Develop the program's marketing mix • Develop the budget, by estimating revenues, expenses, and profits	• Obtain resources • Design marketing organization • Develop schedules • Execute marketing program	• Compare results with plans to identify deviations • Correct negative deviations; exploit positive ones
Information	• Trends for industry and competitors • Project future sales, expenses, and profits	• Market potential studies • Market-product grids, with targets • Positioning studies	• Marketing mix (4Ps) actions • Detailed plans to execute the marketing program	• Action memos with deadlines, Gantt charts • Organizational charts • Marketing research	• Tracking reports measuring results • Action memos to correct problems

Plans → Results →

Corrective actions | Corrective actions

FIGURE 22–2

The actions in the strategic marketing process are supported and directed by detailed reports, studies, and memos.

Resource Allocation and the Strategic Marketing Process   Company resources are allocated effectively in the strategic marketing process by converting marketing information into marketing actions. Figure 22–2 summarizes the strategic marketing process introduced in Chapter 2, along with some details of the marketing actions and information that comprise it. Figure 22–2 is really a simplification of the actual strategic marketing process: While the three phases of the strategic marketing process have distinct separations in the figure and the marketing actions are separated from the marketing information, in practice these blend together and interact.

The upper half of each box in Figure 22–2 highlights the actions involved in that part of the strategic marketing process, and the lower half summarizes the information and reports used. Note that each phase has an output report:

Phase	Output Report
Planning	Marketing plans (or programs) that define goals and the marketing mix strategies to achieve them
Implementation	Action memos that tell (1) *who* is (2) to do *what* (3) by *when*
Evaluation	Corrective action memos, triggered by comparing results with plans, often from the firm's marketing dashboards and metrics (measures)

The corrective action memos become feedback loops in Figure 22–2 that help improve decisions and actions in earlier phases of the strategic marketing process.

THE PLANNING PHASE OF THE STRATEGIC MARKETING PROCESS

Three aspects of the strategic marketing process deserve special mention: (1) the varieties of marketing plans, (2) marketing planning frameworks that have proven useful, and (3) some marketing planning and strategy lessons.

The Variety of Marketing Plans

The planning phase of the strategic marketing process usually results in a marketing plan that sets the direction for the marketing activities of an organization. As noted earlier in Appendix A, a marketing plan is the heart of a business plan. Like business plans, marketing plans aren't all from the same mold; they vary with the length of the planning period, the purpose, and the audience. Let's look briefly at two kinds: long-range and annual marketing plans.

Long-Range Marketing Plans Typically, long-range marketing plans cover marketing activities from two to five years into the future. Except for firms in industries such as autos, steel, or forest products, marketing plans rarely go beyond five years into the future because the tremendous number of uncertainties makes the benefits of planning less than the effort expended. Such plans are often directed at top-level executives and the board of directors.

Annual Marketing Plans Usually developed by a marketing or product manager (discussed later in the chapter) in a consumer products firm such as General Mills, annual marketing plans deal with marketing goals and strategies for a product, product line, or entire firm for a single year. This annual planning cycle typically starts with a detailed marketing research study of current users and ends after 42 weeks with the approval of the plan by the division general manager, 10 weeks before the fiscal year starts. Between these points there are continuing efforts to uncover new ideas through key-issues sessions with specialists both inside and outside the firm. The plan is fine-tuned through a series of often excruciating reviews by several levels of management, which leaves few surprises and little to chance.

It is easier to talk about planning than to do it well. The next section describes some marketing planning frameworks to aid the process.

learning review

1. What are the four basic practices "that really work"—that are characteristics of industry-leading firms?

2. What is the significance of the S-shape of the sales response function in Figure 22–1?

3. What are two kinds of marketing plans?

Marketing Planning Frameworks: The Search for Growth

LO2

Marketing planning for a firm with many products competing in many markets is a complex process. Yet in a business firm all these planning efforts are directed at finding the means for increased growth in sales and profits. Three techniques that help corporate and marketing executives make important resource allocation decisions are: (1) Porter's generic business strategies, (2) diversification analysis, and (3) synergy analysis. All three techniques relate to elements introduced in earlier chapters.

Porter's Generic Business Strategies As shown in Figure 22–3 on the next page, Michael E. Porter has developed a framework in which he identifies four basic, or "generic," strategies.[15] A **generic business strategy** is one that can be adopted by any firm, regardless of the product or industry involved, to achieve a competitive advantage.

FIGURE 22–3

SOURCE OF COMPETITIVE ADVANTAGE

Porter's four generic business strategies involve combinations of (1) competitive scope or the breadth of the target markets and (2) a stress on costs versus product differentiation.

Competitive scope	Lower cost	Differentiation
Broad target	1. Cost leadership	2. Differentiation
Narrow target	3. Cost focus	4. Differentiation focus

Although all of the techniques discussed here involve generic strategies, the phrase is most often associated with Porter's framework. In this framework, the columns identify the two fundamental alternatives firms can use in seeking competitive advantage: becoming the low-cost producer within the markets in which it competes or differentiating itself from competitors by developing points of difference in its product offerings or marketing programs. In contrast, the rows identify the competitive scope: a broad target by competing in many market segments or a narrow target by competing in only a few segments or even a single segment. The columns and rows result in four generic business strategies, any one of which can provide a competitive advantage among similar business units in the same industry:

1. A **cost leadership strategy** (cell 1) focuses on reducing expenses and, in turn, lowers product prices while targeting a broad array of market segments. One way is by securing raw materials from a lower-cost supplier. Also, significant investments in capital equipment may be necessary to improve the production or distribution process and achieve these lower unit costs. The cost leader still must have adequate quality levels. Wal-Mart's sophisticated systems of regional warehouses and electronic data interchange with its suppliers have led

Which of Porter's generic strategies are Wal-Mart and Toyota using? For the answers and a discussion of the strategies, see the text.

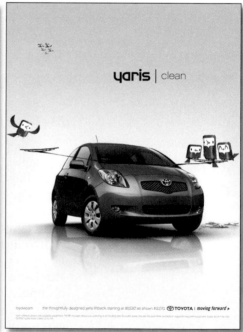

to huge cost savings and its cost leadership strategy that results in lower prices for customers.

2. A **differentiation strategy** (cell 2) requires products to have significant points of difference in product offerings, brand image, higher quality, advanced technology, or superior service to charge a higher price while targeting a broad array of market segments. This allows the firm to charge a price premium. Delphi Automobile Systems has used this strategy to use satellite communications to connect you and your car to 24-hour-a-day emergency services, directions to a destination, and the opportunity to order a movie while on the road.

3. A **cost focus strategy** (cell 3) involves controlling expenses and, in turn, lowering product prices targeted at a narrow range of market segments. Retail chains targeting only a few market segments in a restricted group of products—such as Office Max in office supplies—have used a cost focus strategy successfully. Southwest Airlines has been very successful in offering low fares between restricted pairs of cities.

4. Finally, a **differentiation focus strategy** (cell 4) requires products to have significant points of difference to target one or only a few market segments. The average age of today's Toyota owner is 47. So a concerned Toyota product planning group visited cities where young people are buying and renting loft apartments. The planners discovered these young city dwellers need smaller cars they can park in cramped spaces. This suggests offering a new Toyota model with an important point of difference for a narrow segment of buyers—a differentiation focus strategy.[16]

These strategies also form the foundation for Michael Porter's theory about what makes a nation's industries successful, as discussed in Chapter 7.

Diversification Analysis Our market–product grid analysis covered in Chapter 9 shows firms often view growth opportunities in terms of markets and products. This idea underlies **diversification analysis**, which is the search for growth opportunities from among current and new markets as well as current and new products.[17] To illustrate diversification analysis, we can view some very specific market and product decisions General Mills recently made and their strategy implications.

For any market, there is both a current product (what the firm is now selling) and a new product (something the firm might sell in the future). And for any product there is both a current market (consisting of existing customers) and a new market (consisting of potential customers). To increase sales revenues, General Mills uses all four of the market–product strategies shown in Figure 22–4 on the next page.

For example, it can try to use *market penetration*—a marketing strategy of increasing sales of present products in existing markets. In this case General Mills might try to increase sales of its flagship brand of Cheerios to its current customers by stressing the cereal's cholesterol-lowering benefit in a broad band across the front of the package (Figure 22–4). In this market–product combination there is no change in either the basic product line or the market served. But increased sales are possible—either by selling more of the product (say, by having the Cheerios package highlight an important benefit) *or* by selling the same amount of it at a higher price to its existing customers.

Market development, a marketing strategy of selling existing products such as cereals to new markets, is a reasonable alternative for General Mills. Europe is potentially a good market where it might sell its cereals through its Cereal Partners Worldwide joint venture with Swiss-based Nestlé. This is how it successfully introduced Cini Minis to Polish consumers, the brand Americans know as Cinnamon

PRODUCTS

Markets	Current	New

Market Penetration

 Finding ways to make current products appeal to current customers: stress reduced-cholesterol benefit on Cheerios box

Product Development

 Reaching current customers with a new product: 100 calorie Curves granola bar, mainly for women

Current

Market Development

 Reaching new customers with a current product: Cini Minis for Polish consumers—known as Cinnamon Toast Crunch in the United States

Diversification

 Reaching new customers with a new product: 8th Continent Soymilk, for those who can't drink milk or are health conscious

New

FIGURE 22–4

For General Mills to continue its growth it finds opportunities in all four strategies shown in this diversification analysis.

Toast Crunch (Figure 22–4). The potential downside to this market development strategy for General Mills in Europe is its lack of experience there—overcome by its joint venture with Nestlé, which has decades of experience marketing products in Europe.

Product development is a marketing strategy of selling new products to existing markets. Figure 22–4 shows that General Mills can leverage its joint venture with Curves International, a fitness center chain serving American women, to introduce its Curves Chocolate Peanut granola bar. The bar has 5 grams of fiber with only 100 calories, the number of calories burned in a typical Curves workout.[18] In this case General Mills incurs extra product development costs but knows the existing U.S. market very well.

Diversification is a marketing strategy of developing new products and selling them in new markets. This is a potentially high-risk strategy for General Mills, and for most firms, because it has neither previous production nor marketing experience on which to draw. If General Mills wants to enter a new milk-substitute market, its diversification strategy must overcome *both* its extra product development costs *and* the difficulties of gaining distribution in a new market. In the case of the 8th Continent Soymilk shown in Figure 22–4, General Mills is exploiting innovative new technology in a joint venture with DuPont. The result offers both regular and light soymilk versions, giving nutritious new options for breakfast.

Synergy Analysis **Synergy analysis** seeks opportunities by finding the optimum balance between marketing efficiencies versus R&D–manufacturing efficiencies. Using the market–product grid framework introduced in Chapter 9, we can see two kinds of synergy that are critical in developing corporate and marketing strategies: (1) marketing synergy and (2) R&D–manufacturing synergy. While the following example involves external synergies through mergers and acquisitions, the concepts apply equally well to internal synergies sought in adding new products or seeking new markets.

Marketing Matters > > > > > customer value

A Test of Your Skills: Where Are the Synergies?

To try your hand in this multibillion-dollar synergy game, assume you are vice president of marketing for Great States Corp., which markets a line of nonpowered, powered walking, and powered riding lawn mowers. A market–product grid for your business is shown. You distribute your nonpowered mowers in all three market segments shown and powered and walking powered mowers only in suburban markets. However, you don't offer powered riding mowers for any of the three markets.

Here are your strategy dilemmas:

1. Where are the marketing synergies (efficiencies)?
2. Where are the R&D–manufacturing synergies (efficiencies)?
3. What would a market-product grid look like for an ideal company that Great States could merge with in order to achieve both marketing and R&D–manufacturing synergies (efficiencies)?

To consider these questions, read the text and study Figure 22–5 and the figure below.

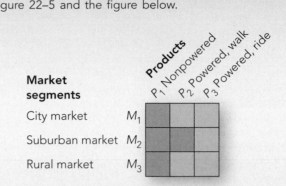

A critical step in the external analysis is to assess how these merger and acquisition strategies provide the organization with synergy, the increased customer value achieved through performing organizational functions more efficiently. The increased customer value can take many forms: more products, improved quality on existing products, lower prices, improved distribution, and so on. But the ultimate criterion is that customers should be better off as a result of the increased synergy. The firm, in turn, should be better off by gaining more satisfied customers resulting in increased sales and profits.

As noted in the Marketing Matters box, assume you are vice president of marketing for Great States Corp.'s line of nonpowered lawn mowers and powered walking mowers sold to the consumer market. You are looking for new product and new market opportunities to increase your revenues and profits.

You conduct a market segmentation study and develop a market–product grid to analyze future opportunities. You identify three major segments in the consumer market based on geography: (1) city, (2) suburban, and (3) rural households. These market segments relate to the size of lawn a consumer must mow. The product clusters are: (1) nonpowered, (2) powered walking, and (3) powered riding mowers. Five alternative marketing strategies are shown in the market–product grids in Figure 22–5 on the next page.[19] As mentioned in Chapter 9, the important marketing synergies, or efficiencies, run horizontally across the rows in Figure 22–5. Conversely, the important R&D–manufacturing synergies, or efficiencies, run vertically down the columns. Let's look at the synergy effects for the five combinations in Figure 22–5.

A. *Market–product concentration.* The firm benefits from focus on a single product line and market segment, but it loses opportunities for significant synergies in both marketing and R&D–manufacturing.

B. *Market specialization.* The firm gains marketing synergy through providing a complete product line for the city market segment, but R&D–manufacturing has the difficulty of developing and producing three different products.

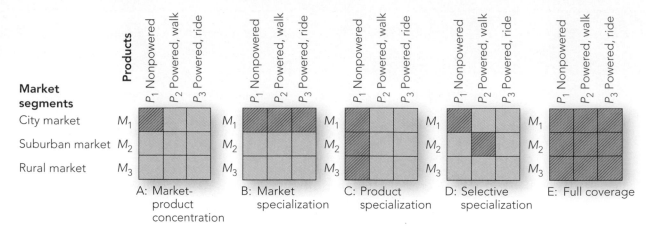

FIGURE 22–5

Market–product grids show alternative strategies for a lawnmower manufacturer. Try to find synergies in each strategy—if any exist.

C. *Product specialization.* The firm gains R&D–manufacturing synergy through producing only a nonpowered lawnmower, but gaining market distribution in the three different geographic areas will be costly.

D. *Selective specialization.* The firm doesn't get either marketing or R&D–manufacturing synergies because of the uniqueness of the market–product combinations.

E. *Full coverage.* The firm has the maximum potential synergies in both marketing and R&D–manufacturing. The question: Is it spread too thin because of the resource requirements needed to reach all market–product combinations?

The Marketing Matters box poses the question of what the ideal partner for Great States would be if it merged with another firm, given the market–product combinations shown in the box. If, as vice president of marketing, you want to follow a full-coverage strategy, then the ideal merger partner is shown in Figure 22–6. This would give the maximum potential synergies—if you are not spreading the resources of your merged companies too thin. Marketing gains by having a complete product line in all regions, and R&D–manufacturing gains by having access to new markets that can provide production economies of scale through producing larger volumes of its existing products.

Often the search for synergies is within the company itself. Ford Motor Company, fighting for survival, plans to reduce its number of car platforms—on which the car body sits—from the 30 it had in 2007 down to five or six like its competitor Honda. The result should be greater manufacturing synergies and efficiencies that in turn will lead to better quality control and happier customers.[20] Similarly, Procter & Gamble concluded the world didn't really need 31 varieties of its Head & Shoulders shampoo. Cutting the number in half, P&G also reduced its expenses and increased profits in the bargain.[21]

FIGURE 22–6

This is the ideal merger for Great States to obtain full market–product coverage. The ideal partner offers lawn mower products to the exact segments of customers *not* now served by Great States.

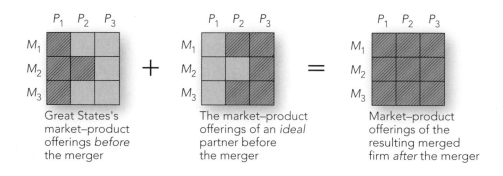

Great States's market–product offerings *before* the merger

The market–product offerings of an *ideal* partner before the merger

Market–product offerings of the resulting merged firm *after* the merger

4. Describe Porter's four generic business strategies.

5. What are four alternative ways to increase a firm's revenues when using the diversification analysis framework?

6. Where do (a) marketing synergies and (b) R&D–manufacturing synergies appear when using the synergy analysis framework?

Some Marketing Planning and Strategy Lessons

Applying these frameworks is not automatic but requires a great deal of managerial judgment. Common sense requirements of an effective marketing plan are discussed next, followed by problems that can arise.

Guidelines for an Effective Marketing Plan President Dwight D. Eisenhower, when he commanded Allied armies in World War II, made his classic observation, "Plans are nothing; planning is everything." It is the process of careful planning that focuses an organization's efforts and leads to success. The plans themselves, which change with events, are often secondary. Effective planning and plans are inevitably characterized by identifiable objectives, specific strategies or courses of action, and the means to execute them. Here are some guidelines in developing effective marketing plans:

- *Set measurable, achievable goals.* Ideally, goals should be quantified and measurable in terms of what is to be accomplished and by when. So "Increase market share from 18 percent to 22 percent by December 31, 2011" is preferable to "Maximize market share given our available resources." Also, to motivate people the goals must be achievable.
- *Use a base of facts and valid assumptions.* The more a marketing plan is based on facts and valid assumptions, rather than guesses, the less uncertainty and risk are associated with executing it. Good marketing research helps.
- *Utilize simple, but clear and specific, plans.* Effective execution of plans requires that people at all levels in the firm understand what, when, and how they are to accomplish their tasks.
- *Have complete and feasible plans.* Marketing plans must incorporate all the key marketing mix factors and be supported by adequate resources.
- *Make plans controllable and flexible.* Marketing plans must enable results to be compared with planned targets, often using precise marketing metrics and dashboards. This allows replanning—the flexibility to alter the original plans based on recent results.

Problems in Marketing Planning and Strategy From postmortems on company plans that did work and on those that did not work, a picture emerges of where problems occur in the planning phase of a firm's strategic marketing process. The following list explores these problems:

1. Plans may be based on very poor assumptions about environmental forces, especially changing economic conditions and competitors' actions. A Western Union plan failed because it didn't reflect the impact of deregulation and competitors' actions on business.
2. Planners and their plans may have lost sight of their customers' needs. But not at the Papa John's pizza chain. The "better ingredients, better pizza" slogan makes the hair stand up on the back of the necks of competing Pizza

Hut executives. The reason is that this Papa John's slogan reflects the firm's obsessive attention to detail, which is stealing market share from much-bigger Pizza Hut. Sample detail: If the cheese on the pizza shows a single air bubble or the crust is not golden brown, the offending pizza is not served to the customer.

3. Too much time and effort may be spent on data collection and writing the plans. Westinghouse cut its planning instructions "that looked like an auto repair manual" to five or six pages for operating units.

4. Line operating managers often feel no sense of ownership in implementing the plans. Andy Grove, when he was CEO of Intel, observed, "We had the very ridiculous system . . . of delegating strategic planning to strategic planners. The strategies these [planners] prepared had no bearing on anything we actually did."[22] The solution is to assign more planning activities to line operating managers, the people who actually carry them out.

Big G: Global Strategies to Find Synergies, Segments, and Partners Competing in today's global marketplace, General Mills is concerned *both* with selling its products and brands in countries around the world *and* also obtaining ideas for new products from anyone, anywhere who has a great product or technology. The Marketing Matters box gives examples of this two-way street.

General Mills' successful introduction of French-developed Yoplait Yogurt to U.S. consumers led the way to its global initiatives today.

Easy to understand is the benefit for General Mills of moving its existing U.S. products into foreign markets. The company's joint venture with Swiss-based Nestlé in Cereal Partners Worldwide provides General Mills access to European, Latin American, and Asian consumers—offering everything from cereals to ice cream bars. This joint venture has achieved great success.

Less clear is the reason for Big G's current global search for new ideas, products, and technologies. The success of Yoplait Yogurt ("The Yogurt of France") has led to bringing other products developed outside the United States to our shores. As mentioned in the Marketing Matters box, Wanchai Ferry™ brand dinner kits are coming to the United States through a collaboration managed by General Mills of scientists on three continents. The dinner kits, which do not require freezing or refrigeration, are an adaptation of frozen dumplings developed by Madame Kin Wo Chong, a Hong Kong entrepreneur.[23]

Have a great idea for a new technology or product General Mills might use? Under its Worldwide Innovation Network, the company wants your idea to help accelerate its innovation efforts. You can contact General Mills online through an Internet portal at www.generalmills.com/win to submit your idea. But there's a wrinkle: The new product or technology must (1) have a patent or patent pending and (2) be on the market somewhere in the world![24]

Balancing Value and Values in Strategic Marketing Plans Two important trends are likely to influence the strategic marketing process in the future. The first, *value-based planning,* combines marketing planning ideas and financial planning techniques to assess how much a division or strategic business unit (SBU) contributes to the price of a company's stock (or shareholder wealth). Value is created when the financial return of a strategic activity exceeds the cost of the resources allocated to the activity.

The second trend is the increasing interest in *value-driven strategies,* which incorporate concerns for ethics, integrity, employee health and safety, and environmental safeguards with more common corporate values such as growth, profitability, customer service, and quality. Some experts have observed that although many corporations cite broad corporate values in advertisements, press releases,

Big G's Global Search for Products and Markets: Sweet & Sour Chicken from China and Nature Valley Granola Bars to India

With the huge success of its French-developed Yoplait Yogurt, international business is now a two-way street for General Mills. It is not only concerned with selling its products globally but also in finding product ideas from around the world.

New Product Ideas from Around the World

Now known as Hong Kong's "dumpling queen," Madame Kin Wo Chong started selling her dumplings in 1977 from a cart on the city's Wanchai Ferry pier. "My vision is to bring Chinese traditional dim sum and dumplings to every part of the world . . .," she says through an interpreter. She is well on her way, and her story shows the lengths General Mills goes to find ideas for new products.

Her Chinese business is mostly for frozen dumplings. Working with research teams in China, Europe, and the United States, General Mills intro-

duced her Wanchai Ferry brand dinner kits in the United States in 2006 and in Europe a year later. The technical challenge was to keep the ingredients fresh because the kits aren't refrigerated or frozen. General Mills hopes Madame Chong's kits will take advantage of the popularity of Chinese food among Americans.

Reaching New Global Markets

Revenues from international operations at General Mills reached $1.8 billion in 2006—up fivefold from five years earlier. Much of this results from its Cereal Partners Worldwide joint venture with Switzerland's Nestlé, which recently introduced Trix & Yoghurt in Latin America and Uncle Tobys cereals in Australia. Häagen-Dazs ice cream sandwiches are hits in Japan and Europe. And Nature Valley granola bars reached Indian consumers in 2006.

and company newsletters; they have not yet changed their strategic plans to reflect the stated values. U.S. firms, like firms and governments around the world, are increasingly called on to be good global citizens and to support sustainable development.[25]

THE IMPLEMENTATION PHASE OF THE STRATEGIC MARKETING PROCESS

The Monday morning diagnosis of a losing football coach often runs something like "We had an excellent game plan; we just didn't execute it."

Is Planning or Implementation the Problem?

The planning-versus-execution issue applies to the strategic marketing process as well: When a marketing plan fails, it's difficult to determine whether the failure is due to a poor plan or poor implementation.[26]

Effective managers tracking progress on a struggling plan first try to identify whether the problems involve: (1) the plan and strategy, (2) its implementation, or (3) both, and then they try to correct the problems. But as discussed earlier in the chapter, research on what really works shows that successful firms have excellence

What are some of the benefits General Electric achieved in its "ecomagination" initiative? For the answer, which shows GE's world-class program planning and implementation, see the text.

General Electric Company
www.ge.com

on both the planning and strategy side and the implementation and execution side. For example, General Electric's continuing leadership in lighting combines strong innovative products (planning and strategy) with excellent advertising and distribution (implementation and execution).

At the other extreme, most of the hundreds of dot-com firms that failed in the late 1990s had both planning *and* implementation problems. Their bad planning often resulted from their focus on getting start-up money from investors and not providing real value to customers. Bad implementation by the dot-coms frequently led to their spending huge sums on wasteful ads to try to promote their failing websites. While some Internet firms may have had good ideas for delivering physical products like toys and groceries to their customers' doors, they didn't understand key implementation issues that involved inventories, warehouses, and physical distribution.

Increasing Emphasis on Marketing Implementation

In the new millennium, the implementation phase of the strategic marketing process has emerged as a key factor to success by moving many planning activities away from the duties of planners to those of line managers.

General Electric's Jack Welch became a legend in making GE more efficient and far better at implementation. When Welch became CEO in 1981 he faced an organization mired in red tape, turf battles, and slow decision making. Further, Welch saw GE bogged down with 25,000 managers and close to a dozen layers between him and the factory floor. In his "delayering," he sought to cut GE's levels in half and to speed up decision making and implementation by building an atmosphere of trust and autonomy among his managers and employees.

In terms of implementation and meeting key goals, Jack Welch also insisted General Electric's departments be "winners"—or #1 or #2 in their industry in terms of revenues and profits. Welch had another mantra for these departments: "Fix, close, or sell!" Under his leadership, more than 100 GE businesses were closed or sold. An example is GE's small appliance division that was sold to Black & Decker. The remaining GE businesses were either running well or were "fixed"—in Welch's terms. Although there are debates on some Welch strategies, businesses around the world are using GE's focus on implementation as a benchmark.

One measure of GE's global impact: In 2007 *Fortune* magazine named General Electric America's most admired company, the seventh time in nine years that GE attained this distinction.[27] An example of where GE combines both planning and implementation is its much-publicized "ecomagination" initiative. This campaign includes goals of doubling its investment in research and development, reducing greenhouse gas emissions, and increasing revenues from its ecomagination

Papa's Signature Pizzas

Core value 4—"PAPA"—makes very clear to all Papa John's Pizza employees what its priorities are!

products that aid the environment—such as more efficient lighting, lower-emission aircraft engines, and solar-energy hybrid locomotives. This ecomagination program led GE to re-lamp 62 of its facilities using the products from its Lighting Division, both to reduce greenhouse emissions and lower its energy costs.[28]

Improving Implementation of Marketing Programs

No magic formula exists to guarantee effective implementation of marketing plans. In fact, the answer seems to be equal parts of good management skills and practices, from which have come some guidelines for improving program implementation.

Communicate Goals and the Means of Achieving Them Those called on to implement plans need to understand both the goals sought and how they are to be accomplished. Everyone in Papa John's—from founder John Schnatter to telephone order takers and make-line people—is clear on what the firm's goal is: to deliver better pizzas using better ingredients. The firm's orientation packet for employees lists its six core values that executives are expected to memorize. Sample: Core value 4 is "PAPA," or "People Are Priority No. 1, Always."[29]

Have a Responsible Program Champion Willing to Act Successful programs almost always have a **product or program champion** who is able and willing to cut red tape and move the program forward. Such a person often has the uncanny ability to move back and forth between big-picture strategy questions and specific details when the situation calls for it. Program champions are notoriously brash in overcoming organizational hurdles. The U.S. Navy's Admiral Grace Murray Hopper not only gave the world an early computer language but also the word *bug,* meaning any glitch in a computer or computer program. This program champion's famous advice for moving decisions to actions by cutting through an organization's red tape: "Better to ask forgiveness than permission."

Reward Successful Program Implementation When an individual or a team is rewarded for achieving the organization's goal, they have maximum incentive to see a program implemented successfully because they have personal ownership and a stake in that success.

Take Action and Avoid Paralysis by Analysis Management experts warn against "paralysis by analysis," the tendency to excessively analyze a problem instead of taking action. To overcome this pitfall, they call for a "bias for action" and recommend a "do it, fix it, try it" approach.[30] Conclusion: Perfectionists finish last, so getting 90 percent perfection and letting the marketplace help in the fine-tuning makes good sense in implementation.

Lockheed Martin's Skunk Works got its name from the comic strip *L'il Abner* and its legendary reputation from achieving superhuman technical feats with a low budget and ridiculously short deadlines by stressing teamwork. Under the leadership of Kelly Johnson, in 35 years the Skunk Works turned out a series of world-class aircraft from the world's fastest (the SR-71 Blackbird) to the nation's most untrackable aircraft (the F-117 Stealth fighter). Two of Kelly Johnson's basic tenets: (1) make decisions promptly and (2) avoid paralysis by analysis. In fact, one U.S. Air Force audit showed that Johnson's Skunk Works could carry out a

Great teamwork and communications at Lockheed Martin's Skunk Works have led to state-of-the-art aircraft like this F-117 Stealth fighter. The text gives some examples.

program on schedule with 126 people, whereas a competitor in a comparable program was behind schedule with 3,750 people.[31]

Foster Open Communication to Surface Problems Success often lies in fostering a work environment that is open enough so employees are willing to speak out when they see problems without fear of recrimination. The focus is placed on trying to solve the problem as a group rather than finding someone to blame. Solutions are solicited from anyone who has a creative idea to suggest—from the janitor to the president—without regard to status or rank in the organization.

Two more Kelly Johnson axioms from Lockheed Martin's Skunk Works apply here: (1) When trouble develops, surface the problem immediately, and (2) get help; don't keep the problem to yourself. This latter point is important even if it means getting ideas from competitors.

In Saturn, General Motors created a new company where participatory management and improved communications led to a successful product. For example, to encourage discussion of possible cost reductions, each employee receives 100 to 750 hours of training, including balance sheet analysis. Saturn sought to avoid the "NIH syndrome"—the reluctance to accept ideas "not invented here" or not originated inside one's own firm. Saturn engineers bought 70 import cars to study for product design ideas and selected options that would most appeal to their target market so that they could leapfrog competitors with their new design.

Schedule Precise Tasks, Responsibilities, and Deadlines Successful implementation requires that people know the tasks for which they are responsible and the deadline for completing them. To implement the thousands of tasks on a new aircraft design, Lockheed Martin typically holds weekly program meetings. The outcome of each of these meetings is an **action item list**, an aid to implementing a marketing plan consisting of four columns: (1) the task, (2) the person responsible for completing that task, (3) the date to finish the task, and (4) what is to be delivered. Within hours of completing a program meeting, the action item list is circulated to those attending. This then serves as the starting agenda for the next meeting. Meeting minutes are viewed as secondary and backward looking. Action item lists are forward looking, clarify the targets, and put strong pressure on people to achieve their designated tasks by the deadline.

Related to the action item lists are formal *program schedules,* which show the relationships through time of the various program tasks. Scheduling an action program involves: (1) identifying the main tasks, (2) determining the time required to complete each, (3) arranging the activities to meet the deadline, and (4) assigning responsibilities to complete each task.

Suppose, for example, that you and two friends are asked to do a term project on the problem, "How can the college increase attendance at its performing arts concerts?" And suppose further that the instructor limits the project in the following ways:

1. The project must involve a mail survey of the attitudes of a sample of students.
2. The term paper with the survey results must be submitted by the end of the 11-week quarter.

To begin the assignment, you need to identify all the project tasks and then estimate the time you can reasonably allocate to each one. To complete it in 11 weeks,

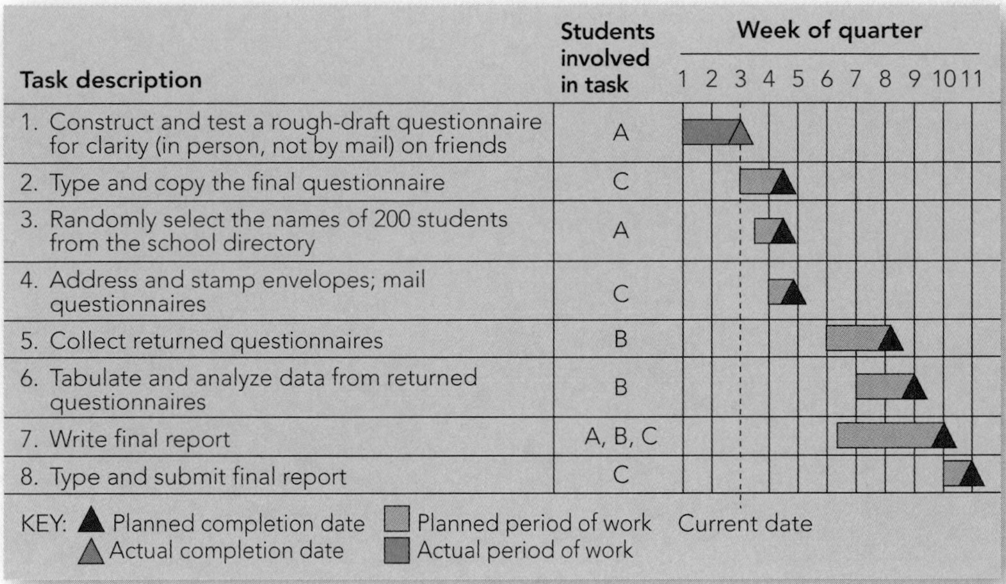

Task description	Students involved in task	Week of quarter 1 2 3 4 5 6 7 8 9 10 11
1. Construct and test a rough-draft questionnaire for clarity (in person, not by mail) on friends	A	
2. Type and copy the final questionnaire	C	
3. Randomly select the names of 200 students from the school directory	A	
4. Address and stamp envelopes; mail questionnaires	C	
5. Collect returned questionnaires	B	
6. Tabulate and analyze data from returned questionnaires	B	
7. Write final report	A, B, C	
8. Type and submit final report	C	

KEY: ▲ Planned completion date ☐ Planned period of work Current date
△ Actual completion date ■ Actual period of work

FIGURE 22–7

This Gantt chart for scheduling a student term project distinguishes the tasks that *must* be done sequentially from those that *can* be done concurrently.

your team must work on different parts at the same time, and some activities must be independent enough to overlap. This requires specialization and cooperation. Suppose that of the three of you (A, B, and C), only student C can type. Then you (student A) might assume the task of constructing the questionnaire and selecting samples, and student B might tabulate the data. You must also figure out which activities can be done concurrently to save time.

Scheduling production and marketing activities—from a term project to a new product rollout to a space shuttle launch—can be done efficiently with a *Gantt chart,* which is a graphical representation of a program schedule. Figure 22–7 shows one variation of a Gantt chart used to schedule the class project, demonstrating how the concurrent work on several tasks enables the students to finish the project on time. Developed by Henry L. Gantt, this method is the basis for the scheduling techniques used today, including elaborate computerized methods. The key to all scheduling techniques is to distinguish tasks that *must* be done sequentially from those that *can* be done concurrently. As in the case of the term project, scheduling tasks concurrently often reduces the total time required for a project. Software programs, such as Microsoft Project, simplify the task of developing a schedule or Gantt chart.

learning review

7. What is the meaning and importance of a program champion?

8. Explain the difference between sequential and concurrent tasks in a Gantt chart.

Organizing for Marketing

LO5

A marketing organization is needed to implement the firm's marketing plans. Basic issues in today's marketing organizations include understanding (1) how line versus staff positions and divisional groupings interrelate to form a cohesive marketing organization and (2) the role of the marketing or product manager.

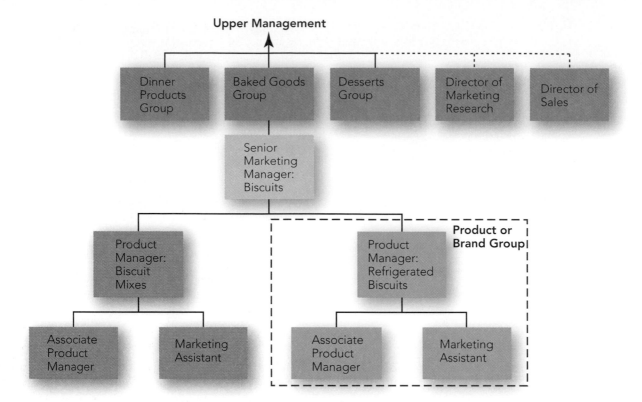

FIGURE 22–8

This organization of a business unit in a typical consumer packaged goods firm shows two product or brand groups.

Line versus Staff and Divisional Groupings Although simplified, Figure 22–8 shows the organization of a typical business unit in a consumer packaged goods firm like Procter & Gamble, Kraft, or General Mills. This business unit consists of the Dinner Products, Baked Goods, and Desserts groups. It highlights the distinction between line and staff positions in marketing. Managers in **line positions**, such as the senior marketing manager for Biscuits, have the authority and responsibility to issue orders to the people who report to them, such as the two product managers shown in Figure 22–8. In this organizational chart, line positions are connected with solid lines. People in **staff positions** (shown by dotted lines) have the authority and responsibility to advise people in line positions but cannot issue direct orders to them.

Most marketing organizations use divisional groupings—such as product line, functional, geographical, and market-based—to implement plans and achieve their organizational objectives. Only the first of these appears in the organizational chart in Figure 22–8. The top of the chart shows organization by **product line groupings** in which a unit is responsible for specific product offerings, such as Dinner Products or Baked Goods.

At higher levels than shown in Figure 22–8, grocery products firms are organized by **functional groupings**—such as manufacturing, marketing, and finance—that represent the different departments or business activities within a firm.

Most grocery products firms use **geographical groupings** in which sales territories are subdivided according to geographical location. Each director of sales has several regional sales managers reporting to him or her, such as western, southern, and so on. These, in turn, have district managers reporting to them, with the field sales representatives at the lowest level.

A fourth method of organizing a company is to use **market-based groupings**, which utilize specific customer segments, such as the banking, health care, or manufacturing segments. When this method of organizing is combined with product groupings, the result is a *matrix organization.*

A relatively new position in consumer products firms is the *category manager* (senior marketing manager in Figure 22–8). Category managers have profit-and-loss responsibility for an entire product line—all biscuit brands, for example. They attempt to reduce the possibility of one brand's actions hurting another brand in the same category. Procter & Gamble uses category managers to organize by "global business units" such as baby care and beauty care. Cutting across country boundaries, these global business units implement standardized worldwide pricing, marketing, and distribution.[32]

Role of the Product Manager The key person in the product or brand group is the manager who heads it. As mentioned in Chapter 10, this person is often called the *product manager* or *brand manager.* This person and the assistants in the product group are the basic building blocks in the marketing department of most consumer and business product firms. The function of a product manager is to plan, implement, and evaluate the annual and long-range plans for the products for which he or she is responsible.

There are both benefits and dangers to the product manager system. On the positive side, product managers become strong advocates for the assigned products, cut red tape to work with people in various functions both inside and outside the organization, and assume profit-and-loss responsibility for the performance of the product line. On the negative side, even though product managers have major responsibilities, they have relatively little direct authority, so they must use persuasion rather than direct orders.[33]

THE EVALUATION PHASE OF THE STRATEGIC MARKETING PROCESS

The essence of evaluation, the final phase of the strategic marketing process, is to compare results with planned goals for the marketing program in order to take necessary corrective actions.

The Marketing Evaluation Process

Ideally, quantified goals from the marketing plans developed in the planning phase have been accomplished by the marketing actions taken in the implementation phase (Figure 22–9 on the next page) and measured as results in the evaluation phase. A marketing manager then uses *management by exception,* which means identifying results that deviate from plans to diagnose their causes and take new actions.

Often results fall short of plans, and a corrective action is needed. For example, after 50 years of profits Caterpillar accumulated losses of $1 billion. To correct the problem, Caterpillar focused its marketing efforts on core products and reduced its manufacturing costs. When results are better than plans, the marketing manager tries to identify the reason and move quickly to exploit the unexpected opportunity.

Evaluation Involves Marketing ROI, Metrics, and Dashboards

In the past decade measuring the performance of marketing activities has become a central focus in many organizations. This boils down to some form of the question, "What measure can I use to determine if my company's marketing is effective?"

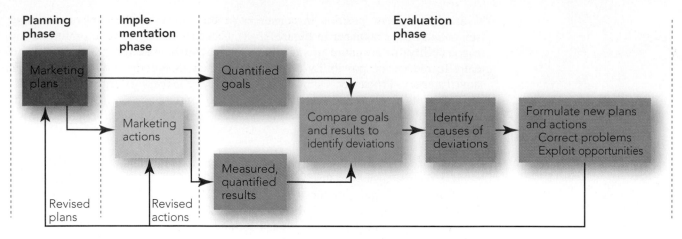

| Planning phase | Implementation phase | Evaluation phase |

Marketing plans → Quantified goals

Marketing actions

Quantified goals → Compare goals and results to identify deviations → Identify causes of deviations → Formulate new plans and actions / Correct problems / Exploit opportunities

Measured, quantified results

Revised plans

Revised actions

FIGURE 22–9

The evaluation phase of the strategic marketing process ties results and actions to goals, often using marketing dashboards.

No single measure exists. In finance, the return on investment (ROI) measure relates the total investment made to the total return generated from the investment. The concept has been extended to trying to measure the effectiveness of marketing expenditures with **marketing ROI**, the application of modern measurement technologies to understand, quantify, and optimize marketing spending.[34]

The evaluation phase of the strategic marketing process tries to improve marketing ROI through the effective use of marketing metrics and dashboards:

- *Marketing metrics.* Depending on the specific objective sought, one or a few key marketing metrics are chosen, such as market share, cost per lead, retention rate, cost per click, sales per square foot, and so on.[35] This is the "quantified goals" step in Figure 22–9.
- *Marketing dashboards.* If the financial resources and technology are available, the marketing metrics are displayed—often hourly or daily on the manager's computer. With today's syndicated scanner data, Internet clicks, and TV viewership tracking, the typical manager faces information overload. So effective marketing dashboard displays highlight—often in color—where actual results vary significantly from plans. This alerts the manager to potential problems.[36]

These highlighted exceptions, or deviations from plans in Figure 22–9, are the immediate focus of the marketing manager. Marketing managers then try to improve their marketing ROI by correcting shortfalls and exploiting results that exceed plans.

Taking Marketing Actions The sole reason for marketing metrics and dashboards is to provide managers useful, timely information that leads to logical actions. Beaten badly for years in the U.S. toothpaste market by P&G's Crest, in the late 1990s Colgate went on the offensive. It used new technology and aggressive marketing actions to introduce its Total toothpaste, the first "oral pharmaceutical" ever approved by the U.S. Food and Drug Administration. Not only does Total clean teeth, but also its germ-fighting feature helps heal gingivitis, a bleeding-gum disease. This has helped Colgate achieve the highest market share in the U.S. toothpaste market.[37]

Colgate launched a successful marketing campaign for its Total toothpaste, obtaining the first ever "oral pharmaceutical" approved by the U.S. Food and Drug Administration.

Strange. It's only breakfast and your toothpaste has already called it a day.

Unless you use Colgate Total. Most toothpastes can't fight plaque after you eat or drink, when teeth become more vulnerable to bacteria. But Colgate Total is different. Its unique formula has an antibacterial ingredient that attaches to teeth to protect for 12 hours. Even after eating and drinking.

Colgate Total
12-Hour Protection

A Dashboard Look at a Career in Marketing

Let's see how marketing dashboards and metrics affect the everyday work life of a marketer.

If you choose a career in marketing, you will soon find that the on-the-job strategic marketing process discussed in the book is really a whirlwind of ideas, issues, and concerns that are volunteered to you by your bosses, the salesforce, market research analysts, operations professionals, your distributor partners, happy and unhappy customers, and even friends and family. These people are all genuinely interested in giving their opinion. More importantly, they all want to help you and your business succeed. Let's apply the challenge–findings–action steps from the book's Using Marketing Dashboards boxes to what your life will look like if you choose a career in marketing.

Your Challenge Most of the issues and concerns that will be shared with you as a marketing professional are *not* carefully researched, evaluated, or considered. There simply isn't time. And your colleagues will ask you, "Isn't that your job?"

The exciting challenge you have, as a marketing professional, is to evaluate what you hear, distill out important themes, and set in motion actions that grow the business. Almost always the problem starts in some way with increasing revenues and profits, or "growing the business." For example, as marketing manager for Nike, you discover sales of your new, just-launched sneakers aren't up to company expectations.

Your Findings Many factors impact your business, including pricing, distribution, sales velocity, new products, other marketing variables, and competition. Analyzing sales by region, you discover other regions are doing well but the Midwest region is lagging badly. Further research shows that many Midwest retailers are out of stock.

Your Action In many marketing positions, you will find that you have little time to reflect and ponder in your busy workday. Many marketplace changes are simply out of your control, and your opinion and decisions will be sought quickly on what to do. In growing your sneaker business, you make calls and write e-mails to overcome your distribution problems in the Midwest region and get your sneakers on those shelves—ASAP!

After all the data collection and analysis, marketing professionals always ask the same question: "What's our action?"

Marketing Careers Are Exciting

What does it take to be a good marketer? If you are considering going into marketing, Appendix C gives a practical guide to career alternatives, résumés, information steps, and the job search process.

A career in marketing is exciting but is not for everyone. It can take the patience of a career counselor, the mathematical rigor of an economist, and an undying passion to understand and provide what the consumer wants to buy. And let's not forget the confidence to make decisive decisions on incomplete information, learning from past mistakes, and having a continuing focus on the consumer.

And . . . it's always a challenge!

learning review

9. What are four groupings used within a typical marketing organization?

10. What two components of the strategic marketing process are compared to evaluate a marketing program?

LEARNING OBJECTIVES REVIEW

LO1 *Explain how marketing managers allocate their limited resources.*

Marketing managers use the strategic marketing process and marketing information, such as marketing plans, sales reports, and action memos, to effectively allocate their scarce resources to exploit the competitive advantages of their products. Marketers may use techniques like sales response functions or market share (share point) analysis to help them assess what the market's response will be to additional marketing efforts.

LO2 *Describe three marketing planning frameworks: Porter's generic business strategies, diversification analysis, and synergy analysis.*

Porter identifies four generic business strategies that firms can adopt: a cost leadership strategy, which focuses on reducing expenses to lower product prices while targeting many market segments; a differentiation strategy, which requires products to have significant points of difference to charge a premium price while targeting many market segments; a cost focus strategy, which involves controlling costs to lower prices of products targeting only a few market segments; and a differentiation focus strategy, which requires products to have significant points of difference to reach one or only a few market segments.

With the diversification analysis framework, a firm can seek increased revenues by using one or a combination of four strategies to focus on present or new products or markets: market penetration (selling more of a product to existing markets); market development (selling an existing product to new markets); product development (selling a new product to existing markets); and diversification (selling new products to new markets).

The synergy analysis framework focuses on two kinds of synergies: marketing synergies (efficiencies), which run horizontally across the row of the various products offered by the firm to a single market segment; and R&D–manufacturing synergies (efficiencies), which run vertically down a column of the various market segments targeted for a given product or product class. This results in five alternative combinations: market–product concentration, market specialization, product specialization, selective specialization, and full coverage.

LO3 *Explain what makes an effective marketing plan.*

An effective marketing plan has measurable, achievable goals; uses facts and valid assumptions; is simple, clear, and specific; is complete and feasible; and is controllable and flexible.

LO4 *Use a Gantt Chart to schedule a series of tasks.*

Successful implementation of a marketing plan requires that people know the tasks, responsibilities, and deadlines needed to complete it. Once the information for these three areas is generated, a program schedule can be developed. A Gantt chart is a graphical representation of this schedule. The key to this scheduling technique is to identify those tasks that must be done sequentially from those that can be done concurrently.

LO5 *Describe the alternatives for organizing a marketing department and the role of a product manager.*

First, marketing departments must distinguish between line positions, those individuals who have the authority and responsibility to issue orders to people that report to them and staff positions, those individuals who have the authority and responsibility to advise but not directly order people in line positions to do something.

Second, marketing organizations use one of four divisional groupings to implement marketing plans: product line groupings, responsible for specific product offerings; functional groupings that represent the different departments and business activities within a firm; geographical groupings, in which sales territories are subdivided on a geographical basis; and market-based groupings, which utilize specific customer segments.

Product managers interact with many people and groups both inside and outside the firm to coordinate the planning, implementation, and evaluation of the marketing plan and its budget on an annual and long-term basis for the products for which they are responsible.

LO6 *Explain how marketing ROI, metrics, and dashboards relate to evaluating marketing programs.*

The evaluation phase of the strategic marketing process involves measuring the results of the actions from the implementation phase and comparing them with goals set in the planning phase. The marketing manager then takes action to correct negative deviations from the plan and to exploit positive ones. Today, managers want an answer to the question "Are my marketing activities effective?" One answer is in using marketing ROI, which is the application of modern measurement technologies to understand, quantify, and optimize marketing spending. Identifying a marketing objective with a carefully defined marketing metric and tracking this metric on a marketing dashboard can improve marketing ROI.

FOCUSING ON KEY TERMS

action item list p. 590
cost focus strategy p. 581
cost leadership strategy p. 580
differentiation focus strategy p. 581
differentiation strategy p. 581
diversification analysis p. 581

functional groupings p. 592
generic business strategy p. 579
geographical groupings p. 592
line positions p. 592
market-based groupings p. 592
marketing ROI p. 594

product line groupings p. 592
product or program champion p. 589
sales response function p. 576
share points p. 577
staff positions p. 592
synergy analysis p. 582

APPLYING MARKETING KNOWLEDGE

1 Assume a firm faces an S-shaped sales response function. What happens to the ratio of incremental sales revenue to incremental marketing effort at the (*a*) bottom, (*b*) middle, and (*c*) top of this curve?

2 What happens to the ratio of incremental sales revenue to incremental marketing effort when the sales response function is an upward-sloping straight line?

3 Assume General Mills has to decide how to invest millions of dollars to try to expand its dessert and yogurt businesses. To allocate this money between these two businesses, what information would General Mills like to have?

4 Suppose your Great States lawn mower company has the market–product concentration situation shown in Figure 22–5A. What are both the synergies and potential pitfalls of following expansion strategies of (*a*) market specialization and (*b*) product specialization?

5 The first Domino's Pizza restaurant was near a college campus. What implementation problems are (*a*) similar and (*b*) different for restaurants near a college campus versus a military base?

6 A common theme among managers who succeed repeatedly in program implementation is fostering open communication. Why is this so important?

7 Parts of tasks 5 and 6 in Figure 22–7 are done both concurrently and sequentially. How can this be? How does it help the students meet the term paper deadline?

8 In the organizational chart for the consumer packaged goods firm in Figure 22–8, where do product line, functional, and geographical groupings occur?

9 Why are quantified goals in the planning phase of the strategic marketing process important for the evaluation phase?

building your marketing plan

Do the following activities to complete your marketing plan:

1 Draw a simple organization chart for your organization.

2 Develop a Gantt chart to schedule the key activities to implement your marketing plan.

3 In terms of the evaluation, list (*a*) the four or five critical factors (such as revenues, number of customers, variable costs) and (*b*) how frequently (monthly, quarterly) you will monitor them to determine if special actions are needed to exploit opportunities or correct deviations.

4 Read Appendix A, "Building an Effective Marketing Plan." Then write a 600-word executive summary for your marketing plan using the numbered headings shown in Appendix A.

video case 22 General Mills Warm Delights™: Indulgent, Delicious, and Gooey!

Vivian Callaway, vice president for the Center for Learning and Experimentation at General Mills, retells the story for the "indulgent, delicious, and gooey" Warm Delights™. She summarizes, "When you want something that is truly innovative, you have to look at the rules you have been assuming in your category and break them all!"

When a new business creates a breakthrough, it looks easy and obvious to an observer. The creators of Betty Crocker Warm Delights highlight that if the marketing decisions had been based on the traditions and history of the cake category, a smaller, struggling business would have been the outcome. The team chose to challenge the assumptions and expectations of accumulated cake category business experience. The team took personal and business risks and Warm Delights is a roaring success.

Let's use this behind-the-scenes look to see how you can apply their marketing frameworks to your own business ideas.

PLANNING PHASE: INNOVATION, BUT A SHRINKING MARKET

In the typical grocery store, the baking mix aisle is a quiet place. Shelves sigh with flavors, types, and brands. Prices are low, but there is little consumer traffic. Cake continues to be a tradition for birthdays and social occasions. But, consumer demand declines. The percentage of U.S. households that bought at least one baking mix in 2000 was 80 percent. Four years later, the percentage of households was 77 percent, a very significant decline of 3 percentage points.

Today, a promoted price of 89 cents to make a 9×12 inch cake is common. Many choices, but little differentiation, gradually falling sales, and low uniform prices are the hallmarks of a mature category. But it's not that consumers don't like cake-like treats. In contrast, indulgent treats are growing. The premium prices for ice cream ($3.00 a pint) and chocolate ($3.00 a bar) are not slowing consumer purchases.

The Betty Crocker marketing team challenged the food scientists at General Mills to create a great tasting, easy to prepare, single-serve cake treat. The goal: make it indulgent, delicious, and gooey. The team focused the scientists on a product that would have:

- Consistent great taste.
- Quick preparation.
- A single portion.
- No clean-up.

The food scientists delivered the prototype! Now, the marketing team began hammering out the four P's. They started with a descriptive name "Betty Crocker Dessert Bowls" (see photo) and a plan to shelve it in the "quiet" cake aisle. This practical approach would meet the consumer need for a "small, fast, microwave cake" for dessert. Several marketing challenges emerged:

Betty Crocker
New! Dessert Bowls
Single-Serve 1-pack

Included: • Microwave-safe bowl with pouch of dry mix or fruit slices
• Topping Pouch such as fudge, caramel or crisp topping
Servings: 1 pack – each bowl is single serve
Store Location: Baking aisle
Suggested Retail Price: $1.89

- The easy shelf price comparison to 9×12 inch cakes selling for 89 cents would make it harder to price Dessert Bowls at $2.00.
- The communication problem. The product message "a small, faster-to-make cake" wasn't compelling. For example, after-school snacks should be fast and small, but "dessert" sounds too indulgent.
- The quiet aisle problem. The cake-aisle shopper is probably not browsing for a cake innovation.
- The dessert problem. Consumer's on-the-go, calorie conscious meal plans don't generally include a planned dessert.
- The microwave problem. Consumers might not believe it tastes good.

In sum, the small, fast-cake product didn't resonate with a compelling consumer need. But it would be a safe bet because the Dessert Bowl positioning fit nicely with the family-friendly Betty Crocker brand.

IMPLEMENTATION PHASE: LEAVING THE SECURITY OF FAMILY BEHIND

The consumer insights team really enjoyed the hot, gooey cake product. They feared that it would languish in the cake aisle under the Dessert Bowl name since this didn't capture the essence of what the food delivered. They explored who really are the indulgent treat customers. The data revealed that the heaviest buyers of premium treats are women without kids. This focused the team on a target consumer direction: "What does she want?" They enlisted business partners (an ad agency and consultants) to come up with a name that would appeal to "her." Several different experts independently suggested the "Warm Delights" name.

Targeting the on-the-go women who want a small, personal treat had marketing advantages:

- The $2.00 Warm Delight price compared favorably to the price of many single-serve indulgent treats.
- The product food message "warm, convenient, delightful" is compelling.
- On-the-go women's meal plans do include the occasional delicious treat.

One significant problem remained: the cake-aisle shopper is probably not browsing for an indulgent, single-serve treat.

The marketing team solved this shelving issue by using advertising and product displays outside the cake aisle. This would raise women's awareness of Warm Delights. Television advertising and in-store display programs are costly, so Warm Delights sales would have to be strong to pay back the investment. The risk of failure on any new product is very high. A product flop is extremely costly to the company.

The team turned to market research to fine-tune the plan. The research put Warm Delights (and Dessert Bowls) on the shelf in real (different) stores. A few key findings emerged. First, the name "Warm Delights" beat "Dessert Bowls." Second, the Warm Delights with nuts simply wasn't easy to prepare, so nuts were removed. Third, the packaging with a disposable bowl beat the typical cake-mix packaging involving using your own bowl. Finally, by putting the actual product on supermarket shelves and in displays in the stores, sales volumes could be analyzed.

EVALUATION PHASE: TURNING THE PLAN INTO ACTION!

The marketing plan isn't action. Sales for "Warm Delights" required the marketing team to: (1) get the factory to produce enough product to meet anticipated demand; (2) get the salesforce to secure distribution on store shelves; (3) get the ad agency to produce fabulous ads and run them; and (4) get the retailers to display the product somewhere other than the cake aisle. Lastly, the consumer had to buy, like, and re-buy the product.

The team's marketing metrics compared actual results to planning goals. For example, if the production schedule calls for 1,000 cases, are 1,000 cases actually being shipped from the factory? And if orders from the national salesforce are expected to be 1,000 cases, are these being booked as expected? The salesforce also secures display commitments from retailers. A display will increase sales and must be accommodated in the production and shipping estimates. A constant juggling of orders, production, and inventory is the nitty-gritty side of a marketing manager's job, who often performs a general management role on a new product roll-out and is responsible for the product's profit and loss (P&L).

The initial acceptance of a product by retailers is important. The next step is for Warm Delights to get on the shelf. The distribution measure shows what percent of stores have Warm Delights available for sale. While a retailer's decision to carry the product may have been made, each store manager has to rearrange the shelf and stock Warm Delights from the case in the backroom. Another problem is success. If the product sells well in the first week, there will be a void on the shelf, which may inadvertently be filled with a different product such as the old one that was there. In the same way, display activity in the store can be monitored. Are the displays occurring as expected? Do the sales increase when a display is present? Watching distribution and display execution on a new product is very important so that sales shortfalls can be addressed proactively.

Did the customer buy one or two Warm Delights? Did the customer return for a second purchase a few weeks later? The syndicated services that sell household panel purchase data provide the answer. The team evaluates these reports to see if the number of people who tried the product matches with expectations and how the repeat purchases occur. Often, the "80/20 rule" applies. So, in the early months, is there a group of consumers that buys repeatedly and will fill this role?

For ongoing feedback, calls by Warm Delights consumers to the free consumer information line are monitored. This is a great source of real-time feedback. If a pattern emerges and these calls are mostly about the same problem, that is bad. However, when consumers call to say "thank you" or "it's great," that is good. This is an informal quick way to identify if the product is on track or further investigation is warranted.

GOOD MARKETING MAKES A DIFFERENCE

The team took personal and business risks by choosing a Warm Delights plan over the more conservative Dessert Bowl plan. Today, General Mills has loyal Warm Delight consumers who are open to trying new flavors, new sizes, and new forms. What would you do to grow this brand?

Questions

1 (*a*) In what stage of the product life cycle is cake mix in the U.S.? (*b*) What is the competitive set of desserts in which Warm Delights is located and (*c*) at what stage of the product life cycle are these desserts in?

2 (*a*) Who is the target market? (*b*) What is the point of difference on the positioning for Warm Delights? (*c*) What are the potential opportunities and hindrances of the target market and positioning?

3 (*a*) What marketing research did Vivian Callaway execute? (*b*) What were the critical questions that she sought research and expert advice to get answers to? (*c*) How did this affect the product's marketing mix price, promotion, packaging and distribution decisions?

4 (*a*) What initial promotional plan directed to (*i*) consumers in the target market and (*ii*) the distributors (or trade) did Callaway use? (*b*) Why did this make sense to Callaway and her team when Warm Delights was launched?

5 If you were a consultant to Vivian Callaway, what product changes would you recommend to increase sales of Warm Delights?

6 What 5 or 6 marketing metrics would you think Vivian Callaway could use to measure progress after Warm Delights was launched?

PLANNING A CAREER IN MARKETING

GETTING A JOB: THE PROCESS OF MARKETING YOURSELF

Getting a job is usually a lengthy process, and it is exactly that—a *process* that involves careful planning, implementation, and evaluation. You may have everything going for you: a respectable grade point average (GPA), relevant work experience, several extracurricular activities, superior communication skills, and demonstrated leadership qualities. Despite these, you still need to market yourself systematically and aggressively; after all, even the best products lie dormant on the retailer's shelves unless marketed effectively.

The process of getting a job involves the same activities marketing managers use to develop and introduce products and brands into the marketplace.[1] The only difference is that you are marketing yourself, not a product. You need to conduct marketing research by analyzing your personal qualities (performing a self-audit) and by identifying job opportunities. Based on your research results, select a target market—those job opportunities that are compatible with your interests, goals, skills, and abilities—and design a marketing mix around that target market. *You* are the "product";[2] you must decide how to "position" yourself in the job market. The price component of the marketing mix is the salary range and job benefits (such as health and life insurance, vacation time, and retirement benefits) that you hope to receive. Promotion involves communicating with prospective employers through written and electronic correspondence (advertising) and job interviews (personal selling). The place element focuses on how to reach prospective employers—at the career services office or job fairs, for example.

This appendix will assist you in career planning by (1) providing information about careers in marketing and (2) outlining a job search process.

CAREERS IN MARKETING

The diversity of marketing opportunities is reflected in the many types of marketing jobs, including product management, marketing research, and public relations. While many of these jobs are found at traditional employers such as manufacturers, retailers, and advertising agencies, there are also many opportunities in a variety of other types of organizations. Professional services such as law, accounting, and consulting firms, for example, have a growing need for marketing expertise. Similarly, nonprofit organizations such as universities, the performing arts, museums, and government agencies are developing marketing functions. Event organizations such as athletic teams, golf and tennis tournaments, and the Olympics are also new and visible sources of marketing jobs.

The diversity of marketing jobs is also changing because of changes in the marketing discipline. The growth of interactive marketing has created a variety of new jobs such as data miners and permission marketing managers. The growth of multichannel marketing has led to the need for communication channel managers and integration specialists. The increasing involvement and control by consumers has required public relations personnel to become social networking experts and consumer-generated content managers. In a recent survey of fast-growing jobs, marketing positions were three of the top 10![3]

Examples of companies that have opportunities for graduates with degrees in marketing include Bank of America, Best Buy, Coca-Cola, Ford, Johnson & Johnson, Lowe's, State Farm, T-Mobile, and Target. Many of these companies also appear on *BusinessWeek's* list of the "The Best Places to Start a Career."[4] Most of these career opportunities offer a chance to work with interesting people on stimulating and rewarding problems. Comments one product manager, "I love marketing as a career because there are different challenges every day."[5]

Recent studies of career paths and salaries suggest that marketing careers can also provide excellent opportunities for advancement and substantial pay. For example, about one of every five chief executive officers (CEOs) of the nation's 500 most valuable publicly held companies have a career history that is heaviest in marketing.[6] Similarly, reports of average starting salaries of college graduates indicate that salaries in marketing compare favorably with those in many other fields. The average starting salary of new marketing undergraduates in 2007 was $40,161, compared with $31,515 for journalism majors and $33,831 for advertising majors.[7] The future is likely to be even better. The U.S. Department of Labor reports that employment of advertising, marketing, promotions, public relations, and sales managers is expected to increase faster than the average for all occupations through 2014, spurred by intense domestic and global competition in products and services offered to consumers.[8]

Figure C–1 on the next page describes marketing occupations in seven major categories: product management and physical distribution, advertising and promotion, retailing, sales, marketing research, global marketing and nonprofit marketing. One of these may be right for you. (Additional sources of marketing career information are provided at the end of this appendix.)

Product Management and Physical Distribution

Many organizations assign one manager the responsibility for a particular product. For example, Procter & Gamble (P&G) has separate managers for Tide, Cheer, Gain, and Bold. Product or brand managers are involved in all aspects of a product's marketing program, such as marketing research, sales, sales promotion, advertising, and pricing, as well as manufacturing. Managers of similar products typically report to a category manager and may be part of a *product management team* to encourage "interbrand cooperation."[9]

College graduates with bachelor's and master's degrees—often in marketing and business—enter P&G as brand assistants, the only starting position in its product or brand group. Each year students from campuses throughout the United States accept positions with P&G.[10] As brand assistants, their responsibilities consist primarily of selling and sales training. After one to two years of good performance, the brand assistant is promoted to assistant brand manager and after about the same period to brand (product) manager. These promotions often involve several brand groups. For example, a new employee might start as brand assistant for P&G's soap products, be promoted to assistant brand manager for Crest toothpaste, and subsequently become brand manager for Folger's coffee, Charmin, or Pampers.

Several other jobs related to product management (Figure C–1) deal with physical distribution issues such as storing the manufactured product (inventory), moving the product from the firm to the customers (transportation), and engaging in many other aspects of the manufacture and sale of goods. Prospects for these jobs are likely to increase as wholesalers increase their involvement with selling and distribution activities and begin to take advantage of overseas opportunities.[11]

Advertising and Promotion

Although we may see hundreds of advertisements in a day, what we can't see easily is the fascinating and complex advertising profession. The entry-level advertising positions filled every year include jobs with a variety of firms. Advertising professionals often remark that they find their jobs appealing because the days are not routine and they involve creative activities with many interesting people.

Advertising positions are available in three kinds of organizations: advertisers, media companies, and agencies. Advertisers include manufacturers, retail stores, service firms, and many other types of companies. Often they have an advertising department responsible for preparing and placing their own ads. Advertising careers are also possible with the media: television, radio stations, magazines, and newspapers. Finally,

Product Management and Physical Distribution

Product development manager creates a road map for new products by working with customers to determine their needs and with designers to create the product.

Product manager is responsible for integrating all aspects of a product's marketing program including research, sales, sales promotion, advertising, and pricing.

Supply chain manager oversees the part of a company that transports products to consumers and handles customer service.

Operations manager supervises warehousing and other physical distribution functions and often is directly involved in moving goods on the warehouse floor.

Inventory control manager forecasts demand for goods, coordinates production with plant managers, and tracks shipments to keep customers supplied.

Physical distribution specialist is an expert in the transportation and distribution of goods and also evaluates the costs and benefits of different types of transportation.

Sales

Direct or retail salesperson sells directly to consumers in the salesperson's office, the consumer's home, or a retailer's store.

Trade salesperson calls on retailers or wholesalers to sell products for manufacturers.

Industrial or semitechnical salesperson sells supplies and services to businesses.

Complex or professional salesperson sells complicated or custom-designed products to businesses. This requires understanding of the product technology.

Customer service manager maintains good relations with customers by coordinating the sales staff, marketing management, and physical distribution management.

Nonprofit Marketing

Marketing manager develops and directs marketing campaigns, fund-raising, and public relations.

Global Marketing

Global marketing manager is an expert in world-trade agreements, international competition, cross-cultural analysis, and global market-entry strategies.

Advertising and Promotion

Account executive maintains contact with clients while coordinating the creative work among artists and copywriters. Account executives work as partners with the client to develop marketing strategy.

Media buyer deals with media sales representatives in selecting advertising media and analyzes the value of media being purchased.

Copywriter works with art director in conceptualizing advertisements and writes the text of print or radio ads or the storyboards of television ads.

Art director handles the visual component of advertisements.

Sales promotion manager designs promotions for consumer products and works at an ad agency or a sales promotion agency.

Public relations manager develops written or video messages for the public and handles contacts with the press.

Internet marketing manager develops and executes the e-business marketing plan and manages all aspects of the advertising, promotion, and content for the online business.

Retailing

Buyer selects products a store sells, surveys consumer trends, and evaluates the past performance of products and suppliers.

Store manager oversees the staff and services at a store.

Marketing Research

Project manager for the supplier coordinates and oversees the market studies for a client.

Account executive for the supplier serves as a liaison between client and market research firm, like an advertising agency account executive.

In-house project director acts as project manager (see above) for the market studies conducted by the firm for which he or she works.

Competitive intelligence researcher uses new information technologies to monitor the competitive environment.

Data miner compiles and analyzes consumer data to identify behavior patterns, preferences, and user profiles for personalized marketing programs.

Source: Adapted from Lila B. Stair and Leslie Stair, *Careers in Marketing* (New York: McGraw-Hill, 2001), p. 100; and David W. Rosenthal and Michael A. Powell, *Careers in Marketing*, ©1984, pp. 352–54.

FIGURE C–1

Seven major categories of marketing occupations

advertising agencies offer job opportunities through their use of account management, research, media, and creative services.

Starting positions with advertisers and advertising agencies are often as assistants to employees with several years of experience. An assistant copywriter facilitates the development of the message, or copy, in an advertisement. An assistant art director participates in the design of visual components of advertisements. Entry-level media positions involve buying the media that will carry the ad or selling airtime on radio or television or page space in print media. Advancement to supervisory positions requires planning skills, a broad vision, and an affinity for spotting an effective advertising idea. Students interested in advertising should develop good communication skills and try to gain advertising experience through summer employment opportunities or internships.[12]

Growing interest in integrated marketing programs has increased opportunities for sales promotion managers, public relations managers,[13] and Internet marketing managers. These positions require an understanding of the potential synergy of all promotional tools. Responsibilities include the design and implementation of sweepstakes, sampling programs, events and partnerships, newsletters, press releases and conferences, e-mail promotions, web-content management, and permission marketing campaigns.

Retailing

There are two separate career paths in retailing: merchandise management and store management (Figure C–2). The key position in merchandising is that of a buyer, who is responsible for selecting merchandise, guiding the promotion of the merchandise, setting prices, bargaining with wholesalers, training the salesforce, and monitoring the competitive environment. The buyer must also be able to organize and coordinate many critical activities under severe time constraints. In contrast, store management involves the supervision of personnel in all departments and the general management of all facilities, equipment, and merchandise displays. In addition, store managers are responsible for the financial performance of each department and for the store as a whole. Typical positions beyond the store manager level include district manager, regional manager, and divisional vice president.[14]

Most starting jobs in retailing are trainee positions. A trainee is usually placed in a management training program and then given a position as an assistant buyer or assistant department manager. Advancement and responsibility can be achieved quickly because there is a shortage of qualified personnel in retailing and because superior performance of an individual is quickly reflected in sales and profits—two visible measures of success. In addition, the growth of multichannel retailing has created new opportunities such as website management and online merchandise procurement.[15]

Sales

College graduates from many disciplines are attracted to sales positions because of the increasingly professional nature of selling jobs and the many opportunities they can provide. A selling career offers benefits that are hard to match in any other field: (1) the opportunity for rapid advancement (into management or to new territories and accounts); (2) the potential for extremely attractive compensation (the average salary of all sales representatives is $119,637);[16] (3) the development of personal satisfaction, feelings of accomplishment, and increased self-confidence; and (4) independence—salespeople often have almost complete control over their time and activities. Many

FIGURE C–2

Two common retailing career paths include merchandise management and store management.

Occupation	2004 Employment	2014 Employment	Percentage Change 2004–2014	Average Annual Growth
Insurance sales agents	399,700	425,900	7%	2,620
Real estate brokers and sales agents	459,800	519,700	13	5,990
Retail sales-persons	4,256,100	4,991,900	17	73,580
Manufacturers' sales representatives	1,851,000	2,095,400	13	24,440
Securities and financial services sales agents	280,900	313,200	12	3,230

Source: "The 2004–2014 Job Outlook in Brief," *Occupational Outlook Quarterly* (Washington, DC: U.S. Department of Labor, Bureau of Labor Statistics, Spring 2006).

companies now offer two sales career paths—one for people who want to go into management, and another for those who want to remain in sales for their entire career.[17]

Employment opportunities in sales occupations are found in a wide variety of organizations, including insurance agencies, retailers, and financial service firms (Figure C–3). In addition, many salespeople work as manufacturer's representatives for organizations that have selling responsibilities for several manufacturers.[18] Activities in sales jobs include *selling duties,* such as prospecting for customers, demonstrating the product, or quoting prices; *sales-support duties,* such as handling complaints and helping solve technical problems; and *nonselling duties,* such as preparing reports, attending sales meetings, and monitoring competitive activities. Salespeople who can deal with these varying activities and have empathy for customers are critical to a company's success. According to *Business-Week,* "Great salespeople feel for their customers. They understand their needs and pressures; they get the challenges of their business. They see every deal through the customer's eyes."[19]

One of the fastest areas of growth in sales is in the direct marketing industry. Interest in information technology, customer relationship management (CRM), and integrated marketing has increased the demand for contact with customers. For many firms this means new or additional telemarketing efforts; for other firms it means increasing the amount of time salespeople spend with clients; for still others it means sophisticated e-mail marketing. "E-mail is the most valuable channel companies have to be interactive with their customers," says Gina Lambright, vice president for client services at marketing consulting firm Quris in San Francisco. At Dell Computer, the company selected by *Sales & Marketing Management* magazine for its Best E-Business Strategy award, online communication allows salespeople to concentrate on "value-added functions" and "the ultimate direct relationship with no intermediary."[20]

Marketing Research

Marketing researchers play important roles in many organizations today. They are responsible for obtaining, analyzing, and interpreting data to facilitate making marketing decisions. This means marketing researchers are basically problem solvers. Success in the area requires not only an understanding of statistical analysis, research methods, and programming, but also a broad base of marketing knowledge, writing and verbal presentation skills, and an ability to communicate with colleagues and clients.[21] Individuals who are inquisitive, methodical, analytical, and solution oriented find the field particularly rewarding.

The responsibilities of the men and women currently working in the market research industry include defining the marketing problem, designing the questions, selecting the sample, collecting and analyzing the data, and, finally, reporting the results of the research. These jobs are available in three kinds of organizations. *Marketing research consulting firms* contract with large companies to provide research about their products or services.[22] *Advertising agencies* may provide research services to help clients with questions related to advertising and promotional problems. Finally, some companies have an *in-house research staff* to design and execute their research projects. Online marketing research, which is likely to become the most common form of marketing research in the near future, requires understanding of new tools such as dynamic scripting, response validation, intercept sampling, instant messaging surveys, and online consumer panels.[23]

Although marketing researchers may start as assistants performing routine tasks, they quickly advance to broader responsibilities. Survey design, interviewing, report writing, and all aspects of the research process create a challenging career. In addition, research projects typically deal with such diverse problems as consumer motivation, pricing, forecasting, and competition. The marketing research field has experienced a shortage of qualified candidates in recent years. Successful candidates, however, "like what they're doing and get excited over their work, whether it be listening to a focus group or running a complex datamining model," according to Carolyn Marconi, director of marketing research for the Vanguard Group, Inc.[24]

International Careers

Many of the careers just described can be found in international settings—in large multinational U.S. corporations, small- to medium-size firms with export business, and franchises. The international consulting firm, Accenture, for example, has 38,000 consultants around the world. Similarly, many franchises such as Blockbuster Entertainment, which has 8,000 locations, are rapidly expanding outside of the United States.[25] The changes in the European Union, BRIC (Brazil, Russia, India, China), and other growing markets are likely to provide many opportunities for international careers. Several methods of gaining international experience are possible. For example, some companies may alternate periods of work at domestic locations with assignments outside of the United States. In addition, working for a firm with headquarters outside of the United States at one of its local offices may be appealing. In many organizations, international experience has become a necessity for promotion and career advancement. "If you are going to succeed, an expatriate assignment is essential," says Eric Kraus of Gillette Co. in Boston.[26]

Applicants for international positions need language skills and an ability to adapt to different business models, management styles, and local practices. In addition, as multinational firms use worldwide communication technologies to build global teams of people who have never met, collaboration skills become increasingly important. Each year Accenture puts 400 of its managers into international groups who meet virtually and in many international locations to learn how to utilize the company's worldwide resources. Similarly, IBM uses Internet-based services to make it possible for its 360,000 employees to "work as one virtual team."[27]

Activities you should consider during your job search process include assessing yourself, identifying job opportunities, preparing your résumé and related correspondence, and going on job interviews.

Assessing Yourself

You must know your product—you—so that you can market yourself effectively to prospective employers. Consequently, a critical first step in your job search is conducting a self-inquiry or self-assessment. This activity involves understanding your interests, abilities, personality, preferences, and individual style. You must be confident that you know what work environment is best for you, what makes you happy, the balance you seek between personal and professional activities, and how you can be most effective at reaching your goals. This process helps ensure that you are matching your profile to the right job, or as business consultant and author Jim Collins explains, "Finding the right seat on the bus."[28]

FIGURE C–4

Questions to ask in your self-analysis

Asking Key Questions A self-analysis, in part, entails asking yourself some very important and difficult questions (Figure C–4). It is critical that you respond to the

Interests

How do I like to spend my time?
Do I enjoy working with people?
Do I like working with tangible things?
Do I enjoy working with data?
Am I a member of many organizations?
Do I enjoy physical activities?
Do I like to read?

Abilities

Am I adept at analysis?
What are my hardware, software, and operating system skills?
Do I have good verbal and written communication skills?
What special talents do I have?
At which abilities do I wish I were more adept?

Education

How have my courses and extracurricular activities prepared me for a specific job?
Which were my best subjects? My worst?
Is my GPA a good indication of my academic ability? Why?
Do I aspire to a graduate degree? Before beginning my job?
Why did I choose my major?

Personal Goals

What are my short-term and long-term goals? Why?
Am I career oriented, or do I have broader interests?
What are my career goals?
What jobs are likely to help me achieve my goals?
What do I hope to be doing in 5 years? In 10 years?
What do I want out of life?
What work–life balance do I prefer?

Personality

What are my good and bad traits?
Am I competitive?
Do I work well with others?
Am I outspoken?
Am I a leader or a follower?
Do I work well under pressure?
Do I work quickly, or am I methodical?
Do I get along well with others?
Am I ambitious?
Do I work well independently of others?

Desired Job Environment

Am I willing to relocate? Why?
Do I have a geographical preference? Why?
Would I mind traveling in my job?
Do I have to work for a large or nationally known firm to be satisfied?
Must my job offer rapid promotion opportunities?
If I could design my own job, what characteristics would it have?
How important is high initial salary to me?

Experience

What previous jobs have I held? What were my responsibilities in each job?
What internships or co-op positions have I held? What were my responsibilities?
What volunteer positions have I held? What were my responsibilities?
Were any of my jobs or positions applicable to positions I may be seeking? How?
What did I like the most about my previous jobs? Like the least?
If I had it to do over again, would I work in these jobs? Why?

Strengths	Weaknesses
I enjoy being with people.	I am not adept at working with computers.
I am an avid reader.	I have minimal work experience.
I have good communication skills.	I have a mediocre GPA.
I am involved in many extracurricular activities.	I am sometimes impatient.
I work well with others.	I resent close supervision.
I work well independently.	I work methodically (slowly).
I am honest and dependable.	I will not relocate.
I am willing to travel in the job.	I anger easily sometimes.
I am a good problem solver.	I lack a customer orientation.
I have a good sense of humor.	I have poor technical skills.

questions honestly, because your answers ultimately will be used as a guide in your job selection.[29] A less-than-candid appraisal of yourself might result in a job mismatch.

Identifying Strengths and Weaknesses After you have addressed the questions posed in Figure C–4, you are ready to identify your strengths and weaknesses. To do so, draw a vertical line down the middle of a sheet of paper and label one side of the paper "strengths" and the other side "weaknesses." Based on your answers to the questions, record your strong and weak points in their respective column. Ideally, this cataloging should be done over a few days to give you adequate time to reflect on your attributes. In addition, you might seek input from others who know you well (such as parents, close relatives, friends, professors, or employers) and can offer more objective views. They might even evaluate you on the questions in Figure C–4, and you can compare the results with your own evaluation. A hypothetical list of strengths and weaknesses is shown in Figure C–5.

What skills are most important? The answer, of course, varies by occupation and employer. Recent studies, however, suggest that problem-solving skills, communication skills, interpersonal skills, analytical and computer skills, and leadership skills are all valued by employers. Personal characteristics employers seek in a job candidate include honesty, integrity, motivation, initiative, self-confidence, flexibility, and enthusiasm. Finally, most employers also look for work experience, internship experience, or co-op experience.[30]

Taking Job-Related Tests Personality and vocational interest tests, provided by many colleges and universities, can give you other ideas about yourself. After tests have been administered and scored, test takers meet with testing service counselors to discuss the results. Test results generally suggest jobs for which students have an inclination. The most common tests at the college level are the Strong Interest Inventory and the Campbell Interest and Skill Survey. Some counseling centers and career coaches also use the Myers-Briggs Type Indicator personality inventory and the Peoplemap assessments to help identify professions you may enjoy.[31] If you have not already done so, you may wish to see whether your school offers such testing services.

Identifying Your Job Opportunities

To identify and analyze the job market, you must conduct some marketing research to determine what industries *and* companies offer promising job opportunities that relate

to the results of your self-analysis. Several sources that can help in your search are discussed next.

Career Services Office Your career services office is an excellent source of job information. Personnel in that office can: (1) inform you about which companies will be recruiting on campus; (2) alert you to unexpected job openings; (3) advise you about short-term and long-term career prospects; (4) offer advice on résumé construction; (5) assess your interviewing strengths and weaknesses; and (6) help you evaluate a job offer. In addition, the office usually contains a variety of written materials focusing on different industries and companies and tips on job hunting. One major publication available in most career services offices is the National Association of Colleges and Employers publication *Job Choices,* which contains a list of employers, kinds of job openings for college graduates, and whom to contact about jobs in those firms. Another publication for students is *jobpostings,* which is published seven times during the academic year and distributed to more than 350 colleges and universities across the United States.

Online Career and Employment Services Many companies no longer make frequent on-campus visits. Instead, they may use the many online services available to advertise an employment opportunity or to search for candidate information. The National Association of Colleges and Employers, for example, maintains a site on the Internet called JobWeb (www.jobweb.org). Similarly, Monster.com and Careerbuilder.com are online databases of employment ads, candidate résumés, and other career-related information. Some of the information resources include career guidance, a cover letter library, occupational profiles, résumé templates, and networking services.[32] Employers may contact students directly when the candidate's qualifications meet their specific job requirements. The advantage of this system for students is that regardless of the size or location of the campus they are attending, many companies have access to their résumé. Some job boards even allow applicants to post audio and video clips of themselves. One advantage for recruiters is that some of the job boards utilize software for performing background verification.[33] Your school's career center may also have a homepage that offers online job search information and links to other Internet sites.

Library The public or college library can provide you with reference material that, among other things, describes successful firms and their operations, defines the content of various jobs, and forecasts job opportunities. For example, *Fortune* publishes a list of the 1,000 largest U.S. and global companies and their respective sales and profits, and Dun & Bradstreet publishes directories of all companies in the United States with a net worth of at least $500,000. The *Occupational Outlook Handbook* is an annual publication of the U.S. Department of Labor that provides projections for specific job prospects, as well as information pertaining to those jobs. A librarian can indicate reference materials that will be most pertinent to *your* job search.

Advertisements Help-wanted advertisements provide an overview of what is happening in the job market. Local (particularly Sunday editions) and college newspapers, trade press (such as *Marketing News* or *Advertising Age*), and business magazines (such as *Sales & Marketing Management*) contain classified advertisement sections that generally have job opening announcements, often for entry-level positions. Reviewing the want ads can help you identify what kinds of positions are available and their requirements and job titles, which firms offer certain kinds of jobs, and levels of compensation.

Employment Agencies An employment agency can make you aware of several job opportunities very quickly because of its large number of job listings available through computer databases. Many agencies specialize in a particular field (such as sales and marketing). The advantages of using an agency include that it: (1) reduces the cost of a job search by bringing applicants and employers together, (2) often has exclusive job listings available only by working through the agency, (3) performs much of the job search for you, and (4) tries to find a job that is compatible with your qualifications and interests.[34] In the past, some employment agencies have engaged in questionable business practices, so check with the Better Business Bureau or your business contacts to determine the quality of the various agencies.

Personal Contacts and Networking   An important source of job information that students often overlook is their personal contacts. People you know often may know of job opportunities, so you should advise them that you're looking for a job. Relatives and friends might aid your job search. Instructors you know well and business contacts can provide a wealth of information about potential jobs and even help arrange an interview with a prospective employer. They may also help arrange *informational interviews* with employers that do not have immediate openings. These interviews allow you to collect information about an industry or an employer and give you an advantage if a position does become available. It is a good idea to leave your résumé with all your personal contacts so they can pass it along to those who might be in need of your services.

Student organizations (such as the student chapter of the American Marketing Association and Pi Sigma Epsilon, the professional sales fraternity) may be sources of job opportunities, particularly if they are involved with the business community. Local chapters of professional business organizations (such as the American Marketing Association and Sales and Marketing Executives International) also can provide job information; contacting their chapter president is a first step in seeking assistance from these organizations. Creating a network of professional contacts is one of the most important career planning activities you can undertake.[35]

State Employment Office   State employment offices have listings of job opportunities in their state and counselors to help arrange a job interview for you. Although state employment offices perform functions similar to employment agencies, they differ in listing only job opportunities in their state and providing their services free.

Direct Contact   Another means of obtaining job information is direct contact— personally communicating to prospective employers (either by mail, e-mail, or in person) that you would be interested in pursuing job opportunities with them. Often you may not even know whether jobs are available in these firms. If you correspond with the companies in writing, a letter of introduction and an attached résumé should serve as your initial form of communication. Your major goal in direct contact is ultimately to arrange a job interview.

Writing Your Résumé

A résumé is a document that communicates to prospective employers who you are. An employer reading a résumé is looking for a snapshot of your qualifications to decide if you should be invited to a job interview. It is imperative that you design a résumé that presents you in a favorable light and allows you to get to that next important step. Personnel in your career services office can provide assistance in designing résumés.

The Résumé Itself   A well-constructed résumé generally contains up to nine major sections: (1) identification (name, address, telephone number, and e-mail address); (2) job or career objective; (3) educational background; (4) honors and awards; (5) work experience or history; (6) skills or capabilities (that pertain to a particular kind of job for which you may be interviewing); (7) extracurricular activities; (8) personal interests; and (9) personal references.[36] There is no universally accepted format for a résumé, but

FIGURE C–6

A chronological résumé presents your education and work experience in the sequence in which they occurred.

SALLY WINTER

Campus address (until 6/1/2008):
Elm Street Apartments #2B
College Town, Ohio 44042
Phone: (614) 424-1648
swinter@osu.stu.edu

Home address:
123 Front Street
Teaneck, NJ 07666
Phone: (201) 836-4995

Education
B.S. in Business Administration, Ohio State University, 2008, cum laude—3.3 overall GPA—3.6 GPA in major

Work Experience
Paid for 70 percent of my college expenses through the following part-time and summer jobs:

Legal Secretary, Smith, Lee & Jones, Attorneys at Law, New York, NY—summer 2006
- Took dictation and transcribed tapes of legal proceedings
- Typed contracts and other legal documents
- Reorganized client files for easier access
- Answered the phone and screened calls for the partners

Salesclerk, College Varsity Shop, College Town, Ohio—2005–2007 academic years
- Helped customers with buying decisions
- Arranged stock and helped with window displays
- Assisted in year-end inventories
- Took over responsibilities of store manager when she was on vacation or ill

Assistant Manager, Treasure Place Gift Shop, Teaneck, NJ—summers and Christmas vacations—2004–2007
- Supervised two salesclerks
- Helped select merchandise at trade shows
- Handled daily accounting
- Worked comfortably under pressure during busy seasons

Campus Activities
- Elected captain of the women's varsity tennis team for two years
- Worked as a reporter and night editor on campus newspaper for two years
- Elected historian for Mortar Board chapter, a senior women's honorary society

Computer Skills
- Word, Excel, PowerPoint, Outlook

Personal Interests
- Collecting antique clocks, listening to jazz, swimming

References Available on Request

three are more frequently used: chronological, functional, and targeted. A *chronological* format presents your work experience and education according to the time sequence in which they occurred (i.e., in chronological order). If you have had several jobs or attended several schools, this approach is useful to highlight what you have done. With a *functional* format, you group your experience into skill categories that emphasize your strengths. This option is particularly appropriate if you have no experience or only minimal experience related to your chosen field. A *targeted* format focuses on the capabilities you have for a specific job. This alternative is desirable if you know what job you want and are qualified for it. In any of the formats, if possible, you should include quantitative information about your accomplishments and experience, such as "increased sales revenue by 20 percent" for the year you managed a retail clothing store. A résumé that illustrates the chronological format is shown in Figure C–6.[37]

Technology has created a need for a new type of résumé—the digital résumé. Although traditional versions of résumés may be visually appealing, today most career experts suggest that résumés accommodate delivery through mail, e-mail, and fax machines. In addition, résumés must accommodate employers who use scanning technology to enter résumés into their own databases or who search commercial online databases. To fully utilize online opportunities, an electronic résumé with a popular font (e.g., New Times Roman) and relatively large font size (e.g., 10–14 pt.)—and without italic text, graphics, shading, underlining, or vertical lines—must be available. In addition, because online recruiting starts with a keyword search, it is important to include keywords, focus on nouns rather than verbs, and avoid abbreviations. Related to this use of technology, don't forget that many employers may visit social networking sites such as Facebook and MySpace, or may simply "Google" your name, to see what comes up. Review your online profiles before you start your job search to provide a positive image![38]

Letter Accompanying a Résumé The letter accompanying a résumé, or cover letter, serves as the job candidate's introduction. As a result, it must gain the attention and interest of the reader or it will fail to give the incentive to examine the résumé carefully. In designing a letter to accompany your résumé, address the following issues:[39]

- Address the letter to a specific person.
- Identify the position for which you are applying and how you heard of it.
- Indicate why you are applying for the position.
- Summarize your most significant credentials and qualifications.
- Refer the reader to the enclosed résumé.
- Request a personal interview, and advise the reader when and where you can be reached.

A sample letter comprising these six factors is presented in Figure C–7 on the next page.

Interviewing for Your Job

The job interview is a conversation between a prospective employer and a job candidate that focuses on determining whether the employer's needs can be satisfied by the candidate's qualifications. The interview is a "make or break" situation: If the interview goes well, you have increased your chances of receiving a job offer; if it goes poorly, you probably will be eliminated from further consideration.

Preparing for a Job Interview To be successful in a job interview, you must prepare for it so you can exhibit professionalism and indicate to a prospective employer that you are serious about the job. When preparing for the interview, several critical activities need to be performed.

Before the interview, gather facts about the industry, the prospective employer, and the job. Relevant information might include: the general description for the occupation; the firm's products or services; the firm's size, number of employees, and financial and competitive position; the requirements of the position; and the name and personality of the interviewer. Obtaining this information will provide you with additional insight into the firm and help you formulate questions to ask the interviewer. This information might be gleaned, for example, from corporate annual reports, *The Wall Street Journal,* Moody's manuals, Standard & Poor's *Register of Corporations, Directors, and Executives, The Directory of Corporate Affiliations,* selected issues of *BusinessWeek,* or trade publications. If information is not readily available, you could call the company and indicate that you wish to obtain some information about the firm before your interview.[40]

Sally Winter
Elm Street Apartments, #2B
College Town, Ohio 44042
January 31, 2008

Mr. J. B. Jones
Sales Manager
Hilltop Manufacturing Company
Minneapolis, MN 55406

Dear Mr. Jones:

Dr. William Johnson, Professor of Business Administration at the Ohio State University, recently suggested that I write to you concerning your opening and my interest in a sales position. With a B.S. degree in business administration and courses in personal selling and sales management, I am confident that I could make a positive contribution to your firm.

During the past four years, I have been a salesclerk in a clothing store and an assistant manager in a gift shop. These two positions required my performing a variety of duties including selling, purchasing, stocking, and supervising. As a result, I have developed an appreciation for the viewpoints of the customer, salesperson, and management. Given my background and high energy level, I feel that I am particularly well qualified to assume a sales position in your company.

My enclosed résumé better highlights my education and experience. My extracurricular activities should strengthen and support my abilities to serve as a sales representative.

I am eager to talk with you because I feel I can demonstrate to you why I am a strong candidate for the position. I have friends in Minneapolis with whom I could stay on weekends, so Fridays or Mondays would be ideal for an appointment. I will call you in a week to see if we can arrange a mutually convenient time for a meeting. I am hopeful that your schedule will allow this.

Thank you for your kind consideration. If you would like some additional information, please feel free to contact me at (614) 424-1648. I look forward to talking with you.

Sincerely,

Sally Winter

enclosure

Preparation for the job interview should also involve role playing, or pretending that you are in the "hot seat" being interviewed. Before role playing, anticipate questions interviewers may pose and how you might address them (Figure C–8). Do not memorize your answers, though, because you want to appear spontaneous, yet logical and intelligent. Nonetheless, it is helpful to practice how you might respond to the questions. In addition, develop questions you might ask the interviewer that are important and of concern to you (Figure C–9). "It's an opportunity to show the recruiter how smart you are," comments one recruiter.[41]

When role playing, you and someone with whom you feel comfortable should engage in a mock interview. Afterward, ask the stand-in interviewer to candidly appraise your interview content and style. You may wish to videotape the mock interview; ask the personnel in your career services office where videotaping equipment can be obtained for this purpose.

Before the job interview you should attend to several details. Know the exact time and place of the interview; write them down—do not rely on your memory. Get the full company name straight. Find out what the interviewer's name is and how to pronounce it. Bring a notepad and pen along to the interview, in case you need to record anything.

FIGURE C–8
Anticipate questions frequently asked by interviewers to practice how you might respond.

Interviewer Questions

1. How would you describe yourself?
2. What do you consider to be your greatest strengths and weaknesses?
3. Describe your most rewarding college experiences.
4. What do you see yourself doing in 5 years? In 10 years?
5. What are three important leadership qualities? How have you demonstrated these qualities?
6. What do you really want out of life?
7. What are your long-range and short-range goals?
8. Why did you choose your college major?
9. In which extracurricular activities did you participate? Why?
10. What jobs have you enjoyed the most? The least? Why?
11. How has your previous work experience prepared you for a marketing career?
12. Why do you want to work for our company?
13. What qualifications do you think a person needs to be successful in a company like ours?
14. Describe a creative idea you produced that led to the success of a project.
15. What criteria are you using to evaluate the company for which you hope to work?
16. Describe a project where you worked as part of a team.
17. What can I tell you about our company?
18. Are you willing to relocate?
19. Are you willing to spend at least six months as a trainee?
20. Why should we hire you?

FIGURE C–9
Interviewees should develop questions about topics that are important to them.

Interviewee Questions

1. Why would a job candidate want to work for your firm?
2. What makes your firm different from its competitors?
3. What is the company's promotion policy?
4. Describe the typical first-year assignment for this job.
5. How is an employee evaluated?
6. What are the opportunities for personal growth?
7. Do you have a training program?
8. What are the company's plans for future growth?
9. What is the retention rate of people in the position for which I am interviewing?
10. How can you use my skills?
11. Does the company have development programs?
12. What kind of image does the firm have in the community?
13. Why do you enjoy working for your firm?
14. How much responsibility would I have in this job?
15. What is the corporate culture in your firm?

Make certain that your appearance is clean, neat, professional, and conservative. And be punctual; arriving tardy to a job interview gives you an appearance of being unreliable.

Succeeding in Your Job Interview You have done your homework, and at last the moment arrives and it is time for the interview. Although you may experience some apprehension, view the interview as a conversation between the prospective employer and you. Both of you are in the interview to look over the other party, to see whether there might be a good match. When you meet the interviewer, greet him or her by name, be cheerful, smile, and maintain good eye contact. Take your lead from the interviewer at the outset. Sit down after the interviewer has offered you a seat. Sit up straight in your chair, and look alert and interested at all times. Appear relaxed, not tense. Be enthusiastic.

During the interview, be yourself. If you try to behave in a manner that is different from the real you, your attempt may be transparent to the interviewer or you may ultimately get the job but discover that you aren't suited for it. In addition to assessing how well your skills match those of the job, the interviewer will probably try to assess your long-term interest in the firm.

As the interview comes to a close, leave it on a positive note. Thank the interviewer for his or her time and the opportunity to discuss employment opportunities. If you are still interested in the job, express this to the interviewer. The interviewer will normally tell you what the employer's next step is—probably a visit to the company.[42] Rarely will a job offer be made at the end of the initial interview. If it is and you want the job, accept the offer; if there is any doubt in your mind about the job, however, ask for time to consider the offer.

Following Up on Your Job Interview After your interview, send a thank-you note to the interviewer and indicate whether you are still interested in the job. If you want to continue pursuing the job, polite persistence may help you get it. The thank-you note is a gesture of appreciation and a way of maintaining visibility with the interviewer. (Remember the adage, "Out of sight, out of mind.") Even if the interview did not go well, the thank-you note may impress the interviewer so much that his or her opinion of you changes. After you have sent your thank-you note, you may wish to call the prospective employer to determine the status of the hiring decision. If the interviewer told you when you would hear from the employer, make your telephone call *after* this date (assuming, of course, that you have not yet heard from the employer); if the interviewer did not tell you when you would be contacted, make your telephone call a week or so after you have sent your thank-you note. While e-mail is a common form of communication today, it is often viewed as less personal than a letter or telephone call, so be confident that e-mail is preferred before using it to correspond with the interviewer.[43]

As you conduct your follow-up, be persistent but polite. If you are too eager, one of two things could happen to prevent you from getting the job: The employer might feel that you are a nuisance and would exhibit such behavior on the job, or the employer may perceive that you are desperate for the job and thus are not a viable candidate.

Handling Rejection You have put your best efforts into your job search. You developed a well-designed résumé and prepared carefully for the job interview. Even the interview appears to have gone well. Nevertheless, a prospective employer may send you a rejection letter. ("We are sorry that our needs and your superb qualification don't match.") Although you will probably be disappointed, not all interviews lead to a job offer because there normally are more candidates than there are positions available.

If you receive a rejection letter, you should think back through the interview. What appeared to go right? What went wrong? Perhaps personnel from your career services office can shed light on the problem, particularly if they are in the custom of having interviewers rate each interviewee. Try to learn lessons to apply in future interviews. Keep interviewing and gaining interview experience; your persistence will eventually pay off.

SELECTED SOURCES OF MARKETING CAREER INFORMATION

The following is a selected list of marketing information sources that you should find useful during your academic studies and professional career.

BUSINESS AND MARKETING PUBLICATIONS

Business Periodicals Index (BPI) (New York: H. W. Wilson Company). This is a monthly (except August) index of almost 527 periodicals from all fields of business and marketing.

Scott Dacko, *A Dictionary of Marketing: Concepts, Laws, Theories, Effects* (Oxford University Press, 2007). This dictionary of marketing terms focuses on key concepts, grouped into four categories: concepts, laws, theories, and effects. Containing over 500 entries, ranging in length and depth, the book will be the ideal reference guide for practitioners and students.

Don Doman, Dell Dennison, and Margaret Doman, *Market Research Made Easy,* 3rd ed. (Bellingham, WA: Self-Counsel Press, 2006). This practical, easy-to-read book provides a marketing research process to help select appropriate research methods, identify subjects, design questionnaires, use the Internet, and analyze data.

Hoover's Handbook of World Business (Austin, TX: Hoover's Business Press, 2007). A detailed source of information about companies outside of the United States, including firms from Canada, Europe, Japan, China, India, and Taiwan.

Paige Leavitt, John Prescott, Darcy Lemon, and Farida Hasanali, *Competitive Intelligence: A Guide for Your Journey to Best-Practice Processes* (Houston, TX: American Productivity and Quality Center, 2004). This book provides a five-step model for developing and implementing a competitive intelligence effort; it explains how to collect, coordinate, and interpret actionable information.

Barbara Lewis and Dale Littler, eds., *The Blackwell Encyclopedic Dictionary of Marketing* (Cambridge, MA: Blackwell Publishers, 1999). Part of the 10-volume *Blackwell Encyclopedia of Management,* this book provides clear, concise, up-to-the-minute, and highly informative definitions and explanations of the key concepts and terms in marketing management, consumer behavior, segmentation, organizational marketing, pricing, communications, retailing and distribution, product management, market research, and international marketing.

Jean L. Sears and Marilyn K. Moody, *Using Government Information Sources,* 3rd ed. (Phoenix, AZ: Oryx Press, 2001). An easy-to-use manual arranged by topics such as consumer expenditures, business and industry statistics, economic indicators, and projections. Each chapter contains a search strategy, a checklist of courses, and a narrative description of the sources.

Cynthia L. Shamel, *Introduction to Online Market & Industry Research* (Mason, OH: Thomson Learning, 2004). This comprehensive reference provides search strategies and valuable data source information, including rankings of data sources, for industry researchers.

Conor Vibert, *Introduction to Online Competitive Intelligence Research* (Mason, OH: Thomson Learning, 2004). This book provides a step-by-step methodology for competitive intelligence research including planning, data collection, analysis, and dissemination. Typical problem scenarios and cases illustrating search strategies are also included in the book.

Garrett Wasny, *World Business Resources.com* (New York: McGraw-Hill, 2000). A directory of over 8,000 international business, economic, and demographic resources online. Organized by topic and by region, this guide also offers more than 200 tips to speed up Internet searches.

Linda D. Hall, *Encyclopedia of Business Information Sources,* 21st ed. (Detroit: Gale Group, 2006). A bibliographic guide to over 35,000 citations covering more than 1,100 primary subjects of interest to business personnel.

CAREER PLANNING PUBLICATIONS

Richard N. Bolles, *What Color Is Your Parachute? 2008: A Practical Manual for Job-Hunters and Career-Changers* (Berkeley, CA: Ten Speed Press, 2008). A companion workbook is also available. See www.jobhuntersbible.com.

Dennis V. Damp, *The Book of U.S. Government Jobs: Where They Are, What's Available, and How to Get One,* 10th ed. (Moon Township, PA: Bookhaven Press, 2008).

Margaret Riley Dikel and Frances E. Roehm, *Guide to Internet Job Searching* (New York: McGraw-Hill, 2008).

Diane Darling, *Networking for Career Success* (New York: McGraw-Hill, 2005).

Lila B. Stair and Leslie Stair, *Careers in Marketing* (New York: McGraw-Hill, 2001).

Princeton Review: Best Entry-Level Jobs, 2009 Edition (Random House Information Group, 2008).

The National Job Bank, (Avon, MA: Adams Media Corporation, 2007). See www.adamsmedia.com.

Richard Walsh, *The Complete Job Search Book for College Students: A Step-by Step Guide,* 3rd ed. (Holbrook, MA: Adams Media Corporation, 2007).

Martin Yate, *Cover Letters That Knock 'Em Dead; and Résumés That Knock 'Em Dead* (Holbrook, MA: Adams Media Corporation, 2006). See www.adamsmedia.com.

Websites: Resources on job searches, résumé writing, interviewing, U.S. and international job postings, and so forth.

www.accessalesjobs.com	www.studentjobs.gov
www.jobbankinfo.org	www.hotjobs.com
www.truecareers.com	www.monster.com
www.careerXroads.com	www.jobbankusa.com
www.careers.org	www.studentcentral.com
www.careerbuilder.com	www.vault.com
www.careers-in-marketing.com	www.wetfeet.com

SELECTED PERIODICALS

Ad Week, Nielsen Business Media, Inc. (weekly). See www.adweek.com. (subscription rate: $149)

Advertising Age, Crain Communications, Inc. (weekly). See www.adage.com. (subscription rate: $99)

Barron's, Dow Jones & Co., Inc. (weekly). See www.barrons.com. (subscription rates: $150 print; $79 online; $39 online for current print subscribers)

BrandWeek, Nielsen Business Media, Inc. (weekly). See www.adweek.com. (subscription rate: $149)

Business 2.0, Business 2.0 Inc. (monthly). See www.money.cnn.com. (subscription rate: $9.99)

Business Horizons, Indiana University c/o Elsevier Science Publishing (bimonthly). See www.elsevier.com. (subscription rate: $353)

BusinessWeek, McGraw-Hill Companies (weekly). See www.businessweek.com. (subscription rate: $45.97)

Chain Store Age, Lebhar-Friedman, Inc. (monthly). See www.chainstoreage.com. (subscription rate: $105)

eCommerce Times, ECT News Network, Inc. (daily). See www.ecommercetimes.com.

Fortune, Time, Inc. (28 issues). See www.money.cnn.com. (subscription rates: $19.99 online special; $29.98 regular)

Forbes, Forbes Inc. (17 issues). See www.forbes.com. (subscription rate: $59.95)

Harvard Business Review, Harvard University (monthly). See www.hbsp.harvard.edu. (subscription rate: $99)

Industrial Marketing Management, Elsevier Science Publishing (8 issues). See www.elsevier.com. (subscription rate: $148)

International Journal of Electronic Commerce, M. E. Sharpe Publishing (quarterly). See www.mesharpe.com. (subscription rate: $87)

Journal of the Academy of Marketing Science, Sage Publications, Inc. (quarterly). See www.sagepub.com. (subscription rate: $112)

Journal of Advertising Research, Advertising Research Foundation (quarterly). See www.arfsite.org. (subscription rate: $155)

Journal of Business and Industrial Marketing, Emerald Group Publishing, Ltd. (7 issues). See www.emeraldinsight.com. (subscription rate: $2,369)

Journal of Consumer Marketing, Emerald Group Publishing, Ltd. (7 issues). See www.emeraldinsight.com. (subscription rate: $1,999)

Journal of Consumer Research, University of Chicago Press (quarterly). See www.journals.uchicago.edu. (subscription rates: $145 nonmembers; $55 members; $25 students)

Journal of Interactive Marketing, Direct Marketing Educational Foundation (quarterly). See www.the-dma.org. (subscription rate: $250)

Journal of Marketing, American Marketing Association (quarterly). See www.marketingpower.com. (subscription rates: $90 nonmembers; $53 members)

Journal of Marketing Education, Sage Publications (three times per year). See www.sagepub.com. (subscription rate: $79)

Journal of Marketing Research, American Marketing Association (quarterly). See www.marketingpower.com. (subscription rates: $105 nonmembers; $53 members)

Journal of Personal Selling & Sales Management, Pi Sigma Epsilon National Education Foundation (quarterly). See www.mkt.cba.cmich.edu/jpssm. (subscription rate: $60)

Journal of Public Policy and Marketing, American Marketing Association (semiannually). See www.marketingpower.com. (subscription rates: $85 nonmembers; $53 members)

Journal of Retailing, Elsevier Science Publishing (quarterly). See www.elsevier.com. (subscription rate: $429)

Marketing Education Review, CTC Press (three times per year). See www.marketingeducationreview.com. (subscription rate: $32)

Marketing Health Services, American Marketing Association (quarterly). See www.marketingpower.com. (subscription rates: $85 nonmembers; $53 members)

Marketing Management, American Marketing Association (six times per year). See www.marketingpower.com. (subscription rates: $80 nonmembers; $53 members)

Marketing News, American Marketing Association (biweekly). See www.marketingpower.com. (subscription rates: $100 nonmembers; $39 members)

Marketing Research, American Marketing Association (quarterly). See www.marketingpower.com. (subscription rates: $85 nonmembers; $53 members)

Media Week, Quantum Business Media (50 issues). See www.mediaweek.co.uk. (subscription rate: $149)

Sales & Marketing Management, VNU Business Publications. See www.salesandmarketing.com. (subscription rate: $99)

Stores, National Retail Federation (weekly). See www.nrf.com or www.stores.org. (subscription rates: $120 nonmembers; free for members)

The Wall Street Journal Interactive, Dow Jones & Company, Inc. (weekly). See www.wsj.com. (subscription rates: $198 print; $79 online; $34.95 (15 weeks) for students, both print and online)

PROFESSIONAL AND TRADE ASSOCIATIONS

American Association of Advertising Agencies
405 Lexington Ave.
New York, NY 10174-1801
(212) 682-2500
www.aaaa.org

American Advertising Federation
1101 Vermont Ave. NW., Suite 500
Washington, DC 20005-6306
(202) 898-0089
www.aaf.org

American e-Commerce Association
2346 Camp St.
New Orleans, LA 70130
(504) 495-1748
www.aeaus.com

American Marketing Association
311 S. Wacker Dr., Suite 5800
Chicago, IL 60606
(800) AMA-1150
www.marketingpower.com

American Society of Transportation and Logistics
1400 Eye St, N.W., Suite 1050
Washington, DC 20005
(202) 580-7270
www.astl.org

Business Marketing Association
   400 N. Michigan Ave., 15th Floor
   Chicago, IL 60611
   (800) 664-4262
   www.marketing.org

Direct Marketing Association
   1120 Avenue of the Americas
   New York, NY 10036-6700
   (212) 768-7277
   www.the-dma.org

Direct Selling Association
   1667 K Street, N.W., Suite 1100
   Washington, DC 20006
   (202) 452-8866
   www.dsa.org

Environmental Defense: Corporate Partnerships
   257 Park Avenue South.
   New York, NY 10010
   (800) 684-3322
   www.environmentaldefense.org

Institute for Supply Management
   P.O. Box 22160
   Tempe, AZ 85285-2160
   (480) 752-6276
   www.ism.ws

International Advertising Association
   World Service Center
   275 Madison Ave., Suite 2102
   New York, NY 10016
   (212) 557-1133
   www.iaaglobal.org

International Franchise Association
   1501 K Street, N.W., Suite 350
   Washington, DC 20005
   (202) 628-8000
   www.franchise.org

Marketing Research Association
   110 National Drive
   Glastonbury, CT 06033
   (860) 682-1000
   www.mra-net.org

Marketing Science Institute
   1000 Massachusetts Ave.
   Cambridge, MA 02138-5396
   (617) 491-2060
   www.msi.org

National Association of Wholesale Distributors
   1725 K St. NW
   Washington, DC 20006-1419
   (202) 872-0885
   www.naw.org

National Mail Order Association
   2807 Polk St. NE
   Minneapolis, MN 55418-2954
   (612) 788-1673
   www.nmoa.org

National Retail Federation
   325 7th St. NW, Suite 1100
   Washington, DC 20004
   (800) NRF-HOW2
   www.nrf.com

Product Development and Management Association
   15000 Commerce Parkway, Suite C
   Mount Laurel, NJ 08054
   (800) 232-5241
   www.pdma.org

Public Relations Society of America
   33 Maiden Lane
   New York, NY 10038-5150
   (212) 460-1400
   www.prsa.org

Sales and Marketing Executives International
   P.O. Box 1390
   Sumas, WA 98295-1390
   (312) 893-0751
   www.smei.org

Society for Marketing Professional Services
   99 Canal Center Plaza, Suite 330
   Alexandria, VA 22314
   (800) 292-7667
   www.smps.org

U.S. Internet Industry Association (USIIA)
   5810 Kingstowne Center Drive
   Suite 120, PMB 212
   Alexandria, VA 22315-5711
   (703) 924-0006
   www.usiia.org

ALTERNATE CASES

case D–1   Nike MaxSight Contact Lenses: Seeing a Need

Nike and Bausch and Lomb have teamed up to offer an exciting new addition to the eyewear market—Nike MaxSight contact lenses.

HISTORY OF CONTACT LENSES

Leonardo da Vinci first illustrated the concept of contact lenses in 1508, but it wasn't until 1887 when contact lenses were actually manufactured. These early lenses were glass and covered the entire eye. In 1948, plastic contact lenses were developed that could cover only the eye's cornea. Soft contact lenses have been around since 1971 providing greater comfort to wearers and expanding the market. Disposable contact lenses were introduced in 1987, addressing the problem of users adequately cleaning the lens to minimize irritation and even infection. What has not been available to this point is a contact lens that can provide the eye with the protection of a pair of sunglasses! Nike MaxSight contact lenses are specially tinted lenses to maximize visual acuity and are available in both prescription and nonprescription form. While designed primarily for athletes and sports participants, the market is not limited to simply those with an active lifestyle.

THE NEED

When Dr. Richard Allen, an experienced ophthamologist and faculty member at the University of Virginia Health System, revealed to his colleague Dr. Richard Edlich in 2000 that he had ocular melanoma—essentially skin cancer of the eye—the two men began researching and publishing articles on skin cancer prevention as well as prevention of ocular melanoma. Dr. Edlich contacted Dr. Reichow and Dr. Citek, two basic researchers that had conducted a comprehensive evaluation of sunglasses. The results revealed that very few brands of sunglasses offered any real protection from the sun's damaging rays and only partially protect the eyes; this despite the fact that the product may be labeled as providing 100 percent protection from the sun.

There are a number of reasons that sunglasses don't do the job. First, they have to be worn to do any good. Many sunglasses have poor quality lens material that does not adequately shield the eyes from the damaging UVA and UVB rays that also cause skin cancer. Design and fit can also minimize the effectiveness of sunglasses. Uncomfortable, unable to adequately cover the eye, and unlikely to stay in place during activity, sunglasses were not the answer.

THE SOLUTION

Doctors Reichow and Citek played a leadership role in coordinating the development of the Nike MaxSight fully tinted soft contact lens. Nike MaxSight contact lenses for athletes come in two tints: gray-green contacts for athletes who play in bright sunlight and want to be comfortable visually (golf, rugby, runners) and amber-tinted contacts for athletes in sports that require tracking of fast-moving objects (baseball, soccer, tennis, softball). The lenses come in both prescription and nonprescription form and as with most daily wear soft contacts, they must be changed monthly.

Benefits of Nike MaxSight lenses are substantial. Not only do wearers have a better field of view with no obstructions from nosepieces or frames, but there's also no fogging. You'll still sweat while exercising but that sweat isn't causing glasses to slip and slide. This lens provides distortion-free optics, whether or not you wear prescription contacts. The lenses filter out more than 90 percent of harmful blue light as well as 95 percent of UVA and UVB rays. Nike still recommends wearing sunglasses whenever possible over MaxSight lenses to protect the rest of the eye.

A box of Nike MaxSight lenses costs about $60 for a two-month supply. Conventional prescription contact lenses sell for around $25 to $70 depending on prescription.

Nike MaxSight lenses are available from selected eye care professionals. The Nike website (www.nikevision.com) provides information on these outlets. Consumers are unable to purchase the product unless they have an eye examination and fitting.

One primary tactic for providing information on the product for both consumers and eye care providers is the Nike website. A downloadable coupon is available for a free trial pair of lenses. In-store product information and displays are provided to eye care professionals to reach potential consumers. Nike also has traditional advertising on the product in selected sports magazines.[1]

Questions

1 How has Nike used an analysis of consumer needs to identify different markets and products for MaxSight? What are these different market–product combinations? Which market segments are likely to be the largest? The most likely to adopt the product?
2 Identify the elements of the marketing mix for Nike MaxSight currently. What marketing mix recommendations do you suggest beyond those Nike has already undertaken?
3 This product is positioned toward athletes who want to improve their performance and visual acuity. However, it may be difficult for anyone who does not already wear contact lenses to be motivated to adopt this product. (*a*) How likely is it that Nike will be able to capture noncontact lens-wearing athletes? (*b*) What can Nike do to encourage the noncontact lens-wearing athlete to adopt the product?

---

case D–2   Daktronics, Inc: Global Displays in 68 Billion Colors

"We were looking for a way to provide jobs and keep our graduates at home," said Dr. Aelred (Al) J. Kurtenbach, board chairman of Daktronics, Inc. So in 1968, Kurtenbach, then an engineering professor at South Dakota State University (SDSU), and fellow professor Duane Sander decided to start a business. "We started a biomedical engineering company, mainly because we'd both done research in this area," continued Kurtenbach.

But even college professors make bad decisions occasionally!

THE DAKTRONICS LAUNCH: DOWNSIDE, UPSIDE

"It was a dismal failure," explains Kurtenbach, "because the electronic thermometer and automated blood-pressure gauge we'd developed worked fine but simply cost too much to produce and sell." Also, he and Sander were concerned that by the time they went through the lengthy process to receive U.S. Food and Drug Administration approval, Daktronics would run out of money.

Enter: A miracle—in the form of the South Dakota State wrestling coach who needed a portable scoreboard near the wrestling mat to tell fans the time and score without blocking their view of action on the mat. At the time, wrestling teams had to use basketball displays that couldn't show the right wrestling information and were too high and far from the mat.

In response, Daktronics designed the Matside®, a pyramid-shaped scoreboard that sits on the floor and is still in use at wrestling matches around the United States today,

35 years later. The Matside also established Daktronics' reputation as a company that could get problems solved, and quickly.

From that low-key launch, Daktronics has emerged as the world-class designer of scoreboards and electronic displays used in the United States and around the globe. The reason for Daktronics' success? "Innovation," says Kurtenbach. *Fortune Small Business* describes the company as a "geek-rich workplace," with more than 230 degreed engineers out of its 900 full-time employees in its plant in Brookings, South Dakota—population 18,504.

To start Daktronics in 1968, Kurtenbach and Sander sold shares to family and friends at $5 per share, raising a bit less than $100,000. That limited initial funding also pushed Kurtenbach and Sander into finding products that customers would buy to generate revenues for Daktronics. The company still must stay alert because it faces global competitors like Barco from Belgium and Mitsubishi from Japan.

TODAY'S MARKET SEGMENTS

Daktronics divides its markets into three segments: sports (70 percent of Daktronics' sales), business (20 percent), and government (10 percent). The company reaches these markets today through 35 U.S. regional sales and service offices and a recently opened office in Frankfurt, Germany, to reach European and Middle Eastern customers.

In the sports segment, if you watched the Kentucky Derby at Churchill Downs or the 2004 Olympics in

Athens on television, you probably saw a sample of Daktronics electronic scoring and display systems. The same goes for 24 of 30 Major League Baseball parks, 22 of 31 National Football League stadiums, 19 of 28 National Basketball Association facilities, and 19 of 30 National Hockey League arenas, where Daktronics has created some or all of the displays. This also is true of election displays at hundreds of colleges, universities, and high schools, where the prices can vary from millions of dollars to a few thousand.

A surprise to many: Advertising on these displays can often pay for themselves in a year or two. Brad Mayne, president of the American Airlines Center in Dallas, where the NBA Mavericks and NHL Stars play, says that Daktronics' scoreboard (shown below) paid for itself in advertising by the second season.

Daktronics' largest scoreboard? It's a 36-by-149-foot giant at the Cleveland Indians' Jacobs Field. The nine full-color displays installed throughout Jacobs Field provide live videos and replays, lineups, scores, pitch information, and so on.

In the business segment, probably the biggest and best known are Daktronics' electronic displays in New York City. It recently installed a 65-foot-high display in Times Square that shows video, animation, graphics, stock quotes, and news headlines in striking shades of color.

While that may be the best-known business display, hundreds of Daktronics programmable displays dot the United States in shopping malls and outside of stores and churches. These displays show everything from current times and temperatures to financial information, gas prices, and motel room rates. James (Jim) B. Morgan, president and chief executive officer of Daktronics, now puts greater emphasis on the business accounts to make the company less dependent on the sports segment.

Less well known are Daktronics displays for the government segment. Suppose that on the way to class today, a freeway sign told you that a crash in the right lane ahead means you should move to a left lane and slow down. It was probably a Daktronics-built sign, something like that for the Cumberland Gap Tunnel that connects Virginia, Kentucky, and Tennessee, shown on the next page. Besides highway signs, the government segment includes airport and train station displays announcing arrival and departure times.

To see what Daktronics sports, business, and government displays have been installed in your state, go to www.daktronics.com.

TECHNOLOGY

Exploiting the latest technology is critical to Daktronics' success. At the level of signage just needed to display words and numbers, a key company innovation is the Glow Cube® pixel, about the size of a Rubik's Cube. Black on one side and reflective yellow on the other, hundreds of these rotate to black or yellow to spell words or create shapes on scoreboards or highway signs. Glow Cube® pixels are the building blocks you also see on traditional signs ranging from those on professional golf tour events to portable soccer scoreboards.

For the giant programmable video displays, the basic building blocks are thousands of LEDs (light emitting diodes). LED color breakthrough in the 1990s led to today's displays capable of showing 68 billion hues of color—largely replacing tiny incandescent lamps in these displays and using only about 10 percent of the electrical power needed for those lamps. Sophisticated computer programs and video and replay systems make these screens come to life at an athletic event. Because of the low power usage and high reliability, the LED pixel has replaced the Glow Cube® pixel in most applications.

COMMUNICATIONS AND MANAGEMENT

With the engineering, manufacturing, and marketing departments housed in the same Daktronics building, many questions can be addressed with simple, direct water-cooler conversations. Kurtenbach sees this open communication as a huge competitive advantage for Daktronics.

Dr. Kurtenbach's transition from academics to business was surprisingly easy. To learn how businesses work and succeed, he checked out histories of large U.S. companies from the library. He uses what he calls his "waterboy" approach in managing—meaning that every manager is like a waterboy for the team, necessary but

not the star. Kurtenbach developed this leadership style growing up as one of 13 children in a farm family that often involved his doing the essential tasks none of his brothers or sisters wanted to do.

STUDENT JOBS AND ECONOMIC DEVELOPMENT

How did Kurtenbach's original goal of starting a local business to help keep South Dakota State University graduates in the state turn out? Kurtenbach and Daktronics

probably get a grade of A+. Not only does the company employ more than 900 full-time people in its Brookings facility, but it also provides more than 450 *paid* internships each year for students—mostly from SDSU. To help Daktronics continue to enhance its cutting-edge technology, SDSU has also responded by enhancing its graphic- and computer-design offerings.

And that $5 per share investment by family and friends in the disastrous Daktronics "biomedical device launch" in 1968? With stock splits, each share is worth about $2,700 today.[2]

Questions

1 What are the reasons or appeals that might cause potential customers in the following markets to buy a Daktronics scoreboard, electronics display, or large-screen video? (*a*) A Major League Baseball team, (*b*) a high school for its football field, (*c*) a local hardware store, and (*d*) a state highway department.

2 (*a*) Do a SWOT analysis for Daktronics. (*b*) For one entry in each of the four cells in your SWOT table (strengths, weaknesses, opportunities, and threats) suggest an action Daktronics might take to increase revenues.

3 Using Figure 2–5 in Chapter 2 as a guide, identify an action Daktronics might take to increase sales in each of the four cells: (*a*) current markets, current products; (*b*) current markets, new products; (*c*) new markets, current products; (*d*) new markets, new products.

---

case D–3 Jamba Juice: Scanning the Marketing Environment

What were you doing in 10th grade? Waiting to get your driver's license? Kirk Perron was thinking about his future and putting together a deal that would help launch the successful Jamba Juice chain. It sounds incredible but Kirk Perron bought the real estate for his first juice bar when he was in 10th grade. He borrowed money from a high school counselor, the librarian, and his school bus driver to put together the $12,000 down payment.

THE COMPANY

Kirk Perron opened up his first operation as The Juice Club in 1990 in San Luis Obispo, California. He hit on the idea for a convenient, delicious, healthful food store on a long weekend bike ride. An avid cyclist with a life-long interest in health and nutrition, he wanted to offer an alternative to typical fast-food fare. The idea was a hit and quickly spread. In 1995, the company changed its name from The Juice Club to Jamba Juice. Today Jamba Juice has more than 445 stores nationwide offering a variety

of healthy drinks and snacks. Jamba Juice is considered the industry leader in the smoothie market, and Perron predicts that one day Jamba Juice will be as big a brand as Coca-Cola.

THE IDEA

Jamba Juice is all about healthy food and fun. Jamba is from an African word that means "to celebrate." Walk into a Jamba Juice store and customers can choose from a wide variety of Jamba Juice specialties including smoothies, fresh-squeezed fruit and vegetable juices, breads, and pretzels. Jamba's commitment to healthy products is reflected in its mission statement, "Enriching the daily experience of our customers, our community, and ourselves through the life-nourishing qualities of fruits and vegetables."

Smoothies are the bulk of Jamba Juice's business. They are made with juice and fruit and often yogurt, sherbet, or ice milk. A typical smoothie gets most of its calories from carbohydrates and protein providing a low- or no-fat, nutritious meal. Jamba smoothies are designed to meet "heart healthy" FDA requirements. Nutritional supplements called "boosts," such as "energy juice boost," containing ginseng and gingko biloba, and "immunity juice boost," with echinacea and antioxidants, are available and can be added to smoothies. Jamba Juice also recently added a new low-calorie drink, the Enlightened Smoothie, to its menu. Learn more about Jamba at www.jambajuice.com.

As you sit at the counter in a Jamba Juice, you can watch friendly, well-trained Jamba Juice employees whip, beat, and blend your smoothie right before your eyes. Stores also feature nutrition centers where customers can get a complete nutritional breakdown for each product. Outlets also feature a merchandising area, which has Jamba Juice juicers, mugs, hats, and T-shirts.

THE COMPETITION

Juice bars have been part of a growing trend. Barriers to entry are fairly low. Single-store outlets and small chains within a city or region are common, although Jamba has several large competitors. New Orleans-based Smoothie King, for example, has 340 locations in 34 states, and Atlanta-based Planet Smoothie has more than 100 stores in 20 states. Other competitors include Juice Stop, Juice It Up!, Surf City Squeeze, and Orange Julius. Jamba Juice has positioned itself as a replacement for typical fast-food fare. This means it also considers fast-food restaurants indirect competitors.

Jamba has had to fight to maintain its trademark in a competitive market. Several years ago a San Francisco Juice bar called Jamm'n Juice was forced to change its name after Jamba complained that Jamm'n Juice and its animated fruit and vegetables were too close to the Jamba trademark and logo.

THE MARKET

Juice bars have existed for decades, often in health-food stores and gyms and were associated with what was a small group of intensely health-conscious customers. That small demographic group boomed in recent years fueling the market for fat-free foods, fitness equipment, and apparel. There has also been an increasing level of health consciousness among society generally. However, "the consumer always talks thin and eats fat," according to Allan Hickock, an industry analyst with Piper Jaffray.

However, Jamba Juice is optimistic about the opportunities for expanding the market by replacing fast food with good-for-you food. Retail sales of juice and smoothies exceeded $1.2 billion in 2004 compared with $552 million in 2000. About two-thirds of Jamba's customers are between the ages of 15 and 25—not exactly the same demographic group as the traditional health-conscious baby boomer. Age and education level are important selection criteria for opening new Jamba Juice outlets. Kirk Perron believes that the more highly educated potential customers are, the more likely they will be to stop in for a nutritious smoothie. In fact, many of current and planned Jamba outlets are in college towns, and partnerships have been formed to open outlets in universities and airports. You can find Jamba in both the Los Angeles and San Francisco airports and on campus at the University of North Carolina, George Washington University, and the University of Nevada–Las Vegas, among others. Jamba also has a licensing agreement with Whole Foods Markets, a partner that shares Jamba's values and commitment to healthy living.

THE ISSUES

Purists insist that the best drinks come from completely fresh produce. Fresh produce can be hard to work with to provide consistent-tasting drinks. Also, the price of fresh produce can change drastically throughout the year.

With fairly limited menus, juice bars are considered great as an add-on rather than a stand-alone retail establishment because they are usually not strong enough to draw customer traffic on their own. Personnel are important to the success of a juice bar—described as "bartenders" they have to be able to put on a good show for the customer.

There is a seasonality effect for smoothie and juice operators. For example, in northern climates, operators in enclosed downtown skyways or mall locations often see their business fall off in the summer when people are outdoors walking around. Business surges in the winter.[3]

Questions

1 Conduct an environmental scan for Jamba Juice as it considers a new juice bar to open near your university. Identify factors that you think have an impact on the juice bar market, and indicate whether these factors would tend to enhance opportunities or represent threats.

2 Given your environmental analysis, which environmental force do you believe is most critical for Jamba Juice and why?

3 Examine the competitive environment for juice bars. Consider the likelihood of new entrants, barriers to entry, existing competitors, and substitutes. How would you summarize the current competitive environment?

4 Do you think that the juice bar phenomenon is a fad or rooted in some fundamental environmental and market forces? Why?

Ford Motor Company and Firestone Tire and Rubber enjoyed one of the longest-running relationships in American business, built upon the friendship and business relationship among the founders, Harvey Firestone and Henry Ford. From 1908 when Firestone first outfitted the Model T Ford until 2000, Firestone was the primary tire supplier to Ford. A well-publicized falling out over the blame for the deaths and accidents occurring in Ford Explorer vehicles equipped with Firestone tires buried the relationship. Firestone variously blamed Ford and consumers while Ford blamed Firestone. Both companies have damaged their credibility and reputation among consumers. What went wrong?

THE FORD EXPLORER

To understand how the entire situation unfolded, it is useful to focus on the development and launch of earlier Ford automobiles. The Ford Pinto was designed in the early 1960s to compete in the lower-priced subcompact segment. Ford engineers located the Pinto's gas tank in a location vulnerable to rear-end collisions to cut costs. A Ford cost-benefit analysis estimated it would cost $11 per car to move the gas tank to a less vulnerable position. Given that it expected to produce 12.5 million Pintos over the life of the model, Ford decided not to redesign the car and spend $137 million to move the gas tank. Using insurance company claim values at the time, Ford estimated that it would "save" about $50 million in insurance claims by relocating the gas tank, netting $87 million loss. Hence, it was cheaper to leave the gas tank in its rear-end position. The decision proved fatal. Ultimately, the recall of the Pinto and related expenses cost Ford at least $1.5 billion.

The Explorer's design was based on the Ford Bronco, essentially a line of light trucks using the twin I-beam suspension to lift up the vehicle to travel over rough terrain. However, this meant that the center of gravity was higher—the vehicle became more prone to stability problems and rollovers. By the late 1980s, Ford faced more than 800 lawsuits from rollovers of the Bronco II and Ranger, forerunners of the Explorer.

Ford developed the Explorer to address a mid-1980s market looking for a rugged vehicle that was primarily image and secondarily performance. Because automobile manufacturing had a four- to five-year lead time for a new model, decisions were made about the Explorer before all the consequences of the earlier decisions on the Bronco and Ranger were in. Among the early decisions made were the use of the same twin I-beam suspension of the Bronco II and manufacturing on the same assembly line used for the Ranger. Internal company documents of tests on the Explorer prototype showed problems with rollovers and a tendency to lift its wheels and tip during turns made at speeds up to 55 mph—even worse performance than the Bronco II. In early 1987 there were calls from designers to make changes in the design of the vehicle that would improve stability and maintain passenger safety.

Consumer Reports came out with a scathing review of the Bronco II in June 1989, advising consumers to "steer clear" of the product. At this point, the Explorer's design, modeled on the Bronco II, was frozen; parts were ordered and facilities were readied for production for 1990 delivery.

Another important design decision was that of the tires for the Explorer. Both Goodyear and Firestone tires were selected for the Explorer. Examining various Firestone models, a Ford engineer reported that there was a good probability of passing the Consumer's Union testing for the Explorer with Firestone P225 tires and less confidence with the Firestone P235. Ford chose the P235. Ford's engineer, Roger Stornant, claimed, "Management is aware of the potential risk with the P235 tires and has accepted that risk. The Consumer's Union test is generally unrepresentative of the real world and I see no 'real' risk in failing except what may result in the way of spurious litigation."

Ford engineers suggested four ways to improve the stability of the Explorer: widening the chassis by two inches, lowering the engine, lowering the tire pressure, and stiffening the springs. Ford chose the latter two, reducing the recommended tire pressure from 30–35 psi to 26 psi. This produced more road gripping, but it also increased friction, increased the heat of the tires, and caused tread separations. The lower tire pressure also reduced fuel economy.

BRIDGESTONE/FIRESTONE

Firestone had its own history of recalls. In 1978, between 13 million and 14 million Firestone "500" tires were recalled due to faulty manufacture, costing the company more than $200 million. The National Highway Traffic Safety Administration (NHTSA) called for tougher new standards for tires and light trucks. If these standards had been in place in the late 1970s, the early and subsequent designs of SUVs would have been quite different, saving lives and money. However, the NHTSA was essentially dismantled by the Reagan administration that slashed the NHTSA's budget and revoked several new regulations, including a warning light for tire inflation problems.

In 1987, Firestone became a subsidiary of Bridgestone Tire Co. Ltd. Bridgestone, a Japanese company, was named for its founder Shojiro Ishibashi, whose name means "stone bridge." Bridgestone was proud of its technological leadership—innovations in tire performance and design—as well as its dedication to quality. The Firestone subsidiary was relabeled the Bridgestone/Firestone Company in 1990, with headquarters in Nashville, Tennessee.

The first tire separation lawsuits hit Firestone in 1992. This was followed by labor disputes and a strike at the Bridgestone/Firestone plant in Decatur, Illinois, following attempts to cut costs. Testing of both Goodyear and Firestone tire models used on the Explorer showed that the Goodyear tires significantly outperformed Firestone. In some instances, Firestone tires wore out twice as fast as Goodyears. The Firestone Wilderness tire earned the lowest-acceptable NHTSA heat resistance rating—a C. The comparable Goodyear tire received a B.

Ford began to pressure Goodyear to lower tire prices in 1995. Goodyear decided it could not manufacture tires at a price that Ford was willing to pay and actually asked for a price increase due to higher material costs. At this point, Ford discontinued using Goodyear tires on its Explorer, relying entirely upon Firestone.

LAUNCH OF THE EXPLORER AND THE LAWSUITS

The Explorer was launched in 1990 and quickly became the best-selling SUV on the market. Granted, few consumers were using it for its off-road capabilities, but they looked adventuresome whizzing down the freeway to the mall. Ford engineers were well aware of the safety risk of the Explorer. Letters to dealerships warned of the dangers of failing to follow precautions on recommended tire usage, stating that ignoring these precautions could lead to loss of control and vehicle rollover, which could result in serious injury or death.

Ford also conducted a survey in 1993 of SUV drivers, finding that these drivers drove faster, were more likely to drive in bad weather, and followed other vehicles more closely, particularly troubling since the Explorer needed 20 to 30 feet more to stop when traveling at 60 mph than a typical family car.

By 1995, a Texas jury found Ford 100 percent at fault for the death of a 20-year-old college student driving a Bronco II that rolled over due to tire separation. The $25 million verdict was the largest SUV rollover verdict at the time. In 1996, a trainee test driver lost control of an Explorer during a lane change at 52.5 mph. The driver, overcorrecting, found the car in a four-wheel slide and then a 360-degree flip.

State Farm Insurance, the largest U.S. automobile insurer, notified Firestone and NHTSA in 1998 that it was experiencing an unusual number of claims on Firestone tires. Ford quietly began replacing Firestone tires on Explorers in Venezuela and Saudi Arabia due to rollover deaths in those countries.

POINTING FINGERS

An investigative report on a Houston television station started to blow the cover off the problems at Ford and Firestone in February 2000. The vice president of public affairs at Firestone accused the television station of unfairly characterizing Firestone Radial ATX tires as dangerous. She stated that the television station would better serve viewers by telling them how to properly maintain their tires and suggested that many of the crashes were caused by external factors such as punctures.

By May 2000, NHTSA belatedly launched an investigation and sent a defect notice to Firestone. Ford accused Firestone of withholding data needed to determine which tires were defective. Ford accused NHTSA of sitting on Firestone data, and it was Ford that pinpointed where the bad tires were being produced and pressed for a recall. By late summer of 2000, the recall was announced.

Ford organized a war room of 500 people dedicated to the crisis—public affairs and media, engineering, legal, regulatory, purchasing, and finance people collecting and analyzing data, operating a 24-hour hotline for the public, and disseminating information with NHTSA and the public.

Meanwhile, Bridgestone executives in Japan had no real appreciation of what was happening with Firestone. There were few Explorers sold in Japan and very few tires subject to recall. The attitude was that the Japanese built better cars, therefore the problem must be with Ford. The first public statement by Firestone's president, Masatoshi Ono, seemed to hold the Ford Explorer responsible and advised car owners to check tire pressure every month, even better, every two weeks.

Ford's CEO, Jacques Nasser, went on the offensive claiming that there were no problems with the design of the Explorer and that there were no data pointing to faults with the Explorer; he insisted that this was a tire problem. Ford rolled out a $5 million advertising campaign to protect its reputation and brand.

In May 2001, a second recall of 13 million Firestone tires was announced by Ford in an attempt to clear the path for the 2002 Explorer. Ford claimed it did not have enough confidence in the Firestone tires, while Firestone countered that the real issue was the safety of the Explorer. Firestone-equipped Explorers accounted for most of the 174 deaths and 700 injuries sustained in accidents reported at that time. In addition, Ford faced lawsuits seeking more than $590 million in damages.

Congressional hearings were launched. Accusations and data flew back and forth. Bridgestone/Firestone announced its intention to close its Decatur, Illinois, plant in December 2001, laying off almost 1,400 people. The president of the local steelworkers union claimed that Ford blamed Firestone and then Firestone made a scapegoat of the Decatur plant.

Ford announced in July 2001 that it had taken an equity position in Top Driver, Inc., the largest chain of driving schools in the country, and would be developing a driver safety course for SUV owners. The implication was that accidents with Ford Explorers were due not only to defective Firestone tires but to driver error as well. Ford was criticized as hypocritical for presenting advertising images of invincible SUVs that can be driven with abandon, weaving in and out of traffic, giving drivers a false sense of security while at the same time claiming that SUV drivers needed safety training.[4]

Questions

1 What moral philosophy appeared to guide the decision making at Ford? At Bridgestone/Firestone? Is there any evidence that either company changed its decision-making model as lawsuits mounted?

2 Do you see Ford's handling of the situation surrounding the development, marketing, and subsequent recall as ethical but illegal, ethical and legal, unethical but legal, or unethical and illegal? Why?

3 What actions would you recommend Ford take to deal with the aftermath of this situation?

---

case D–5   The Jamisons Buy an Espresso Machine

At 4:52 p.m. on Friday, January 28, 2007, Brock and Alisha Jamison bought an espresso machine. There was no doubt about it. Any observer would agree that the purchase took place at precisely that time. Or did it?

When questioned after the transaction, neither Brock nor Alisha could remember which of them first suggested the idea of getting an espresso machine. They do recall that in the summer of 2005 they attended a dinner party given by a friend who specialized in French and Chinese cooking. The meal was delicious, and their friend Brad was very proud of the Krups espresso machine he had used to cap off the evening. The item was expensive, however, at about $900.

The following summer, Alisha noticed a comparison study of espresso machines in *Gourmet* magazine. The performance of four different brands was compared. At about the same time, Brock noticed that *Consumer Reports* also compared a number of brands of espresso machines. In both instances, the Krups brand come out on top.

Later that fall, new models of the Krups were introduced, and a model they liked was selling for $700 in department stores. The Jamisons searched occasionally for Krups in discount houses or in wholesale showroom catalogs, even searching the Internet, hoping to find a lower price for the product. They were simply not offered there.

For Christmas 2006, the Jamisons traveled from Los Angeles to the family home in Michigan. While there, the Jamisons received a gift of a KitchenAid mixer from Brock's grandmother. Although the mixer was beautiful, Alisha immediately thought how much more elegant and useful an espresso machine would be. One private sentence to that effect brought immediate agreement from Brock. The box was (discreetly) not opened, although many thanks were expressed. The box remained unopened the entire time the Jamisons kept the item.

Back home in Los Angeles in January, Alisha again saw that the Krups was sale-priced at $600 at Sur la Table, one of the major gourmet stores in California. Brock and Alisha visited a branch location on a Saturday afternoon and saw the item. The salesperson, however, was not very knowledgeable about its features and not very helpful on explaining its attributes. The Jamisons left, very disappointed.

Two days later, Alisha called a different location for Sur la Table in a more urban location and talked to Dora Mayeur, a seemingly knowledgeable salesperson whose co-worker, Stephanie Wales, claimed to own and love exactly the model the Jamisons had in mind. Furthermore, Dora said that they did carry KitchenAid mixers and would make an exchange of the mixer, which had been received as a gift and for which no receipt was available.

On the following Friday morning, Brock put the mixer in his car trunk when he left for work. That afternoon, Alisha and six-month-old Brock, Jr., rode into town with a friend to meet Brock and make the transaction. After meeting downtown, they drove through uncharacteristic heavy rainy-day traffic to Sur la Table to meet Dora, whom they liked as much in person as they did on the telephone. Dora conducted a brief review of the types and models available.

There was the Nespresso brand, which used Nescafé coffee capsules, for about $400. There were four varieties of the FrancisFrancis brand, priced between $430 and $720. At the top of the price structure, was the multilingual, Swiss-made Jura brand, priced at $2,200. The Krups that they had coveted was also there, selling at $600, but it was much larger than they thought. In fact, the item was the shape (and seemed to be nearly the size) of the Vienna Opera House.

There was a somewhat smaller, less expensive Krups twin-tower model, and the Jamisons toyed with the idea of buying it, but Dora suggested that the more expensive version was well worth the money. The Jamisons then confirmed their initial decision to take the $600 Krups model and asked Dora about exchanging the KitchenAid mixer they had brought with them. "No problem," said Dora.

After making a quick phone call, Dora returned with bad news. Sur la Table had not carried that particular model of mixer. This model mixer was a single-color model that is usually carried at department stores and catalog sales houses. The one carried by the specialized culinary stores, such as Sur la Table, was a two-tone item. She even offered to allow the Jamisons to use her phone to verify the availability of the item. The Jamisons did exactly that.

Alisha dialed several of the suggested stores, looking for a retailer that carried both the Krups and the KitchenAid model, but she quickly learned that they were distributed through different types of retail stores. A young man who answered the phone at one store, however, seemed friendly and helpful, and Alisha was able to obtain his agreement to take the item as a return if she could get there that afternoon.

The store was about one-half mile away. Brock volunteered to brave the elements and return the mixer. He took the shopping shuttle to the store with the still-unopened mixer box under his arm. About an hour later, Brock returned cold and wet, with a refund. Together, the Jamisons bought the Krups espresso machine at 4:52 p.m. and proudly took it home.[5]

Questions

1 Which of the Jamisons decided to buy an espresso machine? The Krups brand?

2 When was the decision to buy made?

3 What were the important attributes in the evaluation of the Krups brand?

4 Would you characterize the Jamisons' purchase decision process as routine problem solving, limited problem solving, or extended problem solving? Why?

case D–6 Motetronix Technology: Marketing Smart Dust

"The next 18 months will be critical in getting the word out about our technology and products," says Ajay Gupta, president of Motetronix Technology. "The Dust Storm is on the horizon and companies that capitalize on it early have huge potential."

THE COMPANY AND TECHNOLOGY

Motetronix Technology is a developer and manufacturer of "smart dust," or tiny wireless microelectromechanical sensors that measure temperature, light, and vibration; analyze chemical compounds, including radiation and air quality; and observe surrounding movement. These sensors are powered by AA batteries and controlled by an operating system called Tiny OS. Called *motes* (short for a re*mote* wireless transceiver that both transmits and receives analog or digital signals), these sensors survey the world around them and communicate with each other wirelessly, grapevining down the line until the data get to a personal computer. The "smart dust" name comes from the ultimate goal of making each mote about one cubic millimeter small, or the size of a grain of sand.

SMART DUST APPLICATIONS

Industry analysts are predicting that smart dust will have a host of commercial, military, security, and ecological applications. Along with the Pentagon, the U.S. Department of Homeland Security has already devoted a large portion of its R&D budget to sensor technology for military and security applications. Commercial and ecological applications are still being studied. According to industry analysts, vibration sensors on a factory floor will tell when a machine is about to fail, saving millions of dollars in downtime. Air-pressure sensors on truck tires will prevent accidents and save on fuel. Sensors dropped in a forest fire's path will predict which areas will flame up next. Motes will be able to determine when a building is safe to reenter after an earthquake, monitor the vital signs (and locations) of elderly people, or monitor power consumption of household appliances. A dispersion of motes 10 to 100 feet apart could monitor traffic on a highway or measure moisture levels on farms.

Applications for motes are expected to increase with decreasing prices and smaller sizes. In 2005, a single mote was priced in the range of $50 to $100, depending on level of sophistication, and was two cubic millimeters in size (smaller than a piece of glitter). By 2010, the price of a mote is expected to fall to $1 and the size will shrink to one cubic millimeter with advances in silicon and fabrication techniques.

MARKETING SMART DUST

Motetronix Technology executives were sensitive to the fact that promising applications of smart dust had to be tempered by the reality of the marketplace and buyer behavior. Therefore, Ajay Gupta charged his marketing team with the responsibility for reviewing buying behavior associated with the adoption of a new technology. The buying process appeared to contain at least six phases: (1) need recognition, (2) identification of available products, (3) comparison with existing technology, (4) vendor or seller evaluation, (5) the decision itself, and (6) follow-up on technology performance. Moreover, there appeared to be several people within the buying organization who would play a role in the adoption of a new technology. For example, top management (such as the president and executive vice presidents) would certainly be involved. Engineering and operations management (e.g., vice presidents of engineering and manufacturing) and design engineers (e.g., persons who develop specifications for new products) would also play a major role. Purchasing personnel would have a say in such a decision and particularly in the vendor-evaluation process. The role played by each person in the buying organization was still unclear to Motetronix. It seemed that engineering management personnel could slow the adoption of smart dust if they did not feel it was appropriate for the products made by the company. Design engineers, who would actually apply fiber-optics in product design, might be favorably or unfavorably disposed to the technology depending on whether they knew how to use it. Top management personnel would participate in any final decisions to use smart dust and could generate interest in the technology if stimulated to do so.

This review of buying behavior led to questions about how to influence an organization's buying process and have its technology used in a company's products or facility. Complicating the discussion was the fact that Motetronix was a comparative unknown in the industry relative to Crossbow Technology and Dust, Inc., two companies that had already commercialized the smart dust technology. In addition, issues still remained related to smart dust reliability, power consumption, and cost/price.[6]

Questions

1 What type of buying situation is involved in the purchase of smart dust, and what will be important buying criteria used by companies considering using smart dust in their products or in their facility?

2 Describe the purchase decision process for adopting smart dust, and state how members in the buying center for this technology might play a part in this process.

3 What effect will perceived risk have on a company's decision of whether to use smart dust in its products or in its facility?

---

case D–7 Callaway Golf: The Global Challenge

THE COMPANY HISTORY

Callaway Golf got its start in 1982 when the late Ely R. Callaway invested $400,000 for half interest in a golf club company called Hickory Stick. Callaway-Hickory, later renamed Callaway Golf, had sales of just $22 million in 1990 and was considered a small player as an OEM (original equipment manufacturer) for golf clubs. Callaway Golf made golf history and truly established itself in 1991 with the introduction of a very popular stainless-steel driver called "The Big Bertha." The Big Bertha driver was soon followed by one of the biggest selling drivers of all time, the titanium headed "Great Big Bertha." The success of the Big Bertha products—drivers, irons, and fairway woods—made Callaway Golf a major player in the golf club business and the oversized titanium driver explosion was on. The Big Bertha name and product line continued with Steelhead, Hawkeye, ERC, C4, and ERC Fusion. Recent additions include the FT-3, FT-5, and FT-i irons and drivers, the Odyssey putter line—the most popular putter in the United States, Europe, and Japan—as well as the Callaway Golf® X Junior set for 8 to 12-year-olds with a manufacturer's suggested retail price of $275.

By 2007 Callaway revenues exceeded $1.0 billion annually, making Callaway Golf one of the major OEMs in the business of golf. Callaway sells drivers and fairway woods, irons, and putters under the Callaway, Odyssey, Ben Hogan, and Top-Flite brands and also markets balls and accessories such as golf bags, gloves, headwear, footwear, and umbrellas. The Callaway trademarks and service marks are also licensed for products such as golf apparel, watches, travel gear, and eyewear. In November 2006, Callaway launched an online store where customers can order pre-owned golf products.

BUYER BEHAVIOR

Golfers, pros and amateurs, experiment with drivers, fairway woods, and putters more than other clubs in their golf bags. Many top professionals and amateurs choose to play with their favorite irons for years before changing. Callaway Golf made a cunning decision to enter the club market the way it did in the late 1980s and early 1990s. By introducing drivers, and uniquely designed fairway woods, clubs that players often change in the constant quest for distance and accuracy, Callaway Golf quickly became a name and force in the golf club equipment business.

THE GLOBAL GOLF MARKET

The golf industry has a broad and diverse global market. The game is popular around the world. The game and the rules are essentially the same everywhere. Golfers share similar characteristics and interests—a beginning golfer or an avid golfer in the United States is not much different from a beginning golfer or an avid golfer in Australia or Germany.

The professional golf tours have done much to link golf as a global sport. Golf enthusiasts from around the world can follow their sport and stars through televised tournaments, daily newspaper coverage, weekly golf journals, monthly golf magazines, and the Internet. Golf-related websites are among the most popular sites on the Internet. The Golf Channel on cable television continues to be a strong venue for direct product marketing as well as international event coverage. Golf is truly a global sport. Courses and competitions exist in many countries and on every continent except Antarctica. Professional and amateur players from around the world compete and interact with a high degree of etiquette and sportsmanship. Golfers at all levels share ideas and experiences from the game.

There are notable differences among global golf markets. Japanese golfers seek out technology and products to compensate for their smaller average stature. Savvy golf equipment manufacturers have developed clubs specifically for the Japanese market with different head shapes, weight, lie angle, and shafts adjusted for the average Japanese golfer's height. And the long or distance ball is very popular. In the United States, distance balls are inexpensive and fairly low-tech. In Japan, distance balls can sell for up to 500 yen each or more than $49 per dozen. While many U.S. golfers—regardless of ability—seek out the equipment used by professional golfers, Japanese golfers often think they are "not worthy" to use top-caliber equipment.

"In the U.S. we talk about the pyramid of influence and how the best players dictate what everyone else wants to buy," says Maki Shinoda of Nike. "But in Japan, you basically need to flip the pyramid upside down." This creates an interesting challenge for golf equipment manufacturers—technology sells but how best to position the product for the market so that it does not appear to be "too professional."

COMPETITION

The golf equipment business is a highly congested and very competitive marketplace. Many merchants exist, and the field is constantly changing with new start-ups, mergers, and acquisitions. Major equipment manufacturers include Titleist, TaylorMade, Callaway, and Ping. Adams, Cleveland, Wilson, Mizuno, Nike, and others also compete for a slice of the multibillion-dollar worldwide golf equipment market. Almost all well-established club manufacturers have followed Callaway's "Bigger is Better" philosophy when it comes to the marketing and manufacturing of popular drivers. In many respects, today's design and engineering for drivers has been a contest of who can make the most forgiving, longest driving club that technology and the rules of golf allow. Premium clubs today not only offer technological innovation, forgiveness, power, distance, and accuracy, but they are also pushing the laws of physics and the rules of golf.

CALLAWAY'S INTERNATIONAL MARKETS

For Callaway Golf, the global market is a very big part of its total market with about 44 percent of all sales coming from golfers in countries outside of the United States in 2006. The global market has grown in importance since the U.S. market—estimated at 28.7 million golfers—is relatively stagnant in terms of participants and number of rounds played (around 500 million annually). In fact, more golf courses closed in the United States in 2006 than opened for the first time since World War II.

The Japanese golf market has yet to recover from a severe economic downturn in the 1990s, and this has hurt Callaway and other golf equipment manufacturers. The typical Japanese golfer is male, spends approximately 480,000 yen ($4,500) per year on golf, and plays 6.8 times a year, practicing 9.5 times a year. Although the cost to golf in Japan has actually fallen as the economy struggled (which should have helped make golf more affordable, boosting rounds played), demographics are now a huge factor. Forecasts predict that Japan will see negative population growth for the first time in its history in 2007. Younger golfers are working more hours to support themselves and the aging Japanese population, leaving them fewer hours on the course to enjoy themselves.

One of the hottest Asian markets is South Korea. More than 30 percent of Korea's 4 million golfers are women, compared to 10 percent of U.S. golfers. Korean women account for the lion's share of the $600 million in golf and apparel/footwear sales tallied at retail compared to hard goods sales of $275 million. The female golf market is also growing faster than the male market in Korea. Pursuing the style-conscious female golfer domestically and internationally would represent a change for most golf equipment manufacturers, including Callaway.

What appeals to style-conscious women golfers? The upscale Shisegae Department Store in Seoul provides some insight. Shisegae devotes nearly an entire floor to golf equipment and apparel and nothing is cheap. Most of the customers are women. The TaylorMade r7 driver retails for 750,000 won ($810). Nearly every shirt costs at least $300! Form-fitting, stylish apparel is the norm. No khakis found here. The sale rack has a plethora of size large items, unlike U.S. stores where small sizes dominate among unsold mechandise.

Nike has a significant head start over many of its rivals in this market. Korean consumers aspire to look and dress like celebrities, and Nike has LPGA stars Michelle Wie and Grace Park endorsing and using Nike golf products.

ISSUES

In sports, it is often said that getting to the top is easier than staying there. Callaway Golf is faced with the burdensome task of sustaining its phenomenal growth and market share against competitors in hot pursuit. Discounting and innovation by competitors are challenges that Callaway now faces. Fast followers like Adams Golf and others have developed and discounted products that cut into Callaway's mainstay, the driver, fairway wood, and specialty club market. Callaway and others were left swimming for higher ground, moving into discount stores such as Target, as discounting and dumping have changed the market share landscape. Callaway has often resisted discounting its premium product line.

Technology does drive the industry. In 2004, Adidas-Soloman A.G. (TaylorMade) released a driver with technological innovation unlike any other on the market. TaylorMade's new driver, the r7 Quad, introduced a unique interchangeable weighting system that allows golfers to customize their driver for different course conditions and desired ball flight. Ratief Goosen's victory at the 2004 U.S. Open, at the hype of the r7 launch, hit the market like a tidal wave. More than three years later, the TaylorMade r7 is still arguably the most popular driver on the market. Even the success of international LPGA tour star, Annika Sorenstam (Sweden), number one in the world, using a bag full of the latest and greatest Callaway clubs has not helped Callaway win back declining market share in the competitive club market. Other big players in the equipment business are also after Callaway's market share and may pose a greater threat to Callaway's long-term success. Titleist, TaylorMade, and Ping are large enough and strong enough to survive any market slump and also have the resources to buy smaller successful companies and the technology to provide popular products.

Steps have been taken by golf's ruling bodies—the United States Golf Association (USGA) in North America and the Royal and Ancient Golf Club of St. Andrews (R&A)—to limit driver head size (larger heads improve forgiveness on off-center hits) and coefficient of restitution (the springiness of the club face surface that creates a trampoline effect producing more distance). Many of the golf greats believe more should be done to protect the game and have bemoaned the fact that technology and equipment advances have changed the game for the worse. Jack Nicklaus says, "It used to be 80 percent shot making and about 20 percent power." Those percentages have been reversed today, according to Nicklaus. Many classic golf courses have been rendered obsolete for professional tournaments by balls and clubs that allow players to reach the greens on par four holes in one shot and par fives in two shots. There are calls to restrict the type of equipment pros can use for tournaments. Equipment manufacturers are not eager to back away from pursuing technological advances. The vast majority of customers are amateurs looking for any edge to improve their games, and one way is through more forgiving equipment. What will happen to the "pyramid of influence" if the pros or even amateur tournaments have to be played with a "handicap" on conforming equipment rather than the latest, greatest, most forgiving equipment? Will it protect the game and put more of the emphasis back on skill?

The newest and potentially biggest golf market is now emerging in China where golf is becoming a popular choice for a growing population of young professionals. Although there are currently only about 1 million Chinese golfers, an annual growth rate of 25 percent is forecast over the next five years. The key to future global growth for the golf equipment industry may be in the budding Chinese market or the growing Indian market, also expected to grow at the same healthy rate as the Chinese market.[7]

Questions

1 What are the pros and cons of a global versus a multidomestic approach to marketing golf clubs for Callaway? Which approach do you feel would have more merit and why?

2 What are some of the significant environmental factors that could have a major impact on the marketing of golf clubs internationally? Describe each factor and what the nature of the impact would be.

3 What marketing mix recommendations would you have for Callaway as it attempts to increase international market share, especially in Asian markets?

"Some ideas are too good *not* to steal!" The speaker isn't a CIA agent but Wayne Johansen, CEO of HOM Furniture, a group of 13 furniture stores in the upper Midwest. Johansen isn't talking about anything illegal but is describing his approach to doing very practical, commonsense marketing research: visiting dozens of first-class retailers and then weaving the best of the ideas into HOM Furniture's operations. But that gets us ahead of the story.

HOW IT ALL BEGAN

Wayne Johansen's life reads like an entrepreneurial case study. Right out of high school, Johansen started JC Imports, a wholesale import business built around jewelry and leather goods. The decision to add water-beds to the merchandise mix proved to be a smart one, and the import business was soon closed to focus on booming waterbed sales. But all good things must come to an end; waterbeds don't wear out and the target audience of baby boomers was aging. When the market became saturated, Johansen, along with his brother, Rod, and Carl Nyberg converted their Water Bedroom stores to Total Bedroom stores. Ultimately, they wanted to expand into a full-line furniture company, but they needed larger store sizes, more warehouse capacity, and more working capital. So they took the first step in 1991 and HOM Oak and Leather stores were born. In 1997, their ultimate dream became reality as HOM Oak and Leather expanded into HOM Furniture, with sales of $30 million in 1996 growing to over $180 million in 2003.

THE CONSUMER BUYING PROCESS

Success at HOM Furniture has been built upon keen understanding of how consumers buy furniture. Furniture is a product category characterized by "complexity and significant risk," explains Johansen. A furniture purchase must fit into the consumer's overall decorating scheme, coordinating with paint, wallpaper, draperies, and floor coverings. Women are the key decision makers and they believe that their home furnishings make a statement about whether they have good taste and social status. They fear a bad decision, relying more on the expertise of the salesperson and the selection available in the store, rather than on brand names.

HOM Furniture has responded with large and inviting stores in highly visible locations, featuring great selection and knowledgeable salespeople who specialize in a given department. The smell of fresh-baked cookies greets customers as they enter the store, drawing them into a race track-shaped layout of the different store departments. This provides maximum exposure to merchandise and creates an airy, open feeling.

MARKETING INFORMATION AT HOM

Very quickly, Johansen and his partners recognized the value of marketing information. Before the launch of HOM Furniture in 1997, they toured 70 of the top 100 U.S. full-line furniture stores to observe the practices that contribute most to success. Some of the successful ideas gleaned from these visits include fresh-baked cookies in the stores, the use of a "house" structure in the center of the stores, and the design of two-level stores.

This benchmarking activity continues today as HOM Furniture participates in a consortium of 14 furniture stores in the United States, Canada, and Mexico. Because the member stores do not directly compete with one another in their geographic area, they are free to share financial statements, sales data, and their best ideas. Meeting three times annually, the participants spend the first day touring the host store and reviewing store advertising. The second day is reserved for the "best idea" contest. Each participant contributes $20 and the best idea takes the pot.

Site location is widely recognized as critical to the success of any retail store. In order to reach a regional audience, HOM Furniture builds stores that are highly visible from the freeways leading into the city from all directions. With analytical assistance from a local newspaper, management can plot the location of all current customers on a map as well as determine the market potential within a given radius for any possible future store location. Assuming that a customer will shop at the HOM store nearest his or her home, HOM management can calculate the extent to which a future store will cannibalize business from existing stores.

This geographic analysis can be merged with MicroVision data from Claritas. MicroVision is a segmentation and consumer targeting system that classifies every U.S. household into 1 of 48 unique market segments, using demographic, lifestyle, socioeconomic, buying, media, and behavioral characteristics. For any given zip code, MicroVision provides a count of the number of households for each of the 48 market segments identified. This allows HOM's management to build stores in areas that are heavily populated with the types of consumers who like to shop at HOM Furniture stores.

Once the store is in operation, sales and productivity information is closely monitored. Management has easy access to a database that tracks sales by store, by department, by day of the week, and by hour of the day. In addition, the sales generated by each salesperson are recorded on a monthly basis. Productivity analysis is made possible through an electronic sensor mounted on the doorframe of the main entrance to each store to measure "door swings"—a very precise measure of customer visits. With door swing data by store, by day, and by hour, management can use sales per door swing as a measure of productivity and also relate door swings to ads, such as a Sunday insert in the local paper.

After the sale is complete, HOM Furniture wants to make sure that the customer is thoroughly satisfied. On average, a person buys $40,000 of furniture during a lifetime. A satisfied customer is more likely to be a repeat customer, worth thousands of dollars in future business. For that reason, HOM monitors the number of customer calls received and also the percentage of product sold that requires service. Expanding the system

for measurement of customer satisfaction is one of Johansen's future priorities.[8]

Questions

1 (*a*) Identify the data sources HOM Furniture uses in its marketing information system. (*b*) Which would you classify as secondary data sources? (*c*) Which would be considered primary data sources?

2 When HOM Furniture advertises, it looks for a resulting spike in sales using an extensive database. (*a*) What are the advantages of this approach? (*b*) What are the possible shortcomings of this approach and how would you address them?

3 Assume that you have been hired as a marketing consultant by HOM Furniture's management. (*a*) What specific types of information should HOM collect to measure customer satisfaction with its stores and services? (*b*) For each type of information you identified in (*a*), how would HOM Furniture make use of that information to improve customer satisfaction?

---

case D–9   Lawn Mowers: Segmentation Challenges

HISTORY

The lawn mower was developed in the 1830s in England. Interest and enthusiasm for lawn care in the United States dates back to the post-World War II boom in suburban living when America's obsession with the perfect lawn began. In the 1950s, the first gas-powered, rotary-motor lawn mowers were introduced, displacing the reel (manual push) lawn mower. The surge in demand for gas-powered mowers was also accompanied by a surge in mower-related injuries, leading to improvements in the safety of these devices. Today, the industry is challenged to come up with more environmentally sound equipment. Although today's gas mowers are 70 percent less polluting than those produced 10 years ago, using a walking gas mower for one hour produces as much hydrocarbon and nitrogen oxide emissions—greenhouse gases—as driving 11 cars for an hour. And a gas-powered riding lawn mower produces as much greenhouse gas as driving 34 cars for an hour.

PRODUCTS

A wide range of products are available for cutting lawns; they vary in terms of power source (manual, electric, gas), operator mode (walking, riding, or automatic/robotic), and additional accessories and features ranging from baggers for grass clippings, cup holders, and power steering to a cooking grill.

An estimated 6 million gas-powered, walking lawn mowers were sold in 2006, the vast majority of all mowers sold in the United States. More Craftsman (Sears) gas-powered walking mowers were sold than any other brand. Prices for gas-powered walking lawn mowers range from $200 to $700 depending on horse power, brand, and features.

Reel mowers, the manual push mowers of old, have been making a comeback. American Lawn Mower Co. of Shelbyville, Indiana, claims to be the only U.S. manufacturer of reel mowers. Estimates are that 350,000 manual mowers were sold in 2006, up almost 100,000 over the previous year. Reel mowers are priced from $100 to $400 and eliminate concerns about gas, repairs, and getting it started. However, *Consumer Reports* cautions that most reel mowers can't cut grass higher than 1½ inches or trim closer than 3 inches around obstacles.

Electric lawn mowers—major brands include Black & Decker and Craftsman—are available in both corded and cordless models. Electric mowers produce no exhaust emissions and require little maintenance besides sharpening. Less adept at tackling tall or thick grass, most electric mowers cut 18 to 19-inch swaths versus 21 inches for most gas mowers. Prices range from $125 to $250 for corded, $400 or more for cordless. Corded versions tether you to within about 100 feet of a power outlet.

Riding lawn mowers share many of the same drawbacks as gas-powered walk-behind mowers. Riding mowers can be less maneuverable and fail to cut close to obstacles. Prices range from $1,600 to $7,200. While the big advantage of riding lawn mowers is the amount of territory that can be covered, they also have a following in the little known sport of lawn mower racing. The U.S. Lawn Mower Racing Association, based in Illinois, claims more than 20 chapters in various states and a slate of regional and national races culminating in a national championship.

LAWN SIZE

According to Bruce Butterfield, research director of the National Gardening Association, it's important to pick the right type of mower for your lawn size. "I've seen people with little yards riding a big riding mower. They spend more time backing up and turning around than cutting the grass." For under a half-acre of lawn (20,000 square feet), consider an electric or battery-powered mower. For lawns up to an acre (43,560 square feet), a gas-powered walk-behind mower is recommended. And if your lawn is from 1 to 3 acres (130,680 square feet), it may be time to consider a riding mower or a lawn tractor.

BENEFITS SOUGHT

What are people looking for in a lawn mower? Is it about speed in mowing the lawn, safety, control, noise reduction, reducing their carbon footprint?

A surprising force in the demand for reel lawn mowers has been women purchasing the mowers for the exercise. Why go to the gym when you can get a workout on your lawn each week? A return to manual mowers has even been touted as a way of addressing the obesity problem in children. Get those inactive kids away from the video games this summer and out there mowing the lawn.

Mower-produced pollution and gas prices have captured the interest of the industry and consumers. Since most gasoline-powered lawn mowers do not have catalytic converters, they produce a tremendous amount of greenhouse gases, not to mention the fact that they are running on a nonrenewable resource—petroleum. Adding catalytic converters to gas-powered mowers is being resisted vigorously by manufacturers just as automobile manufacturers resisted the change in the 1970s. California's proposed regulation of small-engine emissions (which would necessitate the use of a catalytic converter) would cut 22 tons of smog-forming chemicals from the air *per day,* the equivalent of more than 800,000 cars per day.

While a representative for Briggs and Stratton claims that meeting new pollution standards will require a minimum of a 30 percent across-the-board price increase, the Environmental Protection Agency estimates that a catalytic converter and new hoses would cost a company about $20 to $25 per machine on average. Many consumers apparently are willing to pay more for a cleaner machine, especially when educated about the pollution problem.

Home Depot's "Mow Down Pollution" program has been a big success in Canada. Home Depot collected a record 5,000 gas-powered mowers and trimmers in a 10-day period in April, giving consumers a rebate for new manual or electric mowers. The switch was most pronounced in health-conscious urban areas such as Toronto, Montreal, and Vancouver.[9]

Questions

1 Identify at least three bases for segmenting the lawn mower market. Prepare a market–product grid illustrating at least one of these bases.

2 What criteria should a lawn equipment company use in assessing the attractiveness of market segments? What sort of information is needed to fill in the market–product grid and allow the firm to make that target market decision?

3 How might a lawn mower company use segmentation for positioning purposes? At present, the manual reel mower market is rather small but growing. What marketing mix recommendations could be used to significantly expand this market?

---

case D–10 Medtronic in China: Where "Simpler" Serves Patients Better

"I felt tremendous pressure to find markets and technologies to grow the business in other parts of the world," says Bobby Griffin, president of Medtronic Pacing Business.

"Ninety-seven percent of Medtronic's products were being sold to 27 percent of the world. I'd read books on China and *BusinessWeek* articles about the success of

General Electric and other companies that had gone into China with scaled-down products."

THE MARKET AND THE NEED

Medtronic is the world's leading medical technology company and sells products to alleviate heart arrhythmia and neurological disorders, such as heart pacemakers, defibrillators, and angioplasty balloon catheters. But in the early 1990s, Medtronic sold only a few pacemakers in China, a country of 1.3 billion people. So Griffin interviewed a number of Chinese physicians. Their desires were very clear: They wanted a highly reliable, basic pacing device that would allow them to serve more people in need. "These doctors were motivated not by greed but by their desire to help and heal their patients," Griffin concluded. "Their relationships with their patients in the hospitals were touching. Instead of talking down to them from a standing position, they would get down on one knee and whisper in the patient's ear."

Griffin also found that only 4,000 cardiac patients a year were implanted with pacemakers in China, a small minority of the patients who needed them. "It was clear that a certain class of people in China could afford almost anything, while most could afford no treatment at all," Griffin said. "Yet more people in China could afford pacing than the populations of Germany and France combined. Of the millions of people living in the coastal cities and provinces of China, those in the middle class had $2,000 in disposable income. Ten thousand television sets were being sold every week, but health care is also vitally important."

THE NEW PACEMAKER FOR CHINA

As Griffin's plane lifted off from the Hong Kong airport, he recalled, "If we could build a pacemaker we could sell in China for $1,000 and still make our margins, we could serve many more people all over the world with a reliable product and still make a profit. I made up my mind to set an audacious goal. I'd shoot for a *radical* cost reduction in the product design."

Back at corporate headquarters, after a "You're crazy, Griffin!" reaction, Medtronic's head of development agreed to support the project. The project also received support from Medtronic's marketing organization: They liked the idea because the company could lead with an inexpensive product that could leverage sales of higher-end products later.

To meet Bobby Griffin's audacious goal, Medtronic chose its Champion pacemaker, a simplified version of the company's existing pacing systems that could meet specifications of cardiologists in China. Mechanical engineering design manager Bill Hooper had been supporting the

Champion pacing system through Quest, a special program within the company that funded the work of engineers who wanted to develop projects that wouldn't otherwise receive funding. Hooper observed, "My dream was to see patients in less developed countries restored to full life in ways that had been available for years in more developed countries." His efforts exemplified Medtronic's mission: *To contribute to human welfare by application of biomedical engineering in the research, design, manufacture, and sale of instruments or appliances that alleviate pain, restore health, and extend life.*

Hooper and electrical engineer Larry Hudziak had taken the current sophisticated technology and simplified it. "We wanted to reduce the cost to make it affordable in the Chinese market. By using a proven pacing lead technology for the coil, insulator, electrode and tine, we were able to save substantially. One of the most critical parts of the Champion, the lead wire, was needed to flex whenever patients breathed, their hearts beat, or they moved. We chose a lead that had the best reliability of anything we make," Hooper explained.

The Champion design did not include more complex, state-of-the-art features like dual-chamber stimulation, activity sensors, or steroid-eluding leads. The Chinese physicians Bobby Griffin had met with considered these features unnecessary, preferring high quality, low cost, longevity, and ease of use. The design team had to work hard to reduce the cost of the Champion pacemaker, which could translate into a lower selling price. Medtronic engineers also designed the Champion so that it could be programmed externally with a simple magnetic device. By February 1995, the design was complete and the product had been tested.

ON-SITE IN CHINA: A NEW PLANT AND SALESFORCE

Medtronic realized that to ensure quality control, it needed to be directly involved in the production and selling process, and available when physicians implanted the pacemaker. Bill Hooper knew how to design facilities to cut costs, but it required an almost constant presence in Shanghai, where the plant was being built. Over a three-year period, Hooper made 19 trips, and Ron Meyer, vice president of a pacing group, made 26. They reported to each other via e-mail and phone calls. "The routine was grueling," Hooper recalls. "Check into the hotel, unpack, head out to buy water and walk for exercise, then back to your room. It was such a drill."

Building a new plant was not the only challenge facing Hooper and Meyer. Medtronic also needed a salesforce, including experienced heart surgeons, to contact and train Chinese physicians. Furthermore, with the plant located in Shanghai, on the eastern coast of China, they needed a distribution system capable of serving a country roughly the size of the United States (9.6 million square kilometers).

Hooper recalled that these were tough times for both of them: "We both had families. When I was doing algebra with my daughter on the phone in the middle of the night from China, I could remind myself, 'I'm here because of Medtronic's mission and my part in fulfilling that mission.' If I hadn't had that, I would have given up."[10]

Questions

1 Assess Medtronic's decision to develop and market the new Champion heart pacemaker in terms of the following reasons for new-product success: (*a*) points of difference, (*b*) market attractiveness, (*c*) bad timing, and (*d*) economic access to doctors and patients.
2 Discuss the steps of the new-product process as they relate to the Champion pacemaker.

3 New-product development is important to a company like Medtronic, but it is hard work, and often leads to failure. How can a company encourage its employees to take initiative, make a profit, *and* be ethically and socially responsible?
4 Relate Medtronic's decision to sell pacemakers in China to its corporate mission statement. How does the decision relate to these Medtronic stakeholders: (*a*) shareholders of Medtronic stock, (*b*) Medtronic employees, and (*c*) Chinese patients?
5 Medtronic chose to design and build a new low-priced, highly reliable, reduced-feature heart pacemaker in its Shanghai plant. What are the strengths and weaknesses of this decision from (*a*) a marketing viewpoint and (*b*) an ethical viewpoint?

---

case D–11 Pampered Pooches Travel in Style

Can nothing be too good for man's best friend? Pampered pets can dine on Omaha Steaks' Steak Treats for Pets, 100 percent beefsteak with no additives and preservatives, and then finish off with a Frosty Paws soy-based "ice cream" treat for dessert. Fido can recline on a decadent burgundy Versailles love seat for $285 from Awesome Pet Products while wearing a faux mink coat and rhinestone tiara. If that weren't enough, burgeoning pet services include massage, chiropractic, and even liposuction.

The American Pet Products Marketing Association estimated that $40.8 billion would be spent on pets in 2007, $16.1 billion of that on food. To put this in perspective, the nearly $41 billion spent by U.S. consumers on their pets is more than the gross domestic product of all but 64 countries in the world. It's more than U.S. consumers spend annually on movies, video games, and recorded music combined. And pet spending is expected to exceed $52 billion within two years. About 63 percent of all U.S. households now own a pet, more than 71.1 million households.

Who are these pampered pets? And perhaps more importantly, who are their owners? There are 88.3 million cats and 74.8 million dogs in the United States. Pampered pets are often surrogate children for empty nesters and childless-by-choice couples. The vast majority of pet owners consider themselves "mom" or "dad" to their pets. Pets are also considered companions and friends.

American Demographics divides pet owners into four key segments: married boomers with no kids, single/divorced boomer women, young couples with no kids, and seniors. Married boomers without kids are 27 percent more likely than the average American to have a pet and 30 percent more likely than the average American to have more than one pet. More than half (52 percent) of 35-to-45-year-old married couples without children have a pet, 31 percent have two or more. This segment also spends more money on pets than married couples with children. Among the single/divorced boomer women segment, 45 percent own a pet. This group is 18 percent more likely than the average American to own a cat.

Young couples with no kids spend more per year on their pets than any other segment. Of young couples with no kids, 52 percent own a pet and are 33 percent more likely than the average American to own more than one pet.

Among seniors, 39 percent of those 55 to 64 years of age own a pet, and 25 percent of those over 65 own a pet. Seniors are expected to be the group with the fastest rate of growth in pet ownership.

Owners of pampered pooches are likely subscribers to such lifestyle magazines as *Animal Fair, Dog Fancy, Modern Dog,* and *The Bark*—a Berkeley area newsletter started to fight for a leash-free park that has evolved into the *New Yorker* for dog enthusiasts.

One of the hottest parts of the pet market right now is pet travel. An estimated 30 million households travel with their pets, most by car. Air travel with pets is becoming more problematic. At least two North American airlines have banned pets from traveling due to complaints and concerns of passengers with allergies and asthma and because of reduced cargo space as a result of security regulations requiring passengers to check more of their baggage. The majority of those traveling pets are dogs. According to the Travel Industry Association of America, 78 percent of all traveling pets are dogs while 15 percent are cats.

The number of pet-friendly lodgings has increased 300 percent in the past three years, according to Bring YourPet.com. The American Automobile Association has added more than 1,000 pet-friendly lodgings to its 2007 pet travel guide for more than 13,000 total listings. Websites devoted to identifying pet-friendly accommodations such as Pettravel.com and Petsonthego.com, and books such as AAA's *Traveling With Your Pet* are very popular as devoted pet owners make travel plans.

Traditional hotel and motel companies are increasingly catering to pet owners. Hotels and Resorts Worldwide (Sheraton, Westin, and W Hotels) offer oversized pet pillows; plush doggie robes; a check-in gift package that includes a pet toy, dog treat, ID tag, bone, and turn-down treat; and even have a licensed masseuse for dogs on staff. Upscale hotels are more likely to cater to pets and their owners. The Peninsula Chicago has a "pets only" room-service menu. Among other amenities, canine guests get inscribed water bowls at the Beverly Hills Hotel.

According to a survey by TripAdviser, the most pet-friendly hotel chain is Best Western followed by the Holiday Inn and then Red Roof. Among pet owners' biggest concerns when traveling are stress on the pet and care for the pet while they're touring or sightseeing. Look for pet-friendly hospitality services to address these needs.

Or how about a vacation with your best friend at a place such as Camp Unleashed in the Berkshires where you can hike, swim, and camp with your dog at your side?

Pet products companies are expanding their offerings to move into the pet hospitality area. For example, PetSmart is opening PetsHotel next to some of its stores. Starting at $21, PetsHotel provides a private kennel, two walks per day, and supervised playroom time. For a $10 "room" upgrade, you can provide your pet with a television set tuned to *Animal Planet* as well as the "Bone Booth" where pets can take phone calls from their owners.

Kennels can rival four-star hotels—pet aerobics, manicures, swim lessons—and even conventional kennels have added more upscale services. In fact, kennels have restyled themselves as pet country clubs, pet resorts, or pet care centers. Jim Krack, executive director of the American Boarding Kennel Association, put it this way: "A dog doesn't really care if he's in a place with cement walls or one with wallpaper and a brass bed, but owners today expect the same type of accommodations and services they can get for themselves."

Consider the 31-year-old woman who had her 7-year-old black lab, Daisy, as bridesmaid at her wedding. While the newlyweds were on their honeymoon in Italy, Daisy spent two weeks at the luxurious Paradise Ranch Country Club for Dogs in Sun Valley, California, at $45 per night. For this bride, nothing is too good for her best friend.[11]

Questions

1 What product attributes and benefits could an upscale hotel provide a pet owner? Are these the same product attributes and benefits provided by an upscale kennel?

2 What strategy would a company like Petco be pursuing by entering the pet hotel market? What strategy would a company like Marriott be pursuing by entering the pet hotel market?

3 What are the pros and cons of (*a*) a multiproduct branding strategy and (*b*) a multibranding strategy in the pet hospitality industry for companies such as (*a*) Petco and (*b*) Marriott?

4 What stage of the product life cycle is the pet hospitality industry in? An offering such as PetSmart's PetsHotel? Explain and support your answers.

case D–12   DigitalThink: Marketing E-Learning Services

"In 1996, two colleagues and I started discussing the possibilities that the Internet was opening up for corporate training," said Umberto Milletti, vice president of marketing and solutions management at DigitalThink. "We realized that we could harness the power of the same technologies that had revolutionized other parts of the business world to help organizations better disseminate skills and knowledge to their people."

Milletti's observation was very insightful. Over the last several decades, computer technology and, more recently, the Internet have changed the way that companies around the world do business. Increasingly powerful computers and software applications help employees work more productively; processes that once were laborious and manual are lightning fast; and geographically dispersed people can communicate and collaborate in cyberspace faster than ever before.

DigitalThink, a company that has grown from 3 employees to more than 400, and was recently ranked 22nd among the 500 fastest-growing technology companies, is at the forefront of a revolution in corporate training and education services. DigitalThink and other e-learning companies are supplementing, and occasionally replacing, traditional classroom-based training in much of the business world. The effectiveness of e-learning is causing many firms to reconsider their methods of providing training and education to employees, partners, and customers.

MARKET OPPORTUNITIES

Large companies with many locations and dispersed workforces, such as car rental agencies, hotels, airlines, retail stores, banks, and consulting firms, need to train thousands of employees frequently throughout the year. In the past, employees would gather in central locations for training courses that could last anywhere from a few days to one month. This approach to training and education was very costly and time consuming, and its effectiveness was influenced by inconsistencies in the capabilities of the trainers and the difficulty of requiring the trainers and the students to be in the same location. Using technology-based instruction saves the company time and money by increasing the reliability and effectiveness of the service and by putting the learner in control of the location and the pace of the learning experience. DigitalThink is leading the e-learning movement. Its methods have been shown to compress training time by as much as 50 percent and reduce the cost of development, maintenance, and delivery by 64 percent. A recent study reported that the global market for e-learning has grown at a 100 percent annual growth rate to $33.6 billion in 2005.

HOW DOES DIGITALTHINK ACHIEVE THESE MIRACULOUS RESULTS?

DigitalThink e-learning is tied directly to tangible outcomes. Courses are designed to develop the specific knowledge and skills that employees or salespeople need to do their jobs and to give them the opportunity to test their knowledge and apply what they've learned with a real-world situation or problem that they might encounter on the job. "Learning is most effective when students practice and demonstrate performance in a way that closely matches the performance expected of them," explains Shelly Berkowitz, manager of instructional design at DigitalThink. "We design relevant, realistic practice and assessment activities that require students to solve problems that are as complex as those they encounter in actual work situations."

Trainees can go through the courses at their own pace, allowing people to take as much or as little time as they need. Advanced students can skip over material that they already know and go directly to the exercise or assessment section to test their mastery of the material. DigitalThink e-learning can also be delivered to the learner through different media: on a CD, via a company intranet, or through a browser on the Internet. The Web-based versions of DigitalThink's training courses are the most popular—these allow companies to update and maintain the training program easily and cost effectively as well as reach all their employees smoothly and quickly.

THE MARKET

DigitalThink sees its target market as the Global 2000 companies, the largest corporations in the United States and around the world. These companies have the critical mass needed to justify large training programs, as well as continued need for training and retraining. Within these companies, key decision makers with large staffs might include the director of a call center, the vice president of sales, or the chief information officer. Hardware and software manufacturers, travel and leisure companies, major retailers, and other organizations that have typically been dependent on massive instructor-led training efforts are key markets where DigitalThink has had success selling its e-learning products and services. In fact, DigitalThink's current customers include 31 of the Fortune 100 companies and 450 organizations in 158 countries. Specific customer needs vary from ready-made courseware, to custom course development, to comprehensive learning management systems that include virtual classrooms, content management systems, and consulting services.

CUSTOMER EXAMPLES

DigitalThink developed a customized training program for an international airline's baggage and reservations departments. This airline is geographically dispersed, so it did not make sense for it to constantly transport new employees to a central location for training. Also, with the large number of people performing these jobs, training needs are almost constant. The content of the training is process oriented, which is one of the best applications for e-learning. The airline and its employees are pleased with the decision to transition the training program to a technology-based system.

Circuit City is another of DigitalThink's customers. "The e-learning program that we provide to Circuit City is centered around customer service, products that the sales counselors sell, general sales skills, and managerial skills," explains Milletti. DigitalThink has helped Circuit City create effective, interactive training for its 40,000 associates and managers, which has helped the company realize more than $100 million in cost savings. And the retailer expects to see continued improvement in customer satisfaction and sales.[12]

Questions

1 What are (a) the advantages and (b) the disadvantages of DigitalThink's technology-based instruction over conventional classroom-based educational services?

2 Given your answer to question 1 above, (a) what are the key criteria DigitalThink should use in identifying prospective customers for its service, (b) what market segments meet your criteria, and (c) what are possible sales objections these segments might have that you have to address?

3 Suppose a large international hotel chain asks DigitalThink to make a proposal to train its thousands of front-desk clerks and receptionists. (a) How would you design an e-learning program to train them how to check in a customer? (b) How can DigitalThink demonstrate the points of difference or benefits to the hotel chain of its technology-based instruction to obtain a contract to design an e-learning program?

---

case D–13 Health Cruises, Inc.: Estimating Cost, Volume, and Profit Relationships

Health Cruises, Inc., packages cruises to Caribbean islands such as Martinique and the Bahamas. Like conventional cruises, the packages are designed to be fun. But the cruise is structured to help participants become healthier by breaking old habits, such as smoking or overeating. The Miami-based firm was conceived by Susan Isom, 30, a self-styled innovator and entrepreneur. Prior to this venture, she had spent several years in North Carolina promoting a behavior-modification clinic.

Isom determined that many people were very concerned about developing good health habits, yet they seemed unable to break away from their old habits because of the pressures of day-to-day living. She reasoned that they might have a chance for much greater success in a pleasant and socially supportive environment, where good health habits were fostered. Accordingly, she established Health Cruises, Inc., hired 10 consulting psychologists and health specialists to develop a program, and chartered a ship. DeForrest Young, a Miami management consultant, became the chairperson of Health Cruises. Seven of Isom's business associates contributed an initial capital outlay totaling more than $250,000. Of this amount, $65,000 went for the initial advertising budget, $10,000 for other administrative expenses, and $220,000 for the ship rental and crew.

Mary Porter, an overweight Denver schoolteacher, has signed up to sail on a two-week cruise to Nassau, departing December 19. She and her shipmates will be paying an average of $1,500 for the voyage. The most desirable staterooms cost $2,200.

Mary learned of the cruise by reading the travel section of her Sunday newspaper on October 16. On that date, the Pittsford and LaRue Advertising Agency placed promotional notices for the cruise in several major metropolitan newspapers. Mary was fascinated by the idea of combining therapy sessions with swimming, movies, and an elegant atmosphere.

Pittsford and LaRue account executive Carolyn Sukhan originally estimated that 300 people would sign up for the cruise after reading the October 16 ads. But as of November 14, only 200 had done so. Isom and Health Cruises, Inc., faced an important decision.

"Here's the situation as I see it," explained a disturbed Isom at the Health Cruises board meeting. "We've already paid out more than a quarter of a million to get this cruise rolling. It's going to cost us roughly $200 per passenger for the two weeks, mostly for food. Pittsford and LaRue predicted that 300 people would respond to the advertising campaign, but we've only got 200.

"I see three basic options: (1) we cancel the cruise and take our losses; (2) we run the cruise with the 200 and a few more that will trickle in over the next month; or (3) we shell out some more money on advertising and hope that we can pull in more people.

"My recommendation to this board is that we try to recruit more passengers. There are simply too many empty rooms on that ship. Each one costs us a bundle."

At this point, Carolyn Sukhan addressed the board: "I've worked out two possible advertising campaigns for the November 20 papers. The first, the limited campaign, will cost $6,000. I estimate that it will bring in some 20 passengers. The more ambitious campaign, which I personally recommend, would cost $15,000. I believe this campaign will bring in a minimum of 40 passengers.

"I realize that our first attempt was somewhat disappointing. But we're dealing here with a new concept, and a follow-up ad might work with many newspaper readers who were curious and interested when they read our first notice.

"One thing is absolutely certain," Sukhan emphasized. "We must act immediately if there's any hope of getting more people on board. The deadline for the Sunday papers is in less than 48 hours. And if our ads don't appear by this weekend, you can forget it. No one signs up in early December for a December 18 sailing date."

Isom interrupted, shaking her head. "I just don't know what to say. I've looked over Carolyn's proposals, and they're excellent. Absolutely first-rate. But our problem, to be blunt, is money. Our funds are tight, and our investors are already nervous. I get more calls each day, asking me where the 300 passengers are. It won't be easy to squeeze another $6,000 out of these people. And to ask them for $15,000—well, I just don't know how we're going to be able to justify it."[13]

Questions

1 What is the minimum number of passengers that Health Cruises must sign up by November 20 to break even with the cruise? (Show your calculations.)

2 Should Health Cruises go ahead with the cruise, since 200 passengers had signed up as of November 14?

3 Would it be worthwhile for Health Cruises to spend either $6,000 or $15,000 for advertising on November 20? If so, which figure would you recommend?

4 How realistic are Carolyn Sukhan's estimates of 20 more passengers for the $6,000 advertising campaign and 40 more passengers for the $15,000 campaign?

5 Should Health Cruises consider cutting its prices for this maiden voyage health cruise?

---

case D–14 Bagel Bakes: Pricing a New Breakfast Product

"What a Monday morning," thought Kyoshi (Yosh) McNamara. At 8:30 a.m., Yosh expected to leisurely start the fourth and final week of the marketing analyst orientation program at Pristo-Kay, Inc., a medium-size consumer food company. By 11:30 a.m., he had sole responsibility for preparing a pricing recommendation to the vice president of breakfast products for Bagel Bakes, a new line of breakfast foods.

BACKGROUND

Yosh joined Pristo-Kay as a marketing analyst trainee in June 2007 after graduating with a BBA degree in marketing and finance. He had interned with Pristo-Kay the previous summer and worked in the department responsible for prepared breakfast foods. His first three weeks on the job were occupied by software systems training and attending a marketing research boot camp for novice marketing research professionals.

He also spent time with the marketing team for which he was assigned. This team had developed a new line of prepared breakfast foods called Bagel Bakes. These bagels have cream cheese, processed fruit, or peanut butter baked inside and are thin enough to fit in a standard one-slice toaster. Everyone agreed that the development team had done an outstanding job on this project. Consumer tests indicated that Bagel Bakes was the tastiest prepared food developed by Pristo-Kay in recent memory. Management was confident that Bagel Bakes would strengthen Pristo-Kay's breakfast product portfolio, but were aware that it was a departure from existing successful breakfast products. Management was also sensitive to the fact that hundreds of prepared breakfast products are launched annually with a very low percentage (6 percent) of these products still on the market 12 months after launch.

The Bagel Bakes marketing team consisted mainly of Tracy Jackson and Ken Byrne. Tracy was the product manager, having had a hand in developing the product (along with the food science, consumer insights, research and development, and finance teams). She had considerable experience in the food industry over the past 20 years. Ken was an associate product manager and acted as the marketing interface for sales and logistics—a key role for the upcoming product launch. His job was to prepare the sales tools that Pristo-Kay's salesforce needed to ensure that national retailers would carry Bagel Bakes. He also performed all analyses pertaining to stocking fees and point-of-sale promotion for large accounts.

On Friday of the previous week, Yosh heard a rumor that Tracy was interviewing with a competitor for a vice president position. When he arrived on Monday, he learned that Tracy had cleared out her desk over the weekend. Yosh also learned through the office grapevine that Tracy had recruited Ken to work for the competitor. As Yosh contemplated these events, Bob Smith, Pristo-Kay's vice president of breakfast products, approached his cubicle. Bob explained the situation, including the pricing recommendation request. He also said this could be an excellent opportunity for Yosh, if he made the best of it:

> "Tracy and Ken's positions will be filled quickly, but these hiring searches often take several months. Bagel Bakes needs to be launched as quickly as possible—we can't wait to fill these vacancies. The marketing plan is ready with the exception of the pricing plan, which has not yet been finalized. We are going to need you to take the lead on developing pricing recommendations for this product. Clearly, all final decisions will be made by myself and the rest of senior management, but you have a great chance to make an impression on this group. Please put together a pricing analysis and recommendation—include suggested retail prices for discount, grocery, and convenience stores. There are a number of considerations for pricing a new product like this—identify the key ones. Support your decisions well—doing this project properly would score you a lot of points right now and open up many options for your future here.
>
> One final thought for you before you get working on this: Consumer testing shows that the repurchase rate for this product should be very high, which makes me think that

promotional pricing should be used for the first few months, but this is also one of our most expensive breakfast products, in terms of production costs, making it difficult to lower prices substantially. Be sure to also include your recommendation for promotional pricing, both in terms of prices and length of promotion. I know this is a lot to ask given your short time here, but you can handle this."

BAGEL BAKES MARKETING PLAN

The targeting, positioning, promotion, and channel elements of the Bagel Bakes marketing plan had already received approval from senior management. Each element is described below.

Target Market

The primary target market for Bagel Bakes will be young adults looking for a quick, hassle-free hot breakfast. Secondary target markets include two-income families and late-night snackers of all ages.

Positioning

Bagel Bakes was to be positioned . . .

> For busy young people wanting a hot breakfast prepared in a hurry, Bagel Bites is a self-contained, quick and easy start to the day and the most delicious prepared breakfast food available.

Bagel Bakes was intended to capitalize on the growing trend toward "eating on the run" with a traditional breakfast food. In this regard, Tracy crafted a positioning map showing the competitive space for products currently available in the market. The figure below shows the proposed location for Bagel Bakes. The traditional to progressive axis denotes how similarly a product mimics a breakfast consumers could realistically prepare themselves. The sit-down to eat-on-the-run axis denotes the portability of each product. Also shown is whether a product is shelved in the frozen-food section (FRZ) or cereal section (DRY) of food stores, the number of servings per package (count), and the manufacturer's suggested retail price (MSRP). Bagel Bakes would occupy the traditional breakfast, eat-on-the-run competitive space in the frozen-food section and contain five servings (five bagels).

Retail Channels

Bagel Bakes would be sold in the freezer section of grocery, discount, and convenience chain stores currently served by Pristo-Kay. Grocery stores (e.g., Kroger) typically obtained a 23 percent margin based on the MSRP. Discount stores (e.g., Costco) obtained a 15 percent margin. Convenience stores (e.g., 7-Eleven) obtained a 50 percent margin. As a rule, discount stores priced their items 10 percent less than grocery stores.

Packaging

Bagel Bakes would be packaged in two sizes. A five-count (five bagels) package would be sold in grocery

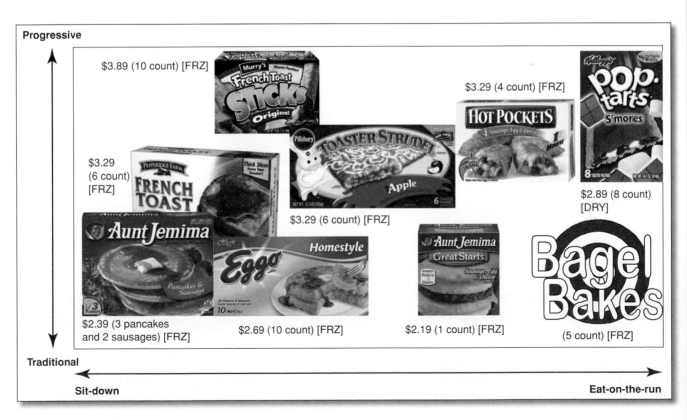

CHANNEL	BAGEL BAKES UNIT VOLUME ESTIMATES BY CHANNEL AND RETAIL PRICE		
	$3.49	$3.99	$4.49
Grocery	1,550,000 (5-count packs)	1,375,000 (5-count packs)	725,000 (5-count packs)
Discount	$3.14 1,550, 000 (5-count packs)	$3.59 1,375,000 (5-count packs)	$4.04 725,000 (5-count packs)
Convenience	$0.99 380,000 (1-count packs)	$1.49 250,000 (1-count packs)	$1.99 90,000 (1-count packs)

and discount stores. A single-count (one bagel) package would be sold in convenience stores.

Advertising and Promotion

The first-year advertising and promotion plan for Bagel Bakes included $2 million for media and $750,000 for slotting fees, necessary to "buy" freezer space in stores. About 70 percent of the media expenditure would be spent in the first four months of the product's launch to create consumer awareness and trial.

Manufacturing and Delivery Costs

Bagel Bakes required specialized baking and food injection equipment. Pristo-Kay purchased this equipment for $450,000. The equipment would be depreciated over five years given frequent advances in food manufacturing technology. In addition, Pristo-Kay leased space for Bagel Bakes production and inventory. The lease expense for the space was $240,000 annually.

Pristo-Kay production personnel estimated that a single Bagel Bake bagel would cost $0.28 per unit to produce, which included the cost of ingredients and labor. Therefore, a five-count Bagel Bake package would cost $1.40 to produce. Packaging cost for a five-count package was estimated to be $0.15 per box. A one-count package would cost $0.10 per box. The delivery cost for a five-count package sold to the grocery and discount channel was $0.10 and $0.07 for a one-count package sold to the convenience channel.

PRICING CONSIDERATIONS

Pristo-Kay's consumer insights group had conducted focus groups and commissioned a simulated market test that included the marketing plan. Three grocery channel retail prices were tested for the five-count package ($3.49, $3.99, and $4.49) and three retail prices were tested for the one-count package ($0.99, $1.49, and $1.99). The test also simulated Bagel Bakes prices for the discount channel, which were 10 percent below grocery retail prices. The simulated test market yielded unit volume estimates by channel and price point. The results are shown above.

As Yosh reviewed the Bagel Bakes situation, he realized that Monday would not be the leisurely day he had expected.[14]

Questions

1 What are the different considerations when setting the price for Bagel Bakes? For instance, competition, costs, and consumer psychology. When studying the impact of Pristo-Kay's costs, be sure to consider all relevant information from the marketing plan, such as retailer margins, fixed and variable costs.

2 What MSRP would you recommend for Bagel Bakes, keeping in mind the various considerations in question 1? Recommend prices for the grocery, discount, and convenience channels, keeping in mind these considerations as well as the respective margins for each retailer category.

3 What other marketing mix tactics would you recommend for Bagel Bakes?

case D–15   Ken Davis Products, Inc.: Finding Success in Retail Channels

"We position Ken Davis Bar-B-Q Sauces, not as something you use for grilling, but as something that adds flavor to ordinary food—a 'spice kit in a jar,'" explains Barbara Jo Davis, president of Ken Davis Products, Inc.

THE COMPANY

Ken Davis Products, Inc., is a small, regional business that develops and markets barbecue sauces. It has succeeded in this fiercely competitive business against corporate giants with this spice-kit-in-a-jar positioning both for its ultimate users and also the food brokers, distributors, and retailers needed to reach them.

The company got its start when Ken Davis, Barbara's late husband, owned a restaurant where he served his grandmother's recipe for barbecue sauce. His grandmother's recipe was a little of this and a little of that—not always the same amounts or ingredients. Customers loved the sauce, but Ken finally realized he needed to standardize the recipe so that consumers would have the same great-tasting sauce every time. He called in Barbara Jo Taylor, a home economist experienced in corporate test kitchens, to help him with the recipe for the sauce. Shortly afterward, Ken married Barbara, closed the restaurant, and began marketing barbecue sauce full time. She now serves as president of Ken Davis Products.

While Ken Davis Products is a market leader regionally, it has not expanded to national distribution. Barbara Davis explains, "What I hear consumers say again and again is the reason they buy Ken Davis barbecue sauces is because it's a local company. I think the reason we're the market leaders is because it's a personal product." Obviously it's not enough just to *be* local, the product has to *appeal* to local tastes, too.

PRODUCTS AND MARKETS

Barbecue sauce is a highly regional business compared with many other condiments because of consumer taste preferences. For example, sweeter sauces are preferred in the Midwest, vinegar-based sauces in the Southeast. Ken Davis Products offers Original, 2 Carb Original, Smooth 'n Spicy, and Sweet & Smoky sauces. Barbara Davis conducts focus groups, solicits comments from shoppers in the supermarket aisles or from testers at an in-store sampling. This allows Ken Davis to continue to be the regional leader.

Barbecue sauces are categorized as base sauces, premium, or super premium brands. Super premium category sauces offer retailers margins over 20 percent; premium (Ken Davis, Bull's Eye, KC Masterpiece) typically provide a retail margin of 18 to 20 percent; and base sauces (Kraft, Heinz) offer a 12 to 15 percent retail margin.

Since consumers do most of their grilling and barbecuing in the summer, the barbecue sauce market is highly seasonal. Retailers will often cut margins on barbecue sauces seasonally and use them as loss leaders during key holidays. Margins and prices are higher "off season."

COMPETITION

The barbecue sauce market is very competitive and Ken Davis Products faces national brands offered by major consumer packaged goods companies such as Kraft and Heinz. These national companies employ their own salesforces to call on grocers and institutional accounts to purchase their products. Local or regional sauce manufacturers rely upon food brokers to represent their products. These food brokers earn a margin of 2.5 to 3.5 percent to represent the manufacturer's products. Typically food brokers demand higher margins for slower moving products and lower margins for faster turn-over items.

It's hard for national manufacturers to cater to local and regional taste preferences and still maintain a consistent brand image as well as manufacturing efficiencies. This is something that regional or local companies such as Ken Davis can do well.

LISTENING TO CONSUMERS

"You have to listen to your consumer because you're not in this business to please yourself—but to please your consumer," says Barbara Davis. Two of her "listen-to-the-consumer" insights relate to brand name and packaging.

In her test kitchen, Barbara Davis developed a sauce that's sweet (but with only 5 grams of carbohydrates per serving) and a tiny bit spicier than the original but that has a definite smoky flavor. The new smoky barbecue sauce needed a name. What to call it? Early candidates included: Original, Part II; Smoky Campfire; Test Batch #19; Sweet Roast; and Crazy Woman Creek. "Give me a break," says Barbara Davis. "Finally, we decided *not* to be cutesy, but to simply describe the flavor." So Ken Davis Sweet & Smoky Bar-B-Q Sauce was born.

Barbara Davis has talked to consumers who used Ken Davis Bar-B-Q

Sauces everywhere from in the kitchen to an outdoor grill to over a campfire. This convinced her that the original cylindrical plastic bottle wasn't easy to grip in all of these places. So in 2004 the new plastic bottle with its easy-to-hold squared shape appeared.

DISTRIBUTION

Gaining access to grocers can be a significant barrier to entry for those trying to break into the market. Many grocery stores purchase from large food distributors such as Supervalu, C&S Wholesale Grocers, and C. H. Robinson. These distributors buy directly from large manufacturers such as Kraft or from food brokers utilized by smaller local and regional manufacturers. Some grocers and institutional accounts do buy directly from Kraft salespeople or from food brokers. But it's not enough to have salespeople calling on distributors and grocery accounts. Slotting allowances are less a factor for gaining access to retail shelf space these days, but are necessary for getting on the shelf at distributors. It is estimated that it may cost $40,000 per SKU (stock keeping unit) to gain entry to a distributor such as Supervalu.

Ken Davis Products pioneered the premium category and has well-established relationships in its regional market with retailers, distributors, and institutions. But as the barbecue sauce category grows more crowded with new entrants, Ken Davis will have to continue to provide not only great flavors for regional tastes but also channel relationships that maintain access to its consumers.[15]

Questions

1 Describe and compare the distribution channel for (*a*) Ken Davis Products and (*b*) Kraft, which offers products in both the base and premium categories. What distribution advantages and drawbacks does each type of channel have?

2 Under what circumstances might Ken Davis change its current distribution strategy?

3 Assume that the retail prices of Ken Davis barbecue sauces are $3.19 per 18.5-ounce bottle, Bull's Eye sauces are $2.59 per 18-ounce bottle, and Kraft Original Barbecue sauce is $1.79 for 18 ounces. (*a*) Compare how much the typical retailer will earn for each brand per bottle. (*b*) What are the implications of these retail profits for Ken Davis and its distribution strategy? (*c*) What other factors will influence retailer profits for a given barbecue sauce brand?

---

case D–16 Dell Inc.: A Foundation Built on Supply Chain Management

THE COMPANY

Dell is the largest direct seller of computers in the world and one of the top global PC manufacturers, though the company has struggled with disappointing performance and product-related problems. Founder Michael Dell returned as CEO in February 2007 to help put Dell back on track. Dell had revenues of $57 billion in 2007, a disappointing 2.1 percent annual increase in sales. Hewlett-Packard (HP) now claims the No. 1 market share position globally while Dell still maintains the market share lead in the United States. While Dell and HP are losing share, Apple and Lenovo are gaining ground. Dell offers PCs, notebooks, network servers, peripherals, and software. Over 90 percent of Dell's sales are to businesses and governmental customers. Recent forays into consumer electronics—digital music players, LCD television/computer monitors—have been discontinued.

SUPPLY CHAIN MANAGEMENT AT DELL

Historically, Dell's success was attributed in large part to its effective use of supply chain management. In a recent interview, Michael Dell stated, "Dell has always had a strength in its supply chain, and I think there is an opportunity to do even better there." Dell has closely aligned its suppliers with its direct channel strategy resulting in dramatic improvements in inventory management and control. Inventories are kept at ultra-low levels, one-tenth that of its competitors. A typical Dell factory runs with about five or six hours worth of inventory on hand. This is important in an industry where component costs can decline 30 to 35 percent per year and helps Dell take advantage of lower anticipated inventory costs in the future as well as minimizing the risk of holding obsolete parts in inventory. In addition, Dell has a very favorable cash conversion cycle—minus 20 days in the most recent cycle. This means that Dell gets paid faster than it pays out to vendors.

No less significant have been Dell's efforts to work with vendors to reduce vendor cycle times—the time that elapses from Dell placing an order to receiving that order in a Dell manufacturing facility. Dell communicates with its suppliers and supply chain partners through "Platinum Supplier" web pages. These pages provide each vendor with information on Dell's forecasted demand for the vendor's products, share production schedules, and allow for e-mail communication to make adjustments and changes.

The Dell website (www.dell.com) allows customers to shop online. Different online "stores" are available for different types of customers such as education, government, home/home office, and businesses. Shoppers can select the items they want and place them in their shopping cart. Once the order has been submitted, the website has the capability to check delivery dates and monitor the status of the order with its online tracking system. More than 50,000 business customers use the Dell online purchasing and information portal. Dell has moved beyond online sales into retail sales both in the United States and globally.

Since 1996, Dell has provided its top corporate customers its "Premier Pages" program. Beyond mere customer service or e-commerce, the Dell Premier Page empowers organizations to take control. The Dell Premier Page is a website that is personalized specifically for your company and includes a customized online computer store where you can configure your system. The prices you see are the contract prices already negotiated with your organization. You will know instantly what the system will cost and you can place your order online.

Dell integrates all its electronic commerce and communication systems. Dell uses browser and Internet/intranet technology as the interface for all applications, so any computer in the world can interact with Dell.

Dell utilizes decision support applications for modeling and simulating materials and factory scheduling to improve supply chain efficiency. For example, Dell can look out hours or days in advance, match this with materials flow, and based on this information, optimize a manufacturing plan to execute in the factory.

And in 2006 Dell introduced its "no charge, no exceptions" free computer recycling program, offering to even pick up your old computer—any brand—while challenging its competitors to offer the same service for their computers. This adds a new dimension in closing the loop on the supply chain—"cradle to grave"—from sourcing raw materials to build and deliver finished products to reclaiming and recycling these components in an environmentally responsible manner.[16]

Questions

1 Explain how Dell's approach to supply chain management satisfies the logistical objectives of minimizing logistics costs while maximizing customer service.

2 What are the supply chain management implications for Dell now that it has followed its competitors by adopting an indirect channel strategy along with its historic direct channel strategy? What supply chain and marketing recommendations do you suggest for Dell given the competitive environment?

3 How does supply chain management relate to the marketing concept at Dell?

---

case D–17 Trader Joe's: Upscale Value

THE COMPANY

With a near cult following, Trader Joe's has carved out a successful position in the competitive grocery market. Started in Los Angeles in 1958 by Joe Coulombe as a convenience store, Trader Joe's was dramatically repositioned in the 1960s as a store with luxurious food at low prices. Trader Joe's has grown to more than 250 stores in more than 20 states. Estimated annual 2006 sales were $900 million with more than 4,500 employees.

THE SHOPPING EXPERIENCE

What makes Trader Joe's a unique grocery shopping experience? Trader Joe's stores are not large—about 10,000 square feet—and carry a limited number of items to keep costs down. While there are fewer items (2,500 to 3,000), the items are often unique. More than 70 percent of the merchandise is private label, including Charles Shaw wine that sells for about $3.29 per bottle! Private label has been part of Trader Joe's product strategy for more than 30 years. According to Trader Joe's president, Doug Rauch, "We went into private label because of the value opportunity, so we could put our destiny in our hands." And over the years, consumers' confidence in these offerings has grown, allowing Trader Joe's to try new things and experiment with other offerings. Private-label offerings allow Trader Joe's to knock at least 20 percent off the cost of its products. And all private-label offerings boast no artificial colors, flavors, or preservatives.

Don't let the low prices fool you—the merchandise quality is upscale. In addition to organic fruits and vegetables and other grocery staples such as milk, cheese, and meat, there are unusual items such as Trader Joe's own chocolate-covered, peanut butter-filled pretzels, and exotic cheeses such as an Indian Paneer and a white Stilton with mango and ginger chunks.

THE SEARCH FOR NEW PRODUCTS

Trader Joe's uses a group of trained employees called "the tasting panel" to evaluate, critique, and improve its varied lines of house brands. New-product ideas have been uncovered in an airport in Thailand and a small restaurant in Italy and brought back to Trader Joe's and the tasting panel. This constant influx of new, tasty, critically reviewed products replaces the bottom 10 percent of products. Rotating out the bottom 10 percent isn't easy, but it ensures a constant flow of new products for customers to try, according to Matt Sloan, vice president of merchandising.

And customers are willing to travel to take advantage of the value provided by Trader Joe's. Trader Joe's has become to Manhattan supermarkets what Wal-Mart is to middle America grocery stores. The values offered by Trader Joe's exceed the convenience of the local market. According to Jon Hauptman of consulting firm Willard Bishop, there are price-gap "tipping points" where consumers are willing to pay more for additional convenience. Hauptman says this price gap typically is around 10 percent. Since Trader Joe's prices are easily more than 10 percent lower for similar items (generally 20 percent lower) and offered in a more upbeat shopping environment, consumers are willing to trade convenience and tote their Trader Joe's shopping bags through the subways of Manhattan.

Sampling is a key promotional tool. For a grand opening in Newport News, Virginia, customers were able to try Atlantic smoked salmon and hot cider in the morning followed by roasted red pepper soup, sweet potato bisque, and Tuscan Italian bread in the afternoon. Employees answer customer questions and offer food suggestions. Hand-written suggestions on labels offer ideas for foods that work well together. Recipe cards are available with additional food preparation ideas.

Looking for a special dessert? How about a frozen pumpkin cheesecake or strawberries dipped in white chocolate? "People will think you've gone through so much trouble, or they'll say 'You got that at Trader Joe's,'" says Trader Joe's Danny Owens.[17]

Questions

1 How would Trader Joe's be classified as a retail outlet in terms of ownership, level of service, and merchandise line?

2 What type of retail position does Trader Joe's occupy? Who do you see as its primary competitors, given this positioning?

3 How do you reconcile Trader Joe's success with the fact that grocery stores as a category are in the maturity stage of the retail life cycle? What are the key factors behind Trader Joe's success, and what steps should it take beyond its current marketing activities to continue to prosper?

---

case D–18 McDonald's Restaurants: An IMC Program to Reach Different Segments

"McDonald's outstanding success in Russia is a tribute to our Russian employees, suppliers, and, of course, our customers," comments George A. Cohon, senior chairman, McDonald's in Russia. It all started in 1976 at the Olympic Games in Montreal with a chance meeting between Cohon, who was then senior chairman of McDonald's Canada, and members of the Soviet Olympic delegation.

Fourteen years and countless meetings later, the 700-seat Pushkin Square restaurant in Moscow opened on January 31, 1990. The Pushkin restaurant still is the busiest McDonald's in the world, having served more than 77 million customers during the first 11 years since its opening. But competition from Russian quick-service restaurant operators, such as Rostiks and Russian Bistro, is increasing. Therefore, the McDonald's team must continue to develop effective means of communicating with present and prospective customers.

ABOUT McDONALD'S IN RUSSIA

The amount of food McDonald's has served in Russia is staggering. Consider that in its first 11 years of operations in Russia, McDonald's has served:

- More than 300 million customers, over twice the 146 million population of Russia.
- More than 66 million Big Mac™ sandwiches, that if put side by side would be longer than the 3,476-kilometer diameter of the moon!

McDonald's currently has over 100 restaurants in Russia, from Moscow and St. Petersburg to Nizhny Novgorod and Samara. McDonald's employs more than 6,000 Russians, or about 100 for each new restaurant that opens. More than 70 managers have successfully graduated from its "Hamburger University" training course held at McDonald's head office in Chicago, part of the 2,000 hours of training they each receive. McDonald's in Russia also operates McComplex, a one-of-a-kind food-processing and distribution facility located in Moscow, which supplies products to restaurants not only in Russia but also in Germany, Ukraine, Belarus, Austria, and the Czech Republic. It features dairy, bakery, pie, liquid, and meat lines and has its own quality assurance laboratories to ensure that McDonald's strict food quality standards are met. McDonald's in Russia sources more than 75 percent of the raw ingredients it needs from over 100 independent suppliers in Russia and the Commonwealth of Independent States (CIS).

McDONALD'S COMMUNITY EFFORTS

McDonald's has a philosophy of "giving back to the communities in which we serve" in the 120 countries in which it operates. In Russia, Ronald McDonald Children's Charities (Russia) operates the Ronald McDonald Centre, a sports and play facility for physically and mentally challenged children. Located in Moscow, the Ronald McDonald Centre hosts more than 1,500 children a week, conducting music, computer, and gym classes. In addition, McDonald's in Russia contributes to various charitable children's organizations to purchase items such as medical supplies and transportation equipment. Since opening 11 years ago, McDonald's in Russia has contributed more than $5 million to benefit Russian children in need.

WHAT McDONALD'S MARKETS AND WHAT CUSTOMERS LOOK FOR

McDonald's restaurants were founded and continue to operate worldwide on the basis of the formula, Q, S, C, and V: quality, service, cleanliness, and value. The simple menu ensures convenience and quick service. McDonald's is the favorite restaurant of many Russian families because McDonald's serves a high-quality meal, in a clean environment, with a smile, at a price families can afford.

Customers all over the world count on McDonald's for consistent taste and high-quality products, no matter where the restaurant is located. The McDonald's quality assurance program ensures that only the best quality products are served to its customers. This program begins with ensuring that only top-quality ingredients are used, that each food item is prepared in a consistent manner, and that the final product meets McDonald's exacting quality standards. For example, the components of a McDonald's Big Mac sandwich in Russia will undergo more than 98 quality checks before the final sandwich is presented to the customer. This ensures that every Big Mac sandwich tastes the same whether it is ordered by a customer in London, Tokyo, or Moscow.

McDonald's offers a curious marketing dilemma. Although the same meals are served to all customers, these same customers may be looking for strikingly different eating experiences on their restaurant visits. For example, a busy manager who only has enough time to "grab a quick lunch" is seeking a different eating experience than a young couple with a six-year-old child who is celebrating a special occasion. McDonald's also practices an "act local" strategy, which allows its restaurants to cater to local tastes and laws. For example, its restaurants in Germany and France can serve beer, something prohibited in the United States.

DESIGNING AN INTEGRATED MARKETING COMMUNICATIONS (IMC) PROGRAM

These diverse customer segments, with their very different reasons for visiting a McDonald's restaurant, pose a special challenge for a McDonald's marketing manager responsible for designing and implementing an effective integrated marketing communications (IMC) program. Some of the key initial questions include:

- What are the key market segments that McDonald's might be trying to reach?
- What might each segment look for when it chooses to visit McDonald's?
- What appeals and messages might be used to attract each of these segments?
- What combination of promotional mix elements (advertising, personal selling, public relations, sales promotion, and direct marketing) could be used to reach each segment?

The decisions a McDonald's marketing manager must make become more complicated because the IMC program may vary from city to city. If McDonald's is entering a new city with its first restaurant, an IMC may be very costly. If McDonald's is adding several more restaurants in Moscow, the IMC costs can be spread across the more than 20 outlets it promotes.[18]

Questions

1 Consider these four distinct market segments for McDonald's meals in Russian cities in which it has outlets: a family with young children, busy businesspeople, an older couple, and foreign tourists who are already familiar with McDonald's. For each segment (*a*) identify the special benefit or appeal McDonald's has to offer and (*b*) compose a 10- to 12-word promotional message that might be used to reach it.

2 For the first McDonald's restaurant to open in a city, what element of an integrated marketing communications (IMC) program might be used to reach (*a*) a family with young children and (*b*) busy businesspeople?

3 For the McDonald's restaurants in Moscow, what element of an integrated marketing communications (IMC) program might be used to reach (*a*) an older couple and (*b*) foreign tourists?

THE COMPANY

Recognized as one of the most respected companies in the United States, noted for its philanthropy, its commitment to health and wellness, the environment, innovation, design, and its shareholders, it is not surprising that Target Corporation is also one of the most savvy retail marketers today. Target has grown from a single Minnesota store in 1962 to more than 1,500 stores in 47 states plus the online Target.com. Estimated 2007 sales are $59.49 billion. Sales growth annually has been a healthy 13.1 percent with net income growth of 15.7 percent. Target is number 33 on the Fortune 500 list. Target is considered the No. 2 discount chain after Wal-Mart.

OBJECTIVES AND STRATEGY

The company embarked on a path of differentiation more than 20 years ago that it still follows today. "We knew we would never be able to compete solely on price," says Michael Francis, senior vice president of marketing. "We knew there was a customer out there who wanted (something different)."

From a communication standpoint, the company has several important and overlapping objectives: the need to deepen the bond with the existing customer who identifies Target as a place for trendy and exclusive merchandise and to keep her coming back. The Target customer has a median age of 41, youngest among major retailers, with a median household income of $58,000; 43 percent have children at home; and 43 percent have completed college. While maintaining its base, Target is also looking to broaden its reach with younger consumers, in large part through advertising.

BREAKTHROUGH ADVERTISING

Target is second to none when it comes to award-winning advertising campaigns that reflect its affordable chic, fun, and friendly image. Its ubiquitous bull's-eye logo is recognized by 96 percent of all U.S. consumers. Not content with such high recognition, Target now wants to "own the color red."

Target has dominated the RAC (Retail Advertising Conference) awards for more than 14 years, winning awards in virtually every possible category and media as well as overall best of show.

In terms of media, Target ads are seen in newspapers, magazines, television, and outdoor billboards. Target even has its own in-store TV network (Channel Red) playing in its electronics departments that shows Target ads and promos for new CD and DVD releases. One of the biggest advertising tactics for Target is the newspaper circular listing featured items for the week.

Target also has cleverly utilized promotional events. One such event was the launch of a new apparel line by a British designer that used a London-style double-decker bus as a boutique to showcase the line around the country. Two years ago, the retailer staged a "vertical fashion show" featuring acrobats in harnesses walking down the side of Rockefeller Center while wearing items from Target's fall collection.

Sometimes the Target advertising itself becomes the story—a two-for-one advertising and public relations bonanza. Target was the sole advertiser for the August 22, 2005 issue of *The New Yorker*. *The New Yorker* is the paragon of style and upscale cool, perhaps the most prestigious magazine in the country, and many thought that the image of Target did not fit the media. The campaign generated controversy and buzz. On the one hand, *The New Yorker* was roundly criticized for permitting a single advertiser, unprecedented in its history, and for not printing some statement saying the advertiser did not have any control over the issue's editorial content. On the other hand, an otherwise jaded *Adweek* columnist gushed about Target's clever illustrations, the beautifully rendered and conceptually coherent design that matched the visual design of the magazine. Describing the effort as the "smartest and most exciting example of branded entertainment I have ever seen," the columnist went on to ask, "How many contemporary American brands have a logo and a visual identity so strong and distinct that it can sustain 21 pages in a single issue without a single product mention or word of text and have it all remain immediately recognizable?"

Target has demonstrated that it is willing to take risks. Michael Francis has been known to say that if an idea sounds a bit scary, it's probably a good idea. One idea that didn't work quite as planned was painting bull's-eyes on white hermit crab shells as a means for Target to brand the Spirit Awards in Los Angeles, the week before the Academy Awards. People thought the crabs were cute until they were bit on their fingers. Well-branded hermit crabs were hanging off fingers in photographs from the event. But the stunt took on a life of its own as people from as far away as Mexico and San Diego called in over the next 18 months with reports of branded crabs on the loose. Undeterred, Target decided it was a great opportunity to send out Target gift cards and turn it into something that was completely unplanned—a find the hermit crab sweepstakes.

EFFECTIVENESS AND ASSESSMENT

What does Target spend on advertising? The Target annual report suggests that Target spent approximately $1,170 million on advertising in 2006. Newspaper circulars and media broadcast made up the bulk of the spending. How does the company evaluate the return on that expense? Winning advertising awards is fine, but what are the key measures for assessing effectiveness?

One example was the Target "Tony Bennett" campaign to leverage Bennett's 80th birthday and his new CD "Duets: An American Classic." Target negotiated an exclusive version of "Duets" featuring four exclusive tracks and a DVD of the making of the CD, sold exclusively at Target. Then the company sponsored a star-studded gala in New York City to celebrate Tony Bennett's 80th birthday and the release of his new CD/DVD complete with branded cocktail napkins and martini glasses distributed to hot New York and Los Angeles clubs. Target ads ran on A&E, TBS, TNT, as well as in *Time, People,* and *Vanity Fair* to support the CD. Target's ad agency also worked with director Rob Marshall to produce an NBC special that aired the week of Thanksgiving that was the No. 1 televised music special of the year. Tony Bennett's CD won three Grammy Awards, breaking sales records for the singer and for Target. Bennett singled out Target during his Grammy acceptance speech, thanking them for their sponsorship and support. Bottom line, it cost Target $6.2 million for the entire program. Target sold an astonishing 28 percent of all U.S. copies of the Bennett CD plus added $2.1 million in incremental non-music sales to its coffers.

ISSUES

It has been said that the best advertising does two things—drives sales and builds brands in the long term. It's tough to do both, and yet Target seemingly has been successful at both.

Some potential areas of concern are a substantial gap between the creativity and excitement of Target's advertising and the store shopping experience. The store shopping experience is just not as much fun as the advertising. Attempts to court the youth market have not been particularly successful. While Target advertising has a very youthful feel and energy, there hasn't been a corresponding surge in the young adult market.[19]

Questions

1 What are Target's primary promotional objectives? Have these objectives changed significantly over the years and if so, how?

2 What do you feel are the most valid measures for assessing the success of Target's advertising? Explain why you feel that these are the best means of determining effectiveness.

3 Many of Target's competitors are attempting to imitate aspects of its advertising and promotional program. (*a*) Does this present a threat to Target? (*b*) Why or why not, and how should Target respond?

---

case D–20   Morgantown Furniture: Making Promotion Trade-Offs

Edward Meadows, president of Morgantown Furniture, met with representatives of Kelly, Astor & Peters Advertising (KAP) and Andrew Reed, Morgantown's vice president of marketing and sales, to discuss the company's advertising program for 2008. The KAP Advertising representatives recommended that Morgantown Furniture increase its advertising in shelter magazines (such as *Good Housekeeping* and *Better Homes and Gardens,* which feature home improvement ideas and new ideas in home decorating) by $300,000 and maintain the expenditures for other promotional efforts at a constant level during 2008. The rationale given for the increase in advertising was that Morgantown Furniture had low name recognition among prospective buyers of furniture, and it intended to introduce new styles of living and dining room furniture. Reed, however, had a different opinion as to how Morgantown Furniture should spend the $300,000. He thought it was necessary to: (1) hire additional salespeople to call on the 30 new retail stores to be added by the company in 2008, (2) increase the funds devoted to cooperative advertising, and (3) improve the selling aids given to retail stores and salespeople.

THE COMPANY

Morgantown Furniture is a medium-sized manufacturer of medium- to high-priced living and dining room furniture. Sales in 2007 were $50 million. The company sells its furniture through 1,000 furniture specialty stores nationwide, but not all stores carry the company's entire line. This fact bothered Meadows because, in his words, "If they ain't got it, they can't sell it!" The company employs 10 full-time salespeople, who receive a $50,000 base salary annually and a small commission on sales. A company salesforce is atypical in the furniture industry because most furniture manufacturers use selling agents or manufacturer's representatives who carry a wide assortment of noncompeting furniture lines and receive a commission on sales. "Having our own sales group is a policy my father established 30 years ago," noted Meadows, "and we've been quite successful having people who are committed to our company. Our people don't just take furniture orders. They are expected to motivate retail salespeople to sell our line, assist in setting up displays in stores, coordinate cooperative advertising plans, and give advice on a variety of matters to our retailers and their salespeople."

In 2007, Morgantown spent $2.45 million for total promotional expenditures, excluding the salary of the vice president of marketing and sales. Promotional expenditures were categorized into four groups: (1) sales expense and administration, (2) cooperative advertising programs with retailers, (3) trade promotions, and (4) consumer advertising. Cooperative advertising allowances are usually spent on newspaper advertising in a retailer's city and are matched by the retailer's funds on a dollar-for-dollar basis. Trade promotion is directed toward retailers and takes the form of catalogs, trade magazine advertisements, booklets for consumers, and point-of-purchase materials such as displays for use in retail stores. Also included in this category is the expense of trade shows. Morgantown Furniture is represented at two trade shows a year. Consumer advertising is directed to potential consumers through shelter magazines. The typical format used in consumer advertising is to highlight new furniture and different living and dining room arrangements. Dollar allocation for each program in 2007 was as follows:

Promotional Program	Expenditure
Sales expense and administration	$ 612,500
Cooperative advertising	1,102,500
Trade advertising	306,250
Consumer advertising	428,750
Total	$2,450,000

THE INDUSTRY

The household wooden furniture industry is composed of more than 5,000 firms. Industry sales at manufacturers' prices were $10 billion. California, North Carolina, Virginia, New York, Tennessee, Pennsylvania, Illinois, and Indiana are the major U.S. furniture-producing areas. Although Ethan Allen, Bassett, Henredon, and Kroehler are well-known furniture manufacturers, no one firm captured more than 10 percent of the total household wooden furniture market.

The buying and selling of furniture to retail outlets centers around manufacturers' expositions at selected times and places around the country. At these marts, as they are called in the furniture industry, retail buyers view manufacturers' lines and often make buying commitments for their stores. However, Morgantown's experience has shown that sales efforts in the retail store by company representatives account for as much as half the company's sales in a given year. The major manufacturer expositions are held in High Point, North Carolina, in October and April. Regional expositions are also scheduled in June through August in locations such as Los Angeles, New York, and Boston.

Company research on consumer furniture-buying behavior indicated that people visit several stores when shopping for furniture, and the final decision is made jointly by a husband and wife in about 90 percent of furniture purchases. Other noteworthy findings are as follows:

- Eighty-four percent of buyers believe "the higher the price, the higher the quality" when buying home furnishings.
- Seventy-two percent of buyers browse or window shop in furniture stores even if they don't need furniture.
- Eighty-five percent read furniture ads before they actually need furniture.
- Ninety-nine percent agreed with the statement, "When shopping for furniture and home furnishings, I like the salesperson to show me what alternatives are available, answer my questions, and let me alone so I can think about it and maybe browse around."
- Ninety-five percent get redecorating ideas from shelter magazines.
- Forty-one percent have written to order a manufacturer's booklet.
- Sixty-three percent feel they need decorating advice for "putting it all together."

BUDGETARY ISSUES

After the KAP Advertising representatives made their presentation, Reed again emphasized that the incremental $300,000 should not be spent for consumer advertising. He noted that Morgantown Furniture had set as an objective that each salesperson would make six calls per year at each store and spend at least four hours at each store on every call. "Given that our salespeople work a 40-hour week, 48 weeks per year, and devote only 80 percent of their time to selling due to travel time between stores, we already aren't doing the sales job," Reed added. Meadows agreed but reminded Reed that the $300,000 increment in the promotional budget was a maximum the company could spend, given other cost increases.[20]

Questions

1 How might you describe furniture buying using the purchase decision process described in Chapter 5?

2 How might each of the elements of the promotional program influence each stage in the purchase decision process?

3 What should Morgantown's promotional objectives be?

4 How many salespeople does Morgantown need to adequately service its accounts?

5 Should Morgantown Furniture emphasize a push or pull promotional strategy? Why?

THE COMPANY

Chicago-based Crate and Barrel started as a one-store operation in 1962. Gordon and Carole Segal returned from their honeymoon in Europe with a variety of unique and affordable designs for their home. Recognizing that there was no one addressing the need for those with "more taste than money," they took out a lease on an old elevator factory and Crate and Barrel was born. The entrepreneurs were so excited about the new venture that only moments before the store opened, they realized that they had forgotten to get a cash register. A simple box had to serve.

Crate and Barrel has grown to over 150 stores with 7,000 sales associates and 2006 sales of more then $2.2 billion, an 11 percent annual increase over 2005. Crate and Barrel stores, catalogs, and its website offer a wide variety of household items—furniture, lighting, rugs, products for bed and bath, dinnerware, flatware, cookware, kitchenware, linens, food, and gifts. In 1998, Hamburg's Otto Group, the world's largest mail-order merchant, acquired a majority stake in Euromarket Designs Inc., which does business as the Crate and Barrel brand.

Crate and Barrel competes in the retail home furnishings and housewares industry with such well-known names as Pottery Barn, Williams-Sonoma, Pier 1 Imports, and Restoration Hardware. What makes Crate and Barrel special? Crate and Barrel carves out its own unique niche with more modern styling and brighter colors than its competitors. About one-third of the merchandise is unique to Crate and Barrel. But the best news is that Crate and Barrel offers a wide selection of well-designed products that provide good customer value.

MULTICHANNELS

Crate and Barrel has successfully utilized multiple channels to make its products available to customers. The company sends out more than 15 million brightly colored catalogs annually. The catalogs are fun to look through. For the most complete selection of products, check out the Crate and Barrel website, www.crateandbarrel.com. Product offerings are arrayed by category so customers can browse or visit the gift ideas or bridal registry pages to select a purchase. Unlike the catalog, the website allows customers to zoom in on items and check out specs. Crate and Barrel customers can opt in to e-mail alerts of product offerings and sales.

Purchases can be made in one of the many retail stores, online, by mail, or by the toll-free phone line. Crate and Barrel even offers its own credit card to facilitate purchase.

The company has made significant investments in enterprise marketing systems to manage its customer database and direct-mail campaigns. The system allows Crate and Barrel to effectively design, execute, and assess the results of cross-channel marketing efforts. A Crate and Barrel customer can spot a set of Marimekko towels in the catalog, order the towels and matching bedding from the website, and easily stop at a Crate and Barrel store to physically test and compare wood and metal beds to complete a purchase.[21]

Questions

1   How does Crate and Barrel facilitate consumer purchases with its multichannel strategy?

2   What are the six "Cs" of e-commerce, and how does Crate and Barrel address each of these?

3   Given that all of its major competitors also attempt to utilize multiple channels, in what ways could Crate and Barrel create a competitive advantage for itself with its multichannel strategy?

Naked® Juice was started in 1983 in Santa Monica, California. Home-squeezed and blended juices and smoothies were peddled from towel to towel on the beaches of Southern California until they caught on with small grocery stores near the beaches, then all over Los Angeles.

Today, Naked Juice is a national brand based in Azusa, California, offering all natural, 100 percent juices and juice smoothies with no added sugar or preservatives. There's "a pound of fruit in every 15.2-ounce bottle!" More than 6 million bottles of Naked Juice are shipped every month and the brand is reportedly the fastest-growing super premium juice brand, growing at a rate of 63.9 percent annually. The top sellers are Green Machine, Protein Zone, and Mighty Mango. *Health* magazine named Mighty Mango the best smoothie, *Progressive Grocer* picked Strawberry

Kiwi Kick "Best New Product" for 2006, and *Gourmet Retailer* selected Naked Juice as the "Editor's Choice" for June 2006. Naked Juice is sold through supermarkets, club stores, health food stores, and neighborhood markets across the country. Suggested retail prices for a 15.2-ounce bottle range from $2.59 for Just Juice products up to $3.19 for the smoothies with special ingredients such as acai.

PRODUCT FAMILIES

Naked Juice organizes its product offerings into "families" or categories. Currently, there are six families: Superfood Family (five different flavors of 100 percent juice smoothies), Just Juice Family (four pure juice flavors), Well Being Family (100 percent juice smoothies with immune boosters such as Vitamin C, potassium, echinacea), Protein Family (soy and whey protein-laced smoothies), Naked Energy Family (100 percent fruit juice smoothies with all-natural energy such as green tea extract, guarana, and B vitamins), and Antioxidant Family (six flavors with boosts of Vitamins A, C, E, and selium).

BEVERAGE INDUSTRY

The beverage industry is a complex and competitive environment with a wide variety of categories. In the nonalcoholic sector, the major segments are carbonated beverages (colas, lemon-lime, root beer, and other flavors), hot beverages (e.g., coffee, tea), and what are referred to as "functional" beverages—energy, sports, health, and nutritional drinks. Functional beverage sales were $7.1 billion in 2005 with a compound annual growth rate of 11.7 percent for the period 2001 to 2005.

Naked Juice competes in the energy, health, and nutritional drinks segment. Key competitors include Hansen Natural, Odwalla (owned by Coca Cola), and Pom Wonderful. Many of these beverages, as well as Naked, are located in the produce department.

SWALLOWED BY PEPSI

Pepsi "got Naked®" in early 2007 with the acquisition of the company to add to its beverage portfolio that also includes Aquafina, Gatorade, SoBe, Lipton, iced Starbucks RTDs (ready to drinks), Propel, and Tropicana. PepsiCo also bought Izze Beverage Co. for $75 million, while Coca-Cola agreed to buy juice and tea maker FUZE Beverage LLC. The reasons for this buying binge of small, successful noncarbonated beverage companies is simple—the cola market is at best in the late stage of the maturity product life cycle, more likely in decline. In the first half of 2006, Pepsi-Cola's U.S. volume fell 7.2 percent while Coca-Cola Classic's fell 4.9 percent in grocery, drug, and mass merchandisers. The diet versions were also down 4.7 percent and 4.9 percent, respectively. According to Tom Pirko, president of BevMark, Coke and Pepsi executives are torn between conflicting demands of supporting declining soda brands and driving growth of noncarbonated coffee and energy drinks that younger consumers crave. The largest consumer group for cola products is not younger consumers, but 35-to-54-year-old householders. Midwesterners and those with less education index are higher on cola consumption.

Further evidence of the upheaval in the beverages market is apparent in media spending. For the first time, media spending for noncarbonated beverages and energy drinks—at $953 million in 2005, up 6.7 percent—topped the $898 million spent on traditional carbonated soft drinks.

JUICES PROSPER

"Consumption of juice may be up because of health benefits and people's interest in whole, natural, or fresh food," according to Gaff Rampersaud, a registered dietician at the University of Florida. "One hundred percent juice and other minimally processed healthy foods are gaining popularity. One benefit is the nutrient density, which means the amount of nutrients per calorie. Citrus juices and other popular juices have higher amounts of nutrients per calorie." There is also growing evidence that citrus juice consumption is beneficial in reducing the risk of oral cancer, colorectal cancer, adenomas, urinary stones, and Alzheimer's disease. Pomegranate juice is getting a lot of attention for its health benefits and has shown up in a number of new juice offerings as is acai, a rain forest berry from Brazil with a very high antioxidant content.

Consumers also continue to demand more upscale, natural and organic products. While the juice category grows, the fastest-growing part of that category is juice smoothies with a 52.4 percent one-year increase.

ISSUES

Major soft drink players have all agreed to cut back on sales of high-sugar beverages to public schools by the 2008 school year, which will further dampen carbonated sales.

The growing importance of the Hispanic market that prefers fruit-flavored beverages is part of the trend away from colas. With the explosion of variety in the beverage industry you can get your caffeine jolt with a Starbuck's latte, a Red Bull energy drink, or the green tea and guarana boosts of a Naked Juice Black & Blueberry Rush.[22]

Questions

1 What strategy(ies) has Naked Juice taken to reach its current market position?

2 Consider PepsiCo's strategy(ies) in its beverage business. What are the implications for Naked Juice in this portfolio?

3 What key marketing metrics do you think PepsiCo should use to evaluate the performance of Naked Juice? Would these measures be different for its traditional carbonated soft drinks, and if so, how?

GLOSSARY

80/20 rule A concept that suggests 80 percent of a firm's sales are obtained from 20 percent of its customers. p. 234

above-, at-, or below-market pricing Setting a market price for a product or product class based on a subjective feel for the competitors' price or market price as the benchmark. p. 364

account management policies Specifies whom salespeople should contact, what kinds of selling and customer service activities should be engaged in, and how these activities should be carried out. p. 538

action item list An aid to implementing a marketing plan, consisting of four columns: (1) the task; (2) the person responsible for completing that task; (3) the date to finish the task; and (4) what is to be delivered. p. 590

adaptive selling A need-satisfaction presentation format that involves adjusting the presentation to fit the selling situation, such as knowing when to offer solutions and when to ask for more information. p. 531

advertising Any paid form of nonpersonal communication about an organization, good, service, or idea by an identified sponsor. pp. 466, 490

all-you-can-afford budgeting Allocating funds to promotion only after all other budget items are covered. p. 477

attitude A learned predisposition to respond to an object or class of objects in a consistently favorable or unfavorable way. p. 127

average revenue (AR) The average amount of money received for selling one unit of a product, or simply the price of that unit. p. 341

baby boomers The generation of children born between 1946 and 1964. p. 73

back translation The practice where a translated word or phrase is retranslated into the original language by a different interpreter to catch errors. p. 180

balance of trade The difference between the monetary value of a nation's exports and imports. p. 167

barriers to entry Business practices or conditions that make it difficult for new firms to enter the market. p. 84

barter The practice of exchanging goods and services for other goods and services rather than for money. p. 331

basing-point pricing Selecting one or more geographical locations (basing point) from which the list price for products plus freight expenses are charged to the buyer. p. 373

beliefs A consumer's subjective perception of how a product or brand performs on different attributes based on personal experience, advertising, and discussions with other people. p. 127

bidder's list A list of firms believed to be qualified to supply a given item. p. 156

blended family A family formed by merging two previously separated units into a single household. p. 75

blog A web page that serves as a publicly accessible personal journal for an individual or organization. p. 562

bots Electronic shopping agents or robots that comb websites to compare prices and product or service features. p. 561

bottom of the pyramid The largest but poorest socioeconomic group in the world consisting of 4 billion people who reside in developing countries and live on less than $2 per day. p. 181

brand equity The added value a given brand name gives to a product beyond the functional benefits provided. p. 293

brand licensing A contractual agreement whereby one company (licensor) allows its brand name(s) or trademark(s) to be used with products or services offered by another company (licensee) for a royalty or fee. p. 294

brand loyalty A favorable attitude toward and consistent purchase of a single brand over time. p. 126

brand name Any word, device (design, shape, sound, or color), or combination of these used to distinguish a seller's goods or services. p. 292

brand personality A set of human characteristics associated with a brand name. p. 293

branding A marketing decision by an organization to use a name, phrase, design, or symbols, or combination of these to identify its products and distinguish them from those of competitors. p. 292

breadth of product line The variety of different items a store carries. p. 443

break-even analysis A technique that analyzes the relationship between total revenue and total cost to determine profitability at various levels of output. p. 346

break-even chart A graphic presentation of the break-even analysis that shows when total revenue and total cost intersect to identify profit or loss for a given quantity sold. p. 348

break-even point (BEP) The quantity at which total revenue and total cost are equal. p. 346

brokers Independent firms or individuals whose principal function is to bring buyers and sellers together to make sales. p. 399

bundle pricing The marketing of two or more products in a single package price. p. 359

business The clear, broad, underlying industry category or market sector of an organization's offering. p. 33

business analysis The stage of the new-product process that involves specifying the product features and marketing strategy and making necessary financial projections needed to commercialize a product. p. 269

business goods Products that assist directly or indirectly in providing products for resale. Also called *B2B goods*, *industrial goods*, or *organizational goods*. p. 255

business marketing The marketing of goods and services to companies, governments, or not-for-profit organizations for use in the creation of goods and services that they can produce and market to others. p. 144

business plan A road map for the entire organization for a specified future period of time, such as one year or five years. p. 54

buy classes Consists of three types of organizational buying situations: straight rebuy, new buy, and modified rebuy. p. 153

buying center The group of people in an organization who participate in the buying process and share common goals, risks, and knowledge important to a purchase decision. p. 151

capacity management Integrating the service component of the marketing mix with efforts to influence consumer demand. p. 319

653

category management An approach to managing the assortment of merchandise in which a manager is assigned the responsibility for selecting all products that consumers in a market segment might view as substitutes for each other, with the objective of maximizing sales and profits in the category. p. 454

cause marketing Occurs when the charitable contributions of a firm are tied directly to the customer revenues produced through the promotion of one of its products. p. 107

caveat emptor The legal concept of "let the buyer beware" that was pervasive in the American business culture before the 1960s. p. 99

central business district The oldest retail setting, usually located in the community's downtown area. p. 453

channel captain A channel member (producer, wholesaler, or retailer) that coordinates, directs, and supports other channel members. p. 408

channel conflict Arises when one channel member believes another channel member is engaged in behavior that prevents it from achieving its goals. p. 407

channel of communication The means (e.g., a salesperson, advertising media, or public relations tools) of conveying a message to a receiver during the communication process. p. 464

channel partnership Consists of agreements and procedures among channel members for ordering and physically distributing a producer's products through the channel to the ultimate consumer. p. 401

choiceboard An interactive, Internet-enabled system that allows individual customers to design their own products and services by answering a few questions and choosing from a menu of product or service attributes (or components), prices, and delivery options. p. 552

code of ethics A formal statement of ethical principles and rules of conduct. p. 101

cognitive dissonance The feeling of postpurchase psychological tension or anxiety consumers may experience when faced with two or more highly attractive alternatives. p. 118

collaborative filtering A process that automatically groups people with similar buying intentions, preferences, and behaviors and predicts future purchases. p. 552

commercialization The stage of the new-product process that involves positioning and launching a new product in full-scale production and sales. p. 272

communication The process of conveying a message to others and requires six elements: a source, a message, a channel of communication, a receiver, and the processes of encoding and decoding. p. 464

community shopping center A retail location that typically has one primary store (usually a department store branch) and often 20 to 40 smaller outlets, serving a population of consumers who are within a 10- to 20-minute drive. p. 453

company forecast The total sales of a product that a firm expects to sell during a specified time period under specified environmental conditions and its own marketing efforts. Also called *sales forecast*. p. 246

competencies An organization's special capabilities, including skills, technologies, and resources, which distinguish it from other organizations and provide value to its customers. p. 35

competition The alternative firms that could provide a product to satisfy a specific market's needs. p. 83

competitive advantage A unique strength relative to competitors, often based on quality, time, cost, or innovation. p. 35

competitive parity budgeting Allocating funds to promotion by matching the competitor's absolute level of spending or the proportion per point of market share. Also called *matching competitors* or *share of market*. p. 477

consideration set The group of brands that a consumer would consider acceptable from among all the brands in the product class of which he or she is aware. p. 117

constraints In a decision, the restrictions placed on potential solutions to a problem. p. 202

consultative selling A need-satisfaction presentation format that focuses on problem identification, where the salesperson serves as an expert on problem recognition and resolution. p. 531

consumer behavior The actions a person takes in purchasing and using products and services, including the mental and social processes that come before and after these actions. p. 116

Consumer Bill of Rights (1962) A law that codified the ethics of exchange between buyers and sellers, including the rights to safety, to be informed, to choose, and to be heard. p. 99

consumer ethnocentrism The tendency to believe that it is inappropriate, indeed immoral, to purchase foreign-made products. p. 180

consumer goods Products purchased by the ultimate consumer. p. 255

consumer socialization The process by which people acquire the skills, knowledge, and attitudes necessary to function as consumers. p. 132

consumerism A grassroots movement started in the 1960s to increase the influence, power, and rights of consumers in dealing with institutions. p. 87

consumer-oriented sales promotion Sales tools used to support a company's advertising and personal selling directed to ultimate consumers. Also called *consumer promotions*. p. 509

convenience goods Items that the consumer purchases frequently, conveniently, and with a minimum of shopping effort. p. 257

cookies Computer files that a marketer can download onto the computer of an online shopper who visits the marketer's website. p. 564

cooperative advertising Advertising programs by which a manufacturer pays a percentage of the retailer's local advertising expense for advertising the manufacturer's products. p. 514

core values The fundamental, passionate, and enduring principles of an organization that guide its conduct over time. p. 31

corporate level The level in an organization where top management directs overall strategy for the entire organization. p. 29

cost focus strategy One of Porter's generic business strategies that involves controlling expenses and, in turn, lowering product prices targeted at a narrow range of market segments. p. 581

cost leadership strategy One of Porter's generic business strategies that focuses on reducing expenses and, in turn, lowers product prices while targeting a broad array of market segments. p. 580

cost per thousand (CPM) The cost of reaching 1,000 individuals or households with the advertising message in a given medium (M is the Roman numeral for 1,000). p. 498

cost-plus pricing Summing the total unit cost of providing a product or service and adding a specific amount to the cost to arrive at a price. p. 360

countertrade The practice of using barter rather than money for making global sales. p. 166

cross-channel shopper A consumer who researches offerings online and then purchases them at retail stores. p. 565

cross-cultural analysis The study of similarities and differences among consumers in two or more nations or societies. p. 177

cross-functional teams A small number of people from different departments in an organization who are mutually accountable to accomplish a task or common set of performance goals. p. 30

cultural symbols Things that represent ideas and concepts. p. 178

culture The set of values, ideas, and attitudes that are learned and shared among the members of a group. p. 76

currency exchange rate The price of one country's currency expressed in terms of another country's currency. p. 183

customary pricing Setting a price that is dictated by tradition, a standardized channel of distribution, or other competitive factors. p. 364

customer contact audit A flowchart of the points of interaction between consumers and a service provider. p. 316

customer experience The internal response that customers have to all aspects of an organization and its offerings. p. 19

customer experience management (CEM) The process of managing the entire customer experience within the company. p. 318

customer relationship management (CRM) The process of identifying prospective buyers, understanding them intimately, and developing favorable long-term perceptions of the organization and its offerings so that buyers will choose them in the marketplace. p. 19

customer service The ability of logistics management to satisfy users in terms of time, dependability, communication, and convenience. p. 423

customer value The unique combination of benefits received by targeted buyers that includes quality, price, convenience, on-time delivery, and both before-sale and after-sale service. p. 14

customerization The growing practice of not only customizing a product or service but also personalizing the marketing and overall shopping and buying interaction for each customer. p. 562

customs What is considered normal and expected about the way people do things in a specific country. p. 177

data The facts and figures related to the problem, divided into two main parts: secondary data and primary data. p. 204

data mining The extraction of hidden predictive information from large databases. p. 217

decision A conscious choice from among two or more alternatives. p. 200

decoding The process of having the receiver take a set of symbols, the message, and transform them back to an idea during the communication process. p. 464

demand curve A graph relating the quantity sold and price, which shows the maximum number of units that will be sold at a given price. p. 339

demand factors Factors that determine consumers' willingness and ability to pay for goods and services. p. 340

demographics Describing a population according to selected characteristics such as age, gender, ethnicity, income, and occupation. p. 71

depth of product line The store carries a large assortment of each item. p. 443

derived demand The demand for industrial products and services is driven by, or derived from, demand for consumer products and services. p. 147

development The stage of the new-product process that involves turning the idea on paper into a prototype. p. 270

differentiation strategy One of Porter's generic business strategies that requires products to have significant points of difference in product offerings, brand image, higher quality, advanced technology, or superior service to charge a higher price while targeting a broad array of market segments. p. 581

differentiation focus strategy One of Porter's generic business strategies that requires products to have significant points of difference to target one or only a few market segments. p. 581

direct forecast Estimating the value to be forecast without any intervening steps. p. 246

direct investment A global market-entry strategy that entails a domestic firm actually investing in and owning a foreign subsidiary or division. p. 188

direct marketing A promotion alternative that uses direct communication with consumers to generate a response in the form of an order, a request for further information, or a visit to a retail outlet. p. 469

direct marketing channels Allowing consumers to buy products by interacting with various advertising media without a face-to-face meeting with a salesperson. p. 395

direct orders The result of direct marketing offers that contain all the information necessary for a prospective buyer to make a decision to purchase and complete the transaction. p. 482

discretionary income The money that remains after paying for taxes and necessities. p. 81

disintermediation Channel conflict that arises when a channel member bypasses another member and sells or buys products direct. p. 407

disposable income The money a consumer has left after paying taxes to use for food, shelter, clothing, and transportation. p. 80

diversification analysis The search for growth opportunities from among current and new markets as well as current and new products. p. 581

dual distribution An arrangement whereby a firm reaches different buyers by employing two or more different types of channels for the same basic product. p. 396

dumping When a firm sells a product in a foreign country below its domestic price or below its actual cost. p. 192

dynamic pricing The practice of changing prices for products and services in real time in response to supply and demand conditions. p. 563

economic espionage The clandestine collection of trade secrets or proprietary informtion about a company's competitors. p. 100

Economic Espionage Act (1996) A law that makes the theft of trade secrets by foreign entities a federal crime in the United States. p. 169

economy Pertains to the income, expenditures, and resources that affect the cost of running a business and household. p. 78

efficient consumer response Inventory management systems that are designed to reduce the retailer's lead time for receiving merchandise, which then lowers a retailer's inventory investment, improves customer service levels, and reduces logistic expenses. Also called *quick response*. p. 423

eight-second rule A view that customers will abandon their efforts to enter and navigate a website if download time exceeds eight seconds. p. 561

electronic commerce Any activity that uses some form of electronic communication in the inventory, exchange, advertisement, distribution, and payment of goods and services. p. 83

electronic data interchanges (EDIs) Combining proprietary computer and telecommunication technologies to exchange electronic invoices, payments, and information among suppliers, manufacturers, and retailers. p. 421

electronic marketing channels Employing the Internet to make goods and services available for consumption or use by consumers or business buyers. p. 394

e-marketplaces Online trading communities that bring together buyers and supplier organizations to make possible the real time exchange of information, money, products, and services. Also called *B2B exchanges* or *e-hubs*. p. 157

emotional intelligence The ability to understand one's own emotions and the emotions of people with whom one interacts on a daily basis. p. 539

encoding The process of having the sender transform an idea into a set of symbols during the communication process. p. 464

environmental forces The uncontrollable factors in a marketing decision involving social, economic, technological, competitive, and regulatory forces. p. 13

environmental scanning The process of continually acquiring information on events occurring outside the organization to identify and interpret potential trends. p. 70

ethics The moral principles and values that govern the actions and decisions of an individual or group. p. 96

evaluative criteria Factors that represent both the objective attributes of a brand and the subjective ones a consumer uses to compare different products and brands. p. 117

everyday low pricing (EDLP) The practice of replacing promotional allowances with lower manufacturer list prices. p. 372

exchange The trade of things of value between buyer and seller so that each is better off after the trade. p. 7

exclusive distribution A level of distribution density whereby only one retail outlet in a specific geographical area carries the firm's products. p. 404

experience curve pricing A method of pricing based on the learning effect, which holds that the unit cost of many products and services declines by 10 percent to 30 percent each time a firm's experience at producing and selling them doubles, resulting in possible rapid price reductions. p. 361

exporting A global market-entry strategy in which a company produces goods in one country and sells them in another country. p. 185

extranets Internet-based technologies used to permit communication between a company and its suppliers, distributors, and other partners. p. 83

failure fee A penalty payment a manufacturer makes to compensate a retailer for sales its valuable shelf space failed to make. p. 273

family life cycle The distinct phases that a family progresses through from formation to retirement, each phase bringing with it identifiable purchasing behaviors. p. 132

feedback In the feedback loop, the sender's interpretation of the response, which indicates whether a message was decoded and understood as intended during the communication process. p. 466

field of experience A mutually shared understanding and knowledge that the sender and receiver apply to a message so that it can be communicated effectively during the communication process. p. 466

fixed cost (FC) The sum of the expenses of the firm that are stable and do not change with the quantity of a product that is produced and sold. p. 345

flexible-price policy Setting different prices for products and services depending on individual buyers and purchase situations. Also called *dynamic pricing*. p. 366

FOB origin pricing The "free on board" (FOB) price the seller quotes that includes only the cost of loading the product onto the vehicle and specifies the name of the location where the loading is to occur (seller's factory or warehouse). p. 372

Foreign Corrupt Practices Act (1977) A law, amended by the *International Anti-Dumping and Fair Competition Act* (1998), that makes it a crime for U.S. corporations to bribe an official of a foreign government or political party to obtain or retain business in a foreign country. p. 178

form of ownership Distinguishes retail outlets based on whether individuals, corporate chains, or contractual systems own the outlet. p. 440

formula selling presentation A presentation format that consists of information that must be provided in an accurate, thorough, and step-by-step manner to inform the prospect. p. 531

four I's of services The four unique elements to services: intangibility, inconsistency, inseparability, and inventory. p. 309

franchising A contractual arrangement between a parent company (a franchisor) and an individual or firm (a franchisee) that allows the franchisee to operate a certain type of business under an established name and according to specific rules. p. 401

frequency The average number of times a person in the target audience is exposed to a message or an advertisement. p. 498

full-service agency An advertising agency that provides the most complete range of services, including market research, media selection, copy development, artwork, and production. p. 507

functional groupings Organizational groupings that represent the different departments or business activities within a firm. p. 592

functional level The level in an organization where groups of specialists actually create value for the organization. p. 30

gap analysis A type of analysis that identifies the differences between a consumer's expectations about and experiences with a service based on dimensions of service quality. p. 316

Generation X Includes the 15 percent of the population born between 1965 and 1976. Also called *baby bust*. p. 73

Generation Y Includes the 72 million Americans born between 1977 and 1994. Also called *echo-boom* or *baby boomlet*. p. 74

generic business strategy A strategy that can be adopted by any firm, regardless of the product or industry involved, to achieve a competitive advantage. p. 579

geographical groupings Organizational groupings in which sales territories are subdivided according to geographical location. p. 592

global brand A brand marketed under the same name in multiple countries with similar and centrally coordinated marketing programs. p. 175

global competition Exists when firms originate, produce, and market their products and services worldwide. p. 173

global consumers Consumer groups living in many countries or regions of the world who have similar needs or seek similar features and benefits from products or services. p. 175

global marketing strategy Transnational firms that employ the practice of standardizing marketing activities when there are cultural similarities and adapting them when cultures differ. p. 174

goals Statements of an accomplishment of a task to be achieved, often by a specific time. Also called *objectives*. p. 34

gray market A situation where products are sold through unauthorized channels of distribution. Also called *parallel importing*. p. 192

green marketing Marketing efforts to produce, promote, and reclaim environmentally sensitive products. p. 106

gross domestic product (GDP) The monetary value of all goods and services produced in a country during one year. p. 167

gross income The total amount of money made in one year by a person, household, or family unit. Also known as *money income* at the Census Bureau. p. 79

gross rating points (GRPs) A reference number used by advertisers that is obtained by multiplying reach (expressed as a percentage of the total market) by frequency. p. 498

hierarchy of effects The sequence of stages a prospective buyer goes through from initial awareness of a product to eventual action (either trial or adoption of the product). The stages include awareness, interest, evaluation, trial, and adoption. p. 476

hypermarket A form of scrambled merchandising, which consists of a large store (more than 200,000 square feet) that offers consumers everything in a single outlet, eliminating the need to shop at more than one location. p. 444

idea generation The stage of the new-product process that involves developing a pool of concepts as candidates for new products. p. 267

idle production capacity Occurs when the service provider is available but there is no demand. p. 311

industrial distributor An intermediary that performs a variety of marketing channel functions, including selling, stocking, delivering a full product assortment, and financing. p. 394

industry potential The maximum total sales of a product by all firms to a segment during a specified time period under specified environmental conditions and marketing efforts of the firms. Also called *market potential*. p. 245

infomercials Program-length (30-minute) advertisements that take an educational approach to communication with potential customers. p. 500

information technology Involves operating computer networks that collect, store, and process data. p. 217

in-house agencies Consists of the company's own advertising staff, who may provide full services or a limited range of services. p. 507

institutional advertisements Advertisements designed to build goodwill or an image for an organization rather than promote a specific good or service. p. 491

integrated marketing communications (IMC) The concept of designing marketing communications programs that coordinate all promotional activities—advertising, personal selling, sales promotion, public relations, and direct marketing—to provide a consistent message across all audiences. p. 464

intensive distribution A level of distribution density whereby a firm tries to place its products and services in as many outlets as possible. p. 404

interactive marketing Two-way buyer–seller electronic communication in a computer-mediated environment in which the buyer controls the kind and amount of information received from the seller. p. 552

internal marketing The notion that a service organization must focus on its employees, or internal market, before successful programs can be directed at customers. p. 318

intertype competition Competition between very dissimilar types of retail outlets. p. 444

intranet An Internet-based network used within the boundaries of an organization. p. 83

involvement The personal, social, and economic significance of the purchase to the consumer. p. 119

ISO 14000 Worldwide standards for environmental quality and green marketing practices developed by the International Standards Organization (ISO). p. 107

ISO 9000 Standards for registration and certification of a manufacturer's quality management and assurance system based on an on-site audit of practices and procedures developed by the International Standards Organization (ISO). p. 149

joint venture A global market-entry strategy in which a foreign company and a local firm invest together to create a local business in order to share ownership, control, and profits of the new company. p. 187

just-in-time (JIT) concept An inventory supply system that operates with very low inventories and requires fast, on-time delivery. p. 431

key account management The practice of using team selling to focus on important customers so as to build mutually beneficial, long-term, cooperative relationships. p. 537

label An integral part of the package that typically identifies the product or brand, who made it, where and when it was made, how it is to be used, and package contents and ingredients. p. 299

laws Society's values and standards that are enforceable in the courts. p. 96

lead generation The result of a direct marketing offer designed to generate interest in a product or service and a request for additional information. p. 482

lead time The lag from ordering an item until it is received and ready for use or sale. Also called *order cycle time* or *replenishment time*. p. 423

learning Those behaviors that result from (1) repeated experience and (2) reasoning. p. 126

level of service The degree of service provided to the customer from three types of retailers: self-, limited-, and full-service. p. 440

lifestyle A mode of living that is identified by how people spend their time and resources, what they consider important in their environment, and what they think of themselves and the world around them. p. 128

limited-service agencies Advertising agencies that specialize in one aspect of the advertising process such as providing creative services to develop the advertising copy or buying previously unpurchased media space. p. 507

line positions Managers who have the authority and responsibility to issue orders to the people who report to them. p. 592

linear trend extrapolation Using a straight line to extend a pattern observed in past data into the future. p. 246

logistics Those activities that focus on getting the right amount of the right products to the right place at the right time at the lowest possible cost. p. 416

logistics management The practice of organizing the cost-effective flow of raw materials, in-process inventory, finished goods, and related information from point of origin to point of consumption to satisfy customer requirements. p. 416

loss-leader pricing Deliberately selling a product below its customary price, not to increase sales, but to attract customers' attention in hopes that they will buy other products as well. p. 364

lost-horse forecast Making a forecast using the last known value and modifying it according to positive or negative factors expected in the future. p. 246

make–buy decision An evaluation of whether components and assemblies will be purchased from outside suppliers or built by the company itself. p. 155

manufacturer's agents Agents who work for several producers and carry noncompetitive, complementary merchandise in an exclusive territory. Also called *manufacturer's representatives.* p. 399

marginal analysis A continuing, concise trade-off of incremental costs against incremental revenues. p. 396

marginal cost (MC) The change in total cost that results from producing and marketing one additional unit of a product. p. 345

marginal revenue (MR) The change in total revenue that results from producing and marketing one additional unit. p. 341

market People with both the desire and the ability to buy a specific product. p. 12

market modification A strategy in which a company tries to find new customers, increase a product's use among existing customers, or create new use situations. p. 288

market orientation An organization that focuses its efforts on (1) continuously collecting information about customers' needs, (2) sharing this information across departments, and (3) using it to create customer value. p. 19

market potential The maximum total sales of a product by all firms to a segment during a specified time period under specified environmental conditions and marketing efforts of the firms. Also called *industry potential.* p. 245

market segmentation Involves aggregating prospective buyers into groups, or segments, that (1) have common needs and (2) will respond similarly to a marketing action. pp. 46, 226

market segments The relatively homogeneous groups of prospective buyers that result from the market segmentation process. p. 226

market share The ratio of sales revenue of the firm to the total sales revenue of all firms in the industry, including the firm itself. p. 34

market testing The stage of the new-product process that involves exposing actual products to prospective consumers under realistic purchase conditions to see if they will buy. p. 271

market-based groupings Organizational groupings that utilize specific customer segments. p. 592

marketing The activity for creating, communicating, delivering, and exchanging offerings that benefit the organization, its stakeholders, and society at large. p. 6

marketing channel Individuals and firms involved in the process of making a product or service available for use or consumption by consumers or industrial users. p. 390

marketing concept The idea that an organization should (1) strive to satisfy the needs of consumers (2) while also trying to achieve the organization's goals. p. 18

marketing dashboard The visual display on a single computer screen of the essential information related to achieving a marketing objective. p. 41

marketing metric A measure of the quantitative value or trend of a marketing activity or result. p. 41

marketing mix The marketing manager's controllable factors—product, price, promotion, and place—that can be used to solve a marketing problem. p. 13

marketing plan A road map for the marketing activities of an organization for a specified future period of time, such as one year or five years. p. 42

marketing program A plan that integrates the marketing mix to provide a good, service, or idea to prospective buyers. p. 15

marketing research The process of defining a marketing problem and opportunity, systematically collecting and analyzing information, and recommending actions. p. 199

marketing ROI The application of modern measurement technologies to understand, quantify, and optimize marketing spending. p. 594

marketing strategy The means by which a marketing goal is to be achieved, usually characterized by a specified target market and a marketing program to reach it. p. 49

marketing tactics Detailed day-to-day operational decisions essential to the overall success of marketing strategies. p. 49

market–product grid A framework to relate the market segments of potential buyers to products offered or potential marketing actions by an organization. p. 237

marketspace Information- and communication-based electronic exchange environment mostly occupied by sophisticated computer and telecommunication technologies and digitized offerings. p. 83

measures of success Criteria or standards used in evaluating proposed solutions to a problem. p. 201

merchandise line Describes how many different types of products a store carries and in what assortment. p. 440

merchant wholesalers Independently owned firms that take title to the merchandise they handle. p. 397

message The information sent by a source to a receiver during the communication process. p. 464

microfinance The practice of offering small, collateral-free loans to individuals who otherwise would not have access to the capital necessary to begin small businesses or other income-generation activities. p. 183

mission A statement of the organization's function in society, often identifying its customers, markets, products, and technologies. Often used interchangeably with *vision*. p. 32

mixed branding A branding strategy where a firm markets products under its own name(s) and that of a reseller because the segment attracted to the reseller is different from its own market. p. 298

moral idealism A personal moral philosophy that considers certain individual rights or duties as universal, regardless of the outcome. p. 104

motivation The energizing force that stimulates behavior to satisfy a need. p. 122

multibranding A branding strategy that involves giving each product a distinct name when each brand is intended for a different market segment. p. 297

multichannel marketing The blending of different communication and delivery channels that are mutually reinforcing in attracting, retaining, and building relationships with consumers who shop and buy in traditional intermediaries and online. p. 395

multichannel retailers Retailers that utilize and integrate a combination of traditional store formats and nonstore formats such as catalogs, television, and online retailing. p. 457

multicultural marketing Combinations of the marketing mix that reflects the unique attitudes, ancestry, communication preferences, and lifestyles of different races. p. 76

multidomestic marketing strategy Multinational firms that have as many different product variations, brand names, and advertising programs as countries in which they do business. p. 174

multiproduct branding A branding strategy in which a company uses one name for all its products in a product class. p. 296

need-satisfaction presentation A presentation format that emphasizes probing and listening by the salesperson to identify needs and interests of prospective buyers. p. 531

new-product process The stages a firm goes through to identify business opportunities and convert them to a salable good or service. p. 266

new-product strategy development The stage of the new-product process that defines the role for a new product in terms of the firm's overall corporate objectives. p. 266

noise Extraneous factors that can work against effective communication by distorting a message or the feedback received during the communication process. p. 466

nonprobability sampling Using arbitrary judgments to select the sample so that the chance of selecting a particular element may be unknown or zero. p. 204

North American Industry Classification System (NAICS) Provides common industry definitions for Canada, Mexico, and the United States, which makes easier the measurement of economic activity in the three member countries of the North American Free Trade Agreement (NAFTA). p. 145

objective and task budgeting Allocating funds to promotion whereby the company: (1) determines its promotion objectives; (2) outlines the tasks to accomplish these objectives; and (3) determines the promotion cost of performing these tasks. p. 477

objectives Statements of an accomplishment of a task to be achieved, often by a specific time. Also called *goals*. p. 34

observational data Facts and figures obtained by watching, either mechanically or in person, how people actually behave. p. 206

odd-even pricing Setting prices a few dollars or cents under an even number. p. 358

off-peak pricing Charging different prices during different times of the day or days of the week to reflect variations in demand for the service. p. 320

off-price retailing Selling brand-name merchandise at lower than regular prices. p. 452

one-price policy Setting one price for all buyers of a product or service. Also called *fixed pricing*. p. 366

online consumers The subsegment of all Internet users who employ Internet-enabled technology to research products and services and make purchases. p. 557

opinion leaders Individuals who exert direct or indirect social influence over others. p. 130

order getter Sells in a conventional sense and identifies prospective customers, provides customers with information, persuades customers to buy, closes sales, and follows up on customers' use of a product or service. p. 525

order taker Processes routine orders or reorders for products that were already sold by the company. p. 524

organizational buyers Those manufacturers, wholesalers, retailers, and government agencies that buy goods and services for their own use or for resale. pp. 21, 144

organizational buying behavior The decision-making process that organizations use to establish the need for products and services and identify, evaluate, and choose among alternative brands and suppliers. p. 154

organizational buying criteria The objective attributes of the supplier's products and services and the capabilities of the supplier itself. p. 149

organizational culture A set of values, ideas, attitudes, and norms of behavior that is learned and shared among the members of an organization. p. 33

packaging A component of a product that refers to any container in which it is offered for sale and on which label information is conveyed. p. 299

partnership selling The practice whereby buyers and sellers combine their expertise and resources to create customized solutions, commit to joint planning, and share customer, competitive, and company information for their mutual benefit, and ultimately the customer. Also called *enterprise selling*. p. 524

penetration pricing Setting a low initial price on a new product to appeal immediately to the mass market. p. 357

perceived risk The anxieties felt because the consumer cannot anticipate the outcomes of a purchase but believes that there may be negative consequences. p. 125

percentage of sales budgeting Allocating funds to promotion as a percentage of past or anticipated sales, in terms of either dollars or units sold. p. 476

perception The process by which an individual selects, organizes, and interprets information to create a meaningful picture of the world. p. 124

perceptual map A means of displaying or graphing in two dimensions the location of products or brands in the minds of consumers to enable a manager to see how consumers perceive competing products or brands and then take marketing actions. p. 244

permission marketing The solicitation of a consumer's consent (called "*opt-in*") to receive e-mail and advertising based on personal data supplied by the consumer. p. 553

personal selling The two-way flow of communication between a buyer and seller, often in a face-to-face encounter, designed to influence a person's or group's purchase decision. pp. 467, 522

personal selling process Sales activities occurring before and after the sale itself, consisting of six stages: (1) prospecting, (2) preapproach, (3) approach, (4) presentation, (5) close, and (6) follow-up. p. 528

personality A person's consistent behaviors or responses to recurring situations. p. 123

personalization The consumer-initiated practice of generating content on a marketer's website that is custom tailored to an individual's specific needs and preferences. p. 553

points of difference Those characteristics of a product that make it superior to competitive substitutes. p. 46

posttests Tests conducted after an advertisement has been shown to the target audience to determine whether it accomplished its intended purpose. p. 508

power center A huge shopping strip with multiple anchor (or national) stores. p. 453

predatory pricing The practice of charging a very low price for a product with the intent of driving competitors out of business. p. 376

prestige pricing Setting a high price so that quality- or status-conscious consumers will be attracted to the product and buy it. p. 357

pretests Tests conducted before an advertisement is placed in any medium to determine whether it communicates the intended message or to select among alternative versions of the advertisement. p. 506

price The money or other considerations (including other goods and services) exchanged for the ownership or use of a good or service. p. 331

price discrimination The practice of charging different prices to different buyers for goods of like grade and quality. p. 374

price elasticity of demand The percentage change in quantity demanded relative to a percentage change in price. p. 343

price fixing A conspiracy among firms to set prices for a product. p. 374

price lining Setting the price of a line of products at a number of different specific pricing points. p. 358

price war Successive price cutting by competitors to increase or maintain their unit sales or market share. p. 368

pricing constraints Factors that limit the range of prices a firm may set. p. 336

pricing objectives Specifying the role of price in an organization's marketing and strategic plans. p. 334

primary data Facts and figures that are newly collected for the project. p. 204

private branding A branding strategy used when a company manufactures products but sells them under the brand name of a wholesaler or retailer. Also called *private labeling* or *reseller branding*. p. 298

probability sampling Using precise rules to select the sample such that each element of the population has a specific known chance of being selected. p. 203

product A good, service, or idea consisting of a bundle of tangible and intangible attributes that satisfies consumers and is received in exchange for money or some other unit of value. p. 254

product advertisements Advertisements that focus on selling a good or service and that take three forms: (1) pioneering (or informational), (2) competitive (or persuasive), and (3) reminder. p. 490

product class Consists of the entire product category or industry. p. 286

product differentiation A marketing strategy that involves a firm using different marketing mix activities to help consumers perceive the product as being different and better than competing products. p. 226

product form Consists of variations of a product within the product class. p. 286

product life cycle Describes the stages a new product goes through in the marketplace: introduction, growth, maturity, and decline. p. 280

product line A group of products that are closely related because they satisfy a class of needs, are used together, are sold to the same customer group, are distributed through the same type of outlets, or fall within a given price range. p. 255

product-line groupings Organizational groupings in which a unit is responsible for specific product offerings. p. 592

product line pricing The setting of prices for all items in a product line to cover the total cost and produce a profit for the complete line, not necessarily for each item. p. 367

product mix The number of product lines offered by a company. p. 255

product modification Altering a product's characteristic, such as its quality, performance, or appearance, to increase the product's value and sales. p. 288

product or program champion A person who is able and willing to cut red tape and move the program forward. p. 589

product placement A consumer sales promotion tool that uses a brand-name product in a movie, television show, video, or a commercial for another product. p. 512

product positioning The place an offering occupies in consumers' minds on important attributes relative to competitive products. p. 243

product repositioning Changing the place an offering occupies in consumers' minds relative to competitive products. p. 244

production goods Items used in the manufacturing process that become part of the final product. p. 257

profit The money left after a business firm's total expenses are subtracted from its total revenues and is the reward for the risk it undertakes in marketing its offerings. p. 28

profit equation Profit = Total revenue − Total cost; or Profit = (Unit price × Quantity sold) − (Fixed cost + Variable cost). p. 333

promotional allowances Cash payments or extra amount of "free goods" awarded sellers in the channel of distribution for undertaking certain advertising or selling activities to promote a product. p. 372

promotional mix The combination of one or more communication tools used to: (1) inform prospective buyers about the benefits of the product, (2) persuade them to try it, and (3) remind them later about the benefits they enjoyed by using the product. p. 464

protectionism The practice of shielding one or more industries within a country's economy from foreign competition through the use of tariffs or quotas. p. 170

protocol A statement that, before product development begins, identifies: (1) a well-defined target market; (2) specific customers' needs, wants, and preferences; and (3) what the product will be and do. p. 261

public relations A form of communication management that seeks to influence the feelings, opinions, or beliefs held by customers, prospective customers, stockholders, suppliers, employees, and other publics about a company and its products or services. p. 468

publicity A nonpersonal, indirectly paid presentation of an organization, good, or service. p. 468

publicity tools Methods of obtaining nonpersonal presentation of an organization, good, or service without direct cost. Examples include news releases, news conferences, and public service announcements. p. 515

pull strategy Directing the promotional mix at ultimate consumers to encourage them to ask the retailer for a product. p. 475

purchase decision process The five stages a buyer passes through in making choices about which products and services to buy: (1) problem recognition, (2) information search, (3) alternative evaluation, (4) purchase decision, and (5) postpurchase behavior. p. 116

push strategy Directing the promotional mix to channel members to gain their cooperation in ordering and stocking the product. p. 474

quantity discounts Reductions in unit costs for a larger order. p. 370

questionnaire data Facts and figures obtained by asking people about their attitudes, awareness, intentions, and behaviors. p. 209

quick response Inventory management systems that are designed to reduce the retailer's lead time for receiving merchandise, which then lowers a retailer's inventory investment, improves customer service levels, and reduces logistic expenses. Also called *efficient consumer response.* p. 423

quota A restriction placed on the amount of a product allowed to enter or leave a country. p. 171

rating The percentage of households in a market that are tuned to a particular TV show or radio station. p. 498

reach The number of different people or households exposed to an advertisement. p. 498

receivers Consumers who read, hear, or see the message sent by a source during the communication process. p. 464

reciprocity An industrial buying practice in which two organizations agree to purchase each other's products and services. p. 151

reference groups People to whom an individual looks as a basis for self-appraisal or as a source of personal standards. p. 132

regional shopping centers Consist of 50 to 150 stores that typically attract customers who live or work within a 5- to 10-mile range, often containing two or three anchor stores. p. 453

regulation Restrictions state and federal laws place on business with regard to the conduct of its activities. p. 86

relationship marketing Linking the organization to its individual customers, employees, suppliers, and other partners for their mutual long-term benefits. p. 15

relationship selling The practice of building ties to customers based on a salesperson's attention and commitment to customer needs over time. p. 524

response In the feedback loop, the impact the message had on the receiver's knowledge, attitudes, or behaviors during the communication process. p. 466

retail life cycle The process of growth and decline that retail outlets, like products, experience. Consists of the early growth, accelerated development, maturity, and decline stages. p. 456

retail positioning matrix A matrix that positions retail outlets on two dimensions: breadth of product line and value added. p. 450

retailing All activities involved in selling, renting, and providing goods and services to ultimate consumers for personal, family, or household use. p. 438

retailing mix The activities related to managing the store and the merchandise in the store, which includes retail pricing, store location, retail communication, and merchandise. p. 451

reverse auction In an e-marketplace, it is an online auction in which a buyer communicates a need for a product or service and would-be suppliers are invited to bid in competition with each other. p. 159

reverse logistics A process of reclaiming recyclable and reusable materials, returns, and reworks from the point of consumption or use for repair, remanufacturing, redistribution, or disposal. p. 432

sales forecast The total sales of a product that a firm expects to sell during a specified time period under specified environmental conditions and its own marketing efforts. Also called *company forecast.* p. 246

sales management Planning the selling program and implementing and controlling the personal selling effort of the firm. p. 522

sales plan A statement describing what is to be achieved and where and how the selling effort of salespeople is to be deployed. p. 534

sales promotion A short-term inducement of value offered to arouse interest in buying a good or service. p. 469

sales quota Specific goals assigned to a salesperson, sales team, branch sales office, or sales district for a stated time period. p. 541

sales response function Relates the expense of marketing effort to the marketing results obtained. p. 576

salesforce automation (SFA) The use of computer, information, communication, and Internet technologies to make the sales function more effective and efficient. p. 542

salesforce survey forecast Asking the firm's salespeople to estimate sales during a coming period. p. 246

sampling Selecting representative elements from a population. p. 203

scrambled merchandising Offering several unrelated product lines in a single store. p. 443

screening and evaluation The stage of the new-product process that involves internal and external evaluations of the new-product ideas to eliminate those that warrant no further effort. p. 269

secondary data Facts and figures that have already been recorded before the project at hand. p. 204

selective distribution A level of distribution density whereby a firm selects a few retail outlets in a specific geographical area to carry its products. p. 404

self-concept The way people see themselves and the way they believe others see them. p. 123

self-regulation An alternative to government control where an industry attempts to police itself. p. 89

selling agents Agents who represent a single producer and are responsible for the entire marketing function of that producer. p. 399

semiotics A field of study that examines the correspondence between symbols and their role in the assignment of meaning for people. p. 178

service continuum The range of offerings companies bring to the market, from the tangible to the intangible or good-dominant to service-dominant offerings. p. 311

services Intangible activities or benefits that an organization provides to consumers in exchange for money or something else of value. p. 308

share points An analysis that uses percentage points of market share as the common basis of comparison to allocate marketing resources effectively for different product lines within the same firm. p. 577

shopping goods Items for which the consumer compares several alternatives on criteria, such as price, quality, or style. p. 257

situation analysis Taking stock of where the firm or product has been recently, where it is now, and where it is headed in terms of the organization's plans and the external factors and trends affecting it. p. 44

situational influences The five aspects of the purchase situation that impacts the consumer's purchase decision process: (1) the purchase task, (2) social surroundings, (3) physical surroundings, (4) temporal effects, and (5) antecedent states. p. 121

skimming pricing When introducing a new or innovative product, setting the highest initial price that customers really desiring the product are willing to pay. p. 356

slotting fee A payment a manufacturer makes to place a new item on a retailer's shelf. p. 273

social audit A systematic assessment of a firm's objectives, strategies, and performance in terms of social responsibility. p. 107

social class The relatively permanent, homogeneous divisions in a society into which people sharing similar values, interests, and behavior can be grouped. p. 134

social forces The demographic characteristics of the population and its values. p. 71

social responsibility The idea that organizations are part of a larger society and are accountable to that society for their actions. p. 105

societal marketing concept The view that organizations should satisfy the needs of consumers in a way that provides for society's well-being. p. 20

source A company or person who has information to convey during the communication process. p. 464

spam Communications that take the form of electronic junk mail or unsolicited e-mail. p. 562

specialty goods Items that a consumer makes a special effort to search out and buy. p. 257

staff positions People who have the authority and responsibility to advise people in line positions but cannot issue direct orders to them. p. 592

standard markup pricing Adding a fixed percentage to the cost of all items in a specific product class. p. 360

statistical inference Drawing conclusions about a population from a sample taken from that population. p. 204

stimulus-response presentation A presentation format that assumes that given the appropriate stimulus by a salesperson, the prospect will buy. p. 530

strategic alliances Agreements among two or more independent firms to cooperate for the purpose of achieving common goals. p. 173

strategic business unit (SBU) A subsidiary, division, or unit of an organization that markets a set of related offerings to a clearly defined group of customers. p. 30

strategic business unit (SBU) level The level in an organization where managers set a more specific strategic direction for their businesses to exploit value creating opportunities. p. 30

strategic channel alliances A practice whereby one firm's marketing channel is used to sell another firm's products. p. 396

strategic marketing process The approach whereby an organization allocates its marketing mix resources to reach its target markets. p. 44

strategy An organization's long-term course of action designed to deliver a unique customer experience while achieving its goals. p. 29

strip location A cluster of neighborhood stores to serve people who are within a 5- to 10-minute drive. p. 453

subcultures Subgroups within the larger, or national, culture with unique values, ideas, and attitudes. p. 135

subliminal perception Seeing or hearing messages without being aware of them. p. 125

supplier development The deliberate effort by organizational buyers to build relationships that shape suppliers' products, services, and capabilities to fit a buyer's needs and those of its customers. p. 149

supply chain A sequence of firms that perform activities required to create and deliver a good or service to consumers or industrial users. p. 416

supply chain management The integration and organization of information and logistic activities across firms in a supply chain for the purpose of creating and delivering goods and services that provide value to consumers. p. 416

supply partnership A relationship that exists when a buyer and its supplier adopt mutually beneficial objectives, policies, and procedures for the purpose of lowering the cost or increasing the value of products and services delivered to the ultimate consumer. p. 151

support goods Items used to assist in producing other goods and services. p. 257

survey of buyers' intentions forecast Asking prospective customers if they are likely to buy the product during some future time period. p. 246

sustainable development Conducting business in a way that protects the natural environment while making economic progress. p. 108

SWOT analysis An acronym describing an organization's appraisal of its internal **S**trengths and **W**eaknesses and its external **O**pportunities and **T**hreats. p. 44

synergy The increased customer value achieved through performing organizational functions more efficiently. p. 229

synergy analysis Seeks growth opportunities by finding the optimum balance between marketing efficiencies versus R&D–manufacturing efficiencies. p. 582

target market One or more specific groups of potential consumers toward which an organization directs its marketing program. p. 13

target pricing Consists of (1) estimating the price that ultimate consumers would be willing to pay for a product, (2) working backward through markups taken by retailers and wholesalers to determine what price to charge wholesalers, and then (3) deliberately adjusting the composition and features of the product to achieve the target price to consumers. p. 358

target profit pricing Setting an annual target of a specific dollar volume of profit. p. 362

target return-on-investment pricing Setting a price to achieve an annual target return-on-investment (ROI). p. 363

target return-on-sales pricing Setting a price to achieve a profit that is a specified percentage of the sales volume. p. 362

tariffs A government tax on goods or services entering a country, primarily serving to raise prices on imports. p. 170

team selling The practice of using an entire team of professionals in selling to and servicing major customers. p. 527

technology Inventions or innovations from applied science or engineering research. p. 81

telemarketing Using the telephone to interact with and sell directly to consumers. p. 448

third-party logistics providers Firms that perform most or all of the logistics functions that manufacturers, suppliers, and distributors would normally perform themselves. p. 425

total cost (TC) The total expense incurred by a firm in producing and marketing a product. Total cost is the sum of fixed cost and variable cost. p. 345

total logistics cost Expenses associated with transportation, materials handling and warehousing, inventory, stockouts (being out of inventory), order processing, and return goods handling. p. 422

total revenue (TR) The total money received from the sale of a product. p. 341

trade name A commercial, legal name under which a company does business. p. 292

trademark Identifies that a firm has legally registered its brand name or trade name so the firm has its exclusive use, thereby preventing others from using it. p. 292

trade-oriented sales promotions Sales tools used to support a company's advertising and personal selling directed to wholesalers, distributors, or retailers. Also called *trade promotions*. p. 513

trading down Reducing the number of features, quality, or price. p. 291

trading up Adding value to the product (or line) through additional features or higher-quality materials. p. 291

traditional auction In an e-marketplace, it is an online auction in which a seller puts an item up for sale and would-be buyers are invited to bid in competition with each other. p. 159

traffic generation The outcome of a direct marketing offer designed to motivate people to visit a business. p. 482

trend extrapolation Extending a pattern observed in past data into the future. p. 246

ultimate consumers The people who use the goods and services purchased for a household. Also called *consumers*, *buyers*, or *customers*. p. 21

uniform delivered pricing The price that the seller quotes includes all transportation costs. p. 372

unit variable cost (UVC) Variable cost expressed on a per unit basis. p. 345

unsought goods Items that the consumer either does not know about or knows about but does not initially want. p. 257

usage rate The quantity consumed or patronage (store visits) during a specific period. Also called *frequency marketing*. p. 232

utilitarianism A personal moral philosophy that focuses on the "greatest good for the greatest number," by assessing the costs and benefits of the consequences of ethical behavior. p. 104

utility The benefits or customer value received by users of the product. p. 22

value The ratio of perceived benefits to price; or Value = Perceived benefits divided by Price. p. 332

value analysis A systematic appraisal of the design, quality, and performance of a product to reduce purchasing costs. p. 155

value consciousness The concern for obtaining the best quality, features, and performance of a product or service for a given price that drives consumption behavior. p. 78

value-pricing The practice of simultaneously increasing product and service benefits while maintaining or decreasing price. p. 332

values A society's personally or socially preferable modes of conduct or states of existence that tend to persist over time. p. 177

variable cost (VC) The sum of the expenses of the firm that vary directly with the quantity of a product that is produced and sold. p. 345

vendor-managed inventory (VMI) An inventory-management system whereby the supplier determines the product amount and assortment a customer (such as a retailer) needs and automatically delivers the appropriate items. p. 432

vertical marketing systems Professionally managed and centrally coordinated marketing channels designed to achieve channel economies and maximum marketing impact. p. 399

viral marketing An Internet-enabled promotional strategy that encourages individuals to forward marketer-initiated messages to others via e-mail. p. 562

warranty A statement indicating the liability of the manufacturer for product deficiencies. p. 302

web communities Websites that allow people to congregate online and exchange views on topics of common interest. p. 562

wheel of retailing A concept that describes how new forms of retail outlets enter the market. p. 455

whistle-blowers Employees who report unethical or illegal actions of their employers. p. 103

word of mouth The influencing of people during conversations. p. 131

workload method A formula-based method for determining the size of a salesforce that integrates the number of customers served, call frequency, call length, and available selling time to arrive at a figure for the salesforce size. p. 537

World Trade Organization (WTO) A permanent institution that sets rules governing trade between its members through panels of trade experts who decide on trade disputes between members and issue binding decisions. p. 171

yield management pricing The charging of different prices to maximize revenue for a set amount of capacity at any given time. p. 359

LEARNING REVIEW ANSWERS

CHAPTER 1

1. What is marketing?

Answer: Marketing is the activity for creating, communicating, delivering, and exchanging offerings that benefit the organization, its stakeholders, and society at large.

2. Marketing focuses on _____ and _____ consumer needs.

Answer: discovering; satisfying

3. What four factors are needed for marketing to occur?

Answer: The four factors are: (1) two or more parties (individuals or organizations) with unsatisfied needs; (2) a desire and ability on their part to be satisfied; (3) a way for the parties to communicate; and (4) something to exchange.

4. An organization can't satisfy the needs of all consumers, so it must focus on one or more subgroups, which are its _____.

Answer: target markets

5. What are the four marketing mix elements that make up the organization's marketing program?

Answer: product, price, promotion, place

6. What are environmental forces?

Answer: Environmental forces are those that the organization's marketing department can't control. These include social, economic, technological, competitive, and regulatory forces.

7. Like Pillsbury and General Electric, many firms have gone through four distinct orientations for their business, starting with the _____ era and ending with today's _____ era.

Answers: production; customer

8. What are the two key characteristics of the marketing concept?

Answer: An organization should (1) strive to satisfy the needs of consumers (2) while also trying to achieve the organization's goals.

CHAPTER 2

1. What is the difference between a business firm and a nonprofit organization?

Answer: A *business firm* is a privately owned organization that serves its customers in order to earn a profit so that it can survive. A *nonprofit organization* is a nongovernmental organization that serves its customers but does not have profit as an organizational goal. Instead, its goals may be operational efficiency or client satisfaction.

2. What are examples of a functional level in an organization?

Answer: The functional level in an organization is where groups of specialists from the marketing, finance, manufacturing/operations, accounting, information systems, research & development, and/or human resources departments focus on a specific strategic direction to create value for the organization.

3. What is the meaning of an organization's mission?

Answer: A statement of the organization's function in society, often identifying its customers, markets, products, and technologies. Often used interchangeably with *vision*.

4. What is the difference between an organization's "business" and its "goals"?

Answer: An organization's business is the clear, broad, underlying industry category or market sector of an organization's offering. Goals (or objectives) are statements of an accomplishment of a task to be achieved, often by a specific time.

5. What is business portfolio analysis?

Answer: Business portfolio analysis studies a firm's business units as though they were a collection of separate investments.

6. What is the difference between a hedgehog strategy and a blue ocean strategy?

Answer: The hedgehog strategy involves developing a simple, excellent offering that captures the imagination of the organization and its customers based on the answers to three questions: (1) What can we be the best at in the world? (2) What drives our economic engine? and (3) What are we deeply passionate about? A blue ocean denotes all industries (1) not yet in existence or (2) that are created by expanding industry boundaries. An organization that follows a blue ocean strategy reduces or eliminates some factors in an industry it competes while raising and creating value to buyers on other factors, resulting in a leap of value for both the organization and its customers.

7. What are marketing dashboards and why are they important?

Answer: A marketing dashboard is the visual display on a single computer screen of the essential information related to achieving a marketing objective. It allows a marketing manager to glance at a graph or table in order to make a decision whether to take action or do more analysis to understand the problem better.

8. What is the difference between a strength and an opportunity in a SWOT analysis?

Answer: Both are positive factors for the organization, but a strength is an internal factor whereas an opportunity is an external one.

9. What is market segmentation?

Answer: Market segmentation involves aggregating prospective buyers into groups, or segments, that (1) have common needs and (2) will respond similarly to a marketing action.

10. What are points of difference and why are they important?

Answer: Points of difference are those characteristics of a product that make it superior to competitive substitutes. They are the single most important factor in the success or failure of a new product.

11. What is the implementation phase of the strategic marketing process?

Answer: This is the phase that involves carrying out the marketing plan that emerges from the planning phase. The implementation phase consists of: (1) obtaining resources; (2) designing the marketing organization; (3) developing schedules; and (4) executing the marketing program designed in the planning phase.

12. How do the goals set for a marketing program in the planning phase relate to the evaluation phase of the strategic marketing process?

Answer: The planning phase objectives are used as the benchmarks with which the actual performance results are compared in the evaluation phase.

CHAPTER 3

1. Describe three generational cohorts.

Answer: (1) Baby boomers are those among the U.S. population born between 1946 and 1964. (2) Generation X are those among the U.S. population born between 1965 and 1976. (3) Generation Y are those among the U.S. population born between 1977 and 1994.

2. Why are many companies developing multicultural marketing programs?

Answer: (1) The racial and ethnic diversity of the United States is changing rapidly due to the increases in the African American, Asian, and Hispanic populations, which increases their economic impact. (2) An accurate understanding of the culture of each group is essential if marketing efforts are to be successful.

3. **How are important values such as "health and fitness" reflected in the marketplace today?**

Answer: Millions of Americans are trying to live a healthier lifestyle. In response, companies have developed vitamins, exercise equipment, fitness drinks, magazines and other products to target these consumers.

4. **What is the difference between a consumer's disposable and discretionary income?**

Answer: Disposable income is the money a consumer has left after paying taxes to use for food, clothing, and shelter. Discretionary income is the money that remains after paying for taxes and necessities.

5. **How does technology impact customer value?**

Answers: (1) Consumers assess value on the basis of other dimensions, such as quality, service, and relationships, due to the decline in the cost of technology. (2) Technology provides value through the development of new products. (3) Technology has changed the way existing products are produced through recycling and precycling.

6. **In pure competition there are a _____ number of sellers.**

Answer: large

7. **The _____ Act was punitive toward monopolies, whereas the _____ Act was preventative.**

Answers: Sherman Antitrust; Clayton

8. **Describe some of the recent changes in trademark law.**

Answer: The *Trademark Law Revision Act* (1988) allows companies to secure rights to a name before its actual use by declaring an intent to use the name. Also, the U.S. Supreme Court recently ruled that a company may obtain trademarks for colors associated with its products.

9. **How does the Better Business Bureau encourage companies to follow its standards for commerce?**

Answer: Companies must agree to follow BBB standards before they are allowed to display the BBB logo.

CHAPTER 4

1. **What are ethics?**

Answer: Ethics are the moral principles and values that govern the actions and decisions of an individual or group. They serve as guidelines on how to act rightly and justly when faced with moral dilemmas.

2. **What are four possible reasons for the present state of ethical conduct in the United States?**

Answer: (1) Pressure on businesspeople to make decisions in a society with diverse value systems. (2) Business decisions being judged publicly by groups with different values and interests. (3) The public's expectations of ethical business behavior have increased. (4) Ethical business conduct may have declined.

3. **What rights are included in the Consumer Bill of Rights?**

Answer: The rights to safety, to be informed, to choose, and to be heard.

4. **Economic espionage includes what kinds of activities?**

Answer: Economic espionage includes trespassing, theft, fraud, misrepresentation, wiretapping, searching competitors' trash, and violations of written and implicit employment agreements with noncompete clauses.

5. **What is meant by moral idealism?**

Answer: Moral idealism is a personal moral philosophy that considers certain individual rights or duties as universal, regardless of the outcome.

6. **What is meant by social responsibility?**

Answer: Social responsibility means that organizations are part of a larger society and are accountable to that society for their actions.

7. **Marketing efforts to produce, promote, and reclaim environmentally sensitive products are called _____ .**

Answer: green marketing

8. **What is a social audit?**

Answer: A social audit is a systematic assessment of a firm's objectives, strategies, and performance in the domain of social responsibility.

CHAPTER 5

1. **What is the first stage in the consumer purchase decision process?**

Answer: problem recognition

2. **The brands a consumer considers buying out of the set of brands in a product class of which the consumer is aware is called the _____ .**

Answer: consideration set

3. **What is the term for postpurchase anxiety?**

Answer: cognitive dissonance

4. **The problem with the Toro Snow Pup was an example of selective _____ .**

Answer: comprehension

5. **What three attitude-change approaches are most common?**

Answer: (1) Change beliefs about the extent to which a brand has certain attributes. (2) Change the perceived importance of the attributes. (3) Add new attributes.

6. **What does *lifestyle* mean?**

Answer: Lifestyle is a mode of living that is identified by how people spend their time and resources, what they consider important in their environment, and what they think of themselves and the world around them.

7. **What are the two primary forms of personal influence?**

Answer: opinion leadership; word of mouth

8. **Marketers are concerned with which types of reference groups?**

Answer: membership groups; aspiration groups; dissociative groups

9. **What two challenges must marketers overcome when marketing to Hispanics?**

Answer: diversity of this subculture; the language barrier

CHAPTER 6

1. **What are the three main types of organizational buyers?**

Answer: industrial firms; resellers; government units

2. **What is the North American Industry Classification System (NAICS)?**

Answer: The NAICS provides common industry definitions for Canada, Mexico, and the United States, which makes easier the measurement of economic activity in the three member countries of NAFTA.

3. **What one department is almost always represented by a person in the buying center?**

Answer: purchasing department

4. **What are the three types of buying situations, or buy classes?**

Answer: straight rebuy, modified rebuy, and new buy

5. **What is a make–buy decision?**

Answer: An evaluation of whether components and assemblies will be purchased from outside suppliers or built by the company itself.

6. **What is a bidder's list?**

Answer: A list of firms believed to be qualified to supply a given item.

7. **What are e-marketplaces?**

Answer: E-marketplaces are online trading communities that bring together buyers and supplier organizations to make possible the real time exchange of information, money, products, and services.

8. **In general, which type of online auction creates upward pressure on bid prices and which type creates downward pressure on bid prices?**

Answer: traditional auction; reverse auction

CHAPTER 7

1. **What is the trade feedback effect?**

Answer: The phenomenon in which one country's imports affect the exports of other countries and vice versa, thus stimulating economic activity in all the nations involved.

2. **What variables influence why some companies and industries in a country succeed globally while others lose ground or fail?**

Answers: (1) factor conditions; (2) demand conditions; (3) related and supporting industries; and (4) company strategy, structure, and rivalry.

3. **What is protectionism?**

Answer: Protectionism is the practice of shielding one or more industries within a country's economy from foreign competition, usually through the use of tariffs or quotas.

4. **The North American Free Trade Agreement was designed to promote free trade among which countries?**

Answer: United States, Canada, and Mexico

5. **What is the difference between a multidomestic marketing strategy and a global marketing strategy?**

Answer: A multidomestic marketing strategy means that firms have as many different product variations, brand names, and advertising programs as countries in which they do business. A global marketing strategy standardizes marketing activities when there are cultural similarities and adapts them when cultures differ.

6. **Semiotics involves the study of _____ .**

Answer: the correspondence between symbols and their role in the assignment of meaning for people

7. **When foreign currencies can buy more U.S. dollars, are U.S. products more or less expensive for a foreign consumer?**

Answer: less expensive

8. **What mode of entry could a company follow if it has no previous experience in global marketing?**

Answer: indirect exporting through intermediaries

9. **How does licensing differ from a joint venture?**

Answer: In licensing, the firm offers the right to a trademark, patent, or trade secret in return for a fee or royalty. In a joint venture, a foreign and a local firm invest together to produce some product or service. The two companies share ownership, control, and profits of the new entity.

10. **Products may be sold globally in three ways. What are they?**

Answers: Products can be sold: (1) in the same form as in its home market (product extension); (2) with some adaptations (product adaptation); and (3) as a totally new product (product invention).

11. **What is dumping?**

Answer: Dumping is when a firm sells a product in a foreign country below its domestic price or below its actual cost.

CHAPTER 8

1. **What is marketing research?**

Answer: Marketing research is the process of defining a marketing problem and opportunity, systematically collecting and analyzing information, and recommending actions.

2. **What are the five steps marketing research uses that help lead to marketing actions?**

Answer: The five steps are: (1) define the problem; (2) develop the research plan; (3) collect relevant data; (4) develop findings; and (5) take marketing actions.

3. **What are constraints as they apply to developing a research plan?**

Answer: Constraints in a decision are the restrictions placed on potential solutions to a problem, such as time and money.

4. **What is the difference between secondary and primary data?**

Answer: Secondary data are facts and figures that have already been recorded before the project at hand, whereas primary data are facts and figures that are newly collected for the project.

5. **What is the difference between observational and questionnaire data?**

Answer: Observational data are facts and figures obtained by watching, either mechanically or in person, how people actually behave. Questionnaire data are facts and figures obtained by asking people about their attitudes, awareness, intentions, and behaviors.

6. **Which survey provides the greatest flexibility for asking probing questions: mail, telephone, or personal interview?**

Answer: personal interview survey

7. **What is the difference between a panel and an experiment?**

Answer: A panel is a sample of consumers or stores from which researchers take a series of measurements. An experiment involves changing a variable in a customer purchase and seeing what happens.

8. **What does a marketing manager mean when she talks about a sales driver?**

Answer: "Drivers" are the factors that influence buying decisions of a household or organization and, hence, sales.

9. **How does data mining differ from traditional marketing research?**

Answer: Data mining is the extraction of hidden predictive information from large databases to find statistical links that suggest marketing actions. Marketing research identifies possible drivers and then collects data.

10. **In the marketing research for Tony's Pizza, what is an example of (a) a finding and (b) a marketing action?**

Answer: (a) Figure 8–9A shows a finding that depicts annual sales from 2001 to 2004. (b) Figure 8–9D shows a finding (the decline in pizza consumption) that leads to a recommendation to develop an ad targeting children 6 to 12 years old.

CHAPTER 9

1. **Market segmentation involves aggregating prospective buyers into groups that have two key characteristics. What are they?**

Answer: The groups should (1) have common needs and (2) will respond similarly to a marketing action.

2. **In terms of market segments and products, what are the three market segmentation strategies?**

Answer: The three market segmentation strategies are: (1) one product and multiple market segments; (2) multiple products and multiple market segments; and (3) "segments of one," or mass customization.

3. **The process of segmenting and targeting markets is a bridge between what two marketing activities?**

Answer: identifying market needs and taking marketing actions

4. **What is the difference between the demographic and behavioral bases of market segmentation?**

Answer: Demographic segmentation is based on some objective physical (gender, race), measurable (age, income), or other classification attribute (birth era, occupation) of prospective customers whereas behavioral segmentation is based on some observable actions or attitudes by prospective customers—such as where they buy, what benefits they seek, how frequently they buy, and why they buy.

5. **What are some criteria used to decide which segments to choose for targets?**

Answer: These criteria include market size, expected growth, competitive position, cost of reaching the segment, and compatibility with the organization's objectives and resources.

6. **In a market–product grid, what factor is estimated or measured for each of the cells?**

Answer: Each cell in the grid can show the estimated market size of a given product sold to a specific market segment.

7. **What is the difference between marketing synergies and product synergies in a market–product grid?**

Answer: Marketing synergies run horizontally across a market–product grid. Each row represents an opportunity for efficiency in the marketing efforts to a market segment. Product synergies run vertically down the market–product grid. Each column represents an opportunity for efficiency in research and development (R&D) and production.

8. **What is product positioning?**

Answer: Product positioning refers to the place an offering occupies in consumers' minds on important attributes relative to competitive offerings.

9. **What are the three kinds of sales forecasting techniques?**

Answer: They are: (1) judgments of the decision maker; (2) surveys of knowledgeable groups; and (3) statistical methods.

CHAPTER 10

1. **Explain the difference between product mix and product line.**

Answer: The product mix is the number of product lines offered by a company. A product line is a group of products that are closely related because they satisfy a class of needs, are used together, are sold to the same customer group, are distributed through the same type of outlets, or fall within a given price range.

2. **What are the four main types of consumer goods?**

Answer: convenience goods, shopping goods, specialty goods, and unsought goods

3. **To which type of good (business or consumer) does the term** *derived demand* **generally apply?**

Answer: business

4. **From a consumer's viewpoint, what kind of innovation would an improved electric toothbrush be?**

Answer: continuous innovation

5. **What does "insignificant point of difference" mean as a reason for new-product failure?**

Answer: The product must have superior characteristics that deliver unique benefits to the user compared to those of competitors.

6. **What step in the new-product process has been added in recent years?**

Answer: New-product strategy development has been added recently by many companies to provide focus for ideas and concepts developed later.

7. **What are the main sources of new-product ideas?**

Answer: Customer and supplier suggestions, employee suggestions, R&D breakthroughs, and competitive products.

8. **What is the difference between internal and external screening and evaluation approaches used by a firm in the new-product process?**

Answer: In internal screening, company employees evaluate the technical feasibility of new product ideas. In external screening, evaluation consists of preliminary testing of the concept (not the actual product) with consumers.

9. **How does the development stage of the new-product process involve testing the product inside and outside the firm?**

Answer: Internally, laboratory tests are done to see if the product achieves the physical, quality, and safety standards; externally, consumer tests are done.

10. **What is a test market?**

Answer: A test market is a city that is viewed as being representative of U.S. consumers in terms of demographics and brand purchase behaviors, is far enough from big markets to allow low-cost advertising, and has tracking systems to measure sales.

11. **What is commercialization of a new product?**

Answer: Commercialization involves positioning and launching new product in-full-scale production and sales and is the most expensive stage for most new products.

CHAPTER 11

1. **Advertising plays a major role in the _____ stage of the product life cycle, and _____ plays a major role in maturity.**

Answer: introductory; sales promotion

2. **How do high-learning and low-learning products differ?**

Answer: A high-learning product requires significant customer education and there is an extended introductory period. A low-learning product requires little customer education because the benefits of purchase are readily understood, resulting in immediate sales.

3. **What are the five categories of product adopters?**

Answer: The five categories of product adopters based on the diffusion of innovation are: (1) innovators—2.5 percent; (2) early adopters—13.5 percent; (3) early majority—34 percent; (4) late majority—34 percent; and (5) laggards—16 percent.

4. **How does a product manager help manage a product's life cycle?**

Answer: A product manager shepherds a product through its life cycle by modifying the product, modifying the market, and repositioning the product.

5. **What does "creating a new use situation" mean in managing a product's life cycle?**

Answer: Finding new uses for an existing product.

6. **Explain the difference between trading up and trading down in repositioning.**

Answer: Trading up involves adding value to the product (or line) through additional features or higher-quality materials. Trading down involves reducing the number of features, quality, or price, or downsizing—reducing the content of packages without changing package size and maintaining or increasing the package price.

7. **What are the five criteria mentioned most often when selecting a good brand name?**

Answer: The brand name should: (1) suggest the product benefits; (2) be memorable, distinctive, and positive; (3) fit the company or product image; (4) have no legal or regulatory restrictions; and (5) be simple and emotional.

8. **What are the three major benefits of packaging and labeling?**

Answer: (1) Communication benefits. (2) Functional benefits. (3) Perceptual benefits.

9. **What is the difference between an expressed and an implied warranty?**

Answer: Express warranties are written statements of liabilities. Implied warranties, which are unwritten, assign responsibility for product deficiencies to the manufacturer even if the retailer sells the product.

CHAPTER 12

1. **What are the four I's of services?**

Answer: intangibility, inconsistency, inseparability, and inventory

2. **Would inventory carrying costs for an accounting firm with certified public accountants be (*a*) high, (*b*) low, or (*c*) nonexistent?**

Answer: (*a*) high because the inventory cost of a service is the cost of paying the person used to provide the service: the salary of the accountant.

3. **To eliminate service inconsistencies, companies rely on _____ and _____ .**

Answer: standardization; training

4. **What are the differences between search, experience, and credence properties?**

Answer: Search properties can be determined before purchase. Experience properties can only be assessed during or after consumption. Credence properties may be impossible to evaluate even after purchase and consumption.

5. **Hertz created its differential advantage at the points of _____ in its customer contact audit.**

Answer: customer interaction

6. **Matching demand with capacity is the focus of _____ management.**

Answer: capacity

7. How does a movie theater use off-peak pricing?

Answer: Movie theaters reduce prices for matinees and often for weekday shows.

8. What factors will influence future changes in services?

Answer: Technology and the global economy.

CHAPTER 13

1. What factors impact the list price to determine the final price?

Answer: discounts, allowances, rebates, and extra fees or surcharges

2. What is the difference between pricing objectives and pricing constraints?

Answer: Pricing objectives involve specifying the role of price in an organization's marketing and strategic plans whereas pricing constraints are factors that limit the range of prices a firm may set.

3. How does the type of competitive market a firm is in affect its range in setting price?

Answer: In a market characterized by pure competition, the marketplace determines the price an individual firm can set. In a market characterized by monopolistic competition, there is some price competition among firms, which allows an individual firm to set a price within a range of prices. In an oligopoly, a firm may either be a price leader and set the market price that other firms follow or be a price follower and set a price based on the prices set by its competitors to aviod a price war. In a pure monopoly, the firm, being the only one in the market, can set any price it wants.

4. What is the difference between a movement along and a shift of a demand curve?

Answer: A movement along a demand curve occurs when the price is lowered and the quantity demanded increases (and vice versa), assuming that other factors remain unchanged. However, if these factors change, then the demand curve will shift.

5. What is total revenue and how is it calculated?

Answer: Total revenue (TR) is the total money received from the sale of product. Total revenue (TR) equals the unit price (P) times the quantity sold (Q) or TR = P × Q.

6. What does it mean if a product has a price elasticity of demand that is greater than 1?

Answer: Elasticities greater than 1 indicate the product is price elastic.

7. What is the difference between fixed costs and variable costs?

Answer: Fixed cost is the sum of the expenses of the firm that are stable and do not change with the quantity of the product that is produced and sold. Variable cost is the sum of the expenses of the firm that vary directly with the quantity of the product that is produced and sold.

8. What is a break-even point?

Answer: A break-even point (BEP) is the quantity at which total revenue and total cost are equal.

CHAPTER 14

1. What are the circumstances in pricing a new product that might support skimming or penetration pricing?

Answer: A firm introducing a new product can use either skimming pricing to set the highest initial price that customers desiring the product are willing to pay or penetration pricing to set a low initial price to appeal immediately to the mass market.

2. What is odd-even pricing?

Answer: Odd-even pricing involves setting prices a few dollars or cents under an even number. Psychologically, a $499.99 price feels lower than $500.00, even though the difference is 1¢.

3. What is standard markup pricing?

Answer: Standard markup pricing entails adding a fixed percentage to the cost of all items in a specific product class.

4. What profit-based pricing approach should a manager use if he or she wants to reflect the percentage of the firm's resources used in obtaining the profit?

Answer: target return-on-investment pricing

5. What is the purpose of loss-leader pricing when used by a retail firm?

Answer: Loss-leader pricing involves deliberately selling a product below its customary price, not to increase sales but to attract customers in hopes they will buy other products as well.

6. Why would a seller choose a flexible-price policy over a one-price policy?

Answer: A flexible-price policy involves setting different prices for products and services depending on individual buyers and purchasing situations in light of demand, cost, and competitive factors instead of setting one price for all buyers.

7. If a firm wished to encourage repeat purchases by a buyer throughout a year, would a cumulative or noncumulative quantity discount be a better strategy?

Answer: cumulative quantity discount

8. Which pricing practices are covered by the Sherman Act?

Answer: horizontal price-fixing and predatory pricing

CHAPTER 15

1. What is meant by a marketing channel?

Answer: A marketing channel consists of individuals and firms involved in the process of making a product or service available for use or consumption by consumers or industrial users.

2. What are the three basic functions performed by intermediaries?

Answer: Intermediaries perform transactional, logistical, and facilitating functions.

3. What is the difference between a direct and an indirect channel?

Answer: A direct channel is one in which a producer of consumer or business goods and services and ultimate consumers or industrial users deal directly with each other whereas an indirect channel has intermediaries that are inserted between the producer and consumers or industrial users and who perform numerous channel functions.

4. Why are channels for business products typically shorter than channels for consumer products?

Answer: Business channels are typically shorter because business users are fewer in number, tend to be more concentrated geographically, and buy in larger quantities.

5. What is the principal distinction between a corporate vertical marketing system and an administered vertical marketing system?

Answer: A corporate vertical marketing system combines successive stages of production and distribution under a single ownership. An administered vertical marketing system achieves coordination by the size and influence of one channel member rather than through ownership.

6. What are the three degrees of distribution density?

Answer: intensive; exclusive; selective.

7. What are the three questions marketing executives consider when choosing a marketing channel and intermediaries?

Answer: The three questions are: (1) Which will provide the best coverage of the target market? (2) Which will best satisfy the buying requirements of the target market? (3) Which will be the most profitable?

8. What is meant by *exclusive dealing*?

Answer: Exclusive dealing exists when a supplier requires channel members to sell only its products or restricts distributors from selling directly competitive products. It is specifically prohibited under the *Clayton Act* when it lessens competition or creates monopolies.

CHAPTER 16

1. **What is the principal difference between a marketing channel and a supply chain?**
   Answer: A supply chain also includes suppliers who provide raw materials to a manufacturer as well as the wholesalers and retailers—the marketing channel—who deliver the finished goods to ultimate consumers.

2. **The choice of a supply chain involves what three steps?**
   Answer: (1) Understand the customer. (2) Understand the supply chain. (3) Harmonize the supply chain with the marketing strategy.

3. **The objective of information and logistics management in a supply chain is to _____.**
   Answer: minimize logistics costs while delivering maximum customer service

4. **How does consumer demand information increase supply chain responsiveness and efficiency?**
   Answer: Demand information improves supply chain responsiveness because customers will find the products when and where they want them. Demand information improves supply chain efficiency because firms are better able to forecast customer needs and to produce, transport, and store the required amount of inventory.

5. **What is the relationship between the number of warehouses a company operates, its inventory costs, and its transportation costs?**
   Answer: As the number of warehouses increases, inventory costs rise and transportation costs fall. Because more inventory is warehoused, it is transported in larger volumes closer to customers. The net effect is to minimize the total costs of logistics.

6. **What are the basic trade-offs between the five modes of transportation?**
   Answer: Each mode of transportation can be evaluated against six service criteria: cost, time, capability, dependability, accessibility, and frequency.

7. **What types of inventory should use storage warehouses and which type should use distribution centers?**
   Answer: Storage warehouses are best suited for goods that will not be needed for substantial periods of time. Distribution centers are used if inventory needs to be in decentralized locations to facilitate sorting or consolidating products from different plants or suppliers, ingredients needs to be blended, or labeling and repackaging need to be done before the goods are shipped to customers.

8. **What are the strengths and weaknesses of a just-in-time system?**
   Answer: A JIT system saves money on inventory if demand forecasting is reliable. However, it is not suitable for inventories that are to be stored over significant periods of time.

CHAPTER 17

1. **When Polo makes shoes to a customer's exact preferences, what utility is provided?**
   Answer: form utility

2. **Two measures of the impact of retailing in the global economy are _____ and _____.**
   Answer: total sales; number of employees

3. **Centralized decision making and purchasing are an advantage of _____ ownership.**
   Answer: chain

4. **What are some examples of new forms of self-service retailers?**
   Answer: Delta Air Line and Hilton self-service kiosk for customer check-in as well as others.

5. **Would a shop for big men's clothes carrying pants in sizes 40 to 60 have a broad or deep product line?**
   Answer: deep product line

6. **Successful catalog retailers often send _____ catalogs to _____ markets identified in their databases.**
   Answer: specialty; niche

7. **How are retailers increasing consumer interest and involvement in online retailing?**
   Answer: Retailers have improved the online retailing experience by adding experiential or interactive activities to their websites through virtual models or the ability to customize a purchase.

8. **Where are direct selling retail sales growing? Why?**
   Answer: Direct-selling retailers are expanding into other global markets due to a lack of effective distribution channels and consumer knowledge about products and brands.

9. **What are the two dimensions of the retail positioning matrix?**
   Answer: breadth of product line and value added

10. **How does original markup differ from maintained markup?**
    Answer: The original markup is the difference between retailer cost and initial selling price whereas maintained markup is the difference between the final selling price and retailer cost.

11. **A huge shopping strip with multiple anchor stores is a _____ center.**
    Answer: power

12. **According to the wheel of retailing, when a new retail form appears, how would you characterize its image?**
    Answer: A low-status, low-margin, low-price outlet.

13. **Market share is usually fought out before the _____ stage of the retail life cycle.**
    Answer: maturity

14. **What is an influence effect?**
    Answer: The complementary role that different communication and delivery channels have on sales.

CHAPTER 18

1. **What are the six elements required for communication to occur?**
   Answer: They are a source, a message, a channel of communication, a receiver, and the processes of encoding and decoding.

2. **A difficulty for U.S. companies advertising in international markets is that the audience does not share the same _____.**
   Answer: field of experience

3. **A misprint in a newspaper ad is an example of _____.**
   Answer: noise

4. **Explain the difference between advertising and publicity when both appear on television.**
   Answer: Since advertising space on TV is paid for, a firm can control what it wants to say and to whom the message is sent. Since publicity is an indirectly paid presentation of a message about a firm or its goods or services, there is little control over what is said to whom or when.

5. **Which promotional element should be offered only on a short-term basis?**
   Answer: sales promotion

6. **Cost per contact is high with the _____ element of the promotional mix.**
   Answer: personal selling

7. **Describe the promotional objective for each stage of the product life cycle.**
   Answer: Introduction—to inform; growth—to persuade; maturity—to remind; and decline—none.

8. **At what stage of the consumer purchase decision is the importance of personal selling highest? Why?**
   Answer: The purchase stage because salespeople can provide sales assistance to prospective customers and negotiate terms of the sale.

9. **Explain the differences between a push strategy and a pull strategy.**
   Answer: In a push strategy, a firm directs the promotional mix to channel members to gain their cooperation to carry the product. In a pull strategy, a firm directs the promotional mix at ultimate consumers to encourage them to ask retailers for the product, who then orders it from wholesalers.

10. What are the characteristics of good promotion objectives?

Answer: Promotion objectives should possess three important qualities. They should (1) be designed for a well-defined target audience, (2) be measurable, and (3) cover a specified time period.

11. What is the weakness of the percentage of sales budgeting approach?

Answer: The major fallacy is that sales cause promotion. By using this method, a company may reduce its promotion budget because of downturns in actual past or projected future sales—situations where promotion may be needed the most.

12. How have advertising agencies changed to facilitate the use of IMC programs?

Answer: Some agencies have adopted: (1) a total communications solutions approach; (2) a long-term perspective in which all forms of promotion are integrated; and (3) an IMC audit to analyze the internal communication network of their clients.

13. The ability to design and use direct marketing programs has increased with the availability of _____ and _____.

Answer: computers; databases

14. What are the three types of responses generated by direct marketing activities?

Answer: They are direct orders, lead generation, and traffic generation.

CHAPTER 19

1. What is the difference between pioneering and competitive ads?

Answer: Pioneering ads tell people what a product is, what it can do, and where it can be found. Competitive ads promote a specific brand's features and benefits to persuade the target market to select the firm's brand rather than that of a competitor.

2. What is the purpose of an institutional advertisement?

Answer: To build goodwill or an image for an organization.

3. What other decisions can advertising objectives influence?

Answer: Advertising objectives can influence the decisions such as selecting media, evaluating an advertising campaign, establishing the importance and sequence of the stages of the hierarchy of effects, and choosing the type and appeal of the advertisement that is designed.

4. What is a potential shortcoming of using a celebrity spokesperson?

Answer: The spokesperson's image may change to be inconsistent with the image of the company or brand.

5. You see the same ad in *Time* and *Fortune* magazines and on billboards and TV. Is this an example of reach or frequency?

Answer: frequency

6. Why has the Internet become a popular advertising medium?

Answer: The Internet offers a visual message, can use both audio and video, is interactive through rich media, and tends to reach younger consumers.

7. What factors must be considered when choosing among alternative media?

Answer: The media habits of the target audience, the product's attributes, and the reach and cost, as measured by CPM.

8. Explain the difference between pretesting and posttesting advertising copy.

Answer: Pretests are conducted before ads are placed in any medium to determine whether the ads communicate the intended message or to select among alternative versions. Posttests are shown to the target audience to determine whether it accomplished its intended purpose.

9. What is the difference between aided and unaided recall posttests?

Answer: Aided recall involves showing an ad to respondents who then are asked if their previous exposure to it was through reading, viewing, or listening. Unaided recall involves asking respondents if they remember an ad without any prompting to determine if they saw or heard its message.

10. Which sales promotional tool is most common for new products?

Answer: samples

11. What's the difference between a coupon and a deal?

Answer: A coupon provides a reduced price for an item based on redemption. A deal is a short-term price reduction.

12. Which trade promotion is used on an ongoing basis?

Answer: trade allowance

13. What is a news release?

Answer: An announcement regarding changes in the company or the product line.

14. What is the difference between government regulation and self-regulation?

Answer: Government regulation involves laws or other controls set by an agency of local, state, or federal government, whereas self-regulation involves ethical guidelines for business practices set by advertising agencies, trade associations, and marketing organizations.

CHAPTER 20

1. What is personal selling?

Answer: Personal selling involves the two-way flow of communication between a buyer and seller, often in a face-to-face encounter, designed to influence a person's or group's purchase decision.

2. What is involved in sales management?

Answer: Sales management involves planning the selling program and implementing and controlling the personal selling effort of the firm.

3. What is the principal difference between an order taker and an order getter?

Answer: An order taker processes routine orders or reorders for products that were already sold by the company. An order getter sells in a conventional sense and identifies prospective customers, provides customers with information, persuades customers to buy, closes sales, and follows up on their use of a product or service.

4. What is team selling?

Answer: The practice of using an entire team of professionals in selling to and servicing major customers.

5. What are the six stages in the personal selling process?

Answer: The six stages in the personal selling process are: (1) prospecting, (2) preapproach, (3) approach, (4) presentation, (5) close, and (6) follow-up.

6. What is the distinction between a lead and a qualified prospect?

Answer: A lead is the name of a person who may be a possible customer whereas a qualified prospect is an individual who wants the product, can afford to buy it, and is the decision maker.

7. Which presentation format is most consistent with the marketing concept? Why?

Answer: The need-satisfaction presentation format of probing and listening by the salesperson to identify needs and interests of prospective buyers and then tailoring the presentation to the prospect and highlighting product benefits, consistent with the marketing concept.

8. What are the three types of selling objectives?

Answer: They are: (1) output-related (dollars or unit sales, new customers, profit); (2) input-related (sales calls, selling expenses); and (3) behavioral-related (product knowledge, customer service, selling and communication skills).

9. What three factors are used to structure sales organizations?

Answer: geography, customer, and product or service

10. How does emotional intelligence tie to adaptive selling?

Answer: Emotional intelligence is the ability to understand one's own emotions and the emotions of people with whom one interacts on a daily basis, qualities that are important for adaptive selling.

CHAPTER 21

1. **The consumer-initiated practice of generating content on a marketer's website that is custom tailored to an individual's specific needs and preferences is called _____.**

   Answer: personalization

2. **Companies produce a customer experience through what seven website design elements?**

   Answer: These design elements are: context, content, community, customization, communication, connection, and commerce.

3. **What is the eight-second rule?**

   Answer: The eight-second rule is a view that customers will abandon their efforts to enter and navigate a website if download time exceeds eight seconds.

4. **Which online consumer lifestyle segment spends the most money online and which spends the most time online?**

   Answer: The "brand loyalists" segment spends the most money online whereas the "hooked, online, and single" segment spends more time online.

5. **What are the six reasons consumers prefer to shop and buy online?**

   Answer: convenience, choice, customization, communication, cost, and control

6. **A cross-channel shopper is _____.**

   Answer: a consumer who researches offerings online and then purchases them at retail stores

7. **Channel conflict between manufacturers and retailers is likely to arise when manufacturers use _____ websites.**

   Answer: transactional

CHAPTER 22

1. **What are the four basic practices "that really work"—that are characteristics of industry-leading firms?**

   Answer: These four basic business and management practices are: (1) strategy; (2) execution; (3) culture; and (4) structure.

2. **What is the significance of the S shape of the sales response function in Figure 22–1?**

   Answer: Different levels of marketing effort will cause different rates of sales revenue growth. In Figure 22–1, an additional $1 million of marketing effort results in far greater increases of sales revenue in the midrange of the curve than at either end.

3. **What are two kinds of marketing plans?**

   Answer: They are long-range and annual marketing plans.

4. **Describe Porter's four generic business strategies.**

   Answer: Porter's four generic business strategies are:

   - *Cost leadership strategy.* Focuses on reducing expenses and, in turn, lowers product prices while targeting a broad array of market segments.
   - *Differentiation strategy.* Requires products to have significant points of difference in product offerings, brand image, higher quality, advanced technology, or superior service to charge a higher price while targeting a broad array of market segments.
   - *Cost focus strategy.* Involves controlling expenses and, in turn, lowering product prices targeted at a narrow range of market segments.
   - *Differentiation focus strategy.* Requires products to have significant points of difference to target one or only a few market segments.

5. **What are four alternative ways to increase a firm's revenues when using the diversification analysis framework?**

   Answer: The four profit enhancement options strategies are:

   - *Market penetration.* Increase market share in existing markets with current products (present markets, present products).
   - *Product development.* Expand product line by introducing new products sold to existing customers (present markets, new products).
   - *Market development.* Find new markets in which to sell existing products (new markets, present products).
   - *Diversification.* Find new markets in which to sell new products (new markets, new products).

6. **Where do (*a*) marketing synergies and (*b*) R&D–manufacturing synergies appear when using the synergy analysis framework?**

   Answer: Using a market-product grid framework, (*a*) marketing synergies run horizontally across the rows and (*b*) R&D–manufacturing synergies run vertically down the columns.

7. **What is the meaning and importance of a program champion?**

   Answer: A program champion is able and willing to cut red tape and move the program forward to get the program implemented.

8. **Explain the difference between sequential and concurrent tasks in a Gantt chart.**

   Answer: In sequential scheduling, certain tasks must be completed before subsequent tasks can be started. In concurrent scheduling, several tasks can be worked on at the same time.

9. **What are four groupings used within a typical marketing organization?**

   Answer: product line, functional, geographical, and market-based

10. **What two components of the strategic marketing process are compared to evaluate a marketing program?**

    Answer: Quantified goals from the marketing plans developed in the planning phase have been accomplished by the marketing actions taken in the implementation phase and measured as results in the control phase.

CHAPTER NOTES

CHAPTER 1

1. The 3M Post-it® Flag Highlighter and Post-it® Flag Pen examples are based on a series of interviews and meetings with David Windorski, 3M, from 2004 to 2007.

2. Evan Ramstad, "Flat-Panel TV Jam," *The Wall Street Journal,* January 3, 2007, p. B9.

3. John Reinan, "Millionaire Whiz Kid," *Star Tribune,* October 13, 2006, pp. A1, A18; John Cloud, "The YouTube Gurus," *Time,* December 25, 2006–January 1, 2007, pp. 66–74; Lev Grossman, "Invention of the Year 2006," *Time,* November 13, 2006, pp. 64–65; and "Two Kings Get Together," *The Economist,* October 14, 2006, pp. 67–68.

4. To compare the 2004 and 2007 American Marketing Association definitions of "marketing," see Shelby D. Hunt, "The 2007, AMA, Committee-Recommended Definition of Marketing" prepared for *AMA Summer* Educators' Conference, August, 2007, p. 1.

5. Richard P. Bagozzi, "Marketing as Exchange," *Journal of Marketing,* October 1975, pp. 32–39; and Gregory T. Gundlach and Patrick E. Murphy, "Ethical and Legal Foundations of Relational Marketing Exchanges," *Journal of Marketing,* October 1993, pp. 35–46.

6. "The Rise of the Creative Consumer," *The Economist,* March 12, 2005, pp. 54–60.

7. Productscan® Online database of new products, from *Marketing Intelligence Service,* December 17, 2003, www.productscan.com.

8. Robert M. McMath and Thom Forbes, "What *Were* They Thinking?" (New York: Times Business, 1998), pp. 3–22.

9. From the New Product Works website, "Favorite Failures," www.newproductworks.com.

10. From the Hot Pockets website, www.chefamerica.com and www.hotpockets.com.

11. From the iRobot website, www.irobot.com; Peter Lewis, "Keep Up With the Jetsons," *Fortune,* February 20, 2006, p. 146.

12. Chad Terhune, "Coca-Cola's Low-Carb Soda Loses Its Fizz," *The Wall Street Journal,* October 20, 2004, pp. B1, B9; "Things Go Worse with Coke," *The Economist,* December 17, 2005, p. 61; and Chad Terhune, "Coke Tries to Pop Back in Vital Japan Market," *The Wall Street Journal,* July 11, 2006, pp. C1, C3.

13. Jonathan Clements, "Dodging the Hazards of Post-College Life: Financial Strategies for New Graduates," *The Wall Street Journal,* December 7, 2005, p. D1; Kara McGuire, "Sweat the Small Stuff," *Star Tribune,* September 9, 2005, p. D6; Amy Hoak, "Debt 101 for College Kids," *Star Tribune,* September 17, 2006, p. D7; John Ewoldt, "Give the Kids Credit: Teach Them About Finances Early," *Star Tribune,* August 20, 2006, pp. E1, E3; and Susan Feyder, "Credit Card Payments to Go Up—for Your Own Good," *Star Tribune,* June 12, 2005, pp. D1, D10.

14. E. Jerome McCarthy, "Basic Marketing: A Managerial Approach" (Homewood, Illinois: Richard D. Irwin, 1960); and Walter van Waterschoot and Christophe Van den Bulte, "The 4P Classification of the Marketing Mix Revisited," *Journal of Marketing,* October 1992, pp. 83–93.

15. Ashish Kothari and Joseph Lackner, "A Value Based Approach to Management," *Journal of Business and Industrial Marketing,* 21, no. 4, pp. 243–49; and James C. Anderson, James A. Narius, and Wouter van Rossum, "Customer Value Propositions in Business Markets," *Harvard Business Review,* March 2006, pp. 91–99.

16. For an examination of both the drivers and outcomes of consumer satisfaction programs, see Leslie M. Fine, "Spotlight on Marketing," *Business Horizons,* 49 (2006), pp. 179–83.

17. Werner J. Reinartz and V. Kumar, "On the Profitability of Long-Life Customers in a Noncontractual Setting: An Empirical Investigation and Implications for Marketing," *Journal of Marketing,* October 2000, pp. 17–35; and "What's a Loyal Customer Worth?" *Fortune,* December 11, 1995, p. 182.

18. Robert W. Palmatier, Rajiv P. Dant, Dhruv Grewal, and Kenneth R. Evans, "Factors Influencing the Effectiveness of Relationship Marketing: A Meta-Analysis," *Journal of Relationship Marketing,* October 2006, pp. 136–53; and William Boulding, Richard Staelin, Michael Ehret, and Wesley J. Johnson, "A Customer Relationship Management Roadmap: What Is Known, Potential Pitfalls, and Where to Go," *Journal of Marketing,* October 2005, pp. 155–66.

19. Susan Foumier, Susan Dobscha, and David Glen Mick, "Preventing the Premature Death of Relationship Marketing," *Harvard Business Review,* January–February 1998, pp. 42–51.

20. Reservations about and elaborations of these simplified stages appear in D.G. Brian Jones and Eric H. Shaw, "A History of Marketing Thought," Chapter 2 in *Handbook of Marketing,* edited by Barton Weitz and Robin Wensley (London: Sage Publications, 2006), pp. 39–65; Frederic E. Webster, Jr., "The Role of Marketing and the Firm," Chapter 3 in *Handbook of Marketing,* ed. Barton Weitz and Robin Wensley (London: Sage Publications, 2006), pp. 66–82; and Frederick E. Webster, Jr., "Back to the Future: Integrating Marketing as Tactics, Strategy and Organizational Culture," *Journal of Marketing,* October 2005, pp. 4–8.

21. Robert F. Keith, "The Marketing Revolution," *Journal of Marketing,* January 1960, pp. 35–38.

22. *Annual Report* (New York: General Electric Company, 1952), p. 21.

23. John C. Narver, Stanley F. Slater, and Brian Tietje, "Creating a Market Orientation," *Journal of Market Focused Management,* no. 2 (1998), pp. 241–55; Stanley F. Slater and John C. Narver, "Market Orientation and the Learning Organization," *Journal of Marketing,* July 1995, pp. 63–74; and George S. Day, "The Capabilities of Market-Driven Organizations," *Journal of Marketing,* October 1994, pp. 37–52.

24. The definition of customer relationship management is adapted from Rajendra K. Srivastava, Tasadduq A. Shervani, and Liam Fahey, "Marketing, Business Processes, and Shareholder Value: An Embedded View of Marketing Activities and the Discipline of Marketing," *Journal of Marketing,* special issue (1999), pp. 168–79.

25. Gary F. Gebhardt, Gregory S. Carpenter, and John F. Sherry Jr., "Creating a Market Orientation: A Longitudinal, Multifirm, Grounded Analysis of Cultural Transformation," *Journal of Marketing,* October 2006, pp. 37–55.

26. Christopher Meyer and Andre Schwager, "Understanding Customer Experience," *Harvard Business Review,* February 2007, pp. 117–26.

27. Michael E. Porter and Claas van der Linde, "Green and Competitive Ending the Stalemate," *Harvard Business Review,* September–October 1995, pp. 120–34; Jacquelyn Ottman, "Edison Winners Show Smart Environmental Marketing," *Marketing News,* July 17, 1995, pp. 16, 19; and Jacquelyn Ottman, "Mandate for the '90s: Green Corporate Image," *Marketing News,* September 11, 1995, p. 8.

28. Shelby D. Hunt and John J. Burnett, "The Macromarketing/Micromarketing Dichotomy: A Taxonomical Model," *Journal of Marketing,* Summer 1982, pp. 9–26.

29. Philip Kotler and Sidney J. Levy, "Broadening the Concept of Marketing," *Journal of Marketing,* January 1969, pp. 10–15.

30. Jim Rendon, "When Nations Need a Little Marketing," *The New York Times,* November 23, 2003, p. BU6.

31. "Marketing Museums: When Merchants Enter the Temple," *The Economist,* April 21, 2001, pp. 64–66; and Lisa Snedeker, "Putting Their Money on Monets," *Star Tribune,* August 16, 2001, p. F16.

32. Bernard Stamler, "Temples of Culture Are Needy, Too. Tai Chi, Anyone?" *The New York Times,* April 23, 2003, p. 2.

33. Based on "The State Hermitage Museum," a case written by Olga Saguinova, Michael J. Vessey, and William Rudelius appearing in Rudelius et al., *Marketing,* 1st Russian ed. (Moscow: DeNovo Publishing Company, 2001), pp. 594–96; and Peter Baker, "Historically Rich Russia Struggles to Attract Tourists," *Star Tribune,* September 9, 2001, p. G5.

34. John A. Byrne, "Caught in the Net," *BusinessWeek,* August 27, 2001, pp. 114–16; and Gary Gentile, "eToast," *Star Tribune,* March 3, 2001, pp. DI, D2.

35. William L. Wilkie and Elizabeth S. Moore, "Marketing's Relationship to Society," Chapter 1 in *Handbook of Marketing,* ed. Barton Weitz and Robin Wensley (London: Sage Publications, 2006), pp. 9–38.

3M's Post-it® Flag Highlighters: This case was written by Michael J. Vessey and William Rudelius and is based on personal interviews with David Windorski and 3M in 2007.

CHAPTER 2

1. Information obtained from selected Web pages and press releases from the Ben & Jerry's website. See www.benjerry.com.

2. Blair S. Walker, "Good-Humored Activist Back to the Fray," *USA Today,* December 8, 1992, pp. 1B–2B.

3. Jim Castelli, "Finding the Right Fit: Are You Weird Enough?" *HR Magazine,* September 1990, pp. 38–39.

4. "Ben & Jerry's Serves Up Cone Contest, Sampling," *PROMO Magazine,* May 25, 2006.

5. Roger Kerin and Robert Peterson, *Strategic Marketing Problems: Cases and Comments,* 11th ed. (Upper Saddle River, NJ: Prentice Hall, 2007), p. 141.

6. Michael E. Porter, "What Is Strategy?" *Harvard Business Review* OnPoint Article, November–December 1996, p. 2.

7. For a discussion on how industries are defined and offerings are classified, see the following resources: the American Marketing Association website, which provides one definition of an industry (www.marketingpower.com/mg-dictionary-view1509.php); and the Census Bureau's Economic Classification Policy Committee Issues Paper #1 (www.census.gov/epcd/naics/issues1), which aggregates industries in the NAICS (www.census.gov/epcd/www/naicsdev.htm) from a "production-oriented" view (see Chapter 6).

8. W. Chan Kim and Reneé Mauborgne, "Blue Ocean Strategy: From Theory to Practice," *California Management Review* 47, no. 3, Spring 2005, p. 105; Porter, "What Is Strategy?" p. 2.

9. Costas Markides, "What Is Strategy and How Do You Know if You Have One?" *Business Strategy Review* 15, no. 2, Summer 2004, p. 5.

10. The definition of *strategy* reflects thoughts appearing in Porter, "What Is Strategy?" pp. 4, 8; a condensed definition of strategy from the American Marketing Association website; Gerry Johnson, Kevan Scholes, and Richard Wittington, *Exploring Corporate Strategy* (Upper Saddle River, NJ: Prentice Hall, 2005), p. 10.

11. Roger A. Kerin, "Strategic Marketing and the CMO," *Journal of Marketing,* October 2005, pp. 12–13; and The CMO Council: Biographies of Selected Advisory Board Members. See www.cmocouncil.org/advisory_board.html.

12. Roger A. Kerin, Vijay Mahajan, and P. Rajan Varadarajan, *Contemporary Perspectives on Strategic Marketing Planning* (Boston: Allyn & Bacon, 1990), chap. 1; and Orville C. Walker, Jr., Harper W. Boyd, Jr., and Jean-Claude Larreche, *Marketing Strategy* (Burr Ridge, IL: Richard D. Irwin, 1992), chapters 1 and 2.

13. Taken in part from Jim Collins and Jerry I. Porras, *Built to Last: Successful Habits of Visionary Companies* (New York: HarperCollins Publishers, 2002), p. 54.

14. Ibid., p. 54; and Jim Collins, *Good to Great: Why Some Companies Make the Leap . . . and Others Don't* (New York: HarperCollins Publishers, 2001), p. 195.

15. Collins and Porras, *Built to Last,* p. 73; Patrick M. Lencioni "Make Your Values Mean Something," *Harvard Business Review,* July 2002, p. 6; and Aubrey Malphurs, *Values-Driven Leadership: Discovering and Developing Your Core Values for Ministry,* 2nd ed. (Grand Rapids, MI: BakerBooks, 2004), p. 31.

16. See www.microsoft.com/smallbusiness/resources/expert/strauss092205.mspx; Louise Lee, "Wizards in the Valley," *BusinessWeek,* April 16, 2007, p. 88.

17. Collins and Porras, *Built to Last,* p. 73; and Lencioni, "Make Your Values Mean Something," p. 6.

18. Catherine M. Dalton, "When Organizational Values are Mere Rhetoric," *Business Horizons* 49 (September–October 2006), p. 345; and Van Lee, pp. 62–63.

19. Collins and Porras, *Built to Last,* pp. 94–95; and Tom Krattenmaker, "Write a Mission Statement that Your Company Is Willing to Live," *Harvard Management Communication Letter,* March 2002, pp. 3–4.

20. See www.editinternational.com/index.php?pag=stories.php?cat=3f550e67b9540.

21. Nikos Mourkogiannis, "The Realist's Guide to Moral Purpose," *Strategy+Business,* no. 41 (Winter 2005), pp. 42, 45, 47.

22. Sheila M. J. Bonini, Lenny T. Mendonca, and Jeremy M. Oppenheim, "When Social Issues Become Strategic," *The McKinsey Quarterly,* 2006, no. 2, pp. 23, 25, 30–31.

23. Kenneth E. Goodpaster and Thomas E. Holloran, "Anatomy of Spiritual and Social Awareness: The Case of Medtronic, Inc.," *Third International Symposium on Catholic Social Thought and Management Education,* Goa, India, 1999, pp. 9–11.

24. Theodore Levitt, "Marketing Myopia," *Harvard Business Review,* July–August 1960, pp. 45–56.

25. Katherine Ellison, "The Bottom Line Redefined," *Nature Conservancy,* Winter 2002, pp. 45–50.

26. George Stalk, Phillip Evans, and Lawrence E. Shulman, "Competing on Capabilities: The New Rules of Corporate Strategy," *Harvard Business Review,* March–April 1992, pp. 57–69; and Darrell K. Rigby, *Management Tools 2007: An Executive's Guide* (Boston: Bain & Company, 2007), p. 22.

27. Michael Arndt, "High-Tech and Handcrafted," *BusinessWeek,* July 5, 2004, pp. 86–87.

28. Roger A. Kerin and Robert A. Peterson, *Strategic Marketing Problems: Cases and Comments,* pp. 2–3; and Derek F. Abell, *Defining the Business* (Englewood Cliffs, NJ: Prentice Hall, 1980), p. 18.

29. Christopher Meyer, *Fast Cycle Time* (New York: Free Press, 1993).

30. Robert D. Hof, "How to Hit a Moving Target," *BusinessWeek,* August 21, 2006, p. 3; and Peter Kim, *Reinventing the Marketing Organization* (Cambridge, MA: Forrester, July 13, 2006), pp. 7, 9, 17.

31. Adapted from *The Experience Curve Reviewed, IV. The Growth Share Matrix of the Product Portfolio* (Boston: The Boston Consulting Group, 1973).

32. Kerin, Mahajan, and Vardarajan, *Contemporary Perspectives,* p. 52.

33. Steve Hamm, "Kodak's Moment of Truth," *BusinessWeek,* February 19, 2007, pp. 42–49.

34. William C. Symonds, "Kodak Rewrites the Book on Printing," *BusinessWeek,* September 4, 2006, p. 83.

35. "Eastman Kodak Company Strategy Review and Outlook," February 8, 2007, p. 59.

36. Jefferson Graham, "Kodak Plans to Sell Inkjet Printers with Cheaper Ink," *USA Today,* February 6, 2007, p. 51; and Stephen H. Wildstrom, "Kodak Moments for Less," *Business Week,* May 14, 2007, p. 24.

37. William M. Bulkeley, "When Neighbors Become Rivals," *The Wall Street Journal,* February 22, 2007, pp. B1, B8.

38. Strengths and weaknesses of the BCG technique are based on Derek F. Abell and John S. Hammond, *Strategic Market Planning: Problem and Analytic Approaches* (Englewood Cliffs, NJ: Prentice Hall, 1979); Yoram Wind, Vijay Mahajan, and Donald Swire, "An Empirical Comparison of Standardized Portfolio Models," *Journal of Marketing,* Spring 1983, pp. 89–99; and J. Scott Armstrong and Roderick J. Brodie, "Effects of Portfolio Planning Methods on Decision Making: Experimental Results," *International Journal of Research in Marketing,* Winter 1994, pp. 73–84.

39. Jim Collins, *Good to Great: Why Some Companies Make the Leap . . . and Others Don't,* pp. 13, 90–91, 93, 95–96, 107.

40. W. Chan Kim and Mauborgne, *Blue Ocean Strategy: How to Create Uncontested Market Space and Make the Competition Irrelevant* (Boston: Harvard Business School Press, 2005), pp. x, 4–5, 8, 13, 16, and 49; and Kim and Mauborgne, "Blue Ocean Strategy: From Theory to Practice," p. 106.

41. Brian Levy, "Value Pioneering—How to Discover Your Own 'Blue Ocean': Interview with W. Chan Kim and Renée Mauborgne," *Strategy & Leadership* 13, no. 6 (2005), p. 14.

42. Kim and Mauborgne, *Blue Ocean Strategy,* pp. 38–40.

43. W. Chan Kim and Renée Mauborgne, "Blue Ocean Strategy," *Harvard Business Review,* October 2004, pp. 7–8.

44. The definition is adapted from Stephen Few, *Information Dashboard Design: The Effective Visual Communication of Data,* (Sebastopol, CA: O'Reilly Media, Inc., 2006) pp. 2–46.

45. *Ibid;* Bruce H. Clark, Andrew V. Abela, and Tim Ambler, "Behind the Wheel," *Marketing Management,* May–June 2006, pp. 19–23; Spencer E. Ante, "Giving the Boss the Big Picture," *Business Week,* February 13, 2006, pp. 48-49; *Dashboard Tutorial,* (Cupertino, CA: Apple Computer, Inc.; 2006).

46. Stephen Few, *Information Dashboard Design: The Effective Visual Communication of Data,* p. 13.

47. Michael Krauss, "Balance Attention to Metrics with Intuition," *Marketing News,* June 1, 2007, pp. 6–8; John Davis, *Measuring Marketing: 103 Key Metrics Every Marketer Needs* (Singapore: John Wiley & Sons (Asia) Pte Ltd., 2007); Paul W. Farris, Neil T. Bendle, Phillip E. Pfeifer, and David J. Reibstein, *Marketing Metrics* (Upper Saddle River, NJ: Wharton School Publishing, 2006); and Marcel Corstjens and Jeffrey Merrihue, "Optimal Marketing," *Harvard Business Review,* October 2003, pp. 114–121.

48. The now-classic reference on effective graphic presentation is Edward R. Tufte. *The Visual Display Of Quantitative Information,* 2nd Edition (Chesire, CN: graphic Press, 2001); also see Stephen Few, *Information Dashboard Design: The Effective Visual Communication of Data,* Chapters 3–5.

49. Linda Swenson and Kenneth E. Goodpaster, *Medtronic in China (A)* (Minneapolis, MN: University of St. Thomas, 1999), pp. 4–5.

50. Bulkeley, "When Neighbors Become Rivals," p. B8.

51. "Has Kodak Missed the Moment?" *The Economist,* January 3, 2004, pp. 46–47.

52. Hamm, "Kodak's Moment of Truth," pp. 45–49.

53. Laura Petrecca, "Filling Up 'Greener,'" Advertising/Marketing section, *USA Today,* April 23, 2007. See http://www.usatoday.com.

54. Adapted from "New Campaign Intended to Show the More Welcoming Side of Gas Stations," *Convenience Store Decisions,* April 5, 2007. See http://www.csdecisions.com/classes/article/articledraw_p.aspx. See also www.bp.com and "The Green Team," p. 23.

The BP video case was prepared by Michael J. Vessey based on interviews with Kathy Seegebrecht and Ann Hand.

APPENDIX A

1. Personal interview with Arthur R. Kydd, St. Croix Management Group.

2. Examples of guides to writing marketing plans include William A. Cohen, *The Marketing Plan,* 5th ed. (New York: Wiley, 2006); and Roman G. Hiebing, Jr., and Scott W. Cooper, *The Successful Marketing Plan: A Disciplined and Comprehensive Approach* (New York: McGraw-Hill, 2003).

3. Examples of guides to writing business plans include Rhonda Abrams, *The Successful Business Plan: Secrets & Strategies,* 4th ed. (Grants Pass, OR: Oasis Press/PSI Research, 2003); Joseph A. Covello and Brian J. Hazelgren, *The Complete Book of Business Plans,* 2nd ed. (Naperville, IL: Sourcebooks, 2006); Joseph A. Covello and Brian J. Hazelgren, *Your First Business Plan,* 5th ed. (Naperville, IL: Sourcebooks, 2005); and Mike McKeever, *How to Write a Business Plan,* 8th ed. (Berkeley, CA: Nolo, 2007).

4. Abrams, *The Successful Business Plan,* p. 35.

5. Some of these points are adapted from Abrams, pp. 35–43; others are adapted from William Rudelius, *Guidelines for Technical Report Writing* (Minneapolis: University of Minnesota, undated). See also William Strunk, Jr., and E. B. White, *The Elements of Style,* 4th ed. (Needham Heights, MA: Allyn & Bacon, 2000).

6. Rebecca Zimoch, "The Dawn of the Frozen Age," *Grocery Headquarters,* December 2002; see www.groceryheadquarters.com.

7. ACNielsen Strategic Planner as reported to the National Frozen & Refrigerated Foods Association for the week ending February 24, 2007; see www.nfraweb.org.

8. Chuck Van Hyning, *NPD's National Eating Trends;* see www.npdfoodworld.com.

9. Jeffery M. Humphreys, "The Multicultural Economy 2006," *Georgia Business and Economic Conditions* 66, no. 3, (Third Quarter 2006), pp. 6, 10–11; see www.selig.uga.edu/forecast.

CHAPTER 3

1. Allison Enright, "Get Clued In: Mystery of 'Web 2.0' Concept Solved," Marketing News, January 15, 2007, p. 20; Jeff Howe, "Your Web, Your Way," Time, December 25, 2006, pp. 60–61; Bob Greenberg, "On Web 2.0's Impact," Adweek.com, January 1, 2007; Robert D. Hof, "There's Not Enough 'Me' in Myspace," BusinessWeek, December 4, 2006, p. 40; and Sebastian Rupley, "You've Heard of Web 2.0. What About Web 3.0?" PC Magazine, December 20, 2006.

2. "Coffee Surpasses Soft Drinks in Daily Market Penetration," National Coffee Association of U.S.A., Inc., April 1, 2007; "Coffee, Tea, or Coffee?" Marketing Management, June 2006, p. 4; and Rebecca Gardyn, "Grounds for a New Strategy," American Demographics, June 2001, pp. 115–17.

3. "Firms Eye Ready-to-Drink Coffee Market," AFX International Focus, January 3, 2007; Deborah L. Vence, "Java Jive," Marketing News, April 1, 2006, p. 3; Ross Sneyd, "Coffee Makers Smell a Trend Brewing," Houston Chronicle, December 18, 2005, p. 7; "Starbucks Automates Espresso Preparation," Restaurant Business, March 12, 2004; and Jeff Cioletti and Sherry Petersen, "Soda Shakeout," Convenience Store News Online, February 9, 2004.

4. "A Quarter-Century of Changes," USA Today, March 26, 2007, p. 8B; "Social Networking, User-Generated Content and Green Technology Are Top Trends for 2007," Wireless News, January 21, 2007; George Ochoa and Melinda Corey, The 100 Best Trends 2006 (Avon, MA: Adams Media, 2006), p. 128; "Future Options," Marketing News, January 15, 2007, pp. 16–17; Top 10 Trend in Tech, Media, and Telecom," Canadian Corporate Newswire, January 15, 2007.

5. World Population Prospects: The 2006 Revision (Geneva: United Nations, Department of Economic and Social Affairs, 2007) 2006 World Population Data Sheet (Washington, DC: Population Reference Bureau 2006).

6. World Population Prospects: The 2006 Revision, Table I.1, p. 1; and "New Facts on Globalization, Poverty, and Income Distribution," International Chamber of Commerce, January 15, 2003.

7. Lawrence A. Crosby, Sheree L. Johnson, and John Carroll III, "When We're 64," Marketing Management, December 2006, p. 14; "U.S. Interim Projections by Age, Sex, Race, and Hispanic Origin," U.S. Census Bureau, Table 1a, Table 2a; and Alison Stein Wellner, "The Next 25 Years," American Demographics, April 2003, pp. 24–27.

8. Kimberly Palmer, "Gen X-ers: Stingy or Strapped?" USNews.com, February 14, 2007; Paul J. Lim, "Baby Boomers Outpace Gen X-ers," USNews.com, March 12, 2007; and Megan Rowe, "Marketing to Gen X," Financial & Insurance Meetings, July 1, 2006, p. 19.

9. Sharon Jayson, "The Goal: Wealth and Fame, but 'the Good Life' Could Elude Gen Y," USA Today, January 10, 2007, p. 1D; Sharon Jayson, "Gen Y Makes a Mark: Their Imprint is Entrepreneurship," USA Today, December 7, 2006, p. 1D; "Millennial Moral," Business-Week, November 6, 2006, p. 13; Richard H. Levey, "Gen Y Phones It In," Direct, September 1, 2006, p. 18; Michael J. Weiss, "To Be about to Be," American Demographics, September 2003, pp. 29–36; Peter Francese, "Ahead of the Next Wave," American Demographics, September 2003, pp. 42–43; and Don O'Briant, "Millenials: The Next Generation," Atlanta Journal-Constitution, August 11, 2003, p. 1D.

10. Pamela Paul, "Global Generation Gap," American Demographics, March 2002, pp. 18–19; and Allyson L. Stewart-Allen, "EU's Future Consumers: 3 Groups to Watch," Marketing News, June 4, 2001, p. 9.

11. "Ocean Village Looks After Single Parents," Travel Trade Gazette, November 24, 2006, p. 13; James Morrow, "A Place for One," American Demographics, November 2003, pp. 25–29; and Michele Conlin, "Unmarried America," BusinessWeek, October 20, 2003, pp. 106–16.

12. "Getting Hitched," National Review, January 24, 2007; Matthew Grimm, "Hitch Switch," American Demographics, November 2003, pp. 34–35; John Fetto, "Till Death," American Demographics, September 2002, p. 8; and Joan Raymond, "The Ex-Files," American Demographics, February 2001, pp. 60–64.

13. Robert Bernstein, "Louisiana Loses Population, Arizona Edges Nevada as Fastest-Growing State," U.S. Census Bureau News, December 22, 2006; Marc J. Perry and Paul J. Mackun, "Population Change and Distribution," Census 2000 Brief: U.S. Bureau of the Census, April 2001; and Paul Campbell, "Population Projection: States, 1995–2025," Current Population Report, U.S. Department of Commerce, May 1997.

14. Thaddeus Herrick, "Aging Areas Around Cities Push Suburban Renewal," The Wall Street Journal, January 31, 2007, p. B1; Stephanie McCrummen, "On the Edge of Va. Sprawl, Labels Crumble, New Lives Thrive," The Washington Post, March 27, 2006, p. A1; Peter Francese, "Top Trends for 2003," American Demographics, December 2002–January 2003, pp. 48–51.

15. Joshua Bolten, "Update of Statistical Area Definitions and Additional Guidance on Their Use," Office of Management and Budget, OMB Bulletin No. 04–03, February 18, 2004; and "About Metropolitan and Micropolitan Statistical Areas," U.S. Census Bureau, www.census.gov/population/www/estimates/aboutmetro.html.

16. Alison Stein Wellner, "Our True Colors," American Demographics, November 2002, pp. S2–S20; Eduardo Porter, "Even 126 Sizes Don't Fit All," The Wall Street Journal, March 2, 2001, pp. B1, B4; and William H. Frey, "Micro Melting Pots," American Demographics, June 2001, pp. 20–23.

17. Robert Bernstein, "Census Bureau Releases Population Estimates by Race," U.S. Bureau News, August 4, 2006; Hikki Hopewell, "U.S. Buying Power by Race," Marketing News, July 15, 2006, p. 29; Brian Grow, "Hispanic Nation," BusinessWeek, March 15, 2004, pp. 58–70; Wellner,

"Our True Colors"; Deborah L. Vence, "You Talkin' to Me? Marketing News, March 1, 2004, pp. 1, 9–11; and Alison Stein Wellner, "The Next 25 Years," American Demographics, April 2000, pp. 24–27.

18. Laurel Wentz, "How Home Depot Plans to Reach Acculturated Latinos," Advertising Age, April 2, 2007, p. 30; and Deborah L. Vence, "Avoid Shortcuts, Hispanic Audience Requires Distinct, Inventive Marketing," Marketing News, February 15, 2006, p. 23.

19. John Fetto, "Does Father Really Know Best?" American Demographics, June 2002, p. 6.

20. Stephanie Thompson, "Ugg, Others Take a Shot at Gender Bending," Advertising Age, May 22, 2006, p. S4; "Female Consumerism: What Women Want," Brand Strategy, December 18, 2006, p. 40; and Allison Enright, "In Friends She Trusts, Seek to Build Relationships with Women Investors," Marketing News, April 15, 2006, p. 16.

21. John Carey and Michael Arndt, "Hugging the Tree-Huggers: Why So Many Companies are Suddenly Linking Up With Eco Groups," BusinessWeek, March 12, 2007, p. 66; David Kiley, "Toyota: How the Hybrid Race Went to the Swift," BusinessWeek, January 29, 2007, p. 58; Stephanie Thompson, "Want That Perfect Body? Have Some More Dannon," Advertising Age, September 25, 2006, p. 3; and Edward B. Keller and Thomas A. W. Miller, "Remapping the World of Consumers," American Demographics, October 2000, pp. S1–S20.

22. Sarah McBride, "How to Haggle Your Way to a Better Price," The Seattle Times, September 16, 2006, p. K14; Nordstrom Rack website, http://about.nordstrom.com/ourstores/rackstores/about.asp, accessed April 9, 2007.

23. Melissa Ludwig, "College Costs Still Going Up," San Antonio Express-News, October 25, 2006, p. 9A; and Jonathan D. Glater, "Weighing the Costs in Public vs. Private Colleges," The New York Times, December 13, 2006, p. 7.

24. James C. Cooper, "The R-Word is 'Rocky,' Not 'Recession,'" Business-Week, March 19, 2007, p. 31; and Michael J. Mandel, "Inventing the Clinton Recession," BusinessWeek, February 23, 2004, p. 48.

25. Richard T. Curtin, Surveys of Consumers (Ann Arbor, MI: Survey Research Center, University of Michigan, October 6, 2006), p. 3; and Michael J. Weiss, "Inside Consumer Confidence Surveys," American Demographics, February 2003, pp. 23–29.

26. Carmen DeNavas-Walt, Bernadette D. Proctor, and Jessica Smith, "Income, Poverty and Health Insurance Coverage in the United States: 2006," Current Population Reports (Washington, DC: U.S. Census Bureau, August 2007), p. 29.

27. Don Carlson, "The Old Economy in the New Economy," Business-Week, November 13, 2000, p. 42H; Owen Ullmann, "Forget Saving, America. Your Job Is to Spend," BusinessWeek, December 28, 1998, p. 54; Gene Koretz, "Savings' Death Is Exaggerated," BusinessWeek, September 14, 1998, p. 26; and Marcia Mogelonsky, "No More Food, Thanks," American Demographics, August 1998, p. 59.

28. "Consumer Expenditures in 2005," U.S. Department of Labor, Bureau of Labor Statistics, February 2007, pp. 1–4; and "Spending on Necessities," Monthly Labor Review, U.S. Department of Labor, Bureau of Labor Statistics, June 24, 2003.

29. Tom Giles, "Tech Trends for 2007," BusinessWeek Online, January 29, 2007; Aili McConnon, "The Mind-Bending New World of Work," BusinessWeek, April 2, 2007, pp. 46–54; and John Carey, "Tiny Smart Bombs vs. Cancer?" BusinessWeek, March 1, 2004, p. 115.

30. Michael Krauss, "Young Net Entrepreneurs Leverage Web Anew," Marketing News, February 1, 2004, p. 6.

31. Leon Jaroff, "Smart's the Word in Detroit," Time, February 6, 1995, pp. 50–52.

32. Clint Willis, "25 Cool Things You Wish You Had and Will," Forbes ASAP, June 1, 1998, pp. 49–60.

33. Jim Carlton, "Recycling Redefined," The Wall Street Journal, March 6, 2001, pp. B1, B4; Stephanie Anderson, "There's Gold in Those Hills

of Soda Bottles," BusinessWeek, September 11, 1995, p. 48; Maxine Wilkie, "Asking Americans to Use Less Stuff," American Demographics, December 1994, pp. 11–12; and Jacquelyn Ottman, "New and Improved Won't Do," Marketing News, January 30, 1995, p. 9.

34. Henry Goldblatt, "The End of the Long Distance Club," Fortune, May 26, 1997, p. 30; and "Wheel of Fortune," The Economist, November 21, 1998, p. 53.

35. DeAnn Welmer, "Don't Be Shocked by Surges in the Price of Power," BusinessWeek, July 27, 1998, p. 33.

36. Jay Greene, "Microsoft: First Europe, Then . . . ?" BusinessWeek, March 22, 2004, p. 86.

37. Michael Porter, Competitive Advantage (New York: Free Press, 1985); and Michael Porter, Competitive Strategy (New York: Free Press, 1980).

38. Bruce H. Clark, Andrew V. Abela, and Time Ambler, "Behind the Wheel," Marketing Management, June 2006, p. 19–23; and Paul W. Farris, Neil T. Bendle, Phillip E. Pfeifer, and David J. Reibstein, Marketing Metrics: 50+ Metrics Every Executive Should Master (Philadelphia: Wharton School Publishing, 2007).

39. Catherine Amst, "For Lucent, a Shining Moment," BusinessWeek, April 21, 1997, p. 126.

40. "Small Business Resources for Faculty, Students, and Researchers: Answers to Frequently Asked Questions," Small Business Administration, Office of Advocacy, March 2004.

41. "A New Copyright Law?" BusinessWeek, August 3, 1998, p. 45.

42. "Highlights of Food Labeling," Marketing News, March 15, 2004, p. 14.

43. Dorothy Cohen, "Trademark Strategy Revisited," Journal of Marketing, July 1991, pp. 46–59.

44. Maxine L. Retsky, "Review Int'l Filing Process for Marks," Marketing News, September 29, 2003, p. 8.

45. Michael Fielding, "Doppelgangers: Monitor Parodies to Measure Brand Value," Marketing News, October 15, 2006, p. 13–15; and Craig J. Thompson, Aric Rindfleisch, and Zeynep Arsel, "Emotional Branding and the Strategic Value of the Doppelganger Brand Image," Journal of Marketing, January 2006, pp. 50–64.

46. Paul Barrett, "High Court Sees Color as Basis for Trademarks," The Wall Street Journal, March 29, 1995, p. A6; Paul Barrett, "Color in the Court," The Wall Street Journal, January 5, 1995, p. A1; and David Kelly, "Rainbow of Ideas to Trademark Color," Advertising Age, April 24, 1995, pp. 20, 22.

47. Maxine L. Retsky, "Dilution of Trademarks Hard to Prove," Marketing News, May 12, 2003, p. 6.

48. Dick Mercer, "Tempest in a Soup Can," Advertising Age, October 17, 1994, pp. 25–29.

49. Maxine L. Retsky, "Stakes Are High for Direct Mail Sweepstakes Promotions," Marketing News, July 3, 2000, p. 8; Catherine Arnold, "Picky, Picky, Picky" Marketing News, February 15, 2004, p. 17; Catherine Arnold, "No Can Spam," Marketing News, January 15, 2004, p. 3; Arundhati Parmar, "Can't Say You Weren't Warned," Marketing News, February 15, 2004, p. 4; and James Heckman, "Laws That Take Effect—and Some Likely to Return in 1999 Mean Marketers Must Change Some Policies," Marketing News, December 7, 1998, p. 1, 16.

50. Mark McFadden, "The BBB on the WWW," HP Professional, September 1997, p. 36.

Geek Squad: This case was written by Steven Hartley. Sources: Mary Ellen Lloyd, "Camp Teaches Power of Geekdom," The Wall Street Journal, July 11, 2007; Dean Foust, Michael Mandel, Frederick F. Jespersen and David Henry, "The Business Week 50—The Best Performers," Business Week, March 26, 2007, p. 58; Jessica E. Vascellaro, "What's a Cellphone For? Businesses are Finding All Sorts of New Uses for Mobile Devices," The Wall Street Journal, March 26, 2007, p. R5; Cade Metz, "Just How Stupid Are You? Geek Squad War Stories," PC Magazine, February 1, 2006; Brad Stone, "Lore of the Geek Squad," Newsweek, February 20, 2006, p. 44; Michelle Conlin, "Smashing the Clock," BusinessWeek, December 11, 2006, p. 60; "Best Buy: How to Break Out of Commodity Hell," BusinessWeek, March 27, 2006, p. 76; Pallavi Gogoi, "Meet Jane Geek," BusinessWeek, November 28, 2005, p. 94; Desiree J. Hanford, "Geek Squad Is Popular at Best Buy," The Wall Street Journal, December 14, 2005, p. 1; Michelle Higgins, "Getting Your Own IT Department," The Wall Street Journal, May 20, 2004, p. D1; and information contained on the Geek Squad website (www.geeksquad.com).

CHAPTER 4

1. www.beeresponsible.com, downloaded April 5, 2007; www.beerinstitute.org, downloaded April 6, 2007; "America's Most Admired Companies," Fortune, March 6, 2006, p. 38.

2. For a discussion of the definition of ethics, see Eugene R. Lazniak and Patrick E. Murphy, Ethical Marketing Decision: The Higher Road (Boston: Allyn & Bacon, 1993), chapter 1.

3. Verne E. Henderson, "The Ethical Side of Enterprise," Sloan Management Review, Spring 1982, pp. 37–47. See also, Joseph L. Badaracco, Jr., Defining Moments: When Managers Must Choose Between Right and Right (Boston: Harvard Business School Press, 1997).

4. "Honorable?" Business 2.0, February 2000, p. 92.

5. Roger O. Crockett, "Hauling in the Hollywood Hackers," BusinessWeek, May 15, 2006, pp. 80–82; "Exporting Death." Time, April 13, 1998, p. 63; Ray O. Werner, "Marketing and the Supreme Court in Transition, 1982–1984," Journal of Marketing, Summer 1985, pp. 97–105; and Jane Bryant Quinn, "Computer Program Deceives Consumers," Dallas Morning News, March 2, 1998, p. B3.

6. The 2005 National Business Ethics Survey (Washington, DC: Ethics Resource Center 2006); "Poll: Ad Execs Are Icky," Advertising Age, January 16, 2006, p. 26; Patrick J. Gnazzo and George R. Wratney, "Are You Serious About Ethics?" Across the Board, July/August 2003, pp. 47–50; and Ronald W. Clement. "Just How Ethical Is American Business?" Business Horizons, July–August 2006, pp. 313–27.

7. See, for example, Lawrence B. Chonko, Ethical Decision Making in Marketing (Thousand Oaks, CA: Sage, 1995).

8. Thomas Donaldson, "Values in Tension: Ethics Away from Home," Harvard Business Review, September–October 1996, pp. 48–62.

9. "Levi Only Comfortable Dealing with Countries That Fit Its Image," Dallas Morning News, January 9, 1995, p. D2.

10. These statistics were obtained from Recording Industry Association of America (www.riaa.com), Motion Picture Association of America (www.mpaa.com), and the Business Software Alliance (www.bsa.org).

11. Internet Piracy on Campus (Washington, DC: IPSOS, September 16, 2003).

12. Vern Terpstra and Kenneth David, The Cultural Environment of International Business, 3rd ed. (Cincinnati: South-Western Publishing, 1991), p. 12.

13. Hukari Kane, "Recall Shows Battery Limits," The Wall Street Journal, August 18, 2006, p. A13; and "Dell Announces Recall of Notebook Computer Batteries Due to Fire Hazard," U.S. Consumer Product Safety Commission Press Release, August 15, 2006.

14. "Three Ad Agencies Settle FTC Charges of Deceptive Car-Leasing Commercials," The Wall Street Journal, January 21, 1998, p. B2.

15. Timothy Muris, "Protecting Consumers' Privacy," www.FTC.gov, downloaded January 3, 2007.

16. For an extensive examination on slotting fees, see Paul N. Bloom, Gregory T. Gundlach, and Joseph P. Cannon, "Slotting Allowances and Fees: Schools of Thought and Views of Practicing Managers," Journal of Marketing, April 2000, pp. 92–109. Also see, "FTC Pinpoints Slotting Fees," Advertising Age, February 26, 2001, p. 52.

17. Hedich Nasheri, Economic Espionage and Industrial Spying (Cambridge, England: Cambridge University Press, 2005).

18. "Coke Employee Faces Charges in Plot to Sell Secrets," The Wall Street Journal, July 6, 2006, p. B6; "Do the Right Thing? Not with a Rival's Inside Info," Advertising Age, July 17, 2006, p. 4; and "You Can't Beat the Real Thing," Time, July 17, 2006, pp. 10–11; and "Former Coke Secretary Sentenced to 8 Years," www.msnbc.com, May 23, 2007.

19. These examples are highlighted in Thomas W. Dunfee, N. Craig Smith, and William T. Ross, Jr., "Social Contracts and Marketing Ethics," Journal of Marketing, July 1999, pp. 14–32; and Andy Pasztor, When the Pentagon Was for Sale: Inside America's Biggest Defense Scandal (New York: Scribner, 1995).

20. www.transparency.org, downloaded January 5, 2007.

21. "U.S. Firms Raise Ethics Focus," The Wall Street Journal, November 28, 2005, p. B4; and Thomas Donaldson, "The Corporate Ethics Boom: Significant, or Just for Show?" Knowledge@Wharton, downloaded February 25, 2002.

22. "Coca-Cola Unit Head Resigns After Rigged Test," www.forbes.com, downloaded August 25, 2003.

23. The 2005 National Business Ethics Survey.

24. "Whistleblowers: Tales from the Back Office," The Economist, March 25, 2006, p. 67; and C. Fred Alford, Whistleblowers: Broken Lives and Organizational Power (Ithaca, NY: Cornell University Press, 2002).

25. For an extensive discussion on these moral philosophies, see R. Eric Reidenbach and Donald P. Robin, Ethics and Profits (Englewood Cliffs, NJ: Prentice Hall, 1989); Chonko, Ethical Decision Making; and Lazniak and Murphy, Ethical Marketing Decisions.

26. "Scotchgard Working Out Recent Stain on its Business," www.mercurynews.com, downloaded June 22, 2003.

27. James O. Wilson, "Adam Smith on Business Ethics," California Management Review, Fall 1989, pp. 57–72.

28. Alix M. Freedman, "Bad Reaction: Nestlé's Bid to Crash Baby-Formula Market in U.S. Stirs a Row," The Wall Street Journal, February 16, 1989, pp. Al, A6; and Alix Freedman, "Nestlé to Drop Claim on Label of Its Formula," The Wall Street Journal, March 13, 1989, p. B5.

29. Harvey S. James and Farhad Rassekh, "Smith, Friedman, and Self-Interest in Ethical Society," Business Ethics Quarterly, July 2000, pp. 659–74.

30. "Cost of Living," The Economist, March 1, 2003, p. 60.

31. "Perrier—Overresponding to a Crisis," in Robert F. Hartley, Marketing Mistakes and Successes, 10th ed. (New York: John Wiley & Sons, 2006), pp. 119–30.

32. "Ford Explorers with Firestone Tires: Ill Handling of a Killer Scenario," in Hartley, Marketing Mistakes and Successes, pp. 105–18.

33. "Pollution Prevention Pays." www.3M.com, downloaded January 10, 2007; www.xerox.com/environment, downloaded January 15, 2007; Elizabeth Royte, "Corn Plastic to the Rescue?" Smithsonian, August 2006, pp. 84–88; Jerry Adler, "Going Green," Newsweek, July 17, 2006, pp. 42–52; and "Hugging the Tree Huggers," Business Week, March 12, 2007, pp. 66–68.

34. The ISO Survey—2005 (Geneva, Switzerland: International Organization for Standardization, 2006).

35. For an extended discussion on this topic, see P. Rajan Varadarajan and Anil Menon, "Cause-Related Marketing: A Coalignment of Marketing Strategy and Corporate Philanthropy," Journal of Marketing, July 1988, pp. 58–74. The examples are found in Nancy Coltun Webster, "Color Coded Causes," Advertising Age, June 13, 2005, pp. 31–35; www.avoncompany.com, downloaded January 10, 2007; and Christine Bittar, "Seeking Cause and Effect," Brandweek, September 11, 2002, pp. 19–23.

36. "The Big Picture," BusinessWeek, November 6, 2006, p. 13; "Cause and 'Affect'," Brandweek, October 7, 2002, p. 16; and Bittar, "Seeking Cause and Effect." Also see Larry Chiagouris and Ipshita Ray, "Saving the World with Cause-related Marketing," Marketing Management, July–August 2007, pp. 48–51.

37. These steps are adapted from J. J. Carson and G. A. Steiner, Measuring Business Social Performance: The Corporate Social Audit (New York: Committee for Economic Development, 1974). See also Sandra Waddock and Neil Smith, "Corporate Responsibility Audits: Doing Well by Doing Good," Sloan Management Review, Winter 2000, pp. 75–84.

38. "Marketers Become Own Watchdogs," Advertising Age, June 12, 2006, p. 57; and "Sweatshops: Finally, Airing the Dirty Linen," BusinessWeek, June 23, 2003, pp. 100–01.

39. Unmesh Kher, "Getting Smart at Being Good... Are Companies Better off for It?" Time, January 2006, pp. A1–A37; and Pete Engardio, "Beyond the Green Corporation," BusinessWeek, January 29, 2007, pp. 50–64.

40. This discussion is based on Wayne D. Hoyer and Deborah J. MacInnis, Consumer Behavior, 4th ed. (New York: Houghton Mifflin Company, 2007), pp. 535–37; "Factoids," Research Alert, December 8, 2005, p. 5; Elizabeth Woyke, "Attention Shoplifters," BusinessWeek, September 11, 2006, pp. 46–50; and "Putting Return Policies to the Test," The Wall Street Journal, February 22, 2007, p. D3.

41. "A Pirate and his Penance," Time, January 26, 2004, p. 60; and Crockett, "Hauling in the Hollywood Hackers."

42. "A Lighter Shade of Green," American Demographics, February 2000, p. 24; and "Schism on the Green," Brandweek, February 26, 2001, p. 18.

43. "FTC Stands by Regs for 'Green' Ad Claims," Advertising Age, October 7, 1996, p. 61.

Source: Starbucks Corporation: this case is based on information on the company website (www.starbucks.com) and the following sources: "Living Our Values ," 2003 Corporate Social Responsibility Annual Report; "Starbucks Annual Shareholder meeting," Starbucks press release, March 30, 2004; Ranjay Gulati, Sarah Haffman, and Gary Neilson, "The Barista Principle: Starbucks and the Rise of Relational Capital," Strategy and Business, 3rd Quarter 2002, pp. 58–69; and Andy Serwer, "Hot Starbucks to Go," Fortune, January 12, 2004, pp. 52ff.

CHAPTER 5

1. Marti Barletta, "Who's Really Buying that Car? Ask Her," BrandWeek, September 4, 2006, p. 20; Joan Voight, "The Lady Means Business," BrandWeek, April 30, 2006, pp. 28ff; and Jennifer Saranow, "Car Dealers Recruit Saleswomen at the Mall," The Wall Street Journal, April 12, 2006, pp. B1, B3.

2. Roger D. Blackwell, Paul W. Miniard, and James F. Engel, Consumer Behavior, 10th ed. (Mason, OH: South-Western Publishing, 2006).

3. For thorough descriptions of consumer expertise, see Joseph W. Alba and J. Wesley Hutchinson, "Knowledge Calibration: What Consumers Know and What They Think They Know," Journal of Consumer Research, September 2000, pp. 123–57.

4. For in-depth studies on external information search patterns, see Brian T. Ratchford, Myung-Soo Lee, and Debabrata Talukdar, "The Impact of the Internet on Information Search for Automobiles," Journal of Marketing Research, May 2003, pp. 193–209; Sridhar Moorthy, Brian T. Ratchford, and Debabrata Talukdar, "Consumer Information Research Revisited: Theory and Empirical Analysis," Journal of Consumer Research, March 1997, pp. 263–77; Joel E. Urbany, Peter R. Dickson, and William L. Wilkie, "Buyer Uncertainty and Information Search," Journal of Consumer Research, March 1992, pp. 452–63; and Sharon E. Beatty and Scott M. Smith, "External Search Effort: An Investigation across Several Product Categories," Journal of Consumer Research, June 1987, pp. 83–95.

5. Consumer Reports Buying Guide Best Buys for 2007 (Yonkers, NY: Consumers Union, 2007).

6. For an extended discussion on evaluative criteria, see Del J. Hawkins, David L. Mothersbaugh, and Roger J. Best, Consumer Behavior, 10th ed. (Burr Ridge, IL: McGraw-Hill/Irwin, 2007).

7. John A. Howard, Buyer Behavior in Marketing Strategy, 2nd ed. (Englewood Cliffs, NJ: Prentice Hall, 1994). For an extended discussion on consumer choice sets, see Allan D. Shocker, Moshe Ben-Akiva, Brun Boccara, and Prakesh Nedungadi, "Consideration Set Influences on Consumer Decision Making and Choice: Issues, Models, and Suggestions," Marketing Letters, August 1991, pp. 181–98.

8. William J. McDonald, "Time Use in Shopping: The Role of Personal Characteristics," Journal of Retailing, Winter 1994, pp. 345–66; Robert J. Donovan, John R. Rossiter, Gillian Marcoolyn, and Andrew Nesdale, "Store Atmosphere and Purchasing Behavior," Journal of Retailing, Fall 1994, pp. 283–94; and Eric A. Greenleaf and Donald R. Lehman, "Reasons for Substantial Delay in Consumer Decision Making," Journal of Consumer Research, September 1995, pp. 186–99.

9. Sunil Gupta and Valarie Zeithaml, "Customer Metrics and Their Impact on Financial Performance," Marketing Science, November–December 2006, pp. 718–39.

10. These estimates given in Jagdish N. Sheth and Banwari Mitral, Consumer Behavior, 2nd ed. (Mason, OH: South-Western Publishing, 2003), p. 32.

11. Frederick F. Reichheld and Thomas Teal, The Loyalty Effect (Boston: Harvard Business School Press, 1996); "What's a Loyal Customer Worth?" Fortune, December 11, 1995, p. 182; and Patricia Sellers, "Keeping the Buyers You Already Have," Fortune, Autumn–Winter 1993, p. 57. For an in-depth examination of this topic, see Sunil Gupta and Donald R. Lehmann, Managing Customers as Investments (Upper Saddle River, NJ: Pearson Education, Inc., 2005).

12. For an overview of research on involvement, see John C. Mowen and Michael Minor, Consumer Behavior: A Framework, 5th ed. (Upper Saddle River, NJ: Prentice Hall, 2001); and Wayne D. Hoyer and Deborah J. MacInnis, Consumer Behavior, 4th cd. (Boston: Houghton Mifflin Co., 2007).

13. Russell Belk, "Situational Variables and Consumer Behavior," Journal of Consumer Research, December 1975, pp. 157–63.

14. A. H. Maslow, Motivation and Personality (New York: Harper & Row, 1970). Also see Richard Yalch and Frederic Brunel, "Need Hierarchies in Consumer Judgments of Product Design: Is It Time to Reconsider Maslow's Hierarchy?" in Advances in Consumer Research, ed. Kim Corfman and John Lynch (Provo, UT: Association for Consumer Research, 1996), pp. 405–10.

15. Joel B. Cohen, "An Interpersonal Orientation to the Study of Consumer Behavior," Journal of Marketing Research, August 1967, pp. 270–78; and Rena Bartos, Marketing to Women around the World (Cambridge, MA: Harvard Business School, 1989).

16. Terry Clark, "International Marketing and National Character: A Review and Proposal for an Integrative Theory," Journal of Marketing, October 1990, pp. 66–79; and John-Benedict E. M. Steenkamp, "The Role of National Culture in International Marketing Research," International Marketing Review 18, no. 1 (2001), pp. 30–44.

17. Myron Magnet, "Let's Go for Growth," Fortune, March 7, 1994, p. 70.

18. This example provided in Michael R. Solomon, Consumer Behavior, 4th ed. (Upper Saddle River, NJ: Prentice Hall, 1999), p. 59.

19. For further reading on subliminal perception, see Anthony G. Greenwald, Sean C. Draine, and Richard L. Abrams, "Three Cognitive Markers of Unconscious Semantic Activation," Science, September 1996, pp. 1699–701; B. Bahrami, N. Lavie, and G. Rees, "Attentional Load Modulates Responses of Human Primary Visual Cortex to Invisible Stimuli," Current Biology, March 2007, pp. 39–47; Dennis L. Rosen and Surendra N. Singh, "An Investigation of Subliminal Embedded Effect on Multiple Measures of Advertising Effectiveness," Psychology & Marketing, March–April 1992, pp. 157–73; and Kathryn T.

Theus, "Subliminal Advertising and the Psychology of Processing Unconscious Stimuli: A Review of the Research," Psychology & Marketing, May–June 1994, pp. 271–90.

20. August Bullock, The Secret Sales Pitch (San Jose, CA: Norwich Publishers, 2004); E. Parpis, "Sex, Crackers and Subliminal Ads," Adweek, March 31, 2003, p. 18; "GOP Commercial Resurrects Debate on Subliminal Ads," The Wall Street Journal, September 13, 2000, p. B10; and "I Will Love This Story," U.S. News & World Report, May 12, 1997, p. 12.

21. Sholnn Freeman, "Brand Breakdown," The Washington Post, March 26, 2006, p. F1ff.

22. Martin Fishbein and I. Aizen, Belief, Attitude, Intention and Behavior: An Introduction to Theory and Research (Reading, MA: Addison-Wesley, 1975), p. 6.

23. Richard J. Lutz, "Changing Brand Attitudes through Modification of Cognitive Structure," Journal of Consumer Research, March 1975, pp. 49–59.

24. "The VALS™ Types," www.sric-bi.com/VALS, downloaded April 1, 2007.

25. This discussion is based on Ed Keller and Jon Berry, The Influentials (New York: Simon and Schuster, 2003).

26. "Word of Mouth Is Where It's At," BrandWeek, June 2, 2003, p. 26.

27. BzzAgent.com, downloaded September 7, 2007; Matthew Creamer, "BzzAgent Seeks to Turn Word of Mouth into a Saleable Medium," Advertising Age, February 13, 2006, p. 12; and "Word on the Street," Time, April 12, 2007, pp. 34–35.

28. For extensive review on consumer socialization of children, see Deborah Roedder John, "Consumer Socialization of Children: A Retrospective Look at Twenty-Five Years of Research," Journal of Consumer Research, December 1999, pp. 183–213. Also see, Gwen Bachmann Achenreinver and Deborah Roedder John, "The Meaning of Brand Names to Children: A Developmental Investigation," Journal of Consumer Psychology 13, no. 3 (2003), pp. 205–19; and Elizabeth S. Moore, William L. Wilkie, and Richard J. Lutz, "Passing the Torch: Intergenerational Influences as a Source of Brand Equity," Journal of Marketing, April 2002, pp. 17–37.

29. J. Paul Peter and Jerry C. Olson, Consumer Behavior and Marketing Strategy, 8th ed. (Burr Ridge, IL: McGraw-Hill/Irwin, 2008). Also see, Rex Y. Du and Wagner A. Kamakura, "Household Life Cycles and Lifestyles in the United States," Journal of Marketing Research, February 2006, pp. 121–32.

30. This discussion is based on Hawkins, Mothersbaugh, and Best, Consumer Behavior: Building Marketing Strategy; www.teenresearch.com, downloaded April 1, 2007; "Teens Rule," MediaBuyer.com, downloaded April 7, 2007; Jennifer Saranow, "This Is the Car We Want, Mommy," The Wall Street Journal, November 9, 2006, pp. D1, D4; and "Trillion-Dollar Kids," The Economist, December 2, 2006, p. 66.

31. Harold R. Kerbo, Social Stratification and Inequality (Burr Ridge, IL: McGraw-Hill, 2000). For an extensive discussion on social class, see Eric Arnould, Linda Price, and George Zinkhan, Consumers, 2nd ed. (Burr Ridge, IL: McGraw-Hill/Irwin, 2004).

32. Jeffrey M. Humphreys, "The Multicultural Economy in 2006," Selig Center for Economic Growth, Terry College of Business, The University of Georgia, downloaded February 14, 2007.

33. The remainder of this discussion is based on Hoyer and MacInnis, Consumer Behavior; "American Demographics," Advertising Age, January 1, 2007, pp. 45–46; and "Hispanic Wanted," BrandWeek, April 12, 2004, p. 22.

34. The remainder of this discussion is based on Peter and Olson, Consumer Behavior and Marketing Strategy; and "Multicultural Marketing: African Americans," Marketing News, October 15, 2006, pp. 19, 22.

35. The remainder of this discussion is based on Hawkins, Mothersbaugh, and Best, Consumer Behavior: Building Marketing Strategy;

and Sonia Reyes, "The Invisible Market," BrandWeek, January 30, 2006, pp. 22–26.

The Best Buy case was written by David P. Brennan of the University of St. Thomas and is based on interviews with Joe Brandt and Best Buy employees and customers, and materials supplied by Best Buy.

CHAPTER 6

1. Interview with Kim Nagele, JCPMedia, January 10, 2007.
2. John Paterson, "Evolution, Innovation are Constants," Purchasing, September 7, 2006, p. 55.
3. Figures reported in this discussion are found in Statistical Abstract of the United States: 2007, 126th ed. (Washington, DC: U.S. Census Bureau, 2007).
4. "Lockheed Wins Major Spacecraft Job," The Wall Street Journal, September 1, 2006, p. A3.
5. This example is based on Dave Nelson, Patricia E. Moody, and Jonathan Stenger, The Purchasing Machine (New York: Free Press, 2003).
6. 2002 NAICS United States Manual (Washington, DC: Office of Management and Budget, 2002).
7. North American Product Classification System (Washington, DC: U.S. Census Bureau, 2006).
8. This listing and portions of the following discussion are based on F. Robert Dwyer and John F. Tanner, Jr., Business Marketing, 3rd ed. (Burr Ridge IL: McGraw-Hill/Irwin, 2005); Michael D. Hutt and Thomas W. Speh, Business Marketing Management, 9th ed. (Mason, OH: South-Western, 2007); and Frank G. Bingham, Jr., Roger Gomes, and Patricia A. Knowles, Business Marketing, 3rd ed. (Burr Ridge, IL: McGraw-Hill/Irwin, 2005).
9. "Siemens Awarded $28 Million Contract for JetBlue Airways' Baggage Handling System with Integrated Security," Siemens USA press release, July 12, 2006.
10. Gwen Moran, The Business Case for Diversity, 5th ed. (Newark, NJ: Diversity Inc., 2006); "The 2007 DiversityInc Top 10 Companies for Supplier Diversity," www.diversity.com, April 2, 2007; and "Supplier Diversity Pays Off," Purchasing, September 7, 2006, p. 28.
11. www.pg.com/supplier_diversity, downloaded January 15, 2007.
12. "Boise Cascade Turns Green," The Wall Street Journal, September 3, 2003, p. B6. Also see Minette E. Drumwright, "Socially Responsible Organizational Buying: Environmental Concern as a Noneconomic Buying Criterion," Journal of Marketing, July 1994, pp. 1–18.
13. For a study of buying criteria used by industrial firms, see Daniel H. McQuiston and Rockney G. Walters, "The Evaluation Criteria of Industrial Buyers: Implications for Sales Training," Journal of Business & Industrial Marketing, Summer–Fall 1989, pp. 65–75.
14. For an overview on ISO 9000 certification, see Thomas H. Stevenson and Frank C. Barnes, "What Industrial Marketers Need to Know about ISO 9000 Certification: A Review, Update, and Integration with Marketing," Industrial Marketing Management, November 2002, pp. 695–703.
15. This example is found in Sandy D. Jap and Jakki J. Mohr, "Leveraging Internet Technologies in B2B Relationships," California Management Review, Summer 2002, pp. 24–38.
16. "America's Most Admired Companies," Fortune, March 8, 2004, pp. 80ff; Brian Milligan, "Medal of Excellence: Harley-Davidson Wins by Getting Suppliers on Board," Purchasing, September 2000, pp. 52–65; and "Harley-Davidson Company," Purchasing Magazine Online, September 4, 2003.
17. "The Smartest Machines on Earth," Fortune, September 18, 2006, pp. 129–36.
18. This discussion is based on www.ibm.com/procurement/html/principles.practices, downloaded January 10, 2007.
19. "EDS Signs $1.7 Billion IT Services Agreement with Kraft Foods," EDS news release, April 28, 2006; and "HP Finalizes $3 Billion Outsourcing

Agreement to Manage Procter & Gamble's IT Infrastructure," Hewlett-Packard news release, May 6, 2003.
20. This discussion is based on James C. Anderson and James A. Narus, Business Market Management, 2nd ed. (Upper Saddle River, NJ: Prentice Hall, 2004); Jeffrey K. Liker and Thomas Y. Choi, "Building Deep Supplier Relationships," Harvard Business Review, December 2004, pp. 104–13; and Joseph P. Cannon and Christian Homburg, "Buyer–Supplier Relationships and Customer Firm Costs," Journal of Marketing, January 2001, pp. 29–43.
21. Thomas V. Bonoma, "Major Sales: Who Really Does the Buying?" Harvard Business Review, May–June 1982, pp. 11–19. For recent research on buying centers, see Morry Ghingold and David T. Wilson, "Buying Center Research and Business Marketing Practices: Meeting the Challenge of Dynamic Marketing," Journal of Business & Industrial Marketing 13, no. 2 (1998), pp. 96–108; Philip L. Dawes, Don Y. Lee, and Grahame R. Dowling, "Information Control and Influence in Emerging Buying Centers," Journal of Marketing, July 1998, pp. 55–68; and Thomas Tellefsen, "Antecedents and Consequences of Buying Center Leadership: An Emergent Perspective," Journal of Business-to-Business Marketing, 13, no. 1 (2006), pp. 53–59.
22. Allison Enright, "It Takes a Committee to Buy into B-to-B," Marketing News, February 15, 2006, pp. 11–13.
23. These definitions are adapted from Frederick E. Webster, Jr., and Yoram Wind, Organizational Buying Behavior (Englewood Cliffs, NJ: Prentice Hall, 1972), p. 6.
24. "Can Corning Find Its Optic Nerve?" Fortune, March 19, 2001, pp. 148–50.
25. Representative studies on the buy-class framework that document its usefulness include Erin Anderson, Wujin Chu, and Barton Weitz, "Industrial Purchasing: An Empirical Exploration of the Buy-Class Framework," Journal of Marketing, July 1987, pp. 71–86; Morry Ghingold, "Testing the 'Buy-Grid' Buying Process Model," Journal of Purchasing and Materials Management, Winter 1986, pp. 30–36; P. Matthyssens and W. Faes, "OEM Buying Process for New Components: Purchasing and Marketing Implications," Industrial Marketing Management, August 1985, pp. 145–57; and Thomas W. Leigh and Arno J. Ethans, "A Script-Theoretic Analysis of Industrial Purchasing Behavior," Journal of Marketing, Fall 1984, pp. 22–32. Studies not supporting the buy-class framework include Joseph A. Bellizi and Philip McVey, "How Valid Is the Buy-Grid Model?" Industrial Marketing Management, February 1983, pp. 57–62; Donald W. Jackson, Janet E. Keith, and Richard K. Burdick, "Purchasing Agents' Perceptions of Industrial Buying Center Influences: A Situational Approach," Journal of Marketing, Fall 1984, pp. 75–83.
26. R. Vekatesh, Ajay Kohli, and Gerald Zaltman, "Influence Strategies in Buying Centers," Journal of Marketing, October 1995, pp. 61–72; Gary L. Lilien and Anthony Wong, "An Exploratory Investigation of the Structure of the Buying Center in the Metal Working Industry," Journal of Marketing Research, February 1984, pp. 1–11; and Wesley J. Johnston and Thomas V. Bonoma, "The Buying Center: Structure and Interaction Patterns," Journal of Marketing, Summer 1981, pp. 143–56. Also see Christopher P. Puto, Wesley E. Patton III, and Ronald H. King, "Risk Handling Strategies in Industrial Vendor Selection Decisions" Journal of Marketing, Winter 1985, pp. 89–98.
27. 2006 Machine Vision Market (Ann Arbor, MI: Automated Imaging Association, 2006).
28. "Machine Vision Looks Well Beyond Inspection," Packaging Digest, August 2005, pp. 32–35.
29. "B2B E-Commerce Headed for Trillions," www.clickz.com, downloaded March 1, 2006.
30. This discussion is based on Jennifer Reinhold, "What We Learned in the New Economy," Fast Company, March 4, 2004, pp. 56ff; Mark Roberti, "General Electric's Spin Machine," The Industry Standard, January 22–29, 2001, pp. 74–83; "Grainger Lightens Its Digital

Load," Industrial Distribution, March 2001, pp. 77–79; and www.boeing.com/procurement, downloaded February 6, 2005.

31. "B2B, Take 2," BusinessWeek Online, November 25, 2005.

32. "New Study Reveals 724,000 Americans Rely on eBay Sales for Income," eBay press release, July 21, 2005; Robyn Greenspan, "Net Drives Profits to Small-Biz," www.clickz.com, March 25, 2004; Michael Krauss, "EBay 'Bids' on Small-Biz Firms to Sustain Growth," Marketing News, December 8, 2003, pp. 6, 7; "Ebay Realizes Success in Small-Biz Arena," Marketing News, May 1, 2004, p. 11; and www.ebaybusiness.com.

33. www.agentrics.com, downloaded January 8, 2007.

34. www.ghx.com, downloaded January 8, 2007.

35. This discussion is based on Robert J. Dolan and Youngme Moon, "Pricing and Market Making on the Internet," Journal of Interactive Marketing, Spring 2000, pp. 56–73; and Ajit Kambil and Eric van Heck, Making Markets: How Firms Can Benefit from Online Auctions and Exchanges (Boston, MA: Harvard Business School Press, 2002).

36. Susan Avery, "Supply Management is Core of Success at UTC," Purchasing, September 7, 2006, pp. 36–39.

37. Shawn P. Daley and Prithwiraz Nath, "Reverse Auctions for Relationship Marketers," Industrial Marketing Management, February 2005, pp. 157–66; Sandy Jap, "An Exploratory Study of the Introduction of Online Reverse Auctions," Journal of Marketing, July 2003, pp. 96–107; and Sandy Jap, "The Impact of Online Reverse Auction Design on Buyer-Supplier Relationships," Journal of Marketing, January 2007, pp. 146–59.

Lands' End: This case is based on information available on the company website (www.landsend.com) and the following sources: Robert Berner, "A Hard Bargain at Lands' End?" BusinessWeek, May 28, 2001, p. 14; Rebecca Quick, "Getting the Right Fit—Hips and All—Can a Machine Measure You Better than Your Tailor?" The Wall Street Journal, October 18, 2000, p. B1; Stephanie Miles, "Apparel E-tailers Spruce Up for Holidays," The Wall Street Journal, November 6, 2001, p. B6; and Dana James, "Custom Goods Nice Means for Lands' End," Marketing News, August 14, 2000, p. 5.

CHAPTER 7

1. Normandy Madden, "P&G Launches Cover Girl in China," Advertising Age, October 31, 2005, p. 22; www.pg.com.cn, downloaded October 11, 2006; and Sheridan Prasso, "Battle for the Face of China," www.cnnmoney.com, December 12, 2005.

2. International Trade Statistics: 2008 (Geneva: World Trade Organization, 2007). Global trade statistics in this chapter come from this source, unless otherwise indicated.

3. Massaki Kotabe and Kristiaan Helsen, Global Marketing Management, 3rd ed. (New York: Wiley, 2004), p. 440.

4. "Bartering Gains Currency in Hard-Hit Southeast Asia," The Wall Street Journal, April 6, 1998, p. A10; and Beatrice B. Lund, "Corporate Barter as a Marketing Strategy," Marketing News, March 3, 1997, p. 8.

5. Michael E. Porter, The Competitive Advantage of Nations (New York: Free Press, 1990), pp. 577–615. For another view that emphasizes cultural differences, see David S. Landes, The Wealth and Poverty of Nations (New York: Norton, 1998).

6. Steven Fink, Sticky Fingers: Managing the Global Risk of Economic Espionage (Chicago, IL: Dearborn Trade, 2002).

7. Dennis R. Appleyard and Alfred J. Field, Jr., International Economics, 5th ed. (Burr Ridge, IL: McGraw-Hill/Irwin, 2005), chapter 15; Patricia Kowsmann, "Banana Growers Find EU Tariff is Mitigated by End of Quotas," The Wall Street Journal, April 26, 2006; and Economic Report of the President (Washington, DC: U.S. Government Printing Office, 2006).

8. This discussion is based on information provided by the World Trade Organization, www.wto.org, downloaded March 25, 2007.

9. This discussion on the European Union is based on information provided at www.europa.eu, downloaded April 19, 2007.

10. This discussion is based on Probable Effect of Certain Modifications to the North American Free Trade Agreement Rules of Origin (Washington, DC: U.S. International Trade Commission, 2006); and Michael Fielding, "CAFTA-DR to Build Options Over Time," Marketing News, February 1, 2006, pp. 13–14.

11. For an overview of different types of global companies and marketing strategies, see, for example, Warren J. Keegan, Global Marketing, 4th ed. (Upper Saddle River, NJ: Prentice Hall, 2005); and Michael Czinkota and Ilka A. Ronkainen, International Marketing, 8th ed. (Mason, OH: South-Western, 2007).

12. Johnny K. Johansson and Ilkka A. Ronkainen, "The Brand Challenge," Marketing Management, March–April 2004, pp. 54–55.

13. Michael Fielding, "Global Brands Need Balance of Identity, Cultural Respect," Marketing News, September 1, 2006, pp. 8–10; and Kevin Lane Keller, Strategic Brand Management, 2nd ed. (Upper Saddle River, NJ: Prentice Hall, 2003), p. 693.

14. Christopher Leporini, "Are U.S. Companies Losing Their Cool Abroad," Marketing Matters Newsletter at www.marketingpower.com, downloaded February 16, 2006; D. Kjeldgaard and S. Askegaard, "The Globalization of Youth Culture: The Global Youth Segment as Structures of Common Difference," Journal of Consumer Research, September 2006, pp. 231–47; www.mtv.com/company, downloaded January 10, 2007; Elissa Moses, The $100 Billion Allowance: Accessing the Global Teen Market (New York: Wiley, 2000); Bay Fong, "Spending Spree," U.S. News & World Report, May 1, 2006, pp. 42–50; and "The Emerging Middle Class," Business 2.0, July 2006, p. 96.

15. "B2B Blossoms," www.clickz.com, downloaded February 10, 2007.

16. For comprehensive references on cross-cultural aspects of marketing, see Paul A. Herbig, Handbook of Cross-Cultural Marketing (New York: Halworth Press, 1998); Jean Claude Usunier, Marketing Across Cultures, 4th ed. (London: Prentice Hall Europe, 2005); and Philip R. Cateora and John L. Graham, International Marketing, 13th ed. (Burr Ridge, IL: McGraw-Hill/Irwin, 2007). Unless otherwise indicated, examples found in this section appear in these excellent sources.

17. This discussion is based on Tipton F. McCubbins, "Somebody Kicked the Sleeping Dog—New Bite in the Foreign Corrupt Practices Act," Business Horizons, January–February 2001, pp. 27–32.

18. "Clash of Cultures," BrandWeek, May 4, 1998, p. 28. Also see R.L. Tung, Business Negotiations with the Japanese (Lexington, MA: Lexington Books, 1993).

19. These examples appear in Del I. Hawkins, David L. Mothersbaugh, and Roger J. Best, Consumer Behavior, 10th ed. (Burr Ridge, IL: McGraw-Hill/Irwin, 2007), chapter 2.

20. "Greeks Protest Coke's Use of Parthenon," Dallas Morning News, August 17, 1992, p. D4.

21. Cateora and Graham, International Marketing.

22. "If Only Krispy Kreme Meant 'Makes You Smarter,'" Business 2.0, August 2005, p. 108.

23. "Marketing by Language: Oracle Trims Teams, Sees Big Savings," Advertising Age International, July 2000, pp. 4, 38.

24. Terrence A. Shimp and Subhash Sharma, "Consumer Ethnocentrism, Construction and Validation of the CETSCALE," Journal of Marketing Research, August 1987, pp. 280–89.

25. Representative research on consumer ethnocentrism includes: Subhash Sharma, Terrence Shimp, and Jeongshin Shin, "Consumer Ethnocentrism: A Test of Antecedents and Moderators," Journal of the Academy of Marketing Science, Winter 1995, pp. 26–37; Joel Herche, "A Note on the Predictive Validity of the CETSCALE," Journal of the Academy of Marketing Science, Summer 1992, pp. 261–64; Srinivas Durvasula, J. Craig Andrews, and Richard G. Netemeyer,

"A Cross-Cultural Comparison of Consumer Ethnocentrism in the United States and Russia," *Journal of International Consumer Marketing* 9, no. 4 (1997), pp. 73–93; John J. Watson and Ken Wright, "Consumer Ethnocentrism and Attitudes Toward Domestic and Foreign Products," *European Journal of Marketing* 34 (2000), pp. 1149–66; Hyokjin Kwak, Anupam Jaju, and Trina Larsen, "Consumer Ethnocentrism Offline and Online: The Mediating Role of Marketing Efforts and Personality Traits in the United States, South Korea, and India," *Journal of the Academy of Marketing Science* 34 (2006), pp. 367–85.

26. Vijay Mahajan and Kamini Banga, *The 86 Percent Solution: How to Succeed in the Biggest Market Opportunity of the Next 50 Years* (Upper Saddle River, NJ: Pearson Education, 2006); and C.K. Pralahad, *The Fortune at the Bottom of the Pyramid: Eradicating Poverty Through Profits* (Upper Saddle River, NJ: Pearson Education, 2005).

27. "Navigating the Labyrinth: Sales and Distribution in Today's China," *Knowledge@Wharton*, October 16, 2006; Mahajan and Banga, *The 86 Percent Solution;* and Cateora and Graham, *International Marketing.*

28. www.wto.org, downloaded January 20, 2007.

29. Pralahad, *The Fortune at the Bottom of the Pyramid;* and Jay Greene, "Taking Tiny Loans to the Next Level," *BusinessWeek,* November 27, 2006, pp. 76–79.

30. "Mattel Plans to Double Sales Abroad," *The Wall Street Journal,* February 11, 1998, pp. A3, A11.

31. These examples are found in Cateora and Graham, *International Marketing,* p. 540; "Honda Takes Currency Hit in Europe," *The Wall Street Journal,* March 28, 2001, p. A16; and "Currency Troubles Halt P&G Shipments to Turkey," *Advertising Age,* March 5, 2001, p. 32.

32. Eric Clark, *The Real Toy Story* (New York: The Free Press, 2007); and Cateora and Graham, *International Marketing.*

33. For an extensive and recent examination of these market-entry options, see for example, Johnny K. Johansson, *Global Marketing: Foreign Entry, Local Marketing, and Global Management,* 3rd ed. (Burr Ridge, IL: McGraw-Hill/Irwin, 2003); A. Coskun Samli, *Entering & Succeeding in Emerging Countries: Marketing to the Forgotten Majority* (Mason, OH: South-Western, 2004); Keegan, *Global Marketing;* and Cateora and Graham, *International Marketing.*

34. Based on an interview with Pamela Viglielmo, director of international marketing, Fran Wilson Creative Cosmetics; and "Foreign Firms Think Their Way into Japan," www.successstories.com/nikkei, downloaded March 24, 2003.

35. *Small and Medium Sized Exporting Companies: A Statistical Handbook* (Washington, DC: International Trade Administration, June 2006).

36. "Made in Taiwan," *Forbes,* April 2, 2001, pp. 64–66.

37. *McDonald's 2006 Annual Report.*

38. "About Us," www.elite.co.il, downloaded January 5, 2007.

39. Cateora and Graham, *International Marketing.*

40. "FedEx Expands Reach in China with Buyout of Joint Venture," *The Wall Street Journal,* January 25, 2006; www.harley-davidson.com, downloaded January 10, 2007.

41. This discussion is based on Keller, *Strategic Brand Management,* pp. 709–10; Todd J. Gillman, "Chip Off the Old Block," *Dallas Morning News,* July 30, 2006, pp. 1A, 22A; "Machines for the Masses," *The Wall Street Journal,* December 9, 2003, pp. A19, A20; "The Color of Beauty," *Forbes,* November 22, 2000, pp. 170–76; "It's Goo, Goo, Goo, Goo Vibrations at the Gerber Lab," *The Wall Street Journal,* December 4, 1996, pp. A1, A6; Donald R. Graber, "How to Manage a Global Product Development Process," *Industrial Marketing Management,* November 1996, pp. 483–98; and Herbig, *Handbook of Cross-Cultural Marketing.*

42. Jagdish N. Sheth and Atul Parvatiyar, "The Antecedents and Consequences of Integrated Global Marketing," *International Marketing Review* 18, no. 1 (2001), pp. 16–29. Also see D. Szymanski, S. Bharadwaj, and R. Varadarajan, "Standardization versus Adaptation of International Marketing Strategy: An Empirical Investigation," *Journal of Marketing,* October 1993, pp. 1–17.

43. Cateora and Graham, *International Marketing.*

44. "With Profits Elusive, Wal-Mart to Exit Germany," *The Wall Street Journal,* July 29, 2006, pp. A1, A6.

45. "Rotten Apples," *Dallas Morning News,* April 7, 1998, p. 14A.

46. For an in-depth discussion on gray markets, see Kersi D. Antia, Mark Bergen, and Shantanu Dutta, "Competing with Gray Markets," *Sloan Management Review,* Fall 2004, pp. 63–69; and Kersi D. Antia, Mark E. Bergen, Shantanu Dutta, and Robert J. Fisher, "How Does Enforcement Deter Gray Market Incidence?" *Journal of Marketing,* January 2006, pp. 92–106.

CNS Breathe Right Strips: This case was prepared by Mary L. Brown based on interviews with Kevin McKenna, vice president, international, and Nick Naumann, senior marketing services manager of CNS, Inc., September 2004.

CHAPTER 8

1. Richard Corliss, "The Year of the 3quel," *Time,* January 15, 2007, pp. 66–68.

2. John Horn, "Studios Play Name Games," *Star Tribune,* August 10, 1997, p. F11; and "Flunking Chemistry," *Star Tribune,* April 11, 2003, p. E13.

3. "2006 U.S. Theatrical Market Statistics—Worldwide Market Research & Analysis." Motion Picture Association of America, p. 12. See www.mpaa.org/2006-US-Theatrical-Market-Statistics-Report.pdf.

4. Based on a cursory analysis of the data presented in "All Time Box Office: Worldwide Grosses." See Box Office Mojo, www.boxofficemojo.com/alltime/world (registration required).

5. Dave McNary, "Shrek 3 Gears Up," *Variety,* March 17, 2007. See www.variety.com/article/VR1117961316.html.

6. The Internet Movie Data Base reference for Daniel Radcliffe and Harrison Ford. See www.imdb.com/name/nm0705356 and www.imdb.com/name/nm0000148; and William Keck, "He Has a Need for Speed." *USA Today,* April 4, 2007.

7. Corliss "The Year of the 3quel," p. 68; and Jehoshua Eliashberg, Anita Elberse, and Mark A. A. M. Leenders, "The Motion Picture Industry: Critical Issues in Practice, Current Research, and New Directions," *Marketing Science,* November–December 2006, pp. 642–43.

8. Corliss "The Year of the 3quel," p. 68; and Nikki Finke, "Sony Acting Extra-Sneaky for 'Spidey 3,'" *Deadline Hollywood Daily,* April 29, 2007, www.deadlinehollywooddaily.com/sony-acting-extra-sneaky-for-spidey-3.

9. Box Office Mojo, www.boxofficemojo.com/alltime/world (registration required).

10. Willow Bay, "Test Audiences Have Profound Effect on Movies," *CNN Newsstand & Entertainment Weekly,* September 28, 1998; see www.cnn.com/SHOWBIZ/Movies/9809/28/screen.test/.

11. Helene Diamond, "Lights, Camera . . . Research!" *Marketing News,* September 11, 1989, pp. 10–11; and "Killer!" *Time,* November 16, 1987, pp. 72–79.

12. Joel Ryan, "Gigli 'Razzed'," att.eonline.com/News/Items, downloaded January 26, 2004.

13. Carl Diorio, "Tracking Projectings: B. O. Calculations an Inexact Science," *Variety,* May 24, 2001; see www.variety.com/index.asp?layout=story&articleid=VR1117799996.

14. For a lengthier, expanded 2004 definition, consult the American Marketing Association's website at www.marketingpower.com; for a researcher's comments on this and other definitions of marketing research, see Lawrence D. Gibson, "Quo Vadis, Marketing Research?" *Marketing Research,* Spring 2000, pp. 36–41.

15. Etienne Benson, "Toy Stories," *Observer* 19, no. 12 (December 2006).

16. Definitions of the three kinds of marketing research are adapted from William R. Dillon, Thomas J. Madden, and Neil H. Firtle, *Marketing Research in a Marketing Environment*, 3rd ed. (Burr Ridge, IL: McGraw-Hill/Irwin, 1994), pp. 40–41.

17. "Behind the Scenes: Toy of the Year Awards 2006," *Family Fun*, http://familyfun.go.com/parties/holiday-seasonal/feature/famf1006_toy_method/famf1006_toy_method.html; and "Toy Industry Association Announces Top Toys of the Year," press release from the Toy Industry Association, February 10, 2007.

18. Lawrence D. Gibson, "Defining Marketing Problems," *Marketing Research,* Spring 1998, pp. 4–12.

19. "Inside TV Ratings" and "National Audience sample" from the Nielsen Media Research website, www.nielsenmedia.com.

20. "Nielsen Media Research Local Market Universe Estimates," Nielsen Media Research Excel spreadsheet from September 23, 2006.

21. "Nielsen Media Research Local Market Universe Estimates" and "Nielsen to Offer Integrated, All-Electronic Television Measurement Across Multiple Media Platforms," Nielsen Media Research press release from June 14, 2006. See http://a2m2.nielsenmedia.com.

22. "Top TV Ratings" from Nielsen Media Research. See www.nielsenmedia.com/nc/portal/site/Public/menuitem.43afce2fac27e890311ba0a347a062a0.

23. Robert Coen, "Insider's Report," *Universal McCann*, December 2006. Data obtained from tables: "The Outlook for 2007 National Advertising" (TV only) and "The Outlook for Total Advertising 2007" (Local TV only), p. 7.

24. David Kiley, "Counting the Eyeballs," *BusinessWeek*, January 16, 2006, pp. 84–85; and "The Ultimate Marketing Machine," *The Economist*, July 8, 2006, pp. 61–64.

25. Mylene Margalinday, "Ad Vantage," *The Wall Street Journal*, June 19, 2006, p. R11.

26. Robert Frank, "How to Live Large, and Largely for Free, Jennifer Voitle's Way," *The Wall Street Journal*, June 9, 2003, pp. A1, A8.

27. Sarah Ellison, "P&G Chief's Turnaround Recipe: Find Out What Women Want," *The Wall Street Journal*, June 1, 2005, p. A1; Mark Maremont, "New Toothbrush Is Big-Ticket Item," *The Wall Street Journal*, October 27, 1998, pp. B1, B6; and Emily Nelson, "P&G Checks Out Real Life," *The Wall Street Journal*, May 17, 2001, pp. B1, B4.

28. Kenneth Chang, "Enlisting Science's Lessons to Entice More Shoppers to Spend More," *The New York Times*, September 19, 2006, p. D3; and Janet Adamy, "Cooking Up Changes at Kraft Foods," *The Wall Street Journal*, February 20, 2007, p. B1.

29. For a more complete discussion of questionnaire methods, see David A. Aaker, V. Kumar, and George S. Day, *Marketing Research*, 8th ed. (New York: John Wiley & Sons, Inc., 2004), pp. 188–272.

30. Jyoti Thottam, "How Kids Set the (Ring) Tone," *Time*, April 4, 2005, pp. 40–45.

31. Jonathan Eig, "Food Industry Battles for Moms Who Want to Cook—Just a Little," *The Wall Street Journal*, March 7, 2001, pp. A1, A10; and Susan Feyder, "It Took Tinkering by Twin Cities Firms to Saver Some Sure Bets," *Star Tribune*, June 9, 1982, p. 11A.

32. Constance Gustke, "Built to Last," *Sales & Marketing Management*, August 1997, pp. 78–83.

33. "Focus on Consumers," *General Mills Midyear Report*, Minneapolis, January 8, 1998, pp. 2–3.

34. Michael J. McCarthy, "Stalking the Elusive Teenage Trendsetter," *The Wall Street Journal*, November 19, 1998, pp. B1, B10; and "Teens Spend $155 Billion in 2000," Teenage Research Unlimited press releases, January 25, 2001.

35. Roy Furchgott, "For Cool Hunters, Tomorrow's Trend Is the Trophy," *The New York Times*, June 28, 1998, p. 10; Patrick Goldstein, "Untangling the Web of Teen Trends," *Los Angeles Times*, November 21, 2000, p. F1; and Lev Grossman, "The Quest for Cool," *Time*, September 8, 2003, pp. 48–54.

36. Clayton M. Christensen and Michael E. Raynor, *The Innovator's Solution: Creating and Sustaining Successful Growth* (Cambridge, MA: Harvard Business School Press, 2003); Clayton M. Christensen, *The Innovator's Dilemma: When Technologies Cause Great Firms to Fail* (Cambridge, MA: Harvard Business School Press, 1997); Clayton M. Christensen and Michael Overdorf, "Meeting the Challenge of Descriptive Change," *Harvard Business Review,* March–April 2000, pp. 67–76; and Clayton M. Christensen and Michael E. Raynor, "Creating a Killer Product," *Forbes*, October 13, 2003, pp. 82–84.

37. The Wendy's questionnaire is adapted from one originally developed by Robert Joffe, now at the University of Redlands.

38. Wendy Zellner, "Look Out, Supermarkets—Wal-Mart Is Hungry," *BusinessWeek,* September 14, 1998, pp. 98–100; Richard McCattery, "Wal-Mart Rumbles in the Supermarket Jungle," The Motley Fool, March 7, 1998; and "Our 1000th Supercenter," Wal-Mart news release, August 22, 2001.

39. Dale Buss, "The Race to RFID," *CEO Magazine*, November 2004, pp. 32–36.

40. The step 4 discussion was written by David Ford and Don Rylander of Ford Consulting Group, Inc.; the Tony's Pizza example was provided by Teré Carral of Tony's Pizza.

Ford Consulting Group, Inc.: This case was written by David Ford of Ford Consulting Group, Inc.

CHAPTER 9

1. Kimberly Weisal, "A Shine in Their Shoes," *BusinessWeek,* December 5, 2005, p. 84.

2. Duff McDonald, "Zappos.com: Success Through Simplicity," *CIO Insight* November 10, 2006.

3. Weisal, "A Shine in Their Shoes," p. 84.

4. McDonald, "Zappos.com."

5. Ibid.

6. See "The Zappos Story" on www.zappos.com.

7. Devin Leonard, "Nightmare on Madison Avenue," *Fortune*, June 28, 2004, pp. 93–108; Anthony Bianco, "The Vanishing Mass Market," *BusinessWeek*, July 12, 2004, pp. 61–65; and Geoff Colvin, "Selling P&G," *Fortune*, September 17, 2007, pp. 163–69.

8. "Special Report on Mass Communication: A Long March," *The Economist*, July 14, 2001, pp. 63–65.

9. Amy Merrick, "Once a Bellwether, Ann Taylor Fights Its Stodgy Image," *The Wall Street Journal*, July 12, 2005, pp. A1, A8.

10. The relation of these criteria to implementation is discussed in Jacqueline Dawley, "Making Connections: Enhance the Implementation of Value of Attitude-Based Segmentation," *Marketing Research*, Summer, 2006, pp. 16–22.

11. The discussion of fast-food trends and market share is based on Simmons Market Research Bureau NCS/NHCS Spring 2007 Adult Full-Year Choices System Crosstabulation Report based on visits within the past 30 days.

12. Jennifer Ordonez, "Taco Bell Chief Has New Tactic: Be Like Wendy's," *The Wall Street Journal*, February 23, 2001, pp. B1, B4; and Jennifer Ordonez, "An Efficiency Drive: Fast-Food Lanes Are Getting Even Faster," *The Wall Street Journal*, May 18, 2000, pp. A1, A10.

13. "Great Expectations: Wendy's Moves Ahead With New Strategic Plan." See www.wendys-invest.com/strategic1206/strategicplan.php.

14. Bruce Horovitz, "Fast-Food Rivals Suit Up for Breakfast War," *USA Today*, February 20, 2007, p. 3B; Janet Adamy, "Wendy's Considers Possible Sale," *The Wall Street Journal*, April 26, 2007, p. A2; and Janet Adamy, "Why No. 3 Wendy's Finds Vanilla So Exciting," *The*

Wall Street Journal, April 6, 2007, pp. B1, B2; and Janet Adamy, "How Wendy's Faltered, Opening Way to Buyout," *The Wall Street Journal,* August 29, 2007, pp. A1, A11.

15. Michael Arndt, "McDonald's 24/7: By Focusing on the Hours Between Traditional Meal Times, the Fast-Food Giant is Sizzling," *Business-Week,* February 5, 2007, pp. 64–72.

16. The discussion of Apple's segmentation strategies through the years is based on information from its website, www.apple.com, and www. apple-history.com/history.html.

17. Dennis Sellers, "Business Journal: Digital Hub Plan Just Might Work," *MacCentral,* January 16, 2001, and Apple's website, www.apple.com.

18. This discussion is based on Roger A. Kerin and Robert A. Peterson, *Strategic Marketing Problems: Cases and Comments,* 11th ed. (Upper Saddle River, NJ: Prentice Hall, 2007), pp. 147–49; John M. Mullins, Orville C. Walker Jr., Haper W. Boyd Jr., and Jean-Claude Larreche, *Marketing Management: A Strategic Decision-Marketing Approach,* 5th ed. (Burr Ridge, IL: McGraw-Hill/Irwin, 2005), p. 216; and Carol Traeger, "What Are Automakers Doing for Women? Part III: Volvo," www.edmund.com, July 26, 2005.

19. Nicholas Zamiska, "How Milk Got a Major Boost by Food Panel," *The Wall Street Journal,* August 30, 2004, pp. B1, B5.

20. Rebecca Winter, "Chocolate Milk," *Time,* April 30, 2001, p. 20.

21. Mark A. Moon, John T. Mentzer, Carlo D. Smith, and Michael S. Garver, "Seven Keys to Better Forecasting," *Business Horizons,* September–October 1998, pp. 44–52.

22. Interview with Bill McKee, manager of corporate communications/ public relations, Xerox Corporation, and annual reports available at www2.xerox.com/go/xix/about_xerox/T_archive,jsp?view-annualreports.

Rollerblade: This case was written by Michael J. Vessey and William Rudelius and is based on personal interviews with Jeremy Stonier and Nicholas Skally in 2005 and Joe Olivas in 2007.

CHAPTER 10

1. Much of the Apple example opening Chapter 10 is based on Lev Grossman, "The Apple of Your Ear," *Time,* January 22, 2007, pp. 48–54.

2. Jefferson Graham, "Apple Earnings Only Expected to Grow," *USA Today,* April 27, 2007, p. 3B; and John Markoff, "Ringing in the Future," *Star Tribune,* January 10, 2007, pp. A1, A6.

3. Ken Belson, "Oh, Yeah, There's a Ballgame, Too," *The New York Times,* October 22, 2006, pp. 3–1, 3–7.

4. Interview with Geek Squad founder Robert Stephens on "60 Minutes," January 28, 2007; also see www.geeksquad.com; Debora Viana Thompson, Rebecca W. Hamilton, and Roland Rust, "Feature Fatigue: When Product Capabilities Become Too Much of a Good Thing," *Journal of Marketing Research,* November 2005, pp. 431–42; and Roland T. Rust, Debora Viana Thompson, and Rebecca W. Hamilton, "Defeating Feature Fatigue," *Harvard Business Review,* February 2006, pp. 98–107.

5. Youngme Moon, "Break Free from the Product Life Cycle," *Harvard Business Review,* May 2005, pp. 86–94.

6. Interview with Geek Squad founder Robert Stephens on "60 Minutes," January 28, 2007.

7. Greg A. Stevens and James Burley, "3,000 Raw Ideas = 1 Commercial Success!" *Research-Technology Management,* May–June 1997, pp. 16–27.

8. R. G. Cooper and E. J. Kleinschmidt, "New Products—What Separates Winners from Losers?" *Journal of Product Innovation Management,* September 1987, pp. 169–84: Robert G. Cooper, *Winning at New Products,* 2nd ed. (Reading, MA: Addison-Wesley. 1993), pp. 49–66; and Thomas D. Kuczmarski, "Measuring Your Return on Innovation," *Marketing Management,* Spring 2000, pp. 25–32.

9. Julie Fortser, "The Lucky Charm of Steve Sanger," *BusinessWeek,* March 26, 2001, pp. 75–76.

10. John Gilbert, "To Sell Cars in Japan, U.S. Needs to Offer More Right-Drive Models," *Star Tribune,* May 27, 1995, p. M1.

11. See Productscan Online at www.productscan.com.

12. The Avert Virucidal Tissues and Hey! There's A Monster in My Room spray examples are adapted from Robert M. McMath and Thom Forbes, *What Were They Thinking?* (New York: Random House, Inc., 1998).

13. Robert Cooper, *The Accelerate to Market—Small-Medium Enterprise: A Stage-Gate Roadmap from Idea to Launch* (Ontario, Canada: Product Development Institute, 2002); and Pierre Loewe and Jennifer Dominiquini, "Overcoming the Barriers to Effective Innovation," *Strategy & Leadership* 34, no. 1 (2006), pp. 24–31.

14. Dan P. Lovallo and Olivier Sibony, "Distortions and Deceptions in Strategic Decisions," *The McKinsey Quarterly,* no. 1 (2006), pp. 19–29; and Byron G. Augusto, Eric P. Harmon, and Vivek Pandit, "The Right Service Strategies for Product Companies, *The McKinsey Quarterly,* no. 1 (2006), pp. 41–51.

15. Isabelle Royer, "Why Bad Projects Are So Hard to Kill," *Harvard Business Review,* February 2003, pp. 48–56; John T. Morn, Dan P. Lovallo, and S. Patrick Viguerie, "Beating the Odds in Market Entry," *The McKinsey Quarterly,* no. 4 (2005), pp. 35–45; Leslie Perlow and Stephanie Williams, "Is Silence Killing Your Company?" *Harvard Business Review,* May 2003, pp. 52–58; Beverly K. Brockman and Robert M. Morgan, "The Moderating Effect of Organizational Cohesiveness in Knowledge Use and New Product Development," *Journal of Marketing Science,* no. 3 (Summer 2006), pp. 295–306; Eyal Biyalogorsky, William Boulding, and Richard Staelin, "Stuck in the Past: Why Managers Persist with New Product Failures," *Journal of Marketing,* April 2006, pp. 108–21; and Irwin L. Janis, *Groupthink* (New York: Free Press, 1988).

16. Jena McGregor, "How Failure Breeds Success," *BusinessWeek,* July 10, 2006, pp. 42–52.

17. Ibid.

18. Micheline Maynard, "Gone but Not Forgotten," *The New York Times,* October 28, 2006, pp. B1, B8.

19. Amy Merrick, "As 3M Chief, McNerney Wastes No Time Starting Systems Favored by Ex-Boss Welch," *The Wall Street Journal,* June 5, 2001, pp. B1, B4; see General Electric's website (www.ge.com) for an in-depth explanation of Six Sigma that 3M and other Fortune 500 companies use to improve quality: "The Road to Customer Impact: What Is Six Sigma?"

20. Janice Griffiths-Hemans and Rajiv Grover, "Setting the Stage for Creative New Products: Investigating the Idea Fruition Process," *Journal of the Academy of Marketing Science,* Winter 2006, pp. 27–39.

21. Kimberly Judson, Denise D. Schoenabachler, Geoffrey L. Gordon, Rick E. Ridnour, and Dan C. Weilbaker, "The New Product Development Process: Let the Voice of the Salesperson Be Heard," *Journal of Product & Brand Management* 15, no. 3 (2006), pp. 194–202.

22. Morgan L. Swink and Vincent A. Mabert, "Product Development Partnerships: Balancing Needs of OEMs and Suppliers," *Business Horizons,* May–June 2000, pp. 59–68.

23. C. K. Prahalad and Venkat Ramswamy, *The Future of Competition* (Boston: Harvard Business School Press, 2004); Steve Hamm, "Adding Customers to the Design Team," *BusinessWeek,* March 1, 2004, pp. 22–23.

24. Anthony W. Ulwick, "Turn Customer Input into Innovation" *Harvard Business Review,* January 2002, pp. 91–97.

25. Sarah Ellison, "P & G Chief's Turnaround Recipe: Find Out What Women Want," *The Wall Street Journal,* June 1, 2005, pp. A1, A16.

26. Adam Aston and Gail Edmonson, "This Volvo Is Not a Guy Thing," *BusinessWeek,* March 15, 2004, pp. 84–86.

27. Joseph Weber, Stanley Holmes, and Christopher Palmeri, "Mosh Pits' of Creativity," *BusinessWeek,* November 7, 2005, pp. 98–100.

28. Bruce Nussbaum, "The Power of Design," *BusinessWeek,* May 17, 2004, pp. 86–94; the article gives many techniques for idea and concept generation, as do Appendixes A, B, and C in Merle Crawford and Anthony Di Benedetto, *New Products Management,* 7th ed. (Burr Ridge, IL: McGraw-Hill/Irwin, 2003).

29. Peter Lewis, "Texas Instruments' Lunatic Fringe," *Fortune,* September 4, 2006, pp. 121–28.

30. Steve Hoeffler, "Measuring Preferences for Really New Products," *Journal of Marketing Research,* November 2003, pp. 406–20.

31. Bruce Hororitz, "Lay's Chips Away at 'Bad' Fat with New Oil," *USA Today,* May 3, 2006, p. 1B.

32. Larry Huston and Nobil Sakkab, "Connect and Develop," *Harvard Business Review,* March 2006, pp. 58–66; "Pringles Announces First-of-Its-Kind Technology that Prints Directly on Individual Crisps," www.pg.com, accessed April 6, 2004.

33. Ely Dahan and John R. Hauser, "Product Development—Managing a Dispersed Process," in *Handbook of Marketing,* ed. Barton Weitz and Robin Wensley (London: Sage Publications, 2006), pp. 179–222.

34. Gary Hammel, "Innovation's New Math," *Fortune,* July 9, 2001, pp. 130–31.

35. Thomas M. Burton, "By Learning from Failures, Lilly Keeps Drug Pipeline Full," *The Wall Street Journal,* April 21, 2004, pp. A1, A12.

36. Ben Elgin, "Managing Google's Idea Factory," *BusinessWeek,* October 3, 2005, pp. 88–90.

37. Jack Neff, "White Bread, USA," *Advertising Age,* July 9, 2001, pp. 1, 12, 13.

38. Tom Molson and George Sproles, "Styling Strategy," *Business Horizons,* September–October 2000, pp. 45–52.

39. Yuhong Wu, Sridhar Balasubramanian, and Vijay Mahajan, "When Is a Preannounced New Product Likely to Be Delayed?" *Journal of Marketing,* April 2004, pp. 101–13.

40. Mark Leslie and Charles J. Holloway, "The Sales Learning Curve," *Harvard Business Review,* July–August 2006, pp. 115–23.

41. Kim Schatzel and Roger Calantone, "Creating Market Anticipation: An Exploratory Evaluation of the Effect of Preannouncement Behavior on a New Product Launch," *Journal of the Academy of Marketing Sciences,* Summer 2006, pp. 357–66.

42. Jennifer Ordonez, "How Burger King Got Burned in Quest to Make the Perfect Fry," *The Wall Street Journal,* January 16, 2001, pp. A1, A8.

43. Kerry A. Dolan, "Speed: The New X Factor," *Forbes,* December 26, 2005, pp. 74–77.

44. Gail Edmonson, "BMW's Dream Factory," *BusinessWeek,* October 16, 2006, pp. 70–80; Steve Hamm, "Speed Demons," *BusinessWeek,* March 27, 2006, pp. 68–76; and Amy Barrett, "J & J: Reinventing How It Invents," *BusinessWeek,* April 17, 2006, pp. 60–61.

45. Peter Burrows, "Architects of the Info Age," *BusinessWeek,* March 29, 2004, p. 22.

3M Greptile Grip Golf Glove: This video case was written by Michael J. Vessey based on interviews with Dr. George Dierberger, 3M personnel, and other published sources.

CHAPTER 11

1. Betsy McKay, "Pepsi Launches Low-Calorie Gatorade," *The Wall Street Journal,* September 7, 2007, p. B6; Cheryl Jackson, "Quaker Acquisition a Big Winner for Pepsi," *Chicago Sun-Times,* December 1, 2006, pp. D1, 5; Darren Rovell, *First in Thirst: How Gatorade Turned the Science of Sweat into a Cultural Phenomenon*

(New York: AMACOM, 2005); "Cindy Alston: CMO, Gatorade and Propel," *Advertising Age,* November 13, 2006, p. S6; and "Gatorade Works on Endurance," *The Wall Street Journal,* March 21, 2005, p. B6.

2. For an extended discussion of the generalized product life cycle, see Donald R. Lehmann and Russell S. Winer, *Product Management,* 5th ed (Burr Ridge, IL: McGraw-Hill, 2008).

3. Jack Neff, "Six-Blade Blitz," *Advertising Age,* September 19, 2005, pp. 3, 53; and Jack Neff, "Fusion's Nuclear Launch Isn't Good Enough—Yet," *Advertising Age,* July 3, 2006, pp. 3, 23.

4. John W. Mullins, Orville C. Walker, Jr., Harper W. Boyd, Jr., and Jean-Claude Larréché, *Marketing Management: A Strategic Decision-Making Approach,* 5th ed. (Burr Ridge, IL: McGraw-Hill/Irwin, 2005), p. 396.

5. Portions of this discussion on the fax machine product life cycle are based on Karen Prema, "Faxes Are Evolving," *Purchasing Magazine Online,* March 16, 2006; "When Your Time Has Come—and Gone," *EDN. Com,* November 27, 2003; and "Atlas Electronics Corporation," in Roger A. Kerin and Robert A. Peterson, *Strategic Marketing Problems: Cases and Comments,* 8th ed. (Upper Saddle River, NJ: Prentice Hall, 1998), pp. 494–506.

6. "How Many Active Email Mailboxes Are There in the World Today?" The Radicate Group, Inc., downloaded January 25, 2007; and "If You Think Fax Is Dead, Think Again," dallasnews.com, downloaded February 10, 2007.

7. Kate MacArthur, "Coke Energizes Tab, Neville Isdell's Fave," *Advertising Age,* August 29, 2005, pp. 3, 21.

8. Julia Boorstin, "Can Fusion Become a Billion-Dollar Razor?" MoneyCentral.msn.com, downloaded January 10, 2007.

9. "Hosiery Sales Hit Major Snag," *Dallas Morning News,* December 18, 2006, p. 50.

10. "How to Separate Trends from Fads," *BrandWeek,* October 23, 2000, pp. 30, 32.

11. *Year-end Marketing Reports on U.S. Recorded Music Shipments* (New York: Recording Industry Association of America, 2007); and "U.S. Music Forecast: 2006–2011," Jupiter Research Reports jupiter.com, January 10, 2007.

12. Everett M. Rogers, *Diffusion of Innovations,* 5th ed. (New York: Free Press, 2003).

13. Jagdish N. Sheth and Banwasi Mitral, *Consumer Behavior: A Managerial Perspective,* 2nd ed. (Mason, OH: South-Western College Publishing, 2003).

14. "When Free Samples Become Saviors," *The Wall Street Journal* August 14, 2001, pp. B1, B4.

15. Nokia.com, downloaded February 7, 2007; and "Wrinkle-Stain-Resistant Apparel Boost Sales," *DSN Retailing,* June 9, 2003, pp. 25–26.

16. Terry Box, "Biker Chic," *Dallas Morning News,* June 24, 2007, pp. 1D, 6D; and "Dried Plum Print Push Paces Prunes," *BrandWeek,* August 12, 2002, p. 6.

17. "Dockers Adds Diversity to Message," *BrandWeek,* September 11, 2006, p. 18.

18. Hilary Cassidy, "Balancing Act," *BrandWeek,* January 23, 2006, pp. 24–28.

19. Sheth and Mitral, *Consumer Behavior;* and Marsha Cohen, *Marketing to the 50+ Population* (New York: EPM Communications, Inc., 2007).

20. John Gourville, "How to Avoid a Price Increase," *Working Knowledge for Business Leaders,* Harvard Business School, June 28, 2004; "The Shrink Wrap," *Time,* June 2, 2003, p. 81; "Don't Raise the Price, Lower the Water Award," *BrandWeek,* January 8, 2001, p. 19; and "More For Less," *Consumer Reports,* August 2004, p. 63.

21. This discussion is based on Kevin Lane Keller, *Strategic Brand Management,* 2nd ed. (Upper Saddle River, NJ: Prentice Hall, 2003). Also see, Susan Fornier, "Building Brand Community on the

Harley-Davidson Posse Ride," *Harvard Business School Note* #5-501-502 (Boston: Harvard Business School, 2001); Tulin Erdem, Joffre Swait, and Ana Valenzuela, "Brands as Signals: A Cross-Country Validation study," *Journal of Marketing,* January 2006, pp. 34–49.

22. Keller, *Strategic Brand Management.*

23. This discussion is based on John Deighton, "How Snapple Got Its Juice Back," *Harvard Business Review,* January 2002, pp. 47–53; and "Can Lender's Get Out of Marketing Pickle? *BrandWeek,* March 5, 2007, p. 6. Also see, Vithala R. Rao, Manj K. Agarwal, and Denise Dahlhoff, "How Is Manifest Branding Strategy Related to the Value of a Corporation?" *Journal of Marketing,* October 2004, pp. 125–41.

24. "Hummer Markets Shoes for Offroad Set," *Advertising Age,* January 12, 2004, pp. 3, 40; "Judge Pooh-Poohs Lawsuit over Disney Licensing Fees," *USAToday.com,* March 30, 2004; and Keller, *Strategic Brand Management.*

25. Rob Osler, "The Name Game: Tips on How to Get It Right," *Marketing News,* September 14, 1998, p. 50; "Porn.com Price May Be Shattered by WallStreet.com," *bloomberg.com,* October 12, 2007; and Keller, *Strategic Brand Management.* Also see Pamela W. Henderson and Joseph A. Cote, "Guidelines for Selecting or Modifying Logos," *Journal of Marketing,* April 1998, pp. 14–30; and Chiranjeev Kohli and Douglas W. LaBahn, "Creating Effective Brand Names: A Study of the Naming Process," *Journal of Advertising Research,* January–February 1997, pp. 67–75.

26. Jack Neff, "Small Ball: Marketers Rely on Line Extensions," *Advertising Age,* April 11, 2005, p. 10.

27. "When Brand Extension Becomes Brand Abuse," *BrandWeek,* October 26, 1998, pp. 20, 22.

28. For an in-depth discussion on co-branding, see Akshay R. Rao and Robert W. Ruekert, "Brand Alliances as Signals of Product Quality," *Sloan Management Review,* Fall 1994, pp. 87–97.

29. This discussion is based on David Aaker, *Brand Portfolio Strategy* (New York: Free Press, 2004); and Ramin Setoodeh, "Barbie vs. Bratz: Which Doll Will Win?" *MSNBC.com,* December 11, 2006.

30. Nikhil Bahadur, "How to Slim Down a Brand Portfolio," *Strategy & Business,* Winter 2006, pp. 15–16.

31. "Private Labels Stock on Growth," *The Wall Street Journal,* July 18, 2007, p. B8; and Lien Lamey, Barbara Deleersnyder, Marnik G. Dekimpe, and Jan-Benedict E. M. Steenkamp, "How Business Cycles Contribute to Private-Label Success: Evidence from the United States and Europe," *Journal of Marketing,* January 2007, pp. 1–15.

32. www.pez.com, downloaded February 1, 2007; David Welch, *Collecting Pez* (Murphysboro, IL: Bubba Scrubba Publications, 1995); and "Elements Design Adds Dimension to Perennial Favorite Pez Brand," *Package Design Magazine,* May 2006, pp. 37–38.

33. "Market Statistics," *Packaging-Gateway.com,* downloaded March 25, 2007.

34. "Green Bean Casserole Turns 50," *Dallas Morning News,* November 19, 2005, p. 10D.

35. "L'eggs Hatches a New Hosiery Package," *BrandWeek,* January 1, 2001, p. 6.

36. Representative recent scholarly research on packaging and labeling perceptions includes: Priya Rgahubir and Eric A. Greenleaf, "Ratios in Proportion: What Should the Shape of the Package Be?" *Journal of Marketing,* April 2006, pp. 95–107; Peter H. Bloch, Frederic F. Brunel, and Todd Arnold, "Individual Differences in the Centrality of Visual Product Aesthetics: Concept and Measurement," *Journal of Consumer Research,* March 2003, pp. 551–65: and Pamela Anderson, Joan Giese, and Joseph A. Cote, "Impression Management Using Typeface Design," *Journal of Marketing,* October 2004, pp. 60–72.

37. Betsy McKay, "Pepsi's New Marketing Dance: Can Can," *The Wall Street Journal,* January 12, 2007, p. B3.

38. "Asian Brands Are Sprouting English Logos in Pursuit of Status, International Image," *The Wall Street Journal,* August 7, 2001, p. B7C.

39. Susanna Hamner, "Packaging that Pays," *Business 2.0,* July 26, 2006, pp. 68–69.

40. "Wal-Mart: Use Less Packaging," *Dallas Morning News,* September 23, 2006, p. 2D. For an overview of Procter & Gamble's environmental efforts, see *Sustainability Report 2005* (Cincinnati, OH: Procter & Gamble Company, 2006).

41. "Packaging," *www.hp.com,* downloaded January 17, 2007.

42. Christian Twigg-Flesner, *Consumer Product Guarantees* (Aldershot, England: Ashgate Publishing, 2003).

BMW: This case was written by Giana Eckhardt and Steven Hartley based on company interviews and the following sources: April Boehm, "BMW Undergoes a Tuneup," *The Wall Street Journal,* September 28, 2007, p. A11; Gail Edmondson, "BMW's Dream Factory," *Business Week,* October 16, 2006, p. 70. Claire Billings, "Continuously Building the BMW Brand for 25 Years," *Compaign,* September 24, 2004, p. 16; Larry Armstrong, "BMW's Brand-new 6-series Convertible is Powerful, Elegant, and Eye-catching," *BusinessWeek,* August 9, 2004, p. 73; "BMW Reaches Out To the Affluent Young Urbanites," "*Campaign,* July 23, 2004, p.18; Gail Edmondson, "BMW: Crashing the Compact Market," *BusinessWeek,* June 18, 2004, p. 36; Troy Dreier, "BMW and iPod: Two Exclusive Names That Now Go Well Together," *PC Magazine,* September 21, 2004, p. 176.

CHAPTER 12

1. Mark Carreau, "With a $25 Million Ticket To Ride, 5th Space Tourist Goes into Orbit," *The Houston Chronicle,* April 8, 2007, p. A17; Kimi Yoshino, "You'll Want a Window Seat, For $200,000, Virgin Galactic Promises Tourists Four Minutes of Zero Gravity and a Perspective-Altering View of Earth," *Los Angeles Times,* March 3, 2007, p. A1; "Now Virgin to Offer Trips to Space," *CNN.com,* September 27, 2004; and "Space Tours for All," *The Gazette,* January 22, 2007, p. A10.

2. Curtis Ross, "Rockin Props Keep Customers Coming," *Tampa Tribune,* December 8, 2006, p. 6; "Hard Rock Café Opens Flagship in Times Square," *Display & Design Ideas,* August 16, 2005; and Lawrence A. Crosby and Sheree L. Johnson, "Manufacturing Experiences: Tapping Emotion Can Create Value for Your Consumers," *Marketing Management,* January–February 2004, p. 12.

3. "Brand Papers—Experience Economy," *Brand Strategy,* July 17, 2006, p. 36; Rana Foroohar and Mac Margolis, "As Luxury Brands Move into the Mass Market They Need a New Way to Make the Superrich Feel Special. Welcome to the Experience Economy," *Newsweek,* July 25, 2005, p. 44; and B. Joseph Pine and James H. Gilmore, *The Experience Economy* (Boston: Harvard Business School Press, 1999).

4. Virginia H. Mannering and Andrew Hodge, "Gross Domestic Product and Corporate Profits," Bureau of Economic Analysis, March 29, 2007; *World Trade Report 2006,* World Trade Organization, Tables 1 and 2, pp. 11–12; and *Monthly Labor Review,* February 2004, Table 1, p. 59.

5. "WhiteTie to Become Official Concierge Partner of Northwest Airlines," *PR Newswire,* January 8, 2007; Lori Becker, "Concierge Firms Cater to Time-strapped Clients," *Palm Beach Post,* January 11, 2007; Larry Armstrong, "Leave Home Without It," *BusinessWeek,* September 11, 2006, p. 108; Nick Timiraos, "New Online Services Tout Low-Cost Medical Tests," *The Wall Street Journal,* p. D4; and Jeffrey M. O'Brien, "What's Your House Really Worth?" *Fortune,* February 19, 2007, pp. 56–68.

6. Janet R. McColl-Kennedy and Tina White, "Service Provider Training Programs at Odds with Customer Requirements in Five Star Hotels," *Journal of Services Marketing* 11, no. 4 (1997), pp. 249–64; Ellyn A.

McColgan, "How Fidelity Invests in Service Professionals," *Harvard Business Review,* January–February 1997, pp. 137–43; and Frederick F. Reichheld and W. Earl Sasser, Jr., "Zero Defections: Quality Comes to Services," *Harvard Business Review,* September–October 1990, pp. 105–11.

7. Christopher Lovelock and Event Gummesson, "Whither Services Marketing?" *Journal of Services Research* 7 (August 2004), pp. 20–41; and Christopher H. Lovelock and George S. Yip, "Developing Global Strategies for Service Businesses," *California Management Review,* Winter 1996, pp. 64–86.

8. "HP Positioned to Lead in New Era of Business Technology; New Solutions and Services to Help Enterprises Optimize Business Outcomes," *Business Wire,* April 24, 2007.

9. Christopher Lovelock and Jochen Wirtz, *Services Marketing* (Englewood Cliffs, NJ: Prentice Hall, 2007), p. 15.

10. Peter C. Honebein and Roy F. Cammarano, "Customers at Work: Self-service Customers Can Reduce Costs and Become Cocreators of Value," *Marketing Management,* January/February 2006, pp. 26–31; and Matthew L. Meuter, Amy L. Ostrom, Robert I. Roundtree, and Mary Jo Bittner, "Self-Service Technologies: Understanding Customer Satisfaction with Technology-Based Service Encounters," *Journal of Marketing,* July 2000, pp. 50–64.

11. Gerard Alexander, "The Nonprofit Industrial Complex," *The Weekly Standard,* April 23, 2007.

12. Jessi Hempl, "Selling a Cause? Better Make It Pop," *BusinessWeek,* February 13, 2006, p. 75.

13. Aaron Baar, "Red Cross Ready to Pump Up Donations," *Brandweek.com,* February 1, 2007; and "Celebrities Commit to Supporting American Red Cross in 2007," *Lab Business Week,* March 18, 2007, p. 92.

14. Larry Chiagouris, "Nonprofits Can Take Cues from Biz World," *Marketing News,* July 15, 2006, pp. 20–22; Hempl, "Selling a Cause? Better Make It Pop"; Deborah L. Vence, "Smart Organizations Use Technology to Spark Dialogue, Cement Relationships," *Marketing News,* July 15, 2006, p. 15; and Jeffrey Gangemi, "Giving Goes Green," *BusinessWeek,* November 27, 2006, p. 84.

15. Diane C. Lade, "Postal Service Learns to Love the Internet," *South Florida Sun-Sentine,* March 15, 2007; Stephen Barr, "Postal Service Feels Heat Over Consolidation Plans," *Washington Post,* August 3, 2006, p. D4; and Allison Enright, "Mail For Sale," *Marketing News,* June 15, 2006, p. 4.

16. Keith B. Murray, "A Test of Services Marketing Theory: Consumer Information Acquisition Activities," *Journal of Marketing,* January 1991, pp. 10–25.

17. Dawn Iacobucci, "An Empirical Examination of Some Basic Tenets in Services: Goods-Services Continua," Teresa Swartz, David E. Bowen, and Stephen W. Brown, eds., in *Advances in Services Marketing and Management,* vol. 1 (Greenwich, CT: JAI Press), pp. 23–52; and Valerie A. Zeithaml, "How Consumer Evaluation Processes Differ between Goods and Services," in James H. Donnelly and William R. George, eds., *Marketing of Services* (Chicago: American Marketing Association, 1981).

18. Michael J. Dorsch, Stephen J. Grove, and William Darden, "Consumer Intentions to Use a Services Category," *Journal of Services Marketing* 2 (2000), pp. 92–117; and Murray, "A Test of Services Marketing Theory."

19. Leonard L. Berry and Neeli Bendapudi, "Clueing in Customers," *Harvard Business Review,* February 2003, pp. 100–6.

20. John Ozment and Edward Morash, "The Augmented Service Offering for Perceived and Actual Service Quality," *Journal of the Academy of Marketing Science,* Fall 1994, pp. 352–63.

21. A. Parasuraman; Valerie A. Zeithaml; and Leonard L. Berry, "Reassessment of Expectations as a Comparison Standard in Measuring Service Quality: Implications for Further Research," *Journal of Mar-

keting,* January 1994, pp. 111–24; and Leonard L. Berry, *On Great Service* (New York: Free Press, 1995).

22. Valerie A. Zeithaml, A. Parasuraman, and Leonard L. Berry, *Delivering Quality Service* (New York: Free Press, 1990); and Stephen W. Brown and Teresa Swartz, "A Gap Analysis of Professional Service Quality," *Journal of Marketing,* April 1989, pp. 92–98.

23. Amy Ostrom and Dawn Iacobucci, "Consumer Trade-Offs and the Evaluation of Services," *Journal of Marketing,* January 1995, pp. 17–28; and J. Joseph Cronin, Jr., and Steven A. Taylor, "Measuring Service Quality: A Reexamination and Extension," *Journal of Marketing,* July 1992, pp. 55–68.

24. James G. Maxham III and Richard G. Netermeyer, "A Longitudinal Study of Complaining Customers' Evaluations of Multiple Service Failures and Recovery Efforts," *Journal of Marketing,* October 2002, pp. 57–71.

25. "Weblogs, Videologs," *Marketing News,* January 15, 2007, p. 21; Michelle Conlin, "Nastiness Online Can Erupt and Go Global Overnight, and 'No Comment' Doesn't Cut It Anymore," *BusinessWeek,* April 16, 2007, p. 54; and "Dell Learns Power of the Blog," *Marketing News,* December 15, 2006, p. 17.

26. Vicki Clift, "Everyone Needs Service Flow Charting," *Marketing News,* October 23, 1995, pp. 41, 43; Mary Jo Bitner, Bernard H. Booms, and Mary Stanfield Tetreault, "The Service Encounter: Diagnosing Favorable and Unfavorable Incidents," *Journal of Marketing,* January 1990, pp. 71–84; Eberhard Scheuing, "Conducting Customer Service Audits," *Journal of Consumer Marketing,* Summer 1989, pp. 35–41; and W. Earl Susser, R. Paul Olsen, and D. Daryl Wyckoff, *Management of Service Operations* (Boston: Allyn & Bacon, 1978).

27. Thorsten Hennig-Thurau, Markus Groth, Michael Paul, and Dwayne D. Gremier, "Are All Smiles Created Equal? How Emotional Contagion and Emotional Labor Affect Service Relationships," *Journal of Marketing,* July 2006, pp. 58–73.

28. Leonard L. Berry, "Relationship Marketing of Services—Growing Interest, Emerging Perspectives," *Journal of the Academy of Marketing Science,* Fall 1995, pp. 236–45; Mary Jo Bitner, "Building Service Relationships: It's All about Promises," *Journal of the Academy of Marketing Science,* Fall 1995, pp. 246–51; Kevin P. Gwinner, Dwayne D. Gremler, and Mary Jo Bitner, "Relational Benefits in Services Industries: The Customer's Perspective," *Journal of the Academy of Marketing Science,* Spring 1998, pp. 101–14; Susan Fournier, Susan Dobscha, and David Glen Mick, "Preventing the Premature Death of Relationship Marketing," *Harvard Business Review,* January–February 1998, pp. 42–51; and John V. Petrof, "Relationship Marketing: The Wheel Reinvented?" *Business Horizons,* November–December 1997, pp. 26–31.

29. Katherine N. Lemon, Tiffany Barnett White, and Russell S. Winer, "Dynamic Customer Relationship Management: Incorporating Future Considerations into the Service Retention Decision," *Journal of Marketing,* January 2002, pp. 1–14.

30. Thomas S. Gruca, "Defending Service Markets," *Marketing Management* 1 (1994), pp. 31–38; and Leonard L. Berry, Jeffrey S. Conant, and A. Parasuraman. "A Framework for Conducting a Services Marketing Audit," *Journal of the Academy of Marketing Science,* Summer 1991, pp. 255–68.

31. Patriya Tansuhaj, Donna Randall, and Jim McCullough, "A Services Marketing Management Model: Integrating Internal and External Marketing Functions," *Journal of Sciences Marketing,* Winter 1998, pp. 31–38.

32. Christian Gronroos, "Internal Marketing Theory and Practice," in Thomas Bloch, G. D. Upah, and V. A. Zeithaml, eds., *Services Marketing in a Changing Environment* (Chicago: American Marketing Association, 1984).

33. Ibid.

34. Yong-Ki Lee, Jung-Heon Nam, Dae-Hwan Park and Kyung Ah Lee, "What Factors Influence Customer-Oriented Prosocial Behavior of Customer-Contact Employees?" *Journal of Services Marketing* 20, no. 4 (2006), pp. 251–64; and Stephen W. Brown, "The Employee Experience," *Marketing Management* 12 (March–April 2003), pp. 12–13; Lawrence A. Crosby and Sheree L. Johnson, "Watch What I Do," *Marketing Management* 12 (November–December 2003), pp. 10–11; and March C.Gilly and Mary Wolfinbarger, "Advertising's Internal Audience," *Journal of Marketing,* January 1998, pp. 69–88.

35. Gabriel M. Gelb and John M. McKeever, "In Their Shoes," *Marketing Management,* July/August 2006, p. 40–45; Lynette Ryals, "Making Customer Relationship Management Work: The Measurement and Profitable Management of Customer Relationships," *Journal of Marketing,* October 2005, pp. 252–61; Bernd H. Schmitt, *Customer Experience Management* (Hoboken, NJ: John Wiley & Sons, 2003); and Shaun Smith and Joe Wheeler, *Managing the Customer Experience* (Englewood Cliffs, NJ: Prentice Hall, 2002).

36. Sandy Allen and Ashok Chandrashekar, "Outsourcing Services: The Contract Is Just Beginning," *Business Horizons,* March–April 2000, pp. 25–34.

37. Dan R. E. Thomas, "Strategy Is Different in Service Businesses," *Harvard Business Review,* July–August 1978, pp. 158–65.

38. Haim Oren, "Branding Financial Services Helps Consumers Find Order in Chaos," *Marketing News,* March 29, 1993, p. 6; and Leonard L. Berry, Edwin F. Lefkowith, and Terry Clark, "In Services, What's in a Name?" *Harvard Business Review,* September–October 1998, pp. 28–30.

39. Frederick H. deB. Harris and Peter Peacock, "Hold My Place, Please," *Marketing Management,* Fall 1995, pp. 34–46.

40. Christopher Lovelock and Jochen Wirtz, *Services Marketing* (Englewood Cliffs, NJ: Prentice Hall, 2007), pp. 260–84.

41. Kent B. Monroe, "Buyer's Subjective Perceptions of Price," *Journal of Marketing Research,* February 1973, pp. 70–80; and Jerry Olson, "Price as an Informational Cue: Effects on Product Evaluation," in A. G. Woodside, J. N. Sheth, and P. D. Bennett, eds., *Consumer and Industrial Buying Behavior* (New York: Elsevier North-Holland, 1977), pp. 267–86.

42. George J. Avlonitis and Kostis A. Indounas, "Pricing Practices of Service Organizations," *Journal of Services Marketing* 20, no. 5 (2006), pp. 346–56; and Tom Abate, "Cellular First Aid," *San Francisco Chronicle,* December 1, 2003, p. El.

43. Leonard L. Berry, Kathleen Seiders, and Dhruv Grewal, "Understanding Service Convenience," *Journal of Marketing* 66 (July 2002), pp. 1–17; and Charles L. Colby and A. Parasuraman, "Technology Still Matters: E-Services Are Alive and Well and Positioned for Growth," *Marketing Management* 12 (July–August), pp. 28–33.

44. Robert E. Hite, Cynthia Fraser, and Joseph A. Bellizzi, "Professional Service Advertising: The Effects of Price Inclusion, Justification, and Level of Risk," *Journal of Advertising Research* 30 (August–September 1990), pp. 23–31; William R. George and Leonard L. Berry, "Guidelines for the Advertising of Services," *Business Horizons,* July–August 1981, pp. 52–56; and Eugene M. Johnson, Eberhard E. Scheuing, and Kathleen A. Gaida, *Profitable Service Marketing* (Homewood, IL: Dow Jones-Irwin, 1986).

45. Kathleen Mortimer, "Services Advertising: The Agency Viewpoint," *Journal of Services Marketing* 2 (2001), pp. 131–46; and Sak Onkvisit and John J. Shaw, "Service Marketing: Image, Branding, and Competition," *Business Horizons,* January–February 1989, pp. 13–18.

46. Joe Adams, "Why Public Service Advertising Doesn't Work," *Ad Week,* November 17, 1980, p. 72.

47. Regina D. Woodall, Charles L. Colby and A. Parasuraman, "E-volution To Revolution," *Marketing Management,* March/April 2007, pp. 29–34; Timothy J. Mullaney, "Online Pics: A Sure Shot," *BusinessWeek*

September 3, 2001, p. EB 12; Ramin Setoodeh, "Technology: Safer Surfing for Love," *Newsweek,* April 19, 2004, p. 66; and Ginny Parker, "Looking for Prince Charming? In Japan Check Your Cell Phone," *Time,* June 4, 2001; p. 88:

48. Stephen J. Grove, Raymond P. Fisk, and Joby John, "The Future of Services Marketing: Forecasts from Ten Services Experts," *Journal of Services Marketing* 17, no. 2 (2003), pp. 107–21; Stephen L. Vargo and Robert F. Lusch, "Evolving to a New Dominant Logic for Marketing," *Journal of Marketing* 68 (January 2004), pp. 1–17; "Model of Exchange Shifts toward Services," *Marketing News,* January 15, 2004, p. 25; and G. Tomas M. Hult, "Think Global, Act Local in Global Services Marketing," *Marketing News,* March 1, 2004, p. 30.

49. See http://asp.usatoday.com/sports/baseball/salaries/totalpayroll.aspx? year=2007.

Philadelphia Phillies: This case was prepared by William Rudelius based on interviews with David Montgomery, David Buck, Marisol Lezcano, and Scott Brandreth; internal company materials; and the Phillies website (www.phillies.com).

CHAPTER 13

1. Steve Stecklow, "StubHub's Ticket to Ride," *The Wall Street Journal,* January 17, 2006, pp. B1, B2.

2. Ibid.

3. See "StubHub," www.wikipedia.org, February 9, 2007.

4. Sarah Lacy, "The Hot Ticket Isn't Ticketmaster," *BusinessWeek,* September 4, 2006, p. 36.

5. Matt Marshall, "eBay Buys StubHub, Online Ticket Reseller, for $310M," www.venturebeat.com, January 11, 2007.

6. See "StubHub," www.wikipedia.org, February 9, 2007.

7. Timothy Matanovich, Gary L. Lillien, and Arvind Rangaswamy, "Engineering the Price-Value Relationship," *Marketing Management,* Spring 1999, pp. 48–53.

8. Lisa Gubernick, "The Little Extras That Count (Up)," *The Wall Street Journal,"* July 12, 2001, pp. B1, B4; and Donald V. Potter, "Discovering Hidden Pricing Power," *Business Horizons,* November–December 2000, pp. 41–48.

9. Sue Zesiger Callaway, "Bachelor Meets Bugatti, *Fortune,* March 19, 2007, pp. 214–215; and www.bugatti.com.

10. Adapted from Kent B. Monroe, *Pricing: Making Profitable Decisions,* 3rd ed. (New York: McGraw-Hill, 2003); and David J. Curry, "Measuring Price and Quality Competition, *Journal of Marketing,* Spring 1985, pp. 106–17.

11. Numerous studies have examined the price-quality-value relationship. See, for example, Jacob Jacoby and Jerry C. Olsen, eds., *Perceived Quality* (Lexington, MA: Lexington Books, 1985); William D. Dodds, Kent B. Monroe, and Dhruv Grewal, "Effects of Price, Brand, and Store Information on Buyers' Product Evaluations," *Journal of Marketing Research,* August 1991, pp. 307–19; and Roger A. Kerin, Ambuj Jain, and Daniel Howard, "Store Shopping Experience and Consumer Price-Quality-Value Perceptions," *Journal of Retailing,* Winter 1992, pp. 235–45. For a thorough review of the price-quality-value relationship, see Valerie A. Ziethami, "Consumer Perceptions of Price, Quality, and Value," *Journal of Marketing,* July 1998, pp. 2–22.

12. Roger A. Kerin and Robert A. Peterson, "Crestfield Furniture Industries, Inc. (A)," *Strategic Marketing Problems: Cases and Comments,* 11th ed. (Upper Saddle River, NJ: Prentice Hall, 2007), pp. 275–86.

13. Thomas L. Friedman, *The World Is Flat* (New York: Farrar, Straus, and Giroux, Expanded Edition, 2006), pp. 5–9; Jason Dean and Peter Wonacott, "Tech Firms Woo 'Next Billion' Users," *The Wall Street Journal,* November 3, 2006, p. A2; Dexter Roberts, "China Mobile's Hot Signal," *BusinessWeek,* February 5, 2007, pp. 42–44; Kerry Capell, "Ikea: How the Swedish Retailer Became a Global Cult Brand," *BusinessWeek,*

November 5, 2005, pp. 96–106; and Mei Fong, "Ikea Hits Home in China," *The Wall Street Journal,* March 3, 2006, pp. B1, B4.

14. Donald L. Bartlett and James B. Steele, "Why We Pay So Much for Drugs," *Time,* February 2, 2004, pp. 44–52; and "The Benefits of Hypertension," *The Economist,* December 6, 2003, p. 14.

15. Mike Dodd, "Cards Hold 50 Years of Memories," *USA Today,* March 27, 2001, pp. 1A, 2A; and J. C. Conklin, "Don't Throw Out Those Old Sneakers, They're a Gold Mine," *The Wall Street Journal,* September 21, 1998, pp. A1, A20.

16. Prices are quoted on ebay.com on October 25, 2007.

17. "Cheap and Cheerful," *The Economist,* May 24, 2003, pp. 66–67; Avery Johnson, "Low-Cost Airlines Raise Fares," *The Wall Street Journal,* April 25, 2006, pp. D1, D3; and Jeff Bailey, "Jet Blue to Try New Route to Profitability: Higher Prices," *The New York Times,* March 1, 2006, pp. C1, C5.

18. Daniel Levy, Mark Bergen, Shautanu Dutta, and Robert Venable, "The Magnitude of Menu Costs: Direct Evidence from Large U.S. Supermarket Chains," *Quarterly Journal of Economics,* August 1997, pp. 791–825.

19. Gordan A. Wyner, "New Pricing Realities," *Marketing Research,* Spring 2001, pp. 34–35.

20. Akshay R. Rao, Mark E. Bergen, and Scott Davis, "How to Fight a Price War," *Harvard Business Review,* March–April 2000, pp. 107–16.

21. Arik Hesseldahl, "For Every Xbox, A Big Fat Loss," *BusinessWeek,* December 5, 2005, p. 13.

22. Ron Winslow, "How a Breakthrough Quickly Broke Down for Johnson & Johnson," *The Wall Street Journal,* September 18, 1998, pp. A1, A5.

23. Adam Cohen, "No Split but Microsoft's a Monopolist," *Time,* July 9, 2001, pp. 36–38.

24. Gina Chon, "Car Industry Brings Back Incentives, *The Wall Street Journal,* May 2, 2006, pp. D1, D3.

25. Frank Bruni, "Price of Newsweek: It Depends," *Dallas Times Herald,* August 14, 1986, pp. S1, S20.

26. Vanessa O'Connell, "How Campbell Saw a Breakthrough Menu Turn into Leftovers," *The Wall Street Journal,* October 6, 1998, pp. A1, A12.

27. Janice Revell, "The Price Is Not Always Right," *Fortune,* May 14, 2001, p. 240; Indrajit Sinha, "Cost Transparency: The Net's Real Threat to Prices and Brands," *Harvard Business Review,* March–April 2000, pp. 43–50; and Walter Baker, Mike Marn, and Craig Zawada, "Price Smarter on the Net," *Harvard Business Review,* February 2001, pp. 122–27.

28. J. Lynn Lunsford, "Boeing's Boom Has Wings," *The Wall Street Journal,* January 5, 2007, p. A8; Daniel Michaels, "Airbus, Boeing Foreclast Clear Skies," *The Wall Street Journal,* November 24, 2006, p. A2; Daniel Michaels and J. Lynn Lunsford, "Airbus Pitch: New A350 Was Worth It," *The Wall Street Journal,* December 4, 2006, p. B2; and J. Lynn Lunsford, "High Design: Boeing Lets Airlines Browse," *The Wall Street Journal,* February 14, 2007, pp. B1, B12.

29. Ethan Smith, "Universal Slashes CD Prices in Bid to Revive Music Industry," *The Wall Street Journal,* September 4, 2003, pp. B1, B8.

30. Peter Coy, "Can't Stop Guzzling," *BusinessWeek,* July 31, 2006, pp. 26–29.

31. Rick Andrews and George R. Franke, "Time-Varying Elasticities of U.S. Cigarette Demand, 1933–1987," *AMA Educator's Conference Proceedings* (Chicago: American Marketing Association, 1990), p. 393.

32. Alex Taylor III, "Ford"s Student Driver Takes the Wheel, *Fortune,* November 13, 2006, pp. 96–100.

33. Linda Himelstein, "Webvan Left the Basics on the Shelf," *BusinessWeek,* July 23, 2001, p. 43.

Washburn Guitar: This case was edited by Steven Hartley. Sources: Burkhard Bilger, "String Theory, Building a Better Guitar," *The New Yorker,* May 14, 2007, p. 79; and the Washburn Guitar website (www. washburn.com).

CHAPTER 14

1. Interview with Erin Patton, The Master Mind Group, June 7, 2007; "Stephon Marbury—Doing the Right Thing," www.sportsbusinessnews.com, December 11, 2006.

2. For the classic description of skimming and penetration pricing, see Joel Dean, "Pricing Policies for New Products," *Harvard Business Review,* November–December 1976, pp. 141–53.

3. Jean-Noel Kapferer, *The New Strategic Brand Management: Creating and Sustaining Brand Equity,* 2nd ed. (London: Kogan Page Ltd., 2004).

4. Stacy Meichtry, "What Your Time Is Really Worth," *The Wall Street Journal,* April 7–8, 2007, pp. P1, P4.

5. "Premium AA Alkaline Batteries," *Consumer Reports,* March 21, 2002, p. 54; Kemp Powers, "Assault and Batteries," *Forbes,* September 4, 2000, pp. 54, 56; and "Razor Burn at Gillette," *BusinessWeek,* June 18, 2001, p. 37.

6. Michael Levy and Barton A. Weitz, *Retailing Management,* 6th ed. (Burr Ridge, IL: McGraw-Hill/Irwin, 2007), pp. 501–2.

7. "Why That Deal Is Only $9.99," *BusinessWeek,* January 10, 2000, p. 36. For further reading on odd-even pricing, see Mark Stiving and Russell S. Winer, "An Empirical Analysis of Price Endings with Scanner Data," *Journal of Consumer Research,* June 1997, pp. 57–67; and Robert M. Schindler, "Patterns of Rightmost Digits Used in Advertised Prices: Implications for Nine-Ending Effects," *Journal of Consumer Research,* September 1997, pp. 192–201.

8. For an overview on target pricing, see Stephan A. Butscher and Michael Laker, "Market Driven Product Development," *Marketing Management,* Summer 2000, pp. 48–53.

9. Thomas T. Nagle and Reed K. Holden, *The Strategy and Tactics of Pricing,* 4th ed. (Englewood Cliffs, NJ: Prentice Hall, 2006), pp. 243–49.

10. Kent B. Monroe, *Pricing: Making Profitable Decisions,* 3rd ed. (Burr Ridge, IL: McGraw-Hill/Irwin, 2003), pp. 420–30.

11. Robert J. Dolan and Hermann Simon, *Power Pricing: How Managing Price Transforms the Bottom Line* (New York: Free Press, 1996), p. 249.

12. Peter M. Noble and Thomas S. Gruca, "Industrial Pricing: Theory and Managerial Practice," *Marketing Science* 18, no. 3 (1999), pp. 435–54.

13. George E. Belch and Michael A. Belch, *Introduction to Advertising and Promotion,* 7th ed. (New York: McGraw-Hill/Irwin, 2007).

14. "In Lean Times, Big Companies Make a Grab for Market Share," *The Wall Street Journal,* September 5, 2003, pp. A1, A6.

15. "Is the Music Store Over?" *Business 2.0,* March 2004, pp. 115–19.

16. "How Dell Fine-Tunes Its PC Pricing to Gain Edge in a Slow Market," *The Wall Street Journal,* June 8, 2001, pp. A1, A8.

17. Rafi A. Mohammed et al., *Internet Marketing: Building Advantage in a Networked Economy,* 2nd ed. (Burr Ridge, IL: McGraw-Hill/Irwin, 2004).

18. "The Web's Role as Equalizer," *BusinessWeek Online,* May 13, 2002; and "Are Minority Shoppers Treated Unfairly? An Expensive Reason to Care," www.diversityinc.com, downloaded May 18, 2002.

19. For an extended discussion on product complements and substitutes, see Allan D. Shocker, Barry L. Bayus, and Namwoon Kim, "Product Complements and Substitutes in Real World: The Relevance of Other Products," *Journal of Marketing,* January 2004, pp. 28–40.

20. Monroe, *Pricing,* pp. 396–97; and "Deciding When the Price Is Right," *Dallas Morning News,* May 23, 2007, pp. 1D, 3D.

21. Jagmohan S. Raju, Raj Sethuraman, and Sanjay K. Dhar, "National Brand-Store Brand Price Differential and Store Brand Market Share," *Pricing Strategy & Practice 3,* no. 2 (1995), pp. 17–24; and Akshay R. Rao, "The Quality of Price as a Quality Cue, *Journal of Marketing Research,* November 2005, pp. 401–5.

22. "The Price Is Not Always Right," *Fortune,* May 14, 2001, p. 240.

23. For an extended discussion about price wars, see Akshay R. Rao, Mark E. Bergen, and Scott Davis, "How to Fight a Price War," *Harvard Business Review,* March–April 2000, pp, 107–16.

24. Monroe, *Pricing,* chapters 16 and 17.

25. Kenneth C. Manning, William O. Bearden, and Randall L. Rose, "Development of a Theory of Retailer Response to Manufacturers' Everyday Low Cost Programs," *Journal of Retailing,* Spring 1998, pp. 107–37; "Everyday Low Profits," *Harvard Business Review,* March–April 1994, p. 13; Stephen J. Hoch, Xavier Dreze, and Mary E. Purk, "EDLP, Hi-Lo, and Margin Arithmetic," *Journal of Marketing,* October 1994, pp. 16–27; and Tibbett Speer, "Do Low Prices Bore Shoppers?" *American Demographics,* January 1994, pp. 11–13. Also see Barbara E. Kahn and Leigh McAlister, *The Grocery Revolution: The New Focus on the Consumer* (Reading, MA: Addison-Wesley Educational Publishers, 1996).

26. Dorothy Cohen, *Legal Issues in Marketing Decision Marking* (Cincinnati, OH: South-Western, 1995).

27. "Six Vitamin Firms Agree to Settle Price-Fixing Suit," *The Wall Street Journal,* October 11, 2000, p. B10.

28. "Price Fixing," *USA Today,* March 7, 2000, p. C1.

29. Ronald A. Cass, "When Price 'Fixing' Makes Sense," *The Wall Street Journal,* March 24–25, 2007, p. A10; and "Price-Floor Ruling May Have Small Effect," *The Wall Street Journal,* June 29, 2007, p. A2.

The Starbury Collection: This case was written by Roger A. Kerin based on interviews and materials provided by Erin Patton, The Master Mind Group.

CHAPTER 15

1. Jerry Useem, "Simply Irresistible," *Fortune,* March 19, 2007, pp. 107–12; Nick Wingfield, "How Apple's Store Strategy Beat the Odds," *The Wall Street Journal,* May 17, 2006, pp. B1, B10; and www.apple.com/retail, downloaded May 20, 2007.

2. Andrew Raskin, "Who's Minding the Store?" *Business 2.0,* February 2003, pp. 70–74.

3. This discussion is based on Bert Rosenbloom, *Marketing Channels: A Management View,* 7th ed. (Cincinnati, OH: South-Western College Publishing, 2004).

4. "Eddie Bauer's Banner Time of Year," *Advertising Age,* October 1, 2001, p. 55.

5. www.generalmills.com, downloaded May 15, 2007; www.nestle.com, downloaded May 15, 2007; and Ian Friendly, "Cereal Partners Worldwide: A World of Opportunity," Nestlé Invester Seminar, Vevey, Switzerland, June 8, 2005.

6. For an extensive discussion on wholesaling, see Anne T. Couglan, Erin Anderson, Louis W. Stern, and Adel I. El-Ansary, *Marketing Channels,* 7th ed. (Upper Saddle River, NJ: Prentice Hall, 2006), chapter 12.

7. For an overview of vertical marketing systems, see Lou Peltson, David Strutton, and James R. Lumpkin, *Marketing Channels,* 2nd ed. (Burr Ridge, IL: McGraw-Hill/Irwin, 2002), chapter 11.

8. Statistics provided by the International Franchise Association, June 15, 2007.

9. For a review of channel partnering, see Jakki J. Mohr and Robert E. Spekman, "Perfecting Partnerships," *Marketing Management,* Winter–Spring 1996, pp. 35–43.

10. "Avon Regains Some Allure," www.businessweek.com, February 6, 2007; "Avon Reports First-Quarter Results," Avon press release, May 1, 2007; and "Avon Calls, China Opens the Door," www.businessweek.com, February 28, 2006.

11. For a thorough discussion of distribution intensity, see Gary L. Frazier and Walfried M. Lassar, "Determinants of Distribution Intensity," *Journal of Marketing,* October 1996, pp. 39–51.

12. Rafi A. Mohammed, Robert J. Fisher, Bernard J. Jaworski, and Gordon J. Paddison, *Internet Marketing: Building Advantage in a Networked Economy,* 2nd ed. (Burr Ridge, IL: McGraw-Hill/Irwin, 2004).

13. Useem, "Simply Irresistible."

14. "Gillette Tries to Nick Schick in Japan," *The Wall Street Journal,* February 4, 1991, pp. B3, B4.

15. Ethan Smith, "Why a Grand Plan to Cut CD Prices Went Off the Track," *The Wall Street Journal,* June 4, 2004, pp. A1, A6; and "Feud with Seller Hurts Nike Sales, Shares," *Dallas Morning News,* June 28, 2003, p. 30.

16. "Dealer Surplus," *Forbes,* October 16, 2006, pp. 50–52; and Kevin Kelleher, "Giving Dealers a Raw Deal," *Business 2.0,* December 2004, pp. 82–83.

17. Representative studies that explore the dimensions and use of power and influence in marketing channels include the following: Kenneth A. Hunt, John T. Mentzer, and Jeffrey E. Danes, "The Effect of Power Sources on Compliance in a Channel of Distribution: A Causal Model," *Journal of Business Research,* October 1987, pp. 377–98; John F. Gaski, "Interrelations among a Channel Entity's Power Sources: Impact of the Exercise of Reward and Coercion on Expert, Referent, and Legitimate Power Sources," *Journal of Marketing Research,* February 1986, pp. 62–67; Gary Frazier and John O. Summers, "Interfirm Influence Strategies and Their Application within Distribution Channels," *Journal of Marketing,* Summer 1984, pp. 43–55; George H. Lucas and Larry G. Gresham, "Power Conflict, Control, and the Application of Contingency Theory in Channels of Distribution," *Journal of the Academy of Marketing Science,* Summer 1985, pp. 27–37; F. Robert Dwyer and Julie Gassenheimer, "Relational Roles and Triangle Dramas: Effects on Power Play and Sentiments in Industrial Channels," *Marketing Letters* 3 (1992), pp. 187–200; Jean L. Johnson, Tomoaki Sakano, Joseph A. Cote, and Naoto Onzo, "The Exercise of Interfirm Power and its Repercussions in U.S.-Japanese Channel Relationships," *Journal of Marketing,* April 1993, pp. 1–10; and Janice M. Payan and Richard G. McFarland, "Decomposing Influence Strategies: Argument Structure and Dependence as Determinants of the Effectiveness of Influence Strategies in Gaining Channel Member Compliance," *Journal of Marketing,* July 2005, pp. 66–79.

18. *Slotting Allowances in the Retail Grocery Industry* (Washington, DC: Federal Trade Commission, November 2003). Also see Paul N. Bloom, Gregory T. Gundlach, and Joseph P. Cannon, "Slotting Allowances and Fees: Schools of Thought and Views of Practicing Managers," *Journal of Marketing,* April 2000, pp. 92–109; and William L. Wilkie, Debra M. Desrochers, and Gregory T. Gundlach, "Marketing Research and Public Policy: The Case of Slotting Fees," *Journal of Public Policy & Marketing,* Fall 2002, pp. 275–89.

19. For a comprehensive treatment of legal issues pertaining to marketing channels, see Dorothy Cohen, *Legal Issues in Marketing* (Cincinnati, OH: South-Western, 1995), chapters 12 and 13.

Golden Valley Microwave foods: This case was written by Thomas J. Belich, Mark T. Spriggs, and Steven W. Hartley based on personal interviews with Jack McKeon and Frank Lynch, company data they provided, and the following sources: "Snagging a Pop Fly," *Snack Food and Wholesale Bakery* (May 2004), p. 48; "Choosing the Right Growth Strategy," *PR Newswire* (November 13, 2003); and "Company Information," from the website (see www.actii.com/company).

CHAPTER 16

1. David Simchi-Levi, Philip Kaminsky, and Edith Simchi-Levi, *Designing and Managing the Supply Chain,* 3rd ed. (Burr Ridge, IL: McGraw-Hill/Irwin, 2007).

2. "The Physical Internet: A Survey of Logistics," *The Economist,* June 17, 2006, special section.

3. Simchi-Levi et al., *Designing and Managing the Supply Chain,* p. 6; and Tim Clark, "Driving at the Speed of Demand," *Consumer Goods Technology,* October 2005, pp. 15–18.

4. Jeffrey McCracken, "Ford Seeks Big Savings by Overhauling Supply System," *The Wall Street Journal,* September 29, 2005, p. All; April Terreri, "Driving Efficiencies in Automotive Logistics," www. inboundlogistics.com, January 2004; and Robyn Meredith, "Harder Than Hype," *Forbes,* April 16, 2001, pp. 188–94.

5. Major portions of this discussion are based on Sunil Chopra and Peter Meindl, *Supply Chain Management: Strategy, Planning, and Operations,* 3rd ed. (Upper Saddle River, NJ: Prentice Hall, 2007), chapters 1–3; and Hau L. Lee, "The Triple-A Supply Chain," *Harvard Business Review,* October 2004, pp. 102–12.

6. David Drickhamer, "Supply-Chain Superstars," *Industry Week,* May 1, 2004, pp. 5–7; "IBM Leans Out Its Supply Chain," *Modern Materials Handling,* November 9, 2005, p. 35; Brian T. Eck and Murry Mitchell, "Transformation at IBM," *Supply Chain Management,* November–December 2003, pp. 56–62; and Thomas A. Foster, "World's Best-Run Supply Chains Stay on Top Regardless of the Competition," *Global Logistics & Supply Chain Strategies,* February 2006, pp. 27–41.

7. This discussion is based on Kathryn Jones, "The Dell Way," *Business 2.0* February 2003, pp. 61–66; Charles Fishman, "The Wal-Mart You Don't Know," *Fast Company,* December 2003, pp. 68–80; "Michael Dell: Still Betting on the Future of Online Commerce and Supply Chain Efficiencies," Knowledge@Wharton, September 7, 2006; and Chopra and Meindl, *Supply Chain Management.*

8. Portions of this discussion are based on Simchi-Levi et al., *Designing and Managing the Supply Chain;* Chopra and Meindl, *Supply Chain Management.* Also, Fan Wu, Sengun Yeniyurt, Daekwan Kim, and S. Tamer Cavusgil, "The Impact of Information Technology on Supply Chain Capabilities and Firm Performance: A Resource-Based View," *Industrial Marketing Management,* October 2006, pp. 593–4.

9. Simchi-Levi et al., *Designing and Managing the Supply Chain,* p. 6.

10. Toby B. Gooley, "How Logistics Drive Customer Service," *Traffic Management,* January 1996, p. 46.

11. Michael Levy and Barton A. Weitz, *Retailing Management,* 4th ed. (Burr Ridge, IL: McGraw-Hill/Irwin, 2001), pp. 335–36; "A&P Bets the Store," *The Industry Standard,* May 14, 2001, pp. 46–49; and Ursula Y. Alvarado and Herbert Kotzab, "Supply Chain Management: The Integration of Logistics in Marketing," *Industrial Marketing Management* 30 (2001), pp. 183–98.

12. "Unisys Selects DHL as Global Lead Provider for Customized Logistics Solutions," DHL press release, May 22, 2006.

13. Robert J. Bowman, "Pursuing 'On Demand,' IBM Shakes Up Its Supply Chain," www.supplychainbrain.com, April 2003.

14. Richard Armstrong and Thomas Foster, "The Top 25 Global 3 PLS: Is Bigger Really Better?" *Global Logistics & Supply Chain Strategies,* May 2006, pp. 28–40.

15. Douglas M. Lambert, *Supply Chain Management: Processes. Partnerships, and Performance,* 2nd ed. (Sarasota, FL: Supply Chain Management Institute, 2006).

16. Kris Maher, "Global Goods Jugglers," *The Wall Street Journal,* June 5, 2005, pp. All, A12.

17. David Simchi-Levi, Philip Kaminsky, and Edith Simchi-Levi, *Managing the Supply Chain: The Definitive Guide for the Business Professional* (New York: McGraw-Hill, 2004), p. 78.

18. Jeffrey Davis and Martha Baer, "Some Assembly Required," *Business 2.0,* February 12, 2001, pp. 78–67.

19. April Terreri, "Driving Efficiencies in Automotive Logistics," www. inboundlogistics.com, January 2004.

20. Jean Murphy, "Better Forecasting, S&OP Support Transformation at Campbell's Soup Co.," *Global Logistics & Supply Chain Strategies,* June 2004, pp. 28–30.

21. Lorraine Woellert, "HP Wants Your Old PCs Back," *BusinessWeek,* April 10, 2006, pp. 82–83; "Hewlett-Packard's Design for Supply Chain Program," *Global Logistics & Supply Chain Strategies,* December 2005, p. 40; and Alan Deutschman, "There's Gold in Them Thar Smelly Hills," *Fast Company,* July/August 2006, pp. 96–98.

22. Brian Hindo, "Everything Old is New Again," *BusinessWeek,* September 25, 2006, pp. 64–70.

23. Doug Bartholomew, "IT Delivers for UPS," *Industry Week,* August 2002, pp. 35–36.

Amazon.com: This case is based on material available on the company website, and the following sources: Robert D. Hof and Heather Green, "How Amazon Cleared That Hurdle," *BusinessWeek* (February 4, 2002), p. 60; Heather Green, "How Hard Should Amazon Swing?" *BusinessWeek* (January 14, 2002), p. 38; Robert D. Hof, "We've Never Said We Had To Do It All," *BusinessWeek* (October 15, 2001), p. 53; and Bob Walter, "Amazon Leases Distribution Center from Sacramento, Calif., Development Firm," *Sacramento Bee* (July 19, 2001).

CHAPTER 17

1. Paige Wiser, "Dressing Rooms of the Future: All Eyes On You," *Chicago Sun-Times,* April 29, 2007, p. A24; Vanessa O'Connell, "Reinventing the Luxury Department Store," *The Wall Street Journal,* July 15–16, 2006, p. P1; Teresa Mez, "High-tech Dressing Rooms Become Virtual Reality," *Christian Science Monitor,* April 20, 2007, p. 11; "Magic Mirror Debuts at NRF Convention & Expo," *Display & Design Ideas,* January 16, 2007; and "Neiman Launches Cusp," www. shopdiary.com, July 27, 2006; Joseph Olewitz, "Facebook Meets the Mall," Icon Nicholson Media Release, http://www.iconnicholson. com/news/press_releases/doc/nrf011407.pdf, January 14, 2007.

2. Kate Betts, "So You Want To Be a Designer," *Time,* May 17, 2004, p. 85.

3. "Fortune 1000 Ranked Within Industries," *Fortune,* April 30, 2007, pp. F-58, 68.

4. *Statistical Abstract of the United States: 2007,* 126th ed. (Washington, DC: U.S. Department of Commerce, Bureau of the Census, 2007), pp. 654–55.

5. "Fortune Global 500," *Fortune,* July 24, 2006, pp. 95–120.

6. "Retail Trade—Establishments, Employees, and Payroll," *Statistical Abstract of the United States: 2007,* 126th ed., (Washington, DC: U.S. Department of Commerce, Bureau of the Census, 2007), pp. 651–652; "County Business Patterns," Bureau of the Census, www. census.gov/epcd/cbp/view/cbpview.html (accessed May 29, 2007).

7. Matthew Boyle, Jenny Mero, and Dana Castillo, "Why Costco Is So Damn Addictive," *Fortune,* October 30, 2006, p. 126; Andrew A. Caffey, "Are You Franchisee Material?" *Entrepreneur,* January 2007; Tanisha A. Sykes, "Prosper With Innovative Business Ideas," *Black Enterprise,* May 2007, p. 132; and Nichole L. Torres, "Turn Up the Crazy," *Entrepreneur,* May 2007.

8. *Economic Impact of Franchised Businesses,* (Washington, D.C.): International Franchise Association Educational Foundation, 2004); Don DeBolt, "Franchises Are Key Segment of Nation's Economy," *Franchising Today,* April 2004; also see "Franchise 500 2007," at www.entrepreneur.com.

9. "Franchise 500," *Entrepreneur,* January 2007; and Scott Shane and Chester Spell, "Factors for New Franchise Success," *Sloan Management Review,* Spring 1998, pp. 43–50.

10. "US Airways Enhancing Customer Service With New Self-Service Check-In Kiosks," *Business Wire,* May 30, 2007; Kyla King, "Self-service Evolves with Technology," *The Star-Ledger,* April 29, 2007, p. 3; Michelle Higgins, "Go Directly to Your Room Key! Pass the Desk!" *The New York Times,* August 20, 2006, p. 6; and Peter C.

Honebein and Roy F. Cammarano, "Customers at Work," *Marketing Management,* January/February 2006, pp. 26–31.

11. Michael A. Wiles, "The Effect of Customer Service on Retailers' Shareholder Wealth: The Role of Availability and Reputation Cues," *Journal of Retailing,* 2007, pp. 19–31; Cate T. Corcoran, "Nordstrom 'Simplifies' Customer Satisfaction," *Women's Wear Daily,* March 22, 2007, p. 8; Vanessa O'Connell, "Posh Retailers Pile on Perks for Top Customers," *The Wall Street Journal,* April 26, 2007, p. D1; Robert Berner, "Retail: This Rising Tide Won't Lift All Boats," *Business-Week,* January 12, 2004, p. 114.

12. Mathew Boyle, "Best Buy's Giant Gamble," *Fortune,* April 3, 2006, p. 68; and Pallavi Gogoi, "Staples Makes Selling Look Easy," *BusinessWeek Online,* December 7, 2006.

13. "Crossroads: Carrefour," *The Economist,* March 17, 2007; Harry Maurer, "Wal-Mart: Deeper Into China," *BusinessWeek,* October 30, 2006, p. 32; and Carrefour website, www.carrefour.com/cdc/group/our-business/our-network-of-stores/, accessed May 31, 2007.

14. Elizabeth Woyke, "Buffett, The Wal-Mart Shopper," *BusinessWeek,* May 14, 2007, p. 66; and Anthony Bianco, Mara Der Hovanesian, Lauren Young, and Pallavi Gogoi, "Wal-Mart's Midlife Crisis," *BusinessWeek,* April 30, 2007, p. 46.

15. Chris Serres, "Your Next-Tech Toy Might Come from a Vending Machine," *Star Tribune,* December 9, 2006, p. 1D; "Zoom Unveils Motorola-Themed Vending Machines," *Airports,* October 31, 2006, p. 2; Elliot Maras, "State of the Vending Industry Report," *Automatic Merchandiser,* August, 2006, pp. 40–56; and "Sony Tests Luxury Vending Machines Nationwide," *Display & Design Ideas,* June 16, 2006.

16. Hisashi Kiyooka Yomiuri Shimbun, "Cell Phones Fast Becoming E-wallets," *Daily Yomiuri,* January 24, 2006, p. 8; "Convenience to the Max," *CSNews Online,* September 7, 2006; "Nation's First Automated Video Rental Store Opens in Reno," *Display & Design Ideas,* January 25, 2007; and Andy Reinhardt, "A Machine-to-Machine Internet of Things," *BusinessWeek,* April 26, 2004, p. 102.

17. "DMA Encourages Catalog & Direct Mail Recycling," *PR Newswire,* May 23, 2007; and "IKEA in the World," www.idkea.com, accessed June 1, 2007.

18. Sandra Guy, "Sears to Light Up Ad Plan, Expands Catalog Concept for New Century," *Chicago Sun-Times,* May 5, 2007, p. 25; Monica Roman, "You Gotta Have a Catalog," *BusinessWeek,* May 14, 2001, p. 56; and Beth Viveiros, "Catalog and Internet Sales Grow More Quickly than Retail," *Direct,* July 2001.

19. Kenneth R. Gosselin, "Store to Offer a 'Sampling' of L.L. Bean; Mail-Order Icon Hoping First Location in State Will Spur More Online, Catalog Sales," *Hartford Courant,* January 9, 2007, p. E4; Robert Berner, "J.C. Penny Get the Net," *BusinessWeek,* June 7, p. 70; see award information at www.multichannelmerchant.com/toolbox/awards/, accessed June 1, 2007.

20. "Corporate Facts," from the QVC website, www.qvc.com, accessed June 1, 2007.

21. "QVC, NFL, and GSI Commerce to Create New, Multichannel, Direct-to-Consumer Opportunity," QVC press release, May 23, 2007; Gina Salamone, "Shopping With the Stars. QVC Viewers Take a Shine to Celeb Lines," *Daily News,* October 1, 2006, p. 14; Ron Grover and Deborah Stead, "Adding Some Sparkle to QVC," *BusinessWeek,* September 25, 2006, p. 16; Stewart Schley, "New Technologies Send Sales Execs Back to School; Reps Bone Up on VOD, Interactive TV, and 'Addressable' Applications," *Multichannel News,* May 7, 2007, p. 5A.

22. "Order Online, Pick Up Items at Local Wal-Mart," *St. Petersburg Times,* May 23, 2007, p. 1D; and Nikki Hopewell, "Marketing Factbook; Online Retail Sales," *Marketing News,* July 15, 2006, p. 37.

23. "Former Cendant Marketing Chief Will Help Company Leverage Core Media Products while Broadening Member Benefit Offerings," *PR Newswire,* February 21, 2001; Tim Mullaney, "And All the Price Trimmings," *BusinessWeek,* December 18, 2000, p. 68; Mary J. Cronin, "Business Secrets of the Billion-Dollar Website," *Fortune,* February 2, 1998, p. 142; Robert D. Hof, Ellen Neuborne, and Heather Green, "Amazon.com: The Wild World of E-Commerce," *BusinessWeek,* December 14, 1998, pp. 106–19; "Future Shop," *Forbes ASAP,* April 6, 1998, pp. 37–52; Chris Taylor, "Cybershop," *Time,* November 23, 1998, p. 142; Stephen H. Wildstrom, "'Bots' Don't Make Great Shoppers," *BusinessWeek,* December 7, 1998, p. 14; and Jeffrey Ressner, "Online Flea Markets," *Time,* October 5, 1998, p. 48.

24. "Jellyfish.com's Smack Shopping Makes Paying Into Play," *TECH-WEB,* February 26, 2007.

25. Roger O. Crocket, "Let the Buyer Compare," *BusinessWeek,* September 3, 2001, p. EB10.

26. Thomas L. Zeller and David R. Kublank, "Focused E-Tail Measurement and Resource Management," *Business Horizons,* January–February 2002, pp. 53–60.

27. Bruce Einhorn, "In China's Net Cafes, Intel Pours It On," *Business-Week,* November 6, 2006, p. 52.

28. "Economic Impact: U.S. Direct Marketing Today Executive Summary—2003," Direct Marketing Association, New York; and Kelly Shermach, "Outsourcing Seen as a Way to Cut Costs, Retain Service," *Marketing News,* June 19, 1995, pp. 5, 8.

29. Deborah L. Vence, "Majority Rules," Marketing News, February 15, 2006, p. 4; Catherine Arnold, "Law Gives Industry a Buzz," *Marketing News,* February 1, 2004, p. 11; Scott Reeves, "Back to (Old) School, 'Do-Not-Call' Revives Door-to-Door Sales," *Marketing News,* December 8, 2003, p. 13; and "Direct Marketing," *Marketing News,* January 15, 2004, p. 16.

30. "Direct Selling by the Numbers," Direct Selling Association, www.dsa.org; and "Need Income? Try Direct Selling," *Grand Rapids Press,* March 18, 2007, p. G1.

31. Nanette Byrnes, "Avon: More Than Cosmetic Changes," *Business-Week,* March 12, 2007, p. 62.

32. Anya Sostek, "It's Not Your Mother's Tupperware Party," *Pittsburgh Post-Gazette,* July 23, 2006, p. C1; and "Avon, The Net, and Glass Ceilings," *BusinessWeek,* February 6, 2006, p. 104.

33. The following discussion is adapted from William T. Gregor and Eileen M. Friars, *Money Merchandizing: Retail Revolution in Consumer Financial Services* (Cambridge, MA: Management Analysis Center, Inc., 1982).

34. Nicole Harris, "Just for Feet Is Making Tracks," *BusinessWeek,* July 20, 1998, pp. 70–72.

35. Francis J. Mulhern and Robert P. Leon, "Implicit Price Bundling of Retail Products: A Multiproduct Approach to Maximizing Store Profitability," *Journal of Marketing,* October 1991, pp. 63–76.

36. Marc Vanhuele and Xavier Dreze, "Measuring the Price Knowledge Shoppers Bring to the Store," *Journal of Marketing,* October 2002, pp. 72–85.

37. Gwen Ortmeyer, John A. Quelch, and Walter Salmon, "Restoring Credibility to Retail Pricing," *Sloan Management Review,* Fall 1991, pp. 55–66.

38. William B. Dodds, "In Search of Value: How Price and Store Name Information Influence Buyers' Product Perceptions," *Journal of Consumer Marketing,* Spring 1991, pp. 15–24.

39. Leonard L. Berry, "Old Pillars of New Retailing," *Harvard Business Review,* April 2001, pp. 131–37.

40. Eric Anderson and Duncan Simester, "Mind Your Pricing Cues," *Harvard Business Review,* September 2003, pp. 96–103.

41. Julie Baker, A. Parasuraman, Dhruv Grewal, and Glenn B. Voss, "The Influence of Multiple Store Environment Cues on Perceived

Merchandise Value and Patronage Intentions," *Journal of Marketing,* April 2002, pp. 120–41.

42. Hyeong Min Kim, "Consumer' Responses to Price Presentation Formats in Rebate Advertisements," *Journal of Retailing,* no. 4 (2006), pp. 309–17.

43. Rita Koselka, "The Schottenstein Factor," *Forbes,* September 28, 1992, pp. 104, 106.

44. Greg Saitz, "Growing Pains for BJ's wholesale." *The Star-Ledger,* November 6, 2007, p. 50; Wendy Zellner, "Warehouse Clubs: When the Going Gets Tough . . ." *BusinessWeek,* July 16, 2001, p. 60; "Warehouse Clubs Fine-Tune Units," *Chain Drug Review,* June 29, 1998, p. 38; James M. Degen, "Warehouse Clubs Move from Revolution to Evolution," *Marketing News,* August 3, 1992, p. 8; Dori Jones Yang, "Bargains by the Forklift," *BusinessWeek,* July 15, 1991, p. 152; and "Fewer Rings on the Cash Register," *BusinessWeek,* January 14, 1991, p. 85.

45. Ira P. Schneiderman, "Value Keeps Factory Outlets Viable," *Daily News Record,* July 20, 1998, p. 10; Stephanie Anderson Forest, "I Can Get It for You Retail," *BusinessWeek,* September 18, 1995, pp. 84–88; and Adrienne Ward, "New Breed of Mall Knows: Everybody Loves a Bargain," *Advertising Age,* January 27, 1992, p. 55.

46. Anne Faircloth, "Value Retailers Go Dollar for Dollar," *Fortune,* July 6, 1998, pp. 164–66.

47. Barry Brown, "Edmonton Makes Size Pay Off in Down Market," *Advertising Age,* January 27, 1992, pp. 4–5.

48. James R. Lowry, "The Life Cycle of Shopping Centers," *Business Horizons,* January–February 1997, pp. 77–86; Eric Peterson, "Power Centers! Now!" *Stores,* March 1989, pp. 61–66; and "Power Centers Flex Their Muscle," *Chain Store Age Executive,* February 1989, pp. 3A, 4A.

49. Pierre Martineau, "The Personality of the Retail Store," *Harvard Business Review,* January–February 1958, p. 47.

50. Julie Baker, Dhruv Grewal, and A. Parasuraman, "The Influence of Store Environment on Quality Inferences and Store Image," *Journal of the Academy of Marketing Science,* Fall 1994, pp. 328–39; Howard Barich and Philip Kotler, "A Framework for Marketing Image Management," *Sloan Management Review,* Winter 1991, pp. 94–104; Susan M. Keaveney and Kenneth A. Hunt, "Conceptualization and Operationalization of Retail Store Image: A Case of Rival Middle-Level Theories," *Journal of the Academy of Marketing Science,* Spring 1992, pp. 165–75; James C. Ward, Mary Jo Bitner, and John Barnes, "Measuring the Prototypicality and Meaning of Retail Environments," *Journal of Retailing,* Summer 1992, p. 194; and Dhruv Grewal, R. Krishnan, Julie Baker, and Norm Burin, "The Effect of Store Name, Brand Name and Price Discounts on Consumers' Evaluations and Purchase Intentions," *Journal of Retailing,* Fall 1998, pp. 331–52. For a review of the store image literature, see Mary R. Zimmer and Linda L. Golden, "Impressions of Retail Stores: A Content Analysis of Consumer Images," *Journal of Retailing,* Fall 1988, pp. 265–93.

51. Mary Jo Bitner, "Servicescapes: The Impact of Physical Surroundings on Customers and Employees," *Journal of Marketing,* April 1992, pp. 57–71.

52. Jans-Benedict Steenkamp and Michel Wedel, "Segmenting Retail Markets on Store Image Using a Consumer-Based Methodology," *Journal of Retailing,* Fall 1991, p. 300; and Philip Kotler, "Atmospherics as a Marketing Tool," *Journal of Retailing* 49 (Winter 1973–74), p. 61.

53. Roger A. Kerin, Ambuj Jain and Daniel L. Howard, "Store Shopping Experience and Consumer Price-Quality-Value Perceptions," *Journal of Retailing,* Winter 1992, pp. 376–97.

54. Kusum L. Ailwadi and Bari Harlam, "An Empirical Analysis of the Determinants of Retail Margins: The Role of Store-Brand Share," *Journal of Marketing,* January 2004, pp. 147–65; Joseph Tarnowski, "And the Awards Went to . . ." *Progressive Grocer,* April 15, 2004; Betsy

Spethmann, "Shelf Sets," *Promo,* May 1, 2004, p. 6; and "Study Shows Continued Support for Category Management," *CSNews Online,* March 17, 2004.

55. John Davis, *Measuring Marketing* (Singapore: John Wiley & Sons, 2007), p. 46

56. Paul W. Farris, Neil T. Bendle, Phillip E. Pfeifer, David J. Reibstein, *Marketing Metrics* (Philadelphia: Wharton School Publishing, 2006), p. 106; Jerry Useem, "Simply Irresistible," *Fortune,* March 19, 2007, pp. 107–12; "Apple 2.0," www.blogs.business2.com; Steve Lohr, "Apple, a Success at Stores, Bets Big on Fifth Avenue," *The New York Times,* May 19, 2006; Jim Dalrymple, "Inside the Apple Stores," *MacWorld,* June 2007, pp. 16–17; Davis, *Measuring Marketing,* pp. 280–81.

57. The wheel of retailing theory was originally proposed by Malcolm P. McNair, "Significant Trends and Development in the Postwar Period," in A. B. Smith, ed., *Competitive Distribution in a Free, High-Level Economy and Its Implications for the University* (Pittsburgh: University of Pittsburgh Press, 1958), pp. 1–25; also see Stephen Brown, "The Wheel of Retailing—Past and Future," *Journal of Retailing,* Summer 1990, pp. 143–49; and Malcolm P. McNair and Eleanor May, "The Next Revolution of the Retailing Wheel," *Harvard Business Review,* September–October 1978, pp. 81–91.

58. Michael Arndt, "McDonald's 24/7," *BusinessWeek,* February 5, 2007, p. 64; "Resolved: No Trans Fats in 2007," *BusinessWeek,* January 15, 2007, p. 27; Kate Macarthur, "McDonald's Coffee," *Advertising Age,* November 13, 2006, p. S-10; Bill Saporito, "What's for Dinner?" *Fortune,* May 15, 1995, pp. 51–64.

59. William R. Davidson, Albert D. Bates, and Stephen J. Bass, "Retail Life Cycle," *Harvard Business Review,* November–December 1976, pp. 89–96.

60. Gretchen Morgenson, "Here Come the Cross-Shoppers," *Forbes,* December 7, 1992, pp. 90–101.

61. Robert A. Peterson and Sridhar Balasubramanian, "Retailing in the 21st Century: Reflections and Prologue to Research," *Journal of Retailing,* Spring 2002, pp. 9–16.

62. Jim Carter and Norman Sheehan, "From Competition to Cooperation: E-Tailing's Integration with Retailing," *Business Horizons,* March–April 2004, pp. 71–8.

63. Ranjay Gulati and Janson Garino, "Getting the Right Mix of Bricks and Clicks," *Harvard Business Review,* May–June 2000, pp. 107–14; Marshall L. Fisher, Ananth Raman, and Anna Sheen McClelland, "Rocket Science Retailing Is Almost Here: Are You Ready?" *Harvard Business Review,* July–August 2000, pp. 115–24; Charla Mathwick, Naresh Malhotra, and Edward Rigdon, "Experiential Value: Conceptualization, Measurement and Application in the Catalog and Internet Shopping Environment," *Journal of Retailing,* Spring 2001, pp. 39–56; Lawrence M. Bellman, "Bricks and Mortar: 21st Century Survival," *Business Horizons,* May–June 2001, pp. 21–28; Zhan G. Li and Nurit Gery, "E-Tailing—for All Products?" *Business Horizons,* November–December 2000, pp. 49–54; and Bill Hanifin, "Go Forth and Multichannel: Loyalty Programs Need Knowledge Base," *Marketing News,* August 27, 2001, p. 23.

64. Robert Berner, "J.C. Penney Gets The Net," *BusinessWeek,* May 7, 2007, p. 70; Multi-Channel Integration: *The New Retail Battleground* (Columbus, OH: PricewaterhouseCoopers, March 2001); and Richard Last, "JC Penney Internet Commerce," presentation at Southern Methodist University, February 12, 2001.

65. Nanette Byrnes, "Secrets of the Male Shopper," *BusinessWeek,* September 4, 2006, p. 44; Simon Brooke, "It's Different for Guys. Retailers Are Rethinking the Shop Floor with Men in Mind," *Financial Times,* April 28, 2007, p. 7; and Velitchka D. Kaltcheva and Baron A. Weitz, "When Should a Retailer Create an Exciting Store Environment?" *Journal of Marketing,* January 2006, p. 107–18.

Mall of America: This case was written by David P. Brennan and is based on an interview with Maureen Cahill and materials provided by Mall of America.

CHAPTER 18

1. Jennifer Netherby, "High-Def Keeps Growing," *Video Business,* January 8, 2007, p. 23; "Rewind," *Promo,* December 1, 2006, p. 30; Gregory A. Quirk, "Rivalry in Consoles Is No Game," *Electronic Engineering Times,* May 14, 2007, p. H92; Lewis Lazare, "Wii Effort Should Inspire More 'Wow,'" *Chicago Sun-Times,* December 5, 2006, p. 57; "Drinks Brands in Wii Promotion," *In Store Marketing,* June 11, 2007, p. 7; Joanne Payne, "Nintendo Plans Live Wii Stunts for Pirates Release," *Brand Republic News,* May 29, 2007, p. 1; "Sony Computer Entertainment America Announces New Marketing Campaign for PlayStation 3: Inspiring Gamers to 'Play Beyond,'" *PR Newswire,* November 15, 2006; Beth Snyder Bulik, "PS3, Wii Get All the Buzz, but Xbox Could Have the Happiest Holidays," *Advertising Age,* October 30, 2006, p. 3.

2. Shu-pei Tsai, "Integrated Marketing As Management of Holistic Consumer Experience," *Business Horizons* 48 (2005), pp. 431–41; and Mike Reid, Sandra Luxton, and Felix Mavondo, "The Relationship Between Integrated Marketing Communication, Market Orientation, and Brand Orientation," *The Journal of Advertising* 34 (Winter 2005), pp. 11–23.

3. Wilbur Schramm, "How Communication Works," in Wilbur Schramm, ed., *The Process and Effects of Mass Communication* (Urbana, IL: University of Illinois Press, 1955), pp. 3–26.

4. E. Cooper and M. Jahoda, "The Evasion of Propaganda," *Journal of Psychology* 22 (1947), pp. 15–25; H. Hyman and P. Sheatsley, "Some Reasons Why Information Campaigns Fail," *Public Opinion Quarterly* 11 (1947), pp. 412–23; and J. T. Klapper, *The Effects of Mass Communication* (New York: Free Press, 1960), chap. VII.

5. Cynthia L. Kemper, "Biting Wax Tadpole, Other Faux Pas," *Denver Post,* August 3, 1997, p. G4.

6. Rik Pieters and Michel Wedel, "Attention Capture and Transfer in Advertising: Brand Pictorial, and Text-Size Effects," *Journal of Marketing,* April 2004, pp. 36–50.

7. Adapted from *Dictionary of Marketing Terms,* 2nd ed., Peter D. Bennett, ed. (Chicago: American Marketing Association, 1995), p. 231.

8. David Robinson, "Public Relations Comes of Age," *Business Horizons* 49 (2006), pp. 247–56; and Dick Martin, "Gilded and Gelded: Hard-Won Lessons from the PR Wars," *Harvard Business Review,* October 2003, pp. 44–54.

9. "RSS, Blogs, Podcast and Social Media Experts to Share Knowledge at PR Online Convergence Conference," *Business Wire,* April 11, 2007; "Business and the Media Forum Focuses on Social Media," *Business Wire,* July 9, 2007; Sarah Murray, "Public Relations: The Ease of Online Communication Is Undermining Companies' Control of Their Image and Reputation," *Financial Times,* November 8, 2006, p. 14; and Matthew Creamer, "Slowly, Marketers Learn How to Let Go and Let Blog," *Advertising Age,* October 31, 2005, p. 1.

10. Marsha d. Loda and Barbara Carrick Coleman, "Sequence Matters: A More Effective Way to Use Advertising and Publicity," *Journal of Advertising Research* 45 (December 2005), pp. 362–71.

11. Amy Johannes, "Made For Each Other," *Promo,* June 1, 2007, p. 16.

12. Kusum L Ailawadi, Scott A. Neslin, and Karen Gedenk, "Pursuing the Value-Conscious Consumer: Store Brands versus National Brand Promotions," *Journal of Marketing,* January 2001, pp. 71–89.

13. B. C. Cotton and Emerson M. Babb, "Consumer Response to Promotional Deals," *Journal of Marketing* 42 (July 1978), pp. 109–13.

14. Robert George Brown, "Sales Response to Promotions and Advertising," *Journal of Advertising Research* 14 (August 1974), pp. 33–40.

15. Adapted from *Economic Impact: U.S. Direct Marketing Today* (New York: Direct Marketing Association, 1998), p. 25.

16. Siva K. Balasubramanian and V. Kumar, "Analyzing Variations in Advertising and Promotional Expenditures: Key Correlates in Consumer, Industrial, and Service Markets," *Journal of Marketing,* April 1990, pp. 57–68.

17. "Multitasking Sports Viewers Engaged With Advertising," *PR Newswire US,* June 28, 2007; Alice Z. Cuneo, "'Yard' Sale? Sprite Talks to Teen with Mobile Promotions, Coca-Cola Launches Interactive Site in Shift from Traditional Media to the 'Critical' Third Screen," *Advertising Age,* June 11, 2007, p. 23; "How is Multitasking Affecting TV Networks and Online Video Sites?" *Business Wire,* February 6, 2007; Greg Lindsay, "Demanding Boomers, MultiTasking Gen Yers Decide What, How, When," *Advertising Age,* January 2, 2006, p. 22; Don E. Shultz, "Include SIMM in Modern Media Plans," *Marketing News,* January 15, 2004, p. 6; and Christopher Vollmer, John Frelinghuysen, and Randall Rothenberg, "The Future of Advertising is Now," *Strategy + Business* 43 (Summer 2006), pp. 38–51.

18. Dunn Sunnoo and Lynn Y. S. Lin, "Sales Effects of Promotion and Advertising," *Journal of Advertising Research* 18 (October 1978), pp. 37–42.

19. John Palmer, "Animal Instincts," *Promo,* May 2001, pp. 25–33.

20. Remco Prins and Peter C. Verhoef, "Marketing Communication Drivers of Adoption Timing of a New E-Service Among Existing Customers," *Journal of Marketing* 71 (April 2007), pp. 169–83.

21. J. Ronald Carey, Stephen A. Clique, Barbara A. Leighton, and Frank Milton, "A Test of Positive Reinforcement of Customers," *Journal of Marketing* 40 (October 1976), pp. 98–100.

22. James M. Olver and Paul W. Farris, "Push and Pull: A One-Two Punch for Packages Products," *Sloan Management Review,* Fall 1989, pp. 53–61.

23. Terry Box, "Pressure's Rising for Ford Dealers," *Dallas Morning News,* February 10, 2007; and Richard Truett, "Ford to Dealers: We'll Support Sales," *Automotive News,* June 18, 2007, p. 3.

24. Fusun F. Gonul, Franklin Carter, Elina Petrova, and Kannan Srinivasan, "Promotion of Prescription Drugs and Its Impact on Physicians' Choice Behavior," *Journal of Marketing,* July 2001, pp. 79–90.

25. Robert J. Lavidge and Gary A. Steiner, "A Model for Predictive Measurement of Advertising Effectiveness," *Journal of Marketing,* October 1961, p. 61.

26. Brian Wansink and Michael Ray, "Advertising Strategies to Increase Usage Frequency," *Journal of Marketing,* January 1996, pp. 31–46.

27. "100 Leading National Advertisers," Advertising Age, June 25, 2007, 51-517.

28. Don E. Schultz and Anders Gronstedt, "Making Marcom an Investment," *Marketing Management,* Fall 1997, pp. 41–49; and J. Enrique Bigne, "Advertising Budget Practices: A Review," *Journal of Current Issues and Research in Advertising,* Fall 1995, pp. 17–31.

29. John Philip Jones, "Ad Spending: Maintaining Market Share," *Harvard Business Review,* January–February 1990, pp. 38–42; and Charles H. Patti and Vincent Blanko, "Budgeting Practices of Big Advertisers," *Journal of Advertising Research* 21 (December 1981), pp. 23–30.

30. James A. Schroer, "Ad Spending: Growing Market Share," *Harvard Business Review,* January–February 1990, pp. 44–48.

31. Jeffrey A. Lowenhar and John L. Stanton, "Forecasting Competitive Advertising Expenditures," *Journal of Advertising Research* 16, no. 2 (April 1976), pp. 37–44.

32. Daniel Seligman, "How Much for Advertising?" *Fortune,* December 1956, p. 123.

33. James E. Lynch and Graham J. Hooley, "Increasing Sophistication in Advertising Budget Setting," *Journal of Advertising Research* 30 (February–March 1990), pp. 67–75.

34. Jimmy D. Barnes, Brenda J. Muscove, and Javad Rassouli, "An Objective and Task Media Selection Decision Model and Advertising Cost

Formula to Determine International Advertising Budgets," *Journal of Advertising* 11, no. 4 (1982), pp. 68–75.

35. Don E. Schultz, "Olympics Get the Gold Medal in Integrating Marketing Event," *Marketing News,* April 27, 1998, pp. 5, 10.

36. Cornelia Pechman, Guangzhi Zhao, Marvin E. Goldberg, and Ellen Thomas Reibling, "What to Convey in Antismoking Advertisements for Adolescents: The Use of Protection Motivation Theory to Identify Effective Message Themes," *Journal of Marketing,* April 2003, pp. 1–18.

37. "GameStop Goes to the Movies with an Extraordinary Line-Up of New Movie-Themed Video Games for Summer," *Business Wire,* June 4, 2007; and Amy Johannes, "Third Time Is a Charm," *Promo,* May 1, 2007, p. 8.

38. Mike Reid, "Performance Auditing of Integrated Marketing Communication (IMC) Actions and Outcomes," *Journal of Advertising* 34 (Winter 2005), p. 41.

39. Jeremy Jullman, "Retooled Starcom Makes Its Own Rules," *Advertising Age,* February 26, 2007, p. S-12; and www.starcomworldwide.com, July 21, 2007.

40. Tom Duncan, "Is Your Marketing Communications Integrated?" *Advertising Age,* January 24, 1994, p. 26.

41. Don E. Schultz, "IMC Is Do or Die in New Pull Marketplace," *Marketing News,* August 15, 2006, p. 7; and Don E. Schultz, "Integration's New Role Focuses on Customers," *Marketing News,* September 15, 2006, p. 8.

42. "Measure for Measure," *Marketing Management,* January–February 2004, p. 7.

43. Don E. Schultz, "Measure IMC's Whole—Not Just Each Part," *Marketing News,* February 15, 2006, p. 8.

44. *Direct Marketing Key Statistics at a Glance, 2006–2007* (New York: Direct Marketing Association, 2006), pp. 1, 5; and *Statistical Fact Book,* 29th ed. (New York: Direct Marketing Association, 2007), p. 17, 18.

45. Deborah L. Vence, "State Farm Ad Campaign Targets Youth, Reinvigorates Brand Image," *Marketing News,* January 15, 2007, p. 13; Michael Fielding, "Direct Mail Still Has Its Place, Marketer Find It Works Best As Part of Integrated Campaigns," *Marketing News,* November 1, 2006, p. 31; Keith Goodman, "Internet Isn't DM's Only Story to Tell," *Marketing News,* November 1, 2006, p. 32; and Alison Masters, "We Have Seen the Future of Marketing and It's Integrated and Direct," *Marketing Direct,* September 4, 2006, p. 61.

46. Robert Berner, "Going that Extra Inch," *BusinessWeek,* September 18, 2000, p. 84.

47. Adapted from *Economic Impact: U.S. Direct Marketing Today* (New York: Direct Marketing Association, 1998), pp. 25–26.

48. Patricia ODell, "Hello, Old Friend," *Promo,* February 1, 2007, p. 26.

49. Julie Tilsner, "Lillian Vernon: Creating a Host of Spin-offs from Its Core Catalog," *BusinessWeek,* December 19, 1994, p. 85; and Lisa Coleman, "I Went Out and Did It," *Forbes,* August 17, 1992, pp. 102–4.

50. Thomas Crampton, "Google to Reduce History of Personal Searches," *The New York Times,* June 13, 2007, p. 3; and Noelle McElhatton, "Search Reveals Mail's Weakness," *Marketing Direct,* June 7, 2007, p. 25.

51. "The Data Dilemma," *Marketing Direct,* February 6, 2007, p. 37; and Marc Nohr, "South Africa—A Worthy Contender," *Marketing Direct,* March 5, 2007, p. 20.

52. Allison Enright, "Direct Mail Challenged," *Marketing News,* April 1, 2007, p. 3; Juliana Koranten, "European Privacy Rules Go into Effect in 15 EU States," *Advertising Age,* October 26, 1998, p. S31; and Rashi Glazer, "The Illusion of Privacy and Competition for Attention," *Journal of Interactive Marketing,* Summer 1998, pp. 2–4.

53. "Spam Is Now 77% of All E-Mail," *The Calgary Herald,* February 1, 2007, p. E1; Randi Schmelzer, "Opt-in E-mail Offers Welcome,

Extended Interactions," *PR Week,* June 11, 2007, p. 11; "Opt-in Plans Could Spell Disaster for DM," *Printweek,* June 7, 2007, p. 24; "Japan to Toughen Regulations on Unsolicited E-mails," *Japan Economic Newswire,* July 17, 2007; LaToya Dream Rembert, "Will CAN-SPAM Affect You?" *Marketing Research,* Spring 2004, p. 8; and Douglas Wood and David Brosse, "Mulling E-Mail Options," *Promo,* September 2001, p. 18.

UPS: This case was written by Steven Hartley based on taped interviews of company personnel and the following sources: Dean Foust, "Big Brown's New Bag," *BusinessWeek,* July 19, 2004, p. 54; David Rynecki, "Does This Package Make Sense?" *Fortune,* January 26, 2004, p. 132; "The UPS Store and Mail Boxes Etc. Expand to 5000 Worldwide Locations," *Business Wire,* September 13, 2004; Charles Haddad, "The Websmart 50," *BusinessWeek,* November 24, 2003, p. 92; and information contained on the UPS website (www.ups.com).

Las Vegas: This case was prepared by Steven Hartley and Roger Kerin. Sources: Bob Garfield, "This Time, Vegas Tourism Gets the Credit It Deserves," *Advertising Age,* August 21, 2006, p. 25; Greg Lindsay, Las Vegas Turns Inward For Next Act," *Advertising Age,* June 5, 2006, p. 10; Hilary Potkewitz, "As Demand Grows, Airlines Say, 'Viva, Las Vegas!" *Crain's New York Business,* September 27, 2007, p. 30; Marc Graser, "Marketers Have A Lot To Learn About Good Integration," *Advertising Age,* February 20, 2006, p. 4; Corey Hajim and Kate Bonamici, "Insider's Guide to Vegas," *Fortune,* January 23, 2006, p 154; Rich Thomaselli, "Las Vegas Ad Slogan Takes On Life Of Its Own," *Advertising Age,* March 8, 2004, p. 6; Joel Stein and Laura A. Locke, "The Strip Is Back!," *Time,* July 26, 2004, p. 22; Julie Rawe, "Vegas Plays to the World," *Time,* July 26, 2004, p. 34; and information contained on the Las Vegas Convention and Visitors Authority website (www.lvcva.com) and the R&R Partners website (www.rrpartners.com).

CHAPTER 19

1. Brooke Capps, "How to Succeed in Second Life," *Advertising Age,* May 28, 2007, p. 6; Jon Fine, "Ready to Get Weird, Advertisers?" *BusinessWeek,* January 8, 2007, p. 24; Andrew Hampp, "Second Life Losing Lock on Virtual-site Marketing," *Advertising Age,* July 9, 2007, p. 10; Aili McConnon and Reena Jana, "Beyond Second Life," *BusinessWeek,* June, 11, 2007, p. 24; Brian Steinberg, "How to Stop Them From Skipping: TiVo Tells All," *Advertising Age,* July 16, 2007, pp. 1, 33; Nat Ives, "Where Have All the Girls Gone?" *Advertising Age,* July 16, 2007, pp. 1, 37; and Todd Wasserman, "15-Second Ads Getting Their Moment," *Brandweek,* September 11, 2006, p. 20.

2. David A. Aaker and Donald Norris, "Characteristics of TV Commercials Perceived as Informative," *Journal of Advertising Research* 22, no. 2 (April–May 1982), pp. 61–70.

3. Larry D. Compeau and Dhruv Grewal, "Comparative Price Advertising: An Integrative Review," *Journal of Public Policy & Marketing,* Fall 1998, pp. 257–73; and William Wilkie and Paul W. Farris, "Comparison Advertising: Problems and Potentials," *Journal of Marketing,* October 1975, pp. 7–15.

4. Jennifer Lawrence, "P&G Ads Get Competitive," *Advertising Age,* February 1, 1993, p. 14; Jerry Gotlieb and Dan Sorel, "The Influence of Type of Advertisement, Price, and Source Credibility on Perceived Quality," *Journal of the Academy of Marketing Science,* Summer 1992, pp. 253–60; and Cornelia Pechman and David Stewart, "The Effects of Comparative Advertising on Attention, Memory, and Purchase Intentions," *Journal of Consumer Research,* September 1990, pp. 180–92.

5. Bruce Buchanan and Doron Goldman, "Us vs. Them: The Minefield of Comparative Ads," *Harvard Business Review,* May–June 1989, pp. 38–50; Dorothy Cohen, "The FTC's Advertising Substantiation Program," *Journal of Marketing,* Winter 1980, pp. 26–35; and Michael Etger and Stephen A. Goodwin, "Planning for Comparative

Advertising Requires Special Attention," *Journal of Advertising* 8, no. 1 (Winter 1979), pp. 26–32.

6. Lewis C. Winters, "Does It Pay to Advertise to Hostile Audiences with Corporate Advertising?" *Journal of Advertising Research,* June–July 1988, pp. 11–18; and Robert Selwitz, "The Selling of an Image," *Madison Avenue,* February 1985, pp. 61–69.

7. Jeremy Mullman, "No Sugar and Spice Here," *Advertising Age,* June 18, 2007, p. 3.

8. Jean Halliday, "Of Hummers and Zen," *Advertising Age,* August 6, 2001, p. 29.

9. "Claritin Springs into Allergy Season with New Consumer Programs," *PR Newswire,* February 20, 2001.

10. Ira Teinowitz, "Self-regulation Urged to Prevent Bias in Ad Buying," *Advertising Age,* January 18, 1999, p. 4.

11. Bob Donath, "Match Your Media Choice and Ad Copy Objective," *Marketing News,* June 8, 1998, p. 6.

12. Award information available at The Magazine Publishers of America Kelly Award website, www.kellyawardsgallery.org.

13. Kate Maddox, "ARF Forum Examines Internet Research Effectiveness," *Advertising Age,* January 11, 1999, p. 28.

14. Demetrios Vakratsas and Tim Ambler, "How Advertising Works: What Do We Really Know?" *Journal of Marketing,* January 1999, pp. 26–43.

15. "It's the Super Bowl, Not the Toilet Bowl," *Advertising Age,* February 5, 2007, p. 1; Claire Atkinson, "Measuring Bowl ROI? Good Luck," *Advertising Age,* January 29, 2007, p. 9; Rama Ylkur, Chuck Tomkovick, and Patty Traczyk, "Super Bowl Effectiveness: Hollywood Finds the Games Golden," *Journal of Advertising Research,* March, 2004, pp. 143–59.

16. "U.S. Market Share Leaders," *Advertising Age,* June 25, 2007, p. S-11; Jean Halliday, "Entry-Lux Gears Up," *Advertising Age,* June 23, 2003, p. S4; and Kate Macarthur, "$50 Million Push: Predictions for Coke's C2," *Advertising Age,* May 31, 2004, p. 8.

17. Michael S. LaTour and Herbert J. Rotfeld, "There Are Threats and (Maybe) Fear-Caused Arousal: Theory and Confusions of Appeals to Fear and Fear Arousal Itself," *Journal of Advertising,* Fall 1997, pp. 45–59.

18. Bob Garfield, "Allstate Ads Bring Home Point about Mortgage Insurance," *Advertising Age,* September 11, 1989, p. 120; and Judann Dagnoli, "'Buy or Die' Mentality Toned Down in Ads," *Advertising Age,* May 7, 1990, p. S12.

19. Cornelia Pechmann, Guangzhi Zhao, Marvin E. Goldberg, and Ellen Thomas Reibling, "What to Convey in Antismoking Advertisements for Adolescents: The Use of Protection Motivation Theory to Identify Effective Message Themes," *Journal of Marketing,* April, 2003, pp. 1–18; Jeffrey D. Zbar, "Fear!" *Advertising Age,* November 14, 1994, pp. 18–19; John F. Tanner, Jr., James B. Hunt, and David R. Eppright, "The Protection Motivation Model: A Normative Model of Fear Appeals," *Journal of Marketing,* July 1991, pp. 36–45; and Michael S. LaTour and Shaker A. Zahra, "Fear Appeals as Advertising Strategy: Should They Be Used?" *Journal of Consumer Marketing,* Spring 1989, pp. 61–70.

20. Stuart Elliot, "Can Beer Ads Extol Great Taste in Good Taste?" *The New York Times,* April 16, 2004, p. C2; and "Operating Strategy," Bebe website, www.bebe.com.

21. Steve McClellan, "The Caveman: Evolution of a Character," *Adweek,* March 12, 2007, p. 78.

22. Theresa Howard, "Thinking Outside the TV Box Ads Get Creative in Midst of New Media Choices," *USA Today,* June 22, 2004, p. 4B; Anthony Vagnoni, "Best Awards," *Advertising Age,* May 28, 2001, pp. S1–18; Dana L. Alden, Wayne D. Hoyer, and Chol Lee, "Identifying Global and Culture-Specific Dimensions of Humor in Advertising: A Multinational Analysis," *Journal of Marketing,* April 1993, pp. 64–75; and Johny K. Johansson, "The Sense of 'Nonsense': Japanese TV Advertising," *Journal of Advertising,* March 1994, pp. 17–26.

23. Campaign information accessed at Berlin Cameron website, www.bc-p.com, July 27, 2007; and Lisa Sanders, "Berlin Cameron Stands on Its Own," *Advertising Age,* January 12, 2004, p. S2.

24. Jeff Manning and Kevin Lane Keller, "Got Advertising That Works?" *Marketing Management,* January–February 2004, pp. 16–20; Stephanie Thompson, "Jacobs Hopes Simpson Can Turn Ice to Gold at Hershey," *Advertising Age,* May 31, 2004, p. 54; "NCP Enlists Simpson Sisters for Ice Breakers," www.Adweek.com, May 18, 2004; "Risky Business: Kobe Sex Scandal Forces Brands to Take a Closer Look," *Business and Industry,* September 29, 2003, p. 1; Alan J. Bush, Craig A. Martin, and Victoria D. Bush, "Sports Celebrity Influence on the Behavioral Intentions of Generation Y," *Journal of Advertising Research,* March 2004, pp. 108–18; "Ronald McDonald Models Milk Mustache," *PR Newswire,* September 11, 2001; "Image of the Week," *Advertising Age,* February 26, 2001, p. 56; Rich Thomaselli, "Air Ball?" *Advertising Age,* October 1, 2001, p. 3; Paul Lukas, "Got Milk? Got Books? Got a Clue?" *Fortune,* September 7, 1998, p. 40; Brian D. Till and Terence A. Shimp, "Endorsers in Advertising: The Case of Negative Celebrity Information," *Journal of Advertising,* March 22, 1998, p. 67; and Alan R. Miciak and William L. Shanklin, "Choosing Celebrity Endorsers," *Marketing Management* 3, no. 3 (1994), pp. 51–59.

25. *2006 Television Production Cost Survey* (New York, New York: American Association of Advertising Agencies, 2006); and Jean Halliday, "Exotic Ads Get Noticed," *Advertising Age*, April 9, 2001, p. jS4.

26. "Ad Spending Totals By Medium," *Advertising Age,* June 25, 2007, p. S-15.

27. Giles D'Souza and Ram C. Rao, "Can Repeating an Advertisement More Frequently than the Competition Affect Brand Preference in a Mature Market?" *Journal of Marketing,* April 1995, pp. 32–42.

28. Vicki R. Lane, "The Impact of Ad Repetition and Ad Content on Consumer Perceptions of Incongruent Extensions," *Journal of Marketing,* April 2000, pp. 80–91.

29. Katherine Barrett, "Taking a Closer Look," *Madison Avenue,* August 1984, pp. 106–9.

30. "Nielsen and Integrated Media Measurement Launch Out-of-Home Television Ratings Measurement Service," *PR Newswire,* April 12, 2007; Holly M Sanders, "You Can Run But You Can't Hide From TV Ads," *New York Post,* July 29, 2007.

31. Brian Steinberg, "McPricey ABC Leads Way With 'Grey' This Fall," *Advertising Age*, October 1, 2007, p. 1, 41.

32. Surendra N. Singh, Denise Linville, and Ajay Sukhdial, "Enhancing the Efficacy of Split Thirty-Second Television Commercials: An Encoding Variability Application," *Journal of Advertising,* Fall 1995, pp. 13–23; Scott Ward, Terence A. Oliva, and David J. Reibstein, "Effectiveness of Brand-Related 15-Second Commercials," *Journal of Consumer Marketing,* no. 2 (1994), pp. 38–44; and Surendra N. Singh and Catherine Cole, "The Effects of Length, Content, and Repetition on Television Commercial Effectiveness," *Journal of Marketing Research,* February 1993, pp. 91–104.

33. Scott Woolley, "Zap," *Forbes,* September 29, 2003, pp. 77–82; Cliff Edwards, "Is TiVo's Signal Fading?" *BusinessWeek,* September 10, 2001, p. 72; Jacqueline M. Graves, "The Fortune 500 Opt for Infomercials," *Fortune,* March 6, 1995, p. 20; and William McCall, "Infomercial Pioneer Becomes Industry Leader," *Marketing News,* June 19, 1995, p. 14.

34. Cara Beardi, "Radio's Big Bounce," *Advertising Age,* August 27, 2001, p. S2.

35. Larry Dobrow, "Parenting Newbie Cookie Is A Friend To Upscale Moms," *Advertising Age*, October 29, 2007, p. S8-9; *The Magazine Handbook: A Comprehensive Guide 2007/2008* (New York, New York: Magazine Publishers of America), p. 5; "Number of Magazines by Category," *Editorial Trends and Magazine Handbook* (New York, New York: Magazine Publishers of America). Kate Fitzgerald, "Launches Crowd Already Tough Field," *Advertising Age,* April 5, 2004, p. S2;

Jon Fine, "Silicon Valley Spawns New Nascar Lifestyle Magazine," *Advertising Age,* January 12, 2004, p. 8; Jon Fine, "Magazine of the Year: Lucky," *Advertising Age,* October 20, 2003, p. S1; *A Magazine for Everyone* (New York: The Magazine Publishers Association, 2003), p. 6; R. Craig Endicott, "Past Performance Is Not a Guarantee of Future Returns," *Advertising Age,* June 18, 2001, pp. S1, S6; and George R. Milne, "A Magazine Taxonomy Based on Customer Overlap," *Journal of the Academy of Marketing Science,* Spring 1994, pp. 170–79.

36. Julia Collins, "Image and Advertising," *Harvard Business Review,* January–February 1989, pp. 93–97.

37. Maureen Morrison, "Revenue At Top U.S. Titles Rises 3.1% But Ad Pages Flat," *Advertising Age,* October 29, 2007, p. S10.

38. Jon Fine, "Newspaper-Industry Slide Worsens," *Advertising Age,* May 10, 2004, p. 59; Jeffery D. Zbar, "Papers Tackling Sprawl," *Advertising Age,* April 30, 2001, pp. S6, S7; Heather Holliday, "Papers, TV Stations Extend War to Web," *Advertising Age,* April 30, 2001, p. S8; Mary Ellen Podmolik, "Urban Tabloids Snare Hipper Young Readers," *Advertising Age,* April 30, 2001, p. S2; and Kim Cleland, "Online Soon to Snare 100-plus Newspapers," *Advertising Age,* April 24, 1995, p. S6.

39. Abbey Klassen, "Here's a $14 Billion Print Business That's Loving the Digital Revolution," *Advertising Age*, August 28, 2006, p. 3; Lisa Sanders, "Major Marketers Turn to Yellow Pages," *Advertising Age,* March 8, 2004, p. 4; "Yellow Pages Still 'Gold Standard' for Searches," *USA Today,* February 16, 2004, p. 10A; Avery M. Abernethy and David N. Laband, "The Impact of Trademarks and Advertisement Size on Yellow Page Call Rates," *Journal of Advertising Research,* March 2004, pp. 119–25; and "Yellow Pages and the Media Mix," Yellow Pages Publishers Association, Troy, MI.

40. Pierre Berthon and James M. Hulbert, "Marketing in Metamorphosis: Breaking Boundaries," *Business Horizons,* May–June 2003, pp. 31–40.

41. Sandeep Krishnamurthy, "Deciphering the Internet Advertising Puzzle," *Marketing Management,* Fall 2000, pp. 35–39; Judy Strauss and Raymond Frost, *Marketing on the Internet: Principles of Online Marketing* (Englewood Cliffs, NJ: Prentice Hall, 1999), pp. 196–249; and Maricris G. Briones, "Rich Media May Be Too Rich for Your Blood," *Marketing News,* March 29, 1999, p. 4.

42. "Search Marketing Fact Pack 2006," *Advertising Age,* November 6, 2006.

43. Brian Grow and Ben Elgin, "Click Fraud," *BusinessWeek,* October 2, 2006, pp. 46–57; Rob Hof, "Is Google Too Powerful?" *BusinessWeek,* April 9, 2007, p. 48; Eric J. Hansen, "Apply Online Market Data for Offline Insights," *Marketing News,* April 1, 2007, p. 30; "Out of Site at AdAge.com," *Advertising Age,* November 6, 2006, p. 12; Michael Fielding, "Click Fraud Settles Down," *Marketing News,* September 1, 2006, p. 4; Brian Grow, "This Mouse for Hire," *BusinessWeek,* October 23, 2006, p. 104.

44. Dana Blankenhorn, "Bigger, Richer Ads Go Online," *Advertising Age,* June 18, 2001, p. T10; Patricia Riedman, "Poor Rich Media," *Advertising Age,* February 5, 2001, p. 26; Heather Green, "Net Advertising: Still the 98-Pound Weakling," *BusinessWeek,* September 11, 2000, p. 36; and Thom Weidlich, "Online Spots—A New Generation," *Advertising Age,* July 30, 2001, p. S10.

45. Arch G. Woodside, "Outdoor Advertising as Experiments," *Journal of the Academy of Marketing Science* 18 (Summer 1990), pp. 229–37.

46. Ronald Grover, "Billboards Aren't Boring Anymore," *BusinessWeek,* September 21, 1998, pp. 86–90; and Marc Gunther, "The Great Outdoors," *Fortune,* March 1, 1999, p. 150–57.

47. "Nokia Ad Business to Power Mobile Advertising for Handmark," *PR Newswire,* November 19, 2007.

48. Charles R. Taylor and Weih Chang, "The History of Outdoor Advertising Regulation in the United States," *Journal of Macromarketing,* Spring 1995, pp. 47–59; Cyndee Miller, "Outdoor Advertising Weathers Repeated Attempts to Kill It," *Marketing News,* March 16, 1992,

pp. 1, 9; Ricardo Davis, "Outdoor Ad Giants Trim Pay to Agencies," *Advertising Age,* January 18, 1993, p. 54; and Patricia Winters, "Outdoor Builds New Areas to Replace Tobacco and Liquor," *Advertising Age,* October 12, 1992, pp. 5–24.

49. Andrew Hampp, "Rise of Out-of-Home Video Sparks Metrics Push," *Advertising Age,* November 19, 2007, p. 8; Ed Brown, "Advertisers Skip to the Loo," *Fortune,* October 26, 1998, p. 64; John Cortex, "Growing Pains Can't Stop the New Kid on the Ad Block," *Advertising Age,* October 12, 1992, pp. 5–28; Allen Banks, "How to Assess New Place-Based Media," *Advertising Age,* November 30, 1992, p. 36; and John Cortex, "Media Pioneers Try to Corral On-the-Go Consumers," *Advertising Age,* August 17, 1992, p. 25.

50. "It's an Ad, Ad, Ad, Ad World," *Time,* July 9, 2001, p. 17; "Triton, Secora in Alliance for Advertising on ATMs," *Marketing News,* June 5, 2000, p. 12; and Joan Oleck, "High-Octane Advertising," *BusinessWeek,* November 29, 1999, p. 8.

51. Sehoon Park and Minhi Hahn, "Pulsing in a Discrete Model of Advertising Competition," *Journal of Marketing Research,* November 1991, pp. 397–405.

52. Peggy Masterson, "The Wearout Phenomenon," *Marketing Research,* Fall 1999, pp. 27–31; and Lawrence D. Gibson, "What Can One TV Exposure Do?" *Journal of Advertising Research,* March–April 1996, pp. 9–18.

53. Rob Norton, "How Uninformative Advertising Tells Consumers Quite a Bit," *Fortune,* December 26, 1994, p. 37; and "Professor Claims Corporations Waste Billions on Advertising," *Marketing News,* July 6, 1992, p. 5.

54. Ivan Pollard, "Agency Model of the Future? Keep an Eye on Media Guys," *Advertising Age,* April 2, 2007, p. 29.

55. The discussion of posttesting is based on William F. Arens, *Contemporary Advertising,* 6th ed. (Burr Ridge, IL: Richard D. Irwin, 1996), pp. 181–82.

56. David A. Aaker and Douglas M. Stayman, "Measuring Audience Perceptions of Commercials and Relating Them to Ad Impact," *Journal of Advertising Research* 30 (August–September 1990), pp. 7–17; and Ernest Dichter, "A Psychological View of Advertising Effectiveness," *Marketing Management* 1, no. 3 (1992), pp. 60–62.

57. David Kruegel, "Television Advertising Effectiveness and Research Innovation," *Journal of Consumer Marketing,* Summer 1988, pp. 43–51; and Laurence N. Gold, "The Evolution of Television Advertising Sales Measurement: Past, Present, and Future," *Journal of Advertising Research,* June–July 1988, pp. 19–24.

58. Kathleen M. Joyce, "Higher Gear," *PROMO 14th Annual Sourcebook,* 2007, p. 5–7.

59. Tom Hansen, "Media Mash," *PROMO,* February 1, 2007, p. 66; Magid M. Abraham and Leonard M. Lodish, "Getting the Most Out of Advertising and Promotion," *Harvard Business Review,* May–June 1990, pp. 50–60; Steven W. Hartley and James Cross, "How Sales Promotion Can Work for and against You," *Journal of Consumer Marketing,* Summer 1988, pp. 35–42; Robert D. Buzzell, John A. Quelch, and Walter J. Salmon, "The Costly Bargain of Trade Promotion," *Harvard Business Review,* March–April 1990, pp. 141–49; and Mary L. Nicastro, "Break-Even Analysis Determines Success of Sales Promotions," *Marketing News,* March 5, 1990, p. 11.

60. "We've Been Clipped," *PROMO,* September 2007, p. AR11; Natalie Schwartz, "Clipping Path," *Promo,* April 1, 2004, p. 4; Mathew Kinsman, "The Hard Sell," *Promo's 11th Annual Source Book* (2004), p. 19; Betsy Spethmann, "Going for Broke," *Promo,* August 2001, pp. 27–31; and Mathew Kinsman, "Bad Is Good," *Promo,* April 2001, pp. 71–74.

61. Kapil Bawa and Robert W. Shoemaker, "Analyzing Incremental Sales from a Direct-Mail Coupon Promotion," *Journal of Marketing,* July 1998, pp. 66–78.

62. Roger A. Strang, "Sales Promotion—Fast Growth, Faulty Management," *Harvard Business Review* 54 (July–August 1976), pp. 115–24; and Ronald W. Ward and James E. Davis, "Coupon Redemption," *Journal of Advertising Research* 18 (August 1978), pp. 51–58. Similar results on favorable mail-distributed coupons were reported by Alvin Schwartz, "The Influence of Media Characteristics on Coupon Redemption," *Journal of Marketing* 30 (January 1966), pp. 41–46.

63. "Competing with Coupons," *Marketing News,* March 15, 1999, p. 2; and Larry Armstrong. "Coupon Clippers, Save Your Scissors," *BusinessWeek,* June 20, 1994, pp. 164–66.

64. Karen Holt, "Coupon Crimes," *PROMO,* April 2004, pp. 23–26, 70.

65. Amy Johannes, "Box Office Buz," *PROMO,* October 1, 2006, p. 34; Carrie MacMillan, "Creature Features," *PROMO,* October 2001, p. 11; and Dan Hanover, "Not Just for Breakfast Anymore," *PROMO,* September 2001, p. 10.

66. Amy Johannes, "Do It Yourself," *PROMO,* September 1, 2007, p. AR14; Patricia Odell, "Hooray For Us," *PROMO,* October 1, 2007, p. 44.

67. Lorraine Woellert, "The Sweepstakes Biz Isn't Feeling Lucky," *BusinessWeek,* March 22, 1999, p. 80.

68. "Eight Ways to Win," *PROMO,* May 1, 2007, p. 42; "Campaign Index," *PROMO,* November 1, 2007, p. 12; Amy Johannes, "Band Wagon," *PROMO,* August 1, 2007, p. 12.

69. Edward Kabak, "Staking out the States," *PROMO,* October 2001, p. 11; Maxine Lans Retsky, "Stakes Are High for Direct Mail Sweepstakes Promotions," *Marketing News,* July 3, 2000, p. 8; Richard Sale, "Sweeping the Courts," *PROMO,* May 1998, pp. 42–45; and Fred C. Allvine, Richard D. Teach, and John Connelly, Jr., "The Demise of Promotional Games," *Journal of Advertising Research* 16 (October 1976), pp. 79–84.

70. Larry Jaffee, "Try It," *PROMO,* September 1, 2007, p. AR25. Lorin Cipolla, "Instant Gratification," *PROMO,* April 1, 2004, p. 4; "Best Activity Generating Brand Awareness/Trial," *PROMO,* September 2001, p. 51; and "Brand Handing," *PROMO's 9th Annual Sourcebook* (2002), p. 32.

71. Amy Johannes, "Top of Wallet," *PROMO,* July 1, 2007, p. 20; Richard Tedesco, "Best is Best," *PROMO,* September 1, 2007, p. AR19. Kathleen Joyce, "Keeping the Faith," *PROMO,* April 2004, p. AR23; and Kelly Shermack, "CPG Marketers Are Developing Loyalty Programs That Benefit Both Manufacturers and Retailers," *Marketing News,* November 10, 2003, p. 13.

72. Patricia Odell, "Shopping List," *PROMO,* September 1, 2007, p. AR23.

73. Jeff Neff, "Floors in Stores Start Moving," *Advertising Age,* August 20, 2001, p. 15.

74. See www.fordcollegegrad.com.

75. Marvin A. Jolson, Joshua L. Wiener, and Richard B. Rosecky, "Correlates of Rebate Proneness," *Journal of Advertising Research,* February–March 1987, pp. 33–43.

76. Patricia Odell, "Star Struck," *PROMO,* April 1, 2007, p. 16; Michael Idato, "A Word from Our Sponsors—Great Moments In Product Placement," *The Age,* October 2, 2003, p. 17; M. Ellen Peebles, "And Now, a Word from Our Sponsors," *Harvard Business Review,* October 2003, pp. 31–42; M. Ellen Peebles, "And Now, a Word from Our Sponsor," *Harvard Business Review,* October 2003, pp. 31–42; Paula Lyon Andruss, "Survivor Packages Make Real-Life Money," *Marketing News,* March 26, 2001, p. 5;

77. Allison Enright, "Apu Buzz, Krusty–Oh My!" *Marketing News,* August 15, 2007, p. 3; Rob Walker, "False Endorsement," *The New York Times,* November 18, 2007, p. 38;

78. This discussion is drawn particularly from John A. Quelch, *Trade Promotions by Grocery Manufacturers: A Management Perspective* (Cambridge, MA: Marketing Science Institute, August 1982).

79. Michael Chevalier and Ronald C. Curhan, "Retail Promotions as a Function of Trade Promotions: A Descriptive Analysis," *Sloan Management Review* 18 (Fall 1976), pp. 19–32.

80. G. A. Marken, "Firms Can Maintain Control over Creative Co-op Programs," *Marketing News,* September 28, 1992, pp. 7, 9.

81. "Safetyforum.com and Public Citizen Report: NHTSA Forces Firestone to Recall Defective Tires, Expand Wilderness ATs Recall," *PR Newswire,* October 5, 2001; and Cindy Skrzycki and Frank Swoboda, "Firestone Refuses Voluntary Recall," www.safetyforum.com, July 20, 2001; and Jim Suhr, "Tire Recall Response Time Defended," www.safetyforum.com, August 10, 2000.

82. Scott Hue, "Free 'Plugs' Supply Ad Power," *Advertising Age,* January 29, 1990, p. 6.

83. David Welch, "Importer's Worst Nightmare," *BusinessWeek,* July 23, 2007, p. 46; Troy Wolverton, "Apple's Backdating Scandal," *San Jose Mercury News,* January 7, 2007, p. 1.

84. Irving Rein, Philip Kotler, and Martin Stoller, *High Visibility* (New York: Dodd, Mead, 1987); and Steven Colford, "Ross Perot: A Winner after All," *Advertising Age,* December 21, 1992, pp. 4, 18.

85. Michael Treacy and Fred Wiersema, "Customer Intimacy and Other Value Disciplines," *Harvard Business Review,* January–February 1993, pp. 84–93.

86. Gerry Khermouch and Tom Lowry, "The Future of Advertising," *BusinessWeek,* March 26, 2001, p. 139; and D. J., "Outlook 2001: Advertising," *Marketing News,* January 1, 2001, p. 10.

87. Betsy Spethmann, "McFallout," *PROMO,* October 2001, pp. 31–38.

88. "Kid Stuff," *PROMO,* January 1991, pp. 25, 42; Steven W. Colford, "Fine-Tuning Kids' TV," *Advertising Age,* February 11, 1991, p. 35; and Kate Fitzgerald, "Toys Star-Struck for Movie Tie-Ins," *Advertising Age,* February 18, 1991, pp. 3, 45.

89. Herbert J. Rotfeld, Avery M. Abernathy, and Patrick R. Parsons, "Self-Regulation and Television Advertising," *Journal of Advertising* 19, no. 4 (1990), pp. 18–26.

Fallon Worldwide: This case was written by Mark T. Spriggs, William Rudelius, Linda Rochford, and Steven Hartley based on interviews with Fallon personnel and material on the Citi and Holiday Inn Express promotional campaigns provided by Fallon Worldwide. Sources: Lori McLeod, "Holiday Inn: A Road-Trip Staple Rebranded," *The Globe and Mail,* November 10, 2007, p. B3; Cecil Johnson, "The Ad Pitch: Creativity, Not Saturation, Is Key," *The Boston Globe,* August 6, 2006, p. D2; "New Campaigns—The World," *Campaign,* May 27, 2005, p. 52; Aaron Baar, "Fallon Showers Intelligence on Hotel Guests," *Adweek,* October 7, 2004; and the Holiday Inn Express website (http://www.ihgplc.com).

CHAPTER 20

1. "Executive Biographies—Anne Mulcahy," www.xerox.com, downloaded July 8, 2007; "Back From the Brink," *The Wall Street Journal,* April 24, 2006, pp. B1, B3; "Xerox—Dedicated to Customer Success," www.sspa.com, February 20, 2007; and "Turning the Page," *Business 2.0,* July 2005, pp. 98–100.

2. "Leading CEOs: A Statistical Snapshot of S&P 500 Leaders," www.spencerstuart.com, February 2007.

3. "Surgical Visits," *Business 2.0,* April 2006, p. 94.

4. Mark W. Johnston and Greg W. Marshall, *Relationship Selling,* 2nd ed. (Burr Ridge, IL: McGraw-Hill/Irwin, 2008).

5. David Kirkpatrick, "Inside Sam's $100 Billion Growth Machine," *Fortune,* June 14, 2004, p. 80ff.

6. Barton A. Weitz, Stephen B. Castleberry, and John F. Tanner, Jr., *Selling: Building Partnerships,* 6th ed. (Burr Ridge, IL: McGraw-Hill/Irwin, 2007), p. 8.

7. "Stop Calling Us," *Time,* April 29, 2003, pp. 56–58.

8. For an overview of team selling, see Eli Jones, Andrea Dickson, Lawrence B. Chonko, and Joseph P. Cannon, "Key Accounts and Team Selling: A Review, Framework, and Research Agenda," *Journal of Personal Selling & Sales Management,* Spring 2005, pp. 181–98.

9. "Group Dynamics," *Sales & Marketing Management,* January/February 2007, p. 8; and Steve Atlas and Elise Atlas, "Team Approach," *Selling Power,* May 2000, pp. 126–28.

10. Scott Sterns, "Cold Calls Have Yet to Breathe Their Last Gasp," *The Wall Street Journal,* December 14, 2006, p. D2.

11. Jim Edwards, "Dinner, Interrupted," *BrandWeek,* May 26, 2003, pp. 28–32.

12. Christopher Conkey, "Record Fine Levied for Telemarketing," *The Wall Street Journal,* December 14, 2005, pp. D1, D4.

13. Paul A. Herbing, *Handbook of Cross-Cultural Marketing* (New York: Halworth Press, 1998).

14. This discussion is based on Weitz, Castleberry, and Tanner, *Selling;* and Johnston and Marshall, *Relationship Selling.*

15. Kapil R. Tuli, Ajay K. Kohli, and Sundar G. Bharadwaj, "Rethinking Customer Solutions: From Product Bundles to Relational Processes," *Journal of Marketing,* July 2007, pp. 1–17.

16. For an extensive discussion of objections, see Charles M. Futrell, *Fundamentals of Selling,* 9th ed. (Burr Ridge, IL: McGraw-Hill/Irwin, 2007), chap. 12.

17. Theodore Levitt, *The Marketing Imagination* (New York: Free Press, 1983), p. 111.

18. Weitz, Castleberry, and Tanner, *Selling.*

19. *Management Briefing: Sales and Marketing* (New York: Conference Board, October 1996), pp. 3–4.

20. Ellen Neuborne, "Know Thy Enemy," *Sales & Marketing Management,* January 2003, pp. 29–33.

21. Alan J. Dubinsky, Marvin A. Jolson, Ronald E. Michaels, Masaaki Katobe, and Chea Un Lim, "Ethical Perceptions of Field Sales Personnel: An Empirical Assessment," *Journal of Personal Selling & Sales Management,* Fall 1992, pp. 9–21; and Alan J. Dubinsky, Marvin A. Jolson, Masaaki Katobe, and Chae Un Lim, "A Cross-National Investigation of Industrial Salespeople's Ethical Perceptions," *Journal of International Business Studies,* Fourth Quarter 1991, pp. 651–70.

22. See Gilbert A. Churchill, Jr.; Neil M. Ford; Orville C. Walker, Jr.; Mark W. Johnson; and Greg Marshall, *Sales Force Management,* 8th ed. (Burr Ridge, IL: McGraw-Hill/Irwin, 2006), pp. 100–4; and William T. Ross, Jr.; Frederic Dalsace; and Erin Anderson, "Should You Set Up Your Own Sales Force or Should You Outsource It? Pitfalls in the Standard Analysis," *Business Horizons,* January–February 2005, pp. 23–36.

23. Eli Jones, et al., "Key Accounts and Team Selling." Also see, Arun Sharma, "Success Factors in Key Accounts," *Journal of Business & Industrial Marketing* 21, no. 3 (2006), pp. 141–50.

24. This discussion is based on William L. Cron and Thomas E. DeCarlo, *Dalrymple's Sales Management,* 9th ed. (Hoboken, NJ: John Wiley & Sons, Inc., 2006).

25. Julia Chang, "Born to Sell?" *Sales & Marketing Management,* July 2003, pp. 34–38.

26. Weitz, Castleberry, and Tanner, *Selling,* p. 19. Also see Dean R. Manna and Alan D. Smith, "Exploring the Need for Emotional Intelligence and Awareness Among Sales Representatives," *Marketing Intelligence & Planning* 22, no. 1 (2004), p. 66ff.

27. *Statistical Abstract of the United States,* 126th ed. (Washington, DC: U.S. Department of Commerce, 2007).

28. Rosann L. Spiro, Gregory A. Rich, and William J. Stanton, *Management of the Sales Force,* 12th ed. (Burr Ridge, IL: McGraw-Hill/Irwin, 2008), chap. 7.

29. Ibid., chap. 8.

30. This discussion is based on Churchill et al., *Sales Force Management,* chap. 11.

31. Vasanth Srihavan, "Riding Sporty in Pink," *Dallas Morning News,* July 16, 2007, pp. 1D, 5D.

32. Gary Hallen and Robert Latino, "Eastman Chemical's Success Story," *Quality Progress,* June 2003, pp. 50–54.

33. Mark Cotteleer, Edward Inderrieden, and Felissa Lee, "Selling the Sales Force on Automation," *Harvard Business Review,* July–August 2006, pp. 18–22.

34. "Corporate America's New Sales Force," *Fortune,* August 11, 2003, special advertising section.

35. www.toshiba.com/technology, downloaded May 15, 2004.

36. "Tools of the Trade," *Sales & Marketing Management,* October 2003, pp. 46–51.

Xerox: This case was written by Steven Hartley and Roger Kerin. Sources: Joseph Kornik, "Table Talk: A Sales Leaders Roundtable," *Sales & Marketing Management,* February, 2007; Philip Chadwick, "Xerox Global Services," *Printweek,* October 11, 2007, p. 32; Kevin Maney, "Mulcahy Traces Steps of Xerox's Comeback," *USA Today,* September 11, 2006, p. 4B; Sarah Campbell, "What It's Like Working for Xerox," *The Times,* September 14, 2006, p. 9; "Anne Mulcahy: How I Compete," *BusinessWeek,* August 21, 2006, p 55; Simon Avery, "CEO's HR Skills Turn Xerox Fortunes," *The Globe and Mail,* June 2, 2006, p. B3; Julia Chang, "Ultimate Motivation Guide: Happy Sales Force, Happy Returns," *Sales & Marketing Management,* March 2006; Chris Taylor, "Changing Gears," www.salesandmarketing.com, October 1, 2005; and resources available on the Xerox website (www.xerox.com) including About Xerox, Executive Biographies, the Xerox 2007 Fact Sheet, the Online Fact Book: Historical Highlights, and the Online Fact Book: How Xerox Sells.

CHAPTER 21

1. Interview with Jennifer Miller, director of marketing at Seven Cycles, Inc., July 20, 2007; and www.sevencycles.com, July 18, 2007.

2. "Where Are All the Online Shoppers Going?" www.emarketer.com, May 16, 2007; and "U.S. Retail e-Commerce Forecast, 2006–2011," www.foresterresearch.com, May 2007.

3. "Statistics: U.S. Online Shoppers," www.shop.org, downloaded June 26, 2005.

4. "The Sky Will Now Have Some Limits," *BrandWeek,* June 18, 2007, pp. S62–63.

5. Rafl A. Mohammed, Robert J. Fisher, Bernard J. Jaworski, and Gordon J. Paddison, *Internet Marketing: Building Advantage in a Networked Economy,* 2nd ed. (Burr Ridge, IL: McGraw-Hill/Irwin, 2004).

6. Ward A. Hanson and Kirthi Kalyanam, *Internet Marketing & Electronic Commerce* (Mason, OH: Thompson Higher Education, 2007).

7. Ibid.

8. Michael Grebb, "Behavioral Science," *Business 2.0,* March 2000, p. 112.

9. Judy Strauss, Adel El-Ansary, and Raymond Frost, *E-Marketing,* 4th ed. (Upper Saddle River, NJ: Prentice Hall, 2006).

10. "Gartner: Nearly $2 Billion Lost in E-Sales in 2006 Due to U.S. Consumers' Security Concerns," www.the-dma.org, downloaded January 6, 2007.

11. This discussion is drawn from Jeffrey F. Rayport and Bernard J. Jaworski, *e-Commerce,* 2nd ed. (Burr Ridge, IL: McGraw-Hill/Irwin, 2004); and *The Essential Guide to Best Practices in eCommerce* (Portland, OR: Webtrends, Inc., 2006).

12. "Demographics of Internet Usage," www.pewinternet.org/trends, downloaded June 10, 2007.

13. "We Can All Get Along," *Marketing News,* May 15, 2007, p. 4.

14. "Women Outnumber Men Online, and It's Likely to Stay that Way," www.emarketer.com, April 9, 2007; and "Demographics of Internet Usage."

15. "The 90/20 Rule of E-Commerce: Nearly 90% of Online Sales Accounted for by 20% of Consumers," Cyber Dialogue press release, September 25, 2000.

16. John B. Horrigan, "A Typology of Information and Communication Technology Users," www.pewresearch.org/pubs, May 7, 2007.

17. "Statistics: U.S. Online Shoppers."

18. "New Study Reveals Internet Is the Medium Moms Rely on Most," Disney Online news release, March 2004; "On a Mission: The New Internet Mom," *FC NOW: The Fast Company Weblog,* May 25, 2004; and "Working Moms Develop Internet Habit," BizReport.com, November 30, 2006.

19. "U.S. Retail e-Commerce Forecast, 2006–2011."

20. Jerry Wind and Arvind Ranaswamy, "Customerization: The Next Wave in Mass Customization," *Journal of Interactive Marketing,* Winter 2001, pp. 13–32.

21. Kenneth Hein, "Shooting Your Mouth Off," *Other Advertising,* December 2005, pp. 20–21. Also see, Kate Fitzgerald, "Blogs Fascinate, Frighten Marketers," *Advertising Age,* March 5, 2007, p. S-4.

22. Quoted in Strauss, et al., *E-Marketing,* p. 357.

23. Hanson and Kalyanam, *Internet Marketing & Electronic Commerce.*

24. Stephen Baker, "The Online Ad Surge," *BusinessWeek,* November 22, 2004, pp. 76–81.

25. "Branding on the Net," *BusinessWeek,* November 2, 1998, pp. 78–86.

26. David Kesmodel, "Marketers Seek to Make Cookies More Palatable," *The Wall Street Journal,* June 17, 2005, pp. B1, B2.

27. Mary Lou Roberts, *Internet Marketing: Integrating Online and Offline Strategies,* 2nd ed. (Mason, OH: Thomson, 2008), chap. 12; Jean Chatzky, "Let the EBuyer Beware," *Time,* April 10, 2006, p. 80; Ben Elgin, "The Plot to Hijack Your Computer," *BusinessWeek,* July 17, 2006, pp. 40–48; and "Gartner: Nearly $2 Billion Lost in E-Sales in 2006 Due to Consumers' Security Concerns."

28. Susan Adams, et al. "This Time It Is Personal: Employee Online Shopping at Work," *Interactive Marketing,* April 2005, pp. 326–36; and "Shop Around the Clock," *American Demographics,* September 2003, p. 18.

29. This discussion is based on "Shop Online, Spend Offline," www.emarketer.com, July 11, 2007; Tamera Mendelsohn, "Are You Prepared for the Cross-Channel Shopper?" *Self-Service World Magazine,* May/June 2006, p. 94; and Tamera Mendelsohn, "The State of Multichannel Consumers in the U.S. and Europe," www.forresterresearch.com, June 25, 2007.

30. "Retailers' Panty Raid on Victoria's Secret," *The Wall Street Journal,* June 20, 2007, pp. B1, B12.

31. Stephanie Kang, "Callaway Will Use Retailers to Sell Goods Directly to Consumers Online," *The Wall Street Journal,* November 6, 2006, p. B5.

32. *The Next Chapter in Business-to-Consumer E-Commerce: Advantage Incumbent* (Boston: The Boston Consulting Group, 2001); and Timothy J. Mullaney, "E-Biz Strikes Again," *BusinessWeek,* May 10, 2004, pp. 80–90.

33. "The State of Multichannel Consumers in the U.S. and Europe."

McFarlane Toys: This case was written by Steve Hartley and Roger Kerin. Sources: www.spawn.com, downloaded July 30, 2007; Bruce Handy, "Small Is Beautiful," *Vanity Fair,* December 2003, p. 208; Wes Orshoski, "McFarlane Adds Hendrix, Elvis to Action-Figure Series," *Billboard,* December 20, 2003, p. 65; and *U.S. Department of Commerce Industry Outlook: Dolls, Toys, Games, and Children's Vehicles* (Washington, DC: International Trade Association, 2007).

CHAPTER 22

1. Personal interview with Vivian Milroy Callaway, August 2007.

2. Ann Merrill, "Feeding the Beast," *Star Tribune,* June 2, 2002, pp. D1, D10; and Richard Gibson, "The Cereal Makers Quest for the Next Grape-Nuts," *The Wall Street Journal,* January 23, 1997, pp. B1, B7.

3. Matthew Boyle, "Kellogg's New Meals," *Fortune,* November 3, 2006, p. 40.

4. Matt McKinney, "General Mills Up Against Cereal Wall," *Star Tribune,* June 29, 2007, pp. D1, D2.

5. Personal interview with Vivian Milroy Callaway, August 2007.

6. Kate Murphy, "Look! We Can Drive and Snack at the Same Time," *The New York Times,* November 2, 2003, p. BU4; Thomas Lee, "Big G Takes the High Road with Whole Grains," *Star Tribune,* October 10, 2004, pp. D1, D4; and Thomas Lee, "More than Just Low Carbs," *Star Tribune,* April 12, 2004, p. D8.

7. *2006 Annual Report* (Minneapolis, MN: General Mills, Inc., 2007), p. 8.

8. Roger A. Kerin, P. Rajan Varadarajan, and Robert A. Peterson, "First-Mover Advantage: A Synthesis, Conceptual Framework, and Research Proposition," *Journal of Marketing,* October 1992, pp. 33–52; and Pankaj Ghemawat, "Sustainable Advantage," *Harvard Business Review,* September–October 1986, pp. 53–58.

9. Nitin Nohria, William Joyce, and Bruce Roberson, "What Really Works," *Harvard Business Review,* July 2003, pp. 42–52; and "Who Gets Eaten and Who Gets to Eat," *The Economist,* July 12, 2003, pp. 61–63.

10. Jack Gordon, "Wall Street Curls Its Lip at Costco's Ungreedy CEO," *Star Tribune,* December 19, 2003, p. A33; and John Helyar, Ann Harrington, and Sol Price, "The Only Company Wal-Mart Fears," *Fortune,* November 24, 2003, pp. 158–63.

11. Kathleen Kerwin and Paul Magnusson, "Can Anything Stop Toyota?" *BusinessWeek,* November 17, 2003, pp. 114–22.

12. Ben R. Rich and Leo Janos, *Skunk Works* (Boston: Little, Brown and Company, 1994).

13. Murali K. Mantrala, Prabhakant Sirha, and Andris A. Zoltners, "Impact of Resource Allocation Rules on Marketing Investment-Level Decisions and Profitability," *Journal of Marketing Research,* May 1992, pp. 162–75.

14. Vanitha Swaminathan, Richard J. Fox, and Srinivas K. Reddy, "The Impact of Brand Extension Introduction on Choice," *Journal of Marketing,* October 2001, pp. 1–15; Deborah Roedder-John, Barbara Loken, and Christopher Joiner, "The Negative Impact of Extensions: Can Flagship Products Be Diluted?" *Journal of Marketing,* January 1998, pp. 19–32; and Akshay R. Rao, Lu Qu, and Robert W. Ruekert, "Signalling Unobservable Product Quality through a Brand Ally," *Journal of Marketing Research,* May 1999, pp. 258–68.

15. Adapted with permission of The Free Press, a Division of Macmillan, Inc., from *Competitive Advantage: Creating and Sustaining Superior Performance* by Michael E. Porter. Copyright 1985 by Michael E. Porter.

16. David Welch, "Staying Paranoid at Toyota," *BusinessWeek,* July 2, 2007, pp. 80–82.

17. H. Igor Ansoff, "Strategies for Diversification," *Harvard Business Review,* September–October 1957, pp. 113–24.

18. Colleen Pierre, "Natural Energy Boosters, " *Diane,* Fall 2006, p. 60.

19. Adapted from Philip Kotler and Kevin Lane Keller, *Marketing Management,* 12th ed. (Upper Saddle River, NJ: Prentice Hall, 2006), pp. 262–263.

20. David Kiley, "The New Heat on Ford," *BusinessWeek,* June 4, 2007, pp. 33–39.

21. Zachary Schiller, Greg Burns, and Karen Lowry Miller, "Make It Simple," *BusinessWeek,* September 9, 1996, pp. 96–104.

22. Stratford Sherman, "How Intel Makes Spending Pay Off," *Fortune,* February 22, 1993, pp. 57–61.

23. Julie Jargon, "General Mills Tries to Convince Americans to Cook Chinese," *The Wall Street Journal,* May 29, 2007, pp. B1, B3.

24. Matt McKinney, "General Public, Meet General Mills," *Star Tribune,* April 6, 2007, pp. D1, D; Julie Jargon, "General Mills Seeks

Help From Iron Chief," *The Wall Street Journal* April 4, 2007, p. B4; and "General Mills Supports Creation of New Food Science Division at Your Encore,™" General Mills press release, July 10, 2007.

25. Bjorn Lomborg, "Prioritizing the World's To-Do List," *Fortune,* May 17, 2004, p. 60; and Alfred Marcus, Donald A. Geffen, and Ken Sexton, "Business-Government Cooperation in Environmental Decision Making," *International Journal of Corporate Sustainability* 9, no. 4 (2002), pp. 345–55.

26. Charles H. Noble and Michael P. Mokwa, "Implementing Marketing Strategies: Developing and Testing a Managerial Theory," *Journal of Marketing,* October 1999, pp. 57–74.

27. Anne Fisher, "America's Most Admired Companies," *Fortune,* March 19, 2007, pp. 88–94.

28. "Ecomagination," see www.ge.com/company/citizenship/ecomagination/index.html, July 24, 2007.

29. Daniel Roth, "This Ain't No Pizza Party," *Fortune,* November 9, 1998, pp. 158–64.

30. Thomas J. Peters and Robert H. Waterman, Jr., *In Search of Excellence: Lessons from America's Best-Run Companies* (New York: Harper & Row, 1982).

31. Tom Peters, "Winners Do Hundreds of Percent over Norm," *Star Tribune,* January 8, 1985, p. 5B; and Rich and Janos, *Skunk Works,* pp. 51–53.

32. Peter Galuska, Ellen Neuborne, and Wendy Zeliner, "P&G's Hottest New Product: P&G," *BusinessWeek,* October 5, 1998, pp. 92–96.

33. Robert W. Ruekert and Orville W. Walker, Jr., "Marketing's Interaction with Other Functional Units: A Conceptual Framework and Empirical Evidence," *Journal of Consumer Marketing,* Spring 1987, pp. 1–19; Shikhar Sarin and Vijay Mahajan, "The Effect of Reward Structures on the Performance of Cross-Functional Product Development Teams," *Journal of Marketing,* April 2001, pp. 35–53; and Amy Edmondson, Richard Bohmer, and Gary Pisano, "Speeding Up Team Learning," *Harvard Business Review,* October 2001, pp. 125–32.

34. James D. Lenskold, *Marketing ROI* (New York: McGraw-Hill, 2003).

35. Michael Krauss, "Balance Attention to Metrics with Intuition," *Marketing News,* June 1, 2007, pp. 6–8; John Davis, *Measuring Marketing: 103 Key Metrics Every Marketer Needs* (Singapore: John Wiley & Sons, 2007); and Paul W. Farris, Neil T. Bendle, Phillip E. Pfeifer, and David J. Reibstein, *Marketing Metrics* (Upper Saddle River, NJ: Wharton School Publishing, 2006).

36. Malcolm Craig, *Thinking Visually: Business Applications of 14 Core Diagrams* (New York and London: Continuum, 2000).

37. Nelson D. Schwartz, "Colgate Cleans Up," *Fortune,* April 16, 2001, pp. 179–80.

Warm Delights: This video case was prepared by David Ford based on interviews with Vivian Millroy Callaway.

APPENDIX C

1. Diane Brady, "Creating Brand You," *BusinessWeek,* August 22, 2007, pp. 72–73; and Denny E. McCorkle, Joe F. Alexander, and Memo F. Diriker, "Developing Self-Marketing Skills for Student Career Success," Journal of Marketing Education, Spring 1992, pp. 57–67.

2. Marianne E. Green, "Marketing Yourself: From Student to Professional," *Job Choices for Business & Liberal Arts Students,* 50th ed., 2007, pp. 30–31; Joanne Cleaver, "Find a Job Through Self-Promotion," *Marketing News,* January 31, 2000, pp. 12, 16.

3. Don E. Shultz, "New Marketing Job Picture Ups Accountability," *Marketing News,* May 15, 2007; and "CareerBuilder.com and PayScale Release Top Ten Picks for Fast-Growing and Higher-Paying Jobs," *PR Newswire,* September 19, 2006.

4. "Opportunities by Occupation," *Job Choices for Business & Liberal Arts Students,* 50th Edition, 2007, pp. 109–111; and Lindsey Gerdes, "The Best Places to Launch a Career," *BusinessWeek,* September 18, 2006, p. 64.

5. Nicholas Basta, "The Wide World of Marketing," *BusinessWeek's Guide to Careers,* February–March 1984, pp. 70–72.

6. Deborah L. Vence, "CEO Job Demands Big Picture View, Integration Skills," *Marketing News,* May 1, 2006, p. 14; and Paula Lyon Andruss, "So You Want to Be a CEO?" *Marketing News,* January 29, 2001, pp. 1, 10.

7. "Average Yearly Salary Offers," *Salary Survey* (Bethlehem, PA: National Association of Colleges and Employers, 2007), p. 3.

8. "Advertising, Marketing, Promotions, Public Relations, and Sales Managers," *Occupational Outlook Handbook* (Indianapolis: JIST Works, 2006–2007), www.bls.gov/oco/pdf/ocos020.pdf.

9. Matthew Creamer, "P&G Primes Its Pinpoint Marketing," *Advertising Age,* May 7, 2007; and Linda M. Gorchels, "Traditional Product Management Evolves," *Marketing News,* January 30, 1995, p. 4.

10. Phil Moss, "What It's Like to Work for Procter & Gamble," *BusinessWeek's Guide to Careers,* March–April 1987, pp. 18–20.

11. Robin T. Peterson, "Wholesaling: A Neglected Job Opportunity of Marketing Majors," *Marketing News,* January 15, 1996.

12. S. William Pattis, *Careers in Advertising* (New York: McGraw-Hill, 2004); and "Advertising," *Career Guide to Americas Top Industries* (Indianapolis, IN: JIST Works, 1994), pp. 142–45.

13. Tanya Lewis, "Talent in Demand," *PR Week Career Guide,* 2006, pp. 4–6.

14. Roslyn Dolber, *Opportunities in Retailing Careers* (New York: McGraw-Hill, 2003); and "The Climb to the Top," *Careers in Retailing,* January 1995, p. 18.

15. "Playing the Retail Career Game," *Careers in Retailing 2001* (New York: DSN Retailing Today, January 2001), pp. 4, 6.

16. Joseph Kornik, "The 2007 Compensation Survey," *Sales and Marketing Management,* May 2007, pp. 27–35.

17. Milan Moravec, Marshall Collins, and Clinton Tripoli, "Don't Want to Manage? Here's Another Path," *Sales & Marketing Management,* June 1990, pp. 62–75.

18. Rebecca Aronaur, "Shaping the Profession of Sales," *Sales & Marketing Management,* July 1, 2006.

19. Jack and Suzy Welch, "Dear Graduate... To Stand Out Among Your Peers, You Have to Overdeliver," *BusinessWeek,* June 19, 2006, p. 100.

20. Daniel Tynan, "CRM on the Cheap," *Sales & Marketing Management,* June 2004, pp. 37–40; Kathleen Cholewka, "Do Not Disturb: A New Way to E-Mail?" *Sales & Marketing Management,* November 2001, pp. 21–22; and "Best E-Business Strategy," *Sales & Marketing Management,* September 2001, p. 28.

21. Edmund Hershberger and Madhav N. Segal, "Ads for MR Positions Reveal Desired Skills," *Marketing News,* February 1, 2007, p. 28.

22. "Market Research Analyst," in Les Krantz, ed., *Jobs Rated Almanac,* 5th ed. (New York: St. Martin's Press, 2000).

23. Deborah L. Vence, "In an Instant, More Researchers Use IM for Fast, Reliable Results," *Marketing News,* March 1, 2006, p. 53; and Joshua Grossnickle and Oliver Raskin, "What's Ahead on the Internet," *Marketing Research,* Summer 2001, pp. 9–13.

24. Carolyn D. Marconi, "Desperately Looking for New Talent Is a Recurring Theme," *Marketing Research,* Spring 2000, pp. 4–6.

25. International Franchise Association, http://franchise.org/Blockbuster_Inc_franchise.aspx, August 20, 2007.

26. Lisa Bertagnoli, "Marketing Overseas Excellent for Career," *Marketing News,* June 4, 2001, p. 4.

27. Pete Engardio, "A Guide for Multinationals: One of the Great Challenges for a Multinational Is Learning How to Build a Productive Global Team," *BusinessWeek,* August 20, 2007, p. 48; and Joann S.

Lublin, "Global Experience Doesn't Have To Mean Going to Live Overseas," *The Wall Street Journal*, August 29, 2006, B1.

28. Barbara Flood, "Turbo Charge Your Job Search, Job Searching and Career Development Tips," *Information Outlook*, May 1, 2007, p. 40.

29. Robin T. Peterson and J. Stuart Devlin, "Perspectives on Entry-Level Positions by Graduating Marketing Seniors," *Marketing Education Review*, Summer 1994, pp. 2–5.

30. "Succeeding in the Job Market For the Class of 2007," *Job Choices for Business & Liberal Arts Students*, 50th ed., 2007, pp. 14–15; and Callum J. Floyd and Mary Ellen Gordon, "What Skills Are Most Important? A Comparison of Employer, Student, and Staff Perceptions," *Journal of Marketing Education*, August 1998, pp. 103–09.

31. Barbara Flood, "Turbo Charge Your Job Search, Job Searching and Career Development Tips," *Information Outlook*, May 1, 2007, p. 40.

32. Barbara Kiviat, "The New Rules of Web Hiring," *Time*, November 24, 2003, p. 57; Karen Epper Hoffman, "Recruitment Sites Changing Their Focus," *Internet World*, March 15, 1999; Pamela Mendels, "Now That's Casting a Wide Net," *BusinessWeek*, May 25, 1998: and James C. Gonyea, *The Online Job Search Companion* (New York: McGraw-Hill, 1995).

33. Peter Cappelli, "Making the Most of On-Line Recruiting," *Harvard Business Review*, March 2001, pp. 139–46.

34. Ronald B. Marks, *Personal Selling: A Relationship Approach*, 6th ed. (New York: Pearson, 1996).

35. Leonard Felson, "Undergrad Marketers Must Get Jump on Networking Skills," *Marketing News*, April 8, 2001, p. 14; and Wayne E. Baker, *Networking Smart* (New York: McGraw-Hill, 1994).

36. Marianne E. Green, "Resume Writing: Sell Your Skills to Get the Interview!" *Job Choices for Business & Liberal Arts Students*, 50th ed., 2007, pp. 39–47.

37. C. Randall Powell, "Secrets of Selling a Résumé," in Peggy Schmidt, ed., *The Honda How to Get a Job Guide* (New York: McGraw-Hill, 1984), pp. 4–9.

38. "If I 'Google' You, What Will I Find?" *Job Choices for Business and Liberal Arts Students*, 50th ed., 2007, p. 16; and Joyce Lain Kennedy, "Computer-Friendly Résumé Tips," *Planning Job Choices: 1999*, 42nd ed. (Bethlehem, PA: National Association of Colleges and Employers, 1998), p. 49; and Joyce Lain Kennedy and Thomas J. Morrow, *Electronic Résumé Revolution* (New York: Wiley, 1994).

39. William J. Banis, "The Art of Writing Job-Search Letters," *Job Choices for Business and Liberal Arts Students*, 50th ed., 2007, pp. 32–38; and Arthur G. Sharp, "The Art of the Cover Letter," *Career Futures* 4, no. 1 (1992), pp. 50–51.

40. Alison Damast, "Recruiters' Top 10 Complaints," *BusinessWeek*, April 26, 2007; and Marilyn Moats Kennedy, "Don't List' Offers Important Tips for Job Interviews," *Marketing News*, March 15, 2007, p. 26.

41. Dana James, "A Day in the Life of a Corporate Recruiter," *Marketing News*, April 10, 2000, pp. 1, 11.

42. Robert M. Greenberg, "The Company Visit—Revisited," *NACE Journal*, Winter 2003, pp. 21–27.

43. Mary E. Scott, "High-Touch vs. High-Tech Recruitment," *NACE Journal*, Fall 2002, pp. 33–39.

APPENDIX D

1. The Nike MaxSight case was prepared by Professor Linda Rochford, University of Minnesota, Duluth, based on the following sources: Bausch and Lomb website, www.bausch.com/en_US/consumer/visioncare/product/softcontacts/nikemaxsight.aspx; Nike website, www.nike.com/nikevision/main.html; "A Brief History of Contact Lenses," Contact Lens Manufacturers Association, February 2007, www.contactlenses.org/timeline.htm; Richard Edlich, "A Tribute to Dr. Robert C. Allen, an Inspirational Teacher, Humanitarian and Friend," *Journal Long Term Effects of Medical Implants*, no. 163 (2006),

pp. 261–64; MayoClinic.com, "Tools for Better Health: Melanoma," www.mayoclinic.com/health/melanoma/DS00439/DSECTION=1; MayoClinic.com, "Tools for Better Health: Eye Melanoma," www.mayoclinic.com/health/eye-melanoma/DS00707; and MayoClinic.com, "Tools for Better Health: Contact Lenses: What to Know Before You Buy," www.mayoclinic.com/health/contact-lenses/WL00010.

2. The Daktronics, Inc., case was prepared by William Rudelius based on conversations with Dr. Al Kurtenbach, internal sources, and these others sources: Bill Syken, "Bright Lights, Little City," *Sports Illustrated*, May 11, 2004; Dick Youngblood, "Signs of Success," *Star Tribune*, April 6, 2003, pp. D1, D2; Marilyn Alva, "Shifting Technology Helps It Score Big Wins," *Investor's Business Daily*, January 12, 2004; and Michael Hiestand, "S.D. Company Lights Up Sports World," *USA Today*, May 4, 2004, pp. C1, C2.

3. The Jamba Juice case was prepared by Professor Linda Rochford, University of Minnesota, Duluth, and Steven Hartley from the following sources: Jamba Juice Corporation website and press releases: www.jambajuice.com; "Juicy Prospects," *Star Tribune*, August 27, 2001, pp. D1–D2; Scott Hume, "Segment Rankings," *Restaurants and Institutions*, July 1, 2004, p. 61; Celeste Ward, "Riney Creates Good Karma for Jamba Juice," *Adweek.com*, March 18, 2004; and John Agoglia, "Squeezing Profits," *Club Industry*, December 1, 2003, p. 12.

4. The Ford and Firestone case was prepared by Professor Linda Rochford, University of Minnesota, Duluth, from the following sources: David Barboza, "Bridgestone/Firestone to Close Tire Plant at Center of Huge Recall," *The New York Times*, June 28, 2001, p. C1; Keith Bradsher, "Ford Intends to Replace 13 Million Firestone Wilderness Tires," *The New York Times*, May 23, 2001, p. C1; John Greenwald, "Tired of Each Other," *Time*, June 4, 2001, pp. 51–56; and Phil Meyerowitz, "SUV Chic: The Rugged and the Reckless," *The New York Times*, July 7, 2001, p. 12.

5. The Jamisons case was prepared by Professor Roy D. Adler, Pepperdine University, Malibu. Used with permission.

6. The Motetronix Technology case was prepared by Roger A. Kerin, based on company sources.

7. The Callaway case was prepared by Professor Linda Rochford, University of Minnesota, Duluth, based on the following sources: James Achenbach, "From Hickory Stick to Callaway, Ely Sought to Please Golfers," *Golfweek*, July 14, 2001, pp. 26–27; "China the Largest Growth Market for Equipment," *Golf Today*, March 2004, www.golftoday.co.uk/news/yeartodate/news04/china.html; "Opportunities in Global Golf Club Market: Market to Grow Over 25% in India and China According to E-Composites, Inc.," PR Newswire, February 18, 2004, www.prnewswire.com; "2006 Participation by Sport," National Sporting Goods Association, www.nsga.org; "Callaway Golf Co.: Company Description, Financial Summary," Reuters, 2007; Bennett Galloway, "Adrift in a Sea of Golf Balls," *Golf In Japan*, June 10, 2006, www.golf-in-japan.com/bennetts; John Steinbreder, "Partnership Could Strengthen NGF's Research," *Golfweek Business*, June 4, 2007; Bradley Klein, "Klein: Remedies for the Malaise," *Golfweek Business*, March 5, 2007; Beth Ann Baldry, "Dispatch from South Korea," *Golfweek Business*, July 20, 2007; Paul Jones, "Japan Golf: The State of the Game," *Golf In Japan*, February 14, 2006, www.golf-in-japan.com/pauls; John Paul Newport, "Golf Journal: Spin Control; Golf's Police Are Tweaking Clubhead Rules, But a Bigger Issue Looms: The Balls," *The Wall Street Journal* (Eastern Edition), March 3, 2007, p. 7; and John Paul Newport, "Golf Journal: Crazy Driver: THE Clubs About to Shake Up Golf; Bizarre New Designs Could Improve Players' Shots—And Many in the Game Worry That's a Bad Thing," *The Wall Street Journal* (Eastern Edition), January 6, 2007, p. 1.

8. The HOM Furniture case was prepared by Kathy Chadwick based on interviews with Wayne Johansen and internal HOM Furniture materials.

9. The Lawn Mowers case was prepared by Professor Linda Rochford, University of Minnesota, Duluth, based on the following sources: Don Babwin, "Reel Mowers Cut in Quietly," *Denver Post,* May 28, 2007, www.denverpost.com; Felicity Barringer, "A Greener Way to Cut the Grass Runs Afoul of a Powerful Lobby," *The New York Times,* April 24, 2006; "It All Adds Up; Lawnmowers," *The Economist,"* June 9, 2007, p. 36; "Lawn and Garden Tractors and Home Lawn and Garden Equipment," *Encyclopedia of American Industries, Online Edition,* Thomson Gale, 2007; "Canadians Switch to Push-Reel Lawn Mowers for Health and Environment," Associated Press Financial Wire, July 2, 2007; Mindy Fetterman, "Compared with Today's Mowers, Yesterday's Just Don't Cut It," *USA Today,* May 4, 2007, p. 4B; Charles J. Murray, "Mowing on Autopilot: With the Introduction of the RoboMower in the U.S., Two Israeli Inventors May Open New Door to the Fledgling Home Robotics Market," *Design News,* June 26, 2006, p. 37; Jonathan Welsh, "Splendor in the Grass; Big, Fast, 'Zero-Turn' Mowers Are Latest Status Symbol; Cruise Control and Cupholders," *The Wall Street Journal,* June 13, 2007, p. D1; Virginia Smith, "A Luscious Lawn's Lure: For Some, It's an Obsession They Never Outgrow," *Philadelphia Inquirer,* May 5, 2006; "Lawn Mowers," *Consumer Reports Buying Guide 2006,* pp. 92–95; Ray Routhier, "Mowers—They're Not Just for Grass Anymore," *Portland Press Herald,* July 15, 2007, p. A1; and Rachel Sauer, "Get Your Mower Runnin'; Speeds Reached: 30 Mph, Goal: To Mow Down the Competition," *Palm Beach Post,* June 5, 2007, p. 1E.

10. The Medtronic in China case was prepared by Mark T. Spriggs and Kenneth E. Goodpaster based on Medtronic annual reports and three Medtronic cases: *Medtronic in China (A), (B),* and *(C)* prepared by research assistant Linda Swenson under the supervision of Kenneth E. Goodpaster (Minneapolis–St. Paul, MN: University of St. Thomas).

11. The Pampered Pooches case was prepared by Professor Linda Rochford, University of Minnesota, Duluth, based on the following sources: American Pet Products Manufacturers Association, Inc., "Industry Trends, 2007–2008," Pet Owners Survey Summary, www.appma.org/press-industrytrends.asp; Diane Brady and Christopher Palmeri, "The Pet Economy," *BusinessWeek,* August 2007; John Woestendisk, "Statistics, Trends Reflect Growing Importance of Pets in the Home," *Baltimore Sun,* July 22, 2007; Sarah Casey Newman "Traveling with Terriers and Tabbies", *St. Louis Post-Dispatch,* July 21, 2007; Leanne Ritchie, "Airline Bans Pets From Travel on Regular Flights," *Daily News,* July 20, 2007; "New Dolce Vita™ Traveler™ Pet Products Let Your Dog Travel in Warmth and Comfort; Take Your Pets Anywhere You Go," PR Newswire, February 22, 2007; "Traveling with Pets for the Dogs, According to TripAdvisor Survey; TripAdvisor Names Top 10 Pet-Friendly Accommodations," PR Newswire, July 18, 2007; Robyn Gardyn, "Animal Magnetism," *American Demographics,* May 1, 2002; "Cool Canines Beg for Frosty Paws; Frozen Treats for Dogs Have Tails Wagging," PR Newswire, October 15, 2003, www.prnewswire.com; Lisa Mclaughlin, "Where Guests With Four Legs Are Pampered," *Time,* February 10, 2003, p. 83; and Joel Stein, Jeanne DeQuine, Jeanne McDowell, Deidre van Dyk, "It's a Dog's Life," *Time,* May 19, 2003, pp. 60–63.

12. The DigitalThink case was adapted by Monica Noordam and Steven Hartley from a case titled "LearningByte International" written by Giana Eckardt. Sources: Personal interviews with Umberto Milletti and Shelly Berkowitz; DigitalThink's website, www.digitalthink.com; Lisa Vaas, "The E-Training of America," *PC Magazine,* December 26, 2001; DigitalThink press release, "DigitalThink Ranked Number 22 Fastest Growing Technology Company in North America on 2003 Deloitte Technology Fast 500," October 14, 2003; and "Making E-Learning More than 'Pixie Dust,'" *Workforce Management,* March 1, 2003, p. 58.

13. The Health Cruises, Inc., case was prepared by Professors Maurice Mandell and Larry Rosenberg. Reprinted with permission.

14. The Bagel Bakes case was prepared by Michael A. Stanko and Matthew Fleming. Michael A. Stanko is a Marketing Doctoral Candidate at Michigan State University. Matthew Fleming is a Certified Management Accountant currently working in Beijing, China. Previously, Matthew was a Senior Financial Analyst at General Mills Canada. © 2007, M. Stanko & M.S.U., All rights reserved. Used with permission.

15. The Ken Davis Products case was prepared by Professor Linda Rochford, University of Minnesota, Duluth, based on the following sources: Ken Davis website: www.kendavis-bbq.com; Kelly Alexander, "'Cue It Up: Taste Testing Barbecue Sauces, From Supermarket to Specialty Brands," *Slate,* May 20, 2002; Hoovers, Food Wholesale Distributors, www.hoovers.com/industry/food-wholesale-distributors/companies; and special thanks to Patrick Miner and Tania New for their assistance with this case.

16. The Dell case was prepared by Professor Linda Rochford, University of Minnesota, Duluth, based on the following sources: Shu-ching Jean Chen, "Dell Going Small in Asia," Forbes.com, July 18, 2007; "Dell 2006 Annual Report," www.dell.com; "Dell Sets Goal of Becoming Greenest Technology Company," www.dell.com/content/topics/global.aspx; "Batteries Burn Benighted Dell," *Client Server News,* August 21, 2006; Brian Caulfield, "What Will Dell Cut Next?" Forbes.com, June 7, 2007; "Factory Floor: Dell Takes Supply Side to Web," *InTech,* September 1, 2002, www.isa.org/InTechTemplate.cfm?Section=InTech&template=/ContentManagement/ContentDisplay.cfm&ContentID=17926; "HP Gains Ground As Dell's Woes Continue," *Information Week,* August 21, 2006; "PC Shipments Rose 12% in Q2, HP Had Top Share," Reuters, July 18, 2007; "Dell Computer Corporation Financial Highlights," Reuters, July 19, 2007; "High Tech Supply Chain: Michael Dell's Memo to Dell Computer Employees Leaked," *Supply Chain Digest,* February 9, 2007; and Louise Lee and Peter Burrows, "Is Dell Too Big for Michael Dell?" *BusinessWeek,* February 12, 2007, p. 33.

17. The Trader Joe's case was prepared by Linda Rochford, Associate Professor of Marketing, University of Minnesota, Duluth, from the following sources: "Trader Joe's Company," www.hoovers.com; David Orgel, "Trader Joe's President Shares Secrets of Success," *Supermarket News,* February 6, 2006; Joy Buchanan, "More Than Just Goat Cheese," Knight-Ridder/Tribune Business News, December 9, 2005; Mark Hamstra "Convenience Only One Small Part of Total Value Equation," *Supermarket News,* July 17, 2006; and "Behind the Scenes at Trader Joe's," *Private Label Buyer* 20, no. 4 (April 2006).

18. The McDonald's in Russia case was prepared by Sarah Casanova of McDonald's Canada and Michael J. Vessey based on internal McDonald's reports and information from the McDonald's website, www.mcdonalds.com.

19. The Target case was prepared by Linda Rochford, Associate Professor of Marketing, University of Minnesota, Duluth, from the following sources: Target Corporation website, www.target.com; "Target Makes Itself Ubiquitous," *MMR* 22, no. 16 (October 3, 2005), p. 16; "Target's Advertising Savvy," *MMR* 24, no. 1 (January 8, 2007), p. 32; Laura Heller, "Target Sweeps Awards Honoring Best Advertising; Office Max Also Wins Nod; Target Stores Inc.," *DSN Retailing Today,* February 25, 2005, p. 6; "Target Dominates RAC Awards," *Chain Store Age,* April 2004, p. 65; Laura Heller, "Target Plans to 'Own' Red to Keep Business in the Black; Campaign Around its Signature Bulls-Eye Has Been Successful, Wins Awards at Retailing Advertising Conference," *DSN Retailing Today,* February 24, 2003, p. 4; "Target Wins RAC's Best of Show, Pushing Ad Bar Even Higher; Retailing Advertising Council Award," *DSN Retailing Today,* February 25, 2002, p. 2; "Top Retailers Recognized With Prestigious 2001 Retail Advertising Conference Awards," *Business Wire,* February 15, 2001; Tedra Meyer, "Best Buy, Target, Sears Cited for Innovative Ad

Campaigns," *Twice,* April 16, 2001, p. 11; "Target Drives Home 'Expect More, Pay Less' Message," *MMR,* 18, no. 5 (March 19, 2001), p. 52; Jim McCartney, "Advertising Age Magazine Gives Target's Ads Top Award," *St. Paul Pioneer Press,* December 12, 2000; "Top Retailers Recognized with Prestigious Retail Advertising Conference—RAC—Awards," *Business Wire,* February 10, 2000; "Top Retailers Recognized with Prestigious International Retail Advertising Conference—RAC—Awards," *Business Wire,* February 10, 1999; "Top Retailers Recognized with Prestigious International Retail Advertising Conference—RAC—Awards," *Business Wire,* February 4, 1998; "Target Sees 'Red' with In-Store TV Network," *DSN Retailing Today,* March 27, 2006, p. 6; and "The New Yorker Is Scolded Over Single-Sponsor Issue," *The New York Times,* September 19, 2005, p. C7.

20. The Morgantown Furniture case was prepared by Roger A. Kerin, based on company sources.

21. The Crate and Barrel case was prepared by Professor Linda Rochford, University of Minnesota, Duluth, based on the following sources: Crate and Barrel website, www.crateandbarrel.com; Crate and Barrel 2007 catalogs; "Home Furnishings Catalogs Freshen Up for Springtime," *Home Furnishings News,* March 22, 2004, p. 20; "Crate and Barrel Selects Unica Corporation's Affinium to Increase Effectiveness of its Multi-Channel Marketing Campaigns," *Business Wire,* April 28, 2004; "Euromarket Design, Inc.," RDS Business and Company Resource Center, 2007; and "Otto Group Takes the Lead in Online Business," Otto Group Media Centre press release, March 28, 2007, www.ottogroup.com/press.

22. The Naked Juice case was prepared by Professor Linda Rochford, University of Minnesota, Duluth, based on the following sources: Anjali Cordeiro, "Beverage Deal Gets Fuel From Desire for Less Fizz," *The Wall Street Journal,* February 14, 2007; Paul Ziobro, "Health Drinks Reward Backers," *The Wall Street Journal,* January 4, 2007, p. B10A; "Naked Juice Company," Hoovers.com; Naked Juice website, www.nakedjuice.com, and promotional materials; Hansen's Natural website, www.hansens.com; Kate MacArthur, "Pepsi Primes Brand Overhauls: Exclusive: $50M effort from BBDO Looks to Restore the Tone and Spirit of the 1970s Work," *Advertising Age* 77, no. 42, p. 1; Bureau of Labor Statistics, *Who's Buying Alcoholic and Nonalcoholic Beverages* (Ithaca, NY: New Strategist Publications, 2005); Odwalla Products website, www.odwalla.com; "A Healthy Glow: Consumers Soak Up the Health Benefits of Juice and Juice Drinks," *Beverage Industry,* January 12, 2007; "Naked Juice Expands DSD, Taps Team of R&D Experts," Beverage Industry, August 8, 2006; "2006 State of the Industry," *Beverage Industry,* July 22, 2006; "Soda Industry to Stop Selling Non-Diet Soft Drinks in Schools," *Food Chemical News* 48, no. 13 (May 8, 2006); and "Beverages," *Media Week,* May 1, 2006, p. SR16.

CREDITS

CHAPTER 1

P. 2, Martin Walter, White Digital Room. P. 4, ©M. Hruby. P. 4, ©M. Hruby. P. 4, Courtesy 3M. P. 5, ©M. Hruby. P. 6, ©Jawed Karim. P. 7, ©Michael Grecco Photography. P. 7, ©Douglas Adesko. P. 10, Courtesy New Product Works. P. 10, Coutesy Nestlé USA (Solon). P. 10, Photo by Business Wire via Getty Images. P. 10, ©M. Hruby. P. 14, Courtesy Costco Wholesale. P. 14, Courtesy Starbucks Coffee Company ©2004. P. 16, ©M. Hruby. P. 16, ©M. Hruby. P. 20, Courtesy Nature Conservancy Communications. P. 21, *No credit*. P. 21, *No credit*. P. 21, *No credit*. P. 25, Martin Walter, White Digital Room.

CHAPTER 2

P. 26, Courtesy Ben & Jerry's. P. 28, AP Photo/Dawn Villella. P. 30, Courtesy Yahoo! Inc. P. 30, Courtesy Motorola, Inc. P. 30, Courtesy FUBU – Thee Collection & FB Entertainment. P. 32, ©CBS Paramount Network Television. P. 33, Courtesy Medtronic. P. 33, Photography by Sean Lamb, 2004. P. 36, ©Rick Armstrong. P. 37, *Both* Courtesy Eastman Kodak Company; Agency Ketchum Communications. P. 37, ©M. Hruby. P. 37, Courtesy Eastman Kodak Company; Agency Ketchum Communications. P. 38, Both Courtesy Eastman Kodak Company; Agency Ketchum Communications. P. 38, ©M. Hruby. P. 38, Courtesy Eastman Kodak Company; Agency Ketchum Communications. P. 39, *Both:* ©Hagadone Photography, Inc. P. 44, *All* ©M. Hruby. P. 48, ©Chris Casaburi. P. 49, Courtesy Eastman Kodak Company; Agency Ketchum Communications. P. 52-53, Courtesy British Petroleum.

APPENDIX A

P. 58-65, ©1996 Paradise Kitchens, Inc. All photos & ads reprinted with permission.

CHAPTER 3

P. 68, ©Jeff Howe. P. 73, ©The Procter & Gamble Company. Used by permission. P. 73, Courtesy Global Hyatt Corporation. P. 73, Courtesy Motorola, Inc. P. 77, Courtesy Saturn Corporation. P. 80, Courtesy Cunard Line Limited/Carnival Corporation. P. 81, Select graphic images reprinted courtesy of ESRI Business Information Solutions, Copyright ©ESRI Business Information Solutions. All rights reserved. P. 82, Courtesy Pioneer Electronics (USA), Inc. P. 82, Courtesy Nuance Communications, Inc. P. 82, ©2001- 2007 Listen.com, a subsidiary of RealNetworks. P. 83, Courtesy Tomra of North America. P. 83, Courtesy of Lever Brothers Company. P. 87, ©M. Hruby.

P. 88, Courtesy American Marketing Association/Marketing News Magazine. P. 92, *Both Photos* by Tim Boyle/Getty Images.

Figure 3-3, UN, World Population Prospects: The 2006 Revision, Online Data (www.un.org/esa/population/unpop.htm, accessed April 2, 2007); and Population Reference Bureau, "Population: A Lively Introduction," Population Bulletin, Vol. 62 (March 2007), p. 24; Figure 3-5, Graph, "Vehicle Buying Attitudes and Total Vehicle Sales (Year-to-year change in series)" from Surveys of Consumers, Sept 2006 Survey, Oct 6, 2006, University of Michigan.

CHAPTER 4

P. 94, Courtesy Anheuser-Busch Companies. P. 99, ©2001 Michael Delsol. P. 100, ©5 Creative, L.P. Illustration C. Tew & J. Robinson. P. 101, Courtesy Transparency International. P. 104, ©M. Hruby. P. 106, Courtesy Susan G. Komen Breast Cancer Foundation. P. 107, AP Photo/Elizabeth Dalziel. P. 108, PhotoDisc Blue. P. 109, Paula Bronstein/Getty Images. P. 113, Michael Newman/PhotoEdit.

Figure 4-11, American Marketing Association Statement of Ethics. Used by permission of American Marketing Association.

CHAPTER 5

P. 114, Courtesy Ford Motor Company. P. 118, Karin Dreyer/Blend Images/Getty Images. P. 119, Courtesy Kimberly-Clark Worldwide, Inc. P. 121, Courtesy McNeil P.P.C. P. 124, The Secret Sales Pitch: An Overview of Subliminal Advertising. Copyright ©2004 by August Bullock. All Rights Reserved. Used with permission. SubliminalSex.com. P. 125, FRESH STEPS® is a registered trademark of The Clorox Pet Products Company. Used with permission. P. 125, ©2001 Mary Kay, Inc. Photos by: Grace Huang for Sarah Laird. P. 127, Courtesy Colgate-Palmolive Company. P. 127, Courtesy The Bayer Company. P. 128, Courtesy SRI Consulting Business Intelligence (SRIC-BI), Menlo Park, CA. VALS™ is a trademark of SRI Consulting Business Intelligence. Reprinted with permission. P. 129, Courtesy SRI Consulting Business Intelligence (SRIC-BI), Menlo Park, CA. VALS™ is a trademark of SRI Consulting Business Intelligence. Reprinted with permission. P. 130, *Both ads,* Courtesy TAG Heuer International SA. P. 131, Courtesy BzzAgent, LLC. P. 134, Courtesy of Haggar Clothing Co. P. 135, Courtesy The Hershey Company. P. 136, Courtesy Bonne Bell, Inc. P. 137, Courtesy McDonald's USA, LLC. P. 140, Gary Conner/Photo Edit Inc.

Figure 5-2, "Flash Memory MP3 Players" Copyright 2007 by Consumers Union of U.S., Inc. Yonkers, NY 10703-1057, a nonprofit organization. Reprinted with permission from the 2007 issue of Consumer Reports for educational purposes only. No commercial use or reproduction permitted. www.ConsumerReports.org; VALS, SRI Consulting Business Intelligence (SRIC-BI), Menlo Park, CA. VALS is a trademark of SRI Consulting Business Intelligence. Reprinted with permission; Figure 5-16, Discussion of VALS reprinted with permission of SRI Consulting Business Intelligence.

CHAPTER 6

P. 142, Courtesy J.C. Penney. P. 145, Courtesy Lockheed Martin Company. P. 146, Courtesy U.S. Department of Commerce/Bureau of the Census. P. 150, Lluis Gene/AFP/Getty Images. P. 152, Daniel Bosler/Stone/Getty Images. P. 156, *No credit*. P. 158, These materials have been reproduced with the permission of eBay Inc. COPYRIGHT ©EBAY INC. ALL RIGHTS RESERVED. P. 163, ©2004 Lands' End, Inc. Used with permission.

CHAPTER 7

P. 164, Courtesy Grey Worldwide/Beijing. P. 169, Courtesy Sharp USA. P. 169, Courtesy of Bruno Magli. P. 171, Frans Lemmens/The Image Bank/Getty Images. P. 174, Courtesy ALMA/BBDO Sāu Paulo. P. 175, Courtesy Diesel S.p.A. P. 176, Courtesy Saatchi & Saatchi/Beijing. P. 178, ©Robert Holmes Photography. P. 178, Antonio M. Rosario/The Image Bank/Getty Images. P. 179, *Both ads:* Courtesy Hewlett-Packard/Canada; Agency: Publicis Hal Riney. P. 180, Courtesy of Nestlé S.A. P. 181, Courtesy The Coca-Cola Company. P. 184, Courtesy The PRS Group, Inc./East Syracuse, NY. P. 186, Courtesy Fran Wilson Creative Cosmetics, Inc. P. 187, *Both* Courtesy McDonald's Corporation. P. 187, Courtesy Elite Industries, Ltd. P. 188, Courtesy Nestlé S.A. P. 190, All Courtesy The Gillette Company. P. 194, Courtesy CNS, Inc.

Figure 7-5, reprinted with the permission of PRIMEDIA Business Magazines & Media, Inc. Copyright 2002. All rights reserved.

CHAPTER 8

P. 196, Courtesy Shooting Star. P. 198, Courtesy Shooting Star. P. 200, Fisher-Price, Inc. a subsidiary of Mattel, Inc. East Aurora, NY 14052 U.S.A. ©2006 Mattel, Inc. All Rights Reserved. P. 201, Fisher-Price, Inc. a subsidiary of Mattel, Inc. East Aurora, NY 14052 U.S.A. ©2006

CHAPTER 9

CHAPTER 10

CHAPTER 11

CHAPTER 12

CHAPTER 13

CHAPTER 14

CHAPTER 15

Braaten. P. 403, An Fu/China FotoPress/Redux. P. 404, Courtesy Jiffy Lube International, Inc. P. 404, ©Amy Etra. P. 405, Justin Sullivan/Getty Images. P. 407, *No credit.* P. 408, ©Joe & Kathy Heiner. P. 412, Courtesy Golden Valley. P. 413, Mark Wilson/Getty Images. P. 413, *Both photos:* Justin Sullivan/Getty Images.

CHAPTER 16

P. 414, Reprinted with permission of Business Week. Illustrated by David Cale. P. 418, Courtesy Volkswagen of America. P. 419, Courtesy IBM Corporation. P. 420, Courtesy Dell, Inc. P. 420, Courtesy Wal-Mart Stores, Inc. P. 421, Courtesy Hewlett-Packard Company. P. 424, PhotoEdit/ Mark Richards. P. 427, Courtesy United Parcel Service, Inc. P. 427, Courtesy Ryder Supply Chain Solutions. P. 429, Courtesy Bax Global. P. 430, Courtesy of United Airlines. P. 430, Courtesy of United Airlines. P. 431, Courtesy Microsoft Corporation. P. 432, ©Digital Vision/ PunchStock P. 435, Courtesy Amazon.com.

APPENDIX B

P. 382 & 386, *Both* Courtesy The Caplow Company.

CHAPTER 17

P. 436, Courtesy IconNicholson LLC. P. 439, Jochen Luebke/AFP/Getty Images. P. 441, Courtesy Entrepreneur Media, Inc. P. 441, Courtesy Doctor's Associates, Inc. P. 442, Courtesy Doctor's Associates, Inc. P. 442, Courtesy Dunkin Brands, Inc. P. 442, Courtesy Jackson Hewitt Tax Service, Inc. P. 442, Copyright © 7-Eleven, Inc. 2007. All rights reserved. P. 442, Courtesy Mail Boxes Etc., Inc. P. 443, Courtesy Staples, Inc. P. 444, AP Photo/Christoiphe Ena. P. 444, AP Photo/Sue Ogrocki. P. 445, Courtesy Get & Go Express. P. 446, Courtesy J.C.Penney. P. 446, Courtesy Lillian Vernon Corporation. P. 446, Courtesy L.L. Bean. P. 447, Photo by Matt Peyton/Getty Images for QVC. P. 447, Courtesy MySimon, Inc. P. 448, Courtesy Connecting Point Communications. P. 449, AP Photo/Jacques Brinon. P. 449, AP Photo/Greg Baker. P. 452, Photo by Tim Boyle/ Getty Images. P. 452, AP Photo/Paul Sakuma. P. 455, Courtesy Taco Bell. P. 461, *Both* Courtesy Mall of America.

CHAPTER 18

P. 462, Fred Prouser/Reuters/Landov. P. 465, Courtesy GM Archives. P. 468, Courtesy

The Coca-Cola Company. P. 468, ©2007 Llewellyn/Frommer's Australia From $60 a Day. Reprinted with permission of John Wiley & Sons, Inc. P. 468, International Dairy Queen, Inc. P. 470, Courtesy of Lebhar-Friedman, Inc. P. 471, Courtesy Nokia North America. P. 472, Courtesy Purina Incredible Dog Challenge. P. 473, Courtesy Gulfstream Aircraft, Inc. P. 473, Courtesy H.J. Heinz Company. Used with permission. P. 475, Courtesy Allergan, Inc. P. 477, Imaginechina via AP Images.P. 479, Courtesy Nintendo of America, Inc. P. 482, Courtesy 4 Seasons Hotels & Resorts. P. 487, Gabriel Bouys/AFP/Getty Images.

CHAPTER 19

P. 488, Courtesy There.com. P. 490, Courtesy Verizon Wireless. P. 490, Courtesy Sony Electronics, INC. P. 490,Courtesy Mars, Inc. P. 491, Courtesy Lorillard Tobacco Company. P. 491, Courtesy The Travelers Companies, Inc. P. 492, Courtesy National Fluid Milk Processor Promotion Board; Agency: Lowe Worldwide/New York. P. 492, Courtesy United States Army. P. 493, *No credit.* P. 494, www.superbowl-ads.com. P. 495, Courtesy Lorillard Tobacco Company. P. 495, Courtesy Diesel S.p.A. P.495, Courtesy GEICO. P. 496, *Both* Courtesy Berlin Cameron United Agency. P. 497, Courtesy Samsung Electronics America. P. 499, Courtesy Speed Channel 2004. P. 501, Oxygen Media, LLC. P. 501, Courtesy Cosmo Girl. P. 502, Reprinted with permission of Wall St. Journal, Copyright ©2007 Dow Jones & Company, Inc. All Rights Reserved Worldwide. P. 503, ©M. Hruby. P. 504, Courtesy Double Click, Inc. P. 505, Courtesy Nationwide Insurance. P. 505, Courtesy ecast. P. 508, Courtesy GfK Custom Research North America. P. 509, Courtesy of Valpak Direct Marketing Systems, Inc. P. 511, Nestle USA/Nestle Crunch Brand. P. 511, Courtesy CIT Group, Inc. P. 512, *No credit.* P. 513, Ron P. Jaffe/CBS/Landov. P. 513, ©M. Hruby. P. 515, John P. Filo/CBS/Landov. P. 518, Courtesy CIT Group, Inc. P. 519, *No credit.*

CHAPTER 20

P. 520, Courtesy Xerox Corporation. P. 523, Courtesy Medtronic P. 525, Courtesy Mitch Kezar/Stone/Getty Images. P. 527, Courtesy Xerox Corporation. P. 529, ©Einzig Photography. P. 530, ©Image Source/Corbis. P. 531, ©Richard Pasley/Stock Boston, LLC. P. 532, Frank Herholdt/Stone/Getty Images. P. 535,

Color Day Productions/Image Bank/Getty Images. P. 537, ©John Boykin/PhotoEdit. P. 541, ©Rex C. Curry. P. 543, *Both* Courtesy of Toshiba Medical Systems & Interactive Media. P. 543, Royalty-Free/Corbis P. 547, Courtesy Xerox Corporation.

CHAPTER 21

P. 548, *Both* Courtesy Seven Cycles, Inc. P. 553, ©Nike. All Right Reserved. P. 554, *No credit.* P. 555, ©2001-2007 H-D. All rights reserved. P. 559, ©Paul Barton/Corbis. P. 561, ©Tom Grill/Corbis. P. 563, Courtesy Diamond Trading Company; Agency: J. Walter Thompson. P. 564, ©Ray Bartkus.

CHAPTER 22

P. 572, Dan Hundley, Token Media. P. 574, ©M. Hruby. P. 575, AP Photo/Don Ryan. P. 575, ©M. Hruby. P. 577, *Both Photos:* ©M. Hruby. P. 580, *Both Photos:* ©M. Hruby. P. 582, *All Photos:* ©M. Hruby. P. 586, ©M. Hruby. P. 587, ©M. Hruby. P. 588, Courtesy General Electric Company. P. 589, Courtesy Papa John's International, Inc. P. 590, Courtesy Lockheed Martin Company. P. 594, Courtesy Cogate-Palmolive Company. P. 599, Warm Delights Courtesy of Vivian Millroy Callaway, General Mills.

APPENDIX C

P. 603, ©Paul Elledge. P. 605, Courtesy The May Department Stores Company. P. 606, Courtesy Xerox Corporation. P. 607, Courtesy Toyota Motor North America, Inc. P. 610, Reprinted from Job Choices 2002, with permission of the National Association of Colleges & Employers. P. 610, Courtesy Monster Worldwide, Inc. P. 616, Thatch cartoon by Jeff Shesol; Reprinted with permission of Vintage Books. P. 616, White Packert/The Image Bank/ Getty Images.

APPENDIX D

P. 622, Courtesy Daktronics, Inc. P. 623, Courtesy Daktronics, Inc. P. 633, Courtesy HOM Furniture. P. 636, Photo by Paul Harris/Online USA/Getty Images. P. 641, *All* ©M. Hruby. P. 643, Courtesy of Ken Davis Products, Inc. P. 643, ©2005 Rick Armstrong. P. 646, Courtesy McDonald's Corporation.

NAME INDEX

A

Aaker, David A., 683, 686, 695, 697
Aaron, Hank, 256
Abate, Tom, 688
Abbott and Costello, 485
Abdul, Paula, 447
Abel, Bill, 353
Abela, Andrew V., 675, 676
Abell, Derek F., 674, 675
Abernathy, Avery M., 696, 698
Abraham, Magid M., 697
Abrams, Rhonda, 55, 701
Abrams, Richard L., 679
Achenbach, James, 702
Achenreinver, Gwen Bachman, 679
Adams, Joe, 688
Adams, Susan, 700
Adamy, Janet, 683
Adler, Jerry, 678
Adler, Roy D., 702
Affleck, Ben, 199
Agarwal, Manj K., 685
Agoglia, John, 702
Ailawadi, Kusum L., 693, 694
Aili, McConnon, 695
Aizen, I., 679
Alba, Joseph W., 678
Alden, Dana L., 696
Alexander, Gerard, 686
Alexander, Joe E., 701
Alexander, Kelly, 703
Alford, C. Fred, 677
Allen, Richard C., 620, 702
Allen, Sandy, 687
Allman, Greg, 352
Allvine Fred C., 698
Alva, Marilyn, 702
Alvarado, Ursula Y., 691
Ambler, Tim, 675, 676, 695
Amst, Catherine, 676
Anderson, Eric, 692
Anderson, Erin, 680, 690, 699
Anderson, James C., 673, 680
Anderson, Kerrii B., 241
Anderson, Pamela, 686
Anderson, Stephanie, 676
Andrews, J. Craig, 681
Andrews, Rick, 689
Andruss, Paula Lyon, 698, 701
Ansoff, H. Igor, 700
Ante, Spencer E., 675
Antia, Kersi D., 682
Appleyard, Dennis R., 681
Arens, William F., 500, 697
Armstrong, J. Scott, 675
Armstrong, Larry, 686, 697
Armstrong, Richard, 691
Arndt, Michael, 674, 676, 683, 693
Arnold, Catherine, 677, 692
Arnold, Todd, 686
Arnould, Eric, 679
Aronaur, Rebecca, 701
Arquette, David, 496
Arsel, Zeynep, 676
Askegaard, S., 681
Aston, Adam, 684

Atkinson, Claire, 695
Atlas, Elise, 698
Atlas, Steve, 698
Augusto, Byron G., 684
Avery, Simon, 699
Avery, Susan, 680
Avlonitis, George J., 688

B

Baar, Aaron, 686, 698
Babb, Emerson M., 694
Babwin, Don, 703
Badaracco, Joseph L., 677
Baer, Martha, 691
Bagozzi, Richard P., 673
Bahadur, Nikhil, 686
Bahrami, B., 679
Bailey, Jeff, 688
Baker, Eric, 329, 330
Baker, Julie, 692, 693
Baker, Peter, 674
Baker, Stephen, 699
Baker, Walter, 689
Baker, Wayne E., 702
Balasubramanian, Siva K., 694
Balasubramanian, Sridhar, 684, 693
Baldry, Beth Ann, 702
Balter, David, 131
Banga, Kamini, 681
Banis, William J., 702
Banks, Allen, 697
Barboza, David, 702
Barich, Howard, 693
Barletta, Marti, 678
Barnes, Frank C., 680
Barnes, Jimmy D., 694
Barnes, John, 693
Barr, Stephen, 687
Barrett, Amy, 685
Barrett, Katherine, 696
Barrett, Paul, 677
Barringer, Felicity, 703
Barrymore, Drew, 513
Bartholomew, Doug, 691
Bartlett, Donald L., 688
Bartos, Rena, 679
Bass, Stephen J., 693
Basta, Nicholas, 701
Bates, Albert D., 693
Bawa, Kapil, 697
Bay, Willow, 682
Bayus, Barry L., 689
Bearden, William O., 689
Beardi, Cara, 696
Beatles, 569
Beatty, Sharon E., 678
Becker, Lori, 686
Belch, George E., 689
Belch, Michael A., 689
Belich, Thomas J., 690
Belk, Russell, 678
Bellizzi, Joseph A., 680, 688
Bellman, Lawrence M., 693
Belson, Ken, 684
Ben-Akiva, Moshe, 678
Bendapudi, Neeli, 687

Bendle, Neil T., 675, 676, 693, 701
Bennett, Peter D., 688, 694
Bennett, Tony, 649
Benson, Etienne, 682
Bergen, Mark E., 682, 688, 689
Berkowitz, Shelly, 638, 703
Berner, Robert, 680, 691, 692, 693, 695
Bernstein, Robert, 676
Berry, Jon, 679
Berry, Leonard L., 687, 688, 692
Bertagnoli, Lisa, 702
Berthon, Pierre, 697
Best, Roger J., 678, 679, 681
Bettencourt, Nuno, 353
Betts, Kate, 691
Bezos, Jeff, 307, 434–435, 562
Bharadwaj, Sundar G., 682, 698
Bianco, Anthony, 683, 691
Bigne, J. Enrique, 694
Bildsten, Bruce, 518
Bilger, Burkhard, 689
Billings, Claire, 686
Bingham, Frank G., Jr., 679
Bittar, Christine, 678
Bittner, Mary Jo, 686, 687, 693
Biyalogorsky, Eyal, 684
Blackwell, Roger D., 678
Blankenhorn, Dana, 697
Blanko, Vincent, 694
Bloch, Peter H., 686
Bloch, Thomas, 687
Bloom, Paul N., 677, 690
Bluestein, Jeff, 150
Boccara, Brun, 678
Bohner, Richard, 701
Bolles, Richard N., 617
Bolten, Joshua, 695
Bonamici, Kate, 695
Bonini, Sheila M. J., 674
Bonoma, Thomas V., 680
Bon Jovi, Jon, 352, 509
Booms, Bernard H., 687
Boorstin, Julia, 685
Boring, Christopher, 452
Boulding, William, 673, 684
Bowen, David E., 687
Bowman, Robert J., 691
Box, Terry, 685, 694
Boyd, Harper W., Jr., 674, 683, 685
Boyle, Matthew, 691, 700
Bradsher, Keith, 702
Brady, Diane, 701, 703
Brandreth, Scott, 326, 688
Brandt, Joe, 679
Branson, Richard, 307, 515
Brennan, David P., 693
Brinegar, Brad, 507
Briones, Maricris G., 697
Brockman, Beverly K., 684
Brodie, Roderick J., 675
Brooke, Simon, 693
Brooks, Garth, 461
Brosse, David, 695
Brown, Barry, 692
Brown, Ed, 697
Brown, Jeff, 543
Brown, Mary L., 682
Brown, Robert George, 694

Brown, Stephen W., 687, 693
Brunel, Frederic F., 679, 686
Bruni, Frank, 689
Bryant, Kobe, 497
Buchanan, Bruce, 695
Buchanan, Joy, 703
Buck, David, 325, 688
Bulik, Beth Snyder, 693
Bulkeley, William M., 675
Bullock, August, 124, 679
Bundchen, Gisele, 496
Burdick, Richard K., 680
Burger, Martin E., 320
Burin, Norm, 693
Burley, James, 684
Burnett, John J., 673
Burns, Greg, 700
Burrows, Carol, 305
Burrows, Peter, 685, 703
Burton, Thomas M., 684
Bush, Alan J., 696
Bush, Victoria D., 696
Buss, Dale, 683
Butscher, Stephan A., 689
Butterfield, Bruce, 634
Buzzell, Robert D., 697
Byrne, John A., 674
Byrne, Ken, 640
Byrnes, Nanette, 692, 693

C

Cahill, Maureen, 460, 461, 693
Calantone, Roger, 685
Callaway, Eli R., 629
Callaway, Sue Zeisiger, 688
Callaway, Vivian Milroy, 572, 573–574, 597, 599, 700, 701
Cammarano, Roy F., 686, 691
Campbell, Paul, 676
Campbell, Sarah, 699
Cannon, Joseph P., 677, 680, 690, 698
Capell, Kerry, 688
Caposella, Alison, 546
Cappelli, Peter, 702
Capps, Brooke, 695
Carey, J. Ronald, 694
Carey, John, 676
Carlson, Don, 676
Carlton, Jim, 676
Carpenter, Gregory S., 673
Carral, Teré, 218–220, 683
Carreau, Mark, 686
Carroll, John, III, 675
Carson, J. J., 678
Carter, Franklin, 694
Carter, Jim, 693
Casanova, Sarah, 703
Cass, Ronald A., 689
Cassidy, Hilary, 685
Castelli, Jim, 674
Castillo, Dana, 691
Castleberry, Stephen B., 698, 699
Cateora, Philip R., 681, 682
Catherine the Great, 21
Caulfield, Brian, 703
Cavusgil, S. Tamer, 691

COMPANY INDEX

SUBJECT INDEX

The **Marketing** student Online Learning

Marketing includes more than just great writing, interesting examples, and helpful pedagogy. We've also prepared a student Online Learning Center loaded with helpful study aids designed to help you study wherever you are.

Visit www.mhhe.com/kerin to find all of the help you need. Here you will find Online Quizzes, Chapter Objectives, and Key Term Flashcards. With these study tools, you'll surely improve your grade!

- Reinforce your reading while it's still fresh with our multiple-choice Chapter Quizzes.
- Review the Chapter Objectives to refresh what you've read before a test.
- The Key Term Flashcards will help you learn all of the terms you need to know to do your best on the next exam!